# WHAT TO EXPECT

# THE TODDLER YEARS

❖ ❖ ❖

*Arlene Eisenberg*

*Heidi E. Murkoff*

*Sandee E. Hathaway, B.S.N.*

❖ ❖ ❖

Foreword by
Morris Green, M.D., F.A.A.P.
Perry W. Lesh Professor of Pediatrics
Indiana University Medical Center

WORKMAN PUBLISHING, NEW YORK

*T*o Elizabeth, the toddler we could always turn to;
and to Emma, Wyatt, Rachel, and Ethan, whose
toddler years are gone but certainly not forgotten.

*To Howard, Erik, and Tim, our partners in parenting,
and our very best friends.*

•••••••••

Copyright © 1994 by
Arlene Eisenberg, Heidi E. Murkoff, and Sandee E. Hathaway
Book illustrations copyright © 1994 by Marika Hahn

**Library of Congress Cataloging-in-Publication Data**
Eisenberg, Arlene. What to expect the toddler years/
Arlene Eisenberg, Heidi E. Murkoff, and Sandee E. Hathaway.
p. cm.
Includes index. ISBN 0-89480-994-6 (paper) 1. Toddlers. 2. Child rearing.
I. Murkoff, Heidi Eisenberg. II. Hathaway, Sandee Eisenberg.
III. Title. HQ774.5.E357 1994 649'.122—dc20 93-8932 CIP

Material in "What Your Toddler May Be Doing Now": Adapted from the
Denver Developmental Materials, W.K. Frankenburg, M.D. By permission of the author.
Toddler Height and Weight Charts, pages 864 to 867: Statistics provided by
the National Center for Health Statistics. Head Circumference Charts,
page 868: Adapted from *Pediatrics* 1986; 41:106.

Book design: Lisa Hollander with Janet Vicario
Cover illustration: Judith Cheng
Book illustrations: Marika Hahn

Workman books are available at special discounts when purchased in bulk
for premiums and sales promotions as well as for fund-raising or educational use.
Special editions or book excerpts can also be created to specification. For details,
contact the Special Sales Director at the address below.

Workman Publishing Company, Inc.
708 Broadway
New York, NY 10003

Manufactured in the United States of America
First printing October 1994
10 9 8 7 6 5 4 3 2 1

**Note:** All children are unique and this book is not intended to substitute for
the advice of your pediatrician or other physician who should be consulted on toddler
matters, especially when a child shows any sign of illness or unusual behavior.

# A Million Thanks

**M**uch like the eight toddlers we've had the pleasure of parenting, *What to Expect the Toddler Years* has presented us with countless challenges. And in the four years that it has taken us to research, write, and produce it, we've been lucky enough to work with many wonderful people who have assisted us in facing those challenges. Now, with the book in hand (make that two hands; at 900 plus pages, one hand won't do), we'd like to take the opportunity to express our thanks to those who have helped put it there:

▲ All the readers of our previous books, not only for their input, insights (keep those cards and letters coming!), and their loyalty (so greatly appreciated), but for their patience as they waited (and waited, and waited) for this book's arrival.

▲ Elizabeth Hathaway, toddler-come-lately, for obligingly posing for countless knock-knee photos, for always doing everything "by the book," and for generally being the right age at the right time.

▲ Dr. Morris Green, our esteemed and distinguished medical advisor, who never flinched (at least visibly) at the endless piles of paper we sent him, who painstakingly crossed our medical t's and dotted our medical i's, who brought not just scientific knowledge, but great sensitivity to the task, and who worked at laser speed no matter how busy he was on other projects.

▲ Suzanne Rafer, our intrepid editor and good friend (she'd have to be), who waded through the sea of manuscript with her usual grace, style, sense of humor, and more "flags" than the United Nations will ever see.

▲ The entire Workman team and extended family, but especially Lisa Hollander and Janet Vicario for their artistic expertise; Shannon Ryan for just about everything (but especially her smile); Helen Zelon for perceptive copy editing, and Deborah Kops and Beth Pearson for attentive proofreading; David Schiller, for copy that lets readers tell our books by their covers; and Peter Workman for his wisdom, understanding, and patience.

▲ Judith Cheng for, as usual, a warm and inviting cover illustration, and Marika Hahn for adorning the inside of the book with so many adorable toddlers.

▲ Elise and Arnold Goodman, for their friendship, and for taking care of business.

▲ Dr. Mark Widome for his invaluable support and assistance, particularly on matters of toddler safety and first aid. And the many others who've lent their expertise, including Carole Marcus, M.D., J. Rutt Reigart, M.D., Kathy Leonard, M.D., Al Mooney, M.D., Shelly Bazes, C.N.P., W.K. Frankenburg, M.D., Beverly Bresnick, Cate D'Amboise, Sara Jacobs, Ann Wimpheimer, Alan Friedman, Sue Kellerman, Wendy Sax, Barbara Braun, Susanna Morgenthau, Mimi Gelb, Eve Coulson, Aliza Cotton, Michael Rand, and the moms and dads who've plied us with questions at our parenting groups and seminars.

▲ The terrific staff at the American Academy of Pediatrics, including Michael Copeland, Carolyn Kolbaba, Leslee Williams, and former staff member Michelle Weber, for helping to keep our books accurate and up-to-date.

▲ The editors of *Contemporary Pediatrics* for invaluable assistance whenever called upon; Juliann Goldman of C.S.P.I.; and N.A.P.N.A.P.

▲ Tameka Hall and Niurka Zameta, crackerjack assistants, who kept up with filing mountains of articles from journals and newsletters, checked phone numbers, and otherwise kept our office going.

▲ Abby and Norman Murkoff and, as always, Mildred and Harry Scharaga for unflagging support.

# *Contents*
·········

# Part Two: Toddler Care, Health, and Safety

## Chapter Seventeen: Toddler Care Primer .................464

## Chapter Eighteen: Feeding Your Toddler .................500

# Chapter Twenty-One: Keeping Your Toddler Safe ....615

Change Your Ways • Change Your Toddler • *Dressing for Safety* • Change Your Toddler's Surroundings • *Lead Can Lead to Trouble* • *Food for Thought* • *Safe Heights* • *No Gun Is a Safe Gun* • *Indoor Pest Control: Sorry for Pests, Still Safe for Toddlers* • *Putting Worry in Perspective* • *JPMA Certified Safe for Kids* • *Poison Control* • *Designed for Safety* • *No Swinging* • *A Safe Place to Play* • *Dress for It* • *Don't Let the Bugs Bite* • *Let It Snow* • *Safe Art* • *Red Light Greenery*

# Chapter Twenty-Two: Treating Toddler Injuries ......658

## FIRST AID FOR THE TODDLER ....................................659

Abdominal Injuries • Bites • Bleeding • Bleeding, Internal • Broken Bones or Fractures • Bruises, Skin • Burns and Scalds • Cat Bites/Scratches • Chemical Burns • Choking • Cold Injuries • Convulsions • Cuts • Dislocations • Dog Bites • Drowning • Ear Injuries • Electric Shock • Eye Injury • Fainting • Finger and Toe Injuries • Foreign Objects • Fractures • Frostbite • Head Injuries • Heat Illness • Hyperthermia • Hypothermia • Insect Bites • Lip, Split or Cut • Mouth Injuries • Nose Injuries • Poisoning • *Post a Warning* • Poison Ivy, Poison Oak, Poison Sumac • Puncture Wounds • Scalds • Scrapes • Seizures • Severed Limb or Digit • *Stocking the Medicine Chest* • Shock • *Making a Boo-Boo Better* • Skin Wounds • *Bandaging a Boo-Boo* • *Tender Loving Care* • Snake Bites • Sprains • Sunburn • Swallowed Foreign Bodies • Teeth, Injury to • Toe Injuries • Tongue, Injury to

## BASIC LIFE SUPPORT FOR TODDLERS ...........................682

1-2-3 and A-B-C • Rescue Breathing for Toddlers • Cardiopulmonary Resuscitation (CPR): Children Over One Year • Basic Life Support for a Choking Toddler

# Chapter Twenty-Three: Your Special-Needs Child ....692

Helping Your Special-Needs Child • *Free Testing* • *Who Can Help?* • Living With and Loving Your Special Child • *It's the Law* • *Residential Care* • *Home Care*

## SOME CHRONIC HEALTH PROBLEMS .............................702

AIDS (Acquired Immunodeficiency Syndrome) and HIV Infection • Allergy • *Helping the Healthy Sibling* • *Life-Threatening Allergies* • *When the Food-Allergic Toddler Steps Out* • Asthma • Autism • Cancer • Celiac Disease • Cerebral Palsy (CP) • Cystic Fibrosis (CF) • Diabetes Mellitus • Down Syndrome • Epilepsy • Fragile X Syndrome • Hearing Impairment • *Hearing Tests* • Juvenile Rheumatoid Arthritis (JRA) • Mental Retardation • Muscular Dystrophy (Duchenne Type) • Phenylketonuria (PKU) • Sickle Cell Disease • Thalassemias • *The Very-Low-Birth-Weight Baby as a Toddler* • Visual Impairment—Legal Blindness

# Part Four: Ready Reference

# A Pediatrician's Prescription

This wonderfully informative book is destined to win blue ribbons for authoritativeness, readability, and usefulness. One of the things that impressed me most as I read it was how thoroughly it prepares parents to understand the needs, behavior, and development of their toddlers, while offering hundreds of valuable suggestions on their care, guidance, and management. (Perhaps that last word should be in quotes. With toddlers, it's never really clear who manages whom.)

But *What to Expect the Toddler Years* is more than a user-friendly technical handbook. The authors present the developmental essentials of the difficult but delightful toddler years in such an accessible and empathic manner that appreciative parents will undoubtedly recommend this book to their friends as a genuine household necessity.

It has become increasingly clear that a child's first three years of life largely determine his or her future developmental trajectory. To a large extent, these early years set the stage for later outcomes in personal health, emotional development, educational attainment, social competence, self-confidence, self-reliance, and positive human relationships. Parental investment in the coin of nurturance, care, love, and understanding during this formative age period brings both short- and long-term dividends.

This latest addition to the *"What to Expect"* series helps parents to achieve these dividends in several ways. It helps parents know what to expect from their toddlers at various ages and stages, and reassuringly maps the wide range of normality. It guides parents in the always challenging, often daunting task of helping the toddler deal successfully with

such key developmental issues as good nutrition, timely immunization, safe play, sound sleep, weaning, speech, separation, self-discipline, good health and hygiene habits, as well as various child care situations.

Considerable attention is given to practical suggestions for the prevention of behavioral and developmental problems. But the authors not only help parents to avoid the negative, they strongly accentuate positive values with innumerable sidebars devoted to the care and nurturing of the toddler's understanding of right, wrong, and the gray areas in between.

Temper tantrums? Breath-holding spells? Sleep disorders? Biting? Short attention span? Speech delay? Toileting worries? Autonomy? Negativity? Resistance to limits? Along with why such behavioral and developmental problems happen, detailed guidance is offered on ways to get them to stop—or at least to minimize them. These recommendations are developmentally based, in keeping with the child's chronological age, needs, and abilities.

Parents themselves are not neglected. A principal goal of the book is to provide frequently overwhelmed and sometimes despairing parents with the kind of information that promotes confidence, self-esteem, resiliency, and feelings of effectiveness. Common parental questions (including those of parents working outside the home) are posed and comprehensively and reassuringly answered. Parent–toddler interaction and communication are strongly promoted as ways to give a young child and his or her parents a good start. Throughout the book, the toddler is viewed in the context of his or her family, with an emphasis on identifying and augmenting the strengths of both.

The authors' thoughtful advice and suggestions are intended to help readers enjoy their toddlers—to take a positive approach to the challenges of their formative years, to understand what often seem to be (but often aren't) irrational behaviors and to put them in perspective, to accept and respect each child as a unique individual and contribute to the realization of that child's potential.

This book directly responds to the sensible desire of today's parents for information that fits our times, a period characterized by rapid changes in the family and our society. This highly skilled synthesis of childrearing principles, savvy from the social, behavioral, and biologic sciences, and successful medical practice is clearly unsurpassed among child-care guides. It is an outstanding volume—one that will be extremely useful to both parents and professionals.

*Morris Green, M.D., F.A.A.P.*
*Perry W. Lesh Professor of Pediatrics*
*Indiana University Medical Center*

# A Tale of "Two" Toddlers

It was the best of the times, it was the worst of times. It was Emma's toddler years.

Shoes hurled across the room because they didn't "feel good" on her feet. Crackers rejected because they had a corner broken. A swimsuit donned on a frigid January morning, a snowsuit donned on a scorching August afternoon. Sit-down strikes on grimy New York City sidewalks (when there was no bus in sight), lie-down strikes in front of the candy display at the supermarket (when sweets weren't on the shopping list). Daily tantrums, nightly sleep problems; battles fought at the dinner table ("Don't wanna eat that!"), at the closet ("Don't wanna wear that!"), at the playground ("Don't wanna go yet!"). Stubbornness that wouldn't quit, a temper to rival a marine drill sergeant's, ritualistic behavior that bordered on the obsessive–compulsive.

And then, there was that smile — a smile that, in one endearing flash of pearly baby whites, could turn a hardened parental heart into a helpless pool of sentimental slush. And those hugs — spontaneous outbursts of unaffected affection more delicious (and more addictive) than imported chocolate truffles. And that voice — cuter than a voice has a right to be, uttering achingly adorable mispronunciation after mispronunciation ("bia" for banana, "pe-um" for peanut butter, "ga-ga" for daddy). And those moments — those thousand-and-one enchanting moments, the ones that made me forget the tantrums and the negativity, that entertained me, charmed me, and made me feel blessed. The way she "nursed" her teddy bears while I nursed her baby brother. The way she poured "tea" for her dolls, and administered shots to sickly stuffed animals. The way she sang to herself while she swung on the swings, and babbled to herself while she flipped the pages of her picture books. The way she scoured the park for caterpillars and butterflies to catch and observe in her "bug house." The way she moved, the way she cuddled, the way she laughed, the way she played, the way she slept.

If there has yet to be a more difficult time in the raising of Emma, there has also yet to be a more delightful one. Though I've thoroughly enjoyed every era of Emma (from newborn to preteen; I'll get back to you on adolescence), the toddler years — more harrowing than any roller coaster ride, and yet, much more intoxicating; a series of ups and downs that at once confused, captivated, exasperated and exhilarated — were among my favorite years.

Of course, that's easy to say now — now that Emma has evolved from an irrational two-year-old to a reasonable (most of the time), responsible, and responsive eleven-year-old, now that I have nearly a decade of time-heals-all perspective between me and those shoe-hurlings (we never did find that sneaker). It was decidedly less easy to say, or to feel, when Emma was a toddler.

If only I'd understood then what experience has helped me to understand now. That, to paraphrase the popular (but unprintable) aphorism, toddler behavior happens. And it has to happen — as inevitably as those two front teeth, as surely as those first steps. It doesn't happen because you're bad parents, and it doesn't happen because your toddler's a bad child — it happens because it's supposed to happen and because it needs to happen. Toddlers don't do what they do to drive their parents to distraction (though that's often the result); they do what they do to grow, to mature, to come to terms with coming of age.

So it is to those trying, terrific, irrepressible, irresistable, completely con-

founding creatures we call toddlers—
and to the parents who struggle to understand them—that this book is dedicated.
In hopes that it will help parents of toddlers appreciate the best of times, cope

with the worst of times—enjoy all the times that are the toddler years.

*Heidi E. Murkoff*

# Before You Begin

## How to Use WHAT TO EXPECT THE TODDLER YEARS

When it comes to parenting, there are few absolutes (one, of course, being that every child needs to be loved) and there is no one "right way" (with the exception of issues that affect a child's safety and health). Use this book for suggestions, for insights, for explanations, for examples — but use it to supplement and support rather than supplant your own instincts. Let it inspire you, not inhibit you. Different parenting techniques work for different children (even for different children within the same family, and the same child under different circumstances); different parenting styles suit different parents and the same parent at different times of life. Let this book serve as a guide as you use your skills, talents, instincts, and knowledge of yourself and your child (no one knows you and your child as well as you do) to try to discover what works best in your family.

## What Your Toddler May Be Doing Now

Every child is unique; each develops at his or her own pace. Because few children are perfectly average or typical, comparisons are not very useful. And though we may be concerned about the child who lags behind his or her peers,

that child may later make great leaps forward, catching up or even surpassing them.

Nevertheless, most of us want to know how our own child is doing in relation to other children, at least once in a while. To help you determine where your toddler's development fits within the wide range of normal, we've developed a monthly milestone scale of achievements for the second year, and a quarterly milestone scale for the third year into which virtually all toddlers fall. These scales are based on the widely respected Denver II scale, with a few added items from the well-regarded ELM (Early Language Milestone) scale.

Here's how they work: Each "What Your Toddler May Be Doing Now" milestone scale is divided into four categories. The first, "What your toddler *should* be able to do," lists milestones that have been reached by 90% of toddlers by that age. The second, "What your toddler *will probably* be able to do," represents milestones that have been reached by 75% percent of toddlers. The third, "What your toddler *may possibly* be able to do," includes milestones that have been reached by 50% of children. And the fourth, "What your toddler may *even* be able to do," includes milestones reached by 25%.

Most parents will find their toddlers achieving in several different categories at any one time. Some may find that their offspring stay consistently in the same category; others may find their child's overall development uneven—slow one month, vaulting ahead the next.

All of these developmental styles are perfectly normal until proven otherwise. Still, there are times when a doctor should be consulted. For example, when a child consistently fails to achieve what a child of his or her age "should be able to do," or when a parent has a gut feeling that something isn't right with a child's development. Even then, though an evaluation may be a prudent step, it may turn out that no problem exists. Some children keep moving forward but simply have a slower than average developmental timetable.

Use the "What Your Toddler May Be Doing Now" sections of this book to check progress periodically, if you like, but don't use them to make judgments about your toddler's potential — they are not predictive. If you find yourself obsessed with comparing your child to the averages, you may be better off looking at the milestone scales rarely, or not at all. Your child will develop just as well — and you (and your toddler) may be happier.

Keep in mind that the questions and issues discussed in each chapter are less specific to that month or period than was true in our book, *What to Expect the First Year.* Be sure to use the index to help you find the answers to your concerns.

Also remember that toddlers, like babies, don't develop in a smooth, linear progression. There are lots of bumps and humps, spurts and lulls. The period before a big step is often one of disorganization — nothing seems to go right; then all of a sudden, the child is walking or talking up a storm. Seemingly stagnant periods, in which there appears to be no progress at all, are actually spent polishing and expanding new skills; they are necessary to normal development. Progress may slow, too, or even slide backward, during times of stress. With adequate support at such times, toddlers usually get right back on the forward track.

## A Note to Nontraditional Families

There's more than one way to raise a family these days. Though the so-called "traditional" home—where a married couple raise the children together—is still perceived as the norm, half of all American children under eighteen are being raised in nontraditional homes. Sometimes by choice, more often by circumstance, more and more families are headed by single parents, usually mothers. And while they're still a small minority, other types of nontraditional families—including those headed by solo fathers, unmarried heterosexual or same-sex couples, mothers and fathers sharing custody in separate homes, and grandparents raising grandchildren—are also growing in number.

This book is meant for all kinds of families—traditional and nontraditional. For the sake of simplicity as well as syntax, we sometimes refer to the traditional family rather than trying to address every conceivable family configuration. But such references are not meant to exclude or offend those living in less traditional arrangements. For more on nontraditional families, see Chapter Twenty-Five.

# PART ONE

# *The Second and Third Years*

# CHAPTER ONE

# *The Thirteenth Month*

## WHAT YOUR TODDLER MAY BE DOING NOW

*By the end of this month,[1] your toddler*
*. . . should be able to (see Note):*

▲ pull up to standing position
▲ get into a sitting position
▲ cruise (move from place to place, always holding on)
▲ clap hands (play "patty-cake")
▲ indicate wants in ways other than crying

**Note:** If your toddler has not reached these milestones or doesn't use his or her hands for purposeful activities like picking things up, consult the doctor or nurse-practitioner. This rate of development may well be normal for your child (some children are late bloomers), but it needs to be evaluated. Also check with the doctor if your toddler seems unresponsive, doesn't smile, makes few or no sounds, doesn't seem to hear well, is perpetually irritable, or demands constant attention. (Remember, the one-year-old who was born prematurely often lags behind others of the same chronological age. This developmental gap progressively narrows and generally disappears entirely around age two.)

*. . . will probably be able to:*

▲ put an object into a container (by 12½ months)
▲ imitate activities (by 12½ months)
▲ stand alone (by 12½ months)
▲ use 1 recognizable word

*. . . may possibly be able to:*

▲ drink from a cup
▲ use 2 recognizable words (by 12½ months)

---

1. The thirteenth month begins when a child is twelve months old and ends when he or she is thirteen months old.

▲ point to a desired object (by 12½ months)
▲ scribble
▲ walk well

### . . . may even be able to:

▲ use a spoon/fork (but not exclusively)
▲ remove an article of clothing
▲ point to 1 body part when asked
▲ dump an object in imitation

**Intellectual development.** Early in the second year, toddlers are explorers and scientists, picking up, studying, testing, manipulating, maybe still putting in their mouths, everything in their path.

Cause and effect is a major focus. They live in the here and now, and do not show much imagination or abstract thinking as yet.

**Emotional development.** As the world begins to open up, the toddler, who has come a long way from the eat-cry-sleep newborn, opens up, too, displaying a wide range of moods, feelings, and behaviors. Expect them and accept them—they are part of growing up. This range includes displays of affection, independence, frustration, fear, anger, protest, stubbornness, willfulness, sadness, anxiety, and puzzlement.

# WHAT YOU CAN EXPECT AT THE ONE-YEAR CHECKUP[2]

**Preparing for the checkup.** Keep a list of concerns that have come up since the last visit to your child's doctor or nurse-practitioner. Be sure to bring the questions with you to this visit so you will be ready when the doctor asks, "Any concerns?" Also jot down new skills your toddler is displaying (clapping hands, waving bye-bye, throwing kisses, walking, climbing) so you won't be at a loss when you're asked, "What's your toddler been doing?" Bring along your child's home health history record, too, so that height, weight, immunizations, and any other information gleaned from the visit can be recorded.

**What the checkup will be like.** Procedures will vary a bit depending on your child's doctor or the nurse-practitioner who conducts health supervision exams, but in most cases, the twelve-month visit will include:

▲ An assessment of growth (height, weight, head circumference) since the last visit. These findings may be plotted on growth charts (see pages 864 to 867) and the child's weight for height evaluated and compared to previous measurements. You can expect that the rate of growth will slow in the second year.[3]

▲ Questions about your child's development, behavior, eating habits, and health since the last visit. There may also be questions about how the family is doing in general, whether there have been any major stresses or changes, how siblings

2. Your child's doctor may call the regular checkup a "health supervision visit," the term used by the American Academy of Pediatrics.

3. Recent research suggests that children don't grow gradually, but rather in spurts. So your toddler may remain the same height for a couple of months, then suddenly pick up a full inch or more virtually overnight.

(if any) are getting along with your toddler, about how you are coping, about child care arrangements (if any). The doctor or nurse will also want to know whether you have any other questions or concerns.
▲ An informal assessment, based on observation and interview, of physical and intellectual development, and of hearing and vision.
▲ A finger-stick blood test (hematocrit or hemoglobin) if the child is at risk of anemia. The test may be done once routinely between twelve months and four years.
▲ A blood test, usually a finger-stick, to screen for lead, between nine and twelve months.[4]
▲ A Mantoux test for tuberculosis for children at high risk; this simple skin test (which has gained in importance with the recent reemergence of TB), may instead be performed at fifteen months.

**Immunizations.**
▲ Hib (hemophilus influenza b); may be given at 15 months instead.

**Anticipatory guidance.** The doctor or nurse-practitioner may also discuss such topics as good parenting practices; your toddler's emerging struggle for independence; discipline; communicating with your toddler; nutrition, weaning, and fluoride supplementation, if appropriate; injury prevention; ways of stimulating language; and other issues that will be important in the months ahead.

**The next checkup.** If your toddler is in good health, the next visit will be at 15 months. Until then, be sure to call the nurse or doctor if you have any questions that aren't answered in this book or if your child shows any signs of illness (see page 568).

# WHAT YOU MAY BE CONCERNED ABOUT

## FREQUENT FALLS

*"Our year-old daughter can barely stay on her feet for five minutes at a time without falling. Is something wrong with her coordination?"*

A toddler is an accident waiting to happen . . . and happen . . . and happen again. Surefootedness is not characteristic of new walkers (which is why, of course, they are called toddlers); most fledgling toddlers can't even make it across a room without taking a flop.

Part of the problem is a lack of experience with balance and coordination, which take a lot of practice to perfect. (If you've learned to ice-skate or ride a bike

as an adult, you have an inkling of what learning to walk must be like.) Another factor is farsightedness; most children this age can't clearly see what's under their nose (see page 5). Judgment, or rather the lack of it, also contributes. So does preoccupation. A toddler is more likely to be paying attention to what's going on around her than where she's going. And since toddlers are rarely able to concentrate on more than one thing at a time, collisions and spills are the typical result.

---

4. This is a new recommendation of the American Academy of Pediatrics and not every doctor does this test routinely. At this point, there is some disagreement over whether it is cost-effective to screen all children.

*A pair of soft, wide, elasticized pony-tail holders or wrist bands that fit comfortably (never snugly) around the ankles of sleepers will keep floppy feet from slipping up a toddler.*

(obviously this is not feasible if your home isn't carpeted), and to keep her away from such extra-hard surfaces as slate, ceramic tile, stone, and brick. Check any areas she frequents for sharp corners and other protuberances and cover or remove them (see page 624). Keep drawers, furniture doors, and appliances (especially dishwashers) closed when she's around; eliminate or tape down dangling electric cords; and temporarily remove rickety chairs or tables (which she might grab onto for support). Areas where falls could be particularly dangerous, such as stairs and bathrooms, should be made completely inaccessible (see page 618).

Protective clothing can help, too. When practical opt for long pants instead of shorts or dresses. Heavy corduroy and quilted fabrics cushion falls more effectively than do thin cotton knits. And while you're outfitting her, make sure your toddler's footwear isn't contributing to the trouble she's having staying upright. Floor temperature permitting, bare feet are best indoors; if socks or slippers are necessary, they should be nonslip. When only shoes will do, make certain that the soles provide enough traction to prevent slipups and that the shoes fit correctly. (Shoes that are too big, too small, or too clumsy can trip up a toddler. See page 8 for more on toddler shoes.)

If your toddler is a climber, putting some cushions or soft mats at the base of her favorite "mountains" can make for a happier landing should she lose her footing. Remove or block off any furniture (including freestanding bookcases) that could topple if she climbed on it.

After taking appropriate safety measures, relax. A toddler's body is built to take the falls. It's close to the ground and usually still well-cushioned with baby fat. The skull is flexible because the soft spot (or fontanel) hasn't closed completely (it doesn't generally close fully until somewhere around eighteen

Though she will continue to make steady progress in the months ahead, chances are your toddler will be cruising for a bruising for some time to come. It probably won't be until somewhere around her third birthday that she'll have gained the expertise necessary to be able to steer a steady course—most of the time.

Meanwhile, since you can't always prevent her from falling, the best you can do is work toward preventing falls and minimizing injury when she does fall. It makes sense to have your child do most of her walking on carpeted surfaces

---

## SAFETY WARNING

..........

Some particularly adventurous toddlers learn how to climb out of their cribs early in the second year. So if you haven't already lowered your child's crib mattress to its lowest level, do so now. Also be sure to keep out of the crib large stuffed animals or other objects that your toddler can utilize as stepping stones to freedom—and a bad fall.

---

months), so a toddler can generally take slight bumps to the head without damage. Overprotecting your toddler in order to prevent falls (penning her up in a playyard for hours at a time, for example) is unwise. A toddler has to take some falls in order to master staying on her feet.

Overprotecting your toddler and overreacting when she does fall ("Oh, my poor baby!") may also inhibit her natural drive to explore, slow her gross motor development (walking, jumping, climbing), and make her needlessly fearful.

# BUMPING INTO THINGS

*"My son constantly bumps into things—tables, chairs, people. Could something be wrong with his eyesight?"*

Probably not. Typically, the oneyear-old is somewhat farsighted and possesses limited depth perception, so judging distances at this age can be tricky. By age two, normal vision improves to about 20–60; by three to about 20–40. It's not until roughly age ten that normal 20–20 vision is attained. (See page 477 for possible signs of vision problems.)

Even if a toddler did possess perfect vision, chances are he still couldn't see his way clear of collisions. That's because he rarely looks where he's going. Preoccupied with the mechanics of walk-

ing, he often looks at his feet (to make sure one's still going in front of the other) instead of at where they're taking him. Or he focuses his attention on the person or object he's trying to reach—the stuffed giraffe that's lying on the sofa, a parent beckoning from across the room with outstretched arms, the fascinating dials of the television set—and not on the obstacles that may be lying in his path. It's not surprising that he careens into the floor lamp, barrels into the coffee table, or stumbles over the dump truck he's left in the middle of the floor. And even if he does spy a roadblock at the last minute, he may not possess the ability necessary to go around it or stop short of it, especially if he's picked up some speed.

Fortunately, both vision and coordination sharpen with time. Around his third birthday, you can expect your toddler to begin navigating his world more steadily and more safely. True grace, however, will probably elude him until the age of eight or nine—at the earliest.

Until then, you can protect him from some of life's little bumps by making his environment safe (see page 620).

# SLOW GROSS-MOTOR DEVELOPMENT

*"Our little girl was the last one in her play group to roll over and to sit up. Now even though she's a year old, she still hasn't pulled up*

*to standing. Everything else (speech, hand coordination, and all) seems normal. The doctor says 'don't worry,' which is easy for her to say. . . ."*

Just about every parent worries sometimes—it's part of the job description. And usually, being told not to worry—even by your child's doctor—isn't enough to calm parental concerns completely. If, in spite of the doctor's reassurances, your gut feeling tells you to pursue the matter further, explain that you would be more comfortable if your baby had an assessment to rule out any problems. The doctor is likely to agree, if only to set your mind at ease. It may well turn out that your daughter's gross-motor development (the development of the large muscles of the body that are involved in crawling, sitting, standing, climbing) is just on the slow side of normal and that she'll gradually catch up with her playmates on her own. In that case, you may be able to help speed the process along in the ways recommended below. Rarely, such tests uncover a motor problem that would benefit from extra attention. When poor muscle tone is at the root of slow motor development, physical therapy can be very beneficial, especially if started at an early age. In fact, with appropriate intervention (usually consisting of a variety of do-at-home physical-therapy exercises) many children with gross-motor delays eventually catch up and do just fine.

## SLOWPOKE WALKER

*"I really thought that by now my son would have started walking. But he hasn't even tried yet."*

The fact that your son hasn't yet started training for the toddler Olympics doesn't mean he isn't destined to perform great feats on two feet. After all, the average baby doesn't take those first momentous steps until he's somewhere between thirteen and fifteen months of age. And though a few begin toddling around as early as seven or eight months, many completely normal youngsters don't step out on their own until sixteen months or even later.

Where your child falls within this very wide range of normal development doesn't tell you anything about his intelligence or his future athletic ability. Just like most slow talkers, most slow walkers catch up quickly once they get started—often breaking into a run just weeks after they've attempted their first tentative steps.

But while you shouldn't worry about or rush him, you should give your toddler plenty of opportunities to practice his prewalking skills. Encourage him to pull himself up by holding onto your hands, your shins, the bars of the crib, or the coffee table. Help him to cruise from your knees to your partner's, from chair to chair, around the crib. If he doesn't seem inclined to practice on his own—content instead to sit or crawl—play pull-up games with him so he can get the hang of standing on his own two feet while exercising his leg muscles. Be sure your toddler doesn't spend most of his day confined to a high chair, stroller, or playpen. Allow him to go barefoot at home or put slip-proof socks on him when floors are cold. Beware of stiff shoes as they can hamper learning to walk. And avoid using a walker. Not only are walkers associated with frequent accidents, but babies who become "walker-dependent" often take longer to learn to walk independently. If your baby has been using a walker, chuck it out now.

If your toddler isn't pulling up or trying to stand on his own, odds are he's just waiting until he's good and ready to walk. You should, nevertheless, check with his doctor at the next checkup.

# ENSURING A GOOD FIT

*"I know that a good fit is important when it comes to buying my daughter new shoes. But between her squirming, her whining, and my inexperience, I don't know where to begin."*

Trying shoes on a toddler can indeed be a trying experience—so much so that you may be tempted to buy her shoes without her around. Don't. Only a good fitting can ensure a good fit.

Keep these tips in mind when you make your next trip to the shoe store:

▲ Shop where the sales staff knows how to fit young children. Ask other parents for recommendations.

▲ Shop after a meal or a hearty snack. A hungry toddler is an uncooperative toddler and a hungry parent is an impatient one—and you're going to need all the cooperation you can get and all the patience you can muster.

▲ Shop after nap time. Whatever can be said about a hungry toddler can be said doubly for a tired toddler.

▲ Avoid after-school hours, if possible. The more crowded the shoe store, the longer the wait and the more difficult the shoe-buying ordeal.

▲ Arm yourself with toddler distractions. Being accompanied by a favorite teddy bear, doll, or truck can make the expedition to the shoe store more tolerable.

▲ Bring along the right socks. Make sure your toddler is wearing socks that are similar in weight and thickness to the socks that will ordinarily be worn with the shoes you're buying.

▲ Don't assume one size fits all. Since the right foot and the left often differ in size—sometimes significantly—the shoe size selected will have to accommodate the larger foot. So be sure that the sales-person measures both feet and that both shoes are tried on.

▲ Don't fit while your toddler sits. Shoes should be fitted while your toddler is standing with her weight on both feet. When checking toe space, make sure that she isn't curling up her toes inside the shoe—a very common habit among young children, particularly those who aren't used to wearing shoes. Rubbing your hand along your toddler's calf will help relax leg muscles and uncurl toes.

▲ Let your fingers do the testing. Check the width by pinching the side of the shoe at its widest point. If you can grasp a tiny bit of it between your fingers, the width is fine. If you can pinch a good piece of shoe, it's too wide; and if you can pinch none at all, it's too narrow. Another sign of a too-narrow shoe: You can feel the little toe or the outside bone of the foot when you run your finger along the side of the shoe.

Check the length by pressing your thumb down just beyond the tip of the big (or longest[5]) toe. If there's a thumb's width (about half an inch) of room, the length is right. Press down, too, to make sure the toe box has enough height so that toes can be curled and wriggled comfortably.

To check the fit of the heel, slip your pinky finger between your toddler's heel and the back of the shoe. It should fit snugly. If you can't slip your finger in at all, or it's a tight squeeze, the shoe is too small and will rub against your toddler's heel. If you can move your pinky around freely, then the shoe is too large. Gaps around the ankle also indicate a poor fit.

▲ Check the shoes in action. If your toddler can't walk alone yet, assist him or her in taking a few steps so you can

---

5. In some children (and adults), the second or third toe is longer than the "big" toe.

# SELECTING SHOES
# FOR THE WALKER

· · · · · · · · · ·

Young children have gone barefoot for most of human history, and still do in many parts of the world, so the definitive answer to the question, "What is the best shoe for the beginning walker?" is still evolving. Since feet are more flexible, stronger, and healthier in societies where shoes are shunned, most experts believe that no shoe is the best shoe. They recommend that children be allowed to go barefoot even in our society, where wearing shoes is the norm. Of course this is not always practical outdoors, where shoes are usually needed for protection, and in cold weather, when they're needed for warmth. Nor is it always feasible in drafty or poorly heated homes, where floors are chilly. Slip-proof slipper socks are a good indoor compromise; they allow plenty of free movement while keeping feet warm.

The next best thing to no shoes is a shoe that's closest to bare feet. Look for:

**Just-right fit.** Ideally, a shoe should be neither too big nor too small, though a too-tight shoe is apt to cause more problems than a too-roomy one. (See page 6 for shoe-fitting tips).

**Easy on, easy off.** Experts differ about whether high-top or low-cut shoes are preferable. High-tops can be confining and are more difficult for parents to put on and take off. But low-cut shoes come off so easily, a toddler can pull them off at will. What's more, they tend to slip off on their own. What's best for your new walker may depend on his or her foot shape as well as on the fit of a particular pair of shoes.

**Light weight.** Toddlers have a hard enough time putting one bare foot in front of another: The weight of a shoe, especially a heavy one, makes the task even more of a challenge.

**Flexible soles.** You should be able to bend the toe of the shoe up (about 40 degrees) easily.

**Nonslip, nongrip soles.** Soles should be neither so slippery that your toddler slides when trying to walk nor so ground-gripping that it's hard to lift a foot. Ideally, traction should be similar to that of the bare foot. Look for rubber soles that are grooved, like tire treads. If you buy shoes with smooth, slippery soles (the kind you are likely to find on dress shoes), rough up the soles with sandpaper, or tape a couple of strips of masking tape across them to improve traction.

**A shape that matches the foot.** Choose a high, square toe box rather than a pointed one.

**Breathable uppers.** Uppers of leather or canvas rather than plastic or imitation leather will allow feet to breathe and minimize moisture buildup from perspiration.

**No heels.** Even a slightly raised heel can throw a toddler's posture and balance out of kilter.

**Stiff heel counters.** The backs (or counters) of the shoes should offer firm support. Look for padding along the back edge; this feature will prevent the counters from rubbing and thereby increase comfort.

**Bright, appealing colors and designs.** Appearances may not mean much to the average thirteen-month-old. But they can mean everything to older toddlers—who will often refuse to wear shoes that do not suit their taste. Bold colors and designs are favorites; animal and cartoon appliqués generally score extra points.

**Reasonable price.** Shoes will probably have to be replaced four or five times—or even more—in the next year. So although they should be well made for the sake of comfort and safety, they needn't be built to last forever.

If you can manage it, purchase two pairs of shoes at a time. Children's feet perspire a lot, and switching off will allow shoes to dry completely between wearings.

observe how the shoe performs on the go. Be sure the toes don't drag with each step and the heels don't slide up and down.

▲ Be sure you don't see red. When you remove the shoes your toddler has tried on, slip off her socks and check for the kind of red marks that indicate that pressure has been placed on the foot. These marks indicate a poor fit.

▲ Don't buy ahead. Considering the rate at which toddlers outgrow shoes, there's always the temptation to buy shoes "with room to grow." Resist. Extra-large shoes can lead to irritation and blisters, cause unnecessary tumbles, and interfere with walking.

Even shoes that fit perfectly can rub and irritate when the wrong kind of socks are worn with them. According to experts, Orlon, which wicks moisture away from the foot, is the material of choice for socks. Stretch socks are most likely to give a good fit—and for a longer time. Socks should fit smoothly without constricting the foot. Socks that are too large will bunch up or wrinkle and may cause irritation and blisters. Those that are too small can cramp the foot and hinder growth. When socks start leaving marks on the feet, it's time to move up to the next sock size.

## REPLACING SHOES

*"How often do I need to replace my son's shoes?"*

On average, toddlers need a new pair of shoes every three or four months. But normal growth spurts and plateaus could cause one pair to be outgrown in two months and the next in five or six.

Since there's no way to predict the rate at which your toddler's feet will grow, you'll have to rely on monthly (or even more frequent) checks of his shoes at home. Use the fitting methods described on page 8, and consider a new pair when there is less than half a thumb's space at the toes. For confirmation, stop by your child's shoe store. A reputable salesperson will be able to tell you whether it's time to spring for another pair.

And, as much as you may be tempted by the potential savings, don't pass down outgrown shoes from one child to the next. Even if the shoes do not seem badly worn, they have molded to the shape of the first wearer's feet and are not likely to be suitable for the next child. The one exception: party or dress shoes that have been worn, and will be worn, for just a few hours a week.

## TOEING-IN (PIGEON-TOES)

*"Now that my daughter has started walking, I've noticed that her toes turn inward. Is this something that needs attention?"*

At this stage of the walking game, probably not. Toeing-in (or pigeon-toes) early in the second year is usually related to internal tibial torsion, a turning in of the tibia (or shin bone), which generally straightens out on its own.

You should consult your toddler's pediatrician, however, if her toeing-in doesn't take a turn for the better during the next six months, if the problem seems to be interfering with her walking or running, if her toes don't point straight ahead when she's at rest, or if her feet exhibit a half-moon curve when observed from the bottom.

In a small percentage (8% to 9%) of children, toeing-in continues into adult-

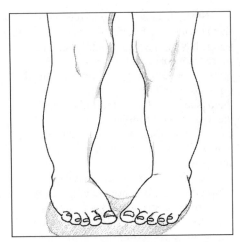

Toeing-in is not uncommon early in the second year.

hood. But as long as the condition doesn't interfere with movement and the feet aren't rigid or painful, it rarely poses a problem.

Children who at this age toe-out rather than in often become pigeon-toed temporarily at about age three or four. That's not a problem either.

# THE INTO-EVERYTHING SYNDROME

*"Our toddler can't pass by any-thing without touching it. When we're in the house, that means nothing is safe; when we're outside, that means he isn't safe. It's driving us crazy."*

A toddler's constant, sometimes maddening, manipulation of his environment isn't the result of malicious-ness, it's the result of curiosity. It's not the devil in him that makes him do it, but the Christopher Columbus and the Isaac Newton. Part explorer, part scien-tist, he views the world around him as both his oyster and his laboratory. But instead of receiving a grant to help fur-ther his discoveries, he receives dozens of

daily reprimands intended to discourage them. "Don't touch!" is probably the single most commonly uttered parental phrase in homes with toddlers. Yet a tod-dler isn't even remotely capable, espe-cially not early in the second year, of suppressing the impulses that drive him to touch—or poke or grab or squeeze or run his hands along something.

You can't—and you shouldn't try to—keep your toddler's hands off every-thing in his environment. To understand the world, toddlers need to lay their hands on it. Of course, some things just aren't meant for a toddler's touch, either because they're dangerous or breakable, or both. So it's necessary to steer a mid-dle course, encouraging safe and dis-couraging unsafe exploration.

**Limit the risk.** Try to make your home as childproof as you can (see page 620). If you don't want to pack away all your valued possessions until your toddler comes of a more responsible age, start training him now in the fine art of touch-ing "fine art" without breaking it (see page 237). When you can, use foresight to head off disaster. If your toddler loves to see what happens when he turns over a cup of milk or juice, keep liquids out of reach and hand him the cup only when he asks for it or when you think he's ready for another sip. Take it back as soon as his thirst is satisfied.

Away from home, avoid elegant sur-roundings filled with expensive break-ables. If Grandma's house falls into this category, she may want to consider putting her best possessions out of reach when her grandchild comes to visit. In stores and supermarkets, buckle your young explorer into a shopping cart or his stroller, and provide him with some interesting tactile objects to keep his hands occupied. If he won't stay put, en-list his help as your assistant, harnessing his potentially destructive energies pro-ductively. Point out the cereal that you want, and have him remove it from the shelf and hand it to you. As you choose the oranges or apples, ask him to drop each into the bag. When he's old enough to recognize the brands of staples (milk, juice, bread) you favor (which will be sooner than you think), challenge him to find what you need on the shelf and point to it. Then have him drop it into the shopping cart.

**Make limits clear and consistent.** Though you don't want to stifle the exploratory urge, you do have to let your toddler know, even at this early age, that some things are off-limits. Every time he reaches for the VCR or the stove or the china closet or any other no-no item, stop him and redirect him immediately. And remember, you may have to repeat the same redirections dozens of times before they sink in.

**Increase the opportunities.** The more opportunities you provide your toddler to explore his world safely, the less temptation there will be for him to do so in a way that will get him into trouble. See page 456 for tips on safe ways to satisfy your toddler's appetite for touch and exploration.

**Provide supervision and training.** He wants to squeeze the toothpaste tube? Teach him how to squeeze it neatly, then appoint him the official toothpaste-squeezer for the family. (But make sure you're there to oversee this operation or your bathroom will be decorated regularly with swirls of toothpaste.) He wants to try out your computer? Sit him on your lap for fifteen minutes (with your work safely stored) and let him tap the keys. He wants to turn the TV on? Show him how and let him do it, but only when you, or another adult, are close at hand. You can also teach your toddler to help you put away the groceries (except for breakables, such as bottles or jars), empty flatware from the dishwasher (after you've safely re-

moved the knives, forks, and other sharp utensils), hand you clothes from the dryer, turn off the lights when leaving a room, and a multitude of other simple daily tasks that will seem exciting to your little scientist.

**Supply substitutes.** When he goes for the freshly folded stack of clothes on the bed, move them out of reach. But give him a couple of towels or T-shirts to drape about him, drag behind him, or play peekaboo with. You might even show him how to fold the towels, then let him practice folding and unfolding to his heart's content. When he wants to program the VCR, give him a toy that has buttons to push and dials to turn. Or let him play with a remote that has no batteries. Does your toddler love to experiment with fluids? Give him plenty of opportunity by supplying a variety of plastic containers to fill and empty during bath time.

**Play down infractions.** While it's important to stop unwanted behavior immediately, it's also important not to make a big issue of it. Toddlers tend to repeat actions that get a major reaction, whether the reaction is positive or negative. When feasible, use low-key distraction techniques, such as humor, rather than scolding.

# BANGING ON EVERYTHING

*"Our son bangs on everything in sight—the kitchen table, the living room curio cabinet, the TV—I'm afraid he'll damage something or hurt himself."*

Many a young toddler seems to be preparing for a career as a rock and roll drummer. And this penchant for banging the day away is as normal as it is common. These pint-size percussionists not only relish the rhythmic sounds they produce, but also delight in the reactions (negative though they may be) their performances elicit from their audience. (Banging is, after all, pretty hard to ignore, particularly in the middle of a phone conversation, a Thanksgiving dinner, or a stressful day.) The young drummer derives pleasure, too, from another potential consequence of his music-making: mess-making. As he bangs, it amuses him to see peas and carrots sailing off his plate, knickknacks dancing in the curio cabinet, magazines flying off the coffee table.

Though you don't want to completely quash your toddler's musical endeavors, there is a limit to how much banging a home and its inhabitants can take. So set some limits:

▲ Stop dangerous drumming promptly. Banging on the television set, a glass-topped table, a dinner plate, or a window can lead to serious injury, damage, or both: Bring this action to a halt without delay. Stop the music, too, before the vibration from your toddler's banging on the table upsets a cup of hot coffee or topples a vase of flowers. "No banging on the . . ." is a good start, but chances are actions will speak louder than words. Hence, you will also need to separate your junior musician from his "instrument of the moment" and quickly provide a substitute instrument or other distraction. Don't succumb to the temptation to shout over the banging; keep your voice soft yet firm and deliberate. Unpleasant behaviors like banging tend to be intensified rather than squelched by parental anger. There's also a chance (albeit a small one) that if he can't hear you over the sound of his one-man band, he'll be intrigued enough by the movement of your lips to stop and listen.

Stopping your toddler from drumming on a forbidden surface once doesn't mean he's going to refrain on his own in the future. It takes more than a few "no"s (and often more than a few hundred) to train a toddler. He'll likely test you many times by trying the wooden spoon out on the coffee table or the truck on the glass doors before he gets the message. Till then, you'll have to stay alert to catch him, and stop him in the act.

▲ Redirect his banging impulses. When you gotta bang, you gotta bang. So let him let loose—on safe surfaces. Offer him an old pot and a wooden spoon, a toy drum and rubber-tipped drumsticks, a child's tambourine, a bang-and-pop toy, a toddler-size hammer and workbench. The tumult will be easier on everyone's ears (and nerves) if your toddler drums in a carpeted room or while sitting on upholstered furniture.

▲ Help him find the rhythmic beat elsewhere. In music of all kinds, live and on tape, at home and in the car; in clapping and foot-stomping games; in the chirping of the cricket, the din of traffic, the tick-tock of a clock; in his own body (encourage him to dance or sway rhythmically to music or song).

▲ No banging in public, please. Parents of toddlers have to be somewhat tolerant (they don't have much choice). The rest of the world doesn't have to be, shouldn't be expected to be, and often isn't. So if your toddler grabs your spoon and starts jamming in a restaurant, for example, stop him promptly—even if he isn't in danger of hurting himself or his surroundings. Better still, think ahead whenever possible. Remove the silverware and the china (especially if it's fragile) from his place setting before you sit him down at the table, and engage him in a socially acceptable activity before he has a chance to start, or even think about starting, to bang. Divert him with a game of peekaboo (use the menu or napkin), a quiet song, a picture book, or a pad and crayons you've cleverly thought to bring along. If necessary, take a break in the foyer or outside until the food arrives.

# DIAPERING DIFFICULTIES

*"There doesn't seem to be any way to get my son to hold still for a diaper change."*

The battle of the bottom—parent strives to cover it, child struggles to keep it bare—is enacted countless times a day in the homes of active toddlers. Though the parents may appear the winners—after all, the bottom ultimately ends up covered—the tension of the battle leaves them feeling ravaged rather than victorious.

For some little ones, revolting against the diaper is a short-lived phase; for others it continues to some degree until potty learning is complete. In the meantime, trying these strategies may help bring about a speedier truce:

**Check for wounds.** Your little rebel may have a diaper rash that hurts more when the diaper is on. If so, follow his doctor's recommendation for treating the condition (or see page 470). If the rash gets progressively worse or doesn't disappear in a couple of days, check with the doctor.

**Choose your gear wisely.** Since speed is of the essence, the fastest methods of diapering should be favored. Instead of cloth, pins, and plastic pants, use a diaper cum Velcro-closing wrap or disposables. This measure also helps eliminate the risk of accidental pin sticks, which can further complicate the diapering process.

**Have everything in readiness.** Don't wait until you've bared your child's bottom to gather your wipes, ointments, corn starch, and diapers. (For safety's sake, arrange them out of his reach.)

**Create a diversion.** The diversions most likely to succeed in capturing baby's attention during diapering are those that are not used in everyday play but are reserved for diaper changes only. But because one toddler's distraction is another's ho-hum, it's usually a matter of trial and rejection until you find the amusements that work for your child. (Of course, avoid anything that might shatter if dropped off the side of the changing table.) Try a plastic hourglass; an unbreakable wind-up musical toy, a sturdy music box, a shakable musicmaker, such as a tambourine; a stuffed animal suspended over the table; a tape of children's songs; or any other appealing diversion that your toddler can manipulate, watch, or listen to during a diaper change. Or, divert with a participatory game, such as "Show me your belly . . . show me your nose . . ." (punctuated by kisses, of course), or by appointing your toddler your "diaper helper," and have him hand you the supplies (make sure tops are tightly screwed on) as you need them.

**Move the offensive.** If the changing table has turned into a battlefield, maybe it's time to retreat to safer ground. Protected by a thick towel or waterproof pad, almost any flat surface can be used for diapering—and the farther away from the despised changing table, the better. Try the living room floor, a hassock or large beanbag chair, the crib (with side railing down), your bed, the bathroom.

**Attack vertically.** Once a child is toddling on his own, it's an affront to be forced down onto his back. So it's often expedient (if not easy) to diaper toddlers where they stand—assuming the diaper is merely wet and the underlying surface can tolerate a sudden flood. Approaching the behind from behind is the wisest tactic. Also helpful is a distracting sight—birds outside the window, changing shadows on the wall, a perpetualmotion machine.

**Forget the element of surprise.** If your toddler is in the middle of an activity, try to wait until he's finished to make the change; or take his toy along to the changing table.

**Try a change of command.** If Mommy with a diaper signals a struggle to your toddler, it may be time to call for reinforcements. Whenever possible, leave the diapering to Daddy or recruit anyone else who's available and willing to tackle the task. With the novelty of a different diaperer, your opponent may be diapered before he knows what hit him.

**Resort to force . . .** If none of the above seems to work, hold your toddler down (or better still, have an ally restrain those swinging feet) and get the job done as quickly as possible. Be friendly but firm. And don't feel guilty. After all, he has to wear a diaper whether he likes it or not.

**. . . but not to brute force.** However, spanking is never a good solution to this or any other parenting problem. Though the shock of a slap on the bottom may quiet a toddler temporarily, it relays a message you don't want to transmit— that hitting is the way to get what you want and to control others. It could also injure your child.

**Try to keep your cool.** If you're noncombative, your little adversary may lose interest in fighting. It takes two, after all, to tussle.

**Look to the future.** The diaper struggles will not last forever. One of these days, your toddler will enter the toilet-learning phase and switch to training pants. To be sure you don't go from the diaper wars to the battle of the potty, prepare yourself and your toddler for this big move by reading Chapter Nineteen.

# APPETITE SLUMP

*"We used to congratulate ourselves on how well our daughter ate. But all of a sudden she's rejecting everything, including all her old favorites. Could she be sick?"*

As long as she isn't exhibiting any other signs of illness (lethargy, weakness, fatigue, fever, weight loss, irritability), rejecting food is not likely to be a sign of illness. Rather, it probably represents four convergent developmental factors:

One, a budding sense of autonomy, is characteristic of normal toddlerhood. This spirit of independence will likely take many forms in the months to come; eventually, you may face it not only at mealtime but at dressing time, bath time, play time, bedtime, and just about every other time.

Two, the normal slowdown in growth—and thus in the need for calories—that occurs at the end of the first year. If your toddler continued consuming calories and gaining weight at the same rate she did in her first year (when she probably better than tripled her birthweight, gaining nearly as much as she'll gain in the next four years combined), she'd weigh as much as a fifth grader before reaching her second birthday.

Three, a newly active lifestyle. Toddlers often become so engrossed in practicing walking and other new skills that they are reluctant to take time out to do anything else, even eat.

Four, an improved memory. A young infant feeds like there's no tomorrow (or no next feeding). But a toddler begins to realize, "They feed me several times a day around here. If I don't eat now, I can eat later." If she's otherwise occupied, she may see no need to stop what she's doing for a meal.

So a drop in appetite now is not only no cause for alarm; it's perfectly normal. Study after study has found that healthy toddlers who aren't pushed or coerced into eating consume enough food for normal growth and development. Children who are force-fed, on the other hand, tend to develop chronic eating problems.

Typically, normal appetites vary from meal to meal, day to day, week to week, month to month. Some children will eat one hearty meal a day and nibble at the rest, other children will satisfy their body's requirements by "grazing" throughout the day. Interest in eating may pick up during a growth spurt, slow down at teething time or with a cold or the flu. Yet calculated over the weeks, the intake of food almost invariably balances out.

To test this theory, keep a record of your child's food intake over a two- or three-week period. Then compare it with the Best-Odds toddler requirements (see page 504). If you're conscientious about recording every bite and about providing only healthy bites (no junk food), you'll probably be surprised to discover how well your toddler is actually eating.

Keep in mind that your toddler's rejection of food is not a rejection of you or a reflection on your parenting skills. You can make the most of what appetite she has by making certain to follow the recommendations for feeding the finicky eater (see page 517).

Sometimes a poor appetite is temporary and related to changes in a child's life or to a cold or other illness. If your toddler isn't gaining weight or seems otherwise out of sorts, discuss your concerns with her doctor or nurse-practitioner.

# MILK ALLERGY

*"Our toddler, who recently was weaned from the breast to cow's milk, has suddenly started having diarrhea off and on, plus she makes sort of a wheezing sound when she breathes, and has a runny nose all the time. She doesn't seem sick, and has no fever. Should I check with the doctor?"*

**A**ny symptom, or group of symptoms, that arrives on the scene suddenly calls for a call to the doctor. Your child may be the victim of a virus, but it's more likely she's developed an allergy to cow's milk.

The symptoms of milk allergy include those your toddler has exhibited (diarrhea, asthma, runny nose) as well as eczema, constipation, irritability, poor appetite, and fatigue. Even the smallest quantity of milk in any form can trigger one or more of these symptoms.

Milk allergy is usually apparent early in the first year if an infant is taking a milk-based formula (and sometimes if a breast-feeding mother is consuming a lot of dairy products). But it often does not show up in a breastfed child or one who has been on a soy or hydrolysate formula until cow's milk is added to the diet at a year.

Milk allergy, which seems to affect about 12% of infants, is usually outgrown by the end of the second year, though a small percentage of children continue to have trouble with milk beyond that time. Children who are allergic to milk generally cannot tolerate *any* milk or milk products. They nevertheless require the calcium that milk provides for healthy growth. This calcium can come from a soy milk that is fortified with calcium or from calcium-fortified orange juice. Goat's milk may also work for a child who is allergic to cow's milk. And there are a variety of other calcium-rich foods (see page 506) that can supplement your toddler's diet. Discuss the options with her doctor so that together you can make certain that your toddler's diet isn't deficient in calcium or in milk's other major nutrients, including protein, phosphorus, vitamin D, and riboflavin. Also see page 355.

# FOOD THROWING

*"After just a few bites or sips, my toddler invariably throws her bowl on the floor or turns her glass over. I can't stand the mess anymore."*

The only sure way to avoid a toddler's mealtime mess is to withhold all food and drink. That being an impossible (if tempting) solution, you'll have to find ways of minimizing this behavior. Try using the sleight-of-hand measures recommended in the next section for dealing with food blowing, as well as the following techniques:

**Rationing.** Many children feel free to squander food when a rich bounty is set before them, so place just a few bites of food in front of your child at a time. Add a few more as those are consumed.

**Distraction.** Using a spoon to feed herself may occupy your toddler's attention so much that she won't feel compelled to overturn her bowl or throw tidbits to the dog. Or try substituting an acceptable game for the objectionable one: "You take a bite of your cereal and then I'll take a bite of mine."

**Fastening.** Use a child's bowl that can be attached to the table or high chair tray with suction cups so that your toddler can't whisk the bowl over the side.

**Bouquets.** Praise your toddler when she's (relatively) neat and make little fuss over her little messes. When the little messes lead to total mealtime mayhem, end the meal.

Though you can't always prevent your toddler from making a mess when she eats, you can reduce some of the work the mess spells for you. Spread some newspaper or a sheet of plastic under her high chair and seat her as far away from walls and nonwashable furniture as possible. To protect her clothing, roll up her sleeves and cover her with an over-the-shoulder large bib. If she balks at the bib, dress her for meals in her most dispensable clothes (or, if the temperature permits, no clothes at all). You may also want to try putting thick terry-like hair bands around her wrists to keep food from trickling down the forearm to clothing (some children will love this novel idea, others reject it out of hand).

If your stomach turns during your toddler's mealtime, turn the other way (wash some dishes, peel carrots, fold laundry). But look back frequently to make sure she's still eating, and that she hasn't gotten herself into any trouble.

# FOOD BLOWING

*"My toddler has developed the habit of blowing his food out as soon as I put it in his mouth. He seems to enjoy the sounds he makes. This habit has left me frustrated (not to mention covered with food). I've tried saying 'no' to him firmly, but he laughs and then I can't help laughing too."*

Nothing brings out the ham in a young performer like an appreciative audience. And, in this case, nothing brings out the oatmeal, junior carrots, and yogurt like one either. At six and seven months of age, babies love to make razzing sounds. Your son's messy habit probably began around this age, when he happened to notice what an intriguing sound he could make by combining razzing and eating. It's likely that this behavior continues because of the reaction it elicits from you. Any reaction, whether it's an angry "No!" or a half-suppressed giggle, signals the toddler that his old material still works—and, as is the case with any comic, as long as it's working he'll keep on using it.

To keep the show from going on indefinitely, try these measures:

**Change the props.** Certain foods lend themselves better to dramatic expulsion than others. Trade in such squishy items as strained fruits and vegetables, baby cereal, and yogurt. Instead, opt for slivers of banana and pieces of well-cooked carrot or sweet potato, healthy teething biscuits, a whole-grain bagel, soft whole-grain bread, and tiny tidbits of sliced cheese. (If you're abandoning iron-fortified baby cereal, be sure to ask your doctor about giving your toddler a vitamin supplement containing iron.) With the source of that wonderfully resonant sound-and-splatter effect elusive, much of your blower's motivation may disappear. If your toddler objects because you withdrew a favorite food, explain your reason. Tell him he can have it again if he doesn't blow it, but if he does you will take it away again.

**Stage a one-man show.** The added responsibility and fun of feeding himself, if he isn't already doing this, may so engage your toddler that he will lose interest in his old tricks. Admittedly, self-feeding takes longer and is often messier than adult-piloted feeding time, but your toddler's got to take this developmental step one of these days, anyway. Just make sure that everything you offer is safe to eat. Steer clear of all chokables (such as hot dogs, peanuts and other nuts, popcorn, raisins, and similar items).

**Let him play to an empty house.** If he doesn't have an audience, your child won't get as much satisfaction out of performing and may not feel compelled to perform at all. Put his food in front of him, then busy yourself in the same room. If you hear a razz, don't turn around. If you accidentally catch him in the act, don't blink an eye and certainly don't smirk.

**Bring down the curtain.** When he blows, he needs to know he's blown it. With a poker-straight face, give him a simple, firm warning, "No blowing." If the blowing continues, repeat, "No blowing," and add, "If you play with your food, I'll have to take it away." The third time he razzes, remove the meal promptly. Even if your toddler doesn't completely understand your words, he'll soon get your meaning.

# MESSY SELF FEEDING

*"I know I'm supposed to let my daughter feed herself so she can gain experience. But I can't stand the mess she makes and I always end up taking her spoon away from her."*

If a toddler with a spoon (or a fork or a bowl or a plate) can be considered armed and dangerous, you're going to have to learn how to live dangerously. There's no denying that disarming her and taking full control of the feeding process will bring any meal to a close more speedily, more efficiently, and much, much more neatly. But for a toddler, eating is not an exercise in speed, efficiency, and neatness. In addition to providing her with some nourishment, eating is an important learning experience—but only if she has the chance to feed herself.

So though she obviously isn't emulating Miss Manners as she smears, crushes, flings, and shovels food toward her mouth, self-feeding—like so many other messy activities in a toddler's life—is something parents have to grin (or grimace) and bear. In the long run, your forbearance will pay off; your toddler will become a child who is a competent self-feeder. Until that happy day dawns, however, the tips in the two previous questions on containing the mess may help. So may offering foods that stick to the spoon, not just to the ribs. Sticky foods are more likely to complete the journey from plate to mouth than foods that can easily be flung where they may. Try mashed potatoes, cottage cheese (the kind that isn't runny), chunky applesauce, oatmeal. It may also help to give your toddler some opportunity every day to play with interesting materials (such as finger paint, water, bubbles, sand, play clay). This may lessen (at least, somewhat) her need to experiment with food at mealtimes.

## CLINGING/ DEPENDENCE

*"My daughter seems too dependent on me. Every time I begin to leave the room, she starts to cry. If I turn my attention to something else, even if it's in the same room, she starts pulling at my leg and complaining."*

To a parent, it's confusing: Just when your child should be needing you less and less, she seems to need you more than ever. She appears eager to step out on her own, but pulls back as soon as she feels any pressure to be self-sufficient. Yet to a young toddler, torn between dependence and independence, between striking out on her own and staying safely by your side, this ambivalence makes perfect sense.

It's somewhat flattering to know that even as your daughter's universe expands, you're still the center of it. But it's also something of a burden—as every parent who has tried to get things

*Torn between a craving for independence and a fear of it, most toddlers still need the sense of security that comes from clinging to a parent.*

done with a leg weighed down by a twenty-pound anchor and a conscience weighed down by plaintive sobs knows. And you're not the only one hampered: Your toddler can't accomplish as much, either—physically, emotionally, socially, or developmentally—when she's clinging to you.

During this sometimes difficult transitional age, you'll need to walk a fine line between providing too much comfort and security and providing too little; between giving her all the support she needs to grow and stifling her growth by overprotecting her. She won't learn to let go overnight—it's a process that begins at birth and continues throughout childhood, adolescence, and young adulthood—but given lots of loving encouragement, she will begin loosening her hold on your leg and start making strides away from your side. Help pave the way for those strides with the following tips:

**Reassure about your return.** Some children this age still worry that when a loved one is out of sight, they're gone for good. Games that teach object permanence (the concept that an object still exists even when it's no longer in sight) may help take some of that uncertainty away—especially if you're the object. Play peek-a-boo with your toddler. Duck behind the door to the next room (or, if that's too upsetting for her, behind the sofa or a chair in the room she's in). Next ask, "Where am I?" And then poke your smiling face out and say, "Here I am!" Over the period of a week or so, gradually extend hiding time from a few seconds to half a minute to a full minute or two.

To maintain comforting contact while you're out of view, talk to your toddler ("Where did Mommy go? Where could she be?") or sing a silly ditty (such as "Where is Mommy? Where is Mommy? Where'd she go? Where'd she go? Where's your loving Mommy? Where's your loving Mommy? Here she is! Here she is!" to the tune of "Frère Jacques"). If, at first, your toddler seems unduly unnerved by this game, try hiding only your face (behind your hands, a napkin, a book) or only part of your body (behind a curtain or a door), or try hiding a teddy bear or doll instead of yourself. When your toddler starts to feel comfortable with your disappearing act, encourage her to play the game, too.[6]

**Make time for togetherness . . .**
Paradoxically, the more attention your toddler gets, the less she's likely to crave. Spending plenty of time with her—singing songs, reading books, shar-

ing tea parties, building block towers, creating collages—will eventually help her feel more secure and thus more able to spend time without you. Be sure, too, that there is plenty of physical contact during the course of the day—hugs, kisses, lap sitting, and so on.

**. . . but don't overdo it.** If you are a constantly hovering presence, you may prevent your toddler from developing independence and learning to play by herself. Start to encourage her to play independently.

**Set her up.** Before you walk away from your toddler (even if you're just walking to the other side of the same room), get her interested in an activity that will (hopefully) occupy her for the brief time you're otherwise occupied ("Why don't you feed your teddy while I make lunch?")

**Keep in touch.** Talk to her occasionally while you work; reach over and pat her head or help her fit a difficult shape into the shape-sorter.

**Keep it casual.** Sometimes parents unwittingly communicate their own feelings of anxiety to their children. Whenever you leave your toddler's side, do it with a convincing smile on your face and a light tone in your voice.

**Stay cool when she's not.** If your toddler starts to unravel when you step away from her, don't react with annoyance ("It makes me so mad when you do that!") or with pity ("Oh, you poor thing—I'm right here!"). Instead, try not to react at all. And don't let her reaction deter you from your mission. Nonchalantly say, "It's okay. I'll be right back." Though

---

6. Although it's important to encourage independence, never leave a young toddler alone in a room—unless she has been safely deposited in a play yard or crib, out of which she can't climb. If you want your toddler to get used to staying in a room without you, attempt basic training only when another adult or responsible child over the age of five is present.

she may not comprehend all the words initially, she's likely to find reassurance in your calm tone. Return with an equally casual, "Here I am, I'm back. Did you have fun?" and she will soon begin to catch on that when you leave, you always come back—as promised. Use the same phrases each time you leave and come back, and your toddler should eventually begin to feel more secure in your comings and goings.

**Let her tail you.** If your toddler insists on following you around the house (even into the bathroom), don't stop her. She has enough conflicted feelings (Do I want to be independent? Dependent?) without your adding rejection.

**Let her leave you.** Even the clingiest of toddlers will often decide to wander off (separation is only traumatic when it's your parent's idea—not when it's your own). If the two of you have been playing together and your toddler wants to go off to do something else, let her—assuming she's still safely in view. She needs to know that it's okay to leave your side.

**Build security by building self-esteem.** Nothing gives a young child a sense of security—and thus independence—like a positive sense of self. Help your toddler feel comfortable by herself by helping her feel good about herself (see page 292 for tips on building self-esteem).

**Make sure you're not dependent on her dependence.** Sometimes, parents secretly relish their children's dependence (who doesn't want to feel needed?) and unconsciously encourage it. They'll hover when they're not needed, barge in on a stuffed animal birthday party uninvited, anticipate clinginess before it occurs ("Don't cry—I'm just going to wash the dishes"). Becoming aware of any part you may be playing in this dependency cycle may make it easier to break.

**Be patient.** Your toddler's fear of being without you is rooted in a normal developmental phase, and with your love and support she will eventually grow out of it.

What if your toddler continues to cling in spite of all your efforts to make her more comfortable with brief physical separations? Let her. Matter-of-factly explain that you have to peel the carrots or there won't be any supper (or sort the laundry or there won't be any clean clothes) and go about peeling (or sorting) with her arms fast around your legs, if need be. When she sees that her attention-getting ploys regularly fail, she's likely to give them up.

Nevertheless, some degree of clinging may continue, possibly well into the preschool years, and even later. It's not unusual for a kindergartner to cling to Mommy or Daddy for a while when being dropped off at school. More exposures to other adults (in play groups, in day care, in preschool, during play dates), along with continued parental attention, will help with the maturation process, which will eventually make clinging a thing of the past.

Not all toddlers are clingy, of course. Some seem to make the leap from dependence to independence with no qualms at all. They don't cling, exhibit no separation anxiety, and love doing things on their own. For more on the independent toddler, see page 387.

# *SEPARATION ANXIETY*

*"My son cries whenever I leave the house. My husband and I left him with a baby-sitter so we could go out and celebrate our anniversary, and he cried for an hour. The baby-sitter finally had to call us to come home."*

From the moment the umbilical cord is cut, life is full of separations. With each new phase of development comes a new one. Taking solid foods eventually leads to weaning from mother's breast, crawling and walking to less need for carrying. On that long road to adulthood, countless other occasions for separation lie ahead: the first morning at nursery school, the first night of sleep-away camp, the first day of college. Helping your toddler learn how to handle separations well now will help both of you handle them better later.

A child experiencing separation anxiety exhibits pronounced distress when one or both parents leave him. This normal phase of development commonly begins in the last quarter of the first year and frequently lasts into the early months of the second year—or beyond. As with all developmental phases, though, there's a wide range of what is normal.

Separation anxiety never touches some toddlers; others develop it closer to the second birthday and suffer the anxiety well into the third year or later. The problem may be more severe in a child who's never been cared for by anyone but his parents and has had little exposure to other adults. It may also be more exaggerated in a child who's experiencing other stress in his life (moving, a new child-care situation, the arrival of a new sibling), is naturally shy and reticent or temperamentally averse to change (see page 201), or has recently been left by his parents overnight for the first time.

The following tips may help both you and your toddler cope with separations better:

▲ Take the anxiety seriously . . . React to it with understanding, patience, and confidence ("I know you don't want me to leave, but I will be back soon. I love you."), instead of with teasing ("Oh, you silly boy!") or annoyance ("You make me feel so mad when you cling like that!"). Of course, there will be times when your understanding and patience will be tested to their limits—as when you're late for an appointment, and you find yourself struggling to pry your toddler's fingers off your legs so you can escape out the door. Do your best, but remember that you're only human (a shortcoming you'll have to concede to your worshipful little toddler sooner rather than later).

▲ . . . but not too seriously. Though a toddler's pleas for you to stay with him can be pretty heart-wrenching, don't join in the melodrama. Instead, stay calm, matter-of-fact, and though sympathetic, unmoved by the histrionics.

▲ Make your toddler feel secure when you're around. Lots of love and attention when you're together makes a child feel better about any separating. During periods of intense separation anxiety (as when upheaval in his life or routine has made him even clingier), provide lots of extra tender, loving care, and don't leave him more often than you must. Don't tell yourself, "He needs to learn—and he's going to learn the hard way." He'll learn faster when you're sensitive to his feelings and needs than when you take a sink-or-swim approach.

▲ Tell him that you love him. But don't add that you'll miss him. If your toddler feels obliged to miss you back, he won't be able to enjoy himself without feeling guilt of his own.

▲ Start with short-term separations. Working on object permanence, with you as the object, will help your toddler begin to view separations as temporary (see page 19). Once he's learned to handle your disappearance behind a door or into another room, gradually work up to leaving the house for brief periods. Follow the tips on pages 22 and 23 for leaving your toddler with a baby-sitter.

## PARTING TIPS

· · · · · · · · · ·

The hardest part of leaving your toddler with a baby-sitter or a caregiver will always be saying good-bye. To make it a little easier, try the following:

▲ Get ready in advance, when possible, so you can spend time together before you separate. If you pass the last half hour before the baby-sitter arrives getting showered and dressed, your toddler may feel neglected while you're still home, and abandoned once you've left. Also try to avoid rushing around frantically at the last minute. This will not only leave you feeling frazzled but could transmit a sense of anxiety and upheaval to your toddler. At least fifteen minutes before you leave, sit down with your child and read a story, do a puzzle, or build a house with blocks. If you simply don't have the time to get ready in advance, get ready together. Set out some toys or dress-up clothes for your toddler to play with while you dry your hair and put on your clothes.

▲ Get your toddler busy before you get going. Set up an engaging activity which your toddler and the baby-sitter can enjoy doing together. Taking this approach may not keep your toddler from crying when you leave, but it will give them something to go back to once you're gone.

▲ Leave your toddler with a reminder of you. Whether it's your pillow, your afghan, a snapshot of you in a lucite frame, or a lipstick-print kiss on the back of the hand, having a little something of yours to keep close may help your toddler deal with the separation. However, if the babysitter reports that the reminder seems to make your toddler miss you more, skip it.

▲ Leave the dramatic farewell scenes to the movies. Keep your exit casual. If you're harboring feelings of apprehension or guilt, keep them well-hidden. As briefly as possible, explain to your child that you are going out, and that you'll be back soon—try to use the same lines you used on practice outings to the next room. Promise a favorite activity when you return, if she'll still be awake ("When I get home, we can read a book") or for the next morning, if she won't be, and plan to keep that promise. Choose a light parting phrase on your way out ("See you later, alligator," is a favorite; eventually, you can teach your toddler to respond, "After a while, crocodile"), and use it every time you leave the house.

▲ Have your toddler wave you on your way. If there's a window in your home that faces the street, the driveway, or the parking lot you'll be leaving from, have the baby-sitter take your toddler to it so they can wave good-bye. Even if there's a lot of sobbing with the waving or your child refuses to wave at all, smile convincingly, wave enthusiastically, and leave.

▲ Arrange for your child and the baby-sitter to leave with you, when feasible. Sometimes that's easier for a toddler. If your baby-sitter takes your toddler to the park or to a play date at a friend's house, and they leave the house with you, your child may not feel so deserted. Be sure to make it clear that you're going out, too. Otherwise, should they get home ahead of you, your toddler may be shocked to find that you're not there. What's more, she may become reluctant to leave the house without you in the future.

▲ Don't be sneaky. Though it may be tempting to slip out of the house when your toddler's not looking or fast asleep—just to avoid a scene—don't. It'll only make him more guarded and insecure next time you try to leave. Instead,

develop a "leaving" ritual that will build your toddler's confidence (see box).

▲ Hold the guilt. If you're leaving your toddler in good hands, you have nothing to feel guilty about. Guilt serves no constructive purpose in such a situation and can intensify a child's separation anxiety by giving him the impression that your leaving him is somehow wrong.

▲ Check your own anxieties. Young children pick up parental anxieties like radar. Be aware that any reluctance you may feel about leaving your toddler is transmitted to him through the expression on your face, your body language, and your tone of voice. If he picks up your anxieties, your toddler's fears will be reinforced. ("If Mommy's feeling sad about leaving me, there must be something wrong with her leaving.") Appearing ambivalent about your departure can also make your child feel guilty later on should he begin having a good time in your absence. See page 24 for tips on dealing with your anxieties.

▲ Remember that separation anxiety won't last forever. Children eventually learn to separate from their parents without a fuss, and sometimes, you may be sorry to hear, with great pleasure. When your once clingy toddler becomes a self-reliant ten-year-old, you'll likely think wistfully of the days when he was reluctant to leave your side.

▲ Don't let yourself be controlled by your child's crying, even if it reaches hysteria. One of the tough lessons to be learned in childhood is that you can't get everything you want by crying. Help your toddler start learning that lesson now by taking your leave as planned, even if he protests vigorously. But be sure that you've taken the steps outlined here and below to gradually accustom your child to being left with someone else.

▲ If the baby-sitter reports that your toddler screams regularly for most or all of the time you're away, if he refuses to go near the baby-sitter, or if he shows other signs of tension (sleep problems, anxiety), perhaps it's time to reevaluate your child-care situation (see page 822).

# THE FIRST SEPARATION

*"Believe it or not, to this point we have not left our daughter with anyone outside our family. We'd like to get a baby-sitter so we can go out together as a couple occasionally, but we're worried about how our child will react."*

Your child may react to being left in the hands of a baby-sitter more positively than you imagine. Having spent the first year of her life in the security of her parents' company, she may not find it very difficult to give up that company once in a while—once she adjusts to the idea. The following plan should help with that adjustment:

▲ First, start preparing your toddler. Vary the company she keeps. Expose her, in your presence, to other adults and children—in your home, at the playground, in a neighbor's home. Accustom her to separating from you when you're at home (see page 19) before working up to more significant separations.

▲ Second, find a baby-sitter. See page 820 for tips on choosing a baby-sitter. You will want someone who is patient, understanding, reliable, responsive, and loving under the most trying conditions. Make it clear that your toddler's never been left with a caregiver before, and that the going may be rough at first: Hire a baby-sitter who's not put off by the prospect of having to weather a few stormy evenings.

▲ Next, orient the caregiver. Spend at least an hour telling her about your toddler. Show her how you diaper her, how you calm her when she cries. Make a list of her favorite storybooks, toys, food, drinks, comfort habits, and rituals.

▲ Then, get baby-sitter and toddler together. If you're concerned about your child's reaction to being left alone, it may be worth paying for one or two practice sessions to familiarize her with her new caregiver, and vice versa. Have the baby-sitter come to the house and play with your child, or read her a story—while you look on. Then busy yourself with a task that doesn't involve your toddler, but stay in the room. When your child and the baby-sitter seem to be getting along well, go into another room. After a few minutes, return. Then leave again periodically, increasing the number of minutes you remain out of the room each time, building up to half an hour or more. If your toddler screams when she's left alone with the baby-sitter— even with you still in the house—start out more slowly, allowing your toddler to get to know the caregiver from the security of your lap before trying to edge your way out of the picture. Remain calm, supportive, and reassuring throughout the process.

If it becomes clear that your toddler's never going to take to the baby-sitter while you're in the house (no matter how many times you try to leave her, her arms remain stubbornly glued around your neck), it may be necessary to move to the next step (see below). Some toddlers won't acquiesce to a parental alternative until Mommy's and/or Daddy's departure has left them with no other choice.

▲ Finally, leave the baby-sitter and your toddler alone. Once they're on fairly good terms (or as good as it's going to get with you around, which in some cases may be awful), take a brief trip out of the house. (See the box on page 22 for parting tips.) Plan on returning in about fifteen minutes, but call first to make sure any crying has stopped. It's preferable to return once your toddler has had a chance to cheer up. If she hasn't stopped wailing after half an hour, head home anyway. Without appearing anxious or upset, calmly comfort her with a reassuring, "See? We went

away, and we came back." Greet the baby-sitter cheerfully, too, and instead of rushing her out the door, say good-bye with some fanfare, waving as she goes down the steps or gets into her car. Once the baby-sitter's gone, quickly divert your toddler with a favorite activity. Message: Parents leave, parents come back, and life goes on normally.

Don't succumb to the easy way out—having the baby-sitter arrive after your toddler is asleep for the night. Should she wake up for any reason (and it can happen on the night you go out even if it doesn't happen routinely), she'll be frightened and feel betrayed. Instead, have the baby-sitter show up while your toddler is awake. You can go through the bedtime ritual yourself with the baby-sitter looking on, and put your toddler to sleep, if you like. But should she call out for you in the middle of the night, she won't be shocked to see an unfamiliar face hovering over her crib.

# YOUR SEPARATION ANXIETY

*"My daughter doesn't seem to have any problem separating from me— I'm the one with separation anxiety."*

Separation anxiety is probably as prevalent among parents as it is among their offspring. But like your toddler, you too can learn to let go.

There are a whole host of reasons why parents are not comfortable being separated from their young children. Some of these reasons are simply instinctive (similar to the instincts that compel lionesses to protect their cubs, and hens to hover over their chicks). Others are more complex. Often, examining why you're reluctant to leave your toddler can help you come to terms with your reluctance. Here are a few of the more common reasons for parental separation anxiety:

▲ Inexperience with separation. If you haven't left your toddler with a baby-sitter until now, the sooner you get the process started, the better for both of you.

▲ Difficulty letting go. Most parents thrive on the parent–child relationship. But sometimes that relationship becomes too important—more so than anything else in the parent's life. Though this bond may make for some splendid times early on, it can eventually stifle the child's growth—as well as the parent's. However difficult it may be for you to accept, you're doing both of you a favor by occasionally leaving your toddler.

▲ Anxiety about the childcare arrangement. Can anyone be as good a caregiver as me? Will that person protect and nurture my child emotionally, physically, and intellectuälly? Actually, if you've chosen your baby-sitter well and prepared her well, your child will almost certainly be in good hands. Keep tabs on the baby-sitter, however—even if she cares for your child only a couple of hours a week—to ensure that the caregiver continues to meet your standards.

▲ Guilt about leaving. Even a parent who feels perfectly justified (for reasons financial, emotional, intellectual, or professional) in leaving a child can feel guilty. But if you give your toddler plenty of love and attention when you're at home, and leave her in a good child-care situation when you're not, you're not a bad parent. Besides, separating from your child at least once in a while can benefit her social development and yours. She'll expand her horizons by learning to interact with others (a skill that can make the transition into preschool a lot smoother), and you'll ex-

pand your horizons by interacting with other adults occasionally or on a regular basis (which will enable you to return to parenting refreshed, and to make more of the time you do spend with her).

▲ Guilt about your child's reaction to your leaving. A toddler's tearful pleas can make parents—especially those experiencing their own separation anxiety—feel guilty. On a subconscious level, your child's crying may be intended to do just that. But those tears are almost always short-lived. Once the parent walks out the door and the child faces the choice between being miserable or having fun, she's likely to opt for fun. The tears, whether real or crocodile, may make leaving harder, but they are rarely a sign that you shouldn't go. Even daily crying, as long as it ends once you've left, is nothing to worry about. If your child's crying raises concern about your child-care situation, see page 822.

▲ Memories of separation anxiety from one's own childhood. Some parents recall fears about going to school or about being left behind by their parents, and assume their own children will experience similar anxieties. That's not necessarily so. All children are different, and yours may handle separation much more easily than you did. Tagging on emotional relics from your childhood to your child's may create a problem where one does not exist.

▲ A history of prematurity, serious illness, or disability. Many parents are loathe to leave a child they feel needs them every moment, though in fact, occasional breaks will benefit everyone. Even when the child has fully recovered, many parents continue to coddle and overprotect; they often harbor the secret fear that their child will suddenly fall ill again.

▲ Jealousy of a caregiver. Though all parents want the best caregiver for their children, many harbor the secret fear that the caregiver will do a better job than they've done—and, worse still, will become the favorite person in their child's life. If that's your concern, relax. Although children almost invariably become attached to a caring substitute caregiver, there's no substitute for the real thing—and even the youngest toddler knows it. Loving parents, even those who work long hours, still manage to remain first in their little ones' hearts. For tips on handling such jealousy, see page 827.

Whatever the reason for your separation anxiety, conquering it is important not only for you but for your toddler. Anxiety is more contagious than the common cold; if you're anxious about leaving your child, your child will be anxious about being left. What's more, your discomfort could signal to her that forming attachments or having fun with other people (baby-sitters, nannies, teachers) is wrong or unsafe—a notion that could hamper her social development.

To make the first separations easier, you may prefer to leave your child with someone you know well and trust implicitly (a grandparent, an aunt, your best friend) before leaving her with a baby-sitter. Discussing your feelings in a parenting group may also help you adapt to separation—you'll find that most parents initially feel uncomfortable leaving their children but that they eventually find ways to adjust.

If your anxieties are so intense that they keep you from ever leaving your toddler with another person, talk to her doctor. Some counseling may be in order.

# RESISTANCE TO THE CUP

*"I don't know how I'm supposed to wean my daughter from the bottle when she won't take a cup."*

**S**ooner or later, all children learn to drink from a cup. The trick is getting them to do it sooner rather than later. The best time is early in the second half of the first year, when babies are still relatively pliable and drinking from a cup is a novelty rather than a necessity associated with weaning.

But even though that ideal time has passed, it's not too late to get your toddler started on the cup. Whether she has always resisted the cup or has just begun to fight it (perhaps in direct response to pressure you've been applying for her to give up her beloved bottle), these tips should help win her over:

▲ Go cup-shopping together. Let your child hold the cups you're considering buying, and allow her to pick her favorite style, color, and design. Some toddlers prefer one handle, some two, some like a spout, others want a cup with a straw built in. Then there are those who want to be grown-up like Mom and Dad and drink from what looks like a real glass. You may have to experiment with a variety of cup styles before you hit on one your child accepts. If you can, buy (or borrow) several so that your toddler can choose which cup she wants at each meal. All cups you choose should be nonbreakable; a weighted bottom, will make tipping less likely.

▲ Let your toddler get acquainted with her cup. Let her use it to feed her dolls, to serve tea to a friend, or to fill and empty in the sink (under your supervision).

▲ Put the cup first. Always offer your toddler a cup before the breast or the bottle—but hold the parental pressure. At each meal and snack, pour a small amount of a favorite beverage into a cup. Place the cup within her reach and offer it to her periodically between bites ("Here's a drink of water"). If she pushes the cup away, don't force the issue. Continue to use this no-pressure approach daily, varying the cup and the beverage. One day, possibly when she's particularly thirsty, she will surprise you and take a sip.

▲ Switch the liquid. Serving a liquid she's unaccustomed to drinking in her bottle may make her less resistant to the cup. Once she's used to the cup, you can start filling it up with her favorite fluids.

▲ Don't make weaning dependent on your toddler's acceptance of the cup. If you do, she will keep rejecting what she considers an unacceptable bottle substitute. Instead, start cutting back on bottle feedings even as she continues to reject the cup. The human body craves fluids, and ultimately your toddler will take them any way she can get them. (If she's consuming less milk during the weaning process, make sure she gets additional calcium from other sources, such as hard cheeses and full-fat yogurt; see page 506.

▲ Cover all bases. Drinking from a cup will be a messy business until your toddler becomes proficient. A large over-the-shoulder bib for your child and a plastic sheet or newspaper spread under the high chair will help handle the spills. Starting out with water or heavily watered-down juice will be less hazardous to clothing and floor. Don't make a fuss about spills, or you might give your toddler another reason to reject the cup.

# WEANING FROM THE BOTTLE

*"I know I'm supposed to start weaning my son from the bottle now that he's a year old, but he doesn't seem ready to cooperate."*

Timing may not be everything, but when it comes to weaning, it's a great deal. And weaning your toddler now would be excellent timing, for several reasons: *Dwindling flexibility.* Though he's

certainly not the putty in your hands he was six or seven months ago, your toddler's still a whole lot less set in his ways now than he will be in the months to come. Once negativity and rebelliousness start kicking in, and every issue becomes a battle of wills, enlisting his cooperation in the weaning process will be more difficult. *Waning appetite.* Bottle drinkers tend to consume unnecessarily large quantities of milk and juice. At a time when toddlers start eating less, drinking more can sabotage appetites and contribute to eating problems. *Continuing health risk.* Infants who drink their bottles flat on their backs have an increased risk of ear infections. The problem can continue for toddlers who aren't weaned from the bottle. *New health risk.* At this age, when most toddlers have at least several teeth, the bottle can start to become hazardous to dental health. Bottle-induced tooth decay, known as "baby-bottle mouth" or "nursing-bottle syndrome," occurs when milk, juice, or another naturally sweet or sweetened liquid is allowed to pool in a child's mouth routinely (as it does when he sucks on a bottle, but not when he sips from a cup), particularly during the time just before he falls asleep. The sugars in the fluids (lactose in milk and fructose in juice) are broken down by bacteria in the mouth. During the process an acid is formed, which feasts on protective tooth enamel, causing decay. Baby-bottle mouth can be severe and extensive enough to require extraction of the baby teeth and installation of a temporary replacement bridge. The cost is high both in money, and often, in self-esteem, since the toddler with missing teeth may develop speech and emotional problems. To prevent baby-bottle mouth, both the American Academy of Pediatrics and the American Academy of Pediatric Dentistry recommend weaning children from bottle to cup when they are a year old.

Of course, convincing your toddler to give up the bottle will take more than scientific evidence, professional pro-

## INTRODUCING COW'S MILK

**· · · · · · · · · ·**

Most toddlers take to cow's milk without a fuss, but an occasional child who's been on formula rejects the taste of plain cow's milk. One way to make the switch easier is to start by diluting the formula with a little cow's milk. Gradually, over a period of a few weeks, increase the proportion of cow's milk and reduce that of formula until your child is drinking pure cow's milk.

nouncements, or simple logic. As a first step, provide your child with a substitute container for his beverages: a cup. By this age, many children are already proficient at drinking from a cup. If yours is, that part of your job will be relatively easy. If not, see page 26.

Once your toddler can drink several ounces of fluid from a cup at a sitting, you can begin saying "bye-bye bottle." Choose one of the following approaches to weaning, keeping in mind how your child handles change—and how hooked he is on the bottle.

**Cold Turkey.** If your toddler is easygoing, doesn't panic in the face of change, makes transitions smoothly, isn't particularly dependent on the bottle, and is proficient with a cup, a cold-turkey approach may work. Pick a time when you anticipate no other major changes in your toddler's life—and when you will have plenty of time to devote to him. Select a day that begins well (if either of you wakes up on the wrong side of the bed, put the project off). Start the day with the announcement, proclaimed with great fanfare, that he's a big boy now, and like all big boys ("just like cousin Josh" or "just like Daddy"), he can drink all his milk and juice from a cup (cheers and applause). Take him to the store and let him help you select several new cups in the style he likes best, with fun designs and bright colors. At home have him help you throw his bottles and nipples into the recycling bin. (Save one or

two bottles to be used for play—as bath tub toys or when "feeding" baby dolls or stuffed animals.) During weaning, your toddler may be a little more cranky and sensitive than usual, and thumb-sucking may increase (or begin). Give him plenty of extra time and attention, and lots of hugs to make up for the comfort he's no longer getting from the bottle. If your toddler remains unfazed at losing his bottle and makes no serious requests for it over the next few days, you can consider yourself lucky and the process complete.

If, however, he starts to have second thoughts and begins begging for a bottle (he might do so at bedtime, or at whatever time of the day taking a bottle has meant a lot to him), borrow back the bottle you've saved for play, wash it, fill it with water, and offer it to him. Tell him that he can have a bottle of water whenever he wants (water won't damage his teeth). Stand tough, though. If he asks for his accustomed milk or juice served up in the bottle, say firmly that those beverages will only be available in a cup from now on.

**Gradual withdrawal.** For most children, this multistep approach works best.[7]

1. Once your toddler is comfortable drinking from a cup, offer him beverages

---

7. If a baby-sitter or other caregiver is with your toddler part- or full-time, involve her in the weaning process as well.

(milk, juice, or water) in a cup and solid foods at meal and snack times before he starts asking for his bottle, not when he's already whining for it. Sometimes a full tummy and a quenched thirst may satisfy him enough and he won't press for the bottle.

2. Make drinking from the bottle less appealing. Insist that your toddler take his bottle while sitting on your lap or in a particular chair instead of allowing him to drink from it as he plays or explores. When he wants to get up, tell him that's the end of the bottle session. Do not allow him to wander off with a bottle in hand.

3. Over the span of a couple of weeks, cut down on the number of bottles given. Drop the one your child shows the least interest in first, and the most beloved bottle last.

4. Make changes in your toddler's routine that help phase out the bottle. Have him spend as much time as possible away from home, in situations that are not likely to remind him of bottle-feeding and in locales that are entertaining enough to keep his mind off it (a children's museum, a mall, the playground, an already-weaned friend's house). At home, keep your youngster busier than usual. Offer him more one-on-one attention and more diverting activities (finger-painting and ring-stacking will give him something to do with his hands; taking a nature walk will engage his mind and his body; free play outdoors will help tire him out). Whenever possible, try changing the rituals that have become associated with bottle-feeding. At nap time, for example, relax your toddler with quiet music instead of with a bottle. If he's always taken a bottle at bedtime, substitute a snack of milk and fruit-juice-sweetened cookies. If you've always comforted him with a bottle after a fall or when he's otherwise upset, put him on your lap for a finger-game session instead.

5. Gradually work down to one bottle a day. The most treasured bottle of the day should be the last to go. If your toddler is like most children, this will be the one he enjoys before going to sleep at night.

Before eliminating this last bottle, be sure you have a comforting bedtime routine in place (see page 68 for more on bedtime routines). Include in this a cup of milk and a nonsugary snack (before brushing the teeth), a bath, and a few quiet stories. Don't offer the bottle automatically. If your toddler asks for it, distract him with an offer of water in a cup ("You can't have milk now because we've already brushed your teeth"). Take a firm stand on the no-milk-in-a-bottle issue. If your toddler pleads for a bottle, give him one filled only with water. There are two benefits to this measure. One, you eliminate the risk of tooth decay because he won't be falling asleep with milk pooled in his mouth. And two, you increase the chances that he will abandon the bottle on his own— most children eventually do when the bottle is no longer filled with milk or juice. If your child is an exception and he seems to like his bottle of water, allow him to continue with it at night for a few weeks. Then change the nipple to one with very tiny holes, so that sucking on it for water will hardly be worth the effort. That should get him to voluntarily abandon the bottle.

Expect your toddler to be cranky and out-of-sorts during the weaning process. He's lost a dear friend and he'll need lots of support as he tries to adjust to the loss and to the changes it brings. Offer him comfort, attention, and distraction in ample amounts, particularly during the times of day when he's likely to miss his bottle the most. Encourage him to take a substitute comfort item to bed—a friendly old teddy bear or doll (or a brand-new one), a cuddly blanket or an old pajama top of yours.

# HOW TO WEAN FROM THE BREAST

• • • • • • • • • •

Sudden weaning from the breast at a year might not be as physically uncomfortable for the nursing mother as earlier weaning would have been. Since a toddler takes in more solids, milk production slows considerably at this time, making engorgement a less likely side effect. Still, gradual weaning generally works best for both members of most nursing teams because it allows mother and child time to adjust to the end of this very special era.

The adjustment will also be easier if you make a concerted effort to give your toddler extra love and attention during weaning. Replace the time you've spent together nursing with other one-on-one activities. Don't show disapproval if your toddler replaces the comfort of breastfeeding with another comfort habit (such as thumb-sucking) or comfort object (such as a blanket or stuffed animal). Children need all the support they can get at this stage.

Weaning now may be relatively easy (if you and your baby are both ready for the step) or relatively difficult (if you're both still strongly attached to nursing). In either case, the following guidelines will help:

**Step One:** Be sure your toddler can drink fairly well from a cup (see page 26).

**Step Two:** Choose the time carefully. Don't begin weaning if your toddler's going through other major changes (meeting a new baby-sitter, starting day care, gaining a new sibling) or when he or she is sick or otherwise out of sorts. Wait until all is relatively calm in your toddler's life before beginning.

**Step Three:** Save the breast for last (except at bedtime). When your child wakes up in the morning or from a nap or is hungry for a meal, offer a beverage from a cup, or a snack, or a meal of solid food first. When the edge is off the appetite, if your toddler still clamors for the breast, oblige. Gradually, milk intake will decrease, which in turn will reduce your milk supply, making you more comfortable as you wean.

**Step Four:** Nurse before, rather than after, the regular bedtime routine (bath, pajamas, story, snack, tooth-brushing, and so on). Try to keep your toddler from falling asleep at the breast—by playing lively music, talking, singing, having other people in the room—and encourage a self-comforting route to dreamland (see page 143).

**Step Five:** Cut back on the number of daily feedings. Start with those in which your toddler shows the least interest, usually the midday ones. This process will probably take several weeks. Changing your daily habits, which means taking your toddler to places where nursing hasn't been routine (shopping, to the playground or a play group, to a museum, and so on), will make it easier. Eventually cut down to just one feeding—the favorite. In most cases, this will be the one at bedtime, though some toddlers are most attached to the first morning feeding. If at any point your breasts become engorged, hand express a small amount to relieve the pressure.

**Step Six:** Drop the remaining feeding. One way to make this final stop easier is have Daddy or Grandma put your toddler to sleep for a couple of nights—while you're out of the house. Or make the switch when the family's visiting relatives or on vacation; if you're in a place your toddler doesn't associate with nursing, he or she may not crave it as much. Distraction—in the form of a new toy, book, tape recording, or special visitor—may also be helpful.

If you're in no hurry to wean, you may prefer to put this final step off for a while. Many women and their toddlers continue to enjoy one breastfeeding a day for weeks or even longer. (In some cases, however, this isn't possible because the milk supply quickly dries up because of inadequate demand.)

# WHEN TO WEAN FROM BREASTFEEDING

*"I thought babies were supposed to wean themselves from the breast when they were ready. My daughter is past her first birthday and doesn't seem to be showing any sign of wanting to stop."*

If you wait until your daughter decides she's ready to graduate to a more grown-up source of liquid nourishment, you may have a very long wait ahead. Though some babies and toddlers cut back on or discontinue breastfeeding on their own, usually near the end of the first year, others never do. So unless you want to see her rush home from school for a snack at the breast, you should consider initiating the weaning process yourself. (See box, facing page).

*"My son seems ready to stop nursing, but I'm not. I don't want to see his baby stage end."*

Watching a child move from one stage of development to another is always a bittersweet experience—filling you at once with pride (how grown-up he is!) and with melancholy (he'll never be a baby again!). Some rites of passage evoke more mixed feelings than do others. For many women, weaning their children from the breast is one of those.

Breastfeeding is an undeniably gratifying experience, but breastfeeding indefinitely because *you're* not ready to give it up isn't fair. If your toddler wants to move on, follow his lead. Don't take his rejection of your breast personally. He isn't rejecting you, he's rejecting the babyhood he's outgrown, and taking another step toward independence. As un-

settling as that may be for you, it's a step he must take.

It's likely that at first you will miss the physical closeness to your toddler that nursing provided. But if you think about it, there are a host of other activities (hugging, cuddling, playing together, reading together before bed, and so on) that reproduce that closeness. Enjoy those more frequently instead.

Because the sadness you're feeling may be intensified by the haywire hormonal changes that weaning can trigger, you should consider weaning gradually over a period of weeks or even months (see box, facing page). Give both your body and your mind plenty of time to recover and they eventually will.

*"I'd really like to continue nursing my son for at least the next year or so. Why should I wean him when neither of us is ready yet?"*

Your feelings and those of your toddler are important factors to consider in deciding when to wean. But other factors merit consideration as well. You will have to weigh these against your own reasons for wanting to continue breastfeeding:

**Expert Opinion.** Most pediatricians and pediatric dentists recommend weaning at a year; their reasons are included in the following list.

**Your toddler's age.** Weaning at a year is ideal. Nutritionally and emotionally the toddler who has nursed for a year has already gotten the optimum benefit from breastfeeding. In addition, he probably has not yet reached the opinionated "terrible twos" and will be easier to wean than an older, more stubborn and set-in-his-ways toddler. Finally, because his year-old memory is less retentive, he is less likely to cling to fond memories of the breast, which could make weaning more painful.

**Your toddler's dietary needs.** Both the composition of breast milk and the nutritional needs of the growing child alter by the end of the first year. Breast milk alone can no longer meet a child's nutritional requirements—in fact, some recent studies indicate that children who are nursed beyond this point may not do as well as those who are weaned. Though more research needs to be done in this area, it does seem clear that there are no nutritional benefits to nursing now. So if you choose to continue nursing during the second year, you can no longer think of your milk as your toddler's main source of nourishment—but rather as a little something extra.

**The effect on his teeth.** Though the problem is apparently more common among children who are bottle-fed, breastfed toddlers are not immune to "baby-bottle mouth." The risk of decay, in this case caused by breast milk pooling in the mouth, is more likely if your toddler falls asleep regularly with the breast still in his mouth, and most likely if he nips on and off through the night (as those who are allowed to sleep in their parents' bed tend to do). If you do continue to nurse, you can reduce the risk of decay by nursing only during the day, and by cleaning your toddler's teeth after each feeding.

**The effect on your toddler's appetite.** Toddlers who feed at the breast (or bottle) frequently may drown their appetites for solid foods, which they need in order to thrive in the second year of life.

**The effect on mother–child interaction.** Sometimes mothers get so much pleasure from breastfeeding that they don't realize that they aren't spending enough time doing other things with their toddler—playing games, reading stories, going to the playground. Once your child is weaned you'll have more time and energy for these fun activities.

**Possible health risks.** There is some evidence that feeding (from bottle or breast) while lying on the back results in an increased incidence of ear infections (otitis media) in babies and toddlers.

**Possible overdependence.** Of toddler on mother, and/or of mother on toddler. This isn't a clear-cut issue. Although there have been no scientific studies to support this concern, it's worth thinking about: Will prolonging nursing keep you and your toddler from "letting go" of each other and moving forward? Also worthy of your consideration: Does this exclusive relationship exclude Daddy, preventing the two of them from growing closer?

**Forestalled development of self-comforting skills.** A toddler who can always turn to Mommy's breast for comfort (when he hurts himself, when he's tired, when he can't have what he wants), may not learn how to make himself feel better when Mommy's not available. Your child will undoubtedly need such skills later in life—particularly after weaning.

**The effect on your spousal relationship.** Breastfeeding that continues well into the second year, especially if it's taking place in your bed, can easily come between you and your spouse. Besides making spousal intimacy inconvenient at best, it may, on a subconscious level satisfy both emotional and physical needs for closeness, diminishing your interest in sex. Your refusal to wean can also be interpreted by your spouse as a way of saying that your toddler is more important to you. (Remember, your spouse is yours for life. Your toddler will grow up, leave home, and eventually find a partner of his own. Save some nurturing for your partner. See page 771.)

# PLAYYARD REJECTION

*"I used to rely on the playyard to keep my son safe and happy while I did some things around the house. Now every time I put him in there he screams to come out."*

To a newly mobile toddler, eager to explore and discover, being relegated to the play yard is like being sentenced to prison—it's no wonder he screams for his freedom. So give it to him. Of course, to do this, you will have to toddler-proof at least one room in your home (and preferably the entire home; see page 620). But even in a toddler-proof setting, you will have to increase your surveillance, providing the supervision that the playyard once did. In other words, with more freedom for him, there will be less freedom for you.

If you find it difficult to get your work done with your toddler on the loose, consider tackling tasks when he's napping or when someone else is on guard duty. (See page 830 for more tips on keeping your toddler busy while you get things done.)

# CAT NAPPING

*"The only time my daughter naps is when she's in the stroller or the car. Not only don't these brief naps give her enough rest, they don't allow me to get anything done while she sleeps."*

Cat naps may be fine for feline moms and their kittens, but they tend not to do the trick for their human counterparts. The average one-year-old isn't able to fill her sleep requirements at night and generally needs two naps of approximately an hour each during the day, one in the morning and one in the afternoon. However, a small percentage of toddlers, much to their parents' dismay, manage very well with a few fifteen-minute snoozes interspersed throughout the day, a few need only one nap, and a few need naps much longer than average.

When children don't get all the shut-eye their bodies need, they are often crankier, more irritable, and more easily frustrated by life's challenges. And their parents, who need the respite their child's nap offers, may also be crankier, more irritable, and more easily frustrated, too.

It isn't easy to nip a cat-napper's habit; sometimes it's impossible. But you have nothing to lose by trying. The following tips may help:

▲ **Start each day at the same time.** Waking your toddler up at the same time each morning may prompt her to tire at about the same time each afternoon. (See page 143 for suggestions on how to regulate morning waking.)

▲ **End each day at the same time.** Erratic bedtimes can lead to erratic napping patterns. Training your toddler to be tired at particular times during the day requires regulating her sleep.

▲ **Head off exhaustion.** Some children become so excited over their new mobility and the opportunities that come with it, that they're reluctant to stop for a rest. Overdoing so overtires that they can't fall asleep easily. Try to keep your toddler from reaching that point. Periodically, encourage her to break from her more-active activities for some less-active ones (drawing, block building, story time)—particularly during the half hour or so before you'd like her to nap.

▲ **Pick a sleepy time.** Examine your toddler's energy pattern during the day to discover when she seems at low ebb and therefore most likely to be able to fall asleep. For most toddlers, this will be the early afternoon.

▲ Create a sleepy mood. Begin developing a nap time routine just as you would a bedtime routine. Start with a soporific snack (milk and a couple of fruit-juice-sweetened cookies or crackers). Then dim her room (install room-darkening shades, if necessary), and in the soft light of a lamp, read her a quiet story or two. With tranquil music playing in the background, tuck her into her crib, sing a lullabye, whisper a few comforting words to her (and a prayer to yourself), and quietly withdraw before the spell is broken. Even if she doesn't fall asleep at all the first few times, stick to this routine for at least a week or two before you give up. She may come to accept the ritual and may eventually learn to fall asleep on cue. Or she may be happy just to rest quietly for twenty minutes or half an hour.

▲ Ease the separation anxiety that naptime may cause. The separation from you that sleep represents may be one reason why your toddler fights her naps. So in addition to her favorite comfort objects, give her a little piece of "you" to take to bed with her: a sweater, T-shirt, or sweatshirt that you wear during the nap time story and then turn over to her, or a pillow or quilt from your bed can be the next best thing to having you next to her in the crib.

▲ If you can't beat her, join her. If you simply can't get your toddler to sleep in her crib, try to get her to sleep longer in the stroller by pushing it for an hour outdoors (many stroller nappers wake up the minute you step into a store or other indoor space). This approach may not only extend her naps but it will give you a healthy dose of daily aerobic exercise (particularly if you keep up a good pace). Of course, you won't be able to get anything else done, but chores should be somewhat less difficult to accomplish later on, with a more rested child about the house.

# LANGUAGE LAG

*"I've heard other one-year-olds saying real words, but my son really doesn't say anything anyone can understand."*

Just because you can't *understand* a word your toddler is saying doesn't mean he isn't *saying* a word. Speech needn't be intelligible to count as legitimate language development, particularly at this tender age, and even well into the second year.

Children use two kinds of "practice" language. One sounds like gibberish, but is actually referred to as "jargon" by professionals. A toddler's jargon may not sound like the parent tongue to parents, but it does to the toddler who utters it. Listen carefully to your child when he rambles on in this seemingly meaningless way, and you'll probably notice that his gibberish has the same rhythmic patterns and inflections as spoken English. Speaking jargon satisfies a toddler's need to have an adult-like conversation (at least to his ear), even with his limited linguistic abilities.

The other kind of practice speech young toddlers use consists of single- or double-syllable sounds. Usually these sounds take on meaning for the child long before his parents have broken the code. "Ba" may mean bottle, "uh" up, "da" that. At first, single syllables may also stand for complete thoughts. For example, "Da" could mean "Give me that" or "What is that?" The first intelligible words may also be multipurpose. "Da-da" may mean Daddy, but it might also be used to call Mommy, the baby-sitter, even the dog. "Ma-ma" could, at different times, mean, "I want Mama," "That is Mama," "Feed me, Mama," or "Pick me up, Mama."

Lend your toddler an attentive ear, and you may be surprised at how much of what he says you can understand. (Or, you may remain just as perplexed by his utterings, and that's okay, too.) Remember, it takes years of practice to make perfect speech, and many toddlers are too busy practicing other skills, especially their newly found mobility, to practice speaking. Verbal conquests often go on the back burner while physical conquests gather steam.

Most children utter their first word sometime between ten and fourteen months. But it isn't unheard of for a child to say a word or two as early as eight months. Nor is it unusual for a child not to have comprehensible speech until eighteen months. Many factors contribute to where within the wide range of normal an individual toddler will fall:

**Heredity.** Children usually follow the speech patterns of one of their parents. Asking your parents about your language development may provide some clues to how your toddler's will develop. Some children have early receptive language (that is, they understand much of what is said to them), but are late talkers because their mouth and tongue muscles are genetically destined to develop more slowly.

**Birth order.** A first child may begin speaking early, both because his parents have more time to encourage him and because he has no siblings to compete with verbally. Sometimes children with older siblings are slower to speak either because they can't get a word in edgewise or because the older sibs anticipate the younger's needs, thereby making speech unnecessary. But this isn't always the case. Sometimes, the extra verbal stimulation provided by older siblings can prompt the younger child to use language sooner rather than later.

**Gender.** On the average, girls speak earlier than boys. This may be due in part to inborn differences and in part to the parental tendency to verbalize more with daughters than with sons (parents often emphasize the acquisition of physical skills over verbal ones with their male offspring). Of course, some girls will end up speaking later than the boys in their play group, and some boys will be the first on the block to put their thoughts into words. Averages, after all, take into account wide variations.

**The language environment.** Children are more likely to speak earlier when they are exposed to a rich verbal environment and given plenty of opportunity and encouragement to hone their verbal skills.[8] If a family speaks more than one language at home, or if a caregiver speaks a different language to your toddler, the child's verbal development is often temporarily slowed (not certain which language to speak, he may hesitate to speak either), though in the long run he may become fluent in both tongues.

**Child-care arrangement.** Where and with whom the child spends most of his day can make a big difference. Children in day care often learn to speak earlier out of necessity; their needs may not be regularly anticipated the way they are when they're in a one-to-one child-care situation. Spending all day socializing with other children, many of whom may be older and more verbal, may also encourage toddlers in day care to begin to talk sooner.

**Receptive language development.** Before a toddler learns to speak he has to be able to understand the words of others. Most children start to understand some of what is said to them well before the end of the first year. It's usually clear from his response that a one-year-old comprehends such statements as, "Do you want a drink?" "Let's go out," and "No, don't touch." So even the child

---

8. Such encouragement is very different from pressure to perform, which is not a good idea (see page 454).

who hasn't uttered a word may be busy building language skills.

**Individual timetables.** Into the pot of factors that affect language development must be stirred a child's individuality. Each child develops verbally, as in all other areas of development, at his own speed. The moment at which the toddler utters his first truly recognizable word can vary from well before the end of the first year to well into the second. Some toddlers spout sentences before they can walk, others don't put two words together until they are about to celebrate their second birthday. Although early talkers tend to be bright, late bloomers aren't necessarily slow. By the time they enter school, some late talkers catch up with and even surpass their verbally precocious peers.

Don't feel anxious or guilty because your child's a late talker. As long as you are exposing him to the spoken word (see the facing page), you're doing your job. The rest must take its natural course.

If your child doesn't attempt to vocalize at all, and especially if he doesn't seem to understand what you're saying, he may have a hearing deficit or other problem. Report your concerns to his doctor or nurse-practitioner.

# CONVERSATION FRUSTRATION

*"We try hard to understand our son, but his jargon is beyond us. This really seems to upset him, and we don't know what to do about it."*

Anyone who's ever visited a foreign country without being able to speak the language can understand the frustration of not being understood. The toddler who can't yet speak your language has an even tougher time communicating than the tourist. He has no phrase book, after all, to help him struggle through, and he has a low

---

## GENERALIZING

Most of the toddler's early words are the "names" of people or things. But because they lack experience, toddlers often overgeneralize (what scientists call "overextending"). If that gray-haired man with wrinkles at the corners of his eyes is "Gra-pa," then all gray-haired men are "Gra-pa." If a cow is a "moo," then all other farm animals are also "moo," or if a four-legged animal with a tail is called a "dog," then so are cats. Do you correct? Or ignore? Actually, a little of both. "That's very good. That animal does have four legs and a tail, just like a cow. And she lives on a farm. But she's a sheep and she says 'baa' instead of 'moo.'" "You're right. That gray-haired man does look like Grandpa, but he has a different name. May-

be he's someone else's grandpa." In time, your little one will start recognizing the differences among similar things and people. But probably not before he or she has thoroughly embarrassed you by pointing to every man in the bank and screeching, "Da-da."

Though most children overextend, some begin language development by doing the opposite: over-restricting. Instead of calling all reading materials (newspapers, magazines, letters) "books," such a child may use "book" to refer only to the bedtime storybook that's read every night. "Stroller" may refer only to the toddler's own stroller. Like overextending, over-restricting disappears as a child's language becomes more sophisticated.

threshold for the frustration that's bound to result when the jargon that seems so clear to him is misinterpreted by others.

As his jargon evolves into distinguishable single words, clumps of words, and finally, sentences, your youngster's frustration—and yours—will ease. In the meantime, as you help him move more speedily toward mastery of his parent tongue, be especially understanding of his need to be understood.

For starters, listen carefully. There may be more to his gibberish than initially meets your ear. Look carefully, too, as you listen. Facial expressions (a smile, a pout, a raised eyebrow) and body language (drooping shoulders, stomping feet, folded arms, pointing fingers) can often be very telling. Avoid interrupting your toddler out of impatience—let him spit out what he has to say no matter how long it takes. Pay attention even if you don't understand. It may help to ask him to "show me what you want with your hands" or "take me where you want to go." If you become frustrated yourself, try not to let it show—this will only compound his own frustrations. And use the tips that follow to encourage language development.

# WHAT IT'S IMPORTANT TO KNOW: Getting Your Toddler Talking

Language is vital. It allows a child to not only communicate with others but to think to himself. It's the primary tool for learning, as well as for creativity.

Fortunately, babies are born communicators. Since their earliest needs are limited to food, sleep, and comfort, crying says it all in the first few weeks: A wail brings breast or bottle, a pair of caressing arms, a dry diaper. Soon, as the infant begins to seek attention and companionship, too, cooing begins to supplement crying. Two effective means of communication have evolved. As the baby's drive to communicate becomes stronger, coos give way to sounds, then groups of sounds uttered singly (most children have one or two at a year), word-like jargon, then real words, groups of real words, and finally complete sentences. In the space of about two years a crying infant becomes a talking toddler, picking up, on average, 200 words[9]—almost half of the 500 words used most frequently in typical adult conversation. By age three, the average toddler's vocabulary has swelled fivefold to an average of some 1,000 words. That number more than doubles by the time a child is ready for kindergarten.

This natural evolution takes place on an individual timetable. From the cradle, some babies spend more time trying to engage those around them in social exchanges than they do trying to master physical feats, and as a result, they're usually early talkers. For others, physical challenges consume more time and attention. These babies are often too busy rolling over, pulling up, climbing, and taking steps to focus on communicating. They'll tackle verbal skills later on in the second and third years, when their fast-talking peers will be focusing on any physical skills they've neglected.

No matter what timetable they're running on, however, children learn to

---

9. The normal range, however, is from a couple of dozen words to 400 or more.

speak faster with a little help. Here are some guidelines for providing such help:

**Expand experiences.** Long before toddlers begin speaking, they build up receptive vocabularies, storing words and concepts in their heads. This means that children understand many words and concepts before using them in speech. So expose your toddler to a wide variety of environments (the supermarket, playground, library, mall, museums, buses, boatyards, farms) and talk about what you both see using simple language. Follow up a new experience with a library book that reinforces it: Reading a book about the zoo ("remember the monkey we saw?") after a visit, for instance, will enhance learning. Build your toddler's grasp of simple concepts (big and little, wet and dry, up and down, in and out, empty and full, standing and sitting, happy and sad, light and dark, good and bad), and cause-and-effect (we put water on the burner and it gets hot, we put it in the refrigerator and it gets cold, we put it in the freezer and it freezes hard). And regularly stimulate the senses, talking about the colors, textures, sounds, and smells found in your child's environment.

**Talk, talk, talk.** For children to use language, they must first understand language. And to understand language, a child must hear it spoken—over and over again. To get your child to talk, you've got to talk. So keep talking, even if you feel silly holding a one-sided conversation, even if you sense that your toddler doesn't have the slightest notion about what you're saying. On a stroll to the park, remark on the blue sky, the red car, the girls playing ball, the man pushing the baby stroller. While you're cooking dinner, give your toddler a blow-by-blow account as you cut the carrots, stir the soup, slice the tomatoes. When you're waiting on line at the bank, give your toddler a running account of people remaining in front of you, counting down

as you move up. When dressing your child in the morning, name his or her body parts as you uncover and cover them; identify each piece of clothing and its color and texture.

But don't get carried away, chattering on endlessly just for the sake of exposing your child to language. Children also need periods of quiet contemplation, a chance to listen to themselves instead of others, to observe what's around them without the help of a tour guide. When you're being tuned out (the eyes are turned elsewhere or glazed), turn it off. There's such a thing as auditory overload.

**Read, read, read.** Reading to your child from picture books—stopping to point out familiar objects in each picture and explain what is going on in the story—provides invaluable exposure to language. Stick to simple stories at first, and to ear-catching rhymes. Toddlers love to hear the same books over and over again, perhaps because they inherently recognize the value of repetition as a way of learning. See page 101 for more on reading to your toddler.

**Sing, sing, sing.** Children naturally love music and will pay close attention to simple songs. Sing to them a cappella or along with a tape recording or an instrument, if you play one, such as a piano or guitar. In particular, toddlers enjoy songs that include hand clapping or finger play (such as "Patty-cake" and "the Itsy Bitsy Spider"). Again, repetition helps a toddler's vocabulary grow, so don't hesitate to sing the same songs over and over. (You probably will be urged to, anyway, whether you like it or not.) And don't worry about your singing ability (or lack of it); your toddler will gladly lend you an ear, even if you do sing out of tune.

**Label, label, label.** There are thousands of words in the English language, and your toddler has to learn them one at a time. The best way to teach them is through labeling. Label things you see on the street (truck, bicycle, traffic light, man, woman, dog), at home (table, chair, sofa, juice, cup, spoon), while reading (cow, girl, farm, duck, frog). Once you've named an object, encourage your toddler to repeat it. ("This is a book. Can you say 'book?'")

**Sound like a grown-up.** Out of the mouths of babes (or rather, toddlers) come some of the cutest words: sketti (spaghetti), ta-too (thank you), ba-bo (apple). The temptation is great to mimic these adorable utterances when conversing with your toddler, but hearing you use baby talk may confuse your toddler and won't help his or her language development. Using such diminutives as "doggy," however, shouldn't be a problem.

**Lend an ear.** Toddlers love chattering to themselves as they play and don't require a full-time audience. But when they direct their chatter at someone else, they (like anyone else) need to feel they're being listened to. When your toddler addresses you, give him the respectful attention he deserves. Don't pick up the phone, turn to speak to your husband, continue to read the newspaper or watch TV, or walk into the next room. Stop, make eye contact, and listen, even if you don't completely understand what's being said (see page 424).

**Sharpen her ear.** Sharpening your toddler's auditory acumen will help with deciphering the nuances of language. Listening to conversation is important, but so is listening to the birds singing, the telephone ringing, the buzzer buzzing, to sirens and running water. Point out these sounds and listen to them together.

**Speak when you're spoken to.** Even you if you don't have the slightest idea of what your toddler has just said, you can respond with, "Hmm, that's very in-

teresting" or "Is that so?" But before you write off what your toddler is saying as gibberish, try to read body language, facial expressions, and other visual clues. If he's headed for the door, sweater in hand, an appropriate response might be: "Would you like to go out? We'll be going out in a few minutes." Is she rubbing her eyes and whining? Then try, "Are you tired? Do you want to take a nap now?" Is he gesturing or pointing at the refrigerator while talking? If so, ask, "Do you want a drink? Do you want a piece of cheese?" Sometimes you'll guess right, and even if you don't, your child will be delighted that you responded. When you just don't get it, there may be frustration and tears. Either way, immediate feedback will provide your toddler with the motivation to keep speaking.

**Provide air time.** Sometimes young children don't speak because they aren't given the opportunity—either because their needs are anticipated before they express them, or because everyone around them is always talking, hogging the air time. So be careful to leave an occasional opening for your littlest conversationalist. Eventually, it will get filled.

**Once more, with feeling.** Repeating what your toddler says in other words ("You want milk?" "Yes, that is a doggy." "You want to go out?") does double duty. It shows you understood what he or she said and also gives you an opportunity to correct mispronunciations in a natural, nonjudgmental way. Using an animated, conversational tone of voice, with plenty of rises and falls, helps to maintain interest.

**Ask away.** Researchers have found that even before toddlers are capable of supplying answers, asking them questions is one of the best ways to spur their language development. A good way to begin is to give a youngster who has few words but can shake yes, nod no, grunt, and point the opportunities to give these simple responses ("Do you want your snack now?" "Show me which book you want to read?").

As your child becomes more verbal, you can try for more verbal responses. If your toddler points at a ball or motions toward a book, don't hand the desired object over immediately. Instead, ask "What do you want?" If any sound is forthcoming, interpret it as a request for the desired object and say, "Oh, you want the ball" or "You'd like to look at this book?" If you don't get a response, don't press for one. Instead, help out with another question: "Do you want this ball . . . or this book?" Accept a grunt, nod, or pointing finger as an answer, but then translate it into words for your toddler: "Ah, you want the book. Here it is."

When your child initiates a conversation, instead of simply restating what you think has been said, ask for more information. "Do you want to go out?" Pause to allow for a reply. "Where would you like to go?" Pause again. "Would you like to go to the park?" But don't put on too much pressure and never insist on getting an answer. If your toddler gets uptight when you ask questions, you're probably overdoing it.

**Get your words' worth.** When you speak to your toddler, try to use each word in several ways. "See the bicycle? The boy is on the bicycle. The boy is riding the bicycle." Or "Look at that bird up in the sky. See, the bird is flying. The bird is flying high in the sky." Do the same when he speaks a word. "Yes, that's a flower. The flower is pink. The flower is pretty. The flower smells so good. (Sniff.) Do you like flowers?" Expand and elaborate by adding descriptive adjectives ("the furry dog," "the big book," "the funny song") and adverbs ("he's walking fast," "they are talking loudly," "she's eating slowly").

**Keep it simple.** Few young toddlers can follow long complicated sentences, comprehend all pronouns, and make sense out of irregular verbs. They also tend to get lost when words come at them fast and furious. Could you understand a movie spoken in French with just a year of high-school French under your belt? Remember, your toddler has had only one year of English. Speaking distinctly, audibly, slowly, and simply makes it easier for a toddler to catch on to meanings and language mechanics—and, eventually, to parrot back speech.

**Act as translator.** Though you may not always understand your toddler as well as you'd like to, you probably understand him or her better than anyone else does. So step in as interpreter in your toddler's verbal exchanges with others, translating what they say into language your toddler can more readily understand, and translating (to the best of your ability) what your toddler says in response. But don't step in unless it's clear that you're needed; let the communicators have a chance to understand each other on their own first.

**Support free speech.** Don't be tempted to turn your toddler into your very own Eliza (or Ezra) Doolittle. Your job is to encourage, not push. Besides, anything that toddlers feel external pressure to do, they feel internal pressure to resist—speaking included. When your child is ready, that spigot of speech will open—and it's likely to flow freely.

Remember that toddlers do the best they can with pronunciation, pronouns, plurals, and other rules of grammar. It will take several years before your toddler comes close to getting it "right." Your carping and correcting not only won't help, it may hurt. Although you should use correct pronunciations when you repeat misspoken words or can explain that the animal jumping over the moon is a cow and not a dog, your tone should be friendly and supportive, not critical. You shouldn't penalize your child for incorrect usage or for nonverbal requests ("Sorry, you can't have that doll unless you ask for it correctly!"). Children who learn to anticipate criticism every time they speak often just decide not to say anything. Your toddler will learn best by hearing the correct speech of others in an easygoing atmosphere.

Remember, too, that your toddler may often hear and repeat words that he or she doesn't fully understand. "I promise" from a toddler probably doesn't mean what *you* think it means. It isn't until the school years that you can count on children to say what they mean and mean what they say.

**Be a cheerleader.** When your toddler says a word you understand or points to the dog in the book and remarks, "Woof-woof," be sure to reinforce positively with a few words of praise ("Very good! That is a dog.") Don't go overboard with adulation, however, or he or she will begin to doubt your sincerity; even a toddler can figure out that being able to say "bottle" or "out," though an important step, isn't the world's greatest achievement. Some may be overwhelmed when their utterances are met by too much fanfare, and may choose to stop uttering.

If your child's language development is within the normal range (see page 34), but is slower than average or slower than that of a sibling or peer, don't worry. Language development is not a sure sign of intellectual ability; in children who are otherwise alert and responsive and have had plenty of verbal stimulation at home, it's more often related to genetic predisposition than intelligence. Of course, if your toddler's language development lags behind normal, you should check it out with his or her doctor or nurse-practitioner. This slower rate of linguistic development may be perfectly normal for your child. If not, early intervention can often help to overcome or reduce language delay.

# WHAT IT'S IMPORTANT FOR YOUR TODDLER TO KNOW:
## Other People Have Rights

The British Empire had nothing on toddlers. The sun rises and sets on them, the world revolves around them. Playmates, parents, grandmas and grandpas, baby-sitters, playmates, even pets—all exist to do the toddler's bidding. Their wishes are paramount, their needs are nonnegotiable, their feelings are the only ones that count.

That these little imperialists have a lot to learn about the rights of others is certain. That it's a tough lesson that will take years to learn is also certain. But you can get started by observing these principles now:

▲ Don't play the martyred parent. Part of being a parent is putting your child's needs before your own—most of the time. Putting his or her needs before your own *all* of the time can have two undesirable outcomes. One, it can make you feel put upon and, eventually, resentful—even if you are the most devoted

## OTHER PEOPLE HAVE FEELINGS, TOO

**I**t may be too early to expect a toddler to stop treating playmates like objects, but it isn't too early to start teaching that these "objects" have feelings of their own. In a play group, when your toddler grabs a toy away from another child, don't just say, "Give that back, it's not yours!" (which doesn't ring true to toddlers, anyway, since they fully believe that everything *is* theirs). Explain: "When you take Jessica's doll away, it makes her sad. Remember how sad you were when Emily took your teddy away?" When your toddler hits a playmate, don't just say, "No hitting!" Say, "Ouch! When you hit Benjamin, it hurts him." When your toddler does choose to act benevolently, introduce feelings again: "Look how happy David feels when you share with him." And add a dose of praise, "That was very nice of you!" Though it'll be years before your toddler is capable of consistently putting someone else's feelings first, showing him or her that other people have feelings is taking a step in the direction of developing empathy.

and selfless of parents. Two, it can reinforce and prolong a toddler's imperial ways. The result: Instead of outgrowing this normal stage of development, the self-centered toddler might grow into an extremely spoiled child.

As a parent, you need to protect your rights, for your own sake as well as for your child's. Though your rights certainly won't be as extensive as they were before parenthood (some, like the right to sleep late on weekends and the right to make love when the mood strikes, necessarily give way to the demands of life with a small child), some of them should remain inalienable. Like the right to read a book occasionally, instead of constantly playing with a demanding toddler; to use the bathroom when you need to, rather than putting it off until your toddler gives you permission; to keep your bedroom unlittered by blocks and shape-sorters; to prevent a little visitor from kicking you out of your own bed at night.

▲ Don't just demand your rights, explain them. Instead of saying, "I can't play now, I'm reading my book," explain, "Reading my book is fun for me, just like playing with blocks is fun for you. Now I'm going to have some fun with my book while you have some fun with your blocks." This lets your toddler know that you're a person with needs and feelings just like him or her.

Similarly, when you need to put off granting your toddler's request for a story until you finish a phone call, don't just say, "You'll have to wait!" Instead, say, "I have to talk on the phone now. I will read you a story when I'm finished." (For more tips on getting a toddler to wait, see page 136.)

Offer an explanation, too, when you ask your toddler to respect the rights of a sibling, a playmate, or a stranger. Telling your toddler, "Your sister is working on a puzzle now. She needs some quiet," teaches more than a brusque, "Stay away from your sister!" Likewise, explaining that, "People are trying to talk in this restaurant, and when you bang on the table, they can't hear," says more than, "Stop banging on the table!"

Of course, toddlers being toddlers, no matter how you phrase your requests, they may well be refused. That's to be expected, and to a certain extent, accepted. What's important is that you've begun to plant in your toddler's mind the idea that other people have rights, too.

▲ Introduce feelings (see box, facing page).

▲ Respect your toddler's rights. Many parents, in a well-intentioned attempt to raise big-hearted offspring, put the rights of their children's playmates ahead of those of their children. Without asking permission, they'll offer their toddler's favorite toy to a visiting peer. Without considering that their toddler might be in the right, they'll automatically side with the other child in a playground dispute over a sand shovel. Unfortunately, instead of teaching a toddler to be more generous, this approach may encourage selfishness. With their own rights constantly taking a back seat or being threatened, toddlers often become even more doggedly determined not to share, not to cooperate, not to take turns.

Respect for your toddler's rights should be maintained, too, when a new sibling comes on the scene. Always asking the toddler to make concessions because "you're bigger" isn't fair, and can build hostility toward the little newcomer. (For more on the subject of siblings, see Chapter Twenty-four.)

▲ Respect your toddler's feelings. Toddlers don't learn to respect the feelings of others if their own feelings are given short shrift. If you embarrass your child in front of others ("Oh, you're so naughty! How could you spill your milk like that?") or never allow his or her opinions to count ("That sweater doesn't go with those pants!") or talk about the child as though he or she is a cipher instead of a person ("This kid is just driving me crazy!"), you not only damage your toddler's self-esteem, but teach that it's all right to ignore the feelings of others.

▲ Set a respectful example. As always, what you say to your toddler doesn't have nearly as much impact as what you do. Asking your toddler to acknowledge the rights or feelings of a playmate, then embarrassing a baby-sitter in public, or snapping at a check-out clerk at the supermarket, or sneaking to the front of the line at the bus stop, sends a message that such behavior is acceptable, and it won't matter what you say to the contrary.

# CHAPTER TWO

# The Fourteenth Month

## WHAT YOUR TODDLER MAY BE DOING NOW

*By the end of this month,[1] your toddler*
*. . . should be able to (see Note):*

▲ wave bye-bye
▲ stand alone
▲ put an object into a container
▲ use mama/dada intentionally
(by 13½ months)
▲ follow 1-step verbal command without gestures (by 13½ months)

**Note:** If your toddler has not reached these milestones or doesn't use his or her hands for purposeful activities like picking things up, consult the doctor or nurse-practitioner. This rate of development may well be normal for your child (some children are late bloomers), but it needs to be evaluated. Also check with

*Toddlers derive much satisfaction from taking things out of where they belong—much more than they derive from putting them back in their place.*

---

1. The fourteenth month begins when a child is thirteen months old and ends when he or she is fourteen months old.

the doctor if your toddler seems unresponsive, doesn't smile, makes few or no sounds, doesn't seem to hear well, is perpetually irritable, or demands constant attention. (But remember, the one-year-old who was born prematurely often lags behind others of the same chronologic age. This developmental gap progressively narrows and generally disappears entirely around age two.)

### . . . will probably be able to:

▲ bend over and pick up an object (by 13½ months)
▲ walk well (by 13½ months)

### . . . may possibly be able to:

▲ dump an object in imitation
▲ use 3 words (by 13½ months)

### . . . may even be able to:

▲ build a tower of 2 cubes (by 13½ months)
▲ use 6 words or more (by 13½ months)
▲ run
▲ walk up steps
▲ follow a 2-step verbal command without gestures

# WHAT YOU MAY BE CONCERNED ABOUT

## NEGATIVISM

*"No matter what we tell him or ask him, our son has the same answer: 'No!' It was funny at the beginning, but now it's straining our patience."*

**"N**o" may not be every toddler's first word, but for many toddlers it quickly becomes their favorite word. Much of this is a matter, at least at the start, of simple physiology: Enunciating the word "no" is easier than enunciating the word "yes," shaking the head side to side is easier than moving it up and down. It may also have something to do with the fact that toddlers tend to hear the word "no" far more often than they hear its positive counterpart.

As time goes on, the explanation for toddler negativity shifts from physiology to psychology. Although now the toddler may be capable of saying "yes," he'd much rather say "no"—not out of orneriness, but because that neat little expression of negativity allows him to demonstrate his new-found identity. Instead of being merely an extension of you, as he was in his baby days, he's now his own little person. By repeating "no" over and over again, he's flexing the muscles of his emerging independence, testing your authority and his autonomy. "No" becomes his declaration of independence, his emancipation proclamation. He'll say "no" to your requests, "no" to your orders, "no" to your limits, "no" to just about anything you offer—sometimes even when it's something he wants. And you won't be the only object of your toddler's negativity; playmates, baby-sitters, and siblings, too, will also be targets. In an effort to preserve his rights as a separate person, he'll suddenly become possessive of his belongings. He will meet anyone who threatens to take them away with a resounding and unequivocally negative response.

Your toddler's negative behavior is not a reflection on you (as a parent) or your child (as a person). All children, usually beginning early in the second year (and occasionally even earlier), go through a negative phase. In some children, it's short-lived and half-hearted; in others, petulance is more persistent. Either way, a toddler can't control his compulsion to resist authority any more than he can control teething or growing. His testing of your authority is healthy and normal, a vital form of self-expression, an essential part of ego building, an important step on the road to personhood.

Knowing that a toddler's negative behavior is healthy and normal, however, doesn't necessarily make it easier to live with. A child who's continually testing authority can sorely try his parents' patience, particularly when he's too young to be reasoned with. Fortunately, negativity is a stage and it does pass in time—the worst of it generally lasts no more than five or six months. By their second birthday, most children start to think and act more positively and cooperatively (though a few may continue to display a thread of rebelliousness in the fabric of their personality). Parents can then breathe a sigh of relief—at least until adolescence propels rebellion to the forefront once more. In the meantime, observing a few basic principles can help to make your toddler's negative stage a little less negative for you:

**Limit your "no's."** Children learn from example much more than they learn from admonitions. When parents who've been hearing nothing but "no" from their toddlers listen to themselves, they often hear "no" more often than "yes." Your own use of negatives can easily put your toddler into a negative frame of mind—so think before you say "no."

**Limit his "no's."** If you don't want to take "no" for an answer, phrase your questions carefully. Instead of "Do you want to put your sweater on?" or even, "Let's put your sweater on," offer a couple of options: "Do you want to wear the sweater with the hood or the sweater with the elephant on it?" Even a nonverbal toddler can point to his choice. Instead of, "Now it's time to wash your hands for dinner," try, "Do you want to wash your hands in the kitchen sink or the bathroom sink? Do you want to use the liquid soap or the bar soap?" Giving the toddler as much decision-making power as possible can help to make him feel that he has some control over his life, and thereby reduce his need to rebel.

**But don't offer a choice when there is none.** When the issue is non-negotiable, make that clear. Asking "Do you want to go home now?" when there's no option but to go home now, is just asking for an insurrection. Better: "It's time to go home."

**Don't laugh at the "no"s.** While it's important to keep a sense of humor about your toddler's negativism (and all his other trying behavior), it's equally important not to laugh it off. As amusing as it might sometimes be to you, his negativity is not a laughing matter to him—it is, in fact, a serious one and one that deserves a respectfully serious response.

**Don't be bossy.** Being ordered around all the time would make anyone consider mutiny. Instead of commanding, "You have to get into your car seat," try, "Now let's get into your car seat." Playing "dumb" and letting your toddler call the shots for you ("Okay, we're in the car. Now what do we do?") often works especially well. So does challenging your toddler ("Where's your car seat?" Then, "Very good, that *is* your car seat." Next, "Can you get into your seat?" And finally," "What a big boy!" with cheers and applause).

**Don't lose your cool.** Getting riled up when your toddler gets rebellious can only make matters worse. Since you're the adult (which it isn't always easy to be consistently), it's up to you to keep the situation from getting overheated (see page 754). Don't punish negativity, either. Respect your toddler's right to say "no," while explaining, when appropriate, that he'll sometimes have to do what you say, even when he doesn't want to.

**Accentuate the positives.** You'll find that reinforcing his positive behavior with words of praise improves a toddler's conduct more effectively than punishing his negative behavior.

**Avoid lose–lose situations.** There's rarely a winner when wills come to blows, particularly when a toddler's in the ring. Keep in mind that good parents don't always wield their authority— sometimes they yield it. The more chances you give your child for self-determination, the less compelled he will feel to fight for his rights by saying "no."

**Be willing to lose occasionally.** It's not all right for your toddler to say "no" when you try to buckle him into his car seat, for example, or when he has to take his vitamins, or when it's time for bed. But there are occasions, when the stakes are low, on which you can meet your toddler's "no" with an "okay." Say you intended to make one more stop on the way home from a shopping trip, but as you pull into the dry-cleaners your toddler screeches, "No! Home!" If that stop can be postponed, you can say, "Okay, I know you're tired. I'm tired, too. We can stop at the cleaners tomorrow. Let's go home now." Letting your toddler win sometimes will make losing sometimes less painful for him. But capitulate *before* the "no" deteriorates into a tantrum. Giving in to a tantrum is almost always a mistake (see page 329).

# SETTING LIMITS

*"I tend to be very relaxed about discipline but my husband feels that we should be setting limits for our toddler. I'm afraid she won't feel loved if we do."*

Score one for Dad. Limits do not make a child feel unloved; they can actually make her feel more loved. Most children crave limits, though some naturally need more outside-imposed structure to govern their behavior than others. For toddlers, who are not yet able to set limits for themselves, knowing that their parents have done this for them brings a particularly comforting sense of security. Although they may not always—or even very often—abide by the rules (at least not willingly), fair and reasonable limits that let toddlers know what to expect and what is expected of them give them a sense of security during this turbulent period of development. Children who learn to live with rules now tend to be happier and better behaved later.

As your child gets older, it will become clearer to her that you've made rules because you care about your home, about other people, and especially about her. When you tell her she has to wear mittens and a hat because it's freezing outside, she'll know you don't want her to be cold or to get sick. When you insist she go to bed at a certain hour, she'll gradually come to realize you want her to feel rested and in good spirits when she gets up in the morning. When you insist that she put her toys away, she'll begin to understand that you want to keep her belongings in good condition and want her to be able to play and live in nice surroundings.

Growing up in an atmosphere where there are limits and rules will do more than make your toddler feel secure and loved. It also will make her more lovable. Children raised in a completely

permissive atmosphere—where everyone's allowed to do whatever they want
whenever they want—are not generally
very popular outside the home.

Of course, too many limits can have
just as negative an effect on a young
child as too few. If you make so many
rules that your home becomes a police
state, your toddler will learn either to
ignore the rules (because they are more
than she can handle), rebel (because they
squelch her natural drive for independence), or knuckle under and become
lethargic (like a disheartened citizen in
a police state). Children who are rigidly
disciplined at home often lack self-discipline whenever they're out from under
their parents' watchful eyes. Those who
are never allowed to make choices of
their own may grow into adults incapable
of making wise choices.

Limits must also be reasonable,
as fair as they are firm. Rules that are
arbitrary ("You can't go out today
because I say so") or unreasonable
(expecting a young toddler to put away
her toys on her own every time, for
example, or to always modulate her
voice level in the house) will only spark
further rebellion. And to be effective,
of course, rules must be enforced (see
page 121).

Just as laws vary from country to
country, state to state, municipality to
municipality, rules vary from family to
family. Tailor limits to your individual
family, so they're comfortable both
for parents and children. For more on
finding the right balance between rules
and freedom for your toddler, see
Disciplining Your Toddler, page 119.

# NOT TAKING "NO"
# FOR AN ANSWER

*"My son says 'no' all the time to
me, but when I say 'no' he com-*
*pletely ignores me or he giggles
and does exactly what I've told him
not to do."*

Toddlers love to give "no" for an
answer, but they hate being on the
receiving end. In their struggle for independence, parental "no's" are a threat to
their self-determination. To your toddler,
obeying your "no's" means admitting
your authority. Instead of making that
admission, he chooses to put your
authority to the test.

While constant testing of authority
is a normal part of toddler growth and
development, it can be admittedly nerve-
racking for parents, particularly as
they strive to keep both toddler and
home safe. Although complete compliance is but a parental pipe dream—not
just in toddlerhood, but at any time in
childhood—you can begin working
toward it:

▲ Know when to say "no"—and when
not to. "No's" have their place in
parenting—especially in matters of
health, safety, and sanity—but too many
can be stifling to a small child, or, as
you've noticed, prompt him to tune out.
To make your "no's" more effective, use
them only when you need to. Avoid "no"
overload without squelching your toddler's exploratory instincts by eliminating as many potential points of conflict
from his environment as possible. Make
your house safe for your toddler and
your toddler safe in your house (see page
620)—put a latch on the bathroom door,
put away your fine breakables, put the
CD player on a higher shelf—and you'll
have fewer reasons to say "no."

By leaving a few "off-limits" items
within your toddler's reach—ones that
won't suffer too terribly under his not-
too-gentle touch—you can begin teaching him the fine art of self-control. When
he heads for these temptations, take the
opportunity to explain, "That's Daddy's;
it's not for you to play with." Offer him

a substitute, "Here, this duck is yours. You can play with this." Occasionally, let him get his hands on something that is off-limits, under your supervision: "You can't play with my music box alone, but we can do it together" (see page 240).

▲ Don't anticipate. Even if he's headed directly that way, wait until your toddler touches the VCR before you tell him, "No touching the VCR!" First of all, anticipating his misdeeds will only fuel them; second of all, everyone, even a toddler, deserves to be trusted until he fails to live up to that trust. Of course, if he's headed toward something that he doesn't know is off-limits or that represents a danger, stop him up front.

▲ Take a positive position. Being positive can achieve positive results more consistently than being negative. For example, "Please stay on the sidewalk" is more likely to elicit compliance than "Don't walk in the mud." And "Try to use the crayon on the paper" will work better than "Don't draw on the table."

▲ When you do say "no," mean it. If you distractedly say "Don't eat the dog food" when your toddler starts sniffing around the dog bowl, but then turn your back as he dives in, he's even less likely to pay attention to your "no" next time. If you say "no", be ready to follow through with action—whether that means removing the dog bowl, or removing or distracting your toddler. Also, suppress that urge to laugh at your toddler's Dennis-the-Menace antics, as adorable as they may be; for your toddler to take your "no's" seriously, you've got to show that you do, too.

▲ Say "no" calmly. Anger or pleading will give your toddler the feeling that he has the upper hand ("If Daddy is getting this upset, I must be in control of the situation"). A firm, "no" gives your authority much more credibility.

▲ Explain your requests and rules. Knowing why rules exist makes them easier to follow. And even at a fairly young age, children can begin to understand that there are reasons for rules. Whenever possible, give your child a rationale: "Wash your hands first so you won't get sand on your cheese stick." "You can't touch the radiator because it's hot and you can get burned." "Don't pull the dog's tail; it hurts the doggy and she might bite you." But *keep it simple*; a toddler will tune out long-winded, overly complex explanations.

▲ Commend compliance. When your toddler does take "no" for an answer— even if it's only one time out of fifty— be ready to acknowledge his compliance ("Thank you for putting that magazine down when I asked").

# FOOD STRIKE

*"Whenever I try to feed my daughter, she clamps her mouth shut and shakes her head. But I can't let her feed herself because she makes such a mess and takes forever."*

Get that bullet and start biting. Yes, it's painful to watch a toddler feeding herself—and the floor, the wall, her clothes—and taking three times as long to get through a meal as when you're in charge of the spoon. But this, like so many aspects of toddler rearing, is a case of no pain, no gain. And the gains to be made here are important ones for your child, bringing her, among other positive rewards, independence, self-feeding skills, and a healthy attitude toward mealtime and eating. Continue feeding your toddler yourself, and you'll save time and a lot of cleaning up but deny her these valuable gains. Fight with her for control over the spoon, and you could set the stage for a future of eating problems.

So leave yourself some extra time for her meals, lay out some extra protection for your floor, and look the other way if you can't bear to watch—but let your toddler feed herself. See the tips on page 17 for how to make the mealtime mess less messy.

# EMPTYING THINGS

*"My son goes around the house emptying everything he sees— drawers, wastebaskets, toy bins. But I can't get him to put anything back."*

It's Mother Nature's perverse sense of humor at work again: slotting the capability to "empty out" months before the capability (and years before the desire) to "put back in." But emptying isn't a laughing matter to your toddler— it's serious developmental work.

How can you help your toddler polish this important fine-motor skill without his demolishing your home? Try these tips for starters:

**Prevent dangerous emptying.** Install childproof locks on cabinets, drawers, and closets that contain items that might harm your toddler or be harmed by him (cleaning fluids, dish detergents, knives, matches, scissors, glass, china, and other breakables). Since it will be a long time before your toddler can control his impulse to touch the forbidden, it's up to you to make sure these objects are completely inaccessible to him. See page 620 for tips on childproofing your home.

**Provide opportunities for safe emptying.** Make available for your toddler's emptying pleasure boxes filled with fabric scraps of bright colors and textures (velvet, silk, mesh, burlap), but no strings or ribbons (which he might choke himself with); baskets of toys; drawers filled with old pots and covers, wooden spoons, measuring cups that nest; low shelves filled with hard-to-destroy board books. Stock the bathtub and the sandbox with plastic cups, bottles, and pails for your child to fill and empty to his heart's content.

**Play the "putting-in" game.** Begin trying to teach your toddler how to "put back in" as well as take out: "You put that toy in the toy box, I'll put this one in" or "Let's see who can fill a basket faster!" Don't expect your toddler to put back with the same diligence he applies to emptying; filling is a much tougher skill, and much less satisfying, too. In fact, even if your toddler does learn to enjoy filling, he'll probably still— to your frustration—end up most play sessions by emptying (empty, refill, empty). Of course, there's the occasional toddler who likes "putting in" so much that Mom finds her car keys in the sock drawer and Dad finds his wallet in the trash bin.

If your toddler doesn't get the hang of putting back in what he empties (or doesn't seem to want to), don't prod, pressure, or punish. Try to keep in mind that emptying is a learning experience for him, even though it's a trying one for you. But to keep chaos under control, and to make clear to your toddler that it's not okay to empty endlessly all over the house, you can refill the container in question and either put it or him out of reaching range.

**Provide reasons.** This won't work until your toddler is at least eighteen months or so, when his comprehension improves. At that age, whenever he dumps a drawer or clears out a cabinet, leaving the contents strewn across the carpet, point out the disadvantages of the mess he's created: one, that people can trip over it; two, that people can step on things and break them; three, that the house looks much nicer when everything's in its proper place. None of this is likely to stop your child from emptying or start him putting back everything he empties—at least not any-time soon. But it will plant in his mind the idea that your rules against emptying aren't arbitrary, they have sound reasons behind them.

# THE DROPSIES

*"My daughter gets enormous pleasure from dropping things— from her crib, her high chair, the supermarket cart. And she seems to get even more of a kick from watching me pick them up."*

When first we saw this behavior, late in the first year, it was a sign that baby had developed enough control over her fingers to release objects she picked up; and as with any other skill, she probably practiced it repeatedly just so she could get it right. She had no in-terest in what happened to the object once it left her pudgy hands. Then, as she got older, dropping became a scien-tific experiment: "What happens when I drop this? Where will it go?" Like a junior Isaac Newton, she watched the object fall all the way to the ground, fas-cinated. She was fascinated still more if it broke on impact.

Eventually many toddlers find enter-tainment value in the dropping skill— as your daughter seems to have. Rapid firing of stuffed animals over the side of your crib or peas from your high chair can be quite a hoot. Watching grown-ups bend over repeatedly to pick up what you've dropped automatically doubles the amusement.

What amuses your toddler, however, can exasperate you, not to mention being hard on your back and knees. Since

numerous other less-annoying routes to amusement are at your toddler's disposal, it's best to encourage her to drop the dropping by taking the following steps:

**Drop the complaints.** For the average toddler, knowing that a particular behavior irks her parents gives her greater motivation to repeat it—and repeat it. So instead of growling about her dropping, pretend that it doesn't bother you in the least.

**Floor her.** Whenever she's in the mood to drop, and you're not in the mood to pick up, put her on the floor so she can drop *and pick up* to her heart's content. Of course, you can be pretty sure she will abandon the activity entirely once she's on the floor.

**End the meal.** If it's food she's flinging, take it away and bring the meal to a quick close.

**Encourage a drop in the bucket.** Let your toddler practice her dropping skills in parent-approved situations and receptacles—drop a block into a bucket, a ball down a slide, a letter down the mail chute, toys into a toy chest, raisins into the cookie batter, and so on.

**Play the pick-up game.** Picking up will never be as much fun as dropping (except, of course, when it's interesting trash she's spied on the sidewalk), but playing a pick-up game may make it less tedious. (For example, "Let's see how fast we can pick up the toys you dropped" or "Can you pick up all those blocks before the music stops?")

**Beware of breakables.** Perhaps it should go without saying, but we'll say it just the same: Those in the habit of dropping things should not be trusted with breakables. No glass, ceramic, or china dishes or cups at mealtime, no del-icate knickknacks, or anything else you would like to remain whole, should be left within your toddler's reach.

# A SHORT ATTENTION SPAN

*"Our daughter doesn't concentrate for more than a few minutes on anything."*

**S**ounds like you have a typical toddler—with a normally short attention span—on your hands. Because a few minutes can seem like an eternity to them, toddlers rarely spend more than a few minutes on anything. In an effort to cover all the ground they can, these pint-size explorers flit endlessly from one pursuit to another. Expecting a fourteen-month-old to concentrate for long periods of time on any one thing— a toy, a puzzle, a book, or an exhibit at a museum—is expecting too much. Like her meals, she'll digest life's experiences better if you let her take them in small bites.

This is not to say that your toddler won't occasionally surprise you by becoming thoroughly engrossed in a single activity. She will, with greater frequency as the months pass and her attention span lengthens. But realistically, it's not until they reach school age (about six years old) that most children develop the ability to concentrate on one project for a long period, shutting out all other stimuli or distractions (see page 170).

# BOWLEGS

*"Our daughter is walking all over the place now, but I'm concerned that she's bow-legged."*

**J**ust about every novice walker has a major gap between the knees, though the size of the gap varies from child to child. As long as your toddler is getting vitamin D from milk or from a supplement (a deficiency in this vitamin can lead to rickets and permanent bowing of the legs), you can assume that her bowlegs are just part of normal development. By the time she toddles into her second birthday party, the bowing will probably have disappeared completely—to be replaced by, if she follows the traditional pattern, knock-knees (see page 322).

If, however, the bowing is severe enough to interfere with her walking, is more pronounced on one side than on the other, or worsens after age two, check with the nurse-practitioner or doctor. Also seek medical advice if the bowing is extreme and your child ranks below the 25th percentile on the height chart for her age (see page 864).

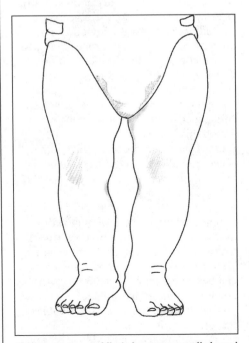

*Not to worry—a toddler's legs are normally bowed until sometime late in the second year. Toeing-out and flat feet are also common in toddlers.*

# TOEING-OUT

*"My son, who has been walking for a few weeks now, walks like a bow-legged duck, with his toes pointing out. Is this normal?"*

**N**ot only normal, but for most fledgling walkers, necessary. By pointing their toes outward, toddlers improve their balance, and thus their staying-up power (even adults tend to broaden their stance and point out when trying to maintain balance). Pointing out also helps compensate for normal toddler bow-leggedness.

Between two and three, children graduate from bow-legs to knock-knees. In an effort once again to maintain balance, they shift the position of their feet to compensate, toeing-in instead of out. At this stage they begin to walk less like ducks and more like pigeons.

By the time they hit school age, most children walk with their feet pointing straight ahead, or almost so. A small number, however, will continue to toe-out for the rest of their lives, almost always without a problem.

# FLAT FEET

*"Both my wife and I have normal arches, but our fourteen-month-old son seems to be completely flat-footed. We're worried this could be a problem."*

**D**on't worry. Your child will almost certainly follow in your foot shape, though probably not for a couple of years at least. In infancy and toddlerhood, flat-footedness is the rule, not the exception. Your toddler's feet are just doing what comes naturally.

There are several reasons toddlers appear flat-footed. For one, bones and joints, including those in the feet, are very flexible in early childhood. For another, the supporting muscles of the foot are not fully developed; it takes a lot of walking, a lot more walking than most toddlers have done, for these to tighten up. The toddler's own weight pushes the loose joints and the weak muscles toward the ground, making the arch disappear. Yet another factor is the baby-fat pad that rounds the arch during this time of life, effectively camouflaging any curve that does exist. And finally, the fact that most beginning walkers toe out to improve their balance putting extra weight on the arch, and causing even a slightly elevated arch to appear flat.

By the time your child marches off to first grade, chances are he'll be the proud owner of two well-defined arches. And if for some reason he isn't (about 10% to 20% of the population remain flat-footed for life), there will still be no reason to worry. Though during World War II, young men with flat feet were ineligible for military service, experts now recognize that being archless is in no way a handicap and that, in some cases, it may even be an advantage. (Because of the superior ability of flat feet to absorb shock, those with such feet are less likely to suffer from sprains and stress fractures than their high-arched counterparts).

While you're waiting for your toddler to develop arches, avoid the urge to "do something." The special shoes, arch supports, and exercises you may hear about or see promoted at shoe stores not only won't help, they may actually do some harm. It's best to just let nature take its course.

If, however, your child's feet seem extremely rigid and unbending, he has limited movement or pain in them, or has trouble walking, do seek medical advice; treatment may be necessary.

# TOE WALKING

*"Our daughter just started walking and seems to think she's a toe-dancer. Her feet are never flat on the ground."*

The sugarplum-fairy style of walking seems to be favored by many toddlers, and not just among those destined for a career in ballet. Toe walking simply feels good, so children do it. But they don't stay on their toes forever; most tiptoers master the normal heel-first stride about midway through the second year.

If your child continues to tiptoe after several months as a walker, or if she can't seem to flatten her foot on the floor even when she's standing still, talk to her doctor about it. In the meantime, don't hold back the applause for her graceful performances *en pointe*.

# POST CRYING-IT-OUT TRAUMA

*"We tried to let our little girl cry it out at night when she woke up, and it seems to have backfired. She became so upset that she now looks terrified when we just talk about it being time to go to sleep. What do we do now?"*

Letting a toddler "cry it out" is meant to help, not hurt. And in most cases it does help, by giving children the opportunity to learn how to fall back to sleep on their own. But once in a while, a very sensitive child is traumatized by being left to cry it out. When this happens, it's best to backtrack a little. If your toddler seems frightened about going to sleep, stay at her side until she dozes off, no matter how long this takes. Quietly talk or sing to her, if she seems

to need it. Otherwise, just be there. If she awakens in the middle of the night, do the same thing. Calm and reassure her and stay with her until she's asleep. But don't pick her up or take her to your bed. Eventually, she will become more relaxed and secure and at that point you will be able to leave her while she's still awake.

# A START IN ART

*"When should I start giving my daughter crayons to draw with?"*

When a toddler's old enough to hold a crayon, she's old enough to draw—or at least to scribble. And chances are, given the opportunity and a little preliminary instruction, yours will prove old enough now.

It's likely that your toddler will find scribbling on paper an exciting new experience. But because the excitement is likely to extend to scribbling on the walls, floors, books, and furniture, and to nibbling on the crayons, allow her to fine-tune her artistic skills only under supervision. Provide crayons rather than pencils or pens, since there's more risk of a toddler falling and poking her eye or pricking her skin with one of the latter two. When the crayon starts to make its way from paper to mouth, intercept it immediately. Demonstrate on paper that "Crayons are for drawing. We don't eat them." Repeat the interceptions as often as it takes, but if your toddler seems interested only in nibbling, end the drawing session and call a snack break. ("See, here's some food. This is for eating.")

Even with constant vigilance, you may not be able to prevent your toddler from taking an occasional nip of crayon or scribbling on your wallpaper, so be sure those you buy are nontoxic and washable. (If your toddler does occasionally use a pencil for scribbling, don't worry if it ends up in her mouth. Pencils are no longer made from lead, and the paint used on them is not toxic.) Thick crayons are sturdier and are often more comfortable for small hands, but some older toddlers may prefer the feel and finer point of the standard crayon size. A large sheet of inexpensive newsprint (buy it in rolls) works best for beginner art—and there's less likelihood the mas-

terpiece will extend beyond its borders. You can also recycle writing paper and junk mail by having your toddler decorate the backs. Taping the paper down to a table, a high-chair tray, or floor will keep it in place, make it easier for your child to succeed at actually making some marks, and reduce the frustration that results when the paper moves each time the child's hand does. (For more ways of encouraging creativity, see page 362.)

# WHAT IT'S IMPORTANT TO KNOW:
## Play Is the Toddler's Work

**B**irds do it, reptiles do it, mammals of all kinds do it. In fact, just about every animal species that's ever been studied does it. Though the name of the game may differ from species to species, culture to culture, generation to generation, play is universal. Whether it's a puppy chasing its tail or a young frog leaping lily pads, an African boy playing with a mancala set his father carved from wood or a North American girl playing with a set of jacks her mother bought at the local toy store, play is an essential part of growing up. Researchers believe that it is critical to growth and vital to future performance. In animals, researchers have actually observed brain connections (synapses) sprouting during periods of play, and theorize that the same kind of brain development takes place when human children play.

Yet many parents today consider play largely a waste of time. Raising children to enter a competitive world, where survival and success often go to the intellectually fittest, they wonder if play time might be put to more constructive use.

*It looks like it's fun—and it is. But for a toddler, play is also work.*

For a child, there is no more constructive pastime than play. No number of flash cards, educational computer games, or gymnastics lessons can provide your toddler with such an amazing spectrum of benefits. Included among them:

▲ Play allows a young child to be omnipotent. In their games, toddlers can be the big fish instead of the tiny guppies. When they play, the frustration of being small and powerless, of being told what to do and when to do it, doesn't exist. Without the adult interference they ordinarily encounter, toddlers get to call the shots, make the choices, formulate the rules, seize control, run the show.

▲ Play helps children learn about the world around them. Through play, toddlers can investigate and discover; test theories; learn about shapes, spatial relationships, and colors; explore cause-and-effect, societal roles, family values.

## *TOYS FOR TOTS EARLY IN THE SECOND YEAR*

· · · · · · · · · ·

Focus on variety when purchasing or borrowing toys for your toddler, selecting one or more items from each of the categories below. Some multipurpose toys appear on two or more lists; these are particularly good choices. Many of these toys will be of interest to your child through this year and even into the next, though the way they are approached may mature as your child does.

▲ Toys that help build small-motor skills: nesting and stacking toys; simple wooden jigsaw puzzles (particularly those with knobs for easier insertion and removal of pieces); shape-sorters; blocks; boxes and containers for filling and emptying; activity boards and pop-up toys with dials, knobs, and buttons to manipulate.

▲ Toys that help build large motor skills: balls of all sizes; pull toys; push toys; riding toys; climbing toys; swings, slides.

▲ Toys that stimulate imagination: stuffed animals; dolls and doll furniture; cars, trucks, and airplanes; board books; kitchen equipment and gadgets (pretend ones and appropriately safe real ones); play household items (telephones, shopping carts); dress-up clothes and accessories (hats, briefcases, handbags); building blocks and building systems (such as Duplo).

▲ Toys that stimulate creativity: crayons and paper; play clay; materials for making collages; poster paints to be used with brushes and pieces of sponge (see page 367).*

▲ Toys that encourage musical play: drums; tambourines; maracas; horns and other wind instruments; xylophones; simple keyboards; cassette players and tapes—made for toddlers.

▲ Toys that encourage learning about the grown-up world: dolls (along with carriages, cradles, strollers, and other gear); cooking paraphernalia (stove, fridge, sink, dishes, fake food); pint-size household and garden tools (pretend brooms, shovels, rakes, lawn mowers); vehicles (cars, trucks, trains, airplanes, fire engines); a work bench or "tool" belt; costumes (firefighter's hat, police-officer's hat, sailor's hat, doctor's bag, dancer's tutu, etc.); toy typewriters, cash registers, and shopping carts.

▲ Toys that encourage discovery and interest in the physical world—that teach about how things work, about cause and effect, about numbers, shapes, patterns: dump trucks; blocks and building systems intended for young toddlers; nesting toys and shape-sorters; boxes and containers for filling and emptying; sandbox and sandbox toys; nonbreakable mirrors; water-play toys (some that float, some that squirt, and some for filling and pouring).

*Be sure all art supplies are nontoxic and safe for use by children your toddler's age.

A toddler at play can be a scientist, a parent, a firefighter, a construction worker, a dancer, a musician, a cowherd; there is virtually no area of life about which play can't teach.

▲ Play builds self-esteem. Children tend to play at what they do well, something that can bring them what they consider success. The fact that they make up

the rules during play time increases their chances of success. With no adults telling them what they're doing wrong toddlers can also feel free to try and fail—and to try and try again—without feeling inadequate.

▲ Play builds social skills. Long before children begin socializing, play prepares them for social experience. Since the

## CONTAINING THE CLUTTER

··········

If there's a down side to toddler's play, it's the disarray and clutter that so often go with it. As beneficial as toys are to your toddler, there will be many days when you'll wish they'd all vanish from your home—days when you'll feel as though you've done nothing but pick up (or step on or trip over) blocks, dolls, puzzle pieces, and miniature cars.

In time and with your persistence, your child can learn to clean up after a day's play; in the meantime, you can help contain the mess by making sure your toddler has:

▲ A play space. Ideally, this should be an area that you can oversee from wherever you spend most of your at-home time (the family room, your home office, the living room, or wherever). Define the space where toys are permissible (the living room carpet, the family room, your toddler's room). At first this won't mean much to your toddler; toys will be dragged all through the house. But if you keep making a point of returning the toys to and setting them up in the same area each day, your toddler will eventually get the message that play should take place in the play area. Ideally, this area should include: a comfy place to cuddle up in—an armchair or small sofa that you and your child can use for reading, telling stories, and so on; two toddler-size chairs (one for your toddler and one for a playmate or a parent) and a small table for doing puzzles and art projects, playing games, and, of course, serv-

ing tea; a safe, efficient, easy-to-reach and easy-to-use storage system; carpeting or an area rug so playing on the floor will be comfortable on chilly days.

▲ A place for everything—so everything can be in its place, at least occasionally. Large, colored baskets on deep shelves are a good way to store toys. Assigning a color for each type of toy (green for blocks, blue for cars, yellow for stuffed animals, and so on) simplifies clean-up and will help your toddler learn to recognize colors. If you use a toy box, see page 625.

▲ A regular clean-up routine. Whether at the end of each play period or the end of each day, make clean-up part of your routine. Though you'll do most of the work, involving your toddler is an important first step in fostering responsibility for caring for his or her own belongings. ("It's time to put the toys away. The blocks go in the green basket. Can you put your blocks in there?") Work on putting away one toy type at a time (blocks, puzzles, books, etc.) to avoid confusion and overload. Playing, singing, or humming a special clean-up tune can make the job more fun. By the second birthday, a challenge to "clean up by the time I count to 100" or "by the time the buzzer rings" can turn a tedious chore into an entertaining game.

For tips on teaching an older toddler to take care of his or her belongings, see page 417.

# BUY RIGHT

· · · · · · · · · ·

There's something about shopping for toys that brings out the kid in every grown-up. And when the kid comes out, it's tough for some grown-ups to keep in mind who they're shopping for. Instead of buying what's appropriate for the child in their lives, they tend to buy what appeals to the child in themselves: an intricate train set for the infant still in the cradle, a computerized alphabet game for the child who hasn't yet spoken his first word, a tricycle for the tot who hasn't taken her first step. Premature purchases that aren't just uninteresting for the young recipients, but often completely unusable, and sometimes even unsafe.

To avoid falling into this toy trap and filling your toddler's toy chest with unsuitable selections, be sure to observe the safety guidelines on page 655 and the specific suggestions that follow:

▲ Don't choose toys your toddler's not developmentally ready for. Overcome with nostalgia, you may be tempted to buy a Barbie for your two-year-old. But she can't possibly dress it, and by the time she can, it'll be ready for the trash bin. Hold off, too, on electric trains, a Monopoly set, or any other tempting toy that appeals to the kid in you. It's the kid in your kid you should try to please. Judge less, however, by what your child demands than by what he or she actually plays with at home. The glitziest toys often have the shortest playing power.

▲ Don't overlook non-toys as playthings— a measuring cup that can be used to mold sand at the playground; a large cardboard box to climb in and out of; a small cardboard box to use as a garage for cars or a table for dolls; paper bags for making masks, costumes, and puppets, and to use for carrying around belongings; a blanket draped over two chairs to create a "tent." Also great: mixing bowls and spoons, small unopened cans of food or empty cereal or cracker boxes, and some plastic flatware, dishes, and cups.

▲ In general, don't buy what offends you or your values. But leave yourself open to compromise when it's something your child is truly yearning for (see page 226).

▲ Avoid excess. Young children are not born with great expectations—the adults in their lives (and, later, their peers and television) generate the expectations. Even if you can afford to go overboard at birthdays and holidays, don't. Children with closets full of toys often bounce from one to the next and don't appreciate or enjoy any of them. If your toddler already has a colossal collection, rotate the toys, making only a few available at a time.

▲ Be a borrower and a lender. Set up a toy co-op with other parents you know, so that you can trade toys, especially big ticket items and toys that are outgrown before they're worn out.

▲ Look for versatility. Toys should offer a variety of play possibilities rather than a variety of elaborate features; they should stimulate children to do, rather than do for them.

▲ Don't discourage originality in your child's play. A child should be allowed to play with a toy his or her own way— even if it's not the way the designers had in mind. The only exception: when originality can lead to danger.

first playmates are usually inanimate and nonthreatening—a teddy bear, a doll, a truck—they're perfect tools with which to practice interactive skills. Later, play with peers builds on this foundation, as children learn (eventually) how to share, wait for a turn, stand up for their own rights, and care about the rights of others. Play with parents hones social skills, too; studies show that children whose parents play with them ultimately do better socially.

▲ Play provides the opportunity for children to work out feelings. A multitude of emotions, including anger, fear, sadness, and anxiety, are often worked through in role play. A toddler who's in a panic about going to the doctor, for example, may deal with the anxiety by setting up a clinic for sickly stuffed animals.

▲ Play spurs language development. Puzzle, truck, doll, blocks. Jump, swing, slide, climb. Mine, yours, ours, share. Up, down, under, on. During play, a toddler uses a vast number of words, many of them repeatedly, fostering language development.

▲ Play allows children to be large beyond their years. All the things a toddler is too small to do in real life, he or she can do in play. Be a parent, a police officer, a doctor. Drive a car, fly an airplane, read a book. Build (and leap) tall buildings. Construct complex roadways and orchestrate car collisions. This kind of power not only exhilarates toddlers but also heightens their self-esteem, teaches them about the world, and helps them identify with adults.

▲ Play stimulates creativity and imagination. Making a castle in the sand or a car garage out of a shoe box, feeding a stuffed lamb from a bottle or setting a bowl of stew in front of a rag doll, dressing up in Mommy's or Daddy's clothes, allows toddlers to stretch the limits of their world and experience the joys of make-believe.

▲ Play develops fine-motor skills (the use of hands and fingers) and eye–hand coordination. During play, the toddler builds a block tower, puts a puzzle together, manipulates clay, scribbles with a crayon.

▲ Play matures large-motor skills. Active play—walking, running, jumping, climbing, skipping, riding, swinging, throwing, catching, pushing, pulling—builds grace, coordination, athletic ability, and a foundation for a future active lifestyle.

In other words, a toddler's play is work—satisfying, energizing, thoroughly worthwhile work. Time spent at play is time well-spent, never wasted.

So let them play, let them play, let them play.

# WHAT IT'S IMPORTANT FOR YOUR TODDLER TO KNOW:
## All About Grandparents

In the old days, it seems that families were almost never far from home. Grandparents, children, grandchildren, aunts, uncles, and cousins all lived, if not in the same house, at least in the same neighborhood. Today, either because of necessity or choice, it's the rare family that stays this close. Only one in ten grandparents live with their children's families—and many grandchildren see their grandparents no more than once or twice a year. The extended family now extends across countries, even oceans.

If some or all the grandparents in your family (some children, because of divorce and remarriage, have as many as eight) live at a distance, helping your toddler develop close ties to them can be tricky. But with the assistance of modern transportation and methods of communication, it can be done. The following tips will help keep your toddler in touch with grandparents (and other dear-but-not-so-near relatives):

**Visits.** At least once or twice a year try to manage a visit to each grandparent or set of grandparents. Keep the costs down by traveling off-season, staying alert for airfare specials, considering rail travel, or driving. (For tips on traveling with a toddler, see page 250.) Or invite the grandparents to come to you (this route can be particularly cost-effective if the grandparents qualify for senior-citizen discounts). To keep togetherness from getting on everyone's nerves (some tension is inevitable when three generations converge under one roof for more than a couple of days), plan plenty of fun outings (to amusement parks, museums, puppet shows, and so on). If all parties (you, your toddler, your parents) seem comfortable with the idea, you and your spouse might even consider taking a night or a weekend away from home while the grandparents toddler-sit.[2]

**The telephone.** Long distance is the next best thing to being there—that is, if your toddler will talk on the telephone. Some toddlers love to babble into the receiver, others won't go near one, especially if they've been spooked by listening to the disembodied voice on the other end of the line. But since you never know when a resistant toddler will suddenly agree to speak into a phone, keep on trying. Each time you speak to the grandparents on the phone, say, "Grandma (and/or Grandpa) is on the phone and wants to speak to you." Place the receiver near your child's ear (if you can) so that special voice can be heard. If you meet with opposition, don't force the issue—just try again next time.

**The photo album.** Make a special album for your toddler (with photos inserted in plastic so they can't be mangled) of grandparents and other family members. Pull out the album often and connect names to the faces in the photos, talk a little bit about them, remind your toddler about gifts they've sent, about past visits, about holidays coming up that you'll be sharing.

**The cassette recorder.** Who says that Grandma can't tuck Junior in with his favorite bedtime story just because she's 2,000 miles away? She can if she records the tale on tape. Exchanged audiotapes are a wonderful way of keeping grandparents and toddlers in touch between visits. Grandparents can read simple books aloud or sing lullabies to younger toddlers; later, they can add stories about when Mommy or Daddy were little, or just talk about something that's going on in their lives (the weather, holiday celebrations, a trip they've just taken). Toddlers can babble, sing, giggle, moo like a cow, or bark like a dog into a tape recorder. Even if the sounds they make are incomprehensible, they're likely to be music to grandparents' ears.

**The video recorder.** Videotapes bring not only the sounds of the sorely missed but the sight of them, too. The home movie doesn't have to be artistic to be appreciated; even the most mundane documentaries earn Oscars from grateful grandparents. You can videotape your toddler eating, bathing, playing, saying

---

2. When you're visiting your parents, be sure their home has been made child-safe (see page 620). Don't put your child to sleep in your old childhood crib unless it meets the safety standards described on page 625. And ask that your parents be particularly careful not to leave medications where your toddler can get hold of them. When your parents are baby-sitting at your home, provide them with all the safety information you usually give to your other baby-sitters.

prayers, singing songs, even crying. (And don't forget to record those monumental milestones: first steps, first haircut, birthdays the grandparents can't attend, and so on.) In turn, your parents can videotape themselves doing what comes naturally: telling or reading stories, singing songs, talking, doing tricks, gardening, baking cookies (they can ship a box of them along with the videotape as an added bonus), making doll's clothes, knitting a toddler-size sweater, working in the wood shop, and so on.

Regularly "seeing" grandparents between visits will make them seem a little more familiar when they show up at your doorstep or you show up at theirs.

**Special gifts.** Many grandparents love giving, and virtually all grandchildren love receiving. But it's important that your toddler knows who sent those gifts. A photo of Grandma and Grandpa attached to the gift wrap or tucked into the present will help. So will reminding your toddler, each time he or she plays with the toy, wears the sweater, eats the cookies, that "Grandma (and/or Grandpa) gave you that."

**Travel with grandparents.** Some toddlers can enjoy spending the night at a hotel or resort with Grandma and Grandpa. (Toddlers experiencing separation anxiety or stranger anxiety aren't good candidates for trips away from their parents; wait until a clingy toddler feels more secure before attempting such a rendezvous.) Preparation should include at least one night, and preferably a few nights, spent together in your home. The first trip should not take the young traveler very far afield, since an attack of homesickness may cause a sudden cancellation. But once a couple of overnighters have been successful, a weekend, or even a long weekend can be attempted. Trips to child-centered resorts are best when children are young because these holiday havens provide child-appropriate food, entertainment, and sometimes even child care.

# CHAPTER THREE
·············

# The Fifteenth Month

## WHAT YOUR TODDLER MAY BE DOING NOW

*By the end of this month,[1] your toddler*
*. . . should be able to (see Note):*

▲ walk well
▲ bend over and pick up an object
▲ use at least 1 word

**Note:** If your toddler has not reached these milestones consult the doctor or nurse-practitioner. This rate of development may well be normal for your child (some children are late bloomers), but it needs to be evaluated. Also check with the doctor or nurse-practitioner if your toddler seems out-of-control, uncommunicative, overly passive, highly negative, doesn't smile, makes few or no sounds, doesn't seem to hear well, is perpetually irritable, or demands constant attention. (But remember, the one-year-old who was born prematurely often lags behind others of the same chronological age.

This developmental gap progressively narrows and generally disappears entirely around age two.)

*. . . will probably be able to:*

▲ use 2 words (by 14½ months)
▲ drink from a cup
▲ scribble
▲ point to a desired object

*. . . may possibly be able to:*

▲ point to 1 body part when asked
▲ use a spoon/fork (but not exclusively)
▲ build a tower of 2 cubes

*. . . may even be able to:*

▲ "feed" a doll

---

1. The fifteenth month begins when a child is fourteen months old and ends when he or she is fifteen months old.

**Emotional development:** At fifteen months, toddlers can be expected to communicate pleasure, warmth, interest in new experiences; to play games with parents; to protest; to begin to accept limits.

# WHAT YOU CAN EXPECT AT THE FIFTEEN-MONTH CHECKUP

**Preparing for the checkup.** Keep a list of concerns that have come up since the last visit. Be sure to bring the questions with you to this visit so you'll be ready when the doctor or nurse asks, "Any concerns?" Also jot down new skills your toddler is displaying (walking, climbing, using a spoon, using new words) so you'll be ready when the doctor asks, "What's your toddler been doing?" Bring along your child's home health history record, too, so that height, weight, immunizations, and any other information gleaned from the visit can be recorded.

**What the checkup will be like.** Procedures will vary a bit depending on your child's doctor or the nurse-practitioner who conducts health supervision exams, but in most cases, the fifteen-month visit will include:

▲ Questions about your child's development, behavior, eating habits, and health since the last visit. There may also be questions about how the family is doing in general, whether there have been any major stresses or changes, how siblings (if any) are getting along with your toddler, about how you are coping, about child-care arrangements (if any). The doctor will also want to know whether you have any other questions or concerns.

▲ An assessment of growth (height, weight, head circumference) since the last visit. These findings may be plotted on growth charts (see pages 864 to 867) and your child's weight for height evaluated and compared to previous measurements.

▲ An informal assessment, based on observation and interview, of physical and intellectual development, and of hearing and vision.

Depending on need, the following may be included:

▲ A finger-stick blood test (hematocrit or hemoglobin), if the child is at risk of anemia. The test may be done once routinely between twelve months and four years.

▲ A blood test, usually a finger-stick, to screen for lead, only if exposure is suspected.

▲ A Mantoux tuberculin test for children at high risk, unless it was performed at twelve months.

**Immunizations**
▲ MMR (measles, mumps, and rubella) vaccine.

▲ Hib (haemophilus influenza b) conjugate vaccine, unless given earlier.

▲ HBV (hepatitis b), if series not completed previously.

▲ DTP (diptheria, tetanus, pertussis) or DTaP; this will be given now or at the eighteen-month visit.

▲ HbOC-DTP (this combination vaccine may be given instead of the HBV and DTP).

▲ OPV (oral polio vaccine); this will be given now or at the eighteen-month checkup.

**Anticipatory guidance.** The doctor or nurse-practitioner may also discuss such topics as good parenting practices; discipline; injury prevention; self-comforting behaviors (such as thumb-sucking, transitional objects); television viewing;

parent support; readiness for toilet-learning; sleep and sleep problems; nutrition, eating habits, weaning, snacks, and vitamin supplementation; day care and child care, if appropriate; and other issues that will be important in the months ahead.

**The next checkup.** If your toddler is in good health, the next visit will be at eighteen months. Until then, call the doctor if you have any questions that aren't answered in this book or if your child shows any signs of illness.

# WHAT YOU MAY BE CONCERNED ABOUT

## DIRTY DOINGS

*"My son has found a fun game: pulling off his dirty diaper and playing with its contents. Needless to say, for me the results are not pleasant."*

Toddlers will play with just about anything they can get their hands on. If it's squishy, squeezable, spreadable, and forbidden—all the better.

Now that your toddler has discovered the delights of diaper-dumping, it won't be easy to keep his hands out of his stash. Until he loses interest in this pastime (which can take a few days to a few months), you can minimize the problem by:

**Limiting access.** Your toddler can't get his hands on his feces if he can't get his hands in his diapers. So try to secure his diaper so it can't be loosened or removed. This may require using diaper pins to fasten cloth diapers (rather than

using a diaper wrap with Velcro closings), pinning the diaper to your toddler's undershirt with diaper pins, or using snug, pull-on plastic pants over the diaper (which might increase the risk of diaper rash, so make sure you change diapers frequently). Be aware, however, that a resourceful toddler intent on dipping into his diaper may well find a way to circumvent such security measures.

**Heading him off.** Many toddlers keep to a fairly predictable bowel-movement pattern (one moves his bowels after each meal, another just once a day after breakfast, others always wake up with a mess in his diaper, and so on). If you've figured out your toddler's pattern, try catching him in the act (or immediately after) as often as possible. That way you can get to his diaper before he does.

**Providing a substitute.** Squishing, squeezing, and spreading are irresistible tactile experiences for toddlers. Supply your toddler with plenty of alternative opportunities for such experiences, and he may not feel as compelled to look for them in his diaper. Try giving him squishy, squeezy toys (make sure they're age-appropriate and that pieces of them can't be chewed off), and opportunities for finger-painting, sand play (especially satisfying when water is mixed with the sand), and playing with nontoxic clay. (Most of these activities will require careful adult supervision.)

**Remaining unfazed.** Chances are excellent that, in spite of all your efforts to discourage or distract, your toddler will still find the will and a way to pursue his diaper probing. And chances are even better that the more attention (either negative or positive) you pay to his dirty little game, the more eager he'll be to keep playing it. So keep both the smiles and the scowls off your face. Simply make it perfectly clear that the behavior is unacceptable ("Don't touch the BM.[2] It's dirty."), without losing your cool.

**Telling him where to put it.** Take this opportunity to introduce the toilet to your toddler. His interest in his feces isn't a sign that he's ready for toilet-learning, but you can take advantage of his natural curiosity about his bowel movements to show him where they ultimately belong. Take him into the bathroom when you empty the contents of his diaper into the toilet, and explain, "BMs go in the potty." You can even let him flush, if he seems interested, and if the noise doesn't frighten him. If, on the other hand, he seems upset or confused in any way by this process, do the clean-up yourself next time. (Always keep the bathroom door locked and the toilet latched not just for safety

---

2. The term BM is usually easy for a toddler to learn and socially acceptable for him to use when he's older. You can also use "poop" or "doo-doo" or whatever term has been traditionally used in your family, if you're more comfortable with it.

but for protection of your belongings. Otherwise you may regularly find keys, letters, paper cups flushed away.)

# NIGHT WAKING

*"Our toddler is still waking up in the middle of the night. We've been cowardly about letting her cry it out up until now. But I think we've reached the end of our rope. We need our sleep."*

And she needs hers—not just now, but in the years of nights ahead. Night waking is normal—everyone wakes up three or four times during the night; what is not normal is not being able to get yourself back to sleep. And this is your child's problem.

Her problem affects the whole family, disturbing not only their sleep but their ability to function during the day. For your toddler, however, there's another downside: If she is always tended to when she wakes during the night, she won't learn to fall back to sleep on her own. Whenever she awakens, she'll stay awake until you provide her with the comfort she's come to expect, whether that comfort is in the form of a bottle, a pacifier, cuddles and lullabies, or a place beside you in bed.

So it's not only in your best interest but also in hers that the wakeful nights end and the restful ones begin. This transition may prove somewhat trickier than it would have been if you'd made it in the second half of the first year, when children are generally more adaptable—after all, your toddler's not only more opinionated now but more verbal about her opinions. But the following tips may make your job easier:

**Start the night right.** Studies show that children who go to sleep alone at night (rather than with a parent at hand to comfort them and keep them company) are more likely to go back to sleep on their own when they wake at night and find themselves alone. If you've been "helping" your child fall asleep by staying with her, you've also been helping to perpetuate her night-waking habit. See page 68 for better ways of getting a toddler to bed.

**Consider her comfort.** Being physically uncomfortable makes it difficult to fall back to sleep. Try to keep the temperature in your toddler's sleeping space neither too hot nor too cold. Wriggly toddlers tend not to stay under the covers long, so keep nighttime shivers in check during the chilly months by outfitting yours in heavy, footed pajamas. Switch to lighter nightwear and coverings in spring and fall. In summer, a diaper may be sufficient on the hottest nights, unless your child's room is air-conditioned, in which case light pajamas and a light cover should be fine. Try to discover whether your toddler prefers sleeping in a dark room or one lit with a night-light, and then adjust the lighting accordingly. If noise tends to disturb her, close the door to insure a quiet room. (You could try running a fan or other appliance in her room. The "white noise" it makes may block out distracting sounds, but this could become another dependency, making it difficult for her to sleep when it's quiet.) If she seems to sleep better

when she hears you going about your business in the evening, leave her door ajar.

**Wait out whimpering.** Many parents make the mistake of responding to the slightest whimper, and end up fully waking a child who was only half-awake and might otherwise have settled down by herself. Toddlers are notoriously noisy sleepers, and it's important to recognize that most of the noises they make during the night don't require a response. (Be sure, of course, that the crib environment is totally safe; see page 625.)

**Check out the situation.** If whimpering escalates into wailing, slip into your toddler's room to be sure she isn't sick or tangled up in the covers. Straighten out her bedding, if necessary. Change her diaper if it's dirty or sopping (preferably without taking her out of the crib and with only a dim night-light on). If she's standing up, lay her down and tuck her in again. Then . . .

**Offer quiet comfort.** Keep the reassurance low-key: The idea is to help your child comfort herself, not to do the job for her. Without talking or picking her up, gently pat or stroke her back for a moment. Add a soothing, "Shhhh . . ." if necessary. Wait until she's calm, but not until she's asleep, and then quietly tell her that you're going back to your bed now and leave the room. If she begins

---

## KEEP IT COOL

• • • • • • • • • •

For sleeping, 65°F is a good goal year-round. If you live in an overheated building, opening the window slightly in cold weather may help keep the room temperature comfortable. In the summer, however, running the air conditioner, if you have one, to achieve 65°F may be wasteful environmentally. Consider setting the air-conditioner temperature somewhat higher and using a fan to circulate the air. A fan will also help if you have no air-conditioning. Be sure neither fan nor air conditioner blows directly on your toddler.

## WHEN THE COW'S THE CULPRIT

**S**ometimes even when parents follow all the recommendations of sleep experts, their toddlers persist in waking up one or more times between bedtime and dawn. In many of those cases, the cause is milk allergy (page 15) or intolerance (page 355), most often associated with the consumption of cow's milk and cow's-milk products. For these toddlers, the elimination of the offending food usually "cures" the insomnia.

You can suspect food allergy or intolerance if these factors are present:

▲ You've tried the techniques on page 65 for helping toddlers sleep through the night and they haven't done the trick.

▲ The sleeplessness began or worsened at about the time your toddler was switched from breast milk or formula to cow's milk.

▲ Your child has gone through a medical work-up and no medical cause (such as sleep apnea) for the sleep disturbances has been found.

▲ There is a family history of food allergy or lactose intolerance.

▲ Your toddler has a history of runny nose, recurrent nose or ear infections, diarrhea, eczema, or nighttime wheezing and/or sweating.

▲ Tests show your toddler has increased blood values of immunoglobulin and anti-lactoglobulins.

crying again (which she probably will), wait five minutes before going back in, and then repeat the comforting process. If the crying resumes, continue this process, each time adding five-minute increments until you're waiting twenty minutes between visits to her room. At some point, she's sure to fall off to sleep on her own. Over the next couple of nights, the number of crying periods should drop, and by the fourth or fifth night the crying will probably cease entirely (although there may be some whimpering when your child awakens and resettles herself).

If your toddler seems to be fearful of being left alone or seems to be having nightmares, you'll have to deal with these issues as well as with the night waking.[3]

If she sleeps fitfully and awakens often during the night, check with the

nurse or doctor to be sure she doesn't have sleep apnea (see page 169).

# NIGHTTIME FEEDINGS

*"Our daughter still wakes us up at least once during the night. Since we both work all day, and we need our sleep, we do the easiest thing to get her back to sleep: give her a bottle. We know it's a bad habit, but we don't know how to stop."*

**I**t's understandable that you've been choosing the path of least resistance in getting your daughter back to sleep. With busy schedules and a demanding toddler draining your patience and your endurance, you probably don't want to deal with any more resistance than you have to—especially at two or three in the morning.

But you're right. Feeding your toddler in the middle of the night at this age

---

3. For more information on dealing with night wakings, see the very helpful *Solve Your Child's Sleep Problems*, by Richard Ferber, M.D.

# *NOW I LAY ME DOWN TO SLEEP*

• • • • • • • • • •

Going to bed can be a pleasant experience—one that's looked forward to as the day draws to a close—or it can be an unpleasant one—dreaded by child and parent alike. It all depends on the trappings. To make bedtime a highlight of the family day and more conducive to sleep, create a nightly routine. Stick to the routine as closely as you can (the predictability of a routine is very comforting to toddlers, and helps facilitate transitions), straying from it only when you have no option. The routine should be aimed at creating a relaxed and calm atmosphere (relegate tickling and roughhousing to an earlier part of the evening). It may include any of the following, and should be individualized to fit your needs and those of your child or children.

**Clean up.** Almost everyone finds comfort in a tub of warm water, children included, so the bath is a perfect beginning for the bedtime ritual.*

**Suit up.** Changing into pajamas (make sure they're cozy and comfortable and cuddly, with no rough seams or scratchy collars, es-

*If your toddler is fearful of water or baths, skip this part of the ritual for now and see page 94. If your toddler has very dry skin, you may need to bathe him or her less frequently; see page 464.

pecially if your child's skin is particularly sensitive) continues the transition from day to night. In the morning, make the change from pajamas to daywear soon after your child gets up so that pajamas become a clear symbol of nighttime, bedtime, and sleeping.

**Snack up.** Especially if your toddler eats dinner early, there's a long stretch of fasting ahead before breakfast. Serving a light snack at bedtime can stave off middle-of-the-night hunger pangs, and if it's chosen carefully, can help induce sleep. A combination of protein and healthful carbohydrates (a little plain yogurt with sliced banana and wheat germ; a piece of cheese, a cracker, and some orange juice; or a juice-sweetened cookie and a cup of milk) make a soporific snack.

**Brush up.** The bedtime brushing is the most important one of the day. If it's not removed, bacteria that's built up on your toddler's teeth can spend the night feasting on tender enamel, causing decay. So make this brushing thorough (see page 492.)

**Read up.** Snuggle up side-by-side in a special place (preferably the same spot each night), and read some stories together. The selections should be serene: no witches, no monsters, no spooky settings, no raucous rhymes.** As your toddler gets a bit older

(whether breast or bottle) is not a good idea. And for several reasons. For one, nighttime feeding is associated with the development of tooth decay (see page 27). For another, your toddler doesn't need nourishment during the night any more than you do;[4] her body is equipped to go the ten or twelve hours of sleep in

a fasting mode. Feeding her when she doesn't need to be fed can lead to overweight, confusion about the purpose of eating, and to eating for the wrong reasons. This in turn can cause weight problems later on in life. Filling up on fluids during the night can also lead to more night waking, a result of uncomfortably wet diapers. What's more, feeding your child too close to waking can easily spoil her appetite for solids at breakfast. And finally, feeding your toddler to get her back to slumber, while undeniably effective, denies her the opportunity to learn

4. Unless she's not growing (in weight and height) as she should be (see the growth chart on page 864), in which case you should go over her daytime menus with her doctor to see where they can be beefed up (see Chapter Eighteen).

and more aware of time and numbers, put a time limit (three books, fifteen minutes, or whatever seems sensible) on your reading. When you get down to the last book or the last few minutes, give fair warning so that your listener won't suddenly be shocked to find the session over.

**Listen up and cuddle up.** A quiet cuddle while listening to a tape of favorite lullabies or other relaxing music can supplement the story hour and provides a perfect prelude to sleep.

**Recap.** At some point in the routine, spend a little time talking to your toddler about the day, about what fun you had together, about how much you love him or her.

**Say good night all around.** This finale is very helpful to a toddler separating from daytime fun and games and entering the quiet solitude of nighttime. Instead of whisking your toddler directly off to bed, take him or her on a "good-night" tour of the house. Together, say "good night" to Mommy, Daddy, siblings, pets, toys, stuffed animals, the sofa, the refrigerator, the stars and moon outside the window—even to your toddler's reflection in the mirror. Limit each encounter to a brief good night, however—otherwise, the tour could go on for hours.

---

**A favorite bedtime classic is *Goodnight Moon* by Margaret Wise Brown.

**Tuck in a few friends.** A beloved blanket or a trusted teddy in hand and a few well-selected sentries (a row of familiar dolls and stuffed animals) standing guard over (but not in) the crib can make a toddler feel more secure about submitting to slumber. Finally, leave your toddler with a hug, a kiss, a cheerful word or two ("See you in the morning" helps the toddler bridge the gap between night and day). Don't tarry, even if requested. Staying with your toddler until sleep comes deprives him or her of the opportunity to learn good sleep habits. It can also increase sleep problems.

Good intentions notwithstanding, there may be times when your toddler dozes off during the bedtime routine. How you handle the situation will depend on what kind of sleeper you have on your hands. If you know that your toddler will wake a bit but be drowsy enough to fall right back into dreamland when tucked in, then do try a polite awakening. If, on the other hand, your toddler will be cranky and have trouble going back to sleep if awakened en route to the crib, you may want to just let your sleeping toddler lie—and make a silent transfer to the crib. If this happens every night, however, you will have to move the bedtime routine to an earlier time slot so that your little one will be able to stay awake until tuck-in time, and thus have the opportunity to fall asleep on his or her own.

how to fall back to sleep on her own, a skill she'll need for the rest of her sleeping life.

Clearly, you and your toddler are caught in a vicious cycle of supply and demand. You supply your toddler's tummy with a nighttime meal, and her tummy wakes her (and you) to demand a repeat each night—just as someone who regularly lunches at noon can expect hunger pangs to strike daily at the stroke of twelve. The only way to train her to sleep through the night without a feeding is to cut off the nighttime food

supply and reset her internal hunger clock.

You're bound to meet up with some pretty heavy resistance—in the form of waking and crying—once you stop taking the path of least resistance. But eventually, both your toddler and you will sleep better for your efforts.

You have a double task: ending the night wakings and the night feedings. You can go at both together, opting to try the techniques for ending night wakings, described above, to end night feedings cold turkey and turn your toddler's sleeping habits around at the same time. Or you can try to wean your toddler from her midnight snacks first, and then work on the sleep problem if it continues. With this approach, when your toddler wakes at night, you substitute a bottle of water for the milk she's been accustomed to. This allows her to use the bottle as a go-back-to-sleep aid a little longer. But more important, it will also reset her appestat (the control center in the brain that oversees appetite) and end her middle-of-the-night need to feed, reducing the risk such feeding poses to her teeth and her weight. Eventually, the bottle of water may end your toddler's night waking, too. Many toddlers decide it's not worth waking up for it.

If your toddler continues to wake for a midnight snack, paltry though it may be, or conversely, if being handed a bottle of water launches her on a temper tantrum, then you'll have no choice but to try option one, cold turkey.

# ANTISOCIAL BEHAVIOR

*"I've got a thirteen-month-old son and recently got together with several neighbors to form a play group. We have five toddlers all between twelve and fifteen months old. They play all right, but not with each other."*

Socializing doesn't come easily to most toddlers—and sometimes it's hard to imagine that it's ever going to come at all. Put a group of average one-and-a-half-year-olds together in a room, and you're more likely to see a free-for-all than cooperative play.

But this typically "antisocial" behavior is as normal as it is natural. Early on in the socializing game, toddlers view fellow toddlers as objects—objects that move and make noise, but objects nonetheless. Objects that can be pushed aside or pushed around as necessary (and that, curiously, often push back), objects whose toys and food are up for grabs, objects that are interesting to observe, poke, and prod, but difficult to interact with.

Playing cooperatively requires not only that your child learn to see these objects as people, but that he also develops the ability to empathize—something a toddler almost invariably finds difficult. Comfortably ensconced at the center of the universe (as he is in his own estimation), he's not ready to recognize or consider the needs, desires, or feelings of those revolving around him.

Still, it's not too early to start getting your toddler ready for the social whirl. Since children aren't born civilized, social beings, and social skills aren't passed on in the genes the way blue eyes or musical ability are (though some children are innately more sociable than others), the art of interaction must be learned. And as with most skills, your toddler will learn best through a combination of practice, exposure, and example.

Being part of a family is a vital first step, and being part of a play group is a good second one (see page 108 for tips on setting one up). But don't expect social etiquette to be mastered quickly. Although most toddlers enjoy the company of other toddlers, they're unlikely to cultivate it. For some time to come, there's likely to be a lot of what appears to be thoughtless and unkind behavior in your toddler's play group. The more aggressive children will try to establish dominance over the more submissive ones. Parallel (side-by-side) play will be the rule, and cooperative play the exception. A good deal of the interactions will take the form of pushing and grabbing. The concept of sharing will probably be nonexistent (though, happily, many fifteen-month-olds lack possessiveness, too, and will give up without

*Most young toddlers are still playing side-by-side (parallel play) instead of with each other. With time and experience, toddler socializing becomes more interactive—jointly-built block structures will then take the place of independently-built ones.*

a fight when a toy is taken from them). A toddler may occasionally seem to become generous and offer a toy or a bagel to a friend or family member, but in most cases he or she will withdraw the offer before giving up the object.

In spite of this lack of true cooperative play, the play group members will be gaining valuable social experience that they'll put to good use one day soon. If the group meets regularly, you'll eventually begin to see the signs of true socializing.

And chances are these signs will start appearing sooner rather than later. It was once believed that children weren't capable of playing cooperatively until the age of three or four, and weren't able to make real friends until somewhere past their fifth birthdays. But after observing toddlers who regularly spent time with their peers, particularly those who attended a day care center or early preschool, some experts have concluded that children can not only learn to play with each other, but in a very rudimentary sense, become friends, sometimes as early as the end of the first year.

Though learning social skills at an early age can give children a head start

in preschool or kindergarten, such a start has not been shown to make them more socially adept as adults. So don't worry if you can't provide your toddler with the opportunity to socialize frequently now; he'll catch up when he gets to school. Nor should you worry if your toddler doesn't seem interested in socializing or if he doesn't seem to be particularly skillful at it. Set a social example yourself. Make the opportunities available to him if you can, but don't push. When he's ready to become a social animal, he will. (Keep in mind, however, that there are many levels of sociability. Some children are by nature much more gregarious than others. Accept and enjoy your child's nature, whatever it may be.)

Harried parents often find that they don't get around to starting or joining a play group or providing other opportunities for group play for second, third, or subsequent children. Yet these children rarely seem to suffer socially— probably because they get their share of socializing at home. After all, a child who has learned to play nicely with a sibling can learn to play with anyone.

# EARLY HITTING

*"I occasionally get together with a friend who also has a toddler. I've been very embarrassed a couple of times when my daughter swung at the other child. She didn't hurt him, but I guess she could have."*

At this age, aggressive behavior is not calculated or malicious. Young toddlers slug out of frustration that they can't cope with or shove to get another child out of their way. They can't be considered callous about hurting others either physically or emotionally, because they haven't yet figured out that others have feelings.

While it's too early to expect truly empathic behavior from your toddler (she's more likely to experience cause-and-effect curiosity than empathy when her slap reduces her playmate to tears), it isn't too early to start planting the seeds. When your child takes a swing at her playmate, say firmly, "Don't hit! Hitting hurts, doesn't it?—ouch!" When your child is the victim, comfort her and say, "Hitting hurts, that's why we don't hit." But realize that your words will almost certainly need to be backed up by actions. Supervise play dates closely and stop aggressive behavior the moment it starts by removing the offender from the victim and quickly distracting both with a new activity—thereby restoring harmony. If necessary, resort to a time out or another disciplining technique (see page 127).

Whatever you do, don't respond to toddler aggression by slapping your child. Hitting a child teaches her that violence is an appropriate response under stress. So keep your temper in check when dealing with hers. For tips on dealing with more serious toddler aggression, see page 189.

# ACQUIRING A PET

*"We had a dog who died before our son was born. We're eager to get another pet. Is this a good time?"*

A dog can not only be a toddler's best friend, it can also be one of his best learning tools. This is true of pets in general, but especially true of dogs. From a dog, a young child can learn about animals and nature, about responsibility, about empathy, about getting along with others, about unconditional love and loyalty. A toddler can help with the care and feeding of a dog— a welcome role reversal for one who is usually on the receiving end of everyone else's caregiving. He can count on his dog to be there for him when he needs it or wants it; unlike parents, dogs are hardly ever too busy for a cuddle or a romp. And since dogs, especially young ones, like to run, jump, frisk, and frolic just as toddlers do, they can join in the toddler games for which parents often lack energy or enthusiasm.

Cats may not be compatible companions for toddlers. Though some cats (particularly those raised in a family with children) are very affectionate and fairly patient with toddlers, many felines prefer the more sedate company of adults. They may be less likely to run around with a toddler than to run away from one. They're also less liable to be tolerant of a toddler's playful roughhousing, which can prove frustrating—and possibly dangerous—to the toddler. If you do choose a cat as a pet, screen candidates carefully with your toddler in tow.

As valuable an addition to a toddler household as a pet can be, pet ownership is a major responsibility that parents should consider seriously. Whether this is the right time to expand your family by one furry member will depend on several factors:

▲ Is your toddler comfortable with animals? If he's afraid or tentative around them, give him some experience with other people's pets and wait until he becomes more relaxed with animals before bringing a pet home. (See page 84 for ways of dealing with fear of animals.)

▲ Is there enough room in your home for pet and toddler? Just as toddlers do, pets, especially puppies, need space in which to play. Consider whether there's enough for child and pet to run around in without having a run-in.

▲ Is there enough room in your schedule for pet and toddler? Pets and toddlers alike need care, attention, and guidance. And unless you acquire a pet that's been obedience-trained already, both have a lot to learn. Think about whether you have the time to feed, groom, entertain, and teach them both.

Choosing the right pet to get is just as important as choosing the right time for getting a pet. So before proceeding to the pet shop or the shelter, consider the following:

**Breed.** Not all breeds are equally good with children. Select one known to be friendly and patient with tots. Often, mixed breeds are less high-strung, more patient, and more intelligent than purebreds. More important than breed is the personality of the individual animal, so spend some time getting to know a prospective pet with your toddler before snapping the leash in place and taking it home. The right pet will be friendly and affectionate, won't shy away from young children, and will not snap if an ear is poked or a tail pulled.

**Gender.** In general, female dogs are more gentle than males. On the other hand, male cats are often more people-loving and affectionate. Neutering tends to make both dogs and cats less aggressive, more gentle, and easier to handle.

It can also help considerably if cats are declawed. But again, individual temperament should be the overriding consideration.

**Age.** The advantage of buying a puppy or kitten is that it can grow up with your toddler, and a strong bond can develop between them. The disadvantage, of course, is that you have two babies in the house, both of whom require a lot of attention and training. A mature animal will usually be housebroken or litter-trained, an advantage. But it will also be set in its ways and may have a difficult time making friends with your toddler. An adult animal who's been raised with young children is a good compromise. A pet on the brink of old age, however, may require more time-consuming care than you can give.

Once you have brought the new pet home, keep in mind these important facts:

▲ Pets need to be toddler-trained. If your new pet is not accustomed to young children, have it spend time with your toddler only under close supervision. Keep these getting-to-know-each-other sessions brief at first so that neither the animal nor your toddler will be overwhelmed.

▲ Toddlers need to be pet-trained. Often overly exuberant, toddlers can hurt or alarm a pet when they actually mean to show affection. See page 85 for tips on training your toddler in pet sensitivity and safety.

▲ Pets and toddlers may need to be protected from each other, at least at first. Since both can be unpredictable, the potential for harm (intentional or not) is great on both sides. In addition to supervising your toddler and pet when they're together, provide a safe play space for your toddler to which your pet can't gain access when you can't oversee (a safety gate across a doorway will usually do the trick).

▲ Pets and toddlers shouldn't eat to-gether. Feed your pet when your little one is napping, has gone to bed for the night, is safely restrained in his high chair, or is busy in another room. Or put the pet's bowl of food down as you head out the door to the store or the playground. Pick the pet bowl up after each meal, unless it's in a space that's inaccessible to your toddler. These steps will not only keep your toddler from nibbling on the puppy chow but also keep your puppy from nibbling on your toddler when it catches his fingers in the chow; even friendly animals can become hostile when someone takes their food.

It also makes sense to keep your pet out of the room when your toddler is eating. Otherwise, feeding will soon dissolve into frenzy, with more food ending up in (and on) your pet than in your toddler.

▲ Pets need their shots, too. Your pet's vaccinations must be kept up to date; rabies is a threat not only in rural areas but also in suburbs; the disease gets passed to pets by neighborhood skunks and raccoons. Cats as well as dogs can contract rabies, and once infected, can become more aggressive and can transmit the disease.

▲ Being kind to animals makes for kinder animals. Disciplining your pet roughly can make him jittery and more apt to snap and sets a bad example for your toddler. Instead, treat a pet firmly but with respect. If possible (and if necessary), invest in obedience training.

## CRAWLING RELAPSE

*"Our daughter started walking a week ago, but has suddenly gone back to crawling. Is something wrong?"*

Development is often a one-step-forward, one-step-back process, particularly when it comes to a developmental milestone as major as walking. Your daughter's sudden return to crawling can probably be attributed to one of the following factors:

▲ Ambivalence about independence. Walking represents a big step toward growing up. As much as most toddlers crave independence and thrive on it, it can sometimes be a worrisome prospect.

▲ Frustration. It takes patience—an attribute most toddlers have in short supply—to perfect walking. Frustration over frequent falls, slow speed, or an inability to turn a corner without bumping into it, may prompt a toddler to take to her knees again until her legs and feet have worked out their kinks.

▲ A nasty fall. Taking a traumatic tumble can cause some cautious toddlers to think twice about getting back on their own two feet again. Until they recover their nerve, crawling may provide the most comforting route from here to there.

▲ An unsettling change. A new child-care situation, a new sibling, a parent going back to work can bring on the kind of emotional stress that can bring back old, baby-like habits.

▲ A new accomplishment. Often, a still-wobbly skill, such as walking, will be temporarily dropped while a toddler focuses her full attention on honing another, such as talking.

▲ An upcoming cold or other minor illness. For a few days before the symptoms of a cold, flu, or other virus become apparent, children often suffer from a rundown feeling that keeps them from running around. In this case, walking, which is still a challenge, might well be dropped in favor of the more familiar and less stressful crawling.

▲ A bad day. Everybody has them—and some toddlers have them quite often. Crankiness and fatigue can temporarily sap a toddler's energy and dampen her enthusiasm for such physical feats as walking.

Of course, if your toddler doesn't want to walk at all, is unusually irritable, or seems to be limping or unable to stand upright, check with her nurse-practitioner or doctor to make sure there is no physical problem, such as an undiagnosed injury or illness.

# LOSS OF VOCABULARY

*"For a while, our son was using a wide variety of words, but in the last week or so, he seems to be using fewer. Shouldn't he be adding to his vocabulary instead of subtracting from it?"*

It's unlikely that your son is losing his vocabulary; he's probably just busy gaining a new skill. Toddlers typically switch off between different kinds of acquisitions and accomplishments: One week they concentrate on verbal skills, the next week physical skills, the following week social skills, the week after that verbal skills again. Often, they're so focused on polishing that skill-of-the-week that they neglect to practice the others.

It's also possible that your child is taking the hiatus from speaking that many young toddlers take after they've mastered their first few words. The break allows beginning speakers the time they need to consolidate their gains and strengthen their receptive vocabularies (the words they understand), so that they can prepare to launch a whole new list of words.

It could be, too, that a change or disruption in your toddler's routine or his life (a new baby-sitter, a new day-care situation, a vacation, a trip out of town taken by Mommy or Daddy) might have left him temporarily speechless. If this seems to be the case, some extra support and reassurance might quickly help get him speaking again.

Or, perhaps, he's simply under too much parental pressure to verbalize. Pushing a toddler to add to his vocabulary is almost certain to trigger resistance. In that case, easing up on the pressure may well get him talking again.

If your toddler stops speaking entirely or doesn't start adding new words to his vocabulary after a week or two, or if his sudden shrinking from speech is accompanied by lethargy, uncharacteristic crankiness, or other symptoms, seek medical advice. He may be ill or upset about something.

# CAVEPERSON LANGUAGE

*"Our fourteen-month-old seems to understand everything, but she only says a half-dozen words. Most of the time she just pushes, pulls, grunts in the direction of what she wants."*

It's pretty remarkable how much a toddler can get across without uttering a recognizable word: Like a little cavewoman, she hauls Mom by the skirt into the kitchen, pushes Dad's legs in the direction of the back door, grunts or nods in response to questions, points to things she wants. And as long as she's actively trying to communicate, you can be impressed by your child's ingenuity rather than worried about her plodding verbal progress.

Although you should make every attempt to comprehend, respond to, and encourage your toddler's primitive language, you should also use it to help her develop modern-day linguistic skills. If she pulls you in the direction of the refrigerator, for example, do a simultaneous translation: "Oh, you want to go to the refrigerator. What do you want? Do you want juice?" If she grunts and points to the stuffed clown on the shelf, ask, "Do you want the clown? Should I get the clown for you?" and then, "Here's the clown." For more tips on stimulating language development, see page 37.

# BIRTHMARKS

*"I thought that by now my son's strawberry birthmark would be less noticeable, but it doesn't seem to be."*

---

## BIRTHMARKS, A YEAR LATER

Newborns can come with a variety of birthmarks—some small, some large, some flat, some raised, some brightly hued, some subdued. Certain birthmarks will fade, others will shrink, others will stick around for a lifetime. Few can, or should, be removed. Chances are that if your toddler has a birthmark it is less noticeable now than it used to be, either because it's grown smaller or because your toddler's grown larger—or just because you've grown accustomed to it. Here's what you can expect from the most common birthmarks a year or so after birth:

**Salmon patch (nevus simplex).** These pale-pink or coral blotches with diffuse borders (sometimes called "stork bites") appear on 40 to 45% of newborns. They are usually located on the eyelids, on the center of the lower forehead (glabellar), and, most often, at the nape of the neck (nuchal). Generally, eyelid lesions fade by a year, those on the forehead take longer, and those on the nape of the neck may not fade at all, but will eventually be covered by hair. Sometimes, even after they seem to have disappeared, stork bites become temporarily visible when a child cries or exercises.

**Port-wine stains (nevus flammeus).** These less-common birthmarks are found on 1 in 200 children, and vary in color from pink to deep purple, though in children with dark skin they may look black. They can appear anywhere on the body and are usually flat (though occasionally they become bumpy) with clearly defined edges. Rarely, they are associated with other anomalies (check with your toddler's doctor if you have any concerns). Port-wine stains may change color somewhat but don't generally fade. Cosmetics, such as Covermark, can be used, if desired, to camouflage port-wine stains early in childhood. Research shows that pulse-dyed laser therapy provides good cosmetic improvement in these birthmarks, with a low incidence of scarring. Unlike argon laser therapy, which often causes scarring in children under sixteen, pulse-dyed laser therapy may be used on infants and young children. Check with a pediatric dermatologist for information.

**Strawberry marks (hemangiomas).** By the end of the first year, about 8 to 10% of children will have developed one of these bright red, rather clearly defined, bumpy birthmarks that resemble strawberries and range from freckle-size to 2 or 3 inches across. During the toddler years these clumps of dilated capillaries in the top layers of the skin begin to fade very gradually, turning grayish in color. Eventually, they disappear entirely—in about half of affected children by age five; in 70% by age seven; and in 90% by

Strawberries are still in season—these colorful birthmarks generally stick around for several years at least. Chances are, however, that your toddler's strawberry mark (clinically known as a hemangioma) is actually looking less and less like its namesake fruit, that it's becoming lighter and grayer, smaller and flatter, but that you are unable to perceive the difference because you see the mark each day. Your toddler's doctor probably checks the birthmark at each visit, though perhaps without commenting on it to you. If you took a photo of it when it first appeared, compare the birthmark in the early photo with the way the mark looks now. You're sure to notice a pronounced change.

To monitor a strawberry mark's changes, take a color photo of it now and measure it at least once a year. The box that begins on the facing page will explain just what you can expect over the next few years.

---

age nine. A strawberry mark is best left untreated, unless it appears on a problem area (such as an eyelid, where, because of lumpiness, it could hamper eyelid movement and interfere with vision) or if it becomes infected, hemorrhages, ulcerates, or continues to grow. A child with numerous hemangiomas also needs medical attention. In the rare instances that treatment is needed, options include surgery, steroids, pressure, argon laser, cryotherapy, and radiation.

**Cavernous hemangiomas.** These birthmarks are composed of larger blood vessels than those that make up strawberry hemangiomas. They are bluish in color, with less clearly defined borders than their cousins. They are less common (only 1 or 2 in 100 children have one) and slower to fade—though most do disappear before the teen years. Occasionally, a scar remains. Treatment, when needed, is similar to that for strawberry marks.

**Mongolian spots.** These bluish black spots, which look like bruises and are most often found on the back or buttocks (and less often on the legs and shoulders) are extremely common among Black (98.8%), Asian (81%), and Hispanic (70%) infants. Most mongolian spots fade by the end of the first year; rarely, they develop later in childhood and persist into adulthood.

**Café-au-lait spots.** These flat patches of darkened skin can range in color from creamy beige (coffee with lots of milk) to dark brown (coffee with just a touch of milk) and usually remain visible for a lifetime. If necessary, makeup can be used to cover them. If your toddler has a number of these spots, mention this to the doctor; they could be related to an hereditary disorder.

**Congenital pigmented nevi, or moles.** Small moles, which can vary in color from light brown to blackish and tend to grow with a child, are fairly common, affecting 1 in 100 children. Although they don't disappear, they are not cause for concern unless they grow rapidly or change in shape or color. Large moles, which can be flat or raised, range from half-dollar to melon-size, and are sometimes hairy, are seen less often than small ones, but do have a greater potential for malignancy. It's usually recommended that large moles and suspicious smaller ones be surgically removed when possible and monitored carefully by a doctor when they can't be removed. Check with your child's doctor.

**Acquired nevi, or moles.** Most light-skinned people develop a number of small moles during their lifetimes, but these don't usually appear before age five. A new mole, however, that appears suddenly on your toddler's skin and is larger than a pencil eraser, has an irregular perimeter, or contains a mixture of shades or colors, should be shown to your child's doctor.

# WHAT IT'S IMPORTANT TO KNOW:
## Accentuating the Senses

Adults take their senses largely for granted. Though we use them every waking hour, we hardly ever use them to their full potential. How many of us, after all, actually stop to smell those roses? Or to listen to the chatter of the birds? Or to savor the taste of the cinnamon in our breakfast muffins? Or let our fingertips revel in the textures of everything we touch, our eyes appreciate every beautiful sight?

Toddlers, on the other hand, not only stop to smell the roses, they stop to look at them, touch them, and more than likely, taste them. They use their senses the way the scientist uses the laboratory. It's through these five miraculous resources that toddlers make their discoveries about the complex world they live in, discoveries that come fast and furious during this intensely curious stage of development.

Even without encouragement, a toddler will instinctively tap into these natural resources. With your encouragement, your child will utilize them even more fully. Use the following as a guide to stimulating your toddler's sensory perceptions and to inspire your own toddler-stimulating strategies.

**Sight.** Because toddlers have not yet developed the ability to pick and choose visually, everything within their range of vision vies for their attention. The park is a kinetic kaleidoscope: tall trees, brightly colored flowers, a little girl circling on a tricycle, a boy zipping past on roller skates, a man pushing a baby carriage, a woman jogging, a squirrel nosing around for acorns, a dog chasing a butterfly. With so much to see, it's not easy for a toddler's untrained eyes to focus on just one part of the picture for more than a fleeting moment.

You can help your toddler practice focusing by calling attention to one object in the scene at a time. At first, keep it simple: "Look at the girl on the pink tricycle. She's riding the tricycle." When your toddler is a bit older, you can begin adding other details: "She's a good rider. Look at the girl's hair—there's a pretty red ribbon in her hair. And her pants have red flowers on them."

Play the "looking" game everywhere you go. Try it in settings that are virtual visual feasts—the beach, the zoo, a crowded city sidewalk—and in settings that seem visually less exciting—the doctor's office, the supermarket parking lot, the post office. Visually explore objects that you and your toddler have seen dozens of times, challenging her to spot something new in the familiar, as well as objects that you've never seen before. The "looking" game will not only be visually invigorating for a toddler but will (as you associate sights with words) help speed her speech development and turn potentially tedious and fussy times (when you're waiting your turn at the deli counter, for instance) into time well-spent.

Your toddler will also enjoy seeing the world from other perspectives: *Through the looking glass,* for example. Toddler's love to look at themselves (most can recognize themselves in a mirror by the end of the fifteenth month) and others in a mirror. You can also show them what their toys and other objects look like in that magic medium. *Through rose-colored glasses.* The distortion of color seen through tinted glasses often captivates young children. So does the distortion of images and shapes viewed through a sheer curtain, a glass block, or a stained-glass ornament.

*Through a magnifying glass.* Older toddlers find investigating their surroundings with a magnifying glass fascinating (make sure the lens is unbreakable). Show your junior scientist how the magnifying glass works, then provide plenty of opportunities to use it in the house and outdoors.

**Sound.** Like your toddler's eyes, your toddler's ears are bombarded daily. Even at home, the auditory competition is fierce: There's music from the radio, a clock ticking, a dog barking in the neighbor's yard, a siren wailing blocks away, an airplane flying overhead, Mommy talking on the telephone, a fan whirling in the kitchen. Encouraging a toddler to focus on a single sound—to shut out the others so that one sound can be fully appreciated—provides a good exercise for young ears.

Flex your toddler's auditory muscles by playing the "listening" game. Call his or her attention to sounds as you sit in the living room, ride in the car, or walk through the park. "Do you hear that siren (whooo, whooo, whooo)? That sounds like a fire engine." "Do you hear the birdie singing (tweet, tweet, tweet)? It sounds pretty." "Do you hear the airplane (vrooom) up in the sky? Isn't it loud?" (Cover your ears with your hands to emphasize the loud noise.) As your child gets older and comprehends more, you can add more details: "We can't see the bird because it's too high up in the tree, but we can hear the singing." "The fire engine is going to a fire." "I wonder where the airplane is going. Maybe to California, where Grandma lives."

When your toddler is older you can intensify the auditory experience and double the fun by turning the listening game into a guessing game. Have your toddler close his or her eyes. Then, one at a time, present a variety of sounds (the ticking of a watch, clanging of a bell, music from a music box) for identification. Some older toddlers enjoy playing this game blindfolded, but others may be frightened by having their eyes covered.

The sound of music can be not only entertaining and tranquilizing for toddlers but it can also teach them to be careful listeners. Expose your child to a variety of musical styles (classical, country, folk, jazz, soft rock[5]) on tape or on the radio. Take in a children's concert together when one comes to your neighborhood. Play music in the background while your toddler plays, or center play around it, through musical games such as "Ring-Around-a-Rosie" and "Farmer in the Dell." Dancing to music (alone, in your arms, or holding your hands) will also help your toddler tune in to the sound of music.

And don't forget to give your toddler a chance to make his or her own "music"—by banging on a pot with a wooden spoon, clanging two spoons together, playing a toy instrument, fingering the keys on the family piano, scratching fingernails across various surfaces (the living room carpet, venetian blinds, the brick on the outside of a building, a piece of paper).

The sound of voices is another fascinating subject for auditory study. Using a tape recorder (there are some especially designed for young children), tape a variety of voices: your toddler's, yours, your spouse's, a sibling's, Grandma's, Grandpa's, a friend's, the baby-sitter's. Then play them back for your toddler and try to identify them together. You can also include other sounds on the tape for identification: a dog barking, a horn honking, the washing machine agitating, the faucet running, the doorbell ringing.

**Smells.** Toddlers' noses are fairly undiscerning—which probably explains why the odor of their own soiled diapers doesn't offend them as much as it does those around them. And why they'll

---

5. But avoid turning the volume up; loud music can damage hearing.

cuddle up without reservation to a parent who's just downed a garlicky Caesar salad when everyone else in the house is staying safely upwind. And why, unfortunately, their noses don't stop them from sampling dangerous substances (such as cleaning fluids or spoiled food) that would smell noxious to an older child or to an adult.

Somewhere around the time toddlers learn to use the toilet, they begin to make sense out of scents, developing the ability to sort smells into those that are esthetically pleasing and those that are not. Exposure to a wide range of sniffing experiences will sharpen these olfactory capabilities, so that your toddler will eventually be able to not only smell those roses but also to differentiate between them and the fertilizer that was used on them.

Taking a sniffing tour of your home will be a nostril-opening experience for your toddler. Sniff the flowers in the vase, laundry fresh out of the dryer, the peaches and bananas ripening on the counter, the chow in the dog's bowl, and the burgers on the family table, identifying each for your toddler. When you're cooking, stop to let your toddler smell the onions you're chopping for stew, the vanilla and the cinnamon you're adding to the muffins, the Parmesan you're grating for the pasta, the tuna you're tossing in the salad. Keeping a watchful eye to prevent sniffing from turning into inhalation, let your toddler's nose have a go at the spice cabinet—from subtle sage to jarring ginger.

Sniff as you go, too. When you're walking through the park, smell the lilacs and the honeysuckle, the pine needles and the freshly mowed grass. When you're at the market, smell the lemons, the oranges, the fresh herbs, the baked goods, the barbecuing chickens.

With older, more adventurous toddlers, "smelling" guessing games can be played blindfolded or with eyes closed. Have your toddler try to identify items

by smell as you hold them up to his or her nose (aftershave, a ripe banana, toasted bread, strawberries).

**Taste.** Most toddlers are somewhat less open to expanding the horizons of their taste buds than they are to other sensory adventures. For a child who won't open wide for anything that doesn't look like a Cheerio, trailblazing gastronomic roadways may be met with tightly clenched teeth instead of eagerly parted lips.

Nevertheless, trying never hurts, and even the most finicky toddler may surprise you by doing just that, especially when the new taste is presented with some fanfare. Experiment with a variety of tastes, textures, colors, and shapes. Occasionally offer a tastefully designed lunchtime sampler on a large plate (but make sure none of the foods "touch" one another; many toddlers dislike mingling flavors). Such a smorgasbord will stimulate not only the sense of taste but, as a bonus, the sense of sight. Introduce some new taste sensations along with some old favorites. As your toddler nibbles, have him or her, with your help, describe the flavor of the fare: banana chunks (sweet and mushy), cheese cubes (salty), minced apple (sweet, crunchy, juicy), cottage cheese (creamy, soft), raisins cooked in juice (sweet, chewy). Never force, pressure, plead, or bribe your toddler to taste a food, however. You'll only encourage more resistance and possibly set up future eating problems.

Toddlers use their sense of taste to explore the nonedibles in their environment, too. Though they may use their mouths less often than they did as babies, some toddlers are still mouthing objects. Which means that special attention must be paid to what your child gets his or her hands on; whatever it is, it's sure to get shoved into a ready mouth.

**Touch.** Toddlers discover so much about their world through their fingertips. Often, from a parent's point of view, too much. They discover, for instance, that tearing pages out of a magazine is fun (and gets the best reaction if that issue hasn't been read yet). And that manipulating the VCR remote is exhilarating (especially after having been told repeatedly to stop).

Considering how much mischief toddlers manage to get into through touching, it's not surprising that they often receive less encouragement to use and develop this sense than any other. But touch can teach toddlers a lot. And encouraging toddlers to touch in a safe, childproofed environment (see page 240) will not only help them build up this tactile sense, it will also help minimize the daily frustration of living in a world where so much is off-limits.

Invite your toddler to feel the roughness of Daddy's unshaven cheeks first thing in the morning, then their smoothness after a shave. The silkiness of a blouse, the nubbiness of a sweater. The fluffiness of a cotton ball, the brittleness of dead leaves. Take your toddler on a fingertip tour in and around the house: the raised embroidery on a pillow, the irregularity of a slate floor, the intricately carved detail on a wooden bannister, the velvety softness of a flower petal, the crew-cut spikiness of a newly cut lawn.

Find textures intriguing to the touch everywhere you go, and let your toddler run his or her fingers along the scratchy surface of burlap, the cold smoothness of steel, the glossiness of wallpaper. Save scraps of fabric (velvet, silk, terry, flannel), carpet, sandpaper, and other interesting textures and keep them in a "touching" box. Help your toddler sort through what feels soft, what feels scratchy, what feels smooth, and so on.

Put your older toddler to the touch test the fun way. With your little one's eyes closed or covered, hold familiar objects (a hairbrush, a toy car, a set of keys, an apple) up for him or her to feel and identify by touch. Or put the objects in a cardboard box, cut a hole in the side, and have your toddler reach inside, finger, and identify an object.

Though there's much you can do to nurture the development of your toddler's senses through stimulating activities, it's important to keep in mind that you can overdo it. Children need time to sit and ponder, time to make their own discoveries. A good clue that you're pushing too hard is your child's reaction. When interest and excitement dwindle and you sense your toddler has tuned out, switch out of your instructive mode.

# WHAT IT'S IMPORTANT FOR YOUR TODDLER TO KNOW: Nobody's Perfect

To the adoring eyes of a small child, it seems that his or her larger-than-life parents know everything, can do anything, are always right. In short, they're perfect. Alas, as those of us who've been around a little longer know all too well, that perception is only an illusion. Even the best and brightest have frailties and imperfections—nobody, but nobody, is perfect.

And it's best that children learn this early on. Because children who are taught that everyone—even a parent, even a grandparent, even a teacher—makes mistakes, can feel free to grow up trying to do their best and to take calculated risks without fearing failure. To help your toddler learn this lesson:

▲ Don't demand perfection in your toddler. Expecting more than your toddler can deliver may be daunting, discouraging, and damaging to his or her self-esteem. Expectations (about behavior, skill mastery, comprehension) should be not only age-appropriate but tailored to your child's temperament and abilities. That doesn't mean, however, that you should set low expectations or none at all. Children who aren't expected to live up to any sort of standard usually fail to learn self-discipline, to meet challenges, and to take risks. They are denied the ego boost that comes with knowing, "I did something I didn't think I could do." And they often become low achievers.

▲ Don't demand perfection in others. Be accepting of the imperfections in those around you. In your spouse (so what if he always leaves the toilet seat up; so what if she always leaves the toothpaste uncapped); in people you work with; in people who work for you; in people at the post office, the supermarket, or the bank. That doesn't mean accepting constant rudeness, incompetence, or sloppiness as a matter of course but practicing patience and tolerance—recognizing that even the best of us slips up or has a bad day occasionally.

▲ Don't hide your mistakes from your toddler. It's important for children to see that parents aren't infallible, and that

they are willing to admit it. So when you lose your temper or forget to buy your toddler's favorite fruit or somehow fail to turn on *Sesame Street* until halfway into the program, admit you goofed and apologize.

▲ Don't demand perfection of yourself. There are no perfect parents. Forgive yourself when you fail to live up to your own expectations. Remember, you're only human. Every parent makes mistakes occasionally and most of us make them fairly often. We need to recognize our mistakes, learn from them, and then move on.

▲ Forgive your child's mistakes fully and completely. Provide unconditional acceptance. Never withdraw love (or pretend to) because a child's behavior or achievements fall short, or for any other reason. (Of course, since you're not perfect either, you won't always be able to react perfectly to your child's imperfect actions. Occasionally losing your cool over messy or destructive mistakes is only human. Just make sure your toddler knows that your *love* never wavers, even when your temper does. See page 751 for more on parental temper.)

You may fear that letting your child know that you don't require perfection will lower both your expectations and his or her performance. But that isn't so. Children who feel free to risk making mistakes, who don't feel pressured to be perfect, actually perform at higher levels than those who are always worried about the need to achieve perfection. Children who feel free to take risks also grow up feeling better about themselves and are less likely to suffer from self-doubt, less likely to turn to substance abuse, less likely to experience severe depression.

# CHAPTER FOUR

# The Sixteenth Month

## WHAT YOUR TODDLER MAY BE DOING NOW

*By the end of this month,[1] your toddler*
*. . . should be able to (see Note):*

▲ imitate activities
▲ scribble (by 16¼ months)

**Note:** If your toddler has not reached these milestones consult the doctor or nurse-practitioner. This rate of development may well be normal for your child (some children are late bloomers), but it needs to be evaluated. Also check with the doctor if your toddler seems out-of-control, uncommunicative, overly passive, highly negative, doesn't smile, makes few or no sounds, doesn't seem to hear well, is perpetually irritable, or demands constant attention. (But

remember, the one-year-old who was born prematurely often lags behind others of the same chronological age. This developmental gap progressively narrows and generally disappears entirely around age two.)

*. . . will probably be able to:*

▲ use 3 words
▲ dump an object in imitation

*. . . may possibly be able to:*

▲ use 6 words
▲ run

*. . . may even be able to:*

▲ kick a ball forward
▲ brush teeth, with help

1. The sixteenth month begins when a child is fifteen months old and ends when he or she is sixteen months old.

# WHAT YOU MAY BE CONCERNED ABOUT

## *FEAR OF DOGS*

*"Whenever my toddler sees a dog—even if it's a block away, he clings to me in terror. It's getting so we can't take a walk anymore."*

**M**any toddlers are a bit cautious around dogs and that's probably a good thing. When children are totally fearless, the consequences can be serious for little fingers and faces, as well as for fluffy tails and floppy ears. But while a little fear can go a long way in keeping your child safe from neighborhood canines (and vice versa) a lot of fear can, in addition to hampering your freedom to walk down the street, deprive him of the many benefits of having four-footed friends.

You needn't aim to eliminate your toddler's fear entirely but only to turn it from an irrational to a rational fear—one that allows him to approach dogs with sensible caution, rather than senseless terror.

Start by spending some time acclimating your toddler to completely non-threatening canines. Cuddly toy dogs he can pet and hug; battery-operated dogs that bark and prance around; picture book dogs of all sizes and breeds. Read stories that center on friendships between children and dogs, and that depict dogs as playmates, as helpers, as heroes. Once your toddler is desensitized to inanimate dogs, try him out on the flesh-and-fur variety. Check with friends, neighbors, and relatives and try to locate an animal who is good tempered (older dogs and dogs who have been spayed or fixed are usually more mellow than puppies), friendly (but not profusely so, since jumping and slobbering can frighten a toddler as much as barking

and biting), and accustomed to children (some dogs are as wary of young children as young children are of them). Secure a snapshot of this dream dog before the face-to-snout introduction takes place, show it to your toddler and talk about the dog with him. Explain that a dog's barking is its way of talking, that wagging its tail is its way of showing it's happy, and that sometimes a dog bumps people with its tail, but it doesn't mean to hurt anyone.

Finally, arrange the actual meeting. Initially, keep the two principals at a distance from each other—your toddler in your arms, the dog held securely by its master. Wave to the dog, talk to it and about it by name, and encourage your child to do the same. If he appears nervous, try to reassure him. Take him out of the room only if he becomes truly upset. If he doesn't seem ready to make contact during the first visit, schedule these not-too-close encounters until he warms up. As his comfort level increases, decrease the distance between him and the dog until he's finally near enough to touch it (but keep him in your arms at first to give him a sense of security and a height advantage). Don't force him, or even urge him, to pet the dog at this point; instead, pet the dog yourself. Say, "See, I'm petting the nice doggy. She's so soft. Do you want to pet the doggy, too?" If he shows interest, have him pet the dog as you hold his hand and show him how to pet gently. If he refuses, let him know, "That's okay, you don't have to pet the doggy." Give him an opportunity to change his mind each time you visit with the dog—and keep up the visits until he finally summons the courage to reach out and pet his new friend.

Allowed to progress through this nonpressured "desensitization" process at his own pace, your toddler should

## PET PRESCRIPTIONS

··········

Whether or not you have a pet at home, toddlers should be pet-proofed as early on as possible. Teach your toddler the following rules for safety's sake:

▲ Let sleeping (and eating) dogs (and cats) lie. Don't touch or go near them when they're napping or dining. And never touch their food; curious fingers can easily be perceived as a threat—retaliation is likely even in a mellow animal.

▲ Never poke an animal's eyes, pull his tail, or tug on its ears. Always pet gently under the chin rather than on top of the head—which implies domination. (Show your toddler how to do this.)

▲ Don't tease an animal. Don't offer a bone and then withdraw it, block its way to the water bowl, pretend you are going to hit it, and so on.

▲ Stay away from dogs, cats, squirrels, raccoons, or other animals you don't know.

▲ Stay away from animals that are sick or behaving strangely. This will have to be your call for now. The signs of rabies in an animal include one or more of the following: limping or staggering (because of paralysis of the hind legs); frothing or foaming at the mouth (due to paralysis of the throat and stiffness of the jaw); aggressive behavior (attacking people, other animals, even objects); behavior changes (a nocturnal animal may come out during the day, a diurnal one at night); disorientation and lack of inhibition. Some infected animals, however, may not have any noticeable symptoms.

▲ Stay away from dogs or cats when they're fighting.

▲ Stay away from a new mother dog or cat who is with her babies; she will fight to protect her offspring.

▲ Never go near any animal without a grown-up around.

▲ Always move slowly when approaching an animal. Don't run toward or ride a riding toy up to an animal; don't make sudden movements or jump around in front of it. (Cats are likely to run from a young child at play, but because toddlers can't necessarily differentiate between dogs and cats—and just to be on the safe side—this rule should apply to both species.)

▲ If a dog growls or is angry, don't run away (the dog might give chase); instead, roll up into a little ball on the ground and cover your face with your arms.

▲ Never put your face near a dog's face. (Because toddlers are small, they are most likely to be bitten in danger areas—face, head, and neck.) The same goes for cats. (Since a feline's claws can do a lot of harm to tender young skin, too.)

overcome his fear of dogs eventually—and perhaps even become a dog lover.

If you have a fear of dogs yourself, you will need to overcome yours before you can help your toddler conquer his. If you try to hide your fear, your anxiety, no matter how subtle, will be transmitted to your child, telling him that there *is* something to be afraid of—no matter how you try to tell him in words and actions that there isn't.

## NO FEAR OF DOGS

························

*"Not only isn't my toddler afraid of dogs, she's completely fearless, even with animals she's never met. And that worries me."*

Dogs and toddlers have a lot in common—they're frisky, exuberant, volatile, impulsive, unpredictable, and often hard to control. Put them together and you've got either the stuff photo opportunities are made of—or a disaster waiting to happen.

To be sure one of your toddler's canine encounters doesn't dissolve into disaster, start instilling a little caution now. Whenever she runs up to a strange dog (or one you know well enough not to trust), stop her before she gets too close. Without alarming her (which could turn her from fearless to fearful), explain, "You can pet a dog only if Mommy or Daddy is with you and says it's okay. And if we don't know the dog, it might be scared of us. So we can't go too close to the dog, and we can't touch it." Also begin making your toddler familiar with the pet prescriptions on page 85.

# POOR EATING HABITS

*"My daughter hardly ever eats, and when she does, she doesn't take more than a bite or two. She's been growing well, according to her doctor, but I don't see how long she can keep that up without nourishment."*

When it comes to eating and growing, a toddler's body works in mysterious ways. Toddlers manage to grow and thrive taking in amounts of food that, from the parental point of view, seem insufficient to nourish a grasshopper. The fact is, in spite of protests from Mom and Dad that they are "living on nothing but air," most kids labeled "poor eaters" actually get adequate nourishment.

Study after study has shown that, given the opportunity, healthy children whose eating habits haven't been thwarted by parental pushiness will neither starve nor overfeed themselves; they will eat just as much as they need for normal growth. It's your job to provide the nourishing food, and then to step back and let your child (and her body's mysterious ways) do the rest.

If you nevertheless harbor some nagging doubts, see page 513 for how to keep a toddler food diary and for Best-Odds feeding tips. Of course, if your toddler's growth starts to slow down or she doesn't seem to be energetic and happy, share your concerns with her doctor.

# ERRATIC EATING

*"One day my son will eat nonstop, the next day he'll eat next to nothing. It's driving me crazy."*

To adults who are accustomed to consuming roughly the same amount of food each day, spread out among roughly the same number of meals and snacks, a toddler's binge-and-starve approach to dining may be disconcerting. But such erratic eating is very common among, and completely normal for, the booster-seat set. A toddler's diet can balance itself out in any number of lopsided and unpredictable equations: One day he may eat a bountiful breakfast but hardly touch lunch and supper; the next day he'll eat a bare-bones breakfast, a lavish lunch, and a paltry dinner; one day he'll eat up a storm at all three meals, the next day nary a drizzle at any of them; one day his total caloric intake may appear to rival a fullback's, the next day it may seem more in line with that of a flea.

Scrutinize each meal, or even each day's worth of meals, and you're certain to see a nutritional roller coaster. Look at the bigger picture—a few days' worth of meals at a time—and you're bound to see at least some semblance of nutritional balance. If you try to force your child into gastronomic conformity—pushing him to eat when he doesn't feel like eating, or to stop eating when you feel he's eaten too much—you'll end up with a child who doesn't know how to respond to his feelings of hunger and fullness and who may eventually develop eating problems. If you overlook his eating eccentricities—letting him eat heartily when hunger strikes, stop when it's abated, and skip a meal when he's not hungry—your child will be more likely to grow up with a healthy approach to eating.

A word of caution: A toddler or young child should not be given complete freedom of choice when it comes to the food he eats. Though allowing a toddler to decide how much to eat at each meal and snack makes nutritional sense, allowing him to decide he's hungry for a doughnut instead of cereal or a bowl of potato chips instead of a bowl of pasta doesn't. Offer your toddler only nutritionally worthy choices—then you'll be safe letting him make his own selections (a meat-and-potatoes dinner or a slice of whole-wheat French toast with sliced banana, not a meat-and-potatoes dinner or a pile of sugary cookies). So be sure to provide your toddler with only the "good stuff" recommended in the "Best-Odds Toddler Diet" (see Chapter Eighteen) and to follow the tips on page 323 to make sure he develops healthful eating habits.

# A CHANGE IN EATING HABITS

*"When my son was younger, he ate everything we offered him. Now I can't get him to even try something new, and he rejects practically all his old favorites. Could he be sick?"*

When a happy, active toddler suddenly develops picky eating habits, it's more likely to be a sign of self-assertion than a sign of sickness. In the golden days of babyhood, your son's philosophy was simple: If it was fun and it felt good, he did it. Eating, fitting that formula, was something he did with plenty of gusto and with little reflection—taking pleasure in a pure and uninhibited sensual experience. Now his philosophy isn't so simple, and feeding him isn't, either.

Since rebellion at the dinner table is a normal accompaniment of toddlerhood, don't try to fight it. Chances are you won't beat it anyway. Instead, give up *without* a fight and let freedom of choice ring for your little rebel (which eventually may decrease his need to rebel). The guidelines on page 517 will help with this and other feeding problems.

If, however, in addition to not eating, your child seems cranky and out of sorts or doesn't seem to be growing or gaining weight, talk with his doctor. Illness or another medical problem may be responsible for the poor appetite.

# SWITCHING SEATS

*"When do we switch our little girl from a high chair to a booster seat?"*

The best seat in the house for a toddler depends on the toddler who's sitting in it. Some toddlers are perfectly happy in their high chairs until they physically grow out of them, but the wriggling and whining of other high-chair captives makes it clear that they're ready—and eager—to be relocated as soon as possible.

If your child does more complaining than eating in her high chair, or if she's indicated a desire to sit at the table with the rest of the family, it's time for a booster seat. Be sure that the seat you buy can be attached securely to a chair or fastened to a tabletop, and that your

*Most toddlers are ready to move out of their high chairs and on to less confining eating–seating arrangements sometime in the middle of the second year.*

*Older toddlers often prefer to dine on their knees rather than in a booster seat. See Safe Seating, page 149.*

toddler can be strapped safely into the seat. If the seat is the kind that attaches to the table, be sure not to place a chair beneath it; a toddler can easily push off against a chair, dislodge her seat, and go flying.

Also be sure that when she's sitting at the table, it isn't one big booby trap. Clear the surfaces she can reach (you may be surprised at how far her boarding-house reach extends) of breakable, spill-able, and dangerous items, including salt and pepper shakers, the sugar bowl, hot beverages, knives, forks, glass vases, and foods that pose a potential choking hazard.

# A TOWERING TODDLER

*"Because my son is very large for his age, he looks much older than he is. So people always expect him to act older and to have more skills than he does."*

**Y**ou can't help what people expect, or what they say. But you can help keep what they expect or what they say from hurting your toddler.

First of all, be quick to volunteer his age, particularly when those careless comments ("My, my—a big boy like you still in a diaper?") start coming. Matter-of-factly set the record straight ("He's actually only fifteen months—he's just big for his age"), not for the edification of the thoughtless commenter, or even to save yourself some embarrassment, but for the preservation of your toddler's self-esteem. Being constantly told that you're not performing up to snuff can erode a tender ego.

Second of all, make sure you don't get caught up in the same trap as these insensitive strangers. Sometimes parents, who on a conscious intellectual level are aware of the limitations their child's age poses, subconsciously expect more. Or weary of hearing "Why doesn't he talk yet?" they may try to push their toddler beyond those limitations—to begin talking or walking or toilet-learning or giving up the stroller before he's ready. Such pressure can bruise a child's ego and impede his natural developmental progress; he's less likely to attempt new skills if he senses that he's already failed at them. So applaud your toddler for what he *can* do and provide the encouragement and support he needs to reach his full potential at each age and stage of development.

And most of all, get used to it. Sizable toddlers often grow into sizable children; your child may well have to face the inflated expectations of others for many years to come. If you learn not to take them personally, your son will probably follow your lead.

# STRANGER SUSPICION

*"Every time someone outside the immediate family approaches my daughter, she hides behind me. Isn't this fear of strangers a little extreme?"*

It isn't extreme—it's extremely appropriate, considering your child's age. Her pronounced fear of strangers, which is known in the child development business as "stranger suspicion," is very common during the toddler years. Unlike "stranger anxiety," which many infants experience as they approach their first birthdays, stranger suspicion is a more rational fear—though it may not seem rational to you. It's a kind of thinking child's paranoia. Because your toddler is capable of more complex thoughts than she used to be, she's also capable of more complex fears. During this suspicious time, every grown-up who isn't

Mommy or Daddy can be viewed as a potential threat: a neighbor, a sitter, a friend or associate of yours, even a once-accepted grandparent or other relative may receive the distrust treatment. While this fearful reaction may sometimes embarrass you and upset others (particularly those who are close to you), it's actually not an altogether bad trait. In fact, if you think about it, knowing that your toddler won't walk off with the first stranger who offers her a cookie should be somewhat comforting.

But fear probably isn't the only thing that keeps your toddler hidden behind your legs in the face of strangers; there may be an element of annoyance, too. Consider how you might react towards a stranger, or someone you barely knew or recognized, who came right up to you, and without permission or hesitation, patted your head, pinched your cheek, tickled your tummy, hugged you, picked you up, or barraged you with silly questions? It's likely that even for you, a grown-up with a highly developed sense of civility, a civil response would be difficult. For a toddler, whose exposure to the world of manners and courtesy has been limited, mustering a civil response to such an assault is often next to impossible.

There's no magical cure for stranger suspicion, but it can be expected to eventually come to an end—sooner in some children, later in others. But since it's impossible, as well as inadvisable, to shelter your toddler from other people completely while she grows out of her suspicious stage, try these tips. They may help her (and you) cope more effectively with it:

**Cut strangers off at the hug.** Try intervening before a stranger makes a move toward your toddler. As with a stranger-suspicious animal, a stranger-suspicious child will be less fearful if the newcomer approaches her gradually, giving her a chance to size him or her up. Without labeling your child as "shy" or "scared," which could perpetuate her wary behavior, explain to the hugger-wannabe that she's more comfortable if people approach her slowly.

**Give physical support.** If your toddler wants to be held while in the company of strangers, hold her—for as long as she needs and wants to be held. When and if she's ready to go it alone, she'll let you know. In the meantime, offer your reassuring support and understanding unconditionally, and without demeaning comments ("You're acting like such a baby") or teasing ("You silly girl").

**Try more exposure.** Your toddler will thaw faster if she's exposed to a wide variety of familiar and unfamiliar people on a regular basis. So take her to the supermarket, mall, museum, zoo, playground, and religious, social, and family gatherings. Travel on buses and subways, go for walks down crowded streets. But be careful not to push your child to interact with the people she'll meet during these outings; always let her take the lead. Just being in the midst of strangers is achievement enough for now.

**Don't push it.** Often parents worry more about the rejected stranger's feelings than those of their child, especially if the "stranger" is a friend or relative they don't want to see rebuffed. So they may push a reluctant child toward an exuberant stranger, with tears and/or tantrum the invariable result. Paradoxically, your child will feel more secure—and more open to the advances of strangers—if you handle her fear with respect and understanding than if you press her to overcome it. As for the stranger's feelings, you can explain that your child's reaction shouldn't be taken personally, that she's at an age when only a parent will do.

For more about toddler fears, see page 207.

# NO FEAR OF STRANGERS

*"Our little boy is very outgoing and will go to any stranger immediately. This worries us."*

Not every toddler is suspicious of strangers; those who are gregarious by nature, or who have been exposed since infancy to many different people in many different settings, may take readily to new faces. So readily, in fact, that it causes their parents to fear for their safety.

Because your toddler's at an age when comprehension of potential dangers is still very limited, your vigilance is his protection. Never let him out of your sight, even for a moment, when you're out and about. If he tends to wander, see the tips on page 181 for keeping him close at hand.

Although it may be too soon to expect your toddler to exercise judicious discretion around strangers, it isn't too soon to start laying the foundation for safe behavior in the future. When your toddler heads for a smiling stranger without first checking with you, say, "If you want to say 'hello' to someone, you have to tell Mommy or Daddy." The concept may not sink in yet, but repeated often it will eventually. Meanwhile, as long as you're there to protect him, your toddler's outgoing personality won't put him in peril.

A word of caution: As you educate your toddler about stranger safety, however, be careful not to send the message that strangers are universally menacing. Don't warn that "strangers might be mean" or that "strangers might steal you." Do tell him, however, that he always needs your okay before talking to a stranger, going to one or with one, or taking something a stranger offers him. Your goal should be to make your child prudently cautious, not unreasonably fearful.

# A PREFERENCE FOR MOMMY

*"Our son won't let anybody else do anything for him when I'm around, even his father. It's tying up all of my time, and making Dad feel like he's not needed."*

A s far as most toddlers are concerned, nobody does it better than Mommy (though for some children it's Daddy who's up there on the pedestal). Nobody fetches a drink, makes sandwiches, puts on shoes, changes diapers, or pushes the stroller in just the same way Mommy does, and as long as Mommy's around, nobody had better try—that is, unless they're fond of rejection.

Mommy is understandably the number one person on most toddlers' short list. In most homes she has been the parent who has met her child's basic needs from infancy. Still, sometimes (especially during stressful times), it may be hard for Mommy to feel flattered by and grateful for her toddler's attention—and easy for her to feel put upon and resentful.

As far as the rejected parent is concerned, it's hard to compete with such unflagging devotion, and sometimes it may not even seem worth the trouble.

But Dad's got to persevere, keep his perspective, and endeavor not to take his toddler's rejections personally. Mommy favoritism is common and developmentally normal for toddlers. In no way does it reflect on a father's parenting capabilities or likeability quotient. Besides, it doesn't last forever. Just as common and normal is the phase of development that often follows sometime in the pre-school years, wherein Daddy becomes the apple of the offspring's eye, leaving Mom on the outside looking in enviously.

In the meantime, with some effort on the part of both parents, some of this single-minded Mommy favoritism can be minimized. Here's what a mother's to do:

**Don't be an accomplice.** Often, deep down, Mom's actually flattered by being the chosen one. Despite her protests, she enjoys the feeling of being wanted and needed, and subconsciously feeds the favoritism—perhaps by monopolizing the child's care, and excluding Dad in the process. An "I'd better do it; he likes it better when I do it," kind of mentality never gives Daddy a chance to prove otherwise or to improve with practice. It also tells the toddler that he's right— Mommy does do it best. If you suspect this might be the case with you, make an effort to stop aiding and abetting your child's desire to play favorites.

**Don't hog all the good jobs.** Sharing the responsibilities of parenting fairly means sharing both the tiresome and the enjoyable. If you dole out to Dad only those jobs that you don't feel like doing (typically, the ones that elicit the most negative response from your child—such as cleaning him up after dinner), keeping all the "good" ones (typically, the ones that elicit the most positive response from your child—such as reading bedtime stories) for yourself, he's never going to be able to compete.

**Step to the sidelines—or even off the field.** At least once in a while, but preferably on a consistent weekly or biweekly basis, take a few hours off, and let Dad take charge. The change will be better accepted if you're not just out of the room, but out of the house, when Dad steps in. Leave your toddler without displaying any trepidation or reservations—and whatever you do, don't call in every five minutes to check on how they're doing without you. Rest assured that when presented with a sink-or-swim situation, most dads do swimmingly; when presented with a Daddy-or-nothing situation, most tots not only pick Papa, but embrace him wholeheartedly.

Even when the three of you are together, try giving Dad as many opportunities to attend to and play with your toddler as possible. The chances that your toddler will accept the Daddy option will be significantly increased if you step away (preferably out of sight) when it's offered.

**Appreciate parental differences.** To each his or her own. Dad's style of parenting may not be the same as yours— it may not be even remotely similar— but that doesn't make it inferior. And though your toddler may not be ready to say *vive la différence* right away, he will say it (or think it) in time; experiencing both your parenting styles will ultimately make his life richer and more fulfilling.

**In Dad we should trust.** Both your spouse and your toddler will sense it if you don't trust Dad's parenting judgment and tactics, whether you deride them out loud or not. The result: Junior won't trust Daddy (if Mommy thinks Daddy doesn't know what he's doing, he probably doesn't); Daddy won't trust his own instincts, and the vicious cycle that keeps Dad on the outside looking in will continue.

**Back him up.** If you and your husband don't see eye to eye on a child-rearing policy, take care not to contradict each other in front of your toddler. If Dad says, "yes" to something you feel strongly should be a "no," or vice versa, back him up for now and then shoot it out later when your youngster's not within earshot. (Since you can't expect to agree on everything, get used to practicing the art of compromise—it'll come in handy in the years of parenting that lie ahead. Sometimes it works best to meet in the middle, other times it works best to let the parent who feels more strongly about an issue win.)

**Flatter the pater.** Rejection can really get a guy down—particularly if he's been trying really hard to win your toddler's favor. Being sensitive to this, and responding with support and empathy,

can help compensate for your toddler's unintentional yet hurtful lack of tact. So can lauding Dad's efforts, and letting him know that you appreciate them even if your toddler doesn't seem to yet.

Of course, there are exceptions to every developmental rule: Though in toddlerhood most children will prefer Mother's company over Father's, some are Daddy's little boys (or girls) from the start. This is true most often in families where dads are responsible for the majority of the child care, either by choice or necessity, but can be the case when Mother's running the show, too. All of the same advice, in reverse, holds true for turning around Daddy favoritism.

# *LEAVING A SLEEPING TODDLER WITH A SITTER*

*"We always wait until our son is asleep to have a sitter come over because we're afraid that if he knows we're going out, he won't let us go."*

In this case, what your son doesn't know could hurt him—and hurt you, too, by turning an evening out into a complicated and worrisome charade. Though your tactic may work for a while, it's bound to backfire when your toddler wakes up one night to find himself with a stranger. The trauma that this kind of rude awakening could cause (suddenly you're gone, he didn't see you go, and he has no inkling of when you're coming back, or whether you're coming back at all) will be compounded by normal middle-of-the-night irrationality. The results: hysteria in the short run, generalized insecurity at bedtime (are Mommy and Daddy going to disappear every night after they tuck me in?) in the long run. Add to this the unsettling complications brought on by your sitter strategy—you'll be showing up late for dinner parties or missing the curtain at the theater because your child didn't fall asleep on time; or turning down invitations to events taking place during the day or early evening—and it should become clear why it should be abandoned altogether.

It certainly won't be as easy to leave when your toddler's awake as it was to sneak out on him asleep, but it will become easier in time. Watching you leave (even if it's through tears) and finding that you always return is a lesson he'll benefit from learning now. See page 23 for tips on leaving your toddler with a sitter.

# CONTINUED MOUTHING OF OBJECTS

*"I thought my son would have stopped putting things in his mouth by now. It's such a dirty habit, how can I break him of it?"*

Using the mouth as a tool of discovery isn't a nasty habit at this age, it's a normal part of development. And like all things developmental, how long it continues varies from child to child. Although the occasional youngster will give up mouthing before his first birthday, most will continue oral exploration of their environment well into toddlerhood. Rather than trying to break your child of the habit, let him grow out of it at his own pace.

Even the most avid mouther will probably start losing his taste for the practice by about twenty-four months, as his primal urge for oral gratification begins to diminish, and he starts tapping into other sensory resources. (For tips on helping accentuate the senses, see page

78.) Voicing displeasure or disapproval when he mouths may prolong the behavior in a rebellious toddler; so look the other way and let development take its natural course.

Of course, before you look the other way, make sure that what your toddler puts in his mouth is safe. Mouthing an object that's been lying around the house and hasn't been washed recently shouldn't be cause for concern (unless the object is, say, a bathroom sponge, a moldy piece of bread dug out of the garbage, or a grimy shoe that's been walking city streets). But mouthing an object that is toxic or small enough to be swallowed or choked on (or that your toddler can bite a small piece off of) should be. Ideally you should try to keep things that are unsafe for your child to mouth out of reach (latch the bathroom door, keep a toddler-proof lid on the garbage can, put shoes in the closet, lock away toxic substances, regularly search the house for coins and other small objects). Since no number of precautions can keep all dangerous items away from your toddler, you'll also need to monitor him and the contents of his mouth closely. And just in case, be sure you know how to handle a choking incident (see page 689).

When your child mouths something unacceptable, say firmly, "No, not in your mouth. Give it to me." If he doesn't hand it over, remove it from his hand or mouth immediately yourself.[2] A child this age is capable of understanding and responding to such a command (though the response isn't always compliance), and will soon begin to learn what's okay to mouth and what's not. (That doesn't mean, however, that you can forgo supervising your child. He is capable of forgetting or ignoring the rules.)

---

2. Some children resist having objects removed from their mouths. Learn in advance how to remove an object safely in such a situation (see page 672).

The teething toddler may gum objects in order to put soothing counter pressure on his painful gums. If that's the case with your toddler, provide him with some interesting and safe teething toys (there's even one that has a built-in shape-sorter for entertainment between bouts of teething pain).

# BATH REJECTION

*"My son has always loved his bath, and he isn't afraid of water at all. So I can't understand why he's suddenly refusing to get into the tub."*

As you've probably already noticed, refusals of every kind are big in the second year. A toddler may refuse to eat, refuse to wear a coat, refuse to go outside, refuse to come back in—simply for refusal's sake, without apparent rhyme or reason. Of course, the reason is his struggle for independence. The following tips may help get your toddler back in the tub—or, at least, help you find other ways to clean up his act:

**Rescind your restraining order.** If you've been using a safety seat in the bathtub, it may be his curtailed movement, and not the tub itself, that your toddler objects to. Giving him free run (or wiggle and splash) of the tub may complicate bath time, but it may also put an end to his resistance. Make sure his newfound freedom doesn't jeopardize his safety, however, by observing the tips on page 641.

**Bring on the bubbles.** And the nontoxic soap foam or soap crayons.[3] And the

fleet of plastic boats. And the funnels and cups. And any other waterproof diversion you can come up with. Let the toys and fun—and not the washing—be the focus of tub experience. Instead of announcing bath time with, "Time to get in the tub," announce it with, "Look at all these bubbles! How are these boats going to get through?" or "Would you like me to paint tiger stripes on you with this funny soap?"

**Schedule a change.** If bath time comes at an unexpected hour, rather than at the accustomed battle time, it's possible that your toddler's surprise may ease his opposition. Admittedly, a change in schedule may mean that your child won't be getting clean when he's his dirtiest (if bath has been switched to mid morning instead of after dinner, for instance), but in the short run that's better than not getting clean at all. Until he becomes more amenable to bathing and bath time can return to a more sensible time slot, a quick session with a washcloth on the more glaringly grimy areas can get him passably clean before he gets into his pajamas.

**Try a little togetherness.** The rub-a-dub-dub may be more appealing if there's more than one in the tub. Mommy or Daddy make perfect tubfellows; if being nude around your toddler makes you uncomfortable, don a bathing suit. (It's important to remember that small children won't—and can't—tolerate the kind of water temperature adults prefer, so don't crank up the heat for your own comfort.) An older sibling or a friend on a play date make ideal bathmates, too (prior parental permission suggested). A companion's enthusiasm for bath time might "spill over" to your toddler.

**Hit the showers.** If it's being in the tub that distresses your toddler, let him accompany you in the shower instead. Wearing a shampoo visor (see page 154)

---

3. Also make sure you use a non-irritating soap, especially if your toddler is female, since girls are more susceptible to vaginal or urinary-tract irritation. Using a liquid baby bath to make bubbles is probably the safest way to go.

will help keep the water out of his eyes and make the overhead stream less threatening. Adjusting the water-flow rate to gentle, if that's possible, will also help, as may holding your toddler until he feels confident enough to stand under the shower on his own. A rousing round of "It's raining, it's pouring" can provide a playful note. As with tub water, shower water should be warm, rather than hot, for toddlers.

**Throw in the towel.** If all your efforts fail to persuade your toddler to get into the tub, don't resort to force—the trauma of which could instill in him a long-lasting antipathy toward bathing. Give up on the bath for the time being, and switch to sponge baths temporarily—using a washcloth, not a sponge (which could pose a choking hazard.)

Occasionally, a child's fear of the tub is rooted in an event—he slipped and banged his head, he got water in his eyes, he urinated into the water and your reaction (or the incident itself) confused and/or frightened him. If you can pinpoint the source of your child's aversion to baths, try to talk to him about the matter, letting him know that you really understand how he feels. And give him a chance to work out his feelings before trying to get him to go back into the tub.

# *READINESS FOR POTTY LEARNING*

*"We started toilet training our daughter at twelve months because she seemed ready. She was cooperative and somewhat successful for over two months, but suddenly she seems to be rebelling. Now she won't go anywhere near the potty and we feel frustrated."*

A t twelve months, the novelty of using a toilet, teamed with your fledgling toddler's still relatively easygoing nature, made her potty putty in your hands. But that was then, and this is now. Now the novelty's over—toileting is no longer a lark she enjoys voluntarily, but a chore she's being pressured into performing. Over too, alas, is the golden age of agreeableness. Instead of being eager to please, your toddler may now be out to displease. It may also be that you were the one who was trained in the first place. You put her on the potty after meals, the minute she squatted or grunted, or when she awoke after a nap. Now she's not as willing to be manipulated.

Trying to control your daughter at an age when she's programmed to resist control is bound to result in failure and frustration for both of you. Coercion won't yield a potty-proficient child any sooner than a laissez-faire attitude will—in fact, coercion could lead to constipation, if your toddler begins to rebelliously withhold the source of conflict in order to retain control of the situation.

Instead of showing concern over her lapsed bathroom skills, accept that toilet learning was initiated prematurely. Drop the matter entirely for now—without even a whisper of parental grumbling. Continue to remind your child about the concept of using the toilet by pointing out that you (and other family members and friends) go on the potty; letting her join you in the bathroom ("See, Mommy—or Daddy, or Brother, or whoever—is . . .[4]); occasionally pointing out to her "big" children who don't wear diapers (without telling her that she's a baby for wearing them); and by reminding her cheerfully that when she's a big girl, she won't wear diapers, either. Continue to keep

---

4. Use any term you're comfortable with to describe this biological function, for example, urinate, sissy, pee-pee, Number one.

her potty-chair available. If she asks to use it, then by all means let her; if she doesn't, wait until she's good and ready—which could be months from now, or a year, or even longer.

*"Every time my daughter soils her diaper, she tells me and wants to be changed right away. Does that mean she's ready to be toilet trained?"*

Just because your toddler tells you that she needs her diaper changed doesn't mean she's saying she's ready for toilet learning. Indicating that she's wet or has dirtied her pants is one of the signs of toilet-learning readiness, but it isn't the only one. And for toilet learning to be successful, all systems should be "go" (so to speak). See Chapter Nineteen for a complete guide to teaching your toddler to stay clean and dry.

## BOOK CONSUMPTION

*"I'd like to encourage my daughter to look at books, but all she seems interested in is chewing on them or ripping out the pages."*

Nobody devours literature or tears through a pile of books or magazines like a toddler. Unfortunately, such behavior is usually spurred on not by a love of words but by a taste for paper or a fascination for ripping. At this age, few children are developmentally ready to sit still for any length of time and quietly appreciate the text and pictures in a book.

However, you should try to take advantage of *any* spark of interest your child shows in books (even nibbling and shredding) and try to fan it into a burn-ing love of literature. To protect the books in your home from destruction while you nurture that fire in your toddler, try these tips:

**Invest in the indestructible.** Sturdy "board" books can withstand almost any assault by teeth, gums, or saliva—and are easy for little fingers to flip through. Keeping a large selection of colorful age-appropriate board books within easy reach will invite your toddler to peruse them frequently—and may discourage her search-and-destroy missions in your own library.

**Shelve the destructible.** On a high shelf. Or wedge those books (or magazines), which might fall prey to curious hands and eager mouths, so tightly into bookshelves that your toddler can't pry them loose. But don't make any reading material (with the exception of rare first editions, antiques, and delicate art books) completely off-limits; let your toddler examine and touch your books under supervision.

**Stop destruction consistently.** Allowing your toddler to shred some magazines and newspapers (for instance, those you've read) but not others sends a confusing message. Since a child this young can't possibly distinguish between reading matter that's ready for recycling and reading material that's hot off the presses, don't permit the ripping of either. Be particularly careful not to allow your child to nibble on newspapers or magazines; the print can be toxic.

**Redirect interest to the printed page.** You don't want to give your toddler the impression that reading material is a "no-no," just that tearing and eating it is. When you catch her in the act of destruction, don't scold her. Instead, entreat, "Please don't hurt the book (or magazine)." Then ask, "Would you like to look at it with me?" Sit down with her and point to and identify a few of the pictures in the book. Read a few sentences to her out loud. If the text is over her head, simplify the words as you read or take the opportunity to bring out a book that's more age-appropriate.

**Redirect the destructive instinct.** If your toddler's interest in the books she's manhandling is definitely not literary, try moving on to an activity that might approximate the satisfaction she gets from ripping (such as sorting the dirty clothes, sliding a zipper up and down, or opening and closing a Velcro closure on an old diaper cover). Or if she's been chewing on the book, ask if she's hungry. Perhaps it's just a snack she's after.

For ways of stimulating a lifelong interest in reading in your child, see page 101.

## CLIMBING CAPERS

*"Since our daughter discovered how to climb, nothing seems safe—even those things we'd tucked away on high shelves and tables."*

Your toddler's moving up in the world. As a crawling baby, most of her discoveries were made close to the ground. Pulling up, and then walking, expanded her world vertically by 2 or 3 feet. Now that she's mastered climbing, the sky (or, at least, the ceiling) is the limit. Take a little ingenuity, add to that your toddler's stacking skills, and almost everything and anything is within her curious reach. Which is gratifying for your toddler, but, understandably, terrifying for you. Nothing is safe anymore—least of all, your toddler.

You can't keep a toddler from climbing, nor should you try. As with any newly chalked up skill, she wants to,

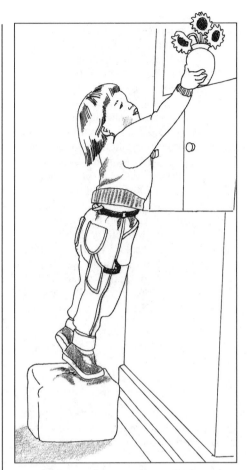

*Toddler Parenting Rule #1: Nothing is safe—even if it's on a high shelf. Creative climbing can put nearly anything at nearly any height within a toddler's reach.*

and should be allowed to, practice it to perfection. But she's got to learn that she can't practice anywhere she likes, that climbing can only take place in safe surroundings and under close supervision. An outdoor play gym is ideal for climbing. So are the scaled-down indoor varieties. Makeshift mountains are more risky, but since you won't be able to ban them entirely, make them as safe as possible. If your toddler likes to climb on chairs, for example, be sure that the rickety ones are put away for the time being. If your toddler is attracted to the kitchen step stool, move it from the hard kitchen floor to the living room carpet when she wants to climb. If she likes to pile up books from lower shelves to get to books on the upper ones, or to climb onto the bathroom vanity to wash her hands, get her a small, stable step stool of her own. Show her how much steadier it is than the stack of books. Scan your home for climbing situations that might be dangerous (an open shelf that could give her a foot up to the stove, for instance, or a table or bookcase that might topple when scaled), and try making them less hazardous. But don't expect to be able to anticipate every possible problem climbing scenario. To protect your little mountaineer, make sure she is always closely supervised. And no matter what she's climbing on, stand by ready to catch her in case she loses her footing.

# CROOKED TEETH

*"I'm concerned that our daughter's going to need braces because her teeth aren't coming in straight."*

N o need to start saving up for the orthodontist yet. Your daughter has years of getting and losing teeth ahead of her before it can be determined whether or not she will need braces.

Often, the first primary teeth are uneven, but straighten out as other teeth push their way through. If they don't, the second teeth give a child a second chance. There is no direct correlation between crooked baby teeth and crooked permanent teeth. But if the irregularities in the baby teeth are due to lack of space (because the child's teeth are large relative to the size of her mouth), it's possible that the problem will recur with the permanent teeth.

If your toddler does end up needing orthodontic work (the decision isn't usually made until age eight at the earliest),

there's good news. Orthodontics are much less expensive than they used to be, are worn for a much shorter time, and are much more esthetically pleasing. What's more, the good news can only get better in the next seven or eight years as more advances are made in orthodontics.

# CRANKINESS FROM TEETHING

*"Our fifteen-month-old seems to be getting molars now. He's a lot more miserable with them than he was with his other teeth."*

H e's miserable for good reason. Because of their large size and double edge, first molars (which usually make their appearance sometime between thirteen and nineteen months) are at least twice as hard to cut as incisors— and for many children that means at least twice as much discomfort. Providing your toddler relief from molar teething pain may be doubly elusive, too. He may be soothed by some of the same standbys that helped him through earlier teething episodes: rubbing the gum with a clean finger; a refrigerator-chilled teething ring (don't use a liquid-filled one, which your child may be able to bite through using his incisors, or a frozen one, which could "burn" his gums) or a partially frozen bagel (once the bagel defrosts, make sure that your toddler can handle the chewed off chunks without choking). Other old standbys are unsafe now that your toddler has teeth: a chilled carrot, for example, because he's capable of biting off a chokable chunk; and teething biscuits, because their high carbohydrate content could lead to tooth decay if they are mouthed all day long. Rubbing a bit of brandy, scotch, or other spirits on the aching gums, a popular folk remedy for teething, is not recommended for children at any age. Even tiny amounts of alcohol can be toxic to a child and repeated exposure to the flavor of alcohol could give him a taste for the stuff. If teething pain interferes with your toddler's eating and sleeping, speak to his doctor about the possibility of administering acetaminophen drops when the pain is at its worst. Don't give your teether medication or rub anything on his gums without his doctor's okay. The benefits of topical ointments last only a few minutes, and are not extremely helpful.

Though many children become cranky and feel out of sorts when teething, and may even exhibit mild signs of illness, report any symptoms (fever, diarrhea, cough, and so on) to the doctor; they could be completely unrelated to teething and may need treatment.

Often, night waking problems begin with molar teething: A toddler wakes with pain, cries out, and finds that waking brings him into Mommy and Daddy's bed or vice versa—so he continues the practice long after the bouts of pain have subsided. If you'd like to avoid such a situation, respond to your child's discomfort with comforting measures but not with extraordinary ones; though you may intend them to be temporary, your toddler almost certainly won't. See page 65 for more on night waking.

# WHAT IT'S IMPORTANT TO KNOW:
## How to Encourage Learning, Thinking, and New Experiences

Children learn more in the first few years of life than in all the years that follow. They learn about relationships and feelings (about trust, caring, and empathy; about anger, fear, jealousy, and resentment), about language (first learning to understand words, then to speak them), about how things work (throw a ball up and it always comes down, turn over a cup of milk and it always spills). One of the most important things they learn—or should learn—is to love learning.

Every child is born curious and this natural curiosity is what propels early learning. But in order for curiosity to continue its creative course, it must be cultivated. When parents encourage a child's search for knowledge, the child will keep searching, as an active and eager participant in the learning process. When parents discourage the search, the child might be less likely to keep the search up—or, at least, to keep it up with the same eagerness.

To fertilize your toddler's curiosity so it can blossom into a lifelong love of learning:

▲ Accept, encourage, and answer questions. With so much to learn, it's not surprising that, once they can speak, toddlers ask so many questions. And though it may be tempting to ignore or put off your toddler after the fiftieth "Wha dat?" of the day, try to resist. All of a young child's questions deserve answers (though sometimes the best answer to a question is another question; see page 199). When toddlers don't receive answers to their questions, or receive unsatisfying ones (such as

"Because" or "You're too young to understand that"), they may stop asking them. Of course, your answers to your child's questions should be tailored to his or her age; keep explanations short and simple.

▲ **Accept and encourage exploration.**
A toddler's explorations may turn out to be a parent's mess. But it's through the exploratory process that toddlers make their discoveries; the world is full of fascinating things and events that your toddler has to experience in order to learn about them. So resist the impulse to restrain your little explorer in the name of cleanliness or tidiness. You may prevent important learning experiences. (Giving your child freedom to explore doesn't mean putting home, hearth, and your toddler's safety in jeopardy, however; see page 241.)

▲ **Accept and encourage experimentation.** The inquiring toddler's mind wants to know. What happens when I remove the leaves from the plant in the foyer? When I throw sand in a playmate's face? Or when I throw a toy car across the room? Of course, while you don't want to allow your budding scientist to destroy your home single handedly while testing hypotheses, you don't want to inhibit the impulse to experiment, either. When experiments take a turn for the destructive or the dangerous, stop them, but make it clear that you object to the result of the experiment, not the process. ("I know that you wanted to see what would happen if you poured water over the side of the tub, but the water has to stay in the tub.") Then redirect the inquiring mind. ("Let's see what happens when you pour water into this boat.") To bring out the scientist in your toddler while saving your home, devise experiments that can be conducted under controlled conditions: Blow the fuzz off of a dandelion, pour sand through a strainer, mix food coloring with sudsy water in the kitchen sink. For more on experiments suitable for toddlers, see page 456.

▲ Expose your toddler to a variety of environments. Museums, playgrounds, supermarkets, malls, toy stores, parks, zoos, a busy city sidewalk—almost any safe and appropriate locale can provide learning experiences for the young. Most toddlers pick up plenty through the power of observation; you can enhance what your toddler picks up by asking questions and adding some observations of your own.

▲ Expose your toddler to a variety of experiences. Swinging on a swing, shimmying down a slide, splashing in wading pool, planting flowers, pulling weeds, playing ball, stirring flour into cake batter, scribbling with a crayon (see page 54), setting the table, ringing the doorbell, pushing the elevator button. The possibilities are endless and everywhere. The experience alone is valuable, but your commentary ("See, the harder you push the swing, the higher up it goes" or "Watch, when you push the button, the red light goes on") can help make them more valuable still.

▲ Expose your toddler to fantasy. For a toddler, there's as much to be learned from fantasy—in books, movies, videos, and the occasional television show—as there is from real life. Encourage make believe in your toddler's play: In the world of fantasy, your child can be a grown-up at a tea party, a squirrel in the forest, the Cat in the Hat or Curious George—just about anyone or anything he or she would like to be (see page 365).

▲ Discourage excessive TV viewing. The fastest way to click off a mind is to click on the television set. True, a child can pick up information by watching carefully selected children's television programs (the alphabet, colors, counting), but the learning is passive. It doesn't encourage children to learn on their own, as active participants in the learning process. Children who learn from TV tend to expect answers to come to them in the form of glitzy, fast-moving graphics, dancing animals, and catchy tunes. They become complacent learners, their natural impulse to make their own discoveries is suppressed. So limit the television viewing, and when your toddler does watch, stay involved yourself (see page 162).

▲ Build learning into everyday activities. With very little effort, you can out-teach the teachers on *Sesame Street*. You can introduce numbers ("Do you want one cracker or two crackers? This is one, this is two"); colors ("Do you want to wear the blue sweater or the red one? This one is blue, this one is red"); letters ("Look at the E on your block. E is for Emily and also for elephant"). The point of these exercises isn't to teach your toddler to count by eighteen months or read by age two, but to spark an interest in these subjects and to create an environment that fosters learning. Also, tap into your toddler's senses as teaching tools; see page 78.

▲ Foster learning by nurturing self-esteem. A child needs to feel good about him or herself to be able to learn. (See page 292.)

▲ Make learning fun. If children feel coerced or pressured into learning, are punished or belittled for failures ("I can't believe you still can't tell an 'A' from a 'B'), or are confronted with formal learning situations prematurely, they'll come to dread learning, not to love it.

▲ Set a curious example. Show your toddler that you're never too old to explore and discover, that learning is a life-long pursuit. Your own excitement about learning—at your own level as well as at your child's—will be contagious.

# WHAT IT'S IMPORTANT FOR YOUR TODDLER TO KNOW: Reading Is *Fund*amental

Reading *is* fundamental. But what a lot of today's television-age children never learn is that it's also *fun*. It's one thing to teach a child to read—with a few primers and a stack of flash cards, just about anybody can do it. But it's quite another thing to teach a child to love reading. And while most experts agree that teaching a child to read—to recognize letters and sound out words and string words into sentences—is a process best left until the child's ready, teaching a child to love reading is a process that can start long before he or she knows an "A" from a "Z." Here are some ways to nurture such a love:

**Be selective.** Choose books with large, clear, bright, realistic, but cheerful illustrations (some very beautifully illustrated books are just too abstract, cluttered, dark, or sophisticated for a toddler to appreciate) and short, simple text. Though most toddlers prefer rhyming books (even if the words don't mean much, the rhythm is appealing), now is a good time to start introducing some very simple stories in prose. Heavy board books, preferably with sturdy spiral bindings, are ideal for your toddler to "read" alone; keep the more delicate paper books for supervised reading sessions. Skip cloth books, which don't seem to bear enough resemblance to the real thing to satisfy most toddlers. Vinyl books are fine for the bathtub (often a good time to get a little reading in), but be sure to dry them thoroughly after each dunking to prevent mildew from taking hold.

**Be persistent.** Many toddlers do little but squirm the first few times they're read to, but persistence usually pays off. Establish a regular story time at least once a day (after the bath and before bed is best); if you have time in the morning, a cuddly reading session in your bed can be nice, too. Even if it lasts just a few pages, and even if your toddler seems more interested in puttering with a new toy or climbing on and off the bed, story time will ultimately become a cherished ritual—one that you'll both continue to treasure long after your child becomes capable of reading to him or herself. Never force your toddler to pay attention to a story while you're reading it. This will make listening seem more like a chore, less like a pleasure.

**Be creative.** You know what interests your toddler better than a book's author does. So don't feel obliged to read the words precisely as written; taking literary license can greatly enhance your toddler's listening pleasure. Abridge long passages, swap simpler words for those your toddler doesn't understand, drop in commentary and explanations as needed. If the text of a story seems to be leaving your toddler cold, concentrate on the illustrations ("Look at that big dog and that little dog" or "I wonder what's in the little girl's basket").

**Be interactive.** Long before your child can read, he or she can participate in the reading process. First by pointing to various characters ("Where's the kitty cat?") and objects in the illustrations ("Where's the cat's hat?"), later by filling in the blanks in sentences or rhymes in books

you've read over and over. When you read a story for the first time, look for characters, objects, colors, and ideas your toddler isn't familiar with, and take the opportunity to introduce them; next time you read the book, encourage (but don't pressure) your child to point them out ("Where's the elephant?") or answer questions about them ("What does the cow say?"). An older and more verbal toddler may even be able to answer such questions as, "What do you think is going to happen next?" or "Why do you think that boy is so sad?" Prompt participation, too, by reading books that are interactive: touch-and-feel books, books with surprises hiding under little flaps, books that have dials to turn, and so on. (Since these kinds of books are usually very fragile, bring them out only when your toddler will be supervised.)

**Be expressive.** No one likes to listen to a monotone. But to a toddler who's just picking up the nuances of language, an expressive reading style makes listening not only more enjoyable, but also more comprehensible. So ham it up.

**Be repetitious.** Toddlers love to hear the same story over and over and over again; and though the repetition may drive you to distraction, it's incredibly satisfying to young ears. Especially if the text is in rhyme, you may be surprised to find after a while that your toddler has memorized some of it.

**Be brief.** Short books and short reading sessions sit best with a toddler who can't sit still. Go from page to page and idea to idea quickly—to keep restlessness from setting in, and your audience from wandering off. And be ready to end story time after just a few minutes, if need be.

**Be cuddly.** Children who come to associate reading with the cozy comfort of being curled up on Mommy or Daddy's lap, almost always enjoy reading books later on.

**Be a good example.** Children of readers are much more likely to end up readers themselves. Try to set time aside each day for your reading—even if you manage just a page or two at a sitting. If you can't fit this into your schedule, or if you just don't like to read, make sure your toddler sees you reading at least occasionally. Make reading material a fixture in your home; keep a book by your bedside ("This is Mommy's [or Daddy's] book"), magazines on the coffee table, newspapers next to your armchair. And minimize the amount of television that's watched by your toddler and by you. Studies have shown that families who watch less, read more.

# CHAPTER FIVE

··········

# *The Seventeenth Month*

··········

## WHAT YOUR TODDLER MAY BE DOING NOW

*By the end of this month,[1] your toddler*
*. . . should be able to (see Note):*

▲ use 2 words (by 16½ months)
▲ drink from a cup

**Note:** If your toddler has not yet reached these milestones consult the doctor or a nurse-practitioner. This rate of development may well be normal for your child (some children are late bloomers), but it needs to be evaluated. Also check with the doctor if your toddler seems out-of-control, uncommunicative, overly passive, highly negative, doesn't smile, makes few or no sounds, doesn't seem to hear well, is perpetually irritable, or demands constant attention. (But remember, the one-year-old who was born prematurely often lags behind others of the same chronological age. This developmental gap progressively

*Most toddlers latch onto at least one comfort habit or object—and some latch on to several.*

---

1. The seventeenth month begins when a child is sixteen months old and ends when he or she is seventeen months old.

narrows and generally disappears entirely around age two.)

### ... will probably be able to:

▲ build a tower of 2 cubes

### ... may possibly be able to:

▲ walk up steps (by 16½ months)
▲ remove an article of clothing

▲ "feed" a doll

### ... may even be able to:

▲ build a tower of 4 cubes
(by 16½ months)
▲ identify 2 items in picture by pointing
▲ combine words
▲ throw a ball overhand
▲ speak and be understood half
the time

# WHAT YOU MAY BE CONCERNED ABOUT

## STRANGE STOOLS

*"Now that my daughter has some teeth, I expected she'd be able to chew up what she ate. But I'm still finding whole pieces of food in her stool."*

You'll continue making dramatic discoveries in your child's diapers, and later, in her potty, for some time to come. Those first few teeth are pretty useless when it comes to chewing—biting (and looking cute) is more their business. Until a set of molars comes in, a toddler chews with her gums, which means that food doesn't get much of a grinding before it's swallowed. And since a toddler's digestive system is relatively immature, what's swallowed passes fairly rapidly through the digestive tract. So it's not surprising that some mouthfuls exit looking more or less the same as when they entered. Among other tidbits you may spy in your child's stool: whole green peas or blueberries, small chunks of cooked carrot, deep-red slivers of tomato skin and golden kernels of corn.

As your child becomes more proficient at chewing and as gastrointestinal transit time slows down, her meals will be more thoroughly digested and her bowel movements less telling. In the meantime, be sure that the food you serve is soft enough to be gummed easily (test a new food by trying to mash it in your mouth without using your teeth) and that it's been cut in very small pieces (the smaller the food particles start out, the smaller they end up). If your child, like many toddlers, doesn't seem to bother much with gumming, preferring the shovel-and-gulp method of eating, try encouraging her to stop and chew before she swallows. Take a bite when she does, and show her how it's done ("See, I'm mushing up the food in my mouth. Can you do that?"). For an older child who's starting to learn numbers, try, "Can you chew that carrot four times?"

But keep in mind that even when your toddler has a full set of teeth, some undigested matter may show up in the stool. That's because chewing mashes food only partly; digestion finishes the job. And your toddler's digestive tract will not be mature enough to do that job thoroughly for another year or two.

# FRIDGE OPENING

*"Our son's discovered how to open the refrigerator—and he does it about 300 times a day."*

It's an open-and-shut case in many toddler households: The toddler opens it, the parent shuts it. Over and over again. It may be the refrigerator, a kitchen cabinet, the bathroom vanity—anything that has a door handle low enough for the toddler to reach. When what's behind these doors poses a danger (the refrigerator, for example, usually contains breakable glass jars and bottles; foods that a toddler could choke on; items that could be toxic to a child or that might trigger an allergic response) or if a child could accidentally get locked behind the door (most refrigerators today can be opened from the inside, but this risk still exists with very old models), it's necessary to install a childproof lock or latch (see page 639) that will assure that the appliance or cabinet cannot be opened by little hands. At least, that is, not in the time it takes you to answer the phone or take a pizza out of the oven.

Your toddler is bound to feel frustrated by his sudden inability to open the refrigerator, so be ready to distract him with something equally attractive but more acceptable, such as a "safe" cabinet filled with plastic containers, wooden spoons, nesting metal measuring cups, and the like. If its food he's looking for, give him a snack.

# THROWING HABIT

*"My son has a habit of throwing everything he picks up. I'm afraid he's going to hurt somebody or break something."*

The acquisition of a new skill is exhilarating for a toddler, but often exasperating for his parents. Though visions of his hurling a no-hitter at Little League may dance through your head the first few times your child hurls a toy across the room, it doesn't take long before those visions are replaced by nightmarish premonitions of lamps shattering and playmates' eyes being blackened.

Banning throwing entirely will only make the activity more tantalizing; worse still, it will deprive your toddler of the opportunity to practice a developmentally appropriate skill. Your job, tricky as it may sound, is to encourage that skill without putting home and hearth in jeopardy. Here's how:

**Start spring training . . . no matter what the season.** Given plenty of opportunities to throw a ball in safe and supervised surroundings, a toddler's itch to pitch may well be satisfied—at least somewhat. Don't expect much in the way of catching yet; a toddler's eye-hand coordination isn't ready for the big leagues. But your child will probably get a kick out of retrieving a ball that's been tossed to him.

**Vary the ball.** A wide range of balls are suitable for toddlers, including beach balls, tennis balls, and small, medium, and large rubber balls. Avoid hard balls, balls small enough for your toddler to put in his mouth, and balls made of spongy material that he could take a bite out of. You can also indulge your toddler's urge to throw by providing a bean bag, a ring toss set, or a frisbee. Or make some paper airplanes for in-house flying.

**Cry foul if it isn't a ball.** Make it clear that some things are meant to be thrown (balls, beanbags, and so on) and others are not (toys, blocks, books, cups): "This is a ball—a ball is for throwing. This is a book. You don't throw a book—a book is for reading."

**One strike, and he's out.** The moment you see your toddler fling (or get ready to fling) an object that is off-limits for throwing, take it away from him. Explain in simple terms the potential consequences of random throwing ("If you throw that block, it can hit someone and give them a boo-boo," or "If you throw that truck, it might break"). Even if a fierce protest ensues, hold your ground. Quickly supply your littlest leaguer with a more appropriate object to throw, or if that doesn't satisfy, try to distract him with an entirely different activity.

Anyone—whether two or thirty-two—may occasionally feel the urge to throw something out of frustration or anger. But although most adults can check such volatile emotions or express them in a way that isn't dangerous or hurtful, most toddlers, not surprisingly, haven't yet learned how to do this. If your toddler's throwing seems more triggered by anger or other feelings than by an interest in sports, try to help him deal with these emotions in more acceptable ways (see page 171). You may not only stop the unwanted behavior, but teach him coping mechanisms that can serve him well all his life.

# CLINGINESS DURING PLAY GROUP

*"The other kids in my son's play group seem happy to go off on their own. Mine clings to me the whole two hours."*

The grass often does seem greener on the other side of the play group—one toddler seems so much more socially adept, another seems so much more verbal, yet another seems so much better behaved. But although comparisons to other people's kids may be irresistible, they really aren't fair. Toddlers are individuals, with distinct personalities and patterns of development. Your expectations should be based on your toddler's temperament and stage of development, not on your observations of his playmates.

Keep in mind that a clingy toddler is no more destined to be a social misfit in adulthood than the gregarious toddler is guaranteed a booked-solid social calendar for life. At this tender age, some toddlers are not yet convinced that it's their time to venture from the nest; they crave the warmth and security that dependency offers more than they lust for the freedom and autonomy that independence promises. Pushing the reticent fledgling into flight before he's ready is likely to increase his clinginess. Instead, try more empathetic measures, such as those listed below, which, along with the gentlest of nudges, should get his wings flapping eventually.

**Try him one-on-one.** If he's had little social contact previously, the full-size play group may be overwhelming your toddler. So set up a series of play dates with individual members of the group. This will give him the chance to get to know the other children one at a time and to learn something about playing with them.

**Encourage gradual integration.** As a first step, try sitting your toddler down near the other children with an appealing activity—a bucket of blocks, a stack of books, a workbench, or a shape-sorter. Get him started playing, then gradually work your way over to the other parents. If he chooses to follow, let him. But after a few minutes on your lap, cheerfully return him to the play area. Repeat this process several times during this and subsequent play sessions, until your child starts to feel secure enough to stay by himself for ten or fifteen minutes. Once he's made it over that hurdle, he may take the next step—joining the

# SETTING UP
# A PLAY GROUP

• • • • • • • • • •

Unless there was a convenient little boy or girl next door, toddlers of previous generations did most of their playing on their own or with family members. Interactions with children of the same age were usually pretty limited until a child started nursery school or kindergarten.

And then along came play groups, greatly widening the social horizons of small children, providing those in this generation of toddlers who aren't in day care or preschool the opportunity for early group play experiences. In a play group, toddlers can practice their social skills while enjoying (or at least learning to enjoy) the company and camaraderie of other children. But play groups are as beneficial for parents as they are for toddlers. Swapping war stories, seeing and hearing that you're not alone—that your toddler is not the only one who's having a hard time sharing, not the only one who's been hitting or biting, not the only one who's been throwing tantrums, or not the only one who won't eat anything but cereal—can be remarkably therapeutic. Exchanging ideas, insights, and tips on dealing with toddler eccentricities can enhance parenting effectiveness and confidence.

Although setting up and maintaining a play group isn't child's play, most parents who've participated in one feel it's ultimately well worth the effort. In launching that effort, remember that there are no hard and fast play group rules; circumstances and the personalities of the toddlers and parents involved will dictate most of the details. But the following guidelines should help you get started:

**Decide on the basic format.** In most playgroups for the very young, toddlers attend with a parent (or other caregiver), allowing adults to talk while children play. This format also permits parents to (hopefully) discipline their own child, making peace keeping (hopefully) less complicated. What it doesn't allow is for parents to get some time off. If this is part of the objective, you might consider a co-op arrangement, which combines a play group situation with child care (see page 808).

**Limit the number of players.** A group of six is probably the ideal—small enough to be accommodated in most homes and large enough to function even if one or two members are under the weather or out of town. Four or five can work well, too, but more than eight can lead to overcrowding, overstimulation, and chaos (not enough toys to go around, not enough room in which to serve a snack). It may help to aim for an even number of members (though inevitably, there will be times when an odd number will show up) so that as children start playing one-on-one, there will be less of a possibility that a single toddler will be left out.

**Look for a good match.** Temperament and interests may be tricky to harmonize, particularly since toddlers tend to fluctuate in those areas from day to day and week to week. But major disparities in development and skills can be avoided by aiming for not much more than three or four months between the oldest child and the youngest. Generally, groups that are all-boy, all-girl, or pretty evenly split between the sexes work better than groups in which one sex overwhelmingly outnumbers the other.

**Match parents, too.** Parents in the group don't have to start out as best friends (although they may end up that way), but all should be compatible, fairly well matched in personality and parenting style. Test the chemistry of potential play group parents by holding a few trial meetings to see how it goes. And only discuss setting up a group when the chemistry seems right. Likewise, if you're joining an established group, attend a couple of sessions on a trial basis before committing to membership.

**Decide where to meet.** Most groups rotate from home to home; others meet regularly in one place, such as a community center, a church, a synagogue. For a change of place, head for a park or playground in pleasant weather, or a child-friendly museum on a rainy day.

**Decide when to meet.** Toddlers are generally jollier at certain times of the day than others. Pick a time when all particpants are relatively well rested (not just before nap time) and well fed (not right before mealtime, unless you plan to serve a sustaining snack). Avoid the very end of the day if parent and toddler stress levels tend to be high at that time. At first, plan to keep sessions short—an hour or so—so that the children can get acclimated to the group gradually. As they start becoming more comfortable, begin lengthening the sessions until you find the children's outer limit for togetherness, probably about two hours.

**Plan to meet regularly.** Once you've chosen a time that fits everyone's schedule, stick to it religiously. Change the time only when absolutely necessary (a winter storm warning is in effect, for example, or three kids are down with the flu). If you start switching around (2 o'clock on Tuesday one week, 11 o'clock on Wednesday the next) or cancelling casually (because one parent has a business meeting or another has social plans), the group could start losing steam. With irregular meetings (or irregular attendance at a play group that meets regularly), children could also lose some of the social momentum they've been building up and tentative ones could take much longer to feel comfortable separating from their parents and joining the play.

**Set basic safety rules.** Most experts agree that it's best to ban children when they are sick; for other suggestions, see Chapter Twenty-One.

**Set etiquette rules.** Try to head off conflict and confusion by discussing and deciding on play group protocol in advance. For example: Who will clean up after each session (kids, host, everyone)? What kind of notice is required if a child won't be attending group? What kinds of behavior will be considered off limits? Who will discipline the children and how quickly will they step in (see page 374 for recommendations)?

**Set a toy policy.** The best toys to provide for the play group set are those that foster cooperation and/or can be easily shared—a bucket of blocks, a toy car and truck collection, a beach ball or other large ball, board books, a doll collection, a tea set, pretend food, arts and crafts materials (crayons, paper, toddler-safe clay and finger paints), dress up items, a sand box, a water table, and so on. Until the children are old enough to start taking turns, you may want to put away riding toys (unless you have enough to go around or everyone brings their own) and other one-of-a-kind items. The host parents should also consider putting away "special" toys that their child might not want to see others play with or that might easily be damaged. They may even want to keep their child's room off limits, if there's another place that's practical for play. See page 267 for more on sharing.

**Set a food policy.** Decide with the other parents what kinds of snacks will be served (for example, crackers, cheese, juice, fruit, milk) and what kinds of snacks will be avoided (for example, sugary cookies and cake, soda, candy).

**Watch, don't hover.** While toddlers need constant supervision for safety's sake, too much parental hovering can stifle the growth of independence. If you want to have a group activity that requires parental participation at each session, balance it with a free play period that allows toddlers to learn how to have a good time on their own as parents watch from the sidelines. When disputes come up (and they will), give the children the chance to work out minor disagreements by themselves. But step in and mediate if they come to blows (or bites, or shoves).

others—on his own. If he doesn't, encourage him to get involved by sitting down with him and with one or two other children and showing him how it's done. Make it look like so much fun that he can't resist playing. Then, as he becomes occupied, step back again. Hopefully, with each passing play-group session, you'll have to spend less time hand-holding.

**Remain unruffled.** He's tugging on your jeans? So what. He's glued to your knee? Who cares! He's hiding between your legs? No problem. Making it clear to your toddler that his participation in the social scene is no big deal (if he mingles, fine; if he clings, fine) will help him relax. If you're having trouble staying cool, try reminding yourself that a play group is supposed to be fun, not torture, for you and your child.

**Be accepting.** Don't lead your toddler to believe that his social shortcomings leave you short on love for him. Be altogether tolerant and unconditionally compassionate. Let him know—through your body language, your facial expression, and your tone of voice—that your love isn't dependent on his independence, that it won't waver, whether he chooses to be the life of the play group or a fixture on your lap. That even if everyone else is nibbling cookies in the middle of the living-room floor, it's okay for him to nibble at your knee.

**Be supportive.** Offer your toddler more support, and he'll ultimately need less. Stay close to your child as long as he seems to want you in the play area. He may feel more confident about participating and interacting when you're there, and eventually feel ready to set off without you.

**But don't smother.** Remember that being there for your toddler when he needs you can mean backing off when he seems to be doing well on his own.

**Keep in touch.** When your toddler manages to meander to the play area without you, don't cut out into the kitchen for coffee; staying close will help your toddler stay comfortable. Continue to offer tangible support—an occasional pat on the head or word of praise ("That's a great tower you built")—and it will become clear to your toddler that becoming part of the play group doesn't mean giving you up entirely. Being quick to give him a hug whenever he wanders your way may give him the confidence jump-start he needs to wander off on his own again.

**Be patient.** It may take many months before your toddler feels ready to join the flock. Chances are that even if he was in full flight by the end of the last play group session, he'll need some time to figure out how to get back in formation at the beginning of the next. Give him all the time he needs. This poky reentry may frustrate parents, but it's perfectly normal for many toddlers.

# ANNOYING HABITS PICKED UP AT PLAY GROUP

*"Every time we go to play group, my daughter comes home with a new annoying habit that she's picked up from one of the other children. One week it was screeching, the next it was making blowing noises, the next it was hitting."*

When toddlers step out into the social scene, they learn a lot from other children—unfortunately, not all of it good. Because they are such excellent mimics, young children tend to pick up the mannerisms and habits—positive and negative—of others. Generally, they test each out for a week or two, then drop it as they pick up a new one that's caught their interest. Sometimes, a habit sticks for longer periods.

Scolding, nagging, or punishing your toddler for the behavior won't get her to give it up and may even make her cling to it more tenaciously. So do your best to ignore what you deplore, or to distract your toddler when she starts pursuing habits that you find especially annoying. When the copy-cat behavior is not only annoying, but unsafe or unacceptable—hitting or biting, for example—deal with it calmly but promptly (see individual behaviors for tips).

It may also help to discuss your concerns with the other parents in the group. Taking a united front against unacceptable or inappropriate conduct may make it easier to deal with.

# SCREECHING AND SCREAMING

*"We've got constant headaches from the screeching and screaming our son does around our house."*

Unfortunately, toddlers don't come equipped with automatic volume controls—or, for that matter, with self-control over their volume. And though you may not enjoy your son's performance, he's certainly enjoying performing. He's suddenly discovered his enormous capacity for creating sound and is gleefully taking advantage of it. Like a recording engineer with a sound control panel at his fingertips, he experiments with levels of pitch and volume. And while everyone around him is developing a migraine, he's having a blast.

You could turn a deaf ear (you may feel as though you're soon going to have two of them) and allow this annoying habit to run its natural course—as, like many toddler habits, it eventually will.

Or, with the help of the following tips, you can make an effort to bring the screeching, if not to a screeching halt, at least to a decibel range that's easier on the ears.

**Don't join him.** Keeping the general noise level in the house low (no blaring television or radio, loud rock music, or shouting matches between parents) will help—at least in the long run—to discourage your toddler's own noise-making. Shouting at him to stop shouting, on the other hand, will rev up the competition and inspire him to greater shouting heights. You will also validate his screaming ("If Mommy and Daddy scream, screaming must be okay").

**Redirect his talents.** When the screeching starts, turn on some lively music and encourage your toddler to sing instead. (If you're outside the house, you can try to engage him in an impromptu sing-along of favorite songs or a recitation of nursery rhymes.) Even if he doesn't want to sing, he may stop screaming, if only so that he can hear you sing. Or suggest other interesting ways your child can use his voice—mooing like a cow, meowing like a cat, barking like a dog, vrooming like a car. Though not voice-box generated, making sounds with musical instruments may also fill your toddler's need for making noise.

**Speak softly.** When the screeching starts, look your toddler straight in the eye and whisper to him. Seeing your lips move but being unable to hear what you're saying may make him curious enough to stop screaming and start listening.

**Help him find his little voice.** Small children have a hard time lowering their voices to a whisper, but they can have fun trying. When your toddler's vocalizing wanders out of bounds, challenge him to a "whisper" match by whispering a word, then having him whisper it back.

Though his will come back more like stage whispers for at least the next couple of years, playing the whisper game shows your toddler that there's fun not just in raising his voice, but in lowering it, too.

**Limit his big voice.** By the time your toddler is in the second half of the second year, he will have an easier time accepting limits, including those put on screeching. He will be able to understand the concept of an "inside voice" and an "outside voice"; see page 288. Or specific rules on when and where his "big" voice can be used ("You can scream in your room, but not in the rest of the house," or "You can screech at the playground but not in a restaurant"). Setting such a limit works better than banning shrieking altogether; behavior generally becomes even more attractive when it's forbidden.

## DIAPER STRIPTEASE

*"My daughter's diaper isn't on for two minutes before she's yanked it off. She finds it funny; I find it incredibly frustrating."*

Given the effort it often takes to diaper a toddler, it's especially upsetting when she undoes all your hard work in short order—and with no effort at all. It's also more than a bit unnerving, since a toddler's little striptease leaves not only the toddler, but the rug, the sofa, the bed, and any other surface of the house she frequents, alarmingly unprotected.

To relieve your frustration you will probably have to increase your toddler's—by making it difficult-to-impossible for her to remove her diapers. Since cloth diapers kept on by Velcro wraps are a snap to remove, consider switching back to diaper-pinned ones until your

toddler's kicked the stripping habit. If she's in disposables, try pinning the flaps closed so she can't rip them open as easily. Further foil her attempts by attaching her diaper or the diaper cover snugly to both sides of her undershirt with diaper pins, and by outfitting her in overalls or one-piece coveralls that she'll have difficulty maneuvering out of.

All these efforts may initially evoke rage from your toddler. But if you stick to your guns (or your pins) and keep your cool, distracting your little complainer whenever possible, this too will pass.

If she continues to wriggle out of her diapers as she gets closer to potty-learning age (near the end of year two), use her penchant for a naked bottom as an opportunity to begin the toileting process. At this point, tell her that if she doesn't like wearing diapers, she can start wearing training pants (see page 544) at home, which she can pull off by herself when she wants to go to the potty. (See Chapter Nineteen for more on potty learning.)

## CONTINUED USE OF A COMFORT OBJECT

*"Our toddler still drags a tattered old crib blanket around with her. Isn't she too old for this sort of thing?"*

Your toddler obviously doesn't think so. And because, by and large, kids are the experts on what's age-appropriate for them, it's her opinion that counts. In fact, though most children form a bond with a security or comfort object before the end of the first year, dependence on it doesn't peak until the second year. The reasons are sound. For one thing, though a toddler can't always take Mommy or Daddy along as she explores her world, she isn't quite ready to go it alone.

A transitional object—whether it's a tattered blanket, a well-worn teddy bear, or a trusty thumb—provides a perfect, portable source of reassurance. For another, fears (of the dark, of strangers, of dogs, of vacuum cleaners, to name just a few) start multiplying in the second year; the moral support a transitional object provides does much to help a toddler face them.

Though we don't usually think about it, adults also often use comfort objects to increase their comfort level in a new or awkward situation. However, we've learned to substitute more socially acceptable objects for the threadbare blankets of our youth: a glass to hold at a cocktail party, a briefcase to clutch at a crucial meeting, or a lucky talisman to rub when negotiating a big deal.

So support your toddler's right to the support of a comfort object.[2] Never tease her about it or pressure her to give it up or leave it at home. And don't be embarrassed for her or for yourself when she drags it around—it's perfectly normal toddler behavior. You can, however, take some steps to make her use of the security object less pervasive— and to make giving it up easier, when she's ready.

▲ Try to limit its use, if possible. If your toddler isn't already in the habit of carrying her comfort object with her everywhere, try to put limits on where it can go. Suggest that it can go in the car, but not into the supermarket. Or that it can be carried around the house, but not to the playground. Offer plausible reasons for the restrictions (it might get lost at the supermarket or dirty at the playground). Volunteer to "take care" of the blanket when she climbs on the jungle gym or holds a tea party at play group. With her help, find a special place where she can leave her blanket when she isn't toting it. But don't make a fuss if she won't negotiate any limits; when the timing's right for her, she'll wean herself off her beloved blanket.

▲ Wash the security object regularly. If you don't, your toddler may become as attached to the gamy odor it develops as she is to the blanket itself; then even washing it will cause an uprising. Since separating a child from her security object can be difficult, you will probably have to launder it after your toddler's gone to bed.

▲ Duplicate it, if you can. Though a baby just starting out with a blanket might not notice (and probably wouldn't object) if you cut the blanket into a couple of pieces (one for you to wash, one for her to cuddle), a toddler who's clutched the same blanket for months is likely to both notice and object. Instead, try buying an identical blanket (if you can find one), washing it a few times so it won't seem too new, and either offering it to your toddler as an extra (she may or may not accept it) or putting it away for emergency use (when, for example, the original blanket is nowhere to be found at bedtime). If the comfort object is a toy or stuffed animal, purchasing a duplicate can accomplish the same objective. If your toddler is only mildly attached to her blanket, however, you might just stick with the one. Should it get lost, she can shed a few tears and get on with her life without it.

▲ Give her something else to do with her hands. Busy hands can't hold onto a blanket or a teddy. Keep your toddler occupied with interesting playthings, arts-and-crafts projects, puzzles, and anything else that will divert her hands, and her attention, from her comfort object, at least some of the time.

▲ Be certain she isn't under excessive pressure. Pressure to achieve too much too soon, to be something she's not, or

---

2. Comfort objects may have pet names, such as "lovey," "goggie," "gigee." Your child's may be totally original; feel free to use her term when referring to the object.

to be independent before she's ready can increase stress and a toddler's need for the support of a security object.

▲ Make sure she's getting enough comfort from you. Sometimes frequent hugs or words of reassurance from a parent can give a toddler the sense of security she craves, lessening her need for a security object. (Some children, however, need all the comfort they can get—both from parents and from their transitional objects; that's okay, too.)

Not all comfort objects are harmless. Toddlers who derive comfort from a bottle of juice or milk can end up with tooth decay (see page 27) or with diarrhea (from drinking too much juice, or from milk gone bad). If a child insists on carrying a security bottle around with her, fill it with plain water. Objects that present a choking or other safety risk (see page 626) can also be classified unsafe.

Problems may arise at day care or preschool if other children want to share your toddler's special blanket or play with her special comfort toy, or if the facility she attends has a policy against children toting them around (many do). Try to head off such problems by persuading your toddler to "tuck" her blanket in at home or to "buckle" it into her stroller or car seat before she goes off to school (promise her that it will be waiting for her on her return, and make sure you keep that promise). If she won't walk into her classroom without it, suggest that she leave it in her cubby ("so it'll be safe") during the day. If you still can't elicit her cooperation, enlist the teacher's help in devising a plan that will work.

It's likely that your toddler will be ready to abandon her blanket, or any other comfort object she's become attached to, somewhere between ages two and five, though she may reach for it again during times of stress and upheaval. In the meantime, as long as she's happy and thriving, relax. If the comfort object

becomes an obsession, however, and your child spends more time stroking and cuddling the blanket than playing with toys, looking at books, or socializing, you may need to look closely for underlying causes—for instance, an unhappy child-care situation, too much stress or pressure at home, or an undetected medical condition. If you can't uncover and remedy the problem yourself, consult your toddler's doctor.

# THUMB SUCKING

*"Our daughter sucks her thumb— usually when she is tired or upset. Is this okay?"*

In a toddler's early forays out of the cozy shelter of infancy and into the cold, cruel, and unfamiliar world that now beckons, it sometimes helps to bring a friend along for support. And whether that friend is an earless stuffed animal, a threadbare blanket, or a trusty thumb, it provides the security a toddler needs to explore the unknown. It also allows her to distance herself from her parents, while still hanging on to a familiar comfort.

Not surprisingly, the toddler craves the thumb most when her inner struggle between independence and dependence is at its most tumultuous, or as with all sources of comfort, when she's tired, cranky, under the weather, or bored. Though many children abandon sucking their thumbs (or fists or fingers) before the end of the first year, many others continue to enjoy the comforting habit well beyond this time.

At this age thumb and finger sucking are normal, and in moderation, not harmful, so there's no need to "do something" about them. In fact, parental pressure tends to increase and intensify the habit. If you're worried about what other people will think, don't be. First of all, the stigma of thumb sucking isn't as great as it used to be. Well-informed parents today are more likely to consider it a normal comfort habit, and not a sign of emotional instability. Second of all, it matters not what others think—your attitude is the one that counts. Just politely disregard any cluck-clucks and tsk-tsks that come from the unenlightened.

Don't worry, either, about thumb sucking interfering with normal development of the mouth and teeth. Most experts say that this shouldn't be a problem, as long as the child isn't sucking day in and day out and the habit is abandoned by age four, which in most cases it is. The redness and irritation that is a side effect of thumb sucking in some children isn't a cause for concern, either.

As with most other comfort habits, thumb sucking usually begins to subside without parental interference by age three. If thumb sucking is so pervasive that it interferes with your child's learning to talk, with her eating, and with her using her hands for playing and learning, see below.

*"Our toddler must be the world's champion thumb sucker. He hardly ever has his thumb out of his mouth. Should we worry?"*

**W**orry isn't called for, but a little action probably is. Since *constant* thumb sucking, unlike *occasional* thumb sucking, can do some permanent damage to the mouth and teeth, you and your toddler will have to work together to see that his habit doesn't wreak oral havoc.

You may be able to help your child cut down on the time he spends sucking his thumb by engaging him in activities that require the use of both hands (such as finger painting, riding a rocking horse or other riding toy, swinging on a swing, playing catch, kneading bread dough); by dressing him in mittens to go out-

doors in cold weather; by doling out extra love and attention; and by being sure that he gets adequate rest and sleep.

If these don't succeed, don't nag or turn up the pressure, but do discuss the situation with your child's pediatrician and, if he has one, his pediatric dentist. For tips on helping an older toddler break the thumb-sucking habit, see page 439.

## CONTINUED PACIFIER USE

*"We didn't have the heart to take away our son's pacifier when he was an infant. Later on, we didn't have the energy. Now he's so attached to it we're afraid he'll never give it up."*

**I**t's a pretty sure bet that your son won't have to pop the pacifier from his mouth in order to kiss the bride on his wedding day. Despite the secret fears harbored by parents of persistent pacifier users, almost all children abandon the beloved plug by age four or five, and most stop sucking well before.

Among experts, pacifier use (both short- and long-term) probably has about as many supporters as detractors. On the positive side, research has shown that the use of a pacifier is beneficial for premature newborns and for colicky babies. On the negative, it has been found that prolonged use of the pacifier can damage the structure of the mouth and the position of the teeth, sometimes causing speech problems and increasing the risk of accidental injury to front teeth. (It is, however, believed that if the habit is nipped early enough, any structural damage that has been done will correct itself. Just what "early enough" means is a matter of debate; some experts say by the end of the second year, others the end of the fourth.) Beyond this, little research has been done on the effects of pacifier use, and the little that has been done hasn't shed much light. As a result, most opinion is based on gut instinct.

Many questions about pacifier use remain unanswered. Does it encourage a need for oral gratification later in life (and thus the use of tobacco or other drugs), or does it reduce such a need? Does it inhibit the development of language or of sociability (smiling, for example)? Does using a pacifier to comfort or calm himself interfere with a toddler's learning to self-comfort and self-calm? Until more research is done, you will have to decide for yourself when you want to pull the plug. Here are some factors to consider in making your decision:

▲ Has pacifier use begun to affect your child's mouth and teeth? This is most likely if your toddler uses the pacifier for lengthy periods every day. Check with a pediatric dentist for the answer. If it's yes, you should consider terminating the pacifier in the near future no matter what your answers to the remaining questions.

▲ Do you use the pacifier to keep your toddler quiet or off your back? Planting a pacifier in the mouth of a child who is upset inhibits self-expression, a valuable human resource. And consider how you would feel if someone shoved a rubber nipple into your mouth every time you opened it to speak your mind.

▲ Does the pacifier seem to be hampering your toddler's language development? Does he grunt and point when it's in his mouth, instead of using words?

▲ Does the pacifier seem to interfere with your toddler's social development by hindering his interactions with others? (Keep in mind, however, that a young toddler's social skills are naturally immature.)

If you feel that the pacifier is having a negative effect on your toddler and you'd like to break him of the habit

sooner rather than later, you can take some steps toward that end.

**Establish limits.** Just what the limits are should depend on how and when your toddler uses the pacifier, and how devastated he would be without it. You might suggest, for example, that now that he's bigger, he use the pacifier only in the house, or only when going to sleep.

**Provide extra comfort.** If your toddler seems dependent on the pacifier for comfort, offer him other sources of solace. Heap on the love and attention, particularly when he's feeling down or insecure. Before he reaches for the pacifier, reach for him with a hug. Or distract him with a story. Or turn on some soothing music and settle down for a cuddle. Or let him pound out his anxieties or anger on a pile of clay, or express them in painting. Also take steps to help boost his sense of control and his self-esteem (see page 292).

**Keep his mouth busy.** Ask questions, strike up conversations, encourage him to recite rhymes, sing, laugh, make funny faces in the mirror, suck juice from a straw, and otherwise use his mouth for non-pacifier purposes. If he tries to talk with the pacifier in his mouth, let him know that you can't understand him, that he has to remove it if he wants you to know what he's saying.

**Don't let him go hungry—or sleepy.** The child who's hungry or overtired tends to lose his ability to cope; it's then that he's likely to turn to a familiar coping mechanism, such as his pacifier. To cut down on your toddler's need for the pacifier, make sure he gets the nourishment (offer a snack before he hits a blood-sugar low) and rest that his body requires.

These measures may help reduce pacifier use, but they aren't likely to end it. More decisive action is usually needed. For how to pull the plug permanently, see page 639.

If you decide to allow your toddler to use the pacifier a bit longer, consult his pediatric dentist about the model to use. Although it is widely believed that the so-called "orthodontic" pacifier is potentially less damaging to the mouth, there are experts in pediatric dentistry who strongly disagree. They recommend one that is shaped like a thumb—if one is used at all. Whatever the shape, look for one-piece construction, which is safest because it can't come apart. (Never use an ordinary bottle nipple as a pacifier since it represents a choking hazard.) The pacifier shield (the flat part between the nipple and the ring) should be rigid, too large to fit in your toddler's mouth (at least 1½ inches across), and it should have ventilation holes. Because the rigid shield could cause a serious cut if your toddler fell on it, don't allow your toddler to run around with the pacifier in his mouth. Tempted as you may be, never hang the pacifier (or anything else) on a string or ribbon around your toddler's neck. Wash the pacifier frequently in the dishwasher, if you have one, or in very hot soapy water. And check it regularly. If you find signs of damage or deterioration, replace the pacifier—or attempt to use its demise as an excuse to break the habit ("Sorry, honey, but your pacifier is broken. We have to throw it away"). If you're lucky it may work. If not, you can always buy a new pacifier.

If all your efforts fail, don't force the issue. While more drastic measures may be needed a year or two from now (when both peer pressure and damage to his mouth and teeth can become problems), they aren't necessary now. Like any comfort object, the pacifier fills a need. It isn't fair to allow a child to become dependent on one, then force him to give it up when he may need it most.

# COMFORT ACTIVITIES

*"When our toddler gets ready for sleep he goes through this ritual where he literally bangs his head against the wall next to his crib. Both my wife and I are very concerned about this."*

A small head banging against the wall. A cribful of toddler bouncing across the room. A tiny fistful of hair yanked from a sweet little head. Who wouldn't be concerned? Yet such disconcerting and seemingly senseless rituals, which understandably bring discomfort to the parents who watch them, actually bring comfort to the children who perform them.

These self-comforting activities, kinetic cousins to the more sedate comfort objects, are seen most commonly among intense children and practiced most commonly at night, when these little fireballs are brimming with energy and tension that need releasing. And being resourceful creatures, release they do: through head banging, rhythmic rocking, hair-pulling, and the like.

Comfort activities, like comfort objects, are normal in toddlers; and when exhibited in a happy, well-adjusted child who relates well to others, they are not reason for concern. Still, they can raise the level of anxiety at home, and even keep a family awake at night as the rocker shimmies his crib across the floor or the head banger plays bongos with his noggin at 2 A.M.

Though it's unwise to try to force an end to these habits (as with any toddler behavior, coercion rarely works and often triggers an increase in the unwanted activity), there are steps you can take to soften their impact on all concerned:

**Reduce stress.** Try to ease any excessive stress there might be in your toddler's life—whether it stems from your going to work; from a new child-care arrangement, a new home, or a new sibling; from being weaned off the bottle or breast; or from another unsettling situation.[3] Be sure, too, that your toddler gets plenty of love, affection, and attention; ample amounts of these will help relax him.

**Provide release.** Supply your toddler with other outlets for his nervous energy: wrestling, pounding with a toy hammer, beating a toy drum, punching a blow-up clown or pillow, tossing a ball around, and playing outdoors. Give a hair puller a long-haired stuffed animal to hang on to and tug. This may reduce the need to pull his own hair. If that doesn't work, a shorter haircut may help.

**Rock around the clock.** Provide plenty of opportunities for more socially acceptable kinds of rhythmic activities. Rocking in a child-size rocker, swinging on a swing, dancing, spinning like an airplane, riding up and down on a teeter-totter, playing lively hand and circle games to music (Patty-Cake, The Itsy Bitsy Spider, Ring-a-Round-a-Rosie, and so on.)

Music itself can also soothe your toddler by satisfying the need for rhythmic activities he's been filling by rocking or banging. Play rousing music during the day, and encourage him to dance to it, clap to it, foot-stomp to it, or accompany it with his own toy instruments. At bedtime, try something softer and more calming. Try rocking or swaying to the music gently as you read a bedtime story, or slow-dancing to it with him in your arms.

**Establish a bedtime routine.** Self-comforting activities generally peak

in the evening; children use them to unwind after a busy day. A regular bedtime routine (see page 68) may help your toddler find more tranquil routes to relaxation.

**Don't bed down your toddler too soon.** Waiting until your toddler's really sleepy before you put him to bed may decrease his need to head-bang his way to dreamland. But don't let him get over-tired to the point of being over-wound. That will make him more likely to bang.

**Protect your toddler and his environment.** If you can't stop your toddler's comfort habit, you can help reduce its potential damage by moving the crib away from the wall; padding the crib or other surfaces your toddler bangs his head against (but be prepared for him to reject the softer surface and look for a harder one); removing the wheels from the crib and wedging a carpet under it so it'll stay put during rocking or head-banging sessions.

In most children, rhythmic comfort activities disappear by age three without parental intervention. If they don't, or if your child is actually hurting himself or seems to enjoy hurting himself, seems perpetually unhappy, doesn't talk or otherwise communicate with others, doesn't like to be held or touched, or spends much of his time engaged in one or more of these activities, talk to his doctor.

# DISINTEREST IN COMFORT HABITS

*"Our son has never had any comfort habits—he doesn't suck his thumb, or carry a blanket or a teddy bear. As a result, he often has a hard time comforting himself, and relies on me. Is this bad?"*

---

3. Tips on how to reduce the stress caused by difficult situations are available under individual topics: going to work (page 770); a new sitter (page 23); a new day-care situation (page 146); moving (page 745); weaning (page 27, 30); a new sibling (page 748). See also, relaxation techniques, page 173.

No, it's just a case of different strokes for different little folks. Some toddlers find security in a totable, inanimate object, others, like your son, find comfort is more satisfying when it takes human form. Such children enjoy playing with teddy bears, and cuddling under blankets, but never develop an attachment to any particular one. That's just their style—and it's perfectly okay.

There are obvious benefits to not being hooked on a comfort object—no dragging around a tattered blanket, no trauma when the treasured teddy can't be found, no thumb or pacifier to be weaned from. When your toddler's only source of security is you, however, there may be drawbacks, too: You may start to feel like an oversized teddy or a ragged blanket yourself, and resent playing the role of comfort object and putting in the time it takes to fulfill that role. But as with any other comfort object, it's important not to push your toddler to give up the extra comfort you provide before he's ready. (See page 386 for more on easing your toddler toward independence gently.)

## WHETHER TO TETHER

*"I never approved of people using leashes to restrain their toddlers until I had a toddler of my own. He's off and running the moment I put him down, and I'm afraid one day I won't be able to catch him. Would a leash be so bad?"*

In some parts of the world, tethers are used routinely to keep toddlers safe. And, indeed, in certain circumstances (in a busy bus, train, or plane terminal, for example, or on a subway) putting a toddler on a leash may make sense. This is especially true when there's only one adult in charge and more than one child (or a lot of luggage) to look after. But a child on a leash, restrained by another person, often doesn't learn self-restraint. So, in most other situations—when walking down the street, playing in front of the house, or shopping in a department store—it's better to keep your toddler nearby using other techniques. See page 181 for dealing with the wandering toddler.

# WHAT IT'S IMPORTANT TO KNOW:
## Disciplining Your Toddler

Discipline. To many minds, it's not a pretty word—summoning up fearful Victorian images of belt-wielding fathers, ruler-plying teachers, angry threats, stinging slaps, and other humiliating punishments.

Yet discipline needn't be *any* of those things; in fact, by definition, it *isn't* any of those things. The word "discipline" actually comes from the Latin word meaning "to teach" and originally had nothing to do with rules, punishment, or the inflicting of pain.

Why discipline a toddler? First of all, to instill an understanding of the concept of right and wrong. Though toddlers aren't ready to fully digest this idea, you can give them a sense of it both from what you do and what you say. Second, to plant the seeds of self-control. These won't sprout immediately, but if nurtured faithfully, they will become the roots of your child's future behavior. Third, to teach respect for the rights and feelings of others, so that your child will grow from a self-centered toddler into a compassionate and caring child and adult. Fourth, to increase your toddler's chances of growing up to be a happy adult; an undisciplined child is often in for a rude awakening—and a lot of unhappiness—when getting out into the real world. And finally, to protect your toddler, your home, and your sanity—now and in the many mischief-laden years that lie ahead.

As you discipline your child, bear the following ideas in mind:

▲ Every child is different, every family is different, each circumstance is different—therefore, there are many different approaches to discipline. But there are universal rules of behavior that apply to everyone, every time.

▲ You can't rely on a toddler's obedience. Until children are old enough to understand what is safe and what is not, or at least which actions are permissible and which are not, their parents and other caregivers have total responsibility for keeping them safe and out of trouble.

▲ Withholding parental love is not an acceptable method of discipline. It threatens a child's self-esteem and sets the stage for a variety of problems later. It's important to let children know that even when their behavior is not lovable, they are still loved. ("I don't like what you're doing," rather than "I don't like you.")

▲ The most effective discipline is neither uncompromisingly rigid nor overly permissive. Discipline that relies entirely on parental policing, rather than on encouraging the development of self-control, usually turns out children who are totally submissive to their parents but often totally out-of-control once out of reach of parental or other adult authority. Overly permissive parents aren't likely to turn out well-behaved children, either. Their overindulged offspring are often selfish, rude, and unpleasant, quick to argue, and slow to comply.

Both extremes can leave a child feeling unloved. Strict parents may seem cruel, and thus unloving; permissive parents may appear apathetic, and thus uncaring. A more nurturing and successful brand of discipline falls somewhere in between—it sets limits that are fair, and enforces them firmly but lovingly.

That's not to say that there aren't normal and acceptable variations in disciplining styles. Some parents are simply more relaxed by nature, and some are more rigid. Be yourself as a parent as long as you avoid the extremes.

▲ Effective discipline is individualized. If you have more than one child, you almost certainly noticed differences in their personalities from birth. You may even have noticed how such differences have influenced the way you discipline each child. One, for instance, will refrain from touching an electric outlet after a gentle remonstrance. Another won't take your warning seriously unless there is a stern tone—or perhaps blind terror—in your voice. A third needs to be removed bodily from the source of danger. A single cross word may reduce one child to tears. Another may tune out (or even laugh in the face of) a thorough scolding. For some children, adult silence or a sharp look may be most effective.

Circumstances can alter a child's response to discipline. A child who ordinarily requires strong admonitions may be crushed if scolded when tired or teething. So tailor your style to the situation as well as to your child.

▲ Children need limits. They often can't control their impulses and become frightened when they lose control. Limits, set by parents and lovingly enforced, let them know what to expect and provide a comforting tether to keep children secure, steady, and safe as they explore and grow. Stretching those limits because your toddler is "just a baby" isn't fair to your child or to anyone whose rights may be violated by his or her action. Tender age shouldn't confer the right to pull a sibling's hair or tear up Mommy's magazine.

Just which limits you set depends on your priorities. In some homes, keeping shoes off the sofa and not eating in the living room are paramount issues. In others, staying out of Mommy's or Daddy's desk drawers is vital. In most families, common courtesy and simple etiquette—using "Please" and "Thank you," sharing, respecting other people's feelings—are primary expectations. Set rules you feel strongly enough about to enforce fully, but keep them to a reasonable number.

Learning to live with limits is necessary for survival in a society that is full of limits—at school, work, and play. Learning to live with limits from an early age can help ease some of the turmoil when "the terrible twos" hits, as well as provide a head start on developing self-control.

Of course, it's one thing to talk about setting limits for toddlers, and another to actually enforce them. It's tempting to give in to an achingly adorable tot who flashes an impish grin in response to your "No!" or to give up and look the other way when your "no" has been boldly disregarded for the fifth time. But it's important to steel yourself and stick to your "no"—for your toddler's sake, as well as for the sake of the table that's about to be crayoned or the vase that's about to be tossed like a football across the living room. While it may not seem vital now to stop your toddler from taking her crackers into the living room (you can always vacuum up the crumbs later, after all), it is. If your child doesn't learn to follow at least a few rules now, the many that come later in life will be that much harder for him or her to live with. You can expect your rules to be met with more defiance than compliance in the beginning, but as time goes on, you'll find that your toddler

will begin to accept the limits you set as a matter of course.

▲ A toddler who gets into trouble isn't "bad." Since young toddlers don't know right from wrong, their misdeeds can't be considered wicked. They learn about the world by experimenting, observing cause and effect, and testing their environment—and the adults in it. What happens when I turn over my glass of juice? Will the same thing happen if I tip it again? And again? What's inside that kitchen drawer, and what will happen if I dump it out? What will Mommy's reaction be?

Repeatedly telling your child that he or she is "bad" or "naughty" can damage a young ego and interfere with the development of self-confidence, which is necessary for achievement down the road. And the child who hears "You're always so bad!" over and over may well fulfill the prophecy in later years ("If they say I'm bad, I must be bad"). Criticize your toddler's actions, but not your toddler ("Hitting is bad," not "You're bad").

Sometimes disobedience is almost incidental. A toddler may appear disobedient when he or she is just distracted. Busy with an activity and unable to focus on more than one thing at a time, your child may shut out what you're saying to avoid overload. Also, a toddler may resist parental authority because he or she lacks the ability to assess options and foresee results in a particular situation. Rather than doing what they're told, they feel compelled to try each possibility, simply to see what will happen. This can appear to be intentional disobedience, but isn't. To top it off, a toddler's impulse control is weak; while they may get the message that dunking the bath towel in the toilet bowl is wrong, they haven't yet learned how to curb the urge to do it.

▲ Consistency is important. If shoes are forbidden on the sofa today but permitted tomorrow, or if hand-washing before dinner was compulsory yesterday but overlooked today, the only lesson learned is that the world is confusing and rules are meaningless. If you fail to be consistent, you'll lose credibility. When you do make an exception, explain why.

▲ Follow-through is crucial. Looking up from your book long enough to mutter "Don't do that" to a toddler who's tugging the television wires, but not long enough to make sure she stops, is not effective discipline. If your actions don't speak at least as loud as your words, your admonitions will lose their impact. When the first "no" is ineffective, take immediate action, especially in such a dangerous situation. Put down your book, pick up your toddler with a firm, "Don't touch the television wires, it's dangerous," and move him or her away from temptation—preferably far away, into another room. Then take your child's mind off the television with a favorite plaything. For most toddlers, what's out of sight is quickly out of mind—though a few may try to return to the scene, in which case you'll have to repeat the relocation process as many times as it takes or, if possible, make the forbidden fruit completely inaccessible. Distraction, when it works, also allows a toddler to save face when "no" is seen as a challenge.

▲ Young toddlers have limited memories. You can't expect them to learn a lesson the first time it's taught, and you can expect them to repeat an undesirable action over and over and over again. Be patient, and be prepared to repeat the same message—"Don't touch the VCR," or "Don't eat the dog food"—every day for weeks, or even months, before it finally sinks in or the fascination is lost. And take nothing for granted when it comes to safety. Don't rely on your toddler having apparently learned a lesson in avoiding danger (running into the street, touching a hot stove, playing with an electric outlet). Supervise him or her closely and follow the safety recommen-

dations in Chapter Twenty-One without fail, no matter how obedient or sage your toddler seems to have become.

▲ Toddlers enjoy the "no" game. Most children savor the challenge of a parent's "No!" as much as the challenge of climbing a flight of stairs or fitting a stubborn circle into a shape-sorter. So no matter how your child goads you, don't let your "No!" dissolve into sport or into a fit of laughter. Your toddler won't take you—or your limits—seriously if you do. (For dealing with the toddler who won't take no for an answer, see page 48.)

Although a certain number of "no's" are necessary, too many "no's" soon lose their effectiveness and can be demoralizing. Just as you wouldn't want to live in a world where everything you did (or tried to do) was censured by the harsh "no" of an unyielding, oversize dictator, your toddler shouldn't live in such a world either. Limit your "no's" to situations that threaten the well-being of your toddler, of another person, or of your home. Remember that not every issue is worth a confrontation. Fewer "no's" will be needed if you create a child-proof environment (see page 620) in your home, and provide plenty of opportunities for safe exploration.

With each "no," always offer a "yes" in the form of an alternative. "You can't pull those leaves off that plant, but you can pull up some weeds; I'll show you which ones" or "You can't play with Daddy's new book, but you can read your board book with the pretty pictures." Try to emphasize the positive. To the child who has already emptied the contents of your desk drawer onto the floor, say, "Those are Mommy's papers. They belong in the desk, not on the floor. Let's see if you can put them back in the drawer and close it" instead of, "Look what a mess you've made with my papers!" scowling as you bend to scoop up your files. Add a dash of praise and a round of applause when your child complies, along with the firm reminder that, "Mommy's papers need to stay in Mommy's desk." This face saving approach gets across the message that emptying the drawer is not okay but it doesn't make your toddler feel "bad."

▲ Parents don't always have to win. Once in a while, when the stakes aren't high or when you realize you've made a mistake, don't be too embarrassed or too impatient to let your child win. An occasional victory will make up for the many "losses" your toddler endures each day.

▲ Children need to be allowed to make some mistakes, and to learn from these mistakes. If you make it impossible for your child to get into trouble (stashing away *all* the knickknacks, for instance), you won't have to say "no" as often, but you'll also miss out on important opportunities to teach. Be flexible, leave room for errors your child can learn from, but not when safety is an issue. For example, if your toddler wants to wear winter boots on a hot day, allowing the fashion *faux pas* so that he or she can learn from it makes more sense than insisting on sandals and triggering a tantrum. (Stash a pair of sandals or sneakers in the diaper bag just in case good sense and sweaty feet triumph over stubborness while you're out.)

▲ Praise and reward are effective disciplinary tools. Use positive reinforcement—praising and rewarding good behavior—often. This will build, rather than knock down, your child's self-confidence as it reinforces good behavior.

▲ Correction is much more effective when it takes place face to face. So rather than call from the other side of the room, "Please stop that banging," walk up to your child, look him or her squarely in the eye, and say your piece. Let your body language, tone of voice, and expression make it clear that you mean business.

▲ Emotional blackmail is unkind. Inducing guilt ("If you loved me, you wouldn't act this way") is hitting below the belt. Children should not be asked to behave just to keep a parent happy.

▲ Uncontrolled anger is ineffective. It clouds your thinking, teaches a poor coping mechanism, can humiliate and frighten young children, and if used repeatedly can damage their self-esteem. Unleashed against older children and adults it generally triggers anger rather then remorse.

When your child has done something that angers you, take a few moments to calm down before responding (see page 751 for tips on dealing with anger). Once your cool is collected, explain to your child that what he or she did was wrong, and why. ("That wasn't a ball you threw, it was Mommy's dish. You broke it and now I'm sad.") This is important to do even if the explanation seems to be sailing clear over your child's head, or if distraction has already set in.

During moments of high anxiety, try to remember (it won't always be easy) that your long-term goal is to teach right behavior, and that screaming or swatting will teach wrong behavior, setting a poor example of what's appropriate when one is angry.

Don't worry, however, if you occasionally find it impossible to put on the brakes. As a human parent, you're allowed your share of frailties, and your child needs to know that. As long as your tirades are relatively few, far between, short-lived, and geared as an attack on your child's actions and *not* your child, they won't interfere with effective parenting. When you do lose your cool, be sure to apologize: "I'm sorry I yelled at you, but I was very angry." Adding "I love you" will let your toddler know that sometimes we get angry at people we love and that such feelings are okay. But don't be so contrite that it sounds as though you're sorry you disciplined at all. (If you find yourself losing your temper at your toddler too often, see page 754.)

▲ Parental use of foul language does nothing but teach children to use it themselves. Many parents spout four-letter words without thinking, and then are shocked to hear the same words coming from the mouths of their babes.

▲ Accidents require different treatment from intentional wrongdoings. Remember, everyone's entitled to make a mistake, and because of their emotional, physical, and intellectual immaturity, toddlers are entitled to make a great many more. When yours knocks over a glass of milk while reaching for a slice of bread, "Oops, the milk spilled. Try to be more careful, honey," is an appropriate response. But when the cup is upended intentionally, it's more fitting to say, "Milk is to drink, not to spill. Spilling makes a mess and wastes the milk—see, now there's no more." In either case, it will also help to fill a drinking cup with very small amounts of liquid in the future, to hand your toddler a rag to help clean up, and to be sure that your little scientist has plenty of opportunity to pursue liquid-pouring experiments in the tub or other acceptable surroundings.

▲ Parents have to be the adults in the family. If you expect your child to act responsibly, you'll have to do the same. Say you promised your toddler a trip to the playground, but then decide you would rather catch up on laundry or have a friend over for coffee. A mature parent keeps the promise and does the laundry later, or chats with the friend on the phone while preparing dinner.

If you expect your child to admit mistakes comfortably, you'll have to lead the way here, too: If you made your toddler cry over spilled milk, then learn later that it was Grandma who spilled it, apologize, and try to avoid jumping to conclusions next time.

If you often find yourself getting down to your child's level, following a toddler tantrum, for example, with one of your own, or demanding things your way when they could just as easily be done your child's way, take some time to reevaluate your own behavior.

▲ Parents should display confidence. If you are constantly moaning, "I don't know what to do with you..." you not only undermine your authority, you could frighten your child by not seeming in control.

▲ Children are worthy of respect. Instead of treating your toddler as an object, a possession, or even "just a baby," treat your child with the respect you would accord any other person. Be polite (say "Please," "Thank you," and "Excuse me") and offer simple explanations (even if you don't think they'll be understood) when you forbid something. Be understanding of and sympathetic to your toddler's wants and feelings (even if you can't permit their acting out), and avoid embarrassing your child (by scolding in front of strangers or playmates).[4] And most of all, really listen to what your child is saying. In the preverbal stage, when grunting, pointing, and monosyllables are the main modes of communication, listening is a challenge, and it continues to be so until speech becomes clear and language is well developed (somewhere around three or four). But making that effort to listen is important. Remember, not being understood is frustrating for your toddler, too.

▲ There should be a fair distribution of rights between parents and children. It's easy, when a child is young, for parents to err in this area, going to one extreme or the other. Some abrogate all their

---

4. Sometimes it's necessary to correct a child in public. It's all right to say, "No throwing" or "No hitting," but any more serious scolding should be done discreetly, by taking the child aside or speaking softly face to face.

---

## WIN-WIN SOLUTIONS

· · · · · · · · · ·

The best solutions to parent–child disputes allow everyone to come up a winner. For example, if your toddler tests you by first touching the flower arrangement on the table, and then gives you a challenging glance and backs off, forget it. He got to touch something off-limits (which is what he wanted), but he didn't go any further or do any damage (which is what you want). You both save face, and you both end up winners. You can create win-win situations by using distraction (he goes for the VCR, you go for the crayons and paper), humor (see page 126), reverse psychology (see page 316), and other creative approaches (such as setting a timer that will ring when the five minutes to dinnertime are up, signaling that it's time to put down the blocks and come to the table). Everybody can end up a winner, too, when you do a little negotiating: "Take your bath right now, and then we'll read your favorite book." Negotiate, but don't bribe. If your toddler is steadfastly refusing to get into the tub, don't promise reading in return for cooperation. Nor should you threaten: "If you don't take a bath right now, we won't read afterward." Later on, when your child's old enough to understand, you can explain that actions have consequences: "If you waste a lot of time now and take your bath late, there won't be any time to read a story."

---

rights in favor of their child—they base their lives on the child's schedule, never go out, forget the value of adult friends, and neglect their personal relationships. Others live their lives as though they were still childless, heedless of their child's needs—they drag an overtired toddler to an adult party, skip giving the child a bath in favor of watching a football game, and miss a pediatrician appointment because of a meeting. Strive for a balance.

▲ Nobody's perfect—and nobody should be expected to be. Avoid setting unattainable standards for your toddler. Children need all the years of childhood to develop to the point at which they can behave as adults. And they need to know that *you* don't expect perfection, now or ever.

▲ Parents aren't perfect either. The parent who has all the answers, never loses control, never yells, and never feels the remotest desire to shake a difficult toddler doesn't exist; even the father of that early television series didn't always

know best. Letting your anger out and clearing the air once in a while is better than keeping frustration bottled up. Bottled-up anger has a way of bursting out inappropriately with an intensity that is far out of proportion to the offense of the moment.

▲ Children need to feel they have some control over their lives. For good mental health, everyone—even a young child—needs to feel as though he or she can call at least some of the shots. It won't always be possible for your toddler to have his or her way, but when it is, allow it. Give your toddler a chance to make choices—the cracker or the piece of bread, the swing or the slide, the T-shirt with the elephant or the one with the clown.

▲ Toddlers are novices at following rules. *You* know what you mean when you tell your toddler to clean up the blocks, but don't take it for granted that your toddler knows what you mean. The most basic tasks must be spelled out,

## MAKE DISCIPLINE A LAUGHING MATTER

· · · · · · · · · ·

Humor is the leavening of life—it raises us up when we're down—and makes a surprisingly effective disciplinary tool. Using humor avoids shouting matches and bad feelings, and allows a toddler to give in without losing face. Use it in situations that would otherwise lead you to exasperation—for instance, when a toddler refuses to get into the stroller. Instead of engaging in fruitless combat amid shrill screams of protest, head off the tantrum and the struggle with some unexpected silliness. Suggest, perhaps, that the dog get in the stroller or pretend to get into it yourself. The incongruity of what you are proposing will probably distract your toddler long enough for you to complete your mission.

Humor can be brought into a variety of disciplinary situations. Give orders pretending you're a dog or a lion, Big Bird, Mickey Mouse, or another of your child's favorites; accompany unpopular procedures with silly songs ("This is the way we wash the face, wash the face . . .") or outlandish play-by-play commentary ("Here comes the clean-up monster," as the washcloth swoops down and "gobbles" the jelly-smeared cheeks); carry your toddler to the dreaded changing table upside down; make silly faces in the mirror to distract your toddler from crying instead of chiding impatiently, "Stop that crying—I can't stand it!"

Taking each other less seriously more often will add sunshine to your days, particularly in this sometimes-stormy second year.

For more ways to make cooperation fun for your toddler, see "A Spoonful of Sugar," page 156.

---

even demonstrated, to be understood. Start by showing your toddler how to put the blocks in the basket and then how to put the basket back on the toy shelf. The next time, encourage your toddler to help you put the blocks away. When your child has gotten the hang of it, try putting the whole job in those capable little hands (while you supervise). You'll eventually be able to say "Please put your blocks away" and get an appropriate response—at least sometimes.

Keep in mind that the directions you give should always be simple and specific. Not "Put those things away," but "Put your blocks in the basket." Avoid a long list, such as, "Put the books away. Then clean up the toys on the floor and put away your clothes. After that, wash your hands and come in to eat." By the time you get to the end of the litany, your toddler will have forgotten the beginning. Instead, give just one direction at a time. When your child has completed one task, then try the next.

Never discipline a child for a task undone unless you're certain he or she has previously been instructed on how to complete it.

▲ Not every task is within a toddler's grasp. Many chores are beyond the physical and intellectual abilities of a toddler. If you expect yours to hang up that winter jacket when coming indoors, be sure the hook is reachable, and that it's possible for a little person to get the coat onto the hook so it will stay there. If you expect clothes to go into the hamper, be sure the hamper isn't too tall, has an easy-to-lift lid that won't slam down on little fingers, and is close to where your child usually undresses. Again, don't discipline a toddler for not doing a task that was difficult or impossible to begin with.

▲ Patience is a necessity when dealing with toddlers. Natural dawdlers with short attention spans, toddlers are easily distracted from the task at hand by almost anything they see or hear; they need frequent gentle reminders to stay with what they are supposed to be doing.

# DISCIPLINING TECHNIQUES THAT WORK

While there's no one right way to discipline a toddler, there are several ways that work well, including the following. Which you choose, and when you choose them, will depend on your toddler's personality, your personality, and the specific set of circumstances.

**Catch your child being good.** Most children learn early on that being good garners them much less parental attention than being naughty. Mommy's not looked up from the checkbook she's been trying to balance for half an hour? It's time to start ripping up her mail. Daddy settles down with the news when he gets home after work and barely says hello? He'll notice me if I dump the dog food bowl over on the carpet. While your toddler's thinking process may not be as clear as all that, the results are.

So the next time your toddler misbehaves to capture your attention, avoid overreacting (a strong reaction, even a negative one, is just what your toddler is playing for). But when your child turns the pages of your book carefully, or plays quietly with a puzzle while you wash the dishes, or picks up a scrap of paper from the floor and hands it to you, be bountiful with your praise. Make a fuss over your toddler's good behavior, not his or her transgressions.

And be sure to give your toddler enough attention (even if you're busy, take a moment to reach over for a hug or to comment on the progress of a block tower) so that there will be little need to try to attract it through intentional misbehavior.

**Make the punishment fit the crime.** It's virtually impossible for a young toddler to understand that television privileges are being revoked because of a crayon masterpiece drawn on the living-room wall. Your child is much more likely to get your point if you take the crayons away immediately and don't return them until after lunch (and then don't forget to include a pad of drawing paper). There is almost always a way to fit the punishment to the crime. If a cup of orange juice is turned over intentionally, the toddler can participate in the clean-up. If blocks are thrown around, they can be confiscated for the rest of the day. If a swipe is taken at another child in the sandbox, the swiper can sit out the next round of shoveling.

**Let your child suffer the natural consequences of the crime.** One of the more important lessons of life (one some adults never learn) is that all actions have consequences. Feed your cookie to the dog, you have no more cookie. Tear pages out of a favorite storybook, Daddy can't read that book to you anymore. Drop your teddy in a mud puddle in the playground and you can't play with it until it goes through the washer. Don't always try to protect your toddler from the consequences of his or her acts and don't consider reparations (another cookie, a new copy of the book, an ice-cream cone to stop the tears) unless the action was an accident. A toddler's period of suffering in such situations is likely to be brief, but a lesson is nevertheless learned—eventually.

**Consider time-out.** Not all experts agree that the "time-out" is a wise disciplinary tool, but some parents swear by it. Its level of effectiveness probably depends on the commitment of the parent and the temperament of the child.

The idea behind time-out is to allow an out-of-control toddler to cool down and regain control; for older children a time-out can also provide a chance (hopefully) for introspection. Often this quiet time can help diffuse a potentially explosive situation before it reaches crisis proportions. Thirty seconds to a minute is a time frame that works with some toddlers (time passes slowly at this age); others require five to ten minutes. Use an egg timer or a minute timer ("when the sand goes through, you can get up") to help define the boundaries of the time-out for your toddler. An older child may be allowed to get up when he or she feels ready to behave. If your child refuses to stay seated (sitting still is rarely a toddler's strong suit), firmly return him or her to the chair or corner as many times as necessary, keeping a hand on the child's shoulder, if need be. If, once the time-out has ended, the child immediately repeats the unwanted behavior, repeat the time-out.

There are several important guide-

## TO SPANK OR NOT TO SPANK

• • • • • • • • • •

Spanking as a means of discipline has been passed on from generation to generation in many families. Nevertheless, most experts agree that spanking is not effective. Children who are spanked may refrain from repeating a misdemeanor rather than risk a repeat spanking, but they obey only out of fear. Instead of learning to differentiate between right and wrong, they only learn to differentiate between what they get spanked for and don't get spanked for. And they rarely learn self-discipline.

Spanking also has many other negative aspects. For one, it sets a violent example. Children who are spanked are more likely to use physical force against peers, and later against their own children. For another, by teaching children that the best way to settle a dispute is with force, spanking denies them the chance to learn alternative, less hurtful, ways of dealing with anger and frustration. It also represents the abuse of power by a very large, strong party (or bully) against a very small, comparatively weak one. Spanking is humiliating and demeaning to both the parent and the child, often shattering self-esteem and morale.

Spanking can also lead to serious injury, particularly when it happens in the heat of anger. Spanking after the anger has cooled may cause less physical damage, but seems even more questionable. It is certainly more cruelly calculated, and in the long run is less effective in correcting behavior, since the punishment is so far removed from the offense.

Sitters and other caregivers should be instructed never to strike your child or to administer any form of physical punishment. If your child is in day care or preschool, be sure that there is a policy that prohibits corporal punishment (though this won't absolutely ensure that a staff member will never strike a child). Any evidence of corporal punishment on the part of a caregiver requires swift and decisive intervention. First, remove your child from his or her care and then report the incident, as appropriate. If you hired the caregiver through an agency or other organization, let them know what happened. If he or she injured your child, this should be reported to the Child Abuse Reporting Hotline (see your phone book or call your child's doctor).

Some experts (and parents) believe that a smack on the hand or the bottom may be warranted in a dangerous situation to get an important message across to a child too young to understand words—for example, when a young toddler wanders into the street or continues to approach a hot stove following a stern warning to stay away. The idea is not to inflict pain, but to quickly call a child's attention to the seriousness of the situation. Such a slap should be followed by an explanation: "If you run into the street, a car could hurt you." Once a child shows that he or she understands what you say, however, physical force is no longer considered justifiable even when safety is an issue.

## WHEN SPANKING BECOMES ABUSE

• • • • • • • • • •

**R**are is the parent who intentionally hurts a child. Most child abusers inflict physical punishment either out of anger or because they believe they are doing it for the child's benefit. Most were disciplined the same way themselves. But anything more than a smack on the bottom (well-padded with a diaper) can injure a child, especially a young one. Even something as seemingly harmless as shaking can cause serious damage in the infant or toddler. Certainly, using a belt, ruler, or other weapon is extremely dangerous.

If you ever feel as though you can't control yourself and want to strike your toddler, get help immediately. Call a neighbor or friend who lives nearby or your local child abuse hotline (it will be listed in the white pages under Child Abuse and may also be listed in a special section, such as Community Services Numbers, in the front of the book). Do the same if anyone who cares for your child or lives in your home attempts to, or actually does hit your child. To have the number handy should you ever need it, fill the number in now under the "Emergency Numbers" listing on the inside back cover of the book.

---

lines to follow when implementing time-out. Dole it out only for actions you've previously warned your toddler are unacceptable, not for first-time offenses. Time-out should be served in a safe place, visible to parent or caregiver (not in isolation in a closet or darkened room), but away from the "fun" of toys and activities. The very young toddler can be deposited in a playpen, reserved only for time-outs (by this age, most children find playpens too restrictive for play, anyway). Don't use your child's crib or room as a time-out location—these are places you want your child to associate with positive experiences. For the child who can climb out of a playpen, a special chair should be set aside for time-out use only; the chair should be placed where nothing of interest (TV, window, books) can be easily seen and nothing that's vulnerable or makes your toddler vulnerable (a plant, a vase, a fragile table) can be easily reached. The toddler should be escorted to the chair, and told to sit in it.[5] He or she should not be allowed to communi-

cate with anyone during the time-out.

The adult who mandated the time-out should be the one to enforce it, and to excuse the child when the time is up. Confusion could result if, for example, Mommy sends Junior to time-out and Grandpa releases him. Junior might conclude that Mommy really wanted him to stay in time-out permanently and/or that Grandpa was rescuing him because Grandpa thought he didn't deserve time-out.

If you're comfortable with the idea of time-out, by all means try it. Be aware, however, that some especially sensitive young children feel rejected or are inconsolably upset when banished to a corner. If that seems the case with your toddler, time-out may not be the best approach to disciplining him or her. The purpose of discipline is to teach good behavior, not to inflict hurtful punishment.

And be careful not to overuse time-outs or to let them become your only form of discipline. Reserve it for an infraction that truly warrants it.

**Give fair warning.** When you catch your toddler in a mischievious act, or on the verge of one, it's legitimate to warn,

---

5. If you think your toddler may have to go to the bathroom or needs a diaper change, attend to that need before beginning time-out.

## NEVER SHAKE A TODDLER

..........

Many parents who would never hit their children feel perfectly comfortable shaking them as a way of showing anger or displeasure. But this isn't a safe practice. Although a toddler's neck muscles are stronger than an infant's, shaking can still, in the second and third years of life, cause serious injury to eyes and/or brain.

---

"If you don't stop by the time I count to three, I will . . ." Then, of course, you must keep your word—or your word won't mean a thing. In situations that involve dangerous consequences—such as hitting, approaching a roaring fire in the fireplace, or banging on the window—it may be necessary to forgo the warning and intervene immediately.

**Explain the sentence.** Even a young toddler can understand, albeit vaguely, that you're confiscating the toy because he threw it at his sister; or that she's being given a time-out because she was found tearing leaves off the ficus tree on the porch. Always offer an explanation when you discipline. Keep it simple, however, or the message will be lost.

**Carry out the sentence immediately.** Toddlers have short memories and even shorter attention spans. Often, by the time you've finished a tirade or taken away a privilege, your toddler has forgotten the reason behind it. Depriving a toddler of dessert at dinner because of an infraction that occurred in the morning pretty much assures that there will be no link whatsoever in the toddler's mind between the misdeed and its consequences.

**Reprise the story.** After a sentence has been carried out, it's a good idea to run briefly over the events that led to it. You can ask a verbal toddler, "Now, why did you need a time-out?" or "Why did I take away the ball?" though in most cases, until your toddler is older, you'll have to answer the question yourself.

**Forgive and forget.** Once your child has paid a fair penalty, life should return to normal. There should be no lingering resentment or lengthy lectures on your part; nor should you go overboard with affection and special privileges, which could transmit the message that you regret having disciplined your toddler.

# WHAT IT'S IMPORTANT FOR YOUR TODDLER TO KNOW: The ABC's of P's and Q's—Introducing Manners

Trying to teach manners to a toddler may sound about as pointless as trying to teach marketing to a German shepherd. After all, there's about as good a chance of getting the toddler to say, "Please, may I be excused from the table?" before darting back to the toy box as there is of getting the German shepherd to write a sales presentation.

But there is a difference—an important difference. Although even the cleverest of canines will never be capable of mastering marketing, toddlers who get a head start in etiquette have an excellent chance of growing up well-mannered.

It's true, as those raised in more genteel times are so fond of reminding us, that children today are not, for the most part, well schooled in their P's and Q's. That's probably because—in understandable backlash against the speak-when-you're-spoken-to school of discipline—their parents have raised them in a relatively permissive say-what-you-like atmosphere.

But raising children to be self-centered self-expressionists isn't much better than raising them to be courteous automatons, quick to say "please" and "thank you" but afraid to say what's on their minds. Children need to learn how to stand up for their rights, and at the same time, learn to consider and respect the feelings and rights of others.

Fortunately, you can have your cake and eat it politely, too (though it may be a while before your toddler can manage this). It is possible to raise mannerly children without subjecting them to the repression of decades past. Start your toddler on the road to civility now, with the following tips:

**Lay the right foundation.** Good manners aren't just a matter of being versed in your "please's" and "thank-you's," knowing when to sit and when to stand, and which utensil to use with which course. The underlying principle of good manners is consideration toward others; in other words, saying "please" and "thank you" should mean that you care, not that you're simply well-bred. So to raise an authentically well-mannered child, you need to teach the "why" of

etiquette along with the "how." The objective: to teach manners that come from the heart (you give up your seat to the elderly man on the bus because he needs to sit more than you do), rather than from the book (you give up your seat because that's what you're supposed to do). The fact is that a child who's raised to be kind can't help growing up to be courteous.

**Set an exemplary example.** The best way to teach manners to your toddler is to display them yourself. So say "thank you" to the toll-taker on the highway; say "please" to the woman behind the deli counter, say "excuse me" when you bump into another shopper in a crowded store; eat with a napkin on your lap and chew with your mouth closed, and ask that the pepper be passed to you rather than reaching across someone's plate for it. But probably most important of all, remember to use your P's and Q's when dealing with your toddler. Say "please" when you've asked your toddler to come to the table. Say "thank you" when your toddler picks up a book as asked, and say "I'm sorry" when you've accidentally knocked over a block project. To teach respect and consideration, respect and consider your toddler's feelings at all times.

**Set an exemplary table.** A toddler can't possibly learn how to use a napkin if one never finds its way onto the table at mealtime, or a fork if you never provide one. Taking the time (it takes very little) to set the table neatly with the proper utensils and napkins, says a mouthful to your toddler about mealtime decorum. Even if your toddler eats like a barbarian now, consistent exposure to civilized eating conditions will eventually instill an appreciation for them.

**Speak for your toddler.** Toddlers don't know enough to say "good-bye" to Grandpa or "thanks for coming" to a visitor or "thanks for having me" to the host of a play group. So it's up to you to say it for them. Hearing you repeat the "magic words" over and over in social situations at home and away from home will teach your toddler much more about common courtesy than any amount of nagging. Being always prodded with "Now what do you say?" can be annoying and humiliating to a toddler—and can make him or her even more reluctant to say what's expected. Occasional reminders are fine, but wait until you're in private.

**Keep the pressure off.** Children who are nagged about their manners or are punished for not saying "thank you" or for not using a fork may learn manners more quickly, or if they are the obstinate sort, may reject them completely. Either way, they won't feel positive about manners and are likely to ignore them completely whenever they are out from under the eye of the enforcing parent.

**But keep the campaign on.** Pressure isn't appropriate, but reminders are. When you're alone and your toddler forgets to say "please," ask "What's the magic word?" When he or she omits a "thank you," try, "Did you forget something?" If you get the appropriate response, fine. If not, fill in the blank for your child. You've at least made clear you think it's important. Again, wage your campaign with a light touch: "What's this? What do we do with a spoon? Wave it in the air? Wear it as a hat?" Challenge rather than chide: "I bet you're not strong enough to pick your chicken up with a fork."

**Listen to your toddler.** Children who are listened to make better listeners—and being a good listener is an important part of being a polite (and considerate) person.

**Have age-appropriate expectations.** Mabel, Mabel may have been able to keep her elbows off the table, but most toddlers are not. Nor are they able to keep their fingers out of the mashed potatoes, their hands out of their cereal, their napkins on their laps, or their juice in their cups. Getting into food is part of the fun of eating when you're a toddler. Messy eating may not become them, but it is them—and it will be with them for some time to come. The same goes for all of the social graces. From remembering to say "thank you" to being willing to share, it will take many years of etiquette exposure (and as many years of reminders) before your child matures into polite company. But if you persevere, one day you will be pleasantly surprised when someone remarks, "My, your child has such good manners."

# CHAPTER SIX

# *The Eighteenth Month*

## **W**HAT YOUR TODDLER MAY BE DOING NOW

*By the end of this month,[1] your toddler*
*. . . should be able to (see Note):*

▲ use 3 words
▲ point to a desired object

**Note:** If your toddler has not reached these milestones or doesn't use symbolic play and words, consult the doctor or nurse-practitioner. This rate of development may well be normal for your child (some children are late bloomers), but it needs to be evaluated. Also check with the doctor if your toddler seems out-of-control or hyperactive; uncommunicative, passive, or withdrawn; highly negative, demanding, and stubborn. (Remember, the child who was born prematurely often lags behind others of the

same chronological age. This developmental gap progressively narrows, and generally disappears entirely around age two.)

*. . . will probably be able to:*

▲ run
▲ use a spoon/fork but not exclusively
▲ point to 1 body part when asked

*. . . may possibly be able to:*

▲ kick a ball forward
▲ follow a 2 step command without gestures

*. . . may even be able to:*

▲ identify 1 picture by naming
▲ use 50+ single words

**Emotional development:** At eighteen months, most children demonstrate a variety of emotions and behaviors,

---

1. The eighteenth month begins when a child is seventeen months old and ends when he or she is eighteen months old.

including pleasure, anger, warmth, assertiveness, and curiosity. They understand a few limits, are able to play and explore away from parents, enjoy parental affection.

**Intellectual development:** At eighteen months, children are able to communicate their wishes and their intentions, and are beginning the imitative and symbolic use of toys.

# WHAT YOU CAN EXPECT AT THE EIGHTEEN-MONTH CHECKUP

**Preparing for the checkup.** Keep a list of concerns that have come up since the last visit. Be sure to bring the questions with you to this visit so you will be ready when the doctor asks, "Any concerns?" Also jot down new skills your toddler is displaying (walking, climbing, running, using a spoon, combining words into phrases, pointing to body parts) so you won't be at a loss when you're asked, "What's your toddler been doing?" Bring along your child's home health history record, too, so that height, weight, immunizations, and any other information gleaned from the checkup can be recorded.

**What the checkup will be like.** Procedures will vary a bit depending on your child's doctor or the nurse-practitioner who conducts health supervision exams, but in most cases, the eighteenth-month checkup will include:

▲ Questions about your child's development, behavior, eating habits, and health since the last visit. There may also be questions about how the family is doing in general, whether there have been any major stresses or changes, how siblings (if any) are getting along with your toddler, about how you are coping, about childcare arrangements (if any). The doctor will also want to know whether you have any other questions or concerns.

▲ An assessment of growth (height, weight, head circumference) since the last visit. These findings may be plotted on growth charts (see pages 864 to 867) and your child's weight for height evaluated and compared to previous measurements.

▲ An informal assessment based on observation and interview, of physical and intellectual development, and of hearing and vision. Gait (the way the child walks) may also be checked.

Depending on need, the following may be included:

▲ A finger-stick blood test (hematocrit or hemoglobin), if the child is at risk of anemia. The test may be done once routinely between twelve months and four years.

▲ A blood test, usually a finger-stick, to screen for lead, only if exposure is suspected.

▲ A Mantoux tuberculin test for children at high risk; this simple skin test, which has gained in importance with the recent reemergence of TB, may be performed at fifteen months instead.

**Immunizations**

▲ DTP (diphtheria, tetanus, pertussis), if not given at the fifteenth month checkup.

▲ OPV (oral polio vaccine), if not given at fifteen months.

**Anticipatory guidance.** The doctor or nurse-practitioner may also discuss such topics as good parenting practices; injury prevention; reading to your child; teaching sharing; good nutrition, eating habits, snacks, vitamin supplementation, weaning (if this hasn't already been accomplished); self-comforting habits (thumbsucking, pacifier use, transitional objects); napping and nighttime sleep problems; night fears; readiness for toilet learning; discipline; day care/child care, if appropriate; parent support; and other issues that will be important in the months ahead.

**The next checkup.** If your toddler is in good health, the next checkup will be at twenty-four months. Until then, be sure to call the doctor if you have any questions that aren't answered in this book or if your child shows any signs of illness (see page 568).

# WHAT YOU MAY BE CONCERNED ABOUT

## ANOTHER BABY— WHEN?

*"Now that our son is a year-and-a-half old, we're starting to think about getting pregnant again. But we're wondering if this is the right time."*

There's no "right" time to have another baby. But there's probably no "wrong" time, either. Having children closely spaced can present a host of challenges in the short run (including: diapers, diapers everywhere), but an efficient use of time in the long run (getting those diapers over with). Having children farther apart may give you more rest between stretches of sleepless nights, but reintroduce those sleepless nights at a time when you may feel less able to handle them. As for having children close together so that they'll be better friends, or farther apart so that they won't fight so much, remember: Sibling friendships are more a matter of fate than family planning. More often they have to do with similarities in temperament and interests than with closeness in age—and there's no age difference that's been proven to guarantee that siblings won't be rivals.

The experts aren't unanimous, but most suggest that less than eighteen months between pregnancies is stressful to the mother's body and may rob the older child of the chance to be the baby of the family for a sufficient period. Others believe that a two-and-a-half- to three-year gap between children is ideal because it is long enough to allow adequate time for number one child to be number one but not so long that the parents feel out of the baby "loop" when number two arrives. Still, this span may not be right for you.

Rather than looking for the answer from an outside source, such as this book or an expert, it's probably better to look for it closer to home. Consider your ages, your health, and how quickly you recovered from your previous pregnancy and delivery; examine your energy level, any special needs your toddler may have, and what life-cycle, family, or professional events (your sister's wedding, moving, a new job) you can predict in the next nine to fifteen months (remember that it takes most couples three to six months to conceive). Then try to determine how these events might affect another pregnancy and another infant—and vice versa. Examine your feelings, too. If both of you feel like the time has come, then perhaps it has—and if both of you feel a need for a little more time, maybe you do. Contemplate, discuss, make lists of pluses and minuses, if you like, but don't overanalyze. Just about any configuration of ages can work and *has* worked for someone, somewhere, sometime.

*"A lot of people have been asking us when we're going to have another baby. Well, we're not sure we want one. We're extremely happy and fulfilled as a threesome, and couldn't ask for a better child than our daughter. Is it wrong to want just one?"*

Children aren't like potato chips; you *can* stop at just one, if you want to. And nobody else is entitled to make that decision for you. Though there may be many valid reasons to have another baby, pressure from friends, family, and society shouldn't be among them.

It used to be that having more than one child was something parents just did automatically, if only because it was expected. Today, more and more parents elect to have only one child. The reasons are many, and include age (older parents may not feel up to rearing another child or up to the idea of having a teenager at home when they are well into their fifties); hectic lifestyle (some parents, finding themselves with precious little spare time, opt to devote all of it to one child); precarious finances (especially with the cost of some college educations skyrocketing into six figures); and concern about overpopulation.

Recent research suggests that one-child families are as happy and fulfilled as families with two or more children, shooting down the old adage that only children always turn out to be lonely or maladjusted. One study found that only children are as likely to be as happy and emotionally healthy as children from larger families. On the average, the study showed, they performed better academically than children with siblings, and were strongly represented among the population of highly successful people—possibly because being the one and only in their parents' hearts brought them more autonomy, greater self-confidence, and less fear of competition.

Which is not to say that families should stick to having a single child just to increase their chances of raising a future president, high-profile attorney, or CEO of a Fortune 500 company. Sibling or no sibling, every child who is raised with love and support has a good chance of growing up to be happy and successful. And when you get right down to it, deciding whether or not to have another child should be a choice based on your feelings and circumstances—not on studies, statistics, or psychosocial rhetoric. Two children may bring twice the joy to some couples (and three thrice, and so on), but one may be the magic number for others. Only you can say which might be the perfect formula for your family.

# IMPATIENCE (NOW!)

*"No matter what it is, my toddler has to have it 'now!' I'm losing my patience with her impatience."*

To young toddlers, a minute can seem like an eternity. In the middle of the second year they still have limited understanding of the passage of time and little concept of past or future. They live for the moment—for "now." And "now" is when they want this cookie or that drink, when they want a story read, when they want to play with a favorite toy. They haven't yet learned that all good things come to those who wait. To them, all good things come to those who demand.

It's not until around the second birthday that the typical toddler is able to comply when asked to "wait a minute." The length of patience continues to expand over the next year or so. By age three, a child can often wait a reasonable time when asked to and may even be able to use self-distraction to help pass the time. Till then, you can expect to continue to hear that chorus of, "Now, now, now."

Be patient while you wait for your toddler to develop patience. To make that wait easier, you can also try the following:

**Make sure it's worth making her wait.** Though it's tempting to make a toddler wait for something she's asked for on principle ("she's got to learn, after all"), it's not always fair or reasonable. Hunger and thirst, for example, are very pressing problems to her, problems that need immediate resolution. If it's a half hour wait for dinner, and she's hungry right now, offer a small, nutritious snack that will take the edge off her appetite without zapping it entirely.

**Create a diversion.** If the wait is legitimate and necessary, try to make it pass more quickly for your toddler with entertainment. For instance, if you're in the car en route home and she wants her lunch "now!" a song, some favorite nursery rhymes, or an ad-lib game—such as "What does the cow say?" or "Can you see a doggy out the window?" —may buy just enough time to get you to your front door.

**Set a timer.** If you need five more minutes in the kitchen before you can take your toddler to the park, set a timer and let her watch it until it dings. Or turn over an hourglass, and let her watch the sand sift through. This will give her a sense of control over you and over time. Just make sure you give yourself enough time to accomplish the task at hand. And when the timer goes off, keep your part of the bargain, or she won't trust your deals in the future.

**Move it.** If you can't get it out of mind, get it out of sight. If your toddler wants something she can't or shouldn't have now (the riding toy on which she wants to scoot across your just-waxed, still-wet kitchen floor), physically separate her from it.

**Be willing to wait yourself.** It's time for your toddler to take her bath or get dressed to go out and she says, *"Not now*—I'm playing." Instead of dragging her from her toys immediately, be willing, when time isn't of the essence, to wait a minute or two. Tell her you will time one minute (or two or more) on your timer and that she doesn't have to stop playing until the timer goes off. If she sees you're patient, she is more likely to learn to be, too.

# TELEPHONE INTERFERENCE

*"Every time the phone rings, it's like a signal for my son to start whining and demanding attention. I never get to complete a conversation."*

A toddler doesn't appreciate anything that competes for your undivided attention—whether it's a letter that needs writing, a meal that needs cooking, or a telephone that needs answering. It's not that he minds fending for himself, it's just that when he does, he wants it to be *his* idea. He may feel threatened and insecure when he loses control of you to the phone. So, acting defensively, he struggles to recoup your attention the best way he knows: by whining and carrying on. Your toddler realizes it's an effective technique—not many parents can manage to carry on a conversation with such shrill distraction at their knees—and he's savvy enough to use it each and every time he sees your ear next to the receiver.

Though the degree of toddler telephone interference will depend to some extent upon your child's temperament and your handling of the situation, you're likely to find that leisurely phone conversations are possible only when your little phone hog is being occupied by another person, is asleep, or out of the house. And though the "static" on your line will eventually clear somewhat, your child may continue to compete with the phone for your attention. Over the years, verbal interference ("Get off the phone, Mom—I'm hungry!") will replace the whimpering. Until, inevitably, the competition *for* you over the phone starts becoming a competition *with* you, and your offspring begins appropriating the line for himself ("Pl . . . ea . . . se get off the phone, Mom—I'm waiting for a call!")

Though no magical or technological solutions exist for your personal telecommunication crisis (no phone company has yet come up with a way to put a child on "hold"), the following may help with your "child-waiting" problem:

**Don't call attention to your toddler's calls for attention.** Anticipate a problem when the phone rings with, "Now I don't want you to bother me while I'm on the phone!" and he's certain to bother you. Instead, when someone rings, head for the phone with a cheerful, "I wonder who that is?"

**Don't blow a fuse.** Understand that your toddler's constant need for attention, though frustrating at times, deserves empathy and not anger. Reacting with rage will only compound your child's need for security and intensify the very behavior that's annoying you.

**Cut the cord.** A portable, cordless phone allows you to move with your toddler as you chat, and allows him to feel less cut off. Granted, it's hard to concentrate on a conversation when you're being whisked from the blocks to the trucks, but that's better than no conversation at all.

**Time your conversations.** Keep an egg timer by the phone, and turn it over when you begin your conversation. Explain to your toddler that when all the sand goes through to the other side, it will be time for you to hang up. Let him hold the timer: Watching the sand sifting through might absorb him and also give your toddler some feeling of control over the situation. Naturally, if you don't hang up as promised, this technique will lose its effectiveness.

**Put him on the line.** Invite your toddler to participate in your conversations when the caller is a close friend or family member, to help make him more comfortable with (and friendly toward) the telephone. You can do this by handing him the receiver for a few minutes with a "Do you want to speak to Auntie Ann?" or by using a speaker phone, if you have one. Be aware, however, that hearing a disembodied voice on the phone may spook or confuse your toddler, and he may not know how to respond. If he pushes the phone away, in effect saying, "No, you talk," don't press the issue. You may have bought yourself a few extra minutes of talking time.

**Add another line.** Having his own play phone may also make a toddler less hostile to the instrument. Buy a toy phone or let him use a real one that's not in use anymore (but be sure to remove both cords and store them out of reach; they can pose a safety hazard). Reserve this toy ploy for when you're on the phone, so that it doesn't lose its novelty. When you're making a call, hand him *his* receiver and suggest that he call someone special—Grandpa, his cousin, someone in his play group, or a favorite storybook or television character. When you're answering your phone, "answer" his first and hand the receiver to him with, "It's a telephone call for you." It doesn't matter if he doesn't speak many words yet—carrying on a one-sided garbled conversation may keep him happily occupied, for at least a few minutes.

**Try a "telephone book."** Or a telephone jack-in-the-box. Or any one of a number of specially stashed distractions, kept out of sight and brought out only when you are called to the phone. Of course, you should avoid in this stash any toys that frustrate your toddler or that require your help.

**Keep in touch.** Maintaining physical contact with your toddler while you speak may take some of the edge off his phone envy. Let him know you're still there for him, even though you're talking to someone else. Rub his arm or shoulder, cuddle him, bounce him on your lap, hold his hand, or stack blocks with him.

**Screen your calls.** If your phone rings a lot, your conversations are bound to cut into your time with your toddler, and he's bound to resent it—possibly rightly so. Use an answering machine to screen your calls when you and your toddler are involved in a game or engrossed in a book. Only take calls that you feel are urgent to make him feel that you value his company over the telephone's intru-

sions; it may make him more tolerant of the calls you do take. If you don't have an answering machine or don't feel comfortable screening calls, just tell callers you'll call them back later—when your toddler is sleeping or occupied by himself. In the long run, if your toddler recognizes that you respect your time with him and don't break into it thoughtlessly, he will gradually come to respect your right to have your time with others unbroken, too.

**Call in the positive reinforcements.** Ultimately, of course, your goal is to get your toddler to recognize that you have a right to talk on the phone—if only for a little while at a time. With that in mind, express your appreciation whenever he allows you to complete a call, even if those occasions are rare. Add to this positive reinforcement by giving him extra attention after such a call and by making a big deal out of it: " That was very good. You let me talk on the phone. Now we can do something special together."

# INTERFERING WITH VISITORS

*"Whenever we have visitors, whether it's friends, relatives, the plumber, or the meter-reader, our daughter won't let us talk to them."*

**M**ost toddlers not only demand center stage but also prefer that the rest of the stage be empty. When another character makes a guest appearance—particularly when that appearance doesn't involve her—the prima donna in your child is liable to speak up, loud and clear.

When a visitor arrives at your home—whether it's a friend or relative with whom you'd like to sit down and chat or a repair person or meter-reader you have to show around—your toddler may resent the intrusion largely because it takes the spotlight off her. So, just as when you're on the phone, she'll do everything she can to try and keep your attention: affix herself to your leg and turn the whine on, crawl all over your lap and pull on your hair, tug on your shirt and whimper, even clamp her hand over your mouth or try to turn your head in her direction.

At this age, when a toddler's own wants and needs are the only wants and needs that matter to her, it's particularly difficult to teach her to respect the wants and needs of others. But though it's a lesson that may take years to learn, it's important to begin the lesson now. With a lot of patience, understanding, careful choreography—and the following tips— your toddler and your visitors may come to share the stage successfully, at least sometimes:

**Do unto your toddler . . .** If you expect your child to learn to respect your time with others, you have to respect your toddler's time with you. Don't, if you can help it, interrupt play time with her to take care of a chore you can just as easily attend to when she's independently occupied or asleep. When duties that can't be put off call, try involving your toddler in them (take a bath together while you wash your hair, let her stack cans on the kitchen floor while you start dinner, have her doodle in her notebook while you prepare a budget in yours. If a friend drops by while you and your child are at play, let the friend know she will have to wait to have your undivided attention until you're finished playing; then turn back to your toddler for five minutes or so. Or, invite your guest to join you and your toddler (assuming your toddler doesn't object to another playmate).

**Time the entrance.** If it's feasible, arrange for your visitor to arrive during your toddler's usual nap time. But be ready to open the door before the bell rings (or leave a note on the door asking the visitor to knock quietly, instead of ringing). And if you have a dog who announces arrivals, either put it out or head off the barking.

**Don't banish her backstage.** If she's awake when a visitor arrives, give your little actress a supporting role in the production. Get her involved, if she's comfortable being sociable, but don't push her to interact with your visitors. Ask her to show her favorite book or doll to your friend. Take her along to "help" show the meter reader where the meter is. Let her watch the plumber open the pipes under the sink—at a safe distance, of course. If you're expecting a special visitor, your child can help with preparations. Clean up the living room together, bake (or shop for) cookies, decorate with pictures in honor of the visit (her ego will get a boost when her artwork is admired).

**Provide special props.** Set up a play area near where you'll be entertaining; stock it with plenty of toys your toddler can enjoy on her own, such as blocks, ring stackers, shape sorters, a pile of picture books, and puzzles (if you don't mind being interrupted once in a while to help her place a stubborn piece). If your toddler likes pretend play, making arrangements for her own tea party (complete with Raggedy Ann and Big Bird) can keep her out of yours. So can appointing her the official "cleaner upper"—equipped with a feather duster, a play broom, and an apron, she can busy herself as you talk.

**Serve refreshments.** Even if you and your guest aren't hungry, putting out a snack to share with your toddler may buy you some quiet time; it's harder to whine with a full mouth. But make sure that refreshments are appropriate: Fruit-juice-sweetened cookies, mini-muffins, and tiny crustless sandwiches cut in various shapes are ideal. (Be sure to avoid very messy foods or possible choking hazards.)

**Break for intermissions.** There's only so long you can realistically expect your toddler to keep herself amused. So if the visit's lengthy, periodically excuse yourself from your company long enough to read your toddler a story or help her with the block tower that keeps collapsing. (But don't break for an intermission when your toddler's playing contentedly; wait until she seems to have exhausted her capacity for independent activity.) Make it clear what the limits of the intermission are before you begin ("Now I'm going to take a break and read you *Curious George*. When I'm done, I'll go back to my friend and you can do a puzzle.") When the intermission is over, set up your toddler with that puzzle or another activity before returning to your guest. Maintain contact between intermissions by taking the time once in a while to call a word or two of encouragement ("I bet you can make that tower even higher!"), praise ("That tea looks so yummy!"), or observation ("You're reading the book about the zoo, aren't you?") over to your toddler as she plays. Make time for physical contact, too. If she's playing at your feet, lean over frequently to squeeze her shoulder, rub her back, or pat her head.

**Don't let her hog the stage.** You have the right to entertain the occasional guest, or to spend a few minutes explaining a problem to the repair person. If you once let your toddler think that you're willing to abdicate those rights in her favor, she won't let you forget it. So when entertaining, be friendly but firm. Remove her hands from your mouth as many times as she puts them there, distract her, involve her, hold her, tickle her as you talk to the visitor—but don't let

her succeed in lowering the curtain on your show. Remember, you're the director. If you let your temperamental little star take over completely, it will only set the stage for years of selfish behavior on her part and selfless denial on yours.

**Know when to bring the curtain down yourself.** If you keep visits short, your toddler will tolerate them better.

**Applaud and reward cooperation.** Even if your toddler was only marginally cooperative while company called (she whined just 75% of the time), reinforce that little bit of positive behavior instead of calling attention to that whole lot of negative behavior. ("I like the way you let me talk to Terry while she was visiting with me. Now you and I are going to do something special together.") A trip to the park, an uninterrupted period of play with you, a collaborative art activity, are all good ways of letting your toddler know how much you appreciated her patience, and how much patience can pay off. Of course, if she did whine 100% of the time, skip the applause and reward.

# NAPPING PROBLEMS

*"Up until last week, my daughter was a wonderful napper—she napped twice a day without fail. Now, all of a sudden, she refuses to go down in the morning."*

Could be your toddler's sending you a message: It's time to give up that morning nap. Most toddlers this age can, and do, get by with just an afternoon snooze. While *you* might still need her morning nap, *she* may not.

As with anyone getting used to a new sleeping schedule, your toddler may seem sleepy and cranky around the time that she has ordinarily napped. This should pass when her body adjusts to the new schedule. Moving her lunch up to 11 or 11:30 A.M. for a little while so that she can take her afternoon nap earlier should help. So should establishing a quiet period—when you can read to her or listen to music together—during the hours she previously napped.

*"It takes me all afternoon to get my daughter to take her second nap. By the time she settles down it's usually close to 5 o'clock. When she wakes up close to 8, she's raring to go for hours, so we can't manage a reasonable bedtime."*

Late naps are not generally popular with parents, for a couple of reasons. For one, late afternoon nappers often skip dinner (substituting a snack when they finally wake) or eat dinner so late that it fuels hours of energy when parents least appreciate it. For another, late afternoon nappers, as you've noticed, tend to be late-to-bedders; their stay-up-till-all-hours ways often leave parents with little evening time to themselves.

The steps you'll need to take in order to adjust your toddler's schedule—so that her nap and her bedtime fall at more convenient times—will depend on the kind of sleep pattern she's fallen into:

▲ Is this evening sleep her only nap? The average toddler at eighteen months needs about one-and-one-half to two hours of nap a day, but it should come earlier in the day so as not to interfere with her night's rest. So try to get your toddler to nap earlier. Begin a calming pre-nap ritual ten or fifteen minutes earlier than she usually beds down in the afternoon. After a few days, when she seems accustomed to the earlier slot, move nap time back another fifteen minutes. Continue this process until she is napping at a reasonable hour. But wake her up after two hours; if she sleeps

longer, she may still have trouble getting to sleep at bedtime.

▲ Are two naps too many? Most toddlers need only one at this age. Try weaning yours from her morning snooze by pushing it later and later (by fifteen minutes a day), until it becomes an early afternoon nap. This will probably eliminate her need for the late nap. (It may, however, trigger a couple of unpleasant temporary side effects; see page 141.)

▲ Is one nap too many? The occasional eighteen-month-old can zoom through the entire day without stopping for a single Z. If this is the case with yours, she may be better off conking out for the day at 7 or 7:30 than sleeping the early evening hours away and then burning the midnight oil. And you may be better off, too. An afternoon "rest period" may stand in well for the nap; see above. If she still needs a nap, she will probably doze off during this rest time.

▲ Is she sleeping late in the morning? Late risers tend to have a late napping schedule. To change this, begin waking her ten or fifteen minutes earlier each morning until she's getting up at what you consider a reasonable time. As you do this, her nap (or naps) and evening bedtime should start to move toward an earlier schedule.

▲ Is she taking a late-morning nap? A nap taken late in the morning could push back her afternoon nap. Try moving the morning nap earlier by fifteen minutes each day. Do the same with the afternoon nap, until both fall at more convenient hours.

▲ Is she sleeping for two or three hours in the morning? Such a long morning nap would almost certainly interfere with her need for an early-afternoon siesta. So wake your toddler fifteen minutes earlier from each morning nap until she is sleeping no more than an hour in the morning.

In some situations, the late nap is a boon to a family's schedule. If both parents get home late from work, for example, they can have a quiet meal together as their toddler sleeps, and can then spend time with her before she's off to bed. If that's the case in your family, leave things the way they are for the moment.

*"Our son used to take a two-hour nap every afternoon. Recently, he's refused to nap at all, no matter what I do. Is he ready to give up his nap?"*

A toddler often needs his nap a lot more than he thinks he does; the problem lies in convincing him of this. With so much to do, and so little time in a day to do it, toddlers understandably balk at taking an hour or two off for sleep; after all, why lie down in a darkened room when you can climb, run, explore, and play in the daylight?

Sometimes, a toddler gives up his nap prematurely because of a one-time event that knocked his schedule out of whack—an afternoon birthday party or trip to the movies, a weekend at Grandma's (where it's too much fun to sleep). Less often, he gives it up because he really doesn't need it. If your child sleeps well at night, seems rested in the morning, is happy and generally good-tempered all day, he probably can drop his nap. If, however, he seems chronically cranky and overtired, easily frustrated and poorly coordinated (tripping over his feet, for example) at his customary nap time or in the evening, try some gentle persuasion to get him napping again. See page 33 for tips on getting your toddler to nap.

At first, your toddler may not fall asleep at the appointed nap time, or may nap only sporadically, no matter what you do. But if you persist with a regular nap-time routine, he may give in. Even

if he doesn't, he will get a much-needed break from his hectic day, and a quiet interlude may turn out to be all he needs. Stick to the nap ritual, whether or not your child actually falls asleep—as long as he doesn't spend the entire time protesting instead of resting.

If your toddler resists both nap and quiet times, and he continues to show signs of fatigue, shoot for an earlier bedtime.

# EARLY RISING

*"Our daughter wakes up before the crack of dawn—usually 5:00 A.M.— every single morning. Either we go to bed at 8:30 in the evening in self-defense, or we're constantly exhausted."*

Like farmers, parents of small children rarely need to set an alarm clock—the rousing call of the average toddler is as difficult to sleep through as the rooster's crow. (And unlike the rooster, who makes his racket and then retreats to the chicken coop, the toddler will persevere loud and long until every member of the household is awake.)

There may well be no rest for the early-morning weary for many years to come; it's usually not until well into the school years (when you *want* them up early) that early risers start sleeping in. Until then, you have nothing to lose by trying the following tips. And, who knows—you might even net yourself a few precious minutes of sleep in the process:

**Regulate the pace of your toddler's life.** Lots of exercise and fresh air during the day plus lots of relaxing and unwinding at night yields the best sleep. Too much stimulation during the day, on the other hand, especially near bedtime, can sabotage peaceful sleep.

**Nix a too-early nap.** If your toddler gets up at 5 A.M. and naps at 8, that 8 o'clock nap may be the problem. Her early morning waking may be more like a middle-of-the-night waking, after which she completes her normal sleep span with the nap. To move her nap time to a later hour, start the nap ten minutes later every morning until she's napping at 10 A.M. or 10:30. She may be cranky for a while, but as her body adjusts to the new nap schedule she should start sleeping later in the morning.

**Establish a waiting period.** Instead of rushing into her room the moment you hear a peep from your toddler in the morning, wait ten or fifteen minutes—even if she's crying. It's possible that she will cry a bit, then turn over and go back to sleep.

**Postpone bedtime.** A too-early bedtime can sabotage your chances of getting your wake-up call at a decent hour. If your toddler's currently hitting the hay at 7 P.M., try tucking her in about ten minutes later each night until her bedtime is at 7:30 or 8 instead. Be aware, however, that overtired toddlers rarely sleep well or late; there's usually no benefit in keeping them up *extremely* late.

**Shut out the dawn.** Some toddlers are more sensitive to incoming light than others, so it's worth a try to darken your daughter's room in an effort to keep her asleep longer. Hang drapes lined with room-darkening fabric, or add a room-darkening shade or blind. If traffic or construction-work racket is the suspected problem, keep your toddler's windows closed. If it's the sound of others in the family who rise early, close your toddler's door.

**Put entertainment at her fingertips.** It's possible that keeping a favorite toy or two in your toddler's crib may encourage her to amuse herself upon waking, giving you an extra few minutes of early morning peace. (Be sure she can't hurt herself on these toys or pile them up to scale the heights of the crib rail.) It's also possible that it won't; some toddlers aren't happy until they've roused some human company.

**Cut down on nighttime liquids.** If your toddler's still taking a bottle of water to bed, a sopping diaper may be waking her up early. Stop that bottle, if possible, as well as other excess fluids, before bed.

**Postpone breakfast.** Feeding your toddler—fluids or solids—as soon as she wakens trains her tummy to wake at daybreak. Instead, try tabling her morning meal until it's less like dawn and more like morning. Again, use the ten-minutes-a-day approach, until you have breakfast time where you want it. If she's really ravenous, give her a very light snack (such as a cracker or some dry cereal) to hold her off until breakfast.

**Accept what you can't change.** Though you may not feel healthier, wealthier, or wiser for your "early-to-bed-and-early-to-rise" routine, you may have to get used to it. Your child may just not need as much sleep as you'd like her to need. Very few parents can count among their blessings a late-sleeping toddler; many, like you, have an early bird in their nest.

# *BEDTIME REBELLION*

*"Bedtime is a battle in our house. Our son doesn't want to go to bed, and once he's there, he drives us crazy with calls and demands."*

**B**ed ranks high on the list of places a toddler would least like to be—right up there with the changing table and the doctor's office. Most toddlers

---

## SLUMBER DIARY

..........

How many times did your toddler get up last night? The night before? What time did you tuck him in? What time did she actually fall asleep? You're probably too groggy to remember. If your child's sleep pattern troubles you, keep a sleep diary for the next two weeks. Jot down bedtimes, actual falling asleep times, night wakings, and night feedings (if any), and keep track of how long wakings and feedings last. Also include naps, when and where they take place and how long they last.

Examining the slumber diary should give you some insight into your toddler's sleep problems, and provide some clues for dealing with them. It should also help you learn just how much sleep your toddler is actually getting and what his or her natural biological clock is like. If this biological clock conflicts with yours or with your family's schedule, try to change your little one's sleep habits (see page 65). If you discuss your toddler's sleep problems with the doctor, take the slumber diary along.

---

are happiest when they're on the go, and coming to a screeching stop at bedtime can be distressing. Going to bed not only requires leaving his toys and his family for ten or twelve hours but also resigning himself to ending his exploits for the day. Add to that what may be budding fears of the dark and of being alone, and it's not surprising that many toddlers make a fuss when bedtime approaches.

To get your toddler into a more sleep-accepting frame of mind at bedtime, set up a regular bedtime routine (as described on page 68), which will help him unwind. Be sure that naps don't interfere with your child's ability to fall asleep. Also try to determine if the scheduled bedtime is unrealistic. The average eighteen-month-old needs one-and-one-half to two hours of napping during the day plus eleven to twelve hours sleep at night (of course, some need more and others less). Pushing a child who's not tired to sleep could lead to bedtime rebellion. If fears are a problem, see page 310. You can also:

▲ Avoid using your toddler's room or his bed as punishment; if you do, he will have a difficult time seeing bedtime as pleasant.

▲ Explain that sleep is necessary for healthy growth, and to be able to play and run and have fun. Remind him of all the other people who sleep at night (friends at day care or preschool, cousins, grandparents, even parents).

▲ Consider a later bedtime. Putting a toddler to bed before he's sleepy is an exercise in futility. If he takes an hour or more to fall asleep, try pushing his bedtime back half an hour or so.

▲ Set a timer to go off about ten minutes before you plan on beginning the nightly bedtime ritual, so that your child will be able to prepare himself. And, in the half-hour or so before bedtime, be sure he doesn't get involved in a lengthy project that he won't want to be dragged from.

▲ Don't insist on your toddler's going to sleep immediately if he says he isn't tired. You can lead a child to bed, but you can't make him sleep. Allow him to listen to tapes in a darkened room, or look at some books while he gets drowsy, if he likes. But insist he stay in bed.

▲ Offer your toddler a comfort object at bedtime. This will ease the transition from being awake and with you to being asleep without you. The object can be anything that works and is safe to leave in the crib, including a teddy or other stuffed animal (an old favorite or a new special-for-bedtime treat), a toy, an old T-shirt of yours.

▲ Beware of becoming the comfort object yourself; resist staying with your toddler until he falls asleep. If you relent even once, he may begin to demand your presence every night.

▲ After you tuck him in tenderly, be tough. Take your time getting him comfy and cozy, doling out hugs and kisses, and bidding good night. But once he's tucked in, become business-like. Don't ignore his questions and requests, but respond quickly and dispassionately, giving the same response over and over, in a monotone. Make communication with you so uncompelling that he won't feel it's worth eliciting. Hopefully he will get tired of the repetition, then tired *from* the repetition. When it's possible, make your remarks from the doorway; if your toddler doesn't get the satisfaction of bringing you back to his side, he may not bother to try. Give him two or three minutes to chatter, then say, "No more questions. I'm leaving now. I love you. Good night. Sleep tight. I'll see you in the morning."[2]

▲ Anticipate his special requests. Have a small cup of water waiting on his nightstand and everything else set up the way he likes it (closet door closed, night-light burning, comfort object at hand, bed covers arranged in an inviting fashion). Also be sure he isn't too warm or too cold, too wet or too hungry. Skipping dessert at dinnertime and serving it as a bedtime snack will help avoid the last problem—but only if it's not high in sugar (see page 502).

▲ If your toddler cries when you leave the room, don't return immediately. He may cry himself to sleep. If after ten minutes or so, he's still at it, return and reassure him with a few soft words ("Shh, go to sleep") and a pat on the back; then promptly leave again. If the crying continues, keep repeating this process at regular intervals until sleep overtakes your toddler. Once you've begun, persist. Don't give in after half an hour and pick him up to rock or feed him—you will give him the message that if he cries long and hard enough he will get what he wants: You.

▲ Retuck as necessary. If your toddler stands up in his crib or gets out of bed, tuck him back in when you return to his room—with as few words and as little contact as possible.

▲ Praise him when he settles down easily. Many toddlers enjoy a sticker chart, and getting gold stars for every night they retire without a fuss. When two rows of gold stars are collected, a reward may be in order.

▲ Don't lose it. The more imperturbable you stay in the face of repeated trips to your toddler's room, the fewer trips you'll ultimately end up making.

# Day-care Separation Problems

*"Every time I drop my daughter at the day-care center, she goes to pieces. The teacher says she's fine all day, and she seems happy enough when I pick her up, but*

---

2. If bedtime rules have been lax until now, don't suddenly start a crackdown when your toddler is teething or sick, when there is another disruption in his life (a new caregiver, a new school, or a new sibling), or when he's learning a new skill, like toilet learning.

*these morning scenes make me
dread saying good-bye to her."*

**Y**ou're not the only one who dreads
saying good-bye. Although your
toddler seems much more grown up than
she did a few months ago, she may still
be torn between independence and dependence. Since she reportedly cheers up
once you've left and seems fine when
you pick her up, she's probably not unhappy with the teacher or the day-care
program. But, since separation anxiety
peaks during the second half of the second year, she could be afraid of being
deserted by you or distressed at being
left out of whatever it is you're doing
without her. This kind of anxiety intensifies as a child becomes mobile; she realizes that not only can you leave her but
that she can leave you.

By about age three, a toddler who
has had plenty of experience with separation and has had any attendant anxiety
met with understanding and support,
finds parting easier. Until then, the following may make day-care drop-offs a
little less miserable for both of you:

**Empathize with your toddler.** Read
about separation anxiety on page 20 to
understand what she's going through and
to learn how you can deal with this phenomenon in general.

**Allow her to tote a security object.** You
can't be with her in day care, but if her
day-care program permits it, her favorite
teddy, blanket, or another comfort object
(see page 112) can be. If such objects
from home are not allowed or are relegated to a cubby, a small memento of
you (a snapshot, a handkerchief of yours)
tucked in her pocket can provide comfort.

**Don't give her any ideas.** Don't drone
on all the way to day care about the impending separation; in fact, don't even
mention it. Even if you dread the worst,
pretend you expect smooth sailing. Talk

about what she will be doing in day care
(if that doesn't upset her) or when you
will pick her up (relate this time to an
event in her day, such as "after nap
time" or "before dinner"), or chat about
the weather, the little dog passing by, or
the big green truck stopped at the traffic
light.

**Don't feed her misery.** If she sees she's
succeeded in upsetting you or in getting
you to feel sorry for her, she will continue to complain. Nothing, after all, succeeds like success. She needs your
*support*, but not your sympathy—you're
not leaving her with the Wicked Witch
of the West.

**Accentuate the positive.** When you arrive, ask the teacher what the group will
be doing first thing, and talk up the activity with your toddler. Try to get her
involved in it while you're still there.
Ask the teacher, too, what the group
will be doing at the end of the day, just
before pick-up time. Pass on the information to your child so she will have a
way to predict when she will see you
again.

**Eliminate the negative.** Don't call her a
baby or otherwise berate her, heaping
humiliation and guilt on top of the pain
she's feeling. Let her know her feelings
are legitimate. Don't threaten or bribe
her, either. Even if these kinds of ploys
work ("If you don't stop crying you
can't watch *Sesame Street* tonight," or
"If you stop crying, I'll bring you a
cookie when I pick you up"), you'll be
setting an undesirable precedent and
teaching her to mask her feelings instead
of working them through.

**Don't look back.** If you do, you won't
turn into a pillar of salt like Lot's wife,
but you may dissolve into a puddle of
conflicted emotions at the sight of your
toddler reaching out to you pathetically,

begging you not to go. Which is exactly what she's hoping for. So make a swift and sure exit. If there's a place from which you can watch her without being seen, do so—you'll almost certainly witness a hasty transition from inconsolable dependent to smiling, independent little girl. If you don't, be sure to ask your child's teacher about her adjustment (in private or on the phone).[3] It's likely the teacher will report that your toddler falls in quickly with the group and the activities most days. If not, discuss the problem and possible remedies with her teacher.

**Make on-time pick-ups.** Even a few minutes of waiting seems an eternity to a toddler, especially when her groupmates are rapidly clearing out with their parents. If she's not sure she can count on you to pick her up at the appointed time, she's not going to feel confident enough to let you leave without a struggle. And when pick-up time comes, don't meet your daughter with a sour look on your face and a lot of remonstrations about that morning's scene. Instead, put on a happy-to-see-you face and accompany it with a good attitude, no matter how miserable she made you when you left her in the morning.

For how to deal with older toddlers and separation anxiety at preschool, see page 395.

# MEALTIME RESTLESSNESS

*"Our son won't sit still for a meal. If we try to buckle him in, he screams. Then he stands up, squirms, and twists in his high chair, usually demanding to be taken out before he's eaten very much."*

For many relatively new walkers, mealtime is not a high priority. Although infants do much of their exploring by mouth—making eating an exciting learning experience—toddlers prefer exploring on foot—making mealtime an exasperating waste of time. While your toddler may tolerate taking a few bites of food, he almost certainly won't sit still for them. And yet, eating is necessary to fuel his other activities. To help your child refuel in spite of himself:

**Consider a new seating arrangement.** It's possible that a seat at your table, in his high chair with the tray removed (strapped in, if necessary), or in a booster or Sassy seat, or at his own child-size table might make your toddler feel less restricted and more grown-up.

**Stop feeding him.** A toddler's hunger for independence and new experiences is a lot greater than his hunger for food. Even if he's not yet skilled at it, letting him feed himself may make him more willing to devote some time to eating (see page 17).

**Keep him company.** Even if you're not dining at the same time, sit down with your toddler while he eats. Make dinner-table conversation, but don't talk about how little he's eating or how much he's squirming. (As if to prove the point that nothing is certain with toddlers, some young toddlers eat better when a grown-up isn't hovering; they find the company distracting. If your child isn't buckled in, however, you should sit next to him anyway until you're pretty confident he won't take a spill.)

**Be ready to call it quits.** When your toddler's had enough, and lets you know this by striving to escape the table or playing with his food, let him go—even

---

3. If you have any doubts about the quality of your child's day-care situation and how he or she is doing during the day, see page 822.

---

## SAFE SEATING

··········

Only you can judge when your toddler is able to sit safely in a booster seat without being belted in. Most children are ready when they fully understand safety directions *and* regularly follow them; and when they are either able to get off the booster seat alone or remember to ask for help. When your toddler starts chafing at the belt and seems mature enough for this transition, test his booster-seat readiness during at least a half-dozen closely supervised meals.

Once the belt is abandoned, don't stand for standing at the table. Though a certain amount of squirming in an active child is acceptable (and unavoidable), standing up in a booster seat, or on any chair, is downright dangerous. Toddlers who ignore warnings not to stand should be belted in. If they refuse to be belted in, they should be removed from the table.

Sometime late in the second year of life, or early in the third, many toddlers can safely kneel on a regular chair at the table when a special seat isn't available. Again, be sure to test your child's readiness under close supervision.

---

if he's eaten very little. Release him with a matter-of-fact "Oh, you've had enough? Okay," rather than a carping "You never eat anything!". And don't follow him to his play area with a forkful of food, pleading, "Just one more bite!" Such pushing of food can not only set up later eating problems, but also give your toddler the idea that "Hey, I don't have to eat at the table. Mom or Dad will feed me while I play." If he gets hungry later, make it clear that he'll have to sit for a snack.

# MEALTIME ENTERTAINMENT

···········································

*"Since our daughter turned one, mealtimes have been disasters. She won't eat anything without being entertained—sometimes my husband and I feel like clowns in a circus act. What can we do?"*

Stop sending in the clowns—and quickly. A toddler who is cajoled into eating by parental acrobatics, jug-gling, songs and dance, stand-up comedy routines, and other variety acts soon comes to expect dinner theater at every meal and balks when her food isn't served up with equal servings of entertainment.

Your goal isn't to "get" your toddler to eat, but to let her eat. In order to avoid future feeding problems, it's important to allow her appetite to guide her food consumption. She needs to associate eating with being hungry ("My tummy's growling, so it must be time for me to eat"), not with being amused ("Daddy's standing on his head again, so it must be time for me to eat").

If when you bring down the curtain on your mealtime performances your daughter stages a few melodramas of her own (in the form of tantrums, table banging, hunger striking) resist the temptation to don your tap shoes and funny hats for "one last show." Stay calm, nonchalant, nonplused—as if her eating, or not eating, didn't matter to you in the least (which it shouldn't, as long as she's growing normally). Rest assured that once hunger triumphs over stubbornness, your toddler will eat again, even if the show doesn't go on.

But just because you're no longer providing your toddler with table-side performances doesn't mean you shouldn't be providing her with companionship while she eats. Sitting down with her (even if you're not eating your meal, join her for a light snack or a beverage), and interacting with her gives her valuable social experiences while making her meals more interesting. Talk with her about anything but how much (or how little) she's eating: about the trip to the park you took this morning, or the play date that's scheduled for this afternoon, or the flowers you saw coming up in the garden. Even if the interaction is initially more like a monologue, it will transmit the message that conversations, not circus acts, are the appropriate accompaniments to a meal.

Putting more "fun" in the food you serve your toddler can also satisfy her appetite for entertainment. See page 522 for suggestions on how to do that.

# MUTINY ON THE HIGHWAY

*"Whenever we put our daughter in the car seat, she arches her back so violently that it's almost impossible to buckle her in."*

Your toddler has no choice but to rebel against this double infringement of her right to freedom. Being strapped into a car seat restricts both her independence (which she is trying so hard to establish) and her mobility (which is so new and exciting). Therefore, it's almost impossible to insure that a toddler won't fight buckling up.

Still, toddlers who are not strapped into car seats (or strollers, feeding chairs, and grocery carts for that matter) can get hurt—or worse. The car seat is required by law in all fifty states; it can make the difference between life and death in even a minor accident. So no ifs, ands, or buts—even if you're just going around the corner, make sure you buckle up your child.[4]

Clearly, in this battle of wills, you must come out the winner. But try to make the it as easy as possible for your little one. These strategies should help:

**Make her comfortable.** If the car-seat straps are too tight over her snowsuit, if the plastic is sticky or the metal buckle hot against her bare skin on a summer's day, if the padding is inadequate or the seat is too cramped, discomfort may intensify her protests.[5] Correcting these problems may help change her tune.

**Approach the issue indirectly.** Instead of commencing each trip with, "Now we have to buckle you into your car seat," which is likely to elicit an immediate protest, distract your toddler with casual chatter ("Look at the snow—see how pretty it is," "Let's go see Grandma and Grandpa this afternoon," "We're going to have such a yummy lunch when we get home"). Or challenge her with questions ("What does the doggy say? The cow? Where's Mommy's nose?") as you carry out the dastardly deed quickly. Try a silly made-up song or rhyme that your toddler can begin to associate with being strapped in: "Let's buckle our belly and eat all our jelly!" Or have a favorite toy or two ready to distract your child and occupy both her head and her hands. Whether these ploys actually make her forget what's happening, or simply allow her a graceful way out of having to make a fuss, doesn't matter. As long as they work.

**Add some music, maestro.** Always have a supply of engaging children's tunes

---

4. To be sure your toddler is buckled up safely, see page 650.
5. By eighteen months, many children are ready for a less-confining toddler booster (see page 652).

ready to soothe your toddler once she's been strapped in. Play them on the car stereo, if you have one, or use a portable cassette player.

**Strap in some entertainment.** Diversion doesn't always work, but it's always worth a try.[6] Keep a rotating selection of toys that can be snapped, Velcroed, or tied (with plastic rings or a ribbon or cord no longer than 6 inches) to her car seat. Unattached toys are potentially dangerous, since they can be thrown into the driver's line of vision and hurled through the air if the car stops suddenly. They can also cause an uproar if they slip out of a toddler's reach. Avoid, too, musical instruments or other noisy toys that might distract the driver.

**Buckle up together.** The buckle-up rule should apply to everyone in your car, including the driver (if the driver is unbuckled, the chance of surviving a crash is greatly diminished)—in the interest not only of fairness but of safety.

**Let her buckle up her "baby."** If there are enough seat belts to go around, let your toddler buckle in a teddy bear, a doll, or a favorite toy before she gets into her car seat. Or use a makeshift "belt" to tie the doll to your toddler's seat. Explain that safety belts are meant to keep her toys from falling out or getting hurt; that's why people need to buckle up, too.

**Put her in charge.** When your toddler is old enough to understand the idea, appoint her the safety-belt monitor, responsible for reminding anyone who enters the car to "buckle up." Once in awhile, "forget" to buckle yourself in so she can have the thrill of scolding you

---

6. Although using food to pacify or distract a child fighting against her car seat can be both tempting and effective, it isn't a wise ploy (unless the child's crankiness is due to hunger), particularly if you do it regularly.

(but don't start driving until she's "jogged" your memory).

**Allow no exceptions.** Even one "Okay, no belt, today" could be a fatal mistake. A simple trip down the street could be deadly for a small child who isn't safely confined in a car seat. And, surrendering once could undermine your authority on the issue, raising the hope in your child's mind that you can be persuaded to surrender again, and again. As every experienced parent knows this is a tactical error.

## STROLLER STRUGGLES

*"I can't get my daughter into the stroller without a fuss, and since I live in the city, sometimes a stroller is absolutely necessary in order to get from one place to another in a hurry."*

Toddlerhood is full of "catch-22's." Typically, toddlers won't let you put on their shoes, even though they can't yet do the job themselves. They won't nap, even though they're tired and cranky. They won't ride in the stroller, even though they can't walk fast enough to get you where you want to go when you need to get there.

Nobody said it was going to be easy (if anybody did, they probably never had a toddler). Toddlers and convenience are often incompatible, and since you're obviously not going to give up the former, you'll need to make concessions in regard to the latter. Though it's worth trying the following tips, it's also worth accepting one of the realities of life with a toddler: Getting there is rarely twice the fun, but it does generally take twice the time.

**Empathize.** When your toddler starts grumbling, "No stroller!" or once in

*Many toddlers resist the confinement of riding in a stroller—that is, unless Mom or Dad has asked them to walk instead.*

yells, "Get out!" be understanding: "I know you don't want to ride in the stroller, but we don't have time for you to walk right now. You can walk when we get near the house (or the store, or the playground)."

**Don't make the stroller a source of conflict.** It's a law of toddler nature: The more an issue appears to mean to parents, the more the child will fight you on it. So come across as cool as you can, unperturbed by your toddler's attempts to resist the stroller, unruffled by her pleas to be released.

**Switch positions.** If your toddler's stroller is reversible and she's riding in the forward position, switch her around so she's facing you—and vice versa. If she's been facing you, switch the other way and give her a chance to view the wide world.

**Stock up on diversions.** Attach a number of little playthings to your toddler's stroller (if you use a ribbon or cord, make sure it's no more than 6 inches long; better still, use plastic links). Miniature musical instruments make for an entertaining ride—if you're not headed to the library, a museum, or another place where quiet is mandatory. Rotate the diversions often; that way, they're more likely to remain pleasant pastimes.

**Keep talking, keep singing.** Point out dogs, pretty flowers, displays in store windows, cement mixers, and tow trucks. Chat about where you're going and what you're going to be doing. Break into a rousing chorus of "The wheels of the stroller go round and round." Nonstop talking and singing may succeed (at least, sometimes) in distracting your toddler—and keep her from complaining. Once she starts recognizing colors, letters, and numbers, you can play the "spotting game": The first one to spot the color red, the letter "A," the number "2," wins.

**Let her walk.** Put yourself in your toddler's shoes: She's only just learned to get around on two feet and she's being denied the pleasure of practicing and exploring. So when it's feasible (even if it means leaving a little earlier or arriving a little later), let your toddler walk. Having her "help" you push the stroller (assuming she'll let you share the task; see below) can keep her in step with you, as will holding hands. Let her walk as long as her little legs hold out; if she gets tired enough, she may even ask longingly for that stroller.

*"My son doesn't want to ride in the stroller anymore—now, he only wants to push it. This wouldn't be so bad, except that he pushes it into everyone and everything. When I try to take it away from*

*him, he has a screaming fit. What can I do?"*

The drive to gain control propels a toddler—whether it's control over what's served for breakfast, over bedtime, or over the steering of his stroller. In the latter case, this drive can propel him (and the stroller) into the heels of a pedestrian, the trunk of a tree, the dairy case at the supermarket, the papers stacked neatly at the newsstand, the flower bed in the park—annoying, destroying, and possibly putting himself in danger.

Although in some areas where toddlers crave control, it's possible (even desirable) to hand it over, it clearly isn't appropriate in the case of the runaway stroller. Instead:

**Leave the source of conflict at home.** Getting around without a stroller may not be easy, but it may be easier than trying to get around with a toddler pushing his own stroller. If necessary, put off walking trips that can't be accomplished without a stroller, or make them car or public-transportation trips.

**Help him sit it out.** If you make *riding* in the stroller attractive enough (see the previous question for how), he may not press so hard to *push* it.

**Lend a helping hand.** Try to sneak a guiding hand onto the stroller (without your toddler noticing, of course), allowing him to "push" without pushing himself into trouble. Distract him from your surreptitious interference with a song or by pointing out interesting sights as you go. If he catches you helping him and protests (as toddlers who want to do it themselves are wont to do), don't make a control issue out of it. Instead of saying "I need to help you push because you're not big enough," which will only irk him more, try something like, "Oh, I'm just

resting my hand because it's tired. You're giving it a nice ride." Maybe he'll buy it, maybe he won't—but it's worth a try. Or tell him he can push, but only with your help.

**Let him push on something his own size.** A child-size stroller or shopping cart is much easier for a toddler to keep on course than a full-size one (and is wonderful for imaginative play at home, too). And since toy strollers are lighter, they're less likely to inflict damage when pushed into someone's heels or a store display. (Remember that he'll still need a hand pushing it across the street, for safety's sake.) Bring the pint-size stroller along only on short trips; otherwise you could end up carrying him and his stroller when his legs give out.

# SHAMPOO STRUGGLES

*"We dread washing our daughter's hair and all the kicking and screaming that goes along with it. Is there any way to get around this struggle?"*

"If only," many a parent has mused, "a child's hair could be slipped off for washing and combing, and then replaced." That being impossible, hair-washing-scarred parents have to resort to other techniques for surviving shampoos. For example:

**Keep it short.** The shorter the hair, the shorter the shampoo. If your toddler's hair is long or hard to deal with, seriously consider an easy-care short cut. (For tips on handling the trip to the barber, see page 309.)

**Make a gentle choice.** Always choose a shampoo that is fragrance-free, and non-irritating to the eyes.

*A shampoo visor keeps water and suds out of the eyes.*

**Start off tangle free.** Baby-fine hair tangles when wet, so comb your child's hair before shampooing to minimize the post-shampoo struggles with tangles. There'll be less tangling, too, if you "pat" the shampoo through the wet hair gently, rather than working up a lather fiercely.

**Streamline.** Make sure at the outset that everything is in readiness (water at the perfect temperature, shampoo and a towel nearby) so that neither of you need to endure the shampooing ordeal any longer than necessary. To reduce the number of hair-washing steps, use a one-step conditioning shampoo instead of shampoo plus conditioner. Or spray on a no-rinse detangler after you've rinsed out the shampoo.

**Keep those eyes covered.** Even a "no-tear" shampoo (even plain water, for that matter) can produce tears. Protect your toddler's eyes with a shampoo visor (it looks like a topless sun hat and is available in many children's speciality stores, as well as through some mail-order catalogs). Or, have your toddler hold a washcloth across her forehead to protect

her eyes or try a child-size snorkeling mask or swimming goggles to keep the eyes dry.

**Control the rinse.** A hand-held spray nozzle offers more control, and less risk of a misdirection mishap. If you don't have a hand-held shower nozzle, use a child's plastic watering can. After shampooing, your toddler can play with the watering can in the tub.

**Give her a turn.** Your toddler may feel less victimized if she's allowed to shampoo someone herself—a doll or a bath toy with hair to shampoo. She can use the watering can, too. Or try the distraction techniques in the box on page 156.

**Let her watch.** Mount an unbreakable mirror in the tub so shampooing can become a spectator sport. Making "suds sculptures" with your toddler's hair (but try to avoid creating tangles) can also be diverting. Encourage her to sculpt her doll's hair into interesting shapes with the suds, too.

**Don't overdo it.** Unless the weather's hot or your toddler's hair is unusually oily (or matted with food), one shampoo a week is enough.

# RESISTANCE TO HAND WASHING

*"Our toddler's hands get unbelievably dirty during a morning of play. But he won't let us wash them before he eats."*

Dirt and toddlers are constant companions. The sandbox set routinely sport blackened knees, filthy forearms, grimy elbows, sticky faces, and dirt-encrusted knuckles. These toddler trademarks develop as surely as temper tantrums and picky eating habits.

But though most of the dirt a toddler attracts during a morning's play can safely remain intact until his nighttime tubbing, the dirt on his hands should be removed before he eats—particularly since he's likely to be using his hands to feed himself. And though most toddlers relish a dunk in the tub, many, like yours, regularly resist hand washing.

Whether your toddler likes it or not, however, he should get into the hand-washing habit. Hand washing is a cornerstone of personal hygiene; it not only helps to keep dirt out of your toddler's food but also to prevent the spread of germs. To make hand washing less onerous and more fun:

**Put hand washing in his hands.** The more control toddlers have over an activity, the less likely they are to have an aversion to it. If you've been washing your toddler's hands, turn the soap and water over to him, and much of his resistance may go down the drain with the dirt. Don't make a fuss about the mess he'll inevitably make—it can be mopped up afterward. Do adjust the water temperature for him, though, to avoid burns. (As a safety precaution, keep your home water heater set below 120°F. And, when your child's old enough to adjust the water himself, teach him to turn on the cold-water faucet first to avoid scalds.)

Check his handiwork when he's finished; if his hands don't look much cleaner than when he started, have him try again. Or let him wash your hands while you wash his.

**Put hand washing within his reach.** One of the most frustrating parts of hand washing for a toddler is the stretch—literally. Providing your toddler with easy access to the bathroom sink (via a steady step stool) and placing accessories (soap and towel) within reach can help him

feel more in control of the process. Another way to make hand washing more fun: Invest in (or borrow) a portable "toddler sink" that can be attached to the side of the bathtub at toddler level.

**Switch to liquid soap.** Bar soap is not only slippery and difficult for little fingers to lather, but it collects almost as much dirt as your toddler's hands and can serve as a breeding ground for bacteria. To keep your toddler from getting carried away with the liquid soap pumping, hand it to him, let him dispense a generous dollop, then return the pump to the sink. As an alternative, you or your toddler can squirt a bit of liquid soap onto a washcloth. After using the cloth to wash his hands, your child can rinse them under the faucet.

**Let him use wipes, when appropriate.** When you're away from home, disposable wipes may be the easiest and most sanitary way of giving hands a quick wash, and even a fairly young toddler can use them. Encourage him to make the wipes as "dirty" as he can, so that more of the grime will come off of him.

# JEALOUSY

*"Our son seems jealous. Every time my husband tries to hug me, he pushes us apart and complains. At first we thought it was cute, but it's getting annoying."*

A lot of toddlers have a little Oedipus in them; they display an excessive and possessive love for their moms, and even talk of marrying them. These feelings are normal, and if handled properly, transient. In fact, by the time they reach three or four, many boys

# A SPOONFUL OF SUGAR

**. . . . . . .**

**M**ary Poppins had the right idea when she prescribed a spoonful of sugar to help the medicine go down. But since sugar is bad for a toddler's teeth (and, questionable for their health in general), it's advisable to choose other methods of making medicine—and having shampoos, getting dressed, putting away toys, washing up, and other necessary routines—palatable. Here are a few that Ms. Poppins (and pediatric dentists) could recommend wholeheartedly:

**Laughable lyrics.** You don't have to be a Rodgers or a Hammerstein to entertain a toddler with an impromptu chorus of "I'm going to wash those elephants right out of your hair" or "This is the way we dress our feet . . ." or a parody of your own making. The more nonsensical and outrageous the lyrics, the more likely your toddler will be distracted by them. Use the same silly song each time you perform an unpopular task and your toddler may come to look forward to the song so much that shampooing, dressing, and washing will be endured without a squabble.

**Mommy's (or Daddy's) mistakes.** As someone small who's always being told what to do and how to do it, nothing gives your toddler more enjoyment than showing you the errors of *your* ways. The object of this game is to give your child that distinct pleasure while giving you the distinct pleasure of his or her compliance. When you want a cup of milk downed, for instance, you might say, "Oh, boy—yum, yum, my milk. I think I'm going to drink it." After you've drawn the bath and your toddler is about to draw a battle line, announce, "I'm all ready for my bath," and proceed to pretend to get into the tub fully dressed. Your toddler will get a kick not only out of correcting you with, "*My* milk!" or "*My* bath!" but out of the goofy incongruity of the situation. And you'll get a kick when your child (you hope) takes the cup and drinks the milk or scrambles into the tub before you do.

**Reverse psychology.** Turning the tables sometimes turns the tide. See page 316.

**Situation-saving sillies.** In this game, you get silly (rather than angry) when trouble is about to erupt. You pretend, for example, to put the mittens on the dog when your toddler refuses to don them, or to struggle into your toddler's coat when he or she's resisting getting dressed to go outdoors. With any luck, the game will not only yield giggles, but results, too: "No, *my* mittens! *My* coat!"

**Funny faces.** Again, it doesn't take much to amuse a toddler. Puffed out cheeks, a scrunched-up mouth, a protruding tongue—improvise until you tickle that funny bone

keep their mothers at arm's length, rejecting hugs and kisses. Instead of reacting angrily (spurning your toddler for Daddy will only fuel jealousy and confirm his fear that Daddy poses a threat) or too sympathetically (spurning Daddy for him will only confuse his notion of family dynamics), try reacting with good humor. So that he won't feel left out, include him in your hugs when he seeks to pry you apart (and remind him, "I love you *and* I love Daddy—I love you both very much"). And be careful not to encourage fantasies because they're cute or you're flattered. (Explain: "You can't marry me, because I'm your Mommy, but you can marry another nice woman when you grow up.")

Make sure, too, that your toddler's getting plenty of loving attention from both of you. If he's wary with Daddy, having them spend time together—"just us boys"—will help them grow closer. Eventually he will realize that he can't

and make your toddler forget what it was he or she didn't want to do.

**Uncharacteristic utterances.** High, low, squeaky, creaky, mouse-like, clown-like—the sound of an unexpected voice can often distract a toddler long enough to enable a parent to get through even the most difficult of routines. If you're one of those talented parents who can produce realistic sound effects (a buzzer, horn, siren, animal imitations, or what have you), use them to amuse and catch a resisting toddler off guard.

**An imaginary setting.** A toddler who's resisting a pair of shoes may relent if you play "shoe store." Line up a few pairs that are obviously not toddler-size and suggest "Let's try these on." After giggling his or her way through a couple of wacky misfits, your toddler may relish trying on a pair that's "just right." Likewise, play "beauty shop" at bath time, "clothing store," at dressing time, "restaurant" at mealtime.

**Giggly games.** Hold a hand-washing contest (who can suds up faster?); a mitten-donning race (who can get their mittens on first?); a pick-up party (who can stash away more toys?).

**Character charades.** Shampoos are much more fun when Big Bird does the sudsing, shoes are much less of a bother to have buckled when Dumbo does the honors. Becoming one of your toddler's favorite storybook or television characters can make it easier to get almost any unpleasant job done.

**Gotcha! gambling.** Everyone loves to win a bet, and older toddlers are no exception. The challenge, "I bet you can't get your shoes on before I get mine on," can motivate a child to move faster than nagging, threatening, pleading, and screaming combined. There's incentive not only to win the bet but to prove you wrong. For variety, you can set your challenges to music, à la musical chairs ("I bet you can't put your books back on the shelf before I finish singing"). Or use a timer's buzz ("I bet you can't wash your hands by the time the buzzer buzzes"). Or, if your toddler is interested in numbers, extend a numerical challenge ("I bet you can't put away your blocks by the time I count to ten"). When he or she's older, try a count down instead. ("Ten, nine, eight . . . three, two, one, blast off!")

An important rule of the game: If your toddler takes you up on your wager, let him or her win—even if it means putting your shoes on at a snail's pace, singing in an exaggeratedly slow fashion, or taking two minutes to count to ten. Without the satisfaction of winning, your toddler's much less likely to accept your wager next time.

It's important that there be no payoff in this game, other than the fun of coming in first. You don't want to start promoting full-fledged gambling.

take Daddy's place, but he can be like him. Then their relationship will blossom.

Many girls also favor Mommy early on. Other children are Daddy's girls (or boys) almost from birth. It's important to remember that favoritism of any kind is not a personal affront to the less-favored parent of the moment but simply a matter of normal development. During later stages, many children shift their loyalties to the other parent—and still later, may swing back again.

# *EARLY TANTRUMS*

*"I've heard of tantrums during the terrible two's; my daughter seems to be starting early. Is that possible?"*

Indeed it is. It's not unheard of for even a twelve-month-old-child to kick and scream when she doesn't get what she wants. And by the middle of the second year, most children exhibit some

## TOYS, PLAYTHINGS, AND ACTIVITIES AT EIGHTEEN MONTHS

..........

At a year and a half, toddlers are a handful and a half. No longer is keeping them busy as easy as putting them in front of a busy box. The typical eighteen-month-old has become more verbal and sociable, is learning the art of pretending, mastering a long list of new skills (stacking three or four blocks in a tower, throwing a ball, pulling a pull toy, opening and closing containers, turning pages and knobs, fitting shapes into a sorter, rocking a "baby"), and is ready for many more challenges. To provide your toddler with those challenges, make sure you provide a wide range of playthings that stimulate the fascinating little person he or she is.

Child-size table and chairs are perfect for games, puzzles, tea parties, coloring, and so on. Look for chairs with legs that get wider at the bottom to reduce the chance of tipping, and check the height of both the table and its chairs to be sure they are right for your toddler. (An 11-inch chair and a 20-inch table usually "fit" until age four.) Also important is adequate and accessible storage space for toys (see page 57 for tips on toy storage). And for carrying toys on outings and trips, a small tote or toddler backpack.

The Toys for Tots recommended on page 56 are suitable for your eighteen-month-old, but they are sure to be used in a more sophisticated way now. Remember to select a few toys from each category so that your toddler will develop a wide variety of interests and skills. And, of course, be sure to check toys for age appropriateness and safety (see page 655).

---

"terrible two's" behavior. Tantrums may be full-blown, very mild, or somewhere in between. Read about how to handle them on page 339.

# DELAYED WALKING
..............................................

*"Our eighteen-month-old son is the only child in his play group not walking on his own. Though he seems normal in every other way, we are very concerned."*

Most children are walking unassisted by eighteen months, but occasionally a perfectly normal toddler refuses to toddle until a bit—rarely, a lot—later. Sometimes fear (because of a previous nasty fall) keeps a toddler from letting go and taking off on his own. Sometimes it's proficiency as a crawler (he knows he can get around more quickly on hands and knees than on two feet). Sometimes a very slow gross-motor developmental timetable is responsible. And sometimes walking is delayed by a problem that needs medical attention.

Your first step in finding out why your son hasn't yet taken his first solo steps is to consult his doctor, who might refer you to a specialist. If a thorough medical work-up rules out a developmental problem, you can breathe easier. But you can also take some steps to encourage your toddler's stepping out:

▲ Give him plenty of opportunity to walk hanging on to one or both of your hands.

▲ Encourage cruising on furniture (but make sure whatever he holds onto for support is sturdy).

▲ Applaud his efforts at cruising, standing alone, and walking but don't belittle him for *not* cruising, standing alone, or walking.

▲ Give him a small, safe toy to hold when he is standing alone or holding your hand; this may distract him enough so that he takes a step without realizing it. Or offer him a favorite toy from a short distance; encourage him to take a step to reach it. A push toy that provides security and stability while he inches forward can also make walking less frightening for him.

▲ If he's been using a walker, get rid of it. A walker is not only dangerous, but it can make it more difficult for a child to walk solo, because it encourages a different walking pattern than that required for walking independently.

# WHAT IT'S IMPORTANT TO KNOW: All About TV and Toddlers

You don't have to look far these days to stumble across startling statistics about children and television; you'll find them in newspapers, magazines, and on television itself. They tell us that children between the ages of two and five watch an average of more than twenty-five hours of television a week—with some staring at the tube for five or more hours a day. That by high school graduation the average American child will have spent a cumulative 15,000 hours (almost two solid years, night and day) in front of a television—a full 4,000 more hours than he or she will have spent in classrooms. And that television has been linked to all of the following among our children:

**The couch potato syndrome.** Kids don't just look like they're vegetating while they're watching TV, they really *are*. They actually enter a trance-like state, with their metabolic rate (the rate at which the body burns calories) dropping as much as 16% below what it is in a normal resting state (when they are just sitting and doing nothing) and even farther below what it is when they are active.

**Inadequate physical, intellectual, social activity.** When the television is on, children aren't generally running around, playing with other kids, looking at books or listening to stories, playing dress-up or make believe, drawing or painting, or exercising their minds and bodies in any other way. Excessive viewing prevents young children from developing skills that are vital to long-term happiness. Chronic TV viewers learn to depend on television for stimulation and satisfaction.

**Obesity.** TV, studies show, is one reason why obesity among children is up 50% in the last couple of decades. The explanation is simple: too many calories. TV addicts consume more calories (they tend to snack while viewing, and tempted by advertising, to snack on the wrong kinds of foods). And they burn fewer of them (because they exercise less and have a slower metabolic rate during TV watching).

**Higher cholesterol levels.** Not only does a heavy diet of TV tend to make young viewers heavier, it also tends to raise their cholesterol level. Researchers suggest that this is due to a combination of factors, including inactivity and a heart-unhealthy diet inspired by TV commercials and junk food snacked on during TV viewing. It's even been suggested that parents who fail to limit TV viewing may be the same parents who also fail to limit fat in the family diet and to take other steps to control cholesterol.

**An increase in aggressive behavior.** Though some continue to dispute it, mounting evidence supports what many parents have long suspected: Watching violence on TV fosters aggressive behavior in children. At the very least, it dulls sensitivity toward violence, and allows young viewers to take it for granted rather than being worried about it. (Why not, when the character splattered across the screen in one episode always snaps right back in the next?)

**Increased fear.** Young children find it difficult, or even impossible, to differentiate between what's real and what's not. They find fantasy as frightening as reality because they tend to take all that they see and hear literally; what they see on TV is, for them, as real as what happens in their living room or playground. Even if they don't seem frightened while watching a scary show, they may later experience nightmares related to it.

As children begin to differentiate between fact and fiction sometime during the preschool years (though they aren't able to make the distinction fully until much later), news shows (with reports on murders, fires, natural disasters, crashes, and so on) become particularly threatening. Young children tend to picture what they see on television happening to themselves or those they love.

**Questionable values.** A few children's shows make a very commendable effort to teach positive values, such as tolerance, sharing, kindness, and honesty. Many programs, however, transmit negative values, such as it's okay to use violence or to lie to get what you want, or

the acquisition of "things" is what makes you important or popular.

**Less effective coping skills.** A toddler is bored, cranky, upset, has a problem? For many parents, the solution is simple: Click on the TV. Experts predict that children whose parents use television in this way may grow up unable to deal with the normal ebbs and flows of life; rather than trying to work out problems or figure a way out of boredom, they may gravitate toward easy fixes, even develop self-destructive habits. You don't have to face reality when *Pinocchio* is on.

**Lagging intellectual and social development.** Not surprisingly, heavy TV viewers tend to score lower on reading tests, and on average, do less well in school than light viewers. There are probably a host of reasons, including: less time (and less inclination) to read and study; overblown expectations (the high-tech, special-effects style of TV learning turns children into passive learners who are bored or unable to concentrate when learning in school is not as exciting and fast-paced as it is on TV). Excessive television viewing in the toddler years can prevent a child from developing a close relationship with books, a relationship crucial to continuing intellectual growth.

**Less imagination and creativity.** Reading provides the paint and the brush but makes your mind do the drawing, visualizing scenes, imagining action, and so on. Television, on the other hand, paints the whole picture and leaves nothing to the imagination. With rare exceptions, TV shows don't challenge children to come up with new ideas and don't encourage creativity.

**Weak independent play skills.** Children who watch a lot of TV often can't entertain themselves and certainly aren't motivated to do so. Spoiled by the ample stimulation of TV, heavy viewers don't want to put effort into free play that requires thought and imagination.

**Weaker family and social ties.** Families that watch TV day in and day out may gradually drift apart. With everyone in a TV trance so much of the time, there is often little interaction, little sharing of ideas, feelings, values.

Have these eye-opening facts prompted us to close our children's eyes to television? For the most part, no—and for a lot of reasons: *Educational value.* TV does have its positive side. When used to advantage, it can be a valuable educational tool, though it rarely reaches its full potential in this role. *Peer pressure.* Even among toddlers, such characters as Big Bird, Lamb Chop, and Mr. Rogers are part of everyday life, and the child who is unfamiliar with them can feel left out. *Convenience.* Busy parents often turn to an electronic "sitter" to occupy their children while they make dinner or open the day's mail or do the laundry. When a favorite film is on, they don't have to make any effort to cheer their children up, find them a project, listen to their problems. *Peace.* There's no surer way of assuring tranquility in a household (assuming everyone agrees to watch the same program) than lining your offspring up in front of a television set. For parents of toddlers, who desperately crave a tranquil moment (if only now and then), the TV option is almost irresistible: click on the TV, click off a high-strung toddler.

# THE TEN COMMANDMENTS OF WISE TV VIEWING

**D**espite its faults, TV does offer access to a wonderland of experiences—sights, sounds, and people—that a child can find nowhere else. It can take children to the far corners of the world or even the universe, expose them to the past and the future, the everyday and the exotic, the arts and the sciences. These Ten Commandments will help your family derive the most benefits from this medium with the least risk:

**1. Establish sensible limits now.** If you wait until your child is in school to enact and enforce such limits, the task will be much more difficult. What limits make sense? Before eighteen months, a toddler can easily do without any TV at all. At eighteen months, half an hour a day is sufficient. Choose the shows for your toddler until he or she is old enough to participate. At that point, you can offer choices: "Do you want to watch *Mr. Rogers' Neighborhood* or *Sesame Street* today?" When your toddler passes his or her second birthday, consider expanding TV viewing to an hour a day, particularly when outdoor play is limited because of inclement weather. But allowing more TV time than that for toddlers, who should be spending most of their time doing rather than watching, is not a good idea.

**2. Enforce limits.** Setting limits is one thing, keeping to them is another. Limits won't work unless you regularly click off the television set when the allotted show is over, and then redirect your toddler's interest elsewhere. Having a favorite activity planned for right after television viewing will help to make for a more pleasant transition.

Of course, as with most rules, there are times when your TV rules will need to be broken, as when a child is sick, and has to be relatively quiet for prolonged periods, or when a children's special is being shown. Just try to make it clear that the rules haven't changed and that this is an exception.

**3. Time television viewing.** Avoid turning the TV on during mealtimes, which should be family time; during play dates, when children should be learning social skills; and during family gatherings and holiday celebrations (except for special holiday shows).

**4. Watch together.** Children are much less likely to sink into a TV trance if they watch with a parent, and if there is a lot of interaction related to what's on the screen: "Isn't that a beautiful horse?" or "That clown is so silly!" or "Oh, what happened to Dumbo?" You can be doing something else while you watch—either with your child (building with blocks, doing a puzzle) or on your own (peeling carrots, working a crossword, paying bills). Allowing your child to watch TV alone is like leaving him or her alone under the influence of strangers; joint viewing allows you to correct misinformation, monitor commercials, and point out values you share as well as those you don't. Of course, there will be times when you will have to let your toddler watch alone, but don't make solitary viewing a habit.

**5. Make TV viewing interactive.** Draw characters from the screen, discuss action and story lines, carry out activities similar to those shown on favorite programs, comment on and ask questions about television shows while they're on. Motivate your toddler to sing or dance and do arts-and-crafts projects along with TV characters. Sing-along or dance-and-movement videos encourage active participation. Getting your toddler to talk about a show (in effect, to critique it) when it's over can turn TV viewing into a valuable educational experience.

**6. Avoid using TV as a substitute for attention.** You wouldn't hire a sitter who talked endlessly, never listened to your child, never responded to questions or fears, and couldn't deal with your child's concerns. But if you use your TV as a sitter, that's just what you're doing.

Employ it in this capacity only when absolutely necessary.

Also avoid using television to calm, soothe, or cheer your child, or to otherwise respond to his or her needs. Try to find out what is bothering your toddler and help him or her deal with the problem instead of sweeping it behind the TV screen. For more on fostering coping skills, see page 384.

**7. Do not offer TV as a bribe or a reward, or take it away as a punishment.** Associating the tube with good behavior (it must be good because only good kids can watch it) or making it more tantalizing by dangling it over your child's head ("If you stop crying now you can watch *Sleeping Beauty*") is sure to make it that much more attractive.

**8. Set a positive example.** Your children will be more likely to do as you do than do as you say, so become a model of responsible TV viewing. Don't keep the TV on for background noise or for round-the-clock entertainment. Except for an occasional special show, save your TV viewing for when your children are safely tucked in for the night. If you don't like total quiet around the house, switch the radio on for periodic weather or news reports, or play background music both you and your toddler enjoy.

**9. Be selective.** Carefully choosing what your children watch on television is as important as controlling how much they watch and how. So:

*Preview.* Before letting your child watch a particular show, try to view it yourself first to determine its appropriateness. (If it's on at a time you are usually with your toddler and you have a VCR, try to tape it for later viewing alone.)

*Choose appropriately.* Look for noncommercial programming designed for young children, with simple language, appealing characters, music, singing, educational value. Ban shows that lean heavily on violence, cartoons included (even a small amount of violence will frighten some children). Prohibit shows that regularly display values you disagree with. If there are older children in the house, don't allow your toddler to sit in on their TV viewing unless the show is toddler-appropriate—and keep your youngest otherwise occupied when it's not. Be careful, too, about the content of shows *you're* watching when your toddler is around. Because of the often violent nature of news stories, try to get your current events on the later evening news shows when children are safely tucked away in bed.

*Videotape.* If you have a VCR, you can tape shows that are on at inconvenient times and show them during your toddler's usual TV time. That way you're not limited to whatever happens to be on. Keep a stash of the best programs—toddlers love "reruns"—and a supply of quality videos, too, around for emergencies. But don't be lulled into believing that just because videos are commercial-free, it's okay for children to watch them for hours on end. Most of the numbing negative side-effects of TV hold true for videos, too. And their ready availability (they can be "on" even when nothing's "on" TV) makes overuse by parents a greater likelihood.

**10. Counteract the negatives.** Television's negative effects can be wiped out or minimized by:

*Turning the family focus away from TV.* Substitute, instead, activities that bring the family together (cooking, gardening, swimming, art projects, a trip to the park or the museum or the zoo). When you do watch TV together, engage in other activities simultaneously (games, for example), and encourage dis-

cussion about what is happening on the screen.

*Building Best-Odds habits.* Adopt a family lifestyle that includes the Best-Odds Toddler Diet (refuse to buy into, or let your children buy into, those junk-food commercials), healthy attitudes toward food and eating, and plenty of exercise.

*Passing on values.* Discuss the values, good and bad, on shows your children do watch ("Do you think those boys were being mean to Dumbo? Wasn't that mouse nice to help Dumbo feel better? Look at the mama and baby hugging; they love each other so much").

*Stimulating creativity and intellectual development.* Use TV to build observation skills ("What did that boy just do?"), creativity ("Can we make a paper bag puppet just like they did on that show?"), intellect ("Why do you think that girl said that? Do you think that was a good idea?"). Work, too, on bringing out your toddler's creative skills and imagination (see page 362), and encouraging thinking and learning (see page 99) in other ways.

*Meeting emotional needs.* Children need more than food, clothing, shelter and TV. They need someone to pay attention to feelings, to teach them how to recognize them, and how to deal with them.

*Talking about violence.* If children are exposed to violence (on the screen, in the newspapers, on the street) and no one talks to them about what it means, and about how to view it, they will be confused and frightened. They may also have distorted views of violence. If an older toddler accidentally catches part of a scary news story and seems upset by it, try to modify the effect with a comforting explanation ("That was a bad fire, but see? All the people are okay"), overlooking, if need be, the fact that some of the people didn't make it. The same would hold true with incidental violence on usually peaceful shows or on otherwise innocent videos (the shooting of the mother deer in *Bambi*, for exam-ple). Sometimes this kind of action passes right over the head of very young toddlers, but if your toddler seems to react to it, you should make an effort to explain ("That was a bad man who shot Bambi's mommy").

# WHAT IT'S IMPORTANT FOR YOUR TODDLER TO KNOW: The Values You Value

Raising children to have decent values certainly isn't easy for parents, especially in a society that sometimes seems short on values. And, though we all have values we want to pass on to our children, we worry that we won't succeed. After all, we remember ourselves as teenagers, rejecting the values our parents so carefully sought to instill in us, insistent on finding our own way.

Studies show, however, that after that predictable period of adolescent rebellion, most of us end up with values that very closely resemble those of our parents. Parents have scant effect on their children's natural temperaments or inborn strengths and weaknesses; nature, in so many ways, has it over nurture. Yet nurture takes the lead when it comes to the development of values. Sometimes consciously, sometimes not, parents can and do strongly influence the way their children treat themselves and others, and the attitudes their children take toward family, charity, honesty, work, environment, and dozens of other moral issues.

Many parents instinctively do a pretty good job of passing on their values, much as their parents did, and their parents before them; good, solid values seem to run in families. Still, the following recommendations (teamed with the details in the other "What It's Important for Your Toddler to Know" sections of this book, where specific values and how to best hand them down are discussed) can help improve the odds that your children will one day value the values you value most.

**Know your own values.** First, decide how far you want to depart from the chain of values that your parents forged when you were growing up. Do you want to add a few links, take away a few, or make more radical alterations in the chain? List the values you would like to pass on to your toddler—in their order of importance—and ask your spouse or partner to do the same. The possibilities are endless: family, health, integrity, religion, work, learning, courtesy, the environment, helping others, tolerance, good taste, political activism, the accumulation of money, of possessions. Then compare your list with your spouse's. Are there areas of disagreement? Can you compromise on them? Once you've reached an accord, you'll be better able to join forces in passing the chosen values onto your toddler.

**Live your values.** As much as they want their children to live by certain values, parents sometimes find it difficult to live by them themselves. They want their offspring to be honest, but they fib about a child's age so he or she can fly for free or get reduced movie or museum admissions. They're determined that their children learn not to abuse their bodies, but *they* fail to show respect for their own bodies—by smoking cigarettes, living on junk food, failing to exercise. They preach tolerance to their children, but they practice close-mindedness in their dealings with those who are different.

To impart values to your children effectively, you must first commit yourself to living them—to following them habitually, not just when your toddler is watching. In the long run, the influences your child is exposed to at home have much greater impact on the person he or she will ultimately become than will any outside influence (including television, the movies, and music). Be an exemplary role model, and your child will likely become an exemplary individual.

**Articulate your values.** Living your values is not enough. Help your children understand *why* you live them. Explain why you believe it's better to be honest than to lie; why taking care of your body is important; why you do unto others as you would have them do unto you.

**Put teaching values in perspective.** By building a framework of values for your toddler to follow, you're heading him or her in the right direction. But realize that this is the best any parent can do. As children grow older, they add their own experiences and the lessons they've learned out in the world to what you've taught them at home, to come up with their own unique set of values. Just as you did.

# CHAPTER SEVEN
·········

# The Nineteenth Month

## WHAT YOUR TODDLER MAY BE DOING NOW

*By the end of this month,[1] your toddler*
*. . . should be able to (see Note):*

▲ perform all previous "should be able to's . . ."

**Note:** If your toddler has not reached these milestones or doesn't use symbolic play and words, consult the doctor or nurse-practitioner. This rate of development may well be normal for your child (some children are late bloomers), but it needs to be evaluated. Also check with the doctor if your toddler seems out-of-control or hyperactive; uncommunicative, passive, or withdrawn; highly negative, demanding, and stubborn. (Remember, the child who was born prematurely often lags behind others of the same chronological age. This developmental gap continues to narrow and

generally disappears entirely around age two.)

*. . . will probably be able to:*

▲ "feed" a doll
▲ use 6 words
▲ walk up steps

*. . . may possibly be able to:*

▲ build a tower of 4 cubes
▲ identify 2 pictures by pointing

*. . . may even be able to:*

▲ name 6 body parts (by 18½ months)
▲ wash and dry hands

---

1. The nineteenth month begins when a child is eighteen months old and ends when he or she is nineteen months old.

# WHAT YOU MAY BE CONCERNED ABOUT

## NIGHT WANDERING

*"Our daughter has been in a big bed since her new brother arrived, and now she wanders around the house in the middle of the night. We're worried about her safety. What should we do?"*

Whether she's learned how to scale the walls of her crib or has been having an easy time escaping from the minimum security of a big bed, the toddler on the prowl at night is a toddler at risk. Minimize the risks by taking these precautions:

**Make her immediate surroundings safe.** Survey your toddler's room or sleeping area to be sure it is child-safe (see page 620). Hot radiators, electric fans that aren't childproof, and other dangers should be *completely* out of reach (remember, your toddler is a good climber). Move out of the way furniture she can bump into, rugs and toys she can trip over, cords she can stumble across (especially if they're attached to lamps she can pull over). Install window guards on all windows, and secure cords from window blinds out of reach. Unless she is more likely to stay in her bed in a darkened room, add a night-light to help your toddler see her way around in the dark and to prevent nocturnal collisions.

**Close the escape route.** To keep your toddler in her room, you can either close the door or use a gate across the open doorway. The gate arrangement is probably less frightening to a child because it allows her to see out and doesn't cut her off completely from the rest of the family. You could start with one gate (be sure it meets safety standards, page 632), but the odds are that a toddler who can climb out of her crib can also clamber over a gate. By adding a second gate directly above the first, you eliminate this possibility. (The gates are easy to set up and are removable in seconds if you must get to your toddler in a hurry.) With an older child you can make a deal: If you stay in your bed, we will keep the door open (or the gate down).

Be sure there's a night-light on in the hall, a gate across any stairs, no access to the kitchen, and a hook-and-eye locking the bathroom door,[2] in case your toddler should somehow slip from her room.

**Go to her instead of letting her come to you.** It often seems easier to allow a toddler who is frightened of staying alone (or who just doesn't want to stay alone) to come into your bed than to risk a major middle-of-the-night battle. But in the long run, since it rewards the child for waking up (and waking you), it could cause more trouble than it prevents. So if your toddler gets out of bed or climbs out of her crib in the middle of the night, return her with little comment, and tuck her back in. Sit near her bed for a bit if she seems frightened, patting her back, and reassuring her that everything's okay. But don't start a conversation, turn on lights, or lie down with her. (If you can, take turns with your spouse to make it a little less wearing.) Your message is that nighttime is for sleeping and that's what you expect her to do. Act as though you believe she can do it, even if you secretly have your doubts.

---

2. Once a child is out of diapers at night, the route to the bathroom will have to be opened. Then safety precautions will have to extend to the hallway and any other accessible spaces.

For the toddler experiencing night-mares or night terrors, see page 312; for a sleep walker, see page 315.

## ESCAPE FROM THE CRIB

*"Our son is very tall for his age and very agile. Now we're afraid he will try to climb out of his crib in the middle of the night. Is that a possibility? What should we do if it is?"*

*For the toddler who's given to night wandering, a tent-like covering for the crib can provide safety and a comfortingly snug environment.*

**A**lthough the average nineteen-month-old is 32 to 34 inches tall, some toddlers of this age are much closer to the 36 inches usually required for a successful escape from the crib. If your child has reached 36 inches or is quickly inching toward it, such an escape is possible any time now.

Since scaling the crib's railing can result not only in freedom for the es-capee but a large bump on his head (or worse), you're wise to start thinking about protective measures now. Be sure that the crib mattress is at the lowest set-ting and that the sides are always safely locked in the "up" position. Never leave in the crib anything (a pile of toys, pil-lows, even a large stuffed animal) that your toddler might use as a stepladder to help him scale the sides of the crib. As an added precaution, pad the escape route with something (an old quilt or sofa cushions, for example) that will soften the landing should your toddler make it over the side. If he does manage an escape, it may be a good idea to dis-mantle the crib and remove everything from the room but the mattress. Place the mattress on the floor, one side wedged up against the wall, until you get a bed set up. Another option is to make the crib escape-proof with a net-covered tent, available through some catalogs and juvenile furnishings stores. The contrap-tion fits over the sides of the crib and contains the toddler while allowing adult access from the outside through a zipper opening. Some toddlers will relish being secured nightly in this cocoon-like set-ting (especially if you emphasize its "co-ziness" and "little-house" qualities), but others will resist the confinement.

A more permanent option is to move up graduation from the crib to a bed. While most children make this transition at around age two, a child who is on the verge of climbing out of the crib is a good candidate for earlier graduation. If you decide to take this option, see page 318 for how to make the transition a happy one.

## NIGHT WAKING DUE TO TEETHING

*"Ever since our daughter started cutting her molars, she's been wak-ing at night. I don't even know if her teeth are bothering her any-*

*more, or if it's just become a bad habit."*

It's possible that teething pain is what started your toddler's night waking habit, but it's likely that the response she got is what kept the habit going strong long after the pain was gone. While everyone awakens three or four times during the night and then drifts back to sleep, a small child who has been conditioned to receive parental attention and comfort when she wakes isn't likely to go back to sleep until she gets it. To reverse that conditioning, and that night waking habit, see the tips on page 65.

# SNORING

*"My son snores in his sleep—so loudly we can hear him down the hallway. I'm concerned that snoring is abnormal for a child."*

When we think of snoring, we usually think of hulking men—not pint-size toddlers. But some of the biggest nocturnal noises actually come from some of the smallest sources; studies show that 7% to 9% of children snore. The rate is higher in homes where parents smoke. Though snoring reaches its peak between ages three and six, it often shows up much earlier.

Snoring is the sound that is created when a child's breathing is partially blocked by enlarged adenoids and/or tonsils. These bits of lymphatic tissue in the nose-throat breathing passage often swell when a child has a cold, flu, or sore throat, sometimes triggering temporary snoring. Persistent allergies and exposure to tobacco smoke may also cause tonsils and/or adenoids to become enlarged. Sometimes, however, they grow excessively for no apparent reason. When this happens, snoring often be-

comes a nightly occurrence, though not all children with enlarged tonsils and adenoids snore (there seems to be an inborn or environmentally induced susceptibility). In addition to snoring, enlarged adenoids may also cause mouth-breathing (both day and night), nasal speech, and noisy breathing, especially during sleep.

Snoring alone is not cause for concern; it tends to diminish as the tonsils and adenoids stop growing and begin to shrink (after age seven or eight). But when it's associated with obstructive sleep apnea (a momentary halt in breathing during snoring or noisy breathing when the child is asleep, which is occasionally the reason for frequent night wakings), it requires immediate medical attention. Suspect this problem, which occurs in a very small percentage of snorers, when snoring is particularly persistent and extremely loud (this may be difficult to judge, since what's loud to one parent may be barely noticeable to another); or when your toddler seems to pause during snoring in an attempt to breathe; appears to be working hard to breathe at night, straining the muscles of the neck and stomach (you can actually see these muscles tighten as the child tries to breathe); seems to choke, gag, or gasp for breath during snoring; thrashes a lot in bed; seems tired or drowsy after a good night's sleep; is not growing and thriving. Any of these symptoms should be reported to your toddler's doctor; a referral to a specialist may be necessary.

Obstructive sleep apnea is generally diagnosed during an overnight observation in a sleep laboratory. The child is tucked into bed in a comfortable, homelike hospital room, and painlessly hooked up to electrodes connected to machines that monitor breathing, heart rate, and blood oxygen levels. Mom or Dad is close by in the next bed. Erratic breathing and heart rate plus oxygen deprivation supports a diagnosis of obstructive sleep apnea. The treatment, successful in more than 95% of children, is removal of tonsils and adenoids. The surgery, in addition to allowing the child to breathe normally, may also reduce or eliminate the frequent colds, chronic ear infections, runny noses, and weepy eyes these children also often experience.

## A CHRONICALLY RUNNY NOSE

*"Our son's nose runs almost constantly. He doesn't seem sick or uncomfortable, but I still worry that something's wrong."*

**A** constantly runny nose is not normal for most toddlers, but is very common among children with allergies. Though the runny nose may only annoy your toddler right now, when he's older it could cause him some embarrassment. In addition, the nasal stuffiness that accompanies it could make his speech less intelligible, which in turn could make him hesitant to speak. To head off such problems, discuss your child's runny nose with his doctor; perhaps a referral to a pediatric allergist is indicated (see page 703).

Because toddlers tend to wipe their runny noses on their sleeves or the backs of their hands, smearing the mucus across their faces, the major side effect of a toddler's chronic runny nose is chapped cheeks. If your child's cheeks, or the area beneath his nose, become raw and red, use a moisturizing ointment or lotion, such as Eucerin, Moisturel, or Baby Magic with Aloe. You can also teach your toddler how to wipe his nose with a clean tissue or a handkerchief instead of his hand or his clothing (though it will likely be years before he regularly remembers to).

## HYPERACTIVITY

*"Our son never stops moving, from the time he wakes up in the morning until he finally falls asleep at night. I suspect he may be hyperactive, but my wife says he's 'just a toddler.' Who's right?"*

**C** hances are pretty good that she is. To most parents, toddlers—with their seemingly endless energy—appear overactive. But only about 1 in 20 will ever be diagnosed with the condition known as "attention deficit hyperactivity disorder," or ADHD.[3]

Children who are ultimately diagnosed with ADHD were often very intense and high strung as infants; they cried and thrashed a lot, and were very sensitive to sound and other stimuli (though far from every high-strung baby becomes a hyperactive child). Most children with ADHD calm down when their nervous systems mature and they are better able to focus their attention for longer periods, usually about the time they enter puberty. Some experts see this condition not as a "disorder" but as the superactive end of the activity continuum, which places the very quiet, least active children at the other end.

Although hyperactive children are sometimes thought to be slow learners, ADHD is not related to intellectual deficits. In fact, children with ADHD usually have average or above average intelligence; they *appear* scattered, however, because of their difficulty screening out distractions and concentrating on anything for more than a few minutes.

---

3. This condition, once simply labeled "hyperactivity," may also be labeled attention deficit disorder with hyperactivity (ADDH). In a variation called attention deficit disorder (ADD) children have difficulty focusing on tasks but are not hyperactive; ADD is more common in girls.

## ENERGY OUTLETS FOR TOTS

**M**ost toddlers are bundles of energy. The challenge is to find outlets for that endless energy that are safe, acceptable, and not too wearying for tired parents trying to keep up. When your toddler starts bouncing off the walls (and the sofa, and the nightstand, and the coffee table), try channeling the little dynamo into one of these energy-expending activities, supervised as necessary:

### Indoors

▲ Punching and kneading bread dough

▲ Punching a punching bag or a pillow

▲ "Drumming" on pots

▲ Pounding or hammering toys

▲ Pounding clay

▲ Dancing to lively music

▲ Kiddie aerobics (lead your toddler in just-for-fun "toe touches," "jumping jacks," and "head-shoulder-knee-and-toe touches")

▲ Pillow fights (but in an area where no lamps or fragile items can be upset)

▲ Bean-bag tossing (ditto, in a safe locale)

▲ Tumbling (on a large mat or carpet, away from sharp corners and other hazards)

▲ Lively circle games and action songs

▲ Running in place (for older toddlers)

▲ Jumping up and down ("How high can you jump?")*

▲ Broad jumps ("How far can you jump?")

▲ Splashing in the tub

### Outdoors

▲ Free play: running, jumping, climbing

▲ Playground play: swings, slide, jungle gym

▲ Ball kicking and throwing (use large, lightweight balls)

▲ "Rolling" on an oversized ball

▲ Pedaling on a trike or other riding toy

▲ Pulling a wagon

▲ Splashing in a kiddie pool (or regular pool, for an older toddler)

▲ On rainy days, splashing in puddles (don slickers and boots first)

▲ Roller (or ice) skating (for an older toddler)

▲ Pulling weeds in the garden (only for toddlers who won't be tempted to taste); digging in the garden

---

*A mini-trampoline that's safety approved for your toddler's age, placed on a soft surface in a clear area away from potential hazards, can make jumping more fun—but this activity must be very closely supervised.

Nor is the hyperactive child "bad." He is overly active because he can't sit still, not because he wants to drive his parents up a wall. And his parents are not bad parents. If your child turns out to have ADHD, it isn't your fault. You didn't cause his condition and shouldn't feel guilty or responsible.

There are many theories as to the cause of ADHD, though at this point, the causes of most cases are unknown. It's likely that there is more than one type of hyperactivity, each with a different set of contributory factors. Such factors may include:

**Immaturity.** Slower development of impulse control, emotional control, and fine motor coordination is common among children with ADHD. As these children mature, their behavior improves.

**Genetics.** The fact that ADHD is seen more often in some families than others indicates that heredity may play a role; in a small percentage of children with ADHD the problem may be an inherited defect in the way the body responds to thyroid hormones.

**Gender.** ADHD is four to seven times more common in boys, who tend to mature more slowly than girls.

**Pre- or Postnatal Environment.** In some children, ADHD can be traced to the mother's alcohol abuse, smoking, or use of other drugs during her pregnancy; in others, to an early-childhood illness, such as encephalitis or meningitis. There are some who believe that sensitivity to certain foods or food additives play a role in certain cases of ADHD.

**Oversensitivity to stimuli.** Some experts suggest that ADHD is the result of a child experiencing a bolt of nervous energy when exposed to seemingly normal stimuli (sights, sounds, people). That nervous energy, or tension, is vented in inappropriate ways, such as wild behavior, emotional outbursts, and recklessness.

Sometimes, a toddler is "hyper" and shows other signs of ADHD, but doesn't actually have the condition. Occasionally the overactivity is a normal manifestation of high intelligence teamed with surplus energy. Or the behavior may be a response to stress in a child's life that he doesn't understand and is unable to cope with. Perhaps his parents have an unsatisfactory relationship; or one or both are overstressed, depressed, or abusing alcohol or drugs; or the family is living in difficult, overcrowded conditions.

If you're concerned about your toddler's behavior, first compare it to that of his peers. Observe him at play group, watch him at the playground with other children, talk with his sitter or teacher at day care. What you will

probably note is that many of the others are just as wild as he. If, however, your child seems more out of control than the others, watch his behavior more closely. The following questions depict behavior that are common in ADHD children. Bear in mind, however, that they are present in all toddlers to some degree; only in the extreme do they point to a potential problem:

▲ Does he seem to have an even shorter attention span and even more difficulty paying attention than his peers? (When a story is being read, for example, does he get up halfway through and move on to another activity, while the others stay put until the end?) Is he more easily distracted from whatever he is doing—whether it's a game, a television show, or a meal?

▲ Does he seem to have more difficulty following simple instructions than do others his age? Does he appear *never* to listen? Keep in mind that language disorders sometimes masquerade as ADHD.

▲ Is he overly talkative, demanding, and emotional, with frequent outbursts of crying, screaming, hitting, or other signs of frustration that seem out of proportion to the triggering event? Does he often interrupt or intrude on others? (This behavior may also surface in toddlers whose mothers or primary caregivers are depressed.)

▲ Does he have more trouble sitting still than most toddlers? Is he constantly "on the go," taking no rest periods? Does he sleep very little? Is his sleep restless, with a lot of flailing and kicking?

▲ Does he often behave recklessly (running into the street, grabbing for a hot cup of coffee, punching a strange dog), without considering the possible consequences of his actions?

▲ Does he demand constant attention?

## RELAXATION TECHNIQUES FOR TOTS

· · · · · · · · · ·

Sometimes, a bundle of energy can become so overwound that constructive channeling is no longer possible. When this happens, it's best to begin the unwinding process promptly. Try relaxing your toddler with any of these soothing techniques:

▲ Hugging, cuddling, or massage

▲ Soft music, with or without lyrics

▲ Selected, low-key video tapes

▲ A relaxing story

▲ A warm bath (only with adult supervision)

▲ A whirlpool bath (only under adult supervision; do not use a hot tub, which is dangerous for young children)

▲ Playing simple puzzles (but only if your toddler doesn't tend to be frustrated by them)

▲ Doodling, painting with a brush or fingers, drawing with crayons or chalk

▲ Clay play

▲ Baking or cooking (with adult supervision)

▲ Water play

▲ Watching fish in fishtank

▲ Petting a gentle pet (if the child isn't afraid) or a stuffed animal

▲ Interaction with a calm parent or caregiver

▲ Simple parent-child meditation, for an older toddler (you both lie down, close your eyes, and picture quiet, pleasant places; you'll need to guide your toddler at first: "I'm thinking about the beach . . .")

Once your child has calmed down, try to determine any underlying cause for the wild behavior and see if you can find a way to deal with it and prevent a repeat.

---

▲ Does he resist adult authority and persist in misbehaving, despite warnings? Is his play with others regularly punctuated by fights and disagreements?

If you responded "yes" to at least three of the above questions, consult your child's doctor. Be aware that it's unlikely that he or she will even consider a diagnosis of ADHD at this age. The possibility of ADHD isn't usually seriously considered until a child is two or three years old, and a diagnosis generally isn't confirmed until age five. Nevertheless, the doctor may want to assess your toddler's behavior by taking a thorough history (including a review of what is going on in the family), observing your child, and performing some standard psychological tests. A thyroid screening

($FT_4$ and thyrotropin) may also be recommended.

Right now you need some help in minimizing the effects of your toddler's out-of-control behavior on himself and on your family more than you need a diagnosis. Preventive management today may help to head off full-blown ADHD and avoid the damage to your child's self-esteem that frequently results from this condition. These suggestions will help with any particularly wild toddler, not just those who are destined for a diagnosis of ADHD:

▲ Examine what's going on in the family to be sure that stress or the illness (emotional or physical) of a family member is not triggering your child's symptoms. Seek help from your doctor or your child's doctor if you or another family member is depressed or otherwise not well.

▲ Emphasize the routine; schedule meals, naps, outings, snacks, bath at the same time each day. Injecting order into your toddler's life may help slow his frenetic pace. So will calm and quiet in the home.

▲ Don't set your toddler up for failure by putting him in impossibly demanding situations (a formal dinner in a fancy restaurant, tea in Aunt Fanny's antique-filled living room, a long movie or live performance, a lengthy religious service) where sitting still and/or keeping quiet are a must and where he is certain to have difficulty.

▲ Avoid using physical punishment or physical restraint, such as tethers (except when life and limb are at risk), but do set limits (see page 47). Even more than most children, the hyperactive child, with his runaway impulses, needs help with control—it is frightening to the child to be out-of-control. Your careful controls will help him begin to develop his own. Limits, of course, should be reasonable. You can't expect any toddler, particularly one who is very active, to sit still for extended periods. Anticipate and allow for plenty of activity, and hold off your commentary unless it spills out of bounds. Discipline should be consistent and firm, but loving (see page 119). State reprimands positively rather than negatively: "Jumping on the bed is not safe. Let's see if we can pretend to sleep on the bed," or "Can you jump on the carpet?" instead of "Stop jumping on that bed!").

▲ Help your toddler to gradually improve his attention span. One way is to set short-term goals and help him meet them. For example, sitting at one task for two minutes. To increase your chances of success, pick a time when your toddler is relatively calm and well rested.

Be sure there are no distractions (radio, TV, other children, an open window, or a favorite action toy). Then say, "Let's see if you can sit in your seat until the buzzer goes off. You can draw or look at a book or do a puzzle or play with a game. When the buzzer goes off, you will get a dinosaur sticker" (or other suitable reward). Set the buzzer for two minutes and encourage compliance. When your toddler shows he can sit and focus for two minutes, increase the time gradually, a minute at a time, up to ten minutes—or even more, if that seems realistic. Make a game of it and your toddler is likely to want to succeed.

▲ Praise quiet play. If your toddler spends a few minutes looking at a book or playing with a puzzle, give him the applause he deserves. Encourage such play, even if it only lasts for brief periods.

▲ Help your toddler improve his basic skills. Frustration often leads to wildness. Learning how to dress himself, ride a tricycle, or catch a ball, for example, will help reduce his frustration with not being able to "do it myself" and help to lower the overall level of frustration.

▲ Give your toddler methods to cope with his feelings. When he's sad (or angry, scared, or frustrated), assure him that it's okay to have strong feelings, and help him find ways he can help himself feel better. Suggest: running, jumping, climbing in the backyard; hitting a punching bag or inflated figure; dancing; lying down to listen to a favorite tape; and some of the other ideas on page 171. Tell him he can always come and cuddle in your arms.

▲ Stress safety. Make sure your toddler has a safe space—preferably a large outdoor area—in which to play and burn off energy several hours each day, and that he is always closely supervised during play. Be sure to keep a sharp eye on him when you go on outings away from home. Dress him in brightly colored clothing so that you can easily spot him in crowded places. Learn first aid (see page 658) so that you'll be prepared for times when even the best preventive measures can't prevent his injuring himself.

▲ When traveling, bring along a plentiful collection of distractions and take frequent activity breaks. Just stopping occasionally for a snack isn't enough. Make some opportunity at each stop for your toddler to run around.

▲ Recognize that your child may not need as much sleep as the typical toddler his age, and don't try to force him to sleep longer than is natural for him. In the evening, discourage roughhousing, overstimulation, and excessive noise. Establish a nightly bedtime routine (see page 68), with plenty of time to unwind, and relaxing activities, such as massage, a warm bath, soothing music, a very gentle story. Be sure his sleeping conditions (room temperature, lighting, noise levels) are ideal. In cold weather, heavy pajamas or blanket sleepers may help to keep your toddler comfortable even when he's kicked off all the covers.

▲ Take charge of your toddler's diet. The issue is controversial, but some parents and physicians believe that removing sugar and additives (and in some cases, certain foods) from a hyperactive child's diet can, at least in some instances, make a big difference in his behavior. Since this dietary treatment is perfectly safe, it's worth a try. If this approach doesn't work in a month or so, try another.

▲ Watch for possible environmental contributors to the problem, including carbon monoxide (is your car's tailpipe leaky, for example? Does your furnace flue need cleaning?) and lead (in tap water or paint, for example). Although it's not clear that such factors are implicated in the development of ADHD, they should be eliminated for other health reasons (see page 628).

▲ Take care of yourself. Parents of very active children often find themselves run ragged, especially if they are at home all day with their highly charged charge. Try to get as much assistance as you can as often as you can from your spouse, another family member or friend, or a baby-sitter. You might also try exercise and/or relaxation techniques to ease the tension. The more relaxed you are, the better equipped you will be to deal with your toddler and to help him to cope.

▲ Love your child as he is (at least he'll never be boring) and don't label him ("Here comes Dennis our Menace"). If you let him know that you expect the worst ("I can't take you anywhere—you always wreck everything!"), that's probably what you'll get. Instead, be positive ("I know you are going to try to play very nicely today"). Help your child to channel his excess energy constructively and chances are that he will be able to use it to accomplish a lot in life.

If the doctor believes that your child is showing early signs of ADHD, more formal treatment may be recommended. If available, a special nursery school program for ADHD children may be suggested. Though controversial because the evidence isn't clear, many parents have found special exercise programs and play therapy helpful in reducing the energy spurts and other symptoms associated with hyperactivity. Medication (because of potential serious side effects in young children) is usually reserved for school-age children; it is only prescribed earlier when a young child is totally unmanageable. Megadoses of vitamins, sometimes touted as an alternative treatment, are not recommended at any time and can be dangerous.

# UNDERACTIVITY

*"I thought toddlers were supposed to be active, but mine just sits and plays quietly, while everyone else her age is running, jumping, and climbing."*

Toddlers are easy targets for stereotypes—probably no other age group (with the possible exception of adolescents) acts as predictably. While generalizations are less easy to make about babies, preschoolers, or schoolchildren, a notorious niche has been carved for toddlers in the annals of child behavior. Say "toddler," and the clichéd associations trip easily off the tongue: negative, rebellious, tantrums, grabby, opinionated, stubborn, perpetual motion.

But as with all stereotypes, there are exceptions that don't fit the mold. While most toddlers are, at times, stubborn and stormy, some are always calm and cooperative. While many are grabby, others are remarkably giving. While some are aggressive in their play, others are gentle and noncombative. And while most toddlers are bundles of ceaseless energy, forever on the go, others are content to sit and watch the world whirl by.

Like all human beings, toddlers are individuals. Your toddler's innate temperament dictates who she is and what she isn't. Nagging about her inactivity, faulting her placid personality, or comparing her to more active toddlers won't change her, but could damage her self-esteem as well as exacerbate her aversion to activity. Instead, accentuate her positive traits—compliment her on her drawing, her choice of books, how carefully she finished a puzzle. And whenever she joins the movers and shakers or does a little moving or shaking on her own, offer her plenty of praise and encouragement.

Keep in mind that even though being a tranquil observer instead of a whirling dervish is perfectly fine most of the time (and probably a lot easier on your nerves and your household), it's important that your toddler gets an adequate amount of physical activity—if only for her health's sake. American children tend, as they reach school age, to become less and less active, spending more and more of their unwinding time in front of televisions instead of outside playing. Encouraging activity now doesn't guarantee that your toddler will end up fit for life, but it's a good place to start. So even if she hears a different drummer, try to get your toddler to do a little marching (and other physical activities, as described on page 296). Instead of running, climbing, and roughhousing, she may prefer dancing, walking, jumping rope, and when she's three or older, dance, movement, or gymnastics classes.

If your toddler chronically resists all activity, check with her doctor to be sure it isn't because she's unwell or depressed. Also be sure the problem isn't inadquate stimulation (see page 78) or lack of opportunity for exercise. If she's being mesmerized by television for hours every day, or is confined to a stroller whenever you leave the house, or is bombarded at home with a continuous barrage of restrictions ("Don't touch that!" "Stay off this!" "Get out of there!"), she may be inactive because she has no other choice.

Assuming she's well and has plenty of opportunities to behave like a toddler, don't be concerned by her calm nature. Continue to cheer on her present behavior, applaud her when she does get energetic, and encourage her, in a nonjudgmental way, to be more active.

## UNCLEAR SPEECH

*"Our toddler has become a regular chatterbox lately. But I don't think there's a word she pronounces correctly. Does she need speech therapy?"*

Faulty (and always adorable) pronunciation at this stage is more the rule than the exception. Few children, even those with large vocabularies, speak clearly in the middle of the second year. Often, no one understands them but their own parents and other regular caregivers. It's not until a child reaches age three that you can expect most people to understand most of what she says.

The reason is the inability of most children to adequately manipulate their tongues and lips at this age, maneuvers needed to produce most consonant sounds. (Try reading this paragraph aloud without using either your tongue or lips and you'll see what your toddler is up against.) When a toddler can't produce a particular sound, she substitutes one she can handle. So a child who has trouble with "d" but no difficulty with "g" may call her father, "gaga." Another may say "dute" for "cute," "ditty" for "pretty," "hewwo" for "hello," and "biper" for "diaper." Consonant blends are also troublesome, so "flower" may become "fower," "tree," "tee," "shoe," "stoo."

Most children continue to mispronounce some consonants and mix up others well into the fourth year; some don't get all the sounds sorted out until they are ready for kindergarten or even first grade.

Support, rather than pick apart, your child's efforts to communicate, no matter how imperfect her speech is. When she says, "I wuv you," you can respond with, "I *love* you, too." But don't try to get her to repeat the word correctly. The more pressure you put on her, the more nervous she will get about speaking. This kind of anxiety can lead to loss of self-esteem and, in some cases, to stuttering (see page 388).

For how to recognize signs of true speech problems in toddlers, see page 178.[4]

## DELAYED LANGUAGE DEVELOPMENT

*"We're concerned that our little girl has only a few words at this age. Most of her playmates seem much further advanced."*

All children learn speech in the same order: first words, then phrases, and finally, sentences. Beyond that, each child's speech development is unique, proceeding according to her own personal timetable, sometimes speeding up, slowing down, or plateauing for a while. Which is why comparisons to other children your toddler's age (and even to your own toddler six months ago) can be misleading. A child who was the first in her play group to use words may *not* be the first to start linking words together in sentences. In fact, a child who was relatively late to speak might accomplish this first.

Sometimes toddlers who are physically precocious—the early walkers, climbers, jumpers, ball-throwers—are later talkers; they put so much of their energy and concentration into physical exploits that they have little left over for verbal exploration. Lack of stimulation (or its opposite, excessive pressure to perform verbally) may also inhibit the

---

4. Children with hearing, neurologic, or other medical problems often have trouble being understood, and this is sometimes mistaken for a sign of a low IQ or learning disability. Appropriate speech therapy, begun early and geared to their interests, allows these children to develop to their full potential.

development of language. So can a well-meaning family that anticipates a toddler's every wish before it is spoken. Whatever the reason, however, once they get started, late talkers often quickly develop mature speech. Because they're older when they begin, they may have better pronunciation, a better intuitive grasp of grammar, and a larger vocabulary (which was quietly building up all along).

It's true that many nineteen-month-olds use a couple of dozen words regularly, but some, like your child, are language beginners. Many late talkers suddenly bloom linguistically over their next few months; others won't, until they're closer to age two. In the meantime, most will use a host of nonverbal language (see page 75) to communicate with others.

To be sure, however, that there isn't something more than a slow timetable at work here, observe your toddler's response to your speech. Does she understand questions ("Do you want a drink?"); follow simple commands ("Put that book back, please"); respond to statements ("We're going bye-bye now")? Also note her ability to communicate nonverbally (through pointing or grunting, for instance) when she wants something to eat, a toy that's out of reach, the TV turned on, her diaper changed. If she understands what is said and is able to communicate her needs and wants (albeit wordlessly), you needn't be concerned about her speech.

Discuss any doubts with your child's doctor to evaluate the advisability of a hearing test or a formal assessment of language skills by a certified speech and language pathologist.[5] If testing confirms either a hearing problem or a significant language delay, it's important to start your toddler on speech therapy as soon as possible, both to protect her self-esteem and to head off any problems that might crop up when she goes to school.

*"I've noticed that most of the toddlers in my son's play group are putting words together. He has a pretty large vocabulary—maybe a hundred words—but he mostly uses just one word at a time. Only occasionally does he throw in a two-word phrase. Shouldn't I worry because he isn't speaking in sentences yet?"*

Not at all. Your son's language development is not only on schedule, it's a bit ahead of schedule. Some children his age are just uttering their first words and most have only a couple of dozen in their repertoire; only a few have begun speaking in complete sentences. It's not until somewhere around the second birthday that most children begin combining words into meaningful sentences. Usually, brief phrases come first, two-word combinations such as, "go out" or "pick up" or "more milk." Then come basic sentences, with subjects and verbs, such as "Bobby go out" or "Dada pick up" or "Brooke wanna drink." On average, more grammatical language doesn't appear until close to the third birthday.

For now, as long as your child uses at least a few words, seems to understand what is said to him, can follow simple instructions (such as, "come here" or "give Mommy the book, please"), and is able to communicate through a combination of single words, sign language, and body language, you can feel confident that his speech development is within the normal range.

You can encourage sentence development by avoiding baby talk and using full sentences in conversation with your son. Rephrase his one-word comments in

---

5. Thanks to a 1986 federal law, affordable testing and treatment for speech, language, and hearing problems are available for developmentally challenged infants and toddlers. Check with your state or local health or education department for information on specific programs.

sentence form: When he says, "Cookie," respond with "Do you want a cookie? Here is a cookie." Ask him questions that require more than a yes or no answer: "Where is the book?" "What are you playing?" Read simple rhyming books to him; once he's heard one several times let him finish the final rhyming word on each page. Then move on to letting him fill in the last two or three words of each rhyme, then finally to the whole last line.

Be careful, however, while you're encouraging your child's language development that you don't communicate the message that he's lacking because he doesn't carry on adult conversations. Pressure to hurry speech development not only won't work, it's likely to backfire. A pressured toddler may simply clam up. Just relax and enjoy talking to your child; before you know it, you'll have the added pleasure of his talking back.

# MEEKNESS

*"Everyone else in my daughter's play group grabs toys. My daughter never does; she just stands there and lets other kids grab from her. I'm afraid she'll never be assertive."*

The meek may inherit the earth, but in a room full of toddlers, they'll always be short on toys.

Although it's part of the typical toddler profile, for some toddlers, grabbiness just doesn't come naturally. And, in most cases, that's okay. Aggressive behavior, while common, is not at all essential to normal toddler development—nor is it required for the development of a strong sense of self. Grabby toddlers don't necessarily end up as grabby adults; neither are the easy-going,

mild-mannered tots of today fated to be the grown-up doormats of tomorrow.

It's important that a toddler be aware that she has rights, not that she be loud and forceful in sticking up for them. As long as your daughter doesn't seem bothered by the grabby behavior of those around her, is content to pick up another toy when someone grabs the one she's been playing with, and seems to feel good about herself and happy with her social lot, there's no reason to try to change her ways. It's possible that, with time and increasing social exposure, and with some encouragement and guidance from you, she'll grow more assertive. Of course, it's also possible that she won't. Many successful people speak softly and get along without a big stick; if your daughter's destined to be among them, accept her gentle ways—even if your personality tends to be more forceful.

If, however, your toddler seems distraught by all the grabbing, yet unable to defend herself against the onslaught of tiny hands, come to her rescue. Step in when she's being confronted by an aggressive peer. If, for example, a playmate is trying to wrestle a toy from her, encourage her to stand up for her rights with: "I'm playing with this now." Chances are that at first you'll need to show her how it's done, and speak for her: "Sarah's playing with that now." If the toy's been grabbed away, don't grab it back (two social wrongs don't make a right; the idea is to teach her to assert her own rights, not to tread on the rights of others). Instead ask for it nicely but firmly, and repeatedly, if necessary: "Sara wasn't finished playing with that doll yet. She would like to have the doll back, please." If the playmate obliges, be generous with the thank you's. And when your child finishes playing with the toy, encourage her to offer it back to the grabber. If the playmate refuses, don't get into a tug-of-war. Instead, find something else for your toddler to play with, and stand by to be sure that isn't purloined as well.

Try this tack whenever your toddler appears to be in social distress: when she's been pushed out of line at the slide, had her shovel commandeered in the sandbox, had her riding toy hijacked at the playground. As you watch from afar, give her the opportunity to speak for herself before you speak for her; your goal is to teach her to handle such encounters on her own. Extra doses of social experience may help; she may be so used to being at home, around those who respect her rights and property, that she finds grappling with life tricky out there in the toddler jungle (or on the toddler jungle gym). While she's learning, let her be herself—and be grateful you don't have other parents complaining that your child is always abusing theirs.

## THE PHYSICAL TODDLER

*"My son is very physical when he gets together with other toddlers. Not in an aggressive way, but he doesn't give the other kids much space—poking and prodding the way he does—and they sometimes get upset."*

Young roughhousers like your son don't mean any harm when they squeeze, jab, or poke another child. They are just busy exploring their environment "first-hand"—and those other children are part of that environment. So they poke and prod away, without a thought to propriety or the feelings of their targets.

An additional developmental factor makes physical contact an integral part of toddler socializing: limited ability to communicate verbally. Instead of "Hello, how are you?" a toddler may greet his

buddy with a poke in the arm. When he wants a playmate to come to his room to see his new truck, he may literally drag him up the stairs. And when he's ready for a friend to leave, he may just push him out the door.

The problem is that this physical "dialect" is neither universally understood nor appreciated by other toddlers. Though their own verbal skills are limited, they are used to having those around them—parents, caregivers, siblings, and so on—communicate with words. A friendly poke can be easily misinterpreted as hostile, demanding retribution, which in turn is often not well received. "Do unto others as you would have them do unto you" is definitely not a toddler credo.

What's a poker's parent to do? Try the following:

▲ Assess the quality of your physical interaction with your toddler. Do you yank him roughly by the arm when he refuses to leave the playground? Do you lead him away by the ear when you find he's been misbehaving at play group? Do you poke and pinch him playfully? Toddlers are great imitators, and such actions on your part could be inadvertently teaching him to do the same to his friends. Modify them if you want your toddler to learn to be gentle with others.

▲ Take a look at what you let him get away with. Many parents allow a fair amount of exuberant physical contact at home, giving the child the confusing message that it's okay to play rough with them, but not with others. When he yanks at your ear or bops you in the belly with his head, let him know you don't like it (even if it really doesn't bother you): "Please don't do that. It hurts." Explain that certain kinds of contact (hugs, pats, handshakes, high-fives) are acceptable, and other kinds won't be well received. And explain that words are the best way to get someone's attention. Practicing with stuffed animals or dolls may help, too.

▲ Help your child develop good social graces to go with his good intentions. Get a little formal with him. When he comes into your room in the morning, greet him with, "Good morning, it's nice to see you," or an equally polite phrase. Greet him graciously, too, perhaps with a handshake, after his nap, after a play date, or when he comes home from the park. Put on your best company manners with other members of the family, too, and encourage your toddler to do likewise. See page 130 for more tips on teaching manners to toddlers.

# WANDERING OFF

*"Whenever we go out with our son, he wanders off to look at this or that, or runs ahead of us toward the street. We're constantly chasing after him, and we're going crazy."*

For many parents of toddlers, the chase is on from the moment they step outdoors. Their young are off and wandering—to the left if their parents want to go right, to the right if their parents want to go left, full speed straight ahead if there's a busy intersection on the horizon—turning outings into ordeals and leaving parents exhausted and frustrated.

A wandering toddler is not propelled by a compulsion to annoy his parents (well, maybe sometimes), but rather by a drive to discover. That his path to discovery often isn't the same as the path to the supermarket doesn't quell his quest; that running off or running ahead might prove hazardous doesn't daunt him.

While it's necessary to protect your toddler's safety and your schedule (the road taken by toddlers inevitably adds an hour to your traveling time), it's also im-

portant to encourage his explorations and start teaching him some basic street smarts. To accomplish all of these goals, you'll need to begin thinking in terms of two kinds of outings:

**Parent-in-charge outings.** Some places can be dangerous to explore: a crowded sidewalk, the middle of the street, a garbage-strewn curb. When safety is at stake or when you've got a lot to do in a little time, your toddler's curiosity has to take a back seat. Make it clear in such situations that he can't run ahead or lag behind, that he must hold your hand or ride in his stroller. He *may* be more willing to agree to these stipulations if you keep him occupied with questions, challenges, or observations about what you see around you, or with a round of silly songs or nursery rhymes (see page 156).

Like a puppy, a toddler doesn't know enough to keep himself safe in potentially dangerous situations. He needs to be taught not to run out into the street or into a crowd without you; to stop, look, and listen at every corner; to never go out into the street alone; to "stay" when and where you ask him to. Your child can only learn these lessons if he has the freedom to walk on his own some of the time. If during a training session he even *looks* as though he's going to head for the street or insists on running off when you've said he must stay at your side, pop him right into the stroller (if you have one along), seat him on a bench for a "time-out," or firmly take hold of his hand. Calmly explain that he can't walk on his own unless he's big enough to obey the rules. Be firm and consistent in enforcing those rules—allowing him to run ahead one day and not the next will doom the lessons to failure. Teaching a toddler to be reasonably street-smart takes a lot of patient but resolute repetition of the same rules, outing after outing, but it's well worth the effort. Children and puppies who don't develop this street sense (and those always on a leash invariably don't) are at the greatest risk of quite literally running into trouble.[6] (Teaching your toddler to obey consistently used "traffic" commands, such as "stop" and "go" or "red light" and "green light" will also help keep him safer.)

Your toddler also needs to know that wandering away from you may result in getting lost. Explain this, but don't frighten him unnecessarily by warning him ominously of strangers who might "steal" him or police officers who might arrest him if he leaves your side.

**Toddler-in-charge outings.** When time permits and the route you're taking is reasonably safe, let your toddler guide the expedition, dawdling to kick a mountain of snow or rushing ahead to see a cat slink under a parked car. Just strap yourself into some running shoes, and be ready to take off when he does. He will get infinitely more satisfaction (and gain more knowledge) out of his explorations if you play co-explorer with him—pointing out that the acorn he found came from that oak tree, or that the dandelion he's smelling is yellow, or that the rock he's proudly displaying in his palm has some shiny spots in it that are called mica. Don't, however, monopolize his investigations or overintellectualize his findings; remember, he's leading the excursion.

And, of course, provide constant supervision—it takes only a second with your head turned away for a toddler to run off into a crowd or dart into the street.

---

6. When your toddler reaches the end of his third year, you can begin letting him race ahead *if* he agrees always to stop at an agreed-upon spot—say, at the corner—and wait for you, and if he can be counted on to keep his word. But it won't be until about age ten—when a child's visual perception is mature enough to be able to judge the speed and distance of an oncoming vehicle—that he will be able to safely cross a busy street by himself.

# RESISTANCE TO NAIL TRIMMING

*"My daughter's fingernails and toenails get very long and dirty. But she screams and struggles whenever I try to trim them."*

The average toddler would rather eat her spinach than have her fingernails trimmed—and for a couple of good reasons. First, having parts of her pared off by a clipper or a pair of scissors (even when they're wielded by a friendly parent) is frightening. A young toddler isn't likely to understand (or remember) that nails don't hurt when they're cut or that they grow back afterwards. Second, the process, for safety's sake, requires restraint. Not only must she sit still (that most dreaded posture), but she must have her hand and fingers held motionless by an enveloping adult hand.

Still, nails need trimming. Not only can long nails harbor dirt and germs even when hands are clean, but they can, both intentionally and inadvertently, cause harm to self and others. Though nail trimming may continue to be a hotly disputed issue for many years to come (until it's replaced by nail biting or cuticle picking), these tips may trim some of the trauma:[7]

**Use a blunt instrument.** Baby scissors, with their blunt safety tips, or small nail clippers, are good for trimming a toddler's nails. Don't trade these in for pointed nail scissors at least until your child's old enough to be counted on to hold still.

**Turn the scissors on yourself, first.** Make a point of trimming your own nails (as well as those of other willing family

---

7. Nibbling a young child's nails off with your teeth is not a good idea; it could tear the cuticles and teach a toddler that nail biting is an acceptable habit.

members) in front of your toddler; it's possible she'll want to be next in line when she sees how much fun you're all having.

**Perform underwater.** Warm water soothes toddlers and softens nails, both of which may make nail trimming less of a trial—so try scheduling your toddler's next manicure when she's fresh out of the tub.

**Try a game.** A made-for-nail-trimming version of "This Little Piggy" may be

distracting and help replace screams with giggles.

**Trim in her sleep.** Chances are your toddler will be most cooperative about nail trimming when she's asleep. Work quickly and quietly, and it's possible she won't wake up during the procedure. If she's a very light sleeper and/or has a hard time going back to sleep once she's been awakened, it will be easier to do the job right before it's time for her to get up—just in case.

# WHAT IT'S IMPORTANT TO KNOW:
## How Toddlers Make Friends

Friends. For many adults, the word summons up dozens of cherished childhood memories: lazy summers at the lemonade stand, after-school games of hopscotch and tag, touch football on a crisp autumn afternoon, sledding and snowball fights after a winter storm, notes passed back and forth in second period math class. Everything good about being a kid.

Others have memories of being on the sidelines, watching the friendships of others blossom, feeling lonely and left out. Everything difficult about being a kid.

Whichever snapshots of their own childhood the word "friends" conjures up, parents are generally eager for their toddlers to make friends and begin experiencing the joys of friendship. They often despair when their toddlers don't play "well" at play group, when they won't share their toys, when an afternoon with a peer at the park turns into World War III.

Hang in there. There are friends in your toddler's future. But the kinds of

friendships you may remember longingly don't form in toddlerhood; at this age, children aren't capable of sociability in the adult sense. Still looking out largely for themselves, the majority of toddlers don't yet possess enough empathy for others to work or play harmoniously in pairs or groups. To most toddlers, the only person who matters is "me." The only part of give-and-take they can relate to is "take." The only agenda that counts—theirs. On top of all that, toddlers are still shaky on matters of right and wrong, almost totally devoid of social graces, and basically unable to control an impulse (to throw a toy at a companion, to knock over someone else's block tower, to pinch the nearest arm when they are irked).

Nevertheless, over the next couple of years these little antisocial beings can learn to share and cooperate, to be sensitive to the feelings of others, to work out disagreements with words instead of aggressive actions, in short, to become friends. You can help your toddler reach that point by doing the following:

**Focus on self-esteem.** Children need to feel good about themselves before they can reach out to others (see page 292).

**Socialize with your child.** The first chance toddlers get to socialize is with their parents—at the dinner table, on outings, at the playground, reading, playing games—so remember to model appropriate social behavior. Don't always be the magnanimous parent, giving your child first choice from the crayon box, first crack at the puzzle, first bite of the muffin you're sharing. And when playing a game, don't always let him or her win. Encourage sharing, sticking to the rules, saying "please" and "thank you." Chat about what you are doing and what you see in a way that elicits your toddler's response and helps develop conversational skills. Without making it obvious, role-play the kind of social situations your child may find him or herself in.

**Start one-on-one.** It's easiest for most toddlers to socialize with only one other child at a time. So arrange frequent one-on-one play dates, especially if your child tends to have difficulty in larger groups. Select children your toddler seems to get along with best, keep the play dates short (limit them to about an hour at first), and be sure there is plenty to occupy both children. Never, however, force a playmate or a play date on your toddler; it's not only unfair, but it's likely to meet with rebellious resistance.

**Stay away from threes.** For toddlers, three isn't just a crowd, it can be a social nightmare. Too often, one of the three (usually the least aggressive and least socially experienced) in the group will suffer at the hands of the other two.

**Don't expect togetherness.** Unless your toddler has been in a play group for a while, most interactions with peers will be what is known as "parallel play"—

they'll play side by side in the same space, but not necessarily together. But look closely, and you'll see that this parallel play really serves as the primitive beginnings of social interaction. While two children may be chattering loudly to themselves, seemingly absorbed in their own play, each is also aware of the other. You can catch them sneaking looks at, observing, imitating, and, of course, often grabbing from their playmate. By the end of the year you can expect to see more actual interaction.

**Encourage cooperative games.** Some activities lend themselves to togetherness more than others. Block play, ball-playing, pretend play (such as "house" and "hospital"), hide-and-seek, tag, joint creative projects (baking, arts and crafts), circle games ("The Farmer in the Dell," "London Bridge"), and games that require taking turns will give toddlers the experience they need to begin fostering friendships. Of course, en route to cooperation there may be an increase in less desirable social behaviors, such as grabbing, hitting, hair pulling, and pinching. (See page 190 for tips on dealing with aggressive behaviors.)

**Stay neutral, and stay nearby.** Since toddlers can be unpredictable and volatile, supervision is critical in early socializing. Keep a constant watch on toddlers at play, even if all seems relatively quiet, and be ready to step in should conflict suddenly break out. Don't take sides, even if it seems to you that one child is clearly in the wrong. Simply break up the skirmish calmly, and march the troops off to a quiet, supervised activity. For more on dealing with play-group combat, see page 190.

**Don't get personally involved.** It's difficult to learn to put your child's feelings first, but that's a big part of what being a parent is all about. Letting your feelings get in the way of your child's social life just isn't fair. If you're gregarious and your toddler is shy, don't let your frustration over this state of affairs make you force socializing on your child or criticize wall-flower behavior. Nor should you let your friendship with another parent, embarrassment that your child is the one acting up, or anger that your child is getting hit, put your toddler at a disadvantage.

**Enlist support.** If your child is in preschool or day care, but is nevertheless hesitant to mix, turn to his or her teacher for help. The teacher can often encourage a more gregarious child to draw the shy child into the group (this usually works better than the teacher trying to do the same job).

**Accept your toddler's social style.** Each child, like each adult, has a very personal approach to socializing. Some are social butterflies from the start, others are destined to be happier with just one or two close friends at a time. Some rush into every new situation with enthusiasm, others hold back and prefer to watch from the sidelines until they're ready to make a move. Remember, too, that some children, the *observers,* never seem to want to make that move at all (see page 215). And that's okay.

**Take note of potential problems.** Annie may want to make friends, but her aggressiveness gets in her way. Jamie may want friends, too, but his shyness is the obstacle he has to overcome. It makes sense to help a child deal with such issues as aggressive behavior (see page 190) and shyness (see page 405) before they cramp his or her socializing style.

**Offer plenty of opportunities for practice.** Children who have lots of early exposure to other children—in a large family, in a play group, on their block, in day care—tend to socialize sooner. If your toddler hasn't yet had such experience, consider joining or forming a play group (see page 108 for ideas on how to do that), or at least making frequent trips to the local playground in addition to arranging single play dates.

**But apply no pressure.** Parental pressure to socialize at an early age doesn't usually help toddlers win friends and influence people. In fact, given the contrary nature of this age group, it could make them more antisocial. Given plenty of time and space your toddler will ultimately discover that child's play is, in fact, fun.

# WHAT IT'S IMPORTANT FOR YOUR TODDLER TO KNOW: Kindness Toward Animals

**W**atch toddlers interact with animals and you might conclude that tykes are indeed made of snips and snails—and created to *pull* puppy dogs' tails. And to torture sleeping cats, chase flocks of pigeons away from their after-noon snack, and squash slugs wriggling their way across the sidewalk.

Unfortunately, toddlers tend to be even less kind to animals than to playmates. Animals—like vegetables, minerals, and peers—are merely objects to be manipulated for a toddler's private entertainment, investigated for his or her personal edification. That these creatures have long ears, tails, fur, feathers, or other interesting appendages or coverings, makes yanking, tugging, squeezing, squishing, pursuing, and tormenting them all the more tantalizing.

But just because animal "torture" is all in fun for toddlers—they certainly don't realize they're doing harm—doesn't mean it's acceptable behavior. Teaching young children to have respect for the rights of animals is as important as teaching them to have respect for the rights of humans. Not teaching your child to be kind to animals can have an adverse effect both on the animals your toddler may encounter (many creatures are defenseless against curious toddlers) and on your toddler (when an animal who *can* defend itself does so). To start your toddler off right:

**Go hunting for animal friends.** Exposing toddlers to different kinds of animals in different settings can help them feel more comfortable around winged or four-footed creatures. And we tend to be kinder to those we are comfortable with. Happy and safe hunting grounds include cousin Jan's house with her four cats, Grandma's with her three dogs and the parakeet, pet shops, the zoo, the park.

Books are another wonderful place to hunt for new and different animal friends. Start with simple books with large, easy-to-distinguish pictures of familiar farm and domestic animals. Then move on to more exotic species. Toddlers particularly love books about baby animals or about animals they are familiar with (such as dogs and cats).

**Bring home your "catch."** Having a pet at home can greatly enhance a child's empathy for animals. If you don't already have a pet, consider adopting one. A couple of goldfish, a guinea pig, or a hamster will be easier to care for than a dog or cat while your toddler is young,

but will be less fun (see page 72). If you're not up to the responsibilities of owning an animal, try hanging a bird-feeder in your backyard, deck, fire-escape, or tree on your street. Your toddler will enjoy watching the feathered friends as they stop for a nibble.

**Teach the fine art of petting.** A toddler's natural inclination is to overwhelm animals with their own special brand of kindness. It's up to you to show your toddler how to safely and humanely hug and pet an animal. Start by using your toddler's stuffed animal collection for demonstration purposes: "See, this is how you pet Big Bird—gently, slowly. That's right. That's the way he likes it." Or have your toddler pretend that he or she's a kitten or a puppy that you can pet and scratch gently (alternatively, *you* can be the pet and let your toddler do the petting).

If your toddler has a fear of animals, take steps to eliminate it (see page 84). And be sure to teach caution with unfamiliar animals (wild or domestic), as described on page 85.

**Tell your toddler where it hurts.** Explain that "animals have feelings, just like people, so we must be careful not to hurt them." That "tail pulling, ear pulling, fur pulling, kicking, dragging, and foot-trampling hurts animals as much as they would hurt you."[8] And that such actions are absolutely off limits.

**Teach the gentle art of observation.** Watch an ant crawl up its hill and disappear, a squirrel cracking open a peanut, a butterfly fluttering from flower to flower. As you watch, talk about the ant going home to its family, the squirrel being hungry for its lunch, the beauty of

---

8. Some animals are more forgiving of physical insult than others, but just about any animal is capable of revenge; for your toddler's sake (as well as the sake of the animals in his or her life), this lesson is vital. See page 85 for more on keeping your toddler safe around pets.

the butterfly. Occasionally, catch an insect in a clean jar to observe it more closely. But always let it go, explaining that it wants to go back to its home. Strongly discourage the kind of wildlife-bashing that is often common among junior naturalists: squashing worms trampling ants, and pulling wings off of captured moths.

**Don't let your toddler tease.** Teasing animals—waving a bone out of a dog's reach, pretending to eat out of the cat's bowl—is not only unkind but potentially dangerous. Explain that it's not nice to interrupt an animal's nap, bother one while it's eating, or take away its toy—animals don't like being treated rudely any more than people do.

# CHAPTER EIGHT

# *The Twentieth Month*

## WHAT YOUR TODDLER MAY BE DOING NOW

*By the end of this month,[1] your toddler
. . . should be able to (see Note):*

▲ dump an object in imitation (by 19½ months)
▲ use a spoon/fork (but not exclusively)
▲ run

**Note:** If your toddler has not reached these milestones or doesn't use symbolic play and words, consult the doctor or nurse-practitioner. This rate of development may well be normal for your child (some children are late bloomers), but it needs to be evaluated. Also check with the doctor if your toddler seems out-of-control or hyperactive; uncommunica-tive, passive, or withdrawn; highly negative, demanding, and stubborn. (Remember, the child who was born pre-maturely often lags behind others of the same chronological age. This develop-mental gap continues to narrow and gen-erally disappears entirely around age two.)

*. . . may possibly be able to:*

▲ combine words
▲ identify 1 picture by naming
▲ name 6 body parts
▲ throw a ball overhand
▲ speak and be understood half the time
▲ use 50+ single words

*. . . may even be able to:*

▲ identify 4 pictures by pointing
▲ build a tower of 6 cubes (by 19½ months)

---

1. The twentieth month begins when a child is nineteen months old and ends when he or she is twenty months old.

# WHAT YOU MAY BE CONCERNED ABOUT

## *AGGRESSIVE BEHAVIOR*

*"Our son seems to be very aggressive with his playmates—hitting, pushing, grabbing. Since we're pretty mild-mannered people, we find this surprising and disturbing."*

It's too early to start worrying about your apple falling far from the tree. Your son's aggressive behavior is more likely a characteristic of his age, and to some extent, his gender, than a predictor of his future personality.

There are a host of reasons why many toddlers tend to be belligerent:

**A drive for independence and identity.** Like a small fish in a pond that keeps getting bigger and bigger (expanding to include play groups, playground sandboxes, day care, tot art and exercise classes, preschool), the toddler asserts himself aggressively in order to feel larger and more important.

**Frustration.** Upset when he can't seem to control his environment as much as he'd like, this little control freak responds the only way he knows how: by biting a playmate in an effort to get her to release the toy he wants, by slugging another who snatches the toy he's playing with, or by pushing a sibling out of the way when she's blocking his view of the television set.

**Egocentricity** and its frequent companion, *lack of empathy.* Most toddlers halfway through the second year still see themselves as the center of the universe and still display an inability to care for others. Many still view their peers as objects (to be handled, mishandled, or discarded as convenient) rather than as equals with feelings.

**Lack of impulse control.** Even once a toddler understands (somewhere around age three) that hitting hurts, he may not be able to stop himself from doing it. You may want to slug someone at the office who is giving you a hard time, but having long ago internalized the restrictions society has put on such behavior, you resist the urge. A toddler has the same impulses when he believes someone is giving him a hard time, but he has not yet learned to control them.

**Inability to foresee consequences.** He may be sorry after he's made a playmate cry, but he doesn't have the foresight yet to avoid that unpleasant result by not hitting his friend in the first place.

**Lack of social proficiency.** Human beings are born with combative tendencies, which help them to survive. But social skills are not inborn; instead, they must be learned through experience, by emulating older role models, by trial and error, and by the repeated instruction of others.

**Lack of verbal facility.** A toddler's actions almost certainly speak more loudly (and more clearly and successfully) than his words. He doesn't yet possess the verbal proficiency required to express his feelings, needs, or desires, or to talk himself out of or through a social problem. So, not surprisingly, he often resorts to more physical means of expression.

**An interest in cause and effect.** An occasional episode of hitting may be no more than a scientific social experiment: "Hmm, when I hit Ryan, he cried; will the same thing happen if I hit Josh?"

# FIGHTING AGGRESSION

**· · · · · · · · · ·**

Children don't learn to tame their aggressive instincts naturally. They need to be taught. Here's how you can help:

**Lay down the law.** When the opportunity arises—a character on a TV show hits another, you see children fighting, your child takes an angry swing at you—make it clear that the use of physical force when you're angry, to settle a dispute, or to get what you want, is unacceptable, and that harming another person is wrong ("We do *not* hit other people!"). This message will take many repetitions to get through, but eventually your child will come to accept it as gospel.

**Avoid a heavy hand.** It's tempting to drag a reluctant-to-leave toddler out of the sandbox, give a sidewalk dawdler a little push when you're late for an appointment, or deliver a quick smack of retribution for kicking a playmate, but such tactics breed toddlers who also get heavy-handed when angry or under stress. Try, instead, to handle your toddler in a firm but gentle way, even when you're annoyed or impatient.

**Opt for middle-of-the-road discipline.** The most aggressive kids usually have aggressive and punitive parents who discipline them physically or push-over parents who don't discipline them at all. Discourage aggressive behavior by avoiding these extremes. For practical disciplining tips, see page 119. If you have an aggressive child, it's particularly important to set limits and supply structure, while providing plenty of opportunity for your child to make choices.

**Pay attention to good behavior.** Hitting, biting, and other aggressive behaviors are often calls for attention by children who are frequently ignored or unappreciated when they're behaving well. A child who feels he or she doesn't get enough attention may do anything to get it, including beating up on playmates. Give plenty of attention (praise, smiles, hugs) for good behavior and very little (other than stopping the behavior and disciplining appropriately but matter-of-factly) for bad.

**Validate your child's feelings.** *All* feelings, unlike some actions, are okay (see page 333).

Acknowledge that it's okay to feel angry when you don't get your way or when a friend grabs a toy from you, but it's not okay to hit.

**Encourage translating feelings into words.** Anger. Disappointment. Jealousy. Sorrow. Fear. Eventually children should learn to express these and other feelings with words rather than through aggressive actions. See "Talking it Out" on page 196.

**Provide opportunities for venting.** Pent-up frustration, energy, or anger can explode in aggressive behavior or be released through a variety of appropriate outlets (see page 171). Teaching your child to express feelings in safe, healthy ways will help lessen his or her need to indulge in physical outbursts.

**Recognize when your toddler's had it.** At any age, a tired child can behave irrationally. During the toddler years, when irrationality reigns even under the best of circumstances, fatigue almost always robs reason. Determine the time of day that your child tends to be overtired (for most toddlers, this is late afternoon and early evening) and avoid play dates then or monitor them closely. For planning play dates to minimize problems, see page 193.

**Banish boredom.** Idle toddlers can do major mischief. Anticipate your toddler's ennui whenever possible, and respond with a challenging game or activity before hellish behavior breaks loose.

**Minimize frustrations.** Much of the aggressive behavior of toddlers is related to frustration. Helping your toddler to learn the skills needed for everyday living—social skills, dressing skills, playing skills, eating skills—may reduce not only frustration but aggression.

**Diffuse with soothing activities.** Take breaks each day (especially during high-stress times) for quiet cuddling, singing, reading, and other pacifying pastimes; these can help diffuse a toddler's aggression. The other plus: They're relaxing for you, too.

**Set a nonaggressive example.** If, over time, your toddler sees you handle your own disagreements maturely, using words instead of actions, compromise instead of confrontation, he or she will be likely to learn to respond the same way. Whenever you can't manage to be a model example—when you lose your temper with your spouse, a friend, or your child—make sure your toddler sees you admit your lapse and apologize for it, too. If you have trouble keeping your own cool, see page 751.

**Know when to stay out of it.** A few harmless rounds of pushing or shoving isn't likely to hurt anyone and doesn't require adult intervention. Step in when you're not needed and you're depriving the children involved of valuable social experience. In such situations, they are learning through experience how relationships work, how to make them work, and what happens when they don't work. If frustrations are building faster than social skills, however, you can try a little lesson in negotiation and compromise. If, for example, two children are fighting over a truck, you can bring over another truck, keeping both parties happy. Or if the dispute is over the one and only riding toy in the house, you can recommend "taking turns." If the children refuse to compromise, impose a settlement: "If you can't take turns, I have to put the tricycle away." Then propose a fun, adult-supervised alternative activity.

**Know when to step in to it.** If a confrontation escalates into outright violence (with hitting, biting, or pinching), or it's clear that someone is going to get hurt, step in and stop it promptly. Focus your immediate attention on rescuing (and if need be, comforting) the victim rather than admonishing the perpetrator. If your child was the attacker, distract the victim with another activity, and take your toddler aside. Calmly, and without anger, explain *briefly* that the behavior— whether it was hitting, biting, punching, kicking, pinching, or pushing—is not acceptable, and why ("You hurt Patrick when you kicked him"). You can warn of consequences if the behavior is repeated ("You'll have to sit next to me on the bench for a time-out," or "We'll have to go home"), but avoid such threats unless you intend to follow through—or your attempts at modifying your toddler's behavior will be futile. (For what to do when the other child is the aggressor, see page 374.)

**Don't take sides.** Some parents tend to side with their offspring in battles with other children, others side with the playmate, and still others try to ascertain who threw the first punch. Though all these parents have good intentions, none of these positions is best. It's unfair to always take one side or the other. And assigning blame when toddlers fight is tricky, since both parties always consider themselves in the right and the first punch you see may not have been the first thrown. So even when intervention is called for, you should play mediator rather than defender or judge and jury. It doesn't matter who started the fray, it's up to you to see that it is brought to an end.

**Don't commence hostilities of your own.** Losing control is frightening enough to a toddler without having to face a scolding—or worse yet, a spanking—by a large, loved authority figure. Bullying your child into obeying creates a bully role model to emulate.

**Skip the lecture.** It's important to let a toddler know that it is wrong to hurt others and to use brute force to resolve conflicts. But droning on and on after a belligerent play date ("You didn't play nicely at all . . . You were so mean to your friend . . . Your friends won't like you anymore if you're so mean") or coaching him for half an hour before a play date ("Now, don't forget not to push. Make sure you share. No hitting or biting") isn't likely to change a child's behavior. In fact, such lectures may cause a toddler to tune out, may increase his inner anger and thus aggressiveness, or, by "rewarding" negative behavior with attention, may encourage more of the same.

**Change the pace.** When aggressive behavior breaks out, peace can often be restored by switching to a parent-supervised activity (such as snack-making, painting, or a circle game) or otherwise redirecting both parties' attention elsewhere. Regularly interspersing parent-supervised activity with one-on-one play often prevents fighting by ending free-play sessions before the players have reached the limits of their good behavior.

**Always supervise.** Even the best-behaved children sometimes get physical with their peers. So all toddler play sessions should be closely supervised.

Normal toddler aggression can be aggravated by external factors. Eliminating or minimizing such factors, when possible, can reduce your child's aggressive behavior. These factors include:

**Lack of sleep.** Perhaps a child recently gave up his nap and hasn't yet adjusted. Or he has been awakening at night a lot because his molars are coming in. Or he simply had trouble settling down the night before.

**Hunger.** Going for long, long stretches between meals and, possibly, consuming foods high in sugar (this last possibility is controversial) can trigger misbehavior.

**Illness.** A suddenly aggressive child may be coming down with a virus or another kind of bug, or may just have gotten over one.

**An unsettling life change.** Anything from a new sitter to his parents taking a vacation without him can make a toddler more edgy than usual.

**Inadequate attention.** Children who don't garner a lot of notice when they are good often "act up" in order to win notice.

**An overly hostile environment.** The violent behavior of people a toddler is close to—parents, caregivers, or sibling—can fuel aggression in that child.

**An overly controlling environment.** When the toddler is never allowed to make choices, his frustrations may increase, and with them, his aggressive tendencies.

**An uncontrolled environment.** Laissez-faire parents who don't set limits may unwittingly encourage out-of-bounds behavior in a toddler, including aggression.

**Impaired parents or caregivers.** When those around a child suffer from depression, abuse alcohol or drugs, or have marital or other problems that interfere with normal parental functioning, the child may display his distress by acting out.

While you may be able to understand where your toddler's behavior is coming from, you certainly can't allow it to continue uncensored. There are a variety of steps you can take to help him control his more aggressive instincts (see page 190).

If, in spite of your best efforts, your toddler's behavior doesn't mellow; if his aggressiveness seems more entrenched than that of his peers; if he seems never to be remorseful when he misbehaves or he seems to enjoy hurting people and animals, talk to his doctor. If a behavior disorder is the problem, delaying treatment could lead to impairment of a child's self-esteem in the short run (problem children do not feel good about themselves) and to more serious difficulties later on.

Sometimes, parents view aggressive behavior as not only normal but desirable. They assume that the aggressive child will grow up to be the successful adult. That's not always so, because aggressive children generally aren't popular either with peers or with teachers and other authority figures. It's the child who is assertive and knows how to get what he wants without stepping on the toes of others who is most likely to do well in life. Some parents also assume that the toddler who seems not to have an aggressive bone in his body is headed for a lackluster future; again, this ain't necessarily so (for a peek at the meek, see page 179).

# PLAY-DATE GUIDELINES

· · · · · · · · · ·

Put two toddlers in the same room together, and anything can happen—and usually does. From tug-of-wars over the plastic shopping cart to enchanted moments in the play kitchen, play-date sessions can represent toddler togetherness at its worst and best.

To bring out more of the best and less of the worst in your toddler's play dates:

**Don't overschedule.** A play date once or twice a week gives toddlers something to look forward to, but play dates every day, or even every other day, may become too much like work. It's hard for toddlers to share and play nicely with peers; asking them to be on their best social behavior every day isn't really fair. If your child is in preschool or day care every day, play dates should probably be even less frequent to avoid socializing burn out. It's simple to tell if you're overscheduling: If your toddler looks forward to play dates and goes off cheerfully, you're doing well; if he or she refuses to plan them with you, is weepy en route, and acts up during the dates themselves, cut back.

**Keep play dates brief.** Most toddlers, especially those under two, have little tolerance for long play sessions. While your toddler's still getting the hang of it, limit sessions to an hour or an hour and a half.

**Time them judiciously.** Avoid socializing at the time of day when your toddler is ordinarily cranky or overtired, at nap time, or just before meals when hunger may trigger a bad mood. Ideally, toddlers should be well rested and well fed before a play date.

**Don't invite a crowd.** Making company out of two is challenge enough for a toddler; making it out of three or more may approach the impossible.

**Make a big deal of hosting.** Kids have a harder time when the play date is in their own homes—they have to share Mommy (or Daddy), as well as their home, room, toys, and food. Be sensitive to this stress factor. Dubbing your toddler "host" and assigning fun responsibilities—answering the door, meeting and greeting, doling out toys (having your toddler set aside some "special" toys that won't have to be shared may make sharing the rest less painful), choosing and preparing the snack (in advance), and planning special activities — will provide a feeling of control and should make hosting play dates easier.

**Start with a snack.** Not only is snack a non-threatening activity (as long as both children receive the same amount of juice and the same number of crackers and cheese cubes), but if it's a nutritious nibble, it'll help curb hunger-induced crankiness.

**Supervise, supervise, supervise.** Overseeing the play date will not only keep the children from hurting each other, but prevent their getting into potentially dangerous mischief.

**Have a contingency plan.** One-on-one play may work well for a while, but in case it dissolves into one-on-top-of-one, be ready to distract the combatants with an adult-directed activity.

**Keep your expectations realistic.** At this age, even a few minutes of harmonious play is an achievement—anything beyond this is gravy. Sometimes you'll get the gravy; other times, you won't.

**Don't push togetherness.** If the kids are happy playing side by side or even in different rooms, leave them be. Don't expect or demand that they play together. You can encourage interaction with the right activities—toddler games, playing "house," building with blocks.

**Be a wary child's home base.** Some children need a lap to crawl back into periodically, or an occasional reassuring touch or friendly smile that says, "I'm here, don't worry."

**Be prepared to deal with conflict.** Read about keeping the peace on page 190 so you'll know what to do when a fight erupts. And if "sharing" is a major cause of friction, regularly use a timer for taking turns.

# HAIR PULLING

*"When my daughter doesn't get what she wants, she pulls hair."*

For many toddlers who lack a grip on vocabulary, gripping and yanking the closest handful of hair is the primitive expressive vehicle of choice. The reasons (see page 189) are the same as for those other primitive forms of expression, hitting and biting, and so are the interventions (see page 190).

With the toddler who pulls hair, it may also help to give her a shaggy stuffed animal to tug at to her heart's content; let her help pull weeds in the garden (put gloves on her and supervise closely to make sure that she doesn't munch on the pickings); allow her to brush your hair; make a fuss over fixing her tresses.

# BITING

*"At the playground, my daughter bites when someone won't share a toy with her."*

The choice of weapon may be different, but a major motive is the same for biters as for the hitter. Frustrated by her inability to manipulate her environment or to make her needs and desires clear, and aware that her words won't have the "bite" she'd like them to have, she simply uses her teeth. Besides, a good bite always seems to get a good reaction.

But toddlers sometimes bite for even more innocent reasons. For the curious toddler, biting may be just another inquisitive sensory experiment ("How will Jessica's shoulder taste? Will it taste the same as Spot's ear? Or Mommy's arm?"). For the affectionate one, biting

*Toddlers often express their frustration as well as demonstrate their considerable lack of social skills with hair pulling, pinching, biting, or another form of aggressive behavior.*

may be her own unique way of saying "I love you." Biting may also be a case of monkey-see, monkey-do. Or a sign that boredom, fatigue, sensory overload, or hunger has set in; that teething pain is provoking the need to nibble on something (or someone); or that a child is ill-at-ease in a new setting. And, as is the case with many other negative behaviors, biting can represent no more than a call for attention.

Probably because biting seems so primal, so animal-like, parents are often more horrified when their toddlers bite than when they hit. Yet the biter is no more vicious than the hitter. In fact, a majority of toddlers engage in some biting sometime between their first and third birthdays. For most, it never becomes chronic; a few experimental chomps seem to satisfy the urge. But for some, the behavior persists, and continues to cause problems.

The following precautions, plus the tips for dealing with toddler aggression

## "TYPE A" KIDS

..........

A recent study suggests that the "type A" personality can surface in early childhood, either as a result of nature or nurture. The study found that one in four children showed "type A" traits—were high-strung, intense, impatient, quick to anger, very competitive. As preschoolers, these children tended to have greater rises in blood pressure under stress; when they hit school age, they were more likely to suffer from headaches, stomachaches, sleeping problems, chronic fatigue. Their behavior sometimes led to low self-esteem, poor listening skills, short attention span, difficulty socializing, and trouble in school (although given their competitiveness, some did do very well in their studies). It's suspected but not confirmed that type A children will grow into type A adults.

More studies will need to be done to confirm this theory. But it certainly couldn't hurt for parents to teach children who seem high-strung how to relax (see page 173), how to cope with the world in non-aggressive ways, and how to delay gratification (see page 136). Parents should also avoid putting pressure on these children to achieve, and instead emphasize the importance of recreation and family as opposed to the work-only ethic. Finally, it will help for parents to set a relaxed example by not running in high gear all the time—though this may be difficult for those who are themselves A types.

---

(see page 190), may help deter the Dracula in your child:

**Provide a nibble to prevent biting.** Sometimes a child bites just because she's hungry. Always give her a meal or snack (without refined sugar, which some believe intensifies aggressive tendencies in some children; see page 502) before letting her loose in a social situation.

**Never bite back.** As with hitting back, biting back is confusing to the toddler. Your bite says that it's okay to bite someone if you're angry at them, while your words say, "Don't bite." Even biting back *once* to show her how it feels isn't likely to help, since she probably isn't yet able to connect her pain with the pain others feel. Being bitten may hurt or frighten her, but it's unlikely to keep her from biting again.

**Nip biting in the bud.** Separate the biter and the victim immediately (if the victim is crying, offer comfort before you disci-

pline the biter). Don't overreact, yell, or embark on a lengthy lecture; simply take your toddler aside and explain calmly but firmly, "Please don't bite. Biting hurts. You hurt Anna when you bit her." When she bites out of an inability to communicate, help her find the words she needs to express her feelings: "I know you feel angry. It's okay to be angry, but it's not okay to hurt someone because you're angry. Let's figure out another way to make the anger go away."

**Avoid a double standard.** Some parents bite their child's toes or fingers playfully or allow their toddlers to take a nip of their shoulder, cheek, or arm occasionally—especially if it doesn't hurt much. Then, when the toddler bites a playmate, they scold. It's best to avoid any confusion by making all biting off limits at all times.

**Take biting seriously.** Some parents can't help laughing the first time their child takes a bite out of them. Almost nothing will encourage biting more. So repress your giggles.

# TALKING IT OUT

· · · · · · · · · ·

You don't have to live in Geneva or be an international diplomat to stage peace talks. And, in fact, if all parents taught their children the importance of verbal conflict resolution—the art of using words instead of physical aggression to work out frustrations and anger and work through differences of opinion—peace talks might end up the option of choice in resolving world conflicts.

Considering the limited verbal skills of toddlers, it might seem hardly worth the effort to try to teach them that words can be effective. After all, it's the fact that their words are ineffective that so often leads them to instead use their fists. But while your message might seem lost on your toddler now, sending it regularly and reinforcing it in years to come will help ensure that one day it will get through.

**Practice as well as preach.** Your toddler will get the message to resolve disputes through words rather than action faster if you send it via actions as well as words. You can set the kind of example that makes a lasting impression dozens of times every day—by discussing a problem with your spouse calmly instead of slamming doors and banging fists, by informing your neighbor that his dog has been getting into your garbage again instead of spreading the refuse on his lawn in righteous retribution, and, especially, by sitting down and explaining to your toddler what's wrong with hitting rather than hitting him for hitting.

**Do the talking for your toddler.** Right now, your toddler is probably not capable of verbally negotiating for a toy that a peer has yanked away from her, or explaining that he's feeling frustrated by his inability to fit the octagon into the shape-

sorter. So, when necessary, you can help by supplying the words. But wait until you're sure your toddler won't be able to speak for him or herself. Step in, for example, when the dispute over a coveted toy begins to escalate dangerously and suggest taking turns (a timer can help make this advanced diplomatic skill easier to carry off). Or sit down and empathize about that hard-to-fit-in shape ("Are you upset? Is that a very tough shape to get in? Maybe if we do it together, we can get it in").

**Encourage your toddler to talk, too.** Children should feel free to express feelings verbally, even negative feelings (such as anger, disappointment, and frustration). Guide your child to examine and verbalize feelings: "Why did you hit him? Are you angry at him? What made you so angry?" And don't squelch attempts at self-expression. Saying "I hate you"—unpleasant as it is for a parent to hear—is far more civilized than reaching out and punching someone. Clamping down on abusive or rude language should come later, when your child is able to discern the difference between self-expression and rudeness. In the meantime, avoiding abusive and rude language yourself will set a good example your child is likely to follow.

**Hold up other role models.** Point out peaceful interactions in the playground ("Look how nicely those children are sharing the sandbox toys"), but don't add judgmental commentary ("How come you can't get along like that?"). Look for, and read to your toddler, books that show the merits of handling disputes by negotiation. Avoid television programs and videos that show differences being resolved through violence (cartoons are notorious in this department) and favor those that try to teach children how to talk out problems.

# HITTING BACK

*"Whenever my toddler hits or bites me it makes me so angry. My immediate reaction is to hit or bite her back. I know that's not mature, but sometimes I just can't control myself."*

**N**othing brings out the child in a parent like a toddler. Even for the ordinarily cool and collected, it's very difficult to remain unruffled in the face of provocative toddler behavior. The impulse to lash back can be strong, sometimes overwhelming.

There's nothing wrong with *feeling* this eye-for-an-eye impulse—most parents experience it at least occasionally. But there are serious problems with *acting* on the impulse. For one thing, it sets a poor example (one you don't want your child to follow) of how to deal with anger and frustration. For another, it's frightening. For yet another, it can escalate into more serious child abuse. So, instead of hitting or biting back, try better responses, such as those described on pages 190 and 196.

If, once in a great while, the child in you gets the best of the adult—and your toddler gets the worst of you, in the form of a slap on the bottom or hand, don't feel guilty. But do apologize immediately and sincerely: "I'm sorry I hit you. I got so angry, I didn't think about what I was doing." If you administered a spanking out of fear for your child's well-being rather than anger, explain that, too: "I spanked you when you ran into the street because I was frightened and wanted you to remember never to do that again."

If, however, responding in kind occurs often—if one slap leads to another; if the slap is hard enough to leave a mark on your child or aims for the face, ears, or head; if you use a strap, ruler, or other object; or if you strike out under the influence of alcohol or drugs, you should talk about your feelings and actions with your child's doctor, your cleric, a family therapist, or another helping professional, or talk to someone at a Child Abuse Hotline as soon as possible.

# AGGRESSIVENESS WITH TOYS

*"Our son seems to be very wild when he's playing. He doesn't hurt anyone, but he throws his teddy bear against the wall for fun, or pummels his sister's doll. We're concerned that this could lead to violence against other children."*

**I**t actually sounds like your son has discovered a *safe* way to deal with his anxiety and the aggressive feelings it can generate. Taking negative feelings out on inanimate objects is relatively socially acceptable, preferable to taking them out on siblings and playmates, and at least as effective and satisfying. Like an adult who relieves frustration with a vigorous game of racquetball or by going a few rounds with a punching bag, your toddler is letting off steam without hurting anyone in the process. (Of course, sometimes such behavior may have nothing to do with frustration and feelings and is just a matter of a little experimentation: "I throw this teddy bear and it bounces off the wall—Wow!")

As long as there continues to be no harm done—either to persons or property—there's no harm if your toddler continues such play. Since making an issue of it is likely to intensify the behavior, it's basically best to leave it alone. But do make a point of following the tips for fighting aggression on page 190, which could prevent your toddler's behavior from escalating. If the escalation does occur, however, and your toddler begins to damage toys, furniture, or other property, or turns his violence against people or animals, you will have to set limits.

Although you shouldn't routinely intrude on your toddler's play, it may be helpful at least once in a while to point out that although the inanimate objects he abuses don't have real feelings, people and real animals do—that the teddy bear doesn't hurt when you throw him against the wall, but that a living bear (or dog, or person) would.

If your toddler's habit seems to mushroom into an obsession—if he spends more time throwing the teddy against the wall than doing anything else—discuss the issue with his doctor.

## AGGRESSIVE FRIENDS

*"The kids in my daughter's play group are very aggressive, and she always ends up being pushed around. I'm not sure whether I should encourage her to fight back or whether I should just be happy she's not aggressive."*

There's a difference between fighting back and standing up for your rights. Teaching a child to fight back is teaching conflict resolution through physical force: someone hits you, you hit back; someone pushes you, you push back; someone bonks you on the head with a toy, you bonk back. And as satisfying as that bonk-for-a-bonk might feel, it rarely eliminates the friction between the sparring parties—all it winds up resolving is which child is brawnier and tougher.

Which is not to say that you should teach your child to roll over and play victim, either. It depends, really, on how

victimized she feels. If she seems perfectly content to let a bully walk away with her booty while she finds something else to play with, there's no reason to step in at all. It's possible that her ego and self-worth aren't dependent on the possessions she's accumulated.

If, on the other hand, your toddler seems upset by the aggressive onslaughts of her playmates, she probably could use a few lessons in pest control (see page 179). And if her playmates start slugging, kicking, biting, or otherwise turn violent, she will need you to intervene. When you do step in, use the distraction of a new activity, a snack, or a change of locale ("How about we go outside for a while?"). See page 190 for ideas on dealing with fighting.

## *BREATH HOLDING*

*"Once in a while, our son will hold his breath during a temper tantrum. Yesterday, he held it for so long that he lost consciousness for a minute. Can he hurt himself?"*

Though watching your child hold his breath until he lost consciousness was undoubtedly traumatic for you, the only real damage done was to your nerves.

Breath holding, most common in the second year and usually gone by the fourth, is a behavior that frequently occurs for the first time during an intense crying spell associated with an injury or, less often, a fierce temper tantrum. At first, the child cries so hard he turns red in the face. As he becomes more distraught, he starts to hold his breath and his lips begin turning blue from lack of oxygen. If he holds his breath long enough, his skin turns blue (an occasional child will turn pale) and he passes out. Rather than being harmful, this loss of consciousness is actually the body's protective response, allowing normal respiration to resume. Thanks to this response, a child can't harm himself by holding his breath.

Besides the wear and tear on your nerves, there is one possible negative effect of breath holding: a spoiled child. Sometimes, in an effort to avoid the conflicts and confrontations that could lead to such a spell, parents invariably give in to their toddler's demands. A perceptive toddler quickly picks up on this, and begins to use breath holding as an effective weapon with which to hold his parents hostage to his whims. Not only can this result in a tyrannical toddler, but one who never learns how to handle frustration, disappointment, controversy, or limits, and is ill-prepared to deal with reality.

Treat breath holding as you would any display of temper; for help, see temper tantrums, page 336.

## *WHAT'S THIS?-ITIS*

*"About three hundred times a day, my toddler says, 'What's this?' She'll ask even when she knows the answer!"*

Curiosity, driven by an overwhelming drive to learn, is one factor that compels a toddler to ask "What's this?" The need to practice her language skills (which often makes her ask about what she already knows) is another. To the novice talker, using a phrase such as "What's this?" is more satisfying than using single words; using the phrase over and over and over again is even more satisfying.

But your toddler has yet another motivation for her broken-record style: attention-getting. It doesn't take long for a toddler to figure out that questions

yield a more substantial and sustained parental response than statements. While she might not receive more than a nod or an absent-minded, "Uh-huh," when she calls out, "Doggy!" she generally receives a full-fledged answer to a query.

Eventually, as your toddler becomes more sophisticated, she will undoubtedly tire of asking "What's this?" and move on to a more challenging (if briefer) question: "Why?" (See page 303 for tips on dealing with that challenge.) In the meantime, be patient with, and respond to, her "What's this?" When you suspect she knows the answer, though, turn the tables and ask her "What do *you* think it is?" This may spare you some tedious repetition, while challenging your toddler to think and figure things out for herself.

## *SHIFT FROM DIFFICULT BABY TO DIFFICULT TODDLER*

*"It was hard enough having a 'difficult' baby—I'm sure our daughter holds the world's record for colic and crying. But now that she's a toddler, she's not just difficult, she's impossible."*

It isn't easy to distinguish between a normally difficult toddler and an especially difficult one. After all, most parents of toddlers would describe their tantrum-throwing, negative, rebellious, ritual-loving offspring as "difficult" at times. But an estimated one in four toddlers go beyond "normal-difficult toddler behavior"—they are *more* prone to tantrums, *more* negative, *more* rebellious, *more* ritualistic.

These extra-difficult toddlers were, like yours, difficult babies who cried and fussed a lot more than other babies did

# LIVING WITH YOUR DIFFICULT TODDLER

**L**iving with a toddler is hardly ever easy; living with a difficult toddler can sometimes border on the intolerable. The stress of coping with a child who can't concentrate, or won't sit still, or won't put up with change, or won't be quiet can be daunting, draining, and debilitating. Worst of all, it can make the best-intentioned parent feel hopelessly inadequate.

Just which children are *unusually* difficult and which *typically* difficult is probably a matter of opinion. Behavior that may seem typical and manageable to some parents may be unusually difficult to others. Either way, if a child's behavior is unbearable to his or her parents, then steps need to be taken to do something about it.

Some children become difficult temporarily as they pass through transitional stages of childhood (the "terrible two's," for example) or because of severe family stress or illness, but their behavior is temporary and not inborn.

The following list describes the basic categories of difficult temperaments and how to handle them in a way that will make your life and the life of your child a lot more pleasant.* Knowing how to handle them will also help your child develop the positive aspects of his or her temperament rather than the negative.

Keep in mind that some difficult toddlers fit neatly into one category and that others display behaviors from two or more. The individual traits are stronger in some children than in others.

**The super-high activity toddler.** These children make the average active toddler seem to be operating in slow motion. They won't sit still, resolutely resist confinement (in a car seat, a high chair, even a crib), and tend to be "wild" and to lose control easily. *The posi-*

---

*This material is based on the book *The Difficult Child* by Stanley Turecki, MD, which many parents of difficult children have found very useful. His work in turn is based on the work of Stella Chase, MD, and Alexander Thomas, MD.

*tives:* Super-high activity children who learn how to harness their energy constructively can grow into adults who get a lot done and never run out of steam. *Best handling techniques:* Allow plenty of opportunity for outdoor play and for burning off energy, but insist on and enforce specific limits for safety and sanity's sake (no jumping on beds, climbing on sofas, racing down stairs, and so on). Try to stop high-energy behavior from escalating into out-of-control behavior. If your toddler seems to be working up to a feverish frenzy, take him or her aside and quietly explain: "You're getting too wild. If you don't calm down, you will have to get off the slide (put the game away, stop playing ball, or whatever)." If the frenzy continues to build, insist on a "cool-down" period, trying one or more of the techniques on page 173. Or, substitute an acceptable excess energy outlet for the unacceptable one (see page 171). Respect your child's inability to sit still, however, and try to avoid situations that require church-mouse decorum. (Also see other tips on handling the overactive child on page 173.)

**The distractible toddler.** Toddlers typically have short attention spans; the distractible toddler seems to have none at all—flitting from activity to activity, distracted by a second before fully engaging in the first. The distractible toddler seems unable to listen or pay attention to parents, teachers, caregivers, or even playmates. Lack of concentration is at its worst when the child is not really interested in an activity or what is being said. *The positives:* Such children, with encouragement, can become fascinating adults with a wide range of interests. *Best handling techniques:* Since most toddlers are pretty distractible, the highly distractible toddler may not need much in the way of special attention at this age. You may, however, be able to gradually extend such a child's ability to concentrate by discovering what subjects or activities best command his or her interest (animals, nature, babies, science, sports, cars, dinosaurs) and using this knowledge when choosing books, games, toys, television programs, videos, and movies). Avoid subjects your child obviously finds boring and don't try to force your distractible toddler to stay focused longer than he or she is able to. Keeping the house quiet and calm may also help your child to be able to pay attention longer.

Insisting on eye contact when you speak to or issue directives to your toddler is a good way of helping him or her shut out the distractions long enough to listen. To elicit full attention, say, "Please come here and sit down with me. I want to talk to you." Then, with your toddler next to you or on your lap, assume a face-to-face position, and say, "Look at me and listen to what I'm going to say." Suggest the same attention-directing technique to anyone else who cares for your child (it may help to demonstrate it as well).

**The slow-to-adapt toddler.** Even more than the typical toddler, this child craves routine, ritual, and the status quo, plays favorites with clothes, foods, and toys, and finds transition and change seriously unsettling and disturbing. Once adjusted to a change, however, these children tend to cling to the new situation fiercely (after having a tantrum when it's time to leave home to go to play group, such a child is likely to explode again when it's time to return home). They can also be stubborn and persistent, prone to prolonged tantrums, and can whine incessantly in pursuit of a desired goal. *The positives:* Slow-to-adapt children often become adults with that rare and valued characteristic of being able to stick with a chosen subject or task. *Best handling techniques:* Whenever possible, prepare your toddler for transitions by giving advance notice: "After lunch, we're going to the playground." Then, at the playground, give notice once again: "You can go down the slide one more time, and then we'll go home." An older toddler may cope better if you provide the entire afternoon's schedule in advance ("After lunch we'll go to the playground, then we'll stop at the supermarket and buy milk and bread, and then we'll go home so you can have a snack). Using a timer ("When the buzzer rings it's time to take a bath") can also help the slow-to-adapt child to better handle change. Further ease a transition by choosing the most opportune moment

to make it (waiting until your toddler has tired of playing with the shape-sorter before moving on to dinner, for instance). When a sudden change in plans is unavoidable, be especially patient and supportive.

For this toddler, changes in surroundings and belongings can be as distressing as changes in schedule. While it isn't feasible or wise to avoid such changes entirely, you should try to avoid those that aren't necessary. Instead of buying all new styles and colors when your child moves up to the next clothing size, select those that are as similar to the old familiars as possible. Let your toddler wear the same outfit every day if he or she wants to—even if it means buying in duplicate (one to wear and one to wash). Let your toddler eat the same foods every day, too, if that provides security; vary meals only as much as you need to in order to ensure good nutrition. When changes must be made—a beloved pair of sneakers must be replaced by a new pair—try to give your slow-to-adjust toddler time to adapt. Talk about the new sneakers for a few days before shopping for them. Allow some time for getting to know the new sneakers (to look at them, handle them, carry them around), instead of insisting they be put on fresh out of the box. Be patient if your toddler is clingy or hesitant in new situations, and provide support as needed. Don't apply pressure or use labels: "Oh, Sam is so shy." For more tips, see shyness, page 405; rituals, page 244; clothing problems, page 279.

**The initial-withdrawal toddler.** When faced with new people, places, situations, food, or clothes, this child withdraws, cries, becomes clingy, and, if pushed, may have a tantrum. *The positives:* Such a child is more likely to grow up to be an adult who carefully analyzes situations before jumping into them and so is more likely to make wise decisions (not likely to be the kind of person to meet someone on Monday and run off to get married on Friday). *Best handling techniques:* As with the slow-to-adapt child, try whenever possible to serve the same foods, buy new sizes of similar clothing, repaint the bedroom the same

*(continued on next page)*

*(continued from previous page)*

color, and so on. If it's necessary to purchase something new, have your toddler help pick the item out and try to allow for an adjustment period before it must be used. Give the initial-withdrawal toddler plenty of time to acclimate to new situations; be as supportive, patient, and understanding as possible. Advance preparation—spending some time talking about an outing beforehand, showing your toddler pictures of the person or place you're going to visit before you actually go—may help lessen the withdrawal reaction in these situations. Also see tips for dealing with the slow-to-adapt child (above) and with shyness (page 405).

**The high-intensity toddler.** This child is always heard—even when not seen. When a high-intensity child is happy, miserable, angry, frustrated, tired, everybody within earshot (and then some) knows it. *The positives:* This "loud" extrovert often does well in careers where being heard is important (such as politics, show business, and sales). *Best handling techniques:* If you can teach your child to have a relatively quiet "indoor" voice and a less-restrained "outdoor" voice, you've accomplished a lot and spared him or her repeated bouts of hoarseness (see page 288 for tips on doing that). If your toddler can't seem to modulate volume at all, try some sound-deadening techniques at home (see page 205). Also provide your toddler with plenty of opportunities for exercising his or her vocal cords in a socially acceptable fashion—singing along with tapes, making animal noises, reciting nursery rhymes.

**The unscheduled toddler.** As infants, these children never settled into a regular feeding or sleeping routine. Their parents never knew when they would waken, go to sleep, nap, or be hungry, cranky, or in good spirits. As toddlers, the guessing game continues. These children, not surprisingly, often have sleep problems. *The positives:* Unscheduled children can handle unpredictable situations well; they may thrive as adults in jobs with the kind of crazy hours that would drive other people crazy (radio and television, print journalism, show business, health services, for example). *Best handling techniques:* First of all, don't count on ever getting the unscheduled child onto a predictable schedule. If schedules aren't important to you, life with this toddler will be considerably easier. If they are important, keep some routines, but bend them as necessary. For example, if your toddler isn't hungry at dinnertime, invite him or her to join you for a snack, but don't force the issue of a main meal. Offer the meal later, when your toddler is finally hungry. Serve breakfast, but if your toddler's not hungry yet and it's time to go to day care, don't push it. (Just let the teachers know that he or she may be ravenous at snack time.) At night, maintain a bedtime routine (vary it a bit each night, if your toddler seems to like it better that way), but when you tuck your child in, don't insist on sleep. Tell your toddler she only needs to lie quietly. Provide a few books, toys, or a tape of lullabyes to enjoy until the sandman makes his irregular appearance.

**The low-sensory-threshold, highly sensitive child.** The socks are bunched up, the sweater itches, the coat is too warm, the clock ticks too loudly, the lamp is too bright, the dog too smelly, the peanut butter too "bumpy," the ice cream too soft. While most toddlers are finicky about some things, low-sensory-threshold children are finicky about almost everything. These children may be super-sensitive to light, sound, colors, tex-

and exhibited an extreme form of colic. They were tough to handle as infants, and are even tougher to handle as toddlers.

Knowing you're not alone—that some 25% of parents are in the same rocky boat—may not help a whole lot. But commiserating with these parents, swapping stories and exchanging tips, may. So look for other parents with difficult toddlers and consider setting up a support group. (Post a notice about starting such a group on the bulletin board at your pediatrician's office—you may find yourself swamped with responses.) Learning what makes your difficult child difficult and what

tures, temperature, pain, tastes, smells; they're disquieted by things that other people may not even notice. *The positives:* These children can utilize their keen senses in a variety of useful and important creative, artistic, and scientific ways. *Best handling techniques:* As with other difficult temperaments, understanding and acceptance are crucial. The bunched-up socks truly *are* uncomfortable, the sweater really is itchy. The irritations aren't imagined or overstated. Acknowledge this in what you say to your child: "I know you can't stand it when the street noises are so loud" or "I know that garbage smells really bad to you." And acknowledge it in what you do, too. Buy stretch socks that fit well but not too tightly and that have no bulky seams at the toe, choose soft cotton clothes that are less likely to itch (and wash them before the first wearing to soften them up), avoid clothes that have scratchy inner seams, rough linings, and high or binding necklines, and remove all labels that might rub against your toddler's super-sensitive skin. If tying and retying shoelaces to get them "just right" takes too long in the morning, opt for Velcro closings on the next pair. Try to remember (or even keep a written record) of how your child likes various foods; the meals you prepare will be less likely to be rejected. If your child continually complains of being "warm," try to dress him or her in layers or more lightly; avoid confining or very heavy coats. If certain colors make your toddler see red, avoid those colors when shopping for clothes or when decorating. If odors are a problem, install an exhaust fan in the kitchen, use unscented products (from bathroom tissue to hair spray and cleaning products). Try, if possible, to adjust the levels of light and sound in your home to your sensitive toddler's comfort. For example, you can substitute an electric clock for one that ticks, put a dimmer on the living-room lamp, keep the volume low on your radio (and TV and tape player), and consider using soundproofing techniques, where practical (see page 205). For more on dressing the difficult toddler, see page 279.

**The unhappy toddler.** These children don't smile a lot as infants; as toddlers, they may whine and complain more than others, and may be said to have "serious" dispositions. *The positives:* The serious, sober child may not be as much fun to be around as the happy-go-lucky tyke, but by nature may be more likely to succeed academically, and later in life, in a wide range of fields where seriousness is appreciated. *Best handling techniques:* The best you can do for a child who's serious and moody is accept him or her, and to recognize it's not anyone's fault.[**] Scolding or punishing your child for a negative frame of mind is unfair—it's out of his or her control—and is only likely to make the mood more solemn. You can, however, minimize problems by dealing with other temperament issues your toddler may have at the same time (such as poor adaptability), which may be contributing to the seeming unhappiness. And smile a lot. Maybe you can rub the edges off your child's negative moods.

---

[**]If, however, a toddler who was a happy baby suddenly seems unhappy or even depressed or one who laughed a lot now rarely smiles, the mood change is more likely to be related to stress rather than temperament. Check with the doctor. Also be sure that your toddler's change in mood isn't in response to harsh or otherwise improper treatment by a caregiver or a recent change in the family.

you can do about it is also helpful. The box starting on page 200 describes the basic difficult-temperament types, as well as some techniques for coping with each.

Keeping the following points in mind may help you learn to live with—and value—the special person she is:

▲ There are many personality "types" and many combinations of types—and there are always some individuals who represent the extremes in each category. Extreme traits need not be viewed as abnormal or negative. The very qualities in a toddler that drive her parents to distraction at age two may make them very proud of her at twenty-two. Extremely difficult children, when handled with wisdom and patience, often end up becoming extremely motivated, hard-working, successful adults.

▲ Your child's inborn temperament is not her fault. She cannot change who she is to any great degree; when she is acting according to her nature, she is not being "bad" or trying to torture you—she's being herself. It's as unfair to punish her or criticize her for behavior that's not within her control as it would be to punish her for her eye color or her inability to carry a tune. (Your child's inborn temperament is *not* your fault, either— even if she seems to have inherited that temperament from you or from someone in your family.)

▲ Accepting a child for what she is rather than constantly struggling to change her into something you'd like her to be will help you to appreciate and nourish her inborn nature, to make it an asset rather than a liability. It will also help your child's self-esteem and sense of worth and value.

# WALL ART AND OTHER DESTRUCTIVE DRAWING

*"My toddler loves to draw with crayons, but not on paper. Today I walked into his room and found that he'd scribbled on the walls with bright red crayon. Should I take the crayons away from him until he's old enough to use them properly?"*

In your toddler's mind, he *is* using them properly—he's drawing with them. By confiscating the crayons you're depriving him of artistic expression. Drawing

should be encouraged, not banned.

This doesn't mean that you should give your mini-Michelangelo the go-ahead to take his crayons and turn your home into his version of the Sistine Chapel. Your toddler needs to know that drawing on walls isn't acceptable.[2] But you do need to be mindful—and respectful—of his intentions, which, in the case of his bedroom mural, were artistic, not malicious. So, aim to redirect his crayon creativity:

▲ When you catch your toddler in the midst of redecorating, count to ten before responding. Remember that he is probably very proud of his work, and expects those who love him to be proud, too; attacking his efforts may not only sting his self-esteem but discourage future artistic endeavors. Or, if he enjoys the attention his wall art stirs up, it may prompt him to repeat the deed.

Instead of assailing your toddler's art work ("Look at the terrible mess you made on the wall!"), calmly explain that his choice of canvas was a mistake ("That's a beautiful picture you drew, but you shouldn't have drawn it on the walls").

▲ Then, while his creative juices are still flowing, sit him down, and show him that "paper is what we draw on." The larger the sheet of paper, the better the chance his crayons will stay on it, rather than straying onto the floor, table—or a nearby wall. A roll of paper, which can be unrolled as he fills up space, can be particularly satisfying to the toddler artist. Taping the paper to the floor, a table, or an easel will keep it from moving out from under his inexperienced touch. Don't hover over him as he works, but do keep an eye on him to be sure he doesn't return to working on the wall.

---

2. Slip-ups will happen. If the walls in your child's room aren't washable, you might consider repainting with nontoxic washable paint (see page 623.)

---

### TRY IT QUIET

· · · · · · · · · ·

Whether the problem is a loud toddler, whose noisiness is driving you to distraction, or a sensitive toddler, who finds any kind of noise disturbing, some in-house sound-proofing can help. Try well-padded carpeting, heavy drapes, cork walls or oversized cork bulletin boards, inside-wall insulation (which can sometimes be blown in), banks of large house plants (such as spider plants and yucca). Re-allocating space in the house so that your sensitive toddler plays far from the sound of dishwasher, washer, and dryer, and so on, may also help. To keep outside noise outside, try insulated drapes or window shades, weather stripping, storm windows or double-paned replacement windows, and plenty of insulation in the building walls, if possible. If you are in a house, hedges, trees, and shrubs can block street sounds.

---

▲ To further reinforce the message that walls aren't for drawing on, have him "help" clean up with his own wet cloth (if you use any cleanser on his cloth, be sure it's nontoxic). Don't have him use a sponge; he might take it into his mind to nibble off and swallow a piece.

▲ Make time every day for supervised drawing, so that your toddler has plenty of opportunity to express his artistic nature. When you can't supervise his art projects, keep crayons out of his reach.

▲ Finally, display his art work proudly on your walls and refrigerator. Appreciation of his "on paper" creations is likely to inspire him to turn his artistic energies in that direction.

## AVERSION TO CLEANLINESS

· · · · · · · · · · · · · · · · · · · · · · · · · · · · · · ·

*"Our daughter can't stay clean for two minutes—no sooner do I change her clothes and wash her up, then she's filthy again. What should I do?"*

Give up. Being a toddler is a dirty job (getting dirty is part of the job description) and your toddler's got to do it. Expecting her to stay clean is like expecting her to stay still; neither is compatible with being a toddler, both would stifle her growth by inhibiting her ability to explore and experiment. And scolding will only fire up a contrary desire to get down and dirty.

So loosen up. Concentrate only on necessary hygiene: hand washing before eating, after toileting, or when she's gotten her hands onto something really raunchy (plain dirt doesn't count); a nightly bath; and the avoidance of such germ breeding-grounds as bird baths, street puddles, and animal droppings. And be sure that her play clothes and shoes are washable and sturdy enough to tolerate rough usage. See page 154 for tips on hand washing.

## PLAYGROUND TIMIDITY

· · · · · · · · · · · · · · · · · · · · · · · · · · · · · · ·

*"Our son refuses to use the slide or swings at the playground. He seems to be frightened and sticks close to the sandbox."*

Your child's caution could be a result of foresight: A sign that he's beginning to recognize the potentially dangerous consequences of letting go and skidding down that slippery slide or flying skyward in a swing. Or it could be hindsight: Perhaps he remembers taking a fall off the slide or the swings during a past playground visit, and hasn't yet regained his confidence. Or a combination of empathy and egocentricity: It's possible that he's seen another child take a bad tumble off the equipment and fears that he may be next. Or perhaps it's simply his nature: Some children are innately more cautious than others.

Whatever the reason, respect your toddler's fears; don't belittle them— or him. Each time you go to the playground, casually offer him the opportunity to try the equipment. Having you go along for the ride (you can hold him securely while you zip down the slide together, or let him cling to you while you swing slowly on the big children's swing) may make the equipment less frightening. If he turns down your offer or wants to call it quits after one trip down the slide or a couple of swings on the swing, don't pressure him to reconsider. Reassure him that the swings and the slides will be there when he's ready to play on them and that in the meantime the sandbox is a perfectly fine alternative. And applaud his sand castles and roadbeds rather than deriding his lack of interest in the rest of the playground.

But while you shouldn't force your toddler to face his fears, a little gentle manipulation may help him to overcome them. The equipment at the playground may be intimidating, but small indoor versions may not be. Borrow such equipment, or let your toddler try it out at a friend's house, at a play gym, or the waiting room at his doctor's office. Again, don't push, but do encourage. Look for books that feature children with similar fears or ones with children playing on slides and swings, jungle gyms and teeter-totters, and read them to your child, but without disparaging comments or comparisons to his own behavior. (For a discussion of the most common toddler fears, see the facing page.)

Be sure you aren't fostering his fears yourself by being hypervigilant and overprotective when he dares to be adventurous. Or by overreacting to his falls. Or by carrying him down a flight of stairs instead of showing him how to climb down by himself. Instead, build your toddler's confidence by arming him with the skills for safely negotiating playground equipment. With you as back-up, encourage (but don't compel) him to practice climbing up and down the ladder to the slide; if its height is too forbidding, launch him on a kitchen stepladder. If he's willing, sit him in the swing and show him how he can make it move a little by himself—by bending his knees; sometimes control can instill courage. Promise you won't push him unless he wants you to, and then keep your word. Let him explore the lowest levels of the jungle gym, again with you at his side. Show him how to grasp the bars and how to move his hands from bar to bar. Help him get the "hang" of horizontal movement before you suggest that he attempt vertical. But, again, let him progress at his own comfortable pace; if he's reluctant to progress at all, accept that.

Even the least adventurous children, with parental patience and support, eventually learn to use basic playground equipment. There will always be some children, however, for whom swings and slides (and later, roller-coaster rides and other daring activities) will never sit that well.

For now, sit back on the park bench, relax, and count the blessings of being a parent to a cautious child. For one, you don't have to sit nervously at the edge of that bench, the way you would overseeing a little daredevil. (For playground safety rules, see page 643.)

# OVERSENSITIVITY

*"Whenever I scold my son, he seems to fall apart. How do I get my point across without hurting his self-esteem?"*

Gently. Every child, like every adult, is an individual—with a temperament all his own. And it's that temperament that determines what kind of disciplinary style will work best. In the case of a tough, aggressive child, an extra-firm approach might be called for (you might even want to make your voice sound more stern than you feel). In the case of a happy-go-lucky child, a balance of humor and firmness is usually successful. And in the case of a particularly sensitive child, a particularly easy-going approach may be the best way to go.

That doesn't mean, of course, that the sensitive child shouldn't be disciplined or required to observe rules, but simply that the person meting out the discipline should speak softly and carry a soft stick. When dealing with a sensitive toddler, use all the guidelines for discipline beginning on page 119, but particularly emphasize the following:

▲ Be sure that rules are consistent and that he knows what they are; this will minimize the need for scolding.

▲ Avoid raising your voice or using a harsh tone when disciplining. Instead, use humor, distraction, or another indirect approach (see page 156), whenever possible. And don't forget the magic power of "touch"—take him on your lap, hold his hand, or pick him up—to let your toddler know that your love is still present even while you're offering correction.

▲ Use constructive suggestions or explanations rather than direct criticism when possible: "You should ask your sister nicely to give you your truck back instead of hitting her." Never make the criticism a put-down of your child; criticize only his behavior: "Hitting your sister is not a nice thing to do" not "You're a bad boy for hitting your sister." Avoid long lectures.

▲ As you should with any child, avoid physical punishment. But go even further in being sure that when you handle your toddler physically, you do it gently, whether you're breaking up a toddler tug-of-war over a toy or trying to keep him from dawdling on your walk to the grocery store.

▲ Let your toddler know that you are correcting him because you love him and know he can do better, but don't expect more from him than he is capable of doing.

# WHAT IT'S IMPORTANT TO KNOW:
## Dealing With Toddler Fears and Phobias

Things that go bump in the night. Things that go woof. Things that get plugged in, make loud noises, suck up everything in sight, or loudly flush down the drain. To an adult, they're routine, harmless, taken for granted. To a toddler, they can be downright terrifying.

Fear is a common phenomenon in early childhood, particularly between the ages of two and six, though the most common fear triggers change with a child's age. For the infant and young toddler, the fear of strangers predominates. In the second half of the second year, fear of sudden noises, strange animals, and doctors comes into prominence. Around age two, the toilet, the dark, and people in masks and costumes (such as clowns and even Santa Claus) top the list of fears. By two-and-a-half, toddlers start worrying about imaginary creatures and possible bodily harm. Of course, there are many children whose fears don't fit these "typical" patterns: Eighteen-month-olds who are already worrying about being flushed down the toilet and three-year-olds who suddenly become afraid of dogs.

Fear is not altogether a bad thing. The completely fearless toddler is the one most likely to get into situations hazardous to health and well-being. Nevertheless, since excessive fear can interfere with the normal functioning of a child and his family, it's important for parents and caregivers to understand the nature of childhood fears and how to handle them.

# THE WHY OF TODDLER FEARS

The infant—innocent, protected, acting largely on instinct and reflex rather than reflection—is a classic example of what-I-don't-know-can't-hurt-me. But sometime in the second year, some developmental changes transform all that:

**A little knowledge.** Getting smarter can make the world seem like a much more dangerous place. The toddler is the proud possessor of hundreds of new thoughts, dozens of new concepts, a mountain of new information—and a more mature thought process that can

synthesize all of these into countless frightening scenarios.

**Too little experience.** Able to grasp the concept of cause-and-effect, but without the experience to sort out the reasonable from the un-, the toddler is now able to ponder possible adverse effects that might seem preposterous to an adult. If a vacuum cleaner sucks up dust and dirt, could it also suck up me? If the dog next door nipped Daddy's leg, won't all dogs bite? If water goes down the bathtub drain, isn't it possible that a person—especially a small one like me—could, too?

**A sense of size differences.** Toddlers recognize how small they are compared to those around them. Picture walking down the street amid people two and three times your size, and you have some notion of why this size difference can engender fear.

**Growing imagination.** As a vehicle that can transport a toddler at play from the dress-up corner to the high seas, or from the block area to a medieval castle, the imagination can be the source of boundless fun. But when it transports a toddler from the safety and security of his or her normally cozy bedroom to a monster's lair or a witch's castle, the imagination can be the source of boundless fear. As imagination grows, fears often do, too.

**Expanding memory.** Babies usually forget a frightening or upsetting experience quickly. But toddlers, like elephants, can retain the memory of such events for a long while. Being scratched by a cat, going too high on a swing, falling down a flight of stairs can trigger a persistent fear of cats, swings, or stairs. Even fictional events can trigger fears: Sleeping Beauty pricking her finger, Dumbo's mommy being locked up, Little Red Riding Hood's grandma being gobbled up by the wolf.

## WHAT'S THAT PITTER PATTER?

**O**lder toddlers may notice that when they are frightened their hearts beat faster or that it's a little more difficult to breathe. Explain to your toddler that these symptoms are okay—they just are how our bodies react to being scared. And show that taking a couple of deep breaths, thinking about something nice (like a favorite song), or climbing onto Mommy's or Daddy's lap for a hug may help.

**Increasing mobility.** A toddler on the go is bound to encounter more fear-provoking situations—a meandering dog, a dangling spider, a lawn mower at work—than will a babe in arms.

**Self-centeredness.** Toddlers are extremely egocentric—all toys belong to them, all attention must focus on them, all experiences happen to them. If a little boy in a book can be chased by a giant, they can be, too. If a little girl on TV can be stung by a bee, so can they. If a sibling can be very ill, so can they.

**Suggestibility.** The emotions of others often rub off on toddlers; if a playmate or a sibling displays a fear of escalators or of monsters, they may become afraid, too. If parents are anxious, the toddler may feel insecure.

## COPING WITH TODDLER FEARS

**T**oddler fears can not only make life miserable for all concerned, but if they get out of hand, they can be crippling to a child's growth and development. To help your toddler deal with fears:[3]

▲ Acknowledge that the fears are real. They may be irrational, but they are—like adult fears—real. Though ignoring

many other kinds of unwanted behaviors may help to banish them, ignoring fear isn't likely to help. In fact, pretending a fear doesn't exist often intensifies it and/or makes it the basis of a lot of other fears (a fear of birds may grow into a fear of all animals; a fear of spiders may beget a fear of all insects).

▲ . . . but don't force your toddler to confront them head-on, either. A sink-or-swim approach is rarely effective when it comes to fears. Forcing a toddler who is afraid of dogs to pet the neighbor's collie, dunking a toddler afraid of water in the swimming pool, or insisting that a toddler afraid of monsters check under the bed and in the closets for that nocturnal nemesis could turn a fear into a phobia. Admonishing, "be brave" or "don't act like a baby" is also bad medicine. Instead, follow a fear-reduction program that combines sensitive support and understanding with gradual exposure (see page 210).

▲ Recognize your toddler's disadvantage in fighting fear. As adults, we can often get around our fears—we can avoid confronting a fear of flying by taking the train or a fear of heights by staying off escalators. Toddlers, less able to control

---

3. Also see specific fears, such as fear of haircuts, page 309; of the bath, page 94; of the dark, page 431; of the dentist, page 308; of the doctor, page 305; of dogs, page 84; of flushing, page 507; of penis loss, page 217; of playground equipment, page 205; of roughhousing, page 285; of sleep, page 310.

# FACING FEARS

• • • • • • • • • •

**M**any fears are simply outgrown as the toddler matures into a more confident and worldly preschooler. But others persist throughout early childhood, and—if they're not dealt with—sometimes into adulthood. Gently helping toddlers face what scares them is the best way to ensure that today's fears won't continue to hold them back tomorrow. Help your toddler work through fears with:

**Illumination.** An older toddler might be reassured by a simple, rational explanation. For example, you may silence a fear of sirens by explaining that: "Fire trucks have to make a loud noise so cars and people will get out of the way and let them get to the fire in a hurry. It's a good, loud noise." For a younger toddler, who may not be able to grasp even a simple explanation, a demonstration may be the route to reassurance. For instance, a toddler who's afraid of going down the drain with the bath water may feel better about bathing after a little display of what can and can't go down drains (water and soap bubbles can, rubber duckies and children can't). A toddler afraid of the vacuum may be relieved to see that though cracker crumbs can be vacuumed up, a toy truck, a block, and Mommy's foot can't be.

**Indirect exposure.** A toddler who's afraid of being flushed down the toilet may gain confidence from being read a storybook about a child who uses the toilet and lives to tell about it. A toddler who's afraid of fire engines may benefit from looking at a picture book about firefighters or a visit to the fire house. A toddler who's afraid of dogs may find four-footers less foreboding after seeing a placid movie about a girl and her dog. Toddlers who are afraid of a natural phenomenon, such as thunder, may become less fearful after being read a simple book that explains it. Avoid books, pictures, or movies, however, that might intensify a toddler's fear. No amount of girl-dog bonding is going to soften a tod-

dler's reaction to a ferocious attack scene—even if it's a bad guy who's being attacked.

**Exposure and desensitization at a distance.** Holding a toddler who's afraid of the vacuum cleaner at the other end of the living room while Daddy vacuums or standing with a toddler who's afraid of draining water at the doorway of the bathroom while the tub empties may help him or her face the fear at a safe distance. Similarly, it may help to let a dog-fearful toddler watch a playmate frolic with a neighbor's dog, near enough to hear the giggles and see the glee, but far enough so that there's no imminent threat.

**Increased control with closer exposure.** Fear tends to make anyone at any age feel out-of-control. So helping your toddler to gain some measure of control over the feared object or situation may take the edge off the fear. For example, experimenting with turning a vacuum cleaner on and off may help the fearful toddler see that the control lies in the human hand, not the dust-sucker. Riding on the vacuum when it's unplugged and silent may also be reassuring.

Set up a toddler who's afraid of the dark or of monsters with a "prop" or two to increase his or her sense of power and control: a flashlight, a friendly night-light, a teddy-bear sentry under orders to chase away unwelcome visitors, a magic word that banishes night creatures, or a magic, monster-repelling potion of water in a spray bottle.

**Ventilation.** We all feel better about our fears when we talk about them. Toddlers are no different. Ask your toddler to talk about his or her fears while you lend an understanding ear.

**A sense of humor.** Though you should never make fun of a child's fears, some of the techniques on page 173 for reducing tension and helping a child relax could in the end reduce fears.

## WHEN LITTLE FEARS GET TOO BIG
· · · · · · · · · ·

Most of the fears (of strangers, of the dark, of dogs, of the bath) that toddlers experience in their second and third years gradually diminish, sometimes to be replaced by more sophisticated fears (such as fear of jails, police, wild animals). By age six fears are generally less prevalent.

If your child's fears interfere with family life or with normal daily activity (he won't leave the house for fear of seeing a dog; she hates to take a bath or wash her hands because of a fear of water), then it may be best to seek professional help.

their environments, aren't always able to keep their fears at bay.

▲ Let your toddler know that everyone has fears. That even grown-ups like Mommy and Daddy are sometimes afraid. Tell an older child what you were afraid of when you were little and how you overcame the fears—endeavoring not to introduce new fears he or she hasn't thought of yet. It always helps to know you're not the only one.

▲ . . . but try your best to control yours. If your toddler sees you take charge of your fears calmly, he or she may eventually learn to do likewise, based on your model. If, on the other hand, you jump three feet in the air every time you spy a spider, you'll be showing your toddler how to let fear take charge.

▲ Don't laugh at or otherwise tease your fearful toddler. Even small people take their own fears very seriously. While a little playful teasing may work wonders on a toddler who's stubbornly refusing to get dressed for day care, teasing a toddler who's afraid of dogs by getting on all fours and barking like a terrier will only feed the terror.

▲ Boost, don't bash, your toddler's ego. Self-confidence can go a long way in overcoming fear. So praise every bit of progress your toddler makes—no matter how small—and avoid criticizing steps taken backwards—no matter how big. And most important, never let your tod-

dler feel that you love or respect him or her any less because of the fear.

▲ Let your toddler lean on you. Fearful toddlers need a strong, supportive hand to hold—one that helps to compensate for the confidence they sometimes lack. Approach difficult situations confidently and calmly, reassuring your toddler that you won't let anything hurt him or her.

▲ . . . but not too much. Beware of letting support foster overdependence. Coddling may reinforce the fearful toddler's belief that there really *is* something to fear. Alternately, it may lead to the discovery that expressing fear is a reliable route to parental attention.

▲ Root out sources of fear in your toddler's life. Scary books (fairy tales can be especially frightening to some children; see page 450), scary movies, scary cartoons, and scary television news reports (even if a toddler doesn't appear to be concentrating on the screen, the fleeting image of an airplane wreck could have a lasting effect) are all capable of generating fear in a toddler. During this fearful stage, it makes sense to stay away from as many of these stimuli as possible. When it's not possible (you go to a children's movie, thinking it will be good family fun, but a scene with a witch leaves your toddler shaken and sobbing; you happen upon a dogfight on your walk to the park), offer a simple, matter-of-fact, but reassuring explanation about what you've witnessed, but don't dwell on it. Instead, distract your toddler.

Even such seemingly harmless items as a stuffed elephant, a set of dancing bears decorating a crib, or charming teddy-bear wallpaper adorning the nursery wall can provoke a fearful reaction in an occasional child and may need to be removed or covered, temporarily or permanently, to ease toddler fears.

▲ Make sure you're not responsible for the fear. Sometimes, fear in children is triggered by repeated parental warnings ("Stay away from strangers—they might try to steal you"), actions (placing a child in a dark room with the door closed), or threats ("If you're not good, we're going to have to send you away"). And while overly harsh discipline can increase fearfulness, paradoxically, so can an absence of discipline; living in a home where there are no external controls can be frightening to a young child.

A parent should also be wary of introducing a fear where none exists or where it hasn't yet been expressed. For example, saying to your toddler, "Don't be afraid," when a cat approaches you is more likely to arouse than allay fear. Better to say, "See the pretty kitty. It wants to say hello to us."

# WHAT IT'S IMPORTANT FOR YOUR TODDLER TO KNOW: The Joy of Giving

Trying to teach charity to a two-year-old may sound futile; toddlers who think "A" is for "altruism" are few and far between. Yet the kind of charity that begins at home can begin a lot sooner than you might think—even as the toddler continues to display age-appropriate self-centeredness and lack of empathy toward others.

It will, of course, be a gradual process, and a subtle one—you may not see results for several years. But planted and periodically nourished, the seeds of charity will grow—and eventually your egocentric toddler will blossom into an altruistic, generous adult. Here's how to begin:

**Build a warm and cohesive family.** Studies show that children who are empathetic come from such homes. But being kind and loving is not enough. Limits are also necessary. Children who grow up without them tend to become selfish adults.

**Make giving a tradition.** Nobody looks forward to traditions more than a child; making giving a family tradition will help make your child eager to give. Giving at times that are traditional for getting—Christmas, Chanukah, or Kwanzaa—sets a powerful example. So when shopping with your toddler for such special events, have him or her help pick out a small gift to give to a less advantaged child. Explain that some children don't have as many toys or clothes as your toddler, and that it makes you feel good to help them have more. In later years, your child may volunteer coins from his or her piggy bank toward the purchase.

**Be a Santa for all seasons.** Anytime is the right time for giving; being open-handed in December and a Scrooge the rest of the year gives your child the message that charity need only be seasonal. So, give throughout the year, and when you do, try to involve your toddler. At this age, children love dropping coins into banks or boxes. So let them drop them into a charity box in a local store, the collection plate at church. Explain briefly—and without going into unnecessarily frightening details—what the money will be used for (to help children who are sick get better, to help build a new Sunday school). Of course, you'll have to subsidize your toddler's giving, but you should encourage older children to drop in some coins of their own from their weekly allowance or "earned" income. When you have outgrown clothes or toys to give away, let your child help pack them up and explain that your family is giving them to children who don't have a lot of toys or clothes. Have your toddler make a drawing to include in the package. When you do your weekly food shopping, ask your child to pick out an extra pound of pasta or a can of soup or beans to give to the hungry or homeless—and take him or her with you when you donate the item to a nearby food pantry.

**Give of yourself.** The less fortunate need your money, true, but they also benefit from your time and effort. And, actually, small children will learn more about giving from your providing an active example than from your writing checks. Bake cookies together and explain that you're going to bring them to the sick children in the hospital; make an extra pie at Thanksgiving and drop it off

at the local soup kitchen (call first to make sure they accept such donations); volunteer to help prepare dinner once a month at the homeless shelter or to deliver holiday meals to those who are housebound. Seeing you get involved will make a lasting impression on your toddler. When your child gets a little older and is better able to participate, he or she is less likely to be intimidated by volunteering. Do it as a family—"adopt" a senior citizen whose own family lives far away and can't visit often, take a shift serving Easter dinner at the Salvation Army before going home to your own, walk together in a fund-raising walkathon, spend an afternoon helping to clean up the local park.

**Give with a smile.** It's fine to "give until it hurts"—as long as you're able to smile through the pain. If your child gets the impression that giving is rewarding and satisfying, rather than an unwelcome obligation, he or she will be more likely to recognize the pleasure inherent in such a deed.

**Don't expect miracles.** There's a reason why there are no patron saints of toddlerhood: virtue just doesn't come that easily to the little tykes. Since they are self-centered by nature, it's unfair to expect them to be models of benevolence. Accept their stage of development, while continuing to make a conscious effort to stretch your own, and—who knows?—one day your child's behavior may give credence to the maxim, "You reap what you sow."

# CHAPTER NINE

# The Twenty-First Month

## WHAT YOUR TODDLER MAY BE DOING NOW

*By the end of this month,[1] your toddler*
*. . . should be able to (see Note):*

▲ build a tower of 2 cubes (by 20½ months)
▲ point to 1 body part when asked

**Note:** If your toddler has not reached these milestones or doesn't use symbolic play and words, consult the doctor or nurse-practitioner. This rate of development may well be normal for your child (some children are late bloomers), but it needs to be evaluated. Also check with the doctor if your toddler seems out-of-control or hyperactive; uncommunicative, passive, or withdrawn; highly negative, demanding, and stubborn. (Remember, the child who was born prematurely often lags behind others of the same chronological age. This devel-opmental gap has probably narrowed by now, and will probably disappear entirely around age two.)

*. . . will probably be able to:*

▲ kick ball forward
▲ identify 2 pictures by pointing
▲ remove an article of clothing (by 20½ months)

*. . . may possibly be able to:*

▲ brush teeth, with help

*. . . may even be able to:*

▲ put on an article of clothing

---

1. The twenty-first month begins when a child is twenty months old and ends when he or she is twenty-one months old.

# WHAT YOU MAY BE CONCERNED ABOUT

## THE OBSERVER

*"We're concerned because our daughter never participates in games or activities with other toddlers. She just watches from the sidelines."*

Just because your daughter isn't an active participant doesn't mean she isn't participating at all. Researchers tell us that about 20% of the average young toddler's waking time is spent "just looking." In fact, more time is spent staring at objects, people, and happenings at this age than is spent in social interaction. As a child approaches her second birthday, time spent socializing increases to about 20% and time spent staring drops to 14%—still a relatively large chunk of time. So it's clear that observation is a very important form of participation for young children—and for some, at least early in their social development, it seems to be the only way.

Though some naturally gregarious children (and adults) jump effortlessly into the thick of things, whether it's a game, a conversation, or another activity, many need to spend time on the outside

*Some toddlers are more comfortable being on the outside looking into a social situation—at least until they've carefully sized it up. Pushing such toddlers to be "joiners" when they'd rather be "observers" may only make them more reluctant to participate.*

looking in before they make a move of any kind. Others are so content watching from afar that they never seem to want to join the crowd. They are the observers.

Your daughter may never turn into a social butterfly, but you can help her to develop her social skills and enable her to come out of her cocoon by giving her plenty of the following:

**Time.** If your toddler needs time to warm up and size up before getting involved in a group, let her have it. What may seem to you like a waste of playing time may to her be time valuably spent.

**Space.** Don't hover over your toddler while she watches her peers at play or urge her to break into the group before she's ready. Pushing her to perform socially is not likely to help; in fact, it may cause her to rebel and withdraw further from the social scene.

**Acceptance.** Your toddler's personality is an important part of her identity. Try to change it and you'll send the message that she is in some way inadequate ("There must be something wrong with me if I can't be the way Mommy and Daddy want me to be"). Instead, let her know that you value and respect her by accepting her the way she is. Make it clear by your words and actions that you consider her approach to socializing as acceptable as that of the gregarious child. Outgoing children may become tomorrow's politicians and executives, but observers like your child may become the journalists who write about them or the social scientists who study them.

**Support.** Be there for your child when she seems hesitant, embarrassed, or shy in a social situation. Give her nonthreatening social experiences by arranging one-on-one play dates. To help her deal with shyness, see the tips on page 405; to help her adapt to new situations, see page 246.

# SWALLOWED OBJECTS

*"Our son found a penny in the playground, put it in his mouth before I could stop him, and swallowed it before I could get it out. He seems okay. What should I do?"*

Wait. As long as your toddler doesn't seem to be having difficulty breathing or swallowing, isn't coughing or choking, and isn't complaining about chest pain, the best course is to observe his stools over the next few days. Most often, swallowed coins or other small objects exit via that route.

If your child develops a fever over the next few days, or if, after four or five days, the coin hasn't shown up in a diaper or the potty, check with his doctor. An x-ray to find just where it's lodged may be in order. In some cases, removal—with the help of an endoscope (a flexible instrument inserted down the esophagus that allows doctors to see what's inside)—may be necessary. If a fairly large object has lodged in the digestive tract, then surgery may be needed.

Anytime, however, your toddler ingests a foreign object and is coughing, has difficulty swallowing, or seems to be experiencing chest pain, immediately call his doctor or take him to the emergency room. (For how to handle choking on an inhaled object, see page 689.) Get prompt medical attention, too, if the object is sharp (a pin or needle, a fish bone, a toy with sharp edges) or otherwise dangerous (a button battery, for example). Sometimes toddlers put small objects in their mouths unbeknownst to parents or caregivers and subsequently swallow them or choke on them. If your child exhibits any of the above symptoms, you should suspect this possibility, and call the doctor.

## POKING OBJECTS IN ORIFICES

*"Our daughter is always sticking something that doesn't belong there (a piece of food, a toy, a crayon) into her nose, her mouth, her ears. I'm afraid she'll hurt herself."*

Any opening that promises to lead somewhere is enticing to a curious young toddler. And though the exploration of ears, nose, and mouth (and occasionally, other body orifices[2]) may be disconcerting to parents, it is completely normal.

Normal, but not risk-free, however. Shoving an object into the ear can damage the eardrum; into the nose can cause bleeding and even infection; into the mouth can cause choking or poisoning; into the vagina, infection. If the object is hot or caustic, burns can result.

While it's important to encourage exploration, it's also important to protect toddlers from the consequences of their own curiosity. If you find your toddler putting an object in any body opening, explain that this is dangerous and comment on the proper use of the object ("Raisins are for eating, not for pushing into your nose"). Take it away if the behavior is continued or if the object is one that your child shouldn't be playing with at all (a letter opener or a marble, for example), but don't make her feel guilty or bad about what she's done.

Sometimes a child will insert a foreign object into the nose, ears, or less often, the vagina without being observed by an adult. Suspect the possibility that such an object might have become stuck if you note a foul odor or an unexplained discharge (bloody or not) from the ori-

fice, or if your child begins complaining about pain in the area. For instructions on how to safely remove an inserted foreign object that you can't get a grip on and how to treat any resultant injury, see page 669.

## PENIS WORRIES

*"Ever since our son saw his new baby sister naked and saw that she didn't have a penis, he's been expressing the fear that he's going to lose his."*

This is an extremely common concern, especially in boys with baby sisters. Such a fear can be quickly allayed with a simple but reassuring biology lesson: Explain to your son that all boys are born with penises, which they never lose, and that girls are born with vaginas, which they never lose. A very simple children's book about the human body, showing the fundamental genital differences between little girls and little boys and between women and men, will help illustrate these facts for your toddler and put his mind at ease.

## PENIS ENVY AND CURIOSITY

*"I took a bath with our son last night, and he got upset because his penis is much smaller than mine. We didn't know what to tell him."*

Tell him the truth—that his penis is little because he's a little boy. Show him that his hands, feet, legs, arms, nose, and mouth are smaller, too, for the very same reason. Show him in the mirror the difference in size between your nose and

2. Very rarely, children of either sex may explore the anus (see page 826).

# *TEACHING TIME*

· · · · · · · · · ·

To a toddler, there's no time like the present. In fact, there's no time *but* the present. *Yesterday, this morning, tomorrow, tonight, in a second, later on* are all relatively meaningless terms. Minutes are no different from hours, and hours no different from days. You can't expect a toddler to rush when you say "hurry" or be patient when you say "wait." A child this age simply doesn't have the understanding or the capability—yet.

Midway through the second year, most toddlers are focusing on "now." Past and future are still beyond their comprehension. "Now" is when they want lunch, want Mommy to come home, want to go out, want to get to Grandma's house. But as the second birthday approaches, there's a big jump in time savvy, and toddlers begin to understand when you say "soon" or "later." By age three, there's further progress, as such concepts as "today," "yesterday," and "tomorrow" become separate (though fuzzy) entities. Many toddlers use "last night" to refer to anything that happened in the past; some will also glibly talk about "tomorrow," but a true comprehension of tomorrow doesn't usually come for another year or two. And since it isn't until about age six that the concept of time as a continuous line really becomes clear, it won't be until the early school years that a clock will hold any significance for your toddler. In the meantime, you can help the learning process along with these timely tips:

**Be a two- (or three-) timer.** When talking time with your toddler use more than one way to describe the same time whenever possible: "We'll go to the playground in the afternoon, right after your nap." Or, "Jessica is coming over to play this morning, after breakfast." With the older toddler, you can begin to add the hour: "We'll go to the playground this afternoon at 1 o'clock, right after lunch."

**Work on order.** Present your toddler with your planned schedule of activities in order: "*First* we'll go to the store, *then* we'll go to the library, and *last* we will have lunch." Or, "*First* we'll have a bath, *then* we'll have some cookies and milk, and *last* we'll have a story." You can also begin introducing the concepts of "before" and "after" ("We'll have a snack *before* we go to the park," "Sara and her mother will come over *after* breakfast") and "soon" and "later" ("*Soon*, it will be time to clean up the blocks in your room," or "*Later*, we'll make a cake"). But don't expect your toddler to comprehend the nuances of these words just yet.

**Use visual aids.** Concrete examples will help to put the passing of time in perspective for your toddler. Show your toddler pictures of him or herself before ("*Before*, you were this little") and now ("*Now*, you're this big"). When you've read a story, go back and outline it in chronological order ("*First*, the little boy went swimming; *then*, he played at the park; *later*, he went home and ate ice cream"). When your toddler is going to have to wait for something, try setting a timer to illustrate the passing of time ("I'm going to set the timer for five minutes; when the timer rings, I'll be ready to paint with you").

**Take the daze out of days.** The days of the week will be less of a blur to your toddler if he or she associates each with a particular activity: "On Monday, we have play group. On Tuesday, we go to the library. On Sunday, we go to Grandma's." A large weekly calendar with pasted-on pictures or other visual reminders of regular activities may also help get the idea across. Make a point to discuss the tangible events of yesterday ("Yesterday, we went out to lunch"), today ("Today we had a good time at the museum"), and tomorrow ("Tomorrow, we'll go over to Brandon's house"). If your toddler is anxiously awaiting a favorite aunt's arrival two days hence, make the arrival day tangible: "Aunt Anne will come for her visit after two long nights' sleep."

his, your teeth and his. Compare your foot sizes, fingernail sizes, and hand sizes.

Explain that as he grows, all these parts of him will also grow, and that when he's a fully grown man they will be just about the same size as yours. A simple picture book that illustrates the physical differences between little boys and grown men as well as photographs of you when you were a little boy will also help him understand the growth process.

*"The last time my daughter went to her play group, she watched one of the little boys have his diaper changed. She seemed disturbed when she saw his penis—and now she's upset that she doesn't have one, too."*

To a toddler, possession is ten-tenths of the law—and just about anything that she doesn't possess, she covets. This goes for toys, cookies, space in the sandbox, and body parts. So when a little girl first realizes that there are "haves" and "have-nots" in this last category, it's not unusual for her to be disturbed by the inequity.

A detailed account of "the birds and the bees" isn't called for yet—and won't be until it's asked for (but as soon as the question comes, be ready to answer; see page 420). What is called for is some reassurance and a couple of key facts. Explain that boys (and men, like Daddy) have penises, and that girls (and women, like Mommy) have vaginas. Boys and girls are different—and that's the way they're supposed to be.

A simple illustrated book written for her age level will help reinforce the information you give her.

# KISSING ON THE LIPS

*"Is it okay for us to continue kissing our daughter on the lips once in a while? My mother-in-law worries it isn't 'healthy'."*

Affection that feels just right to one parent may feel all wrong to another. Personality, social conditioning, upbringing, and other assorted baggage picked up along the way to parenthood combine to determine how parents respond to this issue.

If kissing your daughter lightly on the lips (assuming neither of you has anything contagious) feels right to all of you, it is—particularly when your child is this young. Heavy smooching, of course, is inappropriate. And if you feel uncomfortable about even a light buss on the lips, plant your kisses on your toddler's cheek or forehead instead.

# SHOWING AFFECTION

*"Our oldest child is very cuddly, and has always enjoyed being hugged. But our younger child is clearly doing us a favor when he lets us hug him."*

Just another bit of evidence that, even within the same family, no two children are alike. Some children are gregarious and some are shy. Some cry at every little affront; others, hardly ever. Some are cuddly and some are not. Such differences are normal and it's important that adults respect them. So if your toddler (or child of any age) stiffens, cringes, or otherwise shows that he doesn't appreciate these displays of affection, respect his wishes. Some children don't mind hugging at home but object to public displays. This preference, too, should be respected.

---

## YOU'RE NOT ALONE
· · · · · · · · · ·

You're the *only* parent who ever had a toddler collapse, kicking and screaming, in the middle of a busy sidewalk. You're the *only* parent whose toddler ever refused to wear shoes or a coat on a snowy January day. You're the *only* parent whose toddler yanked down an entire candy display at the supermarket.

Or at least it feels that way. But the fact is, toddlers are almost universally difficult at least some of the time. Look beyond your own "terrible two-er", and you'll realize you're not alone in your toddler trials and tribulations. All parents of one- and two-year olds have their share. It's just that you're more likely to be upset by unpleasant behavior in your own child and more likely to dismiss it in someone else's. (After all, when that other child lies kicking and screaming in the middle of the sidewalk, it's no reflection on you.)

If the hundreds of questions in this book, shared by so many parents, aren't enough to persuade you that you aren't alone, you might try joining (or organizing) a support group for parents of toddlers. Meeting with others, watching their toddlers have tantrums or refuse to get their coats on, will be very reassuring. It will also give you a chance to swap not only problems, but solutions.

Recognizing that you aren't alone won't make life with a toddler a breeze, but it can help you weather the storms. Reminding yourself that other people's children have irrational moments, too, is the best way to keep your perspective and your cool when you're dealing with *your* child's moments. It may also keep you from feeling persecuted, punished, or guilty, and asking: "Why me?" or "Where did I go wrong?"

---

If, however, your toddler never wants to be hugged or held, seems distant and untouchable both physically and emotionally, discuss this with his doctor.

*"My wife and I are both unsure just what the limits are in showing affection to our little girl. You hear so much about sexual abuse that you begin to worry that a hug or a pat on the bottom may be out of line."*

Touch is a very important part of a relationship, particularly the parent–child relationship. Even among nonhuman primates, the young do not develop normally without regular physical contact with their mother.

But, there are limits. Touching that makes a child uncomfortable—whether it's a particular type of hug or of a par-

ticular intensity—should always be avoided. And, of course, touching that stimulates you or your child sexually is unhealthy. If you find yourself wanting to touch your child in this way, get professional help immediately. Otherwise relax—and hug and pat away.

## DIFFICULTY LOVING A TODDLER

*"I know I love my toddler. But he seems so disagreeable and unpleasant so much of the time, that sometimes I feel like I can't stand him another minute."*

There is no period of a child's development (besides adolescence) that can try a parent's patience and affection like the toddler years. (But on the bright side: at least he doesn't have a car, acne, or a girlfriend yet.) Contrariness, uncooperativeness, rebelliousness, irrationality—they're all out in full force, testing your resolve to stay calm and controlled, threatening to dissolve your determination to act your age, undermining your ability to keep your perspective. And—worst of all—causing you occasionally to question your love for a child you thought you'd always love without question.

Try to remember that you're not the only parent who struggles with mixed feelings. Some toddlers are easier than others, of course, and some seem a lot tougher. But few parents of young children don't find, at least once in a while, that their offspring are hard to take, and sometimes even hard to love. So don't feel guilty, and don't despair. You will survive these tumultuous times, and you may even look back on them one day with fondness—or at least a chuckle. And just think: you'll have a good decade or so before that adolescent struggle between dependence and independence starts firing up.

In the meantime, try to give more attention to your toddler's good moments (few as they may be) and ignore (as much as possible) his bad ones. If he gets more notice for being good, he may come to conclude it's the better way to go. When he's driving you to distraction, be sure to focus your anger on his behavior rather than on him. This will help both of you cope with your feelings better. Setting and enforcing limits and using the other disciplining techniques beginning on page 127 will also help reduce unwanted behavior, and make your life easier. As time passes, your child will eventually "grow out" of his toddler behavior.

And don't forget that popular bumper-sticker slogan: "Have you hugged your child today?" Daily hug therapy—squeeze as many squeezes (and cuddles, and snuggles, and nuzzles, and back rubs) into your toddler's day as possible. Hug when the impulse strikes, but also when it doesn't. When you're feeling particularly hostile and your child's behavior seems particularly unlovable, reach out and touch him. A rub on the neck, a stroke on the cheek, a sudden and unexpected embrace can often miraculously dissipate anger and bad feelings, heading off a tantrum or turning an afternoon gone awry onto a happier new course. It may not always work, but it's *always* worth a try.

Of course, since some children don't like to be held as much as others, tailor your touch therapy to your child. If he squirms out of your hugs, maybe a "high-five" or some verbal "stroking" would be more appealing. Find something to show him—and remind yourself—that you do love him.

While feeling angry towards your toddler sometimes is normal, always feeling angry, or feeling as though you're on the brink of acting on your anger, isn't. Talk to your toddler's doctor if you sometimes feel angry enough to strike your child or if you feel detached from him. If at any time you feel as though you are about to strike him or even abuse him verbally, see the tips for cooling off on page 754. If you feel you're in danger of losing control and hurting your child, call a parent hotline (keep the number posted near your phone) or ask a neighbor or caregiver to come and stay with your child while you regain control.

## SEXUAL IDENTITY

*"We worry that our son doesn't play with trucks and cars. He seems to prefer make-believe games with dolls and stuffed animals, and little girls for friends."*

At this age, most boys will be boys and most girls will be girls. But it's not unusual for there to be some crossing of traditional gender lines. In some cases, less-aggressive boys prefer to play with girls because the boys they know play "rough." Or they play with girls because they are the only available playmates. They then may favor dolls and stuffed animals because that's what their playmates favor—though they may sometimes use these toys differently than their female peers (pretending a doll is a superhero rather than a newly born baby, for example). Some little boys cross gender lines in the course of emulating older female siblings, others just to satisfy their curiosity.

By the age of three, children begin to have a stronger sense of who they are and who they are going to be; most boys switch over to predominantly male friendships and traditional male toys and games. But even once they have made this switch, today's preschool boys—unlike their predecessors in previous generations—may be content to play "house," at least some of the time. Many of them, in imitation of their fathers, will rock and bathe a baby doll, croon a lullabye and give a bottle, or "cook" a honey stew for Winnie the Pooh. A small boy who displays such nurturing behavior should be encouraged and applauded for being a good daddy, rather than teased or criticized for trying to be a mommy.

Nor should little boys be pressured by their parents into becoming junior jocks. Though all children should be encouraged to be physically active, boys who prefer drawing or books or playing house over tossing a ball around shouldn't be harassed or punished for their preferences. Real men do read, write, paint, and participate in the care of their children and their households. Real men become authors, doctors, researchers, businessmen, artists, and parents—not just professional athletes.

Many parents who see their little boy straddling gender lines immediately jump to the conclusion that he may be showing homosexual tendencies. But it is too early for such a conclusion. It's not until around age three that gender-based behavior becomes more entrenched and even at that point, a child's choice of play things is in no way a sure predictor of future sexual orientation.[3]

*"Our daughter likes to roughhouse with the boys while other little girls her age are pushing dolls around in carriages. She's even said she wants to be a boy."*

Early childhood is a time for discoveries—scientific, social, and intellectual. But possibly the most important discoveries are those a toddler makes about herself. And for the most part, she makes them through experimentation.

While parents are likely to applaud a toddler's experiments with scientific or intellectual theories (unless, of course, they involve large amounts of juice on the living room carpet), they're often disturbed when she experiments with her sexual identity. Yet gender experimentation is just as normal, and sometimes, just as necessary.

Chances are that your daughter just wants to see how the other half lives, not that she wants to live like them forever. It's possible that her curiosity might have been piqued by spending a lot of time with male playmates—she may well have noticed that boys are often allowed to do things that she isn't ("Would Sam like to help me build this new bookcase?"). It's also possible that her gender jealousy stems from being denied traditional "boy" toys that interest her (toy

---

3. If, however, parents have questions about a three-year-old boy who plays only with dolls, shuns male playmates, and/or regularly wants to dress in girl's clothing, a discussion with his doctor may be helpful.

trains, for example, or a block set), or from being forced to wear frilly dresses when she's more comfortable in sweatpants and overalls. It's even possible that she said "I want to be a boy" for the shock value alone—toddlers get a perverse kind of pleasure out of startling their parents—or because her rebellious side has seen that professing that preference raises your ire. Whatever the reason, your daughter's attitude is certainly nothing to worry about.

Don't fight—or even comment on—your daughter's gender experimentation. Provide her with no less freedom than you would give a son. Let her play the way she wants (instead of stifling her with "Girls don't do that"). Encourage her to fraternize with whom she wants (arrange play dates with boys as well as girls, if that's her wish), and wear what she wants. At the same time, give her positive female footsteps to follow in, and she's very likely to discover that she likes being a girl.

If, after she's celebrated her third birthday (children settle into their sexual identities more solidly at around age three), your daughter still regularly expresses displeasure with being a girl, (as opposed to pleasure in being a tomboy), talk to her doctor about your concerns.

*"My son wants to play with cars and trucks, and won't touch the dolls I bought him—except to throw them around."*

You can lead the average two-year-old boy to a doll carriage, but you can't make him play "dolls"—any more than you can lead a two-year-old girl to a toy garage and make her play "cars." (And if the boy does deign to play with a doll, it might be to throw it up in the air to see how it lands; if the girl does play with cars, it might be to take a toy family for a ride.) That's what more and more determined-to-be-enlightened parents, who buy dolls for their sons and cars for their daughters, are discovering—often much to their chagrin. Sexual stereotypes are, in some ways, more valid than we would like to think.

Just how much of what boys and girls are made of comes from nature, and how much from nurture? Certainly, traditional sexual stereotypes receive ample cultural prodding; studies have shown that parents and others tend to pay different kinds of attention to boys than girls from the start, handling newborn girls with a more tender touch than newborn boys, and responding to a baby girl's cry faster than to a baby boy's. Girls are cuddled and cooed to, while boys are roughhoused. Girls hear, "What a sweet little girl you are," while boys hear, "What a big, strong boy you are." Later on, girls activities are more restricted, while boys are given more freedom. Parents are quick to offer problem-solving help to little girls, while boys are encouraged to "figure it out yourself." Conversations with little girls are punctuated with "emotion" words, while conversations with little boys tend to be oriented to "things," rather than feelings.

But while certain societal expectations relate to sex roles, there are also certain biologically based leanings, which have led some experts to suggest that the tendency to nurture girls and boys differently actually stems (at least in part) from the the fact that girls and boys by nature *behave* differently. Differences in the brain and in hormones seem to manifest themselves in differences in temperament and behavior that are visible from birth. In general, newborn boys are more physically active and more vigorous, while newborn girls are quieter, and more responsive to faces and voices. Typically, boys are more aggressive, girls more social; boys respond more to objects, girls to people.

As with all stereotypes, of course, sexual stereotypes are based on generalizations. There are plenty of boys and plenty of girls who don't fit neatly into these stereotypes, or even fit at all. Some girls are particularly skilled at traditional "boy" things (such as mathematics and mechanics), and some boys are better at "girl" things (such as language and nurturing). But most children do fit comfortably into their respective traditional gender molds—no matter how careful their parents are to raise them in a nonsexist environment, with nonsexist books, nonsexist toys, and nonsexist attitudes.

That there is a difference—and some would say, *vive la différence*—in no way means that one sex is better than the other. On the contrary, society is beginning to acknowledge that men and women are equal but different. Nor does the powerful influence of nature mean that nurture has no influence at all.

Continue to offer your son a wide variety of toys, by all means, but don't force or pressure him to play with toys that don't interest him. The more you push, the more likely he is to push back. Give him the opportunity to play with children of both sexes, but don't fret if he rejects girls. Encourage him to express his emotions as readily as you encourage him to scale the jungle gym. Then if possible provide him with another important ingredient in the recipe for a caring, sensitive, nonsexist male: an exemplary role model. A boy who daily observes that a man can do household chores, change diapers, take children to the playground, read stories, give baths, kiss boo-boos, and hug away hurts as well as he can hit a baseball, fix a bike, and bring home the bacon can't help but grow up with positive feelings about both men and women and have an open mind about the roles each should play. If there is no such father figure in your family, look for a role model elsewhere—invite a willing male friend of the family or a relative to spend time with your son, passing on those positive

feelings. Or find an exemplary role model for your child through a community group or your religious community; your child's doctor may be able to help you locate the resource you need.

# STIFLING A SON'S EMOTIONS

*"My husband says that we have to be very tough with our little boy because he doesn't want him to turn out be a sissy or a crybaby. But I think my son is too young for us to try and make a 'man' out of him."*

Despite the fact that the expression of feelings in males has been squelched for many generations in many cultures, men and boys *do* have feelings, and they should not be discouraged from expressing them. In fact, learning in childhood how to express how one feels is important for normal growth and development. The child, male or female, who can say, "I'm sad," "I'm hurt," "I'm disappointed," or "I'm afraid," is more likely to grow into an emotionally healthy adult than the one who covers up feelings.

Experts unequivocally agree that it's not necessary to discourage a boy's sensitivity or to encourage a tough-as-nails, boys-don't-cry mentality to produce a young man who's secure in his male sexual identity. That our culture is beginning to value more nurturing, gentler character traits in men is evidenced by the fact that the hard-hearted, thick-skinned, love-'em-and-leave-'em screen idols of previous generations are being nudged from favor by more sensitive and empathic love-'em-and-stay-with-'em leading men who experience fear and pain—and even cry.

Though there are believed to be some important innate biological differences when it comes to male and female temperament and response (see page 369), it is likely that the ability (or inability) to express emotion stems at least in part from cultural conditioning that begins in the cradle. Studies show that girl babies generally receive much more verbal attention and comforting than do boy babies, an inequitable pattern that continues through childhood. For example, girls are held and soothed when they tumble from a tricycle and boys are checked for wounds, brushed off, and instructed to get back on.

Comforting a child who's hurt or upset and encouraging him to talk about his feelings, both good and bad, will in no way diminish his capacity to grow into a strong and assertive adult. Such an approach can, in fact, build inner strength. Nor does it produce a crybaby. Rather, it produces a sensitive, caring individual, one who's capable not only of receiving tender, loving care, but of giving it to others.[4] In sum, a real man—in the fullest sense of the word.

# CHALLENGING A DAUGHTER

*"Our daughter seems to be very bright. We don't want to limit her by being unconsciously sexist in the way we raise her. How can we be sure we don't make that mistake?"*

You've already taken the first and most important step in raising a daughter whose potential isn't limited by traditional sexist boundaries—and that is acknowledging that it's something you want to do. The second step is to encourage your daughter—as parents

should any child, male or female—in a wide range of areas, intellectual and physical. When she's faced with a problem (how to get the book she dropped behind the sofa or which way to turn that triangle so that it'll fit in the shape-sorter), challenge her to figure out the answer for herself instead of rushing to supply it for her. Broaden her horizons by providing her with stimulating toys and activities—puzzles, simple word and number games, basic science experiments, books that talk about how and why. And don't put special restrictions on her because of her sex ("You can't play in the mud—you'll get your pants all dirty!" or "That hill is too steep for you to climb"). A little girl who is discouraged from touching that "yucky" worm today may be reluctant to participate in "yucky" biology class projects tomorrow; a little girl who's discouraged from playing ball with the boys today may always shy away from sports.

But while you remember to praise her artwork, her fine performance on the jungle gym, and how well she completed a puzzle, don't forget to compliment her on how nicely she dressed herself or how pretty her hair looks. Be supportive of any interests your daughter may have in what are considered more traditionally feminine areas: dolls, doll houses, tea parties, babies, clothes. There's no evidence that girls who play with dolls are less likely to end up in the boardroom than those who play with cars. And belittling "feminine" interests while cheering those in the male sphere will tell your daughter that there is something inherently better about maleness than femaleness—which, of course, there isn't. It will also make her feel guilty about, or try to stifle, her feminine impulses. Or, if she is more rebellious than compliant, she may just decide to become the most feminine female around.

Most important in your daughter's development of self-esteem will be the example set by her mother at home. A

---

4. Beware of coddling or overprotecting a child of either sex, however (see page 206).

## IS IT TIME TO TAKE THEM OUT TO THE BALL GAME (OR A MOVIE, OR PLAY, OR CONCERT)?

. . . . . . . . . .

Family movies, puppet shows, Chopin-for-children recitals, baseball diamonds, and basketball courts all beckon seductively. Older siblings and parents yearn for an occasional family outing. And there's no doubt that many of these extracurricular activities can be beneficial to toddlers, too, broadening their experience and enriching their lives. If only they can get through them. But most toddlers can't sit still for two minutes at a stretch; is it lunacy to even consider taking them anywhere they'll be expected to sit still for two hours or more?

Toddlers being toddlers—predictable only in their unpredictability—there's no telling how they'll respond to or behave during any kind of spectator event, or predicting whether their response and behavior will be consistent from one event to the next. So basically, parents have to follow their instincts, take their chances, and hope for the best. But before you plunk down money for your tickets, it's probably a good idea to mull over the following questions:

▲ Is the event or performance likely to keep your toddler's attention? In general, you probably have a pretty good idea of what kinds of entertainment your child finds amusing. Animated films are more likely to fit that bill than are standard films; puppet shows, musicals, and plays featuring actors in splashy costumes are more liable to engage than a serious drama. Even if your toddler can't yet follow the story line, he or she may be captivated by vibrant colors, engaging characters, eye-catching sets, and lively music. While some children's concerts feature lyrics and sound effects that can involve a toddler, others are geared more to schoolchildren; call before booking seats to determine if a particular program is appropriate for a toddler. Virtually any circus performance will hold your toddler spellbound for a while, but the magic is likely to wear off long before the ringmaster says good night, so be prepared for an early departure. Fast-paced sporting events may keep some toddlers on the edge of their seats, but may have others off their seats and down the aisle before the first play is called.

▲ Is the event or performance likely to frighten your toddler? Some toddlers may

---

little girl who sees that her mother feels good about herself and commands the respect of others, whether she works outside the home or not, will likely grow up feeling good about being female. (For more on sex roles, see page 369.)

## GUNS AND OTHER WAR TOYS

. . . . . . . . . . . . . . . . . . . . . . . . . . . . . . .

*"The idea of our son playing with guns makes us cringe. But a lot of his playmates already play with war toys; it's getting harder and harder to keep him away from such toys and the violent play that goes along with them."*

Little boys have probably emulated men of war ever since there were men and war. But many of today's parents are eager to raise peaceful doves rather than warring hawks. To them, the notion of weaning their sons from rattles to rifles is offensive, most particularly when these parents survey the frighteningly sophisticated war-toy selection available. The "wholesome" toy soldiers and Davy Crockett ensembles of child-

delight in cartoon witches and in whales that gulp little wooden puppet-boys, but others may be terrified by them. Still others may be delighted one day and terrified the next. Some toddlers may revel in being ringside with elephants and clowns; others may be reduced to tears by the experience. Some toddlers are enchanted by puppets and people in character costumes, others are confused and upset by them. Some toddlers clap and cheer along with a roaring crowd, others wail with fright right over the roar. Based on speculation or past experience, try to imagine how your toddler might react to the event or performance you're thinking about attending—and then, of course, be prepared to be proven entirely wrong.

▲ How long is the event or performance? Clearly, the shorter the program, the better. Scheduled breaks (such as intermissions and half-times) can help break longer programs up into bites your toddler is more likely to be able to swallow, while giving him or her a chance to run off some energy between sittings.

▲ Is sitting through the entire event important to you, or to any older children? If it is, get a sitter to care for your toddler at home, or bring someone along who won't care about missing part of the program and will be willing to take your toddler out if necessary.

▲ Will you have an easy way out? When selecting your seat, accessibility to an exit should be a prime consideration, and sometimes that means sitting near the back and on the aisle. Of course, if having a good view will be vital to your toddler's enjoyment (as it is at a circus or a puppet show), you may have to sit closer to the front, but again on the aisle.

▲ Is there somewhere to wait it out? Be sure there is a lobby, grassy area out front, nearby park, a gift shop, a refreshment stand, or some other neutral, child-friendly area where you, another family member, or a sitter can retreat with your toddler.

▲ Is the gamble worth the expense? Unless money is no object, it's usually unwise to bet on your toddler sitting through a very costly program. You may have to leave early or spend much of the performance in the lobby or outside.

As you should anytime you leave the house with a toddler, come prepared with: a good supply of snacks, books, and quiet toys for strategically timed use; an appreciation of your child's normal, age-appropriate limitations; and your sense of humor.

hoods past have given way to death-ray toting robots and perfect replicas of machine guns—making shopping at a toy store reminiscent of shopping at the Pentagon, except that you don't need security clearance.

Where a little boy's natural instincts leave off and society's influences take over is controversial and almost impossible to document. Anyone who has seen a two-year-old male raised by peace-loving parents, sheltered from war toys, violent cartoons, and the evening news, pick up a stick, a broom, or a hairbrush and proceed to wield it as a weapon, has to wonder whether nurture—and the best

pacifist intentions—can completely subdue nature.

Studies are clear about one thing, however. Though parents can rarely prevent their offspring from playing cops and robbers, soldier, and other shoot-'em-up games, they can almost always prevent them from growing into violent adults. With that in mind:

**Remember, war is history.** You can't shield your child from the fact that wars exist—they're etched in the pages of virtually every history book he'll ever read. But though you can't take the war out of history, you can take the glory out of

# MAKING ROUTINES ROUTINE

Routine. For many adults, the word summons up only negative associations: "predictable," "boring," "monotonous," "same-old same-old." Yet for most small children, routines are eagerly anticipated, promising comfort, not tedium. Knowing what they can expect at various times during their day can make children feel more secure and in control. Particularly during the tumultuous toddler years, routines often represent the only calm in life's storm.

Parents, too, can benefit from making routines routine. Routines can help toddlers accept transition more readily, reducing the likelihood of resistance as they switch gears—from story time to lunch, from playground to home, from blocks to bedtime. They also eliminate a lot of time-consuming planning (once a routine is established, you no longer have to give it a second thought), cut down on last-minute panics, and generally make frenetic days run more smoothly.

Routine doesn't work for everyone, and can actually upset children who are by nature "irregular" (see page 202); they can stress some free-spirited families by cramping their spontaneous style. Nor do the same routines work for every family. But most families with small children find that *some* routine in their chaotic schedules—whether a single weekly routine or several daily rituals—makes sense.

**Bedtime routines.** These set the tone for a happy close to a toddler's day. For tips on how to create such a routine, see page 68.

**Good-morning routines.** Start the day off right—with a cozy cuddle first thing in the morning. Set an earliest hour limit—when it's light outside, when the clock-radio goes on, or once your child begins recognizing some numbers, when the clock says 6 or 7— so that your child won't start awakening in the middle of the night ready to cuddle. Or start off with a special greeting—a kiss, a hug, and a favorite song (live or on tape), for example.

**Off-to-work routines.** When one or both parents leave in the morning, a mock bear hug, a special parting phrase, watching and waving from the window, can all make the farewell easier.

**Clean-up routines.** Whether you insist on one toy being put away before the next comes out or call for a thorough clean-up at the end of a play session or the end of the day, getting your toddler into the routine of picking up after him- or herself will pay both short- and long-term dividends.

Linking clean-up time with a particular song or bit of music ("This is the way we pick up our toys, pick up our toys, pick up our toys . . . This is the way we pick up our toys, so early in the evening") will help establish the routine in the first place and make it much more appealing over the long haul. So will making a game of it: For example, setting an hourglass or timer and trying a beat-the-clock clean-up. (See page 417 for more on cleanup.)

**Welcome-home routines.** No matter who is

war. If your toddler seems fascinated with soldiers and fighting, expose him to some history (of the American Revolution, the Civil War, World War II) at a young child's level—avoiding gruesome pictures and descriptions. Explain that war is not a game, real people get hurt when countries choose fighting it out over working it out.

**Take your cue from the garden of Eden.** Forbidding something completely often makes it more seductive—à la Eve and the apple. A child who isn't allowed to play with toy guns may improvise— turning other objects into "weapons."

**If you do ban weapons, don't ban imagination.** If it's important to you that

coming home—from work or from daycare or from preschool—sticking to a predictable unwinding routine—roughhousing, reading a book, watching a favorite TV show together—before starting on meals, mail, and other obligations can help relax all of you after a long day. Or make taking care of these obligations part of the routine—setting the table together, going to the mailbox together, and so on.

**Mealtime routines.** It may take some of the romance out of dining, but knowing that if it's Monday it must be fish and carrots, if it's Tuesday it must be pasta primavera, if it's Wednesday it must be pizza and salad, and so on, can also take some of the last minute stress out of shopping and cooking. Make weekend meals, when there's more time to plan, the adventurous repasts of the week. (Of course, you'll probably have to be more flexible when it comes to feeding your toddler, who may have his or her own dinner routine in mind: macaroni and cheese every night of the week.) If menu routine turns you off, consider other mealtime traditions: saying grace, taking turns talking about the day's activities, listening to music, playing word games.

**Leisure-time routines.** Since having a toddler in the house pretty much scotches any chance of pre-parenthood weekend spontaneity (remember breakfast and lovemaking in bed, and antiquing in the afternoon?), you might as well stick to weekend routines that you *and* your toddler can look forward to. For instance, early-morning cuddle-and-tickle sessions, pancakes with faces for breakfast, Saturday afternoon outings with Mom, Sunday in the park with Dad.

**Hygiene routines.** For the toddler who tends to resist hygiene-related activities, knowing when to expect them can make these tasks less annoying. So establish a predictable routine for tooth brushing, hand washing, baths, and shampooing.

**"Leaving" routines.** Leaving—a friend's house, the playground, or Grandma's—is difficult for many children. Establishing a regular routine for departures (singing a special good-bye song or reciting a poem, then saying individual good-byes, and on the way home, stopping to look at the puppies in the pet shop window, for instance) may decrease resistance.

**Going to day-care/preschool routines.** Always singing the same "this is the way we go to school" song (or another ditty ), always walking or driving the same route, always playing name-those-kids (trying to remember all the children in the class, then trying to remember something distinctive about each child) or find-that-color, or another game that you've made up can help make the transition from home to school more predictable, and therefore less distressing.

Remember that once you establish a routine, sticking to it as closely as possible is important—even when vacations, visitors, and other extenuating circumstances shake up the status quo. Some toddlers are easily unsettled by change, particularly the last-minute variety. So if you must break with a routine, try to prepare your toddler in advance and then muster up that extra patience to help him or her cope with the disruption.

there be no weapons in the house, by all means forbid them. But if your child plays war games—either with makeshift weapons at home or with store-bought toy weapons at a friend's—don't make an issue of it. By not buying toy weapons for your child and making him aware of how you feel on the subject, you're making a strong enough statement.

**Consider compromise.** Some parents, for example, okay innocuous looking water pistols and old traditional favorites (six-shooters, plastic medieval swords and bows and arrows) that aren't part of a modern weapons arsenal and outlaw those that are too realistic or violent (such as water pistols that look like machine guns and super water blasters).

**Verbalize your objections.** Whether or not you decide on a ban, it's important to explain to your child why you feel the way you do about war toys: "I know you like to play with toy guns, but I want you to know that real guns and knives and swords can hurt people." Whenever the opportunity presents itself tell your child that "It's better to talk than to fight" and that "only police officers and soldiers should use guns against other people, and then only to protect you and me and keep us safe."

**Keep the peace at home.** No other factor has more influence on what kind of person a child becomes than the environment in which he grows up. A child who is raised by parental role models who resolve disagreements and disputes verbally instead of physically will almost certainly do the same as an adult—no matter what toys he chooses and games he plays. Lavishing a child with love, emphasizing such values as the rights of others, tolerance, and kindness, and honing communication skills (see page 424) will be much more significant in nurturing a respect for nonviolence than a ban on toy weapons.

**Use literature as an ally.** Look for books that stress peaceful settlement of battles. For the older toddler, Dr. Seuss's wonderful *Butter Battle Book* clearly illustrates the futility and foolishness of war.

**Tune out television, video, and movie violence.** Even cartoons, depicting far more creative and numerous ways to inflict harm than anything your child could ever summon up in imaginative war play, can insidiously desensitize young viewers to violence (see page 160).

# UNREASONABLENESS

*"I know that my daughter is too young to reason with, but her unreasonableness is making me nuts."*

Though it wouldn't seem so to a reasonably rational adult, a toddler has good reasons for being unreasonable. For refusing to wear a coat in cold weather. For not eating a bite of the cereal she asked for five minutes before. For tearing half of a page out of her favorite book and then being angry because the page is no longer intact.

The most obvious reason, of course, is that she's a typical toddler, struggling for independence. She wants to make her own decisions, even if they are wrong. She wants to find out for herself, even if the process is painful—for her as well as her family. But toddlers are also often unreasonable because they are hungry or tired or otherwise out-of-sorts.

Reasoning with your unreasonable toddler—as you've wisely recognized—is not realistic. Instead, try these techniques:

**Treat with food or rest.** Always think "food" and/or "rest" when considering how to deal with irrational behavior. You won't be able to deal rationally with the toddler who is beside herself because she's hungry or tired until she's been fed or has rested. And while you're at it, make sure that you feed yourself as well—unreasonable toddlers are less exasperating to deal with when you're not cranky with hunger.

**Consider underlying personality differences.** Some toddlers *seem* to be unreasonable but are actually acting in a way that is consistent with their personality type. If you haven't already, check to see if what you think is irrational is just "difficult-child" syndrome (see page 200). If it is, treat accordingly.

**Don't let irrationality rule.** If your toddler refuses to get into the car seat and you must take an older child to school, strap your toddler in kicking and screaming if you must. Or if she decides she wants to empty every bookcase in the house, distract her, take her out to the playground, or otherwise put a stop to her efforts. Don't let a toddler's irrationality run—and ruin—everyone else's life.

**Let cause have its effect.** Except when learning from her mistakes might jeopardize her health or safety, or significantly inconvenience others in the family, allow your toddler to experience the consequences of her unreasonable behavior: When she doesn't put her coat on, she's cold when she goes out (or, if it is bitter cold, she isn't allowed to play outdoors); when she doesn't eat, she goes hungry; when she rips her book, she can't see all the pictures. It'll take plenty of trial and error on her part, but eventually she will begin to realize that parents sometimes have a point.

**Hold the "I told you so's."** It may be tempting, after your toddler has disobeyed the injunction not to step in puddles, to rub her nose in her wet sneakers, at least figuratively. Resist that temptation. The consequence—cold, wet feet—is punishment enough for her faulty judgment; she doesn't need your insults added to her injury. Instead, underline the lesson matter of factly, "Oops, wet feet. That's why stepping in puddles without boots on isn't really such a great idea."

**Get crafty.** There are dozens of tricks to the parents-of-toddlers trade; while none of them work all of the time, one or another of them is likely to work some of the time. When successful, they allow you to achieve your goals while letting your toddler save face. Try a change of activity, a silly incongruity (the old boots-on-the-hands routine), reverse psychology (see page 316), an ad-lib song, a little fast talking ("Do you know what we're doing after lunch today?") to distract your toddler when she's getting irrational.

**And . . . keep your sense of humor.** Instead of letting an irrational toddler drive you up the wall, laugh at her antics—to yourself, of course. Keep them in perspective by reminding yourself over and over again that unbelievable as it may seem, "this too shall pass."

# WHAT IT'S IMPORTANT TO KNOW: The Art of Comforting (Kissing and Making Better)

Your mother did it. Her mother before her did it. And though there may not be any petroglyphs to prove it, chances are cave mothers did it, too. Ever since there have been children in need of comfort (for a scraped knee, a bumped lip, or a bruised ego), there have been mothers (and, more often now than in the past, fathers) around to "kiss the hurt and make it better."

Giving comfort to children is as basic and essential a part of parenting as giving nourishment; in order to thrive, a child needs adequate amounts of both. Much of the comfort comes instinctively—in the form of a quick hug, a touch of the lips, or the brushing away of a few tears—and usually that's enough to get a toddler who's taken a tumble to toddle off happily. But sometimes that kiss alone won't make it better—sometimes you'll need to put a little extra time, effort, and thought into the comforting of your child, particularly as he or she grows older and more complex.

**Be aware of your power.** You may feel you're only human—sometimes, only *too* human. But to a two- or three-year-old, you're nothing short of omnipotent. Though your offspring-endowed omnipotence will fade as the years go by, leaving you, a mere mortal again by the time your child enters adolescence, for now your reassuring words and loving touch carry plenty of weight. When you cradle your toddler in your arms and say, "It will be all right," he or she will magically feel at least a little, if not all, better. Which is why your brand of comfort is the best medicine for whatever is ailing your child—whether the bruise is physical or emotional.

**Be an island of calm in the storm . . .** If you regularly respond to everyday tumbles with a calm, "Whoops, you're all right," your toddler is pretty sure to feel all right. If you screech, "Oh, my poor baby! Are you hurt?" your toddler will learn to take the opportunity to answer "Yes" loud and clear. Nothing alarms a child more than a parent who is alarmed; nothing upsets like an upset parent: "If my tower of strength is crumbling, there must really be something wrong." So though it's only natural for you to feel keenly your child's pain, it's best if you don't show excessive concern. You'll be a much more effective source of reassurance if you remain calm—and if you transmit this calm not only in your words and tone of voice, but in your facial expressions and body language. Toddlers whose parents don't overreact become children who pick themselves up from a fall, brush themselves off, and go on their merry way.

**. . . but don't pretend there is no storm.** Though you shouldn't overreact to a child's pain, you shouldn't totally ignore it, particularly when the hurt is emotional. We all need to know that our feelings have validity—and we all have the right, occasionally, to make a mountain out of a molehill. This is particularly true of toddlers, who are so small and vulnerable—and to whom molehills do, truly, loom like so many Mt. Everests. By treating all problems and anxieties as trifles, dismissing every upset with "Oh, you're absolutely okay . . . that's nothing," when it really *is* something to your child, your message is that his or her feelings don't count.

**Comfort unconditionally.** Even when their behavior has been less than sterling, children deserve consolation when injured. Comfort your child even after he or she has fallen off the chair you declared off-limits two minutes before or has caught a finger in the cabinet door you said to stop swinging.

**Lend an ear . . . and a shoulder to cry on.** A wound of the spirit often needs as much comfort as a wound of the body. Encourage your child to talk about it ("You seem upset; do you want to tell me why?) when his or her feelings have been hurt. It may be difficult, while communication skills are still halting, and particularly during times of stress, to figure out what's being said—but your efforts to recognize and validate your child's feelings will be something he or she appreciates.

**Listen, but don't lecture.** Though toddlers who are in physical or emotional pain need someone to listen, to validate their feelings, and to express support, they don't need lectures, put-downs, or I-told-you-so's. But beware of offering too much sympathy. Overdoses can turn out a child who is dependent, self-pitying, and relishes the martyr's role.

**Don't assign blame.** Blaming your child ("If you hadn't left that car in the middle of the floor, you wouldn't have fallen") will neither comfort nor teach a lesson. Better to say, "Let's see if we can figure out why you fell." When your child says, "I fell on the car," you can respond, "How do you think you can make sure you won't fall that way again?"

Putting the blame elsewhere won't be helpful either ("Lisa always makes such a mess of your toys, no wonder you can't find all the pieces to your game").

Instead, ask "What do you think you can do to keep your game pieces from getting lost next time?"

**Don't try to make everything better.** Your child dropped a toy truck out the window, smashing it? It's okay to say, "I'm sorry your truck is broken." But it's not a good idea to run out and buy a new one immediately. If children don't learn from their mistakes, they're likely to repeat them—over and over and over again.

# WHAT IT'S IMPORTANT FOR YOUR TODDLER TO KNOW: All About Right and Wrong

There's a little Pinocchio in every toddler. Like Pinocchio, toddlers are relatively new to the world and inexperienced in its ways. Consequently, like Pinocchio, they're curious, mischievous, fun-loving, sometimes painfully naive—and lacking that internal compass of right and wrong we call a conscience. Except, instead of a charismatic cricket standing by to provide them with the moral guidance they're not yet able to provide themselves, toddlers have parents and caregivers to show them the way.

It's their parents to whom toddlers look when they're uncertain whether that cookie's okay to take from the man behind the bakery counter; whether that toy's okay to play with in the doctor's waiting room. It's their parents who tell them that hitting Jeremy when he's got the truck they want is wrong, and that waiting your turn when three other kids are lined up at the slide is hard but right. It's their parents who prod them to thank Aunt Marie for the jack-in-the-box she brought, and who discourage them from throwing sand at a playmate at the beach.

And like Pinocchio's Jiminy Cricket, the parents of toddlers aren't the permanent purveyors of conscience for their offspring. They're merely moral stand-ins, distinguishing for their toddlers the difference between right and wrong until their toddlers are able to distinguish for themselves.

Young children, researchers believe, are motivated to behave morally by self-interest and fear of negative consequences.[5] In the next stage of life, the motivation moves up a notch: Moral behavior is based on a desire for approval, a respect for higher authority, and an understanding of the need for maintaining the social order ("If everybody did this bad thing, what would happen?").

---

5. This research was pioneered in the U.S. by Professor Lawrence Kohlberg of Harvard University.

Generally, not until the teen years does a true sensitivity to the needs of others or a real concept of justice and fairness develop. Without adequate moral guidance and example, though, many people never reach that stage.

But just because it's too soon to expect consistently ethical behavior from your toddler—or even to expect an understanding of what ethical behavior is—doesn't mean it's too soon to start cultivating a conscience in your child. If you wait until your child is old enough to participate in a philosophical discussion about right and wrong, you've waited too long.

To play your Jiminy Cricket role to the fullest, use the following script:

**Explain that actions have consequences.** While it's important to tell your toddler that it's wrong to throw sand, it's also important to add the reason *why* it's wrong ("When you throw sand, it can get into someone's eyes, and that hurts a lot. See, Danny's eyes are all red, and he's crying.") And while it's important to tell your toddler that it's right to wait your turn instead of pushing your way to the front of the line at the slide, it's also important to add *why* it's right ("When you wait your turn, everybody gets to go on the slide, everybody has a good time, and there's no pushing or fighting to get on first"). Developing empathy is key to developing a conscience.

**Don't lecture or preach.** A simple explanation is all that's required. Go on

and on and your toddler will surely tune you out. And remember: You're there to guide, not to judge.

**Ask the right questions.** Involve your toddler from the start in his or her own moral education, and stimulate thinking about the consequences of actions: After your child swats a playmate, ask "How do you think Sarah felt when you hit her?" When you've read a book that has a moral to it, explain it in words your toddler can understand, and then ask for his or her opinion on it. Ask for your toddler's two cents, too, when a character in a story or on television has done something obviously right or obviously wrong.

**Fault behavior, not people.** Don't shame your toddler or make him or her feel bad or inadequate for doing something wrong or failing to do something right; criticize the behavior, not the child (see page 295). Guide your toddler to do the same in evaluating the behavior of others. Instead of, "Cookie monster is not nice for eating all the cookies and not sharing," try, "Eating all the cookies the way Cookie Monster did, and not sharing, isn't nice."

**Set a conscientious example.** As always, an ounce of example vastly outweighs a pound of instruction. Let *your* conscience be *your* guide—and for the time being, your toddler's—and eventually your child will develop a conscience all his or her own.

# CHAPTER TEN

# The Twenty-Second Month

## WHAT YOUR TODDLER MAY BE DOING NOW

*By the end of this month,[1] your toddler . . . should be able to (see Note):*

▲ use 6 words (by 21½ months)
▲ walk up steps (by 21½ months)

**Note:** If your toddler has not reached these milestones or doesn't use symbolic play and words, consult the doctor or nurse-practitioner. This rate of development may well be normal for your child (some children are late bloomers), but it needs to be evaluated. Also check with the doctor if your toddler seems out-of-control or hyperactive; uncommunicative, passive, or withdrawn; highly negative, demanding, and stubborn.

---

1. The twenty-second month begins when a child is twenty-one months old and ends when he or she is twenty-two months old.

(Remember, the child who was born prematurely often lags behind others of the same chronological age.) This developmental gap has probably narrowed by now and is likely to disappear entirely around age two.

*. . . will probably be able to:*

▲ build a tower of 4 cubes
▲ follow a 2 step command without gestures (by 21½ months)

*. . . may possibly be able to:*

▲ build a tower of 6 cubes
▲ identify 4 pictures by pointing
▲ wash and dry hands

*. . . may even be able to:*

▲ jump up (by 21½ months)

# WHAT YOU MAY BE CONCERNED ABOUT

## TROUBLE WITH TAKING TURNS

*"Our son doesn't seem to get the idea of 'taking turns.' He won't wait his turn at the playground or at play group. And he always pushes his way in and insists on being first."*

That's because in the world according to toddlers, he *should* come first. He is the star, the director, the stage manager of the drama of life—everyone else is just a bit player. Prima donna that he is, he expects and demands certain rights and privileges—including first (or even exclusive) use of the slide, the swings, the rocking horse, the shape-sorter, and the water fountain.

Such self-centered behavior doesn't mean that your child is destined to become a selfish, inconsiderate bully, but that he has a lot of growing up to do (and you have a lot of guidance to give) be-

fore he regularly displays appropriate respect for the rights of others. He will probably learn to take turns sooner if he is in a day-care or nursery school situation, or meets frequently with a play group. You can also help him reach that goal sooner by trying the following tips:

**Take turns together.** Because he's less likely to feel competitive with you than with his peers, your toddler may be more willing to practice turn-taking at home. When you're eating lunch, take turns taking bites of your sandwiches. When he's in the tub, take turns splashing each other. When you're reading him a book, take turns turning the pages.

**Take turns being first.** When taking turns with your toddler, don't always let him go first. Instead, try to alternate: "This morning you put the first block on top; now it's my turn to be first."

**Take turns tactfully.** Practicing turn taking should be fun, not an ordeal. Only

*Sharing is rarely a toddler's forte.*

attempt it when your toddler's in a sporting mood—not when he's tired, hungry, or otherwise cranky. If and when the practice seems to be provoking tension, stop.

**Take turns with a timer.** Using a timer as an impartial referee at play dates and play groups is one of the most effective ways to teach children to take turns. It allows a toddler to relinquish a riding toy, a shovel, a wagon, a doll without losing face. It also reduces arguing—it's tougher to dispute a clock than a parent. Explain "I am going to set the timer. When the timer rings, your turn will be over and it will be Molly's turn." It may take several demonstrations and run-throughs before the children accept the timer idea, but with persistence this technique will pay off.

**Take taking turns patiently.** Remember that your toddler can't be expected to regularly cooperate in the give-and-take of turn taking with playmates until at least his third birthday.

# *PROTECTING YOUR VALUABLES*

*"We collect pottery and other art objects, and it's important to us that our son learn to respect them and their delicate nature. But we're afraid to let him learn at the expense of our collection."*

**V**ery wise. Though it's not too early to begin your toddler's fine arts training, your fine arts collection will, as you fear, be at considerable risk unless you protect it during the training process—which can take a year or two, or even more.

It often appears that the goal of any toddler confronted with a roomful of valuables is to search and destroy. But that's rarely the case. What's behind your child's behavior is much more likely to be the perilous partnership of curiosity and clumsiness. Seeing something interesting, he picks it up to get a closer look, and (oops!) drops it. If it's breakable, it breaks.

Your cherished collectibles will obviously stand the best chance of survival if they're packed safely away for a few years. But keeping breakables safe by keeping them from your toddler teaches him nothing about respect for the possessions, delicate or otherwise, of others. It also deprives you of the enjoyment of your belongings.

The best way to deal with your situation is to follow a four-pronged plan, which includes protecting your valuables, teaching your child to respect the words "don't touch," training him to touch okay touchables gently and carefully, and instilling in him an appreciation of your treasures.

**Safeguarding valuables.** How best to do this depends on what your collection is like, how extensive it is, where it is ordinarily kept, and whether your child generally plays nearby. Whatever the situation, anything that is breakable or dangerous to your toddler *must* be placed out of his reach. (Keep in mind that he is perfectly capable of climbing.) Irreplaceable items should probably be stashed away temporarily, even if you take other precautions. Ideally, try to house the rest of your collection, at least for the moment, in an area that is not accessible to your toddler, and then limit his access to supervised periods only. If your toddler and your collection must frequently share a space, a locked case with safety-glass doors or a high shelf running around the room at a 6- or 7-foot height are possible alternate display solutions.

## SHOPPING WITH TODDLERS:
## MISSION IMPOSSIBLE

··········

It's yet another of the ironies of parenting: Having a toddler makes it necessary to do more shopping, yet that same toddler also makes it almost impossible to get any shopping done at all. Parenting a toddler certainly signals the end of shopping as you knew it. If a toddler isn't disappearing down the frozen-food aisle, he's knocking over a carefully stacked display of cereal boxes. If she isn't vanishing behind a sale rack, she's trying to go up the "down" escalator. If he isn't loudly demanding that you buy a treat or toy he's just spied on the shelf, he's throwing a full-blown tantrum before an audience of disapproving witnesses. If she isn't hungry ("right now!"), she's thirsty ("right now!"), and if she isn't either, she has to go to the potty ("too late!").

Yet shop we must. Following these tips won't make the process entirely painless, stress-free, or a logistical piece of cake, but they may help you get the job done:

▲ Don't leave home *with* "it." A toddler, that is. Unless a fitting is necessary (as it is with shoes), even shopping for toddler clothing is better accomplished without the toddler (chances are, he or she will refuse to try them on, anyway). Seize the opportunity to shop whenever there's someone else around to stay home with your child—at stores with convenient evening, round-the-clock, or weekend morning hours. Or organize a baby-sitting/shopping co-op with a friend who has a toddler: You can take turns watching the kids and shopping. Or alternate shopping duty with your spouse—one of you stays home with the toddler and the other can go off to the store. If you both work outside the home, make plans for one of you to stop at the store while the other

goes home. Or bring a sandwich to eat at your desk, and shop during your lunch hour if you can. Or don't leave home at all: When possible, phone grocery orders in to markets that will deliver. Order clothing through catalogs or department store circulars (or, if you're adventurous, via computer or TV shopping shows).

▲ When you can't leave home without "it," make sure "it" is in a relatively good mood—fed, well rested, and not overstimulated. There's no predicting toddler behavior, but there's no point in writing a script for disaster (suggested title: "Mayhem in the Market") by taking a hungry, tired, and/or cranky toddler to the store. Avoid staging "Showdown at the Children's Shoe Corral," by keeping your saddlebags well packed whenever you stray from home (see page 251).

▲ Enlist help. Almost anyone who is spry enough to chase a toddler down the aisles will do. Even a preteen who isn't old enough to baby-sit alone can do a good job of looking after your toddler while you shop.

▲ Be a list-maker. Before leaving home, make a detailed list of needed groceries. This is easier to do if you make a master inventory list, arranged in the order you typically proceed through the store (or stores), with items found in the same section (or store) grouped together. List frozen foods and other perishables last and leave some blank space for specialty items. Then make a couple of dozen copies of the list for easy checking-off before your weekly marketing. Make lists, too, for clothing, drugstore, housewares, and other shopping excursions. Though all this takes some time at home, it can cut down dramatically on the time spent shopping. It can also eliminate the last-minute dash during checkout for the carton of eggs you forgot, as well as the extra trips to the market when you forget the eggs entirely.

▲ Prepare your toddler positively. Announce just what you will be shopping for (food, sneakers, a book), but don't plant ideas in your toddler's head by saying, "We're *not* going to be buying candy, party shoes, or toys." Toddlers are talented enough at coming up with such ideas on their own. (When they do, of course, you have to be talented enough to know how to say "No.")

Use the positive approach, too, about the behavior you expect. For example, before going through the automatic doors at the supermarket, say "You're going to ride in the shopping cart; you can help me find the foods on our list and put them in the cart," not "You can't walk around inside, and you can't touch anything!" And don't forget positive reinforcement in the form of a few words of praise when your toddler has exercised even a modicum of restraint while you shop.

▲ Provide transportation. You may also be able to cut your shopping time if you can persuade your toddler to ride in the shopping cart at the supermarket rather than toddle down the aisles. (Young toddlers, of course, should be strapped into the cart for safety. Thousands of small children annually sustain injuries that require emergency room care when they tumble out of carts).

Or use a stroller if you only have a few items on your list. Hook a small shopping basket over the handles of the stroller and keep your little one buckled in while you shop. (Avoid overloading the basket—once the groceries outweigh the child, all will topple backwards.) The stroller can also be a boon at shopping malls. Be sure to bring along toys or trinkets to occupy your toddler while you shop. They should be securely attached—so that you won't have to spend half your time looking for what was dropped in the last aisle or three stores back.

▲ Make a run for it. Leave label reading, coupon clipping, comparison shopping, and careful scrutiny of produce for solo trips to the market. Take the time to analyze a unit price, and your toddler could be three aisles away.

▲ Consider the convenience of convenience stores. When all you need is a container of milk and a couple of bananas, the easy in-and-out accessibility of a convenience store may make the higher prices well worth it.

▲ Steer clear of trouble. If you know your regular shopping destinations well, it should be fairly easy to circumvent or at least speed by potential hot spots (such as the toy department, the fine china and crystal section, or displays of marshmallow-laced cereals). Some supermarkets have a candy-free checkout counter to eliminate (at least in theory) the threat of toddler tantrums ("get me that bubble-gum, or I'll scream!"); if your favorite store doesn't, suggest that they set one up.

▲ Engage idle hands and heads. The toddler occupied with helping push the shopping cart, carrying a box of favorite crackers, counting out three containers of yogurt, spotting "A's" or the color red, or choosing between two parent-suggested jellies may not have the time or inclination to wander off or make a scene. The toddler pushing a mini-shopping cart and loading it (under parental supervision) with unbreakable purchases isn't likely to, either. (If your supermarket doesn't supply such a cart— only a few enlightened stores do—you'll have to tote your own.) Though marketing will probably take a little longer with this kind of help, at least you'll have a shot at getting it done. And your toddler will feel good about being useful, and maybe even learn something about shopping.

**Teaching "Don't touch!"** Place one or two display items in a shared room in plain view, within easy reach of your toddler, and declare them off-limits. (Since you can't expect complete compliance immediately, these items should be safe for your toddler to touch and nonbreakable.) Whenever your toddler approaches them, warn, "Don't touch." Explain that they aren't toys and that he mustn't play with them because they are special. If he nevertheless shows an interest in handling them (and he probably will), pick up a piece yourself and let him touch while you hold. If you forbid his touching an object entirely, you will make him that much more eager to get his hands on it. Tell him that any time that he wants to touch, he has to ask a grown-up for help.

**Teaching a gentle touch.** Too often children are taught *not* to touch without ever learning *how* to touch. Training a toddler how to handle things that are delicate, whether inanimate (precious pottery, fragile knickknacks, books) or living (babies, pets, flowers), should start early. Here's how:

▲ Choose a safe spot. Sit together on a carpet or in the middle of a large bed or sofa, for example.

▲ Choose a safe subject. Don't start off with a prized piece of pre-Columbian pottery; instead select something that you could easily live without if you had to (that banana-shaped candy dish Aunt Edna gave you as an engagement gift, perhaps).

▲ Schedule "touching" lessons wisely. Children learn best—and are also less likely to dash a delicate item to bits in a fit of pique—when they're not cranky, hungry, tired, wound up, or more impatient or frustrated than usual.

▲ Teach by example, first. Take the fragile object in your hands with exaggerated caution, as if it were a Ming vase, and repeat the same chosen catch phrases over and over: "Be gentle." "See how I'm being gentle?" "See how I touch it gently?"

▲ Then try some hands-on experience. Put the object down, and let your toddler experience a gentle touch firsthand, stroking him the same way you stroked the object and repeating, "See, gently." Next, show your child how to touch you gently. Take his hand and guide it across your skin, instructing him, "Be gentle." Then, with him in your arms or on your lap, hand over the object and direct him to touch it "gently."

▲ Keep the lessons brief. Always quit while you're ahead—hopefully, before anything's broken.

▲ Repeat the lessons often. You needn't schedule them daily, but they should be frequent enough so that your child doesn't forget what he's learned from lesson to lesson. Also take the opportunity to talk about gentle touching whenever it arises, when your toddler wants to touch a new baby, for example, or pet the neighbor's dog, or when he wants to handle a pretty figurine at Grandma's house or a flower in the garden. Remember that with toddlers, repetition brings results.

▲ Heap praise on your pupil—during and after the lesson. Nothing prompts compliance in a toddler like positive reinforcement.

▲ Trust you must. If you give a child your trust, he's likely to work very hard to be worthy of it. (And it can also do wonders for his self-esteem.) This doesn't mean you should give him free run in a china shop to prove your trust, but that you probably shouldn't jump 10 feet in the air every time he comes within range of Grandma's coffee table.

▲ Don't take chances. No amount of gentle-touch training can guarantee that an "accident" won't happen. So anything that you value—and particularly, anything irreplaceable—should be kept out of your toddler's reach, even once you feel his training is complete.

▲ Try not to overreact when something gets broken or otherwise damaged. Accidents can happen to anyone, and they happen more often to toddlers.

**Teaching appreciation.** Children understand why a Big Bird puppet or a stuffed Dumbo are special, but they have little understanding of why a bowl with funny markings on it or a doll-size porcelain cup or a crystal vase are special. As your toddler's comprehension grows, begin explaining why the items in your collection are special to you. Perhaps, for example, "These bowls and jugs were made very long ago. No one makes them anymore, so they are very special to me." Or, "Those cups come from very far away and my grandma brought them here. I want to keep them safe so that one day, when you have your own house, I can give them to you." Taking your toddler on brief trips to museums where he can see similar items will also enhance his appreciation. If you collect older pieces, explain what the word "antique" means, and point out examples to him when you see them.

# FASCINATION WITH THE MECHANICAL

*"My daughter seems fascinated by anything mechanical or electrical. She's always trying to investigate machines and wires—and that makes me worry for her safety."*

**Y**ou seem to have a budding engineer on your hands. And, as a prudent parent, there are two concerns you have

to deal with immediately: saving for her tuition at M.I.T. and protecting her from her own curiosity.

A toddler's curiosity typically exceeds her good sense; your job is to keep your child's lack of judgment from jeopardizing her safety. Certainly, the easiest way is to forbid any and all exploration of machines and gadgets. But while that would keep your child's body safe from harm it would probably stifle her scientific curiosity. In fact, taking steps to prevent injury doesn't require that you automatically discourage all investigation.

Instead, make the safety rules (beginning on page 617) a routine part of your life. Be sure your toddler knows which tantalizing objects are totally off-limits (electrical outlets, the kitchen range and oven, the microwave) and which can be used with adult supervision. Then nurture your child's interests while protecting life and limb by giving her plenty of safe and supervised opportunities to satisfy her natural curiosity. Let her turn on the radio or TV for you, push the buttons that control the VCR, tap computer keys or manipulate its "mouse" to make letters, numbers, or pictures appear on the screen. Buy or borrow toys that she can take apart, put together, and make work on her own (but be sure they're age-appropriate or frustration may surpass fascination). Present her with projects (construction sets and toddler computer games, for instance) she can collaborate on with a parent or caregiver. Enroll her in a "discovery" type class for toddlers, if one is available in your area. Take her, whenever you can, to a children's museum that has hands-on science exhibits and let her press, pull, and push to her heart's content. Provide her with books that explore the scientific world and any other topics that interest her.

## GETTING CAUGHT IN THE ACT

*"The other night, we were making love in our bedroom when our daughter wandered in from her room. We didn't notice her for a few moments, so she must have seen what we were doing. Could this be damaging to her?"*

**P**robably not. She can't possibly know what you were doing and may even have been too sleepy for anything to register. If she seemed shaken by the experience, it was most likely because she was afraid you were hurting one another. To a child, who has no idea what's going on, sexual positions can look aggressive and lovemaking sounds can sound like reactions to pain rather than pleasure. If she raises the question of violence, reassure her that you weren't hurting each other but just hugging and kissing and loving each other in the special way that parents do. Don't go into any complicated explanations until she specifically asks for them, which won't be for some time to come (see page 420). If you shouted at her or chased her away when you noticed she was there, apologize. Explain that she surprised you and scared you a little bit.

Because catching you in the act at some future point could upset your child and certainly won't do much for your love life, it would be a good idea to lock your door during lovemaking. (If your door doesn't have a lock, consider installing one, or simply put up a hook and eye out of reach of little hands.)

If some day, in the heat of passion, you forget to turn the lock, and your toddler does walk in on you again, keep your cool. Say that you need a little privacy and ask her to wait outside for a minute. Quickly slip into something, and then calmly return her to her bed without making her feel anxious, ashamed, or

guilty. She didn't do anything wrong— and neither did you.

Most children quickly forget such incidents, especially if little is made of them. But if your child wants to talk about it later, let her. Answer any questions she asks at an age-appropriate level.

## EXPLORATION OF THE GENITALS

*"Ever since she got out of diapers, my daughter has her hands in her pants whenever she gets the chance. I know that's supposed to be normal, but it bothers me— especially when she does it in public places."*

**U**p until now, your daughter's private parts have been largely out of her reach—under wraps, so to speak. With the switch to training pants, they have become much more accessible. The potty-learning process has also made them a focus of attention, heightening her awareness of her body.

For the toddler, explorations of all kinds are normal. Her exploration of her genitals is no less innocent than her exploration of her fingers and toes, her belly button and her ears. While curiosity generally prompts the initial rounds of genital exploration, the toddler usually notes that touching her genitals feels good, and it is that discovery that brings her hands back there again and again. This may look like masturbation, but in toddlers it isn't (not even in little boys, who experience erections when they handle their penis). The feeling may be pleasurable but it is not sexual.

Keeping after your child to keep her hands out of her pants will only make the activity appear more enticing. It will also give her the idea that the good feelings she's discovered are wicked or forbidden, instead of normal and healthy. The best approach? At home, ignore the behavior.

If her hand begins meandering into her pants at play group or on a play date and this makes you uncomfortable, try to tempt her into another hands-on activity, such as shape-sorting or building with blocks. If her hand remains steadfastly at its station, give up and look the other way.

Touching in more public settings, however, should be discouraged. Not because there's anything wrong with the behavior but because it's considered inappropriate in public—and because it could trigger dangerous impulses in a pedophile viewing it. So begin early to explain to your toddler the difference between "private" and "public," and that some things that are fine to do in private are not okay in public. If she forgets your admonitions, and slips her hand into her pants when you're on an outing, quietly remind her. Take hold of her hand, give it a squeeze, distract her, and praise her for being "big enough" to save her touching for home.

Some children hold their genitals when they have to urinate, as if they think this will help them to "hold it in." If your toddler's genital handling seems related to potty accidents, routinely ask her if she has to go to the potty when you see her hand wander.

Occasionally, a child will spend most of her waking hours fingering her genitals. Like any other comfort habit that interferes with day-to-day functioning, this behavior could be rooted in fears or anxieties. But just as often they are related to other kinds of stress (a new baby-sitter, moving to a new home, a parent going off to work, and so on). Only rarely, it may be related to sexual abuse. If your child seems obsessed with her genitals, consult with her doctor.

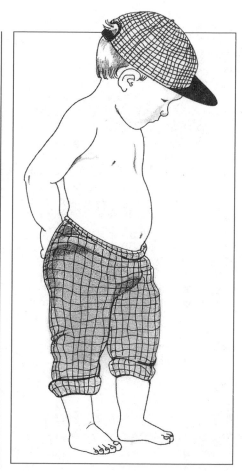

*A tubby tummy is a toddler trademark—not necessarily a sign that your child has been downing too many cookies.*

## POSTURE PROBLEMS

*"Our little girl is slim but she has a pot belly. I keep wanting to tell her to pull her tummy in and stand up straight, but I don't think she'd understand. What can I do?"*

Nothing. At this age, near the end of the second year, the majority of toddlers still have tubby tummies. But by age three or four, when the abdominal muscles gain maturity and strength, most of them sport a slimmer profile—unless they start overdoing the cookies. In the meantime, your toddler doesn't need any tummy tightening exercises or advice on posture, just plenty of opportunities for physical activity.

Keep in mind, too, that while encouraging good posture later on is fine, putting too much emphasis on a slim appearance—or on appearance at all, for that matter—is never a good idea. Setting an elusive goal of physical perfection can threaten a child's self-image, particularly as her body grows and changes, and possibly even lead to eating problems later.

If your toddler's tummy looks much more bulbous than the tummies of most of her playmates, check with her doctor. Very rarely a particularly bulbous tummy could be a sign of a problem.

## FOR-PARENTS-ONLY TEMPER TANTRUMS

*"Our toddler behaves beautifully all day with his baby-sitter. But as soon as we get home from work, he starts with the temper tantrums. Why us?"*

**B**ecause he loves you. Although throwing a tantrum may seem a pretty backhanded compliment, you should actually feel flattered by these outbursts. They suggest that your toddler feels secure enough with you to lose control without worrying that you'll walk out on him. And after a full day of behaving for the baby-sitter (with whom he understandably feels less secure), a fit or two of temper is his way of letting off steam.

A toddler also tends to save up his worst terrible-two's behavior for his par-

ents because his struggle for independence is with them—and not with the baby-sitter, teacher, or day-care provider. It's from those he feels closest to and most dependent on that he feels the need to separate. It's with parents that he has to stake out his territory, take a stand, and assert autonomy.

After-work tantrums can also be a toddler's way of getting parental attention the fastest way he knows how (remember, even negative attention is better than no attention). Nothing prompts a parent to drop everything and focus on a toddler like a tantrum. Sometimes a return-from-work tantrum is a toddler's way of showing his pique at his parents for leaving him every day; he may do this even if he's having a really great time with his substitute caregiver.

Keep in mind, too, that tantrums are most likely to occur during times of fatigue, hunger, stress (yours and your toddler's), and these are in plentiful supply during the after-work period (the sitter, on the other hand, arrives fresh and rested each morning). See page 271 for tips on making this time more peaceful. For tips on handling tantrums, see page 339.

## RITUALISTIC BEHAVIOR

*"Everything's a ritual to my toddler: He always has to have his orange juice in the same cup, he always has to have his sandwich cut up precisely the same way, he always has to wear the same beat-up blue sneakers."*

**T**hough this kind of behavior in an adult might be labeled obsessive or compulsive, in a toddler it's normal. While not every toddler craves ritual—

and that's normal, too—many demand absolute predictability in their food, drink, clothing, and daily routines. Even the slightest deviation from the predictable can set off tirades.

Like negativity and temper tantrums, ritualistic behavior is a toddler's way of trying to gain some measure of control over his life, which—when you're less than two years old, less than 3 feet high, and hopelessly dependent on those much bigger and much more powerful than you—is not easy to do. Being able to control some of the little things in life (which cup he drinks from, how his sandwich is sliced, which sneakers he wears) means a lot to a toddler and his self-esteem.

So instead of trying to talk your child out of his rituals, put up with them—and try to do so with good grace. Let anyone else who cares for him in on what these rituals are and discuss your approach to dealing with them. (A babysitter in your own home will probably be able to indulge your toddler as you do; this may not always be possible at daycare or group home care.) Your toddler may be more open to a change if he is in control of the change. So every once in a while, propose that he pick out a new cup to drink from, show him a fun way of eating a sandwich (use a cookie cutter to cut yours into a star, an animal shape, or a heart and suggest that he do the same with his), propose shopping for sandals just like Daddy's to wear at the beach. But if he shows no interest, don't push. With time and patience, ritual will lose its hold on your toddler.

## FOOD FETISHES

*"Help! My son won't eat any food that is touching another kind of food."*

Try dividing to conquer. Use a divided dish and fill each compartment with a different food. Or serve each food in its own separate bowl. Don't worry that you're catering to your toddler's compulsion. If you humor him and go along with his quirky eating habits, this very common fetish will eventually run its course. If you scold, make sarcastic comments, or roll your eyes, on the other hand, it may very well get worse.

*"My toddler has a fit if the cracker or cookie I give her has a piece broken off. What's her problem?"*

As a toddler, she hasn't yet figured out that nobody (and nothing) is perfect. Though toddlers certainly don't demand perfection in themselves, they often expect perfection (or at least, their perception of it) in everyone and everything around them—including cookies. Popular child psychology sometimes attributes broken-cookie phobia to a fear of being broken or not intact themselves ("If a cookie can break, so can I"). Whether you choose to accept this explanation or to chalk up your toddler's compulsiveness about her crackers and cookies to typical toddler contrariness and desire for control, the best tack to take is to humor her as much as practical. When the age of reason dawns (probably sometime after the third birthday), your child will begin to accept the way the cookie crumbles.

In the meantime, handle cookies and crackers carefully, carry extras to replace casualties, and avoid those varieties or sizes that break too easily. (Whole wheat rolls, bagels, or bread make less fragile carry-along snacks.) Save crumbled cookies for making pie crusts and cracked crackers for breadings and stuffings, rather than finishing them yourself, which could (obviously) lead to other problems.

But don't carry indulging your toddler's eccentricities too far. If your toddler breaks his own cracker, don't provide another one. In such a situation, experiencing the consequences of one's own behavior is the lesson to be learned.

# RESISTANCE TO CHANGE

*"Any little change—a new car seat, a new order in the bedtime routine, new glasses on me—and our daughter gets upset."*

As far as some toddlers are concerned, there's no such thing as a change for the better. Any change is unwelcome.

Like so many toddler trademarks, rigidity has its roots in the toddler's compulsion to try to control her environment as much as she possibly can. When faced with change, even when the change is slight or doesn't affect her directly, she may feel threatened, frustrated, insecure, and uncertain.

While not all toddlers react to change with vehement opposition, most are at least somewhat uncomfortable with it, much more so than babies or older children. Understanding that rigidity is normal and age-appropriate for a toddler and that flexibility is at least a year away should make this phase easier to survive. For now, respect your toddler's wariness in facing the new and different. Keep the status quo "just so"—at least, as much as is practical—to help make your toddler feel more secure and reduce the points of parent-child conflict. Any change that can wait—a new carpet, a new stroller, a new paint color in the nursery, or a new daily routine—should be postponed until your toddler becomes less inflexible. If a major change can't wait—a new child-

care situation suddenly becomes necessary, for instance—take extra pains to give your child plenty of warning (when that's possible) to prepare her for the change, and to help her adjust to it. Anticipate that she will be feeling a little more threatened, a little less secure, and more easily frustrated during a time of upheaval. Instead of reacting angrily to her feelings, respond with extra support and understanding. Being your toddler's calm, steady, stabilizing anchor in the stormy seas of change will help her weather the changes more easily.

If your child seems extremely upset by change or new experiences of *any* kind, her behavior could be more than a passing toddler phase. It could be a sign that this is her inborn temperament. See page 201 for tips on dealing with such a temperament.

# READING REPETITION

*"Every single night, my son wants to hear the same book. Not just once, but two or three times. I'm so bored."*

Toddlers just can't seem to get enough of a good thing—whether it's a favorite food, a favorite blanket, or a favorite book. What seems monotonous to adults is the height of toddler happiness, for several reasons: One, toddlers generally don't like change. They feel more comfortable, secure, and in control with the familiar and the predictable—the book read over and over again becomes a beloved friend. Two, repetition helps them build their vocabularies and comprehension. The first time a story is read, a toddler may not understand every word. With each subsequent reading, more and more words will be picked up.

By the time you've reached nauseam, your toddler's likely to know every word in the book (possibly by heart)—an accomplishment he's sure to feel very good about. Three, knowing a story well allows a toddler to be able to participate in a reading more fully by anticipating what comes next, by filling in words here and there, by pointing out what's familiar in the pictures. Four, the rhythm of the story becomes pleasurable to a toddler (particularly in books that rhyme). And finally, there is often some element of the story that touches a toddler deep down, that helps him deal with his fears and feelings.

In other words, the familiarity that breeds boredom in you breeds contentment in your toddler. And to keep him content (and learning), you'll have to resign yourself to the repetition. While he'll eventually tire of the favorite story of the moment (and probably adopt another immediately), let it be his idea to end the era.

In the meantime, try to make the rereading even more fun for him (and less boring for you) by:

▲ Hamming it up. Though it's tempting to switch onto automatic pilot, you'll both enjoy the story more if you read with animation, even try a different voice or style every night, if you and he like.

▲ Casting your toddler in a co-starring role. Let him fill in as many blanks as he'd like (at the end of rhyme, at the end of a page, and so on). Ask him to predict the plot (even though you both know it backwards and forwards, he'll get quite a thrill out of being so smart) and to identify characters or colors or objects in the illustrations. At each reading, try to point out something as yet unnoticed (the red collar on the puppy, for instance, or the squirrel hidden in the tree), then ask him to find it the next time.

While enhancing the present reading material, don't give up trying for something new. Each night, suggest (but never push) an alternative storybook. Even if your toddler isn't willing to give up his treasured tale, he may be willing to hear a new one as well. You have the best odds of successfully introducing a new book if you try one that is a sequel to his favorite, has the same characters, the same author, or the same illustrator. Help broaden his literary horizons by taking him to the library, exposing him to a variety of different books, and allowing him to select one or two to bring home. Attend story hour at a local bookstore and browse together afterward. When Grandma wants to send a gift, suggest a book. Choose a book as a birthday or holiday gift, selecting one you think your toddler will like rather than one that appeals to you. Or better yet, let him choose his own.

If your toddler is just not open to new books right now and continues to demand the same story every night, give in gracefully. Remember, this stage will not last forever. At some point variety will become appealing, and you will hear, "Not *that* old story again!"

# MUSICAL MONOTONY

*"Our daughter will only listen to one tape, and she wants to listen to it all the time. I'm sick of hearing the same songs over and over—how can I get her to listen to something else for a change?"*

Play it again, Mom (or Dad). Listening to a tape or CD again and again, like reading and rereading a book, can be satisfying to toddlers, who derive comfort from ritual. And as with a book, listening to a tape is a learning experience. If a child listens to the same tape over and over, she will gradually learn its melodies and lyrics, something that would be virtually impossible if she listened to a different tape every day. In addition, for the toddler (as for most listeners of any age) listening to music that is familiar brings the most pleasure. (Remember when you were a teenager and played your favorites over and over?)

That doesn't mean you have to capitulate entirely. For your own sanity and to broaden your toddler's auditory experiences, do try to introduce new tapes occasionally—especially once the old one has pretty well been mastered. You have the best chance of adding a tape to your toddler's hit parade if you select carefully. Ideally, a new tape should include some songs your toddler already knows (from having them heard them sung at home, in daycare, or on a favorite television program or video). It may also help if the performer is the same as on her favorite tape. Once you've chosen the tape, prepare yourself by listening to it on your own, becoming familiar with the songs (there may be a song sheet enclosed), and picking out highlights you think your toddler will like. Before premiering the tape for her, inroduce some of the songs by singing them yourself.

Finally, try slipping a new tape into the cassette player while she's focused on another activity—doing a puzzle, drawing, or building a castle. If she doesn't comment, just let it play. If she seems about to complain, start talking up the new tape—"Listen to that song, that's the one Grandma always sings to you" or "Isn't that song funny—that's the one Cookie Monster sings."

If you've been working on taking turns, you can use that as a vehicle for introducing a new tape. While you're driving to the supermarket (bring along a tape or CD player if you don't have one in the car), give your toddler the chance to pick the first tape, then say, "Okay,

now it's my turn. Now I'm going to pick a tape."

Though it's fine to try to present some other options, don't complain about, put down, or refuse to play your toddler's favorite. Doing so will only make her more determined to listen to it exclusively. Be patient; this broken-record stage will eventually play itself out.

## READINESS FOR POTTY LEARNING NOW

*"One of the children in our play group is almost completely toilet trained. But our daughter doesn't seem a bit interested. Should we be forcing the issue now?"*

Forcing the issue is one sure way to fail at toilet learning (a better term than toilet training because it emphasizes the toddler as learner rather than the parent as teacher). Like other developmental tasks, such as crawling and walking, your child should be allowed to accomplish this skill on her own timetable.

By about twenty months, most toddler excretory systems mature to the point at which they begin to empty less frequently and more predictably, indicating readiness for toilet learning. An occasional child is ready sooner; many others are ready later. But physical maturity alone is not enough to guarantee success. There are a variety of clues that a toddler is ready to begin the process of potty learning. See Chapter Nineteen for a list of these clues (page 539) and much more on toilet learning.

Even once all these signs are present, toilet learning generally won't happen overnight. It took weeks of trial and error (and patience on everyone's part) for your child to learn to walk; expect the same with her learning to use the toilet.

## TOILET LEARNING AND A NEW BABY

*"I'm expecting a second child in two months. Our son hasn't seemed ready for toilet learning, so we haven't pushed the issue, but we're having second thoughts now that we're thinking about all the diapers."*

There's only one timetable that matters to your toddler when it comes to his toilet learning—his own. Though it's tempting to try to tamper with his agenda so that it will be more compatible with your own, it probably isn't wise. As with all developmental milestones, toilet learning is best and most efficiently accomplished when the child—not his parents—is ready. Pressuring a toddler to relinquish his diapers prematurely almost never works, particularly when the pressure coincides with the birth of a new baby. Even a child who's already proficient in using the potty may regress when a sibling appears on the scene; one who's just starting out has even less chance of staying on the toileting track.

Of course, if you find that your toddler shows a genuine interest in learning to use the potty, don't feel compelled to wait until he's comfortable with his approaching status as older sibling before you oblige. Seize the moment, and start the learning process (see Chapter Nineteen). But be especially sensitive, expect relapses, and be ready to retire the potty for a while should you encounter renewed resistance from your toddler.

## GENEROSITY TURNED SELFISH

*"My daughter used to be so generous with her playmates— she'd give them anything they wanted. Now all of a sudden, she's turned selfish."*

It's a toddler-vs.-toddler world out there, and your daughter, like most children in their second year, has suddenly realized it. As a baby, ownership didn't mean much to her, and it was rarely threatened by those around her— consequently, she didn't feel the need to defend it. Now she has a new sense of self ("This is me!") and of ownership ("These are mine!"). Enter other self-centered toddlers—with their curious little hands—and it's no wonder she's taken to protecting her turf and her toys.

It's important to recognize that the impulse to guard what is hers (and to occasionally grab what she wants to be hers) reflects not selfishness but a developmental stage. Real generosity isn't possible until one learns about ownership and feels comfortable enough with it to share. A willingness to share with her playmates—at least part of the time—probably won't be forthcoming for at least a year. You can help speed the time when "give" will be at least as much a part of your child's life as "take" by preparing her to share (see page 267).

# WHAT IT'S IMPORTANT TO KNOW:
## Traveling With Your Toddler

For many parents, staying at home with a toddler is challenge enough; venturing out with one—whether on a day trip or a two-week vacation—is a prospect that can fill even the most adventurous soul with trepidation. A tantrum at home—well, you can always close the windows or call for a time-out. A tantrum at the supermarket—you can always fall back on a quick dash to the car or a speedy retreat back home. But a tantrum aloft at 30,000 feet a full two hours from landing, or speeding along the interstate thirty minutes from the next exit, or on an Amtrak jam-packed with travelers a day away from your destination—this is the stuff that parental nightmares are made of.

Yet the open roads and the open skies still beckon (as do doting grandparents or friends eager for your next visit), vacation days mount up, and toddler or no toddler, the time does come to get up and go. So go—but not before you've planned, planned, and planned some more.

## WHEREVER YOU GO

Although it may seem inherently unfair that one very small person should determine the course of an entire family's vacation, tailoring your trips to the likes, dislikes, and tolerances of your tiny tourist really is the wisest way to go. After all, if your toddler isn't having a good time, no one's going to have a good time. In the interest of all:

**Check with the doctor.** If you are planning a major trip abroad, try to schedule a pediatrician appointment two months before your departure date. If your toddler has a chronic health problem, such as asthma or diabetes, ask what special precautions you need to take while traveling and for the name of a local doctor at your destination, on whom you can call should an emergency arise. If your child regularly takes medication, ask for an extra prescription, in case the medication is lost en route. If you are planning to fly with a toddler who has frequent colds or a respiratory allergy, inquire about taking along an antihistamine and/or decongestant spray. If you're going abroad, request a recommendation for treating traveler's tummy; it's a good idea to take along some packets of ORT solution (such as pedialyte; see page 603), which you can reconstitute with bottled water should your toddler come down with diarrhea. Some foreign destinations require special immunizations or other health precautions. Health information on travel with children is available from your child's doctor or the American Academy of Pediatrics (141 Northwest Point Boulevard, Elk Grove Village, Illinois 60007). For the latest on the health essentials for foreign travel, including immunization requirements[2] and the safety of food and water at your proposed destination, call the Center for Disease Control's (CDC) hotline (404-332-4559) or write or call for a copy of the current *Health Information for International Travel,* available for $6 from the U.S. Government Printing Office (Washington, DC 20402; 202-783-3238). Information is also

---

2. Arrange to get any necessary immunizations at least six weeks prior to departure. Your child should be up-to-date on all basic immunizations (see page 561) and may require other immunizations, depending on your destination.

## *DON'T LEAVE HOME EMPTY-HANDED*

··········

**K**eep a tote bag packed and ready to go with you whenever you leave home.* Include diapers or an extra pair of underpants; diaper wipes for convenient handwashing as well as the more traditional use; a bib, if your toddler will wear one; some tissues or paper towels; a change of clothes and shoes, if a toileting accident is a possibility; some plastic bags for diaper disposal or for carrying home wet clothes or cloth diapers; and, last but hardly least, a selection of portable distractions (books, a small box of crayons and a pad, a favorite stuffed animal, doll, truck, or other toy; avoid those with many pieces).

Regardless of how long you plan to be out of the house and how recent the last meal or the last drink, also carry along a snack (peanut butter sandwiches, with or without bananas, apple butter, or all-fruit

jelly; cheese cubes or sticks; dry cereal; crackers; juice-sweetened cookies or muffins; or fresh fruit**) and a drink (a juice box, or an environmentally preferable thermos or sippy-cup of juice). If any food you're carrying is perishable, be sure to pack it in an insulated bag with an ice pack or ice cubes.

Remember not to offer something to eat or drink as a cure-all for boredom or fussiness, or to end a tantrum. Present it only at meal or snack times, or when your toddler says, "I'm hungry."

---

*For how to pack for trips longer than a day, see page 264.
**All bread, crackers, and cookies should routinely be whole grain. Ideally, after a carbohydrate snack your toddler should munch some cheese (which has some tooth-decay-fighting power) or rinse his or her mouth with water.

---

available from the World Health Organization (49 Sheridan Avenue, Albany, NY 12210) in the booklet, *International Travel and Health: Vaccination Requirements and Health Advice* ($13.50 plus $3.00 for postage and handling).

**Make sleeping arrangements.** Most hotels, motels, and resorts can supply a crib for a young toddler. If your toddler sleeps in a bed, check ahead to be sure that side rails are available, or that the bed supplied for your toddler can be placed between a wall and your own bed. If you're visiting family, see about renting or borrowing a crib or side rails. In a pinch, a children's sleeping bag on the floor will also work for an older toddler (but be sure that the room is childproof; see page 261).

**Limit your itinerary.** One-destination vacations—visiting relatives or sojourns at a family-oriented resort, at a beach

house, or in a single city—are usually the most successful with toddlers. Most cruises and ocean voyages are not recommended for toddlers, both because young children require constant supervision on board and because they could be injured or frightened when the ship begins rolling (but there are some open seas options open to families with toddlers; see page 260). If you're planning a touring vacation, limit the stops so that you're not constantly on the go; in other words, don't try to do seven cities in as many days. Unless you're lucky enough to have an atypically adaptable and agreeable toddler, you'd be asking for trouble.

**Limit your expectations.** The trick to a relatively restful vacation with toddler in tow is to keep expectations low and patience high. True, your toddler may surprise everyone by being agreeable and adaptable, by cheerfully accompanying you on shopping sprees and culture binges, by behaving impeccably on airplanes and in five-star restaurants. But your toddler may, more predictably, act like a toddler. Most toddlers will be bored to tears (literally) by long, overscheduled days in museums, boutiques, and on tour buses. So plan accordingly.

**Limit the sightseeing.** If sightseeing is on your agenda, keep in mind that you won't be able to follow the typical tourist routine. You may want to see everything in the guidebook, but chances are your toddler won't. So unless you're lucky enough to be able to bring along a nanny or a family member who will be willing to baby-sit while you tour, you'll have to alternate adult-interest sightseeing with toddler-interest activities (zoos, children's museums, beaches, parks, amusement parks). And don't try to crowd too much into any one day. In most cases, one destination in the morning and one in the afternoon will be all your toddler can tolerate.

Try to schedule visits to adult-interest museums, churches, historic monuments, and the like when your toddler will (you hope) be napping in the stroller or, at least, less likely to be cranky. If there are two or more adults in your party, consider taking turns touring and baby-sitting. If you're solo, consider hiring an occasional baby-sitter (your requirements for a baby-sitter away from home should be as stringent as those for at-home sitters; see page 820) so that you can do a little adult stuff.

Younger toddlers may be fascinated enough by the forms, colors, and shapes at a museum or gallery to allow you to tour for an hour or so, especially if they are comfortably ensconced in a stroller. Older children may be more cooperative if you build a game into the visit. Try, for example, "Can you find it?" On arrival, head right for the gift shop and have your child pick out postcards of two or three interesting paintings or exhibits

that are in that museum. Then challenge your little sightseer to match the pictures to the real thing: "Can you find this knight in armor and that pretty painting?" Be sure, of course, that your route takes you to the exhibits where the knight and the painting can be found.

For information on attractions attractive to toddlers, pick up a local guidebook that focuses on kids and/or check with the local parenting paper, if there is one (contact Parenting Publications of America, 12715 Path Finder Lane, San Antonio, TX 78230; 210-492-3886).

**Limit the chaos.** On days with busy schedules of visiting or sightseeing, try having breakfast in the room before heading out and/or dinner in the room on your return. This not only reduces the number of times you have to traipse from place to place but also makes the hotel room feel a bit more like home, and fitting in baths and bedtime rituals easier. If you have a room with a refrigerator or a kitchenette, so much the better. You can stock up on familiar foods and beverages and reduce the stress (and expense) of constantly eating out.

**And don't forget to pack your sense of humor.** It's essential to survival when traveling with children. If you're able to laugh when things go wrong—and they will—they won't seem half so bad.

# TRAVELING BY PLANE

**B**ook early. If you can, get your tickets well in advance—this allows you to choose the flight and the seats you want. A travel agent should not only be able to book your seats in advance (at no extra cost), but supply you with boarding passes, which can save time and tension at the airport.

**Travel at off-peak times.** The less crowded a flight is, the more comfortable you will be, the better the service will be, and the less your toddler's behavior will affect other passengers. (On many routes, Monday afternoon through Thursday noon are off-peak.) Try to choose flights at times when your toddler ordinarily sleeps (night flights are great for long trips; nap times for short ones). Maybe, just maybe, he or she will really sleep for a while on the plane.

**Look for "nonstops" on short trips.** The faster you get from here to there, the better for all.

**Consider breaking up a long trip.** On a daytime flight that is going to last five hours or more, a brief stopover may make the trip more tolerable. Look for a "direct" flight, so that the stopover doesn't require changing planes; you'll be able to leave the bulk of your luggage on board when you deplane with your toddler. Use the time at the airport to get a bite to eat, wash up, take care of diapering or toileting, let your toddler run off some energy, watch other planes take off and land, and—if there is one—to visit the airport play center. When a change of planes is involved, make sure that you and your toddler will have enough time to make your way in a leisurely fashion to the next gate, which can be literally miles away in some large airports. When possible, avoid flights that make several stops.

**Consider an extra seat.** Though kids under two can travel for free, parents often choose to purchase a seat for them anyway. Confined to an adult's lap during takeoff, landing, and periods of air turbulence (which can be frequent on some flights), a toddler is likely to twist, turn, and petition loudly for freedom. Paying full fare for a toddler may seem an extravagance (though some airlines offer half price tickets for little

ones), but it will make sitting, playing, and eating less of a hassle for both of you, and at the same time make your child feel more important (with a safety belt, tray, headphones, and armrests of his or her own). Toddlers buckled into a separate seat are also safer in severe turbulence than those restrained only by a parent's arms. (For extra safety, bring along your toddler's car seat.)

If you're traveling with another adult, your travel agent may be able, on uncrowded flights, to book an aisle and window seat with an empty seat between. If you specify that you have a lap child, the airline won't sell that seat unless absolutely necessary. As long as the seat stays unbooked, you've got a free seat for your toddler. If it doesn't, you can be pretty sure the middleman (or woman) will be willing to trade seats with one of you rather than having a toddler passed back and forth over his or her lap during the entire flight.

**Favor the aisle.** Children love window seats—but you'll hate not having access to the aisle. So if you're traveling alone with your toddler on your lap, opt for the aisle—otherwise you're going to end up trying the patience of those you'll have to keep scrambling over in order to take your restless toddler to the lav or for a walk. Of course, if your party fills the entire row, you can have your aisle and your window seat, too. When booking a window seat, be sure to ask for one that doesn't overlook the wing, which will block most of the view. Also be sure that you aren't seated in an emergency exit row; they are restricted to adults only. A seat near the kitchen facilities is noisy and lacks privacy (a problem particularly if you're still nursing), but provides easy access to the toilets and to flight attendants.

Parents often favor bulkhead seats because they provide extra room forward of the seats for a toddler to kick up his or her heels (without annoying the passenger in front) and to play or sleep on the floor when the seat belt sign is off. But these advantages don't stack well against the many disadvantages: Trays unfold over your lap, leaving no room for your child; the armrest usually can't be raised (which means your toddler can't spread out across two seats to nap); you're right on top of the movie screen, if there is one; because there's less oxygen at floor level, a toddler playing or sleeping on the floor is in danger of being deprived of oxygen if the oxygen levels in the cabin drop suddenly; the child on the floor may also be knocked about if there is sudden turbulence; there's no underseat storage so that even your bare necessities must be stored overhead during takeoff and landing.

Smoking is not permitted on flights within the continental United States. But if you're flying abroad, be sure to specify seats as far from the smoking section as possible.

**Don't take meal service for granted.** Airline food is getting lighter and lighter these days in the interest of economy, so what might have once been a meal may now be only a snack. Call ahead to find out exactly what will be served and if special children's or toddler meals are available. Other "special" meals to consider requesting, depending on your toddler's tastes: a fruit and cheese plate or cold cereal. Ask for a description of any snacks, too, since most consist of foods that the typical toddler wouldn't touch with a 10-foot fork (ham and cheese croissants, deli sandwiches). Sometimes a snack means nothing more than a beverage and a bag of peanuts, which, as a choking hazard, are off-limits for twos-and-under. And no matter what fare's been promised, don't ever board without your own supply of toddler-appropriate sustenance (see page 251 for suggestions). Takeoff delays can result in mealtime delays, food service carts can move at a maddeningly slow rate down the aisles, and special meals sometimes don't show up at all.

Since fluids are particularly important when flying (the air in a plane is very dry), be sure to carry your toddler's favorite beverages, just in case the flight doesn't stock them or the beverage service is delayed.

**Dress for the occasion.** Sunday best is not the apparel of choice for travel; dress in comfortable clothing that can accept spills with impunity and look good even when rumpled. If you want everyone spruced up at your destination, change when you get there or bring a "dressy" accessory, such as a hat or vest, to don before deplaning. Because temperatures are unpredictable, dress in layers. For example, for cold weather travel, dress your toddler in a T-shirt topped with a long-sleeved polo and then a sweatshirt or sweater, so that you can add or remove layers as the temperature on the plane or in the airport warrants. Also be sure that your toddler's clothing will allow for easy diaper changes or bathroom use.

**Take advantage of curbside check-in.** To avoid having to lug your luggage through a sprawling airport, check everything but valuables and the essentials (your toddler's backpack of toys, your tote bag) through at the curb. To avoid having to lug your toddler, rent a luggage cart, which has a built-in child seat, at the airport or—if your airline allows you to carry one on—bring a lightweight stroller for getting around the airport. If you're taking a stroller for use at your destination and can't carry it on board, ask the porter to box it for you to prevent it being mangled in the cargo hold by heavy suitcases.

**Don't preboard.** Passengers with small children are generally given this option, but the earlier you board, the longer you have to stay in the plane's cramped quarters. If there are two adults in your party, one can board early with the bags while the other waits with the toddler in the comparatively wide open spaces of the waiting area until the last boarding call is made. Before you board, however, be sure to make a bathroom or diaper-changing stop. Both will be more difficult to accomplish on the plane,[3] especially during taxi and takeoff, which at a busy airport can take upward of half an hour or, in the event of a delay, much longer.

**Know what to ask for.** Pillows, blankets, playing cards, and often fun packs for junior travelers (make sure they're safe for your toddler's age), are all usually there for the asking. It's also sometimes possible to tour the cockpit during boarding or after landing.

**Fear for the ears.** Pressurization of the cabin on takeoff and depressurization on landing is notoriously tough on little ears, with any resultant lusty complaining notoriously tough on any big ears sitting nearby. If your toddler's still on a bottle or breast, sucking during takeoff and landing can help by encouraging swallowing, which helps release the pressure that builds up in the ears. (Start as the plane starts speeding down the runway and again when the pilot announces, "We are beginning our descent.") If not, let your toddler drink from a sippy-cup or a thermos with a built-in straw; munch on a snack that requires a lot of chewing; or, if he or she is old enough to be trusted not to swallow it, chew gum (most aren't until four or five).

One of these popular home remedies for popping the ears when the pressure builds up in the eustachian tube may also help:

▲ Hot towels. Ask the flight attendant to heat two towels. After checking to be sure they are not too hot (touch them to your inner forearm), place one towel over each ear. The heat expands the air in the middle ear, relieving the negative pressure on the eardrum.

▲ Hot cups. Wet a couple of paper napkins or towels with hot, but not scalding, water (ask the flight attendant to do this if you can't; be sure to check that the towels aren't burning hot), wad them into two paper cups, and hold a cup over each ear. Again, the heat relieves the pressure.

▲ Blowing. If your toddler knows how to blow through the nose, have him or her do this while you hold both nostrils closed. Though initially painful, this pops the ears and relieves the pressure.

Blockage of the eustachian tubes due to nasal congestion from a cold or allergy can make ear pain much more likely and more severe. If your toddler has been sick, check with his or her doctor before flying. The doctor may recommend giving an antihistamine and/or decongestant an hour before takeoff and, if the flight lasts longer than the medication, an hour before landing. Or the doctor may suggest postponing the trip entirely.

If all else fails and your toddler screams all the way up and all the way down, ignore the dirty looks from other passengers. (Remember it's likely you'll never see them again.) And keep in mind that the screaming will help reduce the pressure on your toddler's ear drums and ease the pain.

**Put safety first.** If your child is over two and/or is occupying a seat, plan to bring an FAA- (Federal Aviation Administration) approved car seat aboard—it's safer than the seat belt alone. You should encounter no opposition from the plane's crew since the FAA has issued a ruling

---

3. Don't dispose of diapers in airplane rest rooms; airlines prefer you to wrap each in a plastic bag or an airsick bag and hand it to one of the flight attendants when they're not serving food.

## *LEAVING THE COUNTRY*

**· · · · · · · · · ·**

Traveling out of the country alone with a child may require special documentation. Even if you're going only as far as Mexico, some airlines may not allow you to board a flight out of the country with your child unless you can prove that you have permission from the other parent or that you are the child's sole legal guardian. So, in such a situation, bring appropriate documentation along.

requiring airlines to allow families the use of appropriate crash-tested child restraints.[4] Some airlines will allow you to reserve a plane seat for the car seat at 50% off the regular fare. Know how to operate your child's safety seat and how to open it quickly in an emergency. If you're ordered to evacuate, take only your child; leave the car seat and all your other possessions.

If your toddler is on your lap, *do not* belt him or her in with you—serious injury could result from even a mild impact. But do secure your belt and then hold your toddler around the waist with your hands grasping your wrists during takeoffs and landings. Do not allow your toddler to wander around alone in the aisles or to sleep or play on the floor because of the risk of injury if the plane should suddenly hit an area of turbulence.

Also carefully review the use of oxygen masks and know where there are extras in case your child doesn't have a seat (and therefore a mask) of his or her own. Remember, always put on your own mask first and then attend to your child's. If you try to do it the other way around in a low-oxygen emergency, you could lose consciousness before you manage to get either mask on.

---

4. Safety experts warn against the use of booster seats on planes, however, even if they carry FAA approval. Some parents have found the new FAA-approved multipurpose stroller-car-plane seat (for children up to forty pounds) a boon when traveling.

# *TRAVELING BY TRAIN*

**Book in advance.** Ordering train tickets in advance from a travel agent allows you to arrive at the train station with tickets in hand, so you won't have to wait on a long ticket line. If it's possible to make seat or compartment reservations, then do this in advance, too. Remember, however, that coach reservations guarantee a seat for each ticket, but not that those seats are together. Ask if children's meals are available on the train you're planning to take and just what they include; if they sound appealing (they may not), order ahead when possible.

**When possible, travel during off-peak hours.** Peak travel times can be very crowded, especially during holiday seasons. Try to pick off-peak times. A late evening train may be a good choice if your toddler is likely to sleep during the trip.

**Pack appropriately.** For overnight train travel, your carry-on bag should also be an overnight bag—containing pajamas, clean underwear, toiletries, and other basics you and your toddler will need on board. This should make digging into your neatly packed suitcases unnecessary. Better still, it may make it possible to check them through, giving you less to worry about and more room in your compartment or at your seat.

**Arrive early.** Check ahead to find out what time the train ordinarily arrives at your station. If there is a ten or fifteen minute gap between arrival and departure, try to get there before the train arrives rather than just as it's about to leave. The goal: a better chance of seating the family together. If there are two adults, send one ahead, as soon as the platform number is announced, to save seats for all while the other struggles down the platform at a snail's pace with your toddler. Or hire a porter to not only transport your bags but to board you early, for the best choice of seats. When the train isn't crowded, or when four of you are traveling together, the two pairs of seats facing each other at the end of most coaches fills the bill perfectly (as long as two of you don't mind traveling backwards). Just be sure there's a window through which your toddler can watch the scenery go by.

**Take advantage of longer stops.** Even a fifteen minute stop gives you and your toddler a chance to get off the train and stretch your legs, possibly even wander down to see the engine that's been pulling the train (just be sure someone is watching your luggage and that you reboard in time). If the stop is lengthy—as it may be in a hub city like Chicago—try to plan an excursion to a nearby zoo, children's museum, or even a playground or park.

**Supplement the snack car.** Even if there's a dining car, but especially if there's *only* a snack car, be prepared for the worst: not a single food your toddler will eat. To prevent gastronomic catastrophe, bring along enough of your toddler's favorite munchables to last the trip. Plan on filling in with milk and juice purchased on the train.

**Bring bedding on board.** When traveling long distances overnight, it's great if you can book a sleeping compartment, when available. If that's not possible, and the train doesn't supply bedding to coach passengers, bring along a small pillow and blanket from home for your toddler.

**For safety's sake.** Toddlers sometimes go stir-crazy on long train rides, and get the urge to run up and down the aisles. Because a sudden lurch of the train could slam a small toddler against a seat or another passenger, insist that a young toddler go for a stroll only while holding an adult hand.

# TRAVELING BY CAR

**Never start without the car seat.** It's essential for auto travel, no matter how long or short the road ahead. If you're renting the car, ask the rental company to supply you with a safe seat or bring your own. Equip the seat with a cozy cushion to provide head support during naps and provide a variety of distractions (toys, play keys, an unbreakable mirror, a toy steering wheel, all safely attached to the car seat) aimed at making confinement less of a hardship. Suction toys that attach to a car seat tray (if your toddler's seat has one) or to a window (if the car seat is next to one) are also practical for auto travel.

When there are several travelers on a trip, periodically change seats for everyone but the toddler (moving the car seat around is too cumbersome) to give the toddler a change of pace and others in the car a break.

**Don't drive your toddler crazy.** Those glory days of all-day, all-night driving straight through to your destination, fueled by black coffee and the occasional hamburger or doughnut, are gone. While it's wise to do as much driving as you

## TRAVELING TODDLER'S TUMMY

..........

Toddlers, like everyone else traveling abroad, are subject to traveler's diarrhea. You can reduce that risk by giving your toddler only pasteurized milk and bottled juices. When water purity is in doubt, use only boiled or bottled water for drinking (skip the ice cubes unless they're made with boiled water). In countries such as Mexico where fresh fruits and vegetables may be contaminated, be sure you bypass vegetables that aren't well-cooked and haven't been peeled or treated with an iodine/chlorine solution and rinsed with boiling water (ask at the restaurant; if the answer isn't clear, skip the dish). Fruit should be washed and peeled. Also be certain that meats, fish, and seafood are cooked through (skip the ceviche and sushi) and that cheeses, yogurts, and other dairy products are pasteurized. Eat only in restaurants that look as though they follow sanitary food preparation practices (see page 527); avoid food sold by street vendors entirely. Follow sanitary practices yourself by being sure everyone in the family faithfully washes hands after toileting (or changing diapers) and before eating. For information on food and water safety in various parts of the world, contact the Center for Disease Control (see page 250). If toddler tummy does strike, see treatment suggestions for diarrhea, page 601.

Toddlers on the road, at home and abroad, may also be subject to constipation because of dietary and schedule changes and inadequate exercise. To avoid this problem, be sure your little traveler gets plenty of fresh and dried fruits and vegetables (see safety rules above), whole-grain cereals and breads, has an adequate fluid intake, and a chance for some active play every day. Carrying along a portable potty seat from home may make it easier for your toddler and may be more hygienic.

can during toddler nap times, it's also wise to take plenty of breaks for exercise, meals, snacks, and other diversions. A sensible schedule: Start early, while your toddler's still cozily pajama-clad, and get in a couple of hours of driving while he or she gets a couple of hours of sleep (unless he or she tends to stay up once awakened). After a stop for breakfast, a change into day togs, and a little small-fry frolic, pile back into the car for a few more hours of driving (broken up by at least one snack-and-stretch break) before lunch. If possible, stop at a lunch spot that has a playground, mall, or a local attraction nearby that you can explore after eating. Then get on the road again, timing your arrival for late afternoon, so that there's time to unwind at the pool or the playground before dinner and bed. Driving at night is tempting—with your toddler asleep and the road less crowded—but it can also be draining and dangerous, especially if you're already feeling drowsy after a long day.

Some parents prefer to drive when their toddler is asleep and plan driving around nap times and early evening sleeping (you can often carry the sleeping toddler into bed upon arrival). But again, be wary of driving late into the night unless you are well rested.

**Don't use rest stops only for resting.** Sitting in a car for extended periods of time isn't easy for anyone, but it is especially hard for active toddlers. So make sure you break up driving time with plenty of circulation-stimulating breaks. Bring a large beach-type ball (deflatable, if car space is limited) to toss around and chase at rest stops where there is a safe grassy area. (Keep it in the trunk while you're on the road so that there is no chance of it getting in the driver's way.) Then, if you like, line up the family for a brief but rousing round of jumping jacks, bend-and-stretches, or follow-the-leader before buckling back in.

**Entertain.** Carry an ample supply of toys, books, and tapes. Those that aren't attached to your toddler's car seat should be within easy reach of an adult or older child who can dispense them one at a time, as needed. Bringing everything out at once will just mean chaos. Also be prepared to sing songs, recite rhymes, and play spotting games en route. Young toddlers can try to spot a dog, cow, or horse, a truck, a house, a barn, an airplane, a bus, a bridge. Toddlers who know colors can look for a blue car, a red house, a white church. Toddlers who know shapes can look for circles, squares, and triangles. Once they recognize letters and numbers, they can move on to looking for these. Be sure, however, that whoever is doing the driving is not distracted by the fun and games.

**Also carry.** In addition to the supplies needed for any trip (see page 264), you should also take along on car trips: paper towels, several small trash bags, plastic bags in case motion sickness strikes, a blanket and pillow for each child on board, and light sweaters for everyone.

**For safety's sake.** For a safe auto trip, require everyone in the car to be snugly fastened in a seat belt or car seat; don't drive to the point of fatigue (when accidents are more likely to occur); never drive if you've been drinking; prohibit smoking in the car; store heavy luggage or potential flying objects in the trunk, or if you have a station wagon, secure the luggage under a tarpaulin in the rear of the wagon.

# BEDDING DOWN: SELECTING A PLACE TO STAY

**Resorts.** Family-oriented resorts can please the whole family. They provide a single destination, require no moving in and out of motel rooms, no searching out restaurants with children's menus. A full schedule of programs for children free up parents for adult recreation and some much-needed time alone. Family activities allow for togetherness, as desired, and afford a fall-back in case your toddler refuses to stay with the child-care crew. An all-inclusive price eliminates constant digging for the wallet, regrets when Master or Ms. Picky barely touches the three dishes he or she insisted on ordering, and extra charges for activities that your child may or may not end up liking anyway.

**Hotels and motels.** Whether it's just a stop on the road, or your home for the week, there are certain basics parents of small children should look for in a hotel or motel. One, is the availability of a crib, if your toddler still needs one. Two, is a convenient way to satisfy a toddler's hunger and thirst between mealtimes. A room with a refrigerator or—even better—a kitchenette is ideal. Failing that, look for twenty-four-hour room service or a twenty-four-hour coffee shop, or at the minimum, an ice machine so you can refill your own food cooler. Three, on-site entertainment: a toddler-accommodating pool and/or playground, ample indoor play space, a miniature golf course, or a game room, for example. Four, baby-sitting service vouched for by the hotel, if you'd like to plan a toddler-free night on the town. Five, a coin-operated laundry or a reasonably priced laundry service. Six, for really desperate times, video rentals, or at least, cable with programming for children. If there's a choice of room locations available, try to secure one that is not surrounded on all sides by other rooms (or, at least, not by occupied rooms) but is at the end of a row, so that your toddler is less likely to disturb other guests. And finally, don't forget to inquire about special family rates—many hotels and motels offer them.

**House, condominium, or cottage rentals or exchanges.** It's always best to know what you're renting before you make the reservation, but it's particularly important if your vacation rental will be housing a toddler. If you can't check out the rental in person, ask for details (and preferably, photographs—or even a video). Choose a location that's close to shopping, restaurants, baby-sitters, a doctor (or a clinic or hospital); and other conveniences, so that you won't be doing miles of driving each day. A washer and dryer on the premises or very nearby is, of course, a must. Local manmade diversions are a good idea, too; while nature walks may engage you endlessly, they may not hold your toddler's attention for very long. Besides, a couple of days of rain can seem interminable when there's nowhere to hang out but a strange abode.

If the house you're considering is on a heavily trafficked road, make sure it's fenced in. If it's a beach house, make sure that it's not perched on the edge of a cliff—though the views may take your breath away, the potential for accidents may stop your heart entirely. If it's right on the water, be sure the beach you'll be using isn't rocky and doesn't have any sudden drops or unpredictable currents or undertows. If the property has a swimming pool, ask if it's fenced in; unfenced pools pose a serious safety hazard to small children. (You will have to be *extremely* vigilant about supervising your toddler's ventures outdoors if you choose a house with a pool or near water—wading can quickly become submersion when you're 2½ feet tall.) The house should also be able to withstand the wear and tear of a small child and be easily childproofed (see page 620). Avoid a house filled with antiques or other valuables or breakables, one on several levels (with staircases everywhere), and one that doesn't have smoke alarms and other safety equipment.

**Outdoor options.** If the great outdoors beckons, make sure you really want to answer. Even if you're an experienced camper, camping out with a small child can be a grueling experience, especially if the weather doesn't cooperate. If you nevertheless want to try vacationing under the stars, have a fall-back option ready, such as a nearby motel that's likely to have a vacancy. Be sure, too, that you have an ample supply of food and drink, first-aid supplies, and a back carrier for your toddler.

For some vacationing families, a recreational vehicle offers the best of both worlds—a chance to camp in comfort, clean sleeping quarters, refrigeration, cooking facilities, toilet, shower, and even air-conditioning. Such travel holds particular attraction for the parents of toddlers. On the downside: the vehicles may be expensive to rent, unwieldy to handle, guzzle gas, and can drive some people (little ones included) stir-crazy.

**Options at sea.** Until recently cruises were the glamorous domain of vacationing adults. Now more and more lines are offering packages that include activities and meals that appeal to children and even in some cases to toddlers. Before you respond by plunking down your credit card, consider a few points: Will you be able to relax with your toddler running around on deck (check to be sure that rails are toddler safe)? Is your toddler prone to motion sickness? How long is the cruise you're considering (more than a week and your toddler may be climbing the rails)? Is there a supervised activity program designed for toddlers? At what age does it start? How good is it? Ask about playrooms, counselors, food, safety features, medical facilities. Are meals and snacks available at flexible times? Are there special menu selections for the high-chair set?

Wherever you decide to vacation, be certain to do a quick safety check before letting your toddler roam. Check for open windows (open them from the top only); open balconies (keep the door to the outside locked); exposed outlets (bring along safety plugs); loose lamp cords (position furniture in front of them); dangling drapery cords or pulls (knot them out of reach); glassware (put it out of reach). Keep the bathroom door closed (you can block it with a chair or a suitcase, if necessary). Also note fire exits and evacuation procedures, just in case. Set up a play area with your toddler's own toys, imported from home, so he or she will (hopefully) be less tempted to explore and get into trouble. If you are spending a lot of time outdoors, especially in wooded areas, be sure to take the safety precautions recommended on page 643.

# CURBING THE QUEASIES

**M**any young tummies, even those that have no symptoms during the average car ride to the market or the zoo, take a turn for the tumultuous during longer rides in the car, and on airplane, boat, and train trips—particularly if there have been unsettling changes in diet (snack bar French fries and ice cream standing in for lunch, for example). Even if your toddler has never had a problem with motion sickness before, and especially if he or she has, take the following precautions when traveling:

**Get medical advice.** If your toddler has experienced serious motion sickness be-

fore, talk to the doctor about taking along motion-sickness medication—but only as a last resort, since these medications can sometimes have serious side-effects. Never use patch-type medications on children.

**Secure Sea-bands.** Sea-bands are elasticized bracelets that work to curb motion sickness by putting pressure on an acupressure point on the inner wrist. They've been used by sailors for years (but they work on land as well as on sea), are inexpensive, easy to use, safe, comfortable to wear, and frequently effective. Sea-bands are available through marine and camping supply stores, as well as some pharmacies, health food stores and catalogs, and maternity shops. One size theoretically fits all—but if the bands do not fit snugly on your toddler's wrists, take them in with a few stitches.

**Avoid an empty tummy.** Motion sickness is more likely to be a problem when your toddler's stomach is empty. So feed your toddler light, frequent snacks when traveling. Whole-grain crackers, pretzels, and breads are ideal for this purpose.

**Skip acidic fruit and juice.** Oranges, grapefruit, lemons, pineapple, and their juices often upset the traveling tummy. Satisfy vitamin C requirements on the road with less acidic fruit and vegetables (cantaloupe, peppers, vitamin C-enriched apple juice). If the weather is hot or your toddler vomits, be sure to replenish lost fluids with frequent small sips of water or nonacidic juice. Sucking on an ice pop may also be helpful. Avoid bubbly, or carbonated, drinks—even plain seltzer or soda water—since they can worsen stomach distress. Toddlers ordinarily require roughly one ounce of fluid for each pound of body weight daily (so that a thirty pound child needs about thirty ounces, or nearly a quart, of fluid). In hot weather, during air travel (which is dehydrating), or when the child vomits or has

# JUNIOR JET LAG

• • • • • • • • • •

Traveling with a toddler to another time zone can sometimes be compared to traveling with Rod Serling into the Twilight Zone—except that the horror can last for several days, rather than just half an hour.

For toddlers, as for adults, making a transition between time zones isn't easy. Internal body clocks are much more difficult to reset than external ones. Even if we count on an alarm to awaken us on time for work, most of us, accustomed to awakening at a certain time, would continue to wake up at about the same time without the alarm. Our internal clocks tell us when we're tired enough to sleep and when we're not, when we've had enough sleep and when we haven't.

But while an adult is liable to roll over and go back to sleep when a glance at an external clock reveals that her internal alarm has gone off at the right time but in the wrong time zone, a toddler isn't likely to. A toddler is, however, likely to awaken the nearest parent for middle-of-the-night company.

Although experts consider it easier to adjust to a time zone that is behind your own, many parents find that taking young children to a time zone that is ahead is less stressful. A family from Philadelphia visiting Seattle is likely to be awakened long before dawn each morning by their youngest tourist, who will consequently begin to unravel from exhaustion before dark and before dinnertime each evening. But a family from Seattle vacationing in Philadelphia will have only to contend with the logistics of having a midnight-oil-burning, sleep-in-all-morning toddler.

No matter which way in time your trip will be taking you, these tips for traveling three or four time zones may help make the transition smoother (see below for wider time zone jumps):

**Reset your toddler's clock only if it'll be worth the effort.** If you'll be away from home for less than a week, it's wiser to keep your toddler closer to his or her accustomed schedule. Otherwise, by the time you get onto the new schedule, it'll be time to reset the internal clocks for the return home. If you're planning a short trip but must operate on the new time for logistical reasons (for example, you have plans early each morning and can't wait for your little sleep-to-all-hours to wake up), read on.

**Start to reset before you start out.** If you're going west to east, at least three days before your scheduled departure, begin trying to get your toddler to bed a little earlier in the evening and up a little earlier in the morning. If you're going east to west, try to push bedtime forward a little more each evening. Also be sure to keep the few days before departure low-key, especially for your toddler. Avoid a hectic schedule and demanding activities, which could be fatiguing—and fatigue makes jet lag worse.

**Reset your watch.** As you set off on your trip, set your watch to the time at your destination, and continue adjusting meals and sleep patterns to the new time. If your toddler tends to sleep when in motion, napping a lot as you go and making keeping to any schedule impossible, that's okay, too. The scrambled schedule may so confuse your child's body clock that it doesn't know day from night—which will probably ease adjusting to the time zone at your destination.

**Reset gradually, if you can.** If you're driving, or to a lesser extent, traveling by train to your destination, you'll be able to accustom your toddler to the new time zones one zone at a time. It will be even easier if you're taking it slowly, spending a couple of days in each time zone.

**Reset completely.** It's not enough for a traveler to sleep when the locals do. To help reset your toddler's internal clock, you'll also have to work at getting him or her to eat, wake, nap, and play when they do. Start the first day by waking your child at a reasonable hour rather than letting him or her sleep in. Do it gently and be prepared to suffer the grumpy consequences (letting sunlight into the room will help). Breakfast shortly after you get up and continue to stick as closely to the new time as possible for the rest of the day. By the end of the day, exhaustion is sure to have set in and your toddler should be ready for an earlier-than-usual bedtime. Skipping the nap might help a child to adjust to an earlier bedtime more quickly, but it could also backfire. An overtired toddler may welcome sleep less graciously.

In spite of your efforts to reset your toddler's biological clock, he or she may stay tuned in to home-time, at least for a while. Be ready with some quiet entertainment in case your child awakens in the middle of the night and refuses to go back to sleep. Also have a snack handy in case there are pleas for "breakfast" at 3 A.M.

**See the light.** Sunlight appears to play a major factor in helping our bodies reset our biological clocks. So the entire family will adjust more quickly to the new time if you spend as much time as possible in the bright light outdoors as soon after your arrival as possible. Going west to east, you should make a special effort to get out early the next morning; east to west, in the late afternoon. (If you're out in the hot sun, be sure to take appropriate precautions; see page 466.)

When you're traveling through more than four time zones, different factors need to be considered. Going west to east, from Los Angeles to London, for example, entails a radical eight-hour change. Many parents find that taking a late-night flight (10 or 11 P.M.) works well. The children usually sleep a good part of the flight, but their sleep is broken up enough, especially when light streams through the windows at dawn, to leave them exhausted the next day. So exhausted that they are usually willing to go to bed earlier than their accustomed bedtime and closer to nightfall in London.

When flying home from London, a late night flight may again serve well. Although a toddler is likely to spend a somewhat restless night on the plane, it's likely that if you arrive home very early in the morning, he or she will be exhausted enough to go back to sleep. The darkness and the familiar surroundings will help.

On these longer trips, whether west to east or east to west, making an effort to expose everyone in your party to midday (rather than early or late) sun on arrival will make resetting internal clocks easier.

Don't expect to reset your internal clocks overnight. It generally takes at least a few days. It also takes a great deal of patience. Your toddler is likely to be somewhat cranky, clingy, and generally out of sorts at first. Respond with sensitivity and you'll get better results. If possible, avoid major outings during the first couple of days of your trip; these adjustment days are best spent relaxing on a beach, splashing in a pool, or just hanging out. Take it easy again for the first few days on returning home.

In general, be less attached to a schedule while you're away than you are at home—the new schedule is only temporary. Do whatever works. In the end, you may be pleasantly surprised to find that your toddler hardly notices the time change.

diarrhea, that requirement increases 1½ to 1¾ ounces per pound.[5]

**Factor out fats.** Greasy foods can also aggravate motion sickness, so keep your toddler away from fries, chips, burgers, rich desserts, and other fatty foods.

**Add some air.** . . . In a car, fresh air from an open window can minimize motion sickness. On a ship, a walk on deck may help. On a plane, redirecting the overhead air vent is about the best you can do.

**. . . and a seat with a view.** Watching the horizon can help to relieve motion sickness; when possible, seat your toddler next to a window, and periodically call attention to sights in the distance. Discourage looking at books or any other entertainment that requires focusing close up since this can exacerbate motion sickness. Even though the ride in the front seat of a car is smoother than it is in the back (and thus less likely to induce queasiness), for safety reasons, it isn't recommended that a child ride up front until age four.

**Encourage napping.** If your toddler is able to sleep, or at least rest with his or her eyes closed for most of the trip, the chances of motion sickness are greatly reduced. Discourage a lot of moving around; it could make your child feel worse.

**Distract.** Sometimes getting one's mind off one's stomach can help. Use toys, tapes, songs, talk, spotting games, and so on.

**Have a bag handy.** Be prepared for the worst, just in case none of the above do

the trick. Pack some large zip-lock plastic bags within reach if you're driving or traveling by train (planes supply air-sickness bags in the seat pockets)—but keep them out of your toddler's reach. Also have an extra set of clothing, plenty of wipes (they can be used to clean up your child, clothing, seats, upholstery, and carpeting), and air freshener handy, too.

If your child does begin to feel sick, he or she may not know what the sensation is or be able to describe it. Some toddlers just complain about not feeling well, others complain of sore throats or clutch their throats with their hands. Some cough (a reaction to gagging). Some look pale or "green around the gills." There may, however, be no obvious symptoms until your child throws up.

If motion sickness strikes while you're at the wheel, stop at the first opportunity, clean up as best you can, and have your toddler close his or her eyes and rest for a few minutes before you resume driving. Applying a wet cloth to your child's forehead may also help, as can getting some fresh air. Try not to overreact to a bout of vomiting, which may make a toddler feel that he or she has done something wrong.

# PACKING FOR THE ROAD

Among the traveling companions you may want to consider taking along to make your trip more enjoyable for all:

**A carryall.** A single many-compartmented diaper bag, tote, or backpack can hold the basics you will need with you at all times. A shoulder strap will make carrying the bag and a toddler simultaneously easier. Keep your purse or wallet, with most of your cash and/or traveler's checks, credit cards, travel documents,

---

5. Occasionally, a child who vomits as a result of motion sickness becomes dehydrated. This is most likely to happen on a plane or in hot weather when the child is also perspiring. If you note the symptoms (see page 605), take appropriate action.

tickets, and prescriptions, zipped safely inside the main compartment. Tuck some ready cash and one or two credit cards in an easily accessible side pocket or in a pocket of your clothing. The following should also go in your carryall.

**Diapers or training pants.** For the toddler still in diapers, pack enough diapers for your expected hours of travel plus one extra day's worth, so that you will be prepared for unexpected delays, misplaced luggage, or an attack of traveler's tummy. Also carry a supply of plastic bags (reuse supermarket produce bags), with ties or rubber bands (or just knot them closed) for dirty diapers when there is no immediate disposal facility. Be sure to pack the bags in a zippered compartment or make them otherwise inaccessible to your toddler. Pack additional diapers in your luggage. Check in advance to be sure that you will be able to replenish your diaper supply on arrival at your destination; if you are going abroad and disposables won't be available, pack enough for your entire trip.

For the toddler in training pants, tuck in two or three extra pair, just in case. With the happy excitement and upset schedules of travel, there may be more accidents than usual. If your toddler's going to be doing a lot of sleeping while traveling, and he or she ordinarily wears a diaper during naps, consider such protection en route.

**Wipes, wipes, and more wipes.** For dirty hands, grimy faces, stained clothes, soiled car upholstery. When there's no bathroom nearby, or when the bathroom is dirtier than the hands you want to wash, wipes are an excellent stand-in for soap and water.

**A change of clothes.** Keep at least one full extra set of clothing (including socks, underwear, and shoes) with you whenever you travel. To minimize the mess of food spills, carry a wipe-clean plastic bib, if your toddler will wear one.

**Sustenance.** By land, by air, by sea, by rail, even by stroller—traveling with a toddler requires traveling with food and drink, or living to regret it. If you don't have a cooler, take along such neat, nonperishables as quartered peanut-butter sandwiches; whole-grain crackers, pretzels, and bite-size cereals in plastic containers (cereals can also be toted in single-serve boxes); fruit-juice sweetened whole-grain cookies and dried fruit (but only if teeth can be brushed or rinsed right after eating); whole-grain rolls and bagels. Cheese sticks, hard-boiled eggs, fruit-sweetened yogurt, and containers of cut fruit are fine when they're kept cool (in an insulated bag with a frozen ice pack) or when they're going to be eaten within two hours. To wash it all down, bring along a thermos with a twist-out straw and refill it as you go with milk, juice, or water. Also carry your toddler's favorite cup, several plastic spoons, a plastic knife, and a small can opener.

**A mini-medicine chest.** Keep in a zippered (or better still, locked) bag tucked into your carryall any medication your child must take (don't risk leaving it in checked-through luggage); any other travel medications recommended by your child's doctor (see page 250); your toddler's toothpaste and brush; acetaminophen; first-aid supplies (tape, sterile gauze pads, bandage strips, alcohol wipes, and an antibiotic ointment or a first-aid spray); a moisturizer for chapped skin (air travel is dehydrating); diaper rash ointment (an altered diet and irregular diapering increases the risk of diaper rash); sunscreen; and insect repellent (see page 648). It's also a good idea to carry health information about each family member (age, weight, immunization history, regular medicines, allergies, and blood type) with your travel documents.

**Some surprises.** Though old favorites are important to a toddler on the road, magically producing a brand new toy or book when boredom starts to set in can

# TANTRUMS ON THE GO

· · · · · · · · · ·

I f toddlers ever needed excuses to throw tantrums, they've got them during the average vacation: disrupted sleep schedules, erratic eating, long periods of enforced sitting, unfamiliar surroundings. Since tantrums on the road are even tougher to deal with than tantrums at home, it's best to try to prevent them when possible.

Sleepiness, hunger, or boredom can all trigger a tempest. Try to anticipate a toddler's needs before he or she starts screaming for attention; bring on the snacks when meals will be delayed, reschedule a visit to a monument so your toddler won't miss a nap, plan toddler-pleasing activities. Become a master of distraction, pulling tricks out of your little bag to occupy your toddler on the brink. And remember, more isn't always better—underscheduling can prevent overstimulation and possibly prevent a tantrum as well. Building restful time into your schedule, time for reading, listening to music, hugging, may also prevent explosions.

Be patient, however, when explosions do occur. When a child has a tantrum in public, parents tend to put their own embarrassment first. Try not to do that; ignore those around you when your toddler lies down on the floor and starts kicking in the airport, and try to treat your child as you would if you were alone (see page 339 for ways of coping with tantrums).

---

buy you some extra time behind the wheel or buoy your toddler's spirits in flight. Invest in a supply of trinkets, and pace yourself giving them out.

Also take along if needed:

**A travel potty seat.** A light-weight, foldable, portable seat will make it easier for your toddler to use strange toilets, especially if it's a seat he or she is already accustomed to using. Or take along a disinfectant spray to use on public toilets or line the seats with toilet tissue or paper seat covers, if available.

Most toddlers can't yet be counted on to "hold it in" just because the rest stop is still miles away. Some will also refuse to use a restroom that isn't clean or simply "strange." So, if you are planning an auto trip, consider taking a portable potty (and a roll of toilet tissue) for your toddler to use at the side of the road when rest stops are far apart.

**A backpack for your toddler.** Wearing a backpack makes a toddler feel important, and also gives him or her easy access to important personal possessions. Let your toddler pack the pack with favorite toys, books (lightweight paperbacks are best), a pad of paper and crayons. For the little navigator, a map (provide an old one you no longer need) and a child's compass (make sure it's safe) are great diversions. A wallet full of play money and your pretend credit card (expired library cards, health insurance cards, etc.) will also entertain. Avoid pencils, pens, and any other pointed things that could be dangerous at a sudden stop or when a train or plane lurches sharply. Also avoid toy guns or metal toys (especially when traveling by plane—unless they are checked through, they will be confiscated by security); noisy toys; toys or games with numerous pieces; toys that can easily roll away, annoying other passengers; and balloons.

**A "lovey" or comfort object.** If your toddler has a favorite blanket, teddy, or other object, be sure to take it along. On planes or trains, keep it with the carry-on luggage.

**Music and stories to go.** A sturdy, children's cassette player with headphones will keep an older toddler busy for miles on the road (though you may have to help change the tapes). Bring along an assortment of musical favorites and stories on tape (with or without accompanying books). If your toddler won't use the headphones, you'll have to listen to his or her selection, too—it's either that or whining. Your toddler can also listen to tapes on the train—but, unless you're in a private compartment, should use earphones so as not to disturb others. Though you may not be able to use your own tape player on a plane, many airlines supply earphones and have special children's channels for young passengers.

**A travel stroller.** A stroller is invaluable on almost any kind of vacation-with-toddler. It gives your child the option of riding (perhaps napping) when you're walking or touring, and makes it easier for you to get around museums, amusement parks, and other attractions. Depending on your needs, select a light easy-to-fold umbrella stroller (check ahead with the airline to see if it can be carried on or if it must be checked through) or the new car-seat–air-seat stroller combo, which can serve multiple roles.

**A travel wardrobe.** Pack as little as you think you can reasonably get away with. For your toddler, take only easy wash-and-wear items and plan to wash as you go. Mix and match outfits are best, so that if a shirt is covered with chocolate ice cream at lunch, another that also matches the shorts can replace it. Even in warm weather, take a light sweater for your toddler to wear on cool evenings or when the air-conditioning is chilling. Though sandals are fine for the beach (except in areas where parasites are a problem), take along sneakers or other closed shoes for walks in the country and outdoor play, especially in rural areas.

# WHAT IT'S IMPORTANT FOR YOUR TODDLER TO KNOW: All About Sharing

To a toddler, there is no yours, mine, and ours—there is only mine. Just beginning to grasp the concept of ownership, the toddler has not yet grasped that it can apply to others. Not only do toddlers label "mine" those things that are rightfully theirs (their toys, their bed, their chair, their family), but those things that rightfully belong to others (brother's book, Mommy's keys, Auntie's wallet). Even things that are supposed to belong to everyone (the bus, the slide at the playground, the flowers in the park) may be viewed possessively. "Mine" is, for now, the toddler's favorite word.

But possessiveness at this age in no way predicts a lifetime of selfishness. Grabbing from others and holding on to one's own possessions is just another normal manifestation of a toddler's need to establish autonomy and identity, to test boundaries and stand up for his or her rights.

Toddler possessiveness is not only normal, it's a necessary, essential step on the road to sharing. Unless children are given the opportunity to enjoy and appreciate ownership, they have difficulty learning to share. "Owning" comes long before "sharing" on the toddler developmental scale. Most children understand owning by the second half of the second year, but don't learn to share until they are three or four.

Another road block to toddler sharing is the concept of lending and borrowing. They don't grasp the idea that when you let a friend use something (whether it's a toy or the slide you had first dibs on) you get it, or use of it, back. They equate giving with giving up.

While a toddler may offer a favorite teddy to a brother who's crying or share a piece of cookie with Mommy when she's having a rough day, these gestures are more an indication of empathy than generosity. The toddler is comforting, not sharing. Nevertheless, such behavior should be applauded and encouraged. Children tend to repeat acts for which they receive praise. And acts they repeat become habits.

A toddler may also seem to "offer" a toy or other belonging to a friend or family member, but then become indignant if it is actually accepted by the other party. In this situation, the child is usually just showing off the prize rather than sincerely offering it.

But as natural as it is for your toddler to object to sharing, it's also natural for you to want your toddler to learn how to share. Here's how to begin:

▲ Build your toddler's self-esteem. Insecure children have a much harder time learning to share; they often end up hoarders, who use their accumulation of possessions to bolster their feelings about themselves. See page 292 for tips on building self-esteem.

▲ Don't force your toddler to share. Pushing a child to share implies that you consider his or her needs less significant than those of others. But at this sensitive stage of development, when a sense of self and self-esteem are just starting to evolve, your toddler needs to feel as important as the next child. Also, toddlers crave security. Believing that their pos-

sessions are up for grabs can make them feel insecure and unsettled; they need to know that some things are theirs and theirs alone. Finally, forcing children to share teaches them nothing about generosity; when they comply, it's only because they're doing as they're told.

▲ Introduce the concept of other people's ownership. As hard as it is for toddlers to accept, they don't own everything in their surroundings. They need to learn that some things belong to the group or to everybody (toys at day care, equipment at the playground) and that some things belong to other people (a playmate's doll or truck, for example, or your books). They also need to know that children must take turns on the slide, must wait their turn for an empty swing, and can't grab another child's tricycle when she's riding it. Promote these rules regularly. If you encounter resistance to them, you will have to enforce them by bodily removing your toddler from the situation. Be understanding but firm.

▲ Put your toddler's resistance to sharing in perspective. Unwillingness to part with a toy truck for even fifteen minutes (which for a toddler may seem like fifteen hours) may seem unreasonable, but it's actually very valid. Put yourself in your child's sneakers: How willing would you be to part with your car, your favorite shoes, or a special piece of jewelry, just overnight, even to a trusted friend? To toddlers, who don't understand that they'll get back what they lend, sharing possessions is even tougher.

▲ Acknowledge to your toddler that it's hard to share. Instead of scolding, "It's not nice not to let Thomas play with your car", empathize, saying, "I know it's hard to share your car. It's very special to you." Such understanding will help your toddler overcome a reluctance to share sooner. You can also try to help your toddler to empathize with playmates: "Kelly feels sad when you won't let her play with your puzzle."

▲ Don't share *for* your toddler. Your toddler's toys belong to your toddler. Show you recognize that: Always ask permission before offering them to a playmate; if permission isn't granted, don't insist. In the long run this respect will encourage generosity and your toddler will be less likely to guard possessions jealously.

When it's necessary for your toddler to share (you're hosting a play group or a play date, for instance), discuss in advance which special toys should be put away and which he or she is willing share. Until sharing becomes the norm, encourage children to bring one or two playthings of their own—just in case the host is feeling particularly possessive. As they become better negotiators they may start swapping, and this will be the beginning of sharing.

Also see if the principals in a fight over a toy can work it out on their own before you step in—unless, of course, fists start flying. When they settle peacefully or one of the children shows generosity, offer plenty of praise.

▲ Share with your toddler. As usual, the best way for your toddler to learn is from your example. Make a point of sharing with your child often: Offer a piece of your muffin or a chunk of cheese off your plate, a look at your magazine (under supervision, of course), a chance to try on your boots. Explain that, "This is mine, but I like sharing it with you."

Play sharing games, too: "You let me play with your doll and I'll let you play with my deck of cards." Sharing with you will be less threatening than sharing with peers, and it's good practice and invaluable preparation.

▲ Introduce lending and borrowing. Explain that when you lend something, you get it back; when you borrow, you have to give it back. Look for opportunities to illustrate it in your daily life. Borrow a teddy bear for a few minutes, then return it. Let your toddler borrow your sunglasses, then ask for them back. Point out that when children play with the swings at the playground, they don't take them home; when they play with the blocks at a friend's house, they don't take them home. They are just "borrowing" them for a while.

▲ Compliment all efforts at sharing, no matter how small or reluctant. Whenever your toddler agrees to share, commend and praise the act of kindness. Whenever possible, try to help your toddler see that sharing is its own reward: that letting a friend use one of his or her shovels makes a better skyscraper possible; that lending a playmate a truck makes for a more exciting race. With time, experience, and some gentle guidance (when your toddler refuses to share one toy, for example, suggest another), children eventually start to realize that sharing makes play sessions more productive, and that squabbling is a waste of valuable time. This conclusion is often reached sooner by children who have more frequent and more regular exposure to others their own age—whether it's in a child-care situation or in some form of play group.

# CHAPTER ELEVEN

# The Twenty-Third Month

## WHAT YOUR TODDLER MAY BE DOING NOW

*By the end of this month,[1] your toddler*
*. . . should be able to: (see Note)*

▲ kick a small ball forward

**Note:** If your toddler has not reached these milestones or doesn't use symbolic play and words, consult the doctor or nurse-practitioner. This rate of development may well be normal for your child (some children are late bloomers), but it needs to be evaluated. Also check with the doctor if your toddler seems out-of-control or hyperactive; uncommunicative, passive, or withdrawn; highly negative,

demanding, and stubborn. (Remember, the child who was born prematurely often lags behind others of the same chronological age. By twenty-three months, this developmental gap has generally narrowed; it generally disappears by age two.)

*. . . will probably be able to:*

▲ combine words (by 22½ months)
▲ identify 6 body parts by naming
▲ use 50+ single words

*. . . may possibly be able to:*

▲ put on an article of clothing

*. . . may even be able to:*

▲ identify 4 items in a picture by naming
▲ use prepositions

---

1. The twenty-third month begins when a child is twenty-two months old and ends when he or she is twenty-three months old.

# WHAT YOU MAY BE CONCERNED ABOUT

## FIVE O'CLOCK FRAZZLES

*"Every afternoon, when I get home from work, my toddler starts falling apart. She becomes hyper, cranky, and impossible to deal with. I dread this time of day."*

Whoever coined the phrase "Happy Hour" obviously never spent five o'clock with a toddler. This hour, and often the hour or so preceding and the hour or so that follows, is rarely a time for relaxing and unwinding. More typically, the mood is frantic and frazzled. At the end of a long day, toddlers are often overtired, oversensitive, and overwrought, and even more prone than usual to fits of irrationality and negativity. Unfortunately, this hard-to-cope-with behavior happens when parental patience may be stretched to the snapping point— after an average day-in-the-hectic-life-of-a-toddler or after a tough day atwork. It's a time when even the coolest of heads are quick to overheat.

Nothing will guarantee peace, quiet, and intact nerves. But there are ways to take the frazzles out of five o'clock, most of which will work just as well for parents who have been home all day with their toddlers:

**Unwind before you get home.** It's not only the toddler who tends to be high strung at five. With dinner to be made, a toddler-taken-apart house to put back together, and if you've been at work all day, household chores, laundry, mail, and phone calls to attend to, the parental stress level can soar right off the meter. A parent's five o'clock frenzy tends to fuel a toddler's. So try to spend a few minutes unwinding before you pick up

the kids or walk through the front door. Get off the bus or subway ten blocks from home and walk the rest of the way. Listen to soothing music on your Walkman or in your car. Stay in the driver's seat for five minutes longer after you've pulled up to your driveway and practice deep-breathing relaxation techniques. And most of all, avoid putting your mind into overdrive with thoughts of what needs to be done; instead, think tranquil thoughts—they will help calm you before you tread into any potential chaos.

If you've been at home all day with your toddler, you'll probably have to do your unwinding together (see the suggestions below).

**Take a time-out together.** Instead of attacking your chores immediately, try to take a relaxing break (chances are that if you have a whining toddler pulling at your leg, nothing's going to get done anyway). Take a few deep breaths, postpone dinner preparations, put the mail aside, and settle down for a special activity with your toddler— preferably away from the distraction of the work awaiting your attention. Cuddle up with her while you read some nursery rhymes or listen to some soothing children's music (making it the same music each and every night will provide the comfort of consistency, and may even have a Pavlovian effect; you and your toddler will come to associate the music with calming down). Or get involved in an activity that you both enjoy (working on a puzzle, reading a story, looking at baby pictures, resting together in a dark and quiet room, taking a bath together in a tubful of warm water and bubbles, pounding on play clay, crayoning, playing with a toy that requires adult supervision). Or, unwind with a family workout—take a walk to the playground, or a "jog" around the block, or stretch out on the family room rug for a yoga or aerobics session. If you have to get started on dinner, have your toddler help you.

**Set a serene scene.** Take the phone off the hook (or let the answering machine pick up), dim any overly harsh lights, switch the television off, and remove any other agitating influences that might disturb the five o'clock peace—it's tranquillity time. Encourage your toddler to play quietly and to avoid high-energy activities. For more relaxing occupations for toddlers, see page 173.

**Feed the hungry.** A toddler's tummy runs on a different timetable than that of an older child or adult; asking her to hold off her dinner hour until you're ready to eat may be asking too much. And since hunger is a common generator of toddler grumpiness, feeding her early won't just keep her *stomach* from growling—it can help keep *her* from growling, too. Other potential benefits of an earlier supper for your toddler: She'll eat better (like the overtired child who can't sleep, the over-hungry child often can't eat); you'll eat better (sharing the dinner table with an irritable toddler can dampen anyone's appetite); and you'll be able to enjoy some quality time by yourself or with your spouse (particularly if you wait until your toddler's in bed before sitting down to dinner, but even if you just wait until she's calmer).

**Fend off frustration.** During this tense time, try to keep your toddler away from activities that might frustrate her: games or puzzles that are beyond her skill, drawing or coloring (if she's often disappointed by the results), block-building (if seeing her towers tumble upsets her).

# HANDEDNESS

*"My son seems to reach for objects with his left hand. Should I encourage him to use his right hand instead?"*

Hands off that child! Though the right hand is the right hand for a majority of the population, it's the wrong one for the 5% to 10% destined to be lefties. There are a couple of good reasons why you should trust nature and time to reveal your child's handedness.

First of all, persuasive evidence has shown that the hand a child favors is genetically determined. When both parents are lefties, there's more than a 50% chance their children will also be left-handed. When just one parent is left-handed, the chance of a left-handed child drops to about 17%. When neither parent is left-handed, it's down to 2%. Since it's nature, not nurture, at work here, encouraging your toddler to use his right hand won't help and could hurt.

Second, handedness isn't usually apparent until at least the age of three, and some kids keep parents guessing for several years beyond that birthday. During these early years, it's common for children to appear ambidextrous, freely switching back and forth between hands until they decide which is the more facile. About 20% of children never settle exclusively on one hand or the other, but remain to some degree ambidextrous. Some ambidextrous children use both hands equally well and can employ either for almost any task: others switch off for specific tasks—for example, using the right hand for eating, the left for throwing.

Third, research suggests that when parents try to "force" a child into using the hand he's not genetically programmed to use, handwriting and other problems can result. Consider, after all, how tough it is for you to try to write with the "wrong" hand just for fun; imagine how tough it would be if you were required to use that hand all the time.

Although there are no foolproof predictors of which hand a child will eventually favor, parents can sometimes see indications of future handedness even in young toddlers. Some clues (the hand a child uses to draw or throw a ball, for example) are better predictors of handedness than others (the hand he uses to hold a spoon). Some behaviors (which set of fingers a child chooses to scoop up finger food or to reach for toys) are so random that they rarely reveal a permanent preference.

*Toddlers embrace the security that comes from the accumulation of possessions—the more possessions on their person at any given time (stuffed into bags, loaded into backpacks, crammed into pockets), the better.*

In spite of the spurious "sinister" associations that have long been linked to left-handedness, favoring this hand over the right is nothing for either parent or child to be concerned about. Left-handed people, in fact, seem to fare better on average than righties in certain fields, particularly those that require a good sense of spatial relations—such as art, architecture, and athletics. The major negative: Lefties appear to have an increased susceptibility to accidental injury. This is probably due to the problems inherent in living in a world designed for right-handed people. If your child does turn out to be a lefty, stack the odds in his favor by providing him with lefty scissors and other implements, lefty mugs, and furniture and doors that open comfortably with the left hand. And take the safety recommendations in Chapter Twenty-One particularly seriously.

## PACK-RAT SYNDROME

*"My daughter likes to take bags and pack everything she can pick up into them. I'm forever unpacking these bags, and putting things back where they belong."*

"**M**ine" is an important word in the vocabulary of the typical toddler. It may be applied to objects that actually *are* hers as well as to those that are not. Busy trying to build her collection of belongings, this toddler often resembles a squirrel getting ready for winter. She may hoard or hide toys, clothing, books, half-eaten food, household items of an astonishing variety (from the merely mundane to the very valuable), not to mention keys, credit cards, shoes, ties, scarves, and jewelry belonging to other family members. Venture out of the house with the toddler, and little that she can reach will escape her fingers—she'll stash deposit slips and mortgage brochures she's picked up at the bank, twigs and rocks she's collected at the park, and, if you're not careful, candy and gum at the supermarket.

This squirreling syndrome is normal and age-appropriate and in no way predicts a future of kleptomania or compulsive collecting. Acquiring, categorizing, and stockpiling possessions brings a sense of satisfaction and security to the toddler; building a collection can help build her ego, too.

So keep a tolerant attitude towards your little pack rat's pursuits. Aid and abet her by providing her with a tote bag, child-size suitcase, or backpack bag for her collecting. And offer her a special drawer she can dump things into for long-term storage. To minimize battles, go through her bags and her drawer after she's asleep to retrieve contraband. To reduce the need to constantly unpack, take steps to reduce the number of off-limits items available to her. Leave little *you* treasure lying around; have a hook near the door for your keys and handbag, put shoes in the closet, the hairbrush in a drawer, and so on. Lock away valuables at home and watch your toddler's hands closely in stores (you might even want to check her pockets at the register as a matter of course; if you find she's picked up some goodies, see page 444). And, when you find her expropriating an item that isn't hers, gently remind her which items are all right to collect and which items aren't; she will eventually get the message.

# TOOTHBRUSHING TANTRUMS

*"My toddler fusses and clamps his mouth shut when I try to brush his teeth."*

I t's *his* mouth, and he's letting you know that he doesn't appreciate your intrusion into it. The tussle of the toothbrush is just another skirmish in your toddler's valiant struggle for self-determination. Since surrender on his side is unlikely, and surrender on yours isn't wise (even baby teeth need to be protected from cavities; see page 490), a little creative compromise is called for:

**Enlist an ally.** As you may have noticed, an authoritative third voice always has much more impact than the voice of a parent. So turn to the doctor or dentist to explain the importance of brushing his teeth. When your child gives you an argument, remind him: "The doctor (or dentist) said we have to brush your teeth so they'll stay healthy."

**Brush in style.** Let your toddler choose two or three colorful child-size toothbrushes at the drugstore (be sure the bristles are soft and of good quality). Then, each morning and evening, let him select the one he wants to use. This diminishes the control issue and may distract him enough so that he'll forget to protest.

**Let him do it himself, Mom.** Give your toddler his own brush to do some preliminary brushing. Don't worry about his technique or the condition of his toothbrush (the bristles will soon become flattened and misshapen); just let him get the job done the best way he knows how. Heap praise on his efforts, even if they're feeble. As he becomes more proficient, you may be able to let him take over the morning brushing completely, while you continue to help out at bedtime. But don't expect really proficient, independent brushing until somewhere around age seven.

Letting your toddler "brush the teeth" of a stuffed animal or doll (using a toothbrush reserved for play) at brushing time

*Toddlers may be more amenable to toothbrushing when they are allowed to brush a parent's teeth first.*

may make him more amenable to having someone else take a brush to his mouth.

**Then do it yourself.** After you've told your toddler what a great job he's done on his teeth, take your turn—using a different brush (see page 492 for toothbrushing tips). Let him sit in front of the mirror, where he can watch you work, so he feels he's still participating. Approaching him from behind, tilting his head back slightly, may give you the best visibility and maneuverability. Or you can sit on the floor, seat him in your lap, and have him lean back against you. Letting him hold the toothbrush along with you will let him maintain some control over the process (while giving him some experience in the proper technique), as will giving him a complete brush-by-brush as you go ("These two teeth look nice and clean, let's try the next two.") Or try the tooth for a tooth approach: have him brush your teeth after you brush his. Injecting a little levity—"accidentally" brushing his nose or his cheek (with plain water) before moving on to his teeth—may also loosen your toddler up a bit.

**Check each other.** When he's done his brushing, have him open his mouth so you can check to be sure he got all the visible bits of food. When you've done your share, allow him to check your work in the mirror. You can also have him check after you've brushed your own teeth. For tips on good dental care, see page 490.

# TOOTHPASTE CONSUMPTION

*"My daughter would eat a whole tube of toothpaste if I let her. Of course, I don't, but she screams for more every time she sees the tube."*

Swallowing an occasional glob of toothpaste (most toddlers do at one time or another) won't hurt your child, but chronic overindulgence can be toxic.[2] Fluoride, we now know, is one of those good things you *can* get too much of. Although a tiny amount helps strengthen a child's teeth and reduces the risk of decay, large amounts can actually mottle, or stain teeth permanently (a condition called "fluorosis"). And, in fact, the FDA recommends not using fluoride toothpaste at all on a child under two. Since a child between two and five can also swallow enough fluoride to harm teeth, it's important to keep your toddler from indulging in toothpaste binges. Remember:

**A little dab'll do.** It really isn't the toothpaste that cleans your toddler's teeth, it's the elbow grease. Most dentists agree that water does the job just

---

2. Using a saccharine-free toothpaste (there are at least a couple on the market) reduces the theoretical risks, but as long as there's fluoride in the toothpaste, it's unwise to allow a toddler to ingest it in quantity.

as well for toddlers, if not better (without all the foam in the way, you can see what you're doing). Nor is toothpaste necessary for its fluoride content; most children of this age get their fluoride from other sources (see page 493). Still many toddlers won't brush without the flavor kick of toothpaste. If yours is one of them, use just a pea-size dab of toothpaste on her brush. Spread it out and press it into the bristles so that she can't lick it off. And make it clear to her that the toothpaste is for cleaning teeth like soap is for cleaning hands; it's not for eating.

**Rinsing is critical.** Rinsing the toothpaste, as well as loosened bits of food, out of the mouth is an integral part of the brushing process. Teach your toddler how to swish the water around in her mouth, then spit it out. Most toddlers can manage this at around two years of age. A child who isn't yet able to rinse should not use fluoride toothpaste at all.

**Out of sight, out of mind—and mouth.** A toothpaste tube left on the bathroom counter is too great a temptation for your toddler to resist. Instead, keep the toothpaste hidden—even locked away, if necessary—in the medicine cabinet. Apply the toothpaste to her brush, then quickly stash the tube before you invite her into the bathroom, to help avoid cries for second helpings.

Even if you take the precaution of spreading the toothpaste into the brush, your toddler may still manage to suck it off the bristles. If she does this, or if she continues to scream for more, eliminate the toothpaste from the brushing ritual completely for now. Explain that as long as she tries to eat the toothpaste or keeps crying for more, she can't have any on her brush. Or switch to a "baby" gum and tooth cleaner, which does not contain fluorides and is safe if swallowed. Tell her that when she can brush without

swallowing and rinse well she can use the family toothpaste again.

# TOOTHPASTE REJECTION

*"My son can't stand the taste of toothpaste, and resists brushing because of it. Doesn't he need the fluoride in it?"*

Toothpaste adds color, flavor, fresh taste, and suds to the toothbrushing process but brushing with plain water works just as well. And as far as the fluoride is concerned, your toddler probably gets enough right now from drinking water, topical applications at the dentist, and/or his vitamin/mineral supplement (see page 493).

If the taste of the toothpaste you use is turning your toddler off to brushing, try other brands; there are some that come in child-friendly flavors (and packaging). If none appeal, just skip the stuff entirely for the time being.

# HAIRBRUSHING HIJINKS

*"My daughter screams and struggles whenever I try to brush her hair. But when I don't brush it, the tangles just get worse and worse."*

Spine-tingling screams. Wild thrashing. A savage struggle. Is it a scene from an Alfred Hitchcock movie? No, it's even worse: It's a toddler having her hair brushed.

No blood is shed, true, but a fair amount of tears fall—on both sides of the brush—as the chilling drama is played out. That it must be played out, usually at least twice a day, every day, makes the prospect of hairbrushing even more hair raising.

To take some of the terror out of taking out the tangles:

**Open a salon.** Set your toddler up on a chair or highchair in front of a mirror (use a booster seat or pillow if she needs a better view), and play "hair salon." While you're primping your client, allow her to primp one of her own: Supply her with a favorite long-haired doll or stuffed animal, and a hairbrush or comb to style with.

**Take two to untangle.** Your toddler will be less likely to resist hairbrushing if she's participating in it. When she tires of brushing her doll's hair, let her brush her own. You take the left side, and let her take the right. Then switch sides so you can go over what she's done. Or simply take turns brushing ("Now it's my turn to brush"). Just be sure *you* get last licks.

**Tackle tangles gently.** Use a wide-tooth comb or a brush that has bristles with plastic-coated tips; fine-tooth combs can tear and pull. Work upward on one section of hair at a time: Untangle the ends first and work your way up. To reduce pulling, hold the hair at the roots while you work on the ends. Try spray-on, no-rinse cream rinse or untangler to help untangle between shampoos.

**Curtail tangling.** One way to do this is to get your toddler a short, low-maintenance haircut, which should be easier to untangle and require much less attention than long hair. (Of course, this is often easier said than done; see page 309 for tips on getting a toddler to tolerate a haircut.) Another is braiding or tying long hair back into a ponytail or a pair of braids. Hair that's worn loose isn't just vulnerable to tangles, but to sticky globs

of food, mud, paint (or anything else your toddler gets into), all of which can dry into major stumbling blocks for the comb and brush. If you choose to braid or tie back your toddler's hair, however, don't pull it tightly from the scalp; this can cause temporary bald spots. Secure these hairstyles with barrettes, clips, or coated rubber bands specially designed for children. (Don't use ordinary rubber bands, which can break and pull the hair—painful for the child and unhealthy for her hair—when they are removed). Yet another strategy is to braid your toddler's hair before bedtime—assuming she doesn't protest and her hair is long enough—to help ensure trouble-free brushing in the morning.

No matter what your child's hairstyle, combing out tangles before the shampoo will make combing out after the shampoo less of a trial. So will smoothing suds through the hair (instead of vigorously working hair up into a snarl when lathering), and using a tangle-reducing conditioner (or a conditioner-shampoo).

**Take bows (or barrettes) when it's over.** Do her hair up with pretty accessories (let her choose them) as the reward for sitting through the brushing. And don't forget to reward your toddler's "client" the same way.

## SHOE STRUGGLES

*"Every time we try to get shoes on our son, he has a tantrum—he kicks and struggles so that we have to pin him down to get them on."*

Having his shoes put on represents just about everything a toddler resents and resists: being confined, being controlled, having done for him what he'd rather do himself, and, if he is touch-sensitive, being encumbered by uncomfortable clothing. Add a dose of normal toddler negativity and it's not surprising that, for many young children, putting on shoes is one of the most distressing parts of dressing.

Whatever the factors or combination of factors that cause your toddler to buck like a bronco every time you approach him with a pair of shoes, the daily rodeo routine can be debilitating—and can make everyone dread getting ready to leave the house. Though the passage of time will be the ultimate solution to your problem (this phase, like the rest, will eventually be outgrown), the following tips may help get those shoes on your toddler's feet with a minimum of difficulty right now:

**Stay away from laces.** And high tops. And buckles. And any shoe that's tricky to put on. Opt instead for slip-ons, Velcro closures, and other easy-on styles. The exception to this rule: If you have a toddler who likes to take his shoes off anywhere and everywhere, stay away from easy-on styles—they are also easy-off.

**Put his foot in a zebra.** Or a monkey. Or an elephant. Shoes that are designed to look like a favorite animal, or that have intriguing colors or patterns are shoo-ins for toddlers. Since your child is much more likely to cooperate when the shoes are those he's chosen, involve him in the selection of his next pair.

**Let him put himself in his own shoes.** With easy-on shoes, even young toddlers can often manage their shoes solo (lay them out for him with the corresponding shoe in front of each foot). Even if your toddler can't (yet), you can let him secure the Velcro strap, which makes putting shoes on into a participatory sport, greatly increasing the odds of cooperation.

**Be sensitive to the sensitive.** For touch-sensitive children, certain types of cloth-

ing—turtlenecks, snug crew-neck sweaters, snowsuits, and shoes and socks—can feel unbearably uncomfortable and confining. Be patient with this sensitivity; it will lessen with time, though it probably will never disappear entirely (see page 202). To minimize the problem in the interim, make sure shoes fit properly, avoid overly tight closures, rough inner seams, and linings that aren't perfectly smooth. Favor footwear your toddler can get into himself and smooth-fitting socks that meet the requirements outlined in the question that follows.

**Try a little reason.** Point out to your toddler that everyone wears shoes—the letter carrier, the boy next door, Grandma and Grandpa, cousin Sam, Aunt Suzie. Explain that, "We wear shoes to keep our feet clean and warm and safe. Without shoes we could get boo-boos on our feet when we're outside." Don't expect immediate acceptance of your reasoning. But, in time, it will help your toddler to understand the object of footwear.

**Try a little humor.** Pretend to put his shoes on your feet (or your shoes on his feet), on his teddy bear, on his ears, on his hands, then let him correct you; his giggles may get the better of his grumpies. If this sort of attempt at levity backfires the first time you try it (and with some children it does), don't try it again.

**Try a little diversion.** Instead of approaching with, "It's time to put your shoes on now," engage your toddler in a distracting, silly song as you set about your work. Or do some fast talking about the fun you're going to have when you go out. Or divert his attention to something happening outside the window or door; hopefully, he'll be interested enough in what you're saying to not think about what you're doing.

**Try a lot of patience.** Nothing fuels a toddler tirade like a confrontation. So swallow your exasperation and plaster a carefree smile on your face. This will obviously be easier to do if you avoid last minute exits, and start the shoeing process well in advance of a departure.

**Let him find out the hard way.** If your toddler absolutely refuses to wear his shoes, let him venture out in the stroller in socks. But take his shoes along. When his feet get cold, or he wants to get out of the stroller, produce the shoes—matter-of-factly, with no I-told-you-so's: "Oops, you forgot your shoes! Let's put them on fast so you can get out and play."

And of course, don't make matters worse all around by forcing shoes on your child when they aren't necessary. Though it may not always be practical (or safe) to go barefoot in the park, let your toddler go bare at home and any-where else it's possible. Not only be-cause sparing the shoes spares the conflict, but because feet develop best when they're shed.

# SOCK PROBLEMS

*"No matter how carefully I put my daughter's socks on, she complains that they bother her."*

Like the heroine of the story of "The Princess and the Pea" (remember, she couldn't sleep with even the tiniest pea under her stack of mattresses?) your toddler is probably touch-sensitive (or has a low sensory threshold; see page 200). Anything next to the skin that is not extremely soft and smooth can feel uncomfortable to a touch-sensitive child—whether it's a pair of hugging arms or a pair of wrinkled socks. Realizing that this sensitivity is some-thing that a toddler can't control is the first step in helping her to cope with it. The second is anticipating and minimiz-ing those things that might bother her. Avoid bulky cotton socks that can bunch up inside of shoes and socks with thick, rough seams (seams will be less bother-some if they're at the base of the toes rather than at the tip). Instead, choose orlon or orlon-blend stretch socks that are smooth-fitting, but neither too large (they extend beyond the tips of the toes) nor too snug (they leave red marks or lines on your child's feet). Be sure to pull your toddler's socks up so they are completely smooth before putting her shoes on. Choosing socks with fun de-signs and appliqués may also help, as long as the designs won't increase the discomfort.

And as soon as your toddler is able to put on her own socks, let her; she will be able to get them to feel comfortable more easily than you.

# DRESSING DILEMMAS

*"Every time I try to dress my daughter, she has a tantrum. She never wants to wear what I pick out for her."*

Even if it's her favorite sandwich or her favorite sweater, a control-hun-gry toddler is almost sure to resist it if it was chosen without her express approval. Which makes dressing, like feeding, a major challenge for parents of toddlers. Next time you face the challenge:

**Provide choices . . .** Granting her com-plete control over her daily wardrobe isn't practical or sensible, of course (she's liable to select a bathing suit and a pair of sandals on a freezing winter day or a snowsuit and mittens in July), but even a little control can go a long way in preventing dressing disputes. So offer your toddler a choice between two or three outfits. If she comes up with a wild idea of her own (that bathing suit in January), come up with a compromise when possible (she can wear it under her sweats). To reduce the chances of inappropriate choices, you can pack out-of-season clothes away.

When shopping, let her choose the outfits she likes most from several you've preapproved. This won't guarantee she'll want to wear them, but it will improve the odds. (For more on decision making, see page 414.)

**. . . but not too many choices.** Present your toddler with a closet full of choices and you're practically scripting a tantrum. Too many options can overwhelm and frustrate anyone, but particularly an inexperienced young child. So keep the multiple choices down to two or three at the most.

**Compliment her choices.** Praise your toddler's selections when they are suitable, but don't criticize them when they're mismatched and, from your point of view, misguided. Make suggestions if she's open to them ("the blue striped shirt would go nicely with the blue shorts"); don't worry if she's not. She has plenty of time to learn good taste, and to develop a style of her own.

*"My son wants to wear the same pair of pants every single day. Not only is washing them a problem, but they're getting really ratty and we're getting really sick of seeing them. We can just imagine what his day-care teacher thinks."*

Don't worry about what his teachers, other parents, or strangers think. Your toddler isn't the first to insist on wardrobe monotony or on going out looking ragged around the edges. If it makes you feel better, explain the situation to his teacher—she might even be able to make a few subtle comments

about his attire that will move him toward change (after all, *she's* not his parent).

If you can, buy one or two duplicate pairs of your toddler's favorite pants, and try substituting them for his standard garb on alternate days (wash them a few times first, so they won't be rough or noticeably new). Continue to offer your toddler a different option alongside his old standbys, but if he rejects it, accept defeat graciously. He finds comfort and security in the sameness.

And keep your sense of humor— you're going to need it. Though wardrobe eccentricities usually taper off as the toddler years draw to a close, they're almost certain to reappear—with a vengeance—during adolescence.

*"Our toddler struggles with us every morning when we try to get her dressed. It's such an ordeal that we wouldn't even bother if we didn't have to get her to day care."*

The daily dressing-of-the-toddler can be an ordeal for all those concerned—a kicking-and-screaming struggle from shirt to socks. But, unless you move to a nudist colony, it's an ordeal that must be confronted each and every morning. These tips may help make the ordeal a little easier to deal with:

**Have a cuddle.** Before beginning the dressing process, have a cuddle to mellow both your moods. If your toddler becomes really overwrought during dressing, have another cuddle to help her calm down.

**Change the subject.** While you're dressing her, distract her with conversation about what she will be doing in day care, or her play date in the afternoon, or about the rain outside the window.

**Let her dress for her "success."** Your toddler will be much more amenable to dressing if she can do it herself. So do everything you can to make self dressing easier. Choose pants she can pull on by herself, like sweats or elastic-waist leggings, and help her to get the right foot in the right leg, then challenge her to pull them up. Supply her with easy-on, open-necked pullover shirts and sweatshirts. Avoid clothes with a lot of buttons or snaps—not only will they thwart your toddler's attempts to dress herself, but they'll slow things down when you try to get the job done.

**Let her dress someone, too.** Your toddler will feel less persecuted by the dressing process if she's allowed to inflict it on someone else. So make the dressing-of-the-doll (or teddy bear) part of the morning ritual. Provide her with easy-on doll clothes with which to outfit her "child" while you're dressing her. Or have her dress the doll before or after dressing herself. Or, if she prefers an adult's touch, you dress her doll to her specifications.

**Tame with a game.** To reduce resistance, try making a game out of dressing. "Where are you? I can't find you!" can often turn a potentially upsetting shirt-over-the-head moment into a gleeful round of hide-and-go-seek. Likewise, a "What happened to your foot?" (or hand) or "I can't find your fingers. Where could they be?" is likely to produce giggles and cooperation rather than tears and opposition.

**Be sensitive to touch-sensitivity.** Toddlers often do not have adequate language to express their discomfort, or they may not even realize what it is they don't like about the clothes, they simply fuss and cry when an itchy sweater or a stiff pair of jeans is bothering them. If you suspect that your toddler is touch-sensitive, tend to her needs with a wardrobe of soft, comfortable, loose-fitting clothing. Avoid turtlenecks; scratchy

wool, stiff synthetics, and starched cotton; buttons, snaps, or tags that can rub against bare skin; select soft blends or pre-washed cottons (or wash cottons before the first wearing to remove sizing).

*"We have a very active, always busy toddler and getting him dressed for school in the morning is like running a marathon. I chase him into his room to get the T-shirt over his head, then it's into the living room to get one arm into a sleeve, and on to the kitchen for the other arm. Then come his jeans . . ."*

On the positive side, your toddler is probably helping you to keep in shape. The negative side, of course, may be that you are far behind schedule by the time the last leg is in his jeans.

Running from the hand that dresses him may be your toddler's way of getting attention when everyone is busy preparing for the day. If you think that might be the case, then try to work a little "quality time" into the morning schedule—read a story, play a brief game, have breakfast together. Or use one of these special activities as a carrot: "If you hurry up and get dressed, we'll have time to read your favorite book before we . . ."

If it's just exuberance or a mischievous nature at work, try dressing your toddler as soon as he gets out of bed, before he has a chance to get himself into gear. You can also try calming him down for dressing with a tape or a story; if possible, your spouse can do the dressing while you read, or vice versa. If time and patience allow, you could go along with this daily dressing marathon for a while, and make a game of it: "We have one arm in the bedroom . . . Now where do we go to put the other one in?" Your willing participation may take some of the fun out of it for your toddler and even bring him to abandon the chase. If

## A TICKLISH SITUATION

••••••••••

For most kids, nothing brings on the giggles like tickles. But while many gigglers are having a good time during the tickling, others are miserable, especially when the tickling gets too rough or goes on too long. That's because the laughter is involuntary—the body's response to the stimulation of pain receptors in the skin.

The response to tickling, like the response to pain, varies from child to child. While there are children who love being tickled any time any place, and others who like an occasional tickle, there are also some who dread tickling (they actually find it painful), and some who aren't ticklish at all.

How much and how often you tickle—or whether you should tickle at all—depends on how your toddler responds. This isn't always obvious. Watch your toddler's eyes, expression, and body language for signs that he or she wants to continue or to cease and desist. If you sense panic rather than pleasure, stop immediately. If the signs aren't clear, and your toddler is old enough to understand the question, ask directly, "Do you like it when I tickle you?"

---

all else fails, and time is of the essence on busy mornings, simply hold your child down and dress him.

## COAT COMBAT

••••••••••••••••••••••••••••••••••••••••••

*"I can't get my daughter into a coat without a struggle, no matter how cold it is."*

Though having to don any or all items of clothing at someone else's whim may prompt resistance from a toddler, coats and snowsuits probably top the list for wardrobe rebels. And why not? No other piece of apparel so restricts a toddler's freedom of movement. The problem is, while there's usually room for individual expression in other areas of dressing—a toddler who refuses to wear a dress to a birthday party can often get away with wearing play clothes, for instance—there usually isn't with coats. When a coat's necessary, it's necessary.

How can you make getting that coat on your toddler less of a struggle?

**With the right stuff (and stuffing).** Some cumbersome winter jackets make it almost impossible for the wearer to move. Avoid coats that are too tight, too bulky, too itchy, too heavy, or too restrictive. Choose lighter-weight insulating materials over heavy ones.

**With a choice.** You shouldn't fill your toddler's closet with coats to suit her every fancy, of course, but you can make the next coat you buy her a reversible one. That way, she'll be able to choose which side she wants to wear on a particular day. And when the weather is mild enough, give your toddler the option of wearing an extra sweatshirt layer with a heavy sweater instead of the coat.

**With ornamentation.** A tired old coat can become a prized favorite when it's been adorned with whimsical appliques. Muzzle your good taste, and let your toddler's decorating talents and imagination run wild in a notions or souvenir store. (Never sew your toddler's name on the outside of her coat. You don't want to give strangers a means of attracting her attention.) Apply the appliques for her personalized "new" coat.

**With distraction.** Talking fast (and working even faster) distract your toddler with conversation and/or a few props (a toy, an egg timer, your keys) before approaching with the coat.

**With the unexpected.** Do something goofy with your toddler's coat before attempting to put it on her. Put it on yourself (which should look plenty comical), and announce, "Okay, I'm ready to go out." Or drape the coat over her dinosaur or the dog. With any luck, your toddler will find you so amusing that she'll forget to protest when you help her into the coat. She may even become so possessive of the garment, that she'll *insist* you put it on *her.*

**With a little logic.** Before your toddler reaches the point of tantrum, when reasoning will be futile, try talking sense. If you have a window that lets you see pedestrians, put your toddler in front of it and point out people passing by, "See how cold it is outside. Everybody is wearing a coat. Brrr. . . ."

When no number of parental ploys induces your child to put her coat on willingly, you'll have no choice but to put it on her anyway. Be firm, but understanding ("I know you don't like to wear a coat, but when it's cold out, you have to") and quickly distract her once the deed is done ("Let's hurry out and see if we can see our breath today").

# HAT AND MITTENS BATTLES

*"No sooner do I put a hat and mittens on my daughter, than she yanks them off. This goes on for blocks, and she always ends up the winner."*

Almost every toddler has an on-again, off-again relationship with hats and mittens. Fortunately, though bare fingers and a bare head may make a child feel colder (particularly the bare head, since most body heat escapes via the head), they won't make her catch cold—only a virus can do that. And on most days, you needn't panic when the hat and mittens come off.

On very cold days, however, when the wind-chill factor is below 32°F (0°C), frostbite is a distinct possibility. On such days, your child should not play outdoors if she refuses to dress properly. Nor should she be allowed to play in the snow without mittens. This rule shouldn't hamper your activities if you get around by car—your toddler's fingers won't freeze during a quick sprint from house to car to supermarket, for example. But if your outings require walking any distance, you can try fastening a rain cover over her stroller to keep heat in. If that doesn't work, you may have to get a baby-sitter to watch your toddler while you run errands, if she steadfastly refuses to wear her hat and mittens. Having to stay home once or twice may persuade her that covering her hands and head is worthwhile.

Some tactical maneuvers may help you to win her cooperation sooner, however. Allow her to pick out a new hat and mittens. Head coverings that may be more acceptable include: a hat made of orlon or other soft synthetic (such as the fleecy Polartec) instead of an itchier wool one; a roomy hood, which won't be as confining as a tight knit hat; a hat with a fun shape (with puppy ears, for instance); a balaclava, a hood-type hat that slips over the head and covers the neck and chin, doesn't need tying, and eliminates the need for a scarf; a headband or ear muffs, which won't do much about keeping the heat in, but will protect ears from frostbite.

Knit gloves may be more acceptable to your toddler than mittens; they'll be less bulky and allow more movement, though they won't be as warm. Or perhaps mittens shaped like animal puppets (show your child how her hands can converse with each other) or with spaceships or other emblems will do the trick. (Waterproof mittens will allow your toddler to play in the snow.)

Clip mittens or gloves to jacket sleeves so that your toddler can't use "I don't know where they are" as an excuse for not wearing them. It's a good idea to buy a duplicate pair of gloves or mittens so that if one of each is lost, you still have a matching pair. Carry the extra pair along on outings, so small fingers can be kept warm in case a mitten suddenly disappears.

Of course, you shouldn't be surprised if none of these ploys keep your toddler's fingers and head covered. And unless the mercury dips below freezing, this shouldn't be a concern. Just carry the hat and mittens with you, and be ready to offer them should your toddler starts rubbing her fingers or complaining of the cold.

## *SELF-DRESSING FRUSTRATIONS*

*"My daughter wants to dress herself from head to toe—without any help from me. But she usually gets so frustrated that she ends up having a tantrum."*

Unfortunately, the desire to "do it myself" often comes well before the ability to do it (which in the case of self dressing, won't come until closer to the third birthday). The resultant frustration often sets off a tantrum. Although it's impossible to protect your toddler from all frustration (and not advisable, either, since a certain amount of frustration motivates development and achievement), it

is possible to minimize her frustration with dressing by taking these steps:

**Make it easy.** When you're buying clothes or making selections from her current wardrobe, look for easy-to-pull-on pants, shorts, and skirts with elastic waistbands, and clothing without zippers, buttons, and snaps; roomy-necked pullovers and sweatshirts; easy-on jumpers and dresses that won't get stuck halfway up (or down).

**Blame the clothes, not her.** When she runs into a dressing snafu, criticize the clothes instead of her efforts: "This sweater is being so silly today, it just can't figure out what to do. Let's see if we can get this silly sweater on you together."

**Let her finish what you start.** If getting the clothes into position is too tricky for her (she always gets both legs into the same pants leg, for instance, or puts her dresses on backwards), get her started, then let her finish. This can be particularly satisfying for her if you play that you need *her* help ("I can't get these pants up. Can you do it for me?") For more tricks of the dressing trade, see page 498.

*"My son doesn't seem the least bit interested in dressing himself."*

Not every toddler would rather do it himself—there are those who are content to sit back and have it done for them. This is less a matter of innate laziness than of readiness. At almost two, most toddlers aren't yet capable of handling the intricacies of dressing themselves (though most can certainly *un*dress). And until they're able to do it easily and well, some toddlers prefer not to try at all.

Sometimes parents are unwitting accomplices in perpetuating a toddler's disinterest in dressing himself. Either they make his life too cushy, stifling any instinct to help himself by waiting on him hand and foot, or they push him too quickly toward independence, which causes him to cling to his dependence. Or they leave him hungry for attention during those hectic morning hours—and he finds that needing help with dressing is one way to get some of the attention he craves.

Though it will probably be a least a year before your toddler will be capable of completely dressing himself, you can help start him on the long road to self-reliance in the following ways:

**Give him some lessons.** How to get into a shirt or a pair of pants may seem obvious to an experienced hand at dressing but a toddler often doesn't know where to begin, and needs some instruction from you.

**Give him first dibs.** Before you jump in and take over, always give your toddler the chance to dress or undress himself. For example, announce, "Time to get undressed for your bath. I'll fill the tub while you get your clothes off." If there's been no action by the time the tub is filled, offer to lend a hand. Do the same with dressing in the morning. Lay out his clothes, and give him some time to get the process going before offering assistance.

**Try a little friendly challenge.** Position your toddler's pants halfway up his legs, then stand back and say, "Gee, those pants don't look right. What do you think is wrong with them?" In the silliness of the moment, he may forget himself and pull the pants up to his waist. Each time, leave a little more for him to do. Whenever he refuses, just do it yourself without comment.

**Offer praise, avoid criticism.** Even the smallest effort—picking up his socks and handing them to you, zipping up his sweatshirt jacket—should be cheered. Ditto the most bumbling attempts. So

what if the shirt is on backwards? He did it himself. Unless *he* wants to correct a dressing faux pas (or if it might interfere with his functioning—as when he gets two legs in the same pants leg), leave it as is.

Making threats ("If you don't dress yourself, you'll just go out in your pajamas") or belittling a child for failure to dress himself ("Only babies need help to get dressed—big boys get dressed themselves") won't provide your toddler with an incentive to start dressing himself. Such tactics will, however, attach negative associations to dressing, which could make mornings a problem for years to come.

**Practice patience . . .** It's possible that your toddler isn't interested in self dressing because he's interested in too many other things. He may have bigger developmental fish to fry; dressing may seem too mundane for now. So persevere without pressuring him.

**. . . but not forever.** By the time your toddler reaches age two, he should be encouraged to *begin* learning how to dress himself. By the time he's three, he should be able to manage nearly everything himself, except for tricky buttons, suspender clasps, and other such tough closures. At that point, you can begin to insist he do some self dressing, especially when he has a play date he's eager to get to. Let him miss a couple of special events because he failed to get dressed, and he should start self dressing with more enthusiasm.

# ROUGHHOUSING

*"Our son seems frightened by roughhousing, but my father-in-law insists that it'll only make him tougher."*

Roughhousing a child who doesn't like to be roughhoused isn't likely to make him tougher, only more wary of physical contact and/or terrified of the roughhouser. Different children respond differently to roughhousing, just as they respond differently to hugging and cuddling. And with rough-and-tumble play, as with hugging and cuddling, it's important to take note of a child's response and avoid what he finds uncomfortable.

Continued roughhousing could result in exaggerated fears (even nightmares), particularly if the activity takes place shortly before bedtime. It could also compromise your toddler's relationship with his grandfather. Explain this to your father-in-law, and encourage him to switch to activities that your toddler enjoys—playing with cars, for example, or building with blocks.

It's also important to communicate to your father-in-law and anyone else who might get rough with your toddler that there is a risk of serious injury (including retinal detachment and brain damage) if a toddler under three is shaken vigorously or thrown up in the air. (But don't worry about past roughhousing; if damage had been done, there would be obvious signs.)

## *"PLAY-WITH-ME" DEMANDS*

*"Every time I sit down to write a letter, look a the newspaper, or get something else done, my daughter demands that I play with her. How can I get her to play by herself?"*

Toddlers who can play alone for any length of time are a rare breed—with lucky parents. Most toddlers prefer a playmate—either because they are naturally gregarious or because they aren't yet skilled at independent play. And parents make ideal, and often very available, playmates.

While playing with your daughter every day is important for her development and your relationship, and while it can be relaxing, enriching, and fulfilling, you shouldn't feel obligated to be at her beck and call round the clock. For your sake and for hers, your child needs to get some experience playing alone and to recognize that you have pursuits and pastimes beyond block building and toddler tea parties.

By seeing you work on your own, and by seeing you enjoy working on your own, she will learn that solo activities can be fun. When she does spend some time on her own, she will find she can be "good company" and that will make her feel good about herself. Start teaching her how:

**Give her lessons.** We often assume that children are born knowing how to play. But the fact is they often need help using a particular toy or plaything—whether it's advice on how to stack those blocks so they won't tumble, how to turn that triangle so it will fit into the shape-sorter, or how to get started on a jigsaw puzzle. The more time you spend orienting your toddler to the joys of her own toys, the sooner she will be able to play with them on her own.

**Get her started.** Each time you want her to spend some time on her own, get her started on an activity, then tell her she can do her work while you do yours. Be available, of course, if she periodically needs help.

**Keep her company.** Your toddler will be more receptive to playing by herself in your company than all alone. Cuddle up on the bed together with a book for you and a pile of books for her and say, "I'm going to read my book; you can look at your books." Set her up with some crayons and paper at the kitchen table while you catch up on overdue correspondence. Give her a plastic shovel to work the dirt while you do some weeding (but don't let her eat the daises, or the dirt).

**Provide other playmates.** If your toddler is a naturally social being who thrives on playing with others, arrange play dates, join a play group, and visit the playground regularly so that she will become accustomed to peer playmates. Another possible playmate is a mother's helper, who can play with your toddler while you get chores done. Preteens and young teens are often available for such work at reasonable rates, and toddlers usually adore these helpers.

**Demand some rights . . .** Parents of demanding toddlers have a right to demand a thing or two themselves. It's your right to go through the mail or bills, to get around to a thank-you note, to sort the laundry and cook dinner, to occasionally even read the paper or a book (which, in addition, provides a good example for your toddler). Always let your toddler's demands supersede your rights, and you will raise a self-centered child who will think that she can do anything anytime. Make some demands of your own, and your toddler eventually will come to accept that you have rights, too—an important step toward learning to respect the rights of others (see page 41).

**. . . but be realistic.** Let's face it. Many of the rights you enjoyed before you became a parent—the right to flexibility, privacy, and peace and quiet anytime you please—can't be considered inalienable anymore. Though having some occasional time to yourself is a reasonable expectation, time for yourself whenever you want it, at this stage of the game, is not.

**Time your time alone.** If you need to balance the checkbook, make an impor-

tant phone call, or take care of another chore that your toddler can't "participate" in, set a timer for the amount of time you need, and let her watch it tick away. This will not only occupy her while you're busy, but will give her some sense of control over you— which, of course, is what she wants the most. Just be sure that when the timer rings, you're ready to turn your attention to her.

**Be patient.** Teaching a toddler to enjoy playing by herself is a slow process. Getting her to spend even a few minutes on her own should be considered progress, and is an important step on the road to independence.

# CONTINUED CLUMSINESS

*"My toddler has been walking for a year now, but he still falls or trips several times a day. Could he have a problem with his coordination?"*

Most toddlers seem to have a problem with their coordination—but that's only because they're toddlers. Though most have come a long way, with relatively smooth strides taking the place of last year's tentative and awkward first steps, they still have a long way to go. Still absent are the abilities to come to a quick stop and to turn sharp corners—skills that, once they are mastered, will cut down on the number of daily falls dramatically.

But some of the reasons for a toddler's continued clumsiness aren't coordination-related at all. For one, toddlers are apt to be in perpetual motion—motion that doesn't anticipate barriers or slow down for obstacles. For another, they are immensely curious and self-involved—so much so that they don't always look where they're going.

And, of course, toddler judgment still lags behind their motor skills.

As long as your toddler persists in playing the fall guy, continue to take precautions to keep his environment as safe as possible; see page 620. If he seems to have difficulty walking, limps, or is unsteady on his feet, however, check with his doctor.

# REPEATED "NO'S"

*"Sometimes I overhear my daughter saying very sharply to her teddy bear, 'No!' And I wonder if she hears me saying it too often."*

If imitation is the sincerest form of flattery, you should be flattered. And as one of your child's primary role models, you can expect to be the object of frequent flattery: The first attempts at dramatic play almost invariably revolve around family life, with dialogue patterned around the most familiar parental refrains. It is no surprise that "no!" is among them.

But imitation isn't the only reason toddlers like to say "no!" to their dolls and stuffed animals. It's a power trip, their way of turning the tables and taking command, their chance to lay down the law for a change.

All of which is normal and healthy, and nothing to be concerned about. Just make sure you're not saying "no" all the time (see page 48), and that, when appropriate, you're relinquishing some power to your toddler.

# NOISINESS IN PUBLIC PLACES

*"Whenever we go to a restaurant, our son is the noisiest person*

*around. The quieter it is, the louder he talks. It's so embarrassing."*

A toddler loves the sound of his own voice. Put that voice in a quiet space—especially a large, cavernous one with plenty of echoes—and it becomes even more gratifying. Add extra attention—strangers' heads turning, parents turning purple with embarrassment—and you're talking ultimate pleasure.

But there's more than typical toddler mischief behind these noisy outbursts. Toddlers simply don't understand what constitutes proper behavior in public. Even if they did, they would have trouble complying because they're not good at controlling their impulses. Nor have most toddlers learned voice modulation—the difference between an "outside" and "inside" voice. Add to these reasons the fact that children tend to get less parental attention in restaurants (parents are reading a menu, chatting, eating) and acting out is often the fastest way to get noticed and it's easy to understand your toddler's behavior. Others around you, of course, may not, and they have a right to enjoy their meal in relative tranquility—without the crackle of toddler Muzak.

What to do? You could just give up public appearances with your toddler for a while, but that would teach him nothing about public decorum—and it could seriously cramp your lifestyle. Or you could take the steps recommended for successful dining out with toddlers (page 528).

You can also help keep the peace in restaurants by teaching your toddler a modicum of voice modulation:

**Give his voice a name.** Before your next outing, sit your toddler down and explain—with an audio demonstration—that there are two kinds of voices: an "inside" voice, and an "outside" voice. The inside voice is soft; it's the voice to use in the house when people are sleeping or talking or watching television,

## CHEER ACHIEVEMENT . . . BUT HOW MUCH?

..........

Children need praise. But opinions vary on how, and how much, to praise. Some experts recommend bestowing praise freely and lavishly; others warn not to overdo the applause on the premise that your child will find it difficult to judge his or her work accurately. Many recommend that the praise be aimed at the behavior ("Sharing that truck was a very nice thing to do") rather than the child ("You're the best little boy in the whole world"). They believe that constantly telling children they're the best can turn out paralyzed perfectionists who are so afraid of not being able to live up to overblown parental expectations that they stop trying. Others suggest focusing on the effort itself, since the results of a toddler's endeavors are not always successful ("You tried very hard to be quiet while the baby was sleeping; thank you"). Still others suggest phrasing praise (as well as criticism) in the context of "I" sentences ("I like the way you picked up the blocks").

Which approach should you take in praising your child? Pick the one that seems to work best for your toddler. If your child seems upset when you limit yourself to lukewarm accolades such as, "You tried hard to draw a circle," then find something more concrete to praise in the effort, perhaps, "Hey, you made a really cute squiggly line—that's great!" If overlavish and undeserved praise makes your child blasé or sloppy, cut back and try a more honest appraisal: "Putting in all those pieces is very good, but I bet you can finish that puzzle if you try a little harder." (But be sure the goal you're setting is realistic.) Reinforce the feelings of a child who is proud of an accomplishment. Teach self-appreciation ("Aren't you proud of yourself for going up the slide by yourself?") so that your child won't be dependent on you for kudos; he or she will know how to self-applaud. Praise attributes—a sense of humor, kindness, ability to find things, friendliness—as well as actual achievements.

Whichever approach you use, be specific when offering praise ("You did a wonderful job of picking up your toys,") rather than general ("Very good"). Offer praise often enough so that you encourage future efforts, but not so often that it rings false and loses its ego boosting impact. Avoid praise that isn't earned (children usually can tell when you're laying it on thick), but don't set your standards so high that you rarely have anything to praise. If you haven't been offering much praise lately, look hard for something to compliment—this shouldn't be difficult since toddlers are always reaching new milestones.

In spite of the voices of child-care authorities, if you feel like saying, "You were such a good boy today!" or "What a good girl you are to let Lisa take turns riding on your tricycle!" say it. Sincere praise from a parent is much more valuable than praise that is carefully calculated to accord with an expert's opinion.

And don't reserve praise for your toddler alone. Let your child see you expressing sincere and spontaneous appreciation for work well done or for kind or thoughtful gestures to all members of the family, baby-sitters, visiting children, the worker who fixed the television, the sanitation worker who picks up the trash. And keep in mind that praise doesn't always have to be verbal—sometimes a pat on the back, a hug, or a proud smile says it all.

when you're in a restaurant, the library, a museum, at religious services. His outside voice can be louder, and is good for the playground, the backyard, on a noisy street. (Then make sure you stay away from outdoor cafés—at least until he's learned the subtle difference between outdoor places where an outside voice is appropriate and outdoor places that require an inside voice.) Have him practice

## HAPPINESS IS A WARM PARENT . . .

**S**earching for the recipe for a happy life for your child? The single most important ingredient, child development experts agree, is loving, physical contact. One long-term study, in fact, which followed its subjects from early childhood into their thirties, showed that being raised with an abundance of hugs, kisses, and cuddling went further toward producing happy adults than being raised with any other advantage, and even seemed to help negate such potential risk factors as poverty, broken homes, and stress. The study also suggests that kids who are hugged a lot are not only more likely to turn out to be happy adults, but to find more satisfaction in all areas of life, including marriage and family, friendships, and career. So bear in mind that ubiquitous bumper sticker and ask yourself frequently: "Have I hugged my child today?"

Of course, hugging a child doesn't guarantee lifetime happiness. Happiness also stems from satisfying relationships, from helping others, from succeeding at endeavors, from self-esteem, from knowing oneself and one's goals. So it's important to help children to develop all these aspects of their lives. And to stress that ultimately we all make our own happiness—

that it doesn't come from possessions or food or anything else external.

That's not to say that a child must have a pain-free childhood to be happy. In fact, a very sheltered upbringing can lead to culture shock when a child is finally exposed to the real world. It's better for a child to recognize that no one is happy all the time, that life has its good times and bad times, and that, with love, you can cope with the worst of them. Be an upbeat role model when possible; try to be optimistic and satisfied with your lot. Happy parents tend to raise happy children. But don't feel obligated to put on a happy face when you're down (unless you're down all the time; see page 752). It's okay to discuss the fact that you're sad today because something went wrong at work or because your best friend moved away. Talk about the positive things you do to make yourself feel better when you're sad, such as hugging someone you love, listening to your favorite music, playing the piano, reading a book, doing a puzzle, going for a jog, talking to a friend, or helping someone. Avoid suggesting the use of food or money to bring happiness—that would be misleading. (Of course, never turn to alcohol or drugs for a lift—in front of your child or behind closed doors.)

---

the inside voice in the house; tell him he can practice his outside voice when he is playing outside.

**Let him get his outside voice out of his system.** Make sure your toddler has opportunities to scale the decibel range to his ears' content. Let him do plenty of loud singing and screeching at appropriate times and in appropriate places. (But keep in mind that excessive screeching can lead to hoarseness.)

**Praise his choice of the right voice.** Whenever your toddler uses an inside

voice at the appropriate time, even if he's just babbling quietly to himself in the kitchen, don't forget to compliment his good judgment. Positive reinforcement yields better results than criticism. If, however, your toddler is the kind to "get ideas"—when you compliment him on his inside voice, he suddenly remembers what fun he has using his outside voice—save the compliments for when he switches, at your request, from an outside to an inside voice.

**Take an outside voice out.** If your toddler starts jabbering at the top of his lungs in the restaurant, and doesn't respond when reminded to switch to his inside voice, take him and his voice where they belong—outdoors. Do this without much ado, and without raising your own voice.

Finally, keep your expectations realistic when you go to a restaurant. Don't expect your toddler to sit quietly at the table for endless periods of time. When he's reached his limit and starts acting up, it's time for a member of your party to take a walk with your toddler in tow.

# GRAMMATICAL ERRORS

*"My daughter is starting to speak in sentences. She makes a lot of mistakes in grammar. Should I start correcting her so she can get it right from the start?"*

The English language is rife with inconsistencies, with rules made to be broken. What's "right" often makes no sense at all to someone first learning to speak it, and what's "wrong" is often much more logical. Which is why beginners, whether native-born toddlers or newly arrived adults, make so many "mistakes"—adding an "s" to "mouse," for instance, or an "ed" to "bring," or saying "hisself" instead of "himself."

Your toddler has begun feeling comfortable enough with her verbal capabilities to experiment with combining words to form sentences; it's not a good time to bog her down with complicated rules. Rather than enhancing her language development, pressuring her to speak correctly so early in her speaking career would likely make her less inclined to speak at all, for fear of making mistakes. While it's fine to echo back correctly what she says incorrectly (she says, "Stevie did it hisself," you say, "Yes, Stevie did it himself"), it isn't all right to continuously correct her (she says, "The cat catched two mouses," and you say, "No, that's all wrong. You should have said, 'The cat caught two mice'").

Give your toddler time, encouragement, and a good example to follow, and she'll eventually make sense of her nonsensical native tongue.

# PRONOUN MIX-UPS

*"My son has a pretty substantial vocabulary, but he still refers to himself by his name instead of saying 'I' or 'me.' Should I correct him?"*

Although your toddler's vocabulary is shaping up well, many of the subtleties of our language may still elude him for a while yet—pronouns among them. Names, particularly his name, are much clearer in meaning to a young child than are "I" and "me." Most toddlers begin to use pronouns appropriately somewhere between the second and third birthdays; until then, there are plenty of errors.

It's best not to stifle a toddler's urge to communicate with constant grammatical corrections. Instead of criticizing, repeat what he says back to him with the proper pronoun in place (he says, "Her going, too," and you say, "That's great. She's going, too.")

And be wary of avoiding pronouns yourself in an effort to be more clearly understood by your toddler. Say, "Do you want some juice?" instead of "Does Jordan want some juice?" and "I have to cook dinner now," instead of "Daddy has to cook dinner now." If your toddler doesn't seem to grasp the use of pronouns yet, double up until he does ("Daddy has to cook dinner now. I have to cook dinner now.")

# ABC'S AND 1, 2, 3'S

*"Some of the kids my son plays with can recite the alphabet and count. My son doesn't seem interested in learning any of this. Is he going to be behind when he starts school?"*

They're counting, identifying letters—a few are even beginning to recognize words. Is this rampant precocity in today's toddlers a sure sign of giftedness? No. More often, it's a sign that these tots have been watching a lot of television.

Most early alphabet-reciters and counters owe their premature proficiencies to shows like *Sesame Street*, which teach these skills with captivating characters, catchy music, and lots of repetition. Some of these children are actually picking up prereading and number skills; others are just mimicking what they see.

Of course, television isn't the only impetus for this early learning. Intellectual nurturing in the home and innate ability

are factors, too. And although there's probably nothing wrong with this kind of head start, there's nothing necessary about it, either. While children who've had some letter and number experience before school may enjoy a temporary edge, studies show they don't retain it, as other students quickly catch up.

The fact that a child doesn't show an interest in academics at two or three years of age in no way suggests he won't become a good student. Relax and enjoy your toddler as he is. Give him plenty of experiences and stimulation (see page 78); talk to him, read to him, count with him while climbing stairs and doling out crackers, share some fun ABC books, cut sandwiches into triangles, squares, rectangles, circles. If he watches educational TV, watch with him and reinforce what he sees. Make learning exciting and enticing (see page 99), but don't belittle him if he isn't ready to count or learn the alphabet. There's plenty of time ahead for him to master these before first grade. Right now, feeling good about himself is more important than learning specific facts.

# WHAT IT'S IMPORTANT TO KNOW:
## Building Self-Esteem

Looking at most toddlers, it's hard to believe that self-esteem could be in short supply. Imperious and dogmatic, they seem nothing but sure of themselves. Yet, although they may be sure of what they want, toddlers are actually quite unsure of who they are.

It's at this stage that the seeds of self-worth, sown in infancy, must be cultivated and encouraged to grow. Studies show that children who learn to believe early on, "I am a good person, a valuable

person," are more likely to grow up believing in themselves. They have less need to impress others or to receive the approval of others to feel good about themselves; they can have rewarding relationships with others, can better handle peer pressure, and can reject drugs and other self-destructive behaviors. They have high self-esteem.

Though building self-esteem is something a toddler needs to do for him- or herself—one developmental brick at a time—the construction phase will go more smoothly with parental help, support, and patience. To protect your sanity while you protect your toddler's self-esteem, a sense of humor will definitely come in handy. As will these tips:

**Lay on the love . . .** Human beings can't feel good about themselves unless they have known love, the no-strings-attached kind of love that says, "I love you no matter what."

**. . . and the attention.** No matter how confident you are, you would begin to doubt your worth if you were regularly ignored by your spouse, your employer, the hosts at a party, friends at lunch. The toddler, too, needs regular attention in order to feel worthwhile. Talk to your child. Really listen when he or she talks. Pay heed to his or her needs and desires (even when you can't fulfill them, they shouldn't be ignored). Avoid constantly saying, "I'm busy . . ."

**But provide plenty of space.** Hovering over your toddler, always dishing out advice or assistance before it's requested, can squelch self-motivation. It can accustom your toddler to looking to you for answers to questions and solutions to problems, rather than attempting to discover them on his or her own. Lost along with the self-motivation are the self-satisfaction and confidence that come with successfully meeting challenges. It's also confidence building for toddlers to play by themselves occasionally, so that they discover that they can be independent, don't always have to look to others for entertainment, and can be "good company" for themselves (see page 286).

**Hold your toddler in high esteem.** Your toddler's self-esteem, in the long run, depends on the esteem you and others show for him or her. Make your child feel like a valued member of the family—one whose thoughts, feelings, and desires are given equal consideration and are never belittled. Show your respect by being there for your child; don't regularly put your social life, your work, your religious life, your household chores before the needs of your child. This is especially difficult for single parents, but nevertheless necessary.

**Hold yourself in high esteem.** Be a model of self-respect for your toddler; avoid denigrating yourself, doubting your judgment, indulging in self-destructive behavior (smoking, abusing alcohol or drugs, overeating). Having parents who think well of themselves inspires toddlers to think well of themselves, too.

**Be fair—don't compare.** Your toddler is a unique individual. Drawing comparisons in behavior, development, temperament, eating habits, or anything else, from your toddler to siblings, playmates, classmates, the child next door, or your memory of yourself as a child, is unfair and unwise. This goes not only for negative comparisons ("Why can't you behave like Matt?" "Why can't you eat as nicely as your sister does?" "Why can't you go to the potty like all your friends at play group?"), but for positive comparisons, too. Children who are chronically overpraised ("You draw better than anybody!" "Nobody is as pretty as you!" "You know your numbers better than any of your friends!") can find it difficult to live up to this glorified image. And those who come to believe that they are indeed better than everyone else often become unbearably arrogant. As a result, they may be less popular with their peers and with others, which ultimately weakens their inner core of self-esteem (though they may continue to appear cocky on the outside). Accept and appreciate the special individual your toddler is (see page 398), and he or she will be more likely to accept and appreciate that person, too.

**Watch your language.** Be careful not to use derogatory names or labels, even in a playfully teasing way ("Oh, Annie is a fatty!" or "Jason is a baby!") Such taunts can be taken seriously by the literal toddler. Don't exaggerate: Starting every reprimand with, "You *always* . . ." or "You *never* . . ." is unjust and can hardly be accurate. But say it often enough, and your toddler may come to believe it's true. And avoid stirring up guilt: "Oh, if it weren't for you, we'd be able to go to a movie once in a while." Or, "Your nursery school is so expensive we can't go on vacation."

**Balance your expectations.** Pushing your child to achieve early—to speak in sentences or give up diapers or recognize letters—won't necessarily accomplish the desired objective any sooner. But it could make your child feel like a failure for not meeting your expectations. On the other hand, expecting too little gives your toddler no incentive to do his or her personal best. Finding the right balance—having expectations that take into account your toddler's age and abilities, and providing challenges that are realistically within reach—will be most helpful in building self-esteem.

**Make limits and expectations clear and consistent.** If one day you expect your toddler to sit down at the table to eat a snack and the next day you let him or her roam the living room with it, you can generate confusion, which in turn can lower self-esteem. Knowing what's expected makes a child feel confident and secure. Assuming, of course, that what's expected is reasonable. Expecting a two-year-old to make her own bed or sort his own laundry, for example, wouldn't be.

**Validate your toddler's feelings.** As important as accepting your toddler's personality, talents, and abilities is accepting his or her feelings—even if they include such negative and difficult-to-handle emotions as jealousy and anger. Teaching a toddler to express these emotions in socially acceptable ways, rather than criticizing or trying to stifle them, will make your child more comfortable with feelings of all kinds and thus with him- or herself.

**Let your toddler make decisions.** It's not realistic to offer your toddler a choice on everything; if you did, bedtime would be anytime, dinner would be ice cream and soda, and shorts would be *de rigeur* in snowstorms. But it is realistic, and advisable, to give your toddler choices when feasible. Not only is early practice in decision making essential preparation for life in the real world—where options await us at every turn—but it's essential now, for your toddler's self-esteem. As any wise manager recognizes, letting subordinates know that you respect their judgment enough to allow them to make their own choices boosts morale and performance.

When offering choices, however, avoid overloading your toddler with too many (four breakfast choices, for instance), which can overwhelm, frustrate, and result in indecision. For more on decision making, see page 414.

**Let your toddler make mistakes.** Making decisions means making mistakes—at least sometimes. And making mistakes is part of the learning process in becoming a better decision-maker. If you take away the opportunity for your toddler to make mistakes, you take away his or her opportunity to learn from them. Whenever you give your toddler a chance to make a decision, abide by it. If it turns out the decision wasn't such a great one, stand by your toddler—don't attack his or her self-esteem with "I told you so's." Let your child know, and keep in mind yourself, that nobody's perfect (see page 81)—and that's okay.

**Criticize constructively.** Criticism should be used to teach, not wound, to build self-esteem up, not tear it down.

**Criticize the behavior, not the child.** Toddlers need to feel that parental love won't be diminished or withdrawn if they misbehave. To make sure that the message comes across loud and clear, show disapproval of what your toddler's done ("It's not nice to throw toys") rather than of him or her ("You naughty child!"). You can also show you still think well of your child by saying, "I'm surprised you did that. It isn't like you to hit your friend."

**Keep criticism under control.** Having to correct behavior is unavoidable with a toddler. But constantly finding fault can undermine a child's self-esteem— usually without improving behavior. (A child who hears "You're naughty" over and over again may come to believe it and will see no gain in trying to "be good.") If you absolutely need to get something negative off your chest, go into another room and unload it—out of your toddler's earshot.

Avoid cruel and inhuman physical punishment, including spanking, and punishments that embarrass (such as scolding in front of a playmate), frighten ("If you don't behave, I'm going to call the police to come and get you"), or diminish ("You're a nothing!"). In fact, try to avoid punishing at all (see page 127 for better ways to discipline).

**Give your child the gift of empathy.** Helping others helps both adults and children feel good about themselves. See page 42 for tips on developing empathy.

**Nourish the body as well as the ego.** Hungry kids, kids who eat too much of the wrong foods, and kids who don't get enough rest have a hard time working or playing up to their potential and tend to be easily frustrated. These feelings can damage their self-esteem. So can negative reactions of others to their tantrums or other unpleasant behavior.

**Make success a cinch.** Your home should be child-safe, but it should also be toddler-friendly. Provide a stepstool to bring sink handles within reach, a towel bar at toddler-level, and book and toy shelves that aren't a stretch. Clothes that are easy to put on and take off and toys that are challenging but within his or her capability also put success within your toddler's grasp. Which, in turn will bolster self-esteem.

**Put your toddler to work.** By assigning your "little helper" chores around the house, you'll make him or her feel useful, while also expressing confidence in his or her abilities; when you're that little, helping someone much bigger can send your sense of self soaring. Once that confidence is established, though, don't erode it by criticizing your toddler's efforts—even if they're slow, clumsy, and more hindrance than actual help. Remember not to overtax your toddler's capabilities; to avoid crippling frustration, assign only those tasks that you're sure your child can do. Offer assistance when your child needs it to complete a task.

**Learn to take it slow.** Because they're still new at many skills, toddlers can move at a snail's pace when it comes to getting their jobs done. While it might take you fifteen seconds to throw on your clothes, it can take someone who's just learning the ropes closer to fifteen minutes. So don't barrage a child who's taking great pains with a toothbrush or struggling to pull up a pair of pants with impatient choruses of "Hurry up! Hurry up!" Taking the job away and doing it yourself because you can't stand the slow pace demonstrates a lack of confidence that's bound to translate into lowered self-esteem for your toddler.

Instead, let pokey toddlers poke, building the extra time your child take to "do it myself" into your schedules. When you find yourself racing the clock, skip the nagging and speed your toddler along with a challenge that sounds like a game: "Let's see who can get their shoes on first."

# WHAT IT'S IMPORTANT FOR YOUR TODDLER TO KNOW: The Importance of Fitness

We sign our babies up for gymnastics classes before they can roll over, swimming classes before they can walk. We worry about their weight, fret about their flab. Yet despite all of the good intentions and early interventions, American children today are, as a group, less physically fit than any generation of children in our country's history, and less fit than their peers elsewhere in the developed world.

In generations past, fitness came naturally to children; the activities that kept them on the move—stickball, tag, hide-and-seek, touch football, jump rope, hopscotch—were favorite pastimes. Older children helped out at home, in the garden, on the farm, in the family store.

Today, activities that keep children inactive—playing video and computer games and watching television (including videotapes and cable)—predominate. And many children see physical activity as a formal scheduled event (dance classes or gymnastics, phys-ed in school), rather than a natural, spontaneous part of everyday life. When a class isn't on the schedule, exercise doesn't occur to them as an option; given free time to fill, they're more likely to grow roots in front of the television than build muscles out on the front lawn.

As the parent of a toddler, however, you have the opportunity to prevent that inactivity cycle from taking hold by helping your child to enjoy exercise now. You can also greatly increase the odds that exercise will remain a life-long companion. Here's how:

**Unplug the TV.** Don't let cartoons and video games glue your child to the sofa during his or her formative years. Using television as a baby-sitter, as a time-filler, or as a mood-stabilizer not only sabotages any chance to engage in mind-expanding activities like reading and imaginary play, but opportunities for muscle-expanding activities, as well. Experts point to "tube" abuse as one of the major reasons for the decline in fitness among American children—not only because TV watching discourages activity, but because it encourages the consumption of high-salt, high-cholesterol, high-calories snack foods.

**Fit fitness in.** Be sure that from an early age your child spends some time each day outdoors—at a playground, in your backyard, in a nearby park or meadow, anywhere where running, climbing, and jumping are safe and hard to resist. Provide balls in several sizes, a tricycle or other riding toy, a butterfly net, and when feasible, a backyard gym.

**Get up and go with your toddler.** If activity doesn't come naturally to your toddler, encourage it by getting physical together. Supplement sedentary parent–child pastimes (reading, doing puzzles, drawing) with active ones (hide-and-go-seek, follow-the-leader, playing catch, monkey-in-the-middle).

**Set a fit example.** Think about the path you're leaving for your child to follow: Does it lead all too often to the television, the easy chair, or the car? Or does it lead to the running track, the gym, and the bicycle? Your child's future fitness depends a lot more on how you pass *your* free time than on how many exercise, gymnastics, and dance classes you sign him or her up for. One study showed that children whose mothers exercise are twice as likely to be active as children whose parents are sedentary; those whose fathers are active are almost four times as likely to be active. When both parents exercise, their children are six times more likely to be active.

Walk to the supermarket, the library, or a friend's house rather than piling into the car; if it's more than a few blocks take the stroller, but encourage your toddler to walk part of the way. Cheer rather than complain when you have to climb stairs when visiting, or walk a long distance from parking space to store at the mall. Take your toddler along on your morning walks (in the stroller most of the way). Have him or her join you while you do your video workout. Make some family outings active ones (sledding in the park), rather than sedentary ones (gorging on candy at the local cinema).

**Check classes out before you check your toddler in.** There's nothing wrong with signing your toddler up for a weekly exercise, gymnastics, or movement class (but be careful not to overschedule; see page 381)—as long as the teacher's main goal is making fitness fun. Observe a class before you enroll your toddler. Look for instructors who motivate but don't push, equipment that is age appropriate and safe, and formats that favor free play over regimentation.

**Teach respect for the body.** When children learn to respect their bodies, they tend to take care of them. Show that respect by the way you feed the family, by the way you avoid cigarettes, drugs, and the abuse of alcohol, and by seeing that the family exercises together. But also talk about how it's important to take care of our bodies—if we don't our bodies won't take good care of us.

CHAPTER TWELVE

# The Twenty-Fourth Month

## WHAT YOUR TODDLER MAY BE DOING NOW

*By the end of this month,[1] your toddler*
*. . . should be able to (see Note):*

▲ take off an article of clothing
▲ "feed" a doll
▲ build a tower of 4 cubes
▲ identify 2 items in a picture by pointing (by 23½ months)

**Note:** If your toddler has not yet reached these milestones, doesn't follow simple instructions, or if his or her language is always unintelligible, consult the doctor or nurse-practitioner. While this rate of development may well be normal for your child (some children are late bloomers), it needs to be evaluated. Also check with the doctor if your toddler seems out-of-control or hyperactive; ex-

*You can't always get what you want—but, to a toddler's way of thinking, you have a better shot if you demand it loudly in public.*

---

1. The twenty-fourth month begins when a child is twenty-three months old and ends when he or she is twenty-four months old.

tremely demanding, stubborn, or negative; overly withdrawn, passive, or uncommunicative; sad or joyless; unable to interact and play with others. At this age, most children who were born prematurely have caught up to their peers developmentally.

### . . . will probably be able to:

▲ build a tower of 6 cubes
▲ throw a ball overhand
▲ speak and be understood half the time
▲ identify 1 item in a picture by naming
▲ identify 4 items in a picture by pointing

### . . . may possibly be able to:

▲ jump up
▲ put on an article of clothing (by 23½ months)

### . . . may even be able to:

▲ draw a vertical line in imitation
▲ build a tower of 8 cubes
▲ carry on a conversation of 2 or 3 sentences

**Emotional development.** Two-year-olds display a wide range of emotions and behaviors, such as love, pleasure, joy, and anger. Their behavior can be assertive and they tend to protest a lot. They talk, play, and interact with parents and others, can explore new activities, and want to do things for themselves.

**Intellectual development.** Two-year-olds are intellectually light years ahead of where they were a year ago. Now they can form images in their minds, make judgments, categorize (dogs and cats are animals, cups and plates are dishes), and arrange things in order (lining up blocks in size order). Their memories are much more sophisticated and they are beginning to understand more abstract concepts, such as "more" vs. "less" (though they're not likely to be using numbers yet), "later" and "sooner" (but not "next week"), "the same" and "different." Their imaginations are more fertile, their play is creative, not just imitative of what they've seen or heard.

# WHAT YOU CAN EXPECT AT THE TWO-YEAR CHECKUP

**Preparing for the checkup.** Keep a list of concerns (about eating, sleeping, behavior, comfort habits, or anything else) that have come up since the last visit. Be sure to bring the questions with you to this visit so you will be ready when the doctor asks, "Any concerns?" Also jot down new skills your toddler is displaying (climbing stairs alone, using a cup and spoon well, stacking five or six blocks, responding to two-part commands, imitating horizontal or circular strokes with a crayon, washing hands, toilet learning) so you won't be at a loss

when you're asked, "What's your child been doing?" Bring along your child's home health history record, too, so that height, weight, immunizations, and any other information gleaned from the visit can be recorded.

**What the checkup will be like.** Procedures will vary a bit depending on your child's doctor or the nurse-practitioner who conducts health supervision exams, but in most cases, the two-year checkup will include:

▲ Questions about your child's development, behavior, eating habits, and health since the last visit. There may also be questions about how the family is doing in general, whether there have been any major stresses or changes, how siblings (if any) are getting along with your toddler, about how you are coping, about child-care arrangements (if any). The doctor will also want to know whether you have any other questions or concerns.

▲ An assessment of growth (height, weight, head circumference) since the last visit. These findings may be plotted on growth charts (see pages 864 to 867) and the child's weight for height evaluated and compared to previous measurements.

▲ An informal assessment of physical and intellectual development.

▲ A hearing check; a vision check (to see if eyes are properly aligned).

Depending on need, the following may be included:

▲ A finger-stick blood test (hematocrit or hemoglobin) if the child is at risk of anemia. The test may be done once routinely between 12 months and 4 years.

▲ A blood test, usually a finger-stick, to screen for lead.[2]

▲ A Mantoux tuberculin test for children at high risk.

**Immunizations.** Catchup immunizations, if any have previously been missed.

**Anticipatory guidance** The doctor or nurse-practitioner will probably discuss good parenting practices, injury prevention, appropriate toys and play activities, nutrition, sleep, toilet learning, child care, preschool, language development, and other issues that will be important to you in the year ahead.

**The next checkup.** If your toddler is in good health, the next checkup will be at three years. Until then, be sure to call the doctor if you have any questions that aren't answered in this book or if your child shows any signs of illness or other problems.

# What you may be concerned about

## THE SECOND BIRTHDAY PARTY

*"We're planning our daughter's second birthday party. How elaborate should we get at this age?"*

Don't saddle up those ponies or start flipping through the Yellow Pages for merry-go-round rentals yet. To avoid a toddler rendition of "It's my party and I'll cry if I want to," your best bet is to plan the fête around these four "S's": small, simple, sensible, and short. This won't guarantee a perfect party (there are no guarantees when it comes to two-year-olds), but it'll help reduce the risk of disaster and improve the odds of a happy, memorable event.

**The right guest list.** Your best bet for a two-year-old's birthday party is a guest list made up primarily of adults your tod-

_____

2. This is a new recommendation of the American Academy of Pediatrics and not every doctor does this test routinely. At this point, there is some disagreement over whether it is cost-effective to screen all children.

dler knows well and likes. If you plan to include other two-year-olds in the festivities, don't go overboard. The commonly accepted practice of "one guest for every year" may add up to one guest too many at this age. A twosome—your party girl and a single compatible playmate—would make for better company. But if you're obliged to invite more than one toddler (if your child belongs to a play group, for example), try to keep the numbers even, so the children can play in pairs. Since there's no predicting how well your guests will separate from their parents, giving moms and dads the option of staying for all or part of the party will minimize the potential for tears.

If you're hosting other toddlers, one guest you don't want at the party is the family pet. Some children are afraid of dogs or cats, others are allergic, and even the most well-mannered pet can act unpredictably in a roomful of noisy, active children. Confine any pets away from the festivities.

**The right time.** When it comes to planning anything around a toddler—dinner out, a trip to the museum, or a successful birthday party—timing is all. Schedule the party to accommodate your toddler's routine. Avoid nap times (as well as the times right before and right after), hungry times (even if there's going to be food at the party, feed your toddler before the guests arrive so that hunger won't trigger high anxiety), and chronically cranky times. For many children, late morning or early afternoon are best. And remember, keeping the party short (one to one-and-a-half hours) will make it easier for your toddler to stay sweet.

**The right place.** For the two-year-old, a party at home, indoors or out, is the most comfortable. She isn't yet ready for a bash at the museum or the local gymnastics center. Keep safety in mind as you plan the setting. Even if your child is pretty reliable on stairs, other children

might not be, so be sure staircases are blocked. Look around for other potential party dangers—folding chairs that might fold up unexpectedly on a child, lighter fluid or sharp objects (the knife used to cut the cake, for instance) in an easy-to-reach place, bathroom doors left open by guests, and so on.

Another option is to stage a small celebration at your toddler's day-care center or play group, bringing along cupcakes and a few other treats to be served at snack time.

**The right help.** It's difficult to host a party for more than three or four toddlers without help. If your guest list includes more than a couple of children and you're not keen on putting other parents to work, consider hiring a teenager or two to help herd the toddlers and supervise the activities.

**The right supplies.** Use a light hand in decorating; anything else may overwhelm. It's fine to indulge in party paraphernalia that features your toddler's favorite Disney or *Sesame Street* character. But a cloth or washable plastic table covering may be a better idea than a paper one, which could be torn early in the festivities. Add some streamers and, if you like, a few mylar balloons. Do not use latex balloons, which pose a serious choking hazard when popped or deflated (see page 657).[3] Also avoid masks, noisemakers, and anything else that might frighten young guests.

**The right fare.** Serve foods and beverages that are safe for toddlers (see page 538). Many favorite party munchables—nuts, mini-franks, popcorn, whole grapes—are notorious toddler choking hazards; even when they're not meant for toddler

---

3. Balloons also pose an environmental hazard. See page 426 if you want to reduce the negative environmental impact of your toddler's birthday party.

consumption, they can easily get into the wrong hands, and thus, the wrong mouths. Alcohol, a poison for young children, is risky, too; it takes only seconds for a toddler to drain a glass of rum punch set down on a coffee table by an adult. For everyone's good health, limit or eliminate sugary treats. To minimize mess, opt for small cupcakes over sliced cake and serve frozen yogurt or ice cream in mini-cones. To protect your home, avoid purple grape juice and other deeply hued punches and drinks; pear or apple juice will be safer for your home and your guests' clothing.

If you're serving more than cake and ice cream, consider such finger foods as: string cheese sticks, cheese cubes or triangles; toasted cheese, peanut butter and jelly, or plain peanut butter sandwiches cut into circles, triangles, and squares; thin layers of peanut butter spread on thin apple or pear slices; pizza squares or triangles; and small melon cubes.

For safety's sake, make sure that the children eat only while they're sitting down (running around while snacking can lead to choking accidents) and that at least one adult supervises them while they eat. The eating-while-seated rule will also protect your furniture and carpets from spills.

**The right activities.** Magicians, clowns (with scary make-up), storytellers (with scary masks) can all frighten two-year-olds. It's better to avoid such formal entertainment. Try instead:

▲ Games—Stick to games where everybody is a winner (toddlers don't always lose gracefully). Such noncompetitive circle games as London Bridge, the Farmer in the Dell, and Ring-Around-the-Rosie work well.

▲ Dancing—Just turn on the music and let the children dance their excess energy away.

▲ Singing—Lead the group in renditions of "Itsy Bitsy Spider," "The Wheels on the Bus," and other songs from the toddler hit parade.

▲ Story reading—Have someone who loves reading aloud share a favorite storybook.

▲ Arts and crafts—Schedule an activity that's challenging enough to be fun but not so demanding that it's frustrating: decorating placemats or paper hats with markers and stickers, making birthday crowns, coloring on large sheets of newsprint, or making individual collages or a large group mural for the birthday girl. Giving each child a personal box or dish of crayons or markers (washable and nontoxic, of course) will help avoid squabbles.

▲ Free play—Set up the room with blocks, art supplies, riding toys, and dress-up materials (but, again, make sure there's enough of everything to go around).

▲ The highlight activity should be the birthday cake (or cupcakes). Be sure to practice blowing out candles with your toddler before the party. (While the candles are lit, guard them carefully.)

**The right expectations.** Expecting your toddler to be the gracious little hostess—politely greeting her guests, demurely accepting presents (and kisses from Great-Aunt Carol), letting others take first licks at cake and party activities—is unreasonable and unrealistic. Acting her age, at her age, means acting like a toddler: egocentric, unpredictable, and strong-willed, or shy and unsociable—or any combination of the above. The additional stress of being the birthday girl means your toddler is even less likely to demonstrate "proper" social skills.

Expect, too, some minor embarrassments (your toddler gets a present she doesn't like, and lets everyone know it) and some major accidents (a full cup of milk spills on the sofa). And, most important of all, don't be surprised if your pint-sized honoree does not even seem to appreciate her fête very much. That's normal, too.

# WHY? WHY? WHY?

*"Every other word out of my daughter's mouth is, 'Why?' She asks it even when I'm absolutely sure she knows why. Please—tell me why!"*

Why does a toddler ask, "Why?" Sometimes for the most obvious reason—because she needs an explanation. With an insatiable appetite for learning and so much to learn about a very complex world it's no wonder that the "why's" keep coming. Another reason why "why's" (and other questions) are so popular with these novice communicators is the enormous satisfaction they derive out of asking a question and receiving an answer. Even when they already know the answer.

But a thirst for knowledge and a craving for communication aren't the only motivations behind a toddler's "why's." It doesn't take long for a toddler to figure out that the question "Why?" (like the question "What's that?") doesn't only yield information—it gets attention, too. Which makes it worth repeating, and repeating, and repeating. And, like anything that gets repeated and repeated, asking "Why?" soon becomes a habit.

Though it may sometimes be tempting to try to fix a toddler's broken record by ignoring her "why's," it isn't a good idea. Not only because it might suppress her natural curiosity, dampen her appetite for learning, and stifle her desire to communicate, but because it will probably result in added frustration— something no toddler needs. As someone who has very little control over her environment, being unable to obtain answers to her questions will make her feel that she has even less power.

Instead, tap into your inner reserve of patience (you may be able to find them by closing your eyes and silently counting to ten), and keep your answers coming just as long as the questions do. Sometimes, answering your toddler's "why" with a "Why do *you* think . . .?" may help break the monotony and help her to think for herself. But if your question-for-a-question technique seems to irk your toddler (which, occasionally, it probably will), don't push for an answer—just give one yourself.

The meaningless "why" will disappear as your child's communication skills develop, though hopefully she will never stop asking the meaningful questions. In the meantime, try to keep in mind that while curiosity may erode parental patience, it's one of a child's most valuable learning tools.

# POTTY LEARNING REVERSALS

*"Help! Today is my daughter's second birthday and after months of dry training pants and using her potty chair, she suddenly refuses to use it anymore. She's had numerous 'accidents.'"*

There comes a time in the lives of most toddlers when control becomes a major parent–child issue. It comes earlier for some toddlers (soon after their first birthday), later for others (sometime around their second birthday), is short-lived for some, a long haul for others. But almost always, the issue of who's in control comes.

The struggle for control can manifest itself in a thousand different ways: Your daughter refuses to wear what you want her to wear, insisting on something totally different instead; she refuses to eat what's put in front of her, holding out for a completely different menu; she refuses to use the toilet, and has 'accidents' instead. It's a matter of her showing you who's boss.

Some parents try to keep toilet learning from becoming a control issue by waiting until their children are safely out of the contrary second year to begin it; while such a maneuver rarely makes the process effortless, it can make it proceed a bit more smoothly. But even then, resistance and relapses are distinct possibilities. No matter when it comes, however, potty opposition is best overcome with the following strategies:

**Check with the doctor.** Occasionally a toileting relapse has a medical cause, such as a urinary tract infection (see page 548 for other possibilities); be sure to have that ruled out before you go any further.

**Relieve any constipation.** Sometimes constipation snafus the toilet-learning process. Constipation in children, as in adults, can be tackled by stepping up fiber, fluid, and exercise, while easing up on psychological pressure. See page 598 for tips on combating constipation.

**Deal with any stress.** Sometimes, a toddler's regression in toilet learning is not a battle for control but a statement of unhappiness—prompted by anything from a too-cute new sibling to a too-tough new day-care situation. Reducing such unhappiness may get toilet learning back on track.

**Relieve the pressure.** Since your toddler may be reacting to pressure to perform, try relieving that pressure. For the time being, make toileting a nonissue in your home. Make the potty available, but don't make it mandatory. Stress-related toileting accidents are sometimes due to increased urinary frequency. Some children react to stress by feeling the need to urinate as often as three or four times an hour—and getting to the toilet that often can be difficult. This kind of stress-related frequency usually lasts just a few weeks to a few months—but do mention it to your child's doctor. Avoid tsk-tsking, head-shaking, and muttering when you have to change her; make it appear that it couldn't bother you less. As frustrated as you may be having to deal with this apparent regression, it's important that you try not to communicate your feelings, either verbally or nonverbally.

**Make changing her mind a snap.** Dress your toddler in easy-off clothing, so that if she decides to go to the potty herself, she can.

**Reduce the potential damage.** If your child has been having accidents in inconvenient places—in the car, at friends' houses, at preschool—switch to pull-up disposable training pants (see page 544) in such situations. (Cloth diapers, with Velcro closings, would make her more aware of wetting and more uncomfortable than she would be in disposables, but she's not likely to agree to wear them.)

**Try a change of place.** Sometimes a little variety can cajole a toddler out of the potty doldrums. If she's been using a self-contained potty chair, consider buying a potty seat that sits on top of the regular toilet, so your toddler can be more like the rest of the family. Take her with you when you make the purchase, and if there's a choice of styles or colors, let her make the selection. Some seats come with an attached ladder (when you're that little, it's a long way up); alternatively, you can provide her with a steady stepstool. If you started out with a seat on top of the toilet, try switching to the self-contained unit; again, take your toddler along to help shop for it, or borrow one from a friend or neighbor whose family has outgrown it.

**Put her in charge.** A struggle over your toddler's toileting behavior is one you can't win, so give in graciously. For how to put the responsibility in your child's hands, see page 549.

**Offer her more control in other areas.** Toddlers have a fundamental need to assert themselves; give them the opportunity to make their own choices in other areas (what they wear, who they play with, what they eat for lunch), and they may not feel as compelled to oppose you on toileting issues.

**Nix name calling.** Calling your toddler a baby for having accidents will make her more determined to act like one. Ignore this and any other "babyish" behavior, and look for grown-up behavior you can compliment ("You put those shoes on all by yourself? What a big girl you are!").

**Give it time.** Everyone uses a toilet sooner or later; as the old adage goes, "nobody walks down the aisle in diapers." While sooner may be convenient for parents tired of cleaning up accidents later (age three and beyond) is fine, too. There is no correlation between the age of toilet learning and intellectual ability or academic performance; tardy toileters are no less likely to be bright or capable than precocious ones. Your toddler has used the potty in the past, and she will use it again in the future—when *she's* ready. See Chapter Nineteen for more tips on toileting.

# *FEAR OF THE DOCTOR*[4]

"*The last couple of times we visited the pediatrician, we had to drag our son in. He seemed terrified.*"

I n infancy, when experiences generally came and went without leaving a lasting imprint, each trip to the doctor was a new event, no different from going to the supermarket. But, thanks to his newly improved memory, things have changed. Your toddler probably now recollects the probing, prodding, and poking—not to mention the occasional pricking—that went on during previous visits to the doctor, and the thought of enduring more of the same frightens him.

Being sympathetic and recognizing the reasonableness of his feelings are the first and most important steps to take to help him overcome his fear. The next steps:

**Read up.** The more your toddler knows about doctors and doctors' offices, the less trepidation he'll be likely to feel when faced with them. Take an easy-to-follow, clearly illustrated book out of the library that deals with a child's visit to the doctor and read it to your child, offering plenty of comforting commentary along the way. But try not to overexplain or get too complicated or technical. The most important points are that the doctor is a nice person (make sure that your child's doctor comes across that way) whose work is keeping children healthy and that the doctor's office is a safe place.

**Talk up.** Occasionally talk to your toddler about the doctor, about how nice he or she is, about the fun you have at the office, about how the doctor is a friend who helps keep children from getting sick and helps get them better when they do get sick.

**Let him play doctor.** Buy a toy doctor's kit for your toddler, and encourage him to practice playing doctor on you, on friends or older siblings, on his stuffed

---

4. The same tips apply if your child sees a pediatrician or family nurse-practitioner.

animals, on himself. Show him the various instruments and how they are used to examine the ears and throat, to listen for a heartbeat, to take a blood pressure reading. Knowing what to expect will help your child feel more in control of the exam and less like a helpless victim. Let him take the kit along to the doctor's office, if he'd like, and practice on you while he's waiting. When he's ushered into the examining room, ask if your toddler can turn the (examining) tables, and check the doctor's heart before the exam begins.

**Don't make any promises you can't keep . . .** Assuring your toddler that a doctor's exam won't hurt is likely to make him very suspicious. You don't after all, say it won't hurt when you go shopping for a new coat or visit a friend. Simply suggesting the possibility of pain to a highly suggestible toddler could make him more apt to expect and experience it. And, if the exam does hurt, even slightly, he won't accept your assurances next time around.

**. . . and don't make empty threats, either.** "You'd better take your medicine (or your vitamins, or put your hat on), or you'll get sick and I'll have to take you to the doctor for a shot," may be a perennial parental favorite, but its use makes a child equate doctor visits with punishment.

**Schedule for success.** If you can, avoid appointments that coincide with your child's usual nap times, mealtimes, or cranky times, or peak hours at the doctor's office (Saturday mornings or after school), when the staff is less likely to have the time or the patience to coax along reluctant patients.

**Give him something to look forward to.** Planning a treat for after the doctor's visit—a dish of frozen yogurt, or a trip to the playground, the children's museum, or a favorite friend's house—will give your toddler something pleasant to think about during the exam. Follow through with the plan no matter how your toddler handles the visit; withholding the treat because he didn't cooperate isn't fair and might further undermine his cooperation next time. Make a ritual out of the after-visit treat (going to the playground after every visit, for example) so that your toddler will have at least one pleasant association with the doctor.

**Concentrate on comfort.** Offering your toddler comfort when he needs it most can't be considered coddling. So do everything you can to make him feel comfortable. Bring along his favorite blanket to drape over the crackly paper on the examining table. Encourage him to take a favorite stuffed animal or other toy for support during the exam. (Perhaps, time permitting, the doctor will be willing to check the toy animal's ears, nose, eyes—or yours—along with your toddler's.) And if you think your toddler will do better on your lap, let him sit there—at least for as much of the exam as possible. If he cries, don't scold. Let him know it's okay to cry, but that he must sit still when the doctor asks him to, or the exam will take even longer.

**Check your own anxieties.** Fear and anxiety are more contagious than chickenpox. Observing that *you* have no fear of doctors' visits can help your toddler to overcome *his*, so try to appear relaxed and confident. When it's time to leave for the doctor's office, make the announcement a cheerful, "It's time to go visit Dr. Jones now," instead of an ominous, "You *have* to go to the doctor's now" or a resigned, "Guess we have to go to the doctor now." At the doctor's, show your courage. Volunteer to have your heartbeat listened to with the stethoscope first, or your ears checked with the otoscope. Don't cover your eyes (or your toddler's) when the hypodermic needle appears.

Don't let anxiety about your child's possible misbehavior make you ill at

## SHOTS THAT REALLY DON'T HURT?

**I**t looks that way. A new topical anesthetic called EMLA, developed in Sweden and now available to U.S. doctors, appears to be able to eliminate or greatly reduce pain of injections, including immunizations, most of the time. Ask your child's doctor about this "ouch-proof" cream when making an appointment for the next immunization. The cream must be applied at least one hour before the shot in order to be fully effective, so the doctor may want you to pick it up at the office and apply it at home before the visit. Note: Like any other medication, EMLA may trigger some side effects, including slight redness of skin, possible puffiness from water retention, alterations in temperature sensations on the skin, itching, and rash. It should not be used by anyone with a history of drug sensitivities, especially to lidocaine and/or prilocaine. Also keep in mind that the cream is expensive, and though it reduces pain, one study showed it didn't reduce the fears children have about getting shots. It's most valuable when children have to undergo repeated blood tests, shots, or IVs.

For the toddler who knows how to blow, blowing while getting a shot also reduces pain.

ease either. The doctor and the staff have seen it all—and then some—before.

If you're more anxious than most at doctor's visits because your toddler (or a sibling) has experienced serious health problems (low birth weight, chronic illness, surgery, and so on), you will have to try harder than most to mask your feelings.

**Prepare the doctor.** An empathic physician moves through the exam slowly, allowing the toddler to examine the instruments before they're used to examine him, and usually has a few other anxiety-relieving tricks up his or her white-coated sleeve (often including not wearing a white coat). But it can't hurt to call the doctor or nurse ahead of time to discuss your toddler's fears and what can be done to diminish them. In the unlikely event that the physician brushes off your concerns, or is not toddler-friendly during the exam, consider changing doctors.

**Do your waiting in the waiting room.** Many pediatric waiting rooms are play centers, filled with toys, books, and climbing equipment. A wary child may be less anxious if he can wait his turn there rather than in the confining and sterile examining room. So ask the receptionist if it's possible to hold off calling your toddler in until the last possible minute. If it's not, ask if there are toys in the exam room, too. If there aren't, bring along a few diversions from the waiting room or pull some out of your tote bag to keep your child occupied. If undressing is necessary, ask if it can be put off until right before the doctor's arrival; being unclothed can make a child feel more vulnerable.

**Don't hold the applause.** Offer praise when your toddler cooperates, even if it is minimal ("You hardly cried at all"), but don't criticize if he kicks and screams. And don't belittle his fears. Empathize instead ("I know you're not happy about this, but checkups are very important, and everybody has to have them"). Keep in mind that for some children, keeping cool at the doctor's office takes a monumental effort. After the appointment, tell him how well he did, giving specific examples of points at which he really *did* do well; it'll help give him the confidence to do even better next time.

# FEAR OF THE DENTIST

*"I've always dreaded visits to the dentist. Now our daughter has to see the dentist and I'm afraid she's going to respond in the same way."*

Most adults would prefer an encounter with the IRS to one with a DDS. But a young child who's never come face-to-face with a drill has no such negative feelings about dental care. To her, a trip to the dentist's office can just as easily represent a fun adventure as a scary ordeal. Her attitude toward dentists and dentistry is still to be formed and will ultimately depend on parental attitude, prior preparation, and the tone set by the dentist.

Probably the most important factor is the dentist. Look for one who specializes in children's dentistry (a pediatric dentist) or in family care, and whose subspecialties are patience and good humor (get the candidate to chat with your child, if you're uncertain). Look, too, for a friendly office staff and an office furnished and decorated with young patients in mind.

The second most important factor is you. The best predictor of a child who's afraid of the dentist is a parent who's afraid of the dentist. So try to keep your own fear under wraps in front of your toddler.

Prepare your toddler for the visit as you would for a visit to the doctor: Read books about dentists; let her play dentist on you, on dolls, stuffed animals, or other toys; avoid the subject of pain. Ask the office assistant exactly what can be expected at the visit so you can rehearse it in advance with your toddler. You can play the dentist—then reverse roles. Find out what incentives are offered after a visit (toys, stickers, toothbrushes) so you can tell her in advance what's in it for her.

If it's possible, speak to the dentist about your concerns when you make the appointment. Explain that you would like the first visit to be just a get-acquainted session, with some friendly conversation, an introduction to the dentist's office, and a quick exam. Any needed work should wait until another visit. Also discuss whether the dentist prefers you to stay in the room during the exam. Some find they get better results when parents wait in the waiting room (just as teachers usually get better results when parents leave the classroom). Others ask parents to stay.

And remember that although the combination of preplanning, a sensitive dentist, and relaxed parents can do a lot to reduce a toddler's fears, it may not be possible to prevent a scene at the dentist's office. If your toddler does panic, accept her fears, and help her cope with them as well as she can.

# FEAR OF THE BARBER

*"I tried to take my son to the barber for his first haircut, but he wouldn't sit still and seemed really frightened when the barber approached with the scissors. I had to take him home with his hair still uncut."*

If you think about it, a fear of barbers is really quite reasonable. With a perfect stranger aiming straight for his head with a pair of scissors (an implement you've probably warned him is dangerous), is it really any wonder your toddler is squirming, ducking, and generally terrified?

That in perspective, once in a while it is still necessary to get a toddler's hair cut. These tips may help keep the shearing from becoming sheer torture:

## TELL IT LIKE IT IS

· · · · · · · · · ·

Being up front builds trust. Don't spring any surprises, whether it's a visit to the dentist for a checkup, to the doctor for a shot, or the barber for a trim. Be honest about it with your toddler. Don't leave the house as though you're on your way to the playground, then detour to the dentist. Don't tell your child there won't be a shot at the doctor's when you know that there will be. Don't promise that a procedure won't hurt or that it will be over quickly unless you're absolutely certain that's true. Prepare your child for each experience as completely as possible—without risking increasing his or her fears by giving too much information or needless details.

▲ Explain that hair grows back. Some toddlers view hair cutting as they would view cutting any part of the body. Helping such a toddler to understand that it doesn't hurt when hair is cut and that it grows back afterwards may help him to overcome that concern. Snip off a little piece of your own hair, and then encourage him to touch it, bend it, crumple it up ("See, hair doesn't hurt"). Show him pictures of himself as a baby and now as a little boy to illustrate how hair grows ("Your hair was that short when you were a little baby. Then it grew this much . . . and after it's cut, it will grow again").

▲ Open a barber shop for teddy bears. Improvise a play barber kit with a pair of child-safe scissors (he will probably lack the coordination to actually "cut" with the scissors, but may have fun trying), a comb, a brush, and a towel. Set up shop in front of a full-length mirror, and let him "style" his stuffed clients. Do explain that a teddy's hair, unlike his hair, won't grow back after it's cut.

▲ Choose a barber shop that aims to please kids. Such shops tend to be more patient with reluctant customers than those that serve only the occasional child. Some go so far as to provide bright smocks, videos, fun-shaped chairs or boosters, and toys to distract children while waiting.

▲ Watch a barber in action. Visit a barber shop and let your toddler watch (from the safety of your lap) as other children have their hair cut. After seeing them come and go in one piece, hopefully, he'll be convinced that he's not at risk. Even better, have a trim yourself, while your child watches. Take this opportunity to introduce your toddler to the stylist, so he or she won't be a total stranger.

▲ As always, schedule smart. Don't make a haircut appointment at times when your toddler is chronically cranky or tired, when he's likely to be hungry, or when the shop is busy and personnel are both hurried and harried.

▲ Skip the suds. Having to lean back for a salon shampoo can be especially uncomfortable and frightening for a small child (at-home shampoos are trouble enough). A few spritzes of water can dampen hair enough so the stylist can cut right to the cut, without the added trauma of shampooing.

▲ Be your toddler's booster chair. It can be lonely and scary in that big, high seat. Sitting on a parent's lap during the cut may not be easy or comfortable for you or for the stylist (find out in advance if the stylist will okay this strategy), but it may make this first experience more comfortable for your toddler. Hold him on your lap facing the mirror while the front's being cut, then turn him around so he's facing you for the back trim. (Be sure to ask for a smock to cover *your* clothing.)

▲ Plan a reward. Remember, the haircut is your idea, not your toddler's. To sweeten it for him, tie the haircut in with a visit to a favorite park, museum, or a favorite friend or relative, or with something else he considers special ("Today we're going to the Children's Museum, but first we have to stop and get your hair cut"). This will transfer the attention away from the anxiety of a haircut to the anticipation of fun. If your toddler hesitates at the barber shop, remind him: "Let's hurry so we can get to the museum before it closes."

▲ Greet little efforts with big praise. Applaud your toddler's smallest attempts at cooperation. Heap on the praise and spare him the criticism, even if most of the haircut is spent in struggle.

▲ Take up hairstyling yourself. If your toddler resolutely refuses to sit still for a salon cut, try one at home. Check out a book from the library on cutting children's hair, use barber's shears (not regular scissors) and, to minimize the risk of going too far, take off only a little at a time.

# FEAR OF FALLING ASLEEP

*"Our daughter used to fall asleep the moment her head hit the crib mattress. Now she cries, calls out, asks for water, and does everything she can to avoid closing her eyes. It's as if she's afraid of sleep."*

To a toddler, falling asleep doesn't just mean drifting off to dreamland. It means leaving the security and companionship of parents, toys, pets, and activity for darkness, quiet, and solitude. Going to bed is a form of separation—

and for many toddlers, separation is still unsettling. The best way to deal with a fear of falling asleep is to help reassure your child that there's nothing to fear. Make her bedtime ritual cozy, comforting, and secure (see page 68). Let her take her comfort object to bed with her; if she doesn't have one, offer her something of yours (an old T-shirt or nightgown) or get her a special stuffed animal to keep her company. See that she has everything she needs, and then leave her with a reassuring, "See you in the morning," that reminds her that the separation is only temporary. Don't respond right away if she keeps calling you back (for a drink, another kiss, or whatever).

If she cries when you leave, don't go back into her room immediately. Give her fifteen or twenty minutes to comfort herself to sleep. If she's still crying after the alloted time, go in to her, reassure her with a kiss and a pat and a promise that you will see her in the morning, but don't pick her up or sit by her bed. When you leave the room again, don't feel guilty. Tell yourself that it's *your* job to put her to bed and *her* job to get herself to sleep.

Some toddlers, however, develop an extreme panic reaction to being left to cry it out, even for brief periods. If this is the case with your child, see page 54.

# NIGHT WAKING NOW

*"Our toddler had been sleeping through the night for nearly a year when suddenly he started waking up and crying periodically. What's going on?"*

Night waking after months or more of sleeping through could have any number of causes: the eruption of molars (see page 168); nightmares (page 312) or night terrors (page 313); fear of the dark (page 431) or of falling asleep

---

## NIGHTTIME PROTECTION

··········

Fearful toddlers need all the protection they can get when they turn in for the night. This protection can come in the form of a courageous teddy bear, doll, or other favorite figure standing guard over the crib or bed; a flashlight that can be switched on when shadows look menacing; a lucky charm, a "magic" wand or a "monster spray" (an unbreakable spray bottle of water) to banish anything scary; a giant eraser to erase bad dreams or scary visions; something from a parent (a photo, a quilt, a nightshirt) to serve as a stand-in. Some children also enjoy using a "magical" chant ("Monsters, monsters go away; don't come back another day") to scare the demons.

---

(page 310); anxiety brought on by stress in the family; a change in schedule due to travel or other causes; breathing lapses, known as obstructive sleep apnea, usually caused by enlarged adenoids or tonsils (page 169); illness, particularly ear infections (page 605); and rarely, pinworms, which cause itching of the skin around the anus, particularly at night (page 856). To try to discover just which of these factors may be involved in your toddler's waking, see the individual topics. Once you know the cause, deal with it immediately to restore your child's normal sleeping pattern—and yours.

## STRESS-RELATED WAKING

·····································

*"Our daughter always had pretty good sleep habits. But I had to be away from her for a couple of weeks when my mother was critically ill. Ever since then she's had trouble sleeping at night."*

Having one or both parents disappear from her life at this age— even temporarily—is understandably difficult for a toddler to deal with. Nevertheless, such separations are sometimes necessary. And once the traveler returns home, the fallout may be equally difficult to deal with.

Stress-related waking may be a response to a new baby-sitter, a new house, a new school, or a new sibling, as well as an absent parent. To sleep better during the night, the toddler under stress needs extra love and attention during the day, but not to the point of overindulgence. This could lead her to suspect that the treats and presents are hers because you feel bad, or wrong, for going away, which in turn could lead her to think you are securely under her thumb. But do arrange to spend as much fun time with her as possible until she's feeling more secure. Plan some special outings that you know she will enjoy. But most importantly, hug her a lot, and remind her often of your love.

Changes in your toddler's schedule while you were away may also leave her feeling unsettled, and thus, restless at night. Restoring her familiar routine as quickly as possible will help reassure her that everything has returned to normal with your return.

She may especially need reassurance at bedtime. When you tuck her in, relieve any fears that you'll be leaving again any time soon by telling her that you'll see her in the morning (especially if you went off last time after she was in bed). If she seems extremely panicky about you leaving the room and wants you to stay with her until she falls asleep, sit by

*A teddy-bear sentry standing guard in the crib can bring comfort to a fearful toddler.*

her crib or bed (but don't get in with her or take her into your bed) until you can safely slip away. After a few nights, she should feel more secure and you should be able to leave her while she's still awake—your ultimate goal.

If she awakens in the middle of the night, go to her, and reassure her, but don't stay for more than a few minutes. If she cries when you leave, don't return for ten or fifteen minutes—by which point she will probably have fallen asleep. If not, keep returning to reassure her, at ever-longer intervals, until she has.

## NIGHTMARES

*"Lately, our daughter has been waking up in the middle of the night weepy and shaken, as if she's had a nightmare. Is this possible in someone so young?"*

With the possible exception of horror film writers, who may use them as grist for their next grisly production, nobody enjoys a nightmare. As adults, at least, we have the advantage of being able to awaken realizing that it was "only a dream." Young children, with their relatively limited experience, aren't as good at distinguishing between a dream and reality, and don't have this advantage. When a toddler wakes in the middle of the night, the wild animals, ghosts, monsters, or other frightening creatures that may have been besetting her in her dreams are still real and threatening.

Several factors can bring on bad dreams: *stress* (due, for example, to family discord or tension); *change* (nightmares are more common when there is a new baby-sitter, a move, a new school or day-care situation, a new bed or room); *pre-bedtime excesses* (of excitement, activity, or food); *illness* (a fever or certain medications[5] can provoke a frightening dream). But the most common cause of nightmares in young children is an improved memory and a growing imagination unchecked by reason. And as a toddler's imagination becomes more complex, so do her nightmares. The simple, unsettling images of her less-mature

---

5. If your child's nightmares begin when she begins taking a new medication, check with her doctor.

nightmares become more clearly focused, and thus, more frightening. For help on how to identify a nightmare and differentiate it from a night terror, see page 314.

To help reduce the risk of nightmares and ease them when they strike, try the following:

▲ Keep the time before bedtime tranquil. Avoid roughhousing, scary television or videos, scary storybooks. Don't pretend to be a "big bad wolf" when you come to take her to bed, don't play the "tickle monster" when you're tucking her in.

▲ After your toddler awakes, ask her to talk about her bad dream. She may feel better after she's shared it with you. Help her express herself if her vocabulary is limited.

▲ Tell her she's safe. When a toddler awakes from a nightmare, she feels vulnerable and afraid. More than anything else, she needs reassurance that she isn't in danger. Offer your toddler as much comfort as she needs; tell her that she's safe, that you love her, and that her dream wasn't real—it was make-believe, like a story in a book. Explain that everyone has bad dreams sometimes, even grown-ups. Your reassurance will be more credible if you stay calm yourself and don't overreact.

▲ Show her she's safe. Turn on the light to show her that her room at night is just as cozy and secure as it is during the day; if she'd prefer to keep the light on for the rest of the night, let her. Or plug in a night-light. If she's afraid of what might be lurking behind closet doors and under her bed, do a thorough "monster check." If wall hangings, lamps, draped clothing, or other objects in the room take on a sinister shape in the shadows, rearrange or remove them. Taking her fears seriously, while helping her see that there's nothing to be afraid of, should give her the confidence she needs to go back to sleep. If she has trouble going back to sleep, offer her a sip of water, and tell her you will sit with her for a little while.

▲ Make sure she feels safe when you leave her. Your toddler feels very small compared to the nocturnal nasties that frighten her, and needs all the reassurance she can get.

▲ In the morning, reinforce the feeling that she's safe. Nightmares are often more memorable than other kinds of dreams, and even if a toddler doesn't remember all the details, she may wake up next morning with a nagging feeling of anxiety. Let her talk about her bad dream, if she wants to, give her a little extra attention, and be especially sensitive to undercurrents of anxiety. Praise her, too, for having had the courage to fall back to sleep.

▲ If you know of a stressful situation in your child's life that may be contributing to the nightmares, try to do something about it.

# NIGHT TERRORS

*"The other night, our son started crying and screaming in his sleep. He was thrashing around with his eyes open and bulging; his face was contorted and sweaty. We were terrified. But before we could wake him, he was sleeping calmly again. Was this a nightmare?"*

It sounds much more like a night terror (see page 314) than a nightmare. Though frightening to witness, night terrors aren't cause for parental concern or action.

In fact, other than making certain that the house is safe for your toddler should he sleepwalk (see page 315) during a night terror and sitting by to see

## NIGHTMARES VS. NIGHT TERRORS

· · · · · · · · · ·

Your toddler wakes up screaming in the middle of the night. Was it a bad dream or a night terror? It's easy to tell if you know the difference.

**Frequency.** Bad dreams, or nightmares, occur more frequently than night terrors. Still, most children experience at least one episode of night terrors during the toddler or preschool years. When children have frequent night terrors, there's usually a family history of such episodes. Some children appear to have night terrors as early as six months old (usually characterized by extreme restlessness and thrashing during sleep).

**Timing.** Night terrors usually occur in the early hours of sleep, most often between one and four hours after a child goes to bed. Nightmares strike later, during the second half of the night's sleep.

**Stage of sleep.** Nightmares occur during REM (rapid-eye-movement), or dream, sleep, which is the light sleep phase. Though the child sleeps through the dream, he or she awakens after it, usually terrified. Night terrors are a partial arousal from a very deep (non-REM) sleep. Children ex-periencing them usually do not awaken fully, unless they are roused.

**Manifestations.** During a night terror, a child usually perspires profusely, has a very rapid heart beat, and appears frightened and confused. The child may call out for you, yet push you away. He or she may scream, cry, moan, talk, or even seem to hal-lucinate; sit, stand, walk, or thrash around. The eyes may be open, or staring, even bulging, but the child is still asleep. A child having a nightmare, on the other hand, may seem a little restless while dreaming, but it's not until he or she is fully awake that the panic, with plenty of crying and scream-ing, begins. When a parent comes to the res-cue, the child is likely to cling desperately. A verbal child may try to describe a night-mare but will not recall a night terror.

**Duration.** Night terrors can last from ten to thirty minutes, after which the child usually continues to sleep. A nightmare is usually brief, and is followed by wak-ing. The duration of the period of panic following it varies from child to child and episode to episode.

that he doesn't hurt himself while thrashing around, there's little you can do when an episode of night terror strikes. If one strikes again (and it won't necessarily), don't hug your child or hold him down; doing so will only make him more agitated—and he may even push you away. Don't try to wake him up, either, no matter how frantic he seems, as this will only prolong the event. Instead, just watch and wait. Night terrors generally end ten to thirty minutes after they begin, at which time your toddler should calm down (without waking) and you'll be able to tuck him back into bed for a peaceful rest-of-the-night sleep. Blessed-ly, once a night terror is over, it's over. When he gets up the next morning, your toddler will likely have no recollection of the event, though he may seem a bit anxious.

Since night terrors occur more often when a child is overtired, be sure your child's schedule is not too hectic and that he's getting enough sleep. Most children outgrow night terrors by the time they are ready to start grade school, around age six. If yours doesn't, or if he has more than three episodes a year, check with his doctor. There is a very slim possibility that the problem is a nocturnal seizure disorder, which can be controlled with medication if neces-sary. The signs include peculiar, repeti-tive, sometimes violent movements, shaking legs, and flapping arms.

# SLEEPWALKING

*"We sometimes wake up to find our daughter wandering around the house sound asleep. Is sleepwalking considered a problem? Should we get her to stop?"*

Though sleepwalking can be spooky for those awake and watching, it's fairly common and completely normal. The only risk to the sleepwalker is that she'll walk into danger—a flight of stairs, a sharp table corner, a telephone cord, electric wires, or toys left on the floor. For this reason, a sturdy gate at your toddler's doorway is a good idea; if she's able to scale the gate, consider safeguarding with a tower of two gates, one above the other. If you'd rather not put a gate in her doorway, or she becomes very upset if she's confined when sleepwalking, take other safety precautions throughout the house. Lock or latch bathroom doors, block off the kitchen, gate any stairs securely, clear of trippables any pathways that the sleepwalker might travel. If your child does sleepwalk, make a habit of screening your home for potential hazards each night before you climb into bed.

A sleepwalking toddler tends to head either toward a light or her parents' room —so putting a night-light in her room may help to keep her there. If she comes into your room or you happen upon her elsewhere in the house, guide her gently back to bed without waking her.

Besides keeping your sleepwalker safe, there isn't much you can, or need to do about her sleepwalking, which usually stops on its own. Though it's often disruptive to the parents' sleep, it isn't necessarily disruptive to the sleepwalker's. As with the child experiencing night terrors, a low-key bedtime environment and adequate rest may help.

# COLOR-BLINDNESS

*"Our son can't tell the difference between colors. Could he be color-blind?"*

It's too soon to know. It's more likely that he hasn't learned his colors than that he's color-blind. Most children can't identify colors until the age of three or four. Those who can, usually do so because a parent or caregiver has put a lot of time and effort into their color education.

If you'd like to invest that time and effort, there's no harm in trying to teach colors now. But there's also no guarantee that your toddler will catch on right away. Start by pointing out reds, blues, greens, and yellows in clothing, cars, crayons, toys, and other familiar objects. Tackle the subtler shades—pink, brown, and purple, for example—after he's mastered the basic hues, which may not be for another year or two.

When your toddler first begins using color names, he'll probably use them generically—all objects will be red, or blue, or green. That's not an indication of color-blindness, either, just of his inexperience. If he is still confusing colors by the time he turns four, he can be tested to see if he's among the 7% of boys who are color-blind.

Color-blindness, which is usually passed on from mother to son (a girl can be a carrier if she has a color-blind father, but women are rarely color-blind), is due to the partial or complete absence of one of the light-sensitive substances in the cells of the retina. This deficiency limits the ability to distinguish between greens and reds, and occasionally blues. There are different degrees of color-blindness. Some color-blind individuals can see colors normally in good light but have difficulty distinguishing them in dim light. Others can't differentiate certain colors in any light. In the most severe (and least common) form of color-blindness, everything is seen in shades of gray.

Color-blindness does not affect the sharpness of vision, or acuity, at all. Nor does it correlate with low intelligence or future learning disabilities. There is no cure for color-blindness, but beyond being unable to play preschool games that are based on color identification, a color-blind child isn't at any particular disadvantage. Although colored filters on eyeglasses or contact lenses can enhance the ability of color-blind older children and adults to see contrasts, they don't help them to differentiate between colors.

# REVERSE PSYCHOLOGY

*"My typical two-year-old is very defiant and stubborn. Lately, I've tried a little reverse psychology ('Don't you eat that carrot' or 'Don't you dare get into that bathtub'), and it worked like a charm. But is it okay to use?"*

Since there's no cure for toddler negativity but the passage of time, you're wise to look instead for a successful treatment—and it sounds as though you've hit on a winner. Even though they may be wise to their parents' motivations, small children often respond to reverse psychology, simply because they enjoy "playing the game." Using reverse psychology allows both of you to have it your way—he has the satisfaction of doing something that you specifically told him not to do, and you have the satisfaction of seeing him do what you really want. In other words, it's a win–win game. For similar techniques to alternate with reverse psychology—if only to keep predictability or boredom from compromising results—see A Spoonful of Sugar (page 156).

Some caveats should be kept in mind when using reverse psychology, however. For one, don't use it when you aren't certain your child knows what you *really* want—though he knows you want him to eat the carrot or get into the tub, he may not know your true wishes in a new situation and could become confused. For another, be sure it's clear that the game is meant in fun; you don't want your child to develop the notion that it's really okay to do the opposite of what you say. And as with any kind of good-natured teasing, if your child seems disturbed or bewildered by reverse psychology, drop it pronto.

Of course, don't use reverse psychology or similar games with *any* child when health and safety are at risk: getting into the car seat, staying out of the street, keeping dangerous objects out of a toddler's mouth, for example. You don't want to find yourself saying, even in jest, "Do run out in the street" or "Put that knife in your mouth right now."

# GIFTEDNESS

*"My daughter not only started speaking very early, but she recognizes letters and can count. Is she gifted—and if so, what should I do about it?"*

Every child is gifted in some way. Sometimes parents need only look a little more closely to find just where their child's special talents lie. Some have a way with words, others with numbers; still others may be blessed with a prodigious memory. Some are gifted in logic and analytical skills, others in abstract thinking. Some are whizzes at spatial relations and mechanical skills, others have an inborn talent for music or art. There are children who excel in athletics or dance, those who are skilled socially, and those who have an unusual ability to understand the human psyche. There are children who have the kind of smile that lights up a room, those with an aptitude for kindness and caring, and those with a flair for persuading both adults and children to follow their lead. Some exhibit their gifts very early in life, others somewhat later, and many are gifted in ways that traditional evaluation will never demonstrate.

A child who's bright, curious, and quick to learn could very well be gifted intellectually. The question is, is it important to know whether she is at this stage of her young life? Is there a benefit to applying the label "gifted" to a toddler? Probably not.

That's not to suggest you should ignore your child's obvious talents. Instead, you should do what every parent should do: provide stimulation, challenge, encouragement, and attention, as well as ample love and security. That's the best route to helping your child fulfill her potential.

Encourage your child's gifts, but also give her support in areas where she doesn't excel. Your child is good with words and numbers? By all means stimulate her in these areas—read to her frequently, routinely point out to her familiar and unfamiliar letters and words ("Look, the light says 'WALK.' Now we can cross the street."), play number games ("How many slices of banana are left on your plate?"). But also applaud when she reaches a higher rung on the jungle gym than on her last try or sweetly shares her sandwich with a friend.

If you suspect your toddler is gifted, don't rush off to the psychologist for verification. Testing at this age is generally not recommended because results may not be accurate, because testing evaluates only a limited number of skills, and ultimately because there's not much you can do with the results at this point. A high score on an IQ test may, in fact, have a negative effect on your child and on your relationship. Parents who've been told their child is intellectually gifted tend to develop overly high expectations and may push too hard. Frequently, that kind of pushing can lead to tension, unhappiness, uneven development (the child, for example, may have superb reading skills but be slow socially), and early burnout. Attempting to turn a happy toddler into a child prodigy could rob her of the kind of normal childhood every child needs. So avoid trying to create a superchild (see page 454), and enjoy your child's unfolding development with pleasure.

# THE "CARRY ME" SYNDROME

*"For a while, my toddler wanted to walk everywhere. Now, he wants to be carried. Not only is he breaking my back, but I'm concerned that he's getting too dependent."*

Walking was a novelty for your toddler when he first put one foot in front of another. Being independently mobile after so many months of dependency on strollers, baby carriers, and adult arms was exhilarating and compelling; every step he took deepened his tender feelings of pride and accomplishment.

Then the novelty wore off. Walking started to be a responsibility—something that was expected, and often required, of him. True to his two-year-old negativity, he began to respond to parental pressure to perform with refusals and rubber legs. "If *they* want me to walk," he may reason, "that's probably a good enough reason *not* to."

For many toddlers, ambivalence about self-reliance and separation from their parents also prompts them to reject the independence of walking in favor of clinging—both figuratively and literally. To help get your toddler back on his feet again:

**Make walking recreational.** Even if you're out to do some errands, getting there can be more than half the fun. Play games ("Let's see if we can step over all the cracks" or "How many dogs can we see?"), sing songs, point out interesting sights along the way, generally divert him from the task of walking itself. And don't discourage him from stopping to investigate intriguing things that he finds in his path; leave extra time when planning outings so he can explore.

**Appoint him your assistant.** Toddlers love to be "helpers." When you're walking to the market, let yours carry the shopping list (but have an extra in your pocket should he lose his). Coming home from the market, give him a small bag of light (and unbreakable) purchases to carry. Play up his part—tell him you couldn't make it home without his help. Or make him feel "big" beyond his years by letting him wear a backpack or by putting him in charge of holding his "baby"—a favorite doll or stuffed alligator or puppet.

**Get down to his level.** Sometimes part of a toddler's frustration with walking is being so small when everyone else around him is big. Your stooping down to his level now and then will help ease this feeling of being head and shoulders beneath the crowd. So stop periodically—at the traffic light, in front of the store, in the middle of the block—to talk to your toddler eye to eye, or to give him a hug or a tickle. These unexpected, impromptu gestures may also diffuse the pent-up tension that can lead to a whining refrain of "Carry me!"

**Try not to rush or push him.** When your legs are as short as your toddler's, it takes at least twice as many strides to walk a block—which means it can take twice as long, too. It also means that your toddler is going to tire out long before you do. So keep your expectations

reasonable and treks on foot brief. Be ready with a back-up plan: a stroller, a bus, or a shortened trip. And hold the mumbling and grumbling if he doesn't end up walking.

Don't forget that, in this case, your toddler holds the upper hand. You can't, after all, force him to walk. Try it and you will get a lesson in passive resistance. If your toddler goes limp or tries a sit-down-in-the-middle-of-the-sidewalk strike, you can pick him up and carry him or force him into the stroller (which is what he wants anyway), but you can't make him move one foot in front of the other.

**Praise his efforts on two feet.** Use positive reinforcement. After a walk, even a very brief one, congratulate him. Tell him how grown-up he's getting, point out that walking is one of the many fun things he can do now that babes in arms (or strollers) simply can't.

**Don't criticize his failures.** Don't call him a baby, even if he does end up in your arms or in the stroller. And don't fuel any possible existing jealousy by telling him you can't carry him because you're pregnant or because you have to carry an infant sibling.

**Make a deal.** If you're only a few blocks from home, your toddler has had it with the walking, and there's no bus in sight, try cutting a deal: "You walk this block, I'll carry you the next." Alternate until you are home free.

**Set an active example.** If everyone else in the family walks a lot, eventually your child will too—especially if you don't make an issue out of his reluctance now.

# MOVING TO A BED

*"We want to move our daughter to a bed. What's the best way?"*

Odds are that the move to a grown-up bed will thrill your toddler, but there may still be a wee part of her that yearns to hang on to one of her last remaining links to babyhood. So don't just scrap the crib and spring the new bed on her without warning. Instead, carefully lay the groundwork for the transition. Be sure the time is right. If your toddler's life is particularly unsettled—a new sibling has just arrived or is about to, she's just starting day care or preschool, she's in the midst of toilet learning or weaning, or just getting over an illness—it might be wise to postpone the transition to a bed until things are more stable. Look for a book that illustrates a young child's journey from crib to bed, and read it to her several times, stopping frequently during the narrative to personalize it ("See, that boy is getting a new bed just like you will" and "That girl's bed is big, just like your new bed will be," and so on).

Once your toddler adjusts to the idea of switching to a bed, you can start turning the idea into reality. Unless you've opted to accept a hand-me-down, it's a good idea to involve your "big girl" in selecting her "big girl bed." But don't take her along while you do the preliminary scouting; dragging from store to store in search of the right bed will not put your toddler in the right mood. Look for models that are built relatively close to the ground, that will easily accept guard rails,[6] and that come with a firm mattress. When you've narrowed down the candidates to two or three (preferably in the same store), take your toddler along to make the final choice from your picks. Let her get friendly with the bed on the showroom floor (touch it, sit on it,

lie down), so it won't be totally foreign when it's set up at home.

Whether your toddler's big bed is fresh from the showroom or passed on from a friend or sibling, include her in selecting new sheets, a new quilt (unless she's very attached to her old one), and even a new stuffed animal companion to share her new digs with (along with her familiar "old friends," of course). Remember to pick up a rubber sheet or waterproof pad, too, so that the new mattress won't quickly become old.

When it arrives, let your toddler make her bed before lying in it. She can help with putting on the new bedding, then add any number of personal touches (stuffed animals, books, toys that are safe to sleep with, or whatever) to cozy up the place. Make it clear that she can now include bedtime companions that were not able to fit in her crib. Once the bed is set up and made, take your cues from your toddler. If she seems excited about the new bed and doesn't even give her old crib a backward glance, remove the crib from her room and mark another milestone in your child's growing up.

If, on the other hand, she seems hesitant about the move—and assuming there's space for both the bed and the crib in her room—give her the extra time she needs to ease this transition. Let her get to know the bed for a few days (to play in it, cuddle in it, put her teddies to bed in it, have story time in it) before urging her to sleep in it.

Some toddlers like to begin with short sleeps in the big bed before they commit to it full time—napping in it during the day, and retreating to the security of their trusty crib at night. If your toddler feels more comfortable with this kind of arrangement for a few weeks or even longer, there's no harm in it—assuming you've made her crib as safe as possible (see page 625). When it does come time to bid a final farewell to the crib, give it the royal sendoff it deserves. Tell your toddler, "Now that you're so

---

6. A restless sleeper can easily push the bed away from the wall and then slip between the wall and the bed; she could even become wedged between them. So be sure guard rails are installed on both sides of the bed, even if one side is up against the wall. Do not choose a bunk bed; these are not safe for toddlers.

big and you sleep in a big bed, we can put the crib away." Have your toddler say, "Bye-bye" and let her kiss the crib if she wants to. Then store it or give it away.

Of course, once your child is in a bed, a new problem arises: How do you keep her in the bed and out of trouble? Though you may not be able to manage the first (short of enclosing the bed in a stockade fence), you should be able to accomplish the second. For tips on how to keep your toddler out of trouble when she wanders, see page 167.

While your toddler adjusts to sleeping in the wide-open space of a bed, there's always the possibility, unless the guard rails run the bed's full length, of her tumbling out. So for the first weeks, cushion the exit route at night—use a plush area rug, a large mat, a futon, a sleeping bag, an old mattress, a thick comforter, a row of pillows, or even an old down coat. But don't worry if she does fall on the bare floor—an injury in such a fall is very unlikely.

Many toddlers don't handle change easily, and moving from a crib to a bed (even if your child seems happy about the move) can result in some new bedtime problems. Your toddler may try to postpone bedtime *ad infinitum* with requests for drinks, extra hugs, yet another blanket, yet another tucking-in. Respond calmly but firmly to these attempts to put off the inevitable; letting your toddler run the bedtime show even a few times can result in weeks of evening chaos. Stick to her bedtime routine, while providing plenty of attention and reassurance during the daylight hours, and everyone in the family will eventually sleep the better for it.

## UNKIND BEHAVIOR

*"Our two-year-old seems unkind to the other little boys in his play group, and that upsets me."*

**D**on't worry. If your two-year-old hasn't yet developed a taste for the milk of human kindness, he's just acting his age. It's not that his heart's not in the right place, it's just that it's still devoted to more self-centered pursuits. He's not yet capable of loving his neighbor—or his playmate, or another kid in the sandbox—as he loves himself. His needs are paramount; the needs of others are not, for now, his concern. And since he hasn't even begun to do for himself yet (most of his needs are filled by obliging adults), he's not likely to begin doing for others. Especially if those others are other toddlers, who he's noticed also have adults around to tend to their needs.

Toddlers who regularly spend time with other toddlers (as in a day-care situation) or with older siblings tend to show empathy and sympathy (as well as other more mature social traits) earlier, since the group experience gives them more of a "we're-all-in-the-same-boat-together" perspective than does being the center of attention at home.

The teaching of kindness towards others, like the teaching of any value, is a gradual process, not something you impart in an afternoon. And a toddler learns kindness best by the example you set; be kind to others, and eventually he'll respond in kind—at least once he grows out of this normally egocentric age. You can speed the process a bit, and help your child to become kinder and gentler, by following the tips on page 42.

## YOUR BOREDOM WITH TODDLER GAMES

*"My daughter always wants me to join in her play, but I can't sit still two minutes for it—I get too bored. I feel guilty, but I can't help it."*

No guilt necessary. Many adults find a two-year-old's favorite activities tedious—and that's not surprising. After all, they aren't two anymore.

But laying off the guilt doesn't mean you can let yourself off the hook—at least not entirely. Sharing in your child's play says that she's important to you and that you enjoy her company. Here are a few tips on sending that message without driving yourself to distraction:

▲ Give child's play a chance. When it's been decades since you've been a toddler, it's naturally difficult to summon up what it feels like to be a two-year-old at play. Difficult, but not impossible. Join your toddler with your mind already closed to having a good time, and you most assuredly won't have one. Make a conscious effort to shake your staid adult ways and allow yourself to wander into the world of childhood innocence and imagination, and you may actually find yourself enjoying your toddler's games. Of course, you can't expect to get lost in second toddlerhood if you've got half an eye on a movie or are up to the elbows in dishwater. So when you do play with your toddler, give her your complete attention. Hold the phone calls, the trips to the laundry room, the news.

▲ Learn how to play her way. Just because you've been invited to join her game doesn't mean you get to make up the rules. Toddlers and small children have very definite ideas about how they'd like their play to progress (or not progress), so it's important not to interfere. If a game gets unbearably boring or too repetitive, casually suggest a new game plan—but if your toddler resists your suggestions, don't force them on her.

▲ Know your limits, and let her know them, too. Short periods of your wholehearted participation are more rewarding to your toddler than long periods of your grudging attention. If you start squirming and yawning after fifteen minutes of "teddy-bear hospital" or "mommy cat–baby cat," call it quits before resentment kicks in. But give her fair warning—tell her, "We'll take care of just two more sick teddies and then we're going to read a story," or "The mommy cat and the baby cat can have just one more snuggle, and then the mommy cat will have to start dinner."

▲ Pick and choose your games. Some parents get antsy playing make-believe, but love to do science experiments. Some love to read but have little patience for racing cars. Some enjoy doing puzzles but are bored silly by block-building. When your toddler wants to play but hasn't got a game in mind herself, suggest the kinds of things you enjoy doing. Your toddler will probably be happy to go along most of the time.

▲ Try some parallel play. Sometimes a parent's physical presence is enough to satisfy a toddler hungry for a partner in play. So when you can't play with your toddler, "play" alongside her. Tell her that you're going to play your game (balancing the checkbook, answering some letters) next to her on the floor while she plays hers. That way, you'll be there when she needs someone to taste her "soup" or admire her "baby," but you won't have to be a full-time player in her make-believe productions.

▲ Turn the tables. Once in a while, invite your toddler to play with you. Give her a pair of work gloves, a plastic trowel, and a pile of dirt to weed and cultivate while you do some serious gardening alongside her; a pile of fabric scraps to sort through while you do some sewing; a stack of old magazines to flip through while you read the newspaper; an exercise routine of her own to do while you do yours. She may be delighted to participate in your games of choice—or she may be bored. After all, her tea parties aren't always your cup of tea, either.

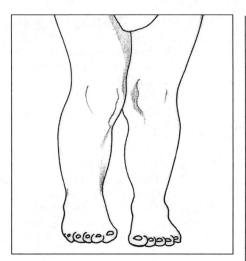

*The bowlegged one-year-old suddenly becomes a knock-kneed two-year-old. And it's perfectly normal.*

# KNOCK-KNEES

*"Our daughter was very bow-legged when she started to walk a year ago; now suddenly, she seems knock-kneed. What's going on?"*

Your toddler is right on schedule: bow-legged at one year, knock-kneed at two. It's not until somewhere between seven and ten that you can expect that her legs will appear truly straight.

In the meantime, there's nothing to worry about or to do. Special shoes, or-thotic supports, and exercises not only won't help, they could be harmful.

If only one leg is affected, or if the curvature is exaggerated, or if your child is way below normal height on the growth charts, discuss this with her doc-tor. Consultation with an orthopedic specialist may be called for. (If growth appears to be a problem, a visit to a specialist in metabolic disorders may be appropriate.)

# DESTRUCTIVE BEHAVIOR

*"Lately, every time we turn our backs, our toddler sets about de-stroying something. He tears up magazines, crayons on the walls, pulls the knobs off the television. Our house is starting to look like a tornado hit it."*

In other words, your house is starting to look like a home occupied by a tod-dler. But though toddlers are certainly frequently destructive, their behavior is not usually intentional. Toddlers tear, break, or otherwise destroy for a variety of reasons: frustration ("I can't get this to do what I want, so I'll toss it against the wall"); poor coordination ("I think I'll put my dish in the dishwasher like the grown-ups do." Crash!); curiosity ("What will happen if I open up the TV remote and take out the insides?"); lack of sophistication ("My juice cup never breaks when I drop it on the floor; no harm in trying it with Daddy's coffee cup"). Occasionally, of course, a tod-dler's destructiveness is deliberate ("I'm so mad at them for not letting me watch TV, I'm going to knock all the books off the coffee table" or "They spend so much time with that baby that I'm going to throw this truck right across the room").

At times you may be able to deter-mine what motivated your toddler's destructive behavior. Other times, his motivation will remain a mystery. Either way, it's important to let him know that destroying things isn't acceptable, and that, whatever his reason, you don't want him to do it again. Don't scold or punish, especially if he destroyed something un-wittingly, but let him know that you'd like him to try to be more careful next time, and why ("Coffee cups can break into sharp pieces when you drop them" or "When you take apart the remote con-trol, it doesn't work anymore"). And have your child help repair the damage when possible (wipe up spills, tape a page back into a torn book, scrub crayon marks off the wall). If frustration was the cause of his destructiveness, give him constructive suggestions for dealing with it ("If you pile the blocks this way, they don't fall over"). If anger was the trigger, remind him of other ways to release his emotions (see page 333). If it was just the junior scientist at work again, provide plenty of opportunities for safe and acceptable experimentation (see page 241) and manipulation (toys to put together and take apart, for example).

If your child continues his destructive behavior despite your intervention, and the destruction seems intentional, think about why. Is he frequently frustrated or angered by too many restrictions or by expectations that exceed his capabilities? Is he going through a difficult period or a tricky transition right now? Does he need additional love and support? Are there family tensions? Could there be a problem in his life you aren't aware of that is causing him distress (an inattentive or cold baby-sitter, unexpressed fears)? If addressing such issues does not lessen intentionally destructive behavior, discuss the problem with his doctor.

# GOOD EATING HABITS

*"I kept my daughter away from sugar and white flour for the first two years of her life, but now that she's around other children more, it's become next to impossible to keep her eating habits 'pure.'"*

A las, the days of gastronomic innocence—when Oreos, M & M's, and frosted cupcakes neither crossed your child's mind nor passed her lips—are gone and gone for good.

Of course, you could protect her nutritional virtue by locking her up in an ivory tower stocked only with healthy foods. But allow her to live in the real world—among the diet-sabotaging influences of peers, television commercials, and gimmicky food packaging—and temptation will never be far away, ever beckoning her to stray from the whole-grain and sucrose-free.

In the face of such temptation, making sure your toddler eats right will undoubtedly be a struggle. But with the solid foundation you've already laid, and the following tips, it's a struggle from which good nutrition can ultimately emerge triumphant.

▲ Make home a nutritional haven. You may not always be able to oversee your child's eating habits when she's out, but you can when she's at home. By keeping your home true to the Best-Odds tradition (see Chapter Eighteen), free—or mostly free—of foods made with white flour, excess fat, sugar, and artificial colors, chemicals, and other nutritionally unworthy ingredients, your toddler will have no choice but to eat right.

▲ Make eating well tempting. If your answer to candy and potato chips is carrot sticks, your toddler will come to associate good nutrition with taste-bud tedium. Respond instead with treats that are both nutritious *and* delicious, such as those beginning on page 832. A toddler whose taste buds haven't been tainted will find them every bit as appealing as the more traditional, empty-calorie treats.

▲ Make a strong statement with your own eating habits. Even a two-year-old will resent, and eventually protest, a double standard at the dining table, at home or away (Daddy washes down his bologna on white with Coke, she is forbidden all three; Mommy has two doughnuts and coffee for breakfast, she's stuck with oatmeal, fruit, and milk). Instead of giving your toddler the message that only little kids have to eat healthy foods and that Mommy and Daddy can eat anything they want, send one that says "our whole family believes eating right is important, and we do our best to eat right all the time."

▲ Make your wishes known. Anyone who will be supervising your toddler's eating when you're not around—her teachers, baby-sitter, playmates' parents, grandparents, or other relatives—should be made aware of your dietary dictums. That doesn't mean your toddler should be denied a birthday cupcake when all the other kids at day care are having one. But it does mean that her teacher should know that you prefer that your toddler not be offered junk food regularly, and that the rare exception not be overdone.

▲ Make a pact. The biggest stumbling blocks in the way of keeping a toddler's eating habits healthy often are the eating habits of peers. Many parents find that making a pact with the parents of their children's friends to avoid junk food at play dates, lunches, snack times, and so on, and to limit it at parties makes it easier for everyone to keep their children's diets healthy. It also eliminates the common parental plaint, "What can I do . . . all the other kids eat that junk."

▲ Make exceptions. The puritanical approach may yield your toddler's compliance when she's with you, but may encourage her defiance when she's not. Allowing the occasional less-than-Best-Odds treat will help satisfy her curiosity and her cravings without undermining her nutritional profile.

## BOOSTER SEAT REJECTION

*"Our son refuses to sit in a high chair or a booster seat, but he's too*

*small to reach the table from an adult seat."*

It's not surprising your son won't sit still for a booster. Not only does sitting in a confining seat significantly curtail a toddler's activity at the table (including his ability to stand up during a meal), it sets him apart from other members of the family, who sit in adult chairs.

You could try a little good-natured manipulation (Daddy tries to sit in the booster seat and Mommy comes to the rescue with, "No, that's Danny's seat"), but it's more than possible your toddler won't fall for it. If he doesn't, give up graciously. Insisting a child sit in a high chair or a booster seat when he doesn't want to can set the table for trouble—ensuring seating problems, and risking eating problems as well. Instead, respect your toddler's need to be active, and offer him some less-confining mealtime alternatives. A small table with toddler-size chairs set up alongside the family table is often acceptable. It gives a toddler the flexibility to move around a bit while eating, to leave when he's finished, and to still feel part of the family meals. If yours prefers to sit at the grown-up table on a grown-up chair, let him kneel on a kitchen chair or sit on a sturdy kitchen stool or a stepladder. Most toddlers like one of these options, but for safety, it's a good idea to seat an adult in the next chair.

## A TODDLER WHO'S A FOLLOWER

*"Instead of choosing things to do on his own, my son tends to follow along with the crowd—particularly if the crowd includes older children."*

Don't write off your son's political future just yet. Though leadership potential may be glimpsed in the sandbox, the followers of today may end up the leaders of tomorrow. It's too early to attach a tag-along tag to a child.

For many toddlers, following—older children in particular—is a great way to learn. Tagging along is also less threatening than taking the lead, and allows a toddler to move into and out of groups and to try new friends without being trailed by a coterie of followers.

As long as your toddler seems happy and secure following the crowd, there's no reason to intervene. It's how he feels about himself, and not who sets the game plan, that matters most. Help build his self-esteem (see page 292), give him plenty of chances to make his own decisions (see page 414), provide the support he needs to be the best he can be, and whether he is following or leading, he'll do just fine.

# SCHOOL-RELATED FATIGUE

*"Our daughter seems exhausted since she started preschool. Could it be too much for her?"*

It's probably not too much—just different. Though your toddler may be accustomed to being on the go all day at home, being on the go at school is different. Even in homes where there are schedules—times for meals, for stories, for bath, for bed—a toddler customarily has plenty of time for the unscheduled and spontaneous. In school or day care, this is usually not the case. Though "free play" is at the core of a good preschool program, most preschools also build in numerous scheduled activities (such as snack time, story time, nap time, arts-and-crafts time, cooking time, dance-and-movement time, outdoor time). To toddlers used to a more relaxed pace at home, this sudden regimentation can

take some getting used to. Until they do get used to it, the preschool experience can be somewhat draining, both physically and emotionally. The program may be wearing, too, because it isn't geared to each child's natural daily rhythms, but rather to what's convenient for the group or the school. So there may be outdoor play when your toddler is accustomed to napping and nap time when she's used to hearing a story. She may not be able to fall asleep at nap time, compounding her exhaustion. Struggling hard to be continuously well-behaved at preschool can also be fatiguing.

It's likely that your toddler just needs more time to adjust to preschool life. In the meantime, keep the remainder of her day free of unnecessary activities. A play date or a class (exercise, dance, art, etc.) at the end of a long school day will probably add to her fatigue, and isn't really needed now. What she needs after school is free unstructured time for unwinding, a healthy snack, and, chances are, a good nap. If she attends an afternoon program, keep her mornings relatively low-key; if it seems she needs it (and it's feasible), get her to nap before she heads for school.

Make certain, too, that separation anxiety—most likely if this is her first experience away from home—isn't contributing to your toddler's fatigue. To counteract this possibility, give her plenty of time, attention, and reassurance when you're with her—and see page 395 for ways of dealing with the anxiety.

If your toddler's exhaustion worsens over the next few weeks, or if her mood is down most of the time, some further exploration may be helpful. Is the program the right one for her? Is it too high-pressure? Could she be missing a needed nap? Is she too excited or too confused to eat her meals and snacks away from home? Look for the answers to these questions at preschool. If you don't find them there, or if she shows any signs of illness in addition to the fatigue, or if the fatigue continues, also check with her doctor.

# BELATED WEANING

*"I just never got around to weaning my son from the bottle. Since he seemed so happy with it, I kept putting it off and putting it off. Now that he's turning two and is so stubborn about everything, I don't know how I'll ever get him off it."*

W eaning at any age is often difficult, and weaning at the typically tyrannical age of two is, as you've guessed, usually considerably more so. But with a lot of patience and determination, and a little friendly persuasion, it can be accomplished. And it should be done as soon as possible to eliminate the risks of prolonged bottle feeding.[7] (See page 27 for more on its drawbacks.) Here's how:

▲ Try the weaning tips on page 27. Although they were designed with a younger toddler in mind, they also work for older children.

▲ Give your toddler some control. The next time your toddler asks for a bottle, give him a choice. Offer a bottle of water in one hand, and a cup of his favorite beverage in the other. If it's his decision, and he realizes that he can't handle holding both at the same time, he may just decide that having his favorite drink is more important than having his favorite container. Even if he doesn't take the cup the first time, keep on trying—eventually, he's likely to reach for it.

---

7. If your toddler has frequent ear infections, prompt weaning is especially important, since swallowing while lying prone (on his back) can allow fluid into the eustachian tube, creating a bacteria-hospitable environment for an impending infection.

▲ Try a little incentive. While a younger toddler probably wouldn't understand the concept of a reward for achievement, an older toddler may. And though regularly offering rewards to a child in order to get him to perform daily chores isn't wise, offering a reward for taking a developmental step can be both wise and effective. Let your toddler know that there's something special in store for him if he gives up his bottle: a new book, a toy, a trip to the zoo. Nothing extravagant—just a little something that may convince him that quitting's worth his while. Also emphasize the fact that giving the bottle up means he's more grown-up, and when he's done it he can be allowed some grown-up privileges— sleeping in a bed instead of the crib, or turning the VCR on and off with supervision, or whatever you think he would consider an important perk. (Realize, however, that emphasizing being "grown-up" may backfire if your toddler has a new sibling and is jealous of the attention "babyish" behavior garners.)

Cheer him on, providing as much support as he needs, as he works towards his goal of giving up the bottle. When he reaches it, provide both the reward he's earned and the heartfelt ovation he deserves.

Expect your toddler to be a little crankier and more out-of-sorts than usual while he's weaning, and possibly, for a few days afterwards. Like anyone who's given up something very special, he'll need some time to adjust. Providing him with plenty of attention and comfort (including a lot of cuddling), and filling his days with fun activities, will help him adjust more quickly.

*"I am still breastfeeding my daughter a couple of times a day. I'm eager to call it quits, especially now that she's old enough to ask for the breast whenever she wants it. But she isn't showing any sign of losing interest."*

## TO GRANDMOTHER'S HOUSE WE GO

Some parents find that weaning works best when they're not around. These parents have had success in shipping their toddlers off for the weekend to a place where they're loved and feel comfortable, but where they don't have access to the breast or bottle they're being asked to give up. This might be grandmother's house, or might just as easily be the house of a favorite aunt, uncle, or family friend. Being in surroundings and around people they don't necessarily associate with breast- or bottle-feeding seems to make weaning less painful (just as a change of locale and activity seems to make kicking the habit less stressful for smokers). Even if the toddler does seem to sense that "something's missing," he or she is usually too busy having a good time to mind much.

By weekend's end, when the toddler returns home, that beloved form of feeding is often no more than a fond memory. If your toddler does come home asking for the bottle or breast, having gone "without" for a few days should make it easier for him or her to accept when you say, "Sorry, sweetie, we have no more bottles" (or, "I have no more milk in my breasts"), "but that's okay because you're so big now." The transition will be smoother still if you're careful to provide lots of extra love and attention and plenty of fun activities to fully take your toddler's mind off those feedings.

For breastfeeding moms, this will only work if you've already cut down to one or two feedings a day; otherwise, painful breast engorgement can result. Don't consider this out-of-sight, out-of-mind approach, either, if your toddler is going through a difficult period or has had to adjust to other major changes, or if you sense that being away from you will increase the stress of weaning rather than decrease it.

It takes two to breastfeed. And when one of the two is ready to call it quits, it's probably time to put the breast to rest—though there are other factors to consider in making the decision (see page 30). Of course, it takes two to *quit* breastfeeding, too, so you need your child's cooperation in the process. Try the tips also on page 30; if they don't work, you might want to add an incentive (see bottle weaning, facing page) to help make giving up nursing more worth her while.

Remember that your toddler won't only be losing a favorite source of nourishment when she's weaned, but a favorite source of comfort. So be sure to compensate by giving her extra comfort and attention; focus on physical contact (hugging, kissing, cuddling), which may be what she will miss most, but also find interesting activities to share. Don't be surprised (and don't object) if she tries to comfort herself—she may increase thumb sucking, adopt a security blanket or another comfort object, and/or seek to spend time stroking or patting you, much as she does while breastfeeding. While she adjusts, she may even want to reach under your shirt now and then for a familiar bare-skin snuggle. Let her—as her memories of nursing fade, she'll lose interest in this comforting technique.

## *EMBARRASSING MOMENTS*

*"Our little girl really embarrassed us today while we were having lunch in a coffee shop. The man at the next table was extremely obese*

*and she practically shouted, "That man fat!" Everyone heard her, including the man. I wanted to crawl under the table. What should I have done?"*

It happens to every parent at least once. It could happen on a crowded commuter bus, in a department store, a restaurant, a museum, or a bank line—just about any public place—but typically, it happens where there's no place to hide. The tiny child (who happens to be undeniably yours) points insistently at someone she's noticed is different (it could be a heavy person, a person of another race, a person in a wheelchair, a person with a cane, a very elderly person), and in a bellow that belies her tiny stature, broadcasts her observation (as in "Why is that woman so fat?" or "Why can't that man walk?"). Every eye and every ear within twenty feet turns to you—the parent, the responsible party—as you, wishing hard for the cloak of invisibility, struggle to think of an appropriate response knowing full well that the response will be important not only to the unfortunate subject of the comment but to your child's future attitudes about people who are different.

Don't worry if you didn't manage to summon up the perfect response this time—or even if you couldn't manage to summon up any at all. But be prepared to react if it happens again (it probably will):

**With understanding.** To you, making remarks in public about a stranger is offensive and decidedly impolite. To your toddler, who knows very little about etiquette and decorum and even less about what hurts people's feelings, remarking on a wide man's girth is as innocent as remarking on a "pretty flower" or a "big red truck." Calling a man fat is, in her mind, an observation, and she has no way of discerning that it's an inappropriate one to express out loud. So put your toddler's remarks in perspective—they

were spoken without malice for the man and without the intention of embarrassing you.

**Without admonishment.** Even if you're feeling mortified by your child's words, and by the disapproving stares or shaking heads they elicited, don't take your embarrassment out on her by scolding. Since your toddler is probably used to having her observations met with parental approval and applause, she likely expected the same approval and applause for this remark. Starting to observe and become curious about the differences between people (and the differences between animals, the differences between cars, the difference between cloudy days and sunny days) is part of a toddler's intellectual development. Chastising a child for making an observation might stifle future questions and comments. It may also give her the impression that differences are "bad"— and that people who are different are also "bad."

**With a quick and quiet explanation.** If it's possible to take your toddler aside to a place where you can talk more freely to her, do so; if it isn't possible (you're on the bus and your stop is a mile away or she's in the middle of her grilled cheese sandwich at the coffee shop), get as close as you can to her and speak quietly. Explain that some people look different because they are fatter or thinner (or have a different color skin, or are very short or very tall, or have weak legs and can't walk), and that saying in front of them that they're fat or thin or old or can't walk might make them feel bad. Let your toddler know that she can ask you anytime she wants to about a difference she's noticed, but that she needs to do it in her "quiet voice" or to wait until later, when the person isn't close by. If you're still within hearing distance of that person, keep your explanation quick and don't encourage further on-the-spot discussion (since your child's side of the discussion will undoubtedly be loud). Promise to talk more about this later, and then quickly distract your toddler.

**With more explanation later.** The point at which your toddler starts to notice differences in people is a good time to begin discussing them at home. Look at picture books about people who are different (people with disabilities, elderly people, people of different nationalities and different cultures). Talk about what makes people different and the same; point out differences in members of your family and among your friends ("You have brown eyes and Megan has blue eyes") as well as similarities ("You and Megan both are good climbers"). For more on helping your toddler learn about differences, see page 342.

**With patience and perseverance.** Chances are it will take several more embarrassing encounters and at least as many explanations and reminders before your toddler learns to be more discreet. But remember that your goal isn't just to keep your daughter from publicly commenting about the differences she sees, but to see differences without intolerance.

**With a good example.** Your attitudes, actions, and words will have more effect on your toddler's future behavior toward others than all the lectures in the world.

# WHINING

*"If there's one thing about my toddler that really gets to me, it's her constant whining. I end up giving in to everything she whines for just so she'll stop."*

Forget a dripping faucet, fingernails on a blackboard, or squeaky brakes.

A young child's whining tops them all on the list of tortures. Like a knife inserted, then slowly twisted, whining, which is really a kind of low-grade crying, can get under a parent's skin as no other behavior can. In fact, given the choice, many parents would rather deal with a full-blown tantrum—which erupts and subsides—than listen to the steady, unrelenting, nerve-grating sound of a whiner in action.

Though we tend to link whiny behavior most closely with the toddler and preschool years, it actually first shows up in infancy as that sort of nondescript crying known as "fussiness." And while some definitely whine more than others, virtually every child whines at one time or another; in and of itself, whining is not a sign that a child is overindulged or spoiled. Typically, children are most prone to whining when they are tired, hungry, bored, overstimulated, sick, upset, or not getting enough attention. Whining may also be triggered by a parental "no"—or by an anticipated parental "no." That this high-pitched harassment often continues until parental desperation has turned the "no" into a "yes" makes it all the more irritating.

Parents are the adults most likely to be on the receiving end of whining; toddlers are often too self-conscious to whine when in the care of others. But if whining is allowed to continue into the preschool years or beyond, the behavior may begin to proliferate, with negative results. The child may take the whining out to play and find that her peers avoid her; she may take it to school and find that teachers limit or withdraw their attention. Some whiny children become whiny adults who find it difficult to make—or keep—friends.

Though there's no sure cure for whining, there are ways of reducing the amount of whining your toddler does. First, take these steps towards preventing whining attacks:

# TOYS FOR TOTS—AT TWO YEARS

· · · · · · · · · ·

Two-year-olds have a lot of energy to burn. You can help your toddler focus some of that energy by providing the appropriate toys and games. Be sure to select toys that will stimulate the wide range of talents—both physical and intellectual—your child is developing. Look for those that develop your child's interest in learning about what grown-ups do (cooking, housekeeping, child care, driving, work, play); those that teach about the physical world (how things work; cause and effect; numbers, shapes, and patterns; how to manipulate dials, knobs, and buttons); for those that stimulate creativity and imagination (see page 362); and for those that encourage intellectual growth (see page 99). Limit playthings that stifle imagination (such as coloring books and dolls that can talk) and those that require no interaction (such as battery-operated toys that are just for watching).

Virtually all the toys that were appropriate at one year are still appropriate at two years (see page 56). Mix and match, to your toddler's delight. But be sure to check toys for age-appropriateness and safety (see page 655). You can also consider adding some more sophisticated items, such as:

▲ Dolls that can be bathed, fed, diapered—but avoid dolls that have extensive wardrobes, since most two-year-olds can't yet manage to dress a doll.

▲ Character figures or plush toys (from storybooks, movies, TV).

▲ More elaborate dress-up items (including handbags, aprons, shirts) plus costumes and pseudo-professional gear (such as a firefighter's hat, police officer's hat, sailor's hat, doctor's bag, dancer's tutu).

▲ Toy typewriters, cash registers, shopping carts, tool chests.

▲ Preschool computer.

▲ Toddler tape player.

▲ Beads or spools to string.

▲ More complex cars, trucks, and airplanes.

**Pay attention.** Many children begin to whine after they have tried and failed at several other ways of attracting adult attention. No matter how busy you are, listen when your toddler talks to you and try not to take too long to respond when she asks for your help. Be sure she's getting not just your ear, but all of you. When possible, take a few moments off from whatever you're doing (while waiting for the pasta water to boil, the washer cycle to finish, or a client to call back), to read a story, work a puzzle together, or just to sit quietly and cuddle.

**Be on the look-out for boredom.** Having "nothing to do" is a common cause of whining. While it's important for small children to begin learning how to entertain themselves, their capacity for independent play is still quite limited. When you sense that your toddler has exhausted her resources, step in with an activity before the whining begins.

**Fend off frustrations.** Some frustration is a necessary part of growing up and of learning new skills. But be sure that you aren't pushing your toddler, demanding a level of performance she's not capable of, or giving her toys and other playthings that are beyond her. When you see she's becoming overly frustrated, help her with what she's doing—or distract her. (See page 384 for more on dealing with frustration.)

▲ Hand and finger puppets, store-bought or handmade.

▲ Books with more words and longer stories.

▲ Simple wooden jigsaw puzzles (four or five pieces).

▲ Toys for water play (some that float, some that squirt, and some for filling and pouring).

▲ Shape-sorters with a wider range of shapes (hexagons, octagons, ovals, and so on).

▲ Pegboards, with pegs of varying shapes and sizes.

▲ Building blocks and systems, such as Duplo. Pieces should be large enough so your toddler can handle them easily and won't choke on them if mouthed. Avoid sets that require building a particular model—if your toddler can't follow the directions (with your help) or build to match the picture, the result could be excessive frustration.

▲ Arts-and-crafts materials, including: play clay; materials for making collages; poster paints to be used with brushes (see page 654).*

▲ Alphabet blocks or magnetic letters; color lotto; very simple number and letter games; an abacus.

▲ All sorts of musical toys, including drums, tambourines, maracas, play horns and other wind instruments, xylophones, simple keyboards, toddler cassette players, and microphones. Favor instruments over music boxes and musical toys that require only the push of a button and offer no real musical challenge.

▲ Climbing toys, such as backyard gyms (the local playground can serve as well, of course).

▲ Sandbox and sand toys.

▲ A real tricycle (check for size before purchasing).

▲ A "balance beam" (a narrow board placed on the ground, on which your toddler can practice walking to improve balance and build confidence).

---

* Be sure all art supplies are nontoxic and safe for use by children your toddler's age.

**Head off hunger and fatigue.** At least when possible—and you're bound to head off some of your toddler's most persistent whining.

**Provide voice lessons.** Children often don't realize the negative effect of whining on other people—until they hear it for themselves. So the next time your toddler whines, take a moment to tape record the awful sounds. Then tape her speaking in her regular voice. When she's in a good mood, sit her down and replay the tape, pointing out the difference between her "whiny" voice and her "regular" voice. Besides getting a good chuckle from the differences in the two voices, your toddler may even discover that she can't bear the sound of her

whiny voice. Reinforce that discovery by explaining "People don't like to hear whining. It hurts their ears, so they stop listening." With that realization fresh in her mind, make a game out of practicing your "regular" voices together.

**Applaud a "regular" voice.** Whenever your toddler asks for something nicely, let her know how much you appreciate her tone of voice (even if you don't appreciate her request). Say, "When you talk so nicely, in your 'regular' voice, it's such a pleasure. You make me and my ears very happy."

**Watch out for whining yourself.** Some parents, without realizing it, make requests of their children (and their spouses) in a nagging, whiny tone. Try always to use a "regular" voice yourself (albeit a firm one when you mean business). After all, if you can't avoid whining, how can you expect your child to?

**Encourage sharing feelings.** A child who can talk about her feelings is less likely to whine (see page 196). Help your toddler to get the words out when she's having trouble.

**Avoid labels.** Don't label your child a "whiner"—children are notorious for living up to parental expectations.

When, despite your best efforts, your toddler starts to whine, you can deal with it more effectively in the following ways:

**Eliminate any obvious trigger.** If the whining toddler is hungry, feed her (but don't reward whining with sweets or other treats); if she's wet, change her; if she's tired, help her to nap or rest; if she's bored, involve her in an activity. If she seems generally out-of-sorts, consider that she may be coming down with something or simply need some extra attention and treat her accordingly.

**Don't yell.** A shrill "Stop that whining!" doesn't get to the root of the problem and often perpetuates it, helping to entrench the habit. For a toddler who's seeking attention, even negative attention spells success.

**Don't capitulate.** When the whining starts, make it clear to your toddler that it won't get her anywhere—you'll listen only if she uses her "regular" voice. As long as the whining continues, avoid eye contact and don't respond. If she switches to a regular voice, do what you can to fulfill her request—at least, discuss it and offer options: "No, you can't have a cookie now, but you can have an apple or a banana." When you can't oblige at all, explain why: "I can't sit down and play with you now because I have to

cook dinner. But you can help me set the table. And we can play after dinner." (Be sure to keep your word.)

Even if the whining continues (and even if it threatens your sanity), don't buckle under to the whined demands. If any giving in is going to be done, it's best to do it immediately. Giving in after twenty minutes of incessant whining teaches your toddler that persistence is the key to successful whining—that if she just whines long enough, she'll always get what she wants. Try to keep yourself calm in the meantime by repeating a meditative mantra to yourself such as, "I will be calm. I will be calm."

**Distract her when reason won't work.** Distraction can often allow a toddler to stop whining without losing face. She's whining for a trinket you've passed at the supermarket? Overlook the request and say, "Did you forget that we get to go to the playground this afternoon? If we don't hurry we won't be able to. Lisa and her mom are going to meet us there . . . Hopefully, the diversion you create will take your toddler's mind off the toy and switch off her whining.

**Try a hug.** Sometimes, a quick cuddle or a back rub can relax your toddler out of a whiny mood. As a bonus, it may make you feel better, too.

**If you can't beat her, join her.** Sometimes the best way to end whininess is to whine along with your toddler. Say, "I feel like whining too. Let's whine together." It's possible that the whining chorus will dissolve into laughter that will relieve the tension that the whining has built up in both of you.

Injecting a little silliness into the situation can sometimes also help deflate the whining. You could pretend, for instance, not to know where the whining is coming from ("Do you hear that squeaky sound? Where do you think it's coming from?"). Proceed to check under the couch, behind the television, and in the closet before stumbling upon the source of the squeak (your toddler's mouth, of course). If that hasn't stopped the whining and started the giggling, offer to "fix that squeak" (an application of friendly tickling usually does the trick.) A dose of good-natured reverse psychology may also reverse the whining process ("I don't think you're whining enough. I think you'd better whine more.")

Be aware that some children, however, move from whining to a full-blown tantrum with this kind of teasing. If that's your child's response, don't try it again.

**Help your child to verbalize.** The toddler who's whining because she can't express herself needs help, not a reprimand. "I know you're upset about something. Let's see if I can help you say what it is." When your child is verbal enough, encourage words rather than whining: "I want to hear what you have to say, but you have to say it without whining." If trying to get your child to verbalize her feelings only makes her more frustrated, try to distract her with a calming activity, like listening to music or a story.

Whining behavior peaks between years three and six, but many children continue to whine occasionally, especially when they are out-of-sorts. Whining is more likely to abate sooner if a child finds it ineffective and unpopular. If your toddler whines all of the time, seems generally unhappy, and none of these interventions help, talk to her doctor about the problem and what needs to be done.

# TODDLER ANGER

*"Our son gets so angry with us sometimes that we have to physically restrain him from punching or biting. What should we do?"*

The first thing you need to do is recognize that anger is a normal, healthy emotion. It's okay that your toddler feels it, and even that he expresses it.

The second thing you need to do is to relay this same message to your toddler. Let him know that feeling angry or saying you're angry isn't wrong, but that expressing anger in aggressive ways—such as hitting, biting, shoving, hair pulling, and parent bashing—is, and won't be tolerated (check the index for finding advice on curbing individual behaviors).

Start teaching your toddler how to deal with his anger in more acceptable ways. When he's angry, acknowledge his feelings ("I can see that you're very angry with me for not letting you go to the park, and that's okay—it's okay to be angry") and then encourage him to talk about them ("Would you like to tell me in words how angry you are? That might help you feel better.") If his vocabulary is limited, as it is for many two-year-olds, help him find the words. If the frustration of searching for words just makes him madder, provide some physical outlets for anger (other than you): a pillow to punch, a bean bag to hurl, clay to pummel, an obstacle course to run in the playroom (see page 171 for more ways to help toddlers release feelings safely). An all-encompassing bear hug can also dissolve the anger in some children (as well as in their parents) and help them regain control (see page 339 for more tips on helping children regain control).

Most importantly, learn to stay calm in the face of your toddler's anger—not only because children tend to mirror their parents' moods, but because it's hard to stay angry with someone who's resolutely unruffled. Instead of responding to his anger with anger of your own, respond with, "I know you're angry. That's okay. I still love you." Even a cry of, "I hate you!" isn't reason for you to scold or punish a toddler, nor is it something you should take personally. When faced with your own anger, strive to handle your emotions in a way that sets a positive example for your toddler (see page 751 for tips on how to do this).

If your toddler can't seem to learn how to control his anger and/or seems angry much of the time, discuss this with his doctor.

# TANTRUMS IN PUBLIC

*"Whenever we go out in public, we can usually count on one thing— our daughter will throw a tantrum. She makes us look like the bad guys—it's so embarrassing, we usually give her what she wants to keep her quiet."*

It doesn't take long for toddlers to figure out that tantrums are most effective when they're thrown in the most inconvenient and inappropriate locales. With parental hands and tongues tied (or at least seriously curtailed by the perceived stares and snickers), toddler kicks and screams are far more likely to yield speedy success.

What's a parent to do? Pretending you don't know the kid anchored to your leg and wailing for candy is always a tempting option, but one you're very unlikely to sustain. Letting her cry it out— a reasonable plan of action at home— becomes impractical with dozens of spectators ready to shake their heads and chorus, "Tsk, tsk" at the child's (and parents') lack of control.

Is the only alternative to giving in to the demands of public tantrums never going out in public? No; here are some others:

**Take preventive measures.** While any toddler is capable of a tantrum, a hungry, tired, bored, or overextended toddler is almost guaranteed to throw one. You can't prevent every public scene, but you can usually prevent those triggered by a missed meal, fatigue, boredom, overstimulation, or an overly taxing agenda. Make sure your toddler is well fed and well rested before an outing, and try not to cram in too many stops. Be fair about making the errand running more tolerable for your toddler; whenever possible, work in a trip to the playground or walk through the pet shop between the post office and the grocery store.

It may also help to have your toddler bring along a stuffed animal or doll and entrust her with the responsibility of "baby-sitting" while you shop or do errands. Not only will this give her something constructive to do (which, in itself, may make her less likely to throw a tantrum), but it will give her someone to wield power over. And feeling in control may help keep her from losing control. (For more on preventing tantrums, see page 338; for more on surviving shopping with children, see page 238.)

**Reinforce good behavior.** At the end of a successful outing (even if they're few and far between), thank your toddler for being well behaved, and tell her how much fun you had with her. You might even consider taking ten or fifteen minutes to read an extra story, listen to a tape, or play a game to show your appreciation. Don't, however, use bribes or material rewards to exact good behavior, or your toddler may begin expecting a treat every time she behaves in a public place.

**Attempt distraction.** If, in spite of your preventive efforts, your toddler starts to explode while you're out, try a quick change of subject ("Let's go see if we can pick out a box of your favorite cereal right now!"). Or implement an out-of-sight, out-of-mind policy by removing her from the trigger, whether it's a bag of potato chips she's campaigning for or the cans of tuna she's pleading to re-arrange and involving her quickly in another activity. Distraction may allow your toddler to gracefully exit from her tantrum. For other approaches to dealing with tantrums, see page 339.

**Resort to isolation.** If distraction doesn't work, try to get your toddler to a relatively private place as soon as possible. The best way to do this is not to drag her by the hand or arm, but to pick her up—handling her firmly, but never violently. Carry her outside (where her voice will carry less) or to your car, to a restroom, a dressing room, or to your home if it's nearby. (If you're out with others, it may be more productive for a well-liked friend or relative to be the one to take your child out for a break; this strategy can distract from the parent–child tug of war.) If your toddler is used to a time-out, give her one in the car, a shopping cart, a park bench, or a chair in the corner of a store, but don't leave her alone. Wait until she's completely calm before attempting to continue your outing—and if she won't calm down, consider ending the excursion and trying again later or another day. Speak to your child softly as you leave. This gives you the appearance of being in control—which will be good for both your child and your pride.

**Ignore the audience.** Your toddler's tantrum is between the two of you—even if it's taking place in the middle of a crowded department store aisle. Concentrate on the task at hand—maneuvering your toddler out of her tantrum in a calm but firm manner—and mentally block out those around you. Try to take your toddler's public displays of temper in stride (or at least pretend to)—after all, tantrums are a normal, predictable part of toddlerhood, and anyone who's ever cared for a toddler knows that. (And those who don't know what it's like and still feel qualified to pass judgment on

your parenting skills don't merit your consideration.) If you can't help being embarrassed, at least don't let on—your child might take advantage of this weakness. And don't bother telling her that she's embarrassing herself—at this stage in her life, she couldn't care less about appearances (if she did, she wouldn't have a public tantrum in the first place).

**Don't give in.** No matter how great the temptation, and even if your toddler refuses to stop her tantrums, don't give in to any demands. Doing so will just feed the next tantrum.

# LAUGHABLE TANTRUMS

*"My son is so cute when he has a tantrum—I can't help laughing."*

**B**ite your tongue, pinch your arm, turn away and hold your breath—but whatever you do, *don't laugh.* Though some toddler tantrums, particularly early ones, are impossibly, achingly adorable, they aren't laughing matters. For some tantrumming toddlers, a parent's laughter is insulting. The feelings of anger and frustration that have triggered the outburst are genuine; having them met with adult giggles can belittle their feelings and may even intensify them. For other children, the laughter serves as positive reinforcement of a habit parents don't wish to reinforce. If it's a behavior a child knows his parents think is cute, he's likely to keep repeating it long after his parents have stopped thinking it cute.

Of course, don't worry about the outright amusement you've already displayed—your toddler won't hold it against you. But, from now on, respect his frustration and treat his "cute" tantrums as you would any other display of anger.

# WHAT IT'S IMPORTANT TO KNOW:
## Taming Tantrums

Webster's Dictionary defines a tantrum simply as "a fit of bad temper." But to parents standing by as their cheerful toddler, one moment all sweetness and smiles, suddenly transforms into a writhing, flailing mound of unrestrained rage, tantrums defy such simplistic definitions. Just what is this force that turns little cherubs into little monsters?

Normal, that's what. Tantrums are a fact of toddler life, a behavior that's virtually universal among members of the sandbox set—beginning for some tots as early as the end of the first year, peaking for most sometime in the second year, and continuing in many children until beyond age four. Toddlers aren't "bad" when they're having tantrums—they're just acting their age.

## WHAT'S BEHIND YOUR TODDLER'S TANTRUMS?

There are a number of reasons why tantrums are "DC" (developmentally correct) for toddlers—a normal part of growing up:

▲ The need to release frustration. The toddler's strong drives for mastery and autonomy are continually stymied, either by adults or by their own limitations (being unable to complete a puzzle, button a shirt, ride an older sibling's bike, say what they mean).

▲ The need to express their feelings, needs, and wishes. Most toddlers don't yet have the language skills to do this. For them, a tantrum speaks louder than words.

▲ The need to assert themselves and to send the message, "*I* am important. What *I* want counts."

▲ Lack of control over their lives. With adults always telling them what to do and what not to do, a tantrum is often the only way toddlers can say "Enough! This is *my* life!"

▲ Lack of control over their emotions. Toddlers are inexperienced at checking their emotions. When emotions get out of control, so do toddlers.

▲ Hunger, exhaustion, overstimulation, boredom.

▲ Too many choices, too few limits or vice versa (see page 47).

Though virtually every toddler has a tantrum now and then, some are especially tantrum-prone. About 14% of one-year-olds, 20% of two- and three-year-olds, and 11% of four-year-olds have what's considered "frequent" tantrums (that is, two or more a day). These children also seem more likely than other children to continue having tantrums well into the preschool and school years.

There are a variety of less common factors that can lead to these more-frequent-than-average tantrums:

▲ Genetic predisposition. Some children are born with temperamental qualities that predispose them to more frequent tantrums. For example, persistence, or stubbornness (great traits when a toddler is working resolutely on a particularly difficult puzzle, but not when it's time to put it aside and get ready for bed); high intensity (these kids react strongly to almost any situation, often with kicking and screaming); slow adaptability (these children are most prone to tantrums in

## TANTRUMS AREN'T JUST FOR KIDS

..........

When most people think of tantrums, they think of the "terrible two's." But the fact is that "kids" of all ages—even adults—throw tantrums.

The same triggers that are responsible for toddler tantrums can set off adult tantrums. Frustration (you've been working on your checkbook for three hours, and your balance is still off). A lack of control over your environment (you miss the train you *had* to make in order to get to an important meeting). Anger (your spouse forgot to make the plane reservations and now the flight's overbooked). Even hunger or fatigue, when teamed with the right set of annoying circumstances, can lead to an adult blow-up.

The difference is that because adults have more control over their environment and have had more practice dealing with frustration, delaying gratification (and a meal or bedtime, when necessary), and annoying circumstances, they often manage to head off a tantrum. And when they can't, they are usually able—thanks to their adult verbal skills—to lose their tempers with angry words rather than with flailing fists and kicking feet.

Realizing that tantrums are not the exclusive province of toddlers—and rather, a behavior we're all susceptible to sometimes—should help to put them in perspective.

the face of unexpected change; see page 201).

▲ Extremes of discipline. In a chronically permissive atmosphere, conspicuously lacking in limits, children may "act out" or misbehave in a cry for external controls. Or they may blow up because they are overwhelmed by too many choices when their parents leave too much of the decision making to them. In an overly strict home, the child may explode in hope of expanding boundaries that are too tight.

▲ A history of illness, chronic disabilities, or health problems. Parents are more likely to treat as "special" the child who has had serious medical problems or who was born after many miscarriages or a long period of trying. Because of lack of limits and discipline, these children can be prone to tantrums. Also particularly subject to tantrums are children who are hearing impaired or have severe speech or other communication problems; who are autistic or have other serious developmental disabilities; who are hyperactive; who have allergies

or recurrent minor illnesses. Certain medications, such as those meant to halt seizures, are also linked to tantrums.

▲ A parent–child personality clash. If you're outgoing and your toddler is quiet and shy, pushing your child to be more like you could lead to unnecessarily frequent tantrums. So could trying to tone down a high-intensity child just because you're laid back.

▲ Divorced or separated parents. The custodial parent may be overwhelmed by solo child-care chores and have little time for the toddler; the visiting parent may be overly permissive. Both may try to "woo" the child with gifts and special privileges. In such situations, the frustrated child is more prone to explode willy-nilly and may learn to use tantrums to control one or both parents.

▲ Parental personal problems, such as depression, overwork, worry, illness, or financial difficulties. When a parent's problems start becoming their child's, frequent tantrums can result. Poor, crowded living conditions can also precipitate a child to erupt more often.

# HEADING OFF TANTRUMS

**P**revention is the best defense against tantrums. Toward this end, begin keeping a record of your toddler's tantrums for a week or two, noting when they occur (time of day; before or after naps, meals, and so on; following a particular event), and, if the cause is apparent, why (hunger, fatigue, restrictions, frustration). After a time, examine the record to uncover your toddler's most common tantrum triggers, then set out to modify or eliminate them, using the following principles. Keep the record as a baseline for future comparison.

▲ Encourage better outlets for the frustration, anger, and other emotions that seem to lead to tantrums (see page 171). Make sure you give your child enough opportunity to let off steam. The child who is perpetually restricted physically and emotionally is like a simmering kettle, always about to boil over. Encourage your toddler to express anger or frustration verbally or to release them in more acceptable ways. If his or her language skills are not up to it yet, help out: "You look like you're mad about not being able to fit that piece in the puzzle. Are you?"

▲ Tailor your toddler's life to his or her personality. For many toddlers, regular meals, regular naps, regular routines for bed and bath will reduce the risk of tantrums. For those who are irregular, loosening up the schedule somewhat may help (see page 202).

▲ Avoid letting your toddler go for long stretches without food. Carry nutritious snacks whenever you go out and don't wait until behavior gets out of hand to offer them.

▲ Reduce the need to say "no." A parent's negativity is often the trigger for a child's tantrums, so take the steps on page 48, including childproofing your home and setting clear and consistent limits, to reduce your need to say "no." To achieve compliance, use more games and challenges (see page 156) and fewer absolute directives, which risk being refused. Avoid setting off too many rebellions by setting too many rules (see page 47). When considering legislation ask yourself: "Is this rule (or this "no") necessary?" Don't lay down the law just because "children have to learn who's the boss." Pick your battles thoughtfully, with an eye to health and safety *and* peace and quiet. Be just as wary, however, of setting too few limits.

▲ When possible, say yes. Instead of issuing an automatic "no" to your toddler every time your toddler asks for something, consider whether there's really any good reason not to say "yes." Giving an okay initially is far better than giving in under duress after a tantrum begins. When you can't give an unconditional okay, try negotiating ("You can't skip your bath, but you can finish looking at that book before you go in").

▲ Don't straddle the line. Either say "yes" or "no" to your toddler immediately or negotiate a compromise. If you say "maybe" when you really mean "no" to avoid a confrontation, you're almost certainly asking for a fight down the road. To most toddlers, "maybe" means "yes."

▲ Don't overcontrol. Heavy-handed parenting (controlling everything a child eats, wears, does) can lead to rebellion. So exert absolute control only when absolutely necessary.

▲ Provide choices when possible. Having opportunities to make decisions of his or her own ("Do you want to read this book or that one?" "Do you want to wear your jeans or your striped pants?") helps a toddler to feel more in control, reducing the potential for tantrums. But avoid offering open-ended choices ("Which shirt do you want to wear?")

because your toddler is sure to pick the one impossible choice, or be flummoxed by the array of options. Also remember to make it clear that some issues are nonnegotiable (wearing a seat belt, holding hands when crossing the street).

▲ Use tips here and on page 334 to prevent tantrums when you're away from home.

▲ Anticipate frustration, when possible. Try hard to listen to and understand what your toddler is saying. Don't eliminate challenges from your toddler's life (they are necessary for growth and development), but do try to limit those that are truly beyond his or her reach. Step in and help when a challenge is turning into a frustration; but instead of taking over the task for your child, offer a little guidance so that he or she can master it independently (turning the triangle ever-so-slightly so your toddler can fit it into the shape-sorter). Expectations and standards, too, should be realistic—not so high that your toddler is constantly failing to meet them.

▲ Keep your toddler from going over the edge. When you see your child tottering on the brink of frustration, exhaustion, overstimulation, boredom or anything else, divert attention toward something calming, soothing, or particularly interesting: a hug, a special song, a special place in the house, a special toy, a special book, a special activity, a phone call to Grandma and Grandpa.

▲ Stick to your principles when a tantrum occurs. If you give in to a tantrum— you relent and buy the candy bar because you can't take the screaming and the stares—you're only reinforcing your toddler's stratagem and setting the stage for the next tantrum.

▲ Commend good behavior, and even behavior that's neutral. Your toddler's been out for an hour of errands without a tantrum? Let him or her know you appreciate the cooperation.

▲ Try to be a model of calm. Seeing you behave in an outwardly cool and rational fashion, even when you're angry or frustrated, will provide an excellent example for your toddler to follow.

# DEALING WITH TANTRUMS

There is no miracle elixir you can give your toddler (or take yourself), no patented parenting technique that magically makes tantrums disappear. Like most of the more trying behaviors of childhood, tantrums pass when they're outgrown, and usually not much before.

But while it isn't possible to vanquish tantrums altogether, it is often possible to moderate or minimize them. The following suggestions for doing so are just that—suggestions. You are likely to find that some will work better than others, and some won't work at all. Once you've discovered which do the trick best, employ them whenever your toddler begins to unravel. Be sure, too, that anyone else (caregivers or relatives, for instance) who may have to deal with your child's tantrums uses them, too:

▲ Stay calm. Nothing fuels a toddler's fire like a fired-up parent; seeing you lose your cool will only make it more difficult for your child to regain his or hers. A parental blow-up can also terrify a toddler, raising the specter of loss of parental love. Already off-balance because of his or her own loss of control, the tantrumming toddler needs your calming influence and the reassurance of your unconditional love. And though the even-tempered approach may not be immediately rewarding, and certainly will not be easy to pull off (the temptation to toss your own tantrum in the face of your toddler's will always be there), you may eventually see your efforts mirrored in your child's increasing self-control. If, during a particularly bad tantrum or on a particularly bad day, you find yourself unable to maintain your composure when the screaming starts, don't feel guilty, take a quick time-out (with your toddler safely in view), and employ some of the tips for cooling down that are on page 751.

▲ Speak softly. Your screaming over the screaming will only encourage your toddler to scream louder, as he or she vies to recapture center stage. A gentle tone of voice, on the other hand, says you're in control, which should help your toddler regain composure. Being unable to hear you over the piercing screams of the tantrum may also induce your toddler to quiet down—if only out of momentary curiosity about what you're saying.

▲ But don't use a big stick. Resorting to physical punishment is a bad idea any time. Resorting to it to try to end a tantrum is a particularly bad idea. It punishes a child for something that he or she can't control and because you too could lose control, it could end up causing serious injury.

▲ Don't try to reason or argue with your toddler during a tantrum. Out-of-control toddlers are simply beyond reason. Logic ("You don't need that doll—you have one just like it at home") is generally lost on them. Save the rational explanations for more rational moments.

▲ Protect your toddler and his or her surroundings. The toddler who does a lot of kicking and thrashing during a tantrum could get hurt (on a sharp corner, a hard floor, or an overturned chair), hurt someone else (a younger sibling nearby or a playmate), or do damage to property (by throwing a dish, kicking a door, tearing a book, pulling down a cereal display in the supermarket). So move the child who is physically out-of-control to a setting that's safer for everyone and everything. If you're at home, the middle of your bed is a good location. If you're out, try a move back to the car or the stroller (and belt in). If that's not possible, you may simply have to hold your toddler snugly to prevent injury to self, to others, or to property. Restrain your toddler, too, when he or she starts swinging at you.

▲ Express empathy. When your toddler's carrying on about something he or she can't have, say, "I know it's hard when you don't get what you want. Sometimes I get angry when I can't get what *I* want."

▲ Try holding your toddler. Being held tightly during a tantrum helps some toddlers "keep it together" when they're falling apart. A tight hold can also help dissolve anger (both in the toddler and the parent), with the hold often turning into a hug as control and composure are regained. Other toddlers, however, particularly those who are older or who generally don't like to be held, will only flail more furiously when an adult tries to restrain them during a tantrum. As always, do what works for your toddler.

▲ Try distraction. Some toddlers can be cajoled out of a tantrum; some easily, some not so easily. Others only get angrier if an adult tries to divert them. If yours is receptive to distraction, get out a favorite book, a puzzle the two of you haven't done in a long time, or another favorite plaything, and try to entice your toddler to sit down with you by starting to read or to put in puzzle pieces (subtlety is important here). Or turn on a favorite tape and start dancing or singing.

If your toddler doesn't seem offended by your responding to an oh-so-serious tantrum with humor, you might want to try a little silliness (stand on your head, put your shoes on your hands, make funny faces) or even a little reverse psychology ("Whatever you do, don't smile . . . No, don't—oh, oh—I think I see a smile"). Or, perform a song and dance (with original lyrics) based on the situation ("Twinkle, twinkle little Joe, this for sure, you surely know. You cannot play with playground rocks, if you do not wear your socks"). See pages 126 and 156 for more ways of using humor with recalcitrant toddlers.

▲ Get down to your toddler's level. Sitting on the floor may help to even out the frustrating size differences between your half-pint and you.

▲ Ignore the tantrum. Often the best course of action is no action at all; a toddler who is left to tantrum may get it out of his or her system faster. This approach, sometimes referred to as the "extinction method" by child-care experts, is especially effective when a toddler's demands are totally outrageous, and even more so if you have a hunch the child knows they are. Continue to go about your business, humming or singing loudly enough to top the screaming and to make it clear you're not paying attention to the tantrum. When you begin to systematically ignore your child's tantrums, they may increase for a while (you can check by comparing their frequency with your baseline records). Eventually, however, as your toddler discovers that it's just not worth getting all worked up when there's no audience, tantrums should become less frequent. Don't use this nonintervention approach, however, on a child who's particularly sensitive, is going through a difficult time, is under some special stress, or seems to get unduly upset by being ignored; instead, try comforting such a child. If you use it on a child who has very physical tantrums, be sure he or she is safe while you're "not paying attention." Keep moving during this period, because it will be harder for your child to thrash you if you're a moving target rather than a sitting duck.

If you can't ignore the tantrum because you're in the middle of a store or you've got to go right out to meet your parents at the station, see page 334.

▲ Call a time-out. For some toddlers, especially older ones, a time-out can give them a chance to "cool off" and regain their composure. See page 127 for how to impose a time-out.

▲ If you're unable to stop a tantrum in its tracks, don't worry—it probably needs to run its course. When your toddler has released the pent up tensions, the hysteria will taper off and end.

However you decide to handle a tantrum, try never to accede to demands made during it. If you do, tantrums will become the route your toddler routinely uses to get his or her way. If you're going to say "yes," it's better to do so before the tantrum gains force.

## AFTER THE STORM

When the tantrum's over, let it go. If your child manages to end a tantrum quickly, offer praise: "You did a good job of helping yourself calm down." But don't rehash the episode or lecture your child about it, or insist on an apology or admission of guilt (though with an older child you may want to discuss later what led to the explosion). And don't administer punishment of any kind (such as taking away a toy or canceling a trip to the park). Your toddler's been through enough, and besides, he or she didn't do anything wrong. If it was hunger, fatigue, or frustration that triggered the tantrum, deal with the cause (with a snack, a nap, or support). If a parental request sparked the tantrum (you asked your child to put away the blocks), you might suggest that the two of you attend to the task together now

that he or she is calm. If it was your refusal to fulfill a request that sparked the
fire, don't give in and meet the demand
now that the flames have died down.
You don't want to give your toddler the
impression that tantrums are an unbeat-
able means towards any end.

Move swiftly to a diverting and enjoyable activity—preferably, one that
won't be frustrating (you don't want to
risk another tantrum). Find something to
applaud or praise in your toddler's behavior or participation in the activity; his
or her ego is likely to have been shaken
by the recent power struggle and needs
your support. Many toddlers appreciate
being held after a tantrum, as reassurance of their parents' continuing love.

Keep in mind that there are tantrums
and there are *tantrums*. If your child's
temper tantrums occur very frequently
(two or more times a day); continue on a
regular basis past age four; seem to be
accompanied by feelings of intense
anger, sadness, helplessness, aggressive
of violent behavior, or other behavior
problems (sleep disorders, food refusal,
extreme difficulty with separation); or if
you are having trouble handling them
(especially if you are responding violently), then talk to his or her doctor.
You may need some extra support yourself—and it always helps to have a situation clarified.

# *WHAT IT'S IMPORTANT FOR YOUR TODDLER TO KNOW:* Everybody's Different

Children don't have to be taught to
notice differences. While a roomful
of infants won't seem to discern a difference between the dark-skinned and light-
skinned, between the chubby, the slender,
the sighted and the visually impaired, a
roomful of older toddlers will begin to
notice what sets individuals apart.

But while the ability to recognize differences comes naturally—as part of a
child's normal intellectual development—
the ability to fear, mistrust, or taunt others
because of these differences doesn't.
Children are very accepting of differences. They have to be taught to hate.

Unfortunately, they are quick studies.
Children exposed to prejudice from the
cradle may begin to express these preju-
dices by the age of two. The foundation
for their attitudes toward those who are
different is usually laid by the age of five,
and those attitudes are cemented—often
for life—by the age of nine.

To raise a child who is as free of
bias and full of tolerance as possible, you
should begin now. Here are some suggestions to help you in your effort. Keep
in mind that the life experiences suggested below are relevant even to a two-
year-old, but that many will not have
meaning until he or she is closer to three:

▲ Build your child's self-esteem. Feeling
good about yourself has a lot to do with
feeling good about others. People who
have poor self-esteem are the ones most
likely to disparage those around them;
they tend to build themselves up by tearing others down. Help your toddler develop positive attitudes about him or
herself, and positive attitudes towards
others should follow. (See page 292 for
tips on building self-esteem.)

▲ Connect your child with his or her
roots. In order to feel good about others,
one must first be comfortable with and

connected to one's own heritage—family, ethnic, religious, and/or racial.

▲ **Meet your child's emotional needs.** Children who lack for love, attention, or caring may become hostile toward others, particularly when they are under stress or feel life is out-of-control—striking out at others makes up for their feeling unloved and unwanted. Make sure your child feels loved, and he or she will be far more likely to have the ability to love others.

▲ **Accept your child.** A child who is accepted unconditionally just the way he or she is—differences, imperfections, and all—is likely to accept others the way they are, too.

▲ **Help your child to develop empathy.** A child who can feel for others will be less likely to do something hurtful, at least consciously. Empathy isn't a quality toddlers can be expected to develop overnight. Even with regular parental encouragement and parental expressions of empathy toward others, it appears only sporadically before the preschool years, and consistently only once a child has reached the age of nine or ten. But it's never too early to begin fostering it; see page 42.

▲ **Expose your toddler to differences.** Children who, from an early age, see many kinds of people from many different backgrounds as part of their lives, are more likely to grow up feeling comfortable with, rather than suspicious of or threatened by, differences. When comparing preschools or day-care facilities, look for one that includes children from different backgrounds, possibly even children who are developmentally or physically challenged. Encourage, too, play dates with children who are socially compatible but not the "same." If possible, visit playgrounds where a diverse group of children gather.

If all your friends tend to fit the same mold, strive to expand *your* horizons, too. Invite to your home people you've become friendly with (either at your toddler's preschool, through your religious community, or at work) who are of a different ethnic, religious, or racial background or who are physically challenged. If you have an elderly neighbor or an elderly relative who lives nearby, consider inviting them over or visiting them with your toddler now and then. This will not only cheer up the senior citizen you're spending time with but help your junior citizen to form healthy attitudes about older folks.

Your efforts to bring more diversity into your life and your toddler's may seem forced at first—gestures that almost border on tokenism. But making those first efforts is an important first step in making diversity a natural part of your lives.

Your options will, of course, be considerably less open if your town is fairly homogeneous, in which case you may need to seek out other ways of exposing your child to a wide range of people; see more below.

▲ **Discuss differences.** Being exposed to many different kinds of people is important, but not enough. As your toddler grows older, it will be useful to talk about the differences he or she sees. Whenever the subject comes up, explain that everyone's different from everyone else, that no two people are exactly alike—some are short and some are tall, some have blue eyes and some have brown, some have curly hair and some have straight, some are young and some are old, some walk and some ride in wheelchairs. Point out that your toddler looks "different" to other people, too. Also explain that in most important ways, all people are the same: We eat, we drink, we love, we work, we play, we laugh, we cry.

▲ **Celebrate differences.** While it's important to teach a child that superficial differences don't make a difference, it's also important to teach a child to appreciate differences. Explain that the world is beautiful not only because it has many different kinds of flowers and trees, but also because it has many different kinds of people. Expose your toddler to this beauty. Attend an exhibit of Indian art at the museum, an Hispanic dance program, a Chanukah festival, a German Oktoberfest celebration, an Italian street fair, an African-American cultural arts event, a Christmas concert.

Bring variety into your home, too. Borrow from the library tapes of music from all over the world, and books that celebrate different cultures and groups. Be sure that the books in your toddler's home library reflect the diversity of the world we live in. Vary the dolls in your toddler's doll collection, too. Watch for television shows about children from backgrounds that differ from yours that you can watch together, or videos about other cultures. Celebrate your own holidays, of course—when possible, inviting your toddler's friends and their parents to share the typical foods and customs. But also try to expose your toddler to the holidays that other people celebrate, attending community celebrations, for instance, on Passover, Easter, Kwanzaa, the Chinese New Year, Cinco de Mayo, and St. Patrick's Day.

▲ Celebrate similarities, too. Show your toddler that as different as people can be from each other, they are the same in many ways. That while your child's best friend goes to synagogue instead of church, they both pray; that while the little boy in day care can't hear, he likes to draw and build tall block towers just like your toddler; that the very large woman she saw at the restaurant has red hair just like Grandma; that the man in the wheelchair has a beard just like Daddy. Finally, even though there are many ways in which she is different from the girl who lives across the street (she has eyes of a different color, different hair,

different skin color, celebrates different holidays), there are also many ways in which they are the same (they're the same age, same height, like to play on the swing, love pizza).

▲ Answer questions about differences. Don't let embarrassment prevent you from answering questions your toddler might have about differences he or she notes in people ("Why is Andrea brown?" or "Why does Carmela's mother talk so funny?" or "Why does Sam's father walk with a stick?"). Instead of changing the subject (which might lead your child to believe that there's something embarrassingly wrong with the difference), provide a simple but complete answer. ("Andrea has dark skin, just like her mommy and daddy and her little sister" or "Carmela's mother comes from Mexico, where they speak Spanish; she's just learning to speak English" or "Sam's father walks with a stick because his leg is weak. The stick is called a cane and it helps him to walk better"). If you find yourself without an answer and need more time or more information to formulate one, say so. Then take an appropriate book out of the library, and find the answer to your toddler's question together.

▲ Avoid stereotypes. If you generalize about racial or ethnic groups, even if the generalizations aren't negative ("Black people are good at basketball" or "Asians are good students"), you risk passing on the message to your child that people can be categorized by *what* they are as a group—instead of *who* they are as individuals. Teach your child to look at people as individuals—not as members of groups. Avoid lumping whole groups together as "those people," talking about "those kinds of kids," and labeling people you meet by their ethnic background, their race, their religious affiliation, or their physical status. If you have family members who frequently stereotype when talking about those of other races or religions, speak to them about keeping their generalities to themselves when they're around your toddler.

▲ Counteract bigotry when you encounter it. If you and your toddler overhear a racial or religious slur, quietly say, "Some people talk that way, but it's not right and it can hurt people's feelings." If you find your toddler repeating a derogatory comment he or she has overheard, don't overreact, but don't ignore it, either. Again, explain that such words are mean and can hurt people.

▲ Check your own biases. It's not enough to preach tolerance—you *must* practice it, too. Before you can instill healthy, unbiased attitudes in your toddler, you need to make sure they're there in you. When children hear ethnic or racial slurs at home (and if slurs are used, children inevitably hear them, whether or not parents think they're listening) or see that those who are different are not treated with respect by their parents, all the brainwashing in the world won't erase the biases they've picked up through osmosis. Examine your attitudes (no one is completely bias-free) and your behavior, and make changes wherever you see room for improvement.

# CHAPTER THIRTEEN

. . . . . . . . . .

# The 25<sup>th</sup> to 27<sup>th</sup> Months

## WHAT YOUR TODDLER MAY BE DOING NOW

*By 2¼ years,[1] your toddler*
*. . . should be able to (see Note):*

▲ use 50+ single words
▲ combine words (by about 25 months)
▲ follow a 2 step command without gestures (by 25 months)

**Note:** If your toddler has not reached these milestones, consult the doctor or nurse-practitioner. This rate of development may well be normal for your child (some children are late bloomers), but it needs to be evaluated. Also check with the doctor if your toddler seems out-of-control or hyperactive; highly demanding, stubborn, negative; overly withdrawn, passive, uncommunicative; sad, joyless; unable to interact and play with

others. At this age, children who were born prematurely have usually caught up to their peers.

*. . . will probably be able to:*

▲ wash and dry hands
▲ jump up
▲ put on an article of clothing
▲ brush teeth, with help

*. . . may possibly be able to:*

▲ build a tower of 8 cubes
▲ use prepositions
▲ carry on a conversation of 2 or 3 sentences

*. . . may even be able to:*

▲ balance on each foot for 1 second
▲ put on a T-shirt
▲ identify a friend by naming

---

1. This chapter covers the period between the time a toddler turns two through two and a quarter (or twenty-seven months).

# WHAT YOU MAY BE CONCERNED ABOUT

## CONSTANT SPILLING

*"As if the accidental spills weren't bad enough, lately my son has decided it's great fun to spill his drinks intentionally—on the floor, the table, himself. I don't know whether to laugh or to cry."*

Don't do either. It's not a good idea to cry—or laugh—over spilled milk (or juice, or water), unless you want your toddler to continue spilling in order to elicit a reaction. Instead, try to swallow your frustration, stifle the giggles, and keep your composure.

As you've noticed, there are two types of spillage perpetrated by toddlers: accidental and intentional. Accidental spills are a result of a child's level of development. Handling a cup without knocking it over or sloshing some liquid out of it may seem a simple task to someone who's been doing it for thirty years or so. But it's a complex task for a relative beginner, whose concentration and fine motor skills still need quite a bit of refining. It generally takes plenty of trials (and just as many errors) before a toddler even begins to get it right.

The intentional spill is generally motivated more by curiosity ("What will happen when I turn this cup over? Hey, look at the milk dripping all over the place. This is great!") than by mischievousness. To adults, it may seem that once a child has discovered the effect of an action, he should no longer need to repeat the experiment. But toddlers are tirelessly enthusiastic and they like to replicate their experiments over and over again. So you can expect to be sponging up spills, at least occasionally, for many months to come.

To end accidental spilling will take practice and effort on your toddler's part;

to end just-for-fun spilling will take his willing cooperation. Either way, on your part, it will take patience, a sense of humor, a good supply of sponges, and these tips:

▲ Prevent accidents that don't have to happen. Some spills can be averted with the right choice of cups. Choose cups that are weighted at the bottom and are small enough for a toddler's hands to grasp comfortably. If your toddler doesn't object, use a cup with a spout and lid. Pour just a small amount into your toddler's cup at a time, and refill as necessary. (If your toddler demands a full cup every time, use a very small cup to avoid very large spills.) Also, try to place the cup out of your toddler's elbow room between sips, so that he will be less likely to knock it over while he's eating. And watch out for other "danger" zones (on the edge of his placemat, near the edge of the table, and so on). Don't permit drinking in areas of your home where spills could do major damage—such as on carpets or upholstered furniture. Confining eating to the kitchen, breakfast area, dining room, and family room may not eliminate spills, but will eliminate their most serious consequences.

The new "spill-proof" cups can end spilling completely (turned on end, they don't even leak), but will teach your toddler nothing about handling an ordinary cup or glass. So use it primarily when spilling would be a major problem (in the car, when visiting, when using your best tablecloth) or when you can't face another spill.

▲ Don't blame your toddler for acting his age. Spilling accidents should be treated as just that—accidents—even when they occur repeatedly during one meal. Eating and drinking can be a struggle when you're two, and your toddler's self-esteem can suffer if his efforts, no matter how awkward, are deprecated. When you're tempted to lose your cool at an accidental spill, remember the times when you—or a guest—accidentally upended a drink.

▲ Give your toddler a sponge instead of a scolding. Enlisting your toddler's help in cleaning up what he's intentionally spilled is a much more positive approach than yelling at him or muttering under your breath and may help to discourage such spilling. Another plus: Having to face the consequences of his actions will help your toddler develop responsibility. (Of course, if he decides he *likes* wiping up so much that he spills intentionally, this isn't the best tactic. Instead, let him play at spilling and wiping up at a play table or in the tub; when he spills where he shouldn't, wipe it up yourself.)

▲ Provide another drink and a gentle reminder. Don't deny your toddler a refill if he spills accidentally. Give him what he's thirsting for, along with a challenge ("Let's see if you can try to be more careful this time") rather than a warning ("If you spill again . . .").

▲ When your toddler spills on purpose, take a stand. Make it clear, without making a big fuss (which will only reinforce the negative behavior) that intentional spills are not acceptable. If he continues to spill intentionally, tell him you will take charge of his cup and give it to him only when he wants to take a sip. If he spills the moment he gets his hands on the cup, take the drink away entirely, with minimal fuss. But make sure he gets plenty of chances to practice filling and pouring in the tub or at a water table.

▲ When you do cry (or scream) over spilled milk, explain why. Seeing milk splatter over a newly mopped floor or grape juice seep into the holiday tablecloth can launch the most even-tempered parent into an uncharacteristic overreaction. Instead of punishing yourself with guilt, explain to your toddler why you got angry ("That's my new tablecloth, and seeing milk spill all over it made me feel mad."), and of course, add an apology ("I'm sorry that I yelled at you. I know it was an accident").

# FAT AND CHOLESTEROL INTAKE NOW

*"Now that my toddler's over two, shouldn't I start limiting her fat intake so she won't have a weight or cholesterol problem later in life?"*

Alas, the days of whole milk, and full-fat cheese and yogurt are gone for your toddler—or at least they should be. The development of artery clogging plaque begins in childhood, and both the American Academy of Pediatrics and the National Cholesterol Education Program (NCEP) suggest that parents begin reducing dietary fat and cholesterol when their children have reached their second birthdays.

The most current recommendations are simple, and the Best-Odds Toddler Diet (see page 500) will help you incorporate them into your family's daily meal planning. The guidelines suggest that children over two should:

▲ Eat a varied diet (or as varied as a toddler's eccentric tastes allow) with sufficient calories for normal growth.

▲ Get less than 30% of their total calories from fat. No more than one-third of these (10% of their total calories) should come from saturated fat (found in dairy products, meats, eggs, coconut, hydrogenated shortening, and coconut, palm, and palm kernel oils). The rest should come from polyunsaturated fats (found in corn, safflower, sunflower, and soybean oils) and especially from monounsaturated fats (found in olive and canola

## CHOLESTEROL LEVELS IN CHILDREN

· · · · · · · · · ·

The following is a summary of the NCEP's recommendations for evaluating cholesterol levels in children:

|  | TOTAL CHOLESTEROL | LOW-DENSITY LIPOPROTEINS (LDLs*) |
| --- | --- | --- |
| Acceptable | less than 170 mg/dL | less than 110 mg/dL |
| Borderline | 170–199 mg/dL | 110–129 mg/dL |
| High | 200 mg/dL or more | 130 mg/dL or more |

*LDLs are considered the "bad," or harmful, substances in the blood cholesterol.

oils), which are believed to be the best fats for heart health.

▲ Get less than 300 milligrams of dietary cholesterol per day. Cholesterol is found only in animal products, such as eggs, meat, poultry, whole milk, cheese, and other dairy products.

To compensate for the reduction in fat, your toddler's diet should be high in filling, fiber-rich whole grains, legumes, fruits, and vegetables, and include moderate amounts of low-fat dairy products, meat, poultry, and fish. And to further reduce the risk of early accumulation of plaque in the arteries, she should be encouraged to be physically active and spend little time watching television. Children who watch a lot of TV tend to have higher cholesterol levels—not only because they snack on high-fat foods while watching, but because they're sitting in front of the TV instead of getting cholesterol reducing, health promoting exercise.

But keep in mind as you go about modifying your toddler's diet, that there's a limit to how much you can, and should, limit a child's cholesterol and fat intake. An overly restrictive diet, in fact, poses several problems. First, children need fat to grow, both physically and in-

tellectually; weight, height, and the ability to learn can be adversely affected by a diet that's too low in fat. Second, a totally fat-free diet can be unappetizing and tough to chew (a definite drawback for those still perfecting the skill). Third, fat-free meals don't stick to the ribs as long, making chronic hunger—and sagging energy between meals—potential problems. Fourth, in severely restricting certain foods that are naturally moderate to high in fat, dairy products, for example, there's the risk that vital nutrients in these foods will also be restricted. And last, as with any overly restrictive diet, a fat-free regimen can lead to mealtime rebellion and unhealthy attitudes towards food, particularly once your child starts seeing that the other kids are eating what she's never allowed.

For a list of high-fat foods appropriate for toddlers, see page 507.

### "Should we have our toddler tested to see if his cholesterol is high?"

Not unless there's a good reason— and concern over your toddler's future cardiac health isn't reason enough. It's presently recommended that a child's cholesterol level be tested *only* when there is a family history of onset of heart disease before age 55, or when at least one parent has an elevated cholesterol reading (240 mg/dL or more).

If there is such a history, or the family history is unknown, talk to your toddler's doctor about testing. Children who have high cholesterol levels (see table, page 349) should, like all over-two's, be put on the low-fat, low-cholesterol diet recommended above. If three months on the diet does not lower a child's cholesterol readings, a "step two" diet is usually prescribed. This diet reduces saturated fat intake to less than 7% of total calories (less than one-quarter of total calories from fat) and limits cholesterol to less than 200 mg a day (less cholesterol than is in one egg yolk).

## STARTING CHEWABLE VITAMINS

*"We've always had trouble getting vitamin drops into our son, but lately he's gotten even more stubborn about it. Our doctor recommends we give him vitamins. What can we do?"*

Young children don't always know what's best for them—and most of the time, they don't care. At this age, they feel invincible, don't understand the concept of present behavior affecting the future, and are unmoved by parental pleas to "take your vitamins so you can stay healthy and not get sick." Like your toddler, most see no good reason to open wide for the medicine dropper.[2]

Which doesn't mean it's time to drop the vitamins, but it might be time to drop the dropper. A sturdy set of teeth and a taste for sweets are the only prerequisites for starting chewable vitamins,

and the vast majority of two-year-olds meet both of these requirements. Not only are the enticing shapes, colors, and fruity tastes and scents of chewables easier for a toddler to take, the dosing process is usually less objectionable; instead of being the unwilling target of a dropper-wielding parent, a toddler can pop and chew his vitamin himself.

When choosing a chewable vitamin, it's a good idea to ask your pediatrician for a recommendation. If you plan to select one yourself, read labels carefully. Some chewables provide *more* nutrients than toddlers require, so look for a formula that provides no more than 100% of the toddler RDA (it is different than the RDA for children four and older) for any one nutrient.

Though most toddlers relish a chewable, and begin looking forward to their daily dose, there are some who find the taste and/or smell objectionable. You can try switching around until you find a brand your toddler will tolerate, although such experimentation can be expensive. In the end, it's likely your toddler will find at least one brand acceptable. If he doesn't, you'll have to try a little sleight of hand: Crush a chewable and fold it into applesauce or mix it in a fruit flavored shake; disguise a liquid preparation[3] in juice (it's best if the flavor of the supplement and the flavor of the juice are the same—both orange, or both cherry, for example), a strong-flavored all-juice punch, or a natural juice spritzer (the bubbles may help disguise the supplement). Dividing the dose (liquid or chewable) in two, and giving the first half in the morning and the second later in the day, may make each less noticeable.

In the end, of course, you can't really force vitamins on a child—particularly not on a daily basis. If you find you are squandering money, effort, time, and your child's good will trying to get the supplement down, give up for a month, then try again. At that point your toddler

---

2. For the pros and cons of vitamin supplementation, see page 508.

3. Excess doses of vitamins can be dangerous.

may have reached a more cooperative stage and/or may have lost his distaste for the taste of vitamins.

Unfortunately, the very properties that can make chewable supplements palatable to many toddlers can also make them dangerous. No bitter pill, these supplements can easily tempt toddlers to overdose. Protect your toddler by keeping the vitamins out of his reach, with the child-guard top secured, and never referring to vitamins as "candy." (These rules should also be observed for over-the-counter and prescription medicines, which often come in palate-pleasing flavors and colors.)

# RESTLESSNESS AT RELIGIOUS SERVICES

*"When we take our toddler to religious services, he can't sit still or be quiet, no matter how many times we tell him to settle down. We don't want to stop taking him, but we can't continue to have him disturbing everyone around us."*

You're asking your toddler to perform two tricks that aren't in his repertoire—sitting still and remaining quiet. Most children his age can't pull these off at a Disney movie, never mind a religious service.

For the time being, you're going to have to accept your toddler's limitations in the decorum department—which are less likely to be indicative of his disposition than of his tender years. As he gains maturity, he'll also gain the ability to control physical and verbal impulses—though he may not resemble the proverbial church mouse in restraint for many years to come. In the meantime, that doesn't necessarily mean you'll have to leave the service—or leave your toddler at home—just that you'll have to practice

a lot of the patience you've been preaching to him. And while you're at it, give these tips a try; they should work in any house of worship or similar environment.

**Seat for success.** And a speedy retreat. Choose a seat that's on the aisle, and as far away from other congregants (in the back or in an unoccupied row) and as close to an exit as possible. Not only will this minimize the disturbance caused by your toddler (and you, if you must slip in and out of the service with him), but your toddler may be less fidgety with more room to spread out.

**Dress him down.** The discomfort of starchy collars, stiff trousers, and binding bow ties and shoes often bring out the squirmies in toddlers. Though he may not be picture-perfect, your child may be much more comfortable and therefore more cooperative in his Monday clothes than in his Sunday best. Of course, some children love dressing up; if yours does, let him.

**Carry more than a prayer book.** A few picture books and quiet toys may occupy your toddler for a short time. So may putting him in charge of keeping a doll or teddy quiet. And don't forget to bring along a drink and a snack for him to enjoy during "intermissions" from the service; hunger and thirst can completely sabotage a child's chances of behaving.

**Practice at home.** Once in a while, play "church" (or synagogue, or mosque) at home. Let your toddler line up stuffed animal "congregants," and make a fun, pressure-free game out of rehearsing a "quiet voice" (small children love to learn how to whisper, though they don't always use what they learn appropriately) and practicing sitting still at services.

**Consider the options.** If your place of worship provides child care or a children's service, take advantage of it as needed. If not, try organizing something for the youngest congregants yourself—possibly a cooperative effort in which parents alternate caring for the children and attending services. Or simply take turns with your spouse or another adult.

**Be fair in your expectations.** Don't threaten your toddler or scold him for acting his age. If he does speak too loudly, gently remind him to use his quiet voice. If he doesn't comply, don't rebuke him, but do remove him; it's important for him to understand that a house of worship is a place where he must be respectfully quiet.

**Play for the long run.** If religion is important to you, try to keep your toddler's experiences at services pleasant, so that he won't grow up with negative feelings toward religion.

## CRANKY DAYS

*"There are some days when my daughter finds fault with everything, from sunup to sundown."*

Everybody has bad days—even bad weeks. But most adults are able to keep much of their melancholy to themselves. Toddlers, however, tend to wear their emotions on their sleeves for all to share. If they're happy, they're all contagious smiles and giggles. If they're proud, they strut like peacocks in full plumage. And if they're grumpy—well, watch out.

Don't join your toddler in the dumps when one of her cranky days dawn (though this may seem the path of least resistance). Instead, try to help her change her mood, with these suggestions:

▲ Bring on the good humor. Crankiness doesn't stand much of a chance when it's bombarded by cheerfulness. Meet your cranky toddler's frowns with smiles, her grumbling with giggles, her sour face with silliness, without making her feel you're making fun of her.

▲ If she baits, don't bite. A cranky child will try to pick a fight over anything and everything—don't give her the satisfaction of putting up your dukes. Respond to her crankiness with friendly detachment.

▲ Simply remember her favorite things. Whether it's a plate full of smiley-face pancakes and some finger painting or a cookie-baking session and a bubble bath, giving your toddler a few of her favorite things when she's feeling grumpy can boost her spirits considerably. If the boost doesn't last long, don't give up hope—and plan some more favorite things for later on.

▲ Take a look at your mood. Bad moods are contagious. If your toddler has caught hers from you, try doing something to improve your mood.

▲ Give her some time and attention. Sometimes crankiness is really a cry for some of the tender, loving care only the uninterrupted time and undivided attention of a parent can provide.

▲ Steer clear of her less favorite things. If possible, put off for a better day any activities that your toddler doesn't enjoy under the best of circumstances—shopping for shoes, for instance, or dragging along while you do errands.

▲ Consider a nap. Lack of sleep can often bring on an episode of crankiness. Being sure your toddler gets a good night's sleep every night and adequate rest during the day may prevent the "crankies" from taking hold.

Children who are morose most of the time need special understanding and possibly a professional consultation. If your toddler's crankiness seems associated with symptoms of illness, check with her doctor (see page 568).

# OVERSTIMULATION

*"Our son gets completely wired whenever he's in a stimulating setting or situation. How can we calm him down?"*

Toddlers, still relatively new to (and unjaded by) the world around them, are often captivated by the sounds, sights, smells, and sensations that older children and adults might overlook or selectively tune out. In settings where these elements all demand their attention at once (the playground, a party, a department store, a museum), bombarding them with more stimuli than they can handle, their sensory circuits overload and, particularly if they are unusually sensitive to stimuli, they become "wired."

Ideally, parents should try to anticipate and prevent high-wire acts. Make sure your toddler has napped and has snacked nutritiously before attending a potentially stimulating event. And try not to line up high-energy events back to back (play group followed by a birthday party, for instance).

If your toddler still becomes overstimulated, don't try to talk him down from his sensory high; the one stimulus that keyed-up toddlers often *won't* tune in is the sound of a parent telling them to slow down. Instead:

▲ Remove him from the madding crowd. Temporarily transfer your toddler from the situation that's become overstimulating.

▲ Once out of the excitement, try relaxation techniques. Different techniques work on different children at different times—try any or all of these to settle your toddler: a great big hug, a gentle hug, a back or neck rub, putting his head in your lap and stroking his hair, singing a quiet song (particularly one with hypnotically repetitive words), reading a favorite story, giving him a glass of milk and a high-protein snack (see page 173 for more ideas).

▲ Once he's calm, try a little logic. Your toddler isn't likely to be able to concentrate on your reasoning when he's wired, but he might be able to once his circuits are clearer. Before returning him to the stimulating situation, ask him to do his best to slow down. But remember that's a lot to ask of someone his age; don't follow your request with threats or a list of demands.

▲ Be ready to repeat. If, on returning to the stimulating scene, your toddler again loses control, promptly remove him again. If he remains out-of-control after several time-outs, consider taking him home. With any luck, he'll get the message before you have to resort to this step.

# NOSE PICKING

*"Our daughter has recently started picking her nose, a habit I really can't stand. How do I get her to stop?"*

Nose picking ranks high on the list of children's habits that irritate parents. And, as with other irksome pursuits, such as thumb sucking and nail biting, parental attempts to nip nose picking in the bud usually succeed only in intensifying the child's passion for the practice.

Toddlers may pick their nose out of curiosity, to relieve stress, to pass the time when bored, or just out of sheer force of habit. But the most zealous nose-pickers are often children with nasal allergies; because of mucus and crusting, they experience a constant feeling of "something" in the nose, which leads them to attempt to get rid of the feeling by clearing their nostrils the only way they know how. (Of course, the discovery of a wonderfully sticky substance, fun to squish between the fingers, often prompts them to continue their excavations long after the discomfort has been relieved.)

Showing your displeasure by scolding, nagging, casting disgusted looks, and yanking your toddler's fingers from her nose will only give her another reason to pick: the satisfaction of defying you. It may also make her feel guilty and "bad" for doing something that's out of her control. Left to pick in peace, she'll eventually find other pursuits for her fingers, though the habit of public picking may continue off and on through the early school years—or at least until she starts to care more about appearances and social form.

In the meantime, it may be possible to reduce the behavior without showing your disapproval by offering her something else to do with her hands or distracting her with a hug or an activity that requires two hands. If her picking is vigorous enough to damage the lining of the nose, and bleeding and scabbing occur, explain to her that picking is causing "boo-boos" in her nose and that she should try to stop (this may or may not work). A visit to the doctor to give the same warning may be more effective. If allergy seems to be at the root of her problem, consultation with her doctor to discuss taking steps to treat the allergy may also be in order.

# DISTASTE FOR NEW FOODS

*"My son eats the same things day in and day out, and refuses to try anything even the slightest bit different. How can I get him to be more adventurous?"*

Even adults vary widely in gastronomic daring: There are those who will gobble down practically anything that isn't moving (and occasionally, a few things that still are) and those who stick stubbornly to their steak and potatoes and ham and eggs. Yet even the most finicky adults have made some strides at the table since toddlerhood. After all, how many grown-ups do you know who still subsist on peanut-butter-and-jelly sandwiches?

So, as hard as it is to believe now, the time will come when your child will expand his gustatory horizons, and begin to be more open to opening wide for new foods. Chances are, though, that the time will come more quickly if you follow the tips for feeding children with a limited dietary repertoire on page 522. And remember, too, that most toddlers are extremely resistant to change. Whether it's a new caregiver at day care, a new hairdo on Mommy, a new sofa in the living room, or a new food on his plate, they're liable to reject it just because it isn't what they're used to. Allow your toddler his inflexibility rather than trying to force him out of it, and he'll gradually become more adaptable. If your toddler is one who has more trouble than most accepting *anything* new (see page 524), introduce unfamiliar foods gradually; once he's seen a food every day for two weeks or so, it won't be as new to him any more and he may be ready to accept it.

Until your toddler becomes more gastronomically daring, don't worry. He won't starve. Most toddlers go through a picky eating stage at one time or another—some eating just a few foods exclusively, others seeming to eat practically nothing at all. But as long as they are presented with only healthy choices, they usually fare pretty well nutritionally. Even a toddler diet that includes nothing but whole-grain cereal, milk, banana, orange juice, peanut-butter-and-jelly on whole wheat, and cantaloupe or carrot sticks, can, with the addition of a vitamin supplement, fulfill the requirements of the Best-Odds Toddler Diet (see page 504).

# LACTOSE INTOLERANCE

*"Our son recently had a stomach virus. He's fine now, but he has started getting stomachaches after drinking his milk. He never had a problem with milk before and always drank lots of it. Could he have suddenly become allergic?"*

It's more likely that he's become intolerant—that is, lactose intolerant. After a bout with a gastrointestinal illness, many young children become temporarily deficient in the enzyme lactase needed to digest the milk sugar lactose. When these children drink milk or eat dairy products they experience such symptoms as bloating, gas, cramps, and diarrhea. (A milk allergic child, on the other hand, may experience eczema, diarrhea, constipation, asthma, runny nose, irritability, poor appetite, and fatigue; see page 15 for more on milk allergy.) Often, the discomfort can induce an avid milk drinker—like your child—to develop an aversion to the beverage.

Though an occasional child is born without the ability to digest lactose, it's rare for permanent lactose intolerance to develop in children under age four. So it's unlikely that your child's difficulties with milk will last more than a few weeks. In the meantime, check with the doctor about temporarily altering your child's diet to reduce the amount of lactose in it. Regular milk, ice cream, ice milk, and such soft cheeses as cottage cheese will probably be the most difficult for your toddler to handle. Switching to lactose-reduced milk (the calcium-fortified type will offer more calcium with less lactose) and cottage cheese may do the trick without taking a nutritional toll. Your child may also be able to tolerate small amounts of hard cheeses (such as Swiss and Cheddar) and yogurt with active cultures (particularly bulgaricus cultures).[4] Limiting dairy products to mealtimes (rather than serving them at snack) will make them easier to digest.

Lactase in tablet or liquid form may also be helpful. Ask your child's doctor about using the tablets (they can be mashed and added to a bit of applesauce or other soft food and eaten before your child consumes a dairy product) or liquids (which can be added to food or drink).

If your child seems not to be able to handle any dairy products at all, not even those that are lactose reduced, or if the discomfort continues even after you've removed dairy from his diet, or if it doesn't disappear entirely in several weeks, check with the doctor to see if there is another problem in the equation.

And remember that your child still needs the nutrients that milk provides. If he can't handle dairy at all, he may temporarily be able to get his calcium from a soy milk that is fortified with calcium (not all soy milk is) or from calcium-fortified orange juice. Be aware that "non-dairy" beverages are usually concoctions of fat and sugar and are *not* nutritious substitutes for milk. Discuss the options with his doctor so that together you can make certain that your toddler's diet isn't lacking in milk's other major nutrients, including protein, phosphorus, vitamin D, and riboflavin.

# MILK REJECTION

*"We never had a problem getting our daughter to drink milk, until now. She won't touch it. I'm afraid she won't get enough calcium without it."*

---

4. Some lactose-intolerant individuals find that certain brands of yogurt are easier for them to handle than others.

Milk is the most popular source of calcium in the American diet, but it's certainly not the only one. An 8-ounce glass of milk contains about 300 milligrams of calcium, but so does 1 ounce of hard cheese, ¼ cup of grated Parmesan cheese, 1 cup of yogurt, ⅓ cup of powdered milk, and ½ cup evaporated milk (the last two of which can be blended into a soup, a pudding, or a shake). There are even a wide variety of non-dairy calcium sources available, including green leafy vegetables, canned salmon and sardines (with the bones), and tofu coagulated with calcium (although, with the exception of the tofu, which is often well-accepted when cubed, breaded, baked or browned in a skillet, and served with a sauce, most nondairy sources of calcium are not popular with the typical toddler). A toddler who doesn't take any milk should probably also be taking a vitamin-mineral supplement that contains the toddler RDA for vitamin D.

So don't insist that your daughter drink her milk; without pressure now, milk may well become a favorite again in the future. Instead, experiment with several other calcium sources until you find some that she'll take without a fight.

Once in a while, a sudden aversion to milk is triggered by lactose intolerance—the child feels unwell after drinking milk, and not surprisingly takes a dislike to it; see the previous question.

# MILK SAFETY

*"I've heard that milk isn't a good food for anyone, children included. Is this true?"*

For those of us raised to refrains of "drink your milk or you won't get dessert!" and "drink your milk or you won't grow!" it seems unthinkable that milk might actually be bad for children. But that's precisely what a small contingent in the medical community has been telling an increasingly confused public. Their main arguments: Drinking milk is linked to diabetes in children, and to high blood cholesterol levels, cataracts, and ovarian cancer in adults.

Though these maligners of milk may be vocal enough to prompt a panic among the millions of parents who, like their parents before them, urge their own children to drain their milk glasses, the data this group has put forth to support their claims have not been convincing enough to alter mainstream medical opinion. While a small body of research has associated milk consumption in infancy with diabetes in children who have an inborn susceptibility to the disease, this work has not been replicated by others. Concern that milk contributes to cholesterol problems is also unwarranted, since children over the age of two can, and *should*, drink skim milk and eat mainly low-fat dairy products. Finally, the evidence for a link between milk and either cataracts or ovarian cancer—both diseases of adults—is lacking.

While the evidence against milk drinking is meager at most, the evidence *for* it is strong. Milk is a bountiful source of many essential nutrients, including calcium, protein, vitamin D, phosphorus, and riboflavin. It's pleasantly palatable (even those children who won't touch plain milk relish a shake; even those who won't drink a drop often eat it in the form of cheese) and far easier to get into a two-year-old than the substitutes milk opponents have proposed. Anyone who has tried to maneuver a few teaspoons of broccoli into the average tyke can only imagine what it would be like to try to maneuver in the 1½ to 2 cups of the green stuff it would take to equal the calcium in just 1 cup of milk. Besides which, these suggested substitutes, while rich in calcium and other nutrients, are lacking many of milk's other vitamins and minerals.

From all that's known, the only children who shouldn't be encouraged to drink their milk are those with a lactose intolerance (although these children can usually tolerate lactose-reduced milk) and those with a true milk allergy (fairly rare). Vegan parents who are philosophically opposed to eating all animal products (including dairy) and wish to raise milk-free children will need to provide essential nutrients in other ways; see the facing page. If you're concerned about the chemicals that might be contaminating the milk supply, see page 534.

But for most parents, the message is clear: milk's okay.

## TOTAL CONCENTRATION ON PLAY

*"Our son really concentrates on his play, which is great sometimes but annoying at other times, like when I need him to take a bath, or eat a meal, or go out, and I can't pull him away from what he's doing."*

Do you enjoy being interrupted in the middle of a good book? Or an engrossing TV movie? Or even a pile of pressing paperwork? Well, your toddler probably feels much the same about being interrupted in the middle of what he's doing. To someone completely absorbed in erecting a monumental block skyscraper, or caring for sick teddy bears, or lining up cars for an exciting race, disruptions ("Time for the tub!") can be irritating and intrusive. And unlike adults, who are generally able to put that book (or that movie, or those papers) on the back burner when obligations call, toddlers have a tough time separating from their interests and pursuits. Partly because they're not yet very good at making transitions and partly be-

cause they have not yet developed much self-discipline or a sense of time.

Since your toddler clearly has his own agenda—no less significant to him than yours is to you—you'll need to figure out how to deal with the inevitable conflicts:

▲ Give him fair warning. Descending on your busy toddler with demands that he stop for lunch or his bath "right now" is both unfair and destined for failure. Instead, start issuing periodic bulletins so that he has time to adjust: *First,* "It's almost time to stop for lunch." *Then,* "In five minutes, your spaghetti will be ready." (Setting a timer at this point will make the time frame more tangible.) *And, finally,* "Okay, time to eat."

▲ Let him finish what he's started. If you haven't given fair warning, and it's possible to wait a few minutes, let your toddler put the finishing touches on that skyscraper, wrap up that race, complete that puzzle. Offer to help him, if he'd like. Show respect for your toddler's agenda and he will be more likely to cooperate with yours. Again, use a timer to set a tangible time limit.

▲ Combine agendas, when feasible, so your toddler won't have to switch gears entirely. Suggest, for example, that he bring his cars into the bath with him, so he can scrub them down while you scrub him down. (This will only be feasible if the toys are waterproof; those that aren't can "watch" from the bathroom vanity.) Or have him put his blocks or sick teddies to bed before he's tucked in. Or, assuming it's portable, let him take what he's playing with, or a part of it, along for the ride to the market.

▲ Make the transition together. The change from one activity to another will be less jarring if you ease into it together. To do this, first get involved—at least, as a spectator—in your toddler's activity. Watch the race, and cheer on your favorite car. Check that flu-ridden teddy's temperature. Begin constructing a tower down the street from his sky-scraper. Then, when it's time to stop, you can quit together. You can even grumble a bit, "I wish we didn't have to stop now, we're having so much fun. But it's time for lunch."

▲ Be patient to a point. If you gave your toddler fair warning, tried easing him through a transition, and he still won't budge, calmly but firmly let him know that the time has come to stop what he's doing and start doing what you've asked. If necessary, physically move him from where he is to where you want him to be.

▲ Once in a while, when it's reasonable, bend *your* agenda. If your toddler's completely immersed in an activity and a planned trip to the market can be postponed, consider postponing it. If lunch can be rewarmed, let it wait until he's done. Then hope that some of your flexibility will rub off on him.

# REFUSAL TO TAKE TIME FOR MEALS

*"Our toddler is always too busy to sit still for meals. And when we force her to sit down with us, she tries to get up again within a few minutes."*

Forget salami and eggs, pizza with the works, a chili dog at the corner snack bar. Nothing brings on indigestion faster than mealtime with an active toddler. You beg, you plead, you nag, you scold to get her seated at the table, and no sooner do you succeed, than she's wriggling out of her seat. The scene plays itself out again and again. She's up, she's down. She's up, she's down. By the time she's had a few perfunctory bites, the food is cold and your stomach is churning.

If this mealtime scenario appears hopeless, that's only because, for the moment, it probably is. Given most toddlers' low tolerance for long stretches of sitting, expecting your child to sit down—and stay down—for meals with the family is unrealistic. Demanding it is likely to turn the table into a combat zone. And though an occasional skirmish may be won, chances are victory will be at the expense of everyone's enjoyment and digestive comfort.

Instead, take steps to make family mealtime more appealing to and more pleasant for your toddler:

▲ Consider a seating change. Whatever her present seat, changing it may help (see page 149).

▲ Keep the conversation flowing in her direction. Adult talk can be boring to a toddler and leave her feeling left out, so postpone it until she's left the table. Hold her attention (and her presence) with toddler-engaging conversation. (But stay off the subject of her eating—or not eating.) When conversation stalls, try a word game, such as "What Do You See?" (Everyone at the table takes turns pointing to and naming something they see.)

▲ Nix the nagging. Don't nag about your toddler's eating or her unwillingness to stay seated.

▲ Allow her to eat and run. When she's finished with her meal, let her leave the table. (But don't allow her to leave the table with food. Done separately, eating and running are fine; eating *while* running is unsafe.)

▲ Save your dinner until later. Sometimes, the problem isn't with the toddler, it's with the dinner hour. Toddlers get hungry a lot earlier than adults do. So try feeding yours earlier, and keeping her company while she eats (munch on some vegetables and dip to take the edge off) so she doesn't feel she's eating alone. Then wait until she's busy playing, or better still, in bed, before you turn to the adult dinner. Your food will stay hotter, your stomach calmer, and as an additional bonus, you'll have the chance to dine—and unwind.

▲ If she skips meals or eats very little of them, make sure she's getting snacks in between. But don't overdo it: Snacks too close to mealtime can sabotage appetite, leaving very little chance for improving dinner table decorum.

## THE "GIMMES"

*"Lately, every time we go into a store my son starts whining for me to buy him something. I don't think we spoil him, but he's certainly got a terrible case of the 'gimmes'."*

You can't always get what you want—but that doesn't keep most toddlers from trying. While the "gimmes" are not universal among toddlers, they are very common. Like the pack-rat syndrome, they seem to stem from the need to accumulate possessions in order to bolster self-importance.

Whether these narcissistic impulses ("I want it, I'm worth it, I should have it"), will run their normal course in toddlerhood or develop into an unhealthy greediness and preoccupation with material possessions and the mistaken belief that happiness comes from these rather than from within, will depend in large part on how they are handled now. The following may help you raise a child who can keep possessions in perspective:

▲ Recognize that you can't buy love. Buying whatever your toddler wants will not win any additional affection in the long run, but it can breed greed. Nor can gifts replace other kinds of attention. The children who feel most loved (and are the happiest) aren't the ones who receive the most gifts, but the ones who receive

the most attention and respect. Give warm hugs, not "cool" presents, to show that you care.

▲ Don't give in to the "gimmes." You won't make your toddler happier by buying him everything he asks for. In fact, if the gifts are standing in for your time and attention, you may achieve just the opposite effect. Even young children know, deep down, when they're being bought.

▲ Don't feel guilty about not giving in. Even though he may complain and call you "mean," you're doing what's best for your toddler—preparing him for the real world, where none of us gets everything we want. You're also helping to preserve the excitement of "special" occasions. If every day is gift day, pretty soon kids start expecting can-you-top-this gift giving binges on birthdays and holidays, and never truly appreciate any gift they get.

▲ Make an effort to teach your child the joy of giving, so that he will learn to associate gifts with giving as well as receiving (see page 212).

▲ Limit his opportunities. When possible, shop when he's in preschool, at a play date, or when he's with your spouse, another adult, or a sitter. When you have to take him along, try to do so when he's not tired, hungry, overstimulated, cranky. Explain before you go into a store that you're going in for shoes, or mittens, or a new toaster, and that's all you'll have time to look at. Don't say you're not buying toys, because on the outside chance he hasn't thought of it, you'll be putting ideas in his head. And keep him occupied by allowing him to help with the project at hand.

▲ Don't give in to a "gimme" tantrum; treat it as you would treat any other show of temper (see page 339).

▲ Once in a while, buy a "little something" that's truly a surprise, and that hasn't been asked for.

## TALKING TO YOUR TODDLER AT TWO

• • • • • • • • • •

All those months of one-sided conversations have paid off. By their second birthdays, most toddlers are talking back to their parents. How much they're talking back depends on the toddler. The average two-year-old has a verbal repertoire of about 200 words, but that's an average that takes into account those who have acquired just a couple of dozen and those who have mastered 500 or more. Some two-year-olds have been combining words to form sophisticated sentences for months, others are just beginning to link theirs into simple phrases. Verbal ability usually burgeons in the third year, with those who were lagging behind often starting to catch up to those who were racing ahead, and with vocabularies multiplying at mind-spinning speed; by the third birthday, the average toddler has 1,000 words to call upon.

At this age, as earlier, talking to your toddler is the best way to get your toddler talking. Though most parents naturally do a pretty good job of promoting their toddler's verbal progress, these suggestions can further foster conversation:

**Put words in your toddler's mouth.** Build on what your toddler says, and your toddler will soon be saying more. When he or she offers, "That building big," add, "It's a big building and it's a tall building. Look how high up into the sky it reaches."

**Be specific.** State your observations as clearly as possible. When you want to show your toddler a cat that's scampering up a tree, don't just say, "Look!" Say "Look! I see a white cat running up that big tree. Maybe he's chasing a bird."

**Get descriptive.** Color your toddler's world with adjectives. Don't just say, "There's a dog." Say, "There's a little brown dog with shaggy fur. He's wearing a pretty red collar."

**Get a little more complicated.** While it was wise to keep your sentences as simple as possible when your toddler was younger, it's time now to start challenging him or her to sort out the meanings of more complex sentences ("We're going to the park with Annie's brother Nelson"), two- or three-part directions ("Please pick up that teddy bear and put it on your bed with the others"), irregular verbs ("When we *went* to the shoe store . . ."), and pronouns. But continue to speak distinctly and audibly, and be prepared to repeat what your toddler doesn't follow the first time around.

**Carry on with the conversations.** Even if your toddler's not using sentences yet, he or she can follow, add to, and eventually, participate fully in conversations with you. Make a point of discussing events that have just taken place, that are currently taking place, or that are going to take place. On the way home from the playground, talk about the adventure: "Remember the sand castle you made in the sandbox?" . . . "That was a pretty blue bird you saw having a bath in a

## WHIMS

• • • • • • • • • • • • • • • • • • • • • • • • • • •

*"Our daughter gets these sudden whims—she wants a puppy, when we don't have room for one in our apartment, or she wants to go to the beach, when it's snowing out. When she doesn't get what she wants, she has a major tantrum."*

Young children are ruled by whim, and not by reason. When an impulse crosses their minds, they don't analyze it for practicality before putting in their demand. And though this is undoubtedly part of their charm, for parents it also presents a challenge.

Not only does a toddler get mad when she doesn't get her way, she often gets even, exploding in a fiery tantrum

puddle." At lunch, talk about the fun your toddler had at that morning's play date, and the nature collage you're going to make together in the afternoon. While waiting for the bus, talk about the people in the cars, where they come from and where they're going. Though your toddler's contributions may be limited to one or two words at first, you'll find it won't be long before he or she is holding up the other end of the conversation.

**Keep asking.** Asking your toddler questions remains a very effective way of building verbal skills. Ask questions that challenge (but don't frustrate) your toddler's vocabulary, rather than ones that require only a "yes" or "no" answer: "What do you think that squirrel is doing?" or "Why do you think that baby is laughing?"

**Keep reading.** Reading teaches a toddler a great deal about language—and it's fun, too. See page 101.

**Play word games.** It's too soon for Scrabble, but it's just the right time for playing "What's That?" The rules are simple: While you're reading a picture book, stop periodically and challenge your toddler to identify specific objects on the page you're reading.* When your toddler gets stuck or gives an incorrect response, offer assistance, not criticism ("That animal is a zebra. It has four feet and a tail just like a horse, but it has black stripes—see?") Or play "What's She Doing?"

_____

*Don't stop so often that you break the flow of the story.

What is the baby in the cradle doing? Or the dog with a bone? Or try "What happens next?"—encourage your toddler to guess where the plot's heading before you turn the page. (If your toddler's stumped, offer a few suggestions: "Do you think the train will make it up the mountain? Or do you think the train will get tired and stop?") Another game that will get your toddler talking is the "In/Out, Up/Down, On/Under" game— in which players use a small toy and a shoe box or carton to demonstrate in-out-up-down-on-under and call out the toy's location. ("The ball was _on_ the box. Now it's _under_ the box.")

**Introduce the ABC's . . .** So that the alphabet won't be a stranger when the process of learning to read begins, and to help pronunciation, sing the alphabet song, read alphabet picture books (start with those that use words your toddler knows; "A is for apple" is better at this age than "A is for antelope"), put your toddler's name up on his or her door and begin looking together for other words that begin with the same letter ("M is for Max, but it's also for Mommy, and merry-go-round, and milk.") But don't be an alphabet-pusher. Let your toddler's own interest (or lack of it) in letters be your guide.

**. . . but hold off on the grammar lessons.** Your toddler will learn lots more about proper grammar from hearing your speech than from having his or hers critiqued. Follow the rules yourself, but don't impose them on your toddler. For now, just let the words flow naturally—mistakes and all.

or resorting to relentless whining—either of which will have you wondering whether refusing her request was really the right way to go.

But, most of the time, it is. A toddler's whims are often not only impractical but not in her best interest, and they will be forgotten in time. Meanwhile, here are some suggested ways to deal with them:

**Weigh the whim.** Some whims are harmless enough—as when your toddler wants to wear boots on a sunny day in July—and aren't worth the effort to deny them or the insult to her ego. Some are unacceptable—as when your toddler wants to don sandals to play in the snow.

**Give in occasionally.** When the whim is harmless (boots in July), acquiesce.

Giving in to an occasional eccentric request will spare you many unnecessary battles, and it will make your toddler feel she has some control of her life. (And when her feet get sweaty and she demands, "boots off," resist, "I told you so." Let her recognize the error of her ways on her own.)

**Say "no" when you must**. When the advisability of giving in to your toddler's whim is clearly outweighed by solid reason (as when she wants to wear sandals in the snow), don't hesitate to turn her down. But explain your reasons. Most adults are subject to wacky whims occasionally, but we usually know when and where to draw the line. Drawing it for

your child now will help her draw it herself later in life.

**Use distraction early on.** To head off a tantrum response to your refusal, immediately provide a diverting alternative to your toddler's wacky wish: "No, you can't have a puppy, but we can go down to the pet store and visit the puppies for a while" . . . "No, we can't go to the beach now, but we can pretend we're there. Let's spread a blanket on the floor, and put on our bathing suits, get out the beach ball, and have a picnic in the living room." If a tantrum's inevitable, however, don't let it change your mind. Instead, let it run its course. (See tips on page 339 for dealing with tantrums.)

# WHAT IT'S IMPORTANT TO KNOW:
## Encouraging Creativity and Imagination

## CREATIVITY

Not every child is born to be a Michelangelo or a Georgia O'Keefe, a Mozart or a Louis Armstrong, an Ernest Hemingway or a Jane Austen, a Madame Curie or a Jonas Salk, a Julia Child or an I.M. Pei. But nearly every child is born with the ability, and the desire, to be creative.

Nurturing that ability and cultivating that desire won't guarantee that your progeny will be prodigies, but it will improve the odds that they'll grow up to fulfill their creative potential—whatever it may be.

So whatever the career in your child's future (artist, banker, author, physician, poet, carpenter, composer, politician, teacher, scientist, ballet dancer) encouraging creativity now will help him or her have a much richer and

more satisfying life. Try these tips, but feel free to be creative yourself and devise your own ways of fostering creativity:

**Let there be mess.** Creative spirits should be free to focus on creating—not distracted by the need to keep their workplace in order. When it comes to toddlers, this is especially true. For them, the medium isn't just the message, but usually the mess, too. Insisting that all the crayons stay in the box, that the clay stay in a contained clump, and fingers, arms, and floor stay immaculate, is asking the impossible. Even in toddlers destined for artistic greatness, fine motor skills are still far from fine tuned. Inherent in any creative effort is a backsplash of splashed paint, scattered clay, smeary globs of glue, spattered flour. Resign yourself to a mess during creative play, and don't let the anticipation prompt you to discourage your child from getting involved in the creative process. Stifling your toddler's urges now in the name of a cleaner house could lead your child to stifle them permanently.

Which isn't to say that a clean home and a creative child are completely incompatible. Taking the proper precautions before your toddler takes to the easel or to the drawing board or to the kitchen counter, will protect both your home and your toddler's wardrobe without interfering with the urge to create. Use an outdoor setting when weather permits—a backyard picnic table (protected by newspaper or an old tablecloth), for example. Indoors, set up, if possible, in an area that has a sink nearby for easy clean-up. Cover the floor and any other assailable surfaces with newspaper (you can recycle it later) or a reusable painters' dropcloth or plastic tarp. Indoors or out, have the *artiste* roll up sleeves and don a large smock or apron. If this idea meets with resistance, let your toddler create in old clothes or, during warm weather or indoors, in just a diaper or underwear.

Now is also a good time to start teaching that clean-up is a part of the artistic process. Arm your toddler with a rag and a spray bottle of water, and ask for help when the creative session is over. Also ask for his or her cooperation in putting all the supplies back where they belong.

**Let freedom reign.** Keep in mind that creativity requires breaking new ground, which means breaking old rules; there's no wrong way to paint a picture, shape a piece of clay, build a structure out of blocks. Hovering over your toddler, directing and suggesting, can inhibit creativity. It's okay to occasionally inquire about a work in progress or make a favorable comment. But offer suggestions only when help is requested. Your child may follow them just to please you—but

may then feel the product is no longer his or her own.

Of course, don't deny assistance when it's asked for or if your child is frustrated simply because you think children should figure things out on their own. And never push your toddler to try or continue an activity he or she doesn't enjoy.

**Don't be a critic.** The process and product need only be pleasing to your toddler, not to you—or to anyone else. Don't say, when he's making a "card" for Grandma, "maybe Grandma won't like those colors." Or when she combines a pink shirt and a red skirt, "That combination doesn't match." Doing what's different is, after all, what creativity is all about. (And don't worry about your toddler developing good taste—that will come with time and your good example rather than through imposing your judgment on your offspring.)

If your toddler is unhappy with a particular creation, show respect for that judgment rather than saying, "Oh, you're wrong, honey—that's great!" Point out some specifics you really think are good ("You made some nice straight lines there"), make some suggestions for improvement ("If you roll the clay between your hands, like this, you'll be able to roll legs for that horse you're making"). And encourage, but don't insist on, another attempt.

**Look past the scribbles.** Find something to compliment in each of your toddler's creative works. Even if the drawing paper's a mass of scribbles, praise the use of colors or space. Even if the toy-horn concert is more cacophony than symphony, praise the lively rhythm and the bouncy beat, or how well your toddler elicits sound from the instrument. But don't be so effusive with your praise that your toddler doubts your sincerity or stops trying to do better.

## COPY CAT

**·········**

Children display the ability to imitate almost from birth; imitation is one of the ways they learn. So while it's important to give them the freedom to be creative, it's also necessary to give them the opportunity to imitate so that they can master basic skills. Show your toddler how to hold a crayon, or pencil, or paintbrush correctly—but if he or she prefers another hold, leave it at that. Once in a while, when the two of you are drawing together, draw a straight line or a circle on your paper, and say, "Can you make that?" When it's time to play with clay, demonstrate rolling the clay to make a string or a ball. When baking cookies, show how to use a cookie cutter. But, never force your toddler to reproduce what you demonstrate, and always allow him or her to do something quite different, if the spirit so moves.

**Become a serious collector.** Enhance your toddler's feeling of accomplishment by hanging pictures and collages around your home—on the refrigerator (with magnets), in the playroom, on his or her bedroom door, on your bedroom mirror, by your night stand. Make a "portfolio" of favorites that he or she can enjoy flipping through or show to visitors. If you work outside the home, periodically take a drawing to work with you and give it a place of honor on your desk, or commission a wallet-size masterpiece to carry around with you. (Taking your toddler's pictures with you when you go to work, or to a meeting, or to see a friend will not only keep you connected during the day, but make it easier for your toddler to separate when you leave.) Give play clay creations positions of prominence on the coffee table, the dining table, or a display shelf. If music rings your toddler's creative bell, make video or audio tapes of his or her musical works, or hold impromptu performances in the living room—and don't forget to be an attentive and appreciative audience. (But never coerce any toddler into performing for you or others.)

**Tell tales.** Make storytelling a family tradition. Instead of relying on books off the shelf at story time, try spinning a few yarns of your own. Your toddler may especially appreciate it if your stories incorporate the same characters each time, and/or if each story begins where the last one left off. As your toddler becomes familiar with the process, he or she may enjoy helping you develop your stories. Offer encouragement by asking, "What do you think should happen next?" or "How can we save Jo-Jo?" If that's too challenging, offer two plot lines and ask your toddler to choose one. Eventually he or she may want to contribute and even create entire stories. Another way to practice the creative process: Leave off the ending of a story, and ask your toddler to offer one (if he or she is willing.)

**Parody old standards.** It's fun to sing songs that everyone knows, but it's also fun to occasionally change them. Collaborate with your toddler to create silly rhymes that fit some of the songs he or she especially enjoys.

**Set a creative example.** You don't have to take up oil painting if your drawing skills stopped developing at stick figures, or start composing sonatas if you can't hum your way through "Twinkle, Twinkle, Little Star." But do look for outlets for your creativity that are within your capabilities—whether that means arranging flowers, leaves, and gourds in an autumnal centerpiece, adding unexpected splashes of color and combinations of patterns to your everyday wardrobe, or making your own party decorations instead of buying out the local party store. You'll be making a creative impression on your toddler.

**Expose your toddler . . .** Early and frequent exposure to the arts will not only stimulate appreciation but application. Go to museums and galleries and view many different types of art (painting, sculpture, collage, and so on). But keep visits brief, to suit a toddler's short attention span, and always call it quits as soon as yours has had enough. Spend time reading well-written and illustrated age appropriate books, to expose your toddler to fine prose, poetry, and art. Attend children's concerts when your toddler seems old enough to sit still; listen to a wide variety of music at home (gospel, jazz, blues, rock, country, and classical, in addition to the usual kids' tapes).

Point out the beauty in the world around you. Creative inspiration is lurking in a vibrant autumn treescape, in a spring flowerbed, in a fruit bowl you've set out for company, in the pattern that a lacy curtain casts in the sunlight, in the dazzling rainbow in a puddle of oil on wet asphalt.

**. . . but don't overexpose.** Too much pressure to appreciate art, music, beauty, and so on ("These paintings are such classics—and you're not even looking at them!") can also turn a toddler off.

**Look beyond the arts.** There are dozens of outlets for your toddler's creative energy that have nothing to do with the fine arts. Your child can be creative in the sandbox (as a budding scientist, architect, engineer), at the kitchen counter (where mundane ingredients can be combined to produce an extraordinary treat),

*Playing dress-up allows a toddler to wear a wide range of different hats—literally, and figuratively.*

even in the closet (many toddlers have a fashion designer in them itching to get out). Encourage creativity in all areas of your toddler's life.

## IMAGINATION

What can make an ordinary broomstick into a galloping stallion? A handful of sticks, stones, and cut grass into a simmering pot of soup? A basket-

## GETTING CREATIVE WITH TECHNIQUES

· · · · · · · · · ·

Toddler art may begin with crayons, finger-paints, and clay, but there are countless other materials and techniques your toddler can explore. Try the following, then create a few of your own.

**Crayons.** For some two-year-olds, chunky crayons are still the easiest to grasp and manipulate, but many prefer the standard "thin" crayon. Taping down the drawing paper still helps to minimize frustration, but you can also use an easel. If you're using a roll of newsprint for drawing paper, you can tape a large sheet of it to the kitchen table and have your toddler create a mural, which you can then hang on the bedroom wall.

**Finger painting.** This old nursery school standby is a favorite with toddlers who derive tactile pleasure from squishing their fingers through gooey paints. Some toddlers, however, resist finger painting because they dislike the messy feeling of paint on their fingers. Don't push it. Another, cleaner option: "finger painting" with shaving cream or a foam soap in the tub (but supervise so

the artist doesn't rub the cream in his or her eyes.)

**Play clay.** Squeeze it, roll it, pull it, shape it make imprints in it with various objects— nontoxic, colorful clay is great fun for toddlers. You can buy it or make your own.* (Toddlers are not yet ready for real modeling clay.)

**Brush painting.** In the third year, many toddlers enjoy painting with a paintbrush and tempera paints. A brush with a thick handle is easier to hold than a slender one, and yields a bolder, more satisfying stroke. If you buy large jars of paint, pour small amounts of each color into small, unbreakable containers that your toddler can dip the

---

*To make a batch of play clay, combine in a pot, 2 cups flour, 1 cup salt, 2 tablespoons cream of tartar, 1 tablespoon vegetable oil, and 2 cups water. Blend well, then stir over medium heat until the mixture thickens. Cool, knead out any lumps, and let your toddler enjoy. Store play clay in an airtight container.

---

ful of ordinary wooden blocks into a bustling city?

Imagination—that fertile force within that enables a young child to be as resourceful as an engineer, as inventive as a scientist, as visionary as an architect, as innovative as a designer, as fanciful as a poet, as caring as a parent.

Historically, the greatest achievers have been the greatest dreamers. But there are many other reasons for nurturing a toddler's imagination: *To end boredom.* Children who learn at an early age to use their imaginations are less likely to always be at a loss for something to do. With even the slimmest of pickings for props, they can create scenario after scenario for pretend or fantasy play. A sailor's hat can transform a bedroom into the open sea, teddy bears into shipmates;

a toy stethoscope can turn the living room into a doctor's office, a bucking-bronco broom can change the kitchen into a wild-west ranch; a baby doll can convert the playroom into a house and toddlers into busy parents. *To promote verbal skills.* Even before speech is intelligible to others, children use it to advance the plots of their fantasy play. Many toddlers "talk" to their toys long before they are ready to test their verbal skills on their parents or peers. *To strengthen social skills.* As toddlers interact with stuffed animals, dolls, and other toys, they gain experience that will serve them well in their interactions with peers. *To improve problem solving.* With their minds constantly challenged during pretend play (what happens next?), children learn to think on their feet and be-

brush into. To minimize spills, cut a hole the size of each paint container in a thick sponge, then place the container in the hole. An upright easel, with a place for the paints, makes painting easier and less messy.

For an intriguing mirror image effect, have your toddler paint just one side of a piece of paper (fold the other side under so paint won't stray). When the work is done and while the paint's still wet, fold the blank side of the page over the painted side and press down.

**Sponge painting.** Sponges that come in animal shapes or ordinary kitchen sponges that you can cut into fanciful shapes, dipped in a bit of tempera paint and pressed onto paper, make an interesting medium that's easy for little fingers to manage. You can also turn a piece of sponge into a "paintbrush" by attaching a clothespin to one end. Other interesting alternatives to paintbrushes: cotton swabs, feathers, old toothbrushes, or nail brushes.

**String painting.** Take several strings of different widths and have your toddler dip them in paint, then drag them across a large sheet of paper.

**Water painting.** For outdoor artistic fun, give your toddler a bucket of plain water and a big brush to use to "paint" the sidewalk, the driveway, even the house.

**Vegetable printing.** Cut root vegetables into chunks your toddler can dip into tempera paint, then press against paper, making interesting prints. This may appeal to older toddlers more than young ones.

**Rubber stamping.** Store-bought rubber stamps in animal and alphabet shapes are fun for older toddlers—but be sure this activity is well supervised, or you may find your entire home "decorated."

**Rubbings.** Place a piece of white paper over an object that has an interesting texture—a piece of bark, for instance. Then have your toddler rub a crayon back and forth firmly on the paper for a fascinating effect.

**Chalk.** Chunky pieces of chalk in bright colors are irresistible to most toddlers. A combination chalkboard-easel enables a child to paint on one side and use chalk on the other. If you don't have a chalkboard, let your tod-

*(continued on next page)*

come better problem solvers. *To provide a taste of the adult world.* By allowing toddlers to experience almost any role, to explore any field (from parent to pilot, from mail carrier to movie star), imaginative play gives children a well-rounded foundation for the future. *Possibly, to reduce violent tendencies.* Studies show that children who are involved in imaginary play tend to be less violent—though it isn't clear whether this is because they watch less TV (which they do) or whether there are other factors at work here. *To deal with fears and problems.* Children can play out their worries in fantasy play—a child afraid of dogs can play with a stuffed one, for example.

While imagination comes naturally to toddlers, a little parental stimulation

can help to fertilize it. To motivate your toddler to use imagination:

▲ Value achievements of the imagination as much as achievements of the intellect. When your toddler hosts an elaborate birthday party for a stuffed giraffe, offer as much enthusiastic appreciation as you would if he or she had learned some letters of the alphabet.

▲ Stay on the sidelines—most of the time. Hovering while your toddler plays can be inhibiting to his or her imagination. So can interrupting the play frequently to ask questions about it or make suggestions. But asking for an occasional drink of "tea" or dish of a favorite "ice cream" flavor, feigning an ailment that requires your good "doctor's" expertise, offering your tresses for a beauty-shop

*(continued from previous page)*

dler create chalk murals on the sidewalk, front step, or on asphalt at the park. Chalk can also be used on construction paper; black paper holds chalk well and your toddler may be thrilled at finding that something finally "shows" on a black background.

**Pencils, pens, and markers.** Part of the appeal of these implements to toddlers is that their parents and older siblings use them. But since pencils can poke eyes and other vulnerable areas, and inks can be tough to wash off should your toddler spontaneously decide to do some body painting, these should be used only under careful supervision. To reduce potential damage, buy only nontoxic, washable markers (again, the thick ones are easier for a toddler to grip), and don't leave any of these tempting implements within your toddler's reach.

**Coloring books.** Traditional coloring books are not recommended for regular use by toddlers. First of all, they do not tend to encourage creativity, except in the use of color. And secondly, though some toddlers enjoy "coloring," others are exasperated by their inability to stay within the lines. For older children, look for the more creative variety of coloring book, such as those that challenge readers to draw a part of the picture. When your toddler does use a coloring book, don't set standards, such as staying in the lines or using conventional colors. Allow and encourage creative freedom.

**Book making.** If children are old enough to scribble, they're old enough to become authors. So fold a few sheets of paper in half, and staple them together to make a book. Add a construction-paper "cover." Then let your toddler illustrate it. You can even offer to write words, dictated by your young author, to go with the pictures. Books can also be filled with a toddler's favorite photos, or with cut-outs from old magazines.

**Cylinder pictures.** Take any drawing your toddler's done, and roll it into a cylinder, taping the two ends together where they meet. Your toddler may enjoy the new perspective this shape gives to his or her art. Of course, if you get objections to the rolling, drop the idea.

**Collages.** With this medium, anything goes. Bits of fabric, feathers, macaroni, beans, seeds, beads and buttons, magazine pictures—just

do, or simply participating in any play when invited will provide enormous satisfaction to your toddler.

▲ Let your toddler's imagination guide the game. As tempting as it might be to fuel your child's play with your ideas, resist. It's important for children to propel their games along with their own ideas, even if those ideas are not as sophisticated as yours. Not only does parental interference prevent children from thinking for themselves, but it can frustrate them if it changes the course of the play.

▲ Occasionally, team your imaginations. Although it's usually best *not* to interfere when a toddler's playing well by him or herself, don't hesitate to suggest joining imaginative forces when your child seems receptive. Be a big train and a little caboose, a grown cat and a baby kitten, a horse and a rider, a doctor and a patient. Play house, farm, hospital, Dumbo, Pinocchio, or whatever—but always let your toddler decide the course you take.

▲ Supply the props. Though imagination comes from within the mind, it may be stimulated from without. Select toys and playthings from the lists on pages 56 and 330, and the above box, that begins on page 366.

*One caution:* Children who consistently live in a fantasy world or who reenact the same fantasy over and over to the exclusion of other play may need some help. Consult your child's doctor about this "imaginary" problem.

about any lightweight household material* can be glued (with supervision and nontoxic washable glue) onto a sturdy piece of construction paper, oaktag, or cardboard to form a collage. A trip to the park can yield innumerable materials for a nature collage: leaves, acorns, small pine cones, twigs, small stones, sand. Large pine cones and rocks, though too heavy for collage use, can be painted or otherwise decorated and/or become a base for a collage. With household discards (cardboard tubes from paper towels and toilet tissue, empty spools, corks, empty matchboxes) glued vertically onto a piece of cardboard or other sturdy base, your child can build a surrealistic city. When the glue is dry, turn your toddler loose with the tempera to paint the town red (or any other favorite colors).

*A note on glue use.* Small children are skilled at overdoing the glue—using so much that their work takes days to dry. Don't spoil the fun by taking over the gluing process; there'll be less mess, but also less learning. You may, however, discourage some of the glue abuse by providing squeeze bottles of glue, paper cups or jars filled with just a little glue (which can be applied with a cotton swab or popsicle stick), jars of paste

that come with an applicator, or a glue stick (probably the least messy).

**Scissors.** Most toddlers don't have the coordination required to use scissors, but many older toddlers like to practice with them anyway. Provide small blunt-edged scissors with cushioned handles, and supervise their use carefully.

**A notebook.** Provide your toddler with an unlined, spiral-bound notebook to scribble in to his or her heart's content—most young artists derive enormous satisfaction from filling the pages. A notebook is easy to tuck into your tote bag, and the end result is easier to save as a memento than a sheaf of loose pages.

**Food.** Let your child's plate be his or her palette. Under your supervision, have your toddler design miniature pizza faces, pancake faces with raisins and banana slices, a landscape with raw vegetables and dips, or create a cottage cheese sundae surrounded by a colorful montage of fruits.

---

*Avoid any objects that might present a choking hazard if your toddler still mouths things (see page 656).

# WHAT IT'S IMPORTANT FOR YOUR TODDLER TO KNOW: What's a Mommy? A Daddy? Sorting Through Gender Roles

A couple of generations ago, gender roles were as clearly defined in most homes as they were on *Father Knows Best* and *Leave It to Beaver.* There were mothers, who wore aprons, wielded a dust cloth and a vacuum cleaner (sometimes simultaneously), and made sure their families had full stomachs and matching socks. And there were fathers, who wore suits and ties or overalls, carried a briefcase or toolbox, and made sure their families had roofs

over their heads and enough bacon for Mom to cook up with the eggs every morning.

Today, the picture's not as clear. On television, and in homes, traditional roles are no longer the norm. They've given way to a potpourri of different, but acceptable, scenarios: Mom works at home, Dad works outside the home; Dad works at home, Mom works outside the home; Mom and Dad both work at home; Mom and Dad both work outside the home; or, in a great many cases, Mom and Dad don't live in the same home, Dad's not in the picture at all, or there are two moms (or dads) instead of a mom and a dad.

Yet, although many of the stereotypes that were popular in the sitcoms of the fifties and sixties have been shattered, the remnants linger in many homes. While Mom may work as many hours as Dad outside of the home, she may still do the Mrs.-Cleaver's-share of the housework. While both parents may have limited leisure time outside of work, Mom may spend more of it cooking, doing laundry and dishes, driving, and providing child care. And if she's a single mom, she may have no time to herself at all.

To be sure, there are homes where gender roles have been completely overhauled with equality in mind—where fathers spend just as much of their free time changing diapers, reading bedtime stories, loading the washing machine, and cleaning the toilet as mothers do, regardless of who works outside the home. But even if you've come a long way, Mom and Dad—and especially if you haven't come quite as far as you feel you should—passing on an egalitarian view of gender roles to your children still poses quite a challenge. To meet this challenge, take some very specific steps:

**Set an equal example.** Making a conscious effort to divide housework and parenting equitably (taking into account what each partner does best) will leave a lasting impression on your child. But in your attempt to raise your child without gender-based stereotypes, be careful not to try and erase in his or her mind the differences between the sexes. Men and women *are* different—in many wonderful ways—and that's to be celebrated.

**Nurture nurturing.** You don't have to be a mommy to offer a shoulder to cry on or a lap to snuggle in—any more than you have to be a daddy to roughhouse or teach kickball. And you don't have to be a little girl to enjoy a good cry or a snuggle, either. Encourage sons as well as daughters to hold the bottle for the baby or offer a toy to a tearful playmate. Children who grow up seeing that both men and women are nurturing have a far better chance of becoming nurturing parents themselves—whether they're girls or boys. Allowing little boys to express their feelings, rather than urging them to "tough it out," will help them to grow into caring, sensitive men—and caring, sensitive spouses and fathers (see page 224).

**Praise courage and strength.** Cheer girls and boys equally when they get to the top of the monkey bars, catch a ball, or go on the merry-go-round. Don't hesitate to play rough with your little girl, as long as she enjoys it. By the same token, avoid such play with a little boy, if he doesn't.

**Take the gender taboos out of toys.** No toy should be considered inappropriate because of traditional sexual stereotypes; girls who want to play with balls, blocks, and trucks should be allowed do so, as should boys who want to play "house" with dolls or teddies. At the same time, don't push a toy on a child (or deny a toy) in an effort to break traditional sexual stereotypes. Boys who favor trucks shouldn't be coerced into playing with dolls; girls who favor dolls shouldn't be pressured to play with trucks (see page 221).

**Look for equality in books.** Try to find storybooks in which both men and women are doctors, engineers, scientists, teachers, and construction workers, and in which daddies and mommies participate fully in parenting and household work. But don't be too zealous about screening stories for sexual stereotypes; your child stands to lose out on some of the world's greatest literature if you do.

**Open your toddler's options.** Help your toddler to grow up feeling there's nothing he or she can't do—that everyone can aspire to the vocation of their dreams. Let them know, too, that being a doctor or a firefighter or an architect doesn't preclude being a parent.

If you're a woman raising a toddler on your own, providing positive male role models will obviously be more difficult. Besides looking for fictional examples of nurturing males in the books you read together, it's also a good idea to try to find a real, live, loving, and caring male role model for your toddler to spend time with. Whether this person is a friend, a relative, or a teacher, spending time with him will make an enormous difference in your toddler's perception of males. The same, of course, in reverse, would hold true for a father raising a toddler without a mother in the home. For more on raising a child on your own, see page 788.

# CHAPTER FOURTEEN

# The 28ᵗʰ to 30ᵗʰ Months

## WHAT YOUR TODDLER MAY BE DOING NOW

*By 2½ years,[1] your toddler
. . . should be able to (see Note):*

▲ identify 1 picture by naming
▲ put on an article of clothing
▲ jump up
▲ name 6 body parts
▲ identify 4 pictures by pointing

**Note:** If your toddler has not reached these milestones, consult the doctor or nurse-practitioner. This rate of development may well be normal for your child (some children are late bloomers), but it needs to be evaluated. Also check with the doctor if your toddler seems out-of-

*In the third year, there's often still a sizable gap between what a toddler wants to do and what a toddler can do. Providing lots of opportunities for practice helps close that gap.*

---

1. This chapter covers the period between the time a toddler turns two and a quarter through two and a half (or thirty months).

control or hyperactive; highly demanding, stubborn, negative; overly withdrawn, passive, uncommunicative; sad, joyless; unable to interact with others. By this age, children who were born prematurely have usually caught up to their peers.

### . . . will probably be able to:

▲ identify 4 pictures by naming

### . . . may possibly be able to:

▲ draw a vertical line in imitation
▲ balance on each foot for 1 second
▲ identify a friend by name

### . . . may even be able to:

▲ balance on each foot for 2 seconds
▲ identify 1 color
▲ describe the use of 2 objects
▲ use two adjectives
▲ broad jump

# WHAT YOU MAY BE CONCERNED ABOUT

## THE CHILD WHO HAS EVERYTHING

*"Our son is the first grandchild on both sides. He has everything a child could ever want in the way of clothes, books, and toys. He's very well behaved and doesn't whine or have tantrums. But we're worried that if we don't say 'no' enough, we'll spoil him and he'll end up a brat."*

There's no doubt that the word "no" has its place in a parent's vocabulary ("*No* hitting!" "*No* more cookies," "*No,* don't touch the hot stove!"). The judicious use of "no"—particularly where health, safety, and fairness are concerned—is essential to raising a caring, responsible individual. Nevertheless, having spared some "no's" doesn't necessarily mean you've been spoiling your child.

In fact, it doesn't sound as though you've got a brat in the making. Signs of overindulgence (or the wrong kind of indulgence) are usually not hard to miss,

and from your description, it doesn't appear that your son's exhibiting any of them. To help keep it that way:

**Don't say "yes" for the wrong reasons.** Giving your son all that he needs—as long as you have the means to do so—isn't an error in and of itself. And saying "yes" to a reasonable request or a justifiable purchase isn't, either. But both giving and giving in, for the wrong reasons—to keep a child happy; to avoid a confrontation; to satisfy your own unrequited childhood longings ("I never had a train set, but by golly, my son's going to have one!"); or to compensate for time you can't spend with him, to name a few—can lead to problems. Giving your child so much so often that getting starts to become a given can not only take the fun out of receiving, but can create a "gimme monster" who doesn't know how to delay gratification. (Which could translate into more serious problems, especially in the teen years.)

**Say "no" for the right reasons.** The arbitrary use of the word "no" can be confusing and ego deflating to a child. By all means, say "no" when there's a good reason to say it (your child wants a swing set and you don't have a backyard; your child wants a new pail and shovel he's spied in the store and he already has a perfectly good one at home; your child wants to watch television all day), not because you have a feeling that you haven't said it enough lately.

**Don't just say "no."** Except when time is of the essence (as when a child runs into the street) don't just say "no"—say "why," too. Though your toddler won't always be able to understand or accept your explanations, he will eventually catch on to their significance, if you make them simple and appropriate to his level of comprehension. Don't, for example, detail your financial troubles to a two-year-old who's requested a life-size stuffed animal you can't afford. Instead explain, "That elephant costs a lot of money. I'm sure you would like to have it, but we need to use our money for food and clothing and can't spend it all on toys."

**Realize that more is sometimes too much.** While the boy who has everything isn't necessarily spoiled, the boy who has more than he needs or can possibly use often becomes either overwhelmed (with so many toys, he doesn't know what to do) or jaded (he has so many toys that they become uniformly boring). And long-term overindulgence can result in a child who can't take "no" for an answer, and who responds to rejection with anger, tears, or acting out. In other words, a spoiled brat.

**Help him to experience the joys of giving.** Since early childhood is a very egocentric stage, young children can't be expected to acknowledge that it's better to give than to receive. But that doesn't mean you can't start modeling this concept through good-hearted example. When you can, include your toddler in your efforts to help others less fortunate

(see page 212); tell him how good you feel when you do these kind deeds. In addition, enable him to experience the joy of giving closer to home: Buying or making a special gift for Grandma's birthday, for example, and watching her face light up when he presents it, or making a Valentine's Day card for Daddy, and surprising him with it at breakfast.

**Give him love.** It's the most important gift anyone can give or receive. And as long as your child's getting plenty of love, and is starting to learn how to give it back, you—and he—are on the right track.

# DISCIPLINING OTHER PEOPLE'S CHILDREN

*"One of the the children who often plays with our daughter tends to hit. When her mother isn't around I'm not sure what my role should be in preventing this child from hurting the other children."*

While it's inappropriate to step in and discipline a child who is misbehaving when her parent or caregiver is present, it's not only appropriate but necessary to do so when you're in charge. When children are in your care, you are responsible for supervising their behavior.

So the next time one of your young guests takes a swing, let her know immediately that hitting won't be tolerated. If the victim is crying or upset, focus your attention there first, then turn to the aggressor. Be firm, but keep your cool—anger is not likely to be productive. Simply explain: "We don't hit in our house. If you keep hitting, you won't be able to play here and you will have to go home." (For more tips for dealing with toddler aggression, see page 190.)

Keep in mind, however, that a child whose parent isn't present may hit because she's uneasy or uncomfortable. Or she may act up because she feels she's not getting enough attention. So be sure that you're not favoring your own child, that there are enough activities to keep your unaccompanied guest busy, and that she gets adequate attention when she's behaving well.

# A HOMEBODY

*"My toddler never wants to go out, not even to the playground. He's perfectly content to stay in his room and play, but I get cabin fever from staying in all the time."*

L  ike adults, toddlers come in all temperaments and personalities. Though most jump up and down with excitement at the mere mention of an excursion, others could just as easily do without them—and an occasional child regularly resists leaving his own home (and his own toys) for the park, the playground, a friend's house, or a trip to the mall or market.

Most stay-at-home behavior can be dealt with successfully if you figure out what it is about going out that a child objects to.

**Change.** Some toddlers are temperamentally opposed to change. That doesn't mean they'll never be able to make any changes in life, but that they'll need a little help with transitions. For example, instead of suddenly announcing at noon, "We're going to the store now," it's better, with such a child, to start dropping hints right after breakfast ("Later on, we'll be going to the store" . . . "Soon, we'll go to the store" . . . "In five minutes, it's time to go to the store"). This allows the child to get used to the idea that he's going out long

before the actual time of departure. (For more support for the child who dislikes changes, see page 246.)

**The proposed destination.** Perhaps your toddler was frightened coming down a slick slide once, or he tumbled off a swing, and now he hesitates to go back to the playground. Or maybe he just isn't into climbing, sliding, and swinging. If it's the chosen destination that is causing your child to rebel, suggest some very different destinations, such as a museum, a zoo, a firehouse, or a playmate's home instead. Try to gear the destination to his interests and you may get a better response. Or perhaps he is bored at the supermarket or the mall; if that's the case, see tips for shopping with toddlers (page 238).

**Separating from his toys and other belongings.** Whether it's a well used toy or a stuffed animal or a favorite comfort object your child is playing with, bringing it along on outings may make venturing outside less objectionable. If it's not feasible to take along his plaything of the moment (you can't pack an entire wooden train set in the stroller basket), help him to select another toy or book to take with him.

**Outdoor play.** Some children enjoy the kinds of solitary activities they can indulge in at home (racing toy cars, drawing, doing puzzles) more than more active playground play. If that seems to be the case with your child, let him know that he can take his cars, or his sketch pad, or a puzzle along when he goes out, and that he doesn't have to run around or play hard, unless he wants to. (Though, of course, it's a good idea to try to entice him into some active play; see page 296.)

**An overly busy schedule.** Some children don't get enough time to spend at home—either they're away from home much of the day (at the baby-sitter's, at

day care), or they're always being shut-
tled from one activity to another. While
always being on the go suits some kids
fine, others crave the comforts, quiet,
and solitude of home. If this may be the
case with your toddler, try to understand
his need for "downtime"—and when
possible, postpone outings after a particularly busy day or week.

**Facing a fear.** If your toddler shows
genuine fear or panic when you suggest
an outing, it's possible he's had a bad
experience of which you're unaware. If
he's very verbal, you can ask him to tell
you why he doesn't want to go out. If
not, you will have to do some sleuthing.
Could it be he was frightened by a
neighbor's dog, or that he heard a story
about someone being hurt by a car, or
saw an automobile on fire? Check with
any baby-sitters or caregivers (including
relatives), and try to get to the bottom of
the problem. If you can't, you should
talk to his pediatrician about it; a child
therapist may be able to use play therapy to discover the object of your
toddler's fear.

**None of the above.** Your toddler's resistance to leaving home may be nothing
more than normal toddler contrariness
and desire for control. Using some win-
win solutions (see page 125) may help
you to get your toddler out without a
parent-toddler struggle. You can try to
coax or cajole him out of the house,
using humor, song ("This is the way we
go to the store, go to the store, go to the
store"), even enticements ("If you like,
we'll stop and see the fire engines after
we're finished at the supermarket").
When he won't willingly leave the
house, and you have an urgent errand
and no one else to stay with him, you
may have no choice but to take him
along against his will. Take a friendly
but firm tone as you carry him out to the
car or the stroller, and make an extra
effort to include a stop you know he'll
enjoy in your itinerary.

While you're trying to discover the
cause of your child's resistance to leaving the house, avoid criticizing or making fun of him or his homebody
tendencies. Comments like "*All* of the
other children love to play at the playground—why do you always want to
stay at home?" are insensitive, can bruise
his ego, and may even make him more
determined to resist going out.

If he steadfastly refuses to go out at
all or becomes upset or panicky when
you insist on taking him along, discuss
the problem with his doctor.

# CONTINUOUS MONOLOGUES

*"Is it normal for a child to talk to
herself? My daughter does it all day
long."*

Everyone talks to themselves—it's
just that by adulthood, we have
learned to do it silently, at least most of
the time. Your toddler, just starting to
formulate her thoughts into words, can do
it more easily when she thinks aloud—
just as a child first learning to read can
comprehend what she's reading better if
she reads aloud. At this age, a toddler
doesn't necessarily know the difference
between silent and verbalized thought.

Toddler monologues are also
prompted by the drive to practice language
skills and by the satisfaction these new
talkers derive from hearing their own
voices, a satisfaction that grows as their
skills improve. And unlike adult monologues, they aren't muted by self-con-
sciousness: Toddlers care little what others
may think. (We'd probably think out loud
ourselves a lot more if we weren't afraid
that others would question our sanity.)

As your toddler becomes more verbally accomplished, she will begin to be

able to think silently more often—though she'll probably continue to talk to herself, at least some of the time, through the preschool years, and if she's like the rest of us, even occasionally after that. In the meantime, instead of fretting over her monologues, enjoy them.

# RESISTANCE TO KISSING

*"Our once-affectionate toddler now hates it when we kiss him—he pushes us away when we try. How come?"*

Silken cheeks, tiny noses, downy heads of hair, pudgy fingers and toes—they all cry out to be kissed. So naturally, when those kisses we can't resist planting are summarily rejected, it's more than a little disheartening. Especially when we've grown so used to having our smooches met with happy acceptance.

While far from every toddler turns his head away to avoid a kiss, many (more often) boys, do. Spurning kisses may be a way to declare their separateness and independence. For some boys, refusing to kiss Mommy may even be a way of handling the strong and sort of scary attraction they feel toward her.

Don't scold your toddler for rejecting your kisses, and don't plead or beg for his. This approach may make him feel guilty but isn't likely to win you the prize you seek. Get a kiss in now and then by chasing him, corralling him, and planting your lips anywhere you can manage to do so. If you keep the chase fun, your toddler will accept it in that spirit and probably even enjoy it (though he may never admit it). And bide your time. One of these days, he's sure to start favoring you with his affection again.

*Many toddlers resist any kind of confinement—even the friendly confinement of a parent's hug. For best results, let your toddler tell you how much loving is "just right."*

# RESISTANCE TO HUGGING

*"My daughter used to like being held when she was a baby, but now she wriggles away whenever I try to hug her. I'm beginning to feel rejected."*

Don't take your toddler's wriggling out of your arms personally. She isn't rejecting you, she's probably just rejecting having her physical freedom limited. Not only do frequent hugs (and strollers, car seats, and high chairs) cramp a toddler's very active style, but they compromise her precious control and autonomy.

But just because your child seems not to welcome your physical affection as much as she once did doesn't mean she doesn't need it. Instead of turning it off entirely, try altering the way you show your love to fit your toddler's present needs:

**Try a light touch . . .** While many toddlers (especially touch-sensitive toddlers, who were probably not very accepting of physical affection even as babies; see page 202) will resist a smothering bear hug, they may be more amenable to a quick and gentle embrace, a shoulder squeeze, or a soft stroke on the cheek—displays of affection that don't limit their mobility or independence.

**. . . or a "macho" one.** Some especially active toddlers find hugging too "mushy." Tickling, wrestling, and slapping a high-five are types of physical contact more up their alley.

**Time hugs well.** A toddler will often be more open to a parent's open arms before and after a nap, at bedtime, and when she's taken a fall (but don't overreact just to get your hugs in) or is otherwise feeling vulnerable. Take advantage of such opportunities to flex your hugging muscles; establishing a regular story-and-cuddle time after her bath, for instance, will likely prove satisfying to both of you.

**Follow her cues.** Let your toddler clue you in to when she's receptive to a hug and when she wants to be released from one. If she knows she won't be imprisoned in your arms any longer than she wishes, she's less likely to reject a hug in the first place.

Don't give up trying. Even if your toddler isn't huggable right now, she's likely glad that you care enough to offer. Most hug-shy toddlers eventually revert to their cuddly selves (albeit with a bit of grown-up dignity). But a few—usually those who are touch-sensitive—will continue to be less amenable to frequent embraces. If your child rejects all physical contact, you might feel better if you talk to her doctor about it.

# LOVE PATS

*"Sometimes, when my son is sitting in my lap, he takes my face in his hands in what promises to be a loving gesture, and then starts slapping my cheeks—hard! Is this some kind of love-hate thing?"*

Toddlers are masters of mixed feelings. They ambivalently straddle the line between confidence and insecurity, independence and dependence, wishful omnipotence and helplessness. So it's not surprising that these mixed feelings sometimes surface in the kind of conflicted behavior you're describing.

Don't be concerned by these love "pats"—they're a way of touching, an important form of toddler communication and exploration, and part of a phase that will pass as your toddler starts to smooth out some of that inner confusion. But don't hesitate to stop your toddler if the pats get out of control. Calmly remove his hands, hold them, and tell him simply "Please don't hit me. That hurts." Then use his hands to stroke your cheeks gently, and say, "See, this is what I like." If that doesn't work, find something else for him to do with his hands—pull out a puzzle, a shape-sorter, some clay. Keep a squishy ball, a small toy, a doll, or a stuffed animal in your tote bag to hand him when he tries these overly enthusiastic love pats while you're out of the house.

# A SECOND LANGUAGE

*"English is a second language for both my husband and myself, which we feel has hindered us somewhat. So we speak only English to our child. But our parents are upset that he doesn't speak*

*Spanish. Will teaching him Spanish now interfere with his English?"*

No, it won't. In fact, your parents have a point. Speaking a second language can be a very valuable asset. When that second language links an individual to his roots and culture, it is even more valuable. But nothing's been lost by waiting until now to start. Many language experts, in fact, recommend two and a half to three years as the perfect age to introduce a child to a second tongue. Introducing it earlier tends to slow down the development of both languages (though in most cases, the child eventually catches up); waiting until the child is reading in English may ultimately limit fluency in the second language.

There are many approaches to teaching a toddler a second language. One parent can speak English to the child, and the other the second language. Both can speak the second language, and the child can continue building his English proficiency in day care or preschool. Or the parents can speak English and the grandparents, if they live nearby, or a full-time caregiver can speak the second language—a method that doesn't seem to work as well. A single parent speaking both languages to the child, interchangeably, is the most confusing approach and makes it harder for the child to sort out which words belong to which language.

Which ever tack you take, be sure that the "teacher" is fluent in the language being introduced and uses it exclusively when speaking to your child. Also be sure that your child is immersed in the second language for hours each day, and that games, books, songs, and videos are used to increase both enjoyment and learning. Once in school, your child should learn to read and write his second language to consolidate his skills. (Since few elementary school curricula include a second language, you'll probably to have to attend to this at home.)

# FAMILY NUDITY

*"We've always been fairly casual about nudity in our home—we let our daughter shower with us, and we've never hesitated to dress or undress in front of her. But now that she's over two, we've started to wonder whether it's healthy to let her see her father nude."*

Many parents have concerns about cross-gender nudity at this age; many others don't give it a thought. Whether you feel comfortable with nudity is, at least partly, a remnant of (or backlash against) your own upbringing. Be sure to factor your feelings into any decision about whether to take undressing behind closed doors.

You also should take cues from your child. Some toddlers are completely oblivious to parental nudity. But at some point, most will become curious about the private parts of others—pointing, asking questions ("What's that Daddy has?), and even tugging at the object of their interest. Such curiosity should be handled with composure, and questions answered simply but accurately. It should also prompt, no matter what the child's age, an end to cross-gender nudity.

Even if a child doesn't show any such interest, family nudity could become a problem by age three, when it's believed that some children unconsciously become sexually stimulated by parental nudity, and are confused and embarrassed by these feelings. So it's probably wise to start donning bathrobes and segregating showers by your toddler's third birthday. You can explain such a change by saying, "Now that you're older, you need to have some privacy, and so do I."

On the other hand, undressing or showering with a same-sex parent may help foster positive feelings in a child about her own sexuality. A mother who's comfortable about undressing in front of her daughter can continue to do so indefinitely, as can a father who's comfortable undressing in front of his son. Some little boys, however, may express anxiety over the size of their penis in relation to their father's. This anxiety can be relieved by explaining that all parts of a child's body (hands, feet, and legs, as well as penises) are small, and that they will all grow as he gets older.

More important than the actual practice of family nudity is the attitude and feelings of parents about their own bodies and those of their children. Probably, both extremes of parental attitudes—the Victorian cover-the-body-at-all-times view and the let-it-all-hang-out stance—are the least desirable in terms of raising children with healthy attitudes about their own bodies. What children need to learn is that the body, naked or covered, should be respected and taken care of; it should be considered beautiful, rather than embarrassing. And most important it should be under the control of the person who inhabits it.

# CHILD NUDITY

*"No sooner do I get my daughter dressed than she's taking her clothes off."*

Your child's partiality for her birthday suit doesn't mean she's destined for lifetime membership in a nudist colony. Spontaneous disrobing is very common between the ages of two and four, and for several reasons. First, toddlers who've just learned how to undress enjoy practicing this new skill. Second, they derive satisfaction from demonstrating control ("You can dress me, but you can't *keep* me dressed"). Third, they relish bucking the system, testing everything and everybody, and, especially, getting a shocked

reaction from onlookers. Finally, they often find running around bare is simply more comfortable.

This penchant for undressing will pass—and as with most phases, it will pass more quickly if your toddler isn't pressed. In the meantime:

▲ Let her practice on someone else. Give your toddler a doll or teddy with easy-to-manipulate clothing so she can try her hand at socially acceptable undressing. Stay close by to help her, though, since redressing is a much tougher task for little fingers, and may result in frustration.

▲ Let her go bare. Temperatures in the house permitting, let your toddler romp in the raw (if she hasn't mastered toileting skills yet and goes without a diaper, be sure she won't soil furniture and carpets[2]) to her heart's content—or at least until it's time to appear in public.

▲ Don't allow her to go bare when it's inappropriate. Explain that people don't walk around with their clothes off outside of the house because they like to keep their bodies private. When it's necessary that your toddler keep her clothes on, try dressing her in outfits that are rather difficult to remove (overalls, blouses that button in the back, jeans with a belt).

▲ Don't let *your* inhibitions inhibit her. Overreacting to your daughter's undressing can convey the message that she should feel ashamed of her body—which could set her up for an unhealthy body image later in life.

▲ But don't laugh at her naked antics, either. Your amusement could prompt her to indulge in more of the same.

Eventually, as new challenges capture her attention, undressing will lose its

---

2. Many parents find that it's easier to teach a naked child to use the toilet than a diapered one; consider taking advantage of your toddler's nudity to begin toilet learning, assuming she's otherwise ready (see page 539).

allure. In fact, by age four or five, you may find that your child takes a turn for the puritanical; many preschoolers are intensely private about their privates. For now, avert your eyes and avoid commenting on her exhibitionism.

# OVERSCHEDULING

*"The other children in my daughter's play group are starting to go to all kinds of classes—art, gymnastics, dance, even science. It seems to me to be overkill. Am I kidding myself and short-changing our child?"*

B eing two years old can be hard work these days—far harder work than it should be. Between gymnastics classes, art classes, music classes, movement classes, play groups and play dates, and often, day care or preschool, some toddlers are carrying schedules that would exhaust the most energetic and organized adult.

For these overworked toddlers, exhaustion is often just one of the potential side effects of their heavy schedules. Others include sleeping problems, eating problems, irritability, and excessive clinginess. Overscheduling also deprives a child of time to do nothing, to play on her own, to relax, to think.

Junior burnout doesn't only affect a toddler in the short term. Being pushed too hard in a particular area, such as music or dance, for example, can cause a child to lose interest, often by the time she's reached school age, even if it's an area in which she is naturally gifted.

What's an appropriate schedule for a toddler? That depends on the child and her parents. For some children, particularly those who attend day care or preschool and/or spend a lot of time socializing in a play group or at play dates, even one class may be too many. For others, one or two short classes a

## INTO THE SWIM? NOT YET.

W hen is the best time for your child to take the plunge and begin formal swimming lessons? According to the American Academy of Pediatrics, not until the age of three. Although splashing in a wading pool (with adult supervision) or in a big pool (in the arms of an adult) can help a toddler gain an important measure of confidence and comfort in the water (a good first step in water safety training), formal swimming instruction can be both unproductive and unsafe. Not only doesn't early swim training make children better swimmers, it doesn't "waterproof" them, either. In fact, children who've had lessons may be at greater risk around water than other children because they feel safe and comfortable in it and because their parents, under the impression their children can "swim," are often lulled into a false sense of security. But there is an important difference between being able to swim and being safe in the water; young children are never safe without adult supervision.

If you do choose to sign your toddler up for swimming lessons before his or her third birthday, be sure that the classes follow the national YMCA guidelines, that the children are never submerged (toddlers, who often swallow water when submerged, are still particularly susceptible to water intoxication, a potentially dangerous condition in which the blood becomes overly diluted), and that instruction is provided one-on-one (usually in parent-child pairings) by instructors certified in resuscitation techniques. See page 646 for more on water safety.

week—even on top of an already active schedule—may be fine. For children who get little stimulation at home and wouldn't otherwise have much contact with peers—and for their parents, who may also benefit from interaction with other adults—two or three weekly classes may happily fill a social void.

Nevertheless, it's commonly agreed that classes are in no way necessary for a toddler's optimum development, and that most toddlers get all the stimulation they need through everyday play. But while classes may not be necessary, there's no harm in them, either—as long as you keep the following guidelines in mind:

▲ The only purpose of a class for toddlers should be enjoyment. Before enrolling your child, make sure that the class she'll be joining promotes fun, not prodigies. Enroll her in a movement class so she can enjoy jumping, and hopping, and swaying to the music—not to get a leaping head start on her training as a prima ballerina. Sign her up for gymnastics so she can climb and tumble—not with an eye to the Olympics.

▲ Classes for toddlers should be completely pressure-free. Reluctant class members should be encouraged but never pressured to participate—by teachers or parents. Teachers should challenge, motivate, and cheer on their young charges, but children who would rather watch from the sidelines should be allowed to do so. (Be sure, however, that a toddler who opts to sit on the sidelines isn't ignored; a little coaxing is generally all that is needed to get a child involved.)

▲ Classes should be age-appropriate and safe. Children should be grouped according to age and ability. Two- and three-year-olds, no matter how talented or precocious, should not be lumped together with five- and six-year-olds. Not only will prodding a two-year-old to perform like a five-year-old lead to burnout, but—because toddlers are neither agile

nor strong enough to keep pace with preschoolers—it can lead to injury. Many materials (such as some paints, craft items, scissors, and so on) that are suitable for older children are not suitable for toddlers; allowing toddlers to use them can be risky.

▲ Classes should focus on developing the whole child, rather than a particular skill. If a child is enrolled in more than one program, the programs should provide different kinds of stimulation. For example, one could promote physical development (dance, gymnastics), another, creativity (music, painting, crafts), or intellectual growth (science, story time).

▲ Discontinue classes that are "too much" for your toddler. If you pick up clues that your toddler is overscheduled (exhaustion, irritability), that the classes she's taking are too demanding (she's reluctant to go or refuses to participate), or that she's just not having fun, it's time to call it quits.

# MIDDLE-OF-THE-NIGHT VISITS

*"We brought our son into our bed a few times because he was running a fever, and now he's started coming in on a regular basis. We're not getting any sleep or privacy, and we're afraid it's become a habit."*

Nocturnal pilgrimages to the parental bed can become a bad habit, one that's tough to kick. They often begin when a child is sick, having a tough time with teething, is experiencing emotional stress (from starting a new school or having a new baby-sitter), or at other times of upheaval (a family vacation, moving). But though the set of circumstances that prompt a child to begin waking at night and cuddling with his parents for comfort may be self-limiting, the visits generally aren't. To put a stop to them, you'll probably have to take action:

▲ Offer your comfort, not your bed. If your child cries for you at night, and you're sure he's awake, go to him. Rub his back, assure him that everything's okay, and then tell him that you're going back to your bed. If he comes into your bed uninvited, carry him back to his bed. Though this approach will definitely cost you sleep in the short term, it should ultimately put a stop to the night visits and eventually earn you uninterrupted sleep. You can minimize the sleep deprivation by taking turns on night duty—one night, Mommy intercepts the night wanderer, the next, Daddy.

▲ Be consistent. Returning your toddler to his bed on Monday night, then allowing him to stay with you on Tuesday (because you're too tired to get up after Monday's nocturnal sojourn) will teach him that it's always worth a try. He's really too young to understand, "Just this once." Be firm, not ambivalent. If there's any inkling in his mind that there's any doubt in yours, he'll be less likely to take "no sleeping in our bed" for the final answer.

▲ Be patient and loving. No matter how tired and grumpy you are, try not to take it out on your toddler. Carry him back to his bed tenderly—rather than muttering and grumbling—so he won't feel that you're rejecting him. What you're rejecting is his presence in your bed.

▲ Give him a light. At this age, fear of the dark (see page 431) is common. Letting your toddler sleep with a night-light, or even a low-wattage lamp, should help him to feel more secure. Comfort can also come in the form of a blanket, pillow, or article of clothing that belongs to Mommy and Daddy.

▲ Play bedtime games during the day. Using your toddler's dolls or stuffed animals, play-act a similar middle-of-the-night visit with him in the light of day. In it, have the "baby" get up out of his bed and try to get into his parents' bed. Then encourage your child to put the baby back in his own bed.

▲ Don't feel guilty. By helping your child learn to sleep on his own again, you're not just ensuring a better night's sleep for yourself. You're teaching your toddler to cope on his own and comfort himself; these skills can help raise his confidence level across the board.

## THE FAMILY BED

*"While our daughter was young and I was breastfeeding, the idea of a family bed seemed appealing. It meant I didn't have to get up to nurse or to comfort her when she awoke. But now that she's two and a half, it's getting a little crowded. Is it time to end this arrangement?"*

The family bed has its supporters: Parents who wouldn't want any other sleeping arrangement, who value the joy of family togetherness that they experience sleeping *en famille,* and who are happy to avoid the ordeal of letting a baby cry it out or of climbing out of bed several times nightly to return a wandering child to her own bed. And certainly there are numerous societies where sleeping as a family is the rule, not the exception.

Still, there's no denying that three can make a crowd. Three can also make for a lot of other problems. Researchers have associated co-sleeping with several potentially negative side-effects, including:

**Less sleep for parents.** Between trying to avoid being kicked or poked by a little set of arms and legs and trying to avoid rolling over on their small bedmate, most parents find it difficult to get a good night's sleep.

**More sleep problems for children.**
Instead of solving sleep problems, as
parents hope, the family bed generally
compounds them. Children who sleep
with their parents wake more often than
children who sleep alone. In addition,
they don't learn how to be content in
their own beds or to fall back to sleep on
their own—vital skills for a lifetime of
restful nights.

**Less lovemaking for parents.** Sleep
isn't all that stands to be lost in the family bed. Parental privacy and intimacy
can be compromised, too. Romance can
be difficult enough to preserve with a
young child in the home; a child in the
bed can make that goal nearly impossible. And lovemaking isn't the only
pleasant pursuit put at peril; having a
child in bed interferes with other kinds
of adult intimacy, such as private conversations and relaxing snuggling.

**Possibly, more separation problems.**
Some researchers suggest that the child
who sleeps in the family bed may have
trouble detaching, both physically and
emotionally, from her parents and seeing
herself as an independent person. They
also suspect that some co-sleepers suffer
from separation anxiety longer than do
other children. For the older toddler, peer
teasing ("Jesse doesn't have her own
bed!") may affect self-esteem.

**Possibly, less daytime attention.** Sometimes, working parents promote (or at
least permit) the family bed as a way of
compensating for inadequate time spent
with their child during the day. Then,
feeling less guilty because they have
nighttime togetherness, they make less of
an effort to try to make extra time for
daytime togetherness. And everybody
loses. (For better ways of making time
for your toddler, see page 770.)

**A difficult time of reckoning.** Since
sleeping with older children is culturally

inappropriate, parents who choose the
family bed have to decide when to tell
their child she has to move to her own
bed. The older the child, the more in-
grained the habit, and the more difficult
the transition may be.

If you think the time for transition is
now—and it sounds as though you do—
use the steps recommended for switching
a child to a bed of her own (see page
318). Introduce your toddler's bed with
great fanfare. Then institute a bedtime
ritual that cozily beds her down in her
new quarters. Alter your present bedtime
ritual somewhat, so that the old cues that
led to your shared bed will not be triggered. If your toddler cries when you
leave her, sit or stand next to her bed
(but don't lie down with her) while she
falls asleep. After a few nights, advance
to leaving before she's soundly asleep; a
few nights later, go while she's just
drowsy. Finally, leave while she's still
awake. If she cries, try offering comfort
at intervals (see page 66). If she attempts to come into your bed in the
middle of the night, try the tips recommended earlier for dealing with nocturnal visits.

If you discover you miss the togetherness of the family bed, invite your toddler into your bed for an early-morning
cuddle, every day or on weekends only,
depending on your schedule.

# FRUSTRATION WITH DIFFICULT TASKS

*"Our son gets so upset when he's
drawing or building with blocks and
he can't get something just the way
he wants it, that he starts to cry.
How can I prevent his frustration?"*

With their desires often exceeding their abilities, frustration is a fact of daily life for toddlers. And though frustration may sometimes upset both the toddler and his parents, a certain amount is actually necessary to spur a child on to achievement and progress. So while trying to protect yours from all frustration may be a normal parental impulse, it not only deprives your child of this impetus to succeed, but ill prepares him for life in a world that's fraught with frustration. A child needs to experience some frustration in order to learn how to deal with it and use it in a constructive way.

Yet it's true that when a child is two and a half years old and hasn't yet developed strong coping skills, *too much* frustration can thwart progress and make the hurdles seem too overwhelming to attempt. It can also trigger tantrums. To minimize frustration in your toddler's daily life:

**Select toys to scale.** Even the brightest of children can become overly frustrated when toys are not appropriate to his age and size. Select playthings that challenge your toddler but won't be very much beyond his capabilities.

**Create a can-do environment.** You can minimize frustration overload by making sure that your toddler can successfully manipulate his immediate environment. For instance, provide him with a stepstool so he can easily reach the sink, a child-sized hairbrush so he can brush his own hair, sneakers with Velcro closures so he can get his shoes on and off independently.

**Teach skills.** The world is much less frustrating when you have the skills to face everyday tasks. For a toddler, that means knowing how to pick up and put away toys (see page 417), how to use art materials, how to put together a construction set, how to get his clothes on. Patiently teach your toddler how to do for himself rather than always doing for

him and you will model independence and self-reliance as important values.

**Respect his frustration.** If your toddler is frustrated because the blocks keep tumbling down, don't pat him on the back with a patronizing "It looks fine just the way it is." It doesn't look fine to him; by disputing his appraisal, you're insulting his judgment. Praise his efforts and validate his frustration ("You worked really hard at building that house, and it keeps falling down. That must make you feel angry").

**Don't add to his frustrations.** Constant criticism and overly high expectations (see page 454) only compound frustration. Your child's trouble meeting his own expectations is trouble enough; he shouldn't feel he has to live up to yours, too.

**Mete out help judiciously.** If your toddler seems to want to work a problem out for himself, don't butt in. Always solving his problems for him will lead him to ask for help before he's even tried. But if he seems frustrated and in need of help or actually asks for aid, offer it without taking over the task. Instead of stepping in and rebuilding his block tower your way ("You see, this is how you do it"), help him to redirect his own efforts ("Let's see, how can we keep that tower from tumbling down again? Do you think it would work better if you put this bigger block under the little blocks?"). Place that puzzle piece in his hand at just the right angle, so *he'll* be able to fit it in. Loosen the jar a little so he'll be able to have the satisfaction of opening it himself. Even if you end up doing most of the job yourself, make sure he does enough himself to take pride in his accomplishment.

**Support him if he wants to try, try, again . . .** Offer plenty of encouragement and praise: "I think it's great that you try so hard, and that you don't give up. You're a very hard worker."

**. . . but if he wants to quit, let him.** Avoid pressuring him to make another attempt: ("Try that again. I know you can do better"). Quitting is a perfectly acceptable way of dealing with an overload of frustration, especially at age two. Knowing *when* to quit is an important skill at any age. So if your toddler decides he doesn't want to keep trying— even if he wants to knock down the tower or tear up his drawing—don't stop him. Let him know you are proud that he tried so hard, but that it's okay to stop trying. Leave the door open, however, for trying again another day: "Maybe we can try that again together another time." If he seems to need comfort and reassurance on abandoning his project, by all means offer it.

**Watch for storm signals.** Frustration can sometimes become so intense that it sets off a tantrum. Try to step in before this happens; give your toddler a bit of help (if he'll take it), or get him to move from the frustrating activity to something less difficult, or simply to a more passive, relaxing activity—such as listening to a story or a tape.

# FEAR OF TRYING

*"Since she isn't satisfied with the way she draws or works a puzzle or puts on her socks, my daughter always wants me to do things for her. It's the same way with everything. I'm afraid she isn't going to learn how to do things for herself."*

It's very frustrating when small hands can't execute what growing minds envision. Some toddlers deal with this frustration by accepting their limitations and moving on to something else, some by expressing their frustration (as a tantrum or by whining, for example), still others by passing the crayon—or the shovel, or the socks—into hands they believe more capable. In this case, yours.

It's often a future perfectionist who chooses this route to frustration relief; since her sensitive esthetic sense tells her that grown-ups produce a better product, it seems logical to have adults do for her rather than to try doing things herself. Sometimes, this perfectionism is part of a child's nature, and sometimes it's bred by the pressures of parents expecting more than their child can deliver. So be sure you're not pushing too hard or setting unrealistic standards (see page 81). Don't buy toys or suggest activities that are way beyond your child's ability. And don't criticize her for failing to perform or achieve at any particular level. Whether you're a toddler or an adult, constant censure can damage self-esteem, hurt feelings, and engender a fear of trying.

If you aren't inadvertently perpetuating your child's fear of trying, she will eventually tire of sitting by as spectator. When she feels more confident, she will start doing for herself. In the meantime, encourage her participation:

**Ask for her opinions.** If your toddler has commissioned a beachscape, ask her to describe the scene while you draw it. When she runs out of ideas, help stimulate new ones ("Do you think there should be a little girl here? What color hair should she have? What could she be doing?") Ask her which puzzle piece you should try to put in next. And get her advice on whether her socks should be pulled straight up, or folded down.

**Give her lessons.** Your toddler may hesitate to try because she doesn't know how. In a low-pressure way, show her how to hold the crayon, hold the sock open for her toes, match the puzzle piece for color and shape.

**Invite her to assist.** Ask her to color in the sun or the waves on the beachscape, or put in the final puzzle piece, or pull her socks up. If she's resistant, don't push. But continue to present opportunities for her to try her hand in small ways that offer her safety and success.

Also make sure your toddler gets plenty of chances during the day to "help" you with simple tasks she is capable of completing. Let her retrieve a book you dropped on the floor, unload cans from the shopping bags into a low cupboard, help you load the laundry into the washing machine or pull it out of the dryer, hold the door open for you while you navigate the stroller through, carry a small item when you're overladen with packages. Assisting you will help her develop the self-confidence she needs to take on tough tasks on her own.

**Commend small contributions as well as large.** When she colors in a blue sky in your drawing or gets the last puzzle piece in by herself or manages to get her toes in her sock before giving up and handing the job over to you, applaud her work. If she carries a cup of juice most of the way from the counter to the table before stumbling and spilling it, compliment her with "That's great, you carried it almost the whole way," rather than criticizing her with "Can't you go two steps without spilling?" Voicing your appreciation of her efforts will boost her ego while prodding her to try harder next time.

**Share the credit.** Whether it's a completed drawing or a toy clean-up, telling her she did it all herself when you did most of it isn't truthful—and is a ploy she'll see right through. Instead, comment on what a wonderful job you did together.

# EXCESSIVE INDEPENDENCE

*"My son wants to do everything himself, even if it's not remotely within his ability. He gets frustrated, and so do I, since he always ends up wasting so much time trying."*

Your toddler isn't wasting time. He's putting time—albeit, time you may not have allotted in your schedule—to valuable use. His determined efforts, though seemingly futile now, give him the practice that will eventually make perfect—or at least, competent.

The next time your toddler doggedly resists your attempts to dress him, cut his food, or wash his hands with an uncompromising, "I wanna do it myself," heed his need. Minimize the mayhem his independence can inflict on your day by allowing extra time in your schedule for his efforts. And be patient, patient, patient, while he practices, practices, practices. Leave fifteen minutes instead of five for dressing if he's going to insist on dressing himself, and thirty minutes instead of fifteen for eating breakfast if he's going to feed himself without your help. You'll feel less pressured, and he will be better able to accomplish his goals if he feels less pressured by you. It will also help if you give some pointers (assuming he'll accept them) about how to accomplish the tasks he insists on taking over. For example: "I know a great trick for getting that jacket on—just watch." If he's resistant to demonstration, try a bit of verbal instruction, offered casually: "Sometimes when I can't get my shoe on, I loosen the laces a little." (For tips on toddler dressing, see page 498.)

The good news is that a toddler who prefers to do everything himself will, with your support, soon be able to do almost everything himself, and quite competently, making your job much easier.

And his self-sufficiency will bolster his self-esteem, making his life easier.

# STUTTERING

*"My son seems to stutter. I've heard the problem is associated with emotional problems. Should I be concerned?"*

No, you should be patient. At this age, stammering and stuttering are not associated with any kind of emotional problem. Commonly, they're caused when a toddler's speech can't keep pace with his thoughts, and/or when he has a verbal vocabulary that isn't yet a match for what he's got on his mind. Stuttering is normal and will likely resolve itself as your toddler becomes more skilled at language and at organizing his thoughts; the less said about it, the better. Pressure of any kind will only make the stuttering worse and longer-lasting. When he stutters, don't ask your toddler to slow down, start over, or take a deep breath before he talks—just let him say what's on his mind the best way he can. And take great pains to understand what he's saying so he doesn't have to repeat himself; frustration can worsen stuttering.

# INTEREST IN ERECTIONS

*"The other day, my son was playing with his penis and he suddenly asked why it got big when he did that. I didn't know what to say."*

Toddlers are nothing if not inquisitive, fascinated by the *how* and *why* and *what* of everything around them. So it's by no means surprising that something so near and dear to your son might pique his curiosity.

A toddler is entitled to an honest response to any question he asks, including this one. But honesty doesn't oblige you to give a medically or sexually complete answer, which would only go over his head and could possibly frighten him. It should suffice to tell him simply and matter-of-factly that sometimes a penis gets bigger when you touch it. It's probably a good idea to add that a penis is private, that any touching is best done when he's alone (see page 242)—and that nobody else should touch his penis (except parents when they're cleaning it and doctors when they are examining it).

# DAWDLING IN THE MORNING

*"Every morning, it's a struggle to get our son out of the house in time for day care. His dawdling makes us late for work and drives us crazy."*

Your toddler isn't dawdling to make you late or drive you crazy. In fact, *he* really isn't dawdling at all. What he's doing is moving at a toddler's pace, which to working parents, frantically getting ready to leave the house in the morning, is painfully slow.

Trying to get him to move at your pace is not only unrealistic but unfair, and for several reasons. *Inexperience.* Chubby, unpracticed fingers work more slowly than adult digits, making getting out of his pajamas and into his clothes a rather long and drawn-out ordeal. *Distractibility.* Between his bed and his clothes he's bound to stumble upon at least a dozen attractions that demand his immediate attention, from the block tower he was building last night, to the teddy bear that needs rocking, to the puzzle he just can't pass by without finishing (and then dumping). With his relatively short attention span and so many temptations spread around him, it doesn't take long for your orders to "Get your clothes on right now!" to fade from his memory. *Lack of time sense.* You want him to hurry up so you can get to day care and work on time—but he can't relate to your concerns about being late, getting stuck in traffic, or missing appointments. At his age, he lives mostly for the here and now, and worrying about "later" is not a priority.

That explains your toddler's perpetual pokiness, but it doesn't solve your problem. To do that, you'll have to work around his turtle-toddler pace:

**Give yourself a head start.** Getting an early bird start on your own routine (showering, dressing, breakfast making, and lunch-box filling up) will allow you to devote more time to getting your toddler ready, eliminating the last-minute rush, or at least making it less rushed.

**Give your toddler a head start.** If you want him to be out of bed, dressed, fed, groomed, toothbrushed, and out the door by 8:15, you'll probably need to wake him at least an hour before that. The more time he has to work with, the better the chance he'll be ready on time—and the less pressure there will be to pressure him to hurry. (Remember that the more you prod, the more he's likely to poke.)

**Give your morning a head start.** Free up more time in the morning (perhaps, even more time for sleep) by organizing everything that can possibly be organized before you go to bed at night. Pick out clothes for yourself and your toddler (pick them out together if your toddler tends to have definite opinions in the dressing department), and lay them out in a convenient spot. Listen to the weather forecast on the evening news and set the appropriate outerwear waiting at the door (including boots and umbrellas, if need be). Have your toddler choose the toy he'd like to bring along for the ride in the morning, and have *it* ready at the door, too (always with the understanding that it's a toddler's prerogative to change his mind). Discuss what he'd like for breakfast (again, if you're willing to take the risk that he might change his mind by morning), and prepare as much of it ahead of time as you can (dry cereal and raisins, for example, can be readied, with milk to be added in the A.M.). Set the table for breakfast, and prepack whatever you can in his lunch box. Try to avoid leaving relatively nonessential chores (reading the mail, glancing at the newspaper, folding laundry) for the morning.

**Set distractions aside.** To keep your toddler on a getting-ready track, help him to dress in your room, or in the bathroom—out of view, if possible, of toys, blocks, books, TV, or the family pet. Or, if it works better, try getting him dressed right after you wake him, while he's still half-asleep and less likely to be distracted or to protest the process (this will also give him some extra play time). Whatever you do, don't try to dress him while he's engrossed in a game or a project. This will understandably upset him and curtail his cooperation.

**Set your morning to music.** Pick a record or tape to play each weekday morning that your toddler will come to associate with getting ready. Something lively and energizing—such as marching music—may help to boost his sluggish pace.

**Set aside time for TLC.** Instead of waking your toddler with "Get up, or you'll be late for day care," wake him with a hug. Set aside a few minutes in your schedule for some quiet cuddling, perhaps even a quick story before you begin your feverish round of preparations. Not only can this help relax both of you, but it may also help to make your toddler more cooperative.

**Set a timer.** Make a game out of getting ready. Set a timer for such tasks as getting dressed and washing up,[3] and let him take the timer with him from room to room so he can have the fun of hearing the minutes tick by or watching the sand slide through. Be sure you leave more than enough time for each procedure, so that he has a good shot at beating the buzzer. Once your toddler recognizes numbers, you can use a digital clock to show him that when "the last two numbers are 2 and 5, it will be time to get dressed," or an analog clock to show him that he'll need to get dressed "when the long hand is touching the 5."

**Set out with what's keeping him.** When a toy he's playing with or a book he's looking at is keeping him from making any progress, suggest that he take it along for the ride (or the walk) to day care.

**Set appropriate expectations.** Don't expect your toddler to stop dawdling immediately or to always be ready to leave on time. Instead of nagging him about his slow pace, offer praise and encouragement when he gets ready on time (or close to it).

On weekends and holidays, when it isn't necessary to get out early, let your toddler dawdle to his heart's content. Everybody needs some time off for good behavior, even toddlers.

---

3. Don't set the timer, however, for breakfast; you don't want your child to think it's a good idea to race through meals.

# DAWDLING WHILE WALKING

*"It takes forever for us to travel the three blocks from our house to the supermarket because of my son's dawdling. I ask him to hurry up, but he seems to tune me out."*

To you, a sidewalk is a path that leads you from one location to another. To your toddler, it leads from one discovery to another. So much to explore! To investigate! To pick up! It's no wonder that walking down the sidewalk is so time-consuming.

The problem is that while your budding geologist is analyzing a pebble specimen, you're running late. Unless you take the car (or a bus, or a taxi, or the stroller), there's no sure way of getting from here to there in a hurry when you have a toddler in tow. These tips, though, may help make your trips on foot less troublesome:

▲ Allow time for lagging, if possible. For a walk that usually takes you five minutes, try to allow at least twenty when your toddler's along. And let him enjoy the extra time to the fullest; don't spoil them with constant reminders to "Hurry up!"

▲ Learn to relax. If the type-A person in you finds the leisurely pace irritating, try some relaxation techniques while you walk (for example, take several deep breaths, and with each repeat to yourself, "I am relaxed").

▲ Bring him up to speed the fun way. Challenge your toddler to a race to the corner (but don't run so fast that he can't keep up); to a hopping, skipping, or jumping competition (every hop, skip, and jump will bring you closer to your destination); to a "don't step on the line" contest. Or get him moving by calling his attention to something interesting ahead —an apple tree in full bloom, a red convertible that's parked up the block, or a busy construction site.

▲ Keep in mind, the next time your toddler's delaying tactics irk you, that time *doesn't* march on for toddlers. Toddlers live in the present; with only very primitive concepts of past and future, rushing makes no sense to them at all.

▲ Remember that you sometimes keep your toddler waiting ("I'll get you a drink when I'm done with these bills." "I'll play with you when I'm finished with the laundry"). That should help put your toddler's keeping you waiting in perspective.

# PLAYGROUND POKINESS

*"My daughter never wants to leave the playground when it's time to go, and I can never convince her to go without a fight and a tantrum. It's gotten to where I don't want to go anymore."*

To a toddler who's happily settled in the sandbox, one hand maneuvering a shovel full of sand, the other patting down the foundation of a castle in the making, "We have to go now" definitely doesn't come as a welcome announcement. "Are you ready to go home?" may seem more politic, but isn't likely to be any more effective. The answer you can expect most of the time is a resounding, "No!"

To entice a two-year-old out of a sandbox, or off the swings, or down from the jungle gym, you have to be cool, calm, and very, very clever:

**Join her in the sandbox.** Transitions are usually easier when you don't have to make them alone. So about ten minutes before your desired time of departure, sidle up next to your toddler in the sand-

box and, taking your cues from her, either act as her assistant or cheer her engineering skills on. Or, if your little Jane is swinging from the jungle gym, walk over and ask her to perform her acrobatics for you. Don't forget to praise her accomplishments. "That flip (or that sand castle) was really great—let's go home now and tell Daddy about it" is a much more gentle segue into the dreaded exit than "Get off that jungle gym right now—we're leaving!"

**Give adequate notice.** Instead of springing a sudden departure on her, give her fair warning. That way she can have a chance to start getting used to the idea and begin to wind down, getting in her last turns on the slide, scrambling to the top of the jungle gym one last time, and finishing her sand creation. Start with a ten minute warning, then give an update at five minutes (but don't issue so many warnings, or make them so threatening, that you spoil the ten minutes you've allotted her). When possible, let her complete whatever she's doing; you don't like to be interrupted in the middle of something either. But make it clear she can't start a new project. If she understands the concept of "one more" or "two more," you can negotiate: "Just two more times on the slide," or "once more to the top of the jungle gym." But be sure that the "two more" doesn't turn into ten more, or such negotiations will lose their effectiveness.

**Make leaving appealing.** "Let's look for pretty leaves on the way home," or "You can play with your new blocks when we get home," or "If we go home now, we can bake muffins" may make leaving the playground less painful. But be wary of out-and-out bribery ("If we leave now, I'll buy you an ice cream cone on the way home"), at least not on a regular basis, or she'll come to expect and demand substantial bribes each time you ask her to leave.

**Give her "one for the road."** A snack, that is. Small children often put hunger on the back burner when they're preoccupied with play and are ravenous by the time they stop. And, as you know, hunger (especially when teamed with disappointment or fatigue) can easily trigger a tantrum. (Make the snack nutritious, but not too filling if you're headed home for a meal.)

**Have toy, will travel.** Sneak one of your toddler's favorite toys into your tote bag; when it's time to leave, produce it magically. Having it in hand while you make your exit may make the transition easier.

**Be ready to provide transportation.** Just because your toddler walked to the park doesn't mean that you can count on her to walk home. Legitimately tired, she may not feel up to the hike. So be sure, if you walk, to bring along a stroller or bus or taxi fare for your return trip. (The fun of riding the bus or taxi may also offer extra incentive for leaving.)

If you can't convince your toddler to leave the playground willingly, remove her physically, but with empathy ("I know you want to stay, but we have to go home now. We'll come back again tomorrow"). You're the parent, and you are still boss, after all.

## POKEY EATING

*"Our son is the slowest eater. He's still eating long after everyone else is done, but wants to keep on until he's finished. How can we speed him up?"*

**S**low and steady may win the race, but it can drive parents to distraction at mealtime. Yet there's little you can do about a toddler who prefers to

amble through his edibles, except practice patience. It's important to give your toddler all the time he needs to eat his fill. Rushing, nagging, threatening, or pressuring him will not only make him pokier, but could keep him from developing healthy attitudes about eating. Instead, allow extra time for his meals. Let him keep nibbling away until he decides to call it quits. Of course, be sure that toys, siblings, the television, or other distractions aren't slowing down his pace. If they are, make some changes.

## COOKING TO ORDER

*"My mother-in-law insists that the only way my toddler will learn how to eat what's put in front of her is to give her no choices. She insists that if my daughter doesn't eat it, I should let her go hungry. But I always end up giving her whatever she wants. Who's right?"*

**W**hen your mother-in-law did her mothering tour-of-duty, toddlers were no less picky, yet catering to their quirks was considered inexcusably indulgent. The dinner table was a tight ship run by the adults of the house; balking at rations of baked chicken and green beans and demanding peanut butter sandwiches instead was considered mutiny. You ate what was put in front of you, or you were denied your just dessert.

But things have changed. It's now accepted by dietary experts (though not necessarily by grandmothers) that you can lead a toddler to the dinner table, but you can't make her eat what's put in front of her, at least not without precipitating an ugly battle. And ugly battles fought over food in childhood, studies show, too often leave scars—in the form of eating disorders, abnormal eating habits, and/or weight struggles—that can last a lifetime. Eating should be a pleasant, unpressured experience for a child, guided not just by an adult's good sense, but to a large extent by her own hunger, tastes, and appetite.

Letting a young child go for months on nothing but cereal, milk, and pasta, or bread and cheese (assuming a few well-chosen fruits and/or vegetables are thrown in for good balance) isn't indulgent or irresponsible, but perfectly acceptable. In fact, there's something inherently unfair about insisting that children eat what's put in front of them, when grown-ups enjoy a great deal of freedom of choice at the table.

So let her eat cake (fruit-sweetened, whole-grain, carrot cake, for example) and milk for breakfast instead of the oatmeal everyone else is having. Or a bowl of cold cereal with bananas and milk for lunch instead of the tuna sandwiches on the menu. Or cottage cheese and cantaloupe for dinner instead of the salad and fish you're eating. Make the foods you're serving an option should your toddler impulsively decide to break from her traditional favorites, but don't pressure her—and don't let anyone else (sorry, Grandma) pressure her, either.

For more tips on feeding a toddler, see Chapter Eighteen.

# CUTTING FOOD

*"My son always wants to cut up his own food; he absolutely refuses to let me cut it. But I'm afraid to give him a knife."*

To help a toddler attain some of the independence he's yearning for, there is much a parent can do—allow him to pick out his own clothes, select his meals, brush his teeth. But putting a knife in his hands, as you have wisely observed, is too risky.

Instead, respect his need to be independent while keeping his fingers intact by serving him food that doesn't need cutting, such as chicken fingers or drumsticks, fish sticks, cooked carrot circles, and English-muffin pizzas he can pick up whole. Or, bring his plate to him with his food already diced. To give him some safe practice with cutting, you can show him how to cut fish sticks or a peanut butter sandwich with a small butter spreader, and then let him try it himself, *under your supervision.* He can also cut sandwiches safely with a cookie cutter.

# A HUNGRY TODDLER

*"Even if she finished eating only an hour earlier, my toddler is always complaining that she's hungry. She's not fat, but if I feed her all day on request, she's bound to end up that way."*

Rare is the toddler who eats just the way her parents would like her to. It's always too little, too much, or all the wrong foods. The problem is, for a child to grow up into an adult who doesn't have an eating hang-up of one kind or another, her parents have to help her learn to regulate her appetite by her internal hunger signals.

So feed her when she's hungry, but be sure she's truly hungry. If she seems to crave food out of boredom, fatigue, frustration, or tension, help her to find better ways of dealing with these—preferably before she starts asking for food. Don't make her eat when she's not hungry or insist she clean her plate, and try not to use food as a reward or a bribe or a pacifier. And never withhold food as a punishment. Avoid getting her into the trap of eating out of habit—don't give her a cookie every time you go into the supermarket, crackers every time you fasten the seat belt, a frozen yogurt whenever you go home from the playground; use toys, conversation, or other diversions to keep her busy instead. And be sure she has enough undistracted time to eat her meals—the child who eats lightly at mealtime tends to snack frequently in between.

Set a good example for her by not obsessing about food or using it yourself to deal with boredom, fatigue, frustration, or tension. If you're in the habit of opening the refrigerator without thinking, taking the first item that appeals, and eating it en route back to whatever you were doing, or absently munching on snacks while watching TV or doing paperwork, try to break those habits. Make eating an event in itself and not an adjunct to other activities. Sit down for meals *and* for snacks—make them a planned part of your day—and your child will tend to do likewise.

Even if she seems to be hungry often, don't chide your toddler for overeating or warn her about getting fat. This will put the focus on food when what you really want is to take the focus off it. However, if your toddler begins gaining weight too quickly, you can take the steps suggested on page 510 for dealing with a tubby toddler, and make sure she gets plenty of exercise (see page 296). Don't, however, underfeed your child because you're afraid she may someday become fat.

When a toddler with an average appetite suddenly begins to eat ravenously, it's usually because of a growth spurt. This eating binge lasts only a few days and is not at all a cause for concern.

If, however, a ravenous appetite continues and is accompanied by excessive thirst and frequent urination, with or without noticeable weight loss, it's important to check with the doctor. Check with the doctor, too, if your child seems obsessed with food to the exclusion of other interests.

# INABILITY TO FOLLOW DIRECTIONS

*"Whether we tell her to clean up her room or get dressed to go outside, our daughter doesn't follow our directions. I don't know how she's going to make it at preschool, where they're going to expect her to cooperate."*

Before you blame your toddler for not following your directions, make sure your directions aren't to blame. Often, parental directions are too vague or too complicated for a young child to comprehend and follow.

To improve your toddler's ability to follow directions, give her a few lessons. Use a game format so she can have fun while gaining expertise. For instance, lay out an assembly line on the kitchen table ("Okay, first pick up the piece of apple. Good. Now, dip it in the yogurt. Great. Now roll it in the granola.") Or set up an obstacle course on the living room floor ("First jump over the sponge. Good. Now, pick up the block. Great. Now hand it to me. Terrific. Now, sit down on the chair.") Even a simplified game of Simon Says ("Simon says, 'Put your hands on your head.' Simon says, 'Lie down on the floor.' Simon says, 'Lift up your legs.'") can get your toddler in the habit of following directions.

Keep directions clear and simple. Sweeping directives (such as "clean up your room," when the room is a hopeless jumble) are way beyond the ability of a toddler to carry out, without further, more specific instructions. Instead, issue very concise instructions for room clean-up one step at a time ("Please put your dirty clothes in the hamper"; "Put your teddy back on the bed"; "Now put all your markers into the red basket"). Be sure she has enough information to follow your directives: for example, which are her dirty clothes, and where the hamper is. Wait until she's satisfactorily completed one step (and you've congratulated her on her success) before sending her on to the next.

Of course, even when a toddler understands and is capable of following directions, she won't always comply. Stubbornness and a desire to march to her own drummer will often prompt your toddler to ignore your instructions. But don't worry about how she's going to do at preschool. She is much more likely to follow directions there—a whole classroom of other children will be following the same directions at the same time, and there will be no parent-child power struggle to engage in—than when she is at home. If she doesn't, and if she continues to be uncooperative at home, see the tips on page 413.

A typical two-year-old should be able to follow a two-step command ("Pick up that book and give it to me, please"), given without any suggestive gestures (such as pointing to the book or putting your hand out to take it), at least some of the time. If your toddler seems unable to do this, talk to her doctor to see if there may be a hearing or developmental problem that needs addressing.

# SEPARATION ANXIETY AT PRESCHOOL

*"Every morning we have the same problem: Our son has to be dragged to his preschool crying. He seems happy when we pick him up, and sometimes even doesn't want to leave. But we're worried that maybe he doesn't like school."*

Chances are your toddler's resistance isn't a sign that he doesn't like school, but rather that the daily transition from home to school is difficult. Even seemingly insignificant transitions (from playing to eating dinner, for instance) can be tough on toddlers; bigger transitions (such as going from home to school) can be even more so.[4]

As long as his arrival protests are short-lived, and your toddler seems to enjoy the time he spends at school, there's nothing to worry about. Typically, there's a gradual decrease in clinginess (and crying) as a child becomes acclimated to his new routine and the school setting. This process takes longer for some children than for others, and some continue having troublesome home–school transitions for a year or two into their school careers. Here's how you can help:

▲ Make sure he has enough time before school to wake up (a tired child tends to be clingier) and to eat a good breakfast (a hungry child will also be clingier). And be sure he doesn't get hurried out of the house without a couple of good, warm hugs and some friendly conversation (as hard as it may be to squeeze these in on hectic mornings).

▲ Let him bring a little piece of home along. A favorite blanket, a special stuffed animal, or a toy to hold onto (it's no coincidence they are often called "transitional objects") can help bridge the gap between home and school, as such items did for many younger toddlers when they first went off to day care. If your toddler's school has a policy against bringing toys from home into the school setting, or if he's uncomfortable about sharing his special possessions with the other children, suggest that he bring them into the school building, but leave them in his cubby. If the school won't even allow that, assure him that his "blankie" or "teddy" or whatever will wait for him in the car or stroller until school is over.

---

4. For help in dealing with the separation anxiety younger toddlers experience when going off to day care, see page 146.

▲ Let him bring a little piece of you along. Separating from you may be easier if you give him something of yours for the day: a handkerchief, a wallet with old credit cards in it, a hat, a photo, a picture you drew, even a "kiss" of lipstick on his hand.

▲ Stay upbeat; don't anticipate trouble. Instead of admonishing your toddler on the way to school with "Now, let's not have any crying today!" (which may only inspire a repeat performance), use the travel time to help get your toddler into the preschool frame of mind, so that he can begin to make the transition before he walks in the door. See who can name the most kids in his class; talk about what he might have for snack; ask him whose cubby is next to his, what's his favorite storybook, with which classmates he likes to play.

▲ Put on a happy face. Give the impression that you're confident about leaving your toddler at school and that you're sure he'll have a good time, even if you're not. Any trace of your nervousness or anxiety will have him wondering "If Mommy's worried about my staying here, there must be something to worry about." If he thinks you're ambivalent about leaving him, he'll be ambivalent about staying.

Don't feel guilty, overly sympathetic, or apologetic (you're not sending him to Siberia). If you waver at all, he'll play to those feelings and you'll feel even worse.

▲ Be supportive, not critical. Your support builds your child's confidence, criticism erodes it.

▲ Arrive early so your toddler can get involved and settled before being overwhelmed by other kids, and so the teacher will be more available to help with his transition.

▲ Linger in his classroom. Usually, spending a few minutes walking around the classroom with your toddler can help him to feel more confident about the transition. It can also give him a sense of pride and ownership about school. Make sure there's extra time in your schedule so that you won't feel or act rushed. Don't concentrate on the clock instead of what your toddler is showing you. Ask questions ("Is this where you play dress-up? What's your favorite costume?"), make observations ("This water table looks like fun!" "Look at all those blocks!"), compliment any of your toddler's art projects that are hanging on the walls ("I really like the beautiful colors in your picture"). After you've made the rounds, ask your toddler which activity he'd like to begin the day with (unless, of course, the activity has been chosen by the teachers) and sit down with him for a couple of minutes while he gets started.

This "tour" approach won't work for all toddlers. Some seem to do better if their parents drop them off and then make a hasty retreat; the longer their parents stay, the clingier they get. They can't seem to join the group until they're completely on their own. If that seems to be the case with your child, turn him over to a teacher, give him a quick hug or kiss (or just wave, if he prefers), and make your exit.

▲ Make your farewell short and sweet. Once you're ready to go, tell your toddler, in terms he can understand, when you or your caregiver will pick him up (after nap, after lunch, or after the playground), say good-bye in a lighthearted but unambiguous manner, and leave, quickly. Don't turn back (no matter how convincingly your toddler pleads), except perhaps to wave cheerfully from the doorway. The sooner you disappear, the sooner he can start his day.

▲ Ask a teacher to join your transition team. The transition will work more smoothly if a cooperative teacher helps out. Make sure your toddler's teachers are aware of the problem, if they're not already, so that one will be ready, as needed, to assist you—whether to take your place at your toddler's side in those first few difficult moments after your departure or to pry your toddler's fingers off your leg so you can walk out the door. If support is not forthcoming, perhaps you should speak with the school director. As a last resort, you can look for a new school as soon as it's feasible.

▲ Try asking a stand-in to drop your toddler off. If your toddler is clingy no matter what you do, have someone else (your spouse, a relative, or a friend) drop him off instead. Separating from you at home may be easier.

▲ Pick him up on time. Eventually, this will relieve him of the daily worry that you might not actually show up. And don't bring up the morning's scene (if there was one) on the way home. Instead, talk about the fun things he did all day and what he's going to do when he gets home.

Occasionally, there's an underlying reason when a child doesn't want to go to school. It may be illness (check for signs, such as fatigue, irritability, pain), change or undue stress (a new baby, for example), or a problem at school (an inappropriate program or an incompatible teacher; see page 822). If you think one of these problems may be operative, deal with it as soon as possible.

# A CALM-AT-SCHOOL, WIRED-AT-HOME TODDLER

*"The teacher at our son's preschool says he's perfectly behaved there, and that she never has any problems with him. But as soon as he gets home, he starts bouncing off the walls. Why?"*

Often a toddler who manages to stay centered long enough to be a model student quickly unravels once he's safely home. This letting loose when school lets out isn't usually a reflection of a parent's inability to control the child (or of the child's lack of self-control), but of several other factors: For one, transitions are often difficult for a young child; the change of pace and locale from school to home may be hard to handle. For another, the structured day at school focuses and directs energies in positive ways; returning to the relative absence of structure at home can leave him at loose ends. For still another, the comparative quiet of home may be jarring after hours of constant activity and stimulation. And probably most important of all, many children are more comfortable acting up at home, where they feel secure that someone will love them no matter what they do, than at school, where they don't feel that absolute security. After a long morning or afternoon on best behavior—no small strain for a two-year-old—it's a relief to be able to let it all hang out.

There are certain advantages to having a child who takes his walks on the wild side at home instead of at school—for example, you don't get calls from irate parents of classmates who have had run-ins with your child and parent-teacher conferences tend to be more pleasant. But if it's a challenge keeping the advantages in perspective when your "model student" is busy climbing the walls of your living room, try these tips for taming the after-school energy in your toddler:

**Stay after school.** When you pick up your toddler at school, don't just grab his things and rush out the door. Instead, ask him to show you some of the day's accomplishments; take time to admire his finger painting, the puzzle he finished, or the collage the whole class put together. Or, if his teacher doesn't object to your staying in the room a few minutes longer, sit down with him in the story corner and read him a quick book. This may help him bridge the formidable gap between school and home and make the transition smoother. En route home, talk about what's on the schedule for the rest of the day. If someone else is picking your child up at school, have him or her follow the same routine.

**Bring along a pick-him-up snack.** Sometimes, hunger brings out the beast in a child. And if all he's had since leaving home is a graham cracker or a few apple slices and juice, it's possible that a high-protein, complex-carbohydrate snack (a cheese stick and a whole-wheat roll) will bring out the calm you crave in him. Administering the snack on the way home will ensure that it kicks in by the time you reach your doorstep.

**Consider a side trip.** Making a stop at the playground on the way home to let your toddler run off some of the energy he's pent up during preschool may reduce his need to release it once you get home.

**Structure his homecoming.** Providing a supervised activity, similar to the ones he's involved in at preschool, is another way to ease his reentry into home life. So before you start tackling lunch or dinner or answering phone calls, try sitting down together with a book, a tape, a puzzle, or a toy—anything that allows you and your toddler to share a little special time.

For more tips on hectic homecomings, see page 271.

# WHAT IT'S IMPORTANT TO KNOW:
## Accepting Individual Temperaments

Popeye said a mouthful when he proudly proclaimed, "I yam what I yam." Yet the question remains, what made Popeye what he was? Was his identity preordained by his genetic blueprint—or was it molded from the cradle on? Was Popeye born to be the tenacious bully beater that he was? Or was his persistent persona a product of his environment?

Chances are, if "toons" are anything like their human counterparts, the responsibility for Popeye's temperament, for his strengths and weaknesses, falls more heavily on the side of genetics, though environment certainly plays a part as well. Most experts agree that each baby is born with a predetermined temperament and set of talents. And, as any parent of more than one child knows, no two children, even in the same family, are alike. One may turn out to be very good with numbers, another may be a whiz with words. One may be shy, another outgoing. One may be a natural athlete, another a natural klutz; one compulsively neat, another a happy slob. While these traits can be influenced in some ways by the home environment and other environmental factors, they are usually inborn.

As biologic children grow and develop, you will be amazed to see certain traits—traits you see in yourself or your spouse, your parents, your siblings, or your in-laws—emerge in different combinations.[5] Some may be traits you're delighted to see carried on, others may be traits you wish had been lost for good. Either way, there is little you can do to alter the inborn nature of your offspring, although you—and teachers, friends, life events, and other factors—will modify it somewhat.

Accepting the fact that a child "yis" what she or he "yis" makes for happier and more productive adults in the long run. To help your child make the most of inborn abilities:

**Shed those expectations.** You expect a "typical" boy to be athletic; yours turns out to be a bookworm. You expect a "typical" girl to be nurturing; yours turns out to love her blocks far more than her dolls. So what? Rid yourself of any preconceived notions of what children *should* be like, and expect yours only to be the best they can be—at being themselves.

**Don't place blame.** Since children come by their traits by chance, not by choice, don't punish or criticize them for being who they are. Nor should you blame yourself, your spouse, or any other family member your child seems to take after.

**Resist labeling.** Anyone who's ever had one affixed knows only too well that labels stuck on in childhood are hard to peel off later. Toddlers tagged "shy" are likely to always doubt their social capabilities; those branded "aggressive" are likely to push and bully their way through life.

**Accept without exception.** Work at understanding and accepting your child's inborn temperament and talents. Take them into account—when making plans, disciplining, buying gifts, deciding on child care (see page 804). Don't push the shy child to be the life of the party or throw a wet blanket on your high-spirited youngster. Don't try to change the musician into a scientist or the scientist into a musician.

**But do direct and modify natural tendencies.** Just because a child is born with a tendency to be shy doesn't mean he can't gain confidence and learn how to socialize comfortably (see page 183). Just because a child's got endless energy, she doesn't always have to be in hot water; her energies can be constructively channeled into sports or dance or other acceptable, active activities. The child who has trouble with numbers may never earn a Ph.D. in math, but he can be helped to succeed at arithmetic in school, to learn how to count his change, balance his checkbook, and keep a budget. Whatever the inborn traits, parental nurturing can influence how a child ultimately turns out.

**Viva those differences . . .** Like hair color, musical talent, or scientific genius, personality isn't always passed on in straight lines—which is why children can be so different from their parents or their siblings. Celebrate the differences, instead of wishing that your toddler was more like you, your spouse, or another family member.

**. . . and those similarities.** Sometimes, there's even more potential for conflict when a child is too much like a parent than when he or she is diametrically different. If your child has inherited an aspect of your personality with which *you* haven't yet come to terms (you're painfully shy, and you've always hoped your child would be outgoing), accept it. And work at accepting yourself so that you can better accept your child.

**Look for your toddler's good qualities.** Every child is special, every child has talents and strengths—as well as weaknesses. There's a silver lining in even the most difficult personality—it's just a

---

5. Adopted children have somebody's traits, too, but you usually can't finger the antecedents.

matter of looking past the clouds to find it. (See page 200 for examples.)

Don't forget that there are many qualities that are not inherited, qualities that parents can instill, such as responsi-bility, a love of learning, kindness, hon-esty, and tolerance toward others. In the long run, these values will have more in-fluence on the kind of person your child grows up to be than all the genes in the family pool.

# WHAT IT'S IMPORTANT FOR YOUR TODDLER TO KNOW: Living by the Rules

Living by the rules isn't always easy. But understanding the reasoning behind the rules usually helps make it easier: If we don't stop at a red light, we may plow into a car or pedestrian; if we burn leaves when there's a smog alert, we will add to a dangerous air-pollution problem; if we don't use a scooper when we walk our dog, someone—maybe even someone in our own family—may be scraping dog deposits off their shoes for days.

But though toddlers have imposed on them their share of rules, more often than not, they have little or no under-standing of why the rules are necessary—which makes living by them far more difficult. Helping your toddler to see the reasons behind rules will not only make rules easier to live by, but will make your toddler easier to live with. So:

**Explain your rules.** The bitter pill of bedtime, for example, may be a little more palatable if it's served up with an explanation ("Your body is still grow-ing—one day it's going to be big and tall. But to grow, it needs sleep.") Like-wise, the edict "Hold my hand when we cross the street," may be resisted less if the rationale is spelled out ("The drivers can't see you because you're smaller. But the drivers can see me because I'm big. If you hold my hand, you will be safe"). Make your point quickly and con-cisely. If you go on and on with a com-plicated explanation of a simple rule, your toddler will probably tune you (and your rule) out.

**Make rules consistent.** Living by the rules is impossible if a child is never sure, from one day to the next, what the rules are. If you scold your toddler for jumping on your bed one day, and you look the other way the next, your toddler won't take your rules seriously and may enjoy testing you to see "What's the rule going to be today?"

**Make rules clear.** When you say "Don't stand on the furniture" to a toddler who is standing on your bed, does that just mean "don't stand on your bed?" On any beds? Or does it mean, don't stand on any furniture, including beds, armchairs, and the sofa? How about the hassock? The kitchen table? Be as specific as you can when setting out your rules, and make sure you use language that is easy for your toddler to understand.

**Make rules reasonable.** Some rules are impossible for a two-year-old to live by: always chewing with his mouth closed, for example, or always cleaning up her toys without being asked. Keep your toddler's abilities in mind when making rules.

**Repeat the rules often.** Toddlers are typically so busy learning and discovering, rules tend to slip their minds. With their still-brief attention span and limited concentration, they have difficulty focusing on more than one thing at a time. So don't assume that stating a rule once, twice, or even a half dozen times is enough.

**Don't make too many rules.** If your toddler can't make a move without breaking a rule, chances are he or she's going to rebel against all the rules—if not now, then later on in life, and if not at home, then outside it.

**Make following the rules easy.** You can't expect a child to follow the rule to put toy cars away unless he or she has been instructed about how to put them away, and has a specific, accessible place to put them. So be sure that each rule you make comes complete with instructions.

**Don't expect perfect compliance.** Toddlers are toddlers; you can expect more rules to be broken than to be followed for a while. Sometimes they'll be broken inadvertently—because your toddler's simply forgotten or because his or her interest or curiosity has superseded everything else. Sometimes they'll be broken because of your child's inability to control his or her behavior. Sometimes they'll be broken because your toddler's testing you and the limits

you've set, and sometimes they'll be broken in a fiery fit of temper. Whatever the reason, once you've carried out any disciplinary measures necessary, be forgiving and understanding.

Realize that some rules are made to be broken, sometimes. When rules are broken in a moment of discovery (excited by the butterfly in the backyard and eager to report the sighting to you, your toddler breaks the "no dirty shoes in the house" rule and tracks fresh mud across the kitchen floor), don't be so quick to condemn the slip-up that you ruin the revelation. Give your attention to your toddler's discovery before turning it to the muddy footprints. At this point, your toddler can be reminded of the "no dirty shoes in the house" rule and handed a wet sponge to help you clean up with.

**Finally, follow the rules yourself.** You hang a U-turn where you know it's illegal, get on a ten-item-or-less line at the market with fourteen items, you cross in between, not at the green. These little everybody-does-it infractions may *seem* harmless enough. But if they become part of your everyday behavior, they tell your child that, when rules are inconvenient or unpalatable, they can be broken. When a role model (and for your child you're the number one role model) breaks rules, it's hard for a child to understand why he or she can't. As usual, your actions speak more eloquently and forcefully than your words.

# CHAPTER FIFTEEN

# *The 31ˢᵗ to 33ʳᵈ Months*

## WHAT YOUR TODDLER MAY BE DOING NOW

*By 2 ¾ years,¹ your toddler . . . should be able to (see Note):*

▲ brush teeth, with help
▲ build a tower of 6 blocks

**Note:** If your toddler has not reached these milestones, consult the doctor or nurse-practitioner. This rate of development may well be normal for your child (some children are late bloomers), but it needs to be evaluated. Also check with the doctor if your toddler seems out-of-control or hyperactive; highly demanding, stubborn, negative; overly withdrawn, passive, uncommunicative; sad, joyless; unable to interact with others.

*Imaginary friends are frequently guests in toddler households—welcome them if they come knocking at your door.*

---

1. This chapter covers the period between the time a toddler turns two and a half through two and three quarters (or thirty-three months).

### ...will probably be able to:

▲ draw a vertical line in imitation
▲ balance on each foot for 1 second
▲ identify a friend by naming
▲ carry on a conversation of 2 or 3 sentences (by 31 months)
▲ build a tower of 8 cubes
▲ wash and dry hands
▲ use prepositions (by 31 months)

### ...may possibly be able to:

▲ identify 1 color
▲ use 2 adjectives
▲ broad jump
▲ put on a T-shirt

### ...may even be able to:

▲ balance on each foot for 3 seconds
▲ count 1 block

# WHAT YOU MAY BE CONCERNED ABOUT

## AN IMAGINARY PLAYMATE

*"Our daughter has come up with an imaginary friend who's with her all the time. She has a family who loves her and friends at play group. Why would she want or need a pretend friend?"*

Between the domineering ways of adults and the grabbiness and pushiness of so many flesh-and-blood peers, what toddler wouldn't want a companion who is completely within her control, completely amenable to her desires, never talks back, and is a threat neither to her person nor her property? And who fits that bill better than a friend of her own creation—an imaginary playmate?

Besides providing the ideal companion, an imaginary friend can serve as an alter ego. This second self can be useful as a scapegoat (to test parental limits, to blame misdeeds on), a conscience (to keep her in line when she loses control), or an outlet for outsize emotions (anger, anxiety, fear, jealousy) she doesn't feel comfortable (or isn't yet capable) of expressing herself. Or the imaginary friend may be a protector (to save her from that big dog down the block or the "monster" lurking under her bed) or simply someone to keep her company when she's lonely or bored.

Imaginary playmates are extremely common. It's estimated that up to two-thirds of children create such companions at some point during early childhood. Most imaginary friends first appear on the scene when a child is between two and a half and three, hang around for a couple of years, and make their exit by the time the child is five or six. The vast majority of children with pretend pals, though they may vehemently deny it, know that their companion is make-believe.

In some families, a young child's unseen playmate pops in for visits only occasionally. In others, the playmate is ever-present. It may take any number of forms (a child, an adult, a smart dog, a powerful fairy godmother), may have a name (plain or fancy), specific characteristics (it's tall or short, fat or thin, pretty or funny), and habits of its own (it always sits in a particular chair, sleeps on the same side of the bed, wears the same color shirt). Some children even have more than one imaginary playmate— these friends may "show up" together or one at a time.

What are the long-term effects of having a pretend playmate? Research reveals that children with imaginary friends tend to have plenty of real friends, to display a rich vocabulary, and to be creative, independent, sociable, cooperative with teachers and playmates. They can distinguish between real and pretend as well as other children, but they are more likely to indulge in imaginary play with pretend objects (zooming around the living room playing "airplane" or handing Mommy a bunch of make-believe daisies picked in a bedroom "garden"). Numerous creative and successful adults recall having dreamed up pretend playmates as children.

To make your child's experience with her pretend friend a positive one for the entire family:

▲ Keep in mind that an imagination is a precious gift—one that helps a child thrive and grow. Let your toddler play out her imaginary-friend fantasy without interference or disparaging remarks. Making fun of her make-believe friend or forbidding her to bring her friend along when she leaves the house isn't likely to persuade her to give it up, only to keep it a secret—which could sink her deeper into her fantasy world than is desirable.

▲ Accept and welcome her friend. Instead of disputing the existence of the imaginary friend (which could upset, and possibly anger, your toddler), be hospitable. Go along with your toddler's wish that her friend have a place at the table, a pillow beside her own, even a bowl of "cereal"— but within the context of an imaginary game, just as you would when playing with dolls or cars with your toddler.

▲ Let your toddler take the lead. Don't offer the friend a place at the table until your toddler's asked for one and don't kiss the friend good-night unless your toddler's asked you to, but do play along when asked.

▲ Be wary of "using" the friend. Some parents use the imaginary friend to try to cajole their toddlers into cooperating. They may say "Dodo wants you to wear your mittens today because it's cold" or they may ask their child to "Show Dodo how nicely you brush your teeth." But this can backfire. Though some toddlers will play along good naturedly when parents try to take over their imaginary playmates, others resent the loss of control over their friend and become angry or uncooperative. Use this technique only if your toddler seems not to mind.

▲ Don't let your toddler use her friend to escape consequences. Using an imaginary friend for support, companionship, and imaginative play is fine. But using it to avoid picking up the box of crayons she's dumped on the floor by asserting "Dodo did it" *isn't*. Don't smile helplessly at this ploy, and end up picking the crayons up yourself later. Instead utter a knowing, "Ahaa," and add, "Well, then since you're her friend, you can help her pick them up." If your toddler balks at joining her pretend pal in the clean-up, stop playing along and insist she do the job herself.

▲ Provide other outlets for your toddler's imagination. Encourage her to play pretend games with dolls (if a baby doll doesn't satisfy her need for companionship, try a toddler-aged doll), stuffed animals, action or character figures, dress-up clothes, and puppets; if she seems unsure how to proceed, join in to get her going. Help feed her imagination by reading her books with varied characters, locales, and plots. (See page 365 for more on stimulating the imagination.)

▲ Provide other outlets for your toddler's negative feelings. If your child seems to use her "friend" to vent anger, jealousy, or other negative emotions, encourage her to talk about them (to the extent that she can) to you instead and to release them in other safe ways; see page 171.

▲ Provide plenty of real-life companion-ship. When the imaginary friend is a stand-in for real-life playmates or for parental attention, making an effort to sup-ply the missing ingredients may decrease a child's need for imaginary companionship.

▲ Remember that your child will eventu-ally give up her pretend playmate. When she becomes more comfortable with the conventional social scene and she is better able to express herself, her need for this extra moral support will likely disappear.

An imaginary friend may sometimes give parents valuable insight into a child's state of mind (for example, the pretend companion's reluctance to go to day care may signal a toddler issue that needs attention). But conjuring up such a friend doesn't, on its own, indicate an emotional problem.

If, however, your toddler becomes so consumed with, or dependent upon, her imaginary playmate that she doesn't interact with anyone else, or if she seems withdrawn or otherwise unhappy, discuss the situation with her doctor; counseling may be needed.

# SHYNESS

*"Our daughter seems terribly shy in social situations. We feel for her, but we don't know what to do to help her."*

Next time your child's in a roomful of toddlers, take an objective look around. Chances are you'll notice that she's not the only shy one in the bunch—and in fact, that many of her peers are as tentative as she is. That's because two- and three-year-olds are rarely outgoing; most show signs of shy-ness at least part of the time. Some are comfortable enough with adults, but not with peers. Others are comfortable with a small group of peers, but won't speak

to an adult outside the immediate family. Still others are shy with anyone they don't know well. By age six, about half of all children are still shy, though half of these will shed their shyness in the teen years. But in about one in five chil-dren the shyness is inborn rather than developmental; these children never completely shake shyness, though they often learn how to overcome it.

At this point, however, it's really impossible to tell whether your toddler's shyness is inborn or whether she's just behaving like a typical toddler. So instead of worrying or looking for a "cure" for her shyness, look for ways of helping her to have good feelings about herself and others, and to feel positively about her interactions with both adults and children. With support, even innately shy children can grow up to be friendly, confident adults (though that shy person will probably always remain somewhere inside). You can help your child reach that goal by:

**Accepting her shyness.** This can be especially hard to do if you are naturally gregarious, but especially important, too. Your child is a separate person—a two-and-a-half-year-old person at that—and she shouldn't be expected to behave the way you do. Viewing her shyness as a shortcoming, and expressing even subtle dissatisfaction with her lack of social prowess, or hinting that her behavior embarrasses you, can cause your toddler to withdraw further. Instead, let her know that you love her the way she is.

**Don't label her.** Calling your toddler "shy"—when talking to her or when talk-ing to others when she is near—will make the label stick in her mind and teach her to accept it as a fact. The label could thus perpetuate her shyness, even if it isn't inborn. Later, it may lead her to use the label as a way of avoiding unpleasant or uncomfortable situations: "I'm shy, so I don't have to." Avoid pointing out or praising more gregarious children, too, and drawing comparisons between their social performance and hers. Not only do you risk hurting her feelings, but her self-esteem as well. And lack of self-esteem can exacerbate shyness.

**Understanding her.** Even if you're not shy, "working the room" (especially when it's a room filled with already paired-off or teamed-up toddlers) is tough. Don't scoff at her very real anxieties and concerns; give her all the reassurance and support she needs. If she's anxious in certain types of situations, don't force her into them. But don't be too quick to come to her rescue either. Give her a chance to succeed before you decide she's going to fail.

**Encouraging her.** While you shouldn't push your toddler into social interactions, you should encourage her to participate in activities with other children, and help to break the ice, when necessary. Initially, she may find it easier to socialize with children who are a bit younger than she is (she will feel less threatened, and as the "big girl," may feel more confident), or a year or two older (if she feels comfortable in the role of follower). No matter their ages, the playmates you select should be laid-back, rather than aggressive. You can also assist her by fostering friendships (see page 183 for tips on how to do this), building her confidence and self-esteem, helping her feel good about herself (see page 292), and by teaching her what to do when she's anxious in a situation (think of something pleasant, or take a couple of deep breaths, for example).

**Rehearsing her.** In the guise of a no-pressure game, encourage relevant role-playing. Sample scenario: A teddy or a doll is hanging around on the edge of the playground, wanting to come and play with the others, but is afraid to try. Ask your toddler for advice, and give the out-sider some good suggestions for joining in, material your toddler can put to use in similar situations later on; children are great imitators. Remember to always conclude your script with a happy ending (teddy joins the group and has a great time).

**Preparing her.** Some children are particularly sensitive to transitions; preparing them well for new situations or giving them a head start can help them to cope better. En route to social events—including school—with your toddler, spend a couple of minutes preparing her, so that she'll know exactly what she's getting into. Go over the names of the children or adults who will be there, the activities that might take place, how she will greet everyone on her arrival. But take note of your toddler's reaction. Overpreparation can increase anxiety rather than decreasing it.

Get your toddler to school a few minutes before the other children arrive, so she can get acclimated and so she can be involved in an activity when other children arrive. Coming in late, with all eyes on you, is embarrassing even for adults. Also try to be among the first arrivals at birthday parties and at play group, rather than walking in once the fun's begun. If you do arrive late, tell your toddler before you walk in just what she can expect and what you're going to do ("We're late, and the party has probably started. So we'll take off your coat and put your gift on the table with the others. Then I'll take you over to where the children are playing"). Once inside, follow through.

**Equipping her.** As every adult party-goer knows, entering a social situation is always easier if you've got something in your hands—a bag, a cold drink, a plate of canapés. Likewise, your toddler may feel more confident striding into a group of peers at play if she's carrying something—a doll or stuffed animal, for instance. Not only will the toy, because it's hers, give her a sense of security, but it may give her an "in" with the other children—whether it's used in the game or just admired. Prepare your child for the possibility, however, that she may need to share the toy she brings and help her select a toy she is willing to share.

**Helping her, if she needs it.** If you see your toddler looking longingly over at a group of children at play, and she seems to want to join but doesn't know how, try giving her a few social pointers. Without pushing her to advance before she's ready, suggest a way in ("Why don't you go over and show those girls your new doll?"). Or if she'd like company when she makes her move, volunteer to move in with her— at least for a while. With her okay, take her hand and enter the circle of play together, asking the permission of the other children before you join in ("Could Jessica and I help you make that sand castle?"). Stay as long as she needs you, but no longer; retreat as soon as she seems comfortable.

Once your toddler has turned three, if you notice that her shyness interferes with her life (she never participates at preschool, always hangs onto you at play group, refuses to go to parties), discuss the problem with her doctor. There are counseling options and early, gentle interventions that can successfully modify extreme shyness in young children.

# UNRESPONSIVENESS TOWARD ADULTS

*"Whenever we're out and someone tries to say 'hello' to my toddler, he's very rude. He refuses to smile or answer their questions, and it gets embarrassing."*

A toddler who doesn't speak when he's spoken to or smile when he's smiled at isn't being rude, he's being normal—for a toddler, that is. Most toddlers are very uncomfortable in social encounters with adults they don't know well (and sometimes even with those they know well but don't see often), and they're usually even more uncomfortable when prodded and prompted ("Come on, silly, say 'hello' to Mrs. Walker"). They reject the kindness of strangers not out of ill will or orneriness, but because of natural timidity, immature social skills, or a lack of common interests (Mrs. Walker doesn't play with Legos or climb the jungle gym). Convincing your toddler to be more sociable won't be easy, and may not even be possible during the next couple of years. But these pointers may help reduce his discomfort (and yours) in such situations:

▲ Care more for your toddler's feelings than for appearances. Sure it's embarrassing to have your child regularly ignore those who greet him. But it's important to keep *your* embarrassment in perspective, to take *his* feelings into account, and to realize that most people understand a toddler's reticence with strangers. So, don't push. Accepting his timid ways and supporting him even when he refuses to be cordial will make it easier for him to become more sociable—when he's ready. And don't label him, by telling him not to be so rude or explaining his behavior to others as "bashful." If you do, he'll have little choice but to live up to the label.

▲ Speak for your toddler, if he's reluctant to speak for himself when addressed by strangers. For example, if he remains mute when a neighbor asks him, "What have you been doing today?" say, "We've just been to the playground, haven't we?" That gives him an easy entry into the conversation. At which point he may nod "yes" or want to share an anecdote, such as "I went on the swings," or he may remain incommunicado. Provide this service ungrudgingly, whenever you sense he needs it, but always give him a chance to answer for himself first.

▲ Try a little play acting. Help your toddler practice his social skills at home, where he feels comfortable and confident. Stage a pretend encounter at the market; you can be the cashier, and he can be the customer. Ask him questions that he might hear from friendly adults ("How old are you?" "What a nice hat you're wearing—is it a baseball hat?" "What's your teddy bear's name?"), and encourage him to answer. If he's hesitant, turn the tables and play the "toddler" yourself. It may be easier for him to be the grown-up asking the questions.

▲ Set a social example. Stop and speak to friends you meet in the street, say "Hello, how are you?" to the check-out clerk in the supermarket, the teller at the bank, the gas station attendant when you stop to refuel. Chat about the weather, the price of coffee, the dropping interest rates, the latest gas tax. Exchange a few pleasantries with his teacher when you pick him up at preschool, with the parents of his friends after play dates, with other parents at the playground. The art of small talk is rarely inborn; most of us learn it from eavesdropping on others.

While it's important to encourage good manners, never give your toddler the sense that you expect him to be unfailingly cordial to every adult or that he must do whatever any adult tells him to do. If he's uncomfortable about something, it's okay to refuse.

# A LACK OF FRIENDS

*"My toddler just started preschool. Other kids in her class seem to have picked up best buddies, but she can't seem to make a friend."*

**P**aired-off play becomes more common in the third year than it was in the second, but it certainly isn't universal. For many toddlers, making friends isn't a priority. They're often just as happy, if not happier, playing *alongside* their peers, playing by themselves, or playing with an older child or an adult (it's more predictable, less risky). Experience—or lack of it—certainly has a lot to do with how actively social a child is. Many of your toddler's classmates may have been in day care for a year or even two, or may at least have participated in a play group regularly from an early age. Children with such experience tend to pair off earlier than those for whom early social encounters are limited.

Sometime during the next couple of years (it may be later than sooner), your child will almost undoubtedly begin to make friends. If she's simply a late social bloomer, she may even end up with a very busy social calendar. Don't push her, but do give her support and help, using the suggestions for building toddler social skills on page 183. Be her friend, even when she doesn't have a peer friend out there. If she's shy, you will need to take this into account in helping her to make friends. If she's aggressive or bossy, either of which can also interfere with friend-making, explain that "Other children don't like to play with children who are bossy (or hit)," and take steps to help her deal with these traits (see pages 411 and 190). Keep in mind that some children (like some adults) tend to want to look over a situation (such as a new school) before entering into it wholeheartedly. If that's her style, let her watch from the sidelines until she's ready to make her move. Remember, too, that some, the *observers*, never seem to want to make that move at all (see page 215).

When you see your toddler on the outside looking in, seemingly eager to join the fun but too shy to try, you can suggest (but not insist on her trying) some ways to make contact: "Annie likes to play with puzzles. Why don't you see if she'd like to help you put some pieces in yours?" Or, "Why don't you ask David if you can play blocks with him?" If your toddler is hesitant to ask, occasionally ask for her so she'll get the idea. Or get her started on a fun project and invite another child to join her. But don't make a habit of intervening, or she may never learn to initiate contacts herself.

Most important of all, let her set her own social pace. If she's happy playing on her own and with family members, accept that; it's not necessary for her to have a circle of friends at this age. If, on the other hand, she seems upset by not having made a friend yet, explain the situation to her teacher (when your toddler's not within earshot); a little skillful intervention on the teacher's part may well get your daughter into the social swing.

# A CRYBABY

*"Our son seems like a pretty happy kid overall, but he's so touchy and sensitive. A dozen times a day, at the slightest provocation, he bursts into tears. This seems extreme, especially for a boy."*

Toddlers, in general, cry a lot. That's true of both girls *and* boys. In fact, studies show that before the age of twelve, crying patterns are pretty much the same in both genders. (After that, girls cry more often—probably, it is now believed, as much because of adolescent hormones as social conditioning.) Current wisdom encourages us to accept the idea that boys cry, and in most quarters, crying is no longer considered a no-no for boys, or even for men.

For the young, crying is often a method of communication. Not yet very facile with language, they cry to express feelings and frustrations. So it's possible that your toddler's crying will lessen as his vocabulary increases. Some toddlers cry more easily than others because their parents have unconsciously encouraged it, either by overreacting to physical or emotional injury ("Oh, you poor thing, did you get hurt?") or by heaping on lavish amounts of attention when the tears begin to flow. Be sure that isn't the case in your home.

It's also possible, however, that your toddler seems sensitive simply because he's a sensitive child. Sensitivity, like shyness, gregariousness, or aggressiveness, is a personality trait that is often inborn. Usually, the sensitive child, like the shy child, acclimates slowly to new people and situations, and has a more difficult time with transitions and changes. He may also be sensitive to sound, light, and/or touch.

While most toddlers experience life intensely, the sensitive child experiences life with *profound* intensity. Whether it's a tiny nick to the knee or to the ego, it's reason enough for a sensitive child to cry—louder and longer than might seem warranted. Instead of taking his tumbles in stride, the sensitive child collapses in a weeping heap after a fall. Instead of grabbing back a toy that's been wrenched from his hands by a playmate, the sensitive child crumples to the floor in tears.

Yet in spite of the fact that he cries easily, a sensitive child is not unhappy. In fact, children who are supersensitive tend not only to cry freely, but to laugh easily as well. And there are other up sides to being sensitive, too: Your child is more likely to be aware of the feelings of other people and even of animals (though at this age, that kind of empathy will probably still be limited). He may also be more perceptive and observant in general, which could serve him well in countless ways throughout his life.

Whatever the reasons behind the tears, crying isn't all bad. The crier usually feels better after a crying jag, possibly, researchers believe, because tears help reduce the build-up of chemicals produced by the brain under stress. Some researchers have also found that people who cry are, in general, emotionally and physically healthier than those who don't. So don't discourage crying entirely.[2]

To reduce it to a level that is more bearable for you and anyone else who cares for your toddler, however, try the following:

▲ Be sensitive to your toddler's sensitivity. The sensitive child feels pain—physical and psychic—more acutely than do others. Making fun of these feelings is unkind and denies their validity. And rather than making a sensitive child less prone to tears, insisting that he "tough it out" can make him feel even more isolated and vulnerable. Respond to his pain with understanding and empathy.

▲ Nuture your toddler's self-esteem . . . Low self-esteem can lead to heightened sensitivity and more crying. So boost your toddler's ego every chance you get by acknowledging good behavior and accomplishments (see page 292). Be sure you aren't demanding too much, or challenging him to perform beyond his capabilities.

▲ . . . but don't feed his crying. Crying should neither be rewarded (with treats, special privileges, or revocation of disciplinary actions) nor punished (with teasing, scolding, or punishment). The parental response to crying should, when possible, be neutral. Distraction may help dry the tears. If it doesn't work, provide just a measured dose of comfort. Too much commiseration will only give your child's crying momentum. If he seems to perk up when you give him a happy hug, use this quick and easy mood-enhancer freely.

▲ Help him replace wails with words. Teach your toddler how to say "It hurts" or "I'm sad" when something's bothering him; being able to express his pain clearly in words may lessen his need to cry it away.

▲ Try to keep your own negative moods in check. Because he's extra-sensitive, your toddler is likely to pick up on your anxiety, tension, anger, depression, or other emotions, even if you're trying to hide them. Use relaxation techniques (see page 173) to help deal with your moods; when you're upset, rather than trying to cover up your feelings, explain them to your child in very simple terms. He will feel better knowing rather than wondering or imagining. But *don't* use him as a therapist and tell all. Children should not have to bear or share parental burdens; sensitive children can be emotionally crushed by even minor parental worries.

▲ Use criticism sparingly. Whenever possible, camouflage it with praise. "You did a great job getting that sweater over your head. Let's look in the mirror, and see if we can figure out what happened to the doggy." When he realizes that the dog that is supposed to be on the front of the sweater is on the back, help him reverse it—if he wants to—but don't insist. Don't criticize a good effort, even if the results are less than what you consider perfect. For example, if he proudly tells you that he washed his own hands, don't criticize him for getting water everywhere, but do enlist his help in mopping up.

▲ Discipline with a light touch. To a sensitive child, a raised eyebrow or a look of shock or disappointment alone is usually enough to communicate your disapproval. Yelling, time-outs, and other more drastic punishments are not normally needed. Humor and other more gentle forms of discipline (see page 156) are likely to be much more effective (and less likely to provoke tears).

---

2.Though a toddler's frequent crying isn't usually a cause for concern, a school-aged child who always cries in response to criticism may lack self-esteem, and may require professional support.

That doesn't mean that you shouldn't require a sensitive child to adhere to standards or explain to him what he did wrong, just that you need to approach discipline in a low-key manner. Be sure to make rules clear to him and to teach him the skills he needs to do things "right," so that you can reduce the need for reprimands.

▲ Don't brand him for life. Tag a child "sensitive" or "crybaby" and he'll wear that label for years to come. If you need to explain his sensitivity to others (teachers or baby-sitters, for example), do so when he's not around.

▲ Don't automatically assume he's crying "wolf." Parents of children who cry easily often assume that there's nothing to cry about; they dismiss the wails even before they've investigated their cause. Remember that even though a sensitive child may cry over a scratch, it's important to respond, at least for a look-see, to every cry—not just for the sake of his self-esteem, but in case there's really a "wolf" this time (for example, a serious injury).

# BOSSINESS

*"Our daughter always wants us to do everything her way. She bosses us around, demanding we do things for her that she's perfectly capable of doing herself."*

Never fear, loyal subjects. Though this royalty complex is common among two- and three-year-olds, it is not usually a predictor of future tyranny, just another manifestation of toddler egocentricity. As the most important person in the world (at least from her point of view), it's only natural that your toddler wants things to run her way. It's also natural that she should want to wrest a little control in a life that often seems totally controlled by others. In other words, bossing you around is her opportunity to give back to you what you give to her.

As your child matures and begins to recognize that the world doesn't truly revolve around her, and as she gains more control over everyday events (as you give her more choices), her imperious manner should temper. And though she may well continue to be a leader, chances are, if you play your cards right, she'll cease to be so demanding. To play this hand:

▲ Treat her as you would like her to treat you. If you'd like your toddler to stop bossing you around, make sure you're not constantly bossing *her* around, and that rules and expectations are fair, age-appropriate, and not excessive.

▲ Give her adequate attention . . . Her demands may represent a need for more of your time; be sure she is getting enough of it without having to ask. And responding to your toddler's requests to "fix this" or for "more juice" as soon as you practically can, rather than continually putting her off, may also reduce her demands. When you can't respond right away, explain why you can't and give her a fair estimate of when you will be able to help her.

▲ . . . but don't let her tyrannize. Don't respond when she's rude. Expect her to say "please" and use a relatively courteous voice when she makes a request (though you may have to make an exception when she is particularly out-of-sorts). When your toddler's demands are excessive, calmly let her know they are and don't feel obligated to fulfill them.

▲ Hand over some control. Giving her choices during the day will help her feel more in control of her environment, and thus less compelled to try to take over completely.

▲ Give her some responsibilities. Start meting out simple jobs that she can handle (see page 416) and when she demands you do something you know she can do herself (pick up the crayon she just dropped or get a book from her room), refuse. Explain that you do a lot of things for her, but some things she can do for herself and some are just too silly to do at all. Don't, however, in an all out effort to defuse her bossiness, suddenly refuse to do anything at all for her. This will only increase her frustration and the bossiness that stems from it.

▲ Reinforce her self-reliance. When she does do something herself instead of demanding you do it, be quick to offer appropriate accolades.

▲ Recognize that the desire to run the show may be a part of your child's natural temperament. You won't be able to—and wouldn't want to—eliminate this trait, but you can help her to develop it in a positive way by teaching her leadership skills, empathy, fairness, and good manners.

*"Whenever our son plays with his friend, he bosses him around. The other kid doesn't seem to mind it, but we do. Bossiness seems like such an undesirable personality trait."*

For some toddlers, having a playmate around who'll let you call the shots presents an opportunity to play the power game. And they'll play it to the hilt—choosing the game, making up the rules, taking the dominant role in every scenario ("I'm the mommy, you're the baby"; "I'm the doctor, you're the sick person"). There are several possible reasons for bossy behavior in a toddler, including: *A sense of powerlessness.* Some toddlers compensate for the lack of power they feel by wielding power over others. Bossing around peers helps make up for their being bossed around by adults and older siblings. *Lack of social skills.* Not yet knowing how to behave with others their own age often contributes to bossiness. *Egocentricity.* At this age, many toddlers still haven't grasped the fact that the world doesn't revolve around them and that others have rights. *Natural temperament.* Some toddlers are born leaders, and early bossiness can be seen as an expression of that tendency.

Whatever the reasons behind your toddler's bossy behavior, you won't be able to change it by fiat or brute force. If it's due to toddlerhood rather than temperament, it's likely to be as transient as the toddler characteristics that cause it. If it's due to temperament, it's likely to persist. But you can ensure that a naturally bossy child turns out to be a leader rather than an obnoxiously bossy adult by nourishing his self-esteem, teaching him social skills and good manners, encouraging turn taking, empathy for others, and cooperation at play dates. (See the subjects individually for tips on how to do this.)

# TEASING

*"We often tease our daughter in fun, and she seems to enjoy it. But a friend said that teasing could hurt a child's self-esteem. Is this true?"*

Some children do indeed feel undermined by even the most playful kidding, but others delight in a good tease. If your child seems to relish the ribbing, there's no reason to deny either of you the fun it generates. As long as teasing is good-natured and not harsh or hurtful, it can actually be beneficial—nurturing a child's sense of humor and preparing her to tolerate teasing later on in life.

Right now, take your cues from your toddler when dishing out the kidding. Be sensitive to her reactions, and know when to quit (*before* she's upset or confused). Keep in mind, too, that small children often take what is said very literally. If you say it's raining "cats and dogs," she might expect to see puppies and kittens falling from the sky, and if you say, "Oh, you told a fib. You're nose is going to grow like Pinocchio's," she might expect to see twigs and a bird's nest projecting from her face. The teasing should be gentle, too. What you see as subtle humor, a toddler may take for a humiliating put-down. And since it's important for a toddler to feel secure in your love and approval, avoid excessive or careless teasing, which can threaten that security.

## *REFUSAL TO LISTEN*

*"Often, when I tell my son to do something or not to do something, he totally ignores me—pretends not even to hear me. I end up screaming at him, something I don't want to do."*

**A**ctions speak louder than words, particularly when you're dealing with toddlers who aren't listening. There are several reasons why a toddler may tune out his parents: For one, they may talk too much in general, or—when trying to get a point across—may sermonize and editorialize until the toddler has little choice but to switch off his audio in self-defense. For another, tuning out can be a toddler's way of avoiding conflict. If he ignores the reprimand when he's just knocked over a pitcher of water, it's as if there isn't one; hear no evil and there is no evil. For still another, not listening can be a toddler's way of testing parental authority and his own autonomy; it's not only enlightening but entertaining for him to see how many times Mommy or Daddy can

repeat themselves ("Aren't you listening? I told you three times to pick up those blocks!") and how angry he can make them get. And, finally, sometimes children become so engrossed in a game or focused on perfecting a skill that they literally block out all background noise—including their parents' voices. They really *don't* hear.[3]

Even when a toddler's reasons for not listening are innocent, being tuned out can be frustrating. To help open your toddler's ears to what you've got to say:

**Listen to *him*.** Parents often don't realize how many times a day they tune out their children. True, what your toddler is saying may not always seem of the utmost importance to you, but it is always important to him. And with his limited powers of self-expression, being ignored is even more frustrating to him than it is to you. He's small; not being heard makes him feel even smaller. Try to always lend him an ear when he asks for it and he is more likely to show you the same courtesy.

**Be realistic.** Parents often issue commands their toddlers don't understand. Or they issue too many at once—the average toddler at this age can handle only two at a time. Or they ask for the impossible: "Hang up your towel!" when a toddler can't reach the towel rod. Or "Put those toys away!" when the child hasn't any idea where or how to begin. Teach the skill before expecting compliance.

**Make contact.** Don't call from the other side of the room or with your back turned. Walk right up to your toddler and look him square in the eye when you speak. If necessary, kneel down so you're on same level.

---

3. Occasionally, a child who seems to have a *listening* problem, actually has a *hearing* problem. See page 488 for how to assess and what to do about such a problem.

**Keep it short and relatively sweet.**
Your toddler's attention span is limited.
Say what you want to say in a few clear
and simple words and you're more likely
to be heard.

**Get physical.** If words don't get a
response, catch your toddler's attention
another way. He's not listening to your
warning to stay away from the VCR?
Pick him up, move him to another room,
and distract him with another activity.
He fails to respond to your invitation to
lunch? Separate him from his playthings:
Pick him up and take him to the table.
He's hurting someone or could hurt himself? Intervene immediately.

Let your toddler know via body
language, tone, and expression that
you mean business, but try to remain
friendly. Don't drag him away from
what he's doing—unless such an action
is necessitated by his kicking and
screaming. Rather, pick him up with an,
"Oops, I don't think you heard me. It's
time for lunch. Tell the trucks you'll see
them later. If you like, you can take one
with you to the table."

**Cheer when your toddler *does* listen.**
Listening, in fact, should get much more
attention than not listening: "You got up
for lunch the minute I called. I really
liked that. Thank you."

# TODDLER DECISION MAKING

*"I know I should let my daughter
make more of her own decisions,
but she always makes such inappropriate choices."*

N obody—not corporate CEOs, not
powerful politicians, not influential
financiers—is called on to make more
(or tougher) decisions than a parent. But
possibly the toughest decision of all is
deciding whether, when, and how often
to let a child make her own decisions.

Letting children make choices is a
little scary, especially during the toddler
years, when they're still short on experience and judgment and long on eccentricities—and when so many decisions
may be (at least in the parental view)
"wrong." Yet having the opportunity to
make decisions is essential to a child's
development—an important part of
growing up. Children who are brought
up in a home where parents make all the
choices are unlikely to develop the skills
needed to help them make responsible
decisions on their own. Later, when
they're away from home—whether for
an afternoon at a friend's house, a day
at school, or a year at college—and face
difficult choices (Should I cheat on a test?
Smoke a cigarette? Drink and drive?),
they often make poor ones, or let others
make the choices for them.

Giving your child decision-making
opportunities will provide a sense of
control now and set her on the road to
becoming a wise decision-maker
later—though you can expect that, at
first, many of her decisions will be far
from sage.

When involving toddlers in decision
making, however, there are some caveats:

▲ **Don't offer open-ended choices.** For
example, ask "What do you want to
eat?" and your toddler could request
something you don't have in the house
or something that is inappropriate, such
as a candy bar for breakfast. If you give
a child free choice and then object to her
choice, she will conclude that she didn't
have a real choice in the first place (diminishing her trust in you) and/or that
her choices are not good ones (diminishing her trust in herself and her decision-
making ability). So set the parameters
when offering choices: "Would you like
cereal and bananas or toast and peanut
butter for breakfast?"

▲ Don't offer choices that can jeopardize health and safety. It needs to be clear to your toddler that there is no choice when it comes to buckling into a car seat, wearing mittens in below freezing weather, or running ahead into the street. But even in such non-negotiable cases, there are usually at least a couple of options you can offer to help bypass a battle: "Do you want me or Grandpa to buckle your belt?" "Do you want to hold Mommy's hand or Daddy's hand when we cross the street?"

▲ Don't burden a toddler with a decision when the consequences are great, as when you're picking a preschool, for example. You can ask for her input, of course; once you've picked out two options that seem equally good, let her help make the final determination. But it's irresponsible to put all of the responsibility for a major decision on a child's shoulders. If the decision turns out to be a poor one, she'll be reminded of it every day, and her sense of failure as a decision-maker may make her hesitant to make future decisions.

▲ Be careful not to overwhelm your toddler with more decisions than she can comfortably handle. Making choices all day long—about food, about clothes, about toys, about playmates, about activities—can be stressful. So don't preface every activity of every day with a "Would you prefer . . ."

Sometimes, you can make joint decisions, based on a blend of your toddler's wishes and whims, and your experience and knowledge. As you share decision making, share with your toddler, in an informal way, the steps that are normally taken in making good decisions. Talk about the choices, what you need to know to make a good decision ("It may rain, so the library may be a better choice than the playground"), whether anyone will be hurt or be sad ("Grandma will be sad if we go to the movie instead of visiting her"), whether

a choice is right or wrong ("We promised Jenny we'd go to the museum with her. It would be wrong to break our promise"). It's too early to discuss the more mature concept of weighing risks against benefits when making a decision (If I walk in front of the swings I get to the sandbox sooner, but I risk getting hit with the swing—is it worth the risk?), but it's not too early for your child to learn to take responsibility for a decision she's made ("We decided to go to the playground. It started to rain and we got all wet, so we have to go home now instead of to the library").

Let your toddler know that even when we try hard to make good decisions, we sometimes make mistakes. If she knows that it's okay to make mistakes sometimes, she will feel freer to risk making decisions. When she makes a less-than-perfect choice, spare her the "I told you so's" and let it speak for itself. Help her, without being critical or judgmental, to see the consequences of each decision, to learn from it, and to think about how the decision could be improved next time around. For example, she insists on wearing a dress to the playground and then falls and scrapes her knee. Instead of "I told you to wear pants . . ." try "I'm sorry you scraped your knee. What do you think you can do next time you come to the playground to keep your knees from getting hurt?"

Don't expect practice to make perfect, however. With experience and maturity, your toddler's decision-making skills will improve, but they (like your own) will never be foolproof. Like her parents before her, she's only human.

# CHORES

*"I'd like my son to be responsible and help out around the house, but I wonder if he's old enough for me to start giving him chores."*

A child who puts his dirty clothes in the hamper instead of leaving them where they drop, who cleans up his room without being told, who clears the dinner table without a murmur, who willingly gives up his Saturday afternoons to mow the lawn. A parent's dream? Yes, indeed. Will this dream come true? Probably not. But it is possible to raise a responsible child—one who will do his fare share of the chores, with only the occasional grumble—if you:

**Start early.** It's certainly too early to require your toddler to perform regular chores, but it isn't too early to give him an occasional taste of responsibility. In fact, since most toddlers enjoy imitating

---

## CHORES TODDLERS CAN TACKLE

· · · · · · · · · ·

While it may be too soon to pass the vacuum cleaner to the next generation, it's just the right time for getting your toddler involved in a few basic chores. You'd be surprised at how many around-the-house tasks the average two- or three-year-old is completely capable of. Sign your toddler up for any of those listed below, or devise your own (keeping his or her safety and skill level in mind). Remember that most jobs will require adult supervision and some will need adult assistance. But try to keep interference to a minimum; a chore that's done "all by myself" is always more satisfying to a toddler.

▲ Pick up and put away toys (see the facing page for tips on making this easier).

▲ Put dirty clothes in the hamper.

▲ Help sort colored and white laundry.

▲ Unload clean clothes from a cooled-down dryer.

▲ Deposit and take mail from mail box.

▲ Dust. Provide a dust cloth or feather duster and give a demonstration, then let your toddler loose. Be sure there are no breakables in the area to be dusted.

▲ Unpack and put away unbreakable groceries (toilet tissue, paper towels, bread, cereal boxes, pasta) in accessible cabinets.

▲ Sweep the floor with a small broom and dustpan (a dustpan that "stands up" and can be held by a long handle makes this task easier).

▲ Set the table with placemats and napkins, unbreakable dishes and cups, and flatware (no knives).

▲ Clear the table of unbreakable items.

▲ Dry unbreakable dishes, pans, spoons, plastic cups.

▲ Wipe water-safe surfaces with a spray bottle of water and a cloth or a damp sponge.

▲ Wash, scrub, and rinse produce in kitchen sink (standing on a sturdy, steady stepstool).

▲ Tear lettuce for salad.

▲ Toss a small salad in a large bowl (until your toddler is proficient, it's probably wise to add the dressing later).

▲ Snap string beans, shell peas, husk corn on the cob, break broccoli or cauliflower into florets.

▲ Cut cookies or sandwiches with a cookie cutter.

▲ Shape meatballs, dumplings, or cookie balls. (Hands should be washed carefully before and after this chore, especially if the mixture contains raw meat or raw egg; your child should also be instructed not to taste such a mixture.)

▲ Mix or stir eggs, pancake batter, cake batter, uncooked pudding. (Again, no licking allowed if raw egg is an ingredient.)

▲ Water plants (use a small watering can).

▲ Pull weeds (under close supervision).

their parents around the house, now might be the perfect time to groom your child for a future of helping out. Assign him safe and simple tasks, such as picking up toys, carrying nonbreakables to and from the table, "dusting" the living room (see box page 416 for more ideas). Also teach him routinely to throw his trash (a drawing he rejected, the wrapping that held his sandwich, the used tissue) right into the wastepaper basket, trash can, or recycling bin.

**Keep chores fun.** Supply placemats with child appeal when you ask him to set the table for lunch, decorate the hamper with a favorite character ("Honey, please give your dirty clothes to Mickey Mouse"), have him pick up his toys to the rhythms of his favorite songs (see page 419 for more ways to enliven picking up).

**Make chores a family affair.** The family that cleans (or cooks or gardens) together gets more done and has a better time doing it. As long as the division of labor is fair and equitable (jobs are apportioned and assigned according to age and ability), this kind of togetherness encourages children to continue to do their share as they grow up.

**Keep your demands reasonable.** Even if your toddler seems enthusiastic about helping out, don't push him to do more than he's capable of or willing to do. If he's overloaded with responsibilities now, he may burn out early and become resentful of helping out later—when his ungrudging help will be much more important.

**Don't grumble yourself.** If you moan and groan every time you have to pick up a dirty dish or push a vacuum cleaner, you're sending a very clear message to your toddler: Chores are the pits. Instead, try to make them less disagreeable for you by playing your favorite music or whistling your favorite tune as you work.

Or, if you hate housework so much that you can't stop grumbling, at least keep your grumbles to yourself.

# ROOM CARE

*"My daughter takes out every toy when she's playing in her room, throws them around, and won't put them away. Isn't it time she started keeping her room clean, or at least cleaning it up after she's finished playing?"*

Clean is in the eyes of the beholder—and what a toddler beholds is usually very different from what her parents view. When you look around your toddler's room, you see a helter-skelter jumble of strewn toys and scattered books, crumpled paper, and broken crayons. When your toddler looks around her room, she sees a soothingly cozy oasis in an otherwise forbiddingly tidy home. It's possible, in fact, that the clutter that you find maddening brings her comfort and pleasure.

*Cleaning up can be almost as easy as ABC when toy bins are toddler-accessible.*

There are a couple of good reasons why most toddlers and preschoolers are happier in a messier room. For one, being surrounded by their possessions, so that they can touch them, feel them, and commune with them, makes them feel more secure. For another, toddler play is often on-going. When your toddler leaves her game of teddy-bear hospital to pick up a puzzle that's caught her eye, it doesn't mean she's done playing doctor. Putting the bears away before they're finished with their treatment—which may well go on for several days—unfairly interrupts her fantasy.

But just because your toddler doesn't see the benefits of keeping her room or play space clean doesn't mean there aren't any. Toys that are put away can't be tripped over, stepped on and broken, or end up in that netherworld under the bed; books that are shelved are less likely to be torn, crushed, or otherwise damaged; puzzles and games that are returned to their proper place are more likely to keep all their pieces (at least for a while). And learning to pick up isn't just good for your toddler's possessions, it's good for her, too. It will prepare her to meet the expectations of preschool, and later elementary school, and, like any skill she learns, help her to feel good about herself.

If you introduced her to a clean-up routine earlier (see page 57), she's already got a head start. But whether you did or not, you can help her to pick up the picking-up habit now by:

**Limiting clean-ups.** It's possible to clean up after a toddler all day long and still be faced with a mess by nightfall. But many parents find it's much more practical to let the messes fall where they may during the day and wait until day's end to start picking up the pieces. That compromise gives a toddler important freedom of play; she can come and go from her games without fearing that they're going to be cleaned up from under her.

By the time a toddler is nearing three, however, it's a good idea to begin encouraging her to put away her playthings as she finishes with them. When you're playing with her, make a point of putting away the game or toy together when play time is up. This concept is especially important if your toddler's play space is in a shared area of the house and/or when dealing with puzzles, games, and other toys with numerous small pieces or bits. You can't expect perfect compliance at this stage, but you can instill an ideal that will, hopefully, become a reality sometime in the future.

**Allowing for continuity.** If your toddler's in the middle of constructing a block city or of setting up a dolls' tea party when clean-up time rolls around, don't insist that she put her things away if she's not finished with them. Gently move the activity-in-progress out of traffic's way, and let her pick it up where she left off in the morning. If she's finished the block city, or another project, but she's not ready to dismantle it yet, respect her desire to leave it in one place for a while. Setting aside a special area for the purpose on the floor or a small table will make this easier to do.

**Sharing the task.** Remember, you're the one who wants the room to be cleaned up—your toddler has a different agenda. It's only fair that you take responsibility for at least some of the job. But instead of routinely doing it all for her (because you want it done quickly and you want it done well), make cleaning up her room a friendly team endeavor. Each of you can contribute your special assets to the effort (you, expertise and experience; your toddler, energy and youthful enthusiasm). Split up the tasks according to ability ("I'll put this puzzle back together, then you can put it away; you put all the books in a pile, and I'll put them on the bookshelf").

**Taking it one step at a time.** A room strewn with toys can be so overwhelming that it can make a toddler want to give up before she's started. So instead of taking on the whole disaster area at once, divide it into more manageable sections—the dress-up corner first; then, the block pile; then, the clutter that's collected on the bed. Tackling a big job in small pieces minimizes frustration and maximizes results. When supervising clean-up, hand out specific tasks one at a time, too: "Put the giraffe on the shelf, then put the piggy next to him," rather than "Pick up all of your stuffed animals and put them on the shelf."

**Making a game of the job.** In true Mary Poppins spirit, try to turn cleaning up into a merry pursuit. Instead of snapping, "Put your toys away this minute!" playfully suggest "It's time for the dolls to go to sleep in their beds . . . for the blocks to go into the block box and have dinner . . . for the cars to have their engines checked in the garage." Challenging your toddler to a race she can win is another way to make cleaning up a lark ("Let's see if you can pick up all of the doll clothes before the buzzer rings" or "Let's see who can put the most crayons in the box by the time I count to ten"). And if you seem to be having a good time yourself (instead of nagging, whining, and complaining), you'll have a much better chance of convincing your toddler that cleaning's not so bad after all.

**Moving the job along with a song.** Many nursery schools play or sing a special "clean-up" song that children come to associate with putting away their toys and moving on to another activity. Adopting the practice at home will give clean-up time the status of a ritual, one your toddler may even look forward to. Choosing a lively song to work by may speed up activity and thus the clean-up process.

**Making the job a learning experience.** Teach colors by saying, "You put away everything that's red, and I'll put away everything that's green." Teach shapes by saying, "You put away all the round blocks and I'll put away all the square ones." Teach numbers by saying, "You put away one-two-three cars, and I'll put away one-two-three-four-five cars" or "See if you can pick up all those dress-up clothes by the time I count to twenty." Keep these clean-as-you-learn sessions fun for your toddler; if they become stressful or your toddler doesn't seem to enjoy them, drop them and try a less academic route.

**Making the job easier.** Unreachable, or otherwise inaccessible, storage makes clean-up impossible for young children. Make it easy for your toddler to help by putting toy storage space within her reach. Shelves should be low and open, bins should be shallow and removable, pegs for clothing shouldn't be a stretch. Labeling shelves and bins with a picture and the clearly printed name of the kind of toy that belongs on it or in it will help; so will using different-colored bins for different types of toys. Avoid using one big toy chest for general toy storage; chests encourage large-scale dumping, which can result in broken toys and frustration when a toddler can't find what she's looking for (toy chests can also be dangerous; see page 625).

**Providing grown-up equipment.** Once she's helped put her toys away, reward your toddler with a small broom and an upright dustpan so she can "sweep" her floor. You can also supply her with her own wastebasket and hamper; if they're colorful, she may be more likely to use them. Of course, always check the contents of the wastebasket before dumping it (it may contain keys, a wallet, several puzzle pieces, and who knows what). And be sure to sort the clothes in the hamper carefully (virtually anything can end up there in the folds of the pajamas and T-shirts).

**Acknowledging her efforts.** Even if she only puts away one crayon for every twenty you put away; even if she gets the toy bin halfway onto the shelf and it falls to the floor (scattering its contents yet again); even if she tosses her dolls in a pile instead of lining them neatly on her dresser—her effort is worth a pat on the back. With plenty of positive reinforcement ("Thank you for putting away those airplanes") and scant negative criticism ("Why can't you put those airplanes away neatly?"), she'll continue to do better and better.

**Not demanding perfection.** If your toddler seems to thrive on disarray, don't insist she keep her room neat as a pin. Strike a happy medium between your standards and hers, keeping in mind that it is *her* room.

# THE FACTS OF LIFE

*"Ever since we told our son that we're having another baby, he's been intensely interested in how babies are made. I've avoided his questions so far because I don't know how to answer them."*

Skip the storks, can the cabbage patch, banish the birds and the bees. Experts now agree that children need real answers to questions about reproduction. No matter how young a child is, if he's old enough to ask, he's old enough for a straightforward answer—albeit, one that's appropriate for his age. So:

**Don't dodge the issue.** Ignoring his questions or putting him off with "I'll tell you when you're older," or "Go ask your mommy (or your daddy)" may make him think that there is something shameful about making babies, or about his curiosity. Don't worry if you're uptight about discussing the subject; most parents are. Try *not* to communicate your anxiety to your toddler, but don't worry if you do. It's better to communicate the anxiety with the facts than the anxiety alone.

**Present a united front.** You, your spouse, or anyone else who may discuss the issue with your toddler should confer and agree on the approach to the subject.

**Give it to him straight.** Toddlers are curious about all bodily functions. Direct, accurate information about those that relate to making babies will satisfy that curiosity. On the other hand, veiling the subject in mystery is likely to make it more fascinating—or frightening. Putting a child off with the traditional myths about conception and delivery will only confuse him now; later on, when he learns the truth, it will shake his faith in you. If you want him to continue to come to you for honest answers, you must answer honestly from the start.

**Give it to him on his level.** A simple, concise explanation should suffice, and in fact, will fulfill his need to know better than a lengthy, complex one. Skip confusing analogies—stick to parents and babies. If a satisfactory explanation eludes you, try the one described below or tell your toddler, "We're going to get a book from the library about how babies are made and read it together." (Be sure the book you check out is geared to toddlers and young preschoolers.) And remember, he isn't asking about "sex," he's asking about "reproduction," about how babies are made.

**Give him the correct terminology.** Your toddler may also be confused by euphemisms for body parts; instead use penis, vagina, uterus, ovum (or egg), sperm.

## THE NEW FACTS OF LIFE

· · · · · · · · · ·

The facts of life used to be simple and predictable—girl met boy, girl married boy, girl and boy went to bed, girl and boy made baby. Variations were few and frowned upon; when they occurred, they were usually kept hush-hush.

Today, the facts of life are sometimes a little more complicated—and consequently, tougher to explain to curious children. Today, girl may meet boy, go to bed with boy, and make a baby with boy, but choose not to marry or even to live with boy. Or girl and boy may find out that they're unable to make the baby in bed, and may end up making it in the laboratory. Or girl may meet girl and decide to bypass boy entirely—except as a sperm donor. To further complicate the detailing of the facts of life, there's nearly a 25% chance that a girl won't deliver in the time-honored way, through her vagina, but through the abdomen instead.

If there's plenty about the "traditional" facts of life that are beyond a toddler's ken, there's even more about the new facts of life that are. For those whose reproductive stories have a twist, the more complicated facts should probably wait until your child is old enough to digest them and mature enough to put them in perspective. Unless you feel strongly that your toddler needs to know the entire truth now (and it may be very difficult to explain it on a level that he or she can grasp), it might be wise to offer an overview of reproduction (based on the question or questions asked) without going into your specific situation. For instance, "Most babies are born through the mother's vagina" will probably satisfy a toddler delivered via cesarean who has asked about the birth process without introducing unnecessarily frightening details about abdomens being cut open. Even if the sperm didn't fertilize the egg in the traditional way (and even if the sperm wasn't actually Daddy's) or if the child was adopted, a toddler will be satisfied in knowing that "A daddy's sperm and a mommy's egg make a baby together." (For more on talking to children about adoption and special families, see Chapter Twenty-Six.)

**Give him only as much as he asks for.** Answer only the questions he asks. If he asks where the baby is, tell him that it's in a special place where babies grow, called the uterus or womb (not stomach or tummy, since he's bound to associate these terms with eating). Explain that as the baby grows, a woman's middle gets bigger. Showing him pictures of what a growing fetus looks like in the uterus in a book for young children will help illustrate your words. If he asks how it's going to get out, tell him that most babies come out through the mommy's vagina. If he asks how it got into the uterus, say that "Mommy and Daddy love each other a lot and love *you* so much, they wanted to make another baby. So Daddy put his sperm into Mommy. And that sperm got together with a tiny egg, called an ovum, that was inside Mommy all along, and they grew into a baby."

Explain the biological part of the process only; for now, stay away from the sexual aspects. If he asks how the sperm got into Mommy, just say, "through the vagina." That should do it. If it doesn't, and he persists in knowing how this neat trick was accomplished, say that, "Daddy's penis put his sperm into Mommy's vagina. The sperm met the egg and a baby began to grow."

Some children express no interest at all in how the baby got inside of Mommy or how it's going to get out—they're more concerned with what it does while it's in there. If your toddler asks how the baby eats or breathes while it's in the uterus, explain simply that it gets everything it needs through the umbilical cord, which is attached to its belly button. A picture of a fetus curled up in the uterus will help illustrate this. Showing your child his own belly button—which he was once fed through—will personalize the concept for him.

**Give him some perspective.** Showing your toddler photos of you when you were pregnant with him, then photos of him as a baby, will help him make some sense of the whole process.

# PARENTAL DISPLAYS OF AFFECTION

*"We're not sure how much affection we should display in front of our son—what's appropriate, what's not?"*

**S**ome—but not all—of what comes naturally can be done in front of your toddler in good conscience. In fact, by showing your toddler the affection you share, you demonstrate your love in a concrete way. Having parents who openly hug, hold hands, cuddle on the couch, pucker up and kiss, indulge in the occasional pat or caress, and don't hesitate to say, "I love you," can increase a child's sense of security. It also sets an important example—one he can follow in his own relationships later on. Not incidentally, such frequent shows of affection can make a marriage more secure (a plus for you *and* your child). Keeping "in touch" is one of the best ways to keep those love lights burning.

There are several cautions, however. Losing your inhibitions entirely (a casual kiss turns into a long, smoldering liplock; cuddling turns to groping; an embrace gets hot and heavy) around your toddler will confuse and possibly frighten him. Parental lovemaking is simply not appro-

priate viewing for children of any age. Any display that makes you feel uncomfortable is probably also inappropriate.

At one point or another, many young children become jealous of their parents' love for each other. To minimize this reaction, be sure your toddler gets his share of hugs and kisses (assuming he enjoys them). If he seems to want to get into the act when you're in the middle of a hug, don't push him away. Bring him in for a family hug, but make it clear that there's more to the family dynamic than just a threesome: "Mommy loves you. Daddy loves you. Mommy and Daddy love you. And Mommy loves Daddy and Daddy loves Mommy. And we like to hug each other, just like we like to hug you." (For more tips on jealousy, see page 155.)

# BRIBES AND REWARDS

*"I often find myself bribing our daughter with special treats so she'll do what I say. But I have the feeling that I'm not doing the right thing."*

**L**ife's full of incentives; around every corner there's someone waiting to offer you X, if you'll just do Y. Work extra hard at the office, and you'll get a bigger holiday bonus. Buy $15 worth of skin care products at the cosmetics counter, and you'll get a free travel tote. Subscribe to the magazine now, and you'll receive an extra six months for free. It's only natural for parents to turn this persuasive technique on their children. Eat your broccoli and you'll get a cookie. Clean up your room and you can watch *Sesame Street*. Come down from the jungle gym right now and we'll stop and buy stickers on the way home. Don't fight with Jonathan and we'll visit the pet store after the play date.

And though the occasional use of incentives is harmless—and, when you consider the stubbornness quotient of the average toddler, sometimes altogether necessary—their habitual use to coax compliance may be unwise. Some studies show that children who are regularly bribed to cooperate or achieve learn to expect rewards and tend to do only as much as they need to in order to collect the prize; eventually, they don't bother to try at all unless a reward is offered. What's more, they often begin to assume that any task for which a reward is offered must be unpleasant or undesirable—otherwise, why would a reward be necessary?

These children don't learn the concept of doing something for its own value (eating the broccoli because it tastes good and helps you grow; cleaning up because a tidy room is more fun to play in; not fighting over toys with a playmate because it makes the play date more pleasant). Later on, in school, experts suggest, creativity and love of learning can be inhibited by the use of too many gold stars and special privileges to reward academic success—on any project, these children tend to expend only the amount of energy necessary to cash in on the incentive, and no more.

Most parents would prefer their children to do what's right not because they are told to or because they expect a reward, but because they have developed inner controls and good values. To help your toddler become that kind of child:

**Reward with praise.** Letting your toddler know (with words, hugs, pats on the back) that you're proud of her accomplishment or cooperation will fuel her inner drive much more effectively than will a more tangible reward. But be sure you praise the behavior ("You did such a wonderful job cleaning up your room!") rather than the child ("You're such a good girl for cleaning up your room!"), and that you don't overdo it; see page 289 for more on praise.

**Offer more tangible rewards occasionally.** Though a toddler shouldn't be rewarded for putting her toys back on the shelf or eating her broccoli, it's okay to offer a special treat (a trip to the playground, a rental video, an ice cream cone) when your child is required to cooperate above and beyond the usual call of duty. For example, when she has to accompany you while you shop around for a new dress and accessories at the mall, it's legitimate to promise a treat at the end in return for good (if not perfect) behavior. Rewards may also be in order when a child is trying to take a major developmental leap forward—staying dry at night, for example, or expanding her food repertoire. Often setting up a chart with gold stars for these kinds of achievement is enough for very young children. Older children like to know that once they've accumulated a certain number of stars, they will be able to choose a gift or special privilege. When you can, it's a good idea to match the reward with the deed: a doctor's kit for the toddler who undergoes medical testing without much complaint; an article of clothing for the toddler who accompanies you to the mall for your shopping spree without squawking; a perky new placemat or cereal bowl for the toddler who has been cooperative about trying new foods.

**Surprise with a reward.** The most satisfying kind of reward—and the one most likely to spark accomplishments and compliance in the future—is the unexpected kind. Occasionally bestowing a surprise reward for particularly fine achievement or for extra-special cooperation can be very effective in reinforcing positive behavior.

**Avoid bribes.** A bribe is used to "buy off" a child who is being contrary or recalcitrant: "Come to the table right now." "No, I'm playing!" "If you come right now, you can have ice cream for dessert." In that scenario, the bribe is offered in order to persuade the child to comply. But resorting to bribery is ultimately a big mistake. Rather than eliciting good future behavior, it encourages a child to say "no" next time so that you will offer her a treat *again* in return for compliance. So if you're going to give a reward anyway (which you should not do routinely), offer it before your child has refused to comply.

**Keep threats to a minimum.** Like bribes, threats tend to stifle any innate drive to achieve and behave responsibly. A child who is threatened may comply, but only to avoid the promised punishment.

**Reinforce the concept of good behavior as its own reward.** Help your toddler see the benefits inherent in doing the right thing. For example, after you've cleaned up the living room, exclaim: "It feels so good to sit in a clean living room; I really didn't feel like cleaning it before, but now I'm glad I did."

Point out some of the benefits of your toddler's good behavior, too. For example, if she stops grabbing toys at play group and then gets a call for a play date, you can say: "I think James really enjoyed playing with you in play group yesterday, and that his mommy appreciated your good manners. That's probably why he wants to play with you today."

# WHAT IT'S IMPORTANT TO KNOW:
## Communicating With Your Child

Articles and books have been written about it. Talk shows address it. Parenting classes are devoted to it. And yet, with all the information available on the importance of parent–child communication, the fact is that parents in America spend far too little time in conversation with their kids—an amazing average of just a few minutes a day, some studies show.

How can your family buck the statistics and make conversation an important part of your lives?

**Start early.** Even children who are barely verbal can participate in conversation, so it isn't too early to begin having two- (or three-) way talks in your family. Building solid communication skills now will lay the groundwork for continuing dialogue as your child grows, and may ultimately make it easier for him or her to talk about sensitive subjects (friends, cheating, bullying, dating, sex, and alcohol and other drugs).

**Set aside a special time for talk.** Though it's valuable to strike up a conversation with your toddler at any time—when you're pushing the stroller or the swing, when you're making dinner, when you're driving to day care, when you're getting ready for work—such conversation isn't enough. Good communication requires a solid stretch of unbroken time. Mealtime generally provides such a stretch, but only if you ban television, newspapers, telephone calls, and other distractions. Even if you don't eat with your toddler, try to sit down for some conversation. A talk, particularly about the day's events, can also be a valuable part of your toddler's bedtime ritual. Make time, too, if you can, for a "good morning" chat (your toddler's bed or yours) before each day begins.

**When your toddler wants to talk, listen.** To a toddler who has no concept of time, being put off with a vague promise of "later" can be enormously frustrating. Not only is "later" a lifetime away, but by the time it rolls around, your toddler is likely to have forgotten that painstakingly formulated thought he or she had been bursting to share. Until your child learns patience and develops the ability to put thoughts on hold (around the age of four), try to avoid keeping him or her waiting for your ear. There will be times when waiting will be unavoidable—as when you're discussing a computer problem with the repair person or you're on an important phone call. Just make certain your toddler's next in line for your attention when you're done. A child who is regularly put off often begins to feel, "No one really wants to hear what I have to say, so I just won't say anything. I'll keep it to myself."

**Make contact when communicating.** Sometimes—when you're driving the car, pushing a stroller across a busy street, dicing carrots with a sharp knife—an ear is all you can lend your toddler. But whenever possible, try to establish an additional avenue of contact (eye-to-eye, hand-to-hand, for example) when you're talking and when you're listening, when you're discussing and when you're disciplining. This connection will communicate love and respect along with the words. If you're busy with something or it's just not practical to sit face-to-face, try to glance at your toddler periodically as you talk and listen, and occasionally offer a pat on the head or a squeeze of the hand; some contact is always better than none.

**Tune in, and stay tuned.** Pretending that you're listening when you're really absorbed in something else is neither honest nor fair and can take a toll not only on your toddler's self-esteem but on the quality of family communications. Focus on your toddler as completely as

you can when he or she is trying to communicate and demonstrate your involvement by making frequent comments. Children need to know that what's important to them is important to their parents. On those occasions when you can't listen, explain why so that your toddler will be reassured that it's nothing personal. Let him or her know that you will lend your ear later.

**Be a patient listener.** Let your toddler take all the time that's necessary to tell a story or collect and express a thought or idea. Even if you're busy, even if steam seems to be coming out of your toddler's ears as he or she struggles to speak, be patient. Unless your help is requested, don't jump in too quickly to put words in your child's mouth or anticipate what's coming next.

**Be an enthusiastic audience.** A blow-by-blow description of your toddler's tea party may not knock your socks off, but if it's exciting to your toddler, it should be worthy of an enthusiastic response from you. Instead of replying "That's nice" or "Uh-huh" to your toddler's tale, show that you're listening and that you care with some sincere repartee, "That tea smelled delicious. Did you drink it all up?"

**Give your toddler space.** If your toddler doesn't want to talk, don't push it. Let your toddler know you would like to hear about what happened in preschool or play group, and leave it at that. If conversation becomes intrusive, an unpleasant third degree, your child may not want to talk at all.

**Listen, but don't judge.** Let your toddler express feelings, good and bad, freely. As difficult as it may be, listen and empathize without judging. If your child says, "I love . . . that toy or book or TV show," say, "I've noticed that. What do you like about it?" rather than, "Well, I think it's silly." Once your child has spoken up, you can say, "That's interesting. I think . . . " Be sure, however, that your comments aren't a put-down.

If your toddler complains, "I get mad when Shauna tries to play with my doll," say, "I know it's hard to share your doll," rather than lecturing about the evils of not sharing. If you criticize or get preachy when your toddler tries to express real feelings now, he or she may never feel free to have an honest conversation with you.

**Help your toddler with self-expression.** Many young children aren't exposed to the vocabulary of feelings, but the feelings are there nevertheless. To help your child express them, provide the words: negative words (like sad, angry, tired, lonely, bored, embarrassed, hurt, worried, afraid, disappointed, and confused) and positive ones (such as happy, proud, excited, strong, confident, eager, loving, satisfied, relaxed). Use them frequently in describing your feelings, your tod-

dler's feelings, as well as the feelings of playmates, family members, and characters in books and on television.

**Listen to body language.** Facial expression (sad eyes, an angry grimace, a frightened look) and body movements (a clenched fist, a shoulder shrug, flailing arms) often say as much as words. And when conversing, especially with toddlers (who often lack an extensive vocabulary), body language has to be taken into account. If body language seems to be saying one thing and your toddler's words another, try to get at the truth with some gentle probing.

**Don't jump to conclusions.** It's always better to hear a person out before you decide what it is he or she is saying. This is particularly important with toddlers, whose conversation can often be circuitous and is rarely organized in a coherent manner.

# WHAT IT'S IMPORTANT FOR YOUR TODDLER TO KNOW: Caring About the Earth—Teaching Environmental Concern

Toddlers love causes. They love to feel helpful and—because it gains them the approval of the adults in their lives—they love doing what's "right." So it's generally easy to recruit them into the environmental crusade.

It's true that many of the concepts of environmental concern are well beyond a toddler's grasp, but early exposure to its three basic precepts—reduce, reuse, and recycle—can help make environmentally correct behavior second nature, and hopefully, help give nature a second chance. Here's how to get your toddler started:

**Model your environmental concern.** Being a good global citizen takes extra time and extra effort—for already overwhelmed parents of young children, the extra burden may not be welcome. But setting an exemplary environmental example serves two important purposes: One, it teaches your toddler to care for and about the Earth; two, it helps ensure that there will be an Earth for your toddler (and the toddlers in coming generations) to care about.

**Recycle as a rule.** And as a family. Put your toddler in charge of collecting recyclable plastics (until your toddler can handle them safely, glass bottles and cans should be the responsibility of adults or older children) and depositing them in the appropriate bin. A toddler can also stack magazines and newspapers (wash hands afterwards to remove the ink) and gather used plastic and paper supermarket bags for deposit in the collection bins (if your supermarket recycles bags; if they don't, suggest that they do).[4] If white-paper recycling is available in your neighborhood (for example, some office supply stores and office buildings offer a recycling service), have your toddler deposit rejected drawings (after both sides have been used) into a special recycling box. When recycling with your toddler, explain the purpose of the undertaking: "Now these old plastic bags (or cans, or bottles) can be made into new plastic bags, and they won't fill up the garbage dumps or dirty the air when they're burned."

Recycle on the go, too. When you take cans, bottles, or other recyclables on an outing, bring them back home for recycling rather than dropping them in the nearest trash bin; this puts more of a load on you, true, but less of a load on the Earth. (Never, ever drop trash on the street or out the car window, or allow your toddler to litter. Use trash cans. When they're not available, hold onto your refuse until one is. Always bring along a bag for this purpose.)

**Reuse as a rule.** Many everyday items can be given new life, reducing the drain on natural resources: supermarket bags (use as garbage bags, or reuse them again and again, instead of getting new bags on each shopping trip); food containers (fill them with leftovers; with grains, nuts, dried fruit; with crayons or

beads); junk mail (the reverse sides can be used for toddler scribbles); catalogs (cut out pictures for collages). Such household items as egg cartons, straws, buttons,[5] bits of cloth, and the like, can be used, in place of store-bought crafts supplies in art projects, collages, and "junk" sculptures. Shoe boxes, decorated by your toddler, can serve as storage containers for crayons, toy cars, doll accessories, or other small items, or can become small doll "beds" or car "garages." Explain the purpose of reusing materials to your toddler, too. For example, "Did you know that paper is made from trees? When you use the back of an old letter to draw on instead of a fresh piece of drawing paper, you help to save a tree."

**Reduce as a rule, too.** The less we take from the environment, the more it will have to give us. Instead of a new paper lunch bag every day, use a reusable lunch box or cloth bag. Instead of packing sandwiches or snacks in disposable plastic baggies, pack them in containers that can be brought home for washing (another way to reuse grocery store plastics). Instead of using individual juice boxes for drinks, use refillable cups and containers (or find out if juice-box recycling is available in your area). Instead of taking home purchases in plastic or paper bags, take them home in a reusable cloth or string shopping bag (give your toddler one, too, so he or she can share the load). Explain to your toddler that every time you use another bag or box or carton it adds to the junk on the Earth, and that if people keep using so many "things" there won't be any place left to keep the trash: "It would be like filling up your room with garbage until there was no room left for you to sleep or play."

---

4. Never let your toddler play with plastic bags or gather them unsupervised; they pose a suffocation risk.

5. Be sure that a toddler who still mouths things doesn't play with buttons or other small items.

Also strive to reduce the use of electricity and water in your home. That means teaching children to always turn lights off when they leave a room, to never let the water run as they brush their teeth or soap up their hands, not to flush the toilet just for fun or take long showers.

**Be a green consumer.** When shopping, choose environmentally responsible products (recycled and recyclable drawing paper, natural cleaning products, products in recyclable packaging, minimally packaged products, refills). Point out the merits of your choices to your toddler.

**Give green parties.** To minimize the negative impact of birthday and other children's parties on the environment, set the table with placemats or a reusable tablecloth and colorful, dishwasher-safe (or recyclable) plastic plates and cups. Or use biodegradable paper plates, home-decorated, if you like. Avoid throwaway plastic forks and spoons (your everyday flatware will be easier for toddlers to handle anyway) or design a menu of "finger foods." Make your own centerpiece to brighten the table instead of buying a commercial paper or plastic one. To avoid unrecyclable plastic goody bags, tuck goodies inside a party favor, such as a plastic drinking mug or pail-and-shovel ensemble, or make your own goody bags from paper lunch bags. Wrap gifts in used gift wrap (carefully salvaged from gifts your family has received); in craft paper made from recycled materials, newsprint, or paper bags (decorated by you or your toddler); or in the newspaper funny pages. After use, recycle the wrappings, if possible. Skip latex balloons entirely; they're hazardous to the environment and to toddlers as well.

**Do a little educating.** The why's of recycling will be easier for your toddler to understand if he or she learns either first hand or from books, television, or videos, how much we depend on nature. Look for age-appropriate books that show, for example, how paper is made from trees so your toddler can start seeing why we have to take care of trees and not waste paper.[6]

Understanding how our food comes from the Earth and not from the supermarket can help a child understand, appreciate, and respect its importance. If you can't plant a vegetable garden, try making that connection by visiting a farm where crops are grown and sold, or take your toddler fruit- and vegetable-picking.

**Start a family compost.** If you have a garden, even if it's just a few window boxes, and room for a compost pile, start saving food and yard wastes for composting.

**Teach your child's day care or pre-school a lesson.** If they aren't already involved in environmental efforts, suggest they start a recycling program. To conserve resources, suggest parents bring in used computer paper for drawing, and other items for crafts projects. Provide a box or boxes in your child's classroom for recyclables. If the school has no easy access to recycling facilities, offer to take home juice cartons or bottles, juice boxes, used foil, plain paper, or any other materials that are recycled in your community. If there are numerous classes, find one or more other parents who will share the task with you.

---

6. Dr. Seuss's *The Lorax* is a wild and wonderful story of the environment gone haywire; both parents and children love it.

# Chapter Sixteen

# *The 34<sup>th</sup> to 36<sup>th</sup> Months*

## **W**HAT YOUR TODDLER MAY BE DOING NOW

*By 3 years old,[1] your toddler
. . . should be able to (see Note):*

▲ identify 4 pictures by naming
▲ wash and dry hands (3.1 years)
▲ identify a friend by naming
▲ throw a ball overhand
▲ speak and be understood half the time
▲ carry on a conversation of 2 or 3 sentences
▲ use prepositions

**Note:** If your toddler has not reached these milestones, consult the doctor or nurse-practitioner. This rate of development may well be normal for your child (some children are late bloomers), but it needs to be evaluated. Also check with the doctor if your toddler still falls frequently or drools persistently, or seems

1. This chapter covers the period between the time a toddler turns two and three-quarters (or thirty-four months) through the third birthday (or thirty-six months).

out-of-control or hyperactive; highly demanding, stubborn, negative; overly withdrawn, passive, uncommunicative; sad, joyless, unable to interact with others. By this age, children who were born prematurely have usually caught up to their peers.

*. . . will probably be able to:*

▲ use 2 adjectives
▲ put on a T-shirt
▲ broad jump

*. . . may possibly be able to:*

▲ balance on each foot for 2 seconds
▲ describe the use of 2 objects

*. . . may even be able to:*

▲ copy a circle
▲ prepare a bowl of cereal
▲ dress without help
▲ identify 4 colors

# WHAT YOU CAN EXPECT AT THE THREE-YEAR CHECKUP

**Preparing for the checkup.** Keep a list of concerns (about comfort habits, appetite, toileting, behavior, speech, or anything else) that have come up since the last visit. Be sure to bring the questions with you to this visit so you will be ready when the doctor asks, "Any concerns?" Also jot down new skills your toddler is displaying (jumping in place, pedaling a tricycle, building a tower of nine or more cubes, speaking intelligibly, self-dressing, self-feeding, copying a circle) so you won't be at a loss when you're asked, "What's your toddler been doing?" Bring along your child's home health history record, too, so that height, weight, immunizations, and any other information gleaned from the visit can be recorded.

**What the checkup will be like.** The procedure will vary a bit depending on your child's doctor or the nurse-practitioner who conducts health supervision exams, but in most cases, the three-year visit will include:

▲ Questions about your child's development, behavior, eating habits, and health since the last visit. There may also be questions about how the family is doing in general, whether there have been any major stresses or changes, how siblings (if any) are interacting with the toddler, about how the parents are coping, about child-care arrangements (if any), or preschool. The doctor or nurse will also want to know whether you have any other questions or concerns and is likely to "interview" your child, too.

▲ An assessment of growth (height, weight, head circumference) since the last visit. These statistics may be plotted on growth charts (see pages 864 to 867) and the child's weight for height evaluated and compared to previous measurements.[2]

▲ An informal assessment, based on observation and interview, of physical and intellectual development. A check of hearing, vision, and speech. Eyes will be checked for strabismus (crossed, wandering, or wall eyes).

▲ A finger-stick blood test (hematocrit or hemoglobin), if your child is at risk of anemia. The test is usually done once routinely between 12 months and 4 years.

▲ A blood test to screen for lead—if exposure is suspected.

▲ A urinalysis may be performed once between 12 months and 4 years.

▲ A Mantoux tuberculin test for children at high risk.

**Anticipatory guidance:** The doctor or nurse-practitioner may also discuss such topics as good parenting practices; injury prevention; appropriate toys and play activities; nutrition; discipline; dental care; and toilet learning (if your child is still in diapers); day care or preschool; and other issues that will be important in the year ahead.

**Immunizations.** None, if immunizations are up-to-date.

**The Next Checkup.** If your toddler is in good health, and there are no problems, the next scheduled checkup will be at four years. Between visits, be sure to call the doctor or nurse-practitioner if your child shows any signs of illness (see page 568) or if you have any questions that aren't answered in this book.

# WHAT YOU MAY BE CONCERNED ABOUT

## SLEEP REQUIREMENTS

*"Our daughter has given up her afternoon nap, and I'm worried she isn't getting enough sleep."*

Sleep needs vary widely from child to child, and even from day to day in the same child. Toddlers sleep an average of twelve hours a day in the third year, but that's an average that takes into account those who sleep only ten hours and those who sleep fourteen, those who nap and those who don't.

If your toddler's recently given up her afternoon nap, you can expect her to be sleepier and crankier than usual until her body adjusts to her new shut-eye schedule. But as long as she's able to function well on the sleep she's getting, you can rest assured she's getting enough. If she isn't functioning up to par, continues to be tired and cranky, consider moving bedtime ahead a bit to compensate for the nap she's nixed.

## FEAR OF THE DARK

*"Our son never had a going-to-bed problem, but now he tells us that he's afraid to go to bed in the dark. What can I do?"*

Your impulse may be to try to tease ("Silly, there's nothing to be afraid of") or shame ("Only babies are afraid of the dark") your child out of his fear; to force him to face it ("Now, I want you to be brave and stay in your dark room"); or even to use logic ("See, there's nothing in your room that's scary, even when we turn off the lights"). But such approaches almost never help a child overcome fear. If anything, they make him more fearful. And by belittling his fears, they can also wound his self-esteem.

Instead, to help your toddler come to terms with his fear of the dark, and ultimately, to conquer it:

**Let there be empathy.** It's often hard for a parent to relate to a fear of the dark—or any other seemingly irrational fear. But it's important to acknowledge and accept your child's fears. When a child feels his fears are given credence, it makes it easier to confront them. Instead of saying, "You're a big boy—big boys aren't afraid of the dark," say, "Sometimes the dark does seem scary." Get him to talk about his feelings about the dark, and listen without judging.

**Let there be light.** For a fearful child, a night-light,[3] or a ceiling light on a dimmer switch, is a welcome compromise between a pitch-black bedroom, which can be scary, and one that's lit up as bright as day and difficult to sleep in. In the dim light, the shapes of toys and furniture often appear familiarly comforting instead of menacing—as they might if the toddler were left to his imagination in the dark. Many children

---

2. Recent research suggests that children don't grow gradually, but rather in spurts. So your toddler may remain the same height for a couple of months, then suddenly pick up a full inch or more virtually overnight.

3. A night-light is particularly appealing when it's in the shape of a favorite animal or character. But be sure that it is UL (Underwriter's Laboratory) approved and is plugged into an outlet away from bedcoverings, clothing, or other flammable materials. Children's rooms have been known to go up in flames because of flammables falling against an overheated night-light. When possible, use a very low-wattage compact fluorescent light, which does not get hot.

no longer need the light by the time they reach five or six, when they begin to realize that there's nothing lurking in the closets and dark shadows. Some, however, need that extra touch of reassurance throughout childhood. And that's okay—as crutches go, a night-light is a pretty harmless one.

**Let there be a search.** Imagination is going full steam at this age. If your toddler keeps talking about the dragons under the bed or the monster in the closet, doing a thorough search before bedtime may help. Or it may not. The imagination is often more powerful than reason, especially in young children. You can also try banishing monsters loudly and dramatically ("Any monsters thinking of coming into this house, STAY AWAY. We will not let you come in."). This will, hopefully, demonstrate to your toddler that you are in control of the house, even when everyone's asleep.

**Let there be a sentry to stand guard.** You can't—and shouldn't—always be there when fear of the dark strikes. So appoint a sentry to stand in for you— a courageous teddy bear or doll, for instance. Make much of this sentry's ability to protect little children ("I know there are no monsters in this room, but if there were, Teddy would take care of you"). Some children are helped by reciting a "magical" sentence or rhyme ("Monsters, monsters go away; don't come back another day") and keeping a flashlight, "lucky charm," and/or a special toy at bedside.

**Let there be comfort.** From time to time, every fearful child needs a mommy or daddy to hide behind. In the right doses, comfort makes children stronger, not weaker. When your child is afraid, provide some extra reassurance—as well as some cuddling and a hug or two. When you leave the room, stay within earshot if possible (the dark is less frightening to young children if they hear their parents puttering around) until your toddler is asleep.

Daytime stress can lead to nighttime fears. If your toddler is going through a difficult time (with a new baby-sitter, a new baby, or some other upheaval), giving him extra time and attention, and helping him to deal with the problem, may reduce nighttime fears.

**. . . but don't overdo it.** Making too much of the fear can have a negative effect. It can lead a child to believe that there really is something to worry about, or teach him to use his fears to pull your strings ("If you read me one more story, I won't be scared of the dark"). Who would want to give up a behavior that nets a lot of attention and extra privileges? Comment little on his fears, but when he shows a bit of bravery, make much of it.

**Put on a brave show.** Children "catch" attitudes from their parents. When their parents seem comfortable in the dark, children usually learn to be comfortable, too. So while you should acknowledge your child's fears, don't feed them. Talk about the dark as a nice, comforting place. Explain to him that his room is just the same in the dark as it is with the light on.

**Let there be pleasant experiences.** Help your toddler to think of his room as a safe haven—never banish him there for time-outs or as a punishment. Also help him to associate the dark with good feelings. When you respond to his calls in the middle of the night, comfort him without turning the light on. In the evening, try turning off the lights in the living room while everyone is holding hands and singing happy songs or listening to a tape. Or lying in his bed in the dark with your toddler, take turns closing your eyes and trying to imagine favorite things (an ice cream cone, the beach,

Grandma's hug). Or roll a glow-in-the-dark ball (or one marked with fluorescent tape) into your child's darkened room and have each family member take a turn at chasing after and retrieving it. (Be sure there is ample room to prevent collisions.) Don't force your toddler to participate in any of these activities, but if you make it fun he may just want to. It may also help to talk about your child's fear of the dark in the light and to read books about children who overcome such a fear.

**Don't let there be frightening experiences.** Scary movies, violent television shows, spooky books can all fire up a child's imagination once he's under the covers. Ban those that you fear can stimulate fear. Also avoid such threats as, "If you're not good, the monster will get you," and harsh punishments or the threat of them. Of course, sometimes children are exposed to scary incidents in real life—as observers or participants—so we can't banish all frightening experiences. But we can minimize them and, afterwards, try to be reassuring.

# *TOILETING SETBACKS*

*"The last couple of days our son has had accidents with bowel movements at preschool. He's been potty-trained for almost a year; why would he regress now?"*

Even the toddler who's been using the toilet for a year is entitled to an accident now and then. But when such accidents happen regularly, there's usually a good reason, such as: *Stress.* A new baby-sitter, a new sibling, a new school (or a new teacher), a trip away from home, or another anxiety-provoking change in a child's life can disrupt his internal timetable and lead to toileting accidents. *A new routine.* Often, a child who's just begun attending preschool has trouble adapting his toileting habits to the new schedule and structure. Some children are also uncomfortable using a toilet that's different from the one they have at home, are uncomfortable asking to use it, or are uncomfortable using it without a parent present. *Anger.* A toddler upset with his parents for any reason may decide to strike back by doing something he knows will really upset them, such as soiling his pants. *Concentration on play.* Toddlers often get so involved in their activities that they ignore their bodily urges until it's too late. This is especially likely at school, where there are so many diversions competing for their attention. *Loose stools.* Softer movements usually give less notice and are tougher for toddlers to contain. These may be due to a change in diet (more fiber than he's used to, or excessive quantities of fruit juice, which children are often served up at preschool), or an intestinal virus (if you suspect the latter, see page 601). *Constipation.* When a young child has had a bout of constipation (see page 598) with painful bowel movements, he sometimes becomes fearful of going to the toilet. In an effort to dodge the pain, he consciously begins withholding his movements, refusing to go when the urge first strikes. And then, all of a sudden—during story time or in the middle of a finger-painting session or halfway down the slide—the bowel movement can wait no more. And out it comes, right into his pants.

But no matter what's precipitating your toddler's toileting accidents, chances are that they are at least as unpleasant and embarrassing to him as they are to you. In most cases the setbacks will be temporary. To help speed an end to these episodes:

**Be sensitive to his situation.** Having an accident can be a real blow to a child's ego, particularly at school. So go out of your way to be understanding, empathetic, and reassuring about what's happened. Don't scold, don't pressure, and don't insist that your child explain or talk about the incident if he's reluctant. A child is often so unnerved by toileting accidents that he'll deny them, even with the evidence in clear view. Don't demand your toddler own up to the accident—you know about it, he knows about it, enough said. If you're with him at the time of the accident, just change his clothes while changing the subject—chat casually about something unrelated and distracting rather than commenting on the mess he made, or worse still, telling him what a baby he is for making it.

**Acknowledge all of his achievements.** Continue to applaud him whenever he does manage a bowel movement in the toilet instead of his pants. But also look for other accomplishments to acclaim—offer praise when he gets his coat on by himself, when he draws a self-portrait, when he remembers to wash his hands before lunch. The better he feels about himself, the better his chances of making it to the toilet next time.

**Ease up on him.** Sometimes too much pressure—whether it's pressure to use the bathroom, to eat what's put in front of him, to have model manners, or to perform academically or socially—can cause a toddler to unravel. And one way that the unraveling can manifest itself is in toileting accidents. So make sure that you're not heaping too many demands or too many expectations on your toddler.

**Counter constipation.** If hard-to-pass bowel movements seem to be the root of the problem, take the steps on page 598 for dealing with constipation.

**Deal with diarrhea.** If frequent soft movements seem to be inducing your

child's potty accidents, examine his diet. The most likely dietary factor is excessive fruit juice. If your child is drinking more than 8 ounces of juice a day, cut back. Dilute the juice with water, substitute all water or milk at some snacks. An excessive amount of dried fruit and high-fiber foods is another possible, though less likely cause of the problem. Cut back some on such foods for a week or two to see if the number of accidents is reduced.

**Get some help at school.** Speak to your child's teacher about his problem, but do so in private, so his embarrassment won't be compounded. Find out if there's been a change in routine that may have triggered the accidents, or if the teacher thinks he may be shy about using the toilet around other children. Ask the teacher to remind him to go and to offer him the opportunity for privacy, if that's what he needs.

**Get up earlier.** If you've been rushing your toddler from the breakfast table out the door each morning, that could be part of the problem. Giving him breakfast (preferably one that contains a high-fiber food and some fruit juice) half an hour earlier than usual and then letting him do something active, maybe even go for a short walk, may enable him to use the bathroom before he leaves home.

If your toddler's bowel movements are loose, watery, bloody, or contain mucus, or if the soiling continues for more than a couple of weeks, discuss the problem with his doctor to see if there is an underlying medical reason (also see page 599).

# *U*RINE ACCIDENTS

*"Our daughter, who's been using the toilet for quite a while, has been*

*wetting her pants almost every day for the last week. We keep trying to remind her to use the toilet, but she always says she doesn't have to; two minutes later, she's wet again."*

Between drawing, trike riding, block building, playing house, and at least a hundred other exciting pursuits, life has become very busy for the toddler. So it's not surprising that being otherwise occupied is the most common reason why young children have toileting accidents. They may also backslide because they are stressed by an upheaval of some kind in their schedule or routine, or because they are emotionally upset. Sometimes, however, a bladder infection is responsible, especially in girls. So it's important to check with your toddler's doctor if the wetting continues or if your child's urine is cloudy, pink, or blood-tinged, or there are other signs of infection or irritation (see page 612); a urine culture may be in order. If infection or another medical problem isn't the cause, you can expect that the accidents will stop in time. Meanwhile:

**Don't blink an eye.** Overreacting to a wetting accident with exasperation ("You wet your pants—again?") or humiliating punishment ("I'm going to put you back in diapers!") will further upset your child and may prompt encores. Instead, respond casually, with a reassuring, "Oh, you didn't make it to the bathroom, did you? Well, next time I bet you'll make it in time."

**Nix name calling.** She's all dressed up for a party and as you're about to walk out the door, a river starts flowing right down your toddler's clean white tights. At moments like these, it's easy to forget you're the adult and to start tossing childish insults ("I thought you were a big girl!"). But insinuating she's a baby won't encourage grown-up behavior, so keep such belittling thoughts to yourself.

**Respond positively.** Tell her that accidents happen to everyone, and that next time she'll use the potty. If she's willing (never force her), foster grown-up feelings by having her help change her clothes as well as clean up the puddle she's leaked on the kitchen floor or to flush away the bowel movement she's produced in her pants.

**Evaluate her fluid intake.** Toddlers, like everyone else, need an adequate fluid intake. But excessive fluids (more than six cups a day[4]) can sometimes lead to an increase in wetting in toddlers. Some kinds of fluids are more likely than others to contribute to incontinence, for example: beverages containing caffeine,[5] because they are diuretic, and citrus juices, because they can irritate the urinary tract in some children.

**Reduce stress.** If you believe the recent spate of potty accidents may be due to excessive stress, examine your child's life and reduce stress as much as possible. Also be sure she's getting adequate attention and affection.

**Keep her bathwater pure.** Bubble baths, bath oils, and harsh bath soaps (as well as harsh detergents used on a child's underpants) can all lead to urinary tract irritation, a common cause of wetting. Avoid them, and see page 465 for safe bathing procedures.

**Cheer her successes.** A few accidents can deliver a major blow to a child's self-esteem. To build her back up again, make a conscious effort to recognize the achievement when she does reach the toilet in time. Bolster her confidence,

---

4. Milk is only two-thirds liquid and each cup your toddler drinks only counts as two-thirds of a cup. Fluid intake may need to be increased when the weather is hot or when a child is running a fever.
5. Beverages containing caffeine are inappropriate for a young child for other reasons as well (see page 534).

# HANDLING SUCKING HABITS NOW

· · · · · · · · · ·

**M**any children abandon sucking on a pacifier, thumb, or bottle somewhere around their third birthdays. If yours doesn't, you will need to decide whether you think it would be best to try to end the habit or habits now or wait another year or two to take action. In making this decision, consider the following:

▲ Does your toddler suck on his pacifier, thumb, or bottle for a good part of the day? All-day sucking is much more deleterious to the mouth and teeth than is occasional sucking.

▲ Is the habit negatively affecting your toddler's oral development? This is a call that only a dentist can make (see page 490). Though mild oral changes will correct themselves when the sucking stops—as long as it stops before the permanent teeth come in—more severe changes may be permanent.

▲ Is the habit interfering with your toddler's communication skills, his pronunciation (the changes in the mouth brought on by sucking can lead to lisping), with social interaction, with learning other ways of coping with stress, or with play? (It's not easy to build a block tower or catch a ball with your thumb in your mouth.)

If the answer to any of the above questions is "yes," then it would probably be wise to try to end your toddler's habit now, or at least to work on cutting it back. Here's how:

**Enlist a professional.** Parents can nag day and night and fail to move a toddler to break any habit; but a pediatrician or pediatric dentist may only need to say, "It's time to stop using the pacifier (or bottle, or thumb) because it is going to make your teeth and mouth crooked," in order to inspire a toddler to quit. Often the pediatrician or dentist will ask the child to call and report in, for example when he or she has abstained for two or three days. It may also be a good idea for the child to call Grandma or another special person with a progress report. The more people involved, the greater the motivation.

**Enlist your toddler.** Children can't be forced to abandon a habit; they have to want to. Motivation can be inspired by the words of a professional, a parent, or another adult, by the teasing of friends, by a sense of embarrassment over the habit, or even by a desire to be more grown-up, but there must be motivation. Ask your child about quitting; discuss with him or her when would be a good time and whether a cold-turkey or a go-slow approach is more appealing.

**Emphasize the grown-up.** Don't put down your toddler's sucking habits as "babyish," but do take every opportunity to call attention to "big boy (or girl)" behavior, such as using the toilet, buttoning a shirt, climbing up the jungle gym without help. The more appreciation garnered for being grown-up, the more incentive to be grown-up—and to kick the habits left over from babyhood.

**Hold the pressure.** Young children are more likely to respond to nagging by rebelling than by knuckling under. Threats, too, ("If you don't stop sucking your thumb, you won't be able to go to preschool") will make your child less likely to cooperate.

**Supply substitutes.** Keeping your toddler's mouth occupied—with conversation, song, a musical instrument that's played with the mouth, juice or milk from a straw (use one of those wild, roller-coaster-shaped ones for extra intrigue, if you can figure out how to get it clean), for example—may satisfy some of that need for oral gratification and will help distract him or her from cravings for the bottle, pacifier, or thumb. At the times of day when your toddler tends to like to suck most, provide nourishing snacks that require a lot of chewing—but be careful that you don't overfeed or replace one oral habit with another.

**Offer a reward.** A three-year-old may be willing to try to give up a sucking habit in exchange for a special treat. But even with the promise of a reward, a toddler needs plenty of help in quitting.

**Begin to limit pacifier use.** Work out a withdrawal plan with your toddler. For example, first limit pacifier use to the house. Then, put the living room off limits; then, one by one, all rooms but the bedrooms. Next, limit use to your toddler's bedroom only, and finally, to when he or she is in bed or sitting on a particular chair. Or set time limitations, limiting pacifier (or bottle) use to only after meals or only before nap and bedtime, then only after breakfast or only before bed. Or limit use to thirty minutes (set a timer) at a stretch, then twenty, then to ten, then five minutes, then two. Limitations will be most effective if they require your toddler to sit while sucking; toddlers find sitting still harder than practically anything—including giving up comfort habits. Present the limitations as a challenging game ("Let's see if you can stop using your bottle and pacifier in the kitchen"), rather than as obligatory restrictions. Whenever your child succeeds in meeting a challenge, be lavish in your praise.

**Take some of the fun out of the bottle.** Fill the bottle with water rather than milk or juice. Explain that sucking on a bottle filled with milk or juice could make cavities (or "holes") in his or her teeth. When offering beverages, give your toddler a choice between a cup of juice or milk and a bottle of water. This may significantly reduce the allure of the bottle.

**Take the air out of the pacifier.** Poke holes in or clip the end off the pacifier nipple; if sucking the pacifier brings no pleasure at all, your toddler may just toss it.

**Lose It.** The bottle or the pacifier, that is. If you're lucky, your toddler's favorite sucking object will disappear on an outing. At that point you can explain that you're not going to buy a new one because the doctor said "you're too old for a bottle (or a pacifier)."

**Replace the comfort of sucking with other comforts.** Children being deprived of a comfort habit need a lot of extra comfort from other sources during the withdrawal period and for a while thereafter. Hold your toddler's hand while he is upset, lavish attention and affection on him or her, spend extra time playing and going on outings together.

The sucking habit that is the most difficult to break is thumb or finger sucking. While you can limit where your toddler can take a bottle or a pacifier, you can't limit where your toddler takes his or her fingers. If your toddler is unable to stop finger-sucking, even with the help of the above measures, don't demand and don't despair. If necessary, more drastic measures may be recommended when your toddler is older—anywhere between three and five, depending on the condition of his or her mouth and your dentist's point of view. Possibilities then will include applying a foul-tasting preparation to the sucking finger (to make the habit unpalatable), and temporarily installing a metal reminder bar across the palate (to make sucking uncomfortable and remind the child not to do it). You can also recommend that when the urge to suck comes on, your toddler make a fist with the thumb inside. Instead of constantly saying, "Take your thumb out of your mouth," develop a silly secret code (such as, "Eeny, meeny, miney, mo" or "Fee, fie, fo, fum") that you can use as a reminder not to suck.

If a child uses a thumb or a pacifier obsessively, and seems withdrawn or depressed, the sucking may represent more than a bad habit. Consult with your child's doctor in such a situation to try to uncover and resolve any underlying problems.

too, by letting her know you admire her other achievements.

**Invite her to join you.** A parent of the same sex can encourage a child to take potty breaks by making toilet going a parent–child activity. If you sense your child is in imminent need of a toilet, but she flatly denies it, ask her to come along with you to keep you company while you go. The camaraderie of sharing the bathroom may move her to participate, too—as may the sight of the toilet and the sound of you using it. If she still refuses to go, however, don't force the issue.

**Make potty stops routine.** Many toddlers refuse to go before they leave the house, but need to go urgently as soon as there's no available toilet. Make it a rule: Everyone in the family uses the toilet before going out. That way, you won't be picking on your toddler alone, and you may even get her to comply.

## DISINTEREST IN POTTY LEARNING

*"We're starting to think that our son is never going to be out of diapers. We've tried, and tried, and tried again, but he's just not cooperating."*

The saying, "If at first you don't succeed, try, try again," applies to many things in life, but potty learning isn't one of them. That's because success must ultimately come from your toddler's efforts, not from yours. In other words, maybe it's time you stopped trying and waited until your toddler is ready to try for himself—which could be days, weeks, or months from now.

There is a saying, however, that does apply to potty learning: "All good

things come to those who wait." Be patient, present your toddler with the option of using the toilet or the potty chair, with no pressure to use it (see potty-learning tips in Chapter Nineteen), and one of these days diapers will be a thing of the past.

Keep in mind that being slow to use the potty in no way reflects on your child's intelligence or on future achievements in other areas. It may, however, reflect the pressure you've been applying. So pull back.

## BED-WETTING

*"Our daughter's been potty-trained during the day for almost a year, but she still wears a diaper at night and, in the morning, wakes up soaking wet. When should we start being more aggressive about getting her to stop wetting at night?"*

Getting aggressive about bed-wetting (medically termed *enuresis*, if it continues well past the toddler years) at any time isn't productive—children don't wet while they're sleeping because they want to, but because they are developmentally unable to stay dry, and threats or punishments won't change that. By about five or six years old, 85% to 90% of children stop bed-wetting on their own, without any adult intervention. Why the remainder (more often boys than girls) continue to wet is uncertain. A variety of contributory factors have been suggested, including heredity, a smaller-than-average bladder, excess urine output at night, and sleep so sound that it's hard to awaken from. The best treatment, usually not recommended until the age of six to eight, is an enuresis alarm, a device which wakes a child when she wets, eventually "conditioning" her to wake when she needs to go.

Pressure to stay dry at night usually only increases the incidence of accidents (both at night and during the day) while wearing down a child's self-esteem. She'll stay dry when she's physiologically ready to; and scolding her, nagging her, or limiting her fluid intake in the evening won't make her ready any sooner.[6] It may help, however, to pick her up to take her to the potty at your bedtime; but don't try this if your suspect it will cause sleep problems.

All of you will probably sleep better if your toddler stays in diapers at night until she's ready to stay dry. Some signs of such readiness are: fewer nighttime wettings (she wakes in the morning barely damp instead of sopping); being upset by nighttime wettings; the ability to stay dry for three to four hours during the day; getting up herself in the middle of the night to urinate; frequently waking up dry from naps, and occasionally waking up dry after a night's sleep.

To protect her ego while you protect her mattress, put her night diaper on without potentially hurtful comments ("When you're a big girl you won't wear diapers.") If she's really uncomfortable about having a diaper put on her (as some children are once they're in underwear during the day), put one on after she's asleep at night. If you find that unwieldly or if it wakes her, consider disposable pull-up training pants (they're as heavy as diapers but are put on like underpants; see page 544). A rubber sheet will help protect the mattress in case of overflow.

## GROWING PAINS

*"Lately, my daughter, who will be three next week, has suddenly begun waking up crying about pains in her legs. The pains don't last long and she falls back to sleep."*

Sounds like a classic case of "growing pains." Most common between the ages of three and six, these pains can be fairly severe and usually are felt in the calf, thigh, or around the knee—mostly at night. They have nothing to do with growing, but are probably due to muscle fatigue after an extremely active day. The attacks usually last no more than twenty minutes. Comfort, reassurance, and a little massage will help get a toddler back to sleep.

Don't tell your toddler that her legs hurt because she's playing too hard or she may just become fearful of playing and refuse to do anything physical. It is a good idea, however, to try to slow her down just a bit without making it obvious to her. Nor should you tell her these are "growing pains"; such an explanation of her pain could instill a fear of growing and even inspire an eating strike.

Seek medical advice, however, if your child has persistent rather than occasional pain at night, pain during the day, pain in just one leg, is limping or has difficulty walking, or has fever or other symptoms along with the pain. If the growing pains continue for several weeks, mention them to your child's doctor. Children who experience such pain before age three also require medical evaluation.

## NAME CALLING

*"I've been very disturbed to hear my daughter calling her friends names. They're harmless enough— mostly things like "poopy-head" or "doo-doo face"—but they still bother me."*

---

6. Be sure, however, your toddler isn't drinking beverages containing caffeine, which—besides being unhealthy—can increase wetting. Citrus juices can, too, in some children.

Once a child starts hanging around with other children, name-calling is as inevitable as struggles over toys. The names that three- and four-year-olds favor most commonly have their roots in the toilet; the potty (and its contents) is still something they're coming to terms with, and playing around with the terminology helps reduce their discomfort.

Don't overreact to name-calling, but don't encourage it—by laughing at it, for example—either. When your toddler hurls a word that you find unacceptable at you or someone else, explain that using mean words can hurt people's feelings just like using your hands to hit can hurt their bodies. Show her more socially acceptable ways of dealing with a confrontational situation, such as saying, "You're making me very angry," or choosing not to play with a child who bothers her. But don't count on complete success; she won't have good control of her tongue for at least a couple of years yet—and name-calling is still preferable to hitting.

Make sure you're not setting a poor example yourself. Many adults use name-calling or foul language to express their annoyance, and though they may do it unconsciously, their children are almost certainly conscious of it. So next time you're tempted to sling an insult at your spouse during a heated argument, at a driver who's cut you off on the highway, or at the phone company when they've made a mistake on your bill, or even just to curse the blankety-blank washing machine for overflowing, think before you speak. If you don't, you're sure to hear your little mimic mouthing the very same expletives one of these days.

Name-calling often has nothing to do with anger but is used just in fun or as an attention-getter. When that's the case, tell your child matter-of-factly that you understand that she wants to hear what the particular word sounds like, and that she's more than welcome to go to her room and say it as many times as she likes, but that it's not nice to say such words in front of people. It's also a good idea to try to encourage her to use silly words that are less offensive: "soup-head" instead of "poop-head" or "loo-loo face" instead of "doo-doo face," for example. But don't make a big fuss—ignore "toilet" language and it's likely to go away more quickly. Keep in mind, however, that no matter what technique parents may use to try to eradicate it, it often lingers well past age four.

As your child gets older you will probably want to set some absolute limits on bad language at home, but at this stage a child's self-control isn't sufficent for her to mind her tongue all the time.

## MEAN-SPIRITED COMMENTS

*"Sometimes, during a play date, my daughter will say something mean to a friend, like: 'I don't like your dress' or 'that drawing doesn't look like a baby.' I'm afraid she's going to end up being a mean-spirited child."*

Such comments from a child as young as yours aren't mean-spirited, just candid. The problem is that most toddlers haven't yet learned that sometimes outright honesty can hurt another person—that you just can't say everything that comes into your head.

Though it wouldn't be right to fault your toddler for her candor, it would be appropriate to explain how saying what she thinks can hurt other peoples' feelings. Next time she speaks up without thinking first, comfort her playmate, but without judgmental comments ("Look how badly you made Rosa feel!"). After the slighted child has been soothed, calmly take your child aside, and ask her if she can try to put herself in her friend's place. "How would you feel if Rosa said she didn't like *your* dress? Or if she said *your* picture wasn't good?" If she doesn't respond, add, "I think you would feel very sad."

This exercise in empathy won't be easy for your toddler—empathy is a very new emotion—so be patient and understanding. Don't scold her for what she said or debate the merits of her sentiments. Let her know that it's okay to not like someone's dress or to think a drawing isn't very good, but that it's *not* okay to say so if it will make that person sad. This message won't sink in the first time, or even the tenth. But if each time she comes out with a thoughtless comment you get her to think about how the other person may be feeling, eventually it will.

But don't make a major issue of this, and don't let her think that it's never okay to express her feelings. Let her know that it is perfectly acceptable to tell someone else that they made her feel bad or hurt her or that what they're doing isn't nice. Make it clear, too, that when what they're doing is dangerous or could hurt her or someone else, that she should also tell the grown-up (parent, caregiver, teacher) in charge.

## SILLY BEHAVIOR

*"Lately, our son has been acting really silly and using silly language. It was cute at first, but now it's getting annoying."*

It's virtually impossible to shake the sillies out of some toddlers. And it's not really fair to try. Let your toddler's sillies run their nonsensical course, not paying them attention of any kind (posi-

tive or negative) rather than trying to stifle them, and they'll play themselves out sooner. And don't let yourself be embarrassed by your toddler's behavior; most people around you will recognize that he's simply acting his age.

Keep in mind that humor is a universal antidote for virtually anything, and kids, coping with the challenging job of growing up, need this special medicine as much as anyone. And though your toddler's brand of humor may not be funny to *you*, it's probably right on target with his friends. Let him enjoy his humor, as long as it isn't played out at inappropriate moments.

When a situation requires at least a modicum of decorum (you're at a religious service, a fancy party, a kiddie concert), explain to your toddler that there's a time and a place for silly behavior, and this situation isn't either. If asking him to quit being silly brings you nothing but another round of giggles, try to distract him with a toy, a book, or a trip to the bathroom. Or just take him outside until he can calm himself down. Don't focus on the silly behavior or threaten to take him home (if you do, you will give him an easy way out of any event he doesn't like: Just be silly).

## MAKING LETTERS

*"I've noticed that some kids in my daughter's preschool can write their names, or at least make some letters, but she hasn't gotten past scribbling yet. Is she behind?"*

In generations past, reading and writing remained a mystery to most children until they entered school—which usually wasn't until the age of five or six. Most kids didn't even recognize letters or words until then. With more children in preschools (where reading readiness and letter recognition are often part of the curriculum), with *Sesame Street* and its letters of the day an influential part of many toddler routines, and with educational videos and toddler computer games, it's not uncommon to see two- and three-year-olds scrawling their names, or at least some letter-like markings, across their finger paintings.

When they enter elementary school, are these early writers ahead of those who take their time picking up these skills? Not necessarily, though they may, at least temporarily, have an added measure of self-confidence that comes from mastering a skill.

For the child who seems to have no interest in letters and numbers, introducing them in the pressure-free ways shown on page 292 will often spark interest. To encourage writing skills: Write your child's name on her pictures and ask "Whose name is that?" Give her plenty of paper and crayons, a chalk board, a metal board (or refrigerator door) with magnetic letters, and read to her regularly. If she's interested, make lines and circles on a paper and ask her to imitate them. If she tries to make a letter and the result is far from accurate, don't criticize. Instead, applaud her attempt ("Good try!"), then make the letter yourself ("See, here's how I make an 'A'").

But remember that each child has her own developmental timetable and priorities. One child may learn to ride a trike while another may put her efforts into learning to make letters; one may concentrate on learning to throw a ball while another practices singing the alphabet. One type of skill isn't necessarily better or more valuable than another, or indicative of future talent or achievement. If, in the months ahead, your daughter continues to show no interest in writing her name or other letters, let it be. There's plenty of time for her to develop these skills.

## SLEEP TALKING

*"My son often talks in his sleep. Should I wake him up when he does it? Does it mean he's upset or has a sleeping disorder?"*

It's a bit eerie to hear a child moaning, murmuring, or laughing in the middle of the night, then go into his room to check on him and find he's fast asleep—but it's not a cause for concern. Sleep-talking is perfectly normal, and isn't a reflection of a child's emotional well-being. Though your toddler may be having a dream or a nightmare (see page 312) when he calls out, it isn't necessary (or advisable) to wake him up. And as long as his sleep isn't seriously disrupted and he isn't chronically fatigued, sleep-talking doesn't signal a need for professional help.

## FRIENDS WHO DON'T SHARE

*"My daughter's pretty good about sharing. But she doesn't understand why she's supposed to share when her best friends won't.*

Trying to explain to a three-year-old why she should share her toys when her friends don't is something like trying to explain to an adult why she shouldn't cheat on her income tax when her colleagues do. Though you may see generosity and honesty as their own reward, your toddler may not.

So rather than attempting to give your toddler a rationale for why she should continue to maintain an open-handed policy with her friends when they are tight-fisted with her, let her

know that her generosity isn't going unnoticed or unappreciated. Take every opportunity to admire it ("I really like the
way you share with your friends").
Hopefully, a well-stroked ego will be
reward enough for her actions, and she'll
keep up her share of the sharing—even
in the company of those who don't share
alike. If it occasionally isn't, and the
selfishness of her friends defensively
brings out the greedies in her, don't
chastise her ("But you always share!").
Generosity should be her idea, and at
this age, no one should pressure her to
give up her belongings, even temporarily
(see page 267).

It's likely that her playmates' grip
on their toys will begin loosening within
the next year or two, especially with
your child's generous example to follow.
Telling her that her friends will learn as
they get older, but that they will probably learn sooner if she continues to set a
good example by sharing, may make it
easier for her to continue her generosity
in the meantime.

## PLAYING DOCTOR

*"A friend told me that she recently
found her nearly three-year-old and
a playmate in his room showing
each other their genitals. I don't
know what I would do if I caught
my son and a playmate doing
that."*

**W**ell, now's a good time to start figuring out what you would do if
you did catch your son "playing doctor"—because chances are you will, one
day soon. Sometime between the ages of
three and six, most children become curious about what's inside other people's
underwear, and will attempt to satisfy
that curiosity with a few rounds of "I'll
show you mine, if you show me yours."

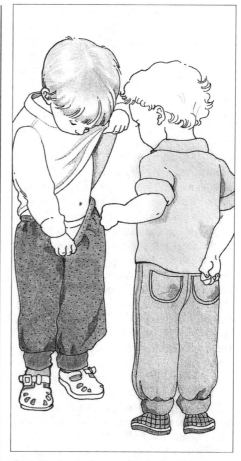

*Curiosity about other people's bodies is just as
normal for toddlers as curiosity about their own.
An occasional game of "doctor" can be expected
as toddlers try to satisfy that curiosity.*

Since a young child doesn't yet
know the rules of modesty or morality,
he's not consciously breaking them
when he plays doctor. His curiosity
about a playmate's genitals is as natural
and as innocent as his curiosity about his
own, and motivated more by scientific
than sexual interest.

Some parents react with shock on
finding their children playing doctor,
others with amusement—but an unruffled, take-it-all-in-stride reaction is best
of all. Punishing, ridiculing, scolding, or
embarrassing a child for acting on a very

natural impulse (whether the "exam" has been boy–boy, girl–girl, or boy–girl) can confuse, demean, and/or make the fruit that's now been "forbidden" all the more intriguing. Such an experience can instill in a child unhealthy feelings about the private parts of his body that can linger through adolescence into adulthood.

If and when you discover your child playing doctor, do try to remain nonplussed—or at least to appear nonplussed. As casually as if you walked in on a game of "school" or "airplanes" remark, "Oh, I see that the two of you are trying to find out about each other's bodies. You can see that both of you have penises." (Or if the other "doctor" is a girl, "that you have a penis because you're a boy, and you have a vagina because you're a girl.") Without launching into any complicated explanations, let the children know that "these parts of our bodies are private, so we don't show them to other people or let other people touch them," and tell your child that you'd be happy to answer any questions he has about the subject later.

Then quickly suggest that the children get their clothes back on and move on to another activity, preferably a supervised one ("Let's read a story—or play ball in the backyard—now"). Often a change of activity actually comes as a relief to children involved in sexual exploration—though they're not exactly sure why, playing doctor often makes them feel uneasy.

After the playmate has left, sit down with your child and encourage his questions; if he doesn't have any, or doesn't seem to want to talk about the subject, don't insist. If you think you may feel awkward talking about it with your toddler or feel uncomfortable using the proper terminology, practice alone or with another adult first. A book or two on the human body, with clear, simple illustrations, may make explanations easier for you to offer and for your toddler to understand. Check with your local library or a good bookstore for recommended titles geared to three-year-olds. If you feel comfortable doing so, let the other child's parents know about what happened so that they can, if they choose, hold a similar discussion in their home.

If you find your child obsessed with the genitals of other children, talk about the problem with his doctor. Occasionally, such interest is a sign of sexual abuse.

# SHOPLIFTING

*"We were out shopping yesterday and I was horrified to find that my daughter had taken a small toy from the store we were in and stuffed it in her pocket."*

This kind of petty pocketing may be a bit shocking for parents, perhaps, but it hardly constitutes a criminal act for a not-quite-three-year-old. In fact, a child this age is incapable of intentionally committing a crime. She saw a toy she liked, picked it up, and took it with her, just as she might a pretty rock she found in the park or a snail's shell she found on the sidewalk—a perfectly normal impulse for a toddler. She might do the same thing with an item she admired at a friend's house, at her grandparents', or at a restaurant.

At the same time, it's a normal impulse that happens to be against the law. So while you shouldn't overreact to your daughter's light fingering, you do need to correct it. Explain to her that people have to pay money for toys or anything else they want from a store before they take them home. But don't introduce the concept of "stealing" or call her a "thief," which would imply that her intentions in taking the toy were dishonest or dishonorable, which they certainly weren't.

To underscore what you're saying, as well as to promote honesty, take the purloined toy back to the store together and return it. Don't buy it, or your daughter will figure out that the way to get a toy is to filch it and then get you to pay for it. Explain that people can't always buy what they want in a store, but they can always enjoy "just looking."

When you find that your toddler has pocketed something from the home of a friend or relative, follow the same procedure—have her return it at the next visit, without any recriminations.

# QUALITY TIME

*"We both spend five days a week at work, away from our toddler, so on weekends we like to spend as much quality time as possible with him. But he never seems to appreciate the special outings we schedule. What are we doing wrong?"*

Probably nothing but trying too hard and expecting too much appreciation. Making an effort to please a toddler doesn't guarantee his pleasure; in fact, given the quirky nature of the toddler, it often has just the opposite effect—especially if you've neglected to consult him about your plans in the first place.

To your child, *any* time you spend with him is quality time. While special outings can be fun if they're tailored to a toddler's interests and limited attention span, scheduled too often, they can become a burden. Children often enjoy and appreciate their parents' company as much, or even more, in the living room constructing a superhighway out of wooden blocks or at the park examining rocks and insects, as they do during ambitious excursions to the museum, a puppet show, or the zoo. And with no monetary investment at stake, stress levels lower, and expectations not as high, a better time is often had by all when simple pleasures are on the agenda. You can greatly improve the odds that everyone will enjoy family time together by including your toddler in your weekend planning.

It's only natural for parents who have less time than they might like to spend with their children to want to make the most of what time there is. But overcompensation is rarely called for; togetherness doesn't have to come in fancy, expensive, or carefully planned packages to be meaningful. Busy parents may not have the time for the more leisurely family fun etched in their memories by reruns of *Father Knows Best*: cookies, milk, and conversation after school; cuddling and cocoa around the fireplace on a winter's day; lazy summer picnics at the lake, complete with watermelon and three-legged races. But even the most hectic day has some time in it for hugs, a story, a tickle-fest, a pillow fight, or splashing in a bathtub of bubbles. Nor do good times need to be scheduled ("Tuesday, 5:35 P.M.: quality time with Junior") to be rewarding; spontaneous fun can be at least as fulfilling. And fun doesn't have to mean play. Family togetherness can be cemented when a toddler helps Mommy set the table or Daddy wash the dishes; when the family spends an hour making holiday cards to send to friends; when everyone works together to clean up the playroom for company.

Chances are you already spend a lot more quality time with your toddler than you realize. You're probably overlooking dozens of special moments a day that are making your toddler feel loved and cared about.

It might help to keep in mind that the plight of parents who work outside the home isn't unique. Even parents who stay home with their children complain that "quality time" is a precious commodity they don't get enough of. So turn off the guilt and the anxiety, and relax and enjoy your toddler in the time you have, scheduled or otherwise.

## TERRIBLE TWOS AD INFINITUM

*"Our daughter's almost three, and she's still having tantrums. Shouldn't she be over the terrible twos by now?"*

The "terrible twos" are a terrible misnomer. They imply a finite time frame for behavior that doesn't necessarily have one. Though the worst of toddler behavior is often concentrated between the second and the third birthdays, the normal range is actually a lot broader. The terrible twos begin surfacing in some children as early as the end of the first year, but don't appear in others until the third year; they wind down within months in some children, but can persist well into the preschool years in others.

Toddler negativism (see page 45) commonly has a two-year course, during which the behavior alters with a child's growing sophistication. The first tentative "no's" are uttered by a child trying to find out what kind of response she will get. By the end of the third year, she's involved in a more serious quest for independence and self-determination and is equipped with a lot more ways of being negative: "Stop!" "I won't!" "I can't!" "I don't!"

Inborn temperament can explain, at least in large part, why the terrible twos last longer in some children—high-intensity or "type A" personalities, for example—than in others. Tantrums are often a necessary release for bottled-up mental energy in these children. Some kids are by nature more rebellious and/or stronger-willed than others; these children, too, tend to have a longer terrible-twos period.

There is no magic strategy guaranteed to instantaneously banish terrible-two behavior. But you can hasten its departure with the following approaches: Continue to deal with negativity in the ways suggested on page 45 and try to avoid power struggles with your child. Set limits, but not too many (see page 47). Give your child opportunities to make decisions (see page 414), but when there is no choice, make that clear ("It's time for lunch," not "Would you like lunch now?"). Discipline fairly, and with the goal of teaching your child self-discipline (see page 119). Try to ward off tantrums (see the techniques suggested on page 338); when they occur, handle them with all the calm you can muster. And, of course, offer plenty of acknowledgement for good behavior.

If the negativity and the fits of temper don't lessen some in the months ahead, talk to your toddler's doctor. It may be time for some extra support from outside the family.

## ICE CHEWING

*"I remember I always chewed ice as a kid, and I never thought twice about it. Now my daughter is doing it, and I'm wondering if it can hurt her teeth."*

From generation to generation, certain pursuits have been favorites with kids. Unfortunately, some that were once considered completely harmless are now known to be potentially harmful. Like playing unprotected all day in the sun, shaking salt on the back of your hand and licking it off, riding a bike barefooted and bareheaded—and chewing ice.

Though a tantalizing sensation (even for many adults), ice chewing can damage the teeth, especially if the teeth are already more vulnerable from fillings. If ice chewing causes a crack in the tooth, nerve damage can result that may require root canal work. Because ice can also be a choking hazard, don't even allow your unsupervised toddler to suck on a cube.

Since ice in the bottom of a glass cries out to be chewed, avoid serving ice to your toddler (or to anyone else, when your toddler's around, if she's likely to seek out a cube from someone else's glass). In restaurants, specify "no ice" before the water is poured or when ordering beverages. If, despite your efforts, your toddler does get her teeth into ice, let her know that she's got to give it up, explaining that the ice can damage her teeth.

# QUESTIONABLE PLAYMATES

*"My son made a friend at preschool whom he always wants to play with. But I'm not crazy about this child. He's destructive, and I don't think he's a good influence."*

You always swore you'd never interfere in your children's social lives the way your parents did in yours, that you'd let them choose their own friends, whether you liked them or not. And then the inevitable happens—your child chooses a friend you don't like, one whose bad habits you're afraid he'll pick up.

What's an enlightened parent to do? First of all, relax. Influences in the home and inborn personality and temperament have far more impact in the long run on your child's behavior than a peer's example. A destructive, wild friend may step up your child's aggressions temporarily, but not permanently—particularly if you provide a calm, nonviolent atmosphere at home.

And second of all, *do* interfere—but just a little. Don't forbid your child to see this objectionable friend; it would probably only make him more determined to pal around with the kid. (You can't keep them from each other at school, anyway.) But do try expanding your child's social horizons a little.

Speak to his teacher (not in front of him) about your concerns, and ask that he or she suggest another child in the class who might make a compatible playmate. The teacher can test out the chemistry during the school day by casually sitting them together at lunch or teaming them up on a project; if the results are positive, you can suggest a play date.

If your son nevertheless continues to want to play with his "wild and crazy" friend, let him—some kids really enjoy the excitement of playing with a live wire. But carefully supervise their play, and plan organized activities when you can. An overly active child often calms down dramatically when engaged in listening to a story, making a collage, or challenged by a game of lotto. And don't hesitate to nip in the bud any behavior you don't approve of or don't feel is safe.

If the child is actually destructive or physically aggressive (hitting, biting, kicking, and so on), let him know that such behavior is not acceptable in your home, that if he wants to come back and play, he will have to behave. Explain this to your child, too, so that he can encourage his friend's compliance. If the warning doesn't work, speak to the child's parents and ask if they have any suggestions. Perhaps one of them or a caregiver could come along on play dates until the behavior improves. If the parents aren't cooperative, you have no choice but to bring an end to the play dates until the child's behavior improves.

# FORGETFULNESS

*"My son is so forgetful. When I ask him what he did at preschool or at his friend's house, he forgets. When I ask him not to walk across the floor I just mopped, he forgets. Why can't he remember anything?"*

Because he's a toddler. Unlike young babies, toddlers do have the ability to store information and experiences in their memory banks. The trouble comes when it's time to make a withdrawal—even when the facts are on file, toddlers often have difficulty retrieving them. Part of the reason is inexperience in retelling experiences. And part is what might be called the "absent-minded professor" syndrome—with his mind so cluttered with "important stuff," the toddler often has no time to focus on the minutiae. He thinks, for example, about the toy at the other side of the room (important to him) and forgets that you said not to walk on the wet floor (important only to you).

As your child grows, so will his powers of recollection. He'll be able not only to remember what he did at school or at his friend's house, but to readily reel off an account of his daily activities as well as countless (and sometimes endless) anecdotes; he'll be able not only to remember that the floor is wet, but how unhappy you get when he tracks muddy footprints across a wet floor.

The more exercise a memory gets, the more facile it becomes. If you'd like to speed your toddler's memory development, regular workouts will help (but *remember* not to take these too seriously; never scold or show frustration with your toddler for not remembering):

▲ Play memory games. Take three different objects, line them up in a row, instruct your toddler to take a good look at where each one is, then cover them up, and then ask if he can remember their location. Or show your toddler three picture cards (make them by gluing magazine or catalog photos on cardboard), then turn them over and see if he can remember the pictures. Or try to recall the names of all the children in his play group (or class) or the names of his cousins.

▲ Remember together. After a visit to the park, sit down together and reminisce about what you saw and did. If your toddler can't seem to remember, refresh his memory ("Do you remember what we saw in the park today? Did we see a squirrel? And what else? Did we see a boy feeding the ducks?"). Prompting him in this way should help get his recollective juices flowing; if it doesn't, do the remembering for him this time—chances are that next time he'll be able to do some recalling of his own. Don't be surprised if what your son remembers isn't the memory you were aiming for (after a boat ride around the harbor he may recall what kind of sandwich he ate rather than the seagull he saw diving for fish).

▲ Recall the day. Make it routine for family members to share the day's events at dinnertime or bedtime, or both. Not only will this replaying of the day sharpen your child's memory skills, but it will become a comforting and cherished tradition.

▲ Ask memory-jarring questions. Eliciting information from a toddler is rarely easy, but it's particularly tough if you ask the wrong kinds of questions. Presented with such overwhelmingly broad inquiries as "What did you do in school today?," a toddler's response is likely to be a shrugged "I dunno." Ask, instead, questions that are specific and geared to shift his memory into playback: "Did you make something in the block corner today?" "Did you paint?" "Who was your partner when you went to the park?" "What did you have for snack?" Try prompting him ("Did you have apple and graham crackers?"), but if he still seems reluctant to part with information about his day or doesn't seem in the mood to talk, don't push him.

▲ Give memorable instructions—and give them as often as necessary. Toddlers don't have as much storage space in their memories as older children do. Until their capacity and concentration increases, they often legitimately "forget" what they're told to do or not do. Just because you tell your child the floor's wet doesn't mean he's going to remember not to walk across it—even five minutes after you've told him—especially if he's gotten involved in a game and he needs the stuffed dog that's across the wet floor. At his age, focusing attention on more than one thing at a time is difficult, and getting distracted is easy. So repeat instructions regularly, and try to be tolerant when he continues to forget to follow them. Limit your directives to no more than one or two at a time, and keep them simple and specific ("Please pick up your book and put it on the table," rather than "Please pick up your toys, put your clothes away, and come in for dinner") to increase the chances that he'll remember to do as you ask. (Keep in mind, however, that your toddler may refuse to do what you want him to do no matter how clearly you spell it out—which is another issue entirely; see page 413.)

▲ Use reminder props. For example, post a do-not-walk-on-the-wet-floor sign when you've washed the floor (paint a bright red line across a picture of a pair of sneakers, clipped from a magazine or hand-drawn on poster paper).

# MUSIC LESSONS

*"I've read that there are piano and violin lessons for children as young as three. Is it a good idea to get our daughter started that young?"*

It depends what you're starting her on. Formal lessons aren't generally recommended until a child reaches at least five or six. What is recommended for toddlers is trying to instill a love of music. Not everyone is musically gifted, but

everyone can learn to appreciate music. You can help your child develop her appreciation by playing music of various kinds in your home, taking her to concerts for very young children, and encouraging her to sing, dance, and play music (on child-size xylophones, triangles, tambourines, harmonicas, recorders, and other toy instruments).

If your child expresses a strong interest in music and is eager to learn to play a "real" instrument, you can consider the Suzuki method, which teaches children as young as three or four to play the violin (small-scale versions of adult instruments are used). As with any kind of lessons or classes you choose for your toddler, don't push. If she expresses an interest in playing the violin, give her a chance to try it, if you can. If she wants to continue, encourage her. If she doesn't, wait a couple of years before trying again—with the violin or another instrument.

# SPEECH THAT'S STILL UNCLEAR

*"Our toddler is still hard to understand—even for us. He mispronounces many consonants and mumbles many words."*

Some children are genetically programmed to speak as clearly as adults long before they are three years old; others are still saying "I wuv you" when they enter kindergarten. Differences in the clarity of speech are most often not a matter of intelligence, but of the rate at which a child develops control over his tongue and lip muscles. So mispronounced consonants and mumbled words themselves are not a reason for concern.

If, however, by your toddler's third birthday you understand what he's saying *less* than half the time, there may be an underlying problem, such as a hearing deficit, that needs addressing. So check with his doctor. Early attention to language delays by a specialist can make a major difference, not just in language development but in learning in general, and most importantly, in a child's self-esteem.

If there doesn't seem to be a problem that requires professional attention, you can try "chewing exercises" to speed development of the structures of the mouth: Have your child chew sugarless gum (if you're sure he won't swallow it) or celery or carrots (cut in thin sticks) or a chewy bagel or similar foods two or three times daily. Since a sucking habit can cause mouth deformities that lead to lisping, getting a child to give up such a habit can also be helpful.

But don't make a fuss about your child's speech deficiencies (remember, they're normal) or try to push him to speak more clearly. Nagging could make your child hesitate to speak, increase shyness and withdrawal, and slow progress—even trigger stuttering. Instead, encourage him to speak freely, try hard to understand what he says, avoid imitating his mistakes (either as a put-down or because they're "cute"), and gradually you can expect his language to become more clear. If he is still mispronouncing some consonants as he approaches school age (many children still are), ask his doctor whether a speech therapist should be consulted.

# FRIGHTENING FAIRY TALES

*"I want to read some of the classic fairy tales to my daughter—like* Little Red Riding Hood, Hansel and Gretel, *and* Snow White.*" But I'm afraid they may frighten her."*

A grandmother is gobbled alive by a bloodthirsty wolf. A clever girl prevents her brother from becoming a witch's dinner; on the way out, they leave the old sorceress to roast in the oven that had been intended for him. A jealous queen-witch orders her huntsman to slaughter her beautiful stepdaughter and remove her heart; when that plan fails, she tricks the innocent maiden into eating a poisoned apple.

Violent? Absolutely! Frightening? Possibly. Inappropriate for young children? Well, probably not. While there's no doubt that fairy tales are chock full of wicked witches, sinister beasts, formidable giants, and other fearsome figures, and that treachery and violence are plentiful, this malice isn't gratuitous. For in each of these time-honored fables, right triumphs over wrong, the evil are punished, and the good enjoy their well-deserved happy ending. And of course, morals abound (for example, when Beauty finally falls in love with the Beast, the young listener comes to realize that you can't judge a person by outward appearance).

Whether these tales, which have been putting children to bed for countless generations, should put your child to bed is a call only you can make—based on your parental instincts, your toddler's personality, and on your evaluation of the expert opinion available. Renowned psychologist and author Bruno Bettelheim gave fairy tales an unambiguous thumbs-up. Not only did he see them as not hazardous to the emotional well-being of children, he saw them as indispensable in their lives. In *The Uses of Enchantment,* his classic examination of the effects of fairy tales on children, Dr. Bettelheim wrote that while most children's literature entertains and arouses curiosity, fairy tales stimulate imagination, develop intellect, clarify emotions, identify with a child's anxieties, problems, and aspirations, and fulfill the need for "magic" in a world that often seems to lack it. In *Little Red Riding Hood,* for example, the child confronts, among other themes, the grandparent (or parent or other caregiver) turned from a gentle nurturing soul into a ferocious beast (a metaphor that may strike a familiar chord) and then back again. *Hansel and Gretel* deals with poverty (the family is so poor that there isn't enough to eat), with greediness (the children set out to devour a stranger's gingerbread house), and with revenge against the witch–mother image (at first she seems kind, then she turns on them). And *Snow White* deals with intrafamily jealousies and rivalries and the struggle to cope with them (this theme, too, may hit home).

Consider, as well, the fact that most children aren't frightened by fairy tales (although some parents are so certain that their children will be, that they never give the classics a chance). When fear does become an issue, it's often the result of parental planting ("Now don't be afraid, the wolf can't get you").

So before you decide to burn your collection of fairy tales along with all the spinning wheels in the kingdom, you might want to try:

**Reading those bedtime stories early in the day.** If you're worried that fairy tales at bedtime may result in nightmares or sleep problems for your toddler, reserve them for the light of day—at least until you're sure she's comfortable with them.

**Starting with *The Emperor's New Clothes*.** Or *The Ugly Duckling*. Or another of the less fearsome fables. If your toddler seems to accept these well, begin working your way up to such spine-tinglers as *Jack and the Beanstalk*.

**Cuddling for security.** Snuggling up under a cozy blanket or in a favorite chair with your toddler while you read the fairy tales will help her to feel more secure and less threatened by any menacing characters.

**Repeating the favorites.** Young children get very little out of a story the first time around, especially stories as complex as fairy tales; it's the repetition that makes the impact. With each telling, they learn more, understand more, internalize more of the story's values.

**Rehashing the stories.** As with any story you read to your child, she'll get much more out of a fairy tale if you discuss it together afterward. To launch a discussion, ask such open-ended questions as: "What do you like about this story?" and "How does this story make you feel?" Then, follow where she leads.

**Doing a little editing.** Don't worry about hurting the author's feelings. If a plot line makes you feel uncomfortable, go ahead and rewrite as you read to your toddler—that's how these stories were shaped in the first place. Tailor any of the venerable old tales to the needs or temperament of your toddler or your family, if you like. Have Granny hide out in the closet until the woodsman comes along and shoos the wolf back into the woods. Have Snow White fall asleep (instead of dropping dead) after eating the apple. Have Hansel and Gretel tie the witch to a kitchen chair before beating their hasty retreat through the forest. (But be sure the story's illustrations can support your revisions.)

If the feminist in you winces at the "handsome prince rescuing the helpless but beautiful princess," weave in some woman-empowering elements (the princess comes up with the plan for defeating the wicked witch, or pulls out a sword of her own and duels with the best of them). If you feel "and they lived happily ever after" paints an unrealistically simplistic picture of relationships between men and women, end your story with "and they loved each other very much, helped each other and shared, and were each other's best friend," implying it takes more than true love to make a lasting marriage. If you'd like to try some of the commercially sanitized (or feminized) versions of fairy tales, feel free to—they're okay for three- and four-year-olds. But don't throw out the originals; when your child is older, she will benefit more from hearing those versions.

**Pointing out the pretend.** Three-year-olds don't fully grasp the difference between reality and fantasy, but they do understand *pretend* (they drink pretend tea from a toy cup, kiss a pretend baby, make a pretend action figure do battle). So when you read a fairy tale to your toddler, make sure she understands that the story is pretend, make believe, not real. Assure her, for example, that wolves don't really dress like grandmothers, that they are just big, wild dogs who can't even talk.

**Taking your cue from your toddler.** If she does seem frightened by a particular story, encourage (but don't force) her to talk about her feelings. And don't read the story again unless she asks for it. (Some children *love* being scared by scary stories, and ask to hear them over and over again.)

# THE THIRD BIRTHDAY PARTY

*"Our daughter's going to turn three in a few weeks, and we were wondering how much more elaborate we can get with the party plans now that she's a little older."*

**D**on't put in that call to Dial-a-Donkey or Magicians Unlimited yet. Three-year-olds can handle a little more party than two-year-olds—but just a *little* more. Too much more can send pint-sized party-goers into celebration overload, with less-than-pleasant results. Besides, three is still an age of relative innocence and relatively low expecta-

tions—even three-year-olds who frequently make the birthday party circuit are perfectly content, and sometimes even happier, with a few games or a craft project, modest decorations, and some ice cream and cake. It's not yet necessary, and it's usually not wise, to try to impress three-year-olds with elaborate plans and presentations.

For a happier third birthday all around:

**Include your toddler in the planning.** A three-year-old can help decide on guests, decorations, simple entertainments, games, and so on. Take the special needs of the invitees into account, too; check with parents for details on allergies, dietary restrictions, limitations on activity, or other problems (such as a fear of dogs).

**Keep it small.** An intimate group of children who know each other well—whether they're preschool classmates or play-group cronies—works best. The one-guest-for-each-year rule (plus your child), which this year would bring the total up to a manageable four, is still a good one to follow. Another, possibly less stressful option, is taking your daughter and one or two guests of her choosing out for a birthday fun-day—a movie and a pizza, for instance, or the zoo and a picnic. If you don't want anyone to feel left out, you can always bring the party to school or day care, serving cupcakes and passing out favors (if they're allowed) at snack time, or hold the party at play group.

**Keep it well supervised.** If your birthday girl insists on having the party at home and you must invite more than three children (because, for instance, your daughter's play group has five members or she wants everyone in her preschool class to come), you will probably need some help. If you can't find enough willing adults, hire a responsible teenager to help out with serving, clean-up, and party games. Or appoint willing older siblings as "helpers."

**Consider inviting parents.** Ask the parents of guests to stay if they'd like to, but only if you're comfortable with the idea. Keep in mind, however, that some children are better behaved when their parents *aren't* around. If you do extend an invitation to parents, have enough cake and other refreshments on hand should they all decide to join the fun.

**Have scheduling savoir-faire.** If most of the children on your guest list still take naps, plan the fiesta around the siestas. Be thoughtful of mealtimes, too; if you're serving cake and ice cream at an afternoon party, for example, don't wait until 4:30 or 5:00 and risk sabotaging your guests' appetites for dinner. Keeping the party shorter will definitely keep the kids sweeter—an hour and a half is party aplenty.

**Set a smart table.** Storybook, TV, and movie character themes are very popular among three-year-olds, and paper party goods very popular among those who have to clean up after them. So take your toddler to the party store and stock up on her choice of paper cups, plates, and napkins. (For environmentally sound alternatives, see page 428.) But instead of buying a matching paper tablecloth—which will be rendered useless by the very first tipped cup of juice—use a colorful vinyl cloth that can stand up to the inevitable spills. Or cover your table with a roll of heavy-duty white butcher paper and provide a cupful of crayons at each place setting for doodling.

**Be a stingy server.** Instead of serving cups with juice filled to the brim, just begging to be upended, pour an inch or so at a time and refill as needed. Instead of cutting huge slabs of cake and doling out double scoops of ice cream, inviting

both waste and food play, start with small portions, and hand out seconds to those who finish firsts and ask for more. An important peace-keeping reminder: If there are special decorations or favors on the cake, either don't serve them at all or make sure that every young guest gets a share.

**Put safety first.** When planning the menu, steer clear of foods children can choke on. While many three-year-olds have the requisite molars and chewing capabilities to handle such foods as hot dogs, popcorn, and grapes, others are still at risk for choking on these items—particularly when they're laughing or running around while eating. To play it safe, don't serve any of the foods listed on page 538, and insist that the children stay seated when eating.

**Eschew formal entertainment.** While some three-year-olds may delight in a pony ride or a sword-swallowing magician, such splashy amusements may reduce others to tears. If you feel compelled to hire someone to perform at your party, an enthusiastic, but not wildly histrionic, storyteller might be the best bet. A singer who specializes in children's music may also be a hit. Avoid costumed performers; no matter how charming they may appear to you, they can spook some of the younger guests. Performers who shape balloons into animals will be popular—until the balloons pop (at which point they can also present a choking hazard).

**Play games—for fun.** Keep games short and avoid those that promote competition; three-year-olds are not known for their sporting attitudes. Some possibilities: Duck, Duck, Goose; London Bridge; Dance the Hokey Pokey; Farmer in the Dell; Musical Statues (everyone freezes when the music stops). Encourage participation, but don't force guests to play. Do have more activities planned than you think you'll need. You don't have to get to them all, but if you run out mid-party—gulp!

**Get crafty.** Crafts projects that are simple enough for all participants to handle are a perfect way to pass party time happily. Letting kids make something that they can take home (rather than having them work on a group project to leave behind) is best, and gives each a personalized party favor. Check with a local crafts or toy store for projects that are appropriate for three-year-olds. Possibilities: making their own puzzles, birthday crowns, mobiles, placemats, nature collages, finger puppets. To avoid nasty struggles over the glue or the markers, make sure to stock ample supplies of everything they'll need to complete the projects.

**Skip prizes.** The only way you can distribute prizes to a group of three-year-olds is to give everyone a prize for each activity. It's easiest and best to enjoy the activity for the fun of it, not the reward.

**Put it in writing.** So that you won't forget anything in the chaos, make a party schedule that includes activities and the times they are slated for. Put the list and all of the supplies you'll need for games and crafts in a carton or basket in a central place, out of reach of curious young guests.

**Think ahead.** Hand out party bags at the very end of the party, as children walk out the door, to prevent guests breaking or misplacing favors before they go. Have extras of edibles, should a slice of cake find its way onto the floor or a scoop of ice cream topple off its cone, and to offer any siblings who might arrive with parents at pick-up time.

# WHAT IT'S IMPORTANT TO KNOW:
## The Superchild Syndrome

**"H**e's doing exactly what he's supposed to be doing for his age," was once music to parents' ears, comforting confirmation that their child was healthy, normal, and developing at just the right rate. But in today's achievement-oriented, competitive society, it seems that many parents want more. They want their children to be healthy and normal, of course, but they also want them to be developing a little faster and a little better than the rest—doing *more* than they're supposed to be doing for their age. They want them to be precocious, gifted, talented, and accomplished, to have an edge. They want them to be *superchildren.*

Is it because these parents want the best for their children that they want them to be the best? Sometimes. But sometimes, there are other motivating factors. Parents who missed getting into an Ivy League college are bent on rearing Harvard-bound children. Parents who were mediocre athletes are intent on their children excelling on the court, the playing field, the slopes. Parents who could never manage more than "chopsticks" on the piano are determined that their children be weaned to Chopin. Parents who were never completely satisfied with their lot want a lot more for their children. Parents who consider their children a reflection of themselves want their

# INTRODUCING THE ABC's AND 1,2,3's

••••••••••

With at least a dozen years of schooling ahead for your child (twenty or more, if college and graduate school are in the cards), there's no reason to rush formal learning. Early childhood should be a time for the unencumbered enjoyment of simple pleasures: running through the sprinkler, playing house, riding a trike around the playground, making snow angels, splashing in the wading pool, collecting pinecones in the park.

Yet many toddlers take a natural, early interest in letters and numbers. And as long as exposure to these building blocks of learning is fun, unpressured, and toddler inspired, there's no reason why parents can't introduce the ABC's and 1,2,3's at this early age. Here's how:

▲ Nurture a love of books and reading (see page 101). As letter identification starts to interest your toddler, look for alphabet books that link letters to familiar objects.

▲ Stimulate an interest in science in your toddler (see page 456).

▲ Post your toddler's name, in simple block letters, on the door of his or her room.

▲ Put posters up on the walls, with lots of colorful pictures and big bright letters.

▲ Label toy shelves: "blocks," "dolls," "books," and so on. By each word, you can also place a picture of the object, so your toddler can begin to associate the two.

▲ Count steps when you climb stairs, cookies and crackers as you dole them out, T-shirts as you fold them, oranges as you select them in the market, blocks as you put them away.

▲ Play lotto, bingo, animal dominoes—all of these teach premath and prereading skills in a fun way. Look for games, puzzles, and other toys for preschoolers that also teach letter and number recognition. Be sure they are age-appropriate or you'll frustrate your toddler's natural curiosity.

▲ Cut sandwiches and cookies into triangles, circles, squares, and rectangles. Learning to recognize shapes is a prereading skill.

▲ In the course of a normal day, casually point out familiar signs, such as: EXIT, WALK, DON'T WALK, STOP, and ONE WAY. But don't go overboard with reading everything that's around you out loud unless your child starts asking, "What's that say?"

▲ Write your child's name on drawings and paintings, and as you write, chant the letters out loud (L-I-Z spells Liz).

▲ When your toddler expresses an interest, show how to write his or her name, starting with one letter at a time. Often children will express particular interest in finding out what words start with the same letter as their name: "R is for Ryan, it's also for rabbit."

▲ Put up and use a message board. Being in a letter-rich environment exposes a toddler to important prereading skills.

---

children to reflect well. Even parents who don't philosophically believe in pushing often end up pushing—if only so their children won't fall behind the rest.

But whatever the reason for pushing a child towards superchild status, experts agree that it's ultimately a mistake. While it might well temporarily net the kind of prodigious progeny these parents dream of—it *is* possible to teach very young children, even babies to read (monkeys can be taught to read, too)—the benefits will be short-lived and the price too great. Studies support the following generalizations about children whose parents impose too much pressure too soon, as compared with less pressured children:

# NURTURING THE SCIENTIST
# IN YOUR TODDLER

· · · · · · · · · ·

There are many little scientists in every toddler. Look closely at yours, and you'll not only see a physicist in the sandbox, but a botanist, entomologist, and geologist in the park, an oceanographer at the beach, a chemist in the kitchen, an inventor in the playroom, an astronomer at the window—all examining, scrutinizing, experimenting, comparing, developing, and testing theories. All for the love of discovery.

Unfortunately, the natural inclination to discover frequently doesn't last much past the toddler years. Often, at about the same time children begin their formal science education, hands-on science becomes hands-off, and the scientists within are suppressed.

It is possible, however, to keep the inner scientists motivated all the way through their school years, or even for life. To start with, try these activities:

**Classify, classify, classify.** Discovering how things are the same and how they are different is a fundamental skill. And though toddlers may not yet know a species from a genus, they can sort out trees that have leaves and trees that have spiky needles, fruits that have edible skins and fruits that have to be peeled, vehicles that have two wheels, four wheels, and more wheels.

**Discover electricity.** Watch the effects of static electricity. Have your toddler rub a balloon against your hair and then place it on the wall, or run a comb through his or her hair and then use the comb to pick up little pieces of paper.

**Grow some roots.** To help your toddler see that many nonhuman things grow, too, plant a root garden. Cut an inch off the top of a few root vegetables (carrots, parsnips, or beets, for instance), then place the vegetables cut-side down on a shallow dish. Pour some water in the dish, put it in a sunny place, and watch it grow roots.

**Plant a dozen seedlings.** Use an empty egg carton as a planter for a seedling garden (use seeds from an orange or other fruit that your toddler's eaten). Show your toddler how to set the seeds in the soil, water them, and give them sunshine; together draw a parallel between what makes plants grow and what makes people grow. If the seeds don't grow, explain that some times that happens.

**Be kitchen chemists.** Some of the most fascinating scientific discoveries can be made in the kitchen. Let your budding scientist watch (from a safe, supervised distance) as heat makes an egg turn from gooey and clear to firm and white; as a piece of bread (soft and light colored) turns into a piece of toast (crispy and dark); as air beaten into egg whites or heavy cream makes them thick and fluffy; as yeast makes bread dough rise; as blowing on hot food cools it off; as vinegar mixed with baking soda (and perhaps a drop of food coloring for drama) in a muffin tin "erupts" in miniature volcanoes; as sugar or salt crystals "disappear" in water; as raisins "dance" in the bubbles in a glass of sparkling water.

**Reinvent the wheel.** What rolls besides a wheel? Have your toddler experiment with an apple and a block, a round rock and a rock that isn't round, a roll of paper towels, a cork, a book, an empty plastic soda bottle. Discuss what the rolling objects have in common.

**Attract some attention.** Let your toddler roam the house (supervised) with a large magnet and see what it will and won't attract. See where your refrigerator magnets will (and won't) cling.

**Have a way with weight.** Select three objects of about the same size (a feather, a spoon, and a banana, for instance) and let your toddler's hands be the scale that determines which is the lightest, the heaviest, and the one in between.

**Make merry with measures.** Can you pour two cups of water into one cup? How many cups can you pour into an empty milk container? How many feet long are you (have your toddler make an outline of his or her foot, cut it out, use it to measure things—including you, lying down)? Or teach your toddler a lesson in how things grow by making a height graph. Every couple of months, mark your child's height on the wall (or on a tall sheet of paper taped onto the wall)—and watch together as the marks grow higher and higher. You can watch the growing of your toddler's feet, too, by making foot outlines on tracing paper, and comparing sizes every six months or so. Now's a good time, too, to explain the things that help children grow bigger—rest, food and drink, fresh air, exercise.

**Be meteorologists.** Get your toddler in the habit of looking out the window each morning and taking note of the weather—and if the vocabulary is within his or her reach, issuing weather bulletins at breakfast. Weather-watching skills come in handy when your child starts preschool; "morning meeting" or "circle time" often begins with a weather report. Becoming weather savvy may also help your toddler become more sensible when it comes to dressing (a rainy day means boots and a slicker, a sunny hot day means shorts and sandals, a cloudy cold day means a warm jacket and mittens). Another weather related activity: On a rainy day, leave a jar outside to collect the rainfall; measure it with a ruler later on. When it snows, measure it, too.

**See the world up close.** An unbreakable magnifying glass can show your toddler the world in an entirely new way. Have your toddler examine a few grains of salt, the peel of a banana, your skin, a strand of hair, a piece of wood, a green leaf and a dried leaf, bubbles in a bubble bath—and anything else that catches his or her scientific fancy. Plastic containers that come with magnifying tops are also fun, especially on nature walks.

**Study nature.** Collect leaves and needles from different trees and compare. Carefully take apart a flower and study its parts (but make it clear to your toddler that this experiment should only be conducted with adult approval; otherwise you're likely to find your entire garden dissected). Dig up a pailful of dirt from the backyard or in the woods when you're hiking, spread it on newspaper, and examine the contents—you may be surprised by the amount of wildlife you can find in just a bucket's worth of dirt. Make a bird feeder by coating a large pine cone with peanut butter mixed with corn meal, then rolling it in bird-

seed; string it outside on a tree or your terrace, and watch the birds fly by for a snack. Follow some animals home: Pick out an ant returning with a mouthful of supplies, and follow it to its hill house; watch a squirrel as it retreats into a tree; spy on a bird flying home to its nest. Talk about the similarities and differences between your home and those of the animals and birds.

**Study water.** In the tub or in a basin of water set up in the bathroom or kitchen, let your toddler fill and empty containers. Or provide a variety of waterproof objects and let your child discover which float and which sink. Together, try to figure out what properties make the floatables float and the sinkables sink. Give your toddler some sponges (cut into fun shapes, if you like; but watch carefully if your toddler is still putting things in his or her mouth); observe as they "grow" when dipped in water, then "shrink" again as they dry. Fill a paper cup with water and have your toddler place it in the freezer; examine the cup's contents periodically, as the water turns to ice. When it's hard, take it out again and let it defrost. Then put the melted water in a pot on the stove and bring it to a boil and let your toddler watch (at a distance) as the water turns to steam.

**Do it in order.** Have your toddler arrange a group of objects in order of smallest to largest. As eye-balling skills improve, have him or her order the objects from largest to smallest, which is trickier.

**Combine science with art.** Lie on your backs in the park and watch the clouds roll by (point out how they move, how they sometimes cover the sun). Then go home and draw pictures of clouds with chalk or paint. Cut open a carrot to examine what's inside, then dip the cross-section in paint and do a vegetable print. Collect dried leaves and pine cones on a nature walk, then preserve the collection in a collage. Pick some flowers in your garden (or, with permission, a neighbor's), then press them inside heavy books until they're dried (explain that they dry as the water that's in them is pressed out). Look for smooth, flat stones or large shells at the beach, then bring them home and paint them (they make great paperweight presents for friends and relatives).

*Watching a colony of ants going about their business is entertaining and educational.*

▲ Their long-term performance is not improved. For example, though children who are taught to read early may have an initial edge, it is quickly lost as children who begin later catch up. It's much wiser to wait until a child *wants* to learn—at which point learning comes more easily. True, some children who are pushed do become highly successful as adults, but often at the cost of a normal childhood and social life, and sometimes even their happiness.

▲ They often suffer from early burnout. The toddler who is dragged to preballet for a couple of years, for example, is often tired of it before she takes her first ballet class, and may rebel by refusing to attend at all.

▲ Their self-motivation is usually weak. Driven by their parents from the start, these children rarely learn to drive themselves.

▲ Though they may be more advanced in learned skills in the short run, they are often behind in reasoning, logic, and conceptualizing in the long run. Able to parrot back what they've been taught, they may not truly understand it.

▲ Their creativity and imagination are often dampened. With early emphasis on structured learning rather than free play, these important qualities may go unnurtured.

▲ Their curiosity may be stifled. In play, young children have the chance to explore the world, repeatedly test it out, and draw their own conclusions— opportunities virtually stolen from those who are given answers before they even have a chance to inquire. As child development authority Jean Piaget said, "Every time we teach a child something, we keep him from inventing it himself."

▲ Their resourcefulness may be diminished. With activities so thoroughly planned for them, they may not learn how to plan for themselves. When left to their own devices, they may not know how to occupy themselves.

▲ When they reach formal schooling, they are often less enthusiastic about learning than less-pressured children, probably because the joy and spontaneity have gone out of their learning, and because they are accustomed to achieving to please their parents rather than themselves.

▲ As a direct result of the constant pressure to perform well, they are afraid of failure and of being wrong, often timid about taking chances.

▲ With the emphasis on achievement and little time for normal childhood socializing, development is lopsided and social skills often lag behind.

▲ They may have trouble finding their own identity. Children who have always been pushed toward achieving goals their parents have set for them instead of goals they've set for themselves are deprived of the chance to discover what their interests are, what makes them happy—in essence, who they are.

▲ Their self-esteem can suffer. Self-esteem grows when children are successful, and children are most successful when the challenges set before them are within their reach. If frequent failures come early—as when children are pushed to achieve tasks that are beyond their ability—self-esteem usually takes a beating. It also suffers when parents run the show,

putting their children in the role of followers: "The things my parents want me to do are important, the things I want to do aren't. So I can't be very important."

▲ In extreme cases, they miss out on childhood pleasures entirely. Because their parents see play time as a waste of time, some "superchildren" never experience what every child needs: a carefree and fun-loving childhood. This deprivation may stunt their growth as adults.

Clearly the case against pushing your child to become a superchild is a strong one. Children grow and develop to be the happiest, healthiest, all-around brightest they can be by being loved and appreciated for the way they are, and by being allowed to develop at a rate that's appropriate for them.

Nevertheless, all children can benefit from being raised in a stimulating and challenging environment, where their innate love of learning is nurtured early on. To encourage without pushing, let your child take the lead. Follow as your child shows you what interests and what doesn't, what satisfies his or her thirst for knowledge and what oversaturates it.

## SIGNS OF THE SUPERCHILD SYNDROME

• • • • • • • • • •

Sometimes it isn't easy for parents to recognize when they've been pushing their child too hard. While a few parents quite consciously set about trying to create a superchild, most parents aren't even aware that they're pushing—much less that the pushing has a negative effect. Watch for warning signs that your child may be under too much pressure:

▲ Little or no time for free, unstructured play.

▲ Anxiety, tension, moodiness, fatigue, irritability, aggressiveness, frequent crying or whining, frequent tantrums, depression, and lack of enthusiasm.

▲ Problems or issues concerning sleeping or eating.

▲ Headaches, stomachaches, tremors, tics, or other (possibly) psychosomatic ailments. (Of course, illness should always be ruled out by the doctor in the case of such symptoms.)

▲ An inability to play well or get along with peers.

Any one of these signs, whether it indicates excessive pushing or another concern in your child's life, deserves attention. If the underlying cause seems to be too much parental pressure, you should reevaluate the situation and consider easing up.

# WHAT IT'S IMPORTANT FOR YOUR TODDLER TO KNOW: The Importance of Being Honest

Your three-year-old accidentally knocks over a box of crayons, and as they scatter across the family room floor, looks you straight in the eye and boldly declares, "I didn't do it."

*A child's first lie.* A bit unsettling to parents? Sure. The end of innocence? Maybe. A predictor of future immoral conduct? Not at all. Just typical toddler behavior. Most toddlers have not yet learned that honesty is the best policy—although by the third year, many have noticed that dishonesty can sometimes get them out of a tight spot.

There are several reasons why toddlers may lie: *The need to retain the illusion of goodness.* By toddler reasoning, denying you did something bad makes the misdeed go away and allows you to remain good. *The wish to avoid facing consequences.* The thinking goes: "If I don't tell Daddy that I knocked the crayons over, maybe I won't have to pick them up." *A still-faulty memory.* When Jonathan accuses Lara of grabbing the truck from him, he may already have forgotten that he grabbed it from her in the first place. *Difficulty distinguishing fully between reality and fantasy.* When Kayla gets a new doll, Hillary sees nothing dishonest in saying, "I got a new doll, too." After all, speaking her fantasy makes her feel better. And Andrew, a very imaginative child, may make up whole stories yet neglect to mention that they're made up—from his point of view, he's telling tales, not lies.

Since toddler fibs aren't malicious or calculated, they're not a cause for concern—or for punishment. Assuming a child lives in an atmosphere of honesty and trust, the fibbing stage will eventually end. As the little voice within grows louder, and as that little voice begins to play a bigger role in decision making and in social interactions, your toddler will outgrow the need to lie. In the meantime, you can deal with untruths and nurture the development of honesty in the following ways:

▲ Don't make it easy for your toddler to tell an untruth. Don't ask "Did you . . . ?" when you know very well the answer is yes. Say instead, "I know that you . . ." or "I saw you . . ."

▲ Make it easy to tell the truth. If you say, "Something happened to this cup of juice. How did it get on the floor? I wonder . . ." you stand a much better chance of securing a confession than if you hurl an accusation. "Look what you did—you spilled your juice again!" is more likely to elicit an indignant "I did not!"

▲ Make telling the truth pay off. If a three-year-old admits to crayoning on the family-room wall and you react to the admission with rage, it's easy to see how the child might be discouraged from admitting future misdeeds. If, on the other hand, you show appreciation for honesty ("I like when you tell me the truth"), the child is more apt to be truthful. (Of course, even when misdeeds are confessed, the appropriate disciplinary action still needs to be taken; for example, if the usual penalty for drawing on the wall is helping to scrub off the scribbles or having drawing privileges suspended temporarily, that penalty should be imposed.)

▲ Help your child to see the whole truth. Often, a toddler will remember only part of what happened, in which case you may have to help extract the full story.

# WHAT ABOUT THOSE LITTLE WHITE LIES?

· · · · · · · · · ·

The most truthful among us have told them—even George Washington probably wasn't above them. They usually seem harmless enough, and sometimes they even seem to prevent hurt feelings. When you're dealing with a young child, they often seem indispensable ("No you can't have another ice cream—it's all gone.")

But the bottom line is that little white lies—like whoppers—are untruths all the same. To impress your toddler with the value of being honest, you have to avoid untruths of any size. Though toddlers may fall for a parent's white lies, at least for a while, they eventually catch on. And when they do, they learn a couple of unfortunate lessons: One, that fibbing is the fastest way out of a sticky situation and an effective way to get what you want, and two, you can't always trust your parents.

White lies are occasionally necessary to avoid hurting someone's feelings. To help your toddler distinguish between the "noble" lie and the self-serving variety, try always to explain when you tell one why you've done so. For instance, "I didn't want to hurt Aunt Mary's feelings, so I told her I liked her cookies, even though I don't like gingerbread. Sometimes it's okay to say something that isn't true to protect someone's feelings. But it's never okay to tell a lie that could hurt somebody." The line between white lies that are permissible and those that aren't is likely to be too fine for your toddler to recognize at first. But with plenty of reinforcement, the message will eventually sink in.

Sometimes, you may have to avoid telling the *whole* truth about something in order to protect your child or because it's beyond his or her comprehension—as when you explain how babies are made or why somebody died (if it was a violent death, for example) or why Aunt Jenny and Uncle Jim don't live together anymore. But even in these cases, try to avoid telling a lie; simply tell only the part of the truth your toddler can digest.

Santa Claus, Easter Bunny, and, later, the Tooth Fairy can also fall into the "little white lie" category. Some parents enjoy perpetuating these myths with young children, others are uncomfortable with the necessary deceit involved. Do what works for you and for your child, continuing the fantasy for as long as you both enjoy it. If somewhere down the line, however, your child asks point blank, "Is Santa real?" he or she deserves an honest answer. Explain that people like to believe in the idea of Santa because it makes them happy, and that the happiness Santa "brings" is real, even if he's only pretend. Let your child know that there's nothing wrong with pretending, and that pretending is not the same as telling a lie, as long as everyone knows you're pretending.

"Sam hit me" may be the truth, but not the whole truth, which may be that your child pinched Sam in the first place. In that context, the accusation looks a lot different, and with a little gentle prodding, your child will come to understand that.

▲ Don't force your toddler to lie. Too much pressure, standards that are too high, punishment that is too severe, all can lead a child to lie in order to avoid extremely unpleasant consequences.

▲ Leave the grilling to the detectives. If you don't get a spontaneous confession, don't give your toddler the third degree. When you and your toddler both know that he or she did something wrong, insisting on an admission of guilt is unnecessary. And when your child maintains, "I didn't do it!" angrily countering with "You did, too!" will only encourage a shouting match or tantrum. Instead, let your child know (even if it's for the twentieth time) that what was done was unacceptable. If there's a punishment due, impose it. If you don't know for sure that your toddler is guilty, however, don't press it. But do say, "I hope you're telling me the truth. If you're not, I'll be very sad."

▲ Trust your child. Truth and trust are inseparable; if you're truthful, you'll be trusted, and if you're trusted, you'll be truthful. Let your child know that you trust him or her (saying before a play date, for instance, "I know you're going to try very hard to play nicely today," rather than warning, "You'd better not hit this time"), and your child will be more likely to live up to that trust. Be sure your toddler can trust you, too; try always to keep your word, and if you can't, be sure to offer an explanation *and* an apology. When the opportunity presents itself (as when your toddler has admitted a transgression), discuss the value of trust—explain that when people tell the truth, other people can trust them and believe what they say. When your child is older, tell him or her the story of *The Boy Who Cried Wolf* to illustrate the connection between truth and trust.

▲ Make honesty *your* policy. Nothing teaches a toddler to be honest better than a parent's example. Be truthful in your dealings—large and small. Don't tell your toddler that taking the splinter out won't hurt, when you know it may; don't tell the train conductor your three-year-old is only two in order to pay a reduced fare; don't tell friends you can't join them for dinner because you're down with the flu, when the truth is you'd rather catch a movie; don't tell a neighbor you have no idea who trampled her flower bed when you know your dog is the guilty party. Even "little white lies" can compromise a child's understanding of the value of honesty; see page 461.

If you do fib, and your child catches you, admit that you've made a mistake—so that he or she will feel free to own up in a similar situation.

# PART TWO

# Toddler Care, Health, and Safety

# CHAPTER SEVENTEEN

# Toddler Care Primer

I t was only yesterday, or so it seems, that you brought that precious little bundle home from the hospital—only yesterday that you gave that first bath, first shampooed that downy head, first trimmed those tiny fingernails. That precious little bundle's not a baby anymore—but though growing up all too fast,

your toddler still requires plenty of care. Besides the baths, shampoos, and trims, you need to attend to your toddler's eyes and ears, skin and teeth, dressing and undressing—and, in the process, begin teaching your child the fundamentals of self-care, too. The tips in this chapter should make it easier.

## FROM SKIN CARE TO DRESSING TIPS

### CARING FOR YOUR TODDLER'S SKIN

#### Defeating Dry Skin

Keeping a baby's skin baby soft isn't always smooth going; keeping a toddler's skin soft can be even rougher. Since the sebaceous glands, which will eventually lubricate and protect the skin, don't kick in until the hormones start flowing just before puberty, young skin is especially prone to dryness. A toddler's skin is even more vulnerable than an infant's, for a couple of reasons. One, being constantly on the go, indoors and out, toddlers are exposed more to skin-chafing elements. Two, toddlers get dirtier—and

both the dirt and the cleaning up can irritate tender skin.

But there are some ways to prevent the moisture loss that causes dryness and to help replenish the moisture when dry skin strikes:

**Avoid overheating.** When the mercury dips outside, it's always tempting to send the mercury soaring inside. But dry, overheated air leads to overdry skin, particularly for toddlers. So during the heating season, try to keep your home between 65° and 68° F during the day and between 60° and 65° at night. Instead of turning up the thermostat, keep the family cozy in heavy sweats or sweaters during the day and flannel pajamas or warm sleepers at night.

**Protect from the elements.** Moisturizer (see next column) or a thin layer of petroleum jelly will protect exposed skin from the drying, irritating effects of severe cold and wind.

**Limit bathing.** Though most toddlers get dirty enough daily to warrant a nightly scrub in the tub, daily bathing can be both trying and drying. If your toddler's skin is very dry, give baths every other day or less often, spot-cleaning or sponge-bathing between tubbings. When you do bathe your toddler, use lukewarm water instead of hot (hotter water is more drying) and do not use bubble bath, which can be irritating as well as drying. Keep baths (and showers, which are even more drying than baths) relatively brief, so your toddler doesn't dry out from the soaking. Though the addition of bath oil can sometimes help prevent drying, they can make the tub slippery—and thus treacherous for a toddler. Also, some toddlers may be sensitive to some of the ingredients in bath oil—perfumes and dyes, for example.

**Be soap savvy.** Use a very mild, superfatted, soap (such as Cetta, Basis, or fragrance-free Dove) or a soapless cleanser (such as Moisturel Liquid or Lowilla Cake). Don't use soaps that contain deodorants or perfumes. Also avoid antibacterial soaps, which don't really wash away more germs than plain soap does (even hospitals, for the most part, use plain soap), and can also be irritating, causing redness or scaling. Long-term use may eventually promote the growth of resistant bacterial strains.

Use even the gentlest of soaps sparingly, soaping up only as needed (where dirt is most obvious, and around the buttocks and genitals).

**Don't rub-a-dub-dub after the tub.** Always *pat* your toddler's skin dry instead of rubbing it.

**Moisturize.** Apply moisturizer after the bath while your child's skin is still slightly moist. It can also be reapplied before bedtime and before going out, if necessary.

The best moisturizers for a toddler's skin contain both water (to replenish moisture) and oil (to seal it in), omit fragrances, and include few if any chemical additives. You can ask your child's doctor to suggest a moisturizer, or use a product such as Eucerin, Moisturel, Neutrogena Emulsion, Vaseline Dermatology, Aveeno Lotion, or Lubriderm Cream. For extremely dry skin, a cream may be more effective than a lotion, although it won't be as easy to apply.

If your child's dry skin becomes worse after you've applied a moisturizer, or if a rash or other eruption develops (even "hypoallergenic" or "natural"[1] products can trigger a reaction in sensitive children), stop using the product immediately. Try a moisturizer with different ingredients, or ask your child's doctor for a recommendation.

**Keep those fluids coming.** Inadequate fluid intake, too, can lead to, among other problems, dry skin. So make sure your toddler gets enough fluids (see page 508). Be especially aware of fluid intake if your toddler has just been weaned and is still working out the kinks of drinking from a cup.

**Be wary in warm weather.** When temperatures soar, the toddler needs protection not from dryness but from heat rash and sun. Lotions, creams, and oils are unnecessary for all but the driest skin in the summer. In fact, especially if they are thick (petroleum jelly, for example), they can make the skin more uncomfortable, and by blocking the evaporation of moisture, lead to heat rash (also known as prickly heat). Both exposure to sun

---

1. Keep in mind that the term "natural" means nothing, since its definition is unregulated by law.

## TAKE A GOOD LOOK AT YOUR TODDLER'S SKIN

· · · · · · · · · ·

Though the skin is by far the body's largest organ, it doesn't usually get its fair share of attention. While an eye infection or an earache is likely to be treated promptly, a skin condition might not even be noticed—a large percentage of our skin, after all, is under clothing most of the time. That's why doctors now recommend routine skin exams that allow parents to become familiar with their children's skin and to be able to note any changes. Make a habit of checking your toddler's skin at bath time at least once a month, observing any changes in moles or birthmarks, and noting any new marks or lesions you hadn't noticed before. If a mole or birthmark has grown instead of fading, if its color has changed, if it is itchy, oozing, bleeding, crusting, scaling, or tender to the touch, report your findings to your child's doctor. Also report any sore that takes longer than two weeks to heal or unexplained rashes or other skin symptoms.

and overdressing can also add to skin distress in hot weather. See below for sun-protection tricks, page 499 for cool dressing ideas, and page 473 for how to treat heat rash, if it does develop.

### Smoothing Chapped Cheeks

On an average day, a variety of substances (ranging from saliva and mucus to jelly and tomato sauce) manage to find their way onto a toddler's face, where they're promptly smeared from cheek to cheek, causing redness and irritation—especially in winter, when skin is already extra dry. Frequent face-washings (as parents strive to remove these substances) often compound the chafing.

If your toddler's cheeks turn apple-red with the first frost and stay that way until the tulips come up, some special attention is needed. To minimize facial chapping:

▲ Pat the face dry with a soft cloth after each washing and whenever there's been excessive drooling.

▲ Avoid using soap on your toddler's face. When more than water is needed, use those recommended on page 465.

▲ Gently wipe your child's face with warm water immediately after meals to remove any traces of food and pat dry promptly. If you notice that a particular food or beverage is especially irritating to the skin (common offenders are those that are high in acid, such as citrus fruits and juices, strawberries, and tomatoes or tomato sauces), avoid serving it to your toddler until the chafing has cleared.

▲ Soothe chapped skin with a mild moisturizer (see page 465). Spreading petroleum jelly on cheeks, chin, and nose before going out in cold weather may also be protective, especially for a teething toddler who is drooling a lot or a toddler with a runny nose.

### Screening Out the Sun

The Australians, who live in a part of the world where the sun's rays are particularly intense, have a word for it, or rather three words: slip, slap, slop (*slip* on a shirt, *slap* on a hat, *slop* on some sunscreen). They've got the right idea.

With the earth's ozone layer shrinking, skin cancer rates soaring, and scientists linking as many as 95% of all skin cancers to ultraviolet radiation from the sun, the days of unprotected sunning should be gone for good. Everyone needs to be shielded from both the sun's ultraviolet A (UVA) rays, which cause tanning, aging of the skin, and skin cancer, and ultraviolet B (UVB) rays, which cause sunburn and skin cancer. But children need special protection. There is some evidence that serious sunburns during childhood may be a more important factor in the development of adult malignant melanoma (skin cancer) than total lifetime exposure to the sun. Sunburns also represent an immediate hazard to young children: Because children have a larger proportion of skin to body mass than adults, severe burns can cause serious fluid and electrolyte imbalances. And although tanning seems innocent enough, there is no such thing as a safe tan. Tanning is a sign of skin damage; contrary to what many people think, it doesn't protect the skin from further harm.

To prevent sun damage, take these precautions whenever your toddler steps outside (and make sure that other caregivers are instructed to do the same):

**Protect year-round.** While we associate sunburn with summer, the sun can also be a threat in winter, especially when there is snow on the ground. In fact, the sun's rays reflected on the snow can be as intense as those from summer sun. And, although less of the burning UVB reaches the earth in winter, the also-harmful UVA rays remain constant year-round. Since the sun's rays also get more intense as you go up in elevation (an increase in 4% with every 1,000 feet above sea level) or get closer to the equator, more precautions need to be taken year-round in high altitudes or equatorial regions.

And don't skip the sunscreen when it's hazy out, especially if you're at the beach; much of the sun's ultraviolet light can penetrate a light cloud cover.

**Schedule outdoor time wisely.** Try to limit your child's exposure to the sun—even when he or she is properly protected—during the hours when its rays are at their most intense, between 10 A.M.

and 3 P.M. or when your shadow is shorter than you are. Think of the sun as a source of radiation or a giant nuclear reactor and you won't feel so guilty about keeping your toddler out of its reach.

**Encourage play in the shade.** Look for playgrounds that are well-shaded, and set up play areas in your own yard, if possible, that are in shade all or part of the day.

**Beware of glare.** On the beach, where you are unlikely to find natural shade, don't rely on a beach umbrella—it can't shield your toddler adequately from the reflected glare of sun on sand. Instead, pitch a beach tent, which will provide shelter from the sun while your toddler plays. Be wary, too, of the sun's reflection on snow, concrete, and water (the toddler who's splashing in the pool is even more vulnerable to sunburn than the one who's playing beside it). And since UVA passes through glass, as any greenhouse gardener can tell you, a child sitting near a car window (unless it's tinted for sun screening) or playing indoors near a broad expanse of window is also susceptible to the damaging rays.

**Cover up.** When you're out and about with your toddler during the hours when the sun is most intense, keep the rays at bay with a stroller canopy or umbrella, a wide-brimmed hat or cap,[2] as much clothing coverage as is comfortable, shoes and socks (bare feet burn quickly), and sunscreen on exposed parts of the body. Keep in mind, however, that the sun's ultraviolet rays can penetrate sheer and lightly woven, light-colored fabrics; the typical T-shirt has a sun protection factor (SPF) of only 7 or 8, which means that most toddlers (darker skinned children excepted) need a layer of sun-

---

2. There is now available, a cap with a brim in the front and a flap in the back to protect the neck. If a toddler with thin, fair hair refuses to wear a hat, spread some sunscreen on his or her head (sprays are easiest to apply).

## AT GREATER RISK UNDER THE SUN

..........

Though all children should be protected from the damaging rays of the sun, some kids are at greater risk than others. These include children with red or blonde hair and fair skin; those with blue, green, or gray eyes; those with a family history of skin cancer; those who live in a tropical or sub-tropical climate or at a high altitude; those with a large number of moles; and those, no matter what their coloring, who burn rather than tan (but don't wait to find out by trial and error whether your child fits this last category). A face full of freckles may be cute, but freckles, too, are a sign that a child is especially vulnerable to sun damage and may have had excessive sun exposure already (in duration or intensity).

Any child who's at greater risk under the sun should routinely wear a sunscreen with an SPF of 20 or more, and spend only limited time in direct midday sunlight.

---

screen under their T's when they are going to spend extended time outdoors. To test a fabric, hold it up to a light; the less light that shows through, the better protection from the sun it affords. Wet fabrics are a third less protective than dry ones, dark colors are more protective than light (but they are more uncomfortable in hot weather); tight weaves are more protective than loose ones. Denims seem to provide the most protection of all (a denim sun hat might be a good idea for a particularly sun-sensitive toddler). If your child takes a medication or has a condition that makes exposure to the sun particularly risky, ask your doctor for information on the special sun-protective apparel that's now available for children.

**Slather up.** No matter what your toddler's wearing, sunscreen is a smart accessory when you're headed for an outing in the sun.[3] Make applying it as routine as donning shoes, and as non-negotiable as sitting in the car seat. You're less likely to face resistance to sunscreen in the future if you make putting it on a habit now. (It's a habit everyone in the family would do well to develop.)

Be sure that a baby-sitter or nanny gets in the habit of applying sunscreen to your toddler, too. If your child goes to day care or preschool, do it yourself every morning (using a long-lasting product); you can't always rely on a teacher to take this task over for you.

When shopping for a sunscreen, look for one that's designed for children (it's more likely to be gentle and—because many children are sensitive to PABA, a common ingredient in sunscreens—PABA-free) and that blocks out both UVA and UVB rays. Choose an SPF of at least 15, unless your toddler's skin is medium to dark, in which case an SPF of 8 should be fine. (See the box that follows for more on SPFs.) Creamy and oily products are less drying and stay on the skin longer. But sprays are usually easier to apply—and since a sunscreen can only be effective for your toddler if you manage to get it *on* him or her, ease of application is a prime consideration (don't use a spray near your toddler's eyes, however). And avoid

---

3. Whether sunscreen protects against melanoma, the most serious type of skin cancer, has been brought into question by recent research—though it's possible that a sunscreen that protects against both UVA and UVB rays may be more effective than one that protects only against UVB. This question increases the importance of other sun protection steps, such as covering up with hat and clothing and limiting time in the sun.

scented sunscreens; they may be attractive to insects. Even once you've chosen a product that's recommended for young skin, it's still a good idea to test your child for sensitivity to it. To do this, spread or spray a thin layer on a small patch of your child's skin; if redness or a rash develops, don't use the product on your child. Instead, try another with different ingredients. Check the expiration date on any sunscreen you're using and be sure to toss what's left after that date has been reached—potency can be affected by age.

Though toddlers are wont to want to do it themselves, applying sunscreen is adult's work, not child's play. A toddler isn't likely to be able to apply the screen evenly (necessary for complete protection), keep it out of eyes and mouth, or off clothing. If it makes an older toddler more cooperative, you might try a little "You cover my back, I'll cover yours." But if you do let your toddler spread a bit of sunscreen on you, be sure to wipe the sticky little hands immediately.

If it's possible, apply the sunscreen thirty minutes before going out into the sun, since it takes that long to be absorbed into the skin. (If you can't manage that, however, applying it right before going out is far better than not applying it at all.) Spread the sunscreen generously and be careful not to miss any exposed skin (including the back of the neck, an area often overlooked). Be careful, too, not to get the sunscreen into your toddler's eyes (there are no-tears formulas available for kids whose eyes are extra-sensitive). Since wind and water both thin out protection, reapply every hour or so if it's windy, if your toddler is sweating a lot, or if he or she has been splashing in a pool or running under a sprinkler. You can reapply it less often—every two hours or so—if you're using a waterproof product (read the label for recommendations). But keep in mind that even a waterproof sunscreen can be rubbed off by a lot of towel drying and will need to be reapplied more often under such conditions.

## DECODING SPF's

· · · · · · · · · ·

The SPF (sun protection factor) tells you just how much protection a sunscreen product offers. An SPF of 15, for example, means that users can remain in the sun fifteen times longer than they could without protection before burning. Just how long that is, of course, depends on the individual. Protected by a product with an SPF of 15, a fair-skinned person who might start to burn within fifteen minutes of unprotected exposure theoretically wouldn't start to burn for 15 × 15 minutes (or 3¾ hours).*

But since you have no way of knowing exactly how long it takes your child to burn, or how intense the sun is on a particular day, it's unwise to stretch sun exposure to this limit. Even slathered with sunscreen, an hour or so at a stretch is long enough in a direct, hot sun for all but darker-skinned toddlers. And don't assume you can safely wait for your toddler's cheeks to start showing some color before you bring him or her under cover. The pinking of the cheeks (or back, or arms, or other exposed areas) is not generally apparent outside in the sun. In fact, most sunburns do not reach their peak color until six to twenty-four hours after sun exposure.

---

* There is some controversy over whether sunscreens with SPFs higher than 15 are of value. Some experts believe they are, but only for children at high risk.

For extra protection on extra-vulnerable areas (nose, cheeks, and the tops of your toddler's ears) you might want to dab on a little zinc oxide or titanium dioxide. These sun*blocks*, which actually let *no* UV rays through, are opaque and not exactly attractive to wear, but offer the strongest protection available. Some blocks come in toddler-pleasing neon colors, and are packaged like lip balm for easy appliction. A few sunscreens feature one or the other of these sun-blocking products in their formulations.

Lips need sun protection, too. Make applying a children's sunscreen lip balm (which should be lick-proof) before going out in the sun as routine as applying sunscreen. Not only will lip balm protect your toddler's lips from the sun, it may also prevent a reactivation of a herpes simplex virus infection in the form of a cold sore or fever blister (see page 494). And it will also shield your toddler's lips from wind and cold in the winter, reducing chapping.

**Make the Best-Odds Diet a habit.**
What does diet have to do with sun protection? Actually, according to recent studies, possibly a lot. It seems that a diet high in beta-carotene (as is the Best-Odds Diet; see page 504) may ward off the ravages of the sun by reducing the detrimental effects of UVA rays.

# THE MOST COMMON TODDLER SKIN PROBLEMS

Once in a while, what looks like chapped skin is actually eczema or another skin condition that needs medical attention. If your toddler's skin is scaly, itchy, blistered, or oozing, check with the doctor.

The most common skin rashes in toddlers include:

**Diaper Rash.** *What is it?* A rash or irritation anywhere in the diaper area. *Who is susceptible?* Babies and toddlers in diapers. Children taking antibiotics are particularly vulnerable to yeast, or fungal, infections. *Signs and symptoms:* These vary, depending on the cause (see chart, facing page); in boys, a diaper rash may appear as a sore on the end of the penis. *Causes:* Again, see the chart on the facing page. *Transmission:* Chafing dermatitis, or simple diaper rash, is not contagious. Diaper rash that is caused by a micro-organism can sometimes spread to other parts of the body if conditions are favorable (for example, yeast infections, which thrive on moisture and warmth, can take hold in skin that is already irritated). When conditions are right and precautions aren't taken, such infections may also be spread from child to child. *Treatment:* For simple chafing dermatitis: 1. Reduce moisture in the diaper area. Change your child's diaper as soon as you know it is wet. As always, *pat* the bottom dry after washing it. Applying cornstarch may help to reduce moisture, and spreading a thick layer of diaper rash ointment can protect the skin from the next flood of urine (ask your child's doctor for a recommendation). This protection is especially important if you use cloth diapers and won't be able to change the next wet one immediately. 2. Increase exposure to air. Allow your toddler to wander about the house bare-bottomed (but only in areas of the house where cleaning up an "accident" will be easy). Keep a potty close by at such times, just in case. If your toddler usually wears waterproof pants with cloth diapers, leave the overpants off whenever feasible. And don't cover the skin with ointment when you are exposing your toddler's bottom to the air—the air can't get through the ointment any more than moisture can. 3. Minimize exposure to irritants. Change wet and soiled diapers immediately. Skip the wipes and use only warm water and cotton balls or

## TYPES OF DIAPER RASH

| TYPE | SIGNS AND SYMPTOMS | CAUSE |
|------|--------------------|-------|
| Chafing dermatitis | Redness where friction is greatest; no discomfort | Moisture, rubbing |
| Atopic dermatitis | Redness with itching | Allergy or sensitivity |
| Seborrheic dermatitis | Deep red rash, often with yellow scales; may start on or spread to scalp; no discomfort | Unknown |
| Candidal (fungal) dermatitis | Bright red, tender rash increases between thighs and abdomen, with satellite pustules spreading from there; uncomfortable | *Candida albicans* (a fungus); *Candida* often infects a skin rash that's around for 3 days or longer |
| Impetigo | See page 473 | Bacteria |
| Intertrigo | Poorly defined reddened areas where skin contacts skin; may ooze white to yellowish matter; may burn when in contact with urine | Rubbing of skin on skin |

soft paper towels for clean-up when changing diapers. Use plain soap (page 465) on your toddler's bottom no more than once a day. Adding a colloidal oatmeal bath product (such as Aveeno) to the bath water may be soothing, especially for a boy with a diaper rash on his penis. 4. Switch diapers. Different children react differently to different diapers. Though diaper rash is slightly less common with disposables, some children do better with cloth diapers; some children do better with one type of disposable than another. If a diaper rash persists in spite of the above measures, try a change of diaper. If you home-launder diapers, rinse them with half a cup of vinegar or a special diaper rinse. 5. For intractable diaper rash in a toddler who shows the signs of being ready for toilet learning, take the steps recommended in Chapter Nineteen to help the learning along. **Do not use:** Boric acid (which is toxic if ingested and is not safe to keep around the home with a toddler); talcum powder or a product containing talc (which, if inhaled, can cause respiratory problems); or medications for other family members, whether prescribed or bought over-the-counter (some ingredients in combination products can cause allergic skin reactions). Call your child's doctor so that the condition can be diagnosed and a topical medication to deal with it prescribed if the diaper rash: gets worse, is painful, or spreads beyond the diaper area; develops blisters, sores, crusts, boils, or pustules or a sore at the end of the penis; doesn't clear in three or four days; or if unexplained fever develops.

(Be sure to ask how long the medication should take to work. Once treatment has begun, call the doctor back if the condition doesn't get better in the specified time, or if it gets worse). Call immediately if your child seems very sick or if large blisters (1 inch or more across) develop. *Prevention:* Keep the diaper area clean and dry (applying cornstarch may help to reduce moisture); don't wait too long between changes of wet diapers and change soiled diapers immediately; avoid giving your toddler foods that seem to irritate (in some children, certain acidic foods, such as citrus, produce irritating stool); and avoid soaps and wipes that seem to irritate. Be sure to wash your hands thoroughly after changing the diaper of a child with an infectious diaper rash, and be sure the same sanitary precautions are taken by your child's other caregivers both at home and preschool.

**Atopic dermatitis** (eczema). *What is it?* The most common skin condition in children under eleven, it has been aptly described as "an itch that rashes." Once the itch begins, scratching or rubbing the area triggers the rash. *Who is susceptible?* Most often, children with a family history of eczema, asthma, or hay fever, or a personal history of allergy. A majority of cases begin in the first year and almost all by age five. *Signs and symptoms:* The itching comes first, sometimes with night waking and crying, face rubbing against crib sheets (crib may shake as child tries to soothe the itch), scratching (sheets may become blood-stained). As the infant or child scratches or rubs the area, bright red scaly patches appear, most often on the cheeks and wrists in infants and young toddlers, and in body creases and folds (at elbows, knees, thigh/groin area) in those over two. It may also spread to the diaper area. Often the skin thickens and in dark-skinned children, it can produce

additional melanin as a protective measure, making the thickened patches look black (hyperpigmentation). Sometimes the rash becomes weepy. Secondary infection, usually with staphylococcus, is common. The papulovesicular lesions (they look like small pimples, or papules) erupt, fill with fluid, then weep and crust over, intensifying itching. Though most children "outgrow" the eczema, they may continue to have sensitive skin as adults. These children are also at extra risk of developing asthma or nasal allergies later. *Causes:* Numerous factors are believed to trigger the itching (most often in children who have inherited a sensitivity) including: dry skin (the major factor), heat or cold exposure (often at change of season), perspiration, wool and/or synthetic clothing, friction, soaps and detergents, certain foods (most often eggs, milk, wheat, peanuts, soy, fish, shellfish, and chicken), and, possibly, inhaled allergens (pollens, dust mites, mold). *Transmission:* Not communicable, though secondary infection of the rash may be. *Treatment:* Medical attention is **essential**: treatment usually includes steroid creams for inflammation, antihistamines for itching (especially to help a child sleep), and antibiotics if secondary infection develops. Skin testing and elimination diet will be recommended if food allergy is suspected. On the home front, it is important to: clip your toddler's nails to prevent scratching; avoid showers, which are particularly drying; limit baths to five minutes three times a week or add a soothing colloidal oatmeal bath product to the daily bath water; use no soap on affected area; use Dove or other gentle soap (see page 465) elsewhere as needed, and instead of shampoo; ban swimming in chlorinated pools and salt water (fresh water is okay); apply any doctor-recommended lubricating skin ointment generously, but do not use vegetable fats or oils; minimize exposure to extremes in temperature, indoors and out, and to dry air indoors (use a humidifier in winter; see page 838); dress your child in cotton (rather than wool or synthetics) and avoid itchy or potentially irritating clothing; protect your child from germs that might infect the open sores by observing scrupulous hygiene practices (see page 606) and being sure that caregivers in any preschool or other group your child attends does likewise; eliminate any food or environmental factor that triggers a breakout (see page 706). A recent study suggests that vitamin C may be helpful as well in treating atopic dermatitis—check with the doctor.

**Impetigo.** *What is it?* A bacterial infection of the skin. *Who is susceptible?* Mostly young children. *Signs and symptoms:* With "staph" infection, large, thin-walled blisters that burst and leave a thin yellow-brown crust. With "strep," a single painless fluid-containing vesicle surrounded by reddened skin develops—often around the nose, mouth, or ears. It may then begin to weep, oozing yellowish fluid, which forms a yellowish crust. It can spread quickly to other areas of skin. *Causes:* Bacteria, such as streptococci or staphylococci, entering the skin through a break, such as a scratch, bite, irritation (e.g.: diaper rash).[4] Both bacteria often infect the same lesion. *Transmission:* Person-to-person; contagious until the rash is gone or until medication is taken for 48 hours and rash improves. *Treatment:* Medical treatment is necessary; **do not** self-treat. Topical antibiotics and hot soaks are usually prescribed for very mild cases (a superficial lesion), oral antibiotics (broad-spectrum type, effective against both strep and staph is best) for multiple lesions. *Prevention:* Avoiding anyone with an active infection; thoroughly cleaning

mild skin wounds with soap and water, and then applying an antibiotic ointment.

**Prickly heat.** *What is it?* Heat rash. *Who is susceptible?* Most commonly, babies; but toddlers, children, and even adults can develop a heat rash. *Signs and symptoms:* Tiny pink pimples on a reddened area of skin; they may blister and then dry up. The rash occurs most often around the neck and shoulders, but it can also appear on back and face, or anywhere skin rubs against skin or clothing constricts. *Causes:* Overheating, overdressing. *Treatment:* Smoothing on cornstarch or adding cornstarch to the bath; dabbing on a solution of 1 teaspoon bicarbonate of soda to 1 cup of water with cotton balls may also be soothing. But avoid products containing talc, which can cause respiratory problems when inhaled. *Prevention:* Protect your toddler from overheating by keeping indoor spaces as cool as possible. (See the tips on dressing your toddler for warm weather on page 499.)

**Ringworm of the body** (tinea corporis). *What is it?* A fungal infection of the skin. *Who is susceptible?* Anyone. *Signs and symptoms:* Itchy, scaly, red patches that grow into red round or oval "rings" surrounding a smooth center. *Causes:* Various types of fungi. *Transmission:* Direct contact with infected people or animals, or items handled by infected individuals. *Treatment:* After diagnosis by examination and, generally, a culture of scrapings from a lesion, topical antifungal medicine is usually prescribed. If the rash doesn't begin to clear in two weeks, an oral preparation may be prescribed. As with other medications, medication for ringworm must be continued for the prescribed period, even if the rash clears sooner. *Prevention:* Avoidance of contact with infected persons or animals, and with any objects they may have handled or touched.

---

4. Very rarely, strep impetigo spreads to kidneys or staph impetigo causes endocarditis or osteomyelitis.

# CARING FOR YOUR TODDLER'S HAIR

Whether it's a mass of ringlets or a fine coating of down, every toddler's hair needs some care. Since most toddlers (and their parents) dread hair care routines, it makes sense to limit them to the bare essentials:

**Choose gentle supplies.** Think "gentle" when you select brushes and combs for your toddler. A brush should be flat, rather than curved, and have bristles with rounded ends. If your child has kinky hair, the bristles should be long, firm, and widely spaced. A comb should have widely spaced, nonscratchy teeth (check for smoothness by running the comb across your inner arm, which is more sensitive than your hand). A wide-tooth comb is especially important for children with extra-thick or frizzy hair. A detangling comb, specially designed for curly, kinky hair, is also useful.

Think "gentle," too, when choosing a shampoo; a mild, no-tears formula that is designed for children is best. Shampoo/conditioner combinations save a step, which makes them perfect for shampooing a squirming toddler. Alternatively, use a children's shampoo plus a spray-on detangling rinse after the shampoo, instead of a conditioner that requires extra rinsing.

**Care for hair gently.** Brushing helps to bring oil to the surface of the scalp and is particularly valuable for children with dry hair. But don't brush hair when it's wet; comb it, instead. Use a light touch when brushing or combing your toddler's hair; avoid tugging or yanking. Detangle with a wide-tooth comb, working from the ends up, one section at a time; keep a bottle of spray-on detangling rinse

around for resistant snags. To prevent hair breakage and loss, don't pull hair tightly, whether in braids, barrettes, or ponytail holders, and never use regular, uncoated rubber bands (use only the soft-coated variety made for hair use). For tips on dealing with the toddler who rejects the comb and brush, see page 276.

Because most African-Americans have hair that breaks easily, be especially gentle when brushing. Start at the nape of the neck and work toward the tips. Do small sections of the hair at a time. Brush downward, rather than up, because brushing up is more likely to break the hair.

**Shampoo only as needed.** Since oil glands on the scalp, like oil glands elsewhere, don't become fully functional until puberty, daily shampoos are rarely necessary, except for toddlers who tend to get a lot of food, sand, or dirt in their hair, or those who have particularly oily scalps. Many toddlers—especially those with very dry hair or scalps—do well with only a weekly shampoo. Others require a shampoo every other day or even every third day. More frequent shampooing is often needed in summer, when hair gets sticky faster. Be sure to rinse well; a soapy residue can become a magnet for grime. For dealing with a shampoo rebellion, see page 153.

**Don't share when it comes to hair.** Most of the time, the ability to share is an admirable trait to encourage in toddlers; but when it comes to hair care equipment, sharing isn't a virtue. Each member of the family should have his or her own comb and brush, and to prevent transmission of head lice or other problems, should keep these to themselves. Combs and brushes should be washed weekly or every other week in suds made with a dash of shampoo and warm water.

---

## GUMMY HAIR

· · · · · · · · · ·

Toddlers don't have to chew gum to get it stuck in their hair; they can pick up a sibling's (or a parent's) leftovers from the trash. When the inevitable happens, put down the panic . . . and bring out the peanut butter. Rub plenty of peanut butter into and around the gum, then gently comb the gum out with a wide-tooth comb, and shampoo.

---

# MOST COMMON TODDLER HAIR/SCALP PROBLEMS

**Hair loss** (alopecia). *What is it?* Abnormal loss of hair. *Who is susceptible?* Anyone, but young children are less susceptible to certain types of hair loss and more susceptible to others. *Signs and symptoms:* It's normal to lose about 40 to 100 hairs a day (more on shampoo days), each of which is replaced by a new hair. But if your child suddenly begins to lose fistfuls of hair and/or develops a bald spot, check with the doctor. *Causes:* A fungus infection, such as ringworm (common in young children; see this page); an underlying medical illness, such as thyroid disease; or alopecia areata (suspected to be an allergic reaction to one's own hair; rare in young children). But balding could also be the result of poor nutrition, stress (though stress-related hair loss is uncommon in toddlers), habits like head-banging (a bare spot develops where the head repeatedly makes contact; see page 177) or hair twisting or pulling or "traction alopecia" (from fastening hair too tightly in barrettes, braids, or ponytails, or pulling it excessively during combing or brushing). *Transmission:* Depends on the individual condition (see below). *Treatment:* Depends on the cause: Ringworm is treated as described in the following section; a thyroid condition is treated with appropriate medication; and alopecia areata is generally left untreated (except in severe cases it is self-limiting[5]). Traction alopecia can be reversed by avoiding barrettes, braids, and other hair styles and accessories that pull at the hair. Whatever the reason for hair loss, keep in mind that the body needs adequate protein intake to restore hair growth.

**Ringworm of the scalp** (tinea capitis). *What is it?* A fungal infection of the scalp. *Who is susceptible?* Anyone, but children between the ages of two and ten are the most vulnerable. *Signs and symptoms:* Thinning hair and balding spots on the scalp, with flaking and itching. (In toddlers, the flaking raises a strong suspicion of ringworm, since young children are unlikely to have either cradle cap or dandruff.) If there is hypersensitivity to the fungus, hair follicles may become inflamed; there may also be blistering, cracking, and tenderness. Some children experience a severe inflammatory reaction, with fever and swollen glands. Ringworm may be confused with other scalp problems, so medical diagnosis is necessary. *Cause:* A fungus, most often *Trichophyton tonsurans*, which infects the hair shaft itself. *Transmission:* Via personal contact, as well as brushes, combs, and barber/hairdresser instruments. *Treatment:* An anti-fungal medication for four to eight weeks combined

---

5. With alopecia areata, 95% of patients have complete regrowth within a year

with a shampoo containing 2.5% selenium sulfide. (The shampoo alone is not effective.)

**Head lice** (pediculosis). *What is it?* An infestation of the hair by lice. *Who is susceptible?* Despite the stigma associated with head lice, they are not choosy;

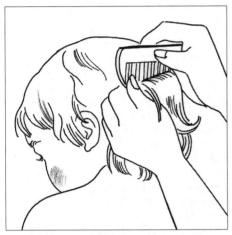

*Using a fine-tooth comb to remove each and every nit, as well as empty nit cases, is necessary following treatment for killing of head lice.*

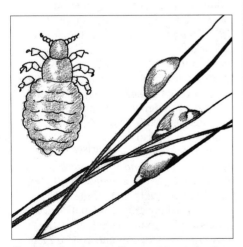

*Head lice, 2 to 4 mm in diameter (shown magnified many times at the left) generally lay their eggs (nits) very close to the scalp. They can survive for no more than ten days on the host; the nits, which are firmly cemented to the hair shaft, survive for about three weeks.*

they will settle comfortably on most any head of hair, clean or dirty, long or short, rich or poor. Lice are more common among children who are in day care or group care situations simply because they're more likely to be exposed. *Signs and symptoms:* Head-scratching or scratch marks behind the child's ears or near the hairline, at the forehead or neck (though many toddlers hardly notice the little visitors and don't scratch at all); sightings of lice or nits in the hair, near the scalp. *Causes:* Infestation by head lice (*Pediculus humanus capitis*), parasites who survive by sucking small amounts of blood from their host's scalp and reproduce by laying eggs (nits) in the host's hair. *Treatment:* Use of a lice-killing product as recommended by your child's doctor; package directions should be followed very carefully. If you have questions about a product, call the manufacturer (most have toll-free numbers on their package inserts). Shampoo over the sink, rather than in shower or tub, to avoid getting the chemical on your child's body. After the treatment, it's necessary to painstakingly remove any remaining lice, as well as each and every little nit or empty nit case, using a special fine-tooth comb (one may be included with the lice-killing product) or your fingernails. A cream product used following the shampoo makes removing the nits easier. *Preventing spread and reinfection:* Prohibit sharing of brushes, combs, towels, pillows or other bedding, clothing, hats, and earphones. Destroy nits or lice that may have ended up in bed linens, towels, clothing, or stuffed animals an infected child has been using by washing the item in hot water (at least 130°F) or tumbling them in the dryer at "high" for at least twenty minutes. Items that cannot be exposed to such heat should be dry-cleaned or stored in air-tight plastic bags for two weeks to allow a full breeding cycle to pass before they are used again. (Remember, lice can live for up to forty-eight hours on clothing, furniture, and so on.) Upholstered furniture, carpets, mattresses, car seats, and such, should be thoroughly vacuumed. (Spraying with an insecticide is probably not necessary.) Hair brushes and combs should be washed in liquid disinfectant, bleach, or the lice-killing product used on the child's hair. Treating family members who are not infected is controversial; check with your child's doctor for advice. But be sure to check all household heads for lice or nits daily for two weeks following the last treatment. Because lice are so easily passed around, a child with lice is generally sent home from day care or preschool until they've been successfully treated; during an outbreak of lice, teachers may check the children's scalps periodically for signs of the parasites.

## CARING FOR YOUR TODDLER'S NAILS

For telling clues to a toddler's daily activities, look no further than the fingernails. There you'll find, among other things, mud (from the morning spent at the park digging), play clay (from that play date), glue (from that collage), remnants of breakfast, lunch, and dinner, and often, even less-savory substances.

Unless you protect them with gloves, there's no way you can keep your toddler's fingernails clean all the time. But since dirty fingernails can harbor germs along with all the collected grime, you'll need to try to:

**Keep them short.** The shorter the fingernails, the less they can collect. Short is also best for toenails, which left to grow ungroomed, can curl under and become ingrown. See page 182 for clipping tips.

**Clean them daily.** Make nail-cleaning part of the regular end-of-the-day routine. Help your child to use a small nail brush in the tub or when washing hands before bedtime. Carefully remove stubborn matter with a rounded wooden toothpick.

## CARING FOR YOUR TODDLER'S EYES

You know how precious eyes and vision are—not just in the toddler years, as children learn about the world, but all through life. Crucial to maintaining your child's eye health and vision are:

**Regular checkups.** It's important to catch vision or eye problems early, so be sure your toddler's eyes are checked by the doctor on schedule. The eyes are usually examined at birth and at six months, and checked informally at all regular well-child visits. If a child is at high risk for eye problems (was under 3.2 pounds at birth, has a family history of retinoblastoma, congenital glaucoma, cataracts, or diseases associated with eye problems), or if any abnormalities are noted, the child may be referred to an eye specialist, or ophthalmologist, for further evaluation. If your child's eyes were not checked during the first year, have them checked as soon as possible. Visual acuity is usually screened again between three and three-and-a-half (earlier if a specific concern arises or if there is a family history of eye disease). The next screening usually takes place sometime before a child enters school, around the age of five. These exams, performed either by the child's doctor or by a pediatric ophthalmologist, are not painful and are rarely upsetting to a toddler. In general, children who were born prematurely are more vulnerable to vision problems, so they need earlier and more frequent eye exams.

# SPOTTING VISION PROBLEMS

· · · · · · · · · ·

Toddlers are rarely able to let parents know that their eyes are bothering them in some way; if their vision isn't what we call normal, *they* certainly aren't aware that it's any different than any one else's. Most often it's a parent's observation that tips off the doctor to a potential vision problem. So keep alert for any of the following behaviors and symptoms, which spell "Check with the doctor:"

▲ An obvious inability to see well, often evidenced by pronounced clumsiness or stumbling (beyond normal toddler clumsiness; see pages 5 and 287), or by seeming not to notice or recognize objects or people—either in the immediate environment or in the distance.

▲ Frequent squinting unrelated to bright sunlight, or face-scrunching when trying to perform a visual task. (Keep in mind, however, that either of these may be a temporary mannerism not linked to vision problems.)

▲ Frequent eye-rubbing, unrelated to sleepiness (eye-rubbing when a child is sleepy is normal), which usually indicates itchy, scratchy, or burning eyes.

▲ Undue sensitivity to light (evidenced, for example, by squinting in discomfort when a light is turned on in a dimly-lit room) or frequent staring at lights.

▲ Excessive tearing, unrelated to crying.

▲ Swelling, redness, or crusting of the eyes (lids may be crusted shut in the morning), or a yellowish-white or yellowish-green discharge (a sign of infection); swollen lids or frequent sties.

▲ Eyes that seem to "bounce" or "dance" in rapid, rhythmic movements, or bulge.

▲ Frequent tilting of the head to one side, as though trying to see better.

▲ Holding the body rigid or at an angle when trying to look at distant objects.

▲ Repeated covering or shutting of one eye in apparent discomfort (as opposed to covering or shutting an eye periodically to see how the world looks with just one eye open).

▲ Holding books, toys, and other objects close to the face in order to see them better; consistently sitting too close to the TV (though in toddlers this may be a normal fascination with seeing things up close rather than a sign of a vision problem).

▲ Avoiding entirely activities (such as looking at books) that require good vision.

▲ Eyes that look crossed or otherwise mismatched, or that don't move in unison (see page 481).

▲ Pupils (the small openings in the center of the eye) that are sometimes or always unequal in size (they should work simultaneously: getting larger in dim light, smaller in bright light) or that appear white instead of black.

▲ Difficulty distinguishing colors (though remember that young toddlers rarely are able to identify colors; see page 315).

▲ Double vision; frequent headaches, dizziness, and/or nausea after doing close work (such as looking at books or television). Only an older and very verbal toddler will be able to alert you to such symptoms.

Keep in mind that a toddler will not be expected to achieve a perfect 20/20 score on an eye exam. The average two-year-old generally scores about 20/60. Vision continues to improve over the next few years to 20/40, but doesn't reach 20/20 until about age ten.

**Protection from the sun.** Long-term exposure of the eyes to the sun appears to increase the risk of cataracts later in life. So get your toddler used to wearing sunglasses or a wide-brimmed hat when outdoors (playing, walking, or riding in the stroller) in strong midday sun for more than a few minutes. Whether children should always wear sunglasses in the sun is controversial; some experts question whether the eye's own sun-protective mechanism will develop properly without some exposure to sun.

When buying sunglasses, look for UV-blocking lenses; they block 99% of both UVA and UVB light. ANSI (American National Standards Institute) ratings on sunglass labels provide a good guide: *general purpose*—medium-to-dark tinted lenses for use in any outdoor activity; *special purpose*—for extra-bright environments (in the snow, at the beach); *cosmetic*—lightly tinted for use around town. Side shields and goggles provide extra protection in extremely bright situations (high-elevation snow fields and tropical beaches, for example). To be most effective, they should screen out 75% to 85% of available light (look for this information on the label). Before purchasing sunglasses, be sure to check the lenses for distortions. (Hold the glasses at arm's length and look through them at a straight line, such as the edge of a door or window, several feet away. Slowly move the lens across the line; if the straight edge becomes distorted, sways, curves, or otherwise seems to move, optical quality is poor.) Tint should be uniform throughout both lenses. Frames should be sturdy and free of rough spots, large enough to block out some side light, and should fit comfortably and stay in place. Coated plastic lenses are the most durable and thus the most practical for toddler use. Gray lenses distort color the least; green or brown are next best. Avoid very dark lenses, which could interfere with a toddler's ability to see what's ahead. Keep the glasses from sliding off during play by attaching them with a special children's headband designed for the purpose.

**Protection from injury.** Whenever there's a risk of eye injury, protective glasses should be worn. The best protective glasses have 3-mm thick polycar-bonate lenses and have frames that are approved for industrial or sports use. Leak-proof goggles are a good investment for toddlers who spend a lot of time in chlorinated swimming pools. Keep in mind, underwater swimming is not recommended.

Though parents have been telling kids otherwise for generations, it's not true that reading or playing in dim light can damage vision. But because not having enough "light on the subject" can cause temporary eye strain and headache, always provide your toddler with adequate lighting.

The major injury risk to a toddler's eyes is from an accident at home, at day care, or at the playground. So be sure to follow the safety recommendations in Chapter Twenty-One. Take particular care to: Keep your child playing with toys that have sharp points or rods, with sticks, or with pencils and pens, except under close supervision (never allow these items in a moving car); cushion sharp corners on furniture (especially tables that are eye-level for your toddler); teach your toddler never to run with toys in hand; keep all toxic substances out of your toddler's reach (many can do eye damage on contact; see page 634); keep your child away when you are mowing the lawn or operating a snow blower (see page 644); use safety guards on power equipment. For a booklet on home eye safety, contact the National Society to Prevent Blindness (see page 482 for address).

**Protection from television.** While no amount of TV will permanently damage a child's eyes, prolonged viewing can induce temporary eye strain. Minimize the risk by limiting television (see page 159); when the TV is on, keep the room adequately lighted, adjust the lighting to minimize glare from the screen, and insist that your toddler take viewing breaks every half hour. Also make sure your child doesn't sit too close to the set (the most desirable distance is at least five times the width of the screen); a child who repeatedly gravitates back closer to the screen may be nearsighted, and should be tested. (Sitting too close also increases the potential risk from electromagnetic fields, or EMFs; see page 633).

**Protection from allergens.** A child who is prone to runny eyes during allergy season should wear wraparound glasses or goggles as often as possible when outdoors to keep pollen and other irritants out. Air-conditioning and air filters can help reduce irritation indoors. Summering in a cool climate, when feasible, is also helpful.

For information on treating eye injuries, see page 667; on eye infections, also see page 667.

# MOST COMMON VISION PROBLEMS IN TODDLERS

Vision problems often go undiagnosed in toddlers because they are too young to complain. Recognizing the warning signs on page 478, should they show up in your toddler, and reporting them to the doctor will allow for prompt diagnosis and treatment, which may help to prevent a condition from getting worse as well as head off related problems (such as learning difficulties, low self-esteem, and so on) that can develop in children when they can't see well.

The eye problems most common to toddlers are:

**Blinking.** *What is it?* Repetitive opening and shutting of the eyes. *Who is susceptible?* Any toddler. *Signs and symptoms:* Generally, just the blinking, though if lack of sleep is the cause, there may also be eye-rubbing. *Causes:* In some toddlers, repetitive blinking is simply a

habit that is picked up when they notice that quickly flicking the eyelids makes for an interesting visual perspective; in others, it's a copy-cat habit, picked up from peers; in still others, it's a result of inadequate sleep (but there will usually be other signs, too, such as crankiness) or of stress overload (though this reaction is much more likely in an older child than a toddler). Very, very rarely, blinking is a manifestation of a petit mal seizure disorder. *Treatment:* When not accompanied by other symptoms, repetitive blinking is generally benign and self-limiting; in most cases, it stops on its own within anywhere from a week to several months. If the blinking seems to be stress-related, reducing the stress in your child's life (see page 173) can often bring the behavior to an end. No matter what the cause, nagging your child about blinking is only likely to make the habit persist. If blinking is accompanied by any of the symptoms on page 478, is virtually nonstop, or seems to bother your child, check with the doctor.

**Nearsightedness** (myopia). *What is it?* An inability to see clearly objects more than a short distance away. *Who is susceptible?* Most often, children who have a nearsighted parent or parents. Though some children become nearsighted in the second or third year of life, the condition more often develops later. *Signs and symptoms:* Squinting, holding books and other objects very close, sitting close to the TV, difficulty identifying distant objects. *Causes:* Most often, an eyeball that is elongated rather than sphere-shaped, causing the image of distant objects to fall short of the retina at the back of the eye and thus to appear blurred. Occasionally, the cornea or lens is responsible for the distortion. Genetics is definitely a factor in the development of myopia; but there may be others that are as yet unknown. *Treatment:* Eyeglasses or contact lenses can correct the visual deficit; because of rapid eye growth in young children, prescriptions may have to be checked (and changed) every six months or so. Clinical trials are presently underway to determine the long-term safety and effectiveness in children of radial keratotomy, a surgery that reshapes the curve of the cornea to correct myopia.

**Farsightedness** (hyperopia). *What is it?* An inability to see clearly objects that are close. *Who is susceptible?* All babies and young children tend to be somewhat farsighted, but in most the vision normalizes eventually. Those who remain farsighted usually have a family history of farsightedness. *Signs and symptoms:* Backing away from close objects, as though trying to see them better; disinterest in close work: looking at books, doing puzzles, stringing beads, or playing with toys that require close vision; eye-rubbing; strabismus (cross-eyes). *Causes:* Most often, a flattened eyeball, which shortens the distance to the retina, causing the observed image to fall behind it and thus to appear blurred. Occasionally, a weakness of the cornea or lens is responsible for farsightedness. *Treatment:* Corrective lenses are considered necessary only when farsightedness is extreme, and interferes with play and other activities, and/or causes discomfort or mild headaches.

**Astigmatism.** *What is it?* Vision that is blurred or wavy; objects look the way they might look when reflected in a funhouse mirror. *Who is susceptible?* Anyone, but children who are either nearsighted or farsighted are the most vulnerable to astigmatism, which is usually present at birth. *Signs and symptoms:* Squinting, holding books and objects close to the face, sitting close to the TV, headaches, eyestrain. The symptoms are similar to those of farsightedness, but the conditons can be differentiated through medical evaluation. *Causes:* An

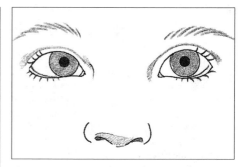

*Cross eyes: When one eye (of both) wanders inward.*

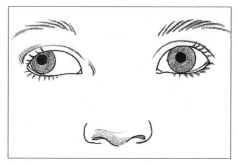

*Wall eyes: When one eye (or both) wanders outward.*

uneven curvature of the cornea and/or the lens of the eye. *Treatment:* Eyeglasses or contact lenses can usually correct an astigmatism; eyeglasses are usually more effective because it is difficult to fit contact lenses correctly to the uneven surface of the eye.

**Strabismus.** *What is it?* Cross eyes— an inability to focus the eyes in unison, which may be present at birth (congenital strabismus) or which may develop later (acquired strabismus). *Who is susceptible?* Children with a family history of strabismus, but the condition can also occur when there is no family history. It occurs in children with normal vision and those with poor vision, but farsighted children are particularly vulnerable. They may develop strabismus in their third year, when they try so hard to focus on near objects that their eyes cross. *Signs and symptoms:* Infants often appear cross-eyed for the first few

## CHECKING YOUR TODDLER'S EYES

**• • • • • • • • • •**

Worried that your child may have a vision problem, but not sure enough to schedule a doctor's visit? Consider some of these home tests, but don't postpone a doctor's appointment if you notice any of the warning signs on page 478. And be sure that your toddler has at least a couple of eye exams by age three; some serious conditions can only be picked up during a thorough exam.

**The red-dot test:** Examine family photos. If your prints show everyone with red dots in both eyes and your toddler has a dot in only one eye, this could indicate a malalignment.

**The at-home eye-chart test:** National Society to Prevent Blindness (500 East Remington Road, Shaumburg, IL 60173) offers an eye chart for testing young children who don't yet know their letters. The chart uses Es facing up, down, left, and right instead of letters.

**The look-who's-coming test:** Walk down the street with your toddler. Ask your spouse, a friend, or another familiar adult to approach from the opposite direction, and prompt your toddler to tell you who's coming. If your child can identify the approaching figure about when you do, his or her vision is probably normal. If it takes much longer for your child to see who's coming, he or she may be nearsighted.

**The reflection test:** Shine a penlight at your toddler's eyes and note where the light is reflected. The reflection should be at the center of the pupil in both eyes (see illustration); if it isn't, strabismus is likely.

---

months of life (pseudostrabismus), and once in a while during this time their eyes seem not to work in unison. But by the middle of the first year both of your child's eyes should move right and left, up and down, and focus together pretty regularly. In about 4% of children, however, the lack of coordination persists. The wandering eye (or eyes) may drift inward toward the nose (cross-eye), or outward (wall-eye), or up or down; the misalignment may always be present, or it may come and go. The child may also rub or cover the weaker eye frequently, tilt the head to try to coordinate vision, and refuse to play games that require judging distances (such as catch). You can test for strabismus yourself at home (see illustration). *Causes:* Strabismus is often related to weakness in the muscles of one or both eyes (six muscles serve each eye). There may also be genetic factors or an association with other eye disorders (such as cataracts or farsightedness) or medical problems (such as

Down syndrome or cerebral palsy), or very rarely, with other serious neurologic problems or eye disease. *Treatment:* Strabismus requires evaluation by a pediatric ophthalmologist; if strabismus develops *suddenly*, call your child's doctor immediately. Except in cases in which the muscle imbalance is so minor that the brain can fuse the images (a condition known as phorias), treatment is imperative to avert amblyopia (see the facing page) and vision loss, and to prevent double vision and restore binocular vision (in which both eyes focus together). Treatment may include medicated eye drops to blur vision in the stronger eye or placing a patch over it (for short periods each day) to force the use of the weaker one; eyeglasses to equalize vision in both eyes; and sometimes, exercises to strengthen the eye muscles. In some cases, surgery may be needed to adjust muscle tension in one or both eyes, remove a cataract, or to correct another contributing condition.

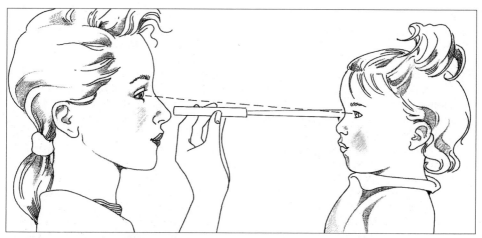

*To test for strabismus, position yourself face to face with your toddler. Shine a penlight at his or her eyes and note where the light reflects (see below).*

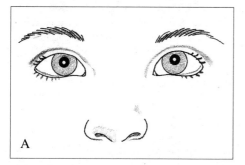

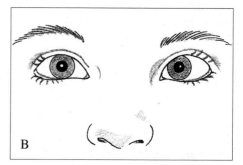

*If the reflection is centered on the pupils in both eyes (A), there is no strabismus—even if the eyes seem crossed. If the reflection is centered in one eye and off-center in the other (B), talk to the doctor about taking your child to see an eye specialist.*

**Amblyopia**. *What is it?* A condition affecting about 4 in 100 children, in which vision in one eye is better than in the other; the eye with the poorer vision becomes "lazy." The brain, confused by the mixed signals and double vision coming in from the eyes, eventually shuts off the signals from the lazy eye and begins to use the better eye exclusively; the lazy eye then begins to lose its visual acuity. *Who is susceptible?* Children with eye problems (sometimes inherited)—such as strabismus, ptosis (see page 484), a cataract, or a refractive error, where vision is different in one eye than the other—or who have sustained an injury to the eye. *Signs and symptoms:* Sometimes, none that a parent can detect, which is why routine vision exams are absolutely essential. *Causes:* Most commonly, strabismus, unequal focus (refractive error), or a cataract. *Treatment:* Treatment for an underlying or associated problem will not cure the amblyopia, which must be treated separately. If it isn't corrected by age five or six, vision in the weaker eye could suffer and loss of vision or even blindness in that eye could result. Treatment may include an eye patch, eye drops, and/or glasses. If an abnormality such as a cataract is responsible for the amblyopia, corrective surgery may be needed.

**Ptosis.** *What is it?* A condition in which one or both eyelids droop. *Who is susceptible?* Some children are born with ptosis (which is often inherited); others develop it later. *Signs and symptoms:* An enlarged, heavy, or drooping eyelid; occasionally, both eyelids are affected. In some cases, the lid totally covers the eye, inhibiting vision, or it distorts the cornea, causing an astigmatism. *Causes:* Generally, the eyelid droops because of weak muscles. Other causes are rare. *Treatment:* Ptosis requires evaluation and treatment by an ophthalmologist to prevent the development of amblyopia (if the child learns to depend on the eye with the normal lid, the lidded eye becomes lazy and its vision begins to deteriorate). When the problem is weak eyelid muscles, surgery (usually performed when the child is three or four) can strengthen them and give the lid a normal appearance. When another medical problem is responsible, treatment of that condition can cure the ptosis.

Other eye conditions (such as glaucoma, cataracts, and retinoblastomas (eye tumors)) are far less common in toddlers, but occur occasionally.

# IF YOUR TODDLER NEEDS GLASSES

Learning that a toddler needs to wear glasses is generally a lot more traumatic for the parents than for the toddler. But it needn't be, if you look at the positives. First of all, the glasses will help your toddler to see better. If they're necessary, wearing them will help prevent the kind of developmental delays—and the diminished self-esteem—that often affects children who can't see well. Secondly, starting to wear glasses at an early age is generally a lot easier than it is later on, when peer opinion becomes a major issue. Third, the need for glasses

is far from uncommon. One in six children between the ages of three and sixteen wears them. In addition, a positive parental attitude about the glasses can go a long way in making a child feel good about wearing them (though, given "typical" toddler behavior, you can expect resistance, at least some of the time.)

**Shopping for glasses.** When choosing glasses, work with an eye specialist who is good with young children (ask your child's doctor for a recommendation). Once you're in capable hands, consider style, quality, and practicality in making your selection. Safety-glass lenses, while relatively scratch-proof, can break. And because they are also generally too heavy for toddlers, they often slide down the nose. Consider, instead, lenses made of regular plastic or of polycarbonate (a lightweight, strong, and shatterproof plastic, which reduces the risk of accidental eye injury). Because plastic lenses scratch easily, however, a scratch-resistant coating may be a good idea. The coating costs a bit extra and can crack, so be sure to ask if a warranty, which provides free replacement for a period of time if the coating becomes damaged, is available. No matter what kind of lens you choose, teaching your toddler careful care of the glasses from the very first day of wear may help them last somewhat longer; see page 486.

When selecting glasses consider, too, how they will be kept in place. For infants, elastic straps are usually substituted for the ear pieces. They hold the glasses in place and allow the child to lie on the side and roll around without discomfort or knocking the glasses off. They may also be practical for a very young toddler, although most year-old children do well with comfort cables (also called cable temples), which secure glasses by earpieces that curl around the ears rather than pressing against the head (*see illustration*). Flexible hinges are also a good idea, since they tolerate more abuse.

*Since active toddlers aren't able to keep ordinary eye glasses in place, their glasses must be specially designed. On infants and young toddlers, glasses are generally kept in place by an elastic strap (left) that substitutes for the ear pieces. Older toddlers do well with comfort cables, which curve around the ears (right).*

**Fitting the glasses.** Glasses can't do their job unless they stay put, so good fit is essential. Because young children have fairly broad, flat nasal bridges and their glasses tend to slide down the nose, special attention is required when fitting the nose bridge. Rolled or flared nose bands (with or without non-skid silicone pads) may help keep glasses in place. The optician may have to drill "rocking" nose pads and arms into the nose bridge to obtain a good fit.

**Helping your toddler adjust.** Many toddlers are reluctant to accept the new and different (especially as a permanent fixture in their lives). But a thoughtful introduction can help a toddler make friends with his or her new spectacles:

▲ Display a positive attitude about the glasses, right from the start. Whisper to others, "The poor kid needs glasses," and your toddler will suspect that wearing them is somehow unfortunate. Instead, try, "Doesn't Jenny look great in those glasses?"

▲ Point out to your toddler others who wear glasses—siblings, playmates, parents, grandparents, favorite characters on television or in books. Explain that all of these people need glasses to see better. Knowing they are not alone in needing glasses helps toddlers feel better about wearing them.

▲ Brief your toddler (briefly) on the expected benefits of glasses. Explain that he or she will be able to see things better and have more fun playing (or won't have headaches or other eye problems anymore). But don't overdo the enthusiasm, or your toddler may become suspicious (nothing could be that terrific) or disappointed (when wearing the glasses doesn't turn out to be that wonderful after all).

▲ Brief older siblings and playmates, too. Let them know about the glasses before your toddler gets them so they'll be more supportive and less likely to make hurtful comments.

▲ Read books to your toddler about children who wear glasses. Check out the library for picture books on the subject; also look for Dr. Seuss's *The Eye Book.*

▲ Invite your toddler's participation in choosing glasses. If you can, make a first trip to the eye-glass store alone to check out the styles, lenses, and prices, and to ask all the questions you may have. Once you're more knowledgeable and aware of what's available, return with your toddler to select from a few prescreened choices.

▲ When the glasses are ready, have your toddler come along to pick them up so the fit can be checked and the optician or optometrist can give instructions on their use. Once the glasses are on your toddler, talk them up a little, comment on how nice they look, and then turn the focus of conversation away from the glasses and move on immediately to a preplanned activity (a visit to a children's museum, a zoo, the playground) that will distract and entertain your toddler for a few hours. Be patient but persistent while your toddler becomes acclimated to the glasses. If the glasses are whipped right off, try again a little later. But don't allow too much leeway; your toddler needs to understand that wearing the glasses, as needed, is as non-negotiable as sitting in a car seat. If you continue to meet with resistance, ask your child's doctor

for some back-up; the voice of a respected nonparental authority may well be more persuasive than yours.

**Teaching your toddler to care for the glasses.** While it's likely to be several years before you'll be able to count on your child to care responsibly for his or her glasses, it's never too early to begin the training process. Teach your toddler how to take off the glasses with two hands, without touching the lenses, and to keep the glasses in their case when they're not in use. An older toddler can learn how to use water and a soft, lint-free cloth to clean them.

# CARING FOR YOUR TODDLER'S EARS AND HEARING

M ost children are supplied at birth with two standard-issue ears which, like their eyes, must last a lifetime. Though other factors can also play

---

## WHAT'S TOO LOUD?

T he ear is a remarkable organ, but also a fairly delicate one; it can tolerate only so much auditory abuse. As a general rule, any noise you have to shout over to make yourself heard is too loud for the ear's comfort and, possibly, its health. Also potentially damaging are noises that leave the ears ringing or buzzing, that cause pain, or that induce temporary loss or muffling of hearing. Just how potentially damaging noise can be to the inner ear depends not only on how loud it is (how many decibels of sound it produces) but on how long the ear is exposed to it. Though, in general, longer exposure increases risk, even momentary exposure to some extremely loud noises, such as the blast of a gun or the roar

of a jet engine, can cause severe pain and injury. Examples of recommended maximum exposure levels to noise (when no protective gear is used) include:

▲ Eight hours of continuous exposure to noises louder than 80 or 90 decibels, such as a lawnmower or truck traffic.

▲ Two hours a day of exposure to noise louder than 100 decibels, such as that from a chainsaw, pneumatic drill, or snowmobile.

▲ Fifteen minutes of continuous exposure to sounds louder than 115 decibels, such as that produced by loud rock music, auto horns, or sandblasting.

## PIERCED EARS

. . . . . . . . . .

For some, piercing a baby daughter's ears is a cultural or family tradition. For others, it's a way of making it perfectly clear to the world—before there's enough hair to clip into a barrette—that their child is a daughter and not a son. Whatever the motivation, it's popular to pierce a little girl's ears when she's barely out of the cradle. But while the practice may fare well in popular opinion, it doesn't fly well in the medical community.

One reason is concern that an infection at the site of the puncture could get out of hand in a young child before the parent is aware of it. Infections are common in the first few months after piercing, and most young children are unable to report that an ear is itchy, sore, or tender (though some will pull at their ears or cry when earrings are inserted). As a result, the early signs of infection can easily go unnoticed.

The earrings themselves can also pose a problem; A young child could take them out to play with (or they could fall off in her hands), then stick herself with or swallow one or more of the parts. So most doc-

tors recommend that the procedure be put off until a child is at least four, and preferably closer to eight years old.

If you nevertheless opt to get your toddler's ears pierced, be sure the procedure is performed under sterile conditions, by someone who is qualified (check with your daughter's doctor for a recommendation). After the procedure, clean the lobes daily by dabbing them with a cotton ball saturated with rubbing alcohol or with hydrogen peroxide (which may be less drying) and rotate the earrings each morning (to keep them from sticking to the holes). If you notice any signs of infection (redness, swelling, pus or crusting, tenderness, or bleeding) call your child's doctor. And do not allow your child to wear dangling earrings: They can be pulled by other children (or by the child herself), possibly tearing the ear lobe. If your child starts trying to remove her earrings or play with them, stop inserting the earrings and let the holes close up. You can always have the ears pierced again when your child is a little older and more responsible.

a part, how well those ears will function depends to a great extent on the care they get in the early years of life.

**Routine Care.** To keep your toddler's ears in the best condition possible:

▲ Be alert to signs of hearing loss (see page 488) and report any such signs to your child's doctor. A parent's observations are extremely important, and can often detect an as yet undiagnosed hearing problem. But medical exams are essential, too. Research is being done to develop a hearing screening test for newborns, but such a test is not yet available. A formal hearing test is not usually performed until age four, unless a hearing problem is suspected earlier, but at each checkup your child's doctor

will note (and ask you) how your child responds to sound. If a hearing deficit is confirmed, be sure it is treated promptly.

▲ At bath time, clean the *outside* crevices of your toddler's ears with a damp, soft cloth or cotton swab, and check ears carefully for foreign objects (toddlers have been known to stick items into their ears; see page 666). Do not probe the inside of the ear with a finger, a cotton swab, or (as the old saying goes) anything smaller than your elbow. Such probing could puncture the eardrum and/or push wax further into the ear.

▲ If you notice a wax build-up (a waxy, yellowish material can be seen in the ear canal), check with the doctor, who will either remove it or recommend drops to

## SIGNS OF A HEARING PROBLEM

．．．．．．．．．．

**M**any toddlers may seem not to hear at least half of what their parents say, but in most cases, it's just a matter of selective listening or inattention. The child who truly doesn't hear well usually exhibits one or more of the following signs of hearing loss (although some of these may also be exhibited by a child with normal hearing):

▲ An apparent inability to hear what is said by others, all or part of the time.

▲ Difficulty hearing when the sound comes from the side or the rear and when not facing the speaker directly; many hearing impaired children instinctively learn some rudimentary lip reading and so understand more when they can see the speaker's lips.

▲ A *consistent* lack of response when spoken to quietly.

▲ A *consistent* inattentiveness to any verbal or other auditory cues.

▲ An apparent inability to follow any directions (more so than is age-appropriate).

▲ A limited vocabulary—both receptive (the words that are understood) and spoken—compared to peers (see the age-appropriate "What Your Toddler Should Be Doing"). The child may be mislabeled "slow" because of this developmental delay.

▲ A lack of response to music—the child doesn't clap, sing along, or move rhythmically to music, or enjoy or recognize frequently played tunes, even those designed especially for children.

▲ Lack of response to the nuances of language (can't seem to tell from the tone of your voice whether you are angry, sad, joking, and so on).

▲ Lack of response to environmental sounds (the ring of the telephone or doorbell, the buzzer on a timer, the song of a bird, the howling of the wind).

▲ Difficulty distinguishing between similar sounding words (door and store, Sue and shoe, fake and shake), particularly when the the words begin with *f*, *sh*, or *s*.

▲ A tendency to give inappropriate answers to questions ("Do you want to play with a puzzle?" "No, I not hungry.")

---

help you remove it at home. Don't, however, try the home removal without explicit instructions and never try to use a cotton swab to remove it.

▲ If you suspect an ear infection, check with the doctor immediately; prompt treatment can protect your child's hearing (see page 605).

▲ Do not allow smoking around your toddler. Exposure to tobacco smoke increases the risk of ear infection.

▲ If your toddler has had previous outer-ear infections (swimmer's ear), limit play time in the water to under an hour, and be sure to have your toddler shake his or her head on emerging from the pool to get rid of excess water. A child who swims often might benefit from the use of ear plugs designed for swimmers. Speak to your doctor for a recommendation.

**Sound defense.** There are numerous reasons to protect your toddler by putting up a sound defense against loud noises. Exposure to excessive noise has been associated with noise-induced hearing loss (NIHL); can hamper a child's ability to learn to communicate through language and to receive other auditory signals (such as the warning honk of a car horn); can quicken pulse and heartbeat, affect other body systems, and interfere with sleep;

▲ A tendency to favor one ear when turning toward a sound.

▲ An inability to hear very low sounds, such as the ticking of a watch.

▲ A tendency to turn the volume of the TV and tape player up too high or to stand very close to them, as if to hear them better (though a toddler with normal hearing may occasionally do this out of curiosity).

▲ Complaints about ringing or pain in ears.

Children who are at high risk for hearing problems should have a formal hearing screening early on, even if they do not display any of these signs. Children are considered to be at risk if:

▲ They have been diagnosed as having a medical problem, such as Franconi syndrome, which is associated with hearing deficit.

▲ There is a family history of inherited or unexplained childhood hearing loss (among siblings, parents, cousins, and so on).

▲ They were exposed in utero to a viral infection known to affect hearing (such as cytomegalovirus [CMV] or rubella), particularly during the first trimester.

▲ They weighed in under 1,500 grams (or 3 pounds, 4 ounces) at birth.

▲ They were born with ear or facial abnormalities (craniofacial anomalies).

▲ They had a low APGAR score (under 4) at birth, or experienced serious problems as newborns—such as asphyxia (oxygen deprivation), seizures, or intracranial bleeding, or if they received prolonged ventilation.

▲ They were given potentially ototoxic (ear damaging) medications (such as Gentamicin) or contracted an illness (such as bacterial meningitis) that can cause ear damage.

Even the smallest suspicion of a hearing problem warrants audiologic testing, especially in a young infant. A child doesn't have to be profoundly deaf to benefit from treatment; in fact, the child with only a mild hearing deficit may benefit most from therapy. Any hearing deficit that goes undetected and untreated can lead to poor language and learning skills, to a bright child being mistakenly labeled "slow" or even "retarded," and to low self-esteem. For a list of the most common forms of hearing loss and the different kinds of treatment available, see page 722.

and can be annoying (for a particularly sensitive child, it can be almost maddening). So it makes sense to keep your toddler's environment as free of loud and extraneous noise as possible, by following these ear-healthy recommendations:

▲ When buying new appliances or power tools, look for those that are quieter.

▲ Monitor the volume of television, radio, and stereo in your home; maximum volume should never be louder than normal speech. A "limiter," available on some such appliances, can be helpful; it allows you to set a maximum volume. Be vigilant, too, when your child is using earphones. If you can hear the sound when the earphones are in use, the volume is probably too high. Keep in mind, however, that if you've spent years listening to loud rock music (or have experienced long-term exposure to other kinds of loud noise), you probably have some hearing loss yourself and may not be a good judge of what is "too loud."

▲ Prohibit very noisy toys, such as cap pistols.

▲ In noisy situations, where you need to shout in order to be heard (when, for example, you're attending rock concerts, fireworks displays, riding the subway, mowing the lawn, blowing snow, or using other power tools), tuck soft foam ear plugs (available at pharmacies) in your toddler's ears or supply him or her with sound-proofing "ear muffs." If you use these yourself, it will probably be easier to persuade your toddler to follow your model. *Do not* rely on wadded-up cotton balls or tissue paper to do the job because these materials allow damaging sound waves to pass through, even if the sound seems muffled.

▲ Teach your child to cover his or her ears when unexpectedly encountering a loud noise (such as a fire engine's blaring siren).

▲ If you live in a high noise area (near an elevated train or an airport, for instance, see page 486), try to reduce noise levels inside your home. When your child plays outdoors, sound-proofing "ear muffs" may be useful (but be sure your child can hear speech, auto horns, and so on, with the ear muffs in place).

▲ Teach your child never to shout in anyone else's ears or to let someone shout in his or her ears. And practice the sound control you preach; try never to scream loudly—at least not in or near your toddler's ears.

# CARING FOR YOUR TODDLER'S TEETH

The toddler years are a busy, busy time in a child's mouth. While some children bite into their first birthday with only a single tooth, most sport a full set of twenty primary teeth by the time they turn three (see page 491). Though these "baby" teeth aren't "for keeps," they must take a child through the next five to ten years of eating; the last of them won't be replaced by permanent teeth until somewhere between ages twelve and fourteen. And since each

tooth is vulnerable to decay from the moment it breaks through the gum, it's important to make good dental hygiene a priority early on.

**Professional care.** There is general agreement that keeping a toddler's teeth healthy requires a three-way partnership of child, parent, and dentist. There isn't complete agreement, however, on when the dentist's involvement becomes necessary. The American Academy of Pediatrics (AAP) currently recommends regular oral checkups by the pediatrician during the toddler years, and a first visit to the dentist at age three. The American Academy of Pediatric Dentistry (AAPD), however, advises that visits to the dentist begin between the ages of six months and a year, asserting that it takes a dentist to catch early signs of decay. To further confuse matters, some pediatric dentists do not schedule appointments for a child who doesn't have a dental problem until age two and a half.

When you decide to schedule that first dental visit will depend on the condition of your toddler's teeth as well as on his or her doctor's advice, the recommendation of the dentist, and your own judgment. Any signs of abnormality (an open, unaligned, or otherwise "bad" bite, misaligned teeth; dark spots or uneven coloration on the teeth) require a prompt dental evaluation. Early attention to dental problems can prevent not only the premature loss of primary teeth from decay, but mouth irregularities (malocclusions) that may interfere with speech development.

When selecting a dentist, keep in mind that a pediatric dentist has had additional training in the treatment of children, is familiar with their special needs, and is better prepared than a general dentist to deal with their fears, questions, and restlessness in the dental chair.[6]

A professional cleaning every six months, once all the teeth are in and regular dental visits begin, will help protect gums as well as teeth from the ravages of plaque (which actually starts forming in a baby's mouth *before* the teeth arrive). Fluoride treatments (see page 493) will help strengthen tooth enamel. Later on, when the first of the permanent molars are in (around the age of six or seven), the dentist may apply a protective sealant (a thin, clear, or light-colored plastic coating) to chewing surfaces. This sealant fills in the pits and crevices in the chewing surfaces and prevents the trapping of debris and the colonization by decay-causing bacteria; its use is not, however, universally endorsed by dentists.

For dealing with a fear of the dentist, see page 308.

**Home care.** Good dental health that lasts a lifetime depends on acquiring the habit of daily dental care. So, if you haven't already done so, get your toddler into the habit of brushing regularly each morning and evening (and after lunch, too, when possible).

Select a toothbrush designed for young children (some brands specify on the box the age group the brush is appropriate for), with a small head and soft, rounded bristles. Some children's shops and catalogs offer a children's brush with a specially contoured handle to make positioning the brush easier; those that are gaily decorated make a child's compliance more likely. Rinse the toothbrush thoroughly after each use, and keep it in a holder, rather than lying around where it can pick up bacteria. Replace the brush after three months, or sooner if it's looking worn—and never allow the sharing of toothbrushes, even among family members. Also replace the brush after your child's been sick so that germs hidden in the bristles won't cause reinfection.

---

6. A safety note: To prevent the spread of infections of any kind at the dentist's office, all instruments must be cleaned ultrasonically and then heat-sterilized between patients. Don't hesitate to ask about sterilizing procedures when you make your first appointment.

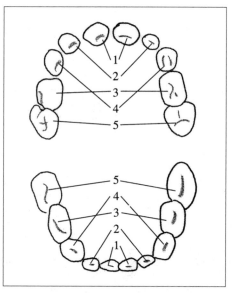

*The full complement of early childhood teeth can be expected by a toddler's third birthday. The teeth usually come in in a specific order, 1 through 20, though occasionally they stray from the standard pattern.*

Brush your toddler's teeth with a gentle back and forth motion across the chewing surfaces; use a circular motion along the sides and the outer gum lines, a back-and-forth motion on inner surfaces, if you can. Lightly brush the gums where teeth haven't yet erupted, or wipe them with a gauze pad, baby finger brush, or washcloth. Skip the toothpaste until your toddler is able to rinse and spit out the residue or use an infant/toddler tooth and gum cleanser that is nonabrasive, nonfoaming, and fluoride-free.

When your toddler begins to show an interest in brushing, encourage him or her. And don't worry about teaching a particular method of brushing; the dentist can offer instruction in the proper technique later on. Until your child's at least seven years old, you should continue to help with the brushing, even if he or she is able to do part of the job solo. If your toddler resists brushing (or your help), see page 274.

## FLUORIDES FOR FIGHTING DECAY

• • • • • • • • • •

Though fluorides have been around for millennia, their cavity-fighting properties weren't discovered until 1945. Since then, many clinical studies have confirmed that fluoride is effective in reducing the incidence of dental caries, or cavities. Because the evidence is so persuasive, both the American Academy of Pediatrics and the American Academy of Pediatric Dentistry recommend fluoride supplementation for infants and children in communities where water is not fluoridated or does not contain enough natural fluoride, or when a child does not get enough water or food containing water in the course of the day.* Fluoridated toothpaste (safe to use once you're sure your child won't swallow it) strengthens enamel but does nothing for teeth not yet erupted; on its own, it's not considered adequate protection. Over-the-counter fluoride rinses are not recommended for young children, since they may swallow harmful amounts.

The fluoride dosages prescribed for a toddler depend on the child's age, how much fluoride is in the local water, and how much water he or she drinks (assuming the child drinks water at all, or consumes drinks—such as reconstituted frozen juice—or food prepared with water). If you use well water or bottled water at home for drinking, or if your toddler never drinks water, let the doctor know, so that this can be taken into account

in deciding on appropriate doses for fluoride supplementation. Fluoride supplementation is important during tooth formation and should continue until all permanent teeth have erupted.

In general, when local water fluoridation levels are below 0.3 parts per million (ppm), it is recommended that children under two take 0.25 mg a day of fluoride, and children between two and three, 0.5 mg daily. When drinking water is fluoridated at levels between 0.3 and 0.7 ppm, those doses are halved. When water is fluoridated at 0.7 ppm or above, no supplementation is needed.

Topical fluoride treatment (in which the dentist applies fluoride directly to the teeth, where it is absorbed by the enamel) is also used to combat dental caries. Though not a substitute for internal fluoride supplements, fluoride treatment strengthens enamel, can attack plaque directly, and can even arrest tooth decay in progress.

If you rely on fluoridated water for your toddler's daily fluoride intake, dilute fruit juices with water to assure some daily water consumption. You can also use soups, sauces, and hot cereals as vehicles for getting water into your child, and thus getting the fluoride down. When cooking pastas, save some of the water for making the sauce (the cooking water contains vitamins as well as fluoride); when a recipe calls for milk, use dry skim milk reconstituted with water (if your toddler is under two, also add a spoonful or two of half-and-half).

---

*If your toddler is still breastfed, don't count on breast milk as a source of fluoride—it contains very little.

---

Rinsing is an essential part of the brushing process. Not only does it remove the toothpaste before it's swallowed, but it eliminates bits of loosened food that would otherwise just resettle elsewhere on the teeth. Children should be taught to rinse their mouths after brushing as soon as they are able to—usually around age two. Each family member should have his or her own cup for rinsing (use different colors to eliminate confusion and territorial disputes); be sure to wash the cups regularly.

When your toddler can rinse and spit, you can begin to put a pea-size amount of fluoridated toothpaste on the brush (do without it or continue using the toddler cleanser if your toddler doesn't like the taste); but watch out for toothpaste eaters (see page 275).

Flossing is as important to good dental health as brushing and rinsing. Just when it should begin, however, is controversial. The American Dental Association says it should begin as soon as all the primary teeth are in. Many dentists, however, recommend waiting until children can floss on their own. Check with your child's dentist for advice and for tips on how to floss, when the time comes. You'll have to be in charge of flossing until your child is at least seven or eight, and is capable of taking the job over. Which is easier said than done, both because it's difficult to maneuver large adult hands in the tiny toddler mouth and because most toddlers will not sit still long enough to get the entire job done.

Unless you have an unusually cooperative toddler, you will probably not be able to floss the entire mouth every night—at best, you may be able to get to the top teeth one night, the bottom the next. It's more important to focus on the molars than the front teeth, so always work from back to front. And remember, getting into the habit is as important as getting the job done.

**Teeth-safe diet.** Cavities form when bacteria found in healthy mouths (especially *Streptococcus mutans*) feed on sugars and starches in food residue in the mouth, producing an acid that wears holes in tooth enamel. It's long been known that foods high in sugar can start this process, but recent research has shown that foods high in other carbohydrates (for example, breads and cereals), which break down to sugar in the mouth, can also contribute to cavity formation. Sticky foods, such as cookies and cakes, containing both sugars and other carbohydrates may do the most damage. Eating cheese, on the other hand, may inhibit cavities and actually strengthen tooth enamel.

How long a food remains on the teeth is more signficant than how much is eaten. For example, a box of raisins nibbled throughout the morning will be more likely to lead to decay than the same box eaten at breakfast with milk and cereal. For much the same reason, children who nip on a breast or on bottles of milk or juice all day long are particularly vulnerable to cavities (see pages 27 and 32). Decay-promoting foods are less likely to do their dirty work if they are eaten with other foods, especially if they're chased with a serving of cheese. (Peanuts and sugarless chewing gum— particularly brands sweetened with xylitol—also can counteract cavity-causing foods, but they're not recommended for toddlers, who might choke on the peanuts or swallow the gum.)

Acid foods can also damage tooth enamel, so have your toddler rinse after eating an orange or pasta with tomato sauce, or chewing a supplement containing vitamin C (ascorbic acid). Drinking acid beverages (citrus juices, tomato or vegetable juices, even sodas), through a straw may help keep more of the liquid off the teeth.

# MOST COMMON TEETH AND MOUTH PROBLEMS

**Dental caries**. *What is it?* Tooth decay. *Who is susceptible?* Most children. Some individuals are particularly susceptible, while others seem to inherit teeth that are resistant to caries. Children whose mothers took fluoride prenatally and who had fluoride supplementation while their teeth were forming tend to be more resistant, too. *Signs and symptoms:* Decay, characterized by black or brown spots, and eventually pain, in teeth. *Causes:* The acid produced by the action of naturally occurring bacteria in the mouth (especially *Streptococcus mutans*) on sugars and starches eats into the tooth enamel, beginning the decay process. *Transmission:* Not contagious. *Treatment:* Prevention is the best treatment, as described above. Once caries are formed, they should be cleaned out and filled by the dentist as soon as possible. Not repairing cavities leaves a child at risk of serious infection and tooth loss. When a tooth is lost to decay, it is usually necessary to maintain the space with a dental appliance to make sure there will be adequate space for the permanent tooth when it erupts.

**Malocclusion**. *What is it?* Irregular positioning of the teeth and jaws, which can affect the bite, the ability to clean the teeth properly, the health of the gums, jaw growth, speech development, and appearance. *Who is susceptible?* Any child, but most often children with an inherited predisposition and those with persistent sucking habits or early tooth loss. *Signs and symptoms:* Teeth are crooked, come up in the wrong places, turn in the wrong direction; often the top and bottom teeth don't meet as they should. *Causes:* Heredity, which determines the shape and size of the mouth, jaws, and teeth (inheriting a small mouth from one side of the family and large teeth from the other, for example, can lead to malocclusion) and environment (having a persistent thumb- or pacifier-sucking habit or losing baby teeth prematurely). *Treatment:* Examination plus plaster models of the teeth, photographs, and/or X-rays may be used to evaluate the problem. A serious malocclusion is usually treated promptly—most often with the insertion of some kind of orthodontic appliance—to keep it from getting worse and affecting new teeth as they erupt, as well as to prevent it from impeding speech development. A minor malocclusion in a toddler can usually go untreated until the permanent teeth are in; in fact, it may actually correct itself.

**Herpes labialis (cold sores, fever blisters)**. *What is it?* An infection that usually strikes the mouth, lips, and area around the lips, but can also affect a facial nerve and the eyes. *Who is susceptible?* Anyone, but most primary infections occur in childhood. *Signs and symptoms:* With the primary, or first-time, infection, there are usually sores on the gums and inside the mouth, often accompanied by fever and irritability, and sometimes, sore throat, swollen glands, bad breath, drooling, and loss of appetite, though some young children display no obvious symptoms. Since the symptoms may mimic those of teething (the sores may even look like teeth about to poke through the gum), fever (sometimes as high as 106°F, or 41.1°C) may be the only tip-off parents have that an infection is brewing. Once the initial infection clears up, the virus generally lies dormant, ready to reappear when the body is under stress. In secondary, or recurrent, eruptions, a welt, which tingles and itches, forms on or near the lip (herpes labialis). The lesion then forms a painful, oozing blister. Finally, it crusts and forms a sometimes itchy scab. In untreated cases, the scab usually falls off within three weeks. The flare-ups can also cause headaches and affect the eyes, causing conjunctivitis or even more serious eye infections. Occasionally, the infection spreads to one or more fingers in the form of a pus-filled inflammation, called an herpetic whitlow. Rare complications include HSV encephalitis, which can be very severe, and HSV meningitis, which is usually mild and self-limited. *Cause:* The herpes simplex virus (HSV). Subsequent flare-ups can be triggered by physical stress (colds, flu, fever, teething), fatigue, emotional stress, or by a period of prolonged exposure of the lips (unprotected by sunscreen) to direct sunlight. *Transmission:* Person to person, year-round, via direct contact with oral or eye secretions or the lesions themselves. It's not clear how long an individual with an active infection is contagious, and the virus can be shed even when no sores are visible, so precautions to avoid transmission should be continued until the lesions have healed. The incubation period is believed to be two to twelve days. *Treatment:* With primary infection, soft, nonacidic foods. For routine flare-ups, topical medications are available without prescription for easing the discomfort of herpes lesions; at the height of an infection, acetaminophen can be used to reduce pain. Applying ice to the sore can also reduce pain, though most children won't tolerate this treatment for long. Some chronic HSV sufferers find that taking acidophilus-lactobacillus tablets or capsules at the first twinge stops a flare-up in its tracks. For toddlers, the chewable tablets can be crushed and served up in yogurt or milk (they taste milky and sweet); check with your child's doctor for dosage. Call the doctor if your child seems ill. When a child has a severe HSV infection or has a compromised immune system (due to another illness or a medication), an antiviral medication (such as acyclovir or vidarabine) is usually prescribed. Because the drugs have not been tested for safety in healthy children, they are not routinely prescribed for them. If there is eye involvement, antiviral eye drops will be given. *Prevention:* Avoiding stress when possible; getting adequate rest; using lip balm with sunscreen in bright sun.

# CARING FOR YOUR LITTLE GIRL'S GENITALS

Keeping a little girl's vaginal area clean and irritant-free is the best way to fend off infection. You can do this in the following ways:

▲ Always wipe your daughter front to back when changing her diaper or after

she uses the toilet. Teach her to do the same as you prepare her to take over the task herself. If she's still in diapers, it may be necessary to spread the labia, or lips, of the vagina to clean up after a particularly messy bowel movement.

▲ Change diapers as soon as they become wet or soiled.

▲ Once she's out of diapers, dress your toddler only in all-cotton underpants to minimize perspiration and maximize ventilation in the area.

▲ Avoid bubble baths, bath oils, perfumes, harsh soaps, and diaper wipes that contain alcohol and/or perfumes, any of which may trigger an allergic reaciton or irritate or "burn" the vagina, predisposing your daughter to vaginal or urinary tract infection. After the bath, rinse your child's body in fresh water. Rinse the vaginal area with a hand-held shower spray, a small watering can, or a dripping washcloth.

▲ Shampoo your daughter at bath's end so that she won't be sitting in potentially irritating shampoo suds. Have her stand as the water drains, and rinse her hair with the shower, a hand-held shower head, or a watering can or plastic cup. Alternatively, you can shampoo her in the sink.

# MOST COMMON GENITAL PROBLEMS IN LITTLE GIRLS

**Vulvovaginitis/vaginitis.** *What is it?* An inflammation of the vagina and/or the vulva (the external female genitalia). *Who is susceptible?* Any female, of any age. *Signs and symptoms:* Vaginal itching, a smelly vaginal discharge, and occasionally, vaginal spotting or bleeding (when the inflammation irritates the delicate vaginal lining). *Causes:* Irritation (from bath water, wet diapers, an inserted object, harsh laundry detergents or soap), which makes the lining of the vagina susceptible to a variety of infectious organisms, such as candida. *Treatment:* Medical consultation is necessary; be certain to call the same day if there is any bleeding. The doctor will probably do an examination and take a culture from the area. Depending on the findings, a topical and/or oral medication may be prescribed. If infection has been caused by a foreign body inserted into the vagina, it will be removed. The doctor should warn the child against putting anything into her vagina, or letting anyone else put something in.

**Vaginal (labial) adhesions.** *What is it?* A condition in which irritated labia become stuck together. *Who is susceptible?* Babies and young girls, because they do not produce estrogen. *Signs and symptoms:* The labia minor (the inner lips of the external female genitalia) adhere to one another; in severe cases, there may be difficulty urinating. *Causes:* Irritation from urine or perspiration makes the labia raw; the raw surfaces then stick together. *Treatment:* If the labia can be separated, the child is able to urinate, and there is no pain involved, adhesions aren't a cause for concern; nevertheless, the doctor will probably prescribe an estrogen cream to promote healing of the labia. In stubborn cases, the cream may have to be applied over a period of time and the labia separated only gradually. Occasionally, the labia must be separated by the doctor with a special instrument. Treatment is important since an inability to urinate or a pooling of urine under the labia could lead to an increase in urinary tract infections (see page 612). Some girls continue to develop adhesions until puberty, when estrogen production starts up. *Prevention:* Keep the vaginal area dry; don't allow a toddler in diapers to stay wet for long; avoid synthetic underwear and pants to help prevent recurrence.

# CARING FOR YOUR LITTLE BOY'S GENITALS

**The circumcised penis**. Routine washing with soap and water is the only care a circumcised penis requires.

**The uncircumcised penis.** No special care is required for the uncircumcised penis, either. It's not only unnecessary but potentially harmful to try to forcibly retract the foreskin or to try to clean under it with cotton swabs, water, or antiseptics. Don't worry about what looks like a cheesy material under the foreskin; this is the normal residue of cells shed as the foreskin and glans begin to separate. These cells gradually work their way out via the tip of the foreskin on their own, and continue to be shed throughout life.

# MOST COMMON GENITAL PROBLEMS IN LITTLE BOYS

**Undescended testicles** (cryptorchidism). *What is it?* A condition in which one testicle (or sometimes both) has not descended down into the scrotum. *Who is susceptible?* Most often, boys who were born prematurely, but the condition can also occur in full-term infants. *Signs and symptoms:* One testicle (or both, in 10% to 30% of cases) cannot be felt in the boy's scrotum; if it has not descended by the child's first birthday, it generally does not do so on its own. The right testicle is more often affected. Most frequently the undescended organ is in the inguinal canal that leads to the scrotum (*see illustration*); but it may also lie elsewhere, just above the scrotum, for example, or higher up, in the abdomen. In about 10% of cases, the testicle is com-

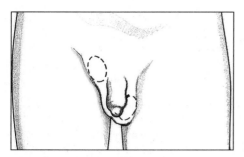

*Most often, an undescended testicle remains in the inguinal canal, though other locations are also possible.*

pletely absent. *Causes:* Hormonal reasons or a physical blockage, such as an inguinal hernia, explain some cases of undescended testicles, but the cause of other cases is unknown. *Treatment:* On examination, the doctor will try to manipulate an undescended testicle down into the scrotum. If this is not possible, and if the parent reports never having seen the testicle in the scrotum, treatment is generally initiated sometime after the first birthday (early treatment appears to be more effective and less traumatic). Treatment is usually a trial of human chorionic gonadotropin (hCG), which is injected, normally two or three times a week for three weeks, followed by testing to check hormone levels. If the hCG does not induce the descent of the testicle (or testicles), surgery (called orchiopexy) to move the testicle into the scrotum is generally recommended. Orchiopexy is performed sooner rather

than later because testicles tend to deteriorate when not descended, increasing the potential for future infertility problems. In some cases, surgery is performed without a trial of hCG. It is believed that hormonal or surgical treatment early in childhood can reduce the likelihood of adult infertility.

**Note:** If a child with an undescended testicle complains of groin pain, call his doctor immediately. It's possible that the testicle has become twisted, cutting off its blood supply. If left untreated, the organ may be damaged permanently.

**Meatal stenosis.** *What is it?* A condition in which the urinary flow is blocked or impeded. *Who is susceptible?* Any young boy, but the condition is more common in boys who are circumcised. *Signs and symptoms:* A narrow urinary stream, difficulty urinating, slow or dribbling urination, and occasionally, repeated urinary tract infections (see page 612). *Causes:* Irritation of the tip of the penis causes the development of scar tissue around the meatus (the opening to the male urethra). The scar tissue reduces the size of the opening. *Treatment:* If the doctor determines that treatment is needed, minor surgery can correct the problem. A general anesthetic may be required for the brief procedure, but the discomfort that follows will disappear fairly quickly. *Prevention:* Avoiding rough underclothes, harsh laundry detergents, prolonged wetness from un-

---

## THE IN-AGAIN, OUT-AGAIN TESTICLE

••••••••••

Sometimes what appears to be an undescended testicle is actually a *retractile* one, which comes down into the scrotum occasionally, only to pull back again when exposed to cold temperatures or other stimulation. The best time to observe whether or not the testicle does come down occasionally is to examine the scrotum in a warm bath; the warmth will often coax a retractile testicle into its proper place. If it does come down, there is probably no reason to worry. Retractile testicles usually settle permanently into the scrotum after puberty, without any treatment.

changed diapers or clothing, or anything else that could, over a period of time, irritate the meatus and lead to scarring.

# DRESSING YOUR TODDLER

**B**athing suits in January. Snowsuits in July. Sweaters put on backwards. Shoes put on the wrong feet. Once a toddler starts getting into the dressing act, the fashion faux pas are as inevitable as the wails of "I wanna pick it myself." Still, self-dressing is an important part of your toddler's growing up, and involving your toddler in the process is an important part of your letting go. And it is possible to invite that involvement while keeping the fashion police at bay (at least, most of the time). See page 279 for dealing with dressing dilemmas.

# TRICKS OF THE DRESSING TRADE

**A**fter dressing ourselves for two or three decades, we grown-ups tend to take the mechanics of putting on clothes for granted. For toddlers, however, even the simplest aspects of self-dressing can present a challenge. Help yours meet that challenge with some practical dressing tricks:

**Set the front and back apart.** Your toddler will have less trouble differentiating the front of garments from the back if outfits have designs only on the front. When they don't, teach your toddler to look for the label, which almost always is in the back of a garment. Garments that don't have labels in the back can be marked with a laundry pen on the inside (if you mark the back with a "B," your toddler will get a headstart on learning

the alphabet). Boys have an easier time with underwear, since briefs and shorts come with a distinctive front; for girls, panties with a design or bow in the front will make their task simpler.

**Button from the bottom up.** Lining up buttons or snaps starting at the bottom is the easiest way to make sure they end up matching all the way to the top. Though buttoning and snapping are beyond the fine-motor capabilities of most toddlers, you can begin teaching this lesson by showing your toddler how you line up the bottom button with the bottom button- hole. Let your toddler practice buttoning, snapping, and zipping skills on his or her own clothing (when time permits) and also provide a doll or book that has buttons, snaps, laces, and zippers for practicing on.

**Teach skillful and careful zippering.** Especially for boys, who risk catching a very sensitive body part, zippers pose a painful threat to tender skin. Even if your toddler isn't doing the zippering solo yet (and especially if he or she is), demonstrate how to hold the zipper away from the skin during the procedure.

**If the shoe's always on the other foot . . .** Matching the right shoe with the right foot (and the left with the left) is one of the trickiest parts of dressing—and most children continue having trouble with this task well past the toddler years. Though you'll need to be patient, you can also help make the task somewhat easier for an older toddler to master by demonstrating that buckles and Velcro straps usually go toward the outside of the shoe. Or you can draw a tiny pattern on the inside of each shoe and tell your child that the picture always goes on the inside or the two pictures go together. It may also help to always leave your child's shoes laid out in ready-to-put-on position.

## Cold-Weather Dressing

When, baby, it's cold outside, take the following dressing precautions, using the wind-chill factor rather than the temperature as your guide, before setting out with your toddler:

**Take it from the top.** When it's below freezing out, a hat is tops at keeping your toddler warm; that's because a great deal of body heat can be lost through a bare head. Find a hat that's comfortable for your toddler to wear, and insist on it being worn when temperatures plummet—if you wear one yourself, you'll be less likely to meet up with resistance. (See page 283 for more on head coverings.) Since heat also escapes through the neck, keep your toddler's neck well covered. Using a balaclava or another type of head gear that covers the neck and possibly part of the face will allow you to dispense with the muffler, and considering how most toddlers resist being bundled, any item that can be dispensed with makes your task easier.

**Layer, layer upon layer.** How do you dress a toddler so that he or she stays warm sitting in the stroller on the way to the playground, but doesn't get overheated once the running around begins? In layers—which insulate when a child's cold (by trapping air between the layers) and can be removed as needed when the child (or the weather) warms up. In really cold weather or when your toddler will be playing in the snow, start with long thermal underwear, move on to a turtleneck (which will keep the neck cozy even when the coat gets unzipped), a sweater and warm pants, sweats, or Polartec, fleece separates, and top it all with a coat or snowsuit. Wool is warming, but may irritate sensitive skin; some especially sensitive toddlers will balk at wearing it even over layers of underclothing.

**Buy mittens (or gloves) in bulk.** Hand coverings (waterproof for snow play) are essential in cold weather because fingers are especially prone to frostbite. Buy duplicate or triplicate pairs when possible, so that when one mitten disappears, you don't have to throw away the mate. Carry a spare pair along on outings so that you can replace lost or wet mittens. For more on mittens, see page 283.

**Keep tootsies toasty.** Not only are cold toes uncomfortable, they can easily become frostbitten, especially when your toddler's walking or playing in the snow. Insulated boots are best for cold weather; make sure they're waterproof, seamless, and snug around the top (so snow is less likely to seep in). Thermal socks (not cotton, which keeps wet feet wet) under the boots will keep your toddler's feet extra comfortable; avoid very heavy socks that completely fill the boots— it's the air space *between* the socks and the boots that increases protection from the cold.

**Check for overheating.** An overheated toddler can be just as uncomfortable as a chilled one. Check your toddler's neck periodically for perspiration; if you detect moisture, consider loosening or removing a layer.

## Warm-Weather Dressing

When it's hot outside, light-colored, light-weight, loose-fitting clothing is the most comfortable. But when playing in the sun, strong, tightly-woven, darker fabrics make for better UV blockers (with denim the best). If you're dressing your toddler lightly, consider applying a layer of sunscreen under the garments. A wide-brimmed hat should be standard issue on hot sunny days.

# CHAPTER EIGHTEEN

# Feeding Your Toddler

## THE BEST-ODDS TODDLER DIET

**B**etween their resistance to change, their suspicion of anything green and leafy, and their intolerance for strange textures, it's hard enough to get three meals into a toddler never mind meet a dozen dietary requirements. And yet, while helping a child learn to eat well may never be more difficult than during toddlerhood, it also may never be as important. For one thing, eating habits (good or bad) formed during these early years are likely to last a lifetime. (No, that doesn't mean that your toddler will still be subsisting on macaroni and cheese as an adult—but it does mean that a preference for sugary sweets or salty, fatty foods adopted in toddlerhood can easily turn into a lifelong preference.) For another, toddlers, busy bundles of endless activity that they are, need a steady infusion of nutrients to fuel their on-the-go lifestyle. Adequate nourishment is also essential for optimal growth and physical and intellectual develop-

ment. Good diet doesn't guarantee good health and long life, but the Best-Odds Toddler Diet will give your child the best odds of starting off in that direction.

## THE BEST-ODDS NINE BASIC PRINCIPLES

**T**he Best-Odds basic principles of healthy eating serve eaters of all ages well; they have been adjusted here only slightly to take into account a toddler's special needs.

**Every bite counts.** With tummies tiny, appetites tender, and tastes limited and fickle, there are just so many bites parents can expect their toddlers to take. And with just so many bites in a day, wasted nutritional opportunities (when the peanut butter and jelly is on white; when the beverage is a "10% juice drink"; when dessert is a cupcake full of empty fat and sugar calories) may not easily be made up. So it's especially important that each bite toddlers take be as nourishing as possible—that the bread be whole grain; the beverage be 100% real juice; and the dessert be wholesome (fresh fruit or a whole-grain fruit-juice-sweetened muffin, for instance).

**All calories are not created equal.** The 110 calories in an ounce of sugar-sweetened, refined breakfast cereal are not nutritionally equivalent to the 110 calories in an ounce of juice-sweetened, whole-grain breakfast cereal. Always keep the quality of the calories in mind when preparing your toddler's meals and snacks.

**Meal-skipping is risky, but it's a toddler prerogative.** Meal-skipping is not recommended at any age, and toddlers who regularly skip meals may not only be deprived of essential energy for get-up-and-go but may be particularly prone to cranky, irrational behavior and temper tantrums. To make sure that your toddler has a steady flow of fuel, serve three meals, as well as snacks in between, each day. But remember that serving a meal to a toddler doesn't necessarily mean it will be consumed. Toddlers don't always eat *what* is put in front of them *when* it's put in front of them. Your toddler may reject an occasional meal, barely eat at others—and that's his or her prerogative. Just be sure to make up for the missed meal with a nutritious snack later on (but not too close to the next meal, or that one may be rejected, too). And don't worry about occasional meal-skipping or pressure your toddler to eat. When healthy children are allowed to eat as much or as little as they like at each meal, the food intake tends to balance out over a week's time.

**Efficiency is effective.** Many toddlers have relatively small stomach capacities, so it makes sense to consider efficiency when selecting your toddler's foods. When possible, offer foods that satisfy more than one nutritional requirement (cheese for calcium *and* protein, cantaloupe for vitamins A *and* C, whole grains for complex carbohydrates *and* iron). Efficiency can also work to curb a too-fast weight gain in an overweight toddler with a voracious appetite (for example, serving filling foods that offer more nutrition for fewer calories, such as fresh fruits and vegetables and whole grain breads and pasta without fattening sauces). Efficiency is effective, too, when feeding a toddler with a pint-sized appetite who is underweight or gaining weight too slowly (foods that pack a lot of nutrition and a lot of calories into small packages, such as peanut butter, meat, avocado, cheese, and beans, are good choices).

**Carbohydrates are a complex issue.** Bread, rolls and bagels, spaghetti and macaroni, cereal—even the most finicky toddler usually enjoys at least one member of the carbohydrate family, and some toddlers like nothing else. But not all carbohydrates are equally nutritious—and some, such as sugars, honey, refined grains, and foods made with them, provide little or nothing but calories. It's true that the white flour sold for home use or used in commercial breads and in some other baked goods is enriched by the addition of a quartet of nutrients (thiamine, riboflavin, niacin, and iron), but it's also true that the flour has lost twenty or more other nutrients in the refining process, which removes the germ and the bran. Such complex carbohydrates as whole-grain flours, breads, and cereals; brown rice, millet, quinoa, and other whole grains; legumes (dried peas and beans); and whole-grain or high-protein pasta, on the other hand, usually provide a wide range of important nutri-

## WHITE WHOLE WHEAT?

· · · · · · · · · ·

To many of us, "white" in flour, breads, cakes, cookies, and other baked goods, means refined and less nutritious. That may not be true much longer. Recently, "white wheat," a strain of wheat long popular in the Far East for making noodles, has begun to appear in the U.S. Whiter and milder than the "red" wheat we are accustomed to, white whole wheat has all the nutrition of other whole wheat. It's available mostly by mail order at present; watch for its appearance on your supermarket shelves. For mail order information and regional availability, call King Arthur Flour, (800) 777-4434.

ents—including protein, vitamins, minerals, and the very important fiber. Always opt for such carbohydrates when shopping, cooking, and ordering in restaurants; use refined carbohydrates only rarely or when there's no other choice. For times when every carbohydrate in sight is refined, carry along a small container of wheat germ to enrich breads, pastas, and pizzas made with white flour. Children who get used to a sprinkling of wheat germ early on, learn to take it for granted.

**Sweet nothings are nothing but trouble.** Parents and teachers have asserted for years that children "under the influence" of sugar exhibit hyperactive behavior. Some studies on the effect of sugar on the behavior of some children have corroborated these claims, and many others have challenged them; much more study still needs to be done before the relationship between sugar and behavior, if any, is fully understood. In the meantime, there are still plenty of reasons to restrict the amount of sugar your toddler consumes. For one, sugar is totally without nutritional value—it provides no vitamins, no minerals, nothing but calories. And the calories that sugar contributes to a toddler's diet can better come from a more worthy source. For another, sugar often keeps bad company; it is frequently found in combination with other nutritional undesirables—unhealthy ingredients, such as fats and refined grains—in largely nutritionally "empty" foods. For yet another, sugar and sugary foods contribute significantly to tooth decay and may contribute to obesity (many of the foods that contain sugar are fattening without being either filling or nutritious). Sugar may also be used to improve the taste of third-rate ingredients (in a tomato sauce, for example, when the tomatoes lack flavor of their own); and ingredients lacking taste are often also lacking in nutrition. And because it increases the body's need for chromium, which is involved in the way the body handles sugar, sugar may also be indirectly implicated in the development of diabetes. But possibly the best reason to keep sugar out of the mouth of your babe—as much as possible—is to help him or her avert a lifelong struggle with a demanding sweet tooth and the problems that come with it. Research shows that children who eat a lot of sugary foods early on are more likely to grow into sugar-craving adults.

In order to minimize the sugar in your toddler's diet, you need to know where to look for it. Sugar goes by many names, including brown sugar, raw sugar, turbinado sugar, fructose, glucose, honey, maple syrup, corn syrup, corn syrup solids, high-fructose corn syrup, corn sweeteners, dextrose and sucrose. Avoid these when shopping for ready-made foods (particularly if they rank high on an ingredients list or if two or more of them are anywhere on a list) and when cooking for your toddler at home. Save exceptions for when there's no other choice—at birthday parties, for instance.

Restricting sugar doesn't have to mean restricting sweets entirely, however. Sweets made with fruit-juice concentrates and fruit sweeteners can be just as satisfying to a toddler as treats made with sugar. Make your own fruit-sweetened treats or look for ready-made ones in your supermarket or health food store. A not insignificant bonus: fruit-sweetened cakes, cookies, and muffins are much more likely to incorporate nutritious ingredients (such as whole-grain flours) than other commercially prepared sweets.

**The best foods remember where they came from.** The days when we ate what we (or our neighbors) grew are gone for most of us. Busy parents can barely manage to remember to buy bread, never mind find the time to bake it. Yet even in these modern times, the closer we stick to the natural food chain, the better; foods that remember their "roots" are much more likely to have retained the nutrients they had when they were harvested. That's not to say that we must grow our own grain and mill our own flour, but that we should buy bread, rolls, and cereals that are made with whole grains rather than their refined counterparts, which have been robbed of so many of their original nutrients. Nor must we grow our own produce, but we

## THE FROSTING ON THE FLAKES

**· · · · · · · · · ·**

When it comes to commercial children's television, parents often have as much to fear from the commercials as from the programming itself. For it is through these commercials that many impressionable young minds get their first "taste" of sugar-coated cereal—a taste that usually sends them down the cereal aisle of the supermarket clamoring for the brands they saw advertised on TV.

But even those parents who try to limit their toddler's viewing to commercial-free television or to shows with responsible sponsors may find that trip down the cereal aisle a harrowing one. After all, the nutritious, low-sugar cereals rarely catch a toddler's attention—their low-key packaging inevitably pales beside the razzle dazzle of sugar-coated-cereal boxes, designed to draw young eyes like so many flies to honey.

Most of these "kids" brands have anywhere from 3 to 7 teaspoons of sugar per serving, with many also containing a laboratory-list of questionable artificial colors and flavors. So, for the sake of your tod-

dler's health, steel yourself against the pleas for sugar-crunchies-cocoa-chunkies and honey-coated-crispies and lay down the breakfast table law: No sugary cereals allowed. Scan nutrition labels carefully (preferably on a market trip sans toddler, since label-reading takes time and concentration), and select brands that are made from whole grains and contain little or no added sugar. The Carbohydrate Information list on the side panel of the box should specify no more than 1 or 2 grams of sucrose and other sugars per serving. The exception: Cereals containing unsweetened dried fruit are okay to use, even though they contain considerably more grams of sugar; such fruits raise the sugar content of cereals dramatically but naturally. (But be sure that these cereals don't also list other sugars, like sugar, corn syrup, fructose, and so on, as ingredients.) And don't be taken in by health-food brands that banner their boxes with "naturally sweetened" but list honey (which is no more healthful than sugar) among their major ingredients.

should select fruits and vegetables that are fresh (or fresh-frozen) rather than highly processed, canned, or overcooked. And we needn't plant fruit trees in our backyards, but we should limit fruit that's been cooked (losing vitamins and fiber) or even juiced (losing much or all of its fiber).

Remember, it isn't just what's *lost* in the processing of foods (vitamins, minerals, and fiber) that poses a threat to growing children—it's what's *gained* in the processing (salt, sugar, chemical additives; see page 534), too.

So, when shopping for or feeding your toddler, choose foods that can remember where they came from—opt for unrefined over refined, and fresh over processed. And do as little processing in your home kitchen as possible: avoid overcooking, long periods of storage, and exposing foods unnecessarily to air, water, or heat, which all rob food of its nutrients.

**Healthful eating should be a family affair.** A double dining table standard (doughnuts for you, cereal and milk for your toddler) isn't fair and rarely works. The Best-Odds Toddler Diet stands the best odds of succeeding when the whole family lives by its principles. If everyone eats whole-wheat bread and unsweetened cereal, everyone opts for nutritious snacks, limits sugar intake, avoids processed foods, then eating right will become a way of family life to your toddler instead of seeming like a "special diet" foisted on him or her alone. And, of course, your toddler's not the only one who stands to benefit when good eating becomes a family affair.

**Bad habits can sabotage a good diet.** Subversive elements are everywhere— they beckon from supermarket shelves with their seductive packaging, they call out from the television screen with enticing commercials. And as your toddler begins getting out a little more—attend-

ing play dates at homes where junk food is the snack of choice, sitting next to kids at preschool whose lunch boxes flaunt white-bread sandwiches, chocolate cookies, and sugar-sweetened fruit punch, and in general seeing how the other half eats—the lure of these subversive elements will be tougher and tougher to ignore. But staying true to the Best-Odds Diet at home will make it easier for your toddler to stay true to it (at least most of the time) outside the home.

For now, junk food represents the biggest threat to your toddler's diet. Down the line, there will be others. Avoid sabotaging your own diet with tobacco, drugs, and excesses of alcohol and caffeine, and your toddler will grow up not only with healthy eating habits, but healthy lifestyle habits as well—thanks to your example.

## THE BEST-ODDS DAILY DOZEN—FOR TODDLERS

Feeding a toddler can be tricky enough without turning food preparation into a laboratory procedure. That's why The Best-Odds Daily Dozen for Toddlers lists dietary requirements not in milligrams, micrograms, and international units of necessary nutrients, but in servings of everyday foods. Small servings, for small appetites. If even these small servings are too much for your toddler to handle, or if your toddler's a grazer who prefers a bite of this and a nibble of that to a full serving of anything, mix and match partial servings to reach the quotas. And remember, too, that many foods can do double nutritional duty (that scant half cup of broccoli meets not only a green leafy vegetable requirement but nearly two vitamin C food requirements, and about a third of a serving of calcium).

## VARIETY IS MORE THAN THE SPICE OF LIFE

**··········**

One- and two-year-olds aren't generally known for their daring at the dinner table (unless you count standing up in the high chair). For many toddlers, dietary variety might mean switching off between peanut butter sandwiches cut into triangles and peanut butter sandwiches cut into squares.

Still, a truly varied diet not only offers the best odds of good nutrition, but minimizes potential exposure to food hazards (both natural and of human fabrication). It also helps keep mealtime monotony from setting in. And introducing variety early on *may* help to expand a toddler's dietary repertoire—or at least increase the possibility that, at some later date, the repertoire will expand.

You can try switching between hot and cold cereals, wheat flakes and oat circles. Top cereals with bananas one day, strawberries the next. Spread sandwich fillings on pita, bagels, or sliced bread; serve Cheddar cheese cubes, string cheese sticks, or Swiss cheese slices; hamburgers, chicken nuggets, or fish sticks. Vary the juice you send for preschool snack: Orange (for vitamin C), apricot (for beta-carotene), mango and papaya (for both), apple and pear (for additional variety).

Measuring servings precisely isn't necessary (the vitamin and mineral police won't serve you with a summons if that serving of tomato juice is 2 ounces scant of ½ cup), but it may help to weigh and measure foods until you've learned to accurately eyeball an ounce of cheese, 1½ tablespoons of peanut butter, ¼ cup of mango cubes. Using measuring spoons and cups for dishing out foods for your toddler will also help you gauge how much you're serving without a lot of extra effort.

The following "Daily-Dozen" requirements should be your dietary goal for your toddler, but don't force, bribe, cajole, or otherwise pressure your child to meet it. As long as you present the Daily Dozen daily and rarely offer empty calorie foods that are not recommended, your toddler is likely to come pretty close to getting the necessary nutrition over the span of several days.

**Calories—an average of 900 to 1,700.**[1]
No need to pull out your abacus or calculator. To determine whether your toddler's getting too many, too few, or just the right number of calories, simply keep track of his or her weight at checkup times. If it's staying on approximately the same curve (see page 865 or 867)—allowing for a jump or dip as a thin toddler fills out or a chubby one slims down, caloric intake is on target. Just how much food your toddler will need to keep gaining at the right rate depends on his or her present size, metabolism, and level of activity. But it's important to keep in mind that too few calories can seriously compromise a toddler's physical and intellectual growth and development (see page 513). And too many calories over the next several years could set a child up for a lifetime of weight problems (see page 510).

**Protein—four toddler servings** (totaling about 25 grams). One toddler serving equals any of the following: ¾ cup milk; ¼ cup nonfat dry milk; ½ cup yogurt; 3 tablespoons cottage cheese; ¾ ounce

---

1. The larger number of calories would probably be appropriate for a very tall, very active three-year-old who weighs about 37 pounds; the smaller number for a small and fairly sedentary one-year-old child who weighs in at 19 pounds.

hard cheese; 1 whole egg or 2 egg whites; ¾ to 1 ounce fish, poultry, or meat; 2 ounces tofu; 1½ tablespoons peanut butter; 1 ounce high-protein pasta or 2 ounces whole-wheat pasta; 1 toddler vegetarian or dairy protein combination (see pages 525 and 526).

**Calcium foods—four toddler servings.**
One toddler serving equals any of the following: ⅔ cup milk;[2] ⅓ cup milk enriched with ⅛ cup nonfat dry milk; ½ cup calcium-added milk; ½ cup yogurt; about ¾ to 1 ounce low-fat hard cheese; 1⅓ ounces full-fat cheese; 4 ounces calcium-fortified orange juice.

Half of a calcium serving equals: 3 ounces tofu (coagulated with calcium; check the label); ⅔ scant cup cooked broccoli; ½ cup cooked kale or turnip greens; 1⅓ ounces canned salmon (mashed with the bones); 1 ounce sardines (mashed with bones).

**Vitamin C foods—two or more toddler servings.**[3] One toddler serving equals any of the following: ½ small orange or ¼ medium grapefruit; ¼ cup fresh strawberries; ⅛ small cantaloupe or ¹⁄₁₂ small honeydew; ¼ cup fresh or frozen reconstituted orange juice; ¼ large guava or ¼ cup papaya; ⅓ large mango or ½ large plantain; ¼ cup broccoli or Brussels sprouts; ½ cup cooked kale or other leafy greens; ½ cup medium green or ⅙ medium red bell pepper; 1 small tomato, skinned; ¾ cup tomato juice or ½ cup sauce; ½ cup vegetable juice.

**Green leafy and yellow vegetables and yellow fruits—two or more toddler servings.**[4] One toddler serving equals any of the following: 1 medium fresh apricot or 2 small dried halves; a sliver of cantaloupe, or about ½ cup cubed; ⅛ large mango; 1 medium nectarine, peeled; ½ large yellow (not white) peach, peeled; ½ medium plantain; 6 asparagus spears; scant ½ cup cooked broccoli; ¾ cup peas; 2 to 3 tablespoons chopped

cooked greens; ¼ small carrot; ½ tablespoon unsweetened pumpkin purée; 2 tablespoons cooked mashed winter squash; 1 tablespoon cooked orange sweet potato; 1 small tomato; scant ½ cup cooked tomatoes or purée; ¾ cup vegetable juice; ¼ large red bell pepper.

**Other fruits and vegetables—one to two or more toddler servings.** One toddler serving equals any of the following: ½ apple, pear, white peach, or large banana; ¼ cup applesauce; ⅓ cup cherries, berries, or grapes; 1 large fig; 2 dates; 3 dried peach halves; 1 dried pear half; ½ slice fresh or canned pineapple; 2 tablespoons raisins, currants, or dried apple rings; 2 or 3 asparagus spears; ¼ medium avocado; ⅜ cup green beans; ½ cup beets, eggplant, or diced turnip; ¼ cup sliced mushrooms, yellow summer squash, or zucchini; 5 okra pods; ⅓ cup green peas; ½ small ear of corn. (Cut corn kernels in half by slicing each row lengthwise, and peel tough-skinned fruit before serving to your toddler.)

**Whole grains and other concentrated complex carbohydrates—six or more toddler servings.** One toddler serving equals any of the following: 1 tablespoon wheat germ; ½ slice whole-grain bread; ½ small (1 ounce) whole-wheat pita; ¼ whole-grain bagel or English muffin; 1 toddler serving Best-Odds muffin (see page 832) or other baked good; 2 to 3

---

2. If your toddler is under two years old, most of the dairy products he or she consumes should be full-fat; toddlers older than two should be switched to skim milk and mostly low-fat (not nonfat) dairy products. But remember that a very low-fat diet is not appropriate for any young child.

3. Increase to four or more servings when your toddler has a cold or flu.

4. Consuming large quantities of fruits and vegetables rich in beta-carotene can tint the skin yellow. It's nothing to worry about, but a sign you're overdoing a good thing. Check with the doctor if your child's skin seems to be yellow for no reason.

## FAT SENSE

· · · · · · · · · ·

Try to vary the sources of fat in your toddler's diet. Though some of it should come from animal sources (whole milk, cheese, meat), especially in the second year, more of it should come from vegetable oils (especially in the third year and beyond). The best oils are those that are highly monounsaturated, such as olive and canola; next best are oils high in polyunsaturates, such as soy, safflower, corn, sunflower. Fair, are margarines high in polyunsaturates, cottonseed, and peanut oils. For toddlers who have passed their second birthday, strictly limit to no more than 10% of calories: coconut, palm, and

palm kernel oils, hydrogenated or partially hydrogenated fats or shortening, chicken or other poultry fat, beef or pork fat (suet or lard), and butter.

Thanks to new nutrition labeling, you will be able to determine the number of grams of fat per seving in virtually all packaged foods you purchase. Since a toddler fat serving is about 7 grams, you can easily calculate how any item fits into your child's fat allowance. Keep in mind that small amounts of fat in many nonfatty foods (low-fat cottage cheese, banana, beans, for example) will probably combine to make a full toddler serving each day.

whole-wheat crackers or breadsticks (about 40 calories); ¼ cup brown or wild rice; ½ serving (see nutrition label for serving size) whole-grain breakfast cereal, unsweetened or fruit-sweetened; ½ ounce whole-wheat or high-protein pasta; ¼ cup cooked lentils, chick-peas, pinto, kidney, navy, or other beans (cooked until soft and mashed or split for a young toddler to prevent choking).

**Iron-rich foods—some every day.** Good sources include: Iron-fortified cereals; beef; blackstrap molasses; baked goods made with carob or soy flour; whole grains; wheat germ; dried peas and beans, including soybeans; dried fruit; liver and other organ meats (serve infrequently because they are high in cholesterol and are storehouses for the many chemical contaminants found in livestock today); sardines; spinach (serve infrequently because of high nitrate and oxalic acid levels). The iron in these foods will be better absorbed if a vitamin C food is eaten at the same sitting. If your toddler doesn't eat a lot of high-iron foods, or if he or she is anemic, the doctor may recommend an iron supplement.

**High-fat foods—five to eight toddler servings daily in the second year; five and a half to eight and a half in the third year.** After the second birthday, this allowance provides about 30% of daily calories from fat. One toddler serving (about 7 grams of fat) equals any of the following (keep in mind that the fat content of prepared foods can vary greatly; ask for nutrition information when available): ½ tablespoon polyunsaturated oil, olive oil, canola oil, butter, margarine, or mayonnaise; 1½ tablespoons cream cheese; 1 tablespoon peanut butter; ¼ small avocado; 1 egg; ¾ cup whole milk; 1½ cups 2% milk; ¾ cup whole-milk yogurt; ½ cup ice cream; 3 tablespoons half-and-half; 1 tablespoon heavy cream; 2 tablespoons sour cream; ⅔ ounce hard cheese; 1½ ounces lean beef, lamb, or pork; 2½ ounces dark meat poultry (no skin); 3 ounces salmon or other fatty fish; ½ small slice of pizza; 9 French fries; ¾ of a kid-size burger; 2 chicken nuggets; ⅓ cup tuna salad.

Each of the following equals one-half toddler serving: 3 slices whole-grain

## MILK MEASURES

· · · · · · · · · ·

A fter weaning (and the elimination of the calibrated baby bottle), many parents wonder if their toddlers are getting enough milk. One easy way to keep tabs is to measure out 3 cups of milk (the 2⅔ cup requirement plus another ⅓ cup to allow for spillage) into a covered pitcher.* Keep the pitcher in the refrigerator and use it for all your toddler's milk needs (drinking, topping cereal, making sauces, casseroles, and puddings). At the end of the day, you'll have an idea how much your toddler consumed. If there's consistently milk left in the pitcher, be sure your toddler gets other forms of calcium (see calcium-rich foods, page 506).

*Do not store milk in a glass or translucent plastic pitcher because exposure to light destroys some of the vitamins. Likewise, don't buy milk in such containers.

---

bread; ¼ cup wheat germ; 1⅔ cup 1% milk; 3 ounces tofu; 3½ ounces white meat poultry (no skin);

**Salty foods—restrict added salt.** Salt. Who needs it? Actually, everyone needs salt—or rather the sodium in sodium chloride, otherwise known as table salt—but no one needs as much as the average American consumes. And since a taste for salt often takes hold in early childhood, restricting your toddler's salt intake now may prevent a salt habit (and the potential health risks that come with it) later.

Children can get all the sodium they require from foods that contain it naturally (milk, yogurt, eggs, carrots, celery, for example) and foods that have salt added during the manufacturing process (bread and most other baked goods, cottage cheese and other cheeses, some cereals). To keep your toddler from overfilling the salty foods requirement and from developing a taste for such foods, add salt to foods rarely or not at all when cooking and limit the consumption of heavily salted foods such as potato chips, pretzels, corn and tortilla chips, pickles, green olives, and salted crackers. When you do tip the shaker, make sure it's filled with iodized salt, to guard against iodine deficiency.

**Fluids—four to six cups daily.** There's water, water everywhere—including in the fruits and vegetables your toddler eats, which are 80% to 95% water. But in addition to the fluids found in these foods, your toddler will still need an *additional* 4 to 6 cups of fluid a day to maintain a healthy fluid balance (toddlers, like the rest of us, are 50% to 75% water). Additional fluids are needed in hot weather or when a toddler has a fever, cold, or other respiratory tract infection, or diarrhea or vomiting. Satisfy your toddler's fluid requirement with fruit juice (preferably diluted with fluoridated tap water[5]), vegetable juice, soups, sparkling water, or plain water. Milk (which is ⅛ milk solids) provides only ⅔ of a fluid serving per cup.

**Supplements.** To supplement or not to supplement—that's the question that's kept parents guessing as the medical community struggles to reach a consensus. Some doctors insist that healthy, thriving children do not need any supplements—that they'll manage to get everything they need through their diet.

---

5. Apple and apple-based juices are best diluted with tap water, both because of their high sugar content (see the facing page) and because fluoridated tap water is a good way to get necessary fluoride into your toddler's diet.

Others, pointing to the eccentric, erratic eating habits of toddlers, suggest that using a supplement as a kind of nutritional insurance makes good sense. Little research has been done on either side, though a few studies have shown a slight but significant increase in IQ in children who take vitamin supplements.

If you have any doubt that your toddler is getting his or her share of daily nutrients, it probably makes sense to invest in the nutritional insurance a daily vitamin-mineral supplement provides. As long as you keep in mind these two caveats. One, no supplement can replace a good diet; dosing your toddler with a supplement doesn't mean you can slacken up on the Daily Dozen or the Nine Basic Principles. There are probably dozens, and possibly hundreds, of nutrients

found naturally in foods that remain undiscovered; they can't be packaged in supplements because scientists don't yet know what they are. In addition, nutrients work better in foods (their natural setting) than they do in drops or pills. Two, the supplement you choose should be appropriate for a toddler and should *not* contain more than 100% of the RDA (Recommended Dietary Allowance) for your child's age (read labels carefully, since different percentages are usually listed for different age groups). Keep in mind that too many vitamins and minerals can be just as dangerous as too few (vitamins A and D, for example, can be toxic when taken at levels not much higher than the RDA). Do not give your toddler cod liver oil, which can contain toxic amounts of vitamin A.

## JUICE FACTS

· · · · · · · · · ·

When a vitamin comes in it's natural package, not only is that vitamin ingested, but so are other nutrients (some of which we aren't even aware of yet) that work with it for good health. For this reason, orange, papaya, and pineapple juice (rich in vitamin C), apricot nectar (rich in vitamin A), mango juice and vegetable juice (rich in both), and other naturally nutritious juices should be your beverages of choice. (Orange juice that has calcium added scores some points over straight O.J.)

Apple juice, still a natural beverage, is a distant second best; it's a better choice if it is enriched with vitamin C.* Though it doesn't naturally contain great quantities of any of the known vitamins, some ingredients in apples are beginning to get scientific attention, and maybe one day soon the reasoning behind the proverb "An apple a day keeps the doctor away" will become clear.

Juice combinations that are comprised mostly of grape juice and/or apple juice fall into the same category as straight apple juice; again, enrichment with vitamin C

makes them a better bet. Sugar-water beverages (vitamin enriched or not), including 10% fruit juice drinks and any other fruit drinks or punches that contain sugar or any of its aliases (see page 502) on the label, are not only least best, they should be scratched from the list of acceptable beverages for your toddler. Your toddler would be better off swallowing some vitamin C drops; at least then there would be no empty calories along for a free ride.

And don't overdo any juice. Too much juice in a toddler's diet can lead to malnutrition, with empty calories replacing nutritious ones, and to chronic diarrhea. Limit your child's intake of apple and other low-nutrition juices to no more than 4 to 8 ounces a day, diluted with an equal amount of water. And be sure that juice, even nutritious juice, doesn't replace milk (your toddler needs 2²/₃ cups daily) or solid foods in your child's diet.

---

*Do not serve fresh cider to your toddler since it could be contaminated with bacteria.

Use a liquid preparation until your toddler's molars are in, then switch to chewables (preferably sugar-free) when your child can be depended upon to chew a tablet thoroughly. (But because the tablet will contain vitamin C—also known as ascorbic acid—it should be chewed just before tooth-brushing, or the mouth rinsed thoroughly after chewing.)

Be careful to keep a childproof cap on the vitamins, to store them well out of your toddler's reach, and never to refer to them as "candy." Their colors and shapes, aroma and taste can be extremely enticing, which is good, since it makes them attractive and palatable to children, and bad, since it can make them *too* tempting. Every year, tens of thousands of children ingest vitamin overdoses—often because the children were tempted by the attractive shapes and pleasant taste of the tablets, which just happened to be within reach.

# WEIGHTY CONCERNS: YOUR TODDLER'S GROWTH

If we're not bemoaning the fact that our toddler is too chubby, we're complaining that he or she is not chubby enough. Either we buy into the advertising industry hype that thin is in or we have an old-fashioned idealized image of the perfect toddler as plump and dimpled. But neither attitude is appropriate; children are individuals who burn calories at different rates. Some are destined to be on the round end of average their entire lives. Others can't be cherubically chubby, no matter how hard their parents try. To further complicate the picture, weight and body build in the first few years of life is no sure predictor of future weight or build. And learned attitudes toward body shape, eating, and exercise habits developed early in life often alter genetic destiny.

## *THE TUBBY TODDLER*

Chubbiness is often in the eyes of the beholders. And when the beholders are parents terrified of turning out a fat child, as many of us are today, evidence of the perceived overweight doesn't always show up on a toddler's growth chart. Many parents tend to confuse normal baby fat and toddler body build with creeping obesity. Chubby cheeks, a round belly, and dimpled elbows and knees are typical toddler trademarks and not necessarily signs of overweight.

So if you suspect you've got a tubby toddler, plan a trip not to the diet foods section of the supermarket but to the doctor's office. There, the possibility that your toddler is truly overweight can be explored and, if necessary, a plan of action mapped out. The doctor will probably consider two questions: One, in his or her medical opinion, does your toddler *look* overweight? And two, is your child's weight 20% or more above the average for age, sex, and height? If the answer to both these questions is no, you can put aside your weighty worries for now; your toddler's rotund physique is likely to eventually slim down to more comfortable proportions. If you'd like to help make a slimmer future more certain, or if you or your spouse has been fighting a weight problem all your life and you'd like your toddler to avoid that fate, you can follow the tips on the facing page, designed for the overweight toddler, but also useful to keep a toddler-on-the-brink from slipping into that category.

## SAMPLE TODDLER MENU

· · · · · · · · · ·

The following is just one way that a toddler's daily dozen can be translated into real meals and snacks—there are literally thousands of other variations that can work just as well (and better for some toddlers). The servings are "average"—what an average toddler can be expected to consume at an average sitting on an average day. That doesn't mean that the same toddler won't want to eat more (the whole slice of bread at snack time, or even a slice and a half one day) or less (just a bite of the bread one day), and that you shouldn't let your child do just that.

*Breakfast*
 ½ cup orange juice
 ½ cup whole-grain breakfast cereal
 ½ sliced banana
 ½ cup milk in cereal

*Mid-Morning Snack*
 ½ slice whole-grain bread with
2 teaspoons peanut butter
 ½ cup milk

*Lunch:*
 ½ grilled cheese sandwich on
whole wheat
 Wedge of cantaloupe
 ½ cup milk

*Afternoon Snack*
 Whole wheat pretzels
 ½ cup apricot juice

*Dinner*
 1 ounce whole-grain or high-protein
pasta (with or without tomato sauce)
 1 tablespoon grated Parmesan cheese
 ¼ cup cooked carrot slices
 ½ cup milk

*Bedtime Snack*
 Pear slices
 Fruit juice-sweetened cookie
 ½ cup milk

If your toddler is truly overweight, getting a hold on eating habits now will be even more important. Though being overweight in the toddler years doesn't seem to increase a child's risk for adult obesity, overweight by age four does. (It's believed that of the estimated 10% to 40% of children who are overweight, 50% to 85% will be overweight as adults.) So now is the time to begin to weight the scales in your toddler's favor. Consider:

**What does your toddler eat?** Right now, it's more important to concern yourself with the eating habits your child is developing than to worry excessively about the fat cells that may be proliferating. Letting your toddler get into the junk food habit now can easily condemn him or her to a never-ending battle with overweight. On the other hand, helping your child acquire a taste for whole grains, fruits and vegetables, low-fat dairy products (after age two), and fruit-sweetened treats will go far in preventing future weight problems (and health problems as well).

Too much dietary fat is usually the major culprit in the accumulation of too much body fat. So while a young toddler shouldn't have his or her fat or cholesterol intake restricted (children under the age of two should continue drinking whole milk and eating eggs; see page 348), it makes sense to limit *excessive* amounts of dietary fat. A diet that's heavy on greasy foods (such as French fries and chips) can tip the scales at any age. Once a child passes the second birthday, heart-smart eating habits are essential, both to long-term health, and normal growth and weight gain. Switch to low-fat or nonfat milk, low-fat cheese,

## THE BROCCOLI CONNECTION

· · · · · · · · · ·

Maybe Popeye should consider switching from spinach to broccoli. Not that spinach isn't a good food. But broccoli and it's *cruciferous* relatives (cauliflower, brussels sprouts, and cabbage) are not only good foods, but evidence is growing that they may protect against cancer. The reason may be sulforaphane, a chemical found in these vegetables, which has been shown to block the growth of tumors, probably by jump-starting the body's output of "phase 2 enzymes, which detoxify cancer-causing substances and help flush them from the body—though some other chemical components of the cruciferous vegetables are also under study. So, like Popeye, you, too, should consider increasing the number of appearances broccoli makes at family meals.

---

yogurt, and other dairy products; keep meat portions small and lean; and limit whole eggs or egg yolks to three a week (serve egg whites, as long as they are cooked, as often as you like). But because too little fat in childhood can also be a problem, even after the second year, don't reduce your toddler's fat intake to below 30% of his or her total calories without the doctor's supervision.

And if you aren't already, start setting the right dietary example for your toddler.

**How much does your toddler drink?** Many toddlers, especially those who still get most of their fluids from a bottle, guzzle a lot of unneeded calories. Most often the fluid at fault is apple juice (which, incidentally, provides little nutrition for the calories). Weaning to a cup, if you haven't already, and diluting juices, particularly apple and apple-based juices, with water will help to cut calories safely.

**When does your toddler eat?** Snacks have a legitimate place in the diets of active young children, most of whom can't go the four or five hours between meals without refueling. But too many such pit stops can be a pitfall when trying to control weight. Provide your toddler with a nutritious, moderate-calorie snack

between breakfast and lunch, another between lunch and dinner, and one more before bedtime. But that should be it.

**How does your toddler eat?** Toddlers who are still being spoon-fed often consume more than they want or need. So give your toddler plenty of opportunity to self-feed—and when he or she loses interest in the meal, end it. And forget trying to enlist your child in the "clean plate club"—studies show that adult members of that society usually weigh more than nonmembers. Fast eaters are often fast gainers. If your toddler shovels food in nonstop, try to slow down the pace at mealtimes with conversation or other distractions.

**Why does your toddler eat?** There's only one good reason for eating: Hunger. Children who learn this vital lesson at an early age rarely have eating (or weight) problems of any kind later in life. It's when eating becomes a source of comfort, a release from tension, an escape from boredom, or a substitute for attention that the trouble begins. Avoid the cookie to make the boo-boo better, the candy to buy quiet in the supermarket aisles, and the chips to fill time while you balance your checkbook. If you don't give food for the wrong reasons, your child won't eat for the wrong reasons.

**How much exercise does your toddler get?** For toddlers who exercise little but their appetite, weight is sure to become a problem, even if it isn't one now. Structured classes aren't necessary, but plenty of opportunities to run, climb, jump, and walk are. And don't forget to practice what you preach. A family that exercises together stays slim for a lifetime, together.

**How much TV does your toddler watch?** While exercise is a proven way to avoid obesity, television viewing has been proven to encourage it. The TV viewing habits your child develops in the toddler years are likely to stick for the rest of his or her life. So limit TV viewing now (see page 159).

Remember, no matter how much you may worry about overweight, you should not put your toddler on a diet. Young children need calories to grow and thrive. The goal is not to get the overweight toddler to lose weight, just to slow down the rate of gain while *maintaining* healthy growth.

# *THE THIN TODDLER*

Thinness, like chubbiness, is often in the eye of the beholder. And, as with chubbiness, when that beholder is a parent, the perspective is often a little skewed. So rather than believing your eyes, check with the doctor to see if your toddler is really abnormally thin from a clinical perspective. If the doctor is satisfied with your toddler's growth and general health, put your concerns aside, and begin to accept and appreciate your toddler's shape as is.

If your toddler is indeed underweight, it will be important for you to work together with the doctor to figure out why. To determine just what your toddler is eating and whether either the quantity or quality of food being consumed (or both) is at the root of the problem, you may be asked to keep a very detailed food and drink diary for a week or two, a diary that lists not just what your toddler eats, but when and in what circumstances. (Keeping track of a toddler's intake won't be easy, of course, considering how much of each meal generally ends up on face, clothing, high chair, floor, and elsewhere, and never makes it to the mouth.) Many factors, some of which are likely to be uncovered when a diary is evaluated, can contribute to a toddler being underweight. Happily, most can be easily remedied:

**Excessive fluid intake.** Many young children fill up on fluids (milk, juice, soft drinks, and/or water), leaving no room for solids. So judiciously limit liquids (see page 521).

**Easy distractability.** The child who is distracted during mealtime by toys, siblings, or television, may leave the table before eating enough. So decrease distraction (see page 518).

**Lack of assertiveness.** Some toddlers never complain when they're hungry; since they never ask for food, their parents may forget to feed them often enough. For these children, it's especially important to provide regular meals and snacks at approximately the same time each day.

**Uncomfortable seating.** The child who isn't comfortable at the table is a child who isn't going to stay at the table long enough to eat a full meal. See page 149 for tips on mealtime seating for toddlers.

**Unpleasant eating conditions.** Mealtime stress can affect the appetites of children as well as adults. So serve up an atmosphere conducive to eating (see page 517).

**Hurried mealtimes.** Many young children are poky eaters. Given the opportunity, they eat a hearty meal. When rushed, they may leave the table before they're done, and go away hungry (see page 519).

**Poor food choices.** Sometimes a child is offered foods that don't adequately fuel growth and weight gain: foods that are too low in fat (see page 348); low in calories (artificially-sweetened "diet" foods, for example); low in nutrition (junk foods, overly processed and refined foods). In planning meals for your underweight toddler, focus on foods that are calorie and nutrient dense, and that will help meet the Best-Odds Daily Dozen requirements (see page 504).

**Self-feeding problems.** Some young toddlers are not yet ready for exclusive self-feeding; when the feeding is left to them, they may not eat enough. Others are eager to self-feed and, when denied the chance, won't eat much at all. So turn the tables (see page 519).

**Continued breastfeeding.** Breast milk itself is not nutritionally adequate for children past the first year, and a toddler who is still nursing may not be getting an adequate intake of other fluids and of solid foods. So limit this liquid, too (see page 521).

**Ill-timed snacks.** Snacking just before meals is sure to dull a child's appetite. So hold the line on snacks (see page 512).

**Ill-timed meals.** Toddlers who wait too long for a meal often lose their appetites altogether. So feed when hunger strikes (see page 517).

**Untimed meals.** Many toddlers need regularity to thrive. So try to serve your toddler's meals and snacks at roughly the same time each day.

**Inadequate eating at day care.** Sometimes, day-care workers are not able to see to it that each of their charges finishes a whole meal. An inattentive (or nutritionally unaware) baby-sitter or nanny may also fail to feed your child adequately—or may be serving the wrong foods. If you suspect your toddler is not eating well enough in another's care, take steps to remedy the situation. Include the caregiver in any attempt to change your toddler's diet.

**Increased activity.** The toddler years are a time of greatly increased activity (and, in the case of some toddlers, of what seems like perpetual motion). Sometimes, parents fail to recognize that all this activity needs to be fueled by ample amounts of high-energy foods. Be sure the very active child gets enough calories to compensate for those that are being burned. Also try to introduce a few quiet activities during the day (reading, puzzles, block-building, and so on) to reduce the overall burning of calories a bit.

**Illness.** A wide range of physical ailments can contribute to underweight, including frequent ear or other infections, asthma or allergies, digestive problems, a metabolic disorder, an iron or zinc deficiency. Certain medications, including some antibiotics, can also dampen a child's appetite. Discuss these possibilities with the doctor.

**Stress.** Stress of all kinds—parental pressure to eat, family problems (such as illness or job loss), family changes (divorce, separation, a new baby, a move), a new or unhappy child-care or school situation, an overly busy schedule—can interfere with a toddler's appetite. When stress affects your child's appetite, try to eliminate or modify that cause, and use stress reduction techniques to relax your toddler (see page 173). If this doesn't help, talk to your toddler's doctor about professional help.

---

## MAYBE THEY REALLY DO GROW OVERNIGHT

· · · · · · · · · ·

Pants that seem to shrink overnight. Skirts that go from knee-length to mini in a week. Shirts that button one day, but not the next. Is your dryer too hot, or is your toddler really growing that fast? A recent study indicates that babies and young children may actually grow in spurts of 0.2 to 1 inch (0.5 to 2.5 cm) over a single 24-hour period rather than at a more gradual pace. And that between these growth spurts, children may not grow at all. (In the study, growth remained stagnant for anywhere from 2 to 63 days.) The study certainly needs confirmation, but it does support that oft-heard observation: "I swear, that child has grown overnight!"

---

# SLOW GROWTH

Growth during the childhood years can be baffling. There's just no predicting future size from newborn size. Some babies are small at birth and start out slowly, but pick up the pace between four months and two years and eventually turn out to be taller than average. Those destined by genetic blueprint to be small may start off with a bang; large at birth, they may grow rapidly during the first few months, but growth slows down as they move toward their genetic norm. When the growing is over, most kids turn out to be about the same size as their parents. If one parent is tall and the other short, the children tend to range somewhere in between.

A downward shift in the growth curve in the first eighteen to twenty-four months of life is generally not cause for concern if a toddler is healthy, active, eats well, and if height and weight tail off together. Concern arises, however, when the growth curve—for both height and weight—does not inch upward in the third year, when growth should start proceeding at a steady, consistent rate.

When both weight and height are below the fifth percentile, or when there's been a drop of two percentiles in weight, when a toddler fails to gain weight for three months or more or suddenly loses weight, and especially when any of these signs is combined with fatigue, listlessness, or behavior changes, there is reason to suspect a syndrome known as failure to thrive (FTT). Some causes the doctor will look for:

**Intrauterine growth retardation.** The child who was born small for gestational age may still not have caught up to peers, though he or she probably will eventually; those children who weighed under four pounds at a full-term birth may always be smaller than average.

**A constitutional growth delay.** Some children are programmed to grow slowly; their bone development lags one to four years behind that of their peers. This kind of delay may run in the family or may just affect a single child; either way, it's nothing to worry about. Though these children may have a difficult time and may need extra emotional support in the early teen years, they eventually reach average height, or taller.

**Illness and disease.** Sometimes illness is behind a child's failure to thrive. It may be diabetes, another endocrine disorder (such as a hormone deficiency), or a disorder affecting the digestive tract, the kidneys, the heart, the lungs, or the bones. The symptoms of early lead poisoning and zinc or iron deficiency may

## HOW DOES YOUR TODDLER GROW?

• • • • • • • • • •

**G**rowth rates are radically different at different times in a child's life. No matter how children start out or how they grew during the first year, the second and third years are a period of weight gain slowdown. Typically, the growth rate behaves as shown on the chart below.

| HEIGHT | |
|---|---|
| **Age** | **Growth** |
| Birth to 1 year | 7 to 10 inches (18 to 25 cm) |
| 1 to 2 years | 4 to 5 inches (10 to 13 cm) |
| 2 to 3 years | 2 to 2½ inches (5 to 6 cm) |
| **WEIGHT** | |
| **Age** | **Gain** |
| Birth to 1 year | 12 to 17½ pounds (5½ to 8 kg) |
| 1 to 2 years | 4 to 6 pounds (1¾ to 2¾ kg) |
| 2 to 3 years | 3½ to 5½ pounds (1¾ to 2½ kg) |

look like those of FTT, so the doctor may check for these.

**Stress and deprivation.** Severe emotional stress or a deprived environment may also contribute to FTT.

**Growth hormone deficiency.** A small percentage of children who exhibit poor growth suffer from a deficiency of growth hormone. Some of these children can be treated with injections of a synthetic form of the hormone. Best candidates for treatment are those growth-hormone-deficient children with short stature, subnormal growth rate, "doll-like" faces, mid-section chubbiness, a history of hypoglycemia (low blood sugar). In boys, who are most frequently affected, there may occasionally be an unusually small penis and undescended testicles.

**"Idiopathic" or FTT of unknown origin.** Sometimes no cause can be found for failure to thrive. But it can still be treated with improved nutrition and feeding regimens. It is important to diagnose and treat FTT because it can interfere with all forms of development (social, emotional, physical, intellectual).

# TACTICS FOR THE TABLE

**W**hen there's a toddler in the house, the best planned menus oft go astray. The toddler refuses to eat what's being served, insists on the same menu meal after meal, suddenly turns fickle (yesterday's favorite food is on today's blacklist). Most parents have seen one or more of these behaviors at least occasionally, and some see all of them all of the time. Fortunately, there are practical ways to deal with toddler eating issues:

# FINESSING THE FINICKY EATER

Every parent who's ever tried to feed a fussy eater knows full well the frustrations. Most toddlers are fussy eaters at least some of the time, and many are always fussy. Like other eccentricities, food fussiness seems to go with the toddler territory. While it may not be possible to turn a finicky two-year-old into a full-fledged gourmand, it is possible to cut down on the frustration of feeding one:

**Offer only the Best.** The Best-Odds, that is. If your toddler doesn't eat all that much, or eats erratically, it's especially important that what he or she *does* eat is as nutritious as possible. A petite appetite is quickly sated; if it's sated by French fries or candy, you've missed an opportunity to provide the nutrients your toddler needs.

If your toddler is underweight, offer such calorie and nutrient dense foods as: meat, poultry, fish, peanut butter, cheese, bananas, beans and peas, dried fruit, and avocado. To increase caloric and protein intake, you can add dry skim milk or canned evaporated whole milk to puddings, custards, soups, cereals, and whole milk. Add grated cheese to soups, pastas, and vegetables. Use some oil, butter, margarine, and mayonnaise in food preparation, but not so much that these fat calories take place of other essential nutrients. The doctor may also prescribe a multivitamin supplement with iron and zinc and recommend increasing your child's calorie and protein intakes beyond the Best-Odds requirements.

**Feed when hunger strikes.** It may sound obvious, but often the reason children don't eat well at meals is because they aren't hungry when they're served. Some toddlers get out of bed in the morning ravenous, ready to dive into their bowl of cereal; others need some time to wake up and work up an appetite. Some toddlers can wait until the working parent or parents are home from work to eat their evening meal, others have lost their appetite by then. Try to tune in to your toddler's individual hunger pattern. For a few days, if it's practical, wait until your toddler actually expresses an interest in eating (or, if your child never complains of hunger, until hunger symptoms, such as crankiness, set in) before presenting a meal. Keep track of when hunger strikes, and if you can identify a pattern, try to set mealtimes a little before each hunger period (on the assumption that a toddler doesn't ask for food until he or she is really starving). Once you've set the mealtimes, try to stick with them; for most toddlers, regular and predictable mealtimes, with food served in the same place at the same time, works best. Don't hold a hungry toddler off until the rest of the family is ready to eat; if necessary, serve your child earlier. Or, serve part of the meal—a raw vegetable or some bread—as a snack to tide your toddler over until the family can sit down together.

**Serve up an atmosphere conducive to eating.** Even the most appetizing meal is hard to swallow when it's offered in a stressful environment. Make certain the eating environment in your home is pleasant and relaxing, free of squabbles, loud voices, and hustle bustle. And leave pressure to eat *off* the menu, allowing your toddler to eat to his or her appetite's content from the nutritious selections you present. When it's clear he or she has had enough, let the meal end without comment; regularly struggling to

## FAST FOOD—FUN OR FOLLY?

· · · · · · · · · ·

It's been a long day at the office, the shop, the day-care center, the park, the mall, the market—or any combination of these. You're too tired to think, never mind cook. Your toddler's too hungry to wait, and too cranky to sit in a restaurant and be waited on. Those golden arches or that drive-through window beckon seductively, promising a quick, inexpensive, and virtually effortless family meal. You waver, and then as the pleas ("I wanna kid's meal! I wanna kid's meal") drown out any remnants of your resolve ("No kid of mine is going to eat fast food"), you relent. As you watch your toddler gleefully dunking greasy fries and chicken nuggets into sugary ketchup and barbeque sauce with the kind of appetite that young children seem to reserve for foods their parents *don't* want them to eat, you silently vow to be stronger next time, to resist the temptation of fast foods—knowing, deep inside, that you're vowing in vain.

But don't be too hard on yourself. Fast-food franchises cater to the most basic human needs, and when you're the harried parent of a toddler, you're only human for responding. But do keep fast-food excursions from compromising your toddler's overall diet—and health—by adhering (at least, most of the time) to these caveats:

▲ Don't make fast-food a habit. Try to limit your visits to fast-food restaurants to a couple of times a month at most. Make these fast-food meals an occasion that you and your toddler can look forward to enjoying together.

▲ Ask for a side of nutrition information. Many fast-food restaurants will provide, on request, a nutritional breakdown of their menu items. This information can help guide your selections.

▲ Cut your nutritional losses, when possible. More fast-food chains are offering "lighter," "leaner," and "healthier" options—everything from less fatty burgers to whole-grain buns to put them on. Pizza is also a nutritionally sound selection (but "blot" any excess grease with a paper napkin first), as is a baked potato stuffed with cheese and broccoli. Selections from a salad bar—most are stocked with grated carrots, shredded cheese, chick-peas (halve or mash for a young toddler), cottage cheese, and other toddler suitable foods in addition to things green and leafy—make worthy accompaniments to a fast-food meal. The occasional toddler who loves salad can even make a meal out of salad for selections, especially when there is pasta or baked potato among the choices. (But avoid drowning salad fixings in ladlesful of high-fat dressings.) Frozen yogurt can make a nutritious dessert (at least when compared to pies and cookies). Ordering a container of milk or orange juice instead of soda or a high-fat milk shake can also help improve the meal's nutritional profile.

▲ Compensate cleverly. Your toddler's had nary a nibble of anything nutritious. No problem—just head home for an after dinner carrot, plateful of cantaloupe cubes, a whole-grain muffin.

▲ Don't spoil the treat with guilt. If you're not overdoing the visits to fast-food restaurants, you're not putting your toddler's health in jeopardy. So hold the guilt, relax, and enjoy.

get a child to eat a little more can set the stage for future eating problems. So ban forcing, bribing, and cajoling "here-comes-the-choo-choo-into-the-tunnel" games, allowing your toddler's appetite to take its natural course instead.

**Decrease distractions.** Eliminate, too, other distractions that may keep your toddler from eating. Television can be distracting, even for a toddler who isn't really watching it. So are siblings or other children playing within view; so be sure that distraction is absent. Toys or other playthings on or near the table also present a problem. If your toddler won't come to the table without a favorite toy, make a deal: "You can take your teddy (or truck, or doll, or giraffe) with you, but you can't play with it. It can watch you eat."

**Let pokey eaters poke.** Many toddlers are slow eaters, particularly once they've started feeding themselves. Each pea must be popped in the mouth individually, strands of spaghetti slithered up one at a time. Give your toddler all the time he or she needs to complete the meal (and be certain that any other caregivers do, too), building the extra time into your schedule, as needed. Sit with your child while he or she eats, if it's necessary to prevent an early departure from the table, keeping up the conversation, and providing company. When eating dissolves into playing, however (the peas are being plopped into the orange juice instead of popped into the mouth, the spaghetti strands are being strung from the high chair like garlands), end the meal promptly.

**Turn the tables.** Stir up some excitement: Switch from finger foods to foods your toddler can eat with a spoon, or the other way around; from a "sippy" cup to a cup with a real straw; from breakfast foods at breakfast to breakfast foods at lunch, and vice versa; from cooked vegetables to raw, from junior foods to table foods.

**Take no captives.** Sometimes it's not the meal itself that a toddler finds objectionable, but the confinement (in a high chair, for instance). See the tips on page 149 for less-confining seating options.

**Let the picky pick.** As long as your toddler is presented with only nutritious selections, let your picky eater pick and choose what appeals—even if it's pizza for breakfast and cereal for dinner.

Encourage him or her to try what everyone else is having, but don't insist, at this point (the preschooler should begin to learn to eat what's set in front of him or her; the toddler simply has to learn how to eat). Of course, when being picky isn't polite (you're at a friend's house and it's waffles for breakfast) or practical (you're at Grandma and Grandpa's and there's no pizza in sight), let your toddler know what the options are: "You can have the waffles (or Grandma's oatmeal), some toast, or these crackers I have in my bag and a glass of milk—or you can leave the table and go play."

**Be sneaky.** Fruits and vegetables don't have to be whole, or even recognizable, to be nutritious. Blend chopped or puréed fruit into stand-by yogurt; serve the yogurt sundae-style, topped with halved berries and a drizzle of warmed fruit-only preserves; serve cereal with a few slices of banana; add chopped or puréed vegetables (cauliflower is hard to spot in an otherwise white dish) or tiny new peas to the macaroni and cheese (if your toddler doesn't object); cook up a vegetable soup (many children especially like minestrone); add a small amount of finely grated carrot to pancake or waffle batter (it won't change the taste or texture significantly enough to bother most children).

Whip up a banana or berry milk shake (sweetened to taste with frozen juice concentrate); serve a variety of vitamin- and mineral-rich juices and blends (apricot, peach, mango, papaya; carrot, tomato, V-8). Though the latter lack the fiber of their fresh counterparts, they may get your child's finicky taste buds acclimated to new flavors, which in turn may make them more accepting of whole fruits and vegetables later. If your toddler has a sweet tooth, satisfy it while satisfying dietary requirements by adding diced dried apricots, puréed dried fruit (soak first in hot fruit juice to soften), ripe bananas, carrots, sweet

# GRATIFYING A SNACK ATTACK

. . . . . . . . . .

How do you keep a toddler happy at snack time without compromising Best-Odds principles? By keeping the following wholesome nibbles on hand:

▲ Whole-grain pretzels, crackers, rice cakes, breadsticks, rolls, and bread

▲ Cheese (sticks, cubes, slices, or coarsely grated)

▲ Whole-grain fruit-sweetened cookies and muffins

▲ *Soft* dried fruit (apricots, raisins, dates, unsweetened pineapple, apples), for older toddlers

▲ Raw vegetable strips (red or green peppers, carrots, zucchini, mushrooms), for older toddlers

▲ Cooked legumes, such as kidney beans or chick-peas (garbanzos); halve them for young toddlers

▲ Fresh cucumber or fruit slices (apples, pears, apricots, bananas, peaches, nectarines, mango, melon, and so on), as appropriate for a toddler's age.

▲ Yogurt (plain, plain with fresh fruit or fruit-sweetened jam added, or fruit-sweetened commercial brands)

▲ Peanut butter and jelly or banana on whole wheat; peanut butter thinly spread on peeled apple slices.

---

potato, or pumpkin into whole-grain bread, cake, muffin, pancake or waffle batter. Look for sorbets or ice pops with nutritious fruit bases (apricot, mango, cantaloupe, berries), or make your own (see page 834).

**Offer choices.** If your toddler rejects new additions you make surreptitiously, try providing some options: "Would you like your yogurt with bananas or with applesauce? . . . berries or peaches in your cereal? . . . peas or broccoli in your macaroni and cheese?" If neither alternative is accepted, you're no worse off than you were before; but if one is, your toddler's taken a giant leap forward. Offering your toddler choices provides some control over dining and often increases the chances that he or she will try something new.

**Vary the options.** In most homes, two or three vegetables and three or four fruits turn up repeatedly on daily menus. But there are literally dozens of fruits and vegetables to try (see page 506 for suggestions) before you decide your toddler won't eat any at all (and don't assume your toddler won't like a particular food because you don't). Remember, vitamins and minerals don't only come in green packages. It's a rare toddler who won't accept at least one food in each Daily Dozen category. And for the moment, that one, eaten daily, is all that's necessary.

**Make food fun.** See page 522 for tips on how to do this.

**Keep the purist happy.** Many toddlers reject stews, casseroles, and other "mixed-up" meals, or even foods that are "touching" each other, preferring instead to keep foods separate on their plate or to eat one food at a time. Keep such a purist happy by serving foods singly or on a plate with built-in dividers.

**Don't make neatness count.** Most toddlers eat more if they're allowed to feed themselves. This is messy business, true, but it puts control over the eating itself where it belongs: in your toddler's hands. Lessons in manners can—and should—come later. See page 17 for more on self-feeding.

**Start small.** Instead of serving mountains of food (which can overwhelm and intimidate, causing a toddler to give up even before beginning or, perhaps, to make the mountain more manageable by unloading half of it onto the floor), start with small portions of each food. If those are finished, you can always offer seconds, then thirds.

**Take "no" for an answer.** Make all kinds of foods available—the more variety the better—but don't make any one food required. When your toddler is finished eating don't keep pressing for "one more bite."

**Limit liquids.** Too much to drink between and during meals can leave a tummy too full of fluids to fit in any solids. This is even more likely to be a problem with bottle drinkers, because it's easier to drink too much from a bottle than a cup (most toddlers are more proficient at it), because the bottle is often more available (many toddlers carry theirs around with them), and because bottle drinkers drink not just to quench thirst but for comfort or out of habit. Make sure your toddler gets adequate fluids, of course, but watch out for excessive drinking. Work on increasing the consumption of solids by offering solid foods first at meals, and bringing on the fluids later. If your toddler insists on a drink with the meal, do serve one, but pour just a small amount at a time. Try to set a limit of no more than three cups of milk and two of juice a day (filling a jar with each allowance first thing in the morning will make the job easier); eliminate water entirely for the time being (except in hot weather).[6] Again, since excessive fluid intake is most com-

mon in toddlers who still use a bottle, it's important to wean the underweight child to a cup as soon as possible (see page 326 for tips on weaning).

If your toddler is still breastfeeding, and you aren't ready to wean, then always serve solids and other fluids before offering the breast so your toddler's appetite won't be prematurely satisfied by your milk. If your toddler is always thirsty, check with the doctor.

**Set an eating example you'd like followed.** If you "nosh" the day away, never sitting down for a meal until dinner (or worse still, never sitting down at all), your toddler may learn to do the same. If you breakfast on coffee cake and lunch on microwave popcorn, your toddler may soon be begging to do likewise. So watch what, when, and how *you* eat as much as you watch what, when, and how your toddler eats. Make your example not only good, but enthusiastic. Your toddler will be more likely to be an appreciative, adventurous eater if he or she sees you doing the same: "Oh, this salad tastes so good!" "This broccoli is so yummy with cheese sauce poured on top!" "This is the best mango I've ever tasted!"

**Be patient.** Your toddler's tastes *will* change—but they'll probably change faster if you don't push.

A persistently poor appetite is sometimes related to changes in a child's life or to a cold or another illness. If your toddler isn't gaining weight or seems otherwise out of sorts, see page 513. A visit to the doctor's office may be in order.

---

6. If your toddler depends on tap water for fluorides, prepare orange and other juices using frozen juice concentrate and tap water.

## FUN WITH FOOD

· · · · · · · · · ·

For many toddlers, eating can be something of a bore. Busy with playing, learning, and generally having a good time, they're often reluctant to leave all that fun for the tedium of the table. But most will be more amenable to sitting down to a meal if it's fun, too. So the next time you prepare food for your toddler, try adding a pinch of merriment. Peruse the tips that follow to get you started, then dare to create some merry meals of your own.

**Shape up.** Cut sandwiches, bread for French toast, even chicken cutlets (pounded flat) into intriguing shapes (circles, diamonds, triangles, animals, hearts, stars) with a knife or a cookie cutter. Spread big, thin pancakes, bread (flatten slightly with a rolling pin first), or whole-grain flour tortillas with preserves, apple butter, cream cheese, tuna salad, or another favorite filling, and roll them up. (You can serve the roll-ups whole, or slice them into pinwheels.) Pour pancake batter (it'll be easier to control from a spoon than a bowl) to form faces, letters, teddy bears, hearts (or shape pancakes after cooking with cookie cutters); decorate with raisins, banana slices, blueberries, dried apricots, or other fruits. Look for intriguing shapes when buying pasta: wagon wheels, shells, twists, and alphabet letters. Mix and match varieties that require the same cooking time.

**Sculpt a dish.** Let loose the artist in you—and in your toddler—as you create masterpieces good enough to eat: a banana boat (with raisin sailors, a date for a mast, jelly waves licking the sides); a cheese "block" tower; a landscape of broccoli and cauliflower "trees" dusted with grated or shredded cheese "snow"; a still life of "ants on a log" (half a banana slightly hollowed out, then filled with cottage cheese, a thin layer of peanut butter, or yogurt, and dotted with dried currants); an abstract of cottage cheese drizzled with fruit-only syrup and studded with an eclectic montage of dried cereals and fresh or dried fruit; a house (whole-wheat bread, with a "door" flap, cheese shutters, broccoli flower beds); a fruit "tree" (a cantaloupe trunk, apple slice or dried apricot sliver branches, halved grape or blueberry leaves) instead of a fruit salad; a skyscape

# A LIMITED DIETARY REPERTOIRE

· · · · · · · · · · · · · · · · · · · · · · · · · · · ·

We may not be able to live on bread alone, but many toddlers seem not only to live but to thrive on such limited fare. And virtually all children will eventually outgrow the self-imposed cereal-milk-and-juice or peanut-butter-jelly and banana regimens they embrace as toddlers. Sometimes craving the same foods day in and day out is related to a toddler's comfort with routine, ritual, and predictability, and discomfort with change. Sometimes it has to do with a child having an extremely sensitive palate; overly keen taste buds can make all but the blandest flavors distasteful. Though such pronounced taste sensitivity is often outgrown (though not necessarily in the early years), it can stubbornly persist (which may explain why some adults *still* won't eat their spinach or *still* turn their noses up at seafood).

As difficult as it may be to ignore your toddler's eating eccentricities, don't make a fuss about what's eaten or not eaten. Strong-arm tactics or even more subtle manipulations will only serve to compound toddler stubbornness and turn mealtime into battle time. There are, however, some steps you can take:

▲ Make certain that your toddler's limited repertoire is unlimitedly healthy and

(mashed potato clouds, with green pea rain or a slice of baked sweet potato sun).

**Think mini.** Bite-size is just the right size for little fists, mouths, and appetites. Cut sandwiches or French toast into tiny squares, chicken cutlets into nuggets or "fingers"; make quarter-size pancakes; serve cooked carrot "pennies"; buy minimuffin pans and make pop-and-eat muffins, miniature meat loaves, single serving carrot cakes. Look for baby carrots, tomatoes, zucchini, squash, corn, and other mini vegetables, and serve steamed, stir-fried, au gratin, or raw.

**Sauce and dip.** While some toddlers prefer their food plain, others like everything sauced or dipped. Many latch onto one particular sauce or dip (tomato sauce, ketchup, cheese sauce, applesauce, yogurt dip), and want everything they eat coated with it. Go along with this idiosyncrasy—even if the combinations disturb your sensibilities (tomato sauce on chicken, applesauce on mashed potatoes, waffles with cheese sauce, yogurt dip on toast). But make sure sauces aren't loaded with salt and/or sugars (look for ketchup and tomato sauces in the health food section).

**Grate great food.** For the toddler who is too young to safely chew a carrot, serve a mound (call it a "hill," if you like) of grated carrot. Apple, cheese, and red cabbage can also be served grated and arranged as a garnish or as a centerpiece on the plate. For young toddlers, grate finely to eliminate a risk of gagging.

**Make the name part of the game.** Just as you'd be more tempted to order "a mélange of baby spring greens tossed in a mustard vinaigrette" than a "house salad," your toddler will be more tempted to eat egg salad if it's scooped up with crackers and called "Eggie Dip," a peanut-butter-and-banana sandwich if it's called a "p, b, and b," a fried egg if it's sunk into the center of a piece of toast and called, "Egg in a Hole," a miniature meat loaf if it's called a "Meat Muffin."

**Try a kebob.** Let your toddler string chunks of fruit (or cooked vegetables) and cheese onto a blunt-tipped skewer; kebobs can then be dipped in a sauce. Blunt-tipped toothpicks are also fun for snaring tasty tidbits.

**Have your toddler join the fun.** Eating food is always more fun when you've had a hand (and some fingers, and maybe an elbow or two) in the preparation. Toddlers are often more willing to try new and different foods when they've helped "cook" them.

---

that what he or she *does* eat meets Best-Odds standards. For example, breads and cereals should be whole grain; pastas should be whole grain or high protein; juices should be chosen from the more nutritious varieties; sugar should be permitted only rarely. Select foods that have been fortified or fortify them yourself: Purchase milk with extra calcium and/or protein or add dry skim milk to regular milk (add the powder to the milk container; mix and chill well before serving); serve orange juice with calcium added, baked goods with added dry skim milk or grated carrots, and meat loaf, burgers, and tomato sauce with grated carrots, chopped cooked cauliflower, or other vegetables added.

▲ Try to broaden the repertoire by building on your toddler's favorites. If bread is a mainstay, for example, try some tempting specialty breads—carrot bread, pumpkin bread, cheese bread. Or turn bread into French toast, grilled cheese sandwiches, or toast spread with cottage cheese and fruit-sweetened jam. If your toddler tends to live on peanut butter sandwiches alone, try to add slices of banana or apple or chopped dried apricots to this favorite.

▲ At each meal, offer options, either from the family meal or from the pantry: a snippet of chicken or tofu, a few strands of pasta, some bits of cheese, half a hard-cooked egg, banana slices, cooked carrot or sweet potato chunks, a banana mini-muffin, a new fruit juice. Make sure that the options you offer are broad enough and interesting enough to really provide a choice. Maybe your toddler would enjoy more finger foods (for example a quartered tuna sandwich instead of a mound of tuna that has to be eaten with a spoon or fork) so self-feeding is easier.

▲ Keep offering. It takes most young children time to warm up to anything new—whether it's a new sofa in the living room or a new food on the table. So don't assume that because your toddler has rejected a new or different food once that he or she will always reject it. Often it takes repeated exposure—making the food available dozens of times on the table—before a finicky eater will decide to take a bite. And keep in mind that biting doesn't always come first; sometimes a toddler needs to get to know a food in other ways—by touching it, studying it, mushing it up, watching other people eat it—before that first bite is taken. (Taking a bite doesn't guarantee that your toddler is going to chew or swallow that new food. Your toddler should always be allowed to spit into a napkin or paper towel a new food that hasn't agreed with his or her taste buds; after all, the idea is to encourage adventurous eating, not to punish a child for trying something new.) Don't force the eating issue, and your toddler may someday surprise you by asking for a serving of something he or she has rejected numerous times before.

Of course, if just the offer of options triggers a tirade, skip it for a while. Continue keeping the foods around should your toddler choose to accept them, but don't press him or her to try them.

▲ Give your toddler a daily vitamin-mineral supplement designed for toddlers (see page 508).

▲ And relax; even the finickiest toddlers outgrow their limited tastes.

# REJECTION OF A FAVORITE FOOD

Just when you think you've finally found a food you can count on your toddler eating without an argument—cereal for breakfast, for example—he or she begins rejecting it. But that's just like a toddler, isn't it? Always keeping you guessing, consistent only in being inconsistent.

Whether it's a whim, boredom, a display of self-assertion, temporary loss of appetite (due to teething or otherwise feeling out-of-sorts), or just plain contrariness that's turned your toddler off to his old favorite, try these tips before you decide to retire it permanently from the menu:

**Don't bring it back for a while.** Matter-of-factly take the rejected food away, and don't try serving it again for at least a week. In the interim serve nutritionally similar foods—whole-grain breads, muffins, or griddle cakes, for instance—in place of the rejected cereal. You may find that soon your toddler is asking, "Where's my cereal?"

**Bring it back with a difference.** When you return the rejected food to the menu, serve it in a different bowl, with a different spoon, or at a different time of day. Cereal for lunch or dinner may be more appealing than cereal for breakfast. If it's the same old cereal that prompts mealtime ennui, try a new variety or presentation (hot instead of cold, dry instead of with milk, topped with chopped dates or apricots or with peaches or blueberries instead of bananas).

**Don't bring it back every day.** Prevent boredom from returning by switching from cereal to pancakes to French toast and back again. That is, unless your toddler latches on to another favorite and refuses to switch off.

**Don't bring it up.** Feign indifference to your child's rejections—of old favorites or new foods. Make a fuss, and temporary rejections could become permanent. It's natural to be annoyed when you prepare food and it isn't eaten, but you'll only fuel the food struggles if you let it show.

# A VEGETARIAN DIET

Whether they're vegetarian by virtue of their own finickiness or household philosophy, many toddlers subsist on a meatless diet. And though this may surprise some people, when the following caveats are observed, a vegetarian diet not only provides all of the nutrients young bodies need to grow and go on, but it can be one of the healthiest dietary lifestyles around.

Whether a vegetarian diet is your idea or your toddler's, make sure it fills the nutritional bill by:

▲ Making every bite count. While this precept is universal when it comes to healthy eating, it's especially important when it comes to feeding young vegetarians. Because vegetarian foods generally are more bulky than other foods (to get the same amount of protein found in a few bites of chicken, a toddler would have to eat nearly a cup of rice and beans), your toddler is likely to get fuller faster on them. And since most toddlers have delicate appetites to begin with, allowing those appetites to be sabotaged by nutritionally vacant foods leaves little or no tummy room for the good stuff.

▲ Monitoring protein intake. Toddlers who eat dairy products and eggs can easily fill their daily requirement for protein. But vegan toddlers, who eat no animal products at all, can easily fall short in this category. And since protein is essential to growth, it's vital for parents to ensure that their vegetarian children get adequate protein (see Dairy and Vegetarian Combinations for Toddlers, below and page 526). It's not clear that it's necessary to get complementary proteins from nonanimal sources (foods that, when taken together, provide all the amino acids found in animal protein) at the same meal, but because it is relatively easy (bean soup with rice, pasta with peas), it makes sense to try to mix vegetable proteins. Though soy protein is complete enough for adults and children over four, it's short on methionine (which is added to infant soy formulas), so soybeans and tofu shouldn't be used as the exclusive protein source for young children. Again, if your toddler eats dairy products and/or eggs, there's no need to worry about combining vegetable proteins at all. Even a small amount of dairy protein will "complete" any vegetable protein in a meal.

---

## DAIRY PROTEIN COMBINATIONS FOR TODDLERS

· · · · · · · · · ·

Combine one of the following with one portion from the Grains or Legumes list in the Vegetarian Protein Combinations for Toddlers box (see page 526) for a Dairy Protein Combination.

*2 tablespoons cottage cheese*
*⅓ cup milk*

*2 tablespoons nonfat dry milk*
*⅙ cup evaporated milk*
*⅓ cup yogurt*
*½ egg or 1 egg white*
*⅓ ounce lower-fat hard cheese (such as Swiss or mozzarella)*
*1 tablespoon Parmesan cheese*

# VEGETARIAN PROTEIN COMBINATIONS FOR TODDLERS

••••••••••

It's preferable for your child to get some of his or her protein from animal sources: meat, fish, poultry, eggs, or dairy products. If your dietary practices make this wholly impossible, or if you occasionally like to serve purely vegetarian meals, the following food combinations will each provide an adequate serving of protein.

For a full toddler protein serving (about 6 grams), combine one portion from the Legumes column with one from the Grains column. **Note:** Nuts are high in protein and can also be combined with legumes to provide vegetable protein servings. But do not serve them to toddlers unless they are finely ground, since nuts are a choking hazard.

## GRAINS
½ ounce soy or high-protein pasta
1 ounce whole-wheat pasta
1½ tablespoons wheat germ
⅙ cup (before cooking) oats
¼ cup cooked wild rice
⅓ cup cooked brown rice, bulgur, kasha (buckwheat groats), or millet*
1 slice whole-grain bread
1 small (1 ounce) whole-wheat pita
½ whole-wheat English muffin or bagel

## LEGUMES**
3 tablespoons lentils, split peas or chickpeas (garbanzos), soybeans, mung, lima, or kidney beans
¼ cup cowpeas, black-eyed peas, white, broad, or Great Northern beans
⅓ cup green peas
1 ounce tofu
¾ tablespoon peanut butter

---

*These grains are protein poor; when serving them, routinely add 1½ teaspoons wheat germ per portion.

**Beans and peas should be split or lightly mashed so they won't be a choking hazard.

---

▲ Supplementing with $B_{12}$, as needed. Toddlers who eat dairy products and eggs shouldn't have a problem getting their fair share of this important vitamin, necessary for growth and development and for a healthy nervous system, but young vegans will. Vegetable sources of $B_{12}$ are rare; the vitamin is found in some seaweed, including nori and spirulina, but in this form it is not absorbed well in children. These foods may also block the absorption of the vitamin from other sources. So a supplement is necessary for vegans. Since the typical toddler multiple vitamin-mineral supplement does not contain $B_{12}$, ask your toddler's doctor for a prescription for a supplement that contains the $B_{12}$ RDA for toddlers.

▲ Watching the iron. Children who don't eat meat, a rich source of iron, often don't get enough of this important mineral. To improve the absorption of the iron that is in your toddler's diet, serve a vitamin-C-rich food each time you serve an iron-rich one (see page 507). Your toddler's doctor may also recommend a vitamin-mineral supplement containing iron.

▲ Pouring on the calcium. On a dairy-free diet, it is difficult (if not impossible) to get adequate calcium from diet alone. It is generally recommended that vegan parents consider giving their children milk, at least through the teen years. If they aren't open to this idea, then calcium supplementation in some form will probably be necessary. Another option is the use of soy milk that is fortified with calcium as well as vitamins A and D. If you plan on giving your toddler soy milk, buy only those brands that are fortified with calcium and vitamins A and D. But read labels carefully: most soy milks are *not* fortified. Calcium-fortified orange juice is another option, but be aware that it is *not* enriched with vitamins A and D and contains negligible amounts of protein.

▲ Giving a vitamin-mineral supplement. Because a variety of other vitamins necessary for toddler growth and development may be missing or in short supply in a vegetarian diet, such as vitamin D and riboflavin, a children's vitamin-mineral supplement is good insurance for vegetarian children (see page 508).

# SAFE FOOD, SAFE WATER

## MONITORING FOOD SAFETY—AT HOME AND AWAY

The media cover a rash of food-poisoning cases involving undercooked fast-food hamburgers; suddenly everyone in the country is cooking their burgers "well." The media report on a poisoning case involving raw seafood; suddenly, everyone's avoiding clams and oysters. They headline a salmonella outbreak; suddenly, everyone's ordering their eggs hard-cooked.

Unfortunately, when the immediate scare is over, the general public's concern over food contamination seems to fade with the headlines. Yet food safety should be an ongoing concern of anyone who prepares food, especially for toddlers. Though only a few make the wire services, there are an estimated 6.5 million cases of foodborne illness in America each year (some estimates go as high as 80 million), resulting in 9,000 deaths.

Protecting your family from contaminated food is not difficult—and it's well worth the effort. Here's how:

▲ Wash hands with soap and warm water before handling food.

▲ When shopping and using foods, pay attention to "sell-by" and "use-by" dates.

Don't use products beyond the "use-by" date.

▲ Don't trust your nose to tell you when food is spoiled. Though you can often smell the decay they cause, you can't smell bacteria; and food can cause illness before it begins smelling "off."

▲ Wash fruits and vegetables thoroughly (see page 534). Wash the rind of a cantaloupe with dish detergent, hot water, and a brush when you bring it into the house (the rind can harbor salmonella, which can cause serious illness). Wash any surface that the melon touched before it was washed and be sure it's been washed before you cut into it. Also wash the brush you used to clean it in hot soapy water or in the dishwasher. Store cut melon in the refrigerator; limit room-temperature exposure to four hours.

▲ Because the bacteria they may harbor present a greater potential risk to young children (as well as pregnant women, the elderly, and those whose immune systems are suppressed), don't serve soft cheeses (such as feta, brie, Camembert, or blue cheeses) to your toddler. Stick to hard cheeses (such as Swiss, Cheddar, Muenster), cottage cheese, and yogurt.

▲ Be wary of mold. When it appears on soft cheese, on baked goods, soft fruits and vegetables (berries, grapes, peaches, cucumbers, tomatoes) or in yogurt, toss the entire food out; on hard cheese, cut

# DINING OUT WITH A TODDLER

·· ·· ·· ··

In generations past, outings to restaurants by highchair habitués were rare; parents were likely to reserve a baby-sitter before they reserved a table in their favorite dining establishment. Today, with more parents apart from their toddlers during the day and reluctant to part with them in the evening, it's common to see under-fours in four-star restaurants. And restaurants of all kinds are responding to their family clientele by becoming more hospitable to younger diners, and more amenable to their special needs.

For a more palatable dining experience with your toddler, consider the following before you set out:

**Cuisine.** You may savor souvlaki or relish rellenos, but your toddler's tastes probably lean more towards pasta (hold the cheese and the green stuff) and chicken fingers (sauce on the side). In the interest of a peaceful meal, let your toddler's palate help guide your selection of a restaurant. Eateries that offer a children's menu are best, of course, but any restaurant that is willing to accommodate bizarre menu substitutions and special requests will probably be just fine. Salad bars and buffets may not make for the most relaxed dining, but they eliminate long waits for food, allow your toddler to participate in selecting the meal, and permit going back for seconds when your toddler demands more. Chinese restaurants are often particularly accommodating to the needs of young eaters and the food (brown rice and noodles of all kinds, particularly cold sesame noodles, which have a peanut-buttery taste) is often appealing. And since stir-fry preparations take but minutes, waits for food are usually blessedly brief. (Always ask for food to be prepared without MSG and heavy-duty spices.) Italian restaurants are big favorites with tots who favor pizza and pasta, but it's also possible to go Mexican if you pick a plain quesadilla (cheese melted on a soft tortilla) for your picky pequeño (be sure to specify no chili or other sauce or garnish). A fish restaurant or steak house that offers baked potatoes that can serve as a meal centerpiece (if your toddler likes them) is also a good choice, especially if they also offer fish sticks or chicken prepared in a way your toddler favors. Any restaurant that offers whole-grain breads is a plus, especially if your toddler tends to fill up on bread.

**Amenities.** Booster seats and high chairs, once found only at family restaurants, are now stocked by more and more elegant dining establishments. Call ahead to make sure there's an ample supply of toddler seating available (unless your child is accustomed to eating kneeling on a chair). If your toddler is fussy about seating, ask if you can bring a booster or toddler seat from home.

**Attitude.** Is the restaurant, and its staff, toddler-friendly? The right equipment doesn't automatically ensure the right experience. Important, too, is the restaurant's attitude towards pint-sized patrons. When you call, you should be able to determine that by asking straight out, "Are children welcome in the restaurant?" The response will undoubtedly be telling—one way or the other.

**Noise level.** A high noise level may inhibit conversation, but it also can drown out toddler whining and fork banging. Lively music or a tableside jukebox (with buttons your toddler can push) are a plus, too, both for entertainment and for camouflaging your young diner's noisy antics.

**Dining time.** Dine unfashionably early. Plan to arrive before the mealtime rush, when the restaurant isn't crowded and the staff's not yet frazzled.

**Waiting time.** Don't leave the wait up to fate. When you can, select a restaurant that takes reservations. An occasional restaurant that doesn't ordinarily take them will make an exception when you plead "toddler." Others, if you explain your situation, will allow you to call and put your name on the list for tables before you come over, which will cut down on the wait. When there is a wait, let your toddler run off some energy outside (weather permitting and under adult supervision, of course). Toddlers don't usually do well when they have to sit and wait for a table and then have to sit and wait for dinner.

**Seating.** Reserve the perfect table, when you can. Location isn't everything, but it counts for a great deal when it comes to dining out successfully with a toddler. So when you call ahead, make sure to specify your requirements and your preferences. Both you and the restaurant will benefit if you're seated in an out-of-the-way area (far enough from other diners so that any excessive noise from your table won't disturb them, far enough from wait stations and the kitchen door so that there won't be a catastrophic collision if your toddler suddenly dashes from the table). Also advantageous is a table close to an exit, which will reduce the potential embarrassment of a hurried exit. For a toddler in the process of learning to use the toilet, easy access to the rest rooms is a good idea. Booths are a best bet for toddlers too big for a high chair; in a booth, they can be safely sandwiched between a parent and the wall, with no chairs to tip backwards.

**Appropriate accoutrements.** Restaurants that provide crayons and paper tablecovers or placemats get extra points; so do that small but growing number that offer a play area. Never head for a restaurant that doesn't offer these amenities empty-handed. You'll need more than a menu to order up a pleasant eating experience—you'll need kiddy entertainment galore. So pack a bag full of books, crayons, a drawing pad or coloring book, and a few small and quiet toys (but plan on offering them one at a time). If you bring a ravenous toddler into a restaurant where you can't be sure of immediate tummy gratification (food from a salad bar or buffet, whole-grain bread on the table, and so on), bring along something to hold your toddler until the meal arrives (such as a whole-grain roll, breadsticks, or crackers). Alternatively, you could give your child a light bite before leaving for the restaurant—but this could completely spoil the appetite for dinner, and for sitting still.

Once you've arrived at the restaurant:

**Go for speed.** There's nothing like a leisurely dinner—if you've left junior home with a baby-sitter. But if he or she's sitting between the two of you, pounding the table for food, climbing over the back of the booth, and clanging the silverware, speed is of the essence—your goal should be to get in, get fed, and get out as expeditiously as possible. Eating at restaurants that specialize in speedy service (but generally avoiding fast-food eateries that specialize in high fat cuisine; see page 518) will help; some that offer take-out (pizza restaurants, for instance) will accept a call ahead to place your order, then serve you when you arrive. When that's not a possibility, peruse the menu before you're seated and order as soon as you are. Ordering all courses at once, rather than placing appetizer and/or beverage orders first, saves time, too. Though, on first consideration, asking that your toddler's meal be brought first sounds like a good idea, consider that he or she may be finished—and halfway out the door—by the time your meal arrives. Unless your toddler is a really slow eater (someone who can be expected to continue nibbling for at least half an hour), ask that everyone's food be brought as soon as possible. If your meal comes with a salad, soup, or appetizer and your toddler's doesn't, either ask to have your toddler's meal served with your first course (so the multiple courses don't slow down the dining process) or ask for something appropriate for your toddler to start with, too. (Or bring out some crackers from home at this juncture.) Bread before dinner should be doled out judiciously to avoid filling up on it, particularly if there are no whole grains in the basket. Best is a fairly hard-to-chew roll or crusty breadstick, on which a toddler will have to work long and hard to make a dent.

When, try as you might to orchestrate the meal so that everyone starts and finishes eating around the same time, you're just lifting that first bite of chicken to your mouth as the youngest member of your party declares

*(continued on next page)*

*(continued from previous page)*

"All done!" you can consider providing a simple dessert (fresh fruit or ice cream, for example, or a few fruit-sweetened cookies brought from home) to occupy your child until *you* are "all done!"

**Pay heed.** Don't wait until your toddler begins literally screaming for attention to give some. Save most of the adult talk for an adult night out, and concentrate on conversation with your child. Begin to offer, one at a time, your selection of distractions to keep your child amused until the food comes. If you've forgotten to pack a goody bag, use the napkin or menu for peek-a-boo, play some finger games, and otherwise improvise entertainment.

**Order favorite foods.** Order dishes you know your child likes—don't attempt taste tests in restaurants, except from your plate. Rely on children's meals if your child likes them; share full meals if there are two or more children in your party (ask that they be split in the kitchen); order an appetizer or half of an entrée as your toddler's main course (or order a full entrée and plan on taking half home); or combine side dishes into a meal (for example, a baked potato, a scoop of cottage cheese, and a dish of broccoli). If your toddler is a purist, warn the server to hold the garnish; explain that even a sprinkling of parsley on plain pasta could spell rejection and a return trip to the kitchen. If your toddler objects to foods touching (see page 245), ask that all things wet and gooey be served on the side.

**Set limits.** It's unreasonable to expect a toddler to sit through a restaurant meal as the model of politeness and decorum. But it's also unfair to subject fellow diners to an hour of uncensored toddler shenanigans. (Consider, after all, that the people at the next table may be paying good money to a baby-sitter so they can relax without their own offspring for an evening.) Go out of your way to keep your toddler relatively quiet and content during your meal; if he or she nevertheless becomes so disruptive that other diners are disturbed, it's high time for some time out. While one adult remains at the table (and enjoys the luxury of a few moments of dining tranquillity), the other should take your toddler outside for a change of scenery and a chance to cool off. If more than one time-out is necessary, take turns; that way, all adults get the opportunity to eat. (But be careful that you're not being led astray by a shrewd toddler who is fussing in order to force you to leave the table.) And don't take your toddler home before your meal is finished; doing this gives toddlers the idea they can change parental dinner plans simply by acting up. *Note:* Make it a rule that your toddler cannot get out of his or her seat during the meal without first asking for permission. Children wandering alone around a restaurant can walk into someone carrying a tray of hot food or beverages and cause a serious accident (not to mention, get hurt themselves).

**Tip well.** The special requests, the pasta ground into the carpet, the tomato sauce splattered across the table, the drinks upturned, and the plates tipped over—five good reasons why anyone who waits on a toddler deserves a little something extra for his or her efforts. Be especially generous if you plan to return to the restaurant.

---

the moldy portion off plus one inch (the rest is safe to use). Never cook with or let anyone in the family eat moldy, discolored, off-tasting, or stale tasting peanuts or peanut butter—they could contain aflatoxin, a dangerous toxin.

▲ Don't use food from unopened cans that are dented, swollen, or leaking, or from jars or bottles with seals that have "popped" before you attempted to open them, or that don't seem to pop when you do open them for the first time.

▲ Though leftovers that have been carefully stored and reheated to at least 165°F are safe for the rest of the family, don't feed them to your toddler. They may contain microorganisms against which a young child has little defense.

▲ To avoid spoilage of stored food, maintain your refrigerator at 40°F or cooler and your freezer at or below 0°F.

▲ Store raw roasts and steaks in the refrigerator for no more than three to five days; hamburger, chicken, and turkey, for no more than one or two days. Refrigerator temperatures should be 40°F or lower.

▲ Thaw meat, poultry, and fish in the refrigerator (or, after protecting it in a sealed plastic bag, in the sink, by running cold water over it) rather than at room temperature.

▲ After handling raw meat, poultry, or fish, wash your hands thoroughly with soap and water. Also wash with soap and water the surfaces and utensils that these raw foods came in contact with. Wipe up drippings with a paper towel to avoid contaminating sponges and dishcloths.

▲ Cook meat, poultry, and fish thoroughly. The center of a piece of meat should reach at least 160°F (use a meat thermometer to test); poultry should reach 180°F; and fish, 160°F. Meats and poultry should not look rare; there should be no pink near the bones of chicken or turkey or at the middle of a hamburger,[7] steak, or roast; juices should run clear, not pink or red. Fish should be opaque and flaky.[8] Hot dogs (not an ideal food for toddlers for both health and safety reasons), though precooked, still need to be heated until steaming.

▲ Don't let cooked food (whether hot or cold) stand at room temperature for more than two hours before eating (one hour if room temperature is 85°F or above); once foods reach room temperature, microorganisms (such as bacteria) begin to multiply. When keeping food warm, be sure to maintain its temperature at 145°F or above (use a meat thermometer to be sure).

▲ Do not use slow cookers for frozen or stuffed foods. When cooking in the oven, keep temperatures at 325°F or higher.

▲ After barbecuing, don't serve up burgers, steaks, franks, chicken, or fish on the same plate the raw food was on before barbecuing. Don't use marinades that the raw meat or fish has been sitting in to baste with near the end of cooking or to serve as a sauce; they contain uncooked juices, which may be contaminated.

▲ Avoid feeding your toddler raw meat, poultry, fish, and seafood (especially clams and oysters); unpasteurized dairy products (milk and cheese); and raw or partially cooked eggs (and products containing them, such as traditionally made eggnog, Caesar salad, and unbaked cake batter or cookie or bread dough).

▲ When eating out, avoid restaurants that have unwashed windows, a heavy fly population, signs of vermin, and so on; that have food (other than bread, cakes, or fresh fruit) sitting around at room temperature for more than short periods; where food-handlers touch food with their bare hands; or where handlers have uncovered open cuts, sores, abrasions.

▲ When packing food for picnics or travel, transfer cold items right from the refrigerator into a thermos or an insulated cooler (kept cool with a plastic bag of ice or a frozen ice pack). Hot food should be hot before it goes into a thermos or insulated bag. Wrap or box all foods separately and well to avoid leakage. Keep the cooler in the shade or in an air-conditioned auto rather than in bright sun or the car trunk. Once the ice has melted or the ice pack defrosted, discard any perishable leftovers. Safeguard picnic fare from flies, other insects, and household pets. Use wipes to wash everyone's hands before digging in.

7. Ground meat and poultry require the most care in preparation and cooking because, being ground, they have more surfaces that can be contaminated.

8. If you have any questions about the safety of meat or poultry, call the Meat and Poultry Hotline (800) 535-4555.

## THE CUTTING BOARD DILEMMA

··········

For centuries, wood was the favored cutting surface in kitchens the world over. As scientists began speculating that the nicks, scratches, and grooves left by the knives in the wood might harbor dangerous bacteria, however, "butcher-block" cutting surfaces fell from grace, replaced by easier-to-wash, harder-to-nick plastic cutting boards. But that's not the end of the story. Now, a study has shown that microorganisms *don't* survive on wooden cutting boards, possibly because of some natural substance in the wood itself. It seems that the supposedly hygienic hard plastic surfaces may actually be more hospitable to germs than wood. Until more research is done, it is unclear which board will stay on the cutting edge. In the meantime, whether you use wood or plastic, play it safer by taking these precautions:

▲ Use one board exclusively for raw meats and poultry and another for bread, vegetables, and fruits.

▲ Wash your cutting boards carefully after each use and between food preparation steps, in hot soapy water—or wash plastic boards in the dishwasher. Periodically sanitize wooden surfaces with a solution of two teaspoons of chlorine bleach to one quart of water, then rinse very thoroughly with clean hot water.

# MONITORING CHEMICAL CONSUMPTION

···········································

The risks to our children from consuming chemicals in food and water has become a consuming concern for many parents, but whether the concern is warranted, however, is unclear. We know less about the effects of chemicals in food than we do about the effects of microorganisms. That's because the effects of a nasty germ in our lunch may make us sick before dinner, while the effects of hazardous chemicals may not show up for years, maybe even decades.

Since young children consume more food per pound of body weight than do adults (eighteen times as much apple juice per pound, for example), process and rid their bodies of many (though not all) potentially dangerous substances more slowly, have immature immune systems, are still growing, and have many more years ahead during which these substances can cause damage, it's believed they are more susceptible to the potential risks of chemical contamination. Whether such damage actually occurs as a direct result of exposure, or when it occurs, however, has not been scientifically proven.

When the alar-apple scare of the 1980s provoked panic over the safety of produce, many parents wondered whether it was safe to continue offering their children nature's bounty. Most experts were quick to point out that to respond to the scare by withholding fruits and vegetables would be folly, because these foods are protective against just the kinds of damage chemicals are suspected of causing.

But while it isn't wise to panic, it is wise to take precautions with each of the following:

**Produce:** Reduce the theoretical risks by taking the following steps:

▲ Buy organic when it's available and when you can afford it. Presently, it is difficult to be sure that "organic" on the label really means that a product was grown without chemical pesticides or fertilizers. Beginning in 1995 such labeling will be regulated by federal law, which will require certification by one of several federally regulated certification organizations (the organization must be identified on the label). In addition, the law states that all packaged foods labeled "organic" must contain at least 95% organic ingredients. Products containing between 50% and 94% organic ingredients may be labeled, for example, "made with organic wheat"; and those that are less than 50% organic may only list the organic ingredients on the ingredients panel. Remember, "all natural" does not mean organic; it doesn't even necessarily mean healthy. Some produce may be labeled "transitional," meaning that the farm on which it was grown is in the process of switching from traditional to organic farming, and that though no chemicals were used in growing the item, the farm has not yet been chemical-free for the three years required for organic certification. (Buying transitional produce helps farmers who are switching to organic weather the difficult transition period.)

Root vegetables (such as turnips, carrots, rutabagas, and potatoes) are among the most important to try to buy in organic form, since they tend to accumulate more pesticide; organic is less of an issue when buying produce with an inedible thick peel or rind (melons, oranges, bananas), since these outer layers offer some protection against chemical infiltration.

If your supermarket doesn't carry a wide variety of organic produce, be persistent in requesting it (and suggest that your friends do the same). The greater the demand for organic products, the more farmers will grow them and the more markets will stock them—and the lower the prices will go. Also inquire if your supermarket chain spot-checks for pesticide residues; if it does, the conventionally grown produce they sell will be safer than most.

Organic produce can also be purchased via mail order. Or you can start an organic food cooperative with friends, play-group parents, or members of any organization to which you belong.

▲ Buy in season, so that what you buy is more likely to be local and less likely to be coated with wax or post-harvest pesticides or fungicides.

▲ Consider the source. Conventionally grown produce of U.S. origin generally has less pesticide residue than produce grown abroad. Produce grown near the point of sale is generally less likely to undergo post-harvest spraying to protect it during shipping. And fruit from the West Coast is generally less likely to be sprayed with fungicide than fruit from the East Coast, where dampness spurs the growth of fungus on foods.

▲ Grow your own organic garden, if possible. Planting such a garden, at home or in your community, won't only ensure safer eating but will provide a valuable learning experience for your toddler. An additional pay-off: Young children are more likely to eat the fruits (and vegetables) of their labors than those purchased in a market.

▲ Avoid or peel fruits and vegetables that have been waxed (most often: peppers, eggplant, cucumbers, and apples), giving them that artificially shiny surface. Though the wax itself may not be hazardous, it is often fortified with carcinogenic fungicides used to prevent mold and rot.

▲ Peel nonorganic potatoes (before or after cooking), say some experts, to remove the sprout-inhibiting chemicals on the skin. These same experts say that, contrary to what has been commonly believed, most of the nutrients will *not* be lost with the skin.

▲ Choose imperfect produce. Fruits and vegetables that aren't completely free of blemishes are more likely to have been grown and shipped with a minimum of chemicals. You don't have to look for worm-eaten apples, but do try to bypass those that look too good to be true.

▲ Wash produce thoroughly before it is eaten. Use a sudsy solution made from water and a few drops of a special produce-washing liquid (sold in health food stores) or dish (*not* dishwasher) detergent to remove as much surface chemical residue as possible along with any microorganisms and dirt. Follow up with a *very* thorough cold-water rinse. Scrub vegetables that can take scrubbing (potatoes, carrots, zucchini, celery) with a sturdy vegetable brush. Break up broccoli and cauliflower, and separate spinach, kale, lettuce, and the leaves of other greens, before washing. Discard the outer leaves of head lettuces and cabbages and peel fruits and vegetables when practical; trim the leaves and tops of celery.

▲ Keep in mind that cooking does reduce chemical residues somewhat; unfortunately, it also reduces the nutritive content of foods to some degree. So alternate between cooked and raw fruits and vegetables.

▲ Feed your toddler as varied a diet as possible in order to reduce the risk of repeated exposure to the chemicals in any one food. (The pesticides, fungicides, and other chemicals used vary from fruit to fruit and vegetable to vegetable.)

▲ If you're still using "junior" foods for your toddler (they're convenient but otherwise unnecessary), buy organic varieties, such as Earth's Best, when possible. Not only are they pesticide-free, but they don't contain the sugar, chicken fat, and sodium found in many other commercial toddler meals.

▲ Be wary of irradiated foods. Though irradiation, which can kill dangerous microorganisms, has been approved by the FDA for use with certain foods, some experts believe more study is needed to prove definitively that foods so treated

are entirely safe. Until more is known, it's your judgment call; you may want to err on the side of caution.

▲ Avoid processed foods containing questionable chemical additives, such as Acesulfame-K, artificial colorings, BHA, BHT, propyl gallate, saccharine, and sodium nitrite. Since some individuals turn out to be sensitive to sulfites, MSG (monosodium glutamate), and HVP (hydrolyzed vegetable protein), it's better not to serve foods containing these additives to young children. Likewise, since young children should not be limiting calories, foods sweetened with aspartame (Equal, Nutrasweet) are not appropriate for children under two. After the age of two, they should be allowed only occasionally—both because the foods they're contained in are rarely nutritionally worthy, and because long-term effects of this sweetener on growing children are not yet known.

▲ Don't serve your toddler beverages containing caffeine. It is a stimulant, and not suitable for young children. Likewise, don't give your toddler sips of beverages or bites of food containing alcohol—alcohol is a drug and can be toxic to children.

**Meat, poultry, fish—and dairy products.** Many of the same chemicals that contaminate our produce also contaminate animal feed, the water animals drink, and the lakes, rivers, and seas fish live in. In addition, meat and poultry may contain residues from antibiotics or hormones fed them during their lifetimes (to prevent or treat illness or to promote growth or milk production). To reduce the risk from animal products contaminated with this mix of chemicals:

▲ When possible, buy meat, poultry, and fish that is certified organic or chemical-free. (Free-range, incidentally, doesn't mean chemical-free.)

▲ Alternate serving meat, poultry, and fish. If the beef has traces of hormones, the poultry of antibiotics, and the fish of PCBs, at least your family will be consuming less of each chemical.

▲ Trim fat from meat and skin from poultry before cooking; chemicals tend to accumulate in fatty tissue. Avoid organ meats, particularly liver, which, because it processes toxins in the animal's body, generally contains high levels of potentially harmful chemicals.

▲ Trim skin, gills, and dark fatty areas from fish and remove innards completely, because contaminants collect in these parts.

▲ After the age of two, give your toddler skim or low-fat dairy products, because chemicals, if any, also tend to accumulate in milk fat. (Even if your toddler does pick up some of these chemicals before the age of two, it's unlikely that enough will accumulate to cause later problems.) When possible, buy milk that comes from cows that are not fed hormones.

▲ Limit fish and seafood intake to three times a week, except when you know it comes from uncontaminated waters. As a rule, it's a good idea to alternate species of fish, especially when feeding young children. Avoid fish from waters known to be polluted (usually lakes and rivers); off-shore fish and farmed fish tend to be the safest. In general, small fish are safer than large, and lean fish are safer than fatty fish. Some experts believe that young children (and pregnant women) should not eat fish caught by sport fishermen for home consumption at all and should eat even commercially caught swordfish, bluefish, and striped bass only rarely, if at all, because of potentially high PCB levels. Limit shellfish, too, which often contains lead, cadmium, chromium, and arsenic. For further information on seafood safety, call the Seafood Hotline, (800) FDA-4010; in D.C., (202) 205-4314; or check with your local Health Department, Fish and Game Department, E.P.A.

# MONITORING COOKING, SERVING, AND STORAGE UTENSILS

As if concerned parents don't have enough worries about the foods they serve their children, every once in a while questions circulate about the safety of the pots, pans, dishes, and glassware that the food is cooked, served, or stored in. Sometimes the concerns raised are unfounded, sometimes they are fully justified.

**Pots and pans.** You've scoured the supermarket for the safest foods for your toddler. But how safe are the pots and pans you'll be cooking them in? In most cases, very:

▲ Nonstick. The material used to make food slide off the surfaces of these pans is not absorbable by humans, so even if bits flake off, there is no danger. Do avoid using high heat with these pans, however; since it's been suggested that the fumes given off might be harmful.

▲ Aluminum. Recent studies indicate the use of this cookware is *not* related to Alzheimer's disease, as was once theorized, and so it is safe to use.

▲ Iron. Though this type of cookware is difficult to maintain, the iron it leaches into acidic foods when they are cooked for long periods is not only innocuous, but can actually be a good source of dietary iron.

▲ Stainless steel. This cookware, too, may leach iron along with chromium and nickel into foods. But since iron and chromium are important nutrients, and nickel is no problem (unless your toddler or someone else in the family has a nickel allergy), it's generally safe to use stainless steel utensils. The older the pots, the fewer minerals leach into foods.

▲ Pyrex, Corningware, other heat-proof glass cooking utensils, and enamel-clad metal. All of these appear safe to use. Always be careful, however, to use according to directions, since excessive heat or direct heat can lead to cracking and breaking.

▲ Copper. The copper in unlined copper pans can dissolve into foods; eating the foods so contaminated can cause nausea and vomiting. So only use lined copper pans. It's safe, however, to beat egg whites in a copper bowl.

▲ Microwave cookware. Always look for the label "Safe for microwave use." Do not use cottage-cheese or yogurt containers or other plastic containers not meant for use in the microwave; the plastics could melt or leach into foods. When heating foods high in fat or sugar (which can reach very high temperatures in the microwave), use glass or ceramic cookware rather than plastic, even if the plastic is microwave-safe.

**Dinnerware and glassware.** Not only is it important to pay attention to what you cook in, it's also necessary to pay attention to what you serve on and store foods in. Be sure all your dinnerware is lead-free (check with the manufacturer or the store where it was purchased or have the items tested); antiques and imports are more likely to contain lead. Do not use lead crystal or tin or aluminum cans soldered with lead for storage, since the lead can leach into foods or beverages.

# MONITORING WATER SAFETY

Most water in the United States is fit to drink, though more still needs to be done to make it safer still. In some municipalities, however, even minimal water protection standards are not met, and the water is contaminated by higher than acceptable levels of chemicals and occasionally by hazardous microorganisms. When water is unsafe, it's important to put community pressure on officials to correct the problem.

The following will help you make sensible decisions concerning the water your family drinks:

**Testing for contaminants.** Unfortunately, you can't tell whether your tap water is safe by looking at it, smelling it, or even tasting it. Most dangerous contaminants don't change the appearance, smell, or taste of water; they are colorless, odor-free, and tasteless. Only testing can give you the lowdown on the water that comes from your tap. Testing, which isn't complicated, should only be done by a disinterested party: a testing service that does not sell filters or bottled water or anything else other than testing. In some municipalities, the water company may come and test for you. Or you can call the Safe Drinking Water Hotline, (800) 426-4791, for the telephone number of the office in your state that certifies labs and can refer you to one. It's usually recommended that you take samples first thing in the morning (*without* first letting the water run) from each tap used for drinking or cooking water. Many testing labs provide plastic bottles for collecting the samples. Tests are generally not very expensive, and the results are often available within two or three weeks.

Well water, once believed to be a reliable source of pure water, is also subject to pollution. If your water comes from a well, it should be checked for run-off contaminants, especially if you live in a farming or industrial area. The water should also be checked periodically for bacterial contamination.

**Dealing with chlorine**. Very long-term ingestion of chlorine, used in most municipalities to keep water safe, has tentatively been linked to some health problems. If your water supply is particularly high in chlorine (sometimes you can actually smell it), boil the water before using, aerate it in a blender, or let it stand uncovered overnight to allow the chemical to dissipate. You can also use an activated carbon system to filter the water.

**Dealing with lead.** Lead in the water presents a serious danger to young children (as well as to pregnant women), so it is especially important for parents to be certain that the family's drinking water is lead-free. Lead in drinking water comes not only from municipal water systems; it also leaches into tap water from lead pipes or lead solder in the plumbing in individual buildings. So each home needs to be tested—unless it was built, completely replumbed, or the water main was replaced, after 1986 when laws outlawing use of lead pipes and lead solder went into effect. Testing, which should be carried out on the water coming from each faucet used for drinking (see facing page for information on finding a testing service), is best done when the water is first turned on in the morning. It's at this time, when water has been sitting overnight, that lead is most likely to accumulate.

If you do find lead in your water, you needn't remortgage your home to put in new plumbing or break your lease and find another apartment. In most cases, all that's needed is to run the water before each use until it's cold (often it will go from cool to warmer before turning really cold) in order to flush out the lead. The water flowing from the street right to your tap will not have time to pick up dangerous levels of lead. To avoid wasting water, you can save the first-run water for washing dishes and other household uses. Once the water is running cold, you can also fill the tea kettle, the coffee pot, and a couple of bottles to store in the refrigerator for drinking. Never use hot tap water for cooking or drinking, since it leaches more lead from pipes.

**Water purification or treatment systems.** In spite of the hype from purveyors of such systems, they are rarely necessary. Never plunk down your money for one without first having your water tested by an independent lab (see facing page ). When a system is needed, the choice will depend on the contaminants in your water. Carbon filters remove a variety of organic chemicals, including pesticides, as well as odors and bad tastes. They may possibly remove radon (which can enter the air from running tap water), but since the radon can disperse from every water source in the house (taps, toilets, washing machines, and so on), the only way to eliminate the problem is to install a point-of-entry carbon filter which purifies from the point at which the city water enters the home).

When tap water is brackish (high in salt), high in nitrates, or loaded with lead, iron, or other heavy metals, a reverse osmosis system is required. But since such systems are very expensive and waste a lot of water, be sure it's really needed before deciding to install one.

Check with the National Sanitation Foundation (NSF; P.O. Box 1468, Ann Arbor, Michigan 48106) before you buy any water filtering system. They can also give you additional information on filtering your water.

**Bottled water.** Though many families, worried about the safety of their local water supply, have turned to bottled water, there is no absolute assurance that water that comes in a bottle is any purer or safer than water that comes from the tap. NSF certification on the bottle offers some security, but something can go wrong with a particular run of water (as drinkers of one popular brand found out a few years ago).

Some bottled water is nothing more than tap water from someone else's tap in a bottle. Some contains little or no fluorides, so it will not protect the teeth of babies or toddlers. (If you use bottled water, check with the manufacturer for information on fluoride content, then check with your dentist to see if it is too little, too much, or just the right amount.)

If you prefer the taste of a particular bottled water to your own tap water, or if the safety of your water is questionable, certainly use bottled water and give it to your toddler. You may, however, want to choose a brand that is NSF-certified and to send a bottle of it off for testing before using it regularly. (Unfortunately, however, there's no guarantee, even if the test turns out fine, that the quality will be uniform in every bottle.)

# CHOKING RISKS

· · · · · · · · · ·

Goodbye baby purée, hello grown-up textures. With a rapidly increasing complement of teeth, most toddlers are ready to enter a whole new world of eating experiences. Yet even with their ever-widening gastronomic horizons, there are still certain foods that must remain off-limits to toddlers, because they can cause choking.

Several factors may combine to make toddlers more subject to choking on food than older children or adults. Even once they have a full set of teeth (usually in the middle of the third year), their chewing and swallowing skills tend to be immature; they are also likely to gulp food when eager to get back to play, and they are inclined to eat on the run (and eat while running).

To minimize choking risks, keep the following foods off-limits to your toddler (with the exceptions noted):

Nuts (especially peanuts, which are best avoided until age seven) unless ground

Round, hard candies*

Hot dogs** (unless sliced lengthwise before slicing crosswise)

Chunks of meat

Grapes (unless peeled, seeded, if necessary, and halved)

Raw cherries (unless peeled, pitted, and halved or quartered)

Raw celery

Whole raw carrots (thin slivers or "carrot fingers" are okay for those with all their teeth)

Peanut butter by the spoonful (it's okay spread lightly on bread or fruit, but should never be eaten by the mouthful, even by adults)

Popcorn

Hard raisins (raisins kept in an airtight container should stay soft enough for a toddler with a full complement of teeth; for a young toddler, squash or halve them before serving)

No matter what your toddler is eating, you can reduce the risk of choking still further by:

▲ Insist that your toddler eat sitting down. Eating on the run, or while walking, playing, lying down, or semi-reclining presents a choking risk.

▲ Prohibiting your toddler from eating any food that can be choked on while in the car, especially if there isn't an adult other than the driver who could handle a possible choking incident.

▲ Being extra cautious when you've applied a teething preparation to numb the gums. Until the anesthetic effects wear off, your child will not be able to chew normally; so only soft foods should be offered.

▲ Discourage talking or laughing with the mouth full.

These rules will be easier to enforce if everyone in the family has to follow them.

---

*These aren't recommended for toddlers, anyway.

**Hot dogs should be served infrequently, because of their high fat, low protein content and because they often contain questionable chemicals. If they are served to a toddler, they should be nitrate-free.

# CHAPTER NINETEEN

# *All About Toilet Learning*

Your child has learned to roll over, to pull up, to cruise, to stand, to walk. Graduated from pablum to peanut-butter sandwiches, from crib gyms to jungle gyms, and (possibly) from crib to bed. Mastered so much, grown and matured in so many ways, come so far, so fast. And yet, like most children his or her age, your child is probably still wearing diapers.

Toileting is far from the last frontier for toddlers, but as you change your 4,326th diaper (give or take a few dozen), it's hard to believe that your toddler will ever cross it and move on to the next. Have faith. Like all other developmental skills, toileting *will* be mastered. This chapter can guide you through the toilet-learning maze and help you to help your child achieve this mastery.

# READY?

Your mother says you were out of diapers by your first birthday; a colleague's son was using the potty by twenty-two months; the little girl across the street seemed closer to four. You don't want to push your toddler into potty learning too soon—yet you don't want to wait too long, either. So what exactly is the right time to begin toilet learning?

As in so many areas of development, look no further than your toddler for the answer. Only your child can tell you (not in words, but through a variety of behaviors) when he or she has attained that magical combination of ability and desire that spells readiness for toileting. And though it's possible to force a child to use the toilet prematurely, it isn't wise and sets the scene for resistance, rebellion, and an unduly long struggle (not to mention more "accidents" to clean up). Letting a child take the lead in toilet learning by waiting for signs of readiness and willingness not only paves the way for swifter success, but can also make the experience an ego-boosting one for your child, an achievement of which to be proud.

Like crawling, walking, and talking, toilet learning is a developmental task, which every child should be allowed to master according to his or her own timetable. The time at which toilet learning is mastered in no way correlates with intelligence or success in other areas of development; an early talker or an early walker doesn't necessarily become an early potty-learner, and an early potty-learner doesn't necessarily become an early reader. Some children are ready for toilet learning before their second birthday, others not until after their third—but most are ready sometime in between.

To make sure the timing's right, look for some of these signs of potty-readiness in your toddler before you start looking for a potty:

▲ **Physiologic readiness.** Before the age of twenty months or so, your child's bladder empties so frequently that it's too difficult to control. A toddler who stays dry for an hour or two at a stretch during the day and occasionally wakes up dry from naps is physically ready to begin toilet learning.

▲ **Regularity.** Bowel movements come at fairly predictable times each day (perhaps first thing every morning, or right after breakfast, or after each meal)—though some children never become that regular.

▲ **Increased awareness of the pertinent bodily functions.** Your toddler lets you know in some way—by grunting, assuming that certain "look," going off to a quiet corner to squat, or possibly even announcing the event—that he or she is having a bowel movement. While a toddler who's not ready for toilet learning might ignore a stream of urine flowing down his or her legs, a toddler who is ready will take note, and perhaps comment on, point to, or be clearly annoyed by the flow.

▲ **An interest in neatness and in being clean and dry.** A sudden finickiness about sticky fingers and face and more tidiness with toys (unfortunately, this is a phase that, in most children, won't last) is often coupled with a new distaste for soggy or soiled diapers and a desire to be changed immediately (which, hopefully, *will* last). Because of a maturing sense of smell, toddlers also become more finicky about smells about the time they're ready for toilet learning—which makes them more aware of the odors associated with dirty diapers.

▲ **An understanding of key concepts:** the difference between wet and dry, clean and dirty, up and down.

▲ **Familiarity with the toilet terminology** used in your household, whatever it may be: pee, poop, BM, urinate, defecate, or whatever, as well as the names of body parts associated with potty use—penis, vagina, bottom, tushy.

▲ **The ability to communicate needs and** to understand and follow simple directions.

▲ **An interest in wearing underpants** instead of diapers.

▲ **The ability to so some simple self-dressing.** To pull down jeans or slacks, lift up a skirt, pull down underpants, and pull them back up.

▲ **Curiosity about the bathroom habits** of others—following others (friends, siblings, parents or other adults) into the bathroom, watching and/or trying to imitate them.

# GET SET . . .

You've checked and rechecked the signs of readiness in your toddler—all systems seem "go." But before you drop your toddler's diapers and dash to the potty for the first time, take a look at what's happening in the family and in your child's life. It's usually better to postpone toilet learning when there's a new baby, a new child-care situation, an imminent move, an illness, or another serious family problem. If there appear to be no major impediments, then gear up for toilet learning by taking the following steps:

**Accentuate the positives of pottying.** Prime your toddler for toilet learning by talking it up: "Won't it be fun when you can wear underpants instead of diapers?" "Soon you can go on the toilet, too—just like Mommy and Daddy!" (But don't denigrate diapers, or you might find yourself with a hostile toileting student.)

**Accentuate, too, the positives of growing up.** To get your toddler interested in taking this significant step forward, compliment any and all "grown-up" behavior—washing hands, drinking from a cup without spilling (too much), putting away toys, being generous to a playmate or sibling—but take no notice of "babyish" conduct. Be wary of demanding or expecting too much maturity, especially if the arrival of a new sibling or going off to preschool has left your toddler yearning for the simpler days of babyhood.

**Read up on potty learning.** Scout out several picture books on the subject geared to toddlers and share them at storytime—but keep the reading light and entertaining and hold off on the editorializing. Hearing about other children learning to use the potty will help prepare your toddler.

**Demonstrate how it's done.** If you haven't before and if you're comfortable with the idea, that is. The excretory processes may come naturally, but the toileting process doesn't. Watching someone else of the same sex use the toilet a few times is better than a thousand explanations.

**Let the student teach, too.** Buy or borrow a doll that drinks and wets, and encourage your toddler to help the doll to "learn" to use the potty and to switch from diapers to training pants.

**Pick a potty.** But not just any potty. Invest in a sturdy, durable potty chair with a stable base that won't tip over when your child gets up to check progress (if your toddler has expressed an interest in using the "big" toilet, see below). If you sense it will help stimulate excitement, either take your toddler along when you shop for the chair or wrap it up as a "present." Print your toddler's name on the chair with indelible marker, and invite him or her to further personalize it with stickers on places that aren't likely to get wet. Explain what the potty is for: "When you're ready, you can use the potty instead of a diaper to urinate and make BMs in (or pee and poop in, or whatever terminology you use)."

**Or, pick a potty seat.** If your toddler shows a preference for using a "grown-up" toilet like everyone else in the family, select a potty seat that fits on top of a regular toilet. Good fit is important (a shaky seat can scare a toddler off), and a built-in footrest will give your toddler something to push against when making a bowel movement. You'll also need a sturdy and steady stepping stool (best are those that come with one built in), so

## POTTY PATIENCE, PLEASE

· · · · · · · · · ·

It probably took weeks of false starts and stumbles before your toddler learned how to walk—and chances are, it'll take at least as long (and at least as many false starts and stumbles) before your toddler learns how to stay clean and dry. This new skill will require awareness, concentration, coordination, muscle control, and, of course, split-second timing.

The majority of children begin to start staying clean about the same time they start staying dry. Of the remainder, most learn to control their bowel movements first. Not surprisingly, boys (who need to master control over both the urge and the apparatus) usually lag a bit behind girls in controlling their urination.

A few toddlers (most often older ones) will learn toileting seemingly overnight and very rarely have an accident. Others, particularly those who are innately resistant to change or for whom transitions are difficult (see page 201), may need to take to the toilet-learning process much more gradually. For parents of these children, patience will be particularly crucial to success.

---

that your toddler can get on and off the potty independently.

**Skip the deflector.** A urine deflector, the plastic shield designed to prevent boys on potty seats from accidentally spraying outside the bowl, can cut or scrape a child getting on or off the seat. To avoid a traumatizing "boo-boo," avoid the deflector. But do provide some lessons on controlling the spray; teach boys to push the penis "down" so the urine will flow down and not out (practicing with toilet paper targets in the bowl helps perfect this tricky skill).

**Do some "dry runs."** Before you put the potty to use, help your toddler get to know it (this is particularly important for children who have a hard time with change). Make the potty available for your toddler to carry from room to room, or to sit on while looking at books (preferably "potty" books) or even watching television. Putting the potty in your toddler's control, rather than putting restrictions on its use from the start, will help motivate independent use by promoting a sense of autonomy ("It's *my* potty!"). Once your toddler has started feeling comfortable with the potty, he or she should feel more comfortable about using it for its intended purpose.

**Change the diaper-changing locale.** Start helping your toddler make the association between what's made in diapers and what's made in the potty by changing diapers in the bathroom (if logistics allow and your toddler is willing). Flushing the solid contents of diapers down the toilet will help make that connection even more tangible. (If your toddler is frightened by the flushing sound of the toilet, just dump the contents in and flush later; if he or she seems unduly upset by the dumping alone, postpone this step as well.)

**Decide on a potty vocabulary.** Whether it's pee and poop or urine and BM, potty learning will be easier if the same terms are used by everyone in your home, and if your toddler is familiar with them before the learning process begins. Some experts recommend using the more formal terminology (bowel movement, defecate, urinate) rather than slang or euphemistic terms so that kids won't have to relearn the terms at a later date or be embarrassed by using "babyish" toilet words. But whatever terms you decide are P.C. (potty correct), use them consistently. And never refer to the contents of your toddler's diapers as "smelly," "stinky," "yucky," or in otherwise unfavorable ways. Treat elimination as a natural process, one without negative connotations, and your toddler will, too.

**Encourage "listening" to body signals.** Help your toddler to recognize body signals. Explain how important it is to listen when your body tells you, "I'm hungry," "I'm thirsty," "I'm sleepy," or "I need to make a BM." Catching your toddler "in the act" of filling his or her diaper is another way to focus attention on body signals: "See, when you have to push like that, that means a BM is coming. Soon you'll be able to sit down on the potty to have one." Then, as casually as you always do, change the diaper.

# Go . . .

Your toddler's ready, you're ready, the potty's ready and waiting for action—it's finally time to get down to the business of toilet learning. Though different approaches may work better for different toddlers, the following "do's and don'ts" apply to most:

## *THE DO'S OF TODDLER TOILET LEARNING*

▲ *Do* switch from diapers to training pants—a combination of traditional cotton underpants and disposables works well (see box, page 544). But never insist your toddler wear the pants—merely suggest. Knowing that the diaper is still an option will make him or her feel more in control of (and less threatened by) the potty process.

▲ *Do* bare your toddler's bottom, once in a while. If the temperature permits and there's an area of your home that's completely washable (or if you have a private yard), letting your toddler go bare-bottomed is an ideal way to help him or her get in touch with body signals (without the security of the diaper, the products of excretion are hard to miss). Keep the potty close by (even outdoors, if possible) so that your toddler will be able to act on those signals at a second's notice. To prevent shoes from getting showered, feet should also be bare (except outdoors), or at least clad in washable shoes.

▲ *Do* make the bottom easily accessible when it's not bare. Until your toddler develops the control necessary to "hold it in," there won't be a moment to lose. To make sure one isn't lost to a stubborn snap or a cumbersome clasp, dress your toddler in easy-off, elastic-waist pants that can be pulled down in a flash, avoiding the extra steps involved in dealing with zippers, overalls, buttons, and suspenders. Training pants will be infinitely easier for a toddler to remove than diapers (but make sure they're not so tight that they make for tough tugging).

▲ *Do* watch your toddler closely. At first, you may be more adept at picking up your child's body signals than your

## TRAINING PANTS

Switching from diapers to a combination of cotton and disposable training pants early in the toilet-teaching process puts a toddler in a new grown-up potty mode. Training pants, which can be pulled on or off by the wearer, usually without adult help, put more control in a toddler's hands and improve the odds of getting to the potty on time. In addition, their more grown-up designs are often appealing to the toddler. Cotton training pants have an added plus: Toddlers wearing them feel uncomfortable or messy when they're wet or soiled, and tend to become more aware of their excretory functions than those children still wearing disposable diapers.

It's generally best to start with disposable training pants and then gradually move toward using the traditional training pants full time:

**Disposable training pants.** This hybrid—a cross between diapers and traditional training pants—is the ideal undergarment for the child about to embark on toilet learning. Disposable training pants look like and are worn like training pants but absorb like a diaper—and often make toddlers and parents happier during early toilet learning. They are thrown out rather than laundered (particularly nice when the results of an "accident" are particularly messy), and because they can be removed for changing (by tearing the side panels) without having to be pulled down over legs and shoes, the unpleasant problem of spreading a messy bowel movement is avoided. However, unlike traditional training pants, they don't allow a child to feel a great deal of wetness and so, if used exclusively, may not move learning along.* So once a toddler begins to exhibit some control over excretion, it's best to use disposables only where accidents could cause serious inconvenience (in the car, in stores, at a friend's house, or any place with carpets or other vulnerable surfaces) and to phase them out as control improves.

**Traditional cotton training pants.** Best are the heavy-duty, extra-absorbent type that promise to hold at least a cup of liquid. These can be used at home during the day in lieu of diapers as soon as a toddler has had a few successes on the potty seat (but not before, or your toddler may be unnerved by numerous early accidents). Eventually, when accidents become few and far between, your toddler can wear them full time.

---

*A couple of additional drawbacks: Like ordinary disposable diapers, disposable training pants contribute to our planet's solid waste disposal problem, so they aren't the most environmentally friendly choice. And many preschools and day-care centers insist on regular diapers rather than pull-ups because getting pull-ups on requires removing other clothing (such as pants and shoes), while diapers can be put on with the pants simply pulled down.

---

child is. So keep an eye out for the telltale signs that say, "I gotta go!" Whenever you notice one of them, ask your toddler, "Do you have to go to the potty?" If your toddler seems willing, lead the way to the bathroom, or if you're using a portable, bring the potty to your toddler. Follow through even if it's too late; just reinforcing the connection between the function and the potty is an important step. Of course, if you find that asking your toddler if he or she has to go always elicits an automatic "No," change the wording of the invitation. Try, "Your potty is waiting for you. Let's hurry up and go." And again, head for the potty.

▲ *Do* watch the clock closely. Most children—like most adults—have regular patterns of elimination: They urinate on waking (from a night's sleep or nap), for instance, or have a bowel movement after breakfast. Determine if your toddler has a pattern and try to take advantage of it. Encourage, but never force, your toddler to sit on the potty at the times of day when success is a good bet.

▲ *Do* let your toddler come and go as he or she pleases. If your toddler senses that he or she is being held prisoner on the potty, resistance and rebellion are inevitable. Some children will sit longer if they're read to (again, potty books can be particularly inspirational), others become so distracted by the reading that they forget why they're there. Keep in mind, too, that "command performances" are still difficult for toddlers, and that just because they're sitting doesn't mean they're going to be able to produce. Until they're able to relax the muscles that control bowel and bladder at will, they may be just as likely to go (all over the floor) after they get up as when sitting down.

▲ *Do* have your toddler take turns on the toilet with a drink-and-wet doll. At this age, going to the potty is more fun when you have a partner.

▲ *Do* try a trickle to start the flow. Turn on the bathroom or kitchen faucet while your toddler sits on the potty; it's an old trick but a good one.

▲ *Do* appreciate your child's reporting after the fact as a step in the right direction. Even recognition of body signals that comes belatedly should be considered a success worth crowing about. It takes plenty of practice before young children are able to recognize impending bladder or bowel activity while there's still time to get to a potty. Don't make the mistake of attributing such accidents to spitefulness or insurgence; it's simply inexperience.

▲ *Do* be an enthusiastic audience. Success at the potty should be cheered and widely admired. But don't get so carried away with your accolades that your toddler starts to question the sincerity of your praise. Overdoing the applause for your toddler's successes can also prompt feelings of failure when he or she has an accident.

▲ *Do* spark motivation. Learning is always more successful when the student is motivated. How you choose to motivate will depend on your toddler, as well as on your own philosophies of child-rearing. For some toddlers, being reminded that using the potty is "grownup" and will make them "just like" their parents, siblings, and older friends is motivation enough. Some eager-to-please toddlers will be motivated simply by parental praise; some eager-to-control toddlers will be motivated by discovering that they wield the power over their bodily functions when they use the potty. For still other toddlers, a tangible incentive works best. Most experts agree that rewards can work for one-time developmental achievements such as toilet learning (the child will ultimately continue using the toilet even when the incentives stop). But keep the rewards small—stickers on a calendar (the toddler gets to apply one for each success on the potty), a penny in the piggy bank, a call to Grandma and Grandpa to brag, a pair of fancy or favorite-character underwear—and plan to phase them out as toileting starts coming naturally to your toddler. (See page 422 for more on the pros and cons of rewards.)

▲ *Do* have your toddler check for dryness. Teaching your toddler how to check his or her pants or diaper for dryness will give an added measure of control over the process. Praise dry pants, but don't criticize wet ones.

▲ *Do* bridge the gap between potty and toilet. Illustrate the connection between the potty chair (if that's what you're using) and the toilet your toddler will eventually graduate to by emptying potty contents into the toilet with your toddler's help. Adding some water to the potty bowl will help a bowel movement slide out more easily. (Don't, however, leave water in the potty itself.) If your toddler enjoys flushing the potty's contents away, assign him or her that honor. If not, flush after your child's left the room.

▲ *Do* be patient with relapses. Remember that learning to use the toilet is a big job for little toddlers, but it's not their only job—it's natural for them to "forget" occasionally, even after they've caught on.

▲ *Do* teach about hygiene (see page 551).

▲ *Do* explain your approach to toilet learning to any other adults who care for your child and ask them to stick to the same strategies. Consistency is especially important.

▲ *Do* be sensitive to your child's feelings and needs. Self-confidence and self-esteem are at issue here, too—not just a clean, dry bottom.

# THE DON'TS OF TODDLER TOILET LEARNING

▲ *Don't* expect too much too soon. Most children take several weeks to master potty proficiency—and at first, you can expect as many steps backward as forward. Setting your expectations too high can dampen your child's enthusiasm and damage self-confidence.

▲ *Don't* scold, punish, or shame. Your child sits at length on the potty without results, then stands up and immediately drenches the carpet. Or asks to use the potty every five minutes while you're busy trying to prepare dinner, but doesn't produce even once. Or refuses to go before leaving the house, then soaks the car seat not two minutes out of the driveway. Your frustration will be great, your impulse to take your frustration out on your toddler greater still—yet staying

calm in the face of toileting setbacks is crucial to ultimate success. Remember, for someone just learning, occasional or even frequent misinterpretations of body signals are to be expected; overreacting to lapses can discourage a toddler from future attempts.

▲ *Don't* deny drinks. Though it might seem logical that withholding liquids would make it easier for a toddler to avoid accidents, this practice is unfair, unwise, unhealthy—and ultimately, ineffective. In fact, stepping up fluid intake means that there will be more opportunities for a toddler to use the potty, and thus, more opportunities for success.

▲ *Don't* use unnatural means to get desired ends. Some parents give laxatives, suppositories, or enemas so that a child will have a convenient or timely bowel movement. But not only is this practice unwise (such products should only be used on a physician's recommendation), it is generally unsuccessful. While it might produce the desired results in the short term, it teaches a child nothing about the bowel control essential for the long term.

▲ *Don't* be a broken record. Nagging almost always backfires with toddlers, who don't like to be told what to do once, never mind over and over again. Occasional, casual reminders of the presence of the potty in the room ("Your potty is here waiting for you whenever you're ready") or invitations ("I'm going to go to the bathroom now; you can come, too, if you like") can help keep a toddler on the toileting track, but incessant carping will almost assuredly derail your efforts.

▲ *Don't* force the issue. Never compel your toddler to sit on the potty when he or she's already refused; don't force your child to stay on the potty when he or she is ready to get up (even if you know that an accident is imminent). Besides hampering toilet-learning efforts, forcing a child can lead to straining, constipation, and even anal fissures (see page 600). The process and the product are your toddler's—and your toddler's alone. You can lead the way, but ultimately the reins must be left in his or her hands. (Read: You can lead your toddler to the potty but you can't make him—or her—use it.)

Don't force, but when appropriate, *do* finesse. For example, your toddler is engrossed in watching a video, one hand holding an apple and the other hand on her crotch. Nonchalantly make an offer: "Here—why don't I hold the apple while you take your pants down." Before your toddler has a chance to compute what is going on, she's on the potty and doing what needs to be done.

▲ *Don't* turn toileting into a moral issue. There is no good or bad when it comes to toileting—only ready and not ready. A toddler who's used the potty successfully shouldn't be called "good" any more than one who's had an accident should be called "bad." Labeling a toddler who's had success on the potty "big" or "grown-up" might stroke his or her ego in just the right way, or, in a toddler who's ambivalent about stepping out of babyhood, might trigger potty regression. As a rule, rather than commending the child ("What a good girl you are!"), commend the act ("You did a great job!").

▲ *Don't* discuss progress (or lack of it) in front of your child. Toddlers usually hear—and understand—much more than their parents give them credit for.

▲ *Don't* take slow progress personally. Slow potty learning is neither a reflection on your toddler (late learners are no less bright) or on you (parents of late learners are no less competent). But be sure that you're not impeding your child's natural progress by stepping up the pressure or by ignoring the subject of potty learning entirely.

▲ *Don't* make the bathroom a battleground. Picking fights over pottying will only prolong the struggle. If you meet with *total* resistance, accept that your toddler's not yet ready, and give up for a while—completely. Don't bring the subject up every day, or point out peers who are in underpants, or display anger or hostility when changing diapers. If you meet *occasional* resistance, pretend you don't care, and continue your toilet-teaching program as before.

▲ *Don't* give up hope. The process of toilet learning may seem like it's going to go on forever—but it won't. Even the most resistant will one day decide that going to the potty beats wearing a diaper—and when that happens, toileting will become as routine for your child as it is for you.

# WHEN ACCIDENTS HAPPEN

Accidents are an inevitable part of learning to use the potty—just as falls are an inevitable part of learning to walk. But whether they're occasional or frequent, sincerely accidental or accidentally-on-purpose, the less said about them, the better. Lecturing, threatening, or otherwise making a fuss will only promote resistance in a rebellious toddler and diminish confidence in a reticent one. Punishment is certainly not warranted; just as you would never have thought of punishing your toddler for falling when learning how to walk, neither should you consider punishing your toddler for having an accident when learning how to use the potty. Don't demand an apology (it was an accident, remember) or a confession (unless there's a renegade puppy on the premises, there will be no doubt who did it).

React to an accident as casually as you possibly can. If your child seems upset, be reassuring, "That's okay—you had an accident. No problem. Maybe next time you'll get to the potty in time." Change your toddler's clothes without negative comment and without delay (forcing your child to stay in wet underpants in order to teach "a lesson" is cruel, and will humiliate and/or anger, not motivate). To foster a feeling of self-sufficiency, encourage your toddler to "help" you in the clean-up, if he or she seems willing (but make hand washing afterwards a required part of the process).

## WHY ACCIDENTS HAPPEN

Even when substantial progress is being made at potty learning, accidents happen; and they may happen frequently. But if they're happening with virtually every urination and bowel movement, consider that the timing for toilet learning may not be right and return to diapers for a while (unless your toddler insists on staying with the potty). After all, there's nothing to be gained from premature toilet learning but dirty laundry.

Though lack of readiness is the most common reason for very frequent accidents and very slow progress, there are others:

▲ Stress. Separation anxiety, a new baby-sitter, a move, a new sibling, and family distress can all trigger accidents, even in children who have been clean and dry for a while.

▲ Fatigue. Tired toddlers often have less control over all their skills, toileting included, and they are also more likely to revert to "babyish" behavior.

▲ Excitement. Children often lose control of their bladder when they're excited.

▲ Concentration. Focusing on an exciting activity or on learning a new skill can disrupt some of the concentration a toddler needs to remember to use the potty. Toddlers are more prone to accidents when they're engrossed in an activity.

▲ Parental pressure. A parent's preoccupation with toileting often turns off an independent-minded toddler.

▲ Conflicted feelings. Some children wet themselves frequently because using the potty represents growing up and they don't feel quite ready to give up their status as the "baby" of the family. Others have "accidents" because they're reluctant to cede control to the older generation by doing what they know their parents want them to do most.

▲ Pokiness. Some toddlers have accidents or mini-accidents (they get slightly wet or soiled en route to the potty) because they wait until the last minute and/or are slow in getting their pants down.

▲ Urinary tract infection. Sometimes, a urinary tract infection can make bladder control tricky for a young child. An infection should always be considered in a toddler who's had no success "holding it in" (but seems eager to try) or has had success followed by sudden regression, particularly if other symptoms are present (see page 612).

▲ A physical problem. Though such problems are very rare, it's wise to be on the lookout for signs that point to the possibility of one: The child who is always a little wet (a sign that urine may be leaking), wets when laughing (a sign of "giggle incontinence"), or has a weak urine stream, painful urination, or blood in the urine should be seen by the doctor.

Often, dealing with these causes of accidents (reassuring a stressed child, gently "reminding" a preoccupied one, seeing to it that a tired one gets more rest, treating an infection, and so on) will put toilet learning back on the fast track.

# WHEN AN OLDER CHILD RESISTS

When a toddler two-and-one-half or older shows all the signs of readiness but, after several months of parental effort, still refuses to cooperate in toileting, a parent may feel like it's time to get tough. But, actually, it's much better—at least in the long run—to let up and:

**Turn it over.** Give your child full responsibility for toilet learning. Explain, "It's your BM and your urine, and you can make them on the potty when you want to. If there's anything I can do to help you, just ask me."

**Present choices.** Diapers or training pants, potty or big toilet, now or later. And keep your own opinions to yourself.

**Stop reminding.** As long as your toddler knows the routine, you needn't say a word about it. Anything you do say is bound to be held against you—and to delay potty learning even further.

**Don't talk about it.** Make potty learning a nonissue for a while—don't discuss it with your child or in your child's presence.

**Sweeten the "pot."** Casually (as though it doesn't matter whether your toddler accepts the challenge or not) offer an incentive for success at the potty. If your child chooses stickers on a calendar, he or she can even chart the toileting "successes" of other family members so it seems like everyone's in it together. Of course, if your toddler demands the stickers or the present even when they haven't been earned, or gets extremely upset when a reward isn't forthcoming, you'll have to shelve this strategy.

**Enlist help.** Often, a few words from a neutral authority figure, such as a nurse, doctor, or preschool teacher, are more effective than a thousand from a parent.

**Give it time.** Eventually your toddler will decide it's time to give up diapers. Stop pushing for that time to come, and it will.

---

## 'TIS THE SEASON?

Potty lore has it that summer is the best time (some members of the older generation would say the only time) to start teaching a toddler to use the toilet. And there's undeniably some wisdom to that tradition: A toddler who's dressed lightly (or better still, not dressed at all) has a better shot at making it to the potty in time than a toddler who's decked out in layers of winterwear. But, seasonal considerations should take a back seat to toddler readiness; spring, summer, winter, or fall, the best time to teach a toddler about toileting is when he or she is ready to learn. If your toddler turns out to be ready in the winter, keep the house a little warmer than usual so that he or she can run around lightly clad. The minimum amount of clothing will allow for maximum success with toileting.

# WHAT YOU MAY BE CONCERNED ABOUT

## SWITCHING TO TRAINING PANTS

*"We're about to begin the toileting process with our daughter. Should we switch to training pants right away, or wait a while?"*

Unless your toddler has put in a request for panties, it's probably better not to push training pants just yet. Since accidents are the rule rather than the exception in the early days of the learning process, putting your toddler in training pants before she's experienced some successes may be asking for failure. Accidents in training pants may be uncomfortable and embarrassing for your toddler and may prompt her to abruptly reject both the training pants and the potty-learning process. Switching to training pants too soon will also make a lot of extra housework—cleaning up after accidents not contained by the underwear and then washing the underwear itself. Instead, until your toddler has met with at least some successes, stick with diapers or—when she's in a room where the floor is easily cleaned and impervious to staining, and when indoor temperatures permit—nothing at all covering her bottom.

If, however, your toddler has seen underpants on a friend or a sibling (or on you) and covets them, don't put her off. Toileting is much more likely to be successful if it's self-motivated; if your toddler is motivated by wearing underpants, by all means, let her wear them. As an alternative, you might try disposable pull-up training pants (see page 544).

Whenever you decide it's time to switch from diapers to training pants, it's best to bring them out on a quiet, low-stress day, when you won't have to be leaving the house, and when you'll be able to devote plenty of one-on-one time and attention to your toddler.

## DIAPER REJECTION

*"Even though my son just started using the potty, he's refusing to wear diapers at all—even when we go out he insists on training pants. But he still has lots of accidents, and I don't want him to walk around wetting—or worse—wherever we go."*

Since toileting is almost always more successful if it's the toddler's idea *and* the toddler's responsibility, making yours wear diapers when he's decided it's time to give them up might compromise that success. If he's determined to make toileting work, you should be determined to support him—even if it means putting up with numerous accidents, at home and away.

Reduce the likelihood of accidents by having your toddler use the potty before leaving the house; by limiting prolonged outings, when possible; by being well-versed in the locations of toilet facilities wherever you go; by stashing an inflatable or regular potty chair in the car trunk (if your toddler is accustomed to a potty chair) or tucking a foldable potty seat in your tote bag (if your toddler is accustomed to using a seat on top of a regular toilet); by dressing your toddler in easy-off clothes; by watching your toddler carefully for signs of urinary urgency; and by suggesting a trip to the toilet at frequent intervals. Life during the early, unpredictable stages of potty learning will be less embarrassing, and

## HYGIENE HYPE

• • • • • • • • • •

There's more to toilet learning than learning to use the toilet. Learning what to do after using the toilet is also important. Get your toddler started now on a lifetime of good bathroom hygiene:

▲ Teach girls to wipe from front to back, to prevent the transfer of bacteria from the anus into the vaginal area, where they could cause infection.

▲ Encourage gentle wiping; rough wiping can irritate sensitive skin and open it up to infection.

▲ Include hand washing in the potty routine. Even if you do the wiping for your toddler, both of you should wash your hands after each toilet use. That way, hand washing will become a habit by the time your toddler takes over the wiping.

▲ Encourage particular care in public toilets. Before sitting on a public toilet (even if it looks clean and dry, there could be lingering germs), be sure to cover it with a paper seat cover or toilet tissue; tell your toddler never to sit on a strange seat without covering it. Also encourage your child to flush using a piece of toilet tissue in order to avoid picking up germs from the flusher. When the roll of toilet paper has been lying on a dirty floor, unroll and dispose of the squares that were exposed before using it.

less stressful, if you avoid (as much as is practical) restaurants, stores, homes, and any other destinations where floors are covered with expensive carpeting or where the only seating is upholstered. When you can't avoid such a destination, insist your toddler wear disposable training pants, just for the occasion.

Make accidents that do happen less traumatic by outfitting your toddler in extra-absorbent training pants (possibly with a disposable night liner, if your child will agree) and always toting along at least one complete change of clothing (including shoes and socks), a good supply of diaper wipes, and several absorbent paper towels (for wiping up the mess). And when your toddler wets or messes, even if it's at an inopportune time and in an inopportune place, don't scold, chide, or say I-told-you-so ("See, you should have worn a diaper!"). Just clean him up quickly and calmly, and hope for better luck next time.

Of course, if your toddler never makes it to the potty on time, makes no attempt to tell you he has to go, and seems oblivious to his excretory functions, tell him he will have to wear disposable training pants until he's ready to go on the potty. This compromise may keep everyone happy.

## WIPING WRANGLES

*"My daughter refuses to let me wipe her after she uses the potty. But she doesn't do a very good job of it herself. What can I do?"*

Fighting a power-hungry toddler for control of the toilet paper can only result in mutiny on the potty. Forced to submit to your wiping, your toddler might well decide to withhold her newly learned toileting skill altogether—in other words, if she can't do it herself, it's possible she'd rather not do it at all.

Instead, try showing her the right way to wipe (see above box for a description of hygienic wiping technique) by demonstrating on a washable-wipeable doll (dab a little oatmeal or jelly on the doll's bottom, so your toddler can see how it needs to be wiped until the tissue comes up clean). Then have her practice on the doll, under your tutelage.

Really proficient wiping may be several years away at least. In the meantime, periodically ask your toddler if you can "check" her work after she's finished wiping, or even if you can get the last wipe in. If she lets you examine her work, make sure you praise it even if you find it less than perfect. If she refuses to let you get your wipes in, drop the issue without a fuss. You can always clean up her act at bath time.

## FEAR OF FLUSHING

*"Our son has just started using the toilet, but he seems terrified every time it flushes. I'm afraid this fear is going to sabotage his toilet learning."*

That's a valid concern. Many a toilet-learning experience has been sabotaged by a fear of flushing. But such sabotage can be averted if the child's fears are respected.

First of all, keep in mind that forcing a toddler to confront a fear of flushing (or any other fear) won't help him overcome it; coercion may even help turn a fear into a phobia (see page 211). So, for now, hold the flushing until your toddler is out of the bathroom. Then gradually try to acclimate him to the sound of the toilet flushing from a distance. Flush the toilet while he's in the next room, where he can hear but not see the event. When that no longer panics him, try holding him in the bathroom doorway while someone else flushes. When he accepts that, try flushing with him in your arms. When he's ready, let

him try pulling the lever himself.

Sometimes it isn't a fear of flushing that upsets a toddler but a fear of losing a part of himself when the stool goes down the drain. In this case, too, it's probably a good idea to flush when your toddler leaves the bathroom and has become occupied with something else. Sometimes waving goodbye to the stool before flushing makes the separation easier. Or it may help to practice flushing toilet tissue down the drain (don't try it with anything that doesn't belong in a toilet, however, because your toddler may decide it's a game that he loves to play—with keys, receipts, gloves, toys).

## WHEN TO TAKE A STAND

*"We just taught our son how to urinate sitting down, and he's pretty good at it. But when will it be time for him to start standing up?"*

If your toddler's just getting the hang of sitting down to urinate, don't rush him into taking a stand. Instituting this change prematurely often leads to confusion and, with not enough sitting time on the potty, to constipation as well. So let a sitting boy sit until basic toilet skills are fairly well-mastered.

The art of urinating in an upright position is a tricky one, requiring a great deal of coordination to direct the penis towards and the flow of urine into the toilet. It's best, if possible, for instruction to come from Dad (the parent with first-hand experience), or another older male, who can pass on some man-to-man tips and even provide a demonstration or two.

Expecting a little boy to stand and aim for the small bowl of a potty chair is asking for trouble. So if yours has been using a potty chair, he will have to become comfortable using the big toilet before trying to stand and deliver. Once that's accomplished, you can start seating him backwards, facing the back of the toilet (the direction he will face when he finally does stand up). In this position, he can sharpen his aim while still in close proximity to his target. Challenging him to "sink" toilet paper "boats" with his stream can make target practice even more fun.[1]

When your child has developed good control over his aim from a sitting position (or sooner if he's noticed his father, an older sibling, or a friend standing to urinate and is eager to rise to the occasion himself), let him try standing. He'll have to stand on a stepstool (some potty seats have steps attached) to get the height he'll need, but make sure it's steady so he doesn't fall off (or in). With your help, have him direct his penis toward the drain hole in the bottom of the toilet; he can also continue trying to sink toilet tissue or other targets for extra practice. You can expect some of the flow to miss its mark, especially if he rejects assistance. It will take plenty of practice—and possibly a year or more—before the floors and walls around the toilet bowl will be free from splashes. In the meantime, be generous with the praise, be patient . . . and keep the spray cleaner handy.

## THE MOVABLE POTTY CHAIR

*"Our son wants to take the potty chair from room to room all day long—he seems to want it with him at all times. Should we make him keep it in the bathroom, so he'll get used to using it in the right place?"*

**A**ny place is the right place, right now. It doesn't matter where your toddler uses the potty chair, just that he uses it—and that he feels good about using it. During potty learning, a friendly, unfettered relationship with the potty is essential; if too many rules and restrictions are attached to the potty, a child may balk at using it.

Eventually, your toddler will graduate to the toilet, which, happily, isn't portable. For now, let the potty perambulations continue.

## A GIRL WHO WANTS TO STAND

*"Ever since our daughter saw her older brother standing up to urinate, she's wanted to do the same. We've tried to explain to her that it won't work, but she's insistent."*

**A**t one time or another, many young children become fascinated by how the other half urinates. Boys who've learned to stand may question why they shouldn't sit; girls who've learned to sit may question why they shouldn't stand. The best person to help a girl who wants to stand is her mother, since she also sits rather than stands.

Explain the reasons for the sitting/standing policy (a boy's stream aims out, a girl's stream aims down), point out the benefits of sitting (girls get to rest and they can make a BM and pee at the same time), and illustrate by example (take her into the bathroom and show her that you always urinate sitting down, too). You can also let her sit on the toilet facing backwards, if that makes her happy.

---

1. Fun targets for toilet training are available through some children's catalogs, or you can make some simple, geometric tissue-paper shapes at home. Just be certain the paper you use is flushable.

These techniques may help, but then again they may not. Sometimes a toddler's curiosity can only be satisfied by learning the hard way. If it comes to that, protect the bathroom floor, remove your toddler's shoes, socks, and below-the-belt clothing, have clean-up supplies at the ready, and give your daughter a shot at urinating standing up.

The experience is not likely to be a comfortable one; with the sensation of urine flowing down her legs fresh in her memory, your toddler may well accept that standing up isn't practical for her. Even if she insists on trying again, and perhaps again, her curiosity should soon be satisfied and start wandering in another direction.

## FASCINATION WITH STOOL

*"We were thrilled when our son started using the potty, until we discovered him smearing his stool all over the walls."*

To an adult, a bowel movement is a bowel movement—the more quickly disposed of, the better. To some toddlers, on the other hand, a bowel movement is a remarkable personal statement, a crowning achievement, something to celebrate, revel in, and if the spirit so moves them, decorate with.

Of course, there's no question who will have to come around to whose way of thinking. For many reasons (hygiene chief among them), you will have to make it clear to your toddler that handling the contents of the potty is not acceptable, that his "stool is not to play with—it belongs in the potty and must stay there until it's dumped in the toilet." But don't scold or make him feel bad or guilty about what he's done (remember, in his mind he's done something great, not

something naughty)—and do your best to keep your cool. The more matter-of-fact your reaction, the more likely your toddler will accept your pronouncement.

Once you've cleaned him up, set him up with a more acceptable creative tactile endeavor, such as finger painting, while you clean up the rest of the mess he made. To prevent repeats, keep a close eye on him when he's using the potty in the future, and dump the contents—or ask him to dump them, if he likes—as soon as he's finished. If that's practical, you could also consider switching him to the toilet.

## SWITCHING TO THE TOILET

*"We started out using the potty chair for our daughter, and she's been pretty successful at it so far. The question is, when should we switch over to the regular toilet?"*

It's more important that your toddler feel secure where she sits than that she move up to the next level of toileting—and most toddlers feel more secure on a low potty chair than on what, to them, is a towering toilet. So wait until your toddler shows some interest in switching over; if she doesn't develop such an interest spontaneously, try to nurture it by having her accompany you on your trips to the bathroom, and occasionally asking her, casually, of course, if she'd like to try using the "grown-up" potty. Buying a child's seat that fits onto the regular toilet seat, and showing her it's available when she's ready, may make the transition more appealing. And getting a seat with an attached stepladder or setting up a small stepstool in front of the toilet may make the big toilet less intimidating and give your toddler a greater sense of control.

# A NEW DIAPER RASH AT NIGHT

*"Our son never had trouble with diaper rash when he was wearing diapers all day. Now that he wears them only at night, he's waking up with a very sore bottom. Why?"*

Some infant bottoms grow accustomed to the acidic assault of urine and build up a certain amount of immunity to diaper rash (although others, of course, seem to be chronically inflamed). Once the bottom gets used to being in dry underpants all day long, it can lose that degree of immunity and become more sensitive to the nightly soakings. Also, because your toddler now tends to "hold in" the urine longer, it becomes more concentrated, and thus, more irritating, when it's finally released. Once he's able to stay dry at night, this diaper rash will be a thing of the past. In the meantime, treat it as you would any diaper rash (see page 470).

# A DIAPER FOR BOWEL MOVEMENTS

*"Our daughter has been using the potty when she urinates for several months now, but she insists on a diaper for a bowel movement. Should we keep letting her?"*

Yes, for the time being. If you make an issue out of it, not only will you get involved in a power struggle you can't win, but your toddler could end up with a serious case of constipation. When she asks for a diaper for her BM, offer her a chance to go on the potty instead; if she refuses, hand over the diaper. With no pressure, but plenty of opportunity, your toddler will eventually come around—especially once all her friends are completely out of diapers.

# TOILET LEARNING AND PRESCHOOL

*"We're thinking of putting our two-year-old son in a half-day nursery school program in the fall, but he's still in diapers. Should we step up the training?"*

With children entering nursery school programs at an earlier age these days—much earlier than many graduate to the potty—some schools are more tolerant of diapered toddlers than they used to be. Check out the programs in your neighborhood to see if any will accept your son in diapers and if they're willing to cooperate in his toilet learning when he's ready to begin it. If there is no such program, you have two choices: You can postpone your child's formal education until his toileting education is complete or you can set the potty-learning process in motion as described earlier in this chapter. Though the first option may be preferable from the point of view of toilet teaching, it may not be feasible if you have to go back to work and do not have an at-home caregiver.

If that's the situation, then your only choice is to step up the toilet teaching. It's also a good choice if your child is showing many of the signs of readiness described on page 540. If you keep pressure to a minimum (which won't be easy with the stakes so high, but is nevertheless vital to the success of the endeavor), put the major responsibility in your child's hands, and offer some incentives (see page 545), there's a good chance your toddler will become potty proficient over the next few months. But don't tell him that he can't go to school unless he starts acting "like a big boy"—this may not only make him more resistant to toilet learning, but resistant to going to school as well.

## STAYING DRY AT NIGHT

*"Our toddler is nearly three and has been staying clean and dry during the day since he was two and a half. But he still wakes up in the morning sopping wet."*

Staying dry during the day—challenging though it may be—is still much easier for most toddlers than staying dry at night. Many are not yet developmentally ready to hold their urine for ten or twelve hours or to wake up in response to the bladder's signal that it is full. While some toddlers automatically begin to stay dry at night once they've mastered staying dry during the day, the majority don't. And since that's normal, nighttime training isn't recommended at this age.

If at any point your toddler begins to regularly wake up dry, you can dispense with the nighttime diaper. Otherwise, don't begin a concerted campaign to teach your toddler to stay dry at night—it's far too early to intervene. If nighttime wetting is still a problem when your child is five years old, offering incentives may be enough to help help him gain nighttime control. When it's not, incentives can be used in combination with other measures (such as an alarm that goes off each time a child begins to wet, eventually conditioning him to wake when his bladder is full).

# CHAPTER TWENTY

# *Keeping Your Toddler Healthy*

**N**obody likes being sick, but nobody hates it quite as much as a toddler. While we adults might secretly relish a day or two of hooky from work or other responsibilities—a chance to curl up in bed with a fat novel or a pile of magazines, to cuddle under a comforter in front of the television with nothing more pressing to attend to than a stuffy nose and the TV remote—young children lack the patience to be good patients. With characteristic obstinacy, toddlers dislike both the symptoms *and* the cures when they're sick; lying still and taking medicine certainly are not their strong suits.

Because when your toddler suffers, you suffer, you have yet another incentive for keeping your toddler healthy, and—when that proves impossible—for treating illness promptly and effectively. This chapter, which describes the most common early childhood illnesses and their treatment and provides information and tips on immunization, fever, calling the doctor, and making the medicine go down, will help.

## IMMUNIZATION: PREVENTING MAJOR COMMUNICABLE DISEASES

**I**n our grandparents' generation, childhood was a risky business. A child born near the turn of the century was lucky to escape falling victim to one or another of the *then* very common and potentially deadly or disabling infectious

# *WHAT YOU SHOULD KNOW ABOUT DTP*

. . . . . . . . . .

## Common Reactions to DTP

The following reactions to DTP are listed in order of frequency. The first three are the most common, and occur in about half of immunized children. Reactions, which generally last only a day or two, are less common when DTaP (with the new acellular pertussis vaccine component) is given.

▲ Pain at the injection site.

▲ Mild to moderate fever (100°F to 104°F [37.8°C to 40°C], rectally).

▲ Fussiness.

▲ Swelling at the site.

▲ Redness at the site.

▲ Drowsiness.

▲ Loss of appetite.

▲ Vomiting.

It is often recommended (particularly when a child has had febrile seizures) that acetaminophen be given just before or just after the immunization to minimize the development of fever and pain. Warm compresses on the injection site may also help to

reduce discomfort. Fever and local soreness may be more of a problem with each subsequent dose of DTP, while fussiness and vomiting may be less so.

## When to Call the Doctor Following DTP

If your toddler exhibits any of the following signs or symptoms within 48 hours of a DTP injection, call the doctor's office, not just for your toddler's sake, but also so that the response can be reported to the Monitoring System for Adverse Events Following Immunization at the Centers for Disease Control.

▲ Persistent crying for more than three hours (probably related to a painful local reaction).

▲ Excessive sleepiness (child may be difficult to wake).

▲ Unusual limpness, paleness, or bluish tinge to skin.

▲ Rectal temperature of 104°F (40°C) or higher.

▲ Convulsions (probably due to the vaccine-induced fever).

---

diseases, including diphtheria, typhoid fever, smallpox, measles, whooping cough, and polio. Today, these diseases—of which parents once lived in dread—are extremely rare in developed countries. Thanks to immunization.[1]

But children are not completely protected against these diseases, even if they've gone through the recommended series of immunizations during the first year of life, until they receive their toddler doses. To safeguard your child, see that he or she is immunized according to the program recommended by the American Academy of Pediatrics (AAP).

# *REQUIRED IMMUNIZATIONS*

. . . . . . . . . . . . . . . . . . . . . . . . . . . .

Children are presently immunized against the following (for the recommended schedule, see page 561):[2]

**DTP (or DTaP).** A reinforcing dose of a combination of diphtheria and tetanus

---

1. For immunization information for travelers, see page 250.

2. If you have any fears about vaccine safety, discuss them with your child's doctor; also see page 563.

### When to Omit the Pertussis Vaccine

The AAP recommends that children who experienced either of the following reactions after a previous DTP injection *not* be given the pertussis vaccine subsequently. Instead, DT, which contains just the diphtheria-tetanus toxoids, should be substituted:

▲ An allergic reaction (with swelling of the mouth, throat, or face, or difficulty breathing) within hours of the shot.

▲ Signs of brain inflammation within seven days, such as alterations in consciousness (including unresponsiveness), or seizures that persist more than a few hours.

The pertussis vaccine is also not generally recommended for a child taking medication (such as cortisone, prednisone, or certain anticancer drugs), or undergoing treatment such as radiation therapy that lowers the body's resistance to infection or with a history of non-febrile convulsions or seizures or suspected neurological disease (such as epilepsy), unless or until such disease has been ruled out. In some circumstances, when the disease is well under control, the pertussis vaccine may be given to a child with neurological disease.

The pertussis component may also be withheld on a case-by-case basis after a consultation between parents and doctor, when a child has experienced any of the following with a previous DTP.

**Within 48 hours:**

▲  A temperature of 104.9°F (40.5°C) or higher, unexplained by any other cause.

▲ Uncharacteristically persistent crying for more than three hours.

▲ Shock-like symptoms (excessive sleepiness, unresponsiveness, limpness, unusual paleness, or bluish tinge to the skin).

**Within 3 days:**

▲ Convulsions, with or without fever.

Policies for the administration of DTP vary slightly from doctor to doctor, so you should discuss any concerns you may have with your child's physician. Most will postpone the vaccination for a child who has a fever (many for as long as a month); some will do so even for a child with a mild cold. Vaccination is generally not postponed if a child suffers from frequent nasal congestion that has been traced to allergy rather than infection.

During an epidemic, even children in high-risk categories may be immunized with DTP, since the risk from whooping cough itself far outweighs any theoretical risk from the vaccine.

---

toxoids and pertussis (whooping cough) vaccine at fifteen months and a booster dose at four to six years are critical to assure that your child develops immunity to these dangerous, often fatal illnesses. If your child did not experience any serious reactions to earlier DTP immunizations (see above box), it's unlikely that there will be a serious reaction to the toddler dose. The use of an acellular pertussis vaccine, which has fewer adverse reactions than the whole-cell vaccine used previously, now licensed for use on children fifteen months to six years of age (but not on infants), is expected to make a reaction even less likely. This vaccine in combination with diphtheria and tetanus toxoids has been labeled DTaP.

**HbOC-DTP.** A combination vaccine, which protects children against hepatitis B (with an oligosaccharide conjugate vaccine) as well as diphtheria, tetanus, and pertussis (with DTP) is now available. HbOC-DTP can be used at two, four, six, and fifteen months, or just for the first three shots, with DTaP and a separate HbCV being substituted for the fourth. The plus for parents, professionals, and es-

---

## DON'T MISS AN OPPORTUNITY

··········

A recent study found that children often miss their immunizations accidentally. A fourteen-month-old is sick, his parents take him to the doctor, he's treated and recovers quickly. The parents think, "Well, the doctor saw Cory last month. I guess we don't have to take him to that fifteen-month checkup." And so the scheduled immunizations are inadvertently missed. Don't let *your* toddler miss an opportunity to be immunized. Keep to the regular well-child checkup schedule, no matter how many sick visits there are in between.

---

pecially toddlers of combining vaccines: fewer bouts with a hypodermic needle.

**Measles, mumps, rubella (MMR).** Like DTP, MMR saves lives and protects health. Measles is a serious disease with potentially fatal complications. While mumps (an inflammation of the parotid gland, also called parotitis) does not usually present a serious threat in childhood, it can have serious consequences (such as sterility or deafness) in male teens or adults. Early immunization prevents not only these future problems, but the spread of the disease from young children to unimmunized adult males. Rubella, also known as German measles, is often so mild that its symptoms are missed. But because it can cause birth defects in the fetus of an infected pregnant woman, immunization in infancy is recommended—both to protect the future fetuses of girl babies and to reduce the risk of infected children exposing their pregnant mothers. MMR vaccine is now given between twelve and fifteen months. There are differing opinions on whether a child who is immunized between twelve and fourteen months needs a booster later; a child who gets a first MMR at fifteen months probably does not.

Reactions to the MMR vaccine are fairly common and generally very mild; they usually don't occur until a week or two after the shot. About 1 in 5 children develops a rash or slight fever lasting a few days, from the measles component.

About 1 in 7 will develop a rash or some swelling of the neck glands, and 1 in 20, aching or swelling of the joints, persisting up to three weeks after the shot, from the rubella component. Occasionally, there is swelling of the salivary glands from the mumps component. Much less common are tingling, numbness, or pain in the hands and feet (all difficult to discern in toddlers), and allergic reactions (see below).

The MMR vaccination should be postponed when a child has a fever. Recent research suggests that it should also be postponed for a mild cold, since a cold seems to interfere with the manufacture of the necessary antibodies to the measles virus. Caution should be taken, too, in administering the vaccine to a child with leukemia, lymphoma, or any other disease that lowers the body's resistance to infection; to one taking a drug that lowers resistance; or to one who has received gamma globulin within the preceding three months. The vaccine could also be dangerous to those who have had an allergic reaction to eggs or to an antibiotic called neomycin that was severe enough to require medical treatment. (Such children can be vaccinated if skin tests with dilute MMR are negative; if skin tests are positive, the vaccine can usually be safely administered in graduated doses.)

**Oral polio vaccine (OPV).** This vaccine has been saving lives and preventing permanent crippling of children for more than thirty years; there have been fewer than a dozen cases of polio a year in the U.S. since widespread immunization was instituted. OPV is usually given at two and four months and then again anytime between six and eighteen months. A fourth dose is recommended between four and six years, before a child begins school.

The vaccine has proven to be quite safe and children rarely have any adverse reactions to it. There is a minuscule risk (about 1 in 8.7 million) of paralysis and a slightly greater (about 1 in 5 million) risk that a susceptible parent or other house-hold member (one who has a suppressed immune system, for example) might con-tract polio from handling the recently immunized child's feces or vomitus.

Administration of live Oral Polio Vaccine is usually postponed for chil-dren ill with anything more serious than a cold. It should not be given to children with cancer, with immune systems that are either naturally deficient or sup-pressed by illness or medical treatment, or who live with someone whose im-mune system is compromised. For these children, an injectable, inactivated polio vaccine (IPV), which goes right into the bloodstream (instead of through the di-

## *AAP IMMUNIZATION RECOMMENDATIONS*

**A**ges are approximate; in some cases, vaccines may be combined. When a vac-cination is delayed, the schedule may vary from these recommendations.

| AGE | DTP | Td | OPV | MMR | Hib | HBV | VZV††† |
|---|---|---|---|---|---|---|---|
| Birth | | | | | | x** | |
| 1 to 2 months | | | | | | x | |
| 2 months | x* | | x* | | x | | |
| 4 months | x | | x | | x | | |
| 6 months | x | | | | x*** | | |
| 6 to 18 months | | | x | | | x | |
| 12 to 15 months | | | | x | x | | |
| 15 to 18 months | x**** | | | | | | |
| 4 to 6 years | x**** | | x | | | | |
| 11 to 12 years | | | | x† | | | |
| 14 to 16 years | | x†† | | | | | |

*May be given earlier during outbreaks. **HBV may be given at 0 to 2 months, and 4 months instead. ***Some Hib vaccines do not require this dose. ****Or DTaP. †Unless two doses were given after the first birthday. ††Given every 10 years through-out life. †††Varicella zoster vaccine; not yet approved for use in healthy children.

gestive tract) should eliminate the risk. As an extra precaution in high-risk homes, meticulous care should be taken in cleaning up the vaccinated child after a bowel movement or after vomiting; the same care should be taken to wash the hands.

**Hemophilus influenzae b (Hib) vaccine.** This conjugate Hib vaccine (HbCV) protects against deadly *Hemophilus influenzae b* bacteria (which has nothing to do with the *influenza virus*) which can cause a wide range of very serious infections in infants and young children, including: meningitis, epiglottitis (the inflamed epiglottis obstructs the airways), septicemia (blood "poisoning"), cellulitis (a skin and connective tissue infection), osteomyelitis (bone inflammation), and pericarditis (an infection of the membrane surrounding the heart). The incidence of Hib infection has dropped dramatically since routine vaccination was instituted in 1990. Your toddler probably was vaccinated at two, four, and six months (or just two and four months, depending on the brand of vaccine), and will get a fourth dose between twelve and fifteen months. A child who hasn't been immunized by a year, will probably be given two doses of Hib vaccine between twelve and fourteen months; a child still unimmunized at fifteen months will probably get just one dose.

The Hib vaccine should not be given to a child who is ill with anything more than a mild cold, or who might be allergic to any of its components (check with the doctor). Though adverse reactions are rare, a very small percentage of children may experience fever, redness and/ or tenderness at the site of the shot, and/or diarrhea, vomiting, or excessive crying after receiving it.

**Varicella zoster vaccine (VZV).** Varicella, or chicken pox, is usually a mild disease without serious side effects in children (adults, especially pregnant women, are at greater risk). About 2% of children develop a secondary skin infection (usually impetigo), and occasionally (1 or 2 cases in 1,000) there can be serious complications, such as Reye syndrome or bacterial infections. Fatalities are rare and occur mostly in high-risk children (such as those with leukemia or immune deficiencies) and those born with chicken pox contracted just prior to birth. But the cost of the disease is nevertheless high in terms of medical expense, lost wages (for parents who must stay home with sick children), and lost school days. For this reason, the FDA is considering licensing the varicella vaccine, presently available for use in high-risk children, for use in healthy children. The expected recommendation: All children routinely receive one dose of the varicella vaccine some time between twelve and eighteen months. Those between eighteen months and thirteen years who have not had chicken pox and have not been immunized should also be vaccinated against the disease with a single dose.

The side effects of the vaccine in children are minimal: sometimes low-grade fever; local pain, reddening, itching, hardening, or rash, or a rash elsewhere on the body. A small percentage of children who are vaccinated are not completely protected, and when exposed, do come down with a modified case of chicken pox, with very few lesions. A booster may be needed between ages seven and nine for those who receive their first VZV in early childhood, but this isn't yet certain.

**Influenza.** Vaccinations against influenza are developed anew each year, based on the educated guesses of epidemiologists and scientists as to which influenza viruses are likely to strike. Flu shots do not offer long-term protection; an individual must be reimmunized each year. The shots are not a guarantee that no flu will strike, just a protection against the predicted main virus strain.

## IF YOU'VE CHOSEN NOT TO IMMUNIZE

· · · · · · · · · ·

In order for immunization to completely wipe out the diseases that once wiped out thousands of children a year here—and are still taking millions of young lives around the world—it must be universal. Every child who can safely be immunized must be.

So if you haven't yet had your toddler immunized because you're afraid that these shots might be harmful, please reconsider. The body of evidence indicates that, for normal, healthy children there is *no* serious risk and very substantial benefit to immunization. It isn't even clear that the few isolated incidents of serious or fatal reactions attributed to vaccines were actually due to the vaccines themselves.

With the risk low and the benefits enormous, it makes sense to see your toddler's doctor for a schedule of "catch-up" immunizations now. Also see about completing your child's schedule of immunizations if they were interrupted at some point for any reason.

---

Flu shots are not routinely recommended for healthy children (although they are safe and are available at parental request). They are, however, recommended for those who are at high risk (including those with chronic lung diseases, such as asthma, cystic fibrosis, or bronchopulmonary dysplasia; children with certain types of cardiac disease; those who are HIV positive or who are receiving immunosuppressive therapy, and those with blood disorders). It may also be recommended for those with chronic kidney or metabolic disorders or diabetes, or those on long-term aspirin therapy. (When flu shots aren't feasible, high-risk children can often be protected by the use of a prophylactic (preventive) dose of an antiviral drug.)

Children are generally given a split-virus vaccine; there are few side effects (possibly a low-grade fever and achy muscles for a day or so). Best time to immunize: mid-October to mid-November. Postpone immunization when a child has a respiratory infection, and because the vaccine is cultured in chicken eggs, don't give flu shots at all if the child is allergic to eggs. A flu shot should not be given to your toddler within three days of a DTP shot.

**Hepatitis B vaccine (HBV).** HBV protects against the hepatitis B virus, which is rare in children but which can become chronic and even lead to cancer in adults. Since immunization of adults has failed, it is recommended that all children be immunized against hepatitis B, usually in the first year. If a child did not receive the full series before age one, HBV will be given between twelve and eighteen months.

**Rabies.** Both human rabies immune globulin (HRIG) and rabies vaccine are available; both are reserved for use when there has been an exposure (by bite, scratch, even lick) to a rabid, or possibly rabid, animal (see page 660).

**Other vaccines.** Vaccines to protect against a wide range of other childhood diseases are being tested or are en route to being adopted. As they are approved, health-care providers, parents, and public-health policymakers will have to decide which should be given routinely and which should be given only to those at high risk or during high-risk situations. The conditions aimed at include: *Hepatitis A virus.* A vaccine for HAV (a seldom fatal form of hepatitis; it does not become chronic but, because it can last six to ten weeks, does take a major toll) is presently being tested. Until it's available, immunoglobulin should be given within two weeks of the exposure to children known to have been exposed to HAV through close contact. *Pneumococcal pneumonia.* A vaccine to prevent this serious disease is available to high-risk adults but is effective in only some (primarily those with diabetes and coronary disease); it isn't effective in those with blood, liver, or kidney diseases, or in children. Work is progressing on a conjugate pneumococcal vaccine that holds out promise for prevention in infants and children. *Lyme disease.* Vaccines are in the process of development both for humans and for the animals that carry the ticks that spread the disease. Until it is available, it is important to take other protective measures (see page 649). *Respiratory syncytial virus (RSV).* This virus is the major cause of respiratory illness in children, and efforts to develop a vaccine are under way. Presently, giving immune globulin (RSV-Ig) during the RSV season (December through April) to children with chronic illnesses that make them more vulnerable to serious RSV infections appears to reduce their risk. *Human immunodeficiency virus (HIV).* Though scientists are hard at work, a vaccine for HIV, which causes the acquired immunodeficiency syndrome, or AIDS, appears to be a long way off.[3] *Tuberculosis.* Vaccination with bacille Calmette-Guérin (BCG) is commonly used in many countries, but—partly because of questions about its efficacy—is used infrequently in the United States. It may be recommended for a child living in a household with individuals who have tested positive for TB but are not

being treated, are being ineffectively treated, or are infected with a drug-resistant strain. It may also be recommended for children living in areas where TB is prevalent. It is not given when a child has a serious burn, skin infection, or a suppressed immune system. *One-shot protection.* On the not too distant horizon is the prospect of a single-dose vaccine, given in infancy, that will protect against all the major childhood diseases.

## BEFORE YOUR CHILD IS IMMUNIZED

Though immunization is basically a safe procedure, it is safer when both parents and professionals take appropriate precautions:

▲ Remind your child's doctor about any previous reactions to earlier vaccinations.

▲ Be sure your child receives a checkup before an immunization to be certain no illness is present that isn't yet apparent. If your child has been showing any signs of illness, inform the doctor.

▲ Observe your child closely for 72 hours after the vaccination (and especially during the first 48), and report severe reactions to the doctor immediately (see page 558). Be on the lookout for a delayed reaction a week or two following an MMR (these are rare). Note any reactions in your child's immunization or health record.

▲ See that the doctor or nurse enters the vaccine manufacturer's name and the vaccine lot/batch number in your child's chart, along with any reactions you report. Bring along your child's immunization record (see page 870) to every checkup so that it can be updated.

▲ Be sure that severe reactions are reported to the Centers for Disease Control in Atlanta.

---

3. Children who are HIV-positive or who have AIDS have a slightly modified childhood immunization program (your toddler's doctor can advise you).

If you believe your child may have been harmed by any vaccine, contact the Vaccine Injury Compensation Program (302-443-6593) for information. This government program protects both those who produce vaccine and those who receive it.

# THE DOCTOR AND THE TODDLER

## THE PARENT– PHYSICIAN PARTNERSHIP

The days when doctors always knew best, when the black bag carried not only a stethoscope and syringes but an aura of unquestioned authority, when patients were seen but rarely heard, are gone. The concept of the physician as more-than-mere-mortal is as outdated as routine tonsillectomies. Today, it is widely recognized that the responsibility for patient well-being doesn't rest in the hands of doctors alone, but that good health and good health care depend on a cooperative partnership between those who provide the care and those who receive it.

But when the recipient of that care is just a year or two old, there's another partnership that's at least as important as the one between patient and physician, and that's the one between the patient's parent and the physician. Parents and doctors must work together to protect the health of children, to keep them safe, and to teach them good health habits, while grooming them to become working members of such a partnership in the future.

As in any good partnership, each partner in the parent–physician partnership brings to it what he or she does best. The doctor contributes invaluable technical medical expertise; parents contribute invaluable insight into their children, illumination that can come only from living with them day in and day out. Parents are also in charge of daily health care, accident prevention, and the teaching (and modeling) of good habits, which, in many ways, makes their role the more critical one.

To make sure that your health-care partnership is serving your toddler's health well:

**Choose the right partner.** The right physician will be willing to work with you to provide your child with the best health care possible. Besides being qualified (certified in pediatrics or family medicine, affiliated with a respected hospital) and having a convenient office location and office hours, he or she should be responsive, empathetic, and accessible—willing to listen to your concerns, encourage your questions (in addition to asking plenty of his or her own), offer easy-to-understand explanations, and not begrudge the extra time that may be necessary to do all of this. And, of course, the right doctor for your child will also be good with children.

Hopefully, you've already found the right physician (or group of physicians, or group of physicians and nurse-practitioners). If you haven't, or you're not sure the parent–provider partnership you're in presently is working well, see Looking for Dr. Right (page 569).

**Give and take philosophies.** Though a partnership usually works better if all partners have similar philosophies, it's unlikely that you and your child's doctor will agree on every issue. Nevertheless, it's important to have some meeting of the minds. In discussions about child care, discipline, nutrition, weaning, the use of antibiotics, the use of comfort objects, the family bed, and other child-rearing topics of concern, express your opinions, then listen to the doctor's. Everyone stands to learn something when there's an open exchange of ideas. If after such an exchange, you find you disagree on most issues, consider finding another provider.

**Agree on protocol.** If more than one individual practitioner is involved in the practice, who will see your toddler at regular checkups? Who will see your toddler when he or she is sick? Will you be able to schedule appointments with the doctor of your choice, or does scheduling depend on availability? Other questions to ask: Should you call in the middle of the night if your toddler runs a fever, or wait until morning? Should you call only during designated call hours, or can you call any time during the day? Will the doctor make a house call when the situation warrants? What should you do in an emergency? Should you go right to the emergency room? Which one? Should you call the doctor to say you're on your way? What if your child's doctor isn't available—who provides backup coverage?

**Always be prepared.** Keep a health history (beginning on page 870) in which you record illnesses, immunizations, developmental milestones, as well as questions, concerns, and observations (regarding your toddler's health, development, eating and sleeping habits, and so on). Remember to bring it to each appointment, and to have it handy when you make a call to the doctor. When your toddler isn't feeling well, be sure to prepare yourself to answer questions prior to calling by reading Before You Call the Doctor (page 572).

**Always tell the truth—the whole truth.** Withholding information, whether intentionally or inadvertently, can make it impossible for the doctor to provide your child the best care possible. To keep up your end of the partnership, make sure you keep your child's doctor well informed. For instance, if you smoke, don't try to hide your habit; this information could be extremely relevant, for example, if your child suffers from recurrent ear infections or bronchitis. If there's a history of high cholesterol in either parent's family, pass that information along, too, alerting your doctor to the possibility that your child may have inherited this tendency. If you missed giving your child several doses of a ten-day course of antibiotics prescribed for a bout with bronchitis, make sure the doctor knows this when you call to say that the cough has gotten worse.

**Ask for explanations.** If the doctor starts talking "medicalese," don't be embarrassed to ask for a translation into easy-to-understand terms. Be clear about just what it is you don't understand.

**Follow the doctor's orders. . .** While you know your toddler best, your toddler's doctor presumably knows medicine best. It's therefore essential to your toddler's health to listen carefully to and follow medical instructions (about sick-child care, about medicine dosage, and so on). Keeping your child's health history with you so that you can take notes when you call the doctor or make an office visit will help ensure that you *remember* the instructions. Briefly review instructions at the end of the visit to be sure you understand them.

**. . . or be clear about why you can't.** Of course, there may be times when the doctor's orders don't tally with what you know to be true about your toddler (for instance, a medication has been prescribed that your toddler refused to take

# THE ROLE OF THE PEDIATRIC NURSE-PRACTITIONER

· · · · · · · · · ·

They dispense shots to squirming tots (and reassurance to their nervous parents), conduct routine checkups, diagnose and treat common illnesses, manage chronic illnesses (like asthma and diabetes), and offer advice on feeding, sleep, development, potty-learning, and just about every other aspect of child care.

They aren't pediatricians or family doctors—they're pediatric nurse-practitioners (PNPs) or pediatric nurse assistants (PNAs). A relatively new hybrid in the medical community, PNPs are registered nurses who have taken additional training in child growth and development, family and cultural issues, pediatric physical and developmental assessment, and common childhood illnesses and problems—through either a Master's degree program in nursing or a formal, accredited continuing education program. As the shortage of primary care physicians (those who take care of the whole patient) grows, so do the numbers of nurse-practitioners. So don't be surprised if many of your child's routine office visits or parts of visits are handled by a PNP or a PNA.

Though no studies have yet been done on the safety and effectiveness of PNPs practicing independently, research has confirmed that when they work with physicians in teams of interdependent professionals, PNPs benefit patients; it is expected that their roles will continue to expand. Exactly what nurse-practitioners can and cannot do (prescribing medications, for example) varies from state to state. They work in clinics, hospitals, schools and day-care centers, health maintenance organizations (HMOs), in and private practice with other nurses or with physicians. Many are certified by either the National Certification Board of Pediatric Nurse-Practitioners and Nurses or the American Nurses Association.

**Note:** In order to make the text less cumbersome, we've opted to use the word "doctor" throughout the book, rather than specifying "doctor or NP." If your child is seeing an NP, substitute NP as appropriate.

---

or had an allergic reaction to last time). Or when they don't correspond with something you've read (as when a recommended procedure has been getting bad press). Don't follow orders in spite of what you know, or ignore them because of what you know—instead, make your concerns known so they can be addressed. If your toddler doesn't tolerate the prescribed medication, the doctor may be able to substitute a more palatable liquid or a chewable (if your toddler can handle it), a suppository, or—if all else is rejected—an injection. If a controversial procedure has you concerned, the doctor may be able to supply evidence to back up the recommendation or may be willing to discuss an alternative.

**Discuss conflicting advice . . .** When the advice of your child's doctor differs from advice you've gotten elsewhere (from family members, friends, books, and other sources), don't hesitate to put the contradictions on the table for discussion.

**. . . but make discussion, not war.** An exchange of ideas (and even a little friendly debate, now and then) can be productive. But when parent and physician are continually at odds, nobody wins—and the child in the middle often loses.

**Ask for recommendations.** Look to your child's doctor's office for recommendations of all kinds. Pediatric and family practices typically have the resources available to refer you to baby-sitters, day care, preschools; to hook you up with other parents interested in forming a play group (or parent's group) or in accepting new members for an established one; to advise you on the best soaps, moisturizers, sunscreens, and equipment for your toddler; and to offer suggestions on stocking your medicine cabinet.

**Practice prevention.** To raise a healthier toddler (who's more likely to grow into a healthier child and a healthier adult), start practicing prevention now. Take your child for routine checkups and immunizations without fail. Be alert to (and ready to report when necessary) the symptoms of illness. Instill a respect for good health habits. Feed your toddler an excellent diet (such as the Best-Odds Toddler Diet). Provide ample opportunity for exercise as well as rest. Take protective measures against infection; in addition to keeping immunizations up to date, make sensible hygienic practices routine; avoid unnecessary exposure to infected individuals, at home or away; and safeguard food from spoilage and bacterial contamination. Keep known chemical residues in your toddler's diet to a minimum (see page 532). Provide an environment as free as possible of controllable hazards, such as tobacco smoke and lead. Safeguard your toddler from accident and injury (always use seat belts and car seats; make your home child-safe; follow safe-toy recommendations; ensure that play areas and playgrounds are safe; and know what to do should an accident or injury occur).

**Don't hesitate to call.** The right physician (and the right office staff) won't mind your calling with questions and concerns. But unless it's an emergency, it's smart to first assess the situation yourself, to the best of your ability with the help of this book (see pages 572 and 658) or another reliable source.

**When you're unhappy, don't keep it to yourself.** If the partnership with your toddler's doctor isn't working, take steps to remedy the situation. First, discuss your discontent and the perceived reasons for it with the doctor. See if you can jointly come up with a solution or solutions. If it doesn't look like the problem can be fixed, if you feel you're not getting anywhere with the doctor, or if you feel your concerns aren't being heard, consider switching to another practice. But make sure to find one you like before giving up what you have; a child should never be without health care.

# WHEN TO CALL THE DOCTOR

New parents tend to call the doctor at the drop of a symptom. By the time a child turns one, these parents, more experienced and more confident, generally pick up the phone less often. Nevertheless, there are still times when a call for medical advice or reassurance is necessary.

Deciding which symptoms say "Call immediately," which say "Call some time today," and which say "Wait and see," isn't always easy. And a call-the-doctor symptom in one child or in one situation may be a wait-and-see symptom in another. That's why you should ask your child's doctor or nurse-practitioner for specific when-to-call recommendations for your child. Jot down these recommendations in the space provided at the end of this list. This is particularly important if your child has a chronic condition (such as heart, kidney, or neurological disease; sickle-cell or other chronic anemia; diabetes or asthma, see Chapter Twenty-Three).

No matter what instructions you've been given, call immediately (or go to the emergency room if the doctor can't be reached), if you feel that there is something very wrong with your

# LOOKING FOR DR. RIGHT

• • • • • • • • • •

**M**any parents of toddlers are fortunate to be in a satisfying partnership with a doctor or group of doctors they consider "right." Others, however—either because the family has relocated, their previous doctor has left town or retired, there has been a change in their insurance coverage, or because of dissatisfaction with their present provider—find themselves once again on the lookout for that special someone (or those special someones) to care for their child's health.

Finding Dr. Right is never easy, but the odds that you'll locate him or her are better if you ask the right people. Look to your obstetrician-gynecologist, midwife, or internist (but only if you're satisfied with the care you're getting from them); to friends and acquaintances (especially any who are pediatric health professionals); other parents at the play group, day care center, or preschool your child attends; members of your religious community; and colleagues at work. Recommendations from people who share a similar lifestyle and temperament as well as many of the same child-rearing philosophies as you do will best serve your search. If you're new to a community, call the local medical society for the name of a doctor. Or try a respected local hospital; they may have a

referral service. If they don't, request the pediatric floor and ask a nurse for a suggestion. If all else fails, turn to the Yellow Pages (but keep in mind that some very busy doctors don't list themselves in the Yellow Pages and some doctors who do list themselves as specialists are not board-certified; so be sure to check out such claims by looking the name up in the Directory of Medical Specialities at the public library or by asking the doctor directly if he or she is board-certified).

Of course, if you belong to an HMO or other health-care group that specifies providers, you will probably be furnished with a list of providers to choose from; asking other group members who they use and what their experiences have been with them can help you make your choice.

Ideally, you should schedule a consultation with a potential candidate before you sign on—to compare philosophies on topics of importance to you, discuss office atmosphere and protocol, and generally test the chemistry. But if you're short on time (a checkup or immunization has come due, or an emergency situation has arisen), you may not have that luxury. If that's the case, you'll need to learn about the physician's approach, style, philosophy, and degree of competence "on the job."

---

child—even if you can't confirm it with the help of the entries on this list and even if you can't quite put your finger on what it is.

If your child develops any of the following symptoms, call as noted. If a symptom that calls for a *call during regular office hours* appears on the weekend, you can wait until Monday to contact the doctor. If a symptom that requires a *call within 24 hours* appears on the weekend, call within that time frame, even if you have to call the doctor's answering service.

### Fever:

▲ over 105°F (40.5°C), rectally, or the equivalent using another method;[4] *call immediately.*

▲ between 104°F and 105°F (between 40°C and 40.5°C); call within 24 hours.

▲ between 102°F and 103.9°F (between 39°C and 39.5°C); call during regular office hours.

---

4. Unless otherwise specified, temperatures given here are for rectal readings. See page 585 for equivalents.

▲ under 102°F (39°C) rectally (low-grade), with mild cold or flu symptoms, that lasts for more than three days; call during regular office hours.

▲ that lasts more than 24 hours when there are no other detectable signs of illness; call within the next 24 hours.

▲ that isn't brought down at all by a fever-reducing medication within an hour; call within 24 hours; *call immediately* if 105°F (40.5°C) or above.

▲ that suddenly rises after being low-grade (under 102°F or 39°C) for a couple of days; that suddenly develops in a child who has been sick with a cold or flu (this may indicate a secondary infection, such as an ear infection or strep throat); call within 24 hours, unless the child appears sick or has a history of febrile seizures, in which case, *call immediately.*

▲ with onset following a period of exposure to an external heat source, such as the sun on a hot day or the closed interior of a car in hot weather; *immediate emergency medical attention* is required (see heat illness, page 671).

▲ that suddenly increases when a child with a moderate fever has been overdressed or bundled in blankets. This should be treated as heat illness; *call immediately.*

### Fever accompanied by:

▲ limpness or unresponsiveness (you can't interest your child in anything, can't elicit a smile); *call immediately.*

▲ convulsions (the body stiffens, eyes roll, limbs flail); *call immediately* the first time. If your toddler has had convulsions in the past, call within 24 hours, unless the doctor has advised you to do otherwise (see page 583).

▲ convulsions that last longer than 5 minutes, *call 911 immediately* for emergency assistance.

▲ inconsolable crying that lasts 2 or 3 hours; *call immediately.*

▲ crying, as if in pain, when your child is touched or moved; *call immediately.*

▲ whimpering or moaning unrelated to behavior; *call immediately.*

▲ purple spots anywhere on the skin; *call immediately.*

▲ difficulty breathing, once the nasal passages have been cleared; *call immediately.*

▲ severe headache (especially with vomiting); *call immediately.*

▲ drooling and a refusal to swallow liquids; *call immediately.*

▲ neck stiffness (the child resists having the head moved forward toward the chest); *call immediately.*

▲ suspected burning or pain during urination (this might be difficult to confirm in a young toddler); *call immediately.*

▲ sore throat (see page 610); call during regular office hours.

▲ a rash (see page 840); call during regular office hours.

▲ repeated vomiting; call within 24 hours.

▲ mild dehydration (see page 605 for typical signs); call during regular office hours.

▲ severe dehydration (see page 605 for signs); *call immediately.*

▲ uncharacteristic behavior—excessive crankiness or crying; excessive sleepiness; lethargy; sleeplessness; sensitivity to light; loss of appetite; ear pulling or clutching; *call immediately.*

### A Cough:

▲ that lasts more than 2 weeks; call during regular office hours.

▲ that disturbs sleep at night; call during regular office hours.

▲ that brings up yellowish or greenish phlegm; call during regular office hours.

▲ that brings up blood-tinged phlegm; *call immediately.*

## A cough accompanied by:

▲ difficulty breathing; *call immediately.*

▲ chest pain; call during regular office hours.

▲ wheezing (a whistling sound on breathing out, as in asthma); call during regular office hours.

▲ retractions (the skin between the ribs appears to be sucked in with each breath); call during regular office hours.

▲ rapid breathing (see page 573); call during regular office hours.

## Sore throat:

▲ following exposure to someone with diagnosed strep infection; call during regular office hours.

▲ in a child with a history of chronic lung disease, rheumatic fever, kidney disease; call within 24 hours.

## Sore throat accompanied by:

▲ fever over 102°F (39°C); call during regular office hours.

▲ discomfort when swallowing; call during regular office hours.

▲ severe difficulty swallowing, drooling; *call immediately.*

▲ white spots or blisters on reddened throat (see page 610); call during regular office hours.

▲ swollen, or tender, glands in the neck (see page 575); call during regular office hours.

▲ a rash; call as soon as rash appears.

▲ hoarseness that lasts 2 weeks; call within 24 hours.

## Bleeding:

Report any of the following symptoms to the doctor *immediately:*

▲ blood in the urine.

▲ blood in the stool (except for streaks of blood that you know are from anal fissures).

▲ blood in sputum or phlegm.

▲ blood leaking from the ears.

## General demeanor:

Also *call immediately* if your toddler displays any of the following symptoms:

▲ Severe lethargy, with or without fever; a semi-awake state from which he or she can't fully be roused; lack of responsiveness.

▲ Crying or moaning as if in pain, when moved or touched.

▲ Restlessness—your child cannot settle down to sleep for more than 30 minutes at a time.

▲ Continuous crying for more than 3 hours; high-pitched crying; faint whimpering or moaning.

▲ Refusal to eat at all for an entire day.

## Other:

▲ Swollen glands (see page 575) that become red, hot, and tender; call within 24 hours.

▲ *Severe* pain anywhere in the body, but especially in the head or chest; *call immediately.*

▲ Abdominal pain that doesn't appear to be related to constipation or lactose intolerance and that lasts more than 3 hours, or is accompanied by vomiting, gets worse, is intermittent, or stops suddenly (see Appendicitis Warnings, page 574); *call immediately.*

▲ Yellowing of the whites of the eyes or of the skin; call during regular office hours.

---

### Special when-to-call recommendations from your toddler's doctor:

_____

_____

_____

_____

_____

_____

_____

_____

_____

_____

_____

_____

_____

_____

_____

_____

_____

_____

_____

_____

_____

---

# BEFORE YOU CALL THE DOCTOR

Whether it's 3 P.M. Monday or 3 A.M. Friday, a Tuesday morning at the office or a Sunday morning at home, the phones of practitioners who care for children are always ringing. In fact, these practitioners spend more time in phone consultations than any other medical specialists—answering questions and dispensing advice about feverish babies, toddlers with ear infections, preschoolers with upset tummies, and first-graders who've just taken their first tumble off a two-wheeler.

Spending so much time on the phone often leaves pediatric doctors short on time to visit, and—despite their good intentions—sometimes a little harried and hurried. To make the most of the time your toddler's practitioner gives you when you call, make sure to do your homework before you pick up the phone.

First of all, using the "When to Call the Doctor" list in this chapter, determine the relative urgency of the situation, whether you must speak to the doctor immediately, whether your call can wait until regular office (or scheduled call-in) hours, or whether you needn't call at all. In an emergency, don't waste time trying to reach the doctor; call 911 immediately or head for the nearest emergency room. Then have someone call the doctor from there.

If you decide that a call *is* necessary, have all of the following ready—in writing—before heading for the phone:

## Information on Your Toddler's Symptoms.

Often, just looking at your toddler is enough to tell you something isn't right. But a physician needs more of an assessment to go on. So before you call to report an illness, check your toddler for these symptoms. Only two or three

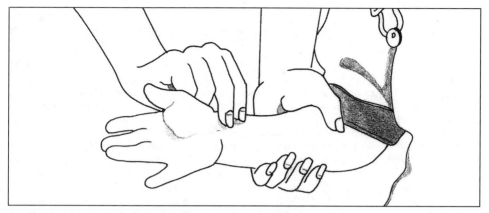

*To take your child's radial pulse, place your index and middle fingers on the inner wrist on the thumb side. Press down slightly until you locate the pulse, then count the beats for 10 seconds and multiply by 6 for the heart rate.*

symptoms will be present in most simple illnesses, but running down this list each time will ensure you haven't missed anything. Make notes as you go so you don't forget your child's temperature by the time you get to counting respirations.

**Temperature.** If your toddler's forehead feels cool to the touch (see page 578), you can assume there's no significant fever; if it feels warm, get a more accurate reading with a thermometer (see page 579). When reporting the temperature to the doctor, mention how, when, and with what kind of thermometer it was taken.

**Heart rate.** A child's heart rate can be affected by illness and may in some cases provide important medical clues. If your child seems very lethargic or has a fever, take the radial pulse (on the wrist; see above illustration) or carotid pulse (on the neck; see page 686). The normal pulse range for toddlers in the second year is between 80 and 140 beats per minute. (It can be up to 20 beats per minute slower during sleep and can get considerably faster during a crying jag.) By age three, the pulse rate ranges from 80 to 120. Report your child's present heart rate to the doctor along with your child's base-line pulse, if you know it. (It's a good idea to determine this baseline pulse rate by taking your child's pulse when he or she is healthy and has been playing quietly for half an hour or so.)

**Respiration.** It's also wise to make a note of your child's baseline respiration rate when he or she is healthy and playing quietly. (You can check respirations by counting how many times in a minute your toddler's chest rises and falls.) Young children normally take about 20 to 40 breaths per minute. Breathing is more rapid during activity (including crying) than during sleep, and may speed up or slow down during illness. If your toddler is coughing or seems to be breathing rapidly or irregularly, check respirations. If your toddler's respiration is faster or slower than usual or is outside the normal range, or if his or her chest doesn't seem to rise and fall with each breath or breathing appears labored or raspy (unrelated to a stuffy nose), report that information to the doctor.

**Respiratory symptoms.** Is your toddler's nose runny or stuffy? Is the discharge watery or thick? Clear, white, yellow, or green? If there's a cough is it dry, hacking, heavy, or crowing? Does it

## APPENDICITIS WARNINGS

· · · · · · · · · ·

An inflamed appendix is very rare in young children. When it does occur, it is exceedingly difficult to diagnose, partly because symptoms often seem to mimic an ordinary stomach upset. In the typical case, pain begins around the umbilicus (the belly button) and several hours later may move to the lower right abdomen (or elsewhere in the abdomen or even the back, if the appendix is in the "wrong" place). There may be tenderness in the area of the pain, and the pain may cause the toddler to limp or walk bent over. After the pain begins there may be a loss of appetite and then vomiting. (Vomiting *before* the pain begins is more likely gastroenteritis, or a stomach ache.) There may be a low-grade fever of 100°F to 101°F (38°C to 38.5°C), and, sometimes, frequent bowel movements (they are gassy, scant, and not watery like diarrhea). If your child's symptoms lead you to suspect appendicitis, even slightly, call the doctor. If the pain stops after several hours don't assume all is well. It could mean a burst appendix and a call to the doctor is still in order.

seem to originate in the throat or in the chest? Is the cough productive—does it bring up any mucus? Has your child vomited mucus during a forceful cough?

**Behavior.** Is there any change from the norm in your toddler's behavior? Would you describe your child as sleepy and lethargic, cranky and irritable, inconsolable or unresponsive? Can you elicit a smile?

**Sleeping.** Is your toddler sleeping much more than usual, or unusually drowsy, or difficult to arouse? Or is he or she having trouble sleeping?

**Crying.** Is your toddler crying more than usual? Does the cry have a different sound or unusual intensity—is it high-pitched, for instance?

**Appetite.** Has there been a sudden change in appetite? Is your toddler refusing fluids and/or solids? Or eating or drinking everything in sight?

**Skin.** Does your toddler's skin appear or feel different in any way? Is it red and flushed? White and pale? Bluish or gray? Does it feel moist and warm (sweaty) or moist and cool (clammy)? Or is it unusually dry or wrinkly? Are lips, nostrils, or cheeks excessively dry or cracking? Are there spots or other lesions anywhere on your toddler's skin—under the arms, behind the ears, on the extremities or trunk, or elsewhere? How would you describe their color, shape, size, texture? Is your child scratching or rubbing them?

**Mouth.** Is there swelling on the gums where teeth might be trying to break through? (Molars, particularly, can cause a lot of discomfort.) Any red or white spots or patches visible on the gums, inside the cheeks, or on the palate or tongue? Any bleeding?

**Throat.** Is the arch framing the throat reddened? Are there white or red spots or patches? (See page 610 for how to examine your toddler's throat.)

**Eyes.** Do your toddler's eyes look different than usual? Do they seem glazed, glassy, vacant, sunken, dull, watery, or reddened? Do they have dark circles under them, or seem partially closed? If there's a discharge, how would you describe its color, consistency, and quantity? Do you notice any "pimples" on the eyelids?

**Ears.** Is your toddler pulling or poking at one or both ears? Is there a discharge from either ear? If there is, what does it look like?

**Lymph glands.** Do the lymph glands in your child's neck seem swollen? (See illustration for how to check them.)

**Digestive system.** Has your toddler been vomiting? How often? Is there a lot of material being vomited, or are your toddler's heaves mostly dry? How would you describe the vomitus—like curdled milk, mucus-streaked, greenish (bile-stained), pinkish, bloody, like coffee grounds? Is the vomiting forceful? Does it seem to project a long distance? Does anything specific seem to trigger the vomiting—eating or drinking, for example, or coughing? Do you know, or suspect, that your toddler has ingested a toxic substance?

Has there been any change in bowel movements? Does your toddler have diarrhea, with loose, watery, mucousy, or bloody stools? Are color and odor different than usual? Are movements more frequent (how many in the last 24 hours?), sudden, explosive? Or does your toddler seem constipated? Is there an increase or decrease in saliva? Excessive drooling? Or any apparent difficulty swallowing?

**Urinary tract.** Does your toddler seem to be urinating more or less frequently? Is the urine different in color—dark yellow, for example, or pinkish—or have an unusual odor? Does urination seem to be painful or burning? (This discomfort could cause a toddler to "hold it in" or to cry on wetting.)

**Abdomen.** Is your toddler's tummy flatter, rounder, more bulging? When you press on it gently, or when you bend either knee to the abdomen, does your child seem to be in pain? Where does the pain seem to be—right side or left, upper or lower abdomen?

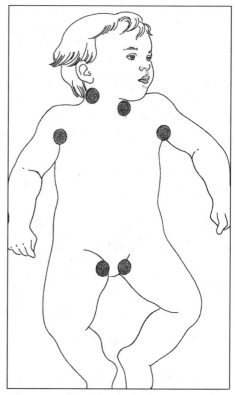

*The lymph glands are part of the body's protection against disease. When there is an infection nearby, they often swell and may sometimes become tender and hot. You can feel for them with your fingertips.*

**Motor symptoms.** Has your toddler been experiencing chills, shakes, stiffness, convulsions, or neck stiffness (can he or she bend chin to chest without difficulty)? Does he or she seem to have difficulty in moving any other part of the body?

**Pain.** Is your child complaining of pain in the arms, legs, abdomen, head, ears, or anywhere else? Or is he or she indicating pain nonverbally—by tugging at an ear, for instance?

**Other unusual signs.** Do you note any unpleasant odor emanating from your child's mouth, nose, ears, vagina, rectum? Is there bleeding from any of these?

## PARENT'S INTUITION

· · · · · · · · · ·

If your toddler just doesn't seem "right" to you, but you can't put your finger on any specific symptom, give the doctor a call anyway. Most likely you'll be reassured, but it's possible that your intuition may have picked up on a subtle problem that needs evaluation. At any rate, it's better to call than to worry.

## The Progress of the Illness So Far

No matter what the illness, there is some general information in addition to the symptoms, that you should have ready when calling the doctor—or when taking your child to the doctor's office or the emergency room:

▲ When did the symptoms first appear?

▲ What, if anything, triggered the symptoms?

▲ What worsens or alleviates the symptoms (sitting up decreases the coughing, for example, or eating increases vomiting)? Are symptoms affected by the time of day (are they worse at night)?

▲ If pain is a symptom, where exactly is it located (if your child can tell you or you can figure that out).

▲ Which over-the-counter or home remedies, if any, have you already tried?

▲ Has your toddler recently been exposed to a virus or infection—a sibling's stomach virus, strep throat at day care, or conjunctivitis at play group?

▲ Has your toddler recently been involved in an accident, in which an unnoticed injury could have occurred?

▲ Has your toddler recently begun taking a new medication?

▲ Has your toddler recently eaten a new or unusual food or a food that might have been spoiled?

## Your Child's Health History

If the doctor doesn't have your child's chart at hand, this information might slip his or her mind. This information is especially important if the doctor has to prescribe medication. Let the doctor know:

▲ Your child's age and approximate weight.

▲ If your toddler has a chronic medical condition and/or is presently taking medication.

▲ If there is a family history of drug reactions or allergies.

▲ If your child has had any previous reactions to medications.

▲ The telephone number of your pharmacy (if a prescription is to be called in).

## Your Questions

In addition to details of your toddler's symptoms, it will also help to have ready any questions you have (about diet, keeping your toddler home from day care, calling back if the symptoms continue, etc.) and a pencil and pad (so you can record any instructions).[5]

---

5. Keeping an illness "diary" (in your child's health history record or just a simple spiral notebook) will give you an important resource for the future when you are trying to remember which medicines your toddler won't tolerate and how many ear infections there were last year.

If the doctor is unavailable when you call, ask when you can expect your call to be returned. Then be sure you're available at that time; don't tie up the telephone or run out to the bank while you're waiting. If you must leave the house, call the doctor's office back and let them know when you can next be reached. If your call isn't returned as expected, try again, just in case there has been a slipup—a misplaced message, for instance.

# ALL ABOUT FEVER

Your toddler's uncharacteristic morning tantrum over what to wear tells you something isn't quite right; a little later the glazed eyes and the too-rosy cheeks say the same thing. When your little one listlessly puts down the spoon and falls asleep at the table at noon, there's further corroboration. A touch to the forehead sends you hunting for the thermometer; within minutes, your suspicions are confirmed: Your toddler is running a fever.

Do you rush to the medicine cabinet to dip into your stash of acetaminophen elixir? To the telephone to call your toddler's doctor? To the bathroom to run a cool tub? To the bedroom for some extra blankets? To the kitchen to warm up some chicken soup—or to pour a glass of orange juice? Do you do all of the above? Or none of the above? Knowing the answers is important to your toddler's health and well-being.

Scientists now believe that fever, in most cases, is not an enemy (even fevers as high as 106°F, or 41.1°C, do no permanent damage), but rather the body's protective response to such invaders as viruses, bacteria, and fungi. When one of these menacing microorganisms makes its way into the body, white blood cells take action and produce a hormone called *interleukin*, which travels to the brain to instruct the hypothalamus, a gland in the brain, to turn up the body's thermostat. It appears that higher body temperatures help the immune system to fight infection and that some microorganisms are unable to thrive at these elevated temperatures. Fever may also

## KNOW YOUR TODDLER

..........

Toddlers, like the rest of us, vary in their responses to pain. Some can tolerate a great deal (the curious climber who falls off the monkey bars, gets up without so much as an "ouch," and climbs right back on) and some very little (the fledgling walker who shrieks with every tumble, even when the landing is cushioned by a plush carpet). It's a good idea to take such differences into account when deciding how sick your toddler is. For example, if a feverish child who is ordinarily a stoic is pulling one or both ears, consider an ear infection—even if he or she doesn't seem to be very uncomfortable—and call the doctor. On the other hand, if you've got a very pain-sensitive child, you might be wise not to fly to the phone at each and every whimper. Be wary, however, of the cry-wolf syndrome; keep in mind that the child who complains a lot will sometimes actually be sick.

lower iron levels in the body while increasing the invaders' need for that mineral—in effect, starving them. When it's
a virus that has launched an attack, fever
enhances the production of interferon and
other antiviral substances in the body.

The chills and shaking that often
occur when body temperature suddenly
rises a couple of degrees above normal
signal the body to turn the heat up still
higher—while encouraging the fever suf-
ferer to take measures that will stoke the
fire even more (drink some hot cocoa or
tea, pile on another blanket, or cuddle up
in a heavy robe).

Normally, body temperature is at its
lowest (as low as 96.5°F, or 35.8°C,
taken orally) between 2 A.M. and 4 A.M.
is still relatively low (as low as 97°F, or
36.1°C) when we get up, then slowly
rises over the course of the day until it
peaks between 6 and 10 in the evening at
about 99°F (37.2°C). Body temperature
tends to be slightly higher in hot weather,
lower in cold, higher during exercise
than at rest. It's more volatile and subject to greater variation in young children than in adults. A toddler is generally
not considered to have a fever until the
rectal temperature reaches 100.5° to
101.1°F (38.1°C to 38.4°C).

Fever behaves differently in different illnesses. In some, the body temperature may remain persistently elevated; in
others it will be lower in the morning
and higher in the evening, or rise, fall,
and spike again with no obvious pattern.
The way the fever behaves sometimes
helps the doctor to make the diagnosis.

When fever is part of the body's response to illness, temperatures above
106°F (41.1°C) are rare, and those beyond 108°F (42.2°C) unheard of. But
when fever results from failure of the
body's heat-regulation mechanism, as in
heat illness, temperatures can soar as
high as 114°F (45.6°C). Such extremes
can occur when the body is producing
too much heat or can't cool itself effectively, either an internal abnormality

or—more commonly—because of overheating caused by an external heat
source, such as a sauna or a hot tub, for
example, or the inside of a parked car in
warm weather (air temperatures inside a
closed car can quickly shoot up to
113°F, or 45°C, even with the windows
open 2 inches and the temperature outside a moderate 85°F, or 29.4°C).
Overheating can also result from strenuous physical activity in hot, humid
weather or from being very overdressed
in very hot weather. (Though toddlers
are less susceptible to heat illness than
they were during the first year of life,
sensible precautions still need to be
taken; see page 499.)

Fever due to the failure of heat regulation is an illness in itself; not only is it
not beneficial, it is dangerous and requires immediate treatment. Temperatures
over 106°F (41.1°C) that are due to illness also require immediate treatment.
It's believed that fever that high ceases
to be helpful and that, at this extreme,
the positive effects of fever on the immune response may be reversed.

# TAKING YOUR TODDLER'S TEMPERATURE

The fastest and easiest way to determine whether your toddler has a
fever is to touch your lips or the back of
your hand to one side of his or her forehead or the nape of the neck. With a little practice, you will quickly learn to
discern the difference between normal
and feverish. If your toddler feels
warmer than normal, use a thermometer
to get a more precise reading. Be aware
that the lip-touch system works less reli-
ably if either you or your toddler has
been outside (in the cold or in the hot
sun) or in a warm bath, or if you recently
sipped a hot or cold drink. A young

child's forehead may also feel toasty when he or she crawls out from under the covers in the morning, whether there's fever or not.

Taking your child's temperature can not only clue you in to an illness in the first place, but taking it during the course of an illness can help to answer questions about your child's progress and response to treatment. In most cases, you can get all the information you need by taking the temperature once in the morning and once in the evening. Take it in-between only if your toddler suddenly seems worse. If he or she seems better, and your lips tell you that the fever is down, you don't really need a second opinion from the thermometer. And both you and your toddler can avoid going through the ordeal of temperature-taking.

The four parts of the body that can most accurately reflect core body temperature are the mouth, the rectum, the axilla (armpit), and the ear canal. Since putting a thermometer in the mouth of a toddler is dangerous (most doctors don't recommend taking temperatures orally until a child is at least four or five and can be counted on to keep the thermometer under the tongue without biting it), oral temperature-taking won't be an option for quite a while, which leaves you with the rectal or axillary route for now. Or you can invest in the new tympanic (or infrared auditory canal) thermometer, which reads body temperature in an instant through the ear.

Oral, rectal, and axillary temperatures can be taken with either standard glass thermometers or digital types; tympanic thermometers all display digital readings. Whether digital thermometers are more or less accurate than the standard glass variety isn't clear (study results differ). But it is clear that they register more quickly (speed varies according to the model) and are easier to read. The same digital can take temperatures through oral, rectal, and armpit routes; a different glass thermometer is usually required for oral and rectal use (the oral has a thin cylindrical tip, the rectal, a stubby, rounded bulb).[6] Fever strips (which are taped to the forehead) are less accurate than other thermometers, though you can use them in a pinch to get an approximate reading. A pacifier-type thermometer, which tells you only whether the temperature is elevated or not, is also of only limited usefulness.

**Preparing your toddler.** Since vigorous activity or crying can raise a child's temperature, try to take your toddler's temperature after a period of about 30 minutes of rest or quiet play (coax a worked-up child to listen to a story or watch a video for a while, if necessary). If there's been crying or screaming, wait until your child has calmed down before pulling out the thermometer. Though an oral temperature (appropriate only for older children) shouldn't be taken within half an hour of consuming hot or cold drinks or foods (since they could affect the readings), this precaution isn't necessary when taking rectal or axillary temperatures. But these readings can be affected by such factors as room or air temperature. So wait, too, if your child has been playing in an overheated apartment (open a window), just came in from the cold, or recently climbed out of a warm bath.

**Preparing the thermometer.** Check the mercury reading on a glass thermometer. If it's above 96°F (35.6°C), shake it down carefully by holding it firmly between your thumb and forefinger (bulb or tip away from you) and shaking with repeated downward snaps of the wrist. Wash it with *cold* soapy water (warm or hot water may cause the mercury to expand enough to burst the thermometer), rinse, then swab it with absorbent cotton

---

6. A flat-tipped thermometer for axillary use is not readily available in the U.S. Rectal and oral thermometers, however, can be used under the arm.

dipped in rubbing alcohol. Thoroughly rinse an oral thermometer again to remove any traces of alcohol before using. Lubricate the bulb end of a rectal thermometer with petroleum jelly (Vaseline) before inserting it.

**Taking a rectal temperature.** Sitting on a bed or sofa, place your bare-bottomed toddler tummy down on your lap (see the illustration below). A pillow to support your child's head may increase comfort. Alternately, place your child's tummy down on a couch, bed, or changing table with a small pillow or rolled-up towel under the hips to help raise the buttocks for easier insertion. The advantage of this position is that the child feels less controlled, and many toddlers will be less likely to fight if they aren't restrained. The disadvantage: You have less control—and for some children, this means they won't lie still.

If your child seems apprehensive, speak reassuringly and try distraction (with a couple of favorite songs, a book, a toy, or even a video). This is easiest to do if you have another person to assist—a spouse, an older child, a grandparent, or a friend. Spread the buttocks with one hand, exposing the rectal opening. With the other, slip about an inch of the bulb

*The axillary thermometer is useful when a child has diarrhea or refuses to allow a rectal thermometer to be inserted.*

end of the thermometer into the rectum. Stop sooner if you meet resistance; don't force. Hold the thermometer in place between your index and middle fingers, with the other fingers of that hand pressing the buttocks together to keep the thermometer from sliding out. Keep the thermometer in place for 2 minutes for a glass thermometer, until it beeps (times vary) for a digital. To avoid accidentally breaking the thermometer, remove it immediately if you get very active resistance and no one is around to help you restrain your toddler. Even if the thermometer has been in for only half a minute or so, it will have registered to within a degree of the actual temperature, giving you a rough figure to use in your assessments and/or report to the doctor. Wipe the thermometer with a piece of tissue before reading. (You may want to put the thermometer down—the reading won't change—to be read after you've rediapered your toddler.)

Rarely, a glass thermometer breaks while inserted. If this happens and you can't find all the pieces, call the doctor. But don't panic: The risk of more than a scratch is slight, the mercury itself is not poisonous. (The mercury used in thermometers is metallic mercury, which ox-

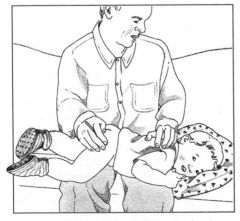

*The rectal thermometer is most often used with toddlers.*

idizes too slowly to yield absorbable mercury ions.) You can avoid cuts from a broken thermometer by using a disposable paper sheath (which won't affect the reading) each time you take a rectal temperature. Sheaths are available at the pharmacy.

**Taking an axillary, or underarm, temperature.** Use this somewhat less precise method of temperature-taking when your toddler won't lie still for a rectal or has diarrhea, which would make the rectal process messy and uncomfortable, or when no rectal thermometer is available. Use either an oral, rectal, or digital thermometer (or an axillary thermometer, if you have one). Remove your toddler's shirt so that no clothing will come between thermometer and skin, and be sure the armpit is dry. Place the bulb end of the thermometer well up into the armpit, holding the arm down snugly over it by pressing the elbow against child's side. Hold this position for at least 4 or 5 minutes (8 minutes is even better) for a glass thermometer and according to directions on a digital. (The digital reading may be more accurate if you keep your child's arm at his or her side for 5 minutes before inserting the thermometer; axillary readings appear to be least accurate when a fever has just begun to rise.) Sing songs, play a tape, put on the television—any activity calculated to keep your toddler still for the duration.

**Taking a tympanic temperature.** Carefully follow the directions that came with the thermometer. Ideally, ask your child's doctor or nurse-practitioner to demonstrate the proper technique for taking a tympanic temperature. Basically, it's just a matter of aiming the instrument correctly into the ear canal; in literally 1 second you get a reading, which is believed to be more accurate than an axillary reading. More study probably needs to be done to determine just how these readings are best interpreted.

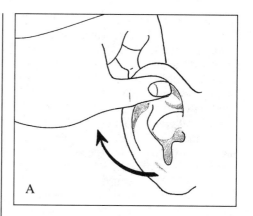

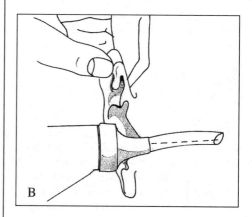

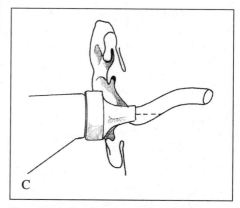

*The ear must be pulled upward (A) to straighten the ear canal (B) and permit a clear "view" for the tympanic thermometer. If the canal isn't straightened (C), the angle may distort the reading.*

**Taking an oral temperature.** You can begin taking oral temperatures when your child can hold the thermometer securely under the tongue with lips closed and can understand *and* follow directions not to bite down on it—usually at about age four or five, but occasionally earlier. For a good oral temperature reading, the thermometer should be tucked well into the pocket under the tongue and held there for 2 to 4 minutes. (If your child is mouth-breathing because of a stuffy nose, it may take 4 minutes or longer for the thermometer to register). When taking an oral reading after hot or cold food or drink, wait about 15 minutes, until mouth temperature returns to normal, before inserting the thermometer.

## READING THE THERMOMETER

A rectal temperature is believed to be the most accurate since it registers core body temperature, but the oral temperature is presently considered the standard. Temperatures obtained rectally, as they are most frequently in toddlers, are usually one-half to a full degree higher than those obtained orally; axillary readings are generally about 1 degree lower, though they can be off even more at the onset of a fever. Generally, 98.6°F (37°C) is considered normal for an oral temperature, 99.6°F (37.6°C) for a rectal, and 97.6°F (36.5°C) for an axillary—although recent studies suggest that "normal" may vary considerably from person to person, and that the average may be a bit lower. A reading of 102.2°F (39°C) taken rectally is the equivalent of 101.2°F (38.4°C) taken orally and 100.2°F (37.9°C) by armpit. A tympanic thermometer can be adjusted to give a reading that is comparable to a rectal or an oral reading.

To read a glass mercury thermometer, hold it in a good light and rotate it until you see the silver column of mercury. Calibrations are marked in full degrees as well as every two-tenths degree. Line up the column of mercury with the calibrations. The point at which the column of mercury ends is the temperature. Write it down, along with the time it was taken. When you report the temperature to the doctor, be sure to indicate how it was taken.

After reading, clean and store the thermometer according to manufacturer's recommendation. A glass thermometer should generally be washed after each use with cold soapy water, rinsed, swabbed with alcohol, and stored away from such sources of heat as a sunny window, a radiator, a fireplace mantel, a clothes dryer, and the kitchen stove.

## EVALUATING A FEVER

In most cases, behavior is a better gauge of how sick a toddler is than body temperature. A young child can be seriously ill, with pneumonia or meningitis for example, and have no fever at all, or have a high fever with a mild cold. So it's important to base your assessment of your child's condition not just on body temperature, but on symptoms that go with it as well. See page 568 for tips on when to call the doctor for a toddler with fever.

## TREATING A FEVER

An estimated 80% to 90% of all fevers in young children are related to self-limiting viral infections (the kind that get better without treatment). Most experts today do not recommend treating such fever in toddlers unless it is at least 102°F (38.9°C), and some suggest waiting until temperatures reach

# FEBRILE CONVULSIONS

• • • • • • • • • •

I t's estimated that 2 to 4 of every 100 young children experience convulsions (eyes roll back, the body stiffens, arms and legs twitch and jerk involuntarily) with a fever, usually at its onset. Though febrile convulsions are frightening for parents, doctors now believe that they are not harmful. Studies show that children who have experienced febrile convulsions show no later neurological or mental impairment, though they have a very slightly increased risk of future epilepsy (but the convulsions, it is suspected, are more likely to be a *result* of an inborn tendency toward the disorder than the cause of it). There appears to be a genetic factor in these convulsions (they run in families); but in most instances the major factor is probably immaturity of the young child's brain. When the brain matures, febrile seizures cease.

## Chance of Recurrence

If your toddler had febrile convulsions as an infant, he or she has a 30% to 40% greater chance of having an episode in the toddler years than does a child who's never had such convulsions; but 7 or 8 out of 10 children who have one episode never have a second. Those most likely to have recurring seizures are children who have had seizures lasting longer than 15 minutes, those whose convulsions came on shortly after the onset of fever, or those whose fevers were not very high at the time of the seizure, and those in whom an underlying cause for the seizures exists.

Ongoing medical treatment for febrile seizures hasn't been found to affect the chances of recurrence. Nor does treatment of a fever seem to reduce the incidence of seizures during an illness in predisposed children, probably because these convulsions almost always occur at the outset of an illness, just as the fever is rising and before treatment can be given.

## Handling Febrile Convulsions

Should your toddler have a febrile convulsion, keep calm (remember, such convulsions are not dangerous) and take the following steps. Check the clock, so that you can time the duration of the seizure. Then hold your child in your arms or place on a bed or another soft surface, lying on one side, with his or her head lower than the rest of the body, if possible. *Don't* try to restrain your child in any way. Loosen any tight clothing. *Don't* try to give food or drink or put anything into your child's mouth; remove anything (like a pacifier or food*) that might be in it. A child may briefly lose consciousness during a seizure, but will usually revive quickly without help. The seizure will probably last only a minute or two.

If your child wants to sleep when the febrile seizure has ended, prop him or her in a side-sleeping position with blankets or a pillow. Then call the doctor (unless this is a repeat and the doctor has told you it isn't necessary to call). If you don't reach the doctor immediately, you can give a sponge bath and acetaminophen (in suppository form if your toddler doesn't seem awake enough to swallow) to try to lower the temperature while you're waiting. But don't put your child in the tub to try to reduce the fever; should another seizure occur, there would be a risk of your child inhaling the bath water.

*Important:* If your child isn't breathing normally after the seizure or if the seizure lasts 5 minutes or more, get immediate emergency help by dialing 911 or your local emergency number. A trip to the emergency room will probably be necessary to determine the cause of this kind of complex seizure.

---

*To remove a bit of food or an object from your toddler's mouth, use a sweep of one finger, rather than a two-finger pincer grasp, which might force the food in further.

104°F (40°C) before reaching for the dreaded medicine dropper. They may, however, recommend the use of acetaminophen even with lower temperatures to relieve aches and pains, improve sleep, generally make a toddler more comfortable, and sometimes, to assuage a nervous parent. On the other hand, illnesses caused by bacteria must always be treated with antibiotics, which lower temperatures indirectly by wiping out the infection. Depending on the illness, the antibiotic being given, the child's level of comfort, and how high the fever is, antibiotics and fever-reducers may or may not be prescribed together.

Unlike most other infection-related fevers, fever associated with shock from a generalized bacterial invasion of the body, as in septicemia (blood poisoning), requires immediate medical treatment to lower the body temperature. So does fever from heat-related illness (see page 671).

If your child has a fever, take these measures as needed, unless the doctor has recommended a different course of action.

**Keep your toddler cool.** Despite what Grandma may say, keeping a feverish child warm with blankets, heavy clothing, or an overheated room is not a safe practice; these measures can actually lead to heat illness by raising body temperature to dangerous levels. (The exception: The child who has chills can be wrapped in a blanket until the shaking subsides.) Dress your feverish child lightly to allow body heat to escape (no more than diaper or underpants may be needed in hot weather), use only a sheet and/or a light blanket as a covering, and maintain room temperature at 68°F to 70°F (20°C to 21.1°C). When necessary, use an air conditioner or fan, if you have one, to maintain this temperature (but keep your toddler out of the path of the air flow or drafts from an open window).

**Up the fluid intake.** Because fever increases water loss through the skin, it's important to be sure a feverish toddler gets an adequate intake of fluids, from diluted juices; juicy fruits, such as citrus

## DOSAGES FOR ACETAMINOPHEN

· · · · · · · · · ·

| Age | Weight (pounds) | Drops (dropperful) | Elixir (teaspoons) | Chewable (tabs) |
|---|---|---|---|---|
| **TYLENOL** | | | | |
| 12 to 23 months | 18 to 23 | 1½ df 1.2 ml | ¾ | |
| 2 to 3 years | 24 to 35 | 2 df 1.6 ml | 1 | 2 |
| 4 to 5 years | 36 to 47 | | 1½ | 3 |
| **TEMPRA** | | | | |
| 12 to 23 months | 18 to 23 | 1½ df | | |
| 2 to 3 years | 24 to 35 | 2 df | 1½ | 2 |
| 4 to 6 years | 36 to 47 | 3 df | 2 | 2½ |

## TYPICAL BODY TEMPERATURES*

· · · · · · · · · ·

| Body Site | Thermometer Type | Normal Range | Fever |
|-----------|-----------------|--------------|-------|
| rectum | mercury glass or electronic | 97.8°F to 100.4°F 36.6°C to 38.0°C | 100.5°F 38.1°C |
| mouth | mercury glass or electronic | 95.9°F to 99.5°F 35.6°C to 37.5°C | 99.6°F 37.6°C |
| axilla (underarm) | mercury glass or electronic | 94.5°F to 99.2°F 34.7°C to 37.3°C | 99.4°F 37.4°C |
| ear | infrared emission | 96.2°F to 99.5°F 35.7°C to 37.5°C | 99.6°F 37.6°C |

*If your child's baseline temperature, taken when well, differs from the normal range, what constitutes a fever may also differ. Discuss this possibility with your child's doctor.

and melons; water; clear soups; healthful gelatin desserts; and ice pops made from fruit juice. Encourage but don't force your child to take frequent sips of favorite beverages. If your child refuses to take any fluids for several hours, inform the doctor.

**Down the fever—with medication.** But only if necessary. Remember, in most cases, fever plays an important role in fighting infection. The doctor may recommend acetaminophen (or sometimes, ibuprofen; see page 594) if your child has a fever of 103°F (39.4°C) or higher (taken rectally); seems very uncomfortable or in pain, or is unable to sleep. Be careful to adhere to recommended doses (see the facing page).

**Down the fever—with sponging.** But only under certain circumstances. Once a routine treatment for fever, sponging (which makes some children *more* uncomfortable) is now recommended only when a child has had an adverse reaction to fever-reducing medication or when such medication isn't working (the temperature isn't down an hour after

medication is given). It may also be recommended, in combination with a fever-reducing medication, such as acetaminophen, when a child has a fever of 104°F (40°C) or higher. Sponging (medication is *not* recommended) is the treatment of choice for heat illness (see page 671).

While cold water is used for sponging with heat illness, only *tepid* or *lukewarm* water (at normal body temperature, neither warm nor cool to the touch) should be used for sponging to bring down illness-induced fevers. Using cool or cold water, or alcohol (once a popular fever-reducing rub) with an illness-induced fever can raise, rather than lower, body temperature by inducing shivering, which provokes the body to turn up the heat instead of turning it down. Alcohol presents an additional risk: The fumes can be harmful if inhaled. Hot water sponging will also raise body temperature and could, like overdressing a feverish child, lead to heatstroke.

If your toddler enjoys a bath, you can sponge in the tub.[7] Alternatively,

---

7. But don't put a child who's recently had a febrile convulsion into the tub.

you can sponge your fevered toddler on a towel-covered, water-proof sheet, pad, or plastic tablecloth. Whether you sponge in the tub or out, the room should be comfortably warm and draft free. If you are sponging in combination with a medication, give the medication half an hour before beginning. Have three washcloths and a tub or basin of tepid water ready before undressing your toddler. If you're sponging out of the tub, cover your child with a light towel. (Do not, however, cover your feverish toddler with a wet towel or wet sheet, since this could prevent the necessary escape of heat through the skin.) Wring out one washcloth so it won't drip, fold it, and place it on your child's forehead; remoisten if it begins to dry out during the sponging. Wet and lightly wring out another cloth and begin gently rubbing your child's skin, one area at a time. Concentrate on the neck, face, stomach, inside of the elbows and knees, but also include the area under the arms and around the groin. The blood brought to the surface by rubbing will be cooled as the tepid water evaporates on the skin. When the rubbing cloth begins to dry out, put it back to soak and switch to the third cloth. Continue rubbing and sponging your toddler, alternating cloths as needed, for at least 20 minutes to half an hour (it takes this long to lower body temperature). If at any time the water in the basin cools to below body temperature, add enough warm water to raise the temperature again. If the bath causes shivering, warm up the water a bit, or if medication was given, wait 20 minutes longer for it to take effect.

**Encourage a slow-down.** A really sick child will want to slow down, but many children with fevers want to keep romping. Allow moderate activity, but discourage strenuous activity, which could raise body temperature further.

**Feed the fever.** The work of running a fever raises the body's caloric requirements; those who are sick actually need more calories, not fewer.

**Don't overtreat.** Do not give an enema (an old fever remedy) or any medication (other than acetaminophen), except under a doctor's directions. Do not give any medication (including acetaminophen) when you suspect heat illness.

**Check with the doctor.** As necessary (see page 569); any fever that lingers for 8 days or more, in the absence of obvious illness, is considered a fever of undetermined origin (FUO), or a fever without a source (FWS), and requires medical evaluation.

# CARING FOR A SICK TODDLER

## AT HOME

**How much rest?** Anyone who's ever tried to inflict bed rest on a toddler who's simultaneously running a fever and running circles around a worried parent knows how difficult it can be to keep a sick toddler down. But the good news is, it isn't necessary to keep a sick toddler down—unless he or she seems to need the rest. There's no evidence that bed rest affects a mild illness one way or the other. And you can almost invariably trust your child to pick up on and comply with his or her body signals. A very sick toddler will readily relinquish playful pursuits in favor of needed rest and relaxation, while one who is only mildly ill will be reluctant to slow down (just as the child on the road to recovery will be eager to pick up the pace). So unless restrictions on activity are "doctor's orders," there's no need to impose restrictions of your own. Keep the home atmosphere as tranquil as possible, however; chaos isn't good for a sick person of any age. And try to discourage vigorous activity when your child has a fever—the activity could raise body temperature even more.

**How much time at home?** Follow the doctor's advice about when to start venturing outside again with your toddler, and when to schedule a return to day care, preschool, or play group. In general, it's recommended that a child who's been running a fever of 101°F (38.3°C) or greater should stay home until the temperature has stayed below 100.2°F (37.9°C) for 24 hours. A child who has some residual symptoms (such as a cough after a cold) can resume normal activities once the fever's gone, though a child who seems "wiped out" probably could benefit from a little extra time at home, if at all possible.

**Dietary guidelines.** Forget the adage, "starve a cold, feed a fever"—it has no foundation in medical fact. Anyone who is ill, fever or no, needs a nutritious diet (in line with any recommendations for the particular illness); if there is fever, extra calories are also important to compensate for the additional calories burned with each increase in body temperature. For most toddler illnesses, you should:

*Stress fluids.* If your toddler has a fever, a respiratory infection (such as a cold, influenza, or bronchitis), or a gastrointestinal illness with diarrhea and/or vomiting, clear fluids and foods with high water content (juices, juicy fruits, soups, fruit-juice-based gelatins, and frozen-juice desserts—but not sugar-sweetened sodas, juices, or punches) will help prevent dehydration. (Sometimes, particularly with diarrhea, an oral rehydration solution may be necessary. Offer fluids frequently throughout the day, even if your toddler takes no more than a sip at a time. If your toddler's appetite is sluggish, fluids should take precedence over solids.

*Emphasize quality.* When your toddler's appetite is dampened by illness, the temptation to put good nutrition aside and allow non-nutritious foods that are ordinarily taboo may be great. Resist it. Since anyone—adult or child—who is sick needs a plentiful supply of nutrients (particularly protein, vitamins, and minerals) to help the immune system fight back, be sure that what little your toddler eats goes a long way nutritionally. And continue to offer a vitamin supplement to your child (unless the doctor advises otherwise or your child has been vomiting it up).

*Think small.* Since appetites may be tender during illness, it's best to feed small amounts of food frequently during the day. Avoid heavy, fatty foods that are difficult to digest.

*Don't force.* Even if your toddler hasn't taken a bite in 24 hours, don't force-feed. Do make sure, however, that your toddler gets enough fluids—you may wish to keep a record of the amounts. Be sure to report inadequate fluid intake and/or serious loss of appetite to the doctor.

*Play favorites.* Skip new foods and foods you know your toddler doesn't love. Instead focus on nutritious favorites. Concern yourself less about balance than about total food intake—six bowls of cereal, milk, and bananas in a day is fine, if that's what your sick toddler craves. If nothing seems to spark the appetite, try tempting your toddler with some of the tasty tricks on page 522. A nutritious shake or juice "smoothie" (made with milk or juice, bananas, berries, or other fruit, fortified with yogurt or a teaspoon or two of wheat germ) may be appealing—and go down more easily than solids.

**TLC.** The best medicine for anyone who isn't well, especially a child, is tender loving care. Dose your toddler with it regularly.

# *IN THE HOSPITAL*

**B**eing around unfamiliar people in unfamiliar surroundings; being poked and jabbed and dosed with medicine; being crib-bound (and sometimes, when mobility has to be rigidly restricted, even physically bound to a crib). When a toddler must be hospitalized—whether for an overnight procedure, a week of testing and observation, or long-term treatment that spans a month or more—no one and nothing can make the experience completely painless or anxiety-free, for the toddler or the toddler's parents. But a positive attitude and the right preparation can make things go more smoothly.

If your toddler must be hospitalized, start preparing as soon as possible (assuming you have the luxury of advance notice) by taking the following steps:

▲ Be sure that a hospital stay is absolutely necessary. Ask if the planned procedure could be performed on an outpatient basis—either in the doctor's office or the hospital—so that your toddler can return home to familiar surroundings the same day.

▲ Check out the hospital before your toddler checks in. If you have a choice of hospitals (this may be restricted by urgency, local availability, finances, or insurance stipulations), investigate the options. A respected pediatric hospital is usually the best choice, with a tertiary hospital (a major medical center) that has a large pediatric department next best. If your toddler requires surgery or another procedure that isn't routine, look for a hospital that has a good track record for that particular procedure (ask the doctor who is to provide the care about his or her experience and results). Sometimes the right hospital for your toddler may end up being far from home, but getting the best care possible, when it's possible, is almost always worth the trip.

Also look for a hospital that has rooming-in arrangements for one or both parents (the doctor may be able to write an order for this if it isn't routinely offered): a play room; a child-friendly atmosphere, and an empathetic staff (stop in and chat for a few minutes, if the hospital is local). Also be sure that you'll be allowed to bring some of the comforts of your toddler's home along to make the hospital accommodations more cozy.

▲ Arrange for some time off. If it's at all possible, at least one parent should be with your toddler around the clock during the hospital stay—not only to provide reassurance and comfort as needed and to serve as his or her advocate, but to afford a sense of security and continuity in the often-unpredictable hospital environment. Most working parents are legally allowed to take time off from their jobs to care for sick children (though, unfortunately, they are not always guaranteed pay for the days they miss). If there are two working parents, alternating bedside shifts can minimize total missed work time for each, and be less physically and emotionally wearing. If you're a single parent, try to find a friend or relative to help relieve you when you need a break, a shower, or some fresh air.

▲ Arrange for child care. If you have other children at home, the logistics of spending time at the hospital become even more complex. Arranging school or day care drop-offs, pick-ups, and hospital visits, as well as daytime and/or nighttime care, will require some advance planning. Depend as much as possible on the kindness of friends and family (most people are happy to help), supplementing as needed with paid help, if necessary and feasible. Be meticulous in your scheduling so that slipups will be less likely; keeping a daily calendar will help. When possible, reconfirm the next day's schedule the night before with those who will be transporting and caring for your family. Some hospitals offer a support program for siblings of young patients; ask if one is available.

▲ Prep yourself. Learn everything you can about your child's condition (ask the doctor to recommend reading material) and about what you can expect at the hospital. If there will be surgery, will your child receive general anesthesia? Can you be present while it is administered? What kind of after-effects can you expect? Will he or she have to be immobile for a while? Will food be limited? Will intravenous lines be connected? Will pain medication be available? If you're still breastfeeding, will you be able to nurse?

▲ Prep your toddler. Though older children may benefit from a very thorough hospital briefing, toddlers generally have no preconceived notions about hospitals. Your most important task will be to avoid passing on to your toddler the burden of any negative baggage you're carrying. Make the preparations as upbeat as possible and gear them to your toddler's level of understanding. Include, as possible:

*Reassurance.* Be sure that you don't give your toddler the impression that you're sending him or her "away" to the hospital; make it clear from the very start that you are going there *together* and you (and/or your spouse or other close family member or friend) are going to be there all the time.

*An explanation.* Explain that a hospital is a place where children go when they are sick (or have "boo-boos"), and that there are doctors and nurses there to help make them better. A brief overview, with a few details, is fine. Avoid potentially frightening terms and explanations. If surgery or another invasive procedure is scheduled, don't say, for example, that "the doctor is going to cut your tummy;" instead, explain that the doctor is going to "fix the boo-boo in your tummy." If your toddler has questions, answer them honestly, but don't provide more information, or more detail, than he or she requests.

*A little reading.* Look in the library or the bookstore for books that are meant to help prepare young children for hospital stays. Read them together in the days before your toddler's hospitalization; use them as a springboard for discussion with an older toddler.

*A little play.* Just as playing "dentist" can help young children prepare for a trip to the dentist and playing "barber shop" helps prepare them for an upcoming trim, playing "hospital" can help them feel more comfortable with hospitalization. Secure a couple of surgical masks and a toy medical kit (some hospitals will provide these at the preadmission exam), and play "hospital" with your child. Becoming familiar with a stethoscope and a blood-pressure cuff and even with play hypodermic needles ("Now give Daddy a shot") will be particularly helpful.

*A look around.* The best way to familiarize your toddler with the hospital is in person. Ask that you and your toddler be taken for a little tour so that the surroundings and facilities won't be so foreign when he or she is admitted (if your toddler needs to go to the hospital for preadmission testing, see if the tour can be arranged then). Be sure to visit the play room (if there is one), the gift shop (promise a special toy when you return to the hospital), the cafeteria (talk up a visit there at some point), and if possible, an *unoccupied* room (so your toddler can see the kind of crib or bed he or she will be sleeping in and where you will be sleeping, too). Stay out of rooms that are occupied (a child may be crying or be hooked up to a lot of scary paraphernalia). Talk to a couple of the pediatric nurses; if they're as good with children as they should be, they'll say just the right thing to your toddler.

▲ Make your toddler at home at the hospital. One of the most difficult aspects of being in the hospital for a toddler is being away from home and routine. Make the transition a little easier by bringing along some favorite and familiar items (be sure to check with the hospital first to see which are allowed). Possibilities include: your toddler's pajamas (if the hospital doesn't supply colorful toddler gowns and if a hospital gown won't be required); crib sheets, quilt, and other comfort items (such as a favorite blanket or stuffed animal); toys (especially ones that your toddler can play with in bed, but avoid those with a lot of pieces that might get lost or that are noisy and might annoy other patients); a pad and crayons (if your toddler normally enjoys drawing); family photos; a tape player and some tapes (preferably with headphones, if your child will be able to wear them); picture books; the pretend medical kit you used for prepping your toddler (being able to play doctor now and then may help the patient in your child feel more in control); some favorite videos, if a VCR is available; snacks and special foods that your toddler particularly enjoys (unless a restricted diet will make this impossible). If a very long stay is predicted, try to bring a few small furnishings from your toddler's room (perhaps a small rocker or some pictures).

▲ Get to know the staff. At no time is the partnership between parent and health-care provider more important than when a child is hospitalized. Be informed and assertive (though not argumentative). Ask direct questions and expect direct answers, and don't hesitate to express concerns and reservations you might have about your child's care or condition to physicians and nurses. If you feel your concerns aren't being heard, consult with the hospital's patient advocate.

▲ Put on a happy face. Anxiety is more contagious than measles. To reassure your toddler about his or her hospitalization, you'll need to project a confident, positive attitude. Though it'll doubtless be difficult at times, being a cheerful, smiling presence at your toddler's side will help ease his or her trepidations— laughter, you know, *is* the best medicine. When you need to release pent-up fears and tension of your own, always leave the room, and unload your feelings on a friend or relative who can handle them.

▲ Fuel recovery with good nutrition. Before, during, and after hospitalization, make nutrition an even greater priority than usual; an ample intake of protein, calories, vitamins, and minerals in the form of nourishing Best-Odds foods can help speed healing and recovery while reducing the risk of complications. If the hospital doesn't serve up enough of the Daily Dozen to satisfy your toddler's requirements, get permission to supplement with foods brought from home.

▲ Be prepared for behavior changes and back-sliding. Hospital stays (and illness) and the period following them can be rough going for young children; expect that your toddler may be clingy, withdrawn, listless, frightened, unhappy— or any combination of these—temporarily. Or that he or she will revert to more babyish behavior, like having toileting accidents or resuming a discarded habit, like thumb-sucking. Be patient and understanding through it all. Having someone *on* their side (as well as *at* their side) helps young patients recover faster, both physically and emotionally.

# WHEN MEDICATION IS NEEDED

Thanks to the availability of modern medicines, the world is a healthier place for toddlers; the use of medicine now routinely prevents serious complications that a century ago were frequently fatal or left a child permanently impaired. No longer need an ear infection lead to hearing loss, a urinary infection to kidney damage, or strep throat to a weakened heart; no longer need an ordinary case of pneumonia take a child's life.

But as invaluable as medications can be in treating illness and preserving health, administered improperly, they also can put health in jeopardy. Misused, overused, or abused, medications can cause more problems than they solve.

So it's important to learn how to use medications safely and effectively when your child is ill.

## *WHAT YOU SHOULD KNOW*

It's important, of course, that the doctor has the information he or she needs to prescribe medication. But it is also important that you become familiar with whatever medication is prescribed for your toddler (or any other family member), including what it is, what it does, and what side effects it might cause. The answers in most cases will come from the doctor and the pharmacist.

When you are given a prescription for your toddler, ask the doctor the following:

▲ If the prescribed medication is to be given three or more times a day, is there an equally effective alternative that can be given just once or twice a day?

▲ If the dose is spit out or vomited up, should you give another?

▲ What if a dose is missed? Should you give an extra, or double, dose? What if an extra dose is inadvertently given?

▲ How soon can you expect to see an improvement? When should you contact the doctor if there is no improvement?

▲ When can the medication be discontinued? Do you need to complete the full prescription?

Most pharmacists now provide an information sheet that answers at least some of these questions. When you pick up the prescription, check the label and any other information you are given, such as a manufacturer's package insert. If any of the following aren't answered in the materials, get the answers from the pharmacist.

▲ What is the generic name of the drug? Its brand name, if any?

▲ What is it supposed to do?

▲ What is the appropriate dose for your toddler?

▲ How often should the medication be given? Should your child be awakened in the middle of the night for it?

▲ Should it be given before, with, or after meals?

▲ Can it be given with milk, juice, or other liquids? Does it interact negatively with any foods?

▲ What common side effects may be expected?

▲ What possible adverse reactions could occur? Which should be reported to the doctor?

▲ Could the medication have an undesirable effect on any chronic medical condition your child has?

▲ If your child is taking any other medication (prescription or over-the-counter), could there be an adverse interaction?

▲ Is the prescription renewable?

▲ What is the shelf life of the medication? If any is left, can it be used again at a later date if the doctor advises use of the same medication?

# GIVING MEDICINE SAFELY

To be sure that your child gains the maximum benefit from medication, with the least risk, always observe these rules:

▲ Do not give your child medication of any kind (over-the-counter, his or her own leftover prescription, or anyone else's prescription) without explicit medical approval. In most cases, this will mean getting an okay to medicate each time your child is ill, except when the doctor has given standing orders (for example, whenever your child runs a temperature over 102°F, or 38.9°C, give acetaminophen; or when wheezing begins, use the asthma medicine).

▲ Unless the doctor specifically instructs you otherwise, give a medication only for the indications listed on the label.

▲ Never give a child a medication (not even in reduced dosages) which does not specifically say it can be given to children (again, unless the doctor so directs).

▲ Do not give your child any product containing aspirin (or "salicylates" or "salicylamides") unless the doctor prescribes it.

▲ Do not give your toddler more than one medication at a time, unless you've checked with the doctor or pharmacist to be sure the combination is safe.

▲ Always make sure the medicine you're giving your child is fresh (see page 595).

▲ Administer medications only according to the directions your child's doctor (or the pharmacist) has given you, or according to label directions on over-the-counter products. (If directions on the label conflict with the doctor's instructions, call the doctor or pharmacist to resolve the conflict before giving the medication.) Observe suggested precautions, including those related to timing, to food, and to beverages. Shake, if required.

▲ Always reread the label before each dose, both to be sure you have the correct medication and to refresh your mind as to dosage, timing, and other instructions; don't rely on your memory. Be particularly careful when administering medicine in the dark; check the label in the light first to make sure that you have the right bottle.

▲ Measure medications meticulously. Use a calibrated medicine spoon, dropper, or cup (usually available at a pharmacy); kitchen spoons are variable and messier to handle. If you don't have a medicine spoon, measure the medication in a measuring spoon, then transfer it to a larger spoon to reduce spillage. A spoon that is gently rounded rather than deep can more easily be licked clean by your child. (If it doesn't come clean during the first pass, turn it over and pull it back over your child's tongue to clean off the dregs.) And remember, more is not better (and less is not more). Never increase or decrease a dosage without your doctor's explicit instructions.

▲ If your child spits out part of a dose of pain relievers or vitamins, it is usually better to err on the side of safety and not give an additional amount—underdosing is less risky than overdosing. If you are administering antibiotics, however, check with the doctor about what to do if your child loses part of one or more doses.

## HERBAL REMEDIES

• • • • • • • • • •

They've been used for centuries to relieve the symptoms of hundreds of ailments. They're available without a prescription. They're natural. But are herbal remedies truly effective and safe?

Unfortunately, we don't know for sure. We *do* know that some herbs have a medicinal effect (some very powerful prescription drugs are actually derived from herbs), and that any substance that has a medicinal effect should be categorized as a drug. Thus the same cautions need to be taken with herbs as with other drugs. But there are additional concerns with herbal remedies: Herbs at the present time are not regulated by the federal government either for effectiveness or safety. So when you pick up an herbal remedy you may not get what you think you're getting, and you may get ingredients or contaminants that you didn't expect and that you certainly don't want. So just as you wouldn't give your toddler a medicine without the doctor's approval, you shouldn't give an herbal remedy without a medical okay either.

Also do not give your child folk remedies from the "old country." They can often be extremely hazardous. For example, *azarcon* and *greta* (used in Mexico for treating digestive problems), *paylooah* (used to treat rash or fever in Southeast Asia), *surma* (an eye cosmetic from India used to improve eyesight), and an ayurvedic medicine from Tibet that is used to improve slow development, have all been linked to lead poisoning.

For safety's sake, avoid anything medicinal that is not approved for your toddler's use by the doctor.

▲ To avoid the possibility of a choking incident (or possibly even aspiration pneumonia from inhaling something other than air) when administering medicine, don't squeeze your child's cheeks, hold the nose, or force the head back. Also be sure your child is in an upright position, rather than lying down.

▲ Follow up a medication with a drink of water (unless you are instructed otherwise).

▲ Keep a record of the time each dose is given on a sheet of paper taped to the refrigerator or over the changing table, so you will always know when you gave the last one. This will minimize the chance of missing a dose or accidentally doubling up. But don't panic if you're a little late with a scheduled medication; just get back on schedule with the next dose.

▲ Always complete a course of antibiotics, as prescribed, unless the doctor advises otherwise, even if your toddler seems completely recovered.

▲ Don't continue giving a medication beyond the time specified in the prescription.

▲ If your toddler seems to be having an adverse reaction to a medication, stop it temporarily and check with the doctor before resuming use.

▲ If another caregiver, at home, in preschool, or at day care, is responsible for giving your child medication during the day, be sure that he or she is familiar with the above recommendations.

▲ Be sure to record the name of any medication you give your toddler, as well as pertinent information (including why it was prescribed, the length of time it was given, and any side or adverse effects you observe), in your child's permanent health history record, to create a ready reference now and in the future.

▲ Never pretend medicine is candy or a special drink. Such subterfuge may work in getting a child to take the medicine, but could also lead to overdose if the child accidentally finds the bottle and decides to have a "snack." Be clear—it's medicine, not a treat.

# HELPING THE MEDICINE GO DOWN

Mary Poppins had the right idea. But for all those parents who can't conjure up Mary's magic, it takes something more than "a spoonful of sugar" to make the medicine go down.

If you're lucky, your toddler is one of those who actually enjoys (or at least doesn't strongly object to) the medicine-taking ritual; who savors the taste of the strange liquids (whether they are vitamins, antibiotics, or pain relievers); and who opens up wide enough to accommodate a double-dip ice-cream cone at the sight of a medicine spoon. If you're not so lucky, you're like most toddler parents; your child possesses a sixth sense that says "clamp your mouth shut" when medicine is anywhere in the vicinity. To outwit the tight-lipped:

▲ Switch delivery systems. If your toddler doesn't take kindly to medicine on a spoon, and a dropper isn't large enough for the prescribed dose, ask the pharmacist for a medicine spoon or plastic syringe (which allows you to shoot the

## ASPIRIN OR NON-ASPIRIN?

· · · · · · · · · ·

When treating toddlers, the answer is easy: non-aspirin. Aspirin, though useful in treating many conditions in adults, is rarely recommended for children since it has a long list of possible side effects. In children with a viral illness, it has been linked to a risk of developing Reye syndrome (see page 860), a very serious illness. So do not give it to your child unless the doctor has specifically prescribed it over an aspirin-free medication.

Like aspirin, acetaminophen (brand names: Tylenol, Tempra, Panadol, Liquiprin, Anacin-3) is an antipyretic (fever reducer) and a pain reliever. But unlike aspirin, it is remarkably free of side effects (though there have been occasional cases of liver damage associated with *heavy* dosing). Acetaminophen comes in liquid form for administration by dropper, measuring spoon, or cup; in chewable tablets for older toddlers; in suppository form for a toddler who can't or won't keep a liquid or chewable down; and in an easy-to-disguise "sprinkle" capsule for the toddler who

casts a suspicious eye on any detectable form of medication.

Ibuprofen (brand names: Advil, Motrin) is as effective as acetaminophen at reducing fever and relieving pain and also has an anti-inflammatory effect. Like aspirin, it can upset the stomach, but its use in children has not been linked to Reye syndrome. Your child's doctor may find it the drug of choice under certain circumstances (it's presently available for children only by prescription).

It takes about half an hour for an antipyretic to reduce fever; the effects last anywhere from 4 to 6 hours with acetaminophen and 6 to 8 hours with ibuprofen. Response to the medication tends to be faster in children under two than in older children.

Since all these medications can be dangerous in larger-than-recommended quantities, never give more than the doctor has ordered (see dosage chart, page 584); and, between doses, keep them (like all medications) safely out of the reach of children.

# OUT-OF-DATE MEDICATIONS

· · · · · · · · · ·

A medication that has expired has likely lost its potency; worse still, it may have become dangerous. The following guidelines will help you assure that the medication you give your toddler is fresh:

▲ Check expiration dates when purchasing over-the-counter medications. If you don't think you will use the entire contents before the expiration date, look for a smaller quantity or another package with a later expiration date. Cough syrups and suppositories, in general, have shorter shelf lives than other products.

▲ Prescription medications are not always dated; if a medication is prescribed for your child for a chronic health problem and there is no expiration date on the container, ask the pharmacist for the date and note it on the label.

▲ Keep in mind that most liquid antibiotics maintain their potency for a very short time after the pharmacist prepares them—many are nothing more than an inert, sugary syrup 2 weeks after purchase.

▲ Don't save any leftovers from a prescribed course of antibiotics "for next time." Most, if not all, should have been used, anyway, unless the medication was stopped mid-course because of an adverse reaction. (Occasionally, when a child has a chronic problem, a medication may be prescribed in bulk, to be used as needed. In such a case, it's fine to save the balance of the medication—just be sure to check the expiration date with each future use.)

▲ Protect the shelf life of any medications you purchase by storing them properly.

Most medications deteriorate when stored at high temperatures or in high humidity—which means that the bathroom medicine cabinet is not the ideal place to store them. Set up a medicine storage area in a cool, dark kitchen cabinet or in a bedroom closet instead. *Wherever* you store medications (including vitamin/mineral supplements), they should be completely inaccessible to your toddler (see page 641).

Some medications must be refrigerated or stored at cool temperatures; follow such instructions. If you're traveling with a liquid medication that must be kept cool, chill it with an ice pack. If you expect to be on the road a great deal, you may be able to get such a prescription switched to a chewable tablet (that can be crushed and fed to your child in a spoonful of applesauce or crushed fruit).

▲ Periodically weed expired medications from your medicine storage area. If a product isn't dated, a change in appearance should clue you in to deterioration. Dispose of liquids that have changed color, gotten cloudy, or whose contents have separated; ointments that have hardened or separated; capsules that have melted or stuck together; and tablets that have crumbled, changed color, or give off an odor they didn't have when fresh. Also discard any prescription products that have been around for a year or more.

▲ Flush expired or deteriorating medications down the toilet; don't throw them in the trash basket, where your toddler could retrieve them.

dose into the child's mouth). If your toddler rejects medication from a dropper, spoon, or syringe and likes a nipple instead, try putting a dose in a hand-held bottle nipple and let your child suck it out. Follow this with water from the same nipple so your child will get any medication remaining in the nipple.

▲ To reduce the assault on your toddler's taste buds, which are concentrated front and center on the tongue, aim a spoon toward the back of the mouth and a dropper or syringe between the molars or rear gum and cheek. To avoid setting off a gagging reflex, try not to let the dropper or spoon touch the very back of the tongue. You can also dull the taste by having your toddler hold his or her nose (but don't hold it yourself) while the medicine is being administered. Or by chilling the medication (if this won't affect its potency; ask your pharmacist)—the taste may be less pronounced when it's cold. Or numb the taste buds by having your toddler suck on an ice pop just before taking the medicine.

▲ Unless you're instructed to give the medication with or after meals, plan on serving it up just before feeding. First, because your child is more likely to accept it when hungry, and second, because if he or she does vomit it right back up, less food will be lost.

▲ Approach your toddler confidently with medicine—even if past experience has taught you to expect the worst. If your child knows you're anticipating a struggle, you're sure to get one. You may get one anyway, of course, but a confident approach could swing the odds in your favor.

▲ For children who reject liquid and chewable forms of acetaminophen, you can try "sprinkle caps." This granular form of the drug is relatively tasteless and can be sprinkled into a spoonful of juice, fruit purée, or applesauce.

▲ As a next-to-the last resort, you can mix an unpalatable medication with a *small* amount (1 or 2 teaspoons) of cold or room-temperature strained fruit or fruit juice—but only if you check with the doctor or pharmacist first (sometimes the temperature or the composition of the food can alter the effectiveness of a medication). Don't dilute a medication in a larger quantity of food or juice since your toddler may not finish it all, and mix only one dose at a time, just before administering. Unless your toddler generally resists new foods, use an unfamiliar fruit or juice for mixing since the medicine may impart an unpleasant taste to a familiar one, causing a future rejection of the once-favored food.

▲ As a last resort, if you can't get the medicine down, talk to your toddler's doctor about such options as suppositories and shots.

# THE MOST COMMON TODDLER HEALTH PROBLEMS

## COMMON COLD (UPPER RESPIRATORY INFECTION, OR URI)

**S**ymptoms: Runny nose (discharge is watery at first, then thickens and becomes opaque and sometimes yellowish or even greenish); nasal congestion, or stuffiness; sneezing; often fever, especially in toddlers; sometimes, sore or scratchy throat, dry cough (which may worsen at night), fatigue, loss of appetite. Most of these, incidentally, are not true "symptoms." They are part of the immune response, the body's way of defending against illness—in this case, the cold virus.

**Season.** A cold can strike anytime, but they occur most often fall through spring.

**Cause.** Almost always a virus. More than two hundred viruses are known to cause colds (including the rhinovirus, the parainfluenza virus, and the respiratory syncytial virus) and it's suspected that there may be as many as 1,500 cold viruses or virus combinations. Because toddlers have had few opportunities to build immunity to any of these viruses through previous infections, they are extremely susceptible to colds. Contrary to popular belief, going bare-headed in the winter, getting the feet wet, exposure to cold drafts, and so on, do *not* cause colds.

**Method of transmission.** Most commonly, it is believed, via hand-to-hand contact (the child with a cold wipes her nose with her hand then holds hands with a playmate at play group; the playmate rubs his eye with his hand and the infection is passed on). Also via droplet transmission from sneezes or coughs, and via contact with an object (such as a toy) contaminated by an infected person—but only as long as the moisture surrounding these droplets remains. Incubation period is usually 1 to 4 days. Colds are often passed along a day or two before symptoms appear; once the runny nose dries up, a cold is less contagious.

**Duration:** Usually 7 to 10 days (with day 3 the worst for most sufferers); a residual nighttime cough may linger longer, however.

**Treatment:** No known cure, but symptoms can be treated, as necessary, with:

▲ Time off. It's a good idea to keep a child home for the first day or two of a cold, when possible (see page 587). It's not necessary, however, to restrict activity; in fact, exercise stimulates production of adrenalin, which is a natural decongestant.

▲ Saline nose drops to soften dried mucus (use those sold over-the-counter in pharmacies rather than making your own solution, but avoid drops containing alcohol, which can burn tender mucous membranes). You can also give warm (not hot) tap-water nose drops (3 drops in each nostril two or three times, until the nose seems clear). Drops may be most useful before your child eats or sleeps. Warm commercial saline drops to body temperature before administering them by tucking them into your pocket or inside your shirt for 15 minutes.

▲ Humidification to help clear nasal passages (see page 838).

▲ Petroleum jelly (Vaseline) or a similar ointment, spread lightly on the rims of the nostrils and under the nose to help prevent chapping and soreness. But be careful not to get the ointment inside the nostrils, where it could block breathing passages.

▲ Elevation of the head of the crib or bed (by placing pillows or books *under* the head of the mattress) to make breathing easier.

▲ Warm slippers or slipper socks; when the feet are cold, the redistribution of blood flow can lead to a stuffy nose.

▲ Decongestants, but only if prescribed by the doctor; they tend to be ineffective in young children.

▲ Cough medicine for a dry cough, but only if the cough is interfering with your child's sleep, and only if prescribed by the doctor.

▲ Non-aspirin fever reducer, but only if fever is high. Check with your doctor for guidelines (see page 594).

▲ Commercial decongestant nose drops or sprays, but only under medical supervision; used for more than 3 days, they can cause "rebound," making stuffiness worse than before.

▲ Antibiotics, only if a secondary bacterial infection (such as a middle ear infection or pneumonia) develops. Antibiotics are *not* effective against cold viruses.

**Dietary changes.** Plenty of fluids, particularly warm ones (chicken soup really is effective), and a nutritious diet. Be sure to offer two or three servings of vitamin C-rich foods (see page 506) each day. Frequent small meals may be more appealing than three squares. It's not necessary to limit milk intake; contrary to popular belief, it doesn't increase mucus production. Also see Dietary Guidelines for the sick child, page 587.

**Prevention.** Good overall health habits. Ban smoking near your child, at home and away, and avoid the use of wood stoves that emit indoor air pollutants. (Tobacco smoke and fumes from wood stoves reduce resistance to colds; check your wood stove if you have one for emissions.) Keep your child away from infected individuals, when possible; make washing hands after touching someone with a cold or handling something they've handled mandatory; promote frequent hand-washing in general. Use a phenol-alcohol solution (such as Lysol) to disinfect surfaces that may be contaminated with cold germs, and follow other tips for preventing the spread of illness (see page 606). But remember that nothing (short of locking your child in a sterile room) will entirely protect your child from cold viruses. The average child has six to eight colds a year; some have nine or ten, and even this is not usually a concern as long as the child is growing and developing well.

**Possible complications.** Ear infection, sinus infection, and—much less often—pneumonia.

**When to call the doctor.** If your child is lethargic, has no appetite, or has diffi-

culty sleeping; has greenish or yellowish, foul-smelling nasal discharge or sputum (phlegm); is wheezing, breathing more rapidly than usual (see page 573), or complaining about chest discomfort; has a cough that's getting worse or continues during the day after other symptoms are gone; seems to be having throat pain, trouble swallowing, or a red throat (especially if there are white or yellowish spots visible (see page 610); has swollen glands in the neck (see page 575); pulls on ears day or night, or is very restless or wakes up screaming in the middle of the night; is running a fever over 102°F (38.9°C) or has a low-grade fever for more than 4 days; gets worse instead of better. Also call if symptoms last longer than 10 days—this usually indicates a secondary sinus infection.

**Note:** If your toddler seems to have a continuous cold or very long-lasting or frequent colds, talk to the doctor about the possibility of allergy being responsible.

## CONSTIPATION

**Symptoms.** Small, hard stools every 3 or 4 days; hard, dry stools (even if they are passed daily) that are difficult or painful to eliminate; abdominal pain relieved by a bowel movement. Infrequent movements alone are not a sign of constipation; some children just go less often than others.

**Season.** Anytime of year, but may be more likely when there is a change in diet and schedule (as during a vacation).

**Cause.** Many possible, including a diet low in fiber and fluids. Temporary constipation may develop during or after an illness; certain medications can also be responsible. In addition, constipation often develops in toddlers going through the toilet-learning process, especially

---

## NOSE BLOWING

• • • • • • • • • •

Toddlers will usually staunchly resist having their noses suctioned, so when they have colds they are often made particularly uncomfortable by stuffiness. The solution: Teach them to blow. Practice when your child is well by having him or her play at blowing over a feather or a light scrap of paper. Then when the nose gets stuffy, have your child blow directly into a tissue.

---

when there is parental pressure to perform (see suggestions for low-key toilet teaching in Chapter Nineteen). Constipation may also develop in a toddler who is uncomfortable using the toilet away from home (at day care, preschool, a friend's house, or a store) or who withholds a bowel movement out of pique, because of being otherwise engaged, or for any other reason. The longer a movement is held, the harder and drier it becomes, and the more difficult and painful it is to pass. Fear of passing these hard, dry stools often prompts a child to continue withholding, and a cycle of withholding and constipation is set in motion. Movements that are withheld too long, in addition to becoming hard, can become very large. When passed, they can stretch the rectum; repeated overstretching can make it more difficult for a child to recognize the urge. This, too, helps to perpetuate the cycle. When constipation becomes chronic and home treatment measures fail, the doctor may look for a medical cause, such as an underactive thyroid gland or a spinal-cord anomaly, though these are very rare.

**Transmission.** Constipation is not contagious, but the poor eating and exercise habits, which often lead to or perpetuate it, can be passed from parent to child.

**Duration.** Anywhere from 1 day to a lifetime.

**Treatment.** When an underlying medical problem is a factor, medical treatment generally focuses on identifying

and dealing with it, as well as on softening and removing (usually with the help of an enema) any impacted stool that has become lodged in the rectum and can't be passed. But home treatment usually plays the most important long-term role in preventing recurrence. Treatment should include plenty of:

▲ Fiber. Be sure your toddler is getting whole-grain breads, cereals, and pastas ("*whole* wheat," not just "wheat"; rolled oats rather than instant; and so on); fresh fruit (ripe apples and pears are particularly effective), and dried fruit (especially raisins, prunes, apricots, and figs); vegetables (cooked until tender but not mushy); and legumes (cooked dried beans and peas).[8] For older toddlers, raw vegetables and salad are a good dietary addition. Give wheat (or miller's) bran, which packs a major laxative wallop, only when the doctor has advised its use. It can be added to cereals, pancakes, muffins, breads, other baked goods, pasta sauce, and almost anything with a gooey texture. Always serve the bran with plenty of liquid, don't exceed the recommended quantity, and use it only for as long as it's necessary.

▲ Fluids. Many toddlers who've been recently weaned off the bottle or breast drink much less than they did before weaning; in some cases, it's less than

---

8. Always be sure, of course, that the foods you offer are age-appropriate; dried fruit, whether cooked or fresh and soft right out of the package, should be diced for younger toddlers, and beans and peas should be mashed or split (see page 538).

they need. Be sure that's not the case with yours. If he or she isn't managing to drink at least a quart (a quart and a half would be better) of fluids a day at meals and snacks, try offering sips of milk, juice, or water frequently in between. Fruit juices are particularly beneficial; limit cow's milk to about 3 cups a day, since the calcium salts in it can harden stools.

▲ Exercise. Although you don't have to sign your toddler up at the local health club to make sure he or she is getting enough constipation-combating exercise, you should see that the whole day isn't spent in the car seat or stroller, with little opportunity for physical activity. Treat your toddler to some outdoor play every day, weather permitting. On inclement days, try an impromptu calisthenics class on the living room floor (jumping jacks, toe touches, upside-down bicycling).

▲ Lubrication. Daubing a bit of petroleum jelly at the anal opening may help the movement slip out more easily. *Do not* use enemas or suppositories for constipation without a doctor's advice. Except in rare instances, these treatments make the problem worse, not better.

▲ Medication. Occasionally, the doctor may recommend a brief course of medication; do not give laxatives, stool softeners, mineral oil, herbal teas, or any other medicines for constipation without the doctor's recommendation.

**Prevention.** Most of the lifestyle changes necessary for treating constipation will also help keep it at bay. Fiber, fluids, and exercise should be part of every child's health routine, but they are especially important for those with a history (or family history) of constipation.

**Complications.** Unchecked constipation can lead to: *Disruption of the toilet-learning process.* A child who expects difficulty, even pain, with a bowel movement may hold it in, then may later have an accident when this self-control fails.

*Fissures.* Anyone, young or old, who regularly strains on the toilet can develop painful cracks around the rectum. Since fissures bleed, there is often blood in or around the stools. *A lifetime of constipation.* Unhealthy toileting habits can lead eventually to such chronic constipation-related problems as hemorrhoids.

**When to call the doctor.** When your toddler has not had a bowel movement for 4 or 5 days; when constipation is accompanied by abdominal pain or vomiting; when bowel movements are dry and hard and/or painful; when constipation is chronic and the home measures described above have been ineffective; when there is blood in or around the stool. The doctor will probably want to rule out the slim chance of an underlying organic problem, as well as determine the best approach to treating the constipation.

# CROUP (LARYNGO-TRACHEOBRONCHITIS, OR LTB)

**Symptoms.** *Spasmodic croup:* Sudden onset in the middle of the night, of gasping for breath, hoarseness, bark-like cough; usually no fever. There may be repeated episodes the same night or the next 2 or 3 nights. *Laryngotracheitis:* Cold symptoms that gradually develop into hoarseness and bark-like cough; noisy, labored breathing; retractions (the skin between the ribs can be seen to be sucked in with each breath) as airway swells and secretions increase and thicken. There may or may not be a fever. *Laryngotracheobronchitis:* Symptoms are similar to laryngotracheitis, but onset is more variable and fever can be as high as 104°F (40°C). Child usually looks sick.

**Season.** Most often, fall and early winter.

**Cause.** Narrowing of the airways below the vocal cords due to inflammation of the larynx and trachea, usually triggered in *spasmodic croup* by a combination of allergy and viral infection (though the mechanism isn't clear); in *laryngotracheitis* by a viral infection (most often with a parainfluenza virus); and in *laryngotracheobronchitis* probably by a viral infection with a bacterial secondary infection.

**Method of transmission.** Depends on the cause. Parainfluenza viruses are believed to be transmitted by direct contact and by contaminated secretions.

**Duration.** Several days to a week. Spasmodic croup may recur.

**Treatment.** Steam inhalation (see page 839). Or cool night air (take the child out into the fresh air for 15 minutes). Humidifying your toddler's sleeping space may help, too (see page 838). Also crucial: comfort and support to minimize crying, which could worsen the problem. In severe cases, medical treatment to open the airways, occasionally, and hospitalization (usually brief) is necessary.

**Dietary changes.** Extra fluids, especially warm ones, such as soup and warm orangeade (made with frozen orange juice concentrate and hot water).

**When to call the doctor.** Immediately, if this is your toddler's first attack of croup. If it's a repeat, follow instructions the doctor has given you previously. Also call if the steam doesn't stop the barky cough or if your child lacks color, seems lethargic or sleepy, refuses to eat or drink, has difficulty catching his or her breath (especially during the day), or you can see retractions. If you can't reach the doctor, take your child to the nearest emergency room. Repeated attacks of croup along with voice changes, abnormal cry, or stridor (a harsh, vibrating, crowing sound on breathing in) may require further inquiry; rarely, they are due to warts (caused by the human papilloma virus) on the larynx.

**Prevention.** None known, but humidification for a cold may help.

# DIARRHEA, WITH OR WITHOUT VOMITING

**Symptoms.** Two or three (your child's doctor's guidelines may differ) or more liquidy stools in a 24-hour period; color and/or odor may vary from usual. Sometimes, an increase in frequency and volume of stool, mucus in the stool, vomiting, and/or redness and irritation around the rectum. Weight loss, when diarrhea continues for several days to a week. Many doctors consider diarrhea that continues for 2 to 3 weeks to be chronic; when it persists for 6 weeks or more, it's termed "intractable." An occasional looser-than-normal stool is not a cause for concern; it is often just a reaction to a dietary indiscretion—too much fruit, for example.

**Season.** Any, but may be more common in warm weather, when more fruit is consumed and food spoils more quickly. Rotavirus-caused gastrointestinal infections, however, are more common in winter, in temperate climates.

**Cause.** Many causes, including microorganisms (viruses, bacteria, parasites) picked up from contaminated food or another person (directly or indirectly); excessive amounts of "laxative" foods (such as fresh fruit, prunes and other dried fruit, or fruit juices, especially pear, apple, prune, and grape); consumption of foods (or chewing of gum) containing sorbitol or mannitol; an intolerance or allergy to a food (often milk) or medication; an infection elsewhere in the body (a cold, ear infection, and so on); a course of antibiotics; and, possibly, teething. Intractable diarrhea may be linked to an overactive thyroid gland, cystic fibrosis, celiac disease, enzyme deficiencies (particularly of en-

## TODDLER TUMMY

··········

**S**ome young children have two or three (or even up to six) loose bowel movements (often peppered with bits of undigested food) a day, every day, but thrive nevertheless. They have no underlying disorder and no specific cause can be found for their diarrhea. The condition (called chronic nonspecific diarrhea of childhood, or "toddler tummy") is unpleasant for parents and any other caregivers, but poses no threat to the children themselves; it is usually outgrown between the ages of three and five. Treatment for two weeks, usually with a bulking agent (psyllium seems to work best), is effective about 80% of the time in reducing or eliminating the problem sooner. Some experts also recommend cutting fluid intake to no more than 100 ml/kg body weight/day (or 4 cups for the 22-pounder, 5 cups for the 27-pounder, and 6 cups for the 33-pounder), and limiting fruit juices (especially apple and pear), sugar-sweetened sodas and drinks, and diet gums and candy containing sorbitol and/or mannitol, while increasing insoluble fiber, such as that in whole grains, which makes stools more bulky and less watery.

zymes that digest sugars, such as lactose or sucrose), and other disorders. Sometimes, diarrhea in toddlers is related to constipation (the feces become impacted and leakage of watery stool around it looks like diarrhea).

**Method of transmission.** Diarrhea caused by microorganisms can be transmitted via the feces-to-hand-to-mouth route or by contaminated foods. Incubation periods vary according to the causative organism.

**Duration.** Acute episodes usually last anywhere from a few hours to several days; some intractable cases can last indefinitely, unless the underlying cause is found and corrected. Chronic nonspecific diarrhea is usually outgrown by age three or four.

**Treatment.** Varies with cause. The most common treatment for diarrhea with no underlying medical problem is dietary (see Dietary changes, facing page). Diarrhea due to an underlying medical problem is treated by dealing with the problem appropriately. Antibiotics may be prescribed for bacterial and parasitic infections, but medication is not rou-

tinely given for simple acute diarrhea. Kaolin-pectin products (such as Kaopectate, Donnagel PG) are not generally recommended, because although they improve stool consistency, they do nothing to reduce frequency, volume, or fluid loss. Products containing atropine sulfate (such as Lomotil) or loperamide hydrochloride (Imodium A-D, Pepto Diarrhea Control) are considered neither effective *nor* safe for children. While a bismuth subsalicylate product (such as Pepto-Bismol) can decrease the water content and number of stools, it should never be given to a child if there is even the suspicion of a viral illness (salicylate is aspirin; see page 594). A recent study suggests that a human *Lactobacillus* strain combined with oral rehydration therapy (described in Dietary Changes below) promotes recovery from acute diarrhea; if confirmed, this may become a routine treatment.

Even with treatment and dietary changes, diarrhea doesn't always stop immediately. To determine if treatment is working, look for gradual improvement (sometimes the first stool of the day will look better, but later ones may be looser again) and for signs of dehydration to disappear (see page 605).

To prevent spread of infectious organisms in the diarrhea to the vagina, be particularly meticulous in cleaning a little girl after a bowel movement; always wipe from front to back.

**Dietary changes.**

▲ Increased fluid intake (at least 3 ounces an hour, while the child is awake). For mild diarrhea with no dehydration (see page 605), milk, juice, or juice and water mixtures may be sufficient. For severe diarrhea (watery bowel movements every 2 hours or more often) or mild diarrhea with vomiting or dehydration, particularly in children under age two, oral rehydration therapy (ORT), using a commercially available electrolyte solution, is recommended. Ask your child's doctor to suggest a specific brand and stock a bottle in your medicine cabinet. Offer a few sips of the solution by spoon, cup, or bottle every 2 or 3 minutes, working up to five 8-ounce cups for a child weighing about 22 pounds, about 5¾ cups for the 27-pounder, and a little more than 6 cups for the 32-pounder. If your child vomits the solution, continue giving it, but in very small sips, or make ice pops (with the solution and a small amount of a favorite juice) for your child to suck on. ORT should be continued for 24 to 48 hours. If your toddler rejects the ORT solution, try using a syringe to direct it to the back of the mouth where the taste will be less noticeable. *Do not* give sugar-sweetened drinks (such as colas or ginger ale), athletic drinks, glucose water, homemade sugar water or sugar-salt-water mixtures, undiluted juices, or boiled milk.[9] They may make the condition worse.

▲ For mild diarrhea. Normal diet, according to the child's appetite. Diarrhea tends to improve more quickly when solids are continued. Cutting back on milk, or stopping it entirely for a day or two, may also be helpful if the diarrhea worsens when your child has dairy products; some children become lactose-intolerant during a bout with diarrhea.

▲ For severe diarrhea. Oral rehydration therapy only (although breast milk is okay) for 24 to 48 hours, followed by a bland diet, unless there is vomiting (see below). Start with easy-to-digest, low-fat, low-sugar complex carbohydrate foods, such as bananas, fruit (apple, pear) sauces, rice, plain pasta, potatoes, cereal, and toast. Small amounts of bland protein foods (chicken, cottage cheese) are also appropriate as soon as your child finds them palatable. Gradually return your child to a normal diet over the next couple of days.

▲ For diarrhea with vomiting. Solid food should be withheld until vomiting has stopped. Diluted juices and oral rehydration preparations (in liquid or ice-pop form) are vital, however, to replace lost fluids. Giving fluids a few sips at a time reduces the chance that they will provoke more vomiting. (If vomiting doesn't cease after 24 hours, call the doctor back.)

**Prevention.** Treatment of any underlying condition causing the diarrhea; avoidance or limitation, when possible, of the foods, beverages, and medications that trigger diarrhea; meticulous adherence to food safety rules (see page 527); thorough hand washing by all family members after bathroom use or after changing diapers. Feeding yogurt containing live cultures during antibiotic therapy may also prove helpful—unless, of course, your toddler is allergic to or intolerant of milk.

**When to call the doctor.** If your toddler shows signs of dehydration (see page 605). Call *immediately* if there is severe

---

9. Boiled milk is not safe for children at any time, since the evaporation of the water content leaves a dangerously high level of salt and minerals in the concentrated remainder.

dehydration; acute diarrhea or the fever or vomiting accompanying the diarrhea lasts longer than 24 hours; your child refuses fluids; stools are bloody or the vomited material is greenish, bloody, or looks like coffee grounds; the abdomen is bloated or swollen or there is severe abdominal pain; there is a rash or jaundice (yellowing of the skin). In such cases, the doctor may want to examine your toddler's stool or send it to the lab, so save a specimen in a plastic bag.

# EAR INFECTION

see Otitis Media (see facing page)

# INFLUENZA (FLU)

**Symptoms.** Sudden onset of headache and fever (often with chills and shaking), fatigue, general achiness, and a dry cough. As the illness progresses, cold-like symptoms (sore throat, nasal congestion) may develop and the cough intensify. There may also be gastrointestinal symptoms (abdominal pain, nausea, vomiting) and "pinkeye," or conjunctivitis (an inflammation of the membrane covering the eye). Sometimes, the flu may be difficult to distinguish from a cold, and sometimes there are no symptoms but fever and fatigue. After several days of flu, some children have calf pain that interferes with walking. Occasionally the influenza virus causes croup or pneumonia.

**Season.** In the northern hemisphere, most often, December through March, with a peak in February. In the southern hemisphere, May through September. And in the tropics, all year round.

**Cause.** Influenza viruses A and B, which occur in epidemic form and of which there are innumerable variations, and virus C.

**Method of transmission.** Direct contact with an infected person; breathing in large (and, sometimes, small) contaminated droplets in the air from coughs or sneezes, which can spray the virus as far as 25 feet; or touching an article recently contaminated by the nose or throat secretions of an infected person. Those with flu are most communicable from the day before symptoms occur until symptoms begin to subside, though children may continue shedding the virus in nasal secretions for a week or longer. The incubation period is most often 1 to 3 days.

**Duration.** Generally 5 to 7 days in healthy individuals.

**Treatment.** General treatment includes fluids, rest, and a nutritious diet. To relieve symptoms: humidified air (see page 838), acetaminophen only as needed for pain or high fever (do *not* give aspirin or any medication containing aspirin or salicylates); cough suppressants, if recommended by the doctor, to aid sleep or improve comfort (although a recent study cast doubt on their effectiveness in children); and, if necessary, decongestants, again, of questionable effectiveness and only if prescribed. An antiviral drug may be prescribed for those children with severe symptoms or at high risk of complications.

**Prevention.** Avoid contact with infected individuals; flu shots (see page 562).

**Complications.** Occasionally, pneumonia; sinusitis; otitis media; Reye syndrome (linked to the use of aspirin in children infected with a flu virus).

## SIGNS OF DEHYDRATION

..........

Children who are losing fluids through diarrhea and/or vomiting may become dehydrated and require prompt treatment with oral rehydration therapy (see page 603). Call the doctor if you note the following in a child who is vomiting, has diarrhea, fever, or has otherwise been ill:

▲ Dry mucous membranes (cracked lips).

▲ Tearless crying.

▲ Decreased urination. If your child is in diapers, fewer than 6 wet diapers in 24 hours or diapers that stay dry for 2 or 3 hours, should alert you to the possibility that urinary output is abnormally scant. If your child uses the toilet, this possibility might be signaled by the child using the potty less often and/or by urine that is darker or more yellow than usual or seems to contain crystals (but be sure what you're seeing isn't the gel from a super-absorbent diaper).

▲ A sunken fontanel—the "soft spot" on the top of the head, which may still be open if your toddler is younger than eighteen months old appears depressed.

▲ A faster than usual heart rate (see page 573).

▲ Listlessness.

Additional signs appear as dehydration progresses. These require *immediate* medical treatment. Do not delay in calling the doctor or getting your child to an emergency room if you note any of the following symptoms. While waiting to reach the doctor or en route to the emergency room, feed your toddler oral rehydration solution (see page 603), if possible.

▲ Coolness and mottling of the skin of the hands and feet.

▲ Reduced skin elasticity/wrinkling of skin.

▲ Decreased capillary refill time; blanch the skin of your child's abdomen or the tip of a finger or toe by pinching and then releasing it; if it takes 2 to 3 seconds or more for normal color to return to the pinched area, there is dehydration. (Note, however, that this will only work in a warm room; in a cool room, the color of even a healthy child may take longer to return to normal.)

▲ Sunken eyes.

▲ No daytime urination for 4 hours or more.

▲ Extreme fussiness or sleepiness; present only sometimes .

# OTITIS MEDIA (MIDDLE-EAR INFLAMMATION)

**Symptoms.** Usually, ear pain, in one or both ears. Pain often worsens at night, because lying down changes pressure in the ear (the child may complain, or tug, rub, or clutch at an affected ear), fever (low-grade to high), fatigue, and irritability. Sometimes, nausea and/or vomiting, loss of appetite, loose stools, muffled hearing due to inability of eardrum to vibrate normally. Occasionally, no symptoms are apparent at all. On examination, the eardrum appears pink early in the illness, then red and bulging (though an eardrum may also appear red if a child's been crying, or because of the type of light being used).

If the eardrum perforates (develops a small hole), pus, often blood-tinged, may spill into the ear canal, relieving the pressure and thus the pain. The eardrum usually heals in about a week, but treatment of the infection helps to prevent further damage, so tell your doctor if you suspect a rupture (crust in and around the ear is a telltale sign).

Sometimes, even after treatment, fluid remains in the middle ear, a condition called otitis media with effusion (see page 609).

**Season.** Any time, but most often winter and early spring.

**Cause.** Usually bacteria, but sometimes viruses, which move up into the tiny middle-ear cavity (it's about the size of a seed from a string bean) from the nose or throat through a eustachian tube that isn't draining properly, usually due to inflammation from a cold, sinusitis, sore throat, or allergies. Behind the inflamed eardrum, the build-up of pus and mucus produced by the body in an attempt to respond to the infection causes the pain of earache. Otitis media is more common in babies and children under six than in adults because their eustachian tubes are shorter (making it easier for them to become blocked and allowing germs to

---

## PREVENTING THE SPREAD OF ILLNESS

∙∙∙∙∙∙∙∙∙∙

Infectious illness tends to spread through a family faster than a wildfire through a forest. Though good hygiene can't halt the spread entirely, it may help to contain it.

▲ When possible, limit exposure. If one child has a communicable disease, try to isolate him or her, if you can, from other family members, at least for the first few days. (In some cases, this will have only limited benefit, however, since many illnesses are passed on before symptoms appear.)

▲ Encourage all family members, sick or well, to be scrupulous about hand washing, especially before eating or handling food, or touching their eyes, nose, or mouth; and after nose blowing or coughing, using the toilet, or contact with someone who is ill. Hand washing is probably the single most effective method of preventing the transmission of illness. Keep antiseptic wipes handy when you can't manage frequent washing or when out of the house.

▲ Have sick family members use disposable tissues instead of handkerchiefs and show them how to dispose of them in a covered trash container immediately after use.

▲ Teach family members to cover their mouths and not to cough or sneeze on each other (or anyone else). And discourage kissing when there's a bug around.

▲ Prohibit the sharing of cups and toothbrushes. Provide separate cups in the bathroom (use a decal or different colors to set cups apart); you can also use small paper cups, but consider the impact on the environment before you do. (To make sure a sick family member doesn't reinfect him or herself, replace toothbrushes after an illness; wash bathroom cups daily with dish detergent and hot water or in the dishwasher.)

▲ Prohibit sharing at the table. Don't let family members share drinks from the same cup or food from the same fork, spoon, or plate.

▲ Don't allow anyone to prepare or handle foods in your home without first washing their hands.

▲ Wash thoroughly, with hot soapy water or in the dishwasher, the eating utensils of any family member who is down with a contagious illness.

▲ Wash or spray possibly contaminated surfaces (such as bathroom faucets, telephones, toys) with Lysol, which can kill many germs.

▲ Change clothing, towels, and bedding frequently.

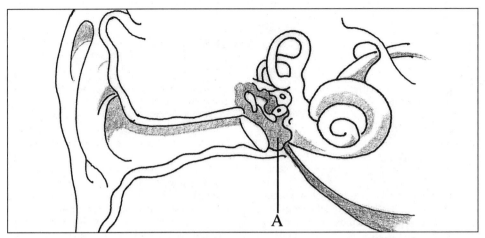

*Most toddler ear infections occur in the middle ear, the tiny chamber (A) at the end of the outer ear canal.*

travel up them more quickly) and horizontal rather than slanted (making drainage poor), and because they get more colds and other respiratory illnesses.

**Method of transmission.** Not direct—otitis media isn't passed from person to person. It often follows a cold or flu. There may be a family predisposition to middle-ear infection.

**Duration.** Although pain usually diminishes or disappears shortly after treatment is begun, it can take 10 days to 8 weeks of antibiotic medication to resolve an acute ear infection; fluid may remain in the middle ear for much longer (see otitis media with effusion, page 609).

**Treatment.** Acetaminophen, as needed, for fever and pain. Heat (applied with a heating pad set on low, warm compresses, or a hot-water bottle filled with *warm* water) or cold (applied with an ice bag or ice wrapped in a wet washcloth) can also be used to relieve pain until the doctor is reached. Elevating the child's head during sleep may also be helpful (see page 837). Do not use ear drops unless the doctor prescribes them for this particular illness; do not use them at all if there is a puncture. And do not rely on

these remedies alone. Because of the risk of serious complications, OM requires medical treatment. Although some physicians will wait 2 or 3 days to treat ear infections (in the hope they will clear on their own), the great majority begin antibiotic therapy promptly and treat for a minimum of 10 days (stopping the medication sooner, even if the patient feels fine after a day or two can lead to a rebound of the infection and eventually to a chronic problem). The doctor may culture a sample of cells drawn from the middle ear in order to pinpoint the culprit microorganism if a child does not seem to be responding to treatment (many doctors check the ears again after 72 to 96 hours of antibiotic therapy) or if it is deemed necessary for another reason. Sometimes, in order to drain infected fluid from the ear, a bulging eardrum may be perforated by the doctor in a procedure called a *myringectomy*. The incision heals in about 10 days, but may require special care until then.

At the end of the course of treatment, the doctor will probably want to recheck your child's ears. Though the infection may clear quickly on antibiotics, in about 1 in 10 children, the ears remain filled with fluid for 3 months or more

## TUBES
## FOR TODDLERS

..........

Tube insertion (myringotomy with tympanostomy) should be considered a treatment of last resort for the child with persistent fluid in the ears (recent research suggests that there is little reason to insert tubes for repeated ear infections). This surgical procedure is performed under general anesthesia, usually by a pediatric ear, nose, and throat specialist (otolaryngologist). A tiny tube is inserted through the eardrum to drain accumulated fluids from the inner ear. Hospitalization for a few hours or overnight is required. The tube falls out on its own after 9 to 12 months, sometimes sooner, and often inhibits future infections.

But there are risks, which should be discussed fully with the child's doctor, and probably a specialist as well, and weighed against possible benefits before a decision is made to go forward. Long term benefits are unclear.

If tubes are inserted, care must be taken to be sure that they don't become a conduit for infection; check with your child's doctor before allowing underwater swimming or submerging in the tub, because water might enter the ear under these conditions. Many children use tot-size ear plugs to protect the tubes when bathing or swimming.

following the resolution of the infection (see otitis media with effusion, page 609).

**When to call the doctor.** During regular office hours if you suspect an ear infection. Call again if your child isn't feeling better after 48 hours of treatment or seems to be getting worse, or if he or she refuses or vomits the antibiotic. Call immediately if there has been an injury to your child's ear, or if ear pain continues and is so bad that your child is screaming, develops a stiff neck or severe headache, seems very sick, or is having unusual difficulty balancing when walking.

**Prevention.** It's not clear whether the use of decongestants during colds and flu is effective in reducing the incidence of otitis media. It is clear, however, that protecting a child from exposure to second-hand tobacco smoke and weaning from the bottle (if the child drinks lying down) can reduce the incidence. Treating allergies that may be contributing to repeated episodes of otitis media may also be helpful (see page 703). Switching from group day care to home day care or

home care may, in some cases, also reduce the number of episodes, since a child in group care will be exposed to many more colds.

When a child has had repeated middle-ear infections (three episodes in 6 months, or four in a year), a low-dose, preventative (or prophylactic) regimen of antibiotics may be given for 3 to 6 months to discourage recurrence. Or the antibiotic may just be given at the height of the otitis media season or when the child has a cold (the antibiotics won't do anything for the cold, but they can help prevent secondary ear infections). When prophylactic antibiotics fail to prevent repeat infections, the insertion of tubes (see box) may be considered. When large adenoids are blocking the eustachian tube, removal of the adenoids may be effective. Most children outgrow the tendency to frequent ear infections by age four or five.

**Complications.** Otitis media with effusion (see facing page). Thanks to antibiotics, other complications, such as mastoid infection, are extremely rare.

# OTITIS MEDIA WITH EFFUSION, OR SEROUS OTITIS MEDIA

**Symptoms.** Usually, hearing loss (temporary, but it can become permanent if the condition continues untreated for many months). Sometimes, clicking or popping sounds on swallowing or sucking; a feeling of fullness or ringing in the ears; or no noticeable symptoms at all.

**Season.** Year-round.

**Cause.** Fluid in the middle ear, which may or may not contain bacteria; sometimes, a lingering viral infection may be involved.

**Method of transmission.** Not person-to-person; usually follows an acute middle-ear infection.

**Duration.** Weeks, months, or even years.

**Treatment.** Watchful waiting for 3 months; if fluid persists, hearing tests and antibiotics. If there is no improvement after 6 months, and especially if hearing is affected, tympanostomy tubes may be recommended (see box, facing page). Recent research suggests that giving steroids with the antibiotics will clear persistent fluid in the ears and reduce or eliminate the need for tympanostomy tubes. Ask your child's doctor about this treatment.

If you are concerned about your child's hearing, you may want to consult a hearing specialist.

**When to call the doctor.** As soon as you note any signs of hearing loss.

**Prevention.** Periodic ear exams, tympanostomy tubes, low-dose prophylactic antibiotics. Treating cold symptoms with decongestants is probably ineffective, but flu shots seem to help.

**Complications.** Possibly, hearing loss, and the verbal, developmental, and emotional issues that often go along with it.

# SINUSITIS[10]

**Symptoms.** In secondary sinus infection: cold symptoms that have continued for more than 10 days, with discharge that is clear, thick and yellowish, or whitish; a cough during the day as well as at night; swelling around the eyes on rising in the morning. Sometimes, bad breath, fever, headache behind or over the eyes (though head and face pain are more common in children over five). There is no fever when sinusitis is the result of allergy or an injury rather than infection.

**Season.** Mostly fall and winter for infections secondary to colds; spring, summer, and fall for cases due to allergy.

**Cause.** Usually bacteria; also allergy or injury.

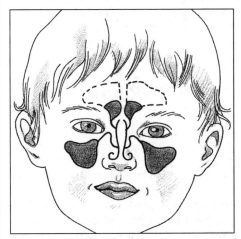

*The sinuses may become inflamed by allergy or infected during a cold. In a young child, the frontal sinuses (above the eyes) are not fully developed.*

10. Sinusitis is uncommon in children under two.

**Method of transmission.** Not transmitted directly.

**Duration.** Most cases begin to improve 10 to 14 days into therapy. With chronic sinusitis, symptoms may not improve for 3 to 4 weeks.

**Treatment.** Antibiotics to treat an infection. When antibiotic therapy isn't effective, the affected sinuses may need to be irrigated and drained; in rare instances, surgery may be necessary. Antihistamines and decongestants for sinusitis in children are not generally recommended. Elimination of allergen is effective when cause is allergy.

**When to call the doctor.** At any signs of acute sinusitis.

**Prevention.** Removal of known allergens from child's environment (see page 706), if the sinusitis is allergy-related.

**Complications.** Rarely, the infection spreads to the central nervous system. Call the doctor *immediately* if there is swelling or redness around your child's eyes, severe headache, sensitivity to light, or increasing irritability.

# SORE THROAT

**Symptoms.** Inflamed tonsils and/or throat, producing pain and difficulty swallowing, and sometimes, fever. A scratchy, sore throat often accompanies a cold. A toddler with a strep infection may have low-grade fever, with irritability, loss of appetite, and swollen glands (see page 575). Older children are more likely to experience high fever, more severe sore throat, and difficulty swallowing with strep.

**Season.** Late fall, winter, and spring.

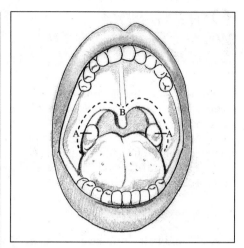

*Ask your toddler to "Stick out your tongue and say Aaah," demonstrating as you do (you probably won't need a tongue depressor or spoon to get a clear view). With a penlight, examine for redness around the edges (the dotted line), white spots, and swelling of the tonsils (A) or the uvula (B).*

**Cause.** Allergy; cold virus or other virus; group A *Streptococcus* bacteria or other bacteria.

**Method of transmission.** Sore throat of a cold is transmitted like a cold; strep is almost always transmitted by direct contact with respiratory secretions from an individual with an active infection. A person can carry strep for months after the acute illness has passed, but is not likely to spread the germ.

**Duration.** Sore throat of a cold usually lasts just a few days; a strep throat usually responds to treatment in a couple of days.

**Treatment.** Warm liquids (see page 587); soothing, nonacidic foods and beverages; humidification; and, if necessary, acetaminophen for pain, but only once the doctor has ruled out or diagnosed strep (giving it sooner could mask pain that would help with diagnosis). A strep throat or other bacterial infection always requires antibiotic treatment.

## TONSILS AND ADENOIDS: TAKING THEM OUT IS NO LONGER IN

••••••••••

At one time, tonsillectomy was as predictable a part of childhood as losing those two front teeth. At some point, virtually every child had tonsils removed (usually along with adenoids). It was believed that this surgical procedure would reduce the risk of sore throats, ear infections, and other upper respiratory illnesses. Now it's recognized that for most children, tonsils help to prevent illness rather than cause it. These bits of tissue in the throat are actually lymph nodes that serve an important role in the immune system. Like lymph nodes elsewhere in the body, the tonsils enlarge when fighting infection nearby; they usually shrink again when the infection is gone.

Today the fact that tonsils and/or adenoids are enlarged is no longer automatically a reason for their removal. Often the doctor will recommend giving them time to shrink on their own or will treat them with antibiotics in hope of reducing the swelling. (Sometimes treating an allergy will gradually reduce the size of enlarged adenoids.)

There are times, however, when surgery is warranted. According to the American Academy of Pediatrics, surgery is recommended when:

▲ The enlarged tonsils and/or the adenoids are interfering significantly with breathing and with the exchange of oxygen and carbon dioxide in the lungs.

Symptoms include drowsiness and exhaustion day after day, in spite of adequate rest, and possibly, sleep apnea (see page 169).

▲ The enlarged tonsils are interfering significantly with swallowing.

▲ The enlarged adenoids are interfering significantly with breathing, making speech sound nasal, and causing distorted pronunciation.

The AAP says surgery is a reasonable option when:

▲ A child has had repeated strep throat infections or other bouts of serious illness (seven in a year, five in each of 2 years, three in each of 3 years).

▲ Tonsillitis or swollen glands have become chronic (for at least 6 months), despite antibiotic treatment.

▲ An abscess forms around or behind the tonsil.

▲ Ear infections continue to recur in spite of the insertion of tympanostomy tubes (see page 608).

▲ There is moderate interference with breathing or swallowing, along with mouth breathing and snoring.

---

**Prevention.** Avoid those with colds or strep infections; see also Common cold, page 596.

**When to call the doctor.** See Sore Throat in the When to Call the Doctor Section, page 571. A throat culture to determine if the sore throat is caused by a streptococcus is usually necessary if: yellowish-white, thick spots are visible on throat or tonsils (see illustration, facing page); fever is over 101°F (38.3°C); a rash develops with or right after the sore throat; the child has been exposed to strep or has had rheumatic fever or rheumatic heart disease or has kidney disease.

**Complications.** Rarely, with strep: rheumatic fever; rheumatic heart disease; scarlet fever. These complications can be virtually eliminated by treating strep throat with antibiotics.

## TREATING YOUR TODDLER'S SYMPTOMS

· · · · · · · · · ·

| SYMPTOM | APPROPRIATE TREATMENT |
|---------|----------------------|
| **Cough\*** | Humidified air\*\*<br>Increased fluids (see page 587)<br>Cough medication, only if prescribed<br>Postural drainage, if recommended and taught to you by the doctor |
| **Croupy cough** | Abundant steam or vapor\*\*<br>A stroller or car ride in the fresh air<br>Possibly, cough medicine, if prescribed<br>In severe cases, medical treatment; sometimes, hospitalization |
| **Diarrhea** | Increased fluids, oral rehydration (see page 603)<br>Antidiarrheal medicine, only if prescribed |
| **Ear pain** | Pain reliever, such as acetaminophen (see page 584)<br>Local dry heat to ear (hot-water bottle made with warm water)\*\*<br>Head elevation<br>Decongestant, only if prescribed<br>Antibiotics, only if prescribed for present infection<br>Ear drops, only if prescribed for present infection |
| **Fever** | Increased fluids (see page 587)<br>Adequate calorie intake<br>Fever reducing medication, such as acetaminophen, but only as recommended by the doctor (see page 584)<br>Tepid bath or sponging, if medication is inappropriate or ineffective (see page 585)<br>Light clothing and cool room temperature (see page 584) |
| **Itching** | Calamine lotion (not Caladryl or other antihistaminic preparation)<br>Comfortably hot bath (test with elbow or wrist)<br>Soothing tepid (body temperature) bath<br>Colloidal oatmeal bath |

# URINARY TRACT INFECTION (UTI).

· · · · · · · · · · · · · · · · · · · · · · · · · · · ·

**Symptoms:** Often, frequent urination, painful urination, incontinence, blood in the urine, pain above the pubic area or on the side, lethargy, and fever; sometimes, no symptoms. Often, what looks like a gelatinous vaginal discharge is not a sign of a vaginal infection or other problem, just a sign that the diaper's absorbent jelly material has oozed out. Not to worry.

**Season.** Any time.

**Cause.** Most often, bacteria that enter through the urethra (the tube that carries

| SYMPTOM | APPROPRIATE TREATMENT |
|---|---|
| **Itching (con't.)** | Prevention of scratching and infection (keep fingernails short and wash with antibacterial soap; cover hands with socks or mittens during sleep) <br> Pain reliever, such as acetaminophen (but not aspirin; see page 584) <br> Oral antihistamine, only if prescribed (but not topical antihistamines or anesthetics) <br> Topical steroids, if prescribed |
| **Nasal congestion** | Humidified air** <br> Salt-water irrigation** <br> Head elevation** <br> Increased fluids (see page 587) <br> Decongestant, only if prescribed <br> Nose drops, only if prescribed |
| **Pain or discomfort from minor injury** | Comfort (cuddling) <br> Distraction (see page 678) <br> Pain reliever, such as acetaminophen <br> Local heat or cold, as appropriate** |
| **Sore throat** | Soothing, nonacid foods and beverages <br> Pain reliever, such as acetaminophen <br> Fever treatment, if needed (see page 582) <br> Saltwater gargle, for older children (most toddlers can't gargle) |
| **Teething pain** | Comfort (cuddling) <br> Local cold, applied to gums (see page 98) <br> Pressure on gums (see page 98) <br> Pain reliever, such as acetaminophen, only if recommended by the doctor |
| **Vomiting** | Increased fluids, in small sips (see page 587) <br> Restricted diet (see page 603) |

*Generally, only a dry cough is treated; a productive cough helps clear mucus and other materials from the chest. Products that contain dextromethorphan as an active ingredient are frequently recommended to suppress a dry cough but recent studies cast doubt on their effectiveness.

**See Common Home Remedies, beginning on page 836 for practical tips on carrying out this treatment.

urine from the bladder for excretion). Because the urethra is shorter in girls and bacteria can travel up it more easily, girls have UTIs more often than boys. Occasionally, bacteria from elsewhere in the body can enter the kidney through the bloodstream. An infection may affect just the urethra (urethritis), the bladder (cystitis), or the kidney (pyelitis, pyelonephritis), or all three. An inadequate fluid intake could encourage UTI. A urine specimen may be obtained and cultured to confirm the diagnosis and determine the causative organism.

**Method of transmission.** Most often via contamination of the urethra by bacteria from the stool (especially in girls).

**Duration.** Varies; most cases clear up quickly on antibiotic therapy.

**Treatment.** Antibiotics; the antibiotic to be used may be determined by a urine culture. It is absolutely necessary for a child to finish the full course of medication prescribed, even if the symptoms have subsided. Also, an ample fluid intake. Cranberry juice, which seems to prevent bacteria from adhering to the lining of the urinary tract, may be particularly helpful. A serious urinary tract infection or repeated milder UTIs should be followed with tests to check the health of the urinary tract; sometimes a urinary tract abnormality or obstruction is present that requires the attention of a specialist.

**Prevention.** Sanitary bathroom habits and diapering techniques: wiping front to back, washing hands after toileting. Also, an adequate fluid intake, regular diaper changes, cotton underwear for children out of diapers, the opportunity to urinate when necessary (no "holding it in"), the avoidance of tight pants in non-breathing synthetic fabrics and of potentially irritating bubble baths and soaps.

**When to call the doctor.** As soon as you notice symptoms of a possible UTI. Prompt treatment is necessary to protect your child's urinary tract from damage.

**Complications.** Kidney damage, although if UTI is treated promptly, it is unlikely.

# CHAPTER TWENTY-ONE

# Keeping Your Toddler Safe

**A**ccidents are rarely truly accidental. In fact, some safety experts believe there are no accidents, or at least that true accidents are extremely rare. And that most of the so-called "accidents" that kill some 10,000 children under 14 in the United States each year and permanently disable another 50,000 don't have to happen. When accidents aren't preventable, the injuries that result from them often are.

Most injuries, however, are as preventable as polio and whooping cough, and implementing what is known about injury prevention can be as effective against injuries as immunization is against childhood diseases. To underscore that injury prevention should be a priority on a par with disease prevention, the Department of Health and Human Services has created the National Center for Injury Prevention and Control as a part of the Centers for Disease Control.

Generally, several factors must come together to "create" an accident that re-

sults in injury: a dangerous object or substance (a bottle of pills, a staircase, a bucket); a vulnerable victim (such as an unsuspecting toddler); and often, environmental conditions (the bottle doesn't have a safety cap, the staircase is ungated, the bucket has a couple of inches of water in it). In the case of childhood accidents, there is an additional factor that can make an injury more likely to happen: insufficient adult vigilance.

To prevent injury, it is necessary to modify each of these factors. Remove the dangerous object or substance from your toddler's reach. Make your toddler less susceptible by gradually instilling good safety habits. Change the hazardous environmental conditions that make an injury more likely—be certain all medicines have childproof caps, that all stairs have gates, that no bucket or other container is left around with water in it. And possibly most important of all in the case of toddlers, you have to be certain that whoever is caring for the child is consistently alert to potential dangers and knows how to avert them.

To minimize the chance that your toddler could be injured:

# CHANGE YOUR WAYS

Though you should begin the education process now, it will be years before your child will be able to take full responsibility for his or her own safety. Right now, *your* behavior has the greatest impact on your child's safety. If you want to greatly reduce the risks of unintentional injury:

▲ Be eternally vigilant. No matter how carefully you attempt to childproof your house, your car, the backyard, the places you visit, it's virtually impossible to make these environments completely safe. Toddlers are curious, impetuous, unpredictable; they lack judgment and need to be protected from their own impulses by the constant, careful supervision of adults.

▲ Don't let your attention be diverted when using household cleaning products, medicines, electrical appliances, power tools, or other hazardous objects or substances when your toddler is on the loose. It takes no more than a second for a toddler to get into serious trouble. If the doorbell or phone rings, or you have to run into the kitchen to check something in the oven while you're involved in a possibly risky activity, be sure to take your toddler with you.

▲ Be particularly alert during times of stress and at stressful (or especially hectic) times of day. It's when you're distracted or preoccupied that you're most likely to forget to put a knife away after using it, to close the medicine bottle and lock it away, or to shut the gate at the top of the stairs.

▲ Never leave your toddler alone in your house, apartment, or backyard. Never leave a young toddler alone in a room except when safely deposited in a playyard, crib, or other safe enclosure—and then only for a few minutes, unless he or she is sleeping (in which case the area should be childproofed and within earshot—in case the child awakens and gets up). Don't leave your toddler alone, even "safely" enclosed in a crib or playpen, awake or asleep, with another young child under five[1] (they often don't know their own strength or realize the possible consequences of their actions) or a pet (even a docile one). It's also unsafe to leave a toddler alone in a car, even for a few moments. You can leave your toddler strapped into a car seat while you close the garage door, as long as you haven't left the key in the ignition (young children have been known to turn the key).

▲ Become familiar, if you aren't already, with emergency and first-aid procedures (see page 659). Take a child cardiopulmonary resuscitation (CPR) course that teaches what to do in case of near-drowning, choking, head injury, and so on. Although you can't always prevent accidents, knowing what to do if a serious one occurs can save lives and limbs.

▲ Give your toddler plenty of freedom. Once you've made the environment as safe as possible, avoid hovering. Though you'll want your child to be safety conscious, it isn't wise to discourage the normal experimentation of childhood. Children, like grown-ups, can benefit by learning from their mistakes; never giving them the chance to make mistakes can retard growth and actually puts them at greater risk. The child who's most likely to be injured at a gymnastics birthday party is the one who's never learned, by trial *and* error, to use the equipment. And the child who is afraid to run, climb, or try new things misses out not

---

1. Sometimes an even older child can not be trusted with a toddler; use your best judgment.

only on the learning experiences that come from free play, but on a lot of the fun of childhood as well.

▲ Set a safe example (and have significant others in your child's life do the same). Keep in mind that when the two are contradictory, your toddler is more likely to do what you do rather than what you say. The best way to teach safe living is to practice it. You can't expect a child to be happy about being strapped into a car seat when you don't buckle up yourself, to obey traffic signals if you dash across the street in spite of a "Don't Walk" light, or to respect the risks fire represents if you leave burning cigarettes all over the house.

# CHANGE YOUR TODDLER

Injuries are much more likely to happen to those who are susceptible to them. And of course, toddlers, with their eagerness to try new things, their shaky motor skills, their relative immaturity, and their lack of judgment, easily fall into that category.[2] Your goal as a parent is to reduce this susceptibility—as much as you can.

To that end, it isn't enough to injury-proof your child's environment, you've got to begin to injury-proof your child by teaching what's safe and what's unsafe (and why), instilling a respect for the body and the risks it faces, and establishing (and modeling) good safety habits. Start by building and using a vocabulary of warning words: ("Ouch," "Boo-boo," "Hot," "Sharp") and phrases ("Don't touch," "That's dangerous," "Be

careful," "That's an ouch," "That could give you a boo-boo"). Your toddler will automatically come to associate these phrases with potentially dangerous objects, substances, and situations. Your dramatic warnings may seem to sail right over your little one's head at first. But in time, your child's brain will begin to store and process the information, until one day, it becomes apparent that your lessons have taken hold. Teach your toddler now about the following:

**Sharp or pointy implements.** Whenever you use a knife, scissors, razor, or letter opener, or other sharp implement, be sure to remind your toddler that it's sharp, that it's not a toy, that only Mommy (and Daddy or other grown-ups) are allowed to use it. Illustrate more tangibly by pretending to touch the point of the implement, saying "Ouch," and pulling your finger away quickly in mock pain. Point out that *you* always carry scissors point down, holding the blades, and that you never run with any sharp object; make it clear that you expect your child to do the same when old enough to use such implements. As your child becomes older and gains better small-motor control, teach cutting with a pair of child's safety scissors and with a butter knife. Eventually, sometime in the school years, you can advance your child to supervised use of the "adult" versions.

**Hot stuff.** By a year, if you've already begun introducing the concept, your toddler will probably understand (albeit in a very rudimentary way) what "hot" means, that the warning "hot!" means don't touch, and that something that's hot can mean a boo-boo. If you haven't taught this yet, start now. Illustrate your point by letting your toddler touch something "hot," but not hot enough to burn, such as the outside of your coffee cup. Whether the concept is novel or old hat, however, continue to consistently remind that your coffee (or the stove, a lit match

---

2. Some toddlers (for example, the risk-takers, who show no fear when on a high slide or getting ready to jump off a wall; kids who seem to thrive on life on the edge) are particularly susceptible. Take this into consideration in setting safety standards, if your toddler has one of these characteristics.

or candle, a radiator or heater, a fire-place, the hot-water faucet) is hot and shouldn't be touched by children. Be particularly careful to provide this warn-ing with something new in your home—a new toaster, or a recently installed wood stove. When your child is old enough to strike a match or carry a hot drink (some time in the mid-school years), he or she should be taught how to do so safely.

**Steps.** True, it's necessary to protect a new walker from serious falls by se-curely gating all staircases in the home. But it is also necessary to help your child learn how to navigate steps safely. The child who has no experience with steps, who knows nothing about them (except that they are off-limits) is at greatest risk of a tumble the first time an open stair-way is discovered. So put a gate at the top of every stairway of more than three steps in your home—going downstairs is much trickier, and thus much more dan-gerous, for the beginner than going up. But when you're downstairs, put the gate three steps up from the bottom so that your child can practice going up and down under controlled conditions. Show your toddler how to hold on to the rail while climbing up or down the stairs. When your toddler becomes proficient, open the gate occasionally so that he or she can tackle the full flight as you stand or crouch a step or two below, ready to provide back-up if necessary. Or hold your child's hand as you walk up to-gether. Once going up is mastered, help your child learn how to come down safely. Many toddlers crawl down on their tummies at first; others bump down on their bottoms. As they become more proficient, they start walking down one step at a time. Continue to keep the gates in place, fastening them when you're not able to stand by, until your child is a very reliable step climber (somewhere around two years old). Even then, putting a gate at the head of the stairs is

still a good idea (especially at night if your toddler is prone to wandering).

If there aren't any stairs in your home or building, find a set (at the home of a friend, a relative, or at some other accessible location) and let your child do some practicing with you close at hand.

**Electrical hazards.** Electrical outlets, cords, and appliances all hold great ap-peal for curious toddlers. And it's not enough to use distraction every time you catch your child on the way to probing an unprotected outlet, or to hide all the visible cords in your home; it's also nec-essary to repeatedly remind the toddler of their "ouch" potential and to teach older children respectful use of electric-ity and the risks of mixing it with water.

**Tubs, pools, and other watery attrac-tions.** Water play is fun and educational; encourage it. But also encourage a healthy respect for water. Teach your toddler basic water safety rules, includ-ing: it's dangerous (and prohibited!) to get into water (the tub, a pool, a pond, or any other body of water) without a par-ent or another grown-up; no running or horsing around near a pool or in it; no playing with wheeled toys near the pool; no diving head first; no going past the shallow end of pool, which should be shallow enough for a toddler to stand in (there should be a "lifeline"—a rope with floats attached—dividing deep and shallow ends). But remember, you can't sufficiently "waterproof" a young child, not even with water wings and swim-ming lessons; never leave a toddler alone near water (see page 646).[3]

**Choking hazards.** When your child puts something in his or her mouth that doesn't belong there (a coin, a pencil, a peanut, a block), take it away and explain, "You

---

3. One rule you *don't* have to teach your toddler: No swimming after meals. In spite of what your mother may have told you, there are no risks re-lated to water activities on a full stomach.

## DRESSING FOR SAFETY

..........

Choose the safest clothing for your toddler. Use only flame-retardant sleepwear (and wash it according to the manufacturer's instructions); be sure that pant cuffs aren't too long or pajama feet too floppy (secure the feet of sleepers by putting large hair elastics that aren't tight enough to restrict circulation around the ankle, see page 4). If your toddler walks around the house in stocking feet, be sure the socks have nonslip bottoms. Soles of slippers and shoes that are slippery smooth should be roughed up with sandpaper or adhesive tape stripes to prevent slipping. Avoid long play scarves or sashes that can trip up your child (or worse, pose a strangling risk) and always shun strings or ties longer than 6 or 7 inches).

can't put those things in your mouth. They might get stuck in your throat and hurt you." Teach your child that it isn't safe to run with food—a lollipop, a teething ring, pencil, pacifier, or a toy—in his or her mouth (a face-first fall could force the toy down the throat, blocking the airways and causing injury and possible suffocation); that food should only be eaten in a seated position; and that it's not only impolite, but unsafe, to talk with one's mouth full.

**Poisonous substances.** You're always meticulous about locking away household cleansers, medicines, and so on. But at a party, one of the guests leaves his vodka and orange juice on the coffee table. Or you're at your parents' house and your father, who's been trying to clear a clogged drain, leaves the drain cleaner on the bathroom counter. You're asking for trouble if you haven't begun to teach your toddler the rules of substance safety. Repeat these messages, over and over and over again:

▲ Don't eat or drink anything unless your parent(s) or another grown-up you know well gives it to you. This is a difficult concept for a young child to grasp, but repetition will make it stick—eventually.

▲ Medicine and vitamin pills are *not* candy, though they are sometimes flavored to taste that way. Don't eat or drink them unless your parent(s) or another grown-up you know well gives them to you.

▲ Don't put anything in your mouth that isn't food; this, too, will bear a lot of repeating.

▲ Only grown-ups are allowed to use scouring powder, spray wax, dishwasher detergent, and other cleaning products. Repeat this every time you scrub the tub, polish the furniture, load the dishwasher, and so on.

There are dangers outside your home, too, that your toddler needs to learn about:

**Street hazards.** Begin teaching street smarts now. Every time you cross a street with your toddler, explain about "stop, look, and listen," about crossing at the green (or the corner), and about waiting for the "Walk" (or green) light. If there are driveways in your neighborhood, be sure to explain that it's necessary to stop, look, and listen before crossing them, too. Explain that drivers can't see little children so little children have to hold the hand of someone big, and insist your toddler always hold your hand (or the hand of another adult) when crossing. Make no exceptions. Teach your child never to step into the street without an adult, even if there's no traffic. Point out the curb as the line a child must never go beyond on his or her own.

It's a good idea to hold hands on the sidewalk, too, but many toddlers revel in the freedom of walking on their own. If you permit this (and you probably will want to, at least some of the time), keep a sharp eye on your child—an instant is all it takes for a child to dart into the path of an oncoming car. Infractions of the don't-go-in-the-street-alone rule demand a swift and stern reprimand.

Be sure, too, that your toddler knows not to leave the house or apartment without you or another adult he or she knows well. Toddlers have been known to toddle, on their own, out the front door and straight into trouble.

It's also important to teach your toddler not to touch refuse in the street—garbage, broken glass, cigarette butts, food leavings. But don't make your child neurotic about touching anything at all—it's okay to touch flowers (without eating or picking them), trees, store windows, light posts, mailboxes, and so on. (But do carry wipes to clean hands before eating—or thumb-sucking.)

**Auto safety.** Be certain that your toddler not only becomes accustomed to being buckled into a car seat, but understands why it's essential. Also explain in simple terms the reason for other auto safety rules: why it's not safe to throw toys around, why it's dangerous to grab the steering wheel when someone is driving, and why children must not play with door locks or window buttons. (Teach school-aged children how to open the locks, in case they should become locked in alone.)

**Playground safety.** A toddler who is old enough to play in a playground is old enough to begin learning playground safety rules. Teach swing safety: Never twist a swing (when it's occupied or even if it's empty), push an empty swing, share a swing meant for one occupant, or walk in front of or behind a moving one. And slide safety: Never climb up the slide from the bottom (always use the ladder) or go down head first; always wait until the child ahead of you is off the slide before going down; and, when you do go down, move out of the way immediately when you reach the bottom.

**Pet safety.** Teach your child how to interact safely with pets—your own, or those of others (see page 85)—and to keep away from strange animals.

**Insect safety.** Teach your toddler to avoid bees when possible, and to stay still (rather than swatting and provoking) when one approaches. Warn your child, too, not to provoke spiders or play with spider webs.

# CHANGE YOUR TODDLER'S SURROUNDINGS

The world of the toddler who is walking and climbing expands rapidly. Virtually overnight, almost everything is within reach. To best protect your toddler, you will have to maintain the same safety precautions you instituted when your child began to crawl, plus several new ones. To make your home as safe as possible for your toddler, start with:

## Changes Throughout the Home

Tour your home looking for potential trouble spots (for a toddler's eye view, get down on your knees), and make changes as necessary:

**Windows.** If windows are above ground level, install window guards according to manufacturer's directions (screens or storm windows *cannot* be relied on to keep a toddler from tumbling out). Or adjust your windows so your toddler can't get out through them: an inexpensive locking device is available for double-hung windows or screws can be screwed into the window frames to keep the lower window from opening more than 4 inches). Be sure, however, that you can open these windows quickly in an emergency, as in case of fire. Even with protections in place, never leave a young child alone in a room with a window that is open from the bottom (a window open from the top is generally safe, unless of course, your child is able to climb to that height). Periodically check the windows in an old house to be sure the panes are not loose and that the putty is not dried out or missing. Never place furniture that your toddler can climb on in front of a window. And don't install a window seat; if you already have one, make sure the window it's under is always locked or is protected by a window guard.

**Venetian blind or drapery cords.** Tie them up so a child can't become entan-

*A glass door can look like an open door. Affix decals to prevent dangerous collisions.*

gled in them. Do not place a crib, a playyard, a chair, or a bed a child can climb on within reach of these (or any other) cords. Cord shorteners, which can put the cords out of reach, are available where child-safety equipment is sold.

**Doors.** Since toddlers are quite capable of toddling out a door without anyone taking notice (a major risk during holiday time and parties, when there's a lot of coming and going) keep all doors, sliders, and screens secured with toddler-proof locks, even in summer. (Some sliders can be locked in a slightly open position, allowing air to enter without allowing a toddler to exit.) Affix decals or hang prisms on large glass doors so that toddlers (or anyone else) will be less likely to walk into them.

**Electrical cords.** Move them behind furniture so that your child will be less tempted to mouth or chew on them (risking electric shock) or tug at them

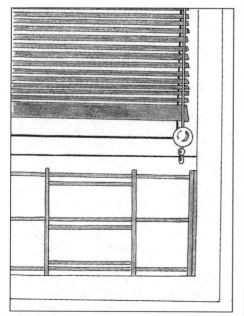

*Window guards and cord shorteners (for venetian blind or drapery cords) make windows safer for toddlers.*

*A door-knob cover, which makes it difficult for a toddler to turn the knob, and a gate can keep your child from leaving a safe area and entering an unsafe one.*

(pulling lamps or other heavy items down). If necessary, fasten the cords to wall or floor with electrical tape or specially designed gadgets. (Do not use nails or staples and do not run cords under carpets, where they can overheat.) Never leave an appliance cord (for a coffeemaker, for example) plugged into an outlet when the cord itself is disconnected from the appliance—this is a major shock risk.

**Electrical outlets.** Cover outlets with caps or with shields (which cover both the outlet and the plug inserted into it) or place heavy furniture in front of them to prevent your child from inserting an object (such as a hairpin or screwdriver) or probing its mysteries with a drooly finger. To reduce the risk of shock, have regular outlets grounded by an electrician, if possible. Since they can't be properly childproofed, avoid using multiple-outlet power strips.

**Lighting.** To prevent nighttime falls, be certain that stairways are well lighted; use night-lights in hallways, bathrooms, and bedrooms, as needed (but remove them by day, if they are within your toddler's reach).

**Lamps and light fixtures.** Don't place a lamp where a toddler could touch a hot bulb, and don't leave a lamp or other light fixture without a bulb within your toddler's reach—probing an empty socket might be irresistible to your child but very unsafe. Avoid using halogen or fluorescent lighting unless there is a glass or plastic shield over the bulb since direct rays may present an environmental hazard.

**Unstable furnishings.** Put rickety or unstable chairs, tables, or other furniture that might topple if leaned on or pulled up on out of the way until your toddler is sure-footed enough not to need furniture for support; securely fasten to the wall bookcases or other wall units that a child might possibly pull down.

**Dresser drawers.** Keep them closed so your child will be less likely to climb into them, possibly upending an unstable dresser; if a dresser isn't stable enough, consider bolting it to the wall.

**Painted surfaces.** Be sure they are lead-free; many homes built before 1960 still harbor paint with high lead concentrations beneath layers of newer applications. As paint cracks or flakes, microscopic lead-containing particles are shed. These can end up in household dust (and outdoor soil) and on a child's hands, toys, clothing—and eventually, of course, in the mouth. Check with your local EPA for information on testing services. If testing shows lead in the paint in your home, discuss with the EPA the benefits of having the lead removed as opposed to painting or papering over it. Removal of lead paint should not be carried out when the family, especially children or pregnant women, is at home. Hand-washing, particularly before meals and snacks, is vitally important in homes where lead dust may be a problem.

Lead isn't the only problem with paint. Paints produced prior to August 1991 may contain mercury, which can be toxic when the fumes are inhaled. If you plan to use some old paint and you aren't sure whether it is mercury-free, call the National Pesticide Telecommunications Network Hotline: (800) 858-7378, or (806) 743-3091 in Texas. Children and pregnant women should not inhale mercury paints while they are being applied or for 48 hours afterward, at which point most of the fumes have dissipated and much of the danger has passed.

**Ash trays.** Put them out of reach so your toddler can't get hold of a hot butt or sample a mouthful of ashes and butts; better still, banish tobacco from your home entirely (see page 628).

**Fireplaces, heaters, stoves, floor furnaces, and radiators.** Put up protective grills, covers, or other barriers to keep small fingers from fire and hot surfaces (even the grill on a floor furnace can get hot enough to cause second-degree burns). And remember, most of these surfaces retain heat long after the heat has been turned off or the fire has died down.

## LEAD CAN LEAD TO TROUBLE

··········

Large doses of lead can cause severe brain damage in children. Even relatively small doses can reduce IQ, alter enzyme function, retard growth, damage the kidneys, as well as cause learning and behavior problems, and hearing and attention deficits. Lead may even have negative effects on the immune system. Ask your toddler's doctor about screening tests for lead, particularly if you live in a high risk area or in a pre-1960s building; if your water supply is contaminated with lead (see page 537); if a sibling, housemate, or playmate has been diagnosed with high blood levels of lead; if you or another adult in your home has a job or hobby involving exposure to lead; or you live near an industry that is likely to release lead into the air, soil, or water (a battery plant or a lead smelter, for example). A diet high in fat and low in calcium, magnesium, iron, zinc, and copper may increase a child's susceptibility to lead poisoning.

If testing shows that your child has high blood lead levels, it may be helpful to consult with a specialist in treating this problem. Chelation therapy and the use of iron and calcium supplementation may be recommended to remove the lead and prevent the damage it can cause.

**House plants.** Keep them out of reach, where your child can't pull them down or sample the leaves or dirt; be especially wary of poisonous plants (see page 656). If you have some favorite plants that are poisonous but which you can't put out of reach, consider asking a neighbor or relative to look after them for you until your toddler can be relied upon not to nibble on the leaves.

**Loose knobs on furniture or cabinets.** Remove or secure any that are small enough to be swallowed or cause choking or get stuck in your toddler's mouth.

**Stairs.** Put gates at the top of any staircase you want to keep your toddler from going down and three steps up from the bottom of any staircase you want to keep your toddler from going up (or move a single gate around, depending on your toddler's whereabouts). But never let a gate substitute for adult supervision. Keep steps clear of toys, clothing, and anything else that could trip up a toddler (or anyone else). Carpeting on the stairs may improve footing and help minimize injury in case a fall does occur. A plush, well-padded carpet or a thick nonskid area rug at the foot of each staircase should also cut down on bumps and bruises.

**Banisters, railings, and balconies.** Be sure that balusters (the upright posts) aren't loose and that the distance between them on stairs or balconies is less than 5 inches, so a toddler can't get stuck or slide through (a 4-inch gap is safer for infants). If the gap is wider, consider a temporary safety "wall" (usually available at stores that sell child safety equipment) of plastic or firm mesh along the length of a balcony. Install railings on both sides of a staircase, if possible; the rail on at least one side should be low enough for your toddler to reach.

**Tablecloths.** When your toddler is around, use placemats, short cloths with little or no overhang, or longer cloths

*Cushions on the sharp edges of furniture help prevent bumps and bruises; caps on electrical outlets prevent shocks.*

held securely in place (with clasps designed to keep outdoor cloths on in windy weather, for instance). If you do use an unsecured tablecloth, limit its use to when your toddler is asleep or very carefully supervised.

**Glass-topped tables.** Either cover a glass top with a heavy table pad or put such tables temporarily out of reach (with some coffee tables, you can remove the glass and replace it with a safer material for the time being). *Never* allow your toddler to stand on a table, even if it's not glass-topped.

**Sharp edges or corners.** If your child could possibly bump into edges on tables, chests, and so on, cover them with homemade or store-bought cushioned strips and corner guards (see above illustration).

**Heavy knickknacks and bookends.** Place them where your child can't pull them over. Never underestimate the strength or ingenuity of a toddler!

**Scatter rugs.** Be sure they have nonskid backings, and don't place them at the top of stairs or allow them to remain rumpled. Rubber matting or two-sided adhesive tape under small rugs and runners helps make them slip-resistant.

**Videocassette recorders.** Place VCRs out of your toddler's reach or install a VCR guard to keep little fingers (or other objects) out of the cassette loader.

**Toy chests.** In general, open shelves and bins are safer for toy storage. But if you still prefer to use a chest, look for one that has a lightweight lift-off lid or a safe hinged lid—one that doesn't snap closed automatically when released. The hinge should allow the lid to remain open at any angle to which it is lifted. If you have an old toy chest that doesn't meet these requirements, remove the lid or the hinges permanently. There should also be air holes in the body of the box (drill a couple on each side, if there aren't) just in case a toddler climbs in and becomes trapped. Like all furniture children spend a lot of time around, a toy chest should have rounded corners or corner padding.

**Your toddler's crib.** Adjust the mattress to its lowest position and remove bulky toys, pillows, bumper pads, and anything else that could be used as a stepping-stone to freedom—and possible disaster. To soften a fall should your toddler get out in spite of your precautions, place a plush rug, an exercise mat, or a couple of cushions next to the crib. Also be sure not to string any toys (such as a crib gym) across the top of the crib—a child could strangle in it. When your toddler is 35 inches tall, it's time for a bed (see page 318).

**Your toddler's bed.** Install safety rails on the bed and place the bed at least 2 feet from windows, heating vents, radiators, wall lamps, or drapery or venetian blind cords. Also, never buy a bunk bed for a toddler or allow one to sleep in the upper bunk of someone else's bunk bed.

**Floors.** To minimize falls: Try to keep clutter out of traffic lanes, wipe up spills and pick up papers immediately, and be sure to repair loose or damaged floor tiles and carpeting promptly.

**Wastebaskets.** Never put anything you don't want your toddler to handle in an open wastebasket. Put potentially hazardous trash in an inaccessible container (see page 640).

**Standing water.** Whether in a pail, bucket (especially a 5-gallon or larger bucket), a diaper pail, an ice chest (in which the ice has melted, for example), or in the more obvious places—tubs, toilets, and home spas—even small amounts of water pose a serious drowning risk to a toddler.

**Lightning.** Since plumbing and phone wires can conduct electricity should lightning strike your home, don't allow family members to shower or bathe (or play in a pool; see page 646) or use the phone during a thunderstorm or the threat of one, unless you know that the building is equipped with a lightning rod.

**Exercise equipment.** It's great for you, but it could be dangerous for your toddler. Don't let your toddler near bikes, ski machines, rowing machines, treadmills, step-machines, weights, and weight machines unless under very close supervision. Even then, it could be risky since toddlers move so fast. If you're buying a new bike, and if you can afford these features, get one with spokeless wheels, an enclosed chain-and-sprocket apparatus, and wheel and pedal locks for when it's not in use. If you exercise with a jump rope, always store it out of reach of your toddler, preferably in a locked cabinet.

**Garage, basement, greenhouse, workshop, and hobby areas.** Since these areas usually contain a variety of hazardous implements and/or poisonous substances,

## FOOD FOR THOUGHT

··········

Although chewing on a pencil is not exactly a recommended activity for toddlers, you needn't panic if yours stops drawing to do a little munching. Pencils are made of graphite, not lead, and are not toxic. The paint finish is nontoxic, too. Large erasers, however, may be bitten off and could present a choking hazard.

---

keep them securely locked and do not allow children unsupervised access.

**Other "sensitive" areas.** Put any room that houses breakable objects—such as a dining room with a collection of fine teacups—off limits to children (set up a gate or another barrier).

**Hazardous objects.** Be alert to the whereabouts of a host of potentially hazardous items typically found at home. If you don't need these things, don't keep them in your home at all. If you do, see that they are safely stored—in drawers, cabinets, chests, or closets with childproof latches, on absolutely out-of-reach shelves (you'd be amazed at how high some toddlers can manage to climb), or behind closed doors your toddler can't open. When you're using such items, be sure your child can't get at them when you turn your back, and always put them away as soon as you've finished with them (or as soon as you discover that one has been left out). Particularly hazardous are:

▲ Sharp implements such as knives, scissors, needles and pins, knitting needles, letter openers, disposable razors and razor blades (don't leave these on the side of the tub or dispose of them in a wastebasket your toddler could get into).

▲ Pens, pencils, and other pointed writing implements (substitute chunky nontoxic crayons or fat washable markers, instead). If your child occasionally wants to "write" with a pencil, pen, or markers "just like a grown-up," allow such use only when he or she is seated and you can supervise closely. (And be sure the ink is washable.)

▲ Small notions, including: thimbles, buttons, marbles, coins, safety pins, button batteries (like those used in hearing aids) and anything else a child might possibly swallow or choke on (see page 618).

▲ Lightweight or filmy plastic bags, such as produce bags, dry cleaning bags, and packaging on new clothing, pillows, and other items. These can suffocate a young child if placed over the face. Remove clothing from dry cleaning bags and new items from their plastic wrap as soon as you get them home; then safely dispose of (or recycle) the plastic. For storage, use zippered garment bags instead of dry cleaning bags.

▲ Incendiary articles, such as matches and matchbooks, lighters, and unextinguished cigarettes.

▲ Tools of a trade or a hobby: paints and thinners if there's an artist in the house; pins and needles if there's a dressmaker; wood-working equipment if there's a carpenter; and so on.

▲ Toys that belong to older siblings. These generally should not be within reach of children under three. Of particular concern are: building sets with small pieces; large trikes, bikes, and scooters; miniature cars and trucks; and anything with sharp corners, small or breakable parts, or electrical connections.

▲ Button batteries. The disk-shaped type used in watches, calculators, hearing aids, cameras, and so on are easy to swallow and can release hazardous chemicals into a child's esophagus or stomach. Store new, unused batteries in an inaccessible place in their original packaging rather than loose. Keep in mind that "dead" batteries are as hazardous as fresh ones; dispose of them promptly and safely. Know what kind of batteries you are using; if your toddler swallows one, the poison control center will want that information.

▲ Fake food. Apples, pears, oranges, and other fake food made of wax, papier-mâché, rubber, or any other substance that isn't safe for children (a wax apple, a candle that smells and looks like an ice-cream sundae, a child's eraser that smells and looks like a ripe strawberry).

▲ Cleaning materials and other household products (see page 635 for a list of those that are toxic).

▲ Glass, china, or other breakables.

▲ Light bulbs. Small ones, such as those in night-lights, are particularly easy for the toddler to mouth and break. Remove your toddler's night-light during the day and put it safely out of reach.

▲ Jewelry. Most risky: beads and pearls, which can be pulled off the strand and swallowed, and small items like rings, earrings, small pins.

▲ Mothballs. They're toxic as well as chokable. Opt instead for cedar blocks (not small balls, which can be mouthed) and store out-of-season clothing in airtight bags or closets. If you do use mothballs, store them in an area not accessible to your toddler, and air clothing and blankets out thoroughly (until the odor has dissipated) before allowing anyone to use these articles.

▲ Shoe polish. If your child gets into it, the results can be messy; if your child eats it, it can cause digestive problems.

▲ Perfumes and all cosmetics. They are potentially toxic.

▲ Vitamins, medicines, and herbal remedies (see page 593).

▲ Whistles. A young child could choke on a tiny toy one, and on the small ball inside any whistle, should it come loose. Not a good toddler toy.

▲ Latex balloons. Uninflated or burst, they can be inhaled and cause choking (see page 657). Condoms pose a similar threat.

▲ Dangerous party foods. Don't serve small, hard finger foods (such as nuts, raisins, popcorn, hard candies, cocktail franks) at parties your child will attend and don't leave them out in candy or nut dishes.

▲ Guns (see page 628).

▲ Strangulation hazards: Strings, cords, cradle gyms, cloth measuring tapes, tape cassettes (which can become unwound),

## SAFE HEIGHTS

• • • • • • • • • •

The "safety line" in your house will move higher as your toddler gets older and more proficient at climbing. Anything above the head of the crawler is usually safely out-of-reach. The early walker can often reach the edge of the dining table, end tables, and low dressers. The young climber can clamber up a chair or other furniture to get to something higher. The competent walker-climber can push the chair (or a box, or a pile of books) over to the kitchen counter, the washing machine, and anything else seemingly out-of-reach—and scale it before you turn around.

## NO GUN IS A SAFE GUN

· · · · · · · · · ·

"**T**OT SHOOTS PLAYMATE WITH FATHER'S GUN." It's a headline we shudder to see, but we see it, or another like it, far too often. Yet tragedies involving young children and the guns they find at home are completely preventable. Not by hiding the weapons (children are capable of seeking out and finding, or simply stumbling into, just about anything their parents try to hide). Not by locking the guns up (all it takes is forgetting to secure the lock just once). Not by teaching children to stay away from guns (curiosity can easily erase parental warnings and overwhelm a toddler's underdeveloped sense of right and wrong). But by keeping guns out of the home—period.

Toddlers are impulsive and incurably inquisitive, perfectly capable of pulling a trigger on a gun, but not capable of comprehending the possible consequences of that seemingly innocent action. Keeping a gun in the home, whether you think your toddler can get to it or not, is leaving open the very real possibility of tragedy. The American Academy of Pediatrics and numerous safety organizations strongly urge: Don't do it.

If you must keep a gun at home, keep it locked up, inaccessible, and unloaded; store the bullets in a separate location (even very young children have figured out how to load a gun—usually by watching the process on TV). And buy a trigger lock or other device to prevent accidental discharge.

---

or anything else that could get wrapped around a child's neck. Toddlers shouldn't sleep with dolls or stuffed animals that contain audio tapes; a child might remove and unravel the tapes on waking and finding nothing else to do.

▲ Holiday hazards. These include: *Decorative and symbolic items.* Check decorations as you would any other household objects for safety (examine for breakability, small parts, toxicity, size; tiny tree ornaments or dreidels, for example, are unsafe) or hang them high, out of the reach of young children. *Gifts.* Don't leave gifts that could be unsafe under the tree or arranged anywhere else (perfumes, cosmetics, hobby kits, liquor, and so on). *Plants.* If you have holiday plants at all, keep them out of reach of children (some are poisonous if ingested; see page 656). For reducing holiday fire hazards, see page 637.

▲ Anything else in your home that would be dangerous if mouthed or swallowed by your child. See list of poisons, page 635. For precautions to take to keep your toddler's food and water safe, see Chapter Eighteen.

## Changes in Indoor Air Quality

The air in the average home looks harmless enough, and chances are it smells harmless enough, too. Yet in some homes, there are substances in the air that can't be seen, can't be smelled, but can be harmful. To make sure the air you and your toddler breathe at home is safe, be alert to the following sources of indoor air pollution:

**Tobacco smoke.** This is the major contributor to indoor air pollution in this country; about 1 in 4 children is exposed to tobacco smoke at home. The risks are many. Tobacco smoke, even secondhand, weakens the airways, making them more vulnerable to germs, poisons, and pollutants, and reduces blood levels of vitamin C (an anti-oxidant important for immunity, which it is believed may protect against such serious health problems as cancer, heart disease, and cataracts). Children who are exposed to secondhand smoke on a regular basis are more susceptible to asthma, tonsillitis, respiratory infections, ear infections, and to bacterial and viral infections severe enough to land them in the hospital. On average, one study found, they are more likely than other children to be in fair or poor health. They also, as a group, score lower on tests of reasoning ability and vocabulary. Children of smokers appear, too, to have an increased risk down the road of developing lung cancer or cancer of the cervix, brain, thyroid, or breast. In addition to these risks, smoking in front of a young child sets a poor example; children who see someone they love smoke are more likely to become smokers themselves, with all the serious risk for a shortened life span that the habit involves. So it's not surprising that the Environmental Protection Agency (EPA) urges parents not to permit smoking at home or in the presence of their children.

**Carbon monoxide.** This colorless, odorless, tasteless, but treacherous gas (it can cause lung ailments, impair vision and brain function, and is fatal in high doses) that results from the burning of fuel can enter your home from many sources. So take steps to keep it out: Be sure that wood stoves and kerosene heaters (if you must use one) are properly vented (ask the fire department to check). Keep your heating system in good working order. Speed up combustion in slow-burning wood stoves by keeping the damper open. Do not permit charcoal fires or propane heaters indoors. Be sure that gas stoves and other gas appliances are properly vented (install an exhaust fan to the outdoors to draw out fumes) and adjusted (if the flame isn't blue, have the adjustment checked). If you're purchasing a new gas range, opt for an electric ignition to reduce the amount of combustion gases released; and *never* use a gas stove for heating your home, or part

of it. Never leave fireplace fires to smolder (douse them with water), and clean chimneys and flues regularly. Never leave a car idling, even briefly, in a garage that is attached to your home (open the garage door before starting the car), and cool off an overheated car before closing the garage door. If your home has a combination of risks for carbon monoxide pollution (an attached garage, a wood stove, and an old heating system, for example, or you use your fireplace a lot), consider having the indoor air checked periodically for carbon monoxide emissions or installing a carbon monoxide detector, which would warn you of increasing levels before they became dangerous.

**Benzopyrenes.** A long list of respiratory problems (from eyes, nose, and throat irritation, to asthma and bronchitis, to emphysema and cancer) can be attributed to the presence of the tar-like organic particles that result from the incomplete combustion of tobacco or wood. To prevent your toddler being exposed, allow no tobacco smoking in your home, be sure the flue that vents smoke from a wood fire doesn't leak, vent combustion appliances (such as dryers) to the outdoors, change air filters on appliances as needed, and increase ventilation (tight weather-stripping keeps heat in more efficiently, but also traps potentially dangerous fumes).

**Particulate matter.** A wide variety of particles, invisible to the naked eye, can pollute indoor air and present a hazard to children. They come from such sources as household dust, tobacco smoke, wood smoke, unvented gas appliances, kerosene heaters, and asbestos insulation and construction materials (which have been linked to a wide variety of illnesses, including some cancers and heart disease). The same precautions discussed above (banning smoking, keeping filters clean, ensuring proper venting and adequate ventilation) can minimize the threat from particulate matter. A reliable air filter unit can remove many particulates and is especially valuable if some- | one in the family has allergies. If you find asbestos in your home, get professional advice on whether it should be

## INDOOR PEST CONTROL: SORRY FOR PESTS, STILL SAFE FOR TODDLERS

• • • • • • • • • •

Ants. Roaches. Mice. Termites. Unwelcome pests infiltrate homes in virtually every part of the country—at least occasionally. And whether the pests where you live are simply annoying or downright dangerous, you'll likely want to keep them out of your home or get rid of them once they enter. But how do you do this without using substances hazardous to your toddler? Try:

**Blocking tactics.** Install window and door screens (don't leave unscreened windows and doors open) and screen or otherwise close off entry points for insects and vermin. Don't count on screens, however, to keep your toddler *in*; see page 620.

**Natural measures.** Check the bookstore or library for a guide that suggests a variety of methods for "natural" pest control, or check the shelves of your local health-food store or supermarket for nontoxic pesticides. But keep in mind that though these products are usually good for the environment, they are not always safe for children. A mix of cayenne pepper and water, for example, may seem relatively harmless, but it could injure a child who tried to eat it or rubbed it in his or her eyes. Ultrasound pest fighters, incidentally, are not effective.

**Sticky insect or rodent traps.** Not reliant on killer chemicals, these snare crawling insects in enclosed boxes (roach traps) or containers (ant traps), flies on old-fashioned fly paper (with no added insecticide), and mice on sticky rectangles. Because human skin can stick to their surfaces (the separation can often be awkward or even painful) these traps must still be kept out of the reach of children or put out after they are in bed at night and taken up before they are up and around in the morning. From a purely humane standpoint, these traps have the disadvantage of prolonging the death of their victims.

**Baited traps.** These traps do contain a poison, but it gives off no chemical fumes and is enclosed in the trap, making it more difficult for a toddler to reach. Still, place the traps out of reach of your child.

**Box traps.** The tenderhearted can catch rodents in box traps and then release them in fields or woods far from residential areas, though this isn't always easy. Because the trapped rodents can bite, the traps should be kept out of the reach of children or put out and carefully monitored when children are not around.

**Safe use of chemical pesticides.** Virtually all chemical pesticides—including the much-touted boric acid—are highly toxic, not just to pests but to people as well. If you opt to use them, *do not* spread them (or store them) where young children can get to them or on food-preparation surfaces. Always use the least toxic substance available for the job.* If you use a spray, keep the children out of the house while spraying and for the rest of the day, at least. Better still, have the spraying done while you're on vacation or otherwise away from home for a time. When you return, open all the windows for a few hours to air out your home.

*For information on safer pest control contact: National Coalition against the Misuse of Pesticides, 701 E Street SE, Suite 200, Washington, DC 20003, (202) 543-5450; National Pesticide Telecommunications Network, (800) 858-7378); or the Environmental Protection Agency (EPA), 401 M Street SW, Washington, DC 20360, (202) 260-2080. For the number of the EPA office nearest you, call (202) 382-4454.

## PUTTING WORRY IN PERSPECTIVE

• • • • • • • • • •

From the moment the pregnancy test comes back positive, worry is an inevitable part of parenting. You worry when they don't sleep through the night—and when they *do* sleep through the night. You worry when they haven't taken their first step yet, and once they have, you worry about what they're going to step into. You worry about them making friends, then you worry about the friends they make.

All parents worry. And a certain amount of worry is healthy—it keeps us on our toes, watchful, thoughtful, careful, and (also inevitably) in close contact with the pediatrician. But too much or the wrong kind of worry—worry that becomes excessive or obsessive—can keep both parents and children from fully enjoying the wonder years of childhood.

It makes sense to worry enough so that you do a good job of keeping your toddler safe—but not so much that you keep your toddler from being a toddler. Enough so that you only frequent playgrounds where safe construction ensures safe fun, and enough so that you keep an eye on your toddler's activities at the playground—but not so much that you make all playground equipment off-limits. Enough so that you take sensible precautions in crowded stores and crowded streets—but not so much that you never let your toddler out of the house. Enough so that you carefully screen baby-sitters and other caregivers before you leave your toddler alone with them—but not so much that you never trust your child with anyone but yourself.

Children pick up on parental anxiety; when it's exaggerated, it can slow the development of skills and compromise their confidence by making them as apprehensive as their parents. Growing requires taking calculated chances, and children whose parents have made them afraid of taking any chances can't move forward.

So don't stop worrying entirely, but try to keep your worry in check and in perspective. Use it to keep your toddler safe, not stifled; to keep your child secure in your love, not suffocated by it.

---

removed or encased, and deal with it before particles become airborne.

**Miscellaneous fumes.** Fumes from some cleaning fluids, from aerosol sprays, and from turpentine and other painting-related materials can be toxic. So, always use the least toxic you can find (such as water-based paints, beeswax floor waxes, paint thinners made from plant oils[4]). Use it in a well-ventilated area and never use it when infants or children are nearby. When possible, use pump sprays rather than aerosols. Store all household products safely out of reach of curious little hands, preferably in an outdoor storage area.

**Formaldehyde.** With so many products in our modern world containing formaldehyde (from the resins in particle-board furniture to the sizing in decorator fabrics and the adhesives in carpeting), it isn't surprising that this gas—which is linked to respiratory problems, rashes, nausea, and other symptoms in humans—is everywhere. The levels of formaldehyde gas released are highest when an item is new, but the gas can continue to be released in decreasing quantities for months or longer. To minimize the potential damage, look for products that are formaldehyde-free (or well-sealed, to prevent its escape) when building or furnishing your home. There are various strategies for dealing with items you already have, but the simplest and nicest

---

4. Avoid paint thinners—or any other product—containing methylene chloride; it is a very strong carcinogen.

# JPMA CERTIFIED SAFE FOR KIDS

· · · · · · · · · ·

Strollers, booster seats, safety gates, and a variety of other equipment designed for children are awarded a Juvenile Products Manufacturers Association (JPMA) Safety Approved Certification Seal once they pass rigorous testing for conformity with tough manufacturing standards. Look for JPMA certification when making the following purchases for your toddler. Try them out for easy use before purchasing.

▲ A stroller. It should have a broad base and be sturdy enough not to tip over if a child moves around in it; if your stroller tips when the handles are overloaded, be certain they never are. Strollers should also be easy to fold and open (be sure a stroller is securely locked into the open position before using), and be free of nooks and joints that could catch and injure small fingers.

▲ A playyard (playpen), if you use one, should have fine mesh sides (less than ¼ inch openings) or vertical slats less than 2⅜ inches apart. Always be sure the playyard is *fully* open before putting your toddler in it, and never leave it partly opened—it could close up on and smother a child who climbed into it.

▲ Gates. These can be used to keep a child in or out of any room in the house as well as away from staircases. Gates can be portable (these usually have to be released and moved for anyone to get through the doorway) or permanent (these usually swing open after unlatching), depending on your needs. Both varieties are generally ad-justable to fit different door frame sizes and can vary from 24 to 32 inches in height. If you are installing a permanent gate, be sure to screw it into wooden wall studs to prevent toppling under the pressure of an eager-to-escape toddler or one rolling along on a riding toy (drywall or plaster won't hold the screws securely). If you use a portable gate with an expandable pressure bar, be sure your little climber can't get a toehold on the bar. Do not use an accordion-style gate with large diamond-shaped openings (in which small hands, feet, or even heads can get caught); opt instead for models with Plexiglas or fine mesh (if the mesh is flexible, it will be even harder for your toddler to climb on the gate) or those with vertical slats (again, no more than 2⅜ inches apart). A gate with a diamond-shaped pattern should have openings no more than 1½ inches wide. Any gate you use should be sturdy, with a smooth nontoxic finish, no sharp parts, no parts that can catch little fingers, and no small parts that can break off and be mouthed. Follow installation directions exactly. Gates are not usually of any use with a toddler over 34 inches tall or over two years old (by then they can usually figure out how to get past them), except perhaps in the middle of the night.

For a free copy of "Safe & Sound for Baby" and the latest directory of JPMA Safety Certified products, write: JPMA Safety Booklets, 2 Greentree Centre, Suite 225, P.O. Box 955, Mariton, NJ 08053.

is strategically placing house plants throughout your home (be sure they are safe plants; see page 656). Fifteen or twenty plants can apparently absorb the formaldehyde gas in an average-size house. If you suspect high levels in your home, contact the 3-M Corporation in St. Paul, Minnesota, which produces a testing device.

**Radon.** This colorless, odorless, radioactive gas, a naturally occurring product of the decay of uranium in rocks and soil, is believed to be the second leading cause of lung cancer in the U.S. Its presence in a home exposes the lungs of those who live there to its radiation. It is suspected that such exposure *over many years* may lead to cancer, particularly when combined with exposure to tobacco smoke.

Radon accumulation occurs when the gas seeps into a home from rocks and soil beneath it and is retained because of poor ventilation in the structure. The following precautions can help to prevent radon exposure:

▲ Before you buy a home, especially in a high-radon area (ask around first), have it tested for the presence of radon. Your local or state EPA can give you information on regional levels and on where to turn for testing.

▲ If you know you live in a high-radon area or are concerned your home may be contaminated, have it tested. Ideally, testing should take place over several months to obtain an average reading, rather than over a span of only a few days. And windows should be closed during testing (levels are usually higher when windows are closed).

▲ If your home turns out to have high levels of radon, consult your local EPA or health department for help in locating a local radon abatement company. These agencies may also be able to supply you with any government or other written material available on the subject of radon reduction. Possible steps include: sealing cracks and other openings in the foundation walls and floors and changing the dynamics of ventilation, perhaps by installing an air-to-heat exchanger.

**Nonstick cookware fumes.** Although pots and pans coated with Teflon or Silverstone are apparently safe for cooking, the fumes given off when they are overheated or scorched may be toxic. So: Never use nonstick drip pans under the burners on your range (they overheat rapidly); never use nonstick cookware at the highest temperature settings (rangetop or oven); don't use it to catch drips on the oven bottom; and take extra care not to let liquids cook out (allowing burning of the nonstick surface).

**Electromagnetic fields (EMFs).** EMFs aren't strictly air pollutants, but they do travel through the air and there is some question as to their safety—though all the scientific answers are far from in. To play it safe until more is known, avoid electric blankets, mattress pads, and waterbed heaters made before 1990, all of which generate significant amounts of EMFs. Or heat the device and turn off the heat once you slip your toddler (or yourself) under the covers. Motor-driven clocks and fans also give off EMFs, so place them at least a foot from the bedside, or use a digital, wind-up, or battery-powered clock. If your toddler uses a computer, be sure the monitor is set about 2 feet back on the desk. Two feet should also be the minimum distance between viewer and television set. If you have a microwave oven, make it a family policy that no one stand in front of it while it is on. If you are considering buying a new home, check the proximity to major power lines.

## Fire-Safety Changes

Like most other "accidental" deaths, fire fatalities need not happen. Most fires can be prevented, but when a fire is not foreseeable, injury can often be prevented by thoughtful preparation. To be sure "it can't happen here:"

▲ Never leave your toddler alone in the house, even for a moment. Should a fire suddenly break out you might not be able to get back in to save your child.

▲ If smoking is permitted in your home (everyone will be better off if it isn't), extinguish and dispose of all cigar and cigarette butts and ashes, pipe ashes, and used matches carefully and never leave them within a child's reach. Any smokers in your home should make a habit of properly disposing of butts immediately after smoking; when guests smoke, be sure to empty ashtrays promptly.

# POISON CONTROL

Every year, some 130,000 children in the U.S. accidentally ingest a hazardous substance. This is not surprising. Children, particularly very young ones, often explore and test their environment orally. Virtually anything they pick up will go right to the mouth, no matter how inappropriate, foul-tasting—or toxic. They don't stop to consider whether a substance or object is safe or edible. Nor do their unsophisticated taste buds or sense of smell warn them, as ours do, that a substance is dangerous because it tastes or smells vile.

To protect your toddler from the perils of poisoning, follow these rules without fail:

▲ Lock all potentially poisonous substances out of reach and out of sight of your toddler; even crawlers can climb up on low chairs, stools, or cushions to get to things left on tables or counters.

▲ Follow all safety rules for administering or taking medicines (see page 592), including not referring to medicine as "candy" and not taking medicine in front of your child.

▲ Be alert for repeat poisonings; a child who has ingested a poison once is statistically likely to make the same mistake again within the year.

▲ Avoid buying brightly colored or engagingly packaged household cleansers, laundry detergents, and other inedibles. If necessary, remove or cover illustrations that might attract your child (but be sure instructions and warnings remain visible). Never transfer toxic substances to other containers (especially not to familiar food containers). Also avoid purchasing potentially toxic substances with appealing fragrances (such as mint, lemon, apricot, almond, or floral).

▲ Purchase products that have childproof packaging, when possible—but don't rely on it to keep your toddler from getting them open; store them safely away.

▲ Make a habit of closing all containers tightly and returning hazardous substances to safe storage immediately after each use; don't put a spray can of furniture polish or a box of dishwasher detergent down "just for a minute" while you answer the phone or the door.

▲ Store food and nonfood items separately, and never put nonedibles in empty food containers (bleach in an apple-juice bottle, for example, or lubricating oil in a jelly jar). Children learn very early where their food comes from, and will assume that what they see is what they'll get without pondering why the "juice" isn't golden or the "jelly" isn't purple.

▲ Never leave alcoholic beverages within your toddler's reach. An amount that merely relaxes you could make your toddler deathly ill. Keep all wine and liquor bottles in a locked cabinet or bar; if you keep beer in the refrigerator, store it on the highest, farthest shelf. Keep a close watch on your toddler at parties where half-finished drinks might be left around, and never offer "just a sip" of your drink for fun. Empty all glasses containing alcohol before retiring for the night; an early riser might just go around sampling leftovers.

▲ When discarding potentially poisonous substances, empty them down the toilet—unless they can harm the septic system or pipes, in which case follow label directions for disposal. Rinse the containers before discarding (unless the label instructs otherwise) and put them out in a *tightly covered* trash can or recycling bin immediately. Never toss them in a wastebasket or an open kitchen garbage can.*

▲ Because of the high level of lead in printing inks, particularly those used in newsprint and four-color illustrations, newspapers and

---

*If you have a hazardous waste disposal program in your community, necessitating storing poisons until a particular day, make absolutely certain these materials are tightly sealed and *in no way* accessible to your toddler or other children.

magazines should not be a regular part of your toddler's diet.

▲ Always choose the less-hazardous household product over the one with a long list of warnings and precautions. Among those products generally considered "less" hazardous: nonchlorine bleaches, vinegar, Bon Ami, borax, baking (or washing) soda, lemon oil, beeswax, olive oil (for furniture), nonchemical flypaper, Elmer's glue, mineral oil (for lubrication), compressed-air drain openers.

▲ To help everyone in your household think "poison" on seeing a potentially poisonous product, put "poison" labels on all such products. If you can't locate commercially printed labels (some poison centers can provide "Mr. Yuk" labels), simply put an "X" of black tape on each product (without covering instructions or warnings). Explain to your family that this mark means "danger." Regularly reinforce the message, and eventually your child will also come to understand that these products are unsafe.

▲ Consider all of the following potentially perilous:

Acid compounds (muriatic acid, acetic acid, etc.)

Alcoholic beverages

Ammoniated mercury (not useful medicinally)

Ammonia

Antidepressants (very high fatality rate)

Antifreeze

Aspirin

Bleaches

Boric acid (not useful medicinally)

Camphorated oil (not useful medicinally)

Cardiac medications (high fatality rate)

Chlorine bleach

Cosmetics (most hazardous: artificial-nail removers containing acetonitrile)

Denture cleaners

Disinfectants

Dishwasher detergents

Drain cleaners (better not to use these; if you do, dispose of any remainder right after use)

Farm chemicals (caustic)

Fertilizers

Fungicides

Furniture polish

Gasoline

Hair straighteners

Iodine (not useful for first-aid purposes)

Insecticides

Iron pills and nutritional supplements containing iron, meant for adults or children (iron overdose is the major cause of fatal poisonings in children)

Kerosene

Laundry detergent powders containing sodium carbonate or silicate

Lighter fluid

Lye (best not to have in the home at all)

Medicines of all kinds

Methyl salicylate (high fatality rate)

Mothballs (switch to cedar products)

Mouthwash containing ethanol or alcohol (not all do)

Oil of wintergreen (not useful medicinally)

Oven cleaners

Pesticides

Rodent poisons

Rust removers

Sleeping pills

Street drugs (all)

Toilet bowl cleaners

Tranquilizers

Turpentine

Vitamins and other nutritional supplements

Weed killers

Windshield washer fluid

Not every household product your child might pick up is toxic. Although the following aren't ideal toddler edibles, occasional accidental ingestion isn't harmful: bubble bath, shaving cream, pet food, shampoo, lipstick, toothpaste, deodorants, dishwashing detergent that you use in the sink (dishwasher detergent, used in the machine, is hazardous, however).

## DESIGNED FOR SAFETY

· · · · · · · · · ·

Literally dozens of products are available through catalogs, in pharmacies, and in juvenile product, department, housewares, and variety stores to keep young children safe at home. But don't rely on them completely; they may slow your toddler down, giving you a bit more time to step in, but they aren't effective for 100% of children 100% of the time. They don't replace constant vigilance. Look for:

▲ Cabinet and drawer locks and latches (to keep kitchen cabinets and drawers closed to prying little fingers)

▲ Stove guards/knob protectors

▲ Doorknob guards (to make it difficult for little ones to open doors)

▲ Door stops

▲ Clear plastic corner cushioning (to soften corners of tables)

▲ Edge cushions (to soften sharp edges)

▲ Hearth cushions

▲ Venetian blind and drapery cord shorteners

▲ Outlet plugs or covers (in addition to plug-in caps, there are hinged shields that can be used even when appliances are plugged in).

▲ VCR guards

▲ Tub spout safety covers

▲ Nonskid decorations for bathtub bottoms

▲ Toilet latches (to keep seat lid down when not in use)

▲ Skid-resistant step stool

▲ Kid-proof patio door locks

▲ Door alarms (to signal when a door to the outside opens)

---

▲ Do not permit anyone (particularly someone who has been drinking), house guests included, to smoke in bed or even while resting on the sofa (a dangling butt can quickly ignite a flammable surface).

▲ Keep matches and lighters out of the reach of children (much easier to do if smoking is totally off-limits in your home)—even a two-year-old may be able to light a lighter, and a three-year-old may be able to strike a match. If you carry matches or a lighter in your bag, be sure that your bag, too, is always out of reach. A lighter can become a very tantalizing object: Never light one in front of your toddler or allow him or her to light one even under your supervision.

▲ Do not allow combustible rubbish (such as solvent-, oil-, or paint-soaked rags or paper towels) to accumulate. Pack such combustibles lightly in a trash container in a well-ventilated area that is not

exposed to heat (from a furnace or space heater, oven, or direct sunlight). If you launder rags or cloths used to wipe up spills of flammables, air-dry them or wash them twice or with a grease-dissolving detergent before drying them in the dryer (otherwise they could catch fire).

▲ Be cautious with hair sprays, nonstick cooking sprays, and other aerosol and non-aerosol products that contain flammable ingredients (check labels); don't use them near a flame or a lighted cigarette and store them away from a heat source.

▲ Store flammables, such as gasoline or kerosene, in containers designed for that purpose outside the home in an area inaccessible to children. Do *not* store these flammables in the basement; the fumes could migrate and be ignited by the pilot light of a furnace or dryer, or another flame source at a seemingly safe distance away. Avoid using flammable liquids, kerosene as well as commercial products, for spot removal on clothing. If you do use such products, do so in a well-ventilated area and wash or dispose of any rags or cloths properly.

▲ Don't cook or work (or let anyone else cook or work) near a fireplace, wood stove, or space heater in clothing with floppy sleeves, loose scarves, or hanging shirt tails, any of which could dangle in a flame and catch fire.

▲ Have your heating system checked and serviced annually.

▲ Be careful not to overload electrical circuits (warm cords are a sign of overload). Always remove plugs from sockets properly (without jerking the cord), and check electrical appliances and cords regularly for scorch marks, which indicate serious trouble in the system, wear, and/or loose connections. Be sure to replace any worn or damaged wiring or plugs promptly. Don't use lightweight extension cords. Use only 15-amp fuses for lighting, and never substitute anything else (such as a coin) for a fuse. It's also a good idea to uncover the reason for a blown fuse or circuit breaker—was there an overload? (Overloaded circuits are a major cause of fire.) If you aren't sure, check with a professional.

▲ Fireplaces should be well-screened to keep any sparks from flying and igniting curtains, furniture, and so on. (A glass screen is safest, but does get hot—so be sure to keep your toddler away when the fire is blazing.) Never use barbecue lighter fluid or gasoline to start the fire (they can explode) or feed a fire with paper (a flake of smoldering paper could drift up the chimney and settle on a shingle or wood-shake roof, possibly igniting it). Also avoid burning magazines or wrapping paper in the fireplace; their inks can emit toxic fumes. The chimney should be checked and cleaned regularly (how often depends on how frequently

the fireplace is used); a creosote build-up or a bird's nest could touch off a fire.

▲ Space heaters are the major cause of home fires in this country. It's best not to use them at all,[5] but if you do, be sure they turn off automatically if toppled or if something is placed against them. (Labels should say that the appliances are laboratory tested to meet industry safety standards.) Don't leave a space heater on when you're not in the room or when you're asleep. Unless a heater stays cool to the touch when in use, keep it safely out of reach of your toddler and at least 3 feet away from possible combustibles, such as curtains. And never use a space heater for drying towels or clothing, since the heat could ignite these items. Kerosene heaters should be refueled outdoors (and only with kerosene) and no heater should be refueled until it has cooled down completely. (For information on the environmental risks of space heaters, see page 629.)

▲ If you use a wood stove, be sure it is set on fire-resistant material; your local fire department can confirm whether the installation is fire-safe. (Wood stoves pose other problems, however; see page 629.)

▲ At holiday time, be especially careful about any of the following you use: *Decorative lights.* Be sure they are UL-approved and are installed according to instructions. Check cords from lights used in previous years to be sure they are not frayed. *Candles.* Place lighted candles where children can't reach them and away from paper decorations; never leave them on a table draped with a cloth that could be pulled off. *Christmas trees.* Dried-out trees pose a serious fire hazard; try to get a fresh one (the needles should bend, not break), then saw a cou-

---

5. Propane heaters, which are intended for industrial use, should definitely not be used in homes, according to the National Fire Protection Association.

ple of inches off the trunk and set it up in a water-filled tree stand. Maintain the water level in the stand while the tree is up, and when the tree begins to dry out, take it down. Or opt for a live tree you can later plant or donate to a local park. If you use a metallic tree, don't decorate with electric lights, as this can present a shock hazard. *Fireworks.* There is no such thing as safe fireworks in the hands of a nonprofessional—even class C fireworks, labeled "safe and sane" by sellers are potentially dangerous; even sparklers, for example, can cause serious burns or blindness. So do *not* use fireworks at home; instead, take the family out to view public holiday fireworks displays. If your family chooses to ignore the no-home-fireworks recommendation of the American Academy of Pediatrics and numerous safety organizations, at least do not allow children within several yards of the person setting off the fireworks, never leave children alone with fireworks, even momentarily, and never allow anyone who has been drinking to handle the explosives.

Prevention isn't enough. Children under five (along with the elderly) are the most likely to be injured or killed in a fire—primarily because they are often unable to sense the danger and to get out of the house quickly. The danger is greatest at night, when a fire can smolder for half an hour or more before it's discovered; by then, it's often too late to evacuate the family. Which is why it's so important to streamline detection and evacuation. Here's how:

▲ Install fire and smoke detectors as recommended by your local fire department (at least one on every floor of your home), if you haven't already. The best type for the kitchen is a photoelectric model, which is most responsive to smoldering fires and less likely to be set off by cooking smoke. Test all smoke alarms monthly to see that they are in good working order and that batteries on

battery-operated models haven't run down (studies show that as many as 1 in 3 home smoke detectors is not in working order). If yours uses batteries, replace them at least once a year (some experts recommend twice a year)—on New Year's Day, your child's birthday, when daylight savings time changes, or on another easy-to-remember date.

▲ Place multipurpose ("ABC") fire extinguishers in areas where fire risk is greatest, such as in the kitchen or furnace room and near the fireplace or wood stove. But be sure they're out of reach of children. In an emergency, bicarbonate of soda (baking soda) can be used for putting out kitchen fires. Attempt to put out a fire *only* if it is small and contained (for example, in your oven [turn off the oven first], a frying pan, or a wastebasket), you have a way out if you don't succeed in extinguishing the fire, you've already evacuated everyone else (or someone else is in the process of doing so), and someone has been instructed to call the fire department. If the fire begins to spread rather than abate, beat a hasty retreat.

▲ Affix stickers (usually available from the local firehouse) on the windows of your children's rooms so that firefighters can locate them quickly, if necessary.

▲ Install escape ladders (various types are available, from simple rope ladders to permanently mounted fold-out ladders that look like drain spouts when closed) at selected upper windows to facilitate escape in a fire, and teach older children and adults how to use them. A couple of times a year, practice getting the entire family down. But install window guards or child-safe locks at the escape windows to make sure children won't be able to make an unsupervised game of "escape."

▲ Hold fire drills periodically so that everyone who lives or works in your household will know how to get out quickly and safely in an emergency and where outside to meet other family members, so that everyone can be accounted for and fire-fighters needn't endanger their lives looking for those already evacuated. Assign each parent or other adult in the household the responsibility to evacuate a specific child (or children). Since fires can start in different areas, plan on more than one escape route from each room, when possible. Teach fire safety to family members, baby-sitters, nannies, housekeepers, and so on. Be sure everyone knows that it's safer to crawl close to the ground than to walk while trying to escape a burning house (most fire-related deaths are due to suffocation or burns from exposure to hot fumes and smoke, rather than from direct flame) and that the priority is to evacuate the premises immediately, without worrying about dressing, tracking down pets, saving valuables, putting out the fire,[6] or calling the fire department. The fire department should be called as soon as possible after any evacuation, from a street phone or a neighbor's house. Do not reenter a burning building for any reason; leave that to the fire-fighters.

## Changes in the Kitchen

Since families generally spend a great deal of time in the kitchen, toddlers do, too. But because it's one of the most intriguing—and dangerous—spots in your home, special precautions should be taken to avoid accidents there. Ensure your kitchen is toddler-safe by taking the following steps:

▲ Rearrange storage areas. Try to move anything off limits to young children—glass and china breakables, food wrap boxes with serrated edges, sharp implements, utensils with slim handles that can poke an eye, utensils and appliances with intricate gears that can pinch little fingers (like an egg beater or electric can opener), hazardous cleaning compounds, medicines, or potentially dangerous food-stuffs (peanuts, peanut butter, hot peppers, and bay leaves[7])—to upper cabinets and drawers. Keep chairs and stepladders away from cabinets to discourage climbing. Keep "safe" pots and pans, wooden and plastic utensils, canned goods, paper goods, unopened food packages that don't present a hazard when opened, and dish towels and cloths in the more accessible lower cabinets and drawers.

▲ Install child-guard latches on drawers or cabinets that house dangerous items or items you don't want your toddler to touch, even if you believe these cabinets are inaccessible to your toddler. If your toddler figures out how to unlatch the safety latches (some toddlers do), you will have to keep your toddler out of the kitchen entirely, when not under close supervision, with a gate or other barrier. Or try doubling the protection by installing two latches per drawer or door, one at the top and one at the bottom (which presumably would be very difficult for a toddler to open at the same time). What your toddler cares to go after and to what lengths (and heights) he or she will go to get it will change over time, so your storage arrangement may have to change as well. Reassess at least every six months, or as needed.

▲ Set aside at least one cabinet (a child's fingers are less likely to be caught in a cabinet than in a drawer) for your toddler to explore and enjoy. Some sturdy pots and pans, wide-handled wooden spoons, strainers, a colander, dish towels, plastic bowls, containers with lids, and so on can provide hours of entertainment and may satisfy your toddler's curiosity enough to keep him or her out of forbidden places. If this cabinet is away from

---

6. The only exception would be a well-contained fire, if the right kind of fire extinguisher is available (see the facing page).

7. Bay leaves should also be removed from food after cooking; if swallowed whole they often get stuck and have to be surgically removed.

*Many dangers lurk in the average kitchen. Protect your toddler with such safety devices as cabinet latches and a range guard.*

major kitchen work areas (not too close to the stove or the sink), your toddler will be less likely to be underfoot when enjoying it.

▲ Use the back burners of the range for cooking, when possible, and always turn the handles of pots toward the rear so they can't be reached (and pulled over) by a curious child. If burner controls are on the front of the range, buy or devise a barrier to keep them untouchable (see above illustration) or snap on commercial stove-knob covers. Appliance latches can keep conventional and microwave ovens inaccessible. Remember that the outsides of some ovens (and of other appliances, such as toasters, coffee makers, and crock pots) can get hot enough to cause burns and that they can stay hot long after they've been turned off—so keep them out of reach.

▲ Keep the refrigerator, and its potentially hazardous contents, off-limits to your toddler with an appliance latch. Also avoid small refrigerator magnets; they are often appealing and—since they may be choking hazards—dangerous.

▲ Don't sit your child on a counter top to play while you work, to have a snack, or to wait while you fill a cup with juice.

Besides the danger of a fall, you risk finding him or her with fingers in the toaster, hands on a hot pot, or a knife heading for an open mouth in the blink of an eye. You also risk imparting the idea that it's okay to climb up on to the counter, something he or she may decide to try when your back is turned.

▲ Don't carry your toddler and hot coffee—or any hot liquid—at the same time. It's just too easy for a child to suddenly startle or bolt, or for you to falter, spilling the liquid and possibly burning you both. Also be sure not to leave a hot beverage or a bowl of soup at the edge of a table or counter, near your toddler's place at the table, or anyplace else small hands can reach it.

▲ Keep garbage and recycling in tightly covered containers that your child can't open or under the sink behind a securely latched door. Children love to rummage through trash, and the dangers—from spoiled foods to broken glass—are numerous.

▲ Clean up all spills promptly—they make for slippery floors.

▲ Follow the safety rules for selecting, using, and storing kitchen detergents, scouring powders, silver polishes, and all other potentially toxic kitchen supplies (see page 635).

▲ Try to avoid heating your toddler's food in a microwave; overheated food or heat pockets in unevenly heated food can scald mouth and tongue. If you do use the microwave, always stir the food thoroughly and test it for temperature yourself before serving it to your child.

▲ Don't let your toddler open a package of just-popped microwave popcorn and don't open one yourself within arm's length of your child—escaping steam can cause serious burns.

▲ Keep your toddler away from toothpicks, sharp skewers, and any other dangerously pointy objects in the kitchen; they can be accidentally or intentionally poked in eyes, nose, ears, and elsewhere, with serious results.

## Changes in the Bath

Nearly as alluring as the kitchen, and potentially equally hazardous, is the bathroom. One way to keep it off limits is to put a hook and eye or other latch high up on the bathroom door, and to keep it latched when not in use. (Once your toddler is using the toilet, the latch will have to go.) Also make your bathroom toddler-safe by taking the following precautions:

▲ Be sure your tub bottom is slip-proof; add nonslip decals if it isn't.

▲ Use nonskid bath rugs on the floor to minimize falls and to cushion them when they do occur.

▲ Install a grab bar over the tub that is low enough for a toddler to grab if necessary; pad the bar if you think it presents a head-bumping risk.

▲ Keep all medications (including over-the-counter ones, such as antacids and aspirin), mouthwashes, toothpaste, vitamin pills, hair preparations and sprays, skin

lotions, and cosmetics safely stored out of your child's reach. (Medicines and vitamins are actually better kept in the bedroom or kitchen, where there is less exposure to moisture, than in the bathroom.) Also be sure razors, scissors, and clippers are well out of reach. Don't leave soaps or shampoos on the edge of the tub; install a high shelf for these items. Never leave any dangerous items on the bathroom vanity or anywhere else your toddler can reach them, even briefly.

▲ Store toilet bowl cleaners and other cleaning supplies out of your toddler's reach in a latched cabinet.

▲ Don't assume the medicine cabinet is out of reach of a climbing toddler. If its contents pose a threat, it should be latched.

▲ Don't leave a sun lamp or heater within a child's reach. It's a burn risk when it's still hot or a shock risk if a child tries to turn it on or plug it in.

▲ Never use, or let anyone else use, a hair dryer near your toddler when he or she is in the bath or playing with water. If you use a hair dryer on your toddler's hair (not a great idea, anyway), put it on the lowest heat setting, hold it 8 or 10 inches away from your child's head, and keep the dryer moving to minimize the risk of burns from focusing on one spot for a period of time.

▲ Never leave a small electrical appliance plugged in when you aren't using it. Just some of the dangers include: electric shock when a child dunks a hair dryer in the toilet or nibbles on the cord; a burn when he or she flicks on the switch on a curling iron; skin irritation from trying to "shave." Even unplugging appliances won't be enough if your child has good manual dexterity or if a curling iron or a hair dryer is still hot (they can cause burns for several minutes after they've been turned off). And the cords themselves present a choking hazard. For optimum safety, put these appliances away promptly after using.

▲ To prevent severe or lethal shocks, install ground fault circuit interrupters in the bathroom and kitchen.

▲ Keep water temperature in your home set no higher than 120°F for energy conservation and to help prevent accidental scalding. (Young children have thin skin; water at 140°F can give a child a third degree burn—serious enough to require a skin graft, in just 3 seconds.) If you can't adjust the heat setting (if you live in an apartment house, for example, and the landlord is uncooperative) install an anti-scald safety device (available from plumbing supply stores) in the tub, which will slow water to a trickle if it reaches a dangerously high temperature. For additional safety, always turn on the cold faucet before the hot and turn off the hot faucet before the cold. And routinely test bath water temperature with your elbow or whole hand, swishing it around to make sure the temperature is even throughout, before letting your toddler climb in. If you're planning to install new bathroom faucets, a single control, which you can set at a comfortable temperature and allow your toddler to turn on and off, is safer than separate hot and cold faucets.

▲ Invest in a protective cover for the tub spout to prevent bumps or burns should a child fall against it.

▲ Never leave your toddler in the tub unattended, even in a special tub seat. This rule should be strictly observed until your child is at least five years old.

▲ Never leave even an inch of water in the tub when it's not in use; a small child at play can topple into the tub and drown.

▲ If you have or visit a sauna, be aware that allowing toddlers, whose bodies are not yet adept at heat regulation, to use a sauna can be dangerous. Hot tubs and whirlpools are also inappropriate.

▲ When the toilet is not in use, keep the lid closed with suction cups or a safety latch made expressly for this purpose. At one time or another, most toddlers find the toilet a fascinating play space. Not only is this unsanitary, but an energetic toddler could topple in head first and be unable to get out.

▲ Use a covered wastebasket that your child can't open easily or take dangerous waste right to the covered receptacle in the kitchen.

▲ Make certain that the bathroom door lock (and interior door locks for other rooms, for that matter) can be opened from the outside, and stash a tool for opening it above the door trim.

## Changes in the Laundry

Whether the washer and dryer are in the kitchen, the basement, a bathroom, or a separate laundry area, these appliances and the laundry products used with them present a serious risk. To reduce that risk:

▲ Limit access to the laundry room; if it has a separate door, keep it closed and latched.

▲ Keep the dryer door closed at all times.

▲ If you can, turn off power to both washer and dryer when they are not in use.

▲ Keep bleach, detergents, and other laundry products in a cabinet out of reach. When containers are empty, rinse them thoroughly, then place them in a toddler-inaccessible recycling or trash bin.

## Changes in the Garage

Most family garages are chock-full of threats to a toddler, so:

▲ If your garage is attached to your house, keep the door between the two locked at all times. If the garage is separate, keep the garage door closed. And, keep any vehicles in the garage locked, too.

▲ If you have a remote-operated automatic garage door, be sure that it's one that automatically reverses if it hits an obstacle (such as your child). Automatic doors manufactured since 1982 are required to have this safeguard; if yours does not, you can get a retrofit kit to upgrade your door. Adding a resilient rubber strip along the bottom of the door offers additional protection. Check your garage door monthly (always on the same date—on the first of the month, for example) by lowering it on a heavy cardboard box or another expendable item to be sure the reverse feature is still operating; if it's not, disconnect the opener until it's been repaired or replaced (having it replaced professionally ensures the best results). The inside button for the door opener should be too high for your toddler to reach and any remote controls should be kept where children can't get to them.

▲ Store pesticides, weed killers, fertilizer; antifreeze, windshield washer fluid, and other car-care products; paints, paint thinners, and turpentine in an out-of-reach cabinet. (An inexpensive metal cabinet installed as high up on the wall as possible and latched with a combination lock is ideal.) These and all other hazardous products should be stored in their original containers so that there is

no mistaking their contents and the directions for their use and safety warnings are visible. If you aren't sure of what's in a particular container, dispose of it as you would hazardous waste.

## Changes for a Safer Out-of-Doors

Though the home is the most dangerous environment of all for a child, serious accidents can also occur in your own backyard—or someone else's—as well as in local streets and the community playground. Many out-of-the-house accidents are, however, relatively easy to prevent:

▲ Never let a toddler play outdoors alone. Even a toddler snoozing in a stroller needs to be checked frequently; some swift toddlers can get out of their safety belts and into mischief within moments of awakening. Even without unbuckling the belt, a toddler standing up in the stroller can overturn it. An unattended toddler is also vulnerable to kidnapping—a remote but horrible prospect.

▲ If possible, enclose a small area of the yard for toddler play. Use fencing that is continuous or has less than 4 inches between its slats and that a toddler couldn't possibly scale. Equip the space with playthings and be sure it doesn't contain any hazardous plants (see page 656), rocks, or potentially harmful debris. A child under eighteen months should be

---

## NO SWINGING

· · · · · · · · · ·

It used to be called "nursemaid's elbow," but a child doesn't have to have a nursemaid to fall victim to a dislocated, or pulled elbow. This condition is common in children younger than four, because their joints are relatively loose and their lack of cooperation often drives caregivers (including parents) to drag them by the arm. When the elbow joint is stretched, nearby soft tissue can slip into it and become trapped, causing severe pain and immobilizing the lower arm. To avoid putting your toddler's elbow out of joint, never drag, lift, or swing him or her by the arm or arms, whether in play or in anger. See first aid tip #17 in the next chapter for how to deal with a pulled elbow.

## A SAFE PLACE TO PLAY

**·········**

Swings, slides, jungle gyms—such are the stuff of a young child's dreams. But dreams can turn into nightmares—in the form of blackened eyes, broken limbs, and worse—if playground equipment isn't as safe as it should be. To ensure the safety of the equipment your toddler plays on at home or away:*

▲ Be sure it is age-appropriate. (Best for home use are adjustable units that are appropriate now and will grow with your child.) For toddlers, equipment should be no higher than 6 feet at its topmost point; play platforms should be no more than 4 feet high, have guard rails, and be easy to get down from. A slide should have no more than a 30° incline, and the platform should be as wide as the slide and at least 22 inches deep; if the slide is more than 4 feet high, it should have raised sides.

▲ Be sure that it is safe. Look for a play system that says the manufacturer followed the guidelines of the American Society for Testing and Materials or of the Consumer Product Safety Commission. This isn't a certification or a guarantee, but it's better than nothing. The play equipment should be sturdily constructed, correctly assembled (follow the manufacturer's directions exactly), firmly anchored in concrete (which should be covered with soft earth or padding), and installed at least 6 feet from fences or walls. All screws and bolts should be capped to prevent injuries from rough or sharp edges; check for loose caps periodically. Avoid S-type hooks for swings (the chains can pop out of them with vigorous swinging). If there's a climbing rope, it should be anchored at both ends. Swings should be bucket-type, of soft, shock-absorbent materials (such as plastic, canvas, or rubber rather than wood or metal) to prevent serious head injuries, and at least 24 inches apart and 30 inches from support posts. All rings and other openings should be designed

supervised on the spot even in such a controlled environment; an older child can be watched from a window.

▲ Since most toddler pedestrian deaths occur in driveways when someone backs up over the child, take extra care never to allow your child to be in a driveway unsupervised; be extra cautious yourself when pulling out. Always walk around (and look under) your car to check for children (yours or someone else's) before you back out.

▲ Don't mow the lawn when your child is in the yard; even if you try to clear all debris from your route before you begin, a pebble or other missed object (such as a nail) could become a dangerous projectile and cause eye or other injury. Opt for a push mower (instead of a more dangerous gas or electric model), if pos-sible. Store the mower, and all other gardening tools, safely out of your toddler's reach.

▲ Be sure that porch and deck railings are sturdy (check them regularly for deterioration or damage) and spaced so that young children won't catch their head or fall through the sides. Any outdoor area with a precipitous drop should be inaccessible to young children.

▲ Check public play areas before letting your toddler loose. Be alert for dog droppings (they can harbor worms), broken glass, rat poison (warnings will be posted), discarded drug paraphernalia, and other perils.

▲ Stop environmental destruction. It's not enough to beseech: "Please don't eat the daisies!" You've got to be sure that your toddler knows that eating plants, into avoid head entrapment (smaller than 3½ inches or larger than 9 inches). Metal should be painted or galvanized to prevent rust; wooden equipment should be weather-treated to prevent rotting. But since wood treated with arsenic-based material is hazardous, it's best to seal treated wood every 2 years with shellac, paint, or poly; if it isn't sealed, be especially careful to have children wash their hands after playing on it.

▲ Be sure that play equipment is in good repair; check regularly for broken parts, loose bolts, missing protective caps, worn bearings, exposed mechanisms that could catch fingers, eroded metal (which could cause cuts), splintered or deteriorated wood. Repair home equipment immediately; if that's not possible, remove any damaged parts or make the play area off limits until repairs are made. If it's park equipment that's in poor repair, report the problems to your local parks department, and avoid that playground until the equipment is fixed.

▲ Be sure that surfaces under play equipment are soft. Remove rocks and tree roots that are exposed or just under the surface of the play area, then spread with 9 to 12 inches of play sand, sawdust, wood chips, or bark; composition rubber mats; or other shock-absorbent material. Do not use concrete, packed earth, or grass, which are all dangerously hard; serious, even fatal, injury is possible on such surfaces should a young child take a fall from as little as a foot up. The surfacing material should extend roughly 6 feet around the play area. Rake sandy surfaces after rain to prevent compacting and add material yearly, as needed.

▲ Be sure that children using play equipment aren't wearing capes, floppy sleeves, flowing dress-up clothes, or any other clothing that might get caught or entangled.

▲ Any play equipment is only as safe as the supervision a child playing on it gets. So be sure to supervise carefully. If the play equipment is taller than your child, supervise from close range.

---

*Avoid public playgrounds that do not meet these standards.

---

doors or out, is forbidden. Avoid planting, or at least fence out, poisonous plants (see page 656) in your own yard and keep an eye out for them when you are in the park with your child.

▲ Don't allow your toddler to play in deep grasses or anywhere poison ivy, poison oak, or poison sumac might lurk, or where—out of sight—he or she might snack on some poisonous plant. If you discover poison ivy, oak, or sumac in your yard, remove it (check with your local cooperative extension or another knowledgeable source about proper removal procedures).

▲ Don't let your toddler routinely ingest fistfuls of soil. It could be contaminated by lead from flaking house paint or industrial residue.

▲ If you have a sandbox, keep it covered when it's not in use (to keep out animal droppings, leaves, blowing trash, and so on). If the sand gets wet, let it dry out in the sun before covering. When filling the sandbox, be sure the sand you choose isn't dusty; dusty sand may contain tremolite fibers. Tremolite fibers float in the air and can cause serious illness if inhaled. To test sand you already have, dump a pailful of it from a foot or so or mix a spoonful of it in a glass of water. If it makes a cloud of dust when dumped or the water in the glass remains cloudy once the sand settles, replace the sand, preferably with ordinary beach sand (a lot of play sand is made from ground stone or marble).

▲ If you have an outdoor fireplace or barbecue, make sure to keep your toddler away from it while it's in use. The fire

*Make bike helmets mandatory for everyone who rides, even a toddler.*

should be attended by an adult from the moment it's lit until it's been doused with water and the coals, if any, have cooled and been disposed of (remember that coals that aren't doused stay hot for a long time after the fire itself is out). If you use a table top grill, be sure to set it on a stable surface that your toddler can't reach or overturn.

▲ If your toddler has a tricycle, be sure that he or she always wears a helmet when riding. Don't assume that because a child is riding the trike in the driveway, on the sidewalk, or in the park that an injury is improbable; many bike injuries occur in just such settings and a helmet can reduce the potential seriousness of an accident. Most important, getting into the helmet habit will not only protect your toddler now but in future years as well. If you ride a bike, set a safety-conscious example: Always wear a helmet yourself. Helmets should be specifically designed for bike riding (don't use one designed for another sport) and labeled as meeting the bicycle helmet safety standards of the American National Standards Institute (ANSI) or the Snell Memorial Foundation—not all helmets do. Most helmets are designed with removable padding, to "grow" with the child so that

you won't have to replace a helmet every year. A helmet that has been involved in a substantial accident, however, is often no longer suitable for use; many manufacturers will test a helmet on request to see if it is still usable, and some offer free lifetime replacement.

▲ If you live in a suburban or rural area, be on the alert for wild animals; skunks, foxes, bats, and raccoons can all carry rabies. An infected animal may behave in an abnormal way, and may be more approachable by humans than a healthy one. Keep garbage can lids on tightly to discourage foraging visitors and don't leave pet food outside.

▲ Limit play outdoors in very hot or subfreezing weather.

▲ In hot weather, always check metal parts on playground equipment, strollers and car seats, outdoor furniture, and so on before letting your toddler come in contact with them. Metal can get hot enough, especially in a scorching sun, to burn a child severely with just a few seconds of contact.

## Water-Safety Changes

Where there is water and a toddler, there is both pleasure and risk. Reduce the risk without reducing the fun by taking these precautions:

▲ Keep swimming or wading pools and any other water catchments, even if filled with as little as an inch of water, inaccessible to unsupervised toddlers. When not in use, keep wading pools overturned, stored away, or covered, so they don't fill with rain water.

▲ If you have a swimming pool, fence it in. The fence should be at least 5 feet high on all sides;[8] vertical posts should

---

8. Some experts maintain that the house can serve as one side of the fence *if* all windows and doors on that side are alarmed. The key pad for turning off the alarm should be out of the reach of a toddler or young child.

---

## DRESS FOR IT

**· · · · · · · · · ·**

Dress your toddler appropriately for outdoor play, keeping in mind that young children are particularly susceptible to *hyper*thermia (dangerously high body temperature; see page 671) when over-dressed in hot weather and *hypo*thermia (dangerously low body temperature; see page 671) when underdressed in very cold weather. For dressing tips, see page 499.

---

be no more than 4 inches apart and not easy to climb (if of chain link design, the openings should be too small to allow a young child's toehold). Entrances to the pool should be kept locked at all times; gates should open away from the pool and be self-closing with a self-latching lock that is well out of reach of children. An alarm that signals that the gate has been opened offers additional protection.

▲ Never allow your child to use a pool with a missing drain until the drain is replaced.

▲ If possible, install an automatic pool cover that meets the standards of the American Society for Testing and Materials (ASTM)—but don't rely on it instead of a fence, and never leave it partly in place (a toddler could slip beneath it unnoticed). Always drain a pool cover that's filled with rain water as soon as possible.

▲ If you have an above-ground pool that's less than 4 feet tall, fence that, too. Steps and/or ladders to an above-ground pool should be inaccessible to children or removed when the pool is not in use.

▲ Be sure there are no trees, chairs, benches, tables, or anything else around that your toddler can climb on to get over a pool fence or into an above-ground pool.

▲ Remove toys from the pool and pool area when not in use—they can lure a toddler or other children toward the water.

▲ Insist on supervision. Children should never be allowed to enter the pool area without a supervising adult, and an adult must continue to be present *and* supervising *every moment* as long as any children are there; a child who falls into a pool generally goes under in a few seconds and is unable to call out for help from the adult who walked around to the other side of the house. The supervising adult should try to maintain frequent eye contact with any children in the pool, should be familiar with CPR and what to do in case of a drowning, and should not be drinking alcohol—even one drink could impair response to an emergency. If there's no stand-in available, and the supervising adult must leave, even for a moment, any young children should be taken along.

▲ Enforce safety rules. Remember that even a child who can swim is not water-safe until he or she also has good judgment (see page 381) and that no one, of any age, should swim without a "buddy."

▲ Don't allow the use of flotation toys, such as inflatable tubes or floats. Not only can a child slip out of or off these devices in a second, but they provide both adult and child with a false sense of security. For added pool safety, a toddler can wear an approved life vest, but never rely on it instead of supervision.

▲ Just in case, know how you will respond to a water emergency. Have a pole and life preserver on each side of the pool and CPR directions posted explain-

# DON'T LET THE BUGS BITE

**· · · · · · · · · ·**

With their jelly-smeared cheeks, their fruit-sticky fingers, and their typically bright-colored clothing, toddlers make appealing targets for insects. Their lack of bug savvy—a young child doesn't usually know enough to steer clear of bees, to come inside when the flies are biting, or to avoid areas where mosquitoes are flitting around—combined with their quick, unpredictable movements (which also attract and provoke bug activity) and their penchant for playing in places where insects happen to congregate, make them easy targets, too.

Though most insect stings and bites are harmless (if often uncomfortable), they can occasionally transmit disease or cause a severe allergic reaction. So it's wise to be wary, and to provide your toddler with as much bug protection as possible. Here's how:

**Protect against all insects.** Though a lot of it is not always practical in very hot weather, the best insect protection is clothing. When insects are swarming, dress your toddler in clothes that cover as much skin as possible: a hat, long sleeves, long pants tucked into socks, and closed shoes. Clothes that are white, pastel, subdued green, or khaki are less attractive to insects than those that are brightly hued, dark, and/or flowered. Since bugs are attracted to scents, opt during bug seasons for unscented detergents, shampoos and soaps, diaper wipes, lotions, and sunscreens, and avoid perfumes, after-shave lotions, and scented hair sprays. And don't plant brightly colored and aromatic flowers in play areas. Since it's difficult to avoid an insect in a car, keep your windows and sunroof closed while your car is parked, and check the car before loading the family onboard.

Insect repellents can be used to deter mosquitoes, biting flies, "no-see-ums," fleas, and ticks. Use only those designed especially for children. Products containing DEET should have concentrations no higher than 10% and should not be used for children under two (except on the advice of a doctor). Stick, roll-on, or spread-on creams or lotions are best (a spray is hard to direct safely). Apply sparingly to exposed skin areas (the more you cover with clothing, the less you will need to cover with repellent), carefully avoiding eyes and mouth and any scrapes or other areas of broken skin. DEET can decompose synthetics and plastics, so don't apply to clothes or skin, that is touch-

---

ing the steps to be taken. When using the pool, keep handy an extension (or a cordless phone), with emergency numbers taped on.

▲ If you install a floating pool alarm, don't depend on it exclusively. These alarms tend to be unreliable and, when they do work, they don't go off until the child is already in the water—far too late for comfort. The best safeguards are ones that keep children away from the pool entirely or warn you before they get into the water.

▲ If you're thinking about installing a swimming pool in your yard, it's best to postpone this step until your toddler is at least five years old and has had swimming instruction.

▲ Be sure any pool your toddler plays or swims in (other than a child's wading pool that is emptied daily) is properly chlorinated. Too little as well as too much chlorine (you can smell it) can be hazardous. Even properly chlorinated pool water may cause problems for the child with asthma and allergies; if your child drinks a lot of it, it can also cause diarrhea. Discourage excessive splashing; chlorinated water in the eyes can cause irritation.

ing clothes. Read labels carefully. Some low-concentration formulas last only a couple of hours and must be reapplied if a toddler remains outdoors longer. Reapplication may also be necessary if your child has been in the water (especially salt water) for long periods. Wash off any repellant once you are back indoors.

**Protect against bees.** Keep your toddler out of areas bees favor (such as fields of clover or wildflowers, around fruit trees, or near garbage cans) whenever possible. If you discover a beehive or wasp's nest in or near your home, have it removed by a professional. When bees are about, avoid serving your toddler sticky, sweet snacks (such as fruit, fruit leather, and fruit juice) outside; when you do, wipe fingers and face promptly with unscented wipes to remove all traces of the snack. (If your toddler has had an allergic reaction to bee stings, see page 707.)

**Protect against mosquitoes.** Since mosquitoes breed in water, fill in puddles, drain rain barrels, and empty bird baths on your property. Keep your toddler indoors at night, when mosquitos are out in large numbers, and be sure screens on doors and windows are kept in good repair and that screens and screen doors are always in place when windows and doors are open. A net cover on

your toddler's stroller will offer protection on walks. If your toddler is two or older, an insect repellent can also be used.

**Protect against deer ticks.** Deer ticks can carry Lyme disease, so it's especially important to protect your toddler from their bite. When your toddler will be playing or hiking in areas where deer ticks are prevalent (you can check with the local department of health for information on their prevalence), cover as much of your child's body area with clothing and apply an insect repellent as described above. Check skin and clothing of family members for ticks when out in infested areas and on returning home; also be sure to check pets, since their fur can pick up ticks and pass them on to family members. It takes about 24 to 48 hours for a tick to transmit a full-blown case of Lyme disease; the sooner you get a tick off (see page 850), the less likely it is that infection will occur.

**Protect against venomous spiders.** Keep children out of warm, dry, dark places (such as closets, attics, unfinished basements, garages, storage sheds), where spiders spend most of their time. Carefully check for spiders on clothing, shoes and boots, and other items that have been taken out of storage, and remove spider webs when you find them.

▲ Do not permit a child who hasn't yet learned to use the potty to play in a pool unless he or she is wearing a securely fastened diaper (feces can contaminate the water, and an accidental bowel movement is likely, especially if several children in diapers use the pool at the same time).

▲ If you have a spa or hot tub, keep curious children out of it with a rigid, lockable cover; a fence is also a good idea.

▲ At the beach, spread your blanket close to the lifeguard station—it's usually set up on the safest strip of beach. But don't rely

on a lifeguard to keep your toddler safe; supervise your child every minute. Neither should you rely on a lifeguard knowing CPR—unfortunately, many do not.

▲ Keep everyone in the family away from pools or other bodies of water during thunderstorms.

▲ If you take your family boating, insist that all children wear child-size life vests (tested by Underwriters Laboratory and approved by the US Coast Guard). But, like lifeguards, life vests are not a substitute for parent (or parent substitute) supervision.

## LET IT SNOW

..........

To adults, a winter snowstorm foretells a hundred headaches—walks and driveways to be salted and shoveled, slippery roads to negotiate, muddy boots and soggy snowsuits to deal with. To children, a snowstorm foretells a hundred pleasures—snow angels to be made, snowballs to be thrown, snow sculptures to create, snow-covered hills begging to be sledded down. But wintry weather and its pursuits pose certain risks that parents need to be aware of. To keep your child's winter wonderland safe:

**Ensure safe sledding.** Slopes for sledding should have a very gentle grade, shouldn't be icy, and should be carefully inspected for hidden rocks, tree roots, or other protuberances that might upset a sled; the path chosen should also be clear of trees and not within skidding distance of traffic. Young children should be supervised at all times when sledding, and should wear a safety helmet. The sled used should be appropriate for the child's age and size. For toddlers, a sled with a seat and seat belt is safest; if such a sled isn't available, a toddler should ride nestled between the legs of an adult or much older child. Never allow head-first sledding or permit your child to slide down on a makeshift sled, such as a garbage can lid or cardboard box. Sleigh rides (being pulled in a sled by an adult or a responsible older child) are probably the best way for young toddlers to enjoy the snow.

**Teach safe snowball "fighting."** A little playful tossing of soft-packed snowballs is harmless fun (assuming all parties have agreed to the sport), but children need to be taught that packing ice or foreign objects in snowballs, or throwing snowballs at moving cars or at anyone's head or face is dangerous.

**Skip skiing.** Though it's possible for toddlers to learn some skiing fundamentals, most safety experts recommend waiting until a child is at least four (when coordination increases significantly) before beginning this potentially dangerous winter sport. For the same reason, ice skating, too, isn't a recommended activity for toddlers.

**Ban snow consumption.** Even the freshest, whitest, cleanest-looking snow may not be as pure as it looks. Snow doesn't have to fall on a city street to be dirty; rural snow can contain a variety of pollutants, including industrial or agricultural runoff, and may be contaminated by animal urine or feces. So while you won't always be able to keep your toddler from sampling a handful of the white stuff (remember how good it tastes?), it's wise to nix snow eating when you see it.

**Know when to call it quits.** When you start to feel chilly outdoors, it's time to bring your toddler in; don't wait until your toddler is cold and cranky. Also retreat to the warm indoors if your child's clothes or gloves get wet.

## Auto Safety Changes

Always buckling up may be the first rule of car safety, but it isn't the only one. To promote auto safety:

▲ Never leave a child in an auto unattended. The possible scenarios are many and frightening. For example: A toddler playing around in a car could set it rolling off on its own, into someone or something; or a stranger could take off with the the car and/or the toddler; or the temperature in the car could dip or rise dangerously.

▲ If you're purchasing a new car seat, select a model that meets Federal Motor Vehicle Safety Standards 213; if you plan on using it for air travel, it should also carry FAA approval. The seat should be appropriate for your child's age and weight now and, for practical purposes, should be designed to serve for

*For safe toddler sledding, try a sled with sides and back—and a safety belt.*

only in a crash), use a locking clip to keep the car seat from shifting when the car turns sharply or stops abruptly. If a locking clip was not supplied with your car or car seat, get one by contacting the auto manufacturer or dealer or (possibly) the store that sold you the car seat.

▲ If you're considering using a second-hand car seat (don't use one manufactured before 1981), be sure that the seat has no missing or broken parts, that it has never been involved in an accident (even a low-impact one), and that you get the instruction booklet along with it so that you can install and buckle it properly.

▲ Since safety seats are occasionally recalled for defects, register a new seat

the next year or two. A 5-point harness may be more trouble to fasten but may give better protection than a 3-point model.[9]

▲ When your toddler outgrows a convertible car seat (these seats usually take children up to 40 pounds), he or she is ready for a booster-style car seat. Which type of booster you should use depends on the type of seat belt in the rear seat of your car (see illustrations, page 652). Shoulder-belt retrofit kits are available from manufacturers for most older cars with only lap belts in the rear seat.

▲ Be sure the car seat is always installed correctly and secured by one of the car's seat belts. Follow the directions that come with the car seat, and with the car, *to the letter.* Don't assume that a new seat is installed just as an old one was. When installed properly, the seat should move very little when you try to shake it. If your car has inertia belts (which lock

*Children who have been facing rearward in a convertible car seat can start facing forward once they weigh twenty pounds and can sit up well alone. When reversing the seat, be sure to install it according to the manufacturer's directions and to readjust the harness as your toddler grows. A child over twenty pounds can also ride in a toddler-only car seat.*

9. The *Family Shopping Guide to Car Seats* is available from the AAP, Safe Ride Program, 141 Northwest Point Boulevard PO Box 927, Elk Grove Village, IL 60009-0927. Enclose a stamped, self-addressed envelope.

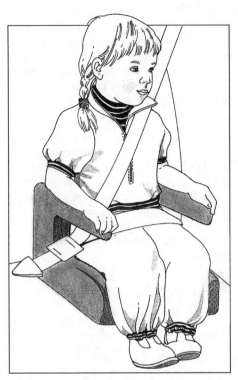

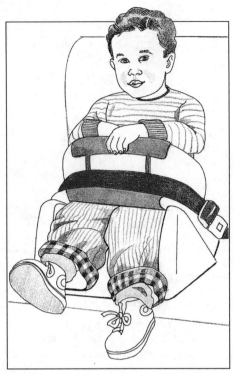

*Children who weigh over thirty pounds can ride in a toddler-only booster seat such as the one above, which raises a toddler up so that lap and shoulder belts fit correctly. Important: Such seats cannot be used with a seat belt unless they come with an optional shield for use when no shoulder belt is available.*

*A booster seat with a shield, like the one shown above, can be used with a seat belt alone for toddlers forty to sixty-five pounds. Keep in mind, however, that though it provides more protection than a seat belt alone, it is somewhat less safe than a booster with both lap and shoulder belts.*

with the manufacturer, so if there's a recall you'll be notified immediately. With older seats, you can check the brand and model against a list of defective car seats available from the Center for Auto Safety—Child Restraints. Send a stamped, self-addressed envelope to 2001 S Street NW, Room 410, Washington, DC, 20009, or call the Auto Safety Hotline, (800) 424-9393.

▲ The safest seat in a car is the middle one in the back seat, so when practical, put your toddler there. If you have a passenger-side airbag, it's okay to put your toddler in the front seat, but *only* in a child restraint system and with the seat moved back as far as possible. An airbag alone is dangerous: The explosive infla-

tion of the airbag during an accident could seriously injure or even kill a child who is not restrained. (A rear-facing infant seat should *never* be placed in a front seat with an airbag.)

▲ Always buckle your child in according to the directions that come with the seat; many children in car seats are injured in accidents because they weren't buckled in properly. The harness should fit snugly but not too tightly. (Adjust the straps as your toddler grows and when switching to or from bulky winter clothes.) If there is a retainer clip, always use it to hold the shoulder straps in place. Position the clip at chest level, as illustrated in your car seat instruction book.

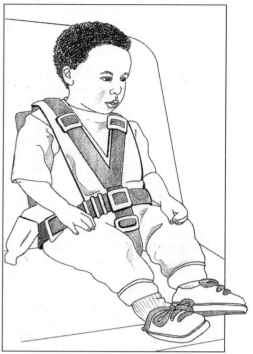

*An ideal traveling companion for a family with a toddler, this contraption converts from a car seat to a stroller to a plane seat and back again with ease—providing car seat protection en route to the airport and at your destination, a safe seat for the flight, and a stroller for vacation enjoyment.*

*These safety restraints, which are particularly convenient for travel, are usually designed for children twenty to twenty-five pounds or more—but check the label, since weight recommendations can vary on these products. As with other safety restraints, these only protect when they are properly installed, so read and follow instructions carefully.*

▲ Never start driving until all the car doors are locked and your child and everyone else in the car is properly buckled in. Every state requires a child to ride in an approved safety seat until at least age four or 40 pounds. Abide by these laws faithfully, even if you're just going for a quick trip from one store to another. For tips on how to keep your toddler happy while buckled up, see page 150.

▲ Don't neglect car safety when you travel. Many parents find a convertible stroller-car seat useful (see above illustration): it can be a car seat in the cab en route to the airport, opened to a stroller for moving around the airport, then strapped into the plane seat for the flight, and finally used both as a car seat in a rented car and as a stroller at your destination. An inflatable travel seat can also be useful. For older toddlers, a simple harness that is worn with a seat belt can also be used for travel (auto or air) or even for short taxi rides (see above illustration).

▲ If your child has special needs, a standard car seat may not be appropriate. Check with your child's doctor or a local children's hospital for information.

▲ If your car has power windows, do not allow young children to control them (control them yourself from the driver's seat, keeping them locked, if possible). And never reach for the button without first checking to be sure no one is leaning out, and no hand, finger, or other body part is in the way.

## SAFE ART

**W**hen purchasing art supplies for your toddler, look for talc-free premixed clays designed for use by children (powdered clay for adult use may contain asbestos); water-based markers, paints, inks; white glues or school pastes (avoid epoxies, instant glues, or solvent-based adhesives). Some older "nontoxic" crayons may not be, in fact, nontoxic. If the crayons your toddler has been using aren't labeled "Conforms to ASTM D-4236," discard them and buy a box that is. Look for the same assurance of safety on other art supplies as well. Keep in mind that a toxic material doesn't have to be ingested to be dangerous; some can cause harm if absorbed through the skin. So don't allow body-painting except with paints designed for that purpose. When an arts and crafts session is over, wash off paint, glue, and other materials from your toddler's skin (be sure to get under the nails). And be sure any day-care or preschool program your child attends also is careful about the use of art supplies, too. For further information, contact the Center for Art Safety, 5 Beekman Street, New York, NY 10028, (212) 227-6220.

▲ Do not permit the use of pens, pencils, or other sharp objects in a moving car or any other vehicle, and prohibit play with toys or other objects that can block the driver's vision—a balloon, for example. And don't leave loose objects on the ledge below the rear window or in the back of a station wagon; they can go flying forward in a short stop.

▲ Don't try to argue with or discipline a child while you're driving; if you're distracted by the behavior, pull over, then deal with it.

▲ Never allow your child to play behind a parked car or near a car that is not locked.

▲ If you take a pet along in a station wagon, have it ride in the back, and put up a removable metal partition so that the animal will not be thrown into passengers on a short stop. Or use an animal restraint system, now available.

▲ Never let your child ride in back of a pickup truck, whether it's open or enclosed. Children can be injured during such an unprotected ride even with just a short stop. The jump seat of an extended pickup is not as safe as a regular auto seat, but is certainly better than riding in the cargo area. Check with the manufacturer on safety features (ask, for example, where would a child's head impact in a crash? Will seat belts hold a car seat?) before letting your child ride in a jump seat and before buying a pickup.

### Pet Safety Changes

Pets can bring a lot of pleasure to a family, but they can also bring some risks. To maximize the pleasure, minimize the risks:

▲ If you're getting a new pet, be sure it's healthy; have it checked by a veterinarian before making your selection final.

▲ Be as careful about your pet's preventive care as you are about your child's. Be sure the pet gets all necessary immunizations (for dogs, and in high rabies areas, cats and some other pets, a rabies vaccination is a must) and treatment for worms and fleas (in dogs, cats, and other pets) according to the schedule recommended by the vet.[10] Checking a cat, particularly one under six months of age,

---

10. Flea collars are not recommended, but brewer's yeast sprinkled on pet food *may* repel fleas.

for *Rochalimeaea henselae* infection (which can be transmitted to humans as cat scratch disease; see page 842) is also a good idea. Antibiotic treatment may rid the cat of the infection.

▲ Wash your hands—and teach your toddler to do so—after playing with or cleaning up after a pet. If your pet contracts a disease that can be transmitted to humans, ask the vet about any special precautions that should be taken to prevent spread.

▲ Do not allow children to touch animal feces. Especially if the stool is loose, it could contain, among other germs, the *Campylobacter* bacterium, associated with severe gastrointestinal infection.

▲ Never allow children to eat pet hair. Some kids get into the habit of pulling out dog hair, for example, and munching on it. A hair ball, or bezoar, can form in the child's stomach; having a bezoar removed can be a very unpleasant experience.

## Toy-Box Changes

Toys are a fundamental part of every toddler's life. But if they aren't carefully chosen, they can become a threat. So as you wander through a toy emporium, overcome at the available games and gadgets, consider not only whether the toys you select will be fun and educational, but also whether they will be safe.[11]

Before loading up your basket (and plunking down your money), check for:

**Age-appropriateness.** For safety's sake, adhere to the label recommendations on toys you buy for your toddler. Toys that aren't labeled for age appropriateness should be avoided or carefully checked for all of the criteria below before being purchased. And keep the toys of any older siblings away from your toddler if they don't meet these standards.

**Developmental appropriateness.** Consider not only your child's age, but his or her behavior and developmental stage when you buy. For example, no matter what age and no matter how bright, children who still explore objects by mouthing them (and are thus at greater risk of choking) should not have toys with small parts. Some children stop putting in their mouths things that don't belong there at twelve months, others, not until three years—or even later.

**Safe size.** Avoid any toy that can fit completely into your toddler's mouth or that has any small parts that can be mouthed (see page 657); also be sure that a larger toy can't be squeezed or molded into a smaller, potentially dangerous size.[12]

**Sturdy construction.** A flimsily fashioned toy not only won't last long, but could also shatter or fall apart, producing dangerously small or sharp parts that could injure your toddler.

**Safe finish.** Paint, if any, should be nontoxic and durable; the finish should be unlikely to peel or splinter.

**Safe ingredients.** Art supplies, which end up in the mouth and on the skin as often as they do on paper, should be nontoxic (see the facing page).

**Washability.** Stuffed animals and other soft toys that can't be tossed in the washing machine may become a breeding ground for germs, so look for "machine-washable" on care tags.

---

11. For information on recalls of toys and on toys with a history of safety problems, call the Consumer Product Safety Commission hotline (800) 638-2772.

12. Another reason for always supervising a toddler. Should an object become stuck in a child's mouth, the child wouldn't be able to cough it out or call for help. Only a parent or another caregiver on the spot could help.

## RED LIGHT GREENERY

· · · · · · · · · ·

Although many toddlers reject the greens on their dinner plate, few have any qualms about taste-testing the greens on house and garden plants. Yet many common house and garden plants are poisonous when eaten. So place houseplants high up, where leaves or flowers can't fall on the floor below, and where your toddler can't get to them. Better still, farm out poisonous houseplants to friends who don't have small children—at least until your child is older. Label with the accurate botanical name any houseplant you do keep, so that if your toddler does accidentally ingest some leaves or flowers, you will be able to supply accurate information to the poison center or your toddler's doctor. Place all plants, even those that are not poisonous, where they can't be toppled with a tug.

Poisonous plants include:
Azalea
Caladium
Daffodil bulbs
Daphne
Dumb cane
English ivy
Foxglove
Holly
Hyacinth bulbs (and leaves and flowers in quantity)
Hydrangea
Iris rootstalk and rhizome
Japanese yew seeds and leaves
Jerusalem cherry
Larkspur
Laurel
Lily of the valley
Mistletoe
Morning Glory seeds
Narcissus bulbs
Oleander
Philodendron
Privet
Rhododendron
Rhubarb leaves
Sweet peas (especially the "peas," which are the seeds)
Tomato plant leaves
Wisteria pods and seeds
Yews

Poinsettia, in spite of its reputation, isn't toxic, though it could cause an upset stomach.

### Avoid toys with:

▲ Removable or loose small parts. Button eyes on teddy bears, shoes on dolls, tiny toy "people" or characters, small beads, tiny building blocks, easily detachable squeakers in or on squeeze toys, and any other toys or parts small enough to swallow, choke on, or be poked into an ear or a nostril are hazardous and should be bypassed.

▲ Strings, ribbons, or cords longer than 6 inches. Toys that come with strings attached (unless the "strings" are made of a stiff plastic) pose a strangulation risk. Avoid these toys or remove or trim the strings before letting your toddler play with them. Also avoid letting your toddler play with audio tapes—unwinding tapes is a favorite occupation for toddlers.

▲ Springs, gears, or hinges that can catch little fingers or long hair.

▲ Sharp points or edges. Watch out for sticks picked up outdoors; allow play with pencils and pens only under supervision.

▲ High noise levels. Toys that produce sounds of 100 decibels or more (such as cap guns, motorized vehicles, and very loud squeeze toys) can damage a toddler's hearing (see page 486).

▲ Heating elements or electrical connections. Battery-operated toys are okay as long as the batteries are completely inac-

*A choke tube, available at many juvenile products stores, as well as through catalogs, can help you determine what's safe for your toddler to handle (and mouthe), and what may pose a choking risk. Any item that fits into the tube (left) is a choking risk and should be kept away from your toddler. Any item that protrudes from the tube (right) does not present a choking risk.*

cessible[13] to curious fingers or the plaything is used only under close adult supervision. Small button batteries are a choking and swallowing risk, and all batteries are dangerous if a toddler chews on them.

▲ Sponge-like construction. Toddlers are often tempted to chew on balls and other items made of spongy material and can gag or even choke on them or on pieces bitten off of them.

▲ Decals or other stickers. Should your toddler manage to remove a sticker (not a very difficult task) and mouth it, it becomes a choking risk. Vinyl stick-ons in design sets (such as Colorforms) can also be choked on.

▲ Projectile parts. Toy bows and arrows, dart guns, and so on, are inappropriate for young children, as they put eyes at risk. Water pistols are okay, but stay away from the high-powered variety, which can do a lot of damage.

---

13. A swath of electrical tape over the battery compartment *may* keep your toddler from prying it open—or it may not.

**Also avoid:**

▲ Latex balloons. Because of their texture, latex balloons are tempting to chew on. A toddler can choke on a deflated balloon, fragments of one that's popped, or a slowly deflating balloon left lying around. And once a toddler has inhaled a balloon, there may not be much anyone can do—even the Heimlich maneuver may not work. Not incidentally, fish and sea mammals are also at risk from balloons, which, after being let loose out-of-doors or dumped as trash, can end up in waterways. If you use latex balloons, closely supervise their use; don't allow young children to blow them up, play with them unsupervised, or chew on them. Deflate and dispose of them carefully and promptly after the party's over. Better still, use mylar balloons, or don't use balloons at all.

▲ Damaged toys. Check your toddler's toys periodically for wear and tear—exposed stuffing bursting from the seam of a teddy bear, cracked plastic on a push toy, splinters on a wooden toy, or anything else that could make a once-safe plaything hazardous. Repair or discard those that are unsafe.

# Treating Toddler Injuries

**Y**ou've made your home as accident-proof as possible. You've trained yourself to be vigilant. You've taught—or tried to teach—your toddler to stay away from electrical outlets, hot stoves, and other hazards at home and away. Still, with a toddler on the loose, accidents are bound to happen once in a while. (One study showed that the typical toddler has three minor bumps or boo-boos a day.) And though you can't avert them all, you can often improve the outcome by taking the appropriate measures when an accident occurs.

Because quick action is often critical, don't wait until your child dunks a hand in your hot coffee or takes a swig of laundry detergent to look up what to do in an emergency. Become as familiar with the procedures for dealing with and treating common injuries as you are with those for bathing your child and taking a temperature. Review the approaches for dealing with less common injuries, as appropriate—the treatment for snake bites, for example, when you're about to go on a camping trip.

Reinforce what you learn in this chapter by taking a course in child CPR, the Heimlich maneuver, and basic first-aid techniques. (Courses are available at many Y's, hospitals, and the American Red Cross, and through fire departments and ambulance corps; check with your child's doctor for information.) Keep your skills current and ready to use with periodic refresher courses (and possibly an AAP- or Red Cross-approved video). See that anyone else who cares for your toddler is also fully prepared to deal with emergencies—from minor to major.

To further prepare yourself for emergencies:

▲ Discuss with your toddler's doctor what the best course of action would be in case of a non-life-threatening injury as well as in a serious emergency: when to call the office, when to go to the emergency room (ER) (and when to do both), when to call 911, and when to follow some other protocol. Remember, for minor injuries, the ER—with its long waits and priority given to life-threatening illnesses—may not be the best place go. If there is a children's hospital in the vicinity, the doctor may recommend heading there when an emergency appears serious, since children's hospitals are generally better equipped to handle pediatric emergencies than are community hospitals.

▲ Keep your first aid supplies (see page 676) in a childproof, easily manageable kit or box so it can be moved as a whole, as needed. If you don't already have one, make the next phone you buy a portable, so that it can be used at the site of an accident in or around your home.

▲ Have handy, near each telephone in your home: *Emergency phone numbers.* The numbers of the doctors your family uses, the Poison Control Center, the hospital emergency room of your choice, your pharmacy, the Emergency Medical Service (911 in most areas), your workplace, your spouse's workplace, as well as the number of a close relative, friend, or neighbor who can be called on in an emergency. *Personal information (updated regularly).* Your child's age; approximate weight; immunization record (including when the last tetanus shot was given); medications, allergies, and/or chronic illnesses, if any. In an emergency, these should be supplied to the EMS and/or taken to the hospital or ER. *Location information.* Home address (include cross streets and landmarks, if necessary), apartment number, telephone number—for use by baby-sitters or other caregivers calling for emergency help

(even a family member might need this in a moment of panic). *A pad and pencil.* For taking instructions from the doctor or emergency medical service.

▲ Be sure there's a clearly distinguishable number on your house and a light that makes it visible after dark.

▲ Know the quickest route to the ER or other emergency medical facility your child's doctor recommends.

▲ Keep some cash reserved in a safe place in case you need cab fare to get to the ER or doctor's office in an emergency. (If you're very anxious, it's best if you don't drive.) Let any sitter who stays with your child know where the stash is, too.

▲ Learn to handle minor accidents calmly, which will help you keep your cool should a serious one ever occur. (Taking a couple of deep breaths before heading for an accident scene will help relax you.) Your manner and tone of voice (or those of another caregiver) will affect how your toddler responds to an injury. If you panic, your child is more likely to be upset or panicky and less likely to be able to cooperate. An uncooperative child is more difficult to treat.

▲ To further relax and reassure, always try to divert your child's attention from the injury by engaging at least three of the senses (stand where your child can *see* you, speak calmly so he or she can *hear* you, and *touch* a part of the body that doesn't seem to be injured).

# First Aid for the Toddler

Following are the most common injuries, what you should know about them, how to treat (and not treat) them, and when to seek medical care for them. Types of injuries are listed alphabetically (abdominal injuries, bites, broken bones, etc.), with individual injuries numbered for easy cross-reference.

A gray bar has been added to the top of these pages, making the chapter easy to locate in an emergency.

# ABDOMINAL INJURIES

**1. Internal bleeding.** A blow to your toddler's abdomen could result in internal damage. The signs of such injury would include: bruising or other discoloration of the abdomen; vomited or coughed-up blood that is dark or bright red and has the consistency of coffee grounds (this could also be a sign of the child's having swallowed a caustic substance); blood (it may be dark or bright red) in the stool or urine; shock (cold, clammy, pale skin; weak, rapid pulse; chills; confusion; and, possibly, nausea, vomiting, and/or shallow breathing). Seek emergency medical assistance (*call 911*). If the child appears to be in shock, treat *immediately* (#48). Do not give food or drink.

**2. Cuts or lacerations of the abdomen.** Treat as for other cuts (#51, #52). With a major laceration, intestines may protrude. Don't try to put them back into the abdomen. Instead, cover them with a clean moistened washcloth or diaper and get emergency medical assistance immediately (*call 911*).

# BITES

**3. Animal bites.** Try to avoid moving the affected part. Call the doctor immediately. Then wash the wound gently with soap and water for 15 minutes. Do not apply antiseptic or anything else. Control bleeding (#51, #52, #53) as needed, and apply a sterile bandage. Try to restrain the animal for testing, but avoid getting bitten yourself. Dogs, cats, bats, skunks, and raccoons who bite may turn out to be rabid, especially if the attack was unprovoked. Infection (redness, tenderness, swelling) is common with cat bites and may require antibiotics. Low-risk dog bites do not usually require antibiotics, but it's important to consult your child's doctor for any animal bite. *Call the doctor immediately* if redness, swelling, and tenderness develop at the site of the bite.

Following cat bites or scratches (especially from a kitten less than six months old) cat-scratch disease may develop. In such a situation, watch for the signs (see page 842), which most often appear between 7 to 12 days after the incident, and call the doctor should they appear. Cat bites are also prone to infection because they tend to be puncture wounds that can't be easily cleaned.

**4. Human bites.** The human mouth contains a variety of infectious organisms. If your child is bitten by a sibling or another toddler, don't worry unless the skin is broken. If it is, wash the bite with mild soap and lukewarm water for about 10 minutes, by running tap water over it if you can, or by pouring water from a pitcher or cup. Don't rub the wound or apply any spray or ointment (antibiotic or otherwise); simply cover the bite with a sterile dressing and *call the doctor*. Use pressure to stem bleeding (#52), if necessary. Antibiotics may be prescribed to prevent infection.

**5. Insect bites.** Treat insect stings or bites as follows:

▲ Scrape off the honeybee's stinger with the blunt edge of a knife or with your fingernail or the edge of a credit card. Don't try to grasp the stinger with your nails or with a tweezer—this could squeeze more of the remaining venom into the wound.

▲ To remove ticks, use blunt tweezers or fingertips protected by a tissue, paper towel, or rubber glove. Swab the area with alcohol, if possible. Grasp the bug as close to the child's skin and to the point of attachment as possible and pull upward, steadily and evenly. Don't twist, jerk, squeeze, crush, or puncture the tick. *Don't* use such home remedies as petroleum jelly, gasoline, or a hot match—they can make matters worse. Save the tick for medical examination if you suspect it's a deer tick; otherwise squash it in a tissue and discard. A deer tick, which can carry Lyme disease (see page 850), is black and brown, pin-head size in the nymph stage and about $\frac{1}{10}$-inch in the adult stage; engorged with blood, it looks larger. Its bite leaves a red, round area that usually develops a clear "bull's eye" center. Removing an infected tick quickly greatly reduces the risk of the victim developing Lyme disease. If you suspect a deer tick bite, call the doctor. Also call the doctor if the head of the tick remains embedded in the skin despite your efforts to remove it.

▲ Wash the site of a minor bee, wasp, ant, spider, or tick bite with soap and water. Apply ice or cold compresses (page 836) if there appears to be swelling or pain. Follow with an application of bug-bite medication, or a paste of baking soda or meat tenderizer and water; a lidocaine spray or a mix of vinegar and salt may also relieve discomfort. If the bite is near an eye or on the eyelid, be careful not to get any medication in the eye.

▲ Apply calamine lotion or another anti-itching medication to itchy bites, such as those caused by mosquitoes. If a child has several bites, a colloidal oatmeal bath may also be soothing (and distracting).

▲ If there seems to be extreme pain, difficulty breathing, or fever after a spider or fire-ant bite, apply ice or cold compresses and *call 911* for emergency help *immediately.* Try to find the spider or ant and put it in a jar (avoid being bitten yourself) so that you can take it to the hospital with you. If you can't find it, be ready to describe it so that the doctor can determine whether it was poisonous.

▲ If you know (or even suspect) your child was bitten by a poisonous spider—a black widow, brown recluse spider, tarantula, or scorpion, for example—get emergency treatment (*call 911*) *immediately,* even before symptoms appear.

Black widow spider bites are graded according to severity. Grade 1: local pain at the site with no other symptoms. Grade 2: muscular pain in the arm or leg bitten, which may spread to the abdomen if a leg is affected or to the chest if an arm is. Grade 3: local diaphoresis (profuse perspiration) at site or on the entire extremity. Grade 4: generalized muscle pain in back, abdomen, and chest; generalized sweating; nausea, vomiting, and headache.

Signs of the bite of a brown recluse spider may include: no initial pain; a round, red spot developing within minutes, which becomes a raised papule (or pimple) within a few hours and then progresses to a painful bruise-like lesion. Over the next few days, a hemorrhagic blister forms around the bite, which develops a white ring and a gray, blue, purple, or black area. An irregular area of redness may also develop around the entire lesion.

▲ Watch for a serious reaction to the sting of a bee, wasp, or hornet. About 90% of children react to an insect sting with short-lived (under 24 hours) redness, swelling, and pain in a 2-inch area at the site of the sting. But the remainder have a much more severe local reaction—with extensive swelling and tenderness covering an area 4 inches or more in diameter that doesn't peak until 3 to 7 days after the sting.

Between 1 and 10 in 200 have a true systemic anaphylactic reaction. Most systemic reactions begin several minutes to several hours after the sting with such allergic symptoms as hives (urticaria; see page 704), reddened patches of skin (erythema), itching (pruritis), and swelling (angioedema) and are rarely life-threatening. Life-threatening anaphylactic reactions (which are uncommon) usually begin within 5 to 10 minutes of the sting. They may include swelling of the face and/or tongue; signs of swelling of the throat (laryngeal edema), such as tickling, gagging, difficulty swallowing, or voice change; bronchospasm (chest tightness, coughing, wheezing, or difficulty breathing); a drop in blood pressure, causing dizziness or fainting; and/or cardiovascular collapse. Fatal outcomes in children are extremely rare, but do report *any* systemic reaction to your child's doctor *immediately*; emergency treatment may be needed. Should your child have a life-threatening system reaction, *call 911 immediately.*

After a systemic reaction, a skin test, and possibly other testing, will probably be performed to determine sensitivity to insect venom. In the unlikely case that it's determined your child is at risk of a life-threatening episode from an insect sting, it will probably be recommended that an Epi-Pen device (see page 707) accompany your child on outings during bee season.

**6. Snake bites.** The four major types of poisonous snakes in the U.S.—rattlesnakes, copperheads, coral snakes, and cottonmouths (or water moccasins)—all have fangs, which usually leave identifying marks when they bite. It's rare that a young child is bitten by a poisonous snake, but such a bite is very dangerous. Because of a toddler's small size, even a tiny amount of venom can be fatal. Following a poisonous snake bite, it is important to keep the child and the affected part as still as possible. If the bite is on a limb, immobilize the limb with a splint if necessary, and keep it below the level of the heart. Use a cool compress if available to relieve pain, but *do not* apply ice or give any medication without medical advice. Sucking out the venom by mouth (and spitting it out) may be helpful if done immediately, but *do not* make an incision of any kind, unless you are 4 or 5 hours from help and severe symptoms develop. If the child is not breathing and/or the heart has stopped beating, give CPR (page 687). Treat for shock (#48) if symptoms (cold, clammy, pale skin; weak, rapid pulse; chills; confusion; and, possibly, nausea, vomiting, and/or shallow breathing) develop. *Get prompt medical help,* and be ready to identify or describe the snake, if you can. If you won't be able to get medical help within an hour for bites to limbs, apply a loose constricting band or tourniquet (use a belt, tie, or hair ribbon) tied loosely enough for you to slip a finger under 2 inches above the bite to slow circulation from the area. (Never tie a tourniquet around a finger or toe, or around the neck, head, or trunk.) Check the pulse (see page 573) on the limb frequently to be sure circulation is not cut off, and loosen the tourniquet if the limb begins to swell. Make a note of the time the tourniquet was tied.

Treat nonpoisonous snake bites as puncture wounds (#54), and notify the doctor.

**7. Marine stings.** The stings of marine animals are usually not serious, but an occasional child will have a severe reaction. Medical treatment should be sought immediately as a precaution. First-aid treatment varies with the type of marine animal involved, but in general, any clinging fragments of the stinger should be carefully brushed away with a diaper or piece of clothing (to protect your own fingers). Heavy bleeding (#52), shock (#48), or cessation of breathing (see page 684) should be treated immediately.

(Don't worry about light bleeding; it may help to purge the toxins). The site of the sting of a stingray, lionfish, catfish, stonefish, or sea urchin should be soaked in hot water, when it's available, for 30 minutes, or until medical professionals take over. The toxins from the sting of a jellyfish or Portuguese man-of-war can be counteracted by applying vinegar, alcohol, or diluted ammonia. (Pack a couple of alcohol pads in your beach bag, just in case.)

# BLEEDING

see #51, #52, #53

# BLEEDING, INTERNAL

see #1

# BROKEN BONES OR FRACTURES

**8. Possible broken arms, legs, collarbones, or fingers.** Though fractures in small children usually mend quickly, medical treatment is necessary to ensure proper healing. Take your child to the doctor or ER even if you only suspect a break. Signs of a break include: a snapping sound at the time of the accident; deformity (although this could also indicate a dislocation, #17); inability to move or bear weight on the part; severe pain (persistent crying could be a clue); numbness and/or tingling (neither of which a young child can be guaranteed to report); swelling and discoloration. If a fracture is suspected, don't move the child before you've checked with the doctor—unless it's necessary for safety. If you must move the child immediately, first try to immobilize the injured part by splinting it in the position it's in with a ruler, a magazine, a book, or another firm object, padded with a soft cloth to protect the skin. Or use a small, firm pillow as a splint. Fasten the splint securely at, above, and below the possible break with bandages, strips of cloth, scarves, or neckties, but not so tightly that circulation is restricted. If no potential splint is handy, try to splint the injured limb with your arm. Check regularly while awaiting help to be sure the splint or its wrapping isn't cutting off circulation. Apply an ice pack to reduce swelling.

**9. Compound fractures.** If a bone is protruding through the skin, don't touch it. Cover the injury, if possible, with sterile gauze or with a clean diaper; control bleeding, if necessary, with pressure (#52); and get emergency medical assistance (*call 911*).

**10. Possible neck or back injury.** If any neck or back injury is suspected, don't move the child *at all*.[1] *Call 911* for emergency medical assistance. Cover and keep the child comfortable while waiting for help, and if possible, put some heavy objects, such as books, around the head to help immobilize it. Don't give any food or drink. Treat severe bleeding (#53), shock (#48), or absence of breathing (see page 684) immediately.

# BRUISES, SKIN

see #49

# BURNS AND SCALDS

> *Important:* If a child's clothing is on fire, use a coat, blanket, rug, bedspread, or even your own body (your clothing won't catch fire) to smother the flames.

---

1. If you must move the child away from a life-threatening situation (such as fire), splint the back, neck, and head as best you can with a flat board, a chair cushion, or your arm, if nothing else is available. Try to move the child as a single unit, without bending or twisting the head, neck, or back.

Teach a child who is old enough to understand never to run if his or her clothing catches on fire, but to *stop, drop, and roll*. Treat any burns as below.

**11. Limited thermal (heat) burns.** Immerse burned fingers, hands, feet, toes, arms, or legs in cool water (50°F to 60°F); apply cool compresses (see page 836) to burns of the trunk or face. Continue until the child doesn't seem to be in pain anymore—usually 15 minutes to half an hour. Do not apply: ice (which could compound skin damage), butter or burn ointments (which could trap the heat in the skin), or baking-soda preparations. And don't attempt to break any blisters that form.

If the burned skin looks normal or only slightly red after soaking, covering it is not necessary. Repeat soaking if pain returns. Apply Bacitracin (or a similar antibiotic ointment) twice a day starting the second day. If redness and pain persist for more than a few hours, however, call the doctor.

*Call the doctor immediately* for: burns that look raw, that blister (second degree burns), or are white or charred looking (third degree burns); burns on the face, hands, feet, or genitals; or burns that are the size of your child's hand or larger.

If the burn looks raw, cover loosely with a material that won't stick to the wound (such as a sterile nonstick bandage, or in a pinch, aluminum foil). If it's oozing, cover only with sterile gauze; if that's not available, leave the area uncovered. If there are blisters, ask the doctor for advice on how to cover the burn until your child gets medical attention.

If a burn you are treating at home doesn't start to heal within a few hours, gets redder, starts to swell, or develops a discharge or bad odor, call the doctor. An infection may have developed.

**12. Extensive thermal (heat) burns.** *Call 911* for emergency medical assistance. Keep the child lying flat. Remove any clothing from the burn area that does not adhere to the wound (cut it away as necessary, but don't pull). Keep the child comfortably warm by covering lightly with a clean sheet. If legs are burned, position them higher than the heart by propping them on pillows or bundled blankets. Apply cool, wet compresses to the injured area (but not to more than 25% of the body at one time). Do not apply pressure, ointments, butter or other fats, powder, or boric-acid soaks to burned areas. If the child is conscious and doesn't have severe burns in the mouth, give water or another fluid (or nurse, if your child is not yet weaned).

**13. Chemical burns.** Caustic substances (such as lye, drain cleaner, and other acids) can cause serious burns. Gently brush off dried chemical matter from the skin (wear rubber gloves or use a towel or clean diaper to protect your hands) and remove any contaminated clothing (again protecting your hands). Immediately wash the skin with large amounts of water and the antidote, if any, recommended on the product container, or soap. Call the Poison Control Center, a physician, or the ER for further advice. Get *immediate* medical assistance if there is difficult or painful breathing, which could indicate lung injury from inhalation of caustic fumes. (If a chemical has been swallowed, see #44.)

**14. Electrical burns.** Immediately disconnect the power source, if possible. Or pull the child away from the source using a dry, nonmetallic object—a broom, wooden ladder, rope, cushion, chair, or even a large book—but not with your bare hands. If the child is not breathing, initiate CPR (page 687) and *call 911*. All electrical burns should be evaluated by a physician, so call your toddler's doctor or go to the ER at once even if your child seems okay.

**15. Sunburn.** Treat by applying cool tap-water compresses (see page 836) for 10 to 15 minutes, three or four times a day, until redness subsides; the evaporating water helps to cool the skin. In between these treatments, apply a sunburn relief spray made just for kids or a moisturizing cream, or give a cool colloidal oatmeal bath. Don't use petroleum jelly on a burn; it seals out air, which is needed for healing. And unless they are prescribed by the doctor, don't give antihistamines. A children's pain reliever (acetaminophen) may reduce the discomfort, but, though there have been some claims to the contrary, giving aspirin won't prevent sun damage to the skin (so don't use it unless the doctor recommends otherwise). When sunburn is severe—there is blistering, pain, nausea, or chills—call the doctor immediately. Steroid ointments or creams may be prescribed, and large blisters may need to be drained and dressed. Calamine liniment may be recommended to help dry out blisters.

# CAT BITES/ SCRATCHES

see #3

# CHEMICAL BURNS

see #13

# CHOKING

see page 689

# COLD INJURIES

see *Frostbite*, #31; *Hypothermia*, #35

# CONVULSIONS

**16.** Symptoms of a seizure or convulsion—caused by abnormal electrical impulses in the brain—vary depending upon the type of seizure, but may include: collapse, eyes rolling upward, foaming at the mouth, stiffening of the body followed by uncontrolled jerking movements, and in the most serious cases, difficulty breathing. Brief convulsions are not uncommon with high fevers (see page 583 for how to deal with febrile seizures). For non-febrile seizures: Clear the immediate area around the child or move the child to the middle of a bed or carpeted area to prevent injury. Loosen clothing around the neck and middle, and lay the child on one side with head lower than hips (elevate them with a pillow). Don't restrain, but do stand by ready to prevent injury. Don't put anything in the child's mouth, including food, drink, breast, or bottle. If the child isn't breathing, begin CPR (see page 687) *immediately*. If someone else is with you, have them *call 911*; if you're alone, wait until breathing has started again to call, or call if breathing hasn't resumed within a few minutes. Also *call 911* if the seizure lasts more than 2 or 3 minutes, seems very severe, or is followed by one or more repeat seizures. If this was a first seizure, call the doctor to arrange for a medical evaluation as soon as possible, even if the child seems fine after the episode has ended.

> *Important:* Seizures may be caused by the ingestion of prescription medicines or other poisons, so check the immediate vicinity for any sign that your child may have gotten into a bottle of pills or another hazardous substance.

# CUTS

see #51, #52

# DISLOCATIONS

**17.** Shoulder and elbow dislocations are common among toddlers (see page 643 for why). A visible deformity of the arm and/or the inability of the child to move it, usually combined with inconsolable crying, are typical indications. A quick trip to the doctor's office or the ER, where an experienced professional can reposition the dislocated part, will provide virtually instant relief. If pain seems severe, apply an ice pack and splint before leaving.

# DOG BITES

see #3

# DROWNING

**18.** Even a child who quickly revives after being taken from the water unconscious should get medical evaluation. For the child who remains unconscious, *have someone else call 911* for emergency medical assistance, if possible, while you begin rescue techniques (see page 683). If the child is not breathing or if no pulse is found, begin CPR immediately. If no one is available to phone for help, call later. Don't stop CPR until the child revives or help arrives, no matter how long that takes. If there is vomiting, turn the child to one side to avoid choking.[2] Also turn the child on one side once breathing is restored. Keep the child warm and dry.

---

2. If you suspect a back or neck injury, do not turn the child— with such an injury is very risky, see

# EAR INJURIES

**19. Foreign object in the ear.** Try to get the toddler to shake the object out by turning the ear down and shaking his or her head gently. If that doesn't work, try these techniques.

▲ For an insect, use a lighted flashlight to try to lure it out.

▲ For a metal object, try a magnet to draw it out (but don't insert the magnet in the ear).

▲ For an object made of plastic or wood that is protruding visibly from the ear, dab a drop of quick-drying glue (that won't bond to the skin) on a straightened paper clip and touch it to the object (*never* probe blindly into the ear). Wait for the glue to dry, then pull the clip out, hopefully with the object attached. Don't attempt this if there's no one around to help hold your child still.

  If the above techniques fail, don't try to dig the object out with your fingers or with an instrument. Instead, take your child to the doctor's office or the ER.

**20. Damage to the ear.** If a pointed object has been pushed into the ear or if your toddler shows signs of ear injury (bleeding from the ear canal, sudden difficulty hearing, a swollen earlobe, or substantial pain), *call the doctor.*

# ELECTRIC SHOCK

**21.** Break contact with the electrical source by disconnecting the appliance involved or turning off the power to the outlet (whichever can be accomplished most quickly), or separate the child from the current by using a dry nonmetallic object (a broom, wooden ladder, robe, cushion, chair, or even a large book or rubber boot) If the child is in contact with water, *do not* touch the water yourself. Once the child has been separated from the power source, *call 911*. If the child isn't breathing, begin CPR (see page 687) *immediately*. If two adults are present, one can disconnect the power source and *call 911* while the other rescues the child.

# EYE INJURY

*Important:* Don't apply pressure to an injured eye; don't touch the eye with your fingers, or instill medications without a physician's advice. Keep the child from rubbing the eye by holding a small cup or glass (or an eyecup) over it or by restraining the child's hands, if necessary.

**22. Foreign object in the eye.** Try to wash the object out by pouring a stream of tepid (body temperature) water into the eye while someone holds the child still, if necessary. If this is unsuccessful, try pulling the upper lid outward and down over the lower lid for a few seconds. Don't be concerned if your attempts provoke crying; the tears may help to wash the object out of the eye.

If after these attempts you can still see the object or if the child still seems uncomfortable, proceed to the doctor's office or the ER; the object may have become embedded or may have scratched the eye. Never try to remove an embedded object yourself. Cover the eye with a sterile gauze pad taped loosely in place, or with a few clean tissues or a clean handkerchief held on by hand, to alleviate some of the discomfort en route.

**23. Corrosive substance in the eye.** Flush the eye immediately and thoroughly with plain lukewarm water[3] (poured from a pitcher, cup, or bottle)

*Giving your toddler an eye bath won't be easy, but it's necessary to wash away a corrosive substance.*

for 15 minutes while holding the eye open with your fingers (see illustration). If only one eye is involved, keep the chemical runoff out of the other by turning the child's head so that the unaffected eye is higher than the affected one. Don't use drops, ointments, or an eye cup, and keep the child from rubbing the eye or eyes. Call the Poison Control Center or the doctor for further instructions.

**24. Injury to the eye with a pointed or sharp object.** Keep the child in a semireclining position while you seek help. If the object is still in the eye, *do not* try to remove it. If it isn't, cover the eye lightly with a gauze pad, clean washcloth, or facial tissue; do not apply pressure. In any case, get emergency medical assistance *immediately* (*call 911*). Though such injuries often look worse than they are, it's wise to consult an ophthalmologist any time the eye is scratched or punctured, even slightly.

---

3. If water isn't available, use a liquid close to it, such as seltzer, a nonacid soft drink, or milk.

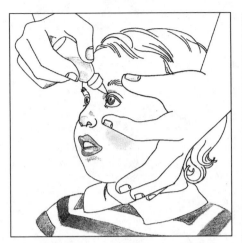

*Do not put drops in your toddler's eyes without the advice of a doctor (they are most likely to be recommended if there is an infection, such as conjunctivitis, see page 844). To administer drops, keep the eye open with two fingers of one hand while steadying the head with the other three.*

**25. Injury to the eye with a blunt object.** Keep the child lying face up. Cover the injured eye with an ice pack or cold compress for about 15 minutes; repeat every hour as needed to reduce pain and swelling (page 836). Consult the doctor if there is bleeding in the eye, if the eye blackens, if the child seems to be having difficulty seeing or keeps rubbing the eye a lot, if the object hit the eye at high speed, or if the child complains of persistent eye pain.

# FAINTING

**26.** Check for breathing. If it is absent, begin CPR *immediately* (see page 687). If you detect breathing, keep the child lying flat, lightly covered for warmth if necessary. Loosen clothing around the neck. Turn the child's head to one side and clear the mouth of any food or objects. Don't give anything to eat or drink. Call the doctor *immediately*.

# FINGER AND TOE INJURIES

**27. Finger or toe bruises.** Young children, ever curious, are particularly prone to painful bruises from catching fingers in drawers and doors. For such a bruise, soak the finger in ice water (see page 836). As much as an hour of soaking is recommended, with a break every 10 minutes (long enough for the finger to rewarm) to avoid frostbite. Unfortunately, few toddlers will sit still for the duration, though you may be able to treat your child for a few minutes by using distraction (see box, page 678) or—if necessary—force. A stubbed toe will also benefit from soaking, but again, lengthy treatment often isn't practical with a young child. Bruised fingers and toes will swell less if they are kept elevated.

If the injured finger or toe becomes very swollen very quickly, is misshapen, or can't be extended or straightened, suspect a break (#8). Call the doctor *immediately* if the bruise is from a wringer-type injury or from catching a hand or foot in the spokes of a moving wheel.

**28. Bleeding under the nail.** When a finger or toe is badly bruised, a blood clot may form under the nail, causing painful pressure. If blood oozes out from under the nail, press on the nail to encourage the flow, which will help to relieve the pressure. Soak the injury in ice water if your child will tolerate it. If pain continues, a hole may have to be made in the nail to relieve the pressure. Your doctor can do the job or may tell you how to do it yourself.

**29. A torn nail.** For a small tear, secure with a piece of adhesive tape or a Band-Aid until the nail grows to the point where the tear can be trimmed. For a tear that is almost complete, trim away along the tear line with a scissors and cover with a Band-Aid until the nail is long enough to protect the finger or toe tip.

**30. A detached nail.** Completely remove the nail if it is still partly attached by clipping with a nail scissors. Soak the finger or toe for 20 minutes in cold water, if possible, then apply antibiotic ointment and cover with a nonstick Band-Aid. For the next 3 days, soak once a day in warm salt water (½ teaspoon salt to 1 pint warm water) for about 15 minutes, applying antibiotic ointment and covering with a fresh Band-Aid after each soak. By the fourth day, dispense with the ointment as long as healing is progressing, but continue the daily soaking for the rest of a full week. Keep the nail bed covered with a Band-Aid until the nail is completely grown in. If the redness, heat, and swelling of infection occur at any point, call the doctor.

# FOREIGN OBJECTS

in the ear, see #19; in the eye, see #22; in the nose, see #42; in the mouth or throat, see #40

# FRACTURES

see #8, #9, #10.

# FROSTBITE

**31.** Young children are extremely susceptible to frostbite (freezing of body tissue), particularly on their fingers, toes, ears, nose, and cheeks. With frostbite, the affected part becomes very cold to the touch and turns white or yellowish gray, sometimes with white spots. In severe frostbite the skin is cold, waxy, pale, and hard. Should you note *any* signs of frostbite in your toddler, immediately try to warm the frosty parts against your body—open your coat and shirt and tuck the parts inside next to your skin (under your arm is best). You can also breathe warm air on your child's skin. Get to a doctor or an emergency room as soon as possible. If that isn't feasible immediately, get your child indoors and begin a gradual rewarming process. Don't massage the damaged parts or put them right next to a radiator, stove, open fire, or heat lamp; the damaged skin may burn. Don't try to quick-thaw in hot water, either; this can further damage the skin. Instead, soak affected fingers and toes directly in water that is about 102°F—just a little warmer than normal body temperature and just *slightly* warm to the touch. For unsoakable parts, such as the nose, ears, and cheeks, use very gently applied warm compresses (apply washcloths or towels soaked in water slightly warm to the touch). Continue the soaks until color returns to the skin—usually in 30 to 60 minutes (add warm water to the soaks as needed to maintain tepid temperature). Also give sips of warm (not hot) fluids. As frostbitten skin rewarms it becomes red and slightly swollen, and it may blister. (Severely frostbitten skin may turn purple or blue, peel, or may become gangrenous.) Gently dry the skin and keep it from rechilling. Application of aloe vera may help healing. If your child's injury hasn't yet been seen by a doctor, it is important to get medical attention now.

If, once the injured parts have been warmed, you have to go out again to take the child to the doctor (or anywhere else), be especially careful to keep the affected areas warm (wrapped in a blanket) en route, as refreezing of thawed tissues can cause additional damage.

# HEAD INJURIES

*Important:* Head injuries are usually more serious if a child falls onto a hard surface from a height equal to or greater than his or her own, or is hit with a heavy object. Blows to the side of the head may do more damage than those to the front or back of the head.

### 32. Cuts and bruises to the scalp.
Because of the profusion of blood vessels in the scalp, heavy bleeding is common with cuts to the head, even tiny ones, and bruises there tend to swell up to egg size very quickly. Treat as you would any cut (#51, #52) or bruise (#49). Check with the doctor for all but very minor scalp wounds.

### 33. Possibly serious head trauma.
Every active toddler experiences an occasional minor bump on the head. Usually such an injury requires no more than a couple of make-it-better kisses. But a severe blow to the head requires more. It's wise to observe a child carefully for 6 hours following a severe blow to the head. Symptoms may occur immediately or not show up for several days—so continue to observe a child who has had a serious head injury even if he or she seems okay initially. *Call the doctor* or summon emergency medical assistance *immediately (call 911)* if your toddler shows any of these signs following a head injury:

▲ Loss of consciousness (a brief period of drowsiness—no more than 2 or 3 hours—is common, however, and nothing to worry about)

▲ Headache that persists for more than an hour (a young toddler may just cry and hold his or her head), that seems to get worse over time, that interferes with normal activity and/or sleep, or that isn't relieved by acetaminophen

▲ Difficulty being roused (check every hour or 2 during daytime naps, 2 or 3 times during the night for the first day following the injury to be sure the child is responsive; if you can't rouse a sleeping child, immediately check for breathing; see page 684)

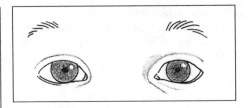

*Eyes should contract (top) in response to a penlight, and expand (bottom) when the light is removed.*

▲ More than 1 or 2 episodes of vomiting

▲ Oozing of blood or watery fluid from the ears or nose

▲ Black-and-blue areas appearing around the eyes or behind the ears

▲ Any depression or indentation in the skull

▲ Difficulty walking or clumsiness (beyond usual toddler clumsiness), or the inability to move an arm, a leg, or another body part

▲ Abnormal speech or behavior (slurred speech, extreme irritability)

▲ Dizziness that persists longer than an hour after the injury (the child's balance may seem off)

▲ Convulsions (seizures; see #16)

▲ Unequal pupil size, or pupils that do not get smaller in response to the light of a penlight or larger when the light is removed (see above illustration)

▲ Unusual paleness that persists for more than an hour or so.

While waiting for help, keep the child lying quietly with his or her head turned to one side. *Do not move* the child if you suspect a neck injury, unless not doing so would be dangerous (see footnote, page 663). If symptoms of shock (cold, clammy, pale skin; weak, rapid pulse; chills; confusion; and, possibly, nausea, vomiting, and/or shallow breathing) develop, treat (see #48). If breathing stops, begin CPR (see page 687). Don't offer any food or drink until you get an okay from the doctor or EMS.

# Heat illness

**34.** *Heat exhaustion,* or mild hyperthermia (high body temperature), is the most common form of heat injury. Signs may include: profuse sweating, thirst, headache, muscle cramps, dizziness or lightheadedness, and/or nausea (a toddler may be cranky and put a hand to the throat, indicating a need to vomit). Body temperature may rise to 101°F to 105°F (38°C to 40°C). Treat heat exhaustion by bringing the child into a cool environment (air-conditioned, if possible) and giving cold beverages (such as diluted, but not full-strength, fruit juice) to drink. Ice packs and a fan may also help. If the child doesn't quickly return to normal, vomits on drinking, or has a high fever, call the doctor.

*Heatstroke,* or severe hyperthermia, is less common and more serious. It typically comes on suddenly after overheating, as when a child has been playing in hot, glaring sunshine or has been enclosed in a car in warm weather. Signs to watch for include hot and dry (or occasionally, moist) skin, very high fever (over 106°F, or 41°C), diarrhea, agitation or lethargy, confusion, convulsions, and loss of consciousness related to overheating. If you suspect heatstroke, wrap your toddler in a large towel that has been soaked in cold water (dump ice cubes, if available, in the sink while it's filling with cold tap water, then add the towel, or use any cool water available)

and summon *immediate* emergency medical help (*call 911*), or rush the child to the nearest emergency room. If the towel becomes warm, repeat with a freshly chilled one.

# Hyperthermia

see #34

# Hypothermia

**35.** After prolonged exposure to cold, when heat loss exceeds heat production, a child's body temperature may drop to below normal levels. A child with hypothermia may seem unusually cold to the touch, be pale and have blue lips, shiver, be lethargic, move stiffly, and/or have trouble speaking. Hypothermia is a medical emergency. In severe hypothermia, shivering ceases and there is loss of muscle control and a decline in consciousness. No time should be wasted in getting a child who appears to have hypothermia to the nearest emergency room (*call 911* if you have no quick transportation). Remove any wet clothing, wrap the child in heavy blankets, and turn on the car heater en route to the hospital. If you are awaiting emergency medical help at home, tuck your toddler under an electric blanket, if you have one, or in a hot bath (not hot enough to burn, of course). If your child is alert, offer warm beverages, such as milk or diluted juices.

# Insect bites

see #5

# Lip, split or cut

see #36, #37

# MOUTH INJURIES

**36. Split lip.** Few toddlers escape their first few years without at least one cut on the lip. Fortunately, these cuts usually heal very quickly. Apply an ice pack to ease pain and control bleeding. Or let the child suck on an ice pop or a large ice cube *only* under adult supervision (switch to a fresh ice cube before the first becomes small enough to choke on). *Call the doctor* if the cut gapes open or if the bleeding doesn't stop in 10 to 15 minutes. Also call if you suspect a lip injury may have been caused by the child chewing on an electrical cord.

**37. Cuts inside the lip or mouth.** Such injuries are also common in young children. To relieve pain and control bleeding inside the lip or cheek, give the child an ice pop or a large ice cube to suck on *only* under adult supervision (again, switch to a fresh ice cube before the first becomes small enough to choke on). To stop bleeding of the tongue that doesn't stop spontaneously, squeeze the sides of the cut together with a piece of gauze, a clean washcloth, or a cloth diaper. *Call the doctor* if the injury is in the back of the throat or on the soft palate (the rear of the upper mouth), if there is a puncture wound from a sharp object (such as a pencil or a stick), or if the bleeding doesn't stop within 10 to 15 minutes.

**38. Dislodged tooth.** If a *permanent* tooth in an older child is knocked out, it should be rinsed gently under running water while being held by the crown (not the root). It can then be reinserted into the gum, if possible, or held in the mouth (or in tap water or milk) en route to the dentist, who may be able to reimplant it if no more than 30 to 45 minutes have elapsed since the accident. But since there is little chance that the dentist will try to reimplant a dislodged *baby* tooth (such implantations often abscess and

rarely hold), precautions to keep a baby tooth alive generally aren't necessary. The dentist will, however, want to see it to be sure it's whole; fragments left in the gum could be expelled and then inhaled or choked on, or the area could become infected. So take the tooth along to the dentist—or to the doctor or ER if you are unable to reach a dentist.

**39. Broken tooth.** Clean dirt or debris carefully from the mouth with warm water and gauze or a clean cloth. Check thoroughly to be sure there are no broken parts of the tooth still in the child's mouth. Place cold compresses (see page 836) on the face in the area of the injured tooth to minimize swelling. *Call the child's dentist immediately* for further instructions; if your child has no dentist as yet, call the doctor for a recommendation.

**40. A foreign object in the mouth or throat.** Removing a foreign object that has already been inserted and can't be grasped easily from the outside is tricky. Unless done carefully, the effort can push the object in even further. Pinch the child's cheeks to open the mouth, and use a tweezer to remove a soft object (such as a piece of tissue paper or bread). For anything else, try a finger swipe: Curl your finger and swipe quickly at the object with a sideways motion. *Do not* attempt a finger swipe, however, if you can't see the object. If a foreign object is lodged in your child's throat, see choking rescue procedures, beginning on page 689.

# NOSE INJURIES

**41. Nosebleeds.** With the child in an upright position or leaning slightly forward (so blood won't drip down the throat), pinch together the outer sides of the nostrils gently between your thumb and index finger, pushing firmly back toward the face, for 5 minutes. (The child will automatically switch to mouth breathing.) Try to keep the child calm; crying increases the blood flow. If bleeding persists, try packing the bleeding nostril with a wad of absorbent cotton and pinch for 10 minutes more and/or apply cold compresses or ice wrapped in a washcloth to the nose to constrict the blood vessels. If this doesn't work and bleeding continues, call the doctor—keeping the child upright while you do. Try to keep your toddler quiet (with stories, videos, games) for several hours following the nosebleed. Frequent nosebleeds, even if easily stopped, should be reported to your child's doctor. Sometimes, adding humidity to the air in your home (see page 838) will reduce the number of nosebleeds.

**42. Foreign object in the nose.** Difficulty breathing through the nose and/or a foul-smelling, sometimes bloody, nasal discharge may be a sign that something has been pushed up the nose. Keep the child calm and encourage mouth breathing. If the object protrudes, remove it with your fingers, but don't probe or use tweezers (or anything else) that could injure the nose if the child were to move unexpectedly, or that could push the object farther into the nasal canal. If you can't remove the object, try to get your child to blow through the nose (have him or her try to move a feather or tiny piece of paper on your hand with the blows). If this fails, take the child to the doctor or emergency room.

**43. A blow to the nose.** If there is bleeding, keep the child upright and leaning forward to reduce the swallowing of blood and the risk of choking on it. Use an ice pack or cold compresses (page 836) to reduce swelling. If swelling persists, check with the doctor to be sure there is no break.

# POISONING

**44. Swallowed poisons.** Any nonfood substance is a potential poison. The more common symptoms of poisoning include: lethargy, agitation, or other behavior that deviates from your child's norm; racing, irregular pulse and/or rapid breathing; difficulty breathing (after inhaling laundry detergent, for example); diarrhea or vomiting; excessive watering of the eyes, sweating, or drooling; hot, dry skin and mouth; dilated (wide open) or constricted (pinpoint) pupils; flickering, sideways eye movements; tremors or convulsions.

If your toddler has some of these symptoms (and their presence cannot be explained in another way), or if you have evidence that your toddler has *definitely* ingested a questionable substance (you saw it happen) or *possibly* has (you found your child with an open bottle of pills or hazardous liquid; found spilled liquid on clothing or loose pills on the floor; smelled a toxic chemical on his or her breath), call (or have someone else call) the Poison Control Center or the hospital emergency room *immediately* for instructions. Call promptly for suspected poisoning even if there are no symptoms—they may not appear for hours.

If your child has severe throat pain, excessive drooling, breathing difficulty, convulsions, or excessive drowsiness after the ingestion (or suspected ingestion) of a dangerous substance, *call 911* for emergency medical assistance. Begin emergency treatment *immediately* if the child is unconscious. Place your toddler face up on a table or another firm surface and check for breathing (see page 684). If there is no sign of breathing, begin CPR promptly. *Call 911* for emergency medical assistance after 2 minutes, then continue CPR until the child revives or until help arrives.

*Do not* try to treat a poisoning on your own. *Do not* follow the directions

## POST A WARNING

· · · · · · · · · ·

**S**yrup of ipecac may sometimes be useful in treating poisoning, but it can also be dangerous when used inappropriately. To be sure you don't accidentally misuse the ipecac in your first-aid supply kit, label it: DO NOT USE WITHOUT INSTRUCTIONS FROM THE POISON CONTROL CENTER OR DOCTOR. Add the phone numbers of the Poison Control Center and your child's doctor.

on a product label—they are often inaccurate, out-of-date, or even outright dangerous. *Do not* give your toddler anything by mouth (including food or drink, the activated-charcoal blend known as universal antidote, or anything to induce vomiting, such as syrup of ipecac, salt water, or raw egg whites) without explicit medical advice.

If you are alone, safely position the child before calling. Set a child who is vomiting on his or her side to reduce the risk of inhaling the vomit; a child who is convulsing should be put in a safe spot, with clothing loosened (see #16).

When calling, have ready your child's illness record (page 872), as well as the name of the product ingested, along with the ingredients and package information, if available (if part of a plant was eaten, supply the name, or at least a description, of the plant); the time the poisoning is believed to have occurred; how much of the substance was ingested (give an estimate if you don't know for sure); any symptoms that have appeared; and any treatment already tried. Have a paper and pen handy for writing down exact instructions.

With many poisons, you will be advised to induce vomiting with syrup of ipecac in order to empty the stomach of as much of the poison as possible.[4] Give the precise dose recommended by the Poison Control Center or the doctor. (If no ipecac is available, ask about using liquid dish detergent—*not* detergent that goes into the dishwasher—to induce vomiting.) If they send you out to buy ipecac, take your toddler along and give the medication at the drugstore to save time. Don't forget to bring along a basin, unbreakable bowl, or bucket for the child to vomit into. If vomiting does not occur within 20 minutes, repeat the dose—but only once. If you succeed in inducing vomiting, keep the vomited material. If you are instructed to go to the emergency room or doctor's office, take it along for analysis. (It may be easier to carry it in a jar with a lid or a heavy ziplock type plastic bag, but bring along an empty basin in case your child heaves again.) Also be sure to take the suspect substance (bottle of pills, container of cleaning fluid, philodendron branch).

Vomiting should not be induced at any age when a corrosive substance (such as bleach, ammonia, or drain cleaner) or anything with a kerosene, benzene, or gasoline base (furniture polish, cleaning fluid, turpentine) has been ingested. Nor should it be induced when the victim is unconscious, drowsy, or having convulsions or tremors. In some cases, special liquid activated charcoal, which absorbs the poison, is the preferred treatment.

**45. Noxious fumes or gases.** Fumes from gasoline, auto exhaust, some poisonous chemicals, and dense smoke from fires can all be toxic. Symptoms of carbon monoxide poisoning include: headache, dizziness, coughing, nausea,

---

4. If you use up your ipecac, be sure to replace it.

drowsiness, irregular breathing, and unconsciousness. Get a child who has been exposed to hazardous fumes to fresh air (open the windows or take the child outside) promptly. If the child is not breathing, begin CPR (see page 687) *at once.* If possible, *have someone else call 911* (and the Poison Control Center), while you proceed. If no one else is around, call 911 yourself after 2 minutes of resuscitation efforts—then return immediately to CPR, and continue until breathing is established or help arrives. Unless an emergency vehicle is on its way, transport the child to a medical facility promptly. Have someone else drive if you must continue CPR or if you were also exposed to the fumes and your judgment and reflexes may be impaired. Even if you should succeed in reestablishing breathing, *immediate medical attention* will be necessary.

## POISON IVY, POISON OAK, POISON SUMAC

**46.** Most children who come in contact with poison ivy, poison oak, or poison sumac will have an allergic reaction (usually a red itchy rash, with possible swelling, blistering, and oozing) that develops within 12 to 48 hours and can last from 10 days to 4 weeks. If you know your child has had such contact, remove his or her clothing. Protect your own hands from the sap (which contains urushiol, the resin that triggers the reaction) with gloves, paper towels, or a clean diaper. To prevent the resin from "fixing" to the child's skin, immediately wash the skin with soap and cool water (for at least 10 minutes) and rinse thoroughly.[5]

Also wash anything else that may have come in contact with the plants (including clothing, pets, stroller, and so on); urushiol can remain active for up to a year on such objects. Shoes can be swabbed with cleaning fluid if they aren't washable.

Should a reaction occur, calamine or another anti-itch lotion will help relieve the itching. Acetaminophen, cool compresses (see page 836), and/or a colloidal oatmeal bath may also offer relief. Cut your toddler's nails to minimize scratching. Contact the doctor if the rash is severe or involves the eyes, face, or genitalia. An antihistamine or oral steroid medication may be prescribed to reduce discomfort.

## PUNCTURE WOUNDS

see #54

## SCALDS

see #11, 12, 13

## SCRAPES

see #50

## SEIZURES

see #16

## SEVERED LIMB OR DIGIT

**47.** Such serious accidents are rare, but knowing what to do should one occur can mean the difference between saving and losing a limb or digit. Take these steps, as needed, immediately:

---

5. The rash itself is not contagious and won't spread from person to person or from one part of the body to another. It may sometimes appear to do this, because the sap was spread originally from the clothing or hands, and because the rash takes longer to appear in areas where the dose of urushiol is smaller.

# STOCKING THE MEDICINE CHEST

· · · · · · · · · ·

Like infants, toddlers have a tendency to get sick or injured late at night, early in the morning, or on weekends—when most stores are closed and help is not readily available. So that you will have necessary supplies on hand in case of an emergency, be sure your medicine chest is well stocked. It should include:

**A nonaspirin product.** \* Acetaminophen (see page 594), in liquid, chewable, suppository, and powdered ("sprinkle") forms, is available over-the-counter under such names as Tylenol, Tempra, Liquiprin, and Panadol. The liquid or elixir form is appropriate for toddlers of any age; the children's chewables can be used for two-year-olds who weigh at least 24 pounds and can be counted on to chew them thoroughly, or on the advice of a doctor, for younger children. See the dosage chart on page 584. In some cases the doctor may prescribe an ibuprofen product, such as Advil.

**Thermometer.** For a description of types of thermometers available, see page 579.

**Medicine spoon.** A specially calibrated spoon with a hollow handle makes for easier handling and administration of medicines.

**Medicine dropper and/or oral syringe.** These, too, can make administering medicine less difficult.

**Tongue depressors.** For facilitating throat examinations.

**Heating pad and/or hot-water bottle.** For relieving muscle soreness (see page 837).

**Saline nasal spray or drops.** For stuffiness due to colds; a commercial preparation is safer than a homemade one.

**An antihistamine.** \*\* For allergic reactions.

**Calamine lotion or ½% hydrocortisone cream.** \* For mosquito bites and itchy rashes. Colloidal oatmeal baths are also helpful for soothing itches.

**Rehydration fluid.** \*\* For dehydration caused by diarrhea, vomiting, fever, or any other problem. Brands include Pedialyte, Infalyte, Naturalyte, and generics.

**Sunscreen.** For time in the sun (see page 468).

**Rubbing alcohol or alcohol pads.** \*\*\* For cleaning thermometers, tweezers, and so on, but *not* for rubdowns for reducing fever (see page 585).

**Petroleum jelly.** For lubricating a rectal thermometer and treating certain minor skin irritations.

---

▲ Try to control bleeding. Apply heavy pressure to the wound with several sterile gauze pads, a fresh sanitary napkin, or a clean diaper or washcloth. If bleeding continues, increase the pressure. Don't worry about doing damage by pressing too hard. Do not apply a tourniquet without medical advice.

▲ Treat shock if it is present (#48).

▲ Check for breathing, and begin CPR immediately if the child isn't breathing (see page 684).

▲ Preserve the severed limb or digit. As soon as possible, wrap it in a wet clean cloth or sponge, and place in a plastic bag. Secure the bag shut and place it in another bag filled with ice (do not use dry ice). Do not place the severed part directly on ice and don't immerse it in water or antiseptics.

▲ Get help. Call or have someone else *call 911* for immediate emergency medical assistance or rush to the ER, calling ahead so they can prepare for your arrival. Be sure to take along the ice-

**Syrup of ipecac.**\*\*\* This should only be used at the recommendation of a poison center or your child's doctor. Carry a bottle with your toiletries when you travel with your toddler; keep one in your tote bag or glove compartment for extra safety.

**Liquified "activated" charcoal.**\*\*\* Recent research suggests that this treatment may be preferable to ipecac in some cases of poisoning. But, as with ipecac, use activated charcoal only when recommended by the Poison Control Center or your child's doctor.

**Sterile adhesive strips and gauze pads.**\*\* Have a variety of different sizes and shapes on hand, including butterfly bandages; look for designs you think your toddler will like or let your toddler help you make the selection. Look, too, for nonstick pads, which make removal easier.

**Antibiotic ointment.**\*\* Some doctors recommend these, others do not.

**A roll of gauze.**\*\*\*

**Elastic bandage.**\*\*\* For sprains.

**A triangular cloth bandage.**\*\*\* For wrapping an injury, making an arm sling, or holding an ice pack in place.

**Adhesive tape.**\*\*\* For securing gauze pads; look for nonirritating adhesive.

**Sterile cotton balls.**\*\*\*

**Small penlight.**\*\*\* For examining your toddler's throat, or to check pupils for signs of head injury or poisoning.

**Scissors with rounded tips.**\*\*\* For cutting tape, bandages, and so on.

**Angle-tip tweezers.** For removing splinters, ticks, or assorted small foreign objects.

**Ice packs.** For reducing inflammation from bruises or other injuries. Keep refreezable ones in the freezer or fill a friendly animal-shaped one with ice as needed. In a pinch, use a can of frozen juice or a pack of frozen vegetables.

---

\*Do not give your child aspirin without explicit instructions from a doctor. A child who has chickenpox, influenza, or another viral infection should not have aspirin at all. Aspirin (acetylsalicylic acid) and other salicylates are contained in many over-the-counter pharmaceutical products, so read ingredients lists carefully for aspirin before giving any medication to your toddler.

\*\*Ask your child's doctor for specific product recommendations before you purchase any of these items.

\*\*\*Keep these first-aid supplies in a portable case (such as a tool box) that can be easily moved to the site of an accident, but that also be locked and stored safely out of a toddler's reach.

---

packed limb or digit; surgeons may attempt to reattach it. During transport, keep pressure on the wound and continue other basic life-support procedures, if necessary.

# SHOCK

**48.** Shock can develop in severe injuries or illnesses. Signs include cold, clammy, pale skin; rapid, weak pulse; chills; convulsions; and, frequently, nausea or vomiting, excessive thirst, and/or shallow breathing. *Call 911 immediately* for emergency medical assistance. Until help arrives, position the child on his or her back. Loosen any restrictive clothing, elevate the legs on a pillow or a folded blanket or garment to help direct blood to the brain, and cover the child lightly to prevent chilling or loss of body heat. If breathing seems labored, raise the child's head and shoulders very slightly. Do not give food or water or use a hot-water bottle to warm a child in shock.

## MAKING A BOO-BOO BETTER

· · · · · · · · · ·

When it comes to being treated for injuries, toddlers are rarely cooperative patients. No matter how uncomfortable the pain of their injuries, they're likely to consider the cure worse.

Except in rare cases, it doesn't help to promise that the ice pack will make the bruise feel better, that soaking will cool down the burn, or that the bandage will keep the cut clean. It may help, however, to use distraction while trying to treat a young child's injury. Entertainment—in the form of a favorite music box, video, or audio tape; a toy dog that yaps and wags its tail; a choo-choo train that can travel across the coffee table; or a parent or sibling who can dance, jump up and down, or sing silly songs—can help make the difference between a successful treatment session and disaster.

Because being forced to sit still (while ice is applied to a bruised knee or while a burned finger is soaked in cold water) is often seen by toddlers as curtailing their freedom, it may help to tie an ice pack on the knee or a cool compress around the burned finger—and allow the child to go about his or her normal activities.

Kid-friendly first-aid supplies may also help ease the pain of treatment. Look for ice packs and bandage strips with interesting designs and shapes (you can find ice packs shaped like bunnies, bandage strips with dinosaurs and cartoon designs and even some shaped like kisses).

How forceful you need to be about treatment depends on the severity of the injury. Treatment may not be necessary for a paper cut, but it may be imperative for a scraped knee filled with playground rubble and dirt. A slight bump on the head may not warrant the trauma of trying to apply an ice pack to a child who's screaming, "NO!" A severe burn, however, will certainly require cold soaks, even if your pint-size patient screams and struggles during the entire treatment. In most cases, try to treat injuries at least briefly—even a few minutes of ice on a bruise will reduce the bleeding under the skin. But abandon the treatment when its benefits are outweighed by the child's upset.

# SKIN WOUNDS

· · · · · · · · · · · · · · · · · · · · · · · · · · · · · ·

*Important:* Exposure to tetanus is a possibility whenever the skin is broken. Should your child incur an open skin wound, check to be sure tetanus immunization is current. Also be alert for signs of possible infection (swelling, warmth, tenderness, and reddening of surrounding area; oozing of pus from the wound), and call the doctor if they develop. Don't apply tincture of iodine or Merthiolate; they can delay healing.

**49. Bruises or black-and-blue marks.**
If the injury is painful, encourage quiet play to rest the injured part. Apply cold compresses, an ice pack, or cloth-wrapped ice (do not apply ice directly to the skin) for half an hour (or for as long as your toddler will sit still). If the skin is broken, treat the bruise as you would an abrasion (#50) or cut (#51, #52). Call the doctor immediately if the bruise is from a wringer-type injury or if it resulted from catching a hand or foot in the spokes of a moving wheel. Bruises that seem to appear from "out of nowhere" or that coincide with a fever should also be seen by a doctor. Also report tiny pinpoint bruises, or under-the-skin hemorrhages. (These are *petechiae,* which may occur on the face and neck when a child has been coughing a lot or crying very vigorously, on

the extremities when clothing has been restrictive, or because of viral infection or other illness.)

**50. Scrapes or abrasions.** In such injuries, most common on the knees and elbows, the top layer (or layers) of skin is abraded (scraped off), leaving the underlying area red, raw, and tender. There is usually slight bleeding from the more deeply abraded areas. Using sterile gauze, cotton, or a clean washcloth, gently sponge off the wound with soap and water to remove dirt and other foreign matter. If the child strenuously objects to this, try soaking the wound in the bathtub. Apply pressure if the bleeding doesn't stop on its own. Apply a spray or cream antiseptic, if your toddler's doctor generally recommends one, then cover with a sterile nonstick bandage that is loose enough to allow air to reach the wound. If there is no bleeding, no bandage is necessary. Most scrapes heal quickly.

**51. Small cuts.** Wash the area with clean water and soap, then hold the cut under running water to flush out dirt and foreign matter. Some doctors recommend applying an antibacterial spray or ointment before taping on a sterile nonstick bandage. A butterfly bandage will keep a small cut closed while it heals. Remove the bandage after 24 hours and expose the cut to air; rebandage only as necessary to keep the wound clean and dry. Check with the doctor about any cuts on your child's hands or face or if a cut shows signs of infection (redness, swelling, warmth, and/or oozing of pus or a white fluid).

---

## *BANDAGING A BOO-BOO*

· · · · · · · · · ·

**A**s a parent, you can expect to apply dozens, possibly hundreds, of adhesive plastic strips and bandages over the years, some large, most small. These tips make bandaging easier while helping boo-boos to get better faster.

▲ Treat the injury appropriately (see individual injuries).

▲ To improve stickability, always apply a Band-Aid or taped bandage to clean, dry skin.

▲ On open wounds, use only *sterile* Band-Aids or gauze pads, which have not been opened prior to use. Don't touch the face of the pad with your fingers; handle only the tape on Band-Aids and only the edges or back of a larger gauze pad.

▲ Use nonstick pads and/or an antibiotic ointment to prevent the bandage from sticking to the wound. If a bandage does stick, soak it in warm water rather than trying to yank it off.

▲ Except for cuts that need to be held closed, bandage loosely to allow air to enter. When using a Band-Aid on a toe or finger, be sure not to make it so tight that it cuts off circulation.

▲ Remove the bandage daily to check how the wound is healing (the best time is during or just after a bath, when the Band-Aid is likely to be wet and loosened anyway, and will slip off without tugging). Rebandage the wound if it still looks raw or open. If a scab has formed on a scrape or a cut has closed up, continued covering is not necessary. Of course, if a Band-Aid-loving toddler disputes this, it's okay to put on a new one. It may prevent the child from picking or scratching the scab and reduce the likelihood of accidental trauma to the boo-boo during play.

▲ Change bandages more often if they become dirty or wet.

---

## TENDER LOVING CARE

. . . . . . . . . .

TLC (tender loving care) is often the best treatment for minor injuries. A kiss and a cuddle can reduce pain. But tailor your comfort to the gravity of the hurt. A smile, a kiss, and a little reassurance ("You're all right") are all a little bump on the knee may need. But a painful pinched finger will probably warrant a heavy dose of kisses and probably some distraction. In most cases, you will need to calm a child before administering first aid. Only in life-threatening situations (which are fortunately rare, and during which children are not usually obstreperous) will taking some time to quiet the child interfere with the outcome of treatment.

---

**52. Large cuts.** With a sterile gauze pad, a fresh diaper, a sanitary napkin, a clean washcloth—or your bare (preferably washed) hand if necessary—apply pressure to try to stop the bleeding; at the same time, elevate the injured part above the level of the heart, if possible. If bleeding persists after 15 minutes of pressure, add more gauze pads or cloth and increase the pressure. (Don't worry about doing damage with too much pressure and don't remove the original gauze pad—you could disturb any clotting that has already begun.) If the wound gapes open, appears deep, is jagged, if blood is spurting or flowing profusely, or if bleeding doesn't stop within half an hour, call the doctor for instructions or take the child to the emergency room. If necessary, keep the pressure on until help arrives or you get the child to the doctor or ER. If there are other injuries, try to tie or bandage the pressure pack in place so that your hands can be free to attend to them. Apply a sterile nonstick bandage to the wound when the bleeding stops, loose enough so that it doesn't interfere with circulation. Do not put anything on the wound, not even an antiseptic, without medical advice. If stitches are needed, ask if self-dissolving sutures can be used to spare your child the added ordeal of having them removed. If the cut is on the face, consider having a plastic surgeon look at it.

**53. Massive bleeding.** If a limb is severed (#47) and/or blood is gushing or pumping out of a wound, get *immediate* emergency medical assistance by *calling 911* or rushing to the nearest ER. In the meantime, apply pressure to the wound with sterile gauze pads, a fresh diaper or sanitary napkin, or a clean washcloth or towel. Increase the packing and pressure if bleeding doesn't stop. Do not resort to a tourniquet without medical advice as it can sometimes do more harm than good. Maintain pressure until help arrives.

**54. Puncture wounds.** Soak a small puncture wound (one caused by a thumbtack, needle, pen, pencil, or nail) in comfortably hot, soapy water for 15 minutes. Then consult the doctor for what to do next. For deeper, larger punctures—from a knife or a stick, for example—take your child to the doctor or ER immediately. (If there is extensive bleeding, see #53.) If the object still protrudes from the wound, do not remove it; this could lead to increased bleeding or other damage. Pad or otherwise stabilize the object, if necessary, to keep it from moving around. Keep your child as calm and still as possible to avoid movement that might make the injury worse.

**55. Splinters or slivers.** Wash the area with clean water and soap, then numb it with an ice pack or ice cube (see page

837) or a commercial teething-pain ointment. If the sliver is completely embedded, try to work it loose with a sewing
needle that has been sterilized with alcohol or in the flame of a match or a gas
burner. If one end of the sliver is clearly
visible, try to remove it with tweezers
(also sterilized by alcohol or flame).
Don't try to remove it with your fingernails, which might be dirty. Wash the
site again after you have removed the
splinter. If the splinter is not easily removed, try soaking in warm, soapy
water (or Epsom salts dissolved in warm
water) for 15 to 30 minutes, three times
a day for a couple of days, which may
help it work its way out or make it easier
to remove. Consult the doctor if the
splinter remains embedded or if the area
becomes infected (indicated by redness,
heat, swelling). Also call the doctor if
the splinter is deeply embedded or very
large and your toddler's tetanus shots are
not up to date, or if the splinter is metal
or glass.

# SNAKE BITES

see #6

# SPRAINS

**56.** A sprain is an injury to the ligaments, which are the tough, fibrous tissues that connect bones to other bones.
Because, during childhood, the ligaments
are strong in comparison to bones and
cartilage, injury to them is less likely
than it is in adulthood, when bones become stronger. Still, a child may occasionally sprain an ankle or, less often, a
wrist or knee. The symptoms (pain,
swelling, inability to use the affected
joint or, if it's an ankle or knee that's injured, to walk on it) are similar to those
for a broken bone, so a sprain often requires medical expertise, and sometimes

an x-ray, to differentiate it from a fracture. Call the doctor if your child develops such symptoms. If there is a
possibility of a fracture, see #8. To treat
a sprain initially, use the traditional
*RICE* treatment: *Rest.* Rest the injured
limb. If the sprain involves a leg, keep
the child off it as much as possible for
the first couple of days, or until the child
seems able to walk without pain. *Ice.*
Apply an ice pack to the injured joint.
*Compression.* Wrap it snugly (but not
so tightly that you restrict circulation)
in an elastic bandage. *Elevation.* Elevate
the injured limb as much as possible.
Your toddler may enjoy resting the limb
on a plump pillow or a large stuffed
animal friend.

Depending on the severity of the injury, the doctor may recommend continuing to use the elastic bandage until the
sprain heals or may immobilize the joint
with a splint (or even a cast). Check
back with the doctor if a sprain hasn't
healed after 2 weeks or if it has gotten
worse. Ignoring a serious sprain can occasionally lead to permanent damage.

# SUNBURN

see #15

# SWALLOWED FOREIGN BODIES

**57. Coins, marbles, and similar small
objects.** When a child has swallowed
such an object and doesn't seem to be in
any distress, it's best to wait for the object to travel through the digestive tract.
You can, however, give your child carbonated water or soda, which may help
dislodge an object that's stuck in the
esophagus. Most children will pass a
small swallowed object within 2 or 3
days (see page 216). Check the stool for
the object until it's passed. If, after in-

gesting such an object, however, a child has difficulty swallowing or complains about chest pain, or if chest or throat pain, wheezing, drooling, gagging, vomiting, or difficulty in swallowing develop later, the object may have lodged in the esophagus. Call the doctor or take the child to the emergency room immediately. In such a case, it is often possible to remove the object with a special instrument or via balloon extraction; if not, surgery may be necessary.

If there is coughing or there seems to be difficulty breathing, the object may have been inhaled rather than swallowed; treat as a choking incident (see page 689). The swallowing of a button battery requires special attention (see #58).

**58. Button batteries.**[6] If your child swallows a button battery of any kind, call the doctor. An x-ray to assure the battery is not lodged in the esophagus may be recommended or a wait-and-see approach suggested. Most children pass a swallowed battery through their digestive systems without problems (61%

pass it within 2 days, 86% within 4 days). If there are any related symptoms, they are usually digestive, though occasionally a rash may develop. Concern arises when the battery lodges in the esophagus (see #57).

**59. Sharp objects.** Get prompt medical attention if a swallowed object is sharp (a pin or needle, a fish bone, a toy with sharp edges). It may have to be removed (see #57).

# TEETH, INJURY TO

see #38, #39

# TOE INJURIES

see #27, #28, #29, #30

# TONGUE, INJURY TO

see #37

# BASIC LIFE SUPPORT FOR TODDLERS

The instructions that follow[7] should serve only to reinforce what you learn in a course on Basic Life Support (BLS) for young children. For your child's sake, you must take such a course. Participating in a formal course is necessary in order to be able to carry

out these life support procedures correctly. Periodically review the guidelines below, and/or the materials you receive from course instructors.

Resuscitation efforts should be begun only on a child who has stopped breathing or on one who is struggling to breathe and turning blue (check around the lips and the fingertips). If your child is struggling to breathe but hasn't turned blue, *call 911 immediately* or rush to the nearest emergency room. Meanwhile, keep your child warm, as quiet as possible, and in the position that seems most comfortable and easiest to breathe in.

---

6. Among button batteries, the most dangerous are larger batteries and those with lithium cells; less hazardous are the very smallest batteries, zinc/air batteries, and batteries containing silver oxide cells.

7. The training you receive may vary somewhat from the protocol described here, and should be the basis for your actions.

To determine if resuscitation is necessary, survey your toddler's condition with the 1-2-3 and A-B-C of life support:

# 1-2-3 AND A-B-C

## 1. Check for Unresponsiveness

Try to rouse a toddler who appears to be unconscious by calling loudly by name several times: "Jason, Jason, are you okay?" If this doesn't elicit a response, try tapping the soles of the child's feet. As a last resort, gently shake or tap the shoulder; don't shake, however, if there is any possibility of head or neck injury.

## 2. Seek Help

If you get no response, have anyone else present *call 911* for emergency medical assistance while you continue to Step 3. If you are alone with the child and feel sure of your CPR skills, proceed to Step 3 without delay. If you can, periodically call out to try to attract help from neighbors or passersby. If, however, you are unfamiliar with CPR or feel overwhelmed by panic, go to the nearest phone immediately—with your child, if there are no signs of head, neck, or back injury. Better still, if a portable phone is available, bring it to your child's side and *call 911*. The dispatcher will be able to guide you as to the best course of action.

> *Important:* The person calling for emergency medical assistance should stay on the phone as long as necessary to give complete information to the dispatcher. This should include: name, age, and approximate weight of child; any allergies, chronic illnesses, or medications taken; present location (address, cross streets, apartment number, best route if there is more than one);[8] condition (is the child conscious? breathing? bleeding? in shock? is there a pulse?); cause of condition

(fall, poison, drowning, etc.), if known; phone number, if there is a phone at the site. Tell the person calling for help *not* to hang up until the EMS dispatcher has concluded questioning and to report back to you after completing the call.

## 3. Position the Child

Move the child, if necessary, to a firm, flat surface (a table will be easier to work on, but the floor will do). Quickly position the child face-up, head level with heart, and proceed with the A-B-C survey below.

If there is the possibility of a head, neck, or back injury—as there might be following a fall or auto accident—go to Step B to look, listen, and feel for breathing before moving the child. If breathing is present, leave the child where he or she is unless there is immediate danger (from traffic, fire, an imminent explosion) at the present site. If breathing is absent and rescue breathing cannot be accomplished in the child's present position, roll the child as a unit to a face-up position, so that head, neck, and body are moved as one, without twisting, rolling, or tilting the head.

## A. Clear the Airway

Use the head-tilt/chin-lift technique described below to try to open the airway, unless there is a possibility of a head, neck, or back injury—in which case, use the jaw-thrust technique (below) instead.

> *Important:* The airway of an unconscious child may be blocked by a relaxed tongue or epiglottis or by a foreign object. It must be cleared before the child can resume breathing.

---

8. Ideally, this information should be kept ready at your home phone; duplicate lists of information should also be carried in your tote (and that of any caregiver).

*Figure 1: Head tilt/chin lift.*

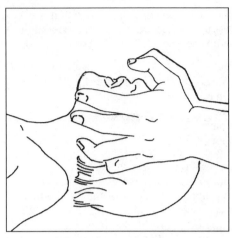

*Figure 2: Jaw thrust.*

**Head tilt/chin lift.** Place the hand nearest the child's head on the forehead and one or two fingers (not the thumb) of your other hand under the bony lower part of the jaw at the chin. Gently tilt the head back slightly by applying pressure on the forehead and lifting the chin to a neutral (facing straight up) or slightly extended (chin pointing up a bit) position. Do not press on the soft tissues of the underchin or let the mouth close completely (keep your thumb in it if necessary to keep the lips apart). See Figure 1.

**Jaw thrust** (for use when neck or back injury is suspected). Approaching from the head, with your elbows resting on the surface where the child is lying, place two or three fingers under each side of the lower jaw, at the angle where the upper and lower jaw meet, and gently lift the jaw upward to a neutral position (facing straight up). See Figure 2.

If, after continuing with Step B (below), it is clear that the jaw thrust did not open the airway, it may be accompanied by a slight head tilt if there is no clear evidence of spinal injury (such as paralysis, stiff neck, muscle weakness). If there is a second adult present, that person should immobilize the cervical

spine (the back of the neck), by surrounding it with rolled up towels, blankets, or clothing.

> ***Important:*** Even if the child resumes breathing immediately, get medical help. Any child who has stopped breathing (even briefly), has been unconscious, or has nearly drowned requires prompt medical evaluation.

## B. Check for Breathing

**B-1.** After performing either the head tilt or the jaw thrust, *look, listen,* and *feel* for 3 to 5 seconds to see if the child is breathing. Can you see the chest and abdomen rising and falling? (This alone isn't proof of breathing; it could mean the child is trying to breathe but isn't succeeding.) Does a mirror placed in front of the child's face cloud up? Can you hear or feel the passage of air when you place your ear near the child's nose and mouth?

If normal breathing has resumed, maintain an open airway with head tilt or jaw thrust.

> ***Activate emergency medical system.*** If breathing has resumed,

and no one has as yet called for help, *call 911* now.

If the child regains consciousness as well (and has no injuries that make moving inadvisable), turn him or her on one side. A spate of coughing when the child starts to breathe independently may be an attempt to expel an obstruction. *Do not attempt to interfere with the coughing.*

If breathing hasn't resumed *or* if the child is struggling to breathe and has bluish lips and/or a weak, muffled cry, you must try to get air into the lungs immediately. Continue with Step B-2 below.

> *Important:* If emergency medical assistance has not yet been summoned and you are alone, continue trying to attract neighbors or passersby as you work.

**B-2.** Maintain an open airway by keeping the child's head in a neutral-plus position (chin pointed slightly upward) with your hand on the forehead. With a finger of the other hand, clear the child's mouth of any *visible* obstructions (vomitus, dirt, or other foreign matter) with a sweep of the finger. Do not attempt a sweep if nothing is visible. Liquids or semi-liquids may be more easily removed if the finger is covered by a piece of cloth.

> *Important:* If vomiting should occur at any point, turn the child on one side and clear the mouth of vomitus with a finger sweep. Reposition child and resume rescue procedure. If there is a possibility of neck or back injury, be very careful to turn the child as a unit, carefully supporting head, neck, and back, as you do; do not allow head to roll, twist, or tilt.

**B-3.** Take a breath through your mouth, then place your mouth over the child's,

*Figure 3: Rescue breathing.*

forming a tight seal. Pinch the child's nostrils closed with the thumb and forefinger of the hand that is maintaining the head tilt. See Figure 3.

**B-4.** Blow two *slow* breaths (1 to 1½ seconds each) into the child's mouth, pausing between them to turn your head slightly and take another breath (the breath is important to maintain an adequate level of oxygen in the air you are delivering). Observe with each breath whether the child's chest rose. If it did, allow it to fall again before beginning another breath. After two successfully delivered breaths, move on to Step C.

**B-5.** If the chest doesn't rise and fall with each breath, your breaths may have been too weak or the child's airway may be blocked. Readjust the child's head to try to open the airway by tilting the chin upward a bit more (Step B-1) and give two more breaths. Blow a bit harder if the chest does not rise with each breath. Continue trying to open the airway by repeating the head-tilt/chin-lift procedure (each time lifting the chin a bit higher) followed by two test breaths, until the chest rises or until the chin is pointing straight up. If the chest still does not rise with each breath, it is possible the air-

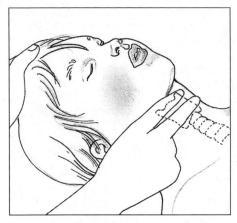

*Figure 4: To locate the carotid pulse, place your index and middle fingers on the Adam's apple while maintaining a head tilt with the other hand.*

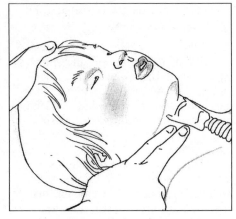

*Figure 5: Slide your fingers down into the groove next to the trachea and locate the pulse.*

way is obstructed by food or by a foreign object—in which case, move quickly to dislodge it, using the procedure described in "Basic Life Support for a Choking Toddler" on page 689. If the chest does rise, indicating the airway is open, move on to Step C.

### C. Check Circulation

**C-1.** As soon as you've determined that the airway is clear, as evidenced by the successful delivery of two breaths, check for a pulse at the carotid artery using your index and middle fingers. (The carotid pulse is located on the side of the neck between the trachea and the neck muscles; see Figures 4 and 5.)

**C-2.** If you can't locate a pulse within 5 seconds, proceed with CPR (see page 687) immediately. If you find a pulse, the child's heart is beating and CPR is not necessary. Return to rescue breathing immediately (next column) if breathing has not resumed spontaneously.

### Activate Emergency Medical System, if Possible

If the EMS has not yet been called and someone is available to make the call,

have them call 911 now. If a call was made before the child's condition was assessed, have the caller contact the dispatcher again with an update on the child's condition. If the child requires rescue breathing or CPR, do not take time to call yourself at this point. Proceed without delay, and if you are alone, periodically call loudly to attract help from neighbors or passersby.

## RESCUE BREATHING FOR TODDLERS

**1.** Breathe into the toddler's mouth as described in B-4, page 685, at a rate of roughly one breath every 3 seconds (or 20 breaths per minute). Watch to be sure the child's chest rises and falls with each breath.

**2.** Check for a carotid pulse after 1 minute of rescue breathing, to see if the heart is beating. If there is no pulse, go to CPR (page 687). If you find a pulse, look, listen, and feel for spontaneous breathing (see B-1) for 3 to 5 seconds. If the child has begun to breathe independently, continue to maintain an open airway and check breathing and pulse frequently while waiting for help to arrive; keep the child warm and as quiet as possible. If there is still no spontaneous breathing, continue rescue breathing, checking for pulse and spontaneous breathing once every minute.

> *Important:* If at any time during rescue breathing the child's abdomen becomes distended, don't push it down—this might cause vomiting, which would introduce the added risk of vomit being aspirated (inhaled) into the lungs. If the abdominal distention seems to be interfering with chest expansion and if there is no possibility of head, neck, or back injury, turn the child on one side, head down if possible, and apply gentle pressure to the abdomen for a second or two.

### Activate Emergency Medical System Now.

If you're alone and emergency medical help has not yet been summoned, *call 911* as soon as independent breathing has been established. If independent breathing hasn't begun within a few minutes, summon help quickly. If one is available, bring a portable phone to the child's side. If not, and the child is small enough and there is no evidence of head or neck injury (see page 663, #10), carry the child to the phone, supporting head, neck, and torso. Continue rescue breathing as you go. Quickly and clearly report to the EMS dispatcher, "My child isn't breathing," and give all pertinent information the dispatcher requests (see page 659). Don't hang up until the dispatcher does. If possible, continue rescue breathing while the dispatcher is speaking; if it's not possible, return to it immediately on hanging up. If you can't move the child, dash to the phone alone and explain the situation, then hurry back to resume rescue breathing.

> *Important:* Do not discontinue rescue breathing until the child is breathing independently or until medical professionals arrive to take over.

# CARDIOPULMONARY RESUSCITATION (CPR): CHILDREN OVER ONE YEAR

**1. Position the child.** Continue with the child face-up on a firm, flat surface. There should be no pillow under the child's head; the head should be level with the heart and in a neutral-plus position (Figure 1, page 684).

**2. Position your hands.** Use the hand nearest the child's head to maintain the neutral-plus position and keep the airway open. With the middle and index fingers of the hand nearest the child's feet, locate the lower edge of the rib cage on the side nearest you; follow the lower edge of the rib cage to the center, to the notch where the ribs meet the sternum (the flat breastbone running down the middle of the chest between the ribs). Place the middle finger of this same hand on this notch; then place the index finger down next to it, making a mental note of the location of the upper edge of the index finger.[9] Then remove the fingers and place the heel of the same hand just above where the index finger was located, with the long axis of the heel parallel to the child's sternum and lined up above where the two fingers were located (Figure 6, page 688).

> *Important:* Do not apply pressure to the tip of the sternum

---

9. If you, or another person present, can very quickly mark the location with a pen or marker this will make it easier to reposition your hand between compressions.

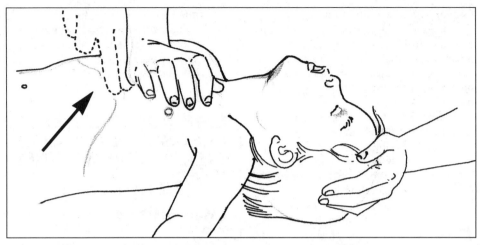

*Figure 6: Locating hand for chest compressions.*

(xiphoid process). To do so could cause severe internal damage.

**3. Begin compressions.** With the heel of your hand, compress the chest to a depth of approximately 1 to 1½ inches. The only contact should be between the heel of your hand and the the flat lower half of the sternum—do not press on the child's ribs during compressions. Allow the chest to return to its resting position after each compression without lifting your hand from the chest. Try to develop a compression–relaxation rhythm that allots equal time to each phase and avoids jerky movements.

**4. Pause and breathe.** At the end of every fifth compression, pause and deliver a slow breath (1 to 1½ seconds). Chest compressions must *always* be accompanied by rescue breathing to ensure a steady supply of oxygen to the brain (a child without a heartbeat is not breathing and is therefore not getting oxygen). Aim for a rate of 80 to 100 compressions a minute, with one breath after every five compressions. Count at a more rapid rate than you would if counting seconds: one and, two and, three and, four and, five and—breathe.

**5. Pause and check.** After about a minute, take 5 seconds to check for a carotid pulse. If there is no pulse, give one slow breath, then continue the compression–ventilation cycles of CPR, checking periodically for a pulse. If a pulse is found, discontinue chest compressions. If the child has not resumed independent breathing, however, continue with rescue breathing alone.

### *Activate Emergency Medical System Now.*

If you are alone, have been unable to attract help by calling out, and have not yet summoned emergency medical assistance, take a moment after a few minutes of CPR to go to a phone and call 911. If one is available, bring a portable phone to the child's side. If not, and the child is small enough and there is no evidence of head or neck injury (see page 663, #10), carry him or her to the phone, supporting head, neck, and torso. Continue rescue breathing as you go. Quickly and clearly report to the EMS dispatcher, "My child isn't breathing and has no pulse," and give all pertinent information the dispatcher requests (see page 659). Don't hang up until the dispatcher does. If possible, continue CPR while the dispatcher is speaking; if it's not possible, return to CPR immediately on hanging up. If you can't move the child, dash to the phone alone and explain the situation, then hurry back to resume basic life support procedures as needed.

> *Important:* Do not discontinue CPR until breathing and heartbeat are reestablished or until emergency medical assistance arrives.

# BASIC LIFE SUPPORT FOR A CHOKING TODDLER

**C**oughing is nature's way of trying to clear the airways (of mucus, dust, smoke) or dislodge an obstruction. A child (or anyone else) who is choking on food or on a foreign object and who can breathe, cry, and cough forcefully should not be interfered with. But if the child continues to cough for more than 2 or 3 minutes, call 911 for emergency medical assistance. If the cough becomes ineffective (it's silent) or the child is struggling for breath, making high-pitched crowing sounds, unable to speak or cry, and/or is starting to turn blue (usually starting around the lips and fingernails), begin the following rescue procedure.

Start these rescue efforts immediately if the child is unconscious and not breathing and if attempts to open the airways (see Steps A and B, beginning on page 683) have been unsuccessful.

> *Important:* An airway obstruction may also occur with such infections as croup or epiglottitis. A child who is struggling to breathe and seems ill—has fever and, possibly, congestion, hoarseness, drooling, lethargy, or limpness—needs immediate medical

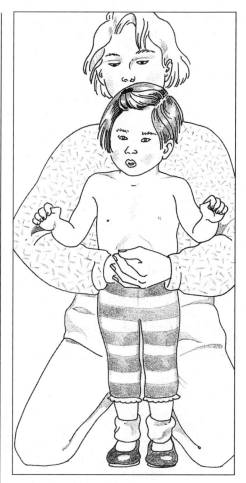

*Figure 7: The Heimlich maneuver on a child is best done from a kneeling position.*

attention at an emergency care facility. Do not waste time in a dangerous and futile attempt to relieve the problem yourself: *Call 911.*

**1. Get help.** If someone else is present, have them *call 911* for emergency medical assistance. If you're alone and unfamiliar with rescue procedures—or if you panic and forget them—take the child with you to the phone (or bring a portable to the child's side) and *call 911* for emergency medical assistance *imme-*

*diately.* It's usually recommended that even if you're familiar with rescue procedures, you take the time to call. That way help can be on the way in case the situation worsens.

*If the child is conscious,* proceed this way:

**2. Position yourself.** Kneel behind the child and wrap your arms around his or her waist (Figure 7, page 689).

**3. Position your hands.** Make a fist with one hand and place the thumb-side in the center of the body slightly above the navel and well below the rib cage. To avoid severe internal damage, do not apply pressure to the tip of the sternum (xiphoid process; see Figure 6, page 688) or to the lower margins of the rib cage.

**4. Administer abdominal thrusts.** Grasp the positioned fist with your other hand and press it into the child's abdomen with a quick inward-and-upward thrust (use less force than you would on an adult or older child). Each thrust should be a separate, distinct movement. Repeat up to five times, or until you see the object ejected or the child begins breathing normally.

> ***Important:*** If the child loses consciousness, attempt to open the airway (Step A, page 683) and, if necessary, attempt rescue breathing. If the airway remains obstructed, perform the Heimlich maneuver for an unconscious child, below.

*If the child is unconscious,* proceed this way:

**1. Position the child and yourself.** Place the child face-up on a firm, flat surface (a floor or a table). Stand or kneel at the child's feet (don't sit astride a small child).

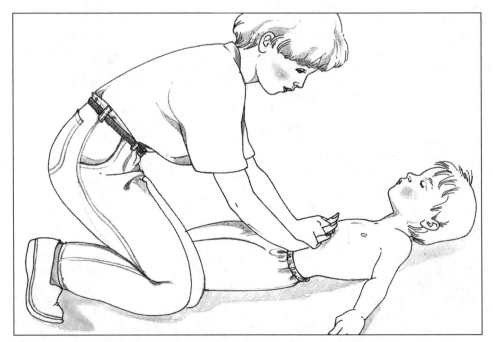

*Figure 8: When administering abdominal thrusts, care must be taken to avoid pressing on the ribs or the tip of the sternum (the xiphoid process).*

**2. Position your hands.** Place the heel of one hand on the abdomen slightly above the navel and well below the rib cage, fingers facing toward the child's face. Place the second hand on top of the first. If you interlace your fingers, as shown in Figure 8, you will have more control. Do not apply pressure over the tip of the sternum (the xiphoid process; see Figure 6) or over the lower margins of the rib cage.

**3. Administer abdominal thrusts.** With the upper hand pressing against the lower, administer a series of up to five inward and upward abdominal thrusts. Thrusts should be delivered to the midline, not to either side, and each should be a separate and distinct movement. These thrusts should be gentler than they would be for an adult or older child.

### After five abdominal thrusts:

If, after *any* thrust, a foreign body is visible in the mouth, use a finger sweep motion to remove it. If you can't see anything, open the child's mouth by grasping both the tongue and the lower jaw between thumb and index finger and lifting (tongue-jaw lift). This action draws the tongue away from the back of the throat and may itself partially clear the obstruction. If the foreign body is seen, remove it with a sweep.

If breathing hasn't resumed, open the airway (Step A, page 683) and attempt rescue breathing. If the airway remains obstructed (the chest does not rise), reposition the head and attempt rescue breathing again. If the airway remains obstructed, repeat the Heimlich maneuver.

Continue repeating this sequence until the airway is clear and the child is conscious and breathing normally or until emergency medical assistance arrives. Don't give up—the longer the child is without oxygen, the more the muscles of the throat will relax, and the more likely the obstruction can be dislodged.

> *Important:* Even if your child recovers quickly from a choking incident, medical attention will be required. Call the doctor or the emergency room immediately.

# CHAPTER TWENTY-THREE

# Your Special-Needs Child

E very child needs special attention. But nearly 10 million children in the United States—and their number is increasing as more very-low-birth-weight babies survive—need somewhat more attention than the rest. Whether the special needs are a result of an allergy, a mild chronic illness, a minor birth defect, or a condition that severely impairs function, providing the extra special attention these children need can make a remarkable difference in the quality of their lives—not just in the toddler years, but in all the years to follow.

If your child's special needs are minor, you may find much of this chapter irrelevant; if they are major, the information that follows can form a foundation for dealing with them now and in the future.

## HELPING YOUR SPECIAL-NEEDS CHILD
..............................................

T hough the well-being of special-needs children depends a great deal on the quality of professional care they receive, it depends even more on parental participation. In most situations no one can help a child more than a parent can, but to be able to help most effectively you will need to:

**Be sure you know what the condition is.** Early diagnosis and early intervention are extremely important. If you have any doubt about the accuracy of a diagnosis or if your child's doctor is unable to come up with a diagnosis at all, don't hesitate to get a second opinion. (To avoid putting your child through duplicate testing, obtain the records from the first round of tests for the second doctor's review.)

In many cases, learning the cause of a condition is also important. Knowing can often help to ease guilt and increase understanding and acceptance. In some cases, it may also help you to prevent a repeat in other children.

**Be sure to listen.** Pay careful attention to what the doctors, therapists, and others involved with your child's care have to say. If hearing the diagnosis initially left you in such a state of shock that you didn't hear anything else that was said, be sure to follow up with a visit or phone call as soon as possible to ask the questions and receive the answers you need to understand your child's condition. You can also ask the medical professionals who are treating your child for a written report or evaluation.

**Be sure you're being heard.** Are the professionals paying attention; do they take your concerns and your input seriously? They should—after all, you know your child better than anyone else and your role is vital in caring for your child. Make sure the lines of communication between you and each care provider stay open *all* of the time, not just during crisis periods.

**Become an expert.** Eventually, most parents of children with special needs become so well educated about their child's condition that anyone eavesdropping on a discussion between them and their child's doctors would find it difficult to pick out the professionals. The sooner you begin your education, the better for your toddler (when you know what you're talking about, you can ask educated questions and make sound judgments about doctors, therapies, and interventions, helping to ensure the best treatment pronto) and for you (you will feel more in control of the situation and have less fear of the unknown). Learn all you can about your child's condition and its care and treatment by keeping track of articles in medical journals, reading books, joining a relevant organization

(see page 694), and/or going on-line with medical computer resources.

Keep up with the latest treatments and technology. Every day new medical procedures, new prosthetics, and new types of support equipment are developed that can turn a child's life around, or at least improve the quality of that life. "Miracle" technologies include everything from surgery that can bring hearing to a deaf ear or correct a disfiguring and/or disabling birth defect to a computer that can help paralyzed children play games, do homework, even "speak" by moving their eyes. Consult with your child's specialist or contact The Foundation for Technology Access (1307 Solano Avenue, Albany, CA 94706) for the latest information specific to your child's condition.

**Be sure you get the best help.** For many chronic childhood conditions, the expertise of a specialist may be needed to make a diagnosis and to recommend treatment. In some cases, the treatment can be supervised by your child's doctor, with or without consultation with a specialist; in others, it's best supervised by a specialist or subspecialist. A specialist affiliated with a children's hospital or a major medical center is most likely to have the resources available to offer the most up-to-date care. Often, a chronic condition is best managed by the combined efforts of a team of medical specialists, other professionals, and parents.

Ideally, anyone treating or working with your child should have a subspecialty

---

## *FREE TESTING*

**U**nder the federal Handicapped Infants and Toddlers Program, through the Individuals with Disabilities Education Act (IDEA), free screening is available for de-velopmental, hearing, and vision problems. Check with your state or local health department for information. Also see the box on page 698.

## WHO CAN HELP?

..........

You're not alone and there are numerous organizations out there ready to help. Information for parents of children with special needs is available from all of the following:

U.S. Department of Education and Office of Special Services Clearinghouse on Disability Information: (202) 205-8241 (for information on disability programs and legislation).

Social Security Administration: (800) 772-1213 (for information on SSI benefits for Children with Disabilities).

National Information Center for Children and Youth with Disabilities: (800) 999-5599 (for information, referrals, respite care).

Administration on Children, Youth and Families, Department of Health and Human Services: (202) 205-8348 (for information on respite care in your area).

March of Dimes Birth Defects Foundation: (914) 428-7100 (for educational materials and referrals).

Resources for Children with Special Needs, Inc. (212) 677-4650 (for information, referrals, advocacy, training, and support services for both parents and professionals).

National Parent Resource Center, Federation for Children with Special Needs: For litera-

ture and referrals, (617) 482-2915.

National Father's Network: (206) 747-4004 or (206) 282-1334 (for information and support for fathers of children with special needs).

National Health Information Center: (800) 336-4797; in Maryland, (301) 565-4167 (for phone numbers of more than 1,000 health-related organizations). For a printed list, send $1 to P.O. Box 1133, Washington, DC 20013-1133.

Information on individual disorders is available from the following national organizations by calling the hotline or writing. In some cases, there is lively educational material for children (activity books, storybooks, comic books); some are suitable for toddlers.

**AIDS.** National AIDS hotline: (800) 342-2437.

**Allergy.** The American Academy of Allergy and Immunology: Tips Order, 611 E. Wells Street, Milwaukee, WI 53202; Food Allergy Network, 4744 Holly Avenue, Fairfax, VA 22030-5647.

**Asthma and Allergy.** Asthma & Allergy Foundation of America: 1125 15th Street NW, Suite 502, Washington DC 20005, (800) 7-ASTHMA; The National Allergy and Asthma Network: 3554 Chain Bridge

---

in pediatrics as well as experience with children who have special needs. In some communities, a case manager (usually a physician, nurse, or social worker) may be available to help you organize your child's care by drafting an Individualized Family Service Plan (IFSP).

**Be persistent.** If you feel strongly that something is amiss with your child and a diagnosis isn't forthcoming, keep trying until you find an answer. (Diagnosis is

sometimes difficult, especially for conditions that are relatively rare, such as carnitine deficiency,[1] but can in many cases make a life-or-death difference.) Like-

---

1. Carnitine is a substance produced by the body that is necessary for cell energy metabolism. Symptoms of deficiency include: feeding problems and failure to grow and thrive; lethargy on waking, perking up on eating; fatigue; late walking; frequent infections; chronic vomiting; seizures; poor muscle tone and coordination and progressive muscle weakness.

Road, Suite 200, Fairfax, VA 22030-2709, (703) 385-4403; National Jewish Center for Immunology and Respiratory Medicine: (800) 222-LUNG (for asthma and other lung diseases); Asthma Information Center, P.O. Box 790, Springhouse, PA 19477-0790.

**Arthritis.** See Juvenile Rheumatoid Arthritis.

**Autism.** Autism Society of America: (301) 565-0433.

**Cancer.** Cancer Information Service of the National Cancer Institute: (800) 4-CANCER (for information on all aspects of cancer).

**Celiac Disease.** The Celiac Sprue Association: (402) 558-0600.

**Cerebral Palsy.** National Cerebral Palsy Association: (800) 872-5827.

**Cystic Fibrosis.** Cystic Fibrosis Foundation: (800) FIGHT CF.

**Diabetes.** Juvenile Diabetes Foundation (JDF): (800) 223-1138.

**Down Syndrome.** National Down Syndrome Society: (800) 221-4602.

**Epilepsy.** Epilepsy Foundation of America: (800) EFA-1000.

**Fragile X Syndrome.** The National Fragile X Foundation: 1441 York Street, Suite 215, Denver, CO 80206, (800) 688-8765.

**Genetic Disorders.** Alliance of Genetic Support Groups: (800) 336-4363.

**Hearing Impairment.** The Deafness Research Foundation: (800) 535-DEAF.

**Juvenile Rheumatoid Arthritis.** Arthritis Foundation: (800) 283-7800; National Jewish Center for Immunology and Respiratory Medicine: (800) 222-5864.

**Language Disorders.** The American Speech-Language-Hearing Association: 10801 Rockville Pike, Rockville, MD 20852; Helpline (800) 638-8255 (voice or TDD).

**Mental Retardation.** Mental Retardation Association of America: (801) 328-1575; American Association on Mental Retardation, 444 North Capitol Street NW, Suite 846, Washington, DC 20001-1570, (800) 424-3688; Voice of the Retarded (a national parents group): 5005 Newport Drive, Suite 108, Rolling Meadows, IL 60008, (708) 253-6020.

**Muscular Dystrophy.** Muscular Dystrophy Association: (602) 529-2000.

**Phenylketonuria.** PKU Parents: (415) 457-4632.

**Sickle Cell Disease.** The National Association for Sickle Cell Diseases: (800) 421-8453.

**Spina Bifida.** Spina Bifida Association of America: (800) 621-3141.

**Thalassemias.** Thalassemia Action Group and Cooley's Anemia Foundation: both (800) 522-7222.

**Visual Impairment.** American Council of the Blind: (800) 424-8666.

---

wise, be persistent in asking questions and seeking answers if you feel the treatment your child is receiving isn't working or isn't the most up-to-date, if your child's doctor (or doctors) aren't keeping you informed, or if you simply have the nagging feeling that more could be done.

**Be a meticulous record-keeper.** Keep a record of all of your child's medical reports, tests, appointments, treatments, medications, doctors, therapists, and so

on—either in a loose-leaf notebook, a file folder, or on the computer (if you use the computer, you will still need a folder for x-rays, test reports, and the like). Put questions in writing, too, so that you'll have them ready when you meet with doctors or other professionals. Emergency numbers (inside back cover) and other pertinent information about your child's condition should be posted at every home phone, carried by anyone who cares for your child, and available to administrators, teachers, and other caregivers at day care, preschool, and intervention centers.

**Be a pair.** When two parents are available, both should be involved in medical consultations, in learning to deal with day-to-day issues, and in day-to-day care. If one parent consistently gets information regarding their child's condition secondhand, he or she may have trouble making sense of it—or accepting it. If one parent consistently has to shoulder the many demands of caring for a special-needs child alone, the stress may be debilitating, and may breed resentment. If you're a single parent, try to enlist a grandparent, another relative, or a friend to share the burden, if possible.

**Be assertive.** If you have questions, ask them. If you don't understand the answers, ask for clarification. Request diagrams, written material, and a list of sources that can help you to learn more. If your child isn't responding to therapy as expected, speak up. If you think something else might work better, say so. If the prescribed amount of medication seems to be too little or too much, report your concerns. If a health care professional does something that you find irritating or worrisome, let him or her know—but avoid slinging angry words. ("I was very upset by what just happened . . ." is better than a torrent of irrational fury.) And when the doctors aren't giving consideration to what you have to say, and the social worker can't improve the situation, try to find another medical team with comparable expertise.

**Be cautious.** Parents of children with special needs of any kind are always hoping and searching for ways of improving the condition and the quality of their child's life. But while it pays to persist in pursuing this goal, it also pays to be wary. For every legitimate advancement or alternative therapy, there are many more that are unproven, or worse still, potentially dangerous. Consider alternatives when the tried-and-true medical treatments aren't working, but proceed with prudence—and always consult with your child's doctor first.

**Be positive.** Don't waste time or energy blaming yourself for your child's condition, or feeling sorry for yourself or your child. For both your sakes, focus on being as upbeat as you can.

**Be realistic.** As important as it is to keep a positive attitude, it's also important—for your sake as well as your child's—to be accepting of the situation. Though you should investigate every avenue when it comes to treatment and management, you should also accept what can't (at least, as yet) be changed.

**Become financially savvy.** Paying for care and treatment of a child with a chronic illness can drain any family's resources. Learn all you can about what support is available from your health insurer, as well as from local, state, and federal sources (see page 694).

# LIVING WITH AND LOVING YOUR SPECIAL CHILD

**E**ach child is an individual unlike any other. Even children who share the same physical or emotional challenge are never exactly alike. But though no two special-needs children are the same, some basic needs are common to them all—and to their families.

**Love.** Focus any anger or frustration you feel where it belongs. Despise the disability, hate the illness, disapprove of the behavior, if you must, but *love your child*—unconditionally. Show your love for your special-needs child in the same ways you would show love for any child—a hug, a kiss, a squeeze of the hand, an offer of help, a moment shared, patience and understanding.

If you find it difficult to love your special-needs toddler or if you find your anger leading to abuse (children with special needs are abused twice as often as other children), seek professional help immediately. Your child's doctor can help you find it.

**Normalcy.** This is a tough but absolutely crucial order for a family with a special-needs child. Strive for a normal family life in as many ways as possible and make every effort to treat your special-needs child as you would any child. Nurture his or her dignity and self-esteem by always being respectful, both in words and deeds. And though this may be most difficult of all, don't withhold discipline. Set limits according to your child's abilities, but be sure there *are* limits. Being overindulgent, overpermissive, or overprotective toward a child with special needs won't help—and may very well impede—his or her development.

Remember that, like all toddlers, a special-needs child is likely to want to "do it myself." Instead of always jumping in and taking over ("Here, let me do that for you"), give your child the chance to try to handle things independently whenever possible. When doing it "myself" leads to mistakes (it inevitably will), encourage your toddler to learn from the mistakes and strive to do better the next time. And no matter what the final result, always praise the effort.

Most special-needs toddlers are also prone to other typical toddler behavior—including tantrums, negativity, self-centeredness, and separation anxiety. Try to respond to these behaviors just as you would with any toddler (check the index for individual behaviors and tips on coping with them).

And as much as is possible, see to it that your child's condition doesn't prevent him or her (or you) from enjoying the simple pleasures—playing with toys, going out, making friends, meeting new people.

**Consistency.** If your child's condition is one that takes getting used to—and friends, neighbors, playmates have already made that leap—it may be a good idea to avoid moving from your community and having to start all over, at least until you are all more secure.

**Clarification.** In the simplest terms, try to explain the situation to your toddler, making it clear that it isn't his or her fault (a typically egocentric older toddler might jump to that conclusion). Explain that nobody knows why, but some children are born with . . . (or without . . .) or have a . . . that doesn't work just the way it should. Empathize with your child as he or she becomes conscious of the negatives ("I know you don't like . . ."), but whenever possible, emphasize the positives ("but you can . . ."). Explain that all the therapy, medications, and other interventions are important to help your child grow to be the best he or she can be. Be upbeat, supportive, and reassuring, but don't dangle false hope (for example, giving a toddler who will never walk—at least not with the present medical technology— the impression that hard work can make it happen). When you don't know the answer to a question your toddler asks, say so; then try to get the answer.

Explain the situation, too, to siblings, grandparents, other family members, and close friends. The more they understand, the more supportive they can be—though some people, unfortunately, never come around to being comfortable and accepting.

**Appreciation.** Every child, even the most severely challenged, needs to feel appreciated. Let your child know that he or she is. Look beyond the condition for

## IT'S THE LAW

··········

The Individuals with Disabilities Education Act (IDEA) assures that children with severe disabilities will have available social, educational, and health services, delivered through a variety of agencies, preschool facilities, and medical and other health programs. Each family with a young child who has a disability or is at risk for disabilities is assured: a family service plan; case management; early identification, screening, and assessment; family training, counseling, and home visits; and selected health and professional services. These programs are administered by the states, which also set eligibility standards. A free appropriate education is guaranteed for the child from the age of three years. The Americans with Disabilities Act (ADA) also guarantees access to public spaces and transportation for those in wheelchairs or otherwise unable to get around; as a result, many more opportunities are now open to people with disabilities than ever before.

---

qualities and character traits that make your child special—a beautiful smile, a kind heart, a way with animals, an indomitable spirit. This appreciation can improve your outlook as well as your child's, and give your family the strength it will need in trying to overcome the obstacles that lie ahead.

Others in your child's life will also need appreciation. Show your gratitude to supportive family members and to those who work with your child (people in the helping professions very often suffer burnout; appreciation can help slow that process while making the hard work more worthwhile). You, too, will benefit from a little appreciation. Since you're unlikely to get all you need from your child (young children aren't usually quick to acknowledge their parents' efforts), look to your spouse, another relative, a good friend, or a support group to build you up when you're feeling underappreciated.

**Courage.** Especially when your child's condition is life-threatening, or when he or she faces a difficult or painful procedure, courage may be in short supply. Don't keep your fears pent-up—talk them out with a professional, or a relative or friend who has a sympathetic ear—but try hard not to air them in front of your child. A parent's fear can heighten a child's apprehension, while a parent's calm can make a child less fearful.

**Relief.** To be effective in what they do, all parents need a break once in a while. But because the demands on parents of children with special needs can be so overwhelming, your need for relief is even greater. Look to respite care (see "General support," below), day care, or friends or relatives who offer to help. Build some private time into your week—go to a movie, relax in the tub, have a massage, jog, enjoy a candlelit supper. And never feel guilty about taking time off; you'll return refreshed, more relaxed, and better able to help your child.

**Fun.** Simple pleasures sometimes vanish from the lives of families with a physically or mentally challenged or chronically ill child; family members often feel guilty at even the thought of having fun. But taking a lighter approach to life can make your child's special needs seem easier to deal with and help you think more positively (which can be contagious). When the going gets tough, try a little laughter, a little silliness, a little frivolity, to get you going again. You all deserve it.

**Early intervention.** Virtually every condition can benefit from early intervention. Make sure your child gets the best available in professional diagnosis and treatment as early as possible. If a daycare or preschool program for children with your child's special needs is available, sign yours up. These programs help children learn valuable coping and social skills and can often make a major difference in a child's life. But you can help, too. You can greatly enhance the benefits of both medical and educational interventions by getting the training you need to extend the stimulation and education to the time your child spends at home.

**General support.** Some states offer respite care, which may include nonmedical care, baby-sitting, in-home care, family counseling, and classes. Check with your doctor, therapist, or caseworker.

**Parent support groups.** Thousands of such groups are active around the country. (If there is no group in your area for parents of children with needs like your child's, consider starting one.) Caring for a special-needs child can be physically demanding and emotionally draining. Meeting regularly with parents who share your concerns can be very therapeutic, and can allow you to vent your feelings of frustration, anger, and resentment in a healthy way and in an empathetic forum, rather than bottling them up or taking them out on your child, on yourself, or on the rest of the family. The swapping of experiences, insights, and coping strategies can also be invaluable. Check with your child's case coordinator, social worker, or doctor, or call a national organization for information (see page 694).

**Relationship support.** While romance is always elusive when there's a young child in the house, it can be even more so when the young child has special

---

## *RESIDENTIAL CARE*

· · · · · · · · · ·

**M**ost children, even those with severe disabilities, can be taken care of at home—if (and this can be a big if) the parents have the physical, financial, and emotional resources to do so, as well as the necessary time. But there are circumstances—for example, when there are other young children at home and/or when there is only one adult in the household and a full-time job is necessary for survival—in which caring for a special-needs child at home is next to impossible. Admitting you can't handle it is often not easy, and putting your child in residential care is even harder, but sometimes there is little choice if the rest of the family is to survive. Sometimes there are compromises: day care in a specialized facility with the child spending evenings and weekends with the family, or weekly care at a facility that allows the child to spend weekends and holidays at home. But sometimes full-time residential care is the only workable option.

Consult with your medical care team, check out the facilities that are available (try to find one that does more than warehouse children, that you can visit regularly, has a good reputation, and seems well run), and then arrange for a trial stay. If it doesn't work out, bring your child home again until a better solution can be found. Perhaps, as your child gets older, you will find it easier for him or her to spend more time, or even live full-time, at home. If you choose residential care for now, don't view the choice as closing the door to other care choices in the future. And don't feel guilty.

# HOME CARE

**M**any children with chronic conditions, who in the past were routinely hospitalized for acute flare-ups or long-term care, can today be cared for at home—reducing costs and improving both outcome and quality of life. A wide range of medical procedures and supportive-care regimens—including monitoring, respiratory therapy and support, intravenous (IV) therapy and feeding—can be handled at home by parents or caregivers with no previous medical training. But the family needs a strong support network, including the backing of the child's physician, who may work along with a specialist in home care and a nurse (either visiting or full-time), to implement and coordinate the details of home care. These details may include: assuring the adequacy of electrical power, storage capacity, and other necessities for a "hospital corner" in the home; obtaining and learning how to use a sickbed and other medical equipment; dealing with issues of treatment, well-child care (including nutrition enhancement, health promotion, and illness prevention), and education and rehabilitation (more often *habilitation,* for young children who have yet to learn basic life skills). Good parental training and certification (if specialized skills are needed and the parent is to provide most of the care) plus written treatment and emergency plans (to assure that emergency services will be immediately available if needed) are also crucial.

In some home-care cases a family member can function as the case coordinator, working in conjunction with a professional case manager (usually a physician, nurse, or social worker); in others, an in-home caregiver (a nurse or home-care aid) tackles this task. (An off-site case manager, though not as helpful, is also a possibility).

In deciding whether home care is right in a particular situation, parents need to weigh possible risks (for example, disruption of family life, added stress, loss of time at work, the chance of a care foul-up) against potential benefits (more family togetherness and a more normal life, less commuting to and from facilities, a happier child). Determine, too, how you can increase benefits and reduce risks in choosing home care (for example, the outcome may be better with a professional nurse, rather than a home-care aid). Financial considerations will also have to come into play; be sure to discuss your plans for home care with your health insurer before you make a final decision.

---

needs. Yet studies show that having a special-needs child doesn't automatically put a marriage at risk; in fact, it's just as likely to strengthen a marriage as it is to weaken it. Buoy your chances of marital success by supporting each other emotionally, sharing responsibilities (no one parent should have to go it alone), setting aside time to spend as a couple (very difficult, but very important), and keeping the lines of communication open so that you can share your feelings—both positive and negative.

**Sibling support.** Siblings stand to suffer when so much attention is necessarily paid to the special-needs child. See page 704 for tips on helping siblings cope.

**Coping strategies.** With help from professionals, support groups, or others who've been through it before you, learn how to cope with your child's special needs, how to meet your needs and the needs of other family members, how to organize your time, and how to forgive yourself for not being perfect (remember, no one is).

Learning stress reduction techniques (see page 173) can also be valuable for everyone in the family, including your special-needs child. It can help to reduce stress that may be aggravating your child's condition as well as stress that results from it.

**A thick skin.** Don't let unfeeling, thoughtless remarks from friends or strangers get you down; don't let their ignorance or intolerance hurt your child. Be as open and matter-of-fact as you can about your child's illness or condition so that you don't give your child (or others) the impression that you're embarrassed or disturbed by it. Make it clear to relatives and friends that you consider your child a person first—that the illness or disability is not the sum total of his or her being—and encourage them to think the same way.

Also encourage your local public schools to develop a program to educate children about people with disabilities— this will make it easier for your child and other special-needs children as they begin to socialize, especially if they will be "mainstreamed" into the system. When your child does attend a program where he or she will stand out as being different, it may help to introduce your child and the condition with a videotape (shown by you or a caseworker) before your child comes on the scene.

**A plan for the future.** You care for your child as no one else could. But though no one likes to think about it, it's important to prepare for the possibility of something happening to you—and your child being left without that care. Most experts recommend a "special-needs trust" rather than an ordinary will. An inheritance can negate SSI disability and Medicaid payments, but the special-needs trust can provide money for special needs while the support payments continue. See a lawyer who specializes in such trusts for advice. One decision you will have to make yourself is who to choose as trustee. A family member you can trust to do what's best for your child is usually an ideal choice; if a lot of money is involved, it may be helpful to choose a corporate co-trustee, who would make financial decisions, but not those related to your child's welfare. Your lawyer can help you find such a person.

**Acceptance.** Most disabilities and chronic conditions are not "curable," though many can be controlled or even greatly improved. You will need to accept the realities of your child's problem and what he or she will and will not be able to do. If your child's condition was only recently diagnosed, you may have to struggle with anger, grief, and guilt before you reach acceptance. You may also focus too hard at first on your child's weaknesses and too little on his or her strengths, but by working at it, you should be able to turn that around. The more accepting you are of your child, the more self-accepting he or she will grow up to be.

**Encouragement.** Accepting your child's limitations doesn't mean that you shouldn't make every effort to help your child reach his or her maximum potential. Encourage intellectual and physical growth (to the extent this is possible) and the development of skills of all kinds (including social skills).

**Hope.** Nor does accepting your child's condition mean that you should abandon hope. For the vast majority of special-needs children, love, support, and appropriate therapy can improve the prognosis, sometimes dramatically. For many, new research tomorrow, or the day after, or the day after that, may even bring the miracle for which parents pray. Recent research suggests that hope itself may also influence how well a child (or anyone with a disability or a chronic illness) does in life. So do keep hoping, and encourage your child to hope, too.

# SOME CHRONIC HEALTH PROBLEMS

## AIDS (ACQUIRED IMMUNODEFICIENCY SYNDROME) AND HIV INFECTION

**What is it?** AIDS is an illness characterized by the breakdown of the body's natural immunity against disease. A child infected with HIV-1 (see "What causes it?" below) may have no apparent symptoms for months or even years; during this time the infection can be diagnosed by blood testing. Not until characteristic symptoms develop is the child considered to have AIDS. Symptoms vary, but may include: fever and night sweats, shaking chills that last for weeks, fatigue, rapid weight loss or inability to gain weight, swollen lymph glands in the neck and underarm areas and/or, rarely, enlarged parotid (salivary) glands, recurrent or chronic diarrhea, white spots or blemishes in the mouth (from persistent thrush, a yeast infection), developmental lags, recurrent bacterial infections, and liver and/or kidney disorders. Patterns of illness are different in children than in adults and can vary, too, from child to child. In some children, AIDS appears to take the form of a chronic disease. For some of the possible manifestations and complications of AIDS, see "Related problems" (next column).

**How common is it?** Very rare in children, particularly those who fit a low-risk profile.

**Who is susceptible?** Mostly, children born to HIV-positive mothers. Though all of these children test positive for HIV as newborns, only 12% to 40% are actually infected with HIV; the most commonly used tests are not accurate until all of the mother's antibodies have cleared the child's body, usually between fifteen and eighteen months. Newer tests appear to provide an accurate diagnosis at six months. The chance of a child turning out to be infected appears to be lowered significantly when the HIV-positive mother is treated prenatally with the drug AZT. Hemophiliacs and other children who receive blood transfusions have in the past been at high risk for infection; today, thanks to improvements in blood screening, the risk that a child will receive blood that contains HIV-1 is minuscule.

**What causes it?** The human immuno-deficiency virus (HIV-1) is transmitted via body fluids (blood, semen, or vaginal secretions, but *not* saliva, sweat, or tears). Most often transmission takes place during sexual intercourse, both homosexual and heterosexual, or when intravenous drug needles are shared. HIV can also be transmitted from mother to child during pregnancy, delivery, or postpartum (during breastfeeding). It is *not* airborne or transmitted by the bite of a mosquito or any other insect, or via household pets or other domestic animals. A child can't get the AIDS virus through casual contact or by playing with an HIV-infected child.

At this point, it appears that not every child who contracts HIV becomes sick with AIDS, though it's not clear why.

**Related problems.** *Pneumocystis carinii* pneumonia (PCP); pneumococcal meningitis; such rare cancers as leiomyosarcoma (Kaposi's sarcoma, common in adults with AIDS, is extremely rare in children), as well as certain types of lymphomas; parasitic infections (such as toxoplasmosis); cardiac abnormalities (especially in children with brain involvement or Epstein-Barr virus); movement disorders and developmental delays; wasting syndrome and failure to thrive; liver disease; kidney disease; anemia; thrombocytopenia (a reduction in blood platelets, which are needed for clotting); dermatitis; tuberculosis.

**Treatment/management.** A multidisciplinary approach is needed. Young children may now be treated with the drug AZT, which though not a cure can sometimes prolong life. Other antiviral drugs are presently being studied for use against AIDS, but none has yet been shown to be effective. Steroids, however, are sometimes useful in treating PCP. Nutrition and pain management are important, as are prevention and the aggressive treatment of any infection. The administration of intravenous immunoglobulin (IVIg) seems to reduce the number of infections in young AIDS patients.

Though a child with AIDS poses no threat to others in a well-run day-care or preschool setting, an HIV-positive child in such a group setting might be exposed to infections that could, because of a weakened immune system, become serious or even fatal. Such placements should be made with caution.

**Prevention.** In children: Treatment of pregnant women who are HIV-positive. Avoidance of contaminated blood or blood components for transfusion (blood that is self-donated or donated by family members who are known to be HIV-negative is usually safest). Good hygienic practices in homes or child-care facilities with infected children (the virus can be eradicated by chlorine bleach and some other household disinfectants). Cleaning up after an infected child who has received a cut requires meticulous cleansing of surfaces the blood touched; the person cleaning up should wear latex gloves and all soiled materials should be disposed of in a sealed plastic bag. Toothbrushes should never be shared— not for fear of spread via infected saliva,

but to avoid potential transmission via blood from bleeding gums. Researchers are trying to develop a vaccine to prevent HIV-infected children from developing full-blown AIDS, but have had no success to this point.

**Prognosis.** Predictions are difficult to make. Though about 1 in 4 babies infected with HIV-1 dies before eighteen months, most HIV-positive children survive beyond age five, and some live into their teens, often showing few or no apparent symptoms. Some children do better than adults, and the hope is that many will live to see a cure or at least more effective treatments.

# ALLERGY

**What is it?** An immune-system–mediated reaction to a substance, or "allergen" (see "What causes it?" page 706 for common allergens). Some allergies can occur any time of the year (food, dust, and drug allergies, for example); others, such as pollen allergies, occur seasonally, usually spring, summer, and/or fall. A single allergic episode can last anywhere from a few minutes to several hours to several days. The symptoms vary, according to the organ or system affected, as follows:

▲ The upper respiratory tract (nose and throat): watery, runny nose (allergic rhinitis); sinusitis (not common in very young children); fluid in the middle ear (otitis media with effusion; see page 609); sore throat (from the allergy itself, but also as a result of mouth breathing when the nose is stuffy); postnasal drip (mucus dripping from the back of the nose into the throat can trigger a chronic cough); spasmodic croup (see page 600). Children with allergic rhinitis often have dark circles, and sometimes, folds under their eyes; they may also do a lot of

# HELPING THE HEALTHY SIBLING

· · · · · · · · · ·

How does growing up in a household with a special-needs sibling affect healthy children? One study of college-age students who had grown up with a mentally retarded sibling found that about half felt they had been harmed and about half felt they had benefitted. Those whose perceptions of their childhood were negative had been ashamed of their sibling and felt they had been neglected by their parents, whom they viewed as having been preoccupied with the care of the special-needs sibling. These healthy siblings also felt overburdened with responsibilities and believed their own opportunities for recreation and growth were unduly restricted. The healthy siblings who felt they had benefitted admired their parents' devotion to their special-needs sibling and felt that this child had brought their family closer; instead of feeling short-changed, they felt lucky. They were, on average, more compassionate and tolerant of others, more understanding and sensitive, and more appreciative of their own good health and intelligence than were their peers in families without special-needs children.

Clearly, although being a healthy sibling in a household with a special-needs child is never easy, it can be an enriching, character-building experience. To improve the odds that your healthy children will benefit from the experience:

**Involve them.** Explain to them in language they can understand just what their sibling's situation is and how the family can work together to take care of him or her and each other. Find small tasks appropriate to their ages. For example, a toddler can dance, sing, and make faces to entertain an asthmatic sibling during nebulizer therapy. A school-age child can share a book or play board games with a bedridden sibling. A teenager can baby-sit occasionally (but don't require this on a regular basis) and perhaps even help with physical therapy or other treatment, if he or she likes.

**Reassure them.** For older children, make it clear that the primary responsibility for caring for their sibling will fall on you, not on them. When the healthy sibling is a toddler, just say, "Yes, Ryan has a problem, but it's not your fault. You didn't do it." In fact, all your children (the special-needs one included) need to be reassured that they are not responsible.* Your healthy children may also need reassurance that the illness or disability is not contagious—that you can't catch it the way you catch a cold, and that if they do come down with a cold or flu, it won't make them sick like their sibling.

**Make time for them.** Though much of your time may be taken up with caring for your special-needs child, your well children need attention, too. Stretch your time as far as you can to make sure that each of your children gets some "one-on-one" with a parent every day. Do whatever works for your family. One option: Stagger bedtimes so that each child can have a chance to talk over his or her day without vying for attention. Perhaps, too, you can plan a special outing once a week for each child—even if it means asking a relative or friend for coverage or hiring someone to stay with your special-needs child. If periods of hospitalization are neces-

---

mouth breathing and have a crease across the top of the nose from frequent wiping (the allergic salute).

▲ The lower respiratory tract (bronchial tubes and lungs): allergic bronchitis, asthma (see page 710).

▲ The digestive tract: gassiness; watery, sometimes bloody, diarrhea; vomiting.

▲ The skin: atopic dermatitis, including eczema (see page 472); urticaria, or hives (a blotchy, itchy, raised red rash); and angioedema (facial swelling, par-

sary, be sure that your well children get to visit and that you take some time away from the hospital to be with them.

**Be a good role model.** Your attitude toward your special-needs child is almost certain to rub off on your other children, so make sure it's a positive one. Get professional help to learn how to deal with any negative feelings—embarrassment, despair, guilt, or anger—that you may have.

**Don't scapegoat.** Often it's easier (and less guilt provoking) to take your anger, frustration, and exhaustion out on your healthy children than on your special-needs child ("I have enough trouble—I don't need any from you!"). But kid gloving your special-needs child and using your well children as scapegoats isn't fair, and can lead to resentment and hostility. If you find yourself frequently taking your feelings out on your family, get some help.

**Be understanding.** Healthy siblings often have mixed feelings: "I am worried (or sad or scared) about my sister"/ "I wish I didn't have a sister—my parents have no time for me." Such ambivalence is normal (even parents are susceptible to it), and you need to make sure your children know that it is. Encourage them to share their feelings by picking up on nonverbal clues (a look of sorrow, or anger, or concern) and asking about them ("Do you feel sad? . . . angry? . . . worried?").

Some well children, feeling the stress, develop the same "symptoms" as their special-needs sibling (of course, never assume the symptoms are sympathetic until you've checked with the doctor). And some may intentionally try to mimic behavior (like a cough, a limp, or a twitch, for example). Most often this is an attempt to either attract attention (after all, that's how the sibling gets it) or to somehow feel at one with the sibling ("I want to know how Geena feels"). Provide some extra attention, lend an understanding ear, and the mimicry is almost certain to disappear. If it upsets your special-needs child, explain that to the sibling and suggest that if he or she wants to continue the imitation, to do so in private.

**Watch for warning signs.** Children who have trouble coping with the stresses generated by having a special-needs sibling may become depressed and withdrawn, or start acting out (having frequent tantrums, for instance, or resisting bedtime). Try to devote some extra time and attention when such signs appear. If that doesn't help, discuss the problem with your children's doctor; individual or family counseling may be helpful.

**Don't stoke up the pressure.** Raising expectations for your healthy children or expecting them to be perfect in order to compensate for their sibling puts an unfair burden on them. Encourage all your children to be the best they can be, but never push, bully, or demand that they be more.

**Provide outside support.** Arranging for your well children to attend a support group, in which they can share feelings and thoughts with other children in similar situations, can be extremely valuable. Some children's hospitals run special groups or classes for siblings of children with particular disabilities or illnesses. If you're unable to locate a group (check with your child's doctor, the hospital, local adult support groups), consider starting one.

---

*Teens may benefit from reading *When Bad Things Happen to Good People,* by Harold Kushner. It can be very helpful for parents as well.

---

ticularly around the eyes and mouth, which is not as itchy as hives, but can be a sign of serious allergy; see page 707).

▲ The eyes: itching, watering, redness, and other signs of eye inflammation.

▲ General: irritability.

**How common is it?** Estimates vary because of different diagnostic criteria, but it is likely that from 10% to 20% of children have or will have allergies at some time in their lives.

**Who is susceptible?** Most often, those with a family history of allergy. The risk is greatest (about 80%) when both parents have allergies. The allergy doesn't develop, however, unless and until the child is exposed to the potential allergen.

**What causes it?** The release of histamine and other substances by the immune system in response to exposure to an allergen (a substance to which the individual is hypersensitive). The tendency toward allergy runs in families. The way allergies are expressed is often different in different family members—one may have hay fever, another asthma; a third may break out in hives on eating strawberries. An allergen can enter a child's system via inhalation (of pollen or animal dander, for example), ingestion (of nuts, milk, wheat, egg whites, soy products, or other food allergens), injection (penicillin shot or bee sting), or skin contact (nickel jewelry, wool garments).

Skin reactions such as urticaria and angioedema as well as anaphylaxis can also be caused by exposure to heat, cold, pressure, vibration, light, water, exercise, and infectious organisms.

**Treatment/management/prevention:** The first step in treating your child's allergy is to get an accurate diagnosis. If your child has a similar reaction every time he or she is exposed to a particular food or other allergen (always throws up after eating fish sticks, for example), check with the doctor. Many suspected food allergies, however, aren't allergies at all and, especially in young children, a clear diagnosis may be difficult. Skin tests are often unreliable in young children (though a negative test is more likely to be accurate than a positive); in-vitro tests, such as RAST (*radioallergosorbent test*), tend to be complicated and expensive. In some cases, a challenge test, in which the suspected food is administered to the child in the doctor's office (where emergency treatment is available if necessary) can be

used to determine if a child is allergic to a particular food. Or the doctor may recommend eliminating a suspected allergen from the child's diet for a few weeks to see if symptoms clear. Alternatively, several items may be eliminated and, once symptoms are gone, restored one at a time to determine the culprit. Such a test can be helpful, but don't attempt one without medical supervision.

It's rare that a child is allergic to more than three foods, so be wary of such a diagnosis. Keep in mind that under-tongue, hair, urine, and skin titration tests have no scientific basis. Once the offending allergen (or allergens) is identified, it's important to treat; untreated children are at increased risk for developing asthma. There are several approaches to treating the allergic child:

*1. Abstinence/removal.* The most successful treatment and prevention for allergy, though also often the most difficult, is elimination of the offending allergen from the life of the allergic individual. If your child turns out to be allergic, here are some ways in which you can remove the offenders from his or her environment:

▲ Food allergens.[2] In infants and young children, the foods most likely to trigger an allergic response are egg whites and cow's milk, followed by wheat and citrus. Many children are also allergic to soy and soy products and some to food additives, such as aspartame, BHA/BHT, certain dyes (Yellow No. 5, for example), monosodium glutamate (MSG), nitrates and nitrites, and sulfites. Fortunately, children are less often allergic to the foods with the greatest potential for triggering a severe response—peanuts, sesame, shellfish, and other fish.

---

2. Not every adverse reaction to a food is allergy. Some people have food "intolerances" or "idiosyncrasies," reactions which do not involve the immune system and are thus not "allergic." If a food bothers your child, even if the doctor determines the response isn't allergic, remove the food from your child's diet.

## LIFE-THREATENING ALLERGIES

• • • • • • • • • •

Most allergy symptoms are just annoy-ing: scratchy throat, runny nose, teary eyes, itchy bumps. But some allergic reactions—primarily anaphylactic responses to a specific food or drug or, rarely, to a bee sting—can be fatal. Serious reactions include any of the following groups of symptoms: wheezing, stridor (noisy breathing, crowing), hoarseness, and difficulty breathing; flushing of the skin, itching, hives along with swelling of the face, lips, and throat (which can interfere with breathing); vomiting, diarrhea (sometimes bloody), and abdominal cramps; a sudden drop in blood pressure, dizziness, light-headedness, fainting, loss of consciousness, and cardiopulmonary failure (anaphylactic shock). *Such reactions require immediate medical treatment.* If a child experiences even a single severe allergic reaction, consultation with a pediatric allergist is in order. Asthmatic children are more likely than other allergic children to experience a serious allergic response.

If, after consultation with the specialist, it's determined that your child is at risk for a life-threatening allergic response, everyone who cares for your child should be alerted to the situation and know what measures are necessary to avoid any possible exposure to the potentially deadly aller-gen. It is also recommended that an epinephrine kit be on hand at all times and that all caregivers (including parents, baby-sitters, day-care workers, teachers) be trained to recognize symptoms and to use the kit.*

Epinephrine, a hormone that counteracts anaphylaxis by raising blood pressure and opening air passages, can be life-saving. It comes in ready-to-use, easy-to-inject, pen-like instruments (Epi-Pen) and should be administered as soon as symptoms are noted, which could be anywhere from a few minutes to a few hours after an exposure. A visit to the doctor or emergency room should follow. Even if the initial reaction is very mild and the child seems to recover spontaneously, he or she should get medical attention and be observed for 24 hours; sometimes there is a secondary reaction that is much more serious than the first. Contact 911 *immediately* if your child has a severe allergic reaction and you do not have epinephrine on hand.

A child with severe allergies should also wear a warning tag (such as a Medic-alert bracelet) that lists the allergy or allergies.

---

*Some state laws do not allow nonmedical personnel to administer epinephrine; discuss this with your child's doctor.

---

Since many allergens are "hidden" in processed foods (nut oil, milk proteins, and hydrolyzed vegetable protein from soy beans, for example), it's necessary to become a relentless label reader; since formulations can change, be sure to check labels every time you buy a product. And, if your toddler is allergic to milk (see page 15), keep in mind that a label that reads "nondairy" or even "pareve" does not guarantee a totally milk-free product (such products can apparently be mislabeled). Ask about ingredients at restaurants and when visiting; be sure that anyone who cares for your child, at home or away, is completely informed about any food allergies. To prevent leaving gaps in your toddler's diet, always use nutritionally equivalent substitutes. Substitute oat, rice, and barley flours for wheat; mangoes, cantaloupe, broccoli, cauliflower, and sweet red peppers for orange juice; meat, poultry, and cheeses for eggs.

Delayed introduction of highly allergenic foods for children with a known family or personal history of allergy may help prevent the development of food allergies. Ideally, it's best to wait until twelve months for introducing cow's milk,

## WHEN THE FOOD-ALLERGIC TODDLER STEPS OUT

. . . . . . . . . .

Parties and play dates don't have to be off limits for toddlers with food allergies or intolerances. But special precautions are necessary when your toddler goes visiting. First of all, begin teaching your child that some foods are forbidden. As he or she becomes more verbal, rehearse such lines as: "I can't have milk, thank you." When it seems appropriate, supply your toddler's meal or snack. When it's not, let your child's host know in advance what foods your child can't have. Either way, be sure that both your child and the host understand the possible consequences of eating "just one bite" of such foods; that such foods are not hidden ingredients (again, careful label reading is a must), and, if your child could have an anaphylactic reaction, that they know what to do in case of an accidental exposure.

---

soy, wheat, corn, and citrus; twenty-four months for eggs; thirty-six months for peanuts and fish.

▲ Pollens. If you suspect pollen allergy (the clue: persistent symptoms when pollen is in the air and the disappearance of symptoms when the season is past), keep your child indoors as much as possible when the pollen count is high (usually in the morning) and when it is particularly windy during pollen season (spring, late summer, or fall, depending on the type of pollen). Give daily baths and shampoos to remove pollen, and use an air-conditioner in warm weather rather than opening the windows and admitting airborne pollen. Cut grass short to reduce pollen output. If you have a pet, the animal can also pick up pollen when out of doors, so it, too, should be bathed frequently. For children with severe pollen allergies, a trip to a pollen-free or low-pollen area during the height of the pollen season, if feasible, may be advisable.

Some people have a reaction to the family Christmas tree or to other evergreens brought into the home. This may be because of the pollen attached to the needles (in which case washing the tree down in the tub before setting it up will help); but more often the reaction is due to a sensitivity to the strong odor. In such instances, it's a good idea to avoid spruce trees or boughs, which are the most fragrant.

▲ Pet dander and other pet allergies. Dander, the tiny scales sloughed off by the skin of animals, is the most common offender. But some people are allergic to the saliva or the urine of animals, in which case, the litter of cats or of small caged animals can be a problem. Cat dander is more often a problem than dog dander, and long-haired pets cause more problems than short-haired ones. If you suspect or have confirmed that your child is allergic to a pet, try to keep your animal and your child in different rooms. It may also help to relegate the animal to the yard, the basement, or the garage as much as possible (if you have these options), bathe it weekly, get rid of wall-to-wall carpets, minimize upholstered furniture and other furnishings that retain dander, and use an air purifier with a high-energy particulate filter. In severe cases, the only solution may be to find the pet another home. Since horsehair can also trigger allergy, don't use horsehair mattresses or brushes; animal-hide and animal-hair rugs, carpets, and ornaments should also be avoided. Some children are allergic to birds, so if you can't figure out your toddler's problem, consider that it might be your feathered friend. Find it a new home, and opt for synthetic rather than goose-down-filled comforters, pillows, and upholstered furniture.

▲ Household dust. It isn't the dust that triggers the sneezes in most dust-allergic people, it's the dust mites. These microscopic insect-like creatures can fill the air in your home and may be inhaled, unseen, by everyone in your family. That's no problem for most people, but for someone who is hypersensitive to these substances, it can mean misery. Limit your toddler's exposure, even if you only suspect this allergy, by keeping the rooms he or she spends the most time in (the bedroom, especially) as dust-free as possible. Dust daily with a specially treated dust cloth, a damp cloth, or a cloth moistened with a bit of furniture polish when your toddler is not in the room; damp-mop floors and thoroughly vacuum rugs and upholstered furniture often.[3] Avoid carpeting, heavy draperies, chenille bedspreads, and other dust catchers in rooms where your toddler sleeps and plays; wash stuffed toys[4] and blankets or comforters frequently (in hot water, if possible[5]) and any curtains, throw rugs, or other such items at least twice a month (or pack them away). Keep such dust collectors as books behind doors, if possible, and store clothing in plastic garment bags. Sheathe mattresses and pillows in airtight casings (crib mattresses usually come with airtight covers). Put filters over forced-air vents; install a central air cleaner, if feasible (table-top models are of questionable effectiveness). And, probably most important, keep humidity in your home moderately low (see page 838); dust mites generally can't survive where humidity is below 50% (some experts recommend keeping humidity levels even lower—between 20% and 30%). For suggestions on sprays or powders that can be used to kill mites in your carpeting and upholstery, and advice on their safety, check with your child's allergist.

▲ Molds. If your toddler is allergic to molds, control moisture in your home by using a well-maintained dehumidifier (sprayed as needed with a mold inhibitor). Provide adequate ventilation and use an exhaust fan vented to the outside to dispose of steam from the kitchen, laundry, and baths. Areas where molds are likely to grow (garbage cans, refrigerators, shower curtains, bathroom tiles, damp corners) should be cleaned meticulously and frequently with a solution of equal parts of chlorine bleach and water or an anti-mold agent. If you have a self-defrosting refrigerator, don't forget to regularly empty and clean the drip pan. Paint basements and other potentially damp areas with a mold-inhibiting paint. Don't allow clothing or shoes to lie around damp or wet. Limit house plants and dried flowers to rooms your child spends little time in, and store firewood outside the house. If you must have a live Christmas tree, which can foster mold, keep it in the house for only a few days. Outdoors, be sure drainage around your home or building is good, that leaves and other plant debris are not allowed to pile up, and that enough sun hits the yard and house to prevent damp areas from spawning mold. If you have a sandbox, keep it covered at night and when it rains; in good weather, let it bask (and bake dry) in the sunshine.

▲ Bee venom. Keep a toddler who is allergic to bee venom away, as much as

---

3. If possible, invest in a vacuum with proven high-allergen containment. Or use a special high-filtration dust bag in your present vacuum so that you don't recirculate dust particles back into the air when you vacuum.

4. Give away stuffed toys that aren't washable.

5. Water over 131°F seems to kill all dust mites, warm water kills some, cold water kills few—but does disable the mites' allergy producing capacity. Blankets, spreads, and similar items that can be washed in hot water should be washed monthly; items that require warm or cold water wash should be laundered more often, about every two weeks.

possible, from outdoor areas known to have bee or wasp populations (flower gardens, for instance). (For tips on avoiding insects, see page 630.) And be sure that you or any other caregiver (including day-care or preschool staff) always has a bee-sting kit at hand.

▲ Miscellaneous allergens. Many other allergens can be removed, if necessary, from your child's environment: wool blankets (cover them or use cotton or synthetics) and clothing (cotton sweaters and synthetic-filled parkas will keep your toddler warm); down or feather pillows (when your child is old enough to use one, use foam or hypoallergenic polyester-filled ones); tobacco smoke (allow no smoking in the house at all, and keep your toddler out of smoke-filled rooms, restaurants, and so on, away from home); perfumes (use unscented wipes, sprays, and so on); soaps (use only hypoallergenic types); detergents (switch to a fragrance-free detergent or use Ivory Snow for the laundry).

*2. Immunotherapy, or desensitization.* Since an allergic reaction is a hypersensitive (or oversensitive) reaction of the child's immune system to a foreign substance, desensitization (usually accomplished via gradually increased injected doses of the offending allergen) is sometimes successful in controlling allergies—particularly to pollen, dust, and animal dander. Except in severe cases, however, desensitization is not usually started until a child is at least four years old.

*3. Medication.* Antihistamines and steroids may be used to counteract the allergic response and reduce any swelling of mucous membranes.

*4. Epinephrine injection (see page 707).*

**Prognosis.** About 90% of food allergies (to cow's milk or citrus, for example) are outgrown by age three or four. Even older children and adults can "outgrow"

a food allergy after avoiding the triggering allergen for a year or two. Allergies to nuts, soy, peas, and seafood, however, are usually life-long. While some children outgrow their allergies, others may exchange one allergy (to milk) for another (hay fever).

# ASTHMA

**What is it?** A chronic inflammatory lung disease in which airways are hyperresponsive. On exposure to a particular trigger (see "What causes it?" below), the muscles around the outside of the bronchial tubes tighten and their lining becomes inflamed, swollen, and filled with mucus. The temporarily narrowed air passages restrict air flow to and from the lungs, resulting in shortness of breath, coughing, and/or wheezing (a whistling sound produced by air traveling through the narrowed airways, which can sometimes only be detected by stethoscope but may be felt with a hand on the child's chest).[6] In young children, the only symptom may be a recurrent croupy, "barky" cough that is worse with activity or at night and may sometimes lead to vomiting. But there may also be rapid and/or noisy breathing, retractions (the skin between the ribs appears to be sucked in with each breath), and chest congestion. Some children experience asthma-related chest tightness or chest pain on exercise. The toddler with asthma may feel apprehensive (because of the occasional difficulty breathing) but not understand why. There may also be restlessness, fatigue, and poor appetite.

Since childhood asthma is different from adult-onset asthma, it may take a pediatric specialist familiar with the condition to diagnose it (its symptoms can

---

6. In severe cases of asthma there may be whistling both on exhaling (wheezing) and inhaling (stridor).

be mistaken for signs of infection) and to differentiate it from other possible lung diseases and conditions (such as cystic fibrosis, bronchiolitis, gastroesophageal reflux, or an inhaled foreign object). The degree of illness also varies from child to child; one child may have only one episode of asthma in a lifetime, another a mild case with just one episode a week or less; yet another may have a moderate or severe case, with several weekly incidents and perhaps several visits to the emergency room a year. It may also vary in the same child from season to season and/or year to year. For some, symptoms may improve with age; in others, they may worsen.

**How common is it?** Very. Worldwide, 5% to 10% of the population suffers from asthma. In the United States, estimates for children vary from 4.8% to 7.6%.

**Who is susceptible?** Those with a family history, especially with an asthmatic parent (there appears to be an inherited predisposition); children with allergies; those with bronchopulmonary dysplasia. Asthma is slightly more common in black children. About 40% of cases develop by age three, 90% by age ten.

**What causes it?** Much is not known about what causes asthma. But it is known that a variety of factors may trigger an episode in a susceptible person. Triggers include: common allergens (such as dust mites, animal dander, molds, cockroach leavings, pollens from trees grass, and ragweed, and sometimes foods—see page 703 for more on allergies); viral infections; irritants, including tobacco smoke, strong odors (from household cleaners, paints, and varnishes, for example); air pollutants (outdoors and in; see page 628); weather changes (temperature, humidity, barometric pressure) and strong winds; anxiety and stress; strenuous exercise

(especially in cold weather or after eating certain foods, including shellfish, celery, and melon); sensitivity to drugs or chemicals (coal and chalk dust, food preservatives, such as sulfites, certain food colorings, and other food ingredients, such as MSG). Middle-of-the-night episodes may be triggered by allergens in the bedroom, by cool nighttime temperatures, or even by gastroesophageal reflux (food sloshing back from the stomach up into the esophagus). The fact that airways constrict slightly at night, even in normal children, may also contribute. Episodes may be worse at certain times of the day or night than others because of a child's individual body chemistry, which varies throughout a 24-hour period.

**Related problems.** Recurrent infections affecting the respiratory tract, including pneumonia.

**Treatment/management.** Early detection and pinpointing what it is that triggers an episode (keeping a diary will help you to do this) combined with preventive measures are the best treatment. Prevention for toddlers includes[7]:

▲ Reducing exposure to triggers—such as allergens (consultation with a pediatric allergist can be very helpful in determining what they are) and stress (see page 173).

▲ Reducing the incidence of respiratory infection with optimum nutrition, annual flu shots, and good hygiene (see page 606).

▲ Warding off possible episodes with the use of carefully selected medication, as prescribed—such prophylaxis can be given daily or before anticipated exposure to a known trigger. Medication (which may include bronchodilators, anti-inflammatory medications, and possibly

---

7. The use of a peak flow meter and regular aerobic exercise, often recommended for older children, is not recommended for toddlers.

adrenalin-like oral beta-agonists; antihistamines, if used at all, must be used with caution) should be tailored to the child, with use limited to the minimum amount needed to achieve control over symptoms. Medications may make a child jittery or "hyper" and interfere with sleep. An opportunity to run around before bedtime may help work off this effect and allow better sleep (for the whole family). Restricting chocolate and caffeinated drinks may help. A nebulizer[8] is often recommended as the best way to get the proper dose of medication into a toddler. Though you may feel like a mad scientist when you start using a nebulizer, the use of this device may help to avoid many visits to the emergency room.

▲ Allergy shots for ragweed and possibly for other allergens. These can significantly reduce asthma symptoms, but are rarely appropriate for toddlers.

▲ A nutritious diet (excluding potential triggers, of course) and an adequate fluid intake.

▲ Recent research suggests that the use of intravenous immunoglobulin (IVIg) from nonasthmatic donors may be able to greatly reduce the need for steroids in children, and may even eliminate it entirely.

Once asthma symptoms flare, keep calm (as you become more experienced, this will be easier) and administer medication as instructed. If your child fails to respond to the medication as expected, head immediately for the doctor's office (if the doctor is available) or the emergency room.

**Prognosis.** Many children with mild asthma (fewer than three episodes a year) and many of those who develop

asthma after age three "outgrow" the condition by late adolescence. Such a remission is less likely among children with moderate to severe disease. But even when asthma continues into adulthood, most asthmatics with good medical care can function normally in their chosen endeavors (including professional athletics).

# *Autism*

**What is it?** A syndrome (a group of symptoms) rather than a clinical disease or condition, autism is the most common form of *Pervasive Developmental Disorder*, or PDD, of childhood. Affected children display: impaired verbal communication (they may repeat words, but don't initiate conversations); inability to interpret nonverbal communications (such as an angry voice or a big smile); markedly restricted interests; impaired social interactions (they don't respond to verbal or physical overtures from others, and may resist physical contact—though some are inappropriately affectionate with strangers or may form an exclusive attachment to their mother); inappropriate behavior (some, for example, lick or smell everything they encounter); and limited or intermittent eye contact (but they may gaze into space for hours on end). Autistic children may also be unable to respond to commands or carry out tasks; they may appear to be deaf even when their hearing is clinically fine. They spend less time playing with toys than other children (including those who are mentally retarded) and often use toys in inappropriate ways. They tend to engage less in imitative play and show little imagination. Head banging and self biting to the point of injury (because pain is not perceived), screaming, and other kinds of frenzied behavior are not uncommon. Autistic children often dislike loud noise, but are fascinated by many visual stimuli (a moving fan, for

---

8. A nebulizer is an air compressor, which turns medication into cold steam, attached to a clear plastic mask, which fits over the child's nose and mouth for administering the medication. It often works best to hold the mask up to the child's face as he or she sits on your lap, rather than to simply attach the mask with the elastic band.

example). They are often described as remote, joyless, unreachable, feelingless.

The autistic child sometimes appears to function as if other humans do not exist—parents may seem to matter little more than a broom or a chair. Sometimes it is clear early in infancy that something is wrong (the baby doesn't focus on faces or babble or coo, for example); other times, subtle signs are present but are not detected until later. Almost always, symptoms surface before the age of thirty months.

**How common is it?** An estimated 4 in 10,000 children are affected.

**Who is susceptible?** Autistic children come from all backgrounds and ethnic groups, but are three to four times more likely to be boys. Autism also appears to be more common in children who have phenylketonuria, the fragile X syndrome (a disorder of the X chromosome), or certain structural abnormalities and metabolic diseases of the brain. Autism is slightly more common in siblings of autistic children.

**What causes it?** Poor parenting is *not* a cause. There are probably a variety of causative factors, possibly including maternal rubella during pregnancy, chromosomal abnormalities, and fetal brain damage in late pregnancy (it's uncertain whether problems during birth or just after are also a factor). The fact that many more boys than girls are affected and that siblings of autistic children are at slightly higher risk points to a genetic component. But the details are far from clear and the cause of most cases is unknown.

**Related problems.** Sometimes, mental retardation (though autistic children range from profoundly retarded to extremely gifted, and some experts believe that sometimes the *appearance* of retardation is due to a sense of hopelessness and failure bred by lack of reinforcement for the autistic child's efforts); learning disabilities, even in bright, verbal children; eccentricities in body movement (toe walking, or jumping, grimacing, or arm flapping when excited, for example); epileptic seizures (these are now believed to be an integral part of the syndrome in some autistic children with severe mental deficiencies); in older children, major depression or schizophrenia.

**Treatment/management.** Should be individualized for each child, with the goal of fostering normal development (as much as is possible) and promoting language development, social interaction, and learning. Hearing should be tested at the outset to be certain that hearing loss is not responsible for the symptoms. In most cases, however, an expensive battery of high-tech testing is not necessary for a diagnosis of autism. There are a variety of treatment approaches; some are scientifically based, and others are alternative therapies generally sought by desperate parents. None cures autism; some help modify the condition, others don't. What works for one child may not work for another. Treatments that have shown some success include: behavior modification (with rewards for appropriate behavior, denial of rewards for inappropriate); medication to treat specific symptoms; motivation (finding an area of interest to the child, such as music or art or science, and trying to make contact through this medium).

Excessive pressure to perform and unrealistic expectations are not recommended. Attempts at talking, for example, should be rewarded even if the results are far from perfect. Such positive reinforcement encourages the child to try again rather than slip back into his or her shell of silence. Taking the child's head in your hands and speaking face to face appears to be the best way of obtaining an autistic child's attention.

**Prognosis.** Varies with the degree of autism and the seriousness of related conditions; it is difficult to predict during the toddler period. But with extensive, intensive intervention by both parents and professionals, and with a multifaceted approach (possibly including medical treatment, psychological counseling, speech therapy, physical therapy, and special education), many children are helped to improve their communication and social skills. Though some children require life-long protective care, others make remarkable progress and are able to be mainstreamed in school, get a good education, and hold jobs later in life (though the type of job may be limited by poor social skills and a lingering difficulty dealing with abstractions). A small percentage of high-functioning autistic adults marry and have families, but genetic counseling is advisable to evaluate the risk of the union resulting in an autistic child. Improved treatment may continue to better the outlook for today's autistic children.

# CANCER

**What is it?** Not a single entity, but a group of more than one hundred different diseases, all characterized by the runaway proliferation of abnormal cells. Symptoms vary widely depending on the type of cancer.

**How common is it?** Relatively rare in children, particularly toddlers. Cancers occur in only about 6,000 children under fifteen in the U.S. annually.

**Who is susceptible?** Those with an inherited gene for a specific cancer (such as Wilm's tumor, a cancer of the kidneys[9]); those with a family history of cancer; those with immune deficiencies; those with certain chromosomal disorders (such

---

9. Wilm's tumor occurs in both hereditary and nonhereditary forms.

as Down syndrome) or congenital malformations (such as aniridia, a defect of the iris of the eye); possibly, those who have been exposed to cancer-causing agents (teratogens). Genetic tests are now available that can predict a small number of inherited cancers; such testing allows individuals to take preventive measures and to be on the alert for the development of the particular malignancy.

**What causes it?** Probably 5% to 10% of all cancers are directly inherited (from an affected parent to a child). Genetic mutations, chromosomal abnormalities, and interactions between genes and environmental factors (including certain viruses, such as the human papilloma virus) also come into play. Though environmental factors—including tobacco, alcohol, high-fat/low-fiber diets, and probably to a lesser extent exposure to chemicals (in pesticides, foods, the air)—have been linked to adult cancers, they are unlikely to be responsible for many in childhood, since long-term exposure is generally necessary for a malignancy to develop.

**Related problems.** Suppression of the immune system and a subsequent increased susceptibility to infection are often side effects of treatment.

**Treatment/management.** Depends on the type of malignancy, but may include surgery (conventional or laser), chemotherapy, radiation, and/or bone marrow transplants. In some cases, an experimental procedure undergoing clinical trial may be recommended. The best treatment is usually found in pediatric cancer centers. As an adjunct to treatment, good nutrition (such as provided by the Best-Odds Toddler Diet) may strengthen the immune system in its fight against a malignancy.

**Prevention.** Nothing we presently know will absolutely prevent someone from ever developing cancer, but you can stack the odds in your child's favor by taking sun-protective measures (see page 466); serving a diet high in fiber, appropriately low in fat, and rich in antioxidants (such as vitamins C and E and beta-carotene); and limiting exposure to environmental pollutants (including tobacco smoke; see Chapter Twenty-One) and to potentially risky chemicals in food and water (see Chapter Eighteen).

**Prognosis.** Childhood tumors are much more responsive to therapy than adult tumors. Survival rates for most childhood cancers have risen dramatically in the last decades, but the prognosis in each case depends upon the type of cancer, how early it is diagnosed, and how well it is treated. In general, better than 2 out of 3 children with cancer survive; for some forms of the disease, the survival rate is closer to 90%.

Long-term survivors (five years or more) generally do well once the ordeal of diagnosis and treatment is over; special attention to helping these children catch up socially and academically can help prevent problems in these areas. Since new malignancies are somewhat more common in cancer survivors than in the general population, careful follow-up is also important.

# CELIAC DISEASE

**What is it?** Also called celiac sprue or gluten-sensitive enteropathy (GSE), this is a condition in which there is sensitivity (*not* allergy) to gliadin (found in gluten, a component of wheat, rye, barley, and oats). When the gluten comes in contact with the small bowel during digestion, the bowel loses its villi (tiny hair-like projections that facilitate the absorption of nutrients) and becomes smooth. This interferes with food absorption. GSE can begin anytime in childhood or adulthood. The most common symptom in infants and young toddlers is the passage of frothy, liquidy, foul-smelling stools; a distended abdomen; pallor; and failure to thrive. In older toddlers there may be poor appetite; a cessation of weight gain (or even weight loss); irritability; and bulky, foul-smelling diarrhea-like stools. Fat globules may appear in the stool because fat isn't being absorbed properly. Sometimes there is also a history of vomiting (often forceful) and/or extreme susceptibility to infection. In some children there may only be constipation or recurrent abdominal pain. Occasionally, the only symptom is failure to thrive.

**How common is it?** The estimated incidence in some parts of the U.S. is 1 in 2,000, but it is even rarer in other areas; the rate is highest in Ireland, where the disease affects about 1 in 300. For unknown reasons, the incidence is slowly decreasing.

**Who is susceptible?** It's not clear; children with affected family members have a slightly increased risk.

**What causes it?** Also unclear. Most likely some combination of environmental factors and genetic predisposition is involved.

**Related problems.** Lactose intolerance in some children; malabsorption of fat; fluid retention; developmental delays; late teething; rickets.

**Treatment/management.** Once the diagnosis has been confirmed via a biopsy of the small bowel (intestine), a gluten-free diet is prescribed, along with extra calories and vitamin and mineral supplementation to help the child catch up growthwise. Baked goods and pasta made with rice, corn, soy, potato, or other gluten-free flours replace the traditional grains. Grain by-products such as

malt, hydrolized vegetable protein, modified starches, vegetable gums, MSG,
and vinegar are also avoided. Another
biopsy may be done after six to twelve
months on the diet to see if it is working.
If the bowel appears normal at that time,
gluten may be reintroduced into the diet.
After two years, or as soon as symptoms
reappear, another bowel biopsy is performed. A positive biopsy confirms the
diagnosis, and the gluten-free diet is resumed. Although continuing this diet for
a lifetime has long been recommended,
some experts believe that such an extreme approach may not be necessary.

**Prognosis.** The gluten-sensitive individual can live a perfectly normal life as
long as gluten products are avoided.
Since there are now many gluten-free
products on the market, this is easier to
do than it was in the past. If a mild case
of GSE is missed and untreated in childhood, the individual may not grow to full
genetic height.

# CEREBRAL PALSY (CP)

**What is it?** Also called static en-
cephalopathy, CP is a neuromuscular
disorder. It's nonprogressive (which
means it doesn't get worse, although its
manifestations may change) and is divided into two major types: spastic and
nonspastic. Signs of a problem may not
be noted until a child is six or seven
months old and diagnosis may not be
made until midway through the second
year of life or later.

Symptoms vary from mild to severe
and may differ from case to case, depending on the type of CP. In toddlers symptoms often include: a history of delayed
development (the child didn't sit, stand,
walk, talk at the usual ages); poor motor
control with diminished (floppy) or excessive (stiff) muscle tone; spasticity.

**How common is it?** CP is the most
common movement disorder of childhood, with an estimated incidence of
about 1 to 2 per 1,000 births.

**Who is susceptible?** Very low-birth-
weight babies (under 3½ pounds or 1,500
grams); boys slightly more often than
girls; white infants more often than black;
twins, triplets, and quadruplets more than
singletons; and children with other major
or minor physical malformations.

**What causes it?** Most often, probably
damage to the developing nervous system
during the prenatal period. A wide range
of possible agents have been suggested,
including: maternal smoking or drug or
alcohol abuse; Rh incompatibility; and
maternal hyperthyroidism. Though it's
also been suggested that some cases may
be genetic, this isn't entirely clear. Recent studies have not found an association between CP and a lack of oxygen or
other trauma during childbirth. An estimated 10% to 20% of cases of CP result
from brain damage (due to a head injury
or an illness, such as meningitis) early in
childhood. About 50% of CP cases have
no identifiable cause.

**Related problems.** Sometimes, seizures;
also communication (speech, vision, and
hearing) disorders; dental defects; mental
retardation; learning disabilities.

**Treatment/management.** No cure, but
early detection and therapy can help a
child reach his or her potential. Treatment plans should stress the whole child,
and may include: surgery to reduce spasticity or otherwise improve functioning;
medication; physical therapy, and training in alternative modes of movement;
speech therapy, and training in alternative modes of communication, such as
computer-synthesized communication;
occupational therapy; braces, splints, or
other orthotics; special furniture and
utensils, and training in self-sufficiency.

Reduction of sudden noise in the environment may be helpful when the child is noise-sensitive.

**Prognosis.** When intelligence is normal, a good long-term outcome can be achieved through providing the child with a way to communicate, a way to get around, and the ability to perform the tasks of daily living. When there is a mental or cognitive (learning) handicap, mild or major, outcomes can vary greatly, depending on the individual case.

# CYSTIC FIBROSIS (CF)

**What is it?** A condition in which there is a generalized dysfunction of the exocrine glands—the glands that discharge secretions through the skin, the mucous membranes, and the linings of the hollow organs. Because the sweat glands are affected, perspiration is salty and profuse, and the disease is often first diagnosed when parents note the saltiness of the skin on kissing their child (there may even be salt crystals visible). Also invariably involved, to a lesser or greater degree, is the respiratory system. Thick secretions eventually fill the lungs, causing chronic coughing and increased risk of lower respiratory infection. The pancreas is also generally affected. The pancreatic ducts become blocked, pancreatic enzymes become deficient, and as a result, the child cannot digest fats and proteins properly. Undigested material is excreted in stools that are large, bulky, foul-smelling, pale, and fatty. Though appetite is ravenous, weight gain is poor; the child's abdomen is distended, arms and legs thin, and skin sallow.

**How common is it?** It is the most common serious genetic disorder affecting whites in the U.S. Estimates vary from 1

in 1,600 to 1 in 2,500 for whites in general; the numbers are much lower for black Americans (1 in 17,000) and lower still for Asians and Native Americans.

**Who is susceptible?** Most often, children of white Anglo-Saxon ancestry.

**What causes it?** Autosomal recessive inheritance; both parents must pass on recessive genes for their child to have CF. Since the gene has now been located, testing is often possible to determine whether parents are carriers and whether their unborn children are affected.

**Related problems.** If fluids are not adequately replaced, excessive perspiration can lead to dehydration and shock. Pneumonia and other respiratory illnesses are common with lung involvement; diabetes with pancreatic involvement; sinusitis; liver damage; gastroesophageal reflux and other digestive disorders; malnutrition; infertility in most males, and in some females.

**Treatment/management.** No cure yet, but early diagnosis (most cases can be diagnosed prenatally) and a comprehensive, intensive therapy program are essential to improving the outlook. Depending on the individual case, the program may include many or all of the following: *Nutritional supplementation*, with about 50% more calories than are normally needed (to fuel growth and activity), a high protein and moderate fat intake, vitamin and mineral supplementation, a copious fluid intake (to help thin secretions), and generous salting of food and salt supplements in hot weather (to prevent salt depletion). *Pancreatic enzymes*, given by mouth with meals and snacks, for digestive problems. *Respiratory therapy*, including postural drainage to help loosen and remove secretions, given daily for respiratory problems. *Oxygen therapy*, as needed. *Air control*, to keep room air cool, dry, and smoke-free.

*Medication*, as needed. Infections are treated with large doses of antibiotics, insulin depletion with insulin. *Surgery*, if rectal prolapse becomes a problem.

A variety of experimental treatments hold promise, including: genetic manipulation; the use of an inhaled enzyme to break up thick secretions in the lungs, the use of anti-inflammatory agents, aerosol therapy, immunotherapy, and a vaccine to prevent infection by *Pseudomonas aeruginosa*.

**Prognosis.** Steadily improving. Once, children with CF rarely survived childhood, usually because of respiratory failure. Today, with early diagnosis, aggressive treatment (especially at a major CF center; ask your child's doctor for a referral to the nearest center), and strong family support, more than half live to the age of twenty-eight, and many more are now reaching their thirties, forties, and fifties, and lead busy, active lives. Some have married, and though males with CF are generally sterile, some women with CF have successfully borne children. The outlook for today's toddler is even better.

# DIABETES MELLITUS

**What is it?** Type 1, or insulin-dependent diabetes mellitus (IDDM; also called juvenile-onset diabetes), is an autoimmune disorder in which the body's immune system attacks the insulin-producing beta (or islet) cells of the pancreas. Insulin is needed to turn sugar into energy that can be used by the cells. When there is inadequate insulin, sugar builds up in the blood, spilling over into the urine and making it sweet—thus the name diabetes mellitus ("mellitus" means sweet). The starving cells, not getting their usual energy source, start to burn fat stores instead. This can lead to serious com-

plications, including a potentially fatal diabetic coma.

Symptoms of high blood sugar in a toddler include frequent urination (difficult to judge in one still in diapers), excessive thirst, excessive appetite coupled with poor weight gain, and, sometimes, lethargy.

**How common is it?** Estimates vary from 1.2 to 3 children in 1,000 in the U.S.; incidence is greater in some parts of the world, lesser in others. It is diagnosed most often in older children—incidence peaks at prepuberty—but it sometimes begins in the toddler years.

**Who is susceptible?** Most often, children with a family history of IDDM.

**What causes it?** Destruction of the insulin-producing beta cells. Just which component or components of the immune system are responsible for this destruction is still to be definitely determined. The disease is not passed on via a single gene, but there appears to be an inherited susceptibility toward developing it. Other factors are apparently also involved, though it isn't clear what they are. The theory, suggested by one study, that for susceptible children, cow's milk in the first year of life could be a triggering factor and that breast milk could be protective, has not been confirmed.

**Related problems.** Retinopathy (damage to the retina of the eye); nephropathy (kidney damage); neuropathy (nervous system damage); premature coronary artery disease; poor circulation to hands and feet. The risk of such complications can be greatly reduced with very careful control of blood sugar levels; about 1 in 4 diabetics never develop a complication.

**Treatment/management.** Aimed at keeping blood sugar at normal levels, treatment usually includes: administration of insulin, home glucose monitoring, exercise (which, among other benefits, helps burn excess sugar and maintain normal circulation to the feet), and dietary management. Dietary management is necessary both to keep blood sugar from soaring too high (by limiting the intake of sugary foods) and to keep it from dropping too low (by serving meals and snacks at regular hours and avoiding long periods without food). Though diets must be individually tailored, the recommended diet for children with diabetes is typically 50% complex carbohydrates, 20% protein, and 30% fat. Pancreas transplants, sometimes recommended for adults, are not recommended for children—the surgery and the required immunosuppression are too risky.

Clinical studies in the works that hold promise include: early suppression of the immune cells to prevent further destruction of beta cells; transplantation of beta cells, which might end the need for insulin shots and prevent or reverse many of the serious complications of diabetes; an implantable insulin pump and an automatic glucose sensor, which together will be able to monitor blood sugar and administer insulin as needed. Meanwhile, parents of toddlers (and other caregivers) will have to take charge of this insulin monitoring and administration process—until the children are old enough to take over.

It's important for parents to keep in mind that on beginning treatment, newly diagnosed IDDM patients often seem to get better, even to need less insulin. That's because some insulin-producing cells are still working and when outside insulin is administered, they seem to perk up. But this "honeymoon" period doesn't last more than a year or two (the cells eventually stop producing insulin entirely), and parents should not become lax in attention to treatment during this time.

**Prognosis.** For children who are able to maintain good control of their disease (with adult help during childhood), the prognosis for a normal life is excellent.

**Prevention.** Still experimental. It is hoped that once tests that screen close relatives of diabetics for antibodies that damage insulin-producing beta cells are refined, accurate prediction of who is likely to eventually develop diabetes will be possible. Those who test positive for the antibodies could then be treated with immunosuppressive therapy aimed at preventing the damage they do.

# DOWN SYNDROME

**What is it?** A set of signs and symptoms that usually include delayed development, oval-shaped eyes, an oversized tongue, and a short neck. Children with Down syndrome may also have a flat back of the head, small ears (sometimes folded a little at the tops), a flat, wide nose; short, wide hands; short stature; poor muscle tone; and a sweet, loving, and lovable personality. Characteristics may vay depending on the type of chromosome abnormality. There may also be a variety of related problems (see below). Though it has long been believed that Down syndrome was synonomous with mental retardation, early intervention has shown that some children with Down syndrome have normal IQs; most others have only mild to moderate retardation.

**How common is it?** About 1 in 1,300 children is affected.

**Who is susceptible?** Children of all ethnic groups and socioeconomic levels. But babies of parents who have already produced a child with Down syndrome, babies of a parent with a chromosome rearrangement (see page 720), and babies of mothers (and possibly fathers) over thirty-five are at a higher risk.

**What causes it?** In 95% of cases, an extra chromosome contributed by one of the parents, giving the baby 47 chromosomes instead of 46. The extra chromosome is a number 21 chromosome; since the Down syndrome individual has three number 21 chromosomes instead of the usual two, this arrangement is called trisomy 21.

**Related problems.** About half of the children with Down syndrome have a congenital heart defect and about 5% have a gastrointestinal abnormality. Some have a weak immune system (making them more susceptible to everything from respiratory illnesses to leukemia and other cancers) and/or hearing and vision deficits, thyroid dysfunction, and a tendency toward premature aging. Though children with Down syndrome are inherently at risk of obesity, positive familial and other environmental factors, including dietary control and physical activity, can reduce the risk.

**Treatment/management.** If prenatal diagnosis was not made, chromosome studies need to be done after birth to confirm the diagnosis of Down syndrome and determine the type of chromosome abnormality responsible. Early specialized education programs can dramatically improve the IQs of Down syndrome children, bringing some into the "normal" range. Good medical care can often reduce related problems. Surgery, for example, may be able to correct heart and digestive defects. In some countries, surgery is performed to normalize appearance, but the benefits are debatable.

**Prognosis.** Varies depending on severity of condition. Most children with Down syndrome have greater capabilities than was previously believed, and intervention begun as soon as the condition is diagnosed can make the best of these abilities, leaving fewer than 10% severely retarded. Many children with Down syn-

drome can be mainstreamed for a while in school; most later find places in sheltered homes and workshops; a few are able to live and work independently, and some marry. The average life span, once the hurdles of the first two to ten years are surmounted, is fifty-five, more than twice what it was in the past.

# EPILEPSY

**What is it?** A chronic disorder of the brain that causes recurrent seizures. A seizure is a sudden, temporary, involuntary alteration in physical movement or consciousness. The severity and type of seizure as well as how much and what part of the body is affected vary depending on the portion of the brain involved. Though seizures used to be grouped into "grand mal" and "petit mal" categories, the new classifications are more specific. Seizures can range from involuntary convulsions of the entire body to a sudden and brief lapse of awareness of the environment. An epileptic seizure is a temporary malfunction and does not mean the brain is deteriorating in any way.

**How common is it?** About 1% of the population has epilepsy. It is the most common neurological disorder in children. About 3% to 5% of children experience at least one seizure, but not all seizures are epileptic (febrile seizures, for example, are not). A child who has one seizure has only a 30% chance of having another.

**Who is susceptible?** Possibly someone with a genetic predisposition to epilepsy. Also, an individual who has sustained severe trauma of some sort to the brain (sometimes one that was undetected).

**What causes it?** Abnormal electrical discharges in the brain, due to an insult to the brain from any of a wide range of causes, including: head injury, brain infection, a metabolic disorder, damage during fetal development, severe hypoglycemia (low blood sugar), and (rarely) a tumor. No cause can be determined in about half of those with epilepsy.

**Related problems.** Epileptics may face a slightly increased risk of accidental injury.

**Treatment/management.** The first step is diagnosis; report a first seizure to your child's doctor, including such details as what preceded it, what your child looked like, and how long it lasted (it's often difficult for an observer to be sure a child really is having a seizure, especially when the seizure is very brief). Diagnosis, evaluation, and classification of seizures is best made by a specialist; but the day-to-day medical care of a child with epilepsy can usually be handled by the pediatrician. Medication or a combination of medications, carefully monitored, can often control or reduce the incidence of seizures. When medication doesn't work, surgery may be considered. Rarely, a special diet—usually high in fat, moderate in protein, and low in carbohydrates—is recommended.

Since children with epilepsy are at a potentially higher risk of drowning (if they suffer a seizure in a bathtub or a pool, for example), they should never be left unattended near water, no matter what their age or how well they swim. They are also *slightly* more likely to be injured at play, but this is not a reason to overprotect them and keep them from doing what comes naturally (playing running games, climbing on the jungle gym, riding trikes, and so on). Any restrictions on activities should be placed only in consultation with the doctor, taking into account the risk that such restrictions will hinder normal development.

For handling a febrile seizure see page 583; epileptic and other seizures are usually handled in a similar way (see page 665). Emergency help should be sought for a seizure that lasts more than 15 minutes.

**Prognosis.** Seizures can be completely controlled without serious medication side effects in 8 in 10 children. After two seizure-free years, a child is generally no longer considered epileptic and medication may be stopped. With appropriate management and support, the great majority of children who continue to have epilepsy can become competent and functioning adults.

# FRAGILE X SYNDROME

**What is it?** An X-linked chromosomal disorder. Typically, boys with fragile X syndrome have delayed speech and language development, prominent foreheads and jaws, low-set ears, long and narrow faces, large testicles, and other physical abnormalities. Some have only mild learning disabilities, and it's estimated that 1 in 5 boys with the fragile X chromosome has no symptoms at all. Most female carriers are also symptom free, though 1 in 3 is mildly to moderately mentally retarded or has a learning disability.

**How common is it?** An estimated 1 in 1,000 boys is affected, which makes fragile X syndrome one of the major causes of mental retardation in the U.S. Most cases of fragile X, however, are not diagnosed as such.

**Who is susceptible?** Because the disorder is linked to the X chromosome, males are much more likely to exhibit the full-blown syndrome. (Males have only one X chromosome; unlike women they have no second X chromosome with a normal gene to counteract the fragile X with the defective gene).

**What causes it?** A defect in a gene on a fragile, or thinned-out, section of the X chromosome.

**Related problems.** Problems of motor coordination and balance after age ten. About 14% are also autistic and display many of the symptoms of autism (see page 712).

**Treatment/management.** At present, early intervention to deal with mental retardation is the prime treatment (see page 725). When the specific gene responsible has been identified, it is hoped that it will be possible to correct the defect through biochemical manipulation.

# HEARING IMPAIRMENT

**What is it?** There are several types of hearing loss in children: *Conductive hearing loss.* In this type of hearing loss, sound is not conducted efficiently through the ear canal; the loudness of a sound is reduced. *Sensorineural hearing loss.* In this type of hearing loss, there is damage to the inner ear or to the nerve pathways from the inner ear to the brain. Loudness of sound is reduced, and so is the child's understanding of spoken language. *Combined hearing loss.* Combines both of the above. *Central (or*

*retrocochlear) hearing loss.* Child hears sounds but is not able to decipher words.

There are many degrees of hearing impairment or hearing loss, and not all children with hearing loss are "deaf." The child who is deaf has a profound hearing loss and cannot understand speech through hearing alone, even with the use of a hearing aid.

Toddlers who are hearing-impaired use their hands to "babble" and to talk; the movements, though they are not real sign language, are organized and very much like the jargon of a hearing toddler.

For signs of hearing impairment, see page 488. If you suspect that your toddler doesn't hear well, speak to his or her doctor.

**How common is it?** An estimated 3 in 100 children experience some degree of hearing impairment by school age.

**Who is susceptible?** See page 488.

**What causes it?** *Conductive hearing loss.* Malformation of the outer or middle ear. Also, colds, allergies, otitis media (middle-ear infections), but illness-related hearing loss is usually temporary. *Sensorineural hearing loss.* Malfunction of inner ear or damage to the auditory nerve; such damage becomes more common with age. When the nerve is damaged, hearing loss is

---

## HEARING TESTS

· · · · · · · · · ·

The most common hearing test for children under two years of age is Visual Reinforcement Audiometry (VRA), in which the child is trained to turn toward a sound by rewarding head turns with lighted and moving toys. For children from two to four, the preferred test is Conditioned Play Audiometry (CPA), in which a child is trained to give a "game" response when a sound is presented (drop a block in a bucket, put a puzzle piece in, etc.). If the child is cooperative, this test can provide a great deal more information than the VRA. In some instances, more than one evaluation session may be necessary.

usually permanent. The causes of sensorineural hearing loss may be prenatal, perinatal, or postnatal, acquired or genetic; the incidence has been reduced by the decrease in congenital rubella and Hib meningitis in infants and by better treatment of meningitis when it occurs. *Central hearing loss.* Changes in the auditory centers of the brain due to injury, disease, tumor, heredity, or unknown causes.

**Related problems.** Poor language development, poor learning, lack of self-esteem.

**Treatment/management.** It is important to diagnose a hearing loss early and to determine the level of impairment, which can range from mild to profound. The first step is testing by an audiologist. If the child does not pass the instructions the first time around, a retest may be ordered (sometimes a child misunderstands the first test or has a cold or other infection that temporarily hampers hearing) or the child may be referred to a pediatric otolaryngologist for further testing and treatment.

Treatment of hearing loss, beginning as soon as a diagnosis is made, is very important, not only to maximize a child's future hearing and language development, but to protect self-esteem. Treatment may be provided by both an otolaryngologist and an audiologist, and may include:

▲ Medication.

▲ Surgery. Cochlear implants can often restore limited hearing (sometimes even to the point where conversation can be understood) and improve the ability of totally deaf children to learn spoken language.[10] For a cochlear implant, a child must be at least two years old, have pro-

found bilateral sensorineural hearing loss, and have received limited or no benefit from conventional hearing devices.

▲ Hearing aids (which magnify all sounds) or assistive listening devices (which magnify selected sounds without background noises). There are many types of devices, and the type used will depend on the child's age and the type of hearing loss. Some assistive listening devices are used with hearing aids, others are used independently.

▲ Education. An education program should be begun as soon as hearing loss is diagnosed, and may include teaching a child to use devices that assist in learning to hear and/or to speak; cued speech, in which a system of manual cues is used to supplement speech (or lip) reading; a total communication program, which uses a combination of speech reading, signing, and finger spelling and may also emphasize listening skills and speech production. No one program fits all hearing-impaired children. The child's pediatrician and hearing specialist can help parents find the program that best meets their child's needs.

Whether a child with a hearing impairment is mainstreamed (that is, attends regular classes with hearing children) depends on the individual child, the programs that local schools offer, and the availability of special classes in speech and language development in the mainstream schools. When the hearing-impaired toddler is ready for day-care or preschool, the options should be discussed with his or her doctor and audiologist as well as the school director and/or teachers at the program being considered.

**Prognosis.** With proper treatment, children with hearing impairments can have successful, fulfilling lives. Some may be helped to hear and to speak; others will learn to communicate through signing.

---

10. These implants are opposed by some in the deaf community who see it as a negative approach to dealing with deafness, which they see as a way of life, not a disability.

# JUVENILE RHEUMATOID ARTHRITIS (JRA)

**What is it?** A pediatric connective-tissue disease, or actually, group of diseases. Fatigue, low-grade fever, loss of appetite, weight loss, and failure to grow are common at onset of the disease in children with moderate to severe JRA. Morning joint stiffness, or "gelling" after inactivity, and night pain are also common, but toddlers are often not able to verbalize these symptoms; instead they may just become increasingly irritable, seem to be protective of their joints, and limp and/or refuse to walk. The three most common forms of JRA are:

*Polyarthritis.* In this, the most common form, five or more joints—most often those in the knees, wrists, elbows, and ankles, and possibly the hands—are involved, usually symmetrically (both wrists or both ankles are involved, for example). Joints may be tender and painful, though the child may not complain of the pain, and there may be neck stiffness and loss of rotation (the head can't turn fully from side to side). Systemic involvement (generalized illness, fever; see below) is usually mild.

*Oligoarthritis (pauciarticular disease).* This form of JRA is almost as common; four or fewer joints are involved (sometimes just the knees or the ankles or even just one joint), and there may be chronic uveitis (irritation of the iris of the eye).

*Systemic disease.* This form accounts for about 10% to 20% of JRA cases. A variable number of joints are affected, systemic involvement is prominent, and chronic uveitis is rare; systemic symptoms that include a spiking fever (over 102.2°F or 39°C) once or twice a day that quickly returns to normal or below and a salmon-colored rash that comes and goes are common and may precede joint symptoms by weeks or more. Intermittent episodes of fever may continue for years in some children; in others, severe chronic polyarthritis develops. The spleen and liver may be enlarged and a variety of organs, including the heart, may be affected.

**How common is it?** In the U.S., an estimated 1 in 425 children is affected.

**Who is susceptible?** Though JRA can begin anytime during childhood, the median age is one to three. Polyarthritis is three times more common in girls than in boys, oligoarthritis (pauciarticular disease) is five times more common in girls, and systemic disease is about equally common in girls and boys.

**What causes it?** The cause is unknown.

**Related problems.** Uveitis (inflammation of the iris of the eye), especially with oligoarthritis; disturbances in growth and development.

**Treatment/management.** A wide range of medications, including aspirin,[11] steroids, glucocorticoids, nonsteroidal anti-inflammatory drugs (NSAIDs), methrotraxate, or combinations of these, and/or injections of a medication containing gold. Antibiotics are given for infectious arthritis. Splinting, physical therapy, and exercise are also important (though sometimes unappealing because of the associated pain). Joint replacement may be considered when damage is severe. Steroid eye drops and dilating agents are usually successful for treating uveitis. Treatment can often completely control JRA.

Some procedures (such as joint injection, open synovectomy, and arthroscopic synovectomy) are controversial. In older children, muscle relaxation, guided im-

---

11. If your child is taking aspirin for JRA and comes down with chickenpox, influenza, or another suspected viral illness, stop the aspirin and switch to an NSAID during the illness (see page 594).

agery, and meditative breathing may be adjunct therapies that help reduce pain and improve functioning.

**Prognosis.** *Polyarthritis.* Varies from poor to moderately good. *Oligoarthritis.* Generally excellent (since the disease is usually nondestructive), except for the risk of damage to eyesight (glaucoma or cataracts) from untreated uveitis. *Systemic disease.* Moderate to poor; the systemic disease is self-limiting, but the arthritis becomes chronic and destructive in half of children affected, causing disability. Most children with JRA recover and have normal lives. But JRA can sometimes lead to permanent damage to the joints and to deformities; treatment can often make a major difference in outcome.

# MENTAL RETARDATION [12]

**What is it?** A condition in which there is a slower rate of learning and a limited capacity to learn. Intelligence is below the normal range—usually defined as an IQ below 70 on standard scales. Only 11% of children in this group have IQs below 50 (making them moderately or severely retarded) or under 25 (making them profoundly retarded). The other 89% are mildly retarded and educable.[13] Most mildly retarded children develop large motor skills (sitting, crawling, standing, walking) at the appropriate age, unless they also have cerebral palsy or another motor disorder. Mild retardation may not be evident until it is clear that language is not developing well.

More severely retarded children may not walk until very late, possibly because there is some motor involvement in their condition. Parents may notice overall developmental slowness, motor disability, language disorder, and behavior disturbances early on. Children who consistently do not reach social and language milestones by the time 90% of their peers do need to be evaluated, though they won't necessarily turn out to have intellectual deficits.

**How common is it?** About 7,500,000 Americans are considered mentally retarded. An estimated 3 in 100 children have IQs below 70.

**Who is susceptible?** Preterm or low-birth-weight infants, and children with any of the risk factors listed in "causes," below. In general, boys are affected more often than girls (possibly because they are more susceptible to the fragile X syndrome).

**What causes it?** It is estimated that the cause of some 30% to 60% of cases of retardation are unknown. The major known causes in the U.S. are Down syndrome and fragile X syndrome, both chromosomal abnormalities. Other causes include: the heavy use of alcohol and possibly other drugs during pregnancy; intrauterine infection or infection during childbirth (toxoplasmosis or herpes simplex virus); exposure to lead and possibly other environmental toxins, pre- or postnatally; genetic factors (Hurler syndrome, neurofibromatosis); inborn errors of metabolism that go untreated (phenylketonuria, hypothyroidism, galactosemia); brain damage (due to trauma or lack of oxygen before or during birth); severe childhood trauma (such as near-drowning or head injury); certain childhood diseases; pre- or postnatal malnutrition or placental insufficiency. In some cases, two or more factors may combine to cause the retardation.

---

12. Though some people prefer such terms as "mentally challenged," the medical community still uses the term "mental retardation," and we use it here to be medically correct.

13. Retardation is sometimes assessed somewhat differently: Mild retardation, an IQ of 52 to 67; moderate, 36 to 51; severe, 20–35; and profound, below 20.

Sometimes what appears to be mild retardation is actually due to a lack of attention and inadequate physical and intellectual stimulation in infancy and early childhood or to a hearing or vision deficit. With adequate intervention, the IQs of these children can be brought up into the normal range.

**Related problems.** Sometimes, other neurological deficits, most commonly CP (about 1 in 10 retarded children has CP). Less common, but not unusual, are hearing loss, vision deficits, language problems, seizures, disorders of sensation and perception, malformations of the brain and other organ systems, and motor disability.

**Treatment/management.** Early intervention and training, both by professionals and by parents trained by professionals, can raise the IQs of mentally retarded children and give them a better chance for a more productive future. Often removal of causative factors (such as lead in the water) or treatment of a causative condition (such as phenylketonuria or a hearing or vision deficit) can increase IQs up to inborn potential. Improved nutrition and nutritional supplementation can also raise IQ in some cases.

**Prognosis.** With optimum education begun early, children who are educable can learn basic academic (most often, to the fourth-grade level), social, and vocational skills, and are able to function independently as adults. Many marry, have children (who, unless a genetic disorder is involved, are no more likely to be retarded than other children), and make satisfying lives for themselves. Those who are trainable can rarely learn useful reading, writing, or spelling skills. With optimal early education they can, however, learn to speak and to complete routine tasks and take care of their personal needs. As adults they can usually function well in a sheltered environment (either within their family or in a group home). Those who are subtrainable (severely and profoundly retarded) are not able to achieve this level of learning and may communicate only nonverbally; their ultimate mental age is no more than six years and they are often unable to take care of even their simplest needs. Most, however, do learn to walk, unless they have CP. Profoundly retarded individuals require constant care and supervision throughout their lives.

# MUSCULAR DYSTROPHY (DUCHENNE TYPE)

**What is it?** Duchenne-type muscular dystrophy (DMD) is the most severe form of progressive primary muscular degeneration. Though the condition, which generally affects only boys, is present at birth, symptoms don't usually appear until sometime between ages three and five. Thereafter there is rapid deterioration and most children with DMD are confined to wheelchairs by the time they're ten or twelve years old. (Other types of muscular dystrophy are much less common; they are also less severe.)

**How common is it?** About 1 in 3,000 boys is born with the condition.

**Who is susceptible?** Mostly males, who inherit the faulty gene. Occasionally, a female child develops DMD, usually because of a chromosomal aberration.

**What causes it?** X-linked inheritance, passed on from mother to son on the X chromosome. In about a third of cases there is no family history of the problem because the genetic defect is a mutation.

**Related problems.** Cardiac and nervous system involvement; musculoskeletal deformities; respiratory failure.

**Treatment/management.** Presently only supportive treatment is available, but much research is under way. One controversial study suggests that injecting immature muscle cells, called myoblasts, into the muscles of a DMD patient may improve muscle strength.

**Prognosis.** At this time, the prognosis is poor. Muscular weakness becomes progressively worse; most children with DMD do not survive their teen years. Hopefully, medical research will find a way to improve the prognosis in the future.

# PHENYLKETONURIA (PKU)

**What is it?** A metabolic disorder in which the affected individual is unable to metabolize a protein called phenylalanine. The buildup of phenylalanine in the bloodstream can interfere with brain development and cause serious retardation.

**How common is it?** 1 in 14,000 newborns in the U.S. is affected.

**Who is susceptible?** The child of parents who both carry the trait has a 1 in 4 chance of being born with PKU. The incidence is low among Finns, Ashkenazi Jews, and those of African descent.

**What causes it?** Autosomal recessive inheritance; both parents must pass on recessive genes for their child to have PKU.

**Related problems.** Without treatment, children with PKU are irritable, restless, and destructive; they may have a musty odor, dry skin or rashes, and possibly convulsions. They are usually physically well developed, and often blonder than others in their family.

**Treatment/management.** If the blood test for PKU, routinely performed shortly after birth, is positive, treatment with a diet low in phenylalanine (breast milk, cow's milk and regular cow's milk formula, meat, and the artificial sweetener aspartame are high in phenylalanine) will be instituted. The diet should, recent studies indicate, be started before three months and be continued for at least twelve years to maximize IQ. Some studies suggest that continuing the diet through the reproductive years may be particularly beneficial for women. At any rate, the diet should be resumed when a woman with PKU becomes pregnant. Blood levels of phenylalanine are monitored periodically during treatment. Researchers are trying to find a medication that can help individuals with PKU metabolize phenylalanine. Until then, careful dietary control in childhood and pregnancy is critical.

**Prognosis.** Usually, a completely normal life for those who are treated; serious retardation for those who aren't.

# SICKLE-CELL DISEASE

**What is it?** A form of anemia in which red blood cells contain hemoglobin S rather than normal hemoglobin (hemoglobin is a major component of the oxygen-carrying red blood cells). Hemoglobin S has the ability, especially when oxygen is short, to change the usually disc-shaped red blood cells to a sickle shape. These abnormal cells do a poor job of delivering oxygen to the cells throughout the body and often clump together, blocking blood vessels and causing a sickle-cell "crisis." Children with sickle-cell disease may be chronically fatigued and have difficulty breathing. Painful swelling of joints, especially in fingers and toes, is common. There are several types of sickle-cell crisis; the most common type is characterized by excruciating pain. Carriers of the sickle-cell trait (those with just one gene for sickle cell) may sometimes show mild signs of the disease.

**How common is it?** In the U.S., 1 in 100 to 300 children of African descent has sickle-cell anemia (as many as 8 to 14 in 100 carry the trait); the incidence is much lower in children from other backgrounds.

**Who is susceptible?** Primarily children of African descent, but also those of Mediterranean/Middle Eastern/Continental Indian heritage. Risk of sickle cell is 1 in 4 if both parents are carriers; however, if both parents have sickle cell, *all* their children will have the disease.

**What causes it?** Autosomal recessive inheritance: Both parents must pass on recessive genes for a child to have full-blown sickle-cell anemia. Periodic crises can be triggered by infection, stress, dehydration, and inadequate oxygen (from overexertion or high altitude).

**Related problems.** Poor growth, delayed puberty, narrow body, curved spine, and barrel chest; increased susceptibility to infection, particularly pneumococcal; eventual damage to organs denied blood during a crisis (including liver, kidneys, gall bladder); stroke.

**Treatment/management.** Folic acid and other nutritional supplementation to help control the anemia and improve growth and development; pain relievers, oxygen,

and fluids to keep the patient comfortable when a sickle-cell crisis occurs; steroids, which a recent study suggests may actually shorten a crisis; transfusions of healthy blood in a severe sickle-cell crisis; prophylactic antibiotic therapy to help prevent the development of pneumonia in young children. Pneumococcal vaccine to prevent infection is useful in some adults, but not yet effective in children. Bone marrow transplants are experimental. They do improve the child's condition, but it's not yet clear that the benefits outweigh the risks. Ultrasound evaluation may be able to predict children who are at high risk for stroke, and allow for possible preventive measures to be taken. Other experimental procedures are currently under investigation, including high-dose IV corticosteroids to relieve pain.

**Prevention.** Avoidance of factors that may reduce oxygen supply (including overexertion, cold, stress, and high altitude) may reduce the number of crises.

**Prognosis.** Fair; while some do not live past young adulthood, others reach middle age. Those with high levels of fetal hemoglobin tend to do best.

# THALASSEMIAS

**What is it?** A group of hereditary anemias, in which there is a defect in the process necessary for the production of hemoglobin (a major component of the oxygen-carrying red blood cells). The most common form, thalassemia B, can range from thalassemia minima, which has no visible symptoms but can be detected through blood and genetic testing, to the very serious Cooley's anemia. Even with serious illness, infants appear normal at birth, but gradually become listless, fussy, and pale, and begin to lose

## THE VERY-LOW-BIRTH-WEIGHT BABY AS A TODDLER

··········

The premature baby who weighed at least 3½ pounds (1,500 grams) at birth is quickly catching up developmentally with his or her chronological peers during the second year. But the very-low-birth-weight (VLBW) child, who weighed in below 3½ pounds, and especially the extremely-low-birth-weight (ELBW) child, who weighed in below 2.2 pounds (1,000 grams), may continue to lag behind peers in the toddler and preschool years. In preschool these children may be behind in the development of visual and motor skills as well as the ability to concentrate (they are often easily distracted). But parents and teachers can help nurture the development of these skills, enabling many VLBW and ELBW children to catch up later.

Though most of these children have no major impairments, a minority, most often those who weighed under 2.2 pounds at birth, do have problems. They may grow more slowly, suffer from respiratory and/or neurological problems, and be at greater risk for many conditions, from hernias to CP, from poor vision to hearing loss (early screening is therefore important). Some have mental deficits, often due to obvious neurological impairment; others are of normal intelligence but have learning disabilities and difficulty with certain kinds of tasks (involving sequencing, for example). The children who are most likely to have continuing problems and who most need intervention to improve school performance and behavior are those who are raised in a high-risk social environment (living with poverty, lack of maternal education, overcrowding, and so on) or face stressful life events. But all VLBW children can benefit from early attention to their special needs.

---

their appetites. Growth and development are slow.

**How common is it?** About 1 in 100 has the beta-thalassemia trait; not all have symptoms.

**Who is susceptible?** Most often those from Mediterranean backgrounds.

**What causes it?** Autosomal recessive inheritance; both parents must pass on a recessive gene for a child to have the trait.

**Related problems.** Bone weakness and fractures; iron overload, which can cause a variety of problems.

**Treatment/management.** Transfusions; bone marrow transplants may be warranted in severe cases; sometimes, prophylactic antibiotics to prevent infection; removal of excess iron through chelation therapy, when necessary.

**Prognosis.** Excellent for those with minor forms of the disease; children with moderate disease also do well, though puberty may be delayed. Of those with severe disease, more children are now living into their teens and twenties, though the threat of heart failure and infection are still significant.

# VISUAL IMPAIRMENT— LEGAL BLINDNESS

··········

**What is it?** An inability to see well, even with corrective lenses. See page 478 for clues to vision problems.

**Who is susceptible?** Anyone who sustains an injury to the eye or suffers from a condition (present at birth or acquired later) that can damage vision.

**What causes it?** Injury, infection, genetic disease, eye diseases (such as cataracts and glaucoma).

**Related problems.** The myriad educational and social problems related to being unable to see.

**Treatment/management.** Depends on the cause, but in all cases prevention is the best treatment. Sometimes surgery can restore partial vision. There are many modern approaches to educating those who are visually handicapped, including voice-activated computers and machines that translate print into voice. Controversial is the teaching of Braille, which has been dropping in recent years, but knowledge of which many experts insist is necessary for building a successful future.

**Prevention.** Good eye care and proper safety precautions (see page 477); prompt treatment of infection or other eye problems, such as cataracts.

**Prognosis.** Children who cannot see can, with the use of modern teaching technology, be educated and prepared for successful careers and fulfilling lives.

# PART THREE

# *The Toddler in the Family*

# CHAPTER TWENTY-FOUR

# *The Toddler as Sibling*

They can go from archenemies to best friends—and back again—in the space of a single morning; hurling insults at each other one moment, playing a companionable game of catch the next. They compete with each other, support each other, attack each other, defend each other, alternatively love, like, hate, and tolerate each other. They share the same toys, the same table, the same parent or parents, and often the same bedroom. They are siblings.

The relationship between siblings can be stormy, satisfying, or more likely, a confusing combination of the two. But when one (or both) of the siblings is a toddler, still short on social skills (including the ability to share, to compromise, to empathize, to cooperate) and long on egocentricity and possessiveness (the toddler wants center stage—and everything on it), the relationship can be more complex still.

Whether your toddler's sibling (or siblings) is older, younger, or yet-to-be-born, there will be a variety of sibling-related issues to deal with. As parents, you'll need to decide when to intervene, when to mediate, and when to turn your back and hope for the best. The following scenarios are a few of the most common that present themselves when a toddler is a sibling; use the advice as a guide to helping you deal with the hundreds of others that are sure to come along.

## WHAT YOU MAY BE CONCERNED ABOUT

### SIBLING RIVALRY

*"We want so much for our two daughters to be friends—that's why we had them so close together. But we're worried about sibling rivalry."*

Don't worry about sibling rivalry, but do expect it. It's one of those facts of life that's pretty much inevitable; it isn't so much a matter of whether, but of when and how much. Your daughters are probably the only two people in the house who *didn't* choose to live together (as, when they are older, they will probably remind you). And while they may very well grow to love each other, and even (this may be the hard part) to like each other, they may not grow to be best friends. The fact that they're related doesn't guarantee that they'll ultimately have a lot in common besides family. (And even if they do, there can still be conflict—being too much alike can pose just as much of a problem in a sibling relationship as being altogether different.)

Remember, rivalry is the natural outcome when two people compete for the same prize—in this case, the attention and love of their parents. You can help minimize the competition, and thus the rivalry, by being sure to show love and appreciation for each child the way she is (by never comparing her—positively or negatively—to her sibling), by regularly spending time alone with each child, by making sure that policies and privileges are equitable (though not necessarily precisely the same), and by not showing favoritism (the child who feels her sibling is preferred is likely not only to feel the need to fight harder for parental attention, but to fight harder with her sibling, too). No matter how fairly you treat your two offspring, however, you can't possibly eliminate all rivalry; it exists in even the best of sibling relationships. In fact, the only sure way to prevent sibling rivalry is to have just one child. (Keep in mind that there are many positive effects of sibling quibbling; see page 737.)

Your children will have a better chance of forging a good relationship without undue parental pressure or interference. Give them plenty of opportunities to play together and share outings together, but also make sure they both have some time apart—time to be alone, time to be alone with you, and time to be with their own friends. If your children end up being best friends, great. If not, that's okay, too. Don't push it. If they learn to respect and support each other,

they will have learned a lot, and they'll have established a good foundation for a sound future relationship.

# EVEN-STEVEN

*"Our son and our daughter, who are only a year and a half apart, always insist on having exactly the same amount of everything—from slices of apple to our time and attention. If one gets something the other doesn't, it's always 'not fair!'"*

Life isn't a bowl of cherries, nor is it always fair (six cherries for you and six for me). That's a lesson that small children often have difficulty swallowing, but one they eventually do need to digest. Though you can try to protect your children from some of the inevitable inequities of life, you shouldn't try to protect them from all of them.

Not only does always trying to make life completely fair for your children set them up for a let-down when they step out into the world, it's also ineffective in fending off family rivalries. Though a policy of "even-Steven" (Shauna gets a new book, so Jamal gets a new book) may seem to subdue sibling skirmishes in the short term, it's bound to step them up in the long term, intensifying the competition and comparisons instead of tempering them (as when Shauna discovers that Jamal's new book is bigger than hers.)

So what's a fair-minded parent to do?

▲ Treat your children as the individuals they are. Since no two children (not even identical twins) are exactly alike, no two children should be treated in exactly the same way. Each requires an individualized approach to affection, discipline, criticism, and praise. If you acknowledge the differences between your children (Shauna loves to look at books; Jamal loves to draw) without making comparisons or judgments, your children are more likely to come to appreciate both their individuality and being treated somewhat differently rather than always insisting on identical treatment.

▲ Give individually. Whether it's presents or hugs, what you give your children doesn't have to be appraised for parity before it's doled out. Jamal doesn't necessarily need a new pair of sneakers just because Shauna outgrew hers; Shauna doesn't necessarily need a new pair of mittens because Jamal's got lost; one child doesn't necessarily need fifteen minutes on Mom's lap just because the other child got it. Give according to the individual needs of each child at the particular moment, and tailor gifts to a child's own special interests (a storybook for Shauna, a drawing pad for Jamal), not to what you're giving a sibling.

▲ Make time alone for each child. If your children don't always have to compete for your attention, they're less likely to feel compelled to compete for everything else.

▲ Be equally loving. If there's one parental commodity that has to be handed out in equal amounts, it's love (even if you don't always feel it equally). How you choose to give that love may be different for each of your children, but how much you give shouldn't be. (No matter how you try, however, you may find that your children still complain about inequities.)

▲ Keep that yardstick handy. Even with all your efforts to eliminate the competitive atmosphere in your home, apples (and cookies and slices of pizza) will have to be pretty evenly divided until your children have gained the maturity needed not to care about who gets what. As they get older, the larger slice may be less important than who gets to stay up later or who gets to watch a favorite show.

You can, however, use some techniques to defuse these even-Steven conflicts. If your children always fight over who gets the larger piece of pie (or anything else), let them take turns choosing the first piece. (Tell them that people with good manners always take the smaller piece if they choose first—but don't expect them to show such courtesy yet.) Or let them take turns doing the dividing. Or, with older children, set aside a quota of cookies each week for each child, for example, and let them take as many as they like at snack or dessert time. When they're all gone, they're gone—until next week.

Keep in mind, however, as you try to be equitable, that you won't always succeed in making your children happy. They don't really care how many cookies or apple slices or cherries they get (they may not even finish what they insisted on); complaining about favoritism toward a sibling is a matter of principle.

## ADORING TODDLER, INTOLERANT SIBLING

*"Our two-year-old just adores his older sister. He follows her everywhere, wants to do everything she does. In the beginning, our daughter seemed to like it, but lately she's been begging me to keep him away."*

He worships the ground she walks on; she wishes he'd walk somewhere else . . . like maybe in another hemisphere. He wants to help her build her block tower, push her baby in the stroller, pour tea for her tea party; she wants him to get lost. He decides to imitate her technique in her favorite coloring book; she decides to slam him one for his efforts. It's a common sibling scenario.

Older children often find it flattering at first to be shadowed by an adoring groupie. But it isn't long before flattery turns to frustration, as they tire of having their every move tracked and imitated, of never having a moment's privacy or a second's rest, of trying to shield their space (and possessions) from curious fingers and grabby hands. It clearly isn't easy being an older sibling, particularly when your younger sibling is two years old—too old to be cute, crib-bound, and helpless, and too young to be an ideal playmate, but just the right age for being a pest.

For now, you can help by making it easier for your older child, which in turn should make the situation better for your toddler, by:

**Lending a commiserating ear.** Acknowledging that you understand and empathize with your older child's predicament—and letting her know that you're there to listen when she needs to air her sibling grievances—will help immeasurably by removing the guilt factor. Let her know that it's okay to feel angry at her little brother's annoying behavior, and that her being angry at him won't make *you* angry at her. Acknowledge your frequent frustration at his havoc wreaking, but also reinforce that it's possible to feel frustrated by or angry at someone's behavior while still loving him very much. Recount stories about her as a toddler: about the time she knocked over the bookshelf, the time she unraveled a whole roll of toilet paper into the toilet, the times she threw tantrums at the supermarket checkout. Not only will these stories be interesting for her to hear, but they'll give her a new perspective on her sibling's behavior—not to mention hope for the future.

**Protecting your older child's privacy.** Nobody who lives in a family can be guaranteed privacy whenever they want it, but everyone who lives in a family is entitled to privacy sometimes. Making sure your older child gets some uninterrupted time alone each day, while her younger sib is sleeping or kept busy by you or another adult caregiver, may make her more tolerant of him the rest of the time. Occasionally arrange a weekend play date for your toddler at a friend's home so your older child can relish having the house (and her parents) all to herself.

**Protecting your older child's possessions.** She has a right to feel that her toys will be safe from the pint-size demolition force she calls "brother." For her sake, as well as for your toddler's (many toys that are appropriate for older children can present a hazard to him), help keep her things out of his reach. Encourage her to protect her possessions by putting them away when she's finished with them. When your toddler does get his hands on her toys, don't scold (he's just doing what comes naturally), but do explain that he can't play with his sister's toys, or markers, or dollhouse figurines, without her permission (she should likewise need his permission to play with his toys). Since that message probably won't have immediate impact (although hearing it announced will make your daughter feel better), you will have to remove your toddler whenever he tries to get into his sister's belongings. Preferably move him into another room and redirect his attention with something that belongs to him. Of course, when your older child is in a sharing mood and invites her little brother to join her at play, applaud her behavior. (But be sure the playthings are toddler safe.)

**Keeping hands off the handing down.** Even if your older child has clearly outgrown a toy, let *her* be the one to decide when it's time to pass it on. Expropriating her things without her permission is certain to foster bad feelings. When she does decide to pass something on, or when she opts on her own to share her "baby" toys with her baby brother, however, be sure to acknowledge her generosity, rather than taking it for granted.

**Socializing your toddler.** It's possible that setting up play dates for your toddler and keeping him busy with someone his own size will help take some of the strain off of your older child. Of course, when the play date is at your house, be sure that she doesn't have two toddlers to contend with; arranging a play date for her too (preferably, at the other child's home) will help assure that.

**Not expecting a live-in babysitter.** Resentment is bound to build if you require your older child to entertain her little brother on a regular basis—or if you oblige her to include your toddler in play with her friends. By all means commend her when she does take on this chore, but don't expect it.

**Not expecting her to "know better."** Sometimes parents put too much of the responsibility for keeping the peace between siblings on the older child. Constantly pressuring your daughter to "give in" to her little brother because "he's just a baby" or because "you're older, you should know better" isn't fair. Just because she was born first doesn't mean her rights always have to come second.

**Playing up the age advantage.** Your daughter will probably get a kick out of playing with her little brother if she can be the boss. Encourage games in which the older sibling makes the rules and the toddler is happy to follow them; for instance "mommy doggy and puppy," "teacher and student," "mommy and baby," "doctor and patient." Of course, in such play there's always the chance that your toddler will eventually want the upper hand; see the next question.

But don't overmanage the situation. Once you've set some standards (for privacy and protection of property), let your children try to work out some of the issues on their own. Step in only when tears flow or blows fly.

# ADORING SIB, INTOLERANT TODDLER

*"Our six-year-old daughter can't get enough of her toddler sister. But the little one rejects all of her older sister's advances; she doesn't want to be babied, she just wants to be left to do her own thing. And this, of course, upsets the older child."*

Some preschool and school-age children see a younger sibling as a plaything, a real live doll all their own. But often, much to their dismay, the "doll" has a mind of its own, and plans to incorporate the toddler-doll into their play are often not well received. Nor are efforts by the older child to be a junior "parent" always acceptable. Toddlers who are struggling for independence find it difficult enough to live under the domination of adult parents and may be unwilling to accept yet another family boss.

Explain as tactfully as you can to your older daughter her younger sister's reluctance to be her plaything. Show her pictures of herself at her sister's age, and rack your memory bank for a story or two of how she wanted to be her own little person, too. Suggest that her sister might prefer the games if she were allowed to be the one in charge—the parent, the doctor, the teacher, the leader, the instigator. Also propose other activities that the two could work on together that wouldn't threaten the younger's autonomy—painting a mural on a large sheet of paper, playing with modeling clay, making a collage, building with blocks. If your older daughter is beginning to read, having her practice her skills on her younger sibling might also be an acceptable activity for both children.

And if your older child doesn't yet have a baby doll of her own, perhaps having one to care for might satisfy her parental cravings.

## SIBLINGS 101

..........

Today's toddlers are probably the most educated in history. They are exposed to art classes, dancing classes, gym classes, music classes. But among the most valuable of these classes is the "sibling preparation class," which prepares older children for the transition from only child to older child. Such classes are becoming as commonplace as childbirth preparation classes. And according to one study, these classes can make a significant difference in both how a child reacts to the new addition (less sibling rivalry was reported among those who'd taken the classes) and how the parents perceive their ability to cope with their suddenly expanded family. If at all possible, sign up your older-child-to-be before your due date.

# SIBLING SLUGFESTS

"Our two boys are two years apart. I thought that would make them close, but it seems all they do is fight."

Not only is closeness in age no bar to fighting, it may sometimes encourage it—children who are close in age, after all, tend to have more contact with each other, tend to compete more with each other, and, consequently, tend to fight more with each other. But a certain amount of conflict between siblings is almost inevitable no matter what the age difference; while some siblings fight more than others, all fight at least occasionally. And bleak though the situation may seem at times, your battling children are getting more than practice in the martial arts. They are also getting practice in conflict resolution, social skills, and learning to get along with others—valuable preparation for life in the real world.

Fighting with a sibling is a safe way to learn how to settle disputes—since a sibling stays a sibling no matter how angry one is with the other, they don't have to worry that the disputes will end the relationship. It also encourages working things through—while you can walk out on a play date (or even a friendship)

without resolving a difference, you can't walk away from a sibling, at least not for long. As tough as it may sometimes be for the parties involved, it's necessary to settle sibling spats—whether through the use of negotiation, compromise, or, as often happens, fists.

The fighting tends to be physical more often when children are younger, especially when one sibling is a toddler. A toddler, after all, doesn't yet have the capabilities for resolving conflicts verbally. Since his skills and interests are less advanced, he may also feel inadequate and impotent around the older sibling, and have the urge to lash out. (The older sibling may react with impatience and annoyance at this skill gap and also feel like lashing out.) In addition, toddlers usually don't think before they act, and their thoughtless behavior can frustrate older siblings no end (as when the little tyke walks head-on into the Lego city it took big brother all day to erect).

But while you should view the disagreements between your children as normal and natural—which they are—you can help keep the skirmishes from escalating into all-out battles with these diplomatic maneuvers:

**Don't play favorites.** Comparing your children or favoring one over the other will only increase resentment, intensify the fighting, and possibly lead to life-

## STEPPING INTO A STEPFAMILY

· · · · · · · · · ·

While most toddlers gain brothers or sisters the traditional way, an increasing number of young children today take on siblings through "family blending." But though movie and television depictions of stepfamilies (*Yours, Mine, and Ours; The Brady Bunch*) have made the blending look relatively easy (if a bit zany), it rarely is. Getting to know, and learning to get along with, new people is always a challenge; learning to live with them—at the breakfast table, in the bathroom, in the family room, in the backyard—is truly formidable.

There are certainly advantages to introducing a child into a stepfamily during the toddler years rather than later. For one, there are many more years ahead in which to adjust and hit that Brady Bunch stride. For another, younger children, for all their ritualistic behavior, are actually more adaptable than they will be later on. For yet another, the lives of toddlers are somewhat less complicated than the lives of older kids: Though they, too, have to deal with the changing family dynamics when blending takes place, they don't have to deal, as school-age children do, with the unsettling input of peers, or as teenagers do, with raging hormones.

But the changes that the blending of families can bring can take a toll on toddlers. So it's important to keep as much continuity in your toddler's life as possible as he or she struggles to adapt. Maintaining predictability in the little things—the same rituals at bedtime, bathtime, and breakfast, for example—will mean a lot to your toddler in terms of security. So will making time for just-the-two-of-you togetherness, which can help reassure that in the face of gaining a new family, he or she hasn't lost you.

No matter what you do, sibling rivalry in the stepfamily is likely to be at least as intense, and sibling spats as frequent, as in traditional homes. A toddler who becomes a sibling through family blending is likely to experience many of the same emotions (jealousy, anger, and ambivalence) and to exhibit many of the same behaviors (including regression and rebellion) as the toddler who becomes a sibling the traditional way. And all of these can be dealt with by parents in stepfamilies in much the same way as they are dealt with in traditional families. But there are special issues that arise in stepfamilies that require special handling. For help, turn to The Stepfamily Association of America (SAA), (402) 477-STEP.

---

long problems in their relationship. For the child who's not the favorite, a poor self-image and jealousy toward his sibling are the likely results; if it feels "safer" to fight with the sibling than the parent, he may even vent anger on his sibling that he truly feels toward his parents. For the child who *is* the favorite, the burden of being "the best" and having to live up to overblown parental expectations often results in a fear of failure (and ultimately, a fear of trying). No one emerges a winner.

Make sure you're not, consciously or un-, making the rivalry worse—for instance, being less tolerant of one child

because he reminds you too much of yourself, or because he's so very different from you.

**Ease competition.** Don't make comparisons between children (see page 747); comparisons promote competitiveness. Give each child what he needs in terms of time, support, love, material goods, and so on, to make your children less compelled to compete for your love and attention. And remember that treating your children fairly doesn't mean treating them exactly the same (see page 733).

**Lead the way.** Your relationship with

your spouse is a significant model for your children's interactions with each other and with others. Parents teach their children valuable lessons about how to get along with those they care about when they are, for the most part, respectful, responsive, patient, loving, and generous with each other; when they try not to pick on each other or be overly critical or demanding; when they cooperate and compromise. And don't just stop there—set a good example through your relationships with friends and extended family as well.

**Minimize stress.** Excessive stress in the home—no matter the source—can cause sparks to fly in every direction, including from sibling to sibling.

**Fight right.** No matter how much you love and respect your spouse, living together in a perpetual state of perfect harmony isn't possible. Every couple argues sometimes, and that's fine. But avoid the down-and-dirty types of domestic squabbles in front of your children. If they are daily witnesses to these, they're much more likely to handle their own disagreements in an equally nasty style. If, however, they see their parents arguing without name calling, fist banging, or door slamming, they're more likely to learn to resolve conflicts with their siblings (and others) in a mature way—at least eventually.

**Be respectful.** Do unto your children what you would have them do unto each other. Children who are treated with consideration and whose possessions and privacy are respected are more likely to extend the same courtesy to others—even occasionally to their siblings. Children who are constantly picked on and criticized, on the other hand, are liable to be critical and picky with their siblings. And children who are spanked can be expected to use physical force routinely on their siblings.

**Validate their feelings . . .** Acknowledge that it's hard to get along with someone who is *always* around, like a sibling or a parent—even if you love him or her. Assure your children that it's perfectly acceptable to disagree with your sibling, to be angry with him, even to get so mad that sometimes you feel you don't like or love him. Listen to all complaints and feelings (even if they seem overblown or irrational) with an objective and sympathetic ear. Don't discourage the verbal ("He's so stupid!") or artistic ("That picture is my bad brother!") expression of any negative emotions. When you listen without judging, your child will be relieved not only of the bad feelings but of the fear that you'll be angry at him for feeling angry at his sibling.

**. . . but not their unacceptable actions.** Make it clear that it's *not* okay to hit, bite, kick, or otherwise physically abuse a sibling (or anyone else, for that matter). Repeatedly remind your children that things usually work out better when you try to settle them with words and ideas instead of fists.

**Don't instill guilt.** Berating your child with "How could you fight with your brother?" not only won't make the angry feelings go away; it could actually intensify them.

**Identify with the combatants.** If you had a sibling you fought with frequently as a child, tell them about your experiences—especially if you now have a good relationship with that sib.

**Understand their positions.** Each child feels at a disadvantage in the sibling relationship—the elder because he senses he's expected to be the "adult" and to give in more often, while, at least in his perception, little or nothing is demanded from his younger sib; the younger because he is less coordinated, smaller, has less verbal ability, and can't compete (except by being the "baby"). Like anyone who feels at a disadvantage, they both often become frustrated, angry, and explosive in difficult situations.

What can you do? Recognize that it's not fair to expect your older child to act the adult when relating to his toddler sibling, and be sure his seniority grants him plenty of benefits as well as responsibilities (see page 734 for how to help an older child deal with a trying younger sib). And help the younger to improve his skills and express his feelings verbally ("Are you mad because Josh took your truck while you were playing with it?"). Show him that he can do better if he acts in a grown-up way ("Come, ask him to please give you back your truck").

**Set and enforce limits on behavior.** Whatever ground rules you decide on (no hitting, no biting, no pushing, no grabbing, no playing with someone else's toy without asking first), make them clear to both your children and enforce them consistently. Eventually they'll stick. Though you will have to have more stringent rules for the older child, they should nevertheless be fair and achievable. (For tips on discipline and setting limits, see page 47.)

**Don't rush in to mediate . . .** While it's important to keep an eye on your children in the midst of a dispute, don't step in unless they are about to (or have already) come to physical blows or damage to property is imminent. It's best to allow them to work on solving disagreements by themselves, when possible.

**. . . but do mediate when necessary.** Challenge your children to come up with a solution or compromise to deal with their conflict. If they can't seem to reach a resolution by themselves, try helping them reach one. If they're fighting over a particular object (a toy, the tape recorder, the television remote control), suggest a

compromise, such as taking turns with the help of a timer. Praise their achievement if a workable settlement is reached.

Should no amount of parental arbitration lead to a peaceful solution, try to deal with the situation in a very matter-of-fact way by removing the source of conflict. If there's no object involved, have the children take separate time-outs to cool off.

**Don't judge.** When stepping between dueling siblings, be careful not to assign blame (you probably won't really know for certain who's at fault, anyway), which will only increase tension. Except in the most flagrant cases, remain as impartial as possible.

**"Catch" them being good.** Don't wait for a fight to break out to turn your attention your children's way. Fighting is a tried-and-true way to get parental attention. Pay such negative behavior minimum heed (except when it turns physical). And reinforce positive sibling interactions. When your children play well together—even for a brief period— or cooperate with each other, or share, take notice and offer words of praise. Be alert to and acknowledge acts of cooperation—even if they're very infrequent.

And take heart. A history of frequent childhood fighting doesn't seem to jeopardize future friendship between siblings. Fighting siblings have just as good a chance of growing up to be friends as those with a more peaceable childhood. And if they eventually learn how to negotiate their differences verbally, their chances may even be better.

# TWO CHILDREN— TWO BEDTIMES?

*"Our daughter is four, and our son is two-and-a-half. Should our*

*daughter have a later bedtime because she's older, or should we try to get them both to sleep at the same time?"*

For most families, a single bedtime works better when children are so close in age. First of all, it's a time-saver. Between the bathing, the pajama-ing, the bedtime snacking and drinking, the toothbrushing, the cuddling, the read-ing, and the actual bedding down, bed-time rituals can be time consuming. While it may take slightly longer to bed down two children than one (especially if they don't bathe together or don't enjoy the same stories), it's definitely faster than bedding down each sepa-rately, particularly if two parents are par-ticipating. Second, rewarding an older child with the "privilege" of a later bed-time can send the message (to both chil-dren) that sleep is a punishment. It can also set the scene for unnecessary sibling rivalry ("She gets to go to bed later and spend more time with Mommy and Daddy—they must love her more"). In addition, putting both children to bed at once allows for more "adult" time in the evenings—a revitalizing tonic that all parents deserve. Finally, preschoolers put in a long day, often without the ben-efit of a nap; chances are your older daughter needs as much sleep at night as your toddler.

If you do observe a shared bedtime, make sure that each child also has some special time *sans* sibling with you every day; just because their bedtimes are lumped together doesn't mean the children should be lumped together in all they do.

Parents who often or always have to handle bedtime rituals on their own (either because they're single, or because their spouse works long hours, travels a lot, and/or isn't very involved in child care) can easily feel overwhelmed by trying to juggle two children at bedtime. But balanced against the benefit of more

time for themselves, these parents usu-ally find the hassles of a joint bedtime are worth it.

If your older child doesn't seem sleepy at the same time as your younger, consider taking them both through the bedtime routine at the same time, then allowing the elder to look at books or play quietly in bed (by the dim light of a clip-on lamp, if the two share the same room), until she's ready for some shut-eye.

Of course, when the age difference is more than a few years, two bedtimes may be necessary; a nine- or ten-year-old can't be expected to turn in at the same time as a toddler. But then, a much older child doesn't generally need as long or as complicated a bedtime ritual as a young one does—and can usually see to much of it (the bath, undressing, tooth-brushing) independently.

# *TOY SAFETY AMONG SIBLINGS*

*"Though we try to be careful, we keep finding our sixteen-month-old daughter trying to mouth some small piece from her older brother's toys; it makes us very nervous."*

If your toddler is the only (or the old-est) child, keeping her away from toys (at home, at least) that are potentially unsafe is as simple as not bringing them into your home. But if your toddler is a younger sibling, childproofing the toy box is a little more complicated. After all, you can't exactly demand that your older child give up toys that he enjoys just because they're not appropriate for your toddler—at least not if you want to avoid mutiny in the playroom.

But you can try to safeguard your toddler by taking the following steps:

▲ Enlist your older child's help. Explain to him the dangers "big-kid toys" pose to toddlers. Show him what's small enough to pose a choking threat (you can even teach him how to do a choke-tube test; see page 657), what might be broken off of a big toy and swallowed, what toys might catch his sibling's curious little fingers. Then make him a member of the "small-parts patrol," in charge of looking out for unsafe toy parts and keeping them safely stowed. Also teach him to always completely close toy bins and closets after taking toys out or putting them in. Not only will all this help keep your toddler safe, it will make your older child more responsible about caring for his belongings.

▲ Store unsafe toys out of your toddler's reach. If your toddler can go anywhere your older child can, store potentially dangerous toys where only you can reach them, and have your older child ask when he wants to use them. You can also store some of these toys in containers that are difficult for your toddler to open (your older child can always ask you for help, if necessary). If toys are stored in low cabinets, use child-safe cabinet latches (the kind usually used in kitchens) and show your older child how to open and close them (assuming he can be trusted with the contents of similarly latched kitchen cabinets). A hook-and-eye installed out of your toddler's reach may slow down access to toys stashed in a closet, but once she's figured out how to drag a chair or box over to give her height, it's no longer foolproof. A safety gate to block access to the older child's room may be helpful—but, again, only until your little one learns how to scale it.

▲ Keep unsafe toys out of sight. Toys stored on high shelves but that are visible to your toddler may tempt her to try scaling those shelves—which can itself be dangerous. Keeping the toys behind closed closet doors or in opaque bins may help discourage interest.

▲ When your older child plays with unsafe toys in the same room your tod-dler is in, try to get her involved in an engrossing activity. If your older child prefers to play in his room, that's fine, too. If he's old enough not to need super-vision, he can close the door. If not, putting up a gate can let you keep an eye on what he's doing while keeping your toddler out.

▲ Be vigilant. No matter how careful everyone in the family is about keeping potentially dangerous toys from your toddler, bite-size game playing pieces are sure to be overlooked under the sofa and tiny building set pieces are certain to be forgotten behind the bed. So always keep a close eye out for any hand-to-mouth actions on the part of your tod-dler, or for chewing motions when she hasn't been eating—especially when your older child is playing with tiny toys. And make sure you're familiar with the emergency treatment of choking inci-dents (see page 689)—just in case.

# SHORTCHANGING NUMBER TWO

*"We feel terribly guilty that we don't seem to pay as much atten-tion to our second child as we did to our first. It doesn't seem to bother him, but it bothers us a lot."*

It happens in almost every family. The birth of the first child is celebrated with festive parties, heralded with adorable an-nouncements, documented by volumes of snapshots (baby's first bath, baby's sec-ond bath, baby's third bath . . . ) and painstakingly kept journals ("Today, Baby had his first bath," "Today, Baby had his second bath," "Today, Baby had his third bath . . . "). The birth of the sec-ond child—well, it just sort of happens. It's not that it isn't eagerly anticipated and joyously received—it's just that nobody seems to have the time or energy to devote to the fanfare and the recordkeeping. And the excitement that comes with newness has worn off.

Yet, for almost every second-born (and third-, fourth-, and fifth-born), this diminished attention turns out to be a plus. Instead of growing up feeling like a second-class citizen, second-borns seem to thrive. The lack of intensely focused parental attention doesn't make him crave more, and often makes him able to do well with less.

Keep in mind, too, that different children (regardless of birth order) can require completely different amounts and applications of attention and affection and that each child's needs change over time. As long as you give your second child as much love as your first, don't deny either one needed attention, and give each some special time alone with you, you're not shortchanging either child.

## SHARING A ROOM

*"Now that our youngest is old enough for a big bed, we'd planned on moving him out of our room and into his seven-year-old brother's room. But our older son is not happy about this at all; he doesn't want to share a room with a 'baby.'"*

When you're used to living solo, two can be a crowd—especially when your new roommate is a younger sibling. But since parents can't be expected to buy a new house, rent a new apartment, or build a new addition just to satisfy a child's desire to keep his room to himself, your oldest will have to come to terms with the move. Help him by:

▲ Understanding his reluctance. Instead of dismissing his complaints with a dog-matic "Your brother's moving in, and that's that!" or sending him on a guilt trip ("It's not very nice of you not to want to share your room with your brother"), encourage your older child to air his feelings. Explain that you understand that he's upset, but that you don't have a choice about moving his brother in. If you had to "room" with a sibling as a child, share your experience with him—and talk about any mixed feelings you had. Reassure him that you'll do everything you can to protect his space and his belongings, and that he won't be expected to share everything else just because he's sharing his room.

▲ Dividing his room. Even if he can't have a room to call his own, perhaps he can have an area of his own. The use of a room divider, such as a stretch of child-safe railing (see page 624) secured to the floor, separating the two play and sleeping areas, can help your older son feel less unhappy about the impending move. So can allowing him to decorate his side of the room his way, to make it distinctly his. Also make sure that your older child will have enough space to store his toys safely out of his brother's reach (to protect not only his toys, but his brother's safety as well).

▲ Letting him have his room to himself, sometimes. Occasionally, allow your older child to play alone in the bedroom while you keep your toddler occupied in another room. Or set up play dates for the younger child outside of the house on days when the older one's entertaining a friend at home, and vice versa.

▲ Playing up the benefits of sharing—having company at night, having someone to talk to as you fall asleep, having someone who can eventually share in keeping the room neat. But do this only if the sharing will go on for several years more—otherwise, a move to a house with separate bedrooms may lead to another rebellion: "I don't want to sleep alone!"

# A TOO-GOOD-TO-BE-TRUE SIB

*"Ever since we brought home our new son three weeks ago, our toddler has been incredibly patient and good. Does this mean that she's suppressing her true feelings, and that we're in for trouble up the road?"*

Since every child is unique, every child's reaction to a new sibling is likely to be unique, too. While the stereotypical toddler responses to a new baby—regression, jealousy, resentment toward her new sibling and/or her parents—are normal, so is the less-typical response your toddler is having.

Just because your daughter seems to be adapting well to the new addition doesn't necessarily mean she's internalizing anger that will later boil over. It's possible that she's enjoying her new role as older sibling, especially likely if you've been including her in the new baby's care. And it's also possible that she hasn't felt slighted by the baby, especially likely if you've been doing a good job of showing her that your love for her hasn't changed. Be prepared, however, for a possible change of heart when the baby is old enough to become a pest (see page 734).

But there's also the possibility that your concerns are well founded, and that your toddler *is* suppressing her true feelings. Some young children fear that expressing their negative feelings toward a new sibling will jeopardize their parents' love for them; others are natural bottle-uppers who routinely need encouragement to uncap their feelings. To make sure your older child gets a chance to air anything that might be bothering her, be available for impromptu discussion. If she doesn't initiate, bring up the issue yourself: "How does it feel to be a big sister? What do you like about having a baby in the house? What don't you

like?" When the baby spends the whole afternoon crying or when the diapers and nursing seem endless, be honest and open about your own ambivalent feelings: "I love your baby brother, but sometimes I get really tired of listening to his crying" or "Babies need so much taking care of!" If your toddler expresses some not-so-nice sentiments, tell her that you understand how she feels, and that no one is going to get mad at her for having or sharing mad or sad feelings. Be equally patient and understanding if she begins regressing (see next question)—either early on or later as a delayed reaction to the baby's intrusion into her life. Toileting accidents, a return to baby talk, clamoring for the breast or bottle, renewed thumb sucking, are all possible and very normal responses in an older child who feels she's lost her special place in her parents' hearts.

Sometimes an older sibling uses "perfect" behavior as a means of getting the attention she craves from her parents—attention she once had all to herself, but now has to compete for. The greatest risk in such a situation is that the delighted parents begin heaping on responsibilities ("Please fetch me a diaper" . . . "Please play by yourself while I feed the baby". . . "Stand next to the bed so the baby doesn't roll off") long before the child is developmentally or emotionally ready to handle them. When the child is unable to meet the expectations, she loses parental approval. Not only does her self-esteem take a beating in the process, but her feelings of resentment toward the new baby inevitably build.

Don't wait for your older child to become a squeaky wheel before you break out the oil. Even if she doesn't seem to be craving attention, make sure she gets plenty of it, and often. Spend time with her without the baby even if she doesn't ask for it, commend her generous nature and good behavior instead of taking it for granted or coming to expect it, and let her know that her place in your hearts is special and no one else can ever fill it.

# A BACK-SLIDING SIB

*"Our almost-three-year-old son has been clingy and cranky since his baby sister was born. He wants to nurse and to wear diapers and acts more like a baby than the baby does!"*

For a toddler who has enjoyed center stage his entire life, the arrival of a major scene-stealer is often upsetting—and understandably so. Also understandable is the frequent result: a wide range of behavioral issues, including regression (often in toileting, language, behavior); open or covert resentment (toward the new arrival, his parents, or both); sleeping disturbances, eating struggles, stepped-up tantrums, and negativity.

That your toddler's reactions are normal doesn't make them any easier to take; just as understandable as his clinginess and crankiness is the difficult time you have dealing with them. But it's now—when he's hardest to take—that your son needs you the most. You can help him weather the transition from only child to older child if you:

**Let him be your baby.** Let him cling, let him cry, let him curl up in your lap, let him suck his thumb and carry around his blanket, and if he asks, let him drink from the baby's bottle or, if you feel comfortable doing so, take a nip from your breast (he'll soon tire of the effort involved in getting a drink that way, or may not even remember how to suckle). If he wants to drink from a bottle, let him—but fill it only with water. If he complains that the baby gets to drink milk, explain that when she has a lot of teeth she won't get milk in a bottle, either.

Don't criticize him for acting like a baby, but let him know that you and he both know he's only pretending: "It looks like you're having fun playing baby." Denying him his right to take a few steps backward or telling him he has to always act like a big boy will only prolong his second babyhood. Instead, be sensitive to his feelings: "I can understand why you want to be a baby again—after all, it seems like everybody is busy with the baby." Reassure him that he'll always be your "baby," even when he's a much bigger boy, and that he doesn't have to act like a baby for you to want to cuddle him and love him.

**Cheer his grown-up behavior.** Whenever he demonstrates maturity, be quick to acknowledge it. Take the occasional opportunity to point out the benefits of being the big brother, such as being able to eat real food (and getting to help pick the menu), play with fun toys, have play dates, and go on the swings. When you're eating ice cream cones together, remind him: "Poor Amy, she can't have an ice cream cone; she's just a baby." When he's in line for a pony ride at the zoo, point out: "You're lucky you're a big boy; you can ride on the pony." Let him know how great you think it is that he can get his shoes on by himself, put puzzles together, and use a spoon and fork.

**Allow him to vent any resentment.** Letting your toddler know that you understand if he's angry at the baby and giving him a chance to vent that anger will help it to dissipate faster. If he says, "I want to give that baby back," don't contradict him with, "I know you don't really mean that. You love our baby." Instead, acknowledge his feelings, and encourage him to talk about them. Say, "It's okay to be angry. Sometimes I get angry, too. But it helps if I talk about it." Give him some crayons and paper and urge him to draw a picture of how he feels if the words aren't enough.

If you suspect your toddler has hostile feelings that he isn't able to vent verbally (a clue: pinches, squeezes, or hugs that are always a little too forceful), provide other safe ways he can release them (see page 171).

**Give him the attention he's crying for.** One of the prime reasons a toddler wants to be a baby again is because he sees the extra attention that babies get. Providing that attention without his having to cry or whine or tantrum for it may reduce his need to act the baby. Read your toddler a story while nursing your baby; calm your colicky infant in a baby carrier while taking your toddler to the park; help your toddler construct a block tower with one hand while rocking your newborn in an infant seat with the other. If you're in a two-adult household, take turns taking care of the baby and spending time alone with your toddler—time that's devoted entirely to him. When there's only one parent around to care for your twosome, divide your attention to conquer that competitive feeling—call on a friend, relative, or baby-sitter to mind the baby while you focus on your older child. Remember, an infant's needs are much simpler to satisfy than a toddler's, yet most parents are more likely to neglect the latter's than the former's. Be especially attentive to your older child when visitors come to see the new baby. Let him open the presents that are brought for the baby (and even "test" them), let him take the visitor on a tour of the nursery, and make sure that as many pictures are snapped of him as of the baby.

**Get him involved.** Sometimes, toddlers feel less left out and more grown-up if they're invited to lend a hand in the care of a new sibling. Give your toddler "jobs" that he's good at—for instance, entertaining the baby (but only if baby's in a good mood; if your toddler finds he's a flop at cheering a colicky baby it could be a blow to his ego); folding diapers or tiny baby outfits; handing you diapers and wipes at changing time; helping you wash tiny toes at bathtime. Solicit his opinion on baby issues: "Do you think the baby's hungry now?" "Do you think the baby needs a nap?" When the baby coos, ask your toddler for a translation: "What do you think she said?"

A couple of caveats, however. One, never push a toddler to be your "helper" if he's not interested in the position; ask if he'd like to help, but never insist. Two, never give your toddler more responsibility than he can handle, particularly if doing so could put his infant sibling in danger (see page 748)—and never leave the two alone together, not even for a few seconds.

**Minimize other changes in his life.** Becoming a big sibling is unsettling enough without adding any other upheaval. So try to keep your toddler's schedule and rituals as comfortingly the same as possible. If you normally read four stories to him before bed, don't cut back to two so you can bathe the baby; if you've always cuddled for five minutes before getting him dressed in the morning, don't skip or skimp on the hugs now.

# THE EAGER LITTLE HELPER

*"Our two-and-a-half-year-old daughter wants to hold the new baby and help take care of him. But I'm afraid that she might drop him or hurt him."*

New babies, while far from china-doll fragile, do need to be handled with care—care that a young child isn't capable of providing. Toddler hands are too small and not yet coordinated enough to master the tricky physical feat of supporting a newborn's heavy head and underdeveloped neck muscles. Toddlers also have notoriously short attention spans and minds that tend to wander; while the proud sister may be thrilled to hold her sibling one minute, she may become bored and distracted the next and unceremoniously dump the infant on the edge of the couch as she makes a beeline for the blocks.

At the same time, the feelings of older siblings need to be handled with care. Denying your toddler opportunities to bond with her sibling—especially when it's clear she's craving that closeness—will make her feel rejected, left out, and unappreciated, setting the scene for resentment. While your toddler shouldn't pick up or carry the baby around, you can let her have closely supervised cuddles. Sit her down in a comfortable armchair, then position the baby on her lap, a pillow under the arm supporting his head. Stay within arm's reach, so if your toddler suddenly loses interest or the baby starts wiggling, you'll be there to relieve her of her delicate charge.

# DIFFERENCES IN SIBLINGS

*"Our first child was a perfect baby and a near-perfect toddler—she never gave us any trouble. Our second has been different from the day she was born. She's a full-fledged terrible-two now, and has several tantrums a day. It's so hard not to favor our oldest."*

It's always hard to avoid favoring an "easy" child over a "difficult" one—but it's especially hard when the easy one came first, setting parental expectations at hard-to-reach levels, providing the more difficult child with an act that she can't possibly follow.

But while showing favoritism for the easier child is a natural reaction, it's one you'll need to make an effort to resist. Being consistently "second best" in her parent's eyes is likely to make a difficult child more difficult (while being consistently favored and favorably compared is likely to put too much pressure on the easy child to maintain the "straight-A" behavior she's known for). Instead, appreciate your more difficult child for the special person that she is, look for and cultivate her positive traits (everyone has them), and help her deal with her intense personality (see page 336 for tips on coping with toddler temperaments). Your toddler's stubbornness and fiery temper may seem to make her "difficult" now, but properly channeled, strength of will can serve her well later in life. Likewise, the boundless energy that makes her hard to handle today can make her fiercely successful tomorrow.

Instead of bemoaning the differences between your children, learn to respect them. Look for and nurture traits in each that are admirable and distinct.

It's also possible that your second child's difficult behavior is intensified by your response to it. Sometimes, parents unconsciously try to get the younger to conform to the older child's pattern of behavior. Accept your younger child's inborn temperament—appreciate her special personality—and you may find her behavior improving with your attitude.

Though some children tend to be more "difficult" than others, all children, to some extent, go through more and less lovable stages; the easygoing kindergartner can turn into an obstinate third-grader, while the tantrum-tossing two-year-old can grow into a piece-of-cake preschooler. These shifts can easily shift parental feelings of favoritism, too. Keep in mind that it's possible to dislike a child's behavior without compromising your love for the child—and you'll find it easier to love your children even when the going gets tough.

---

## PLAY IT SAFE

..........

E ven the most loving toddler can injure an infant—sometimes just with over-exuberant hugs. So never leave a toddler or a preschooler under five alone with an infant, not even for just a moment. Never allow a young child to rock the cradle unsupervised (he or she might well rock too enthusiastically) or pick up the baby without an adult standing close by.

---

Remember, too, that though it's nearly impossible to love two people in exactly the same way, it is possible to love them equally in different ways. The next time you're tempted to say, "I wish you were more like your sister," bite your tongue, take a moment to think about all the things that make you love your little ball of fire, and give her a hug instead.

# ATTENTION SEEKING BEHAVIOR

*"My two-and-a-half-year-old son has been difficult and contrary since his sister was born six weeks ago. He climbs on me when I'm nursing the baby, and is always trying to get my attention. I have so little time for him that I feel guilty. What can I do?"*

F irst of all, stop being so hard on yourself. You're doing the best you can do, and that's all that a parent can do.

Second of all, you can recognize that your toddler's behavior is not only extremely common but completely normal. It's a manifestation of sibling rivalry, which takes up residence in virtually every house with more than one child.

Third of all, try some of the following:

**Include your toddler at nursing time.** Nursing will be less jealousy provoking for your toddler if there's something special in it for him. Nurse on the couch while reading him a story or listening to (and singing along with) his favorite tapes; nurse on the floor while you help him race cars or complete a puzzle; nurse on his bed while he takes your temperature with his toy doctor's kit; nurse at the table while he eats a snack. Put a pillow under the baby so that you can hold her with one arm and use the other to give your toddler a squeeze or a back rub. (Being at your breast is quality time in and of itself for your infant; but so that there's something special in it for her, too, offer her a smile, a kiss, a coo, or a nuzzle now and then as you nurse and play.)

**Set aside "private time."** Even if it's just half an hour, try to make some time to spend with each child alone. Instead of rushing through chores during baby's naptime (tempting as that may be), spend some of it focusing your entire attention on your toddler. Bake together, read together, sort shapes together, color together—or just lie down and read or talk and snuggle together. When your toddler's napping (if he still does) or is otherwise occupied—by himself or with a play date—spend some quality time with your youngest, cuddling and exchanging coos. When another adult is around (accept offers of help from friends and family, if necessary), take turns spending time alone with each of the children. Or hire a neighborhood teenager to allow you some time alone with each child.

**Spend time as a threesome.** Push your toddler on a swing at the playground while the baby takes in fascinating sights and sounds from the carriage. Put baby in an infant seat on the floor so she can watch you and your toddler roll a big, brightly colored ball back and forth. Build up your son's ego and his brotherly instincts by putting him in charge of singing, dancing, making silly faces, and otherwise amusing his little sister (but *always* under your close supervision).

**Consider an outside life for your toddler.** If he hasn't begun preschool yet, now might be a good time to consider enrolling him for a few mornings or afternoons a week—not just so that you'll have more time alone with the baby, but so that he'll have some time *without* the baby.

# DECORATING DILEMMA

*"We have a two-and-a-half-year-old daughter and are expecting our second child in a few months. We can't decide whether it would be better for our older daughter to move into the third bedroom, which we'd redecorate for her, or to stay where she is, in which case we'd make the other room into a second nursery."*

Since you probably don't have a crystal ball, there's no predicting how your toddler will respond to either option. If you move her, she may love the idea of a new room—or she may feel that the baby pushed her out of her old room. If she stays in her room, she may feel comforted by being in familiar surroundings—or she may be envious

because the baby is getting all the new goodies.

If your toddler is fairly true to the eccentricities of her age group, chances are pretty good that she'll be happier staying in her own room. Two-year-olds tend to favor the status quo over change; they derive security from sameness and ritual, particularly in times of stress. Even major redecorations of her own room could be unsettling to your toddler now. Being surrounded by her old bed and her old drapes and her old bedspread when the new baby arrives is probably most likely to bring her comfort.

On the other hand, given the unpredictability of toddlers, there's also the possibility that yours may actually love having a new room, a new bed, new curtains, and new pictures on the wall. Your best bet (short of a crystal ball) may be to ask her how she feels about the issue: "Where do you think we should put the baby when it comes? Would you like it to go in the baby room, where you sleep now? Then we could make a special big girl room for you in the other bedroom. Would you like that? Or would you like to stay in the room you're in now and give the other room to the baby?" Helping to make the decision will give her a sense of control over the situation, which will help her in dealing with the upheaval that is to come.

Whatever her decision, involve your toddler in the changes that are to be made. While you'll need to pick out the big-ticket items, asking for her input in the selection of sheets, blankets, lamps, wall decorations, stuffed animals, and other accessories for the third bedroom[1] (whether she or the baby will occupy it) will make her feel important—and feeling important will help her feel less

---

1. It's always wise not to give a toddler open-ended choices; pick out acceptable items in advance, then ask her to choose: "Do you think the baby would like the teddy bear sheets or the ones with the ducks?"

threatened. If she's chosen to stay in her old room, have her pick out a few new things to help spruce it up without changing it too much (a new comforter or set of sheets, a new doll or stuffed friend, a new night light, a new rug, a new picture).

Be aware, however, that despite all of your efforts and good intentions, your toddler may still feel resentful of the little bundle in Mommy's tummy that's causing all the excitement. She may also decide to change her mind about which room she wants once the bundle is unwrapped at home. At that point, you'll just have to remind her that she chose her own room and that's where she'll have to stay. A lot of extra support and attention (rather than a chorus of "You made your bed—you lie in it") will help her learn to live with her decision.

# CHAPTER TWENTY-FIVE

# Parenting the Toddler

From the first days after you bring your new baby home from the hospital to the last days before you ship your nearly grown child off to college or another career step, every phase of parenting presents its challenges. Yet there are some phases that, typically, present more challenges than others. For many parents, toddlerhood is one of them.

But while parenting a toddler isn't always easy, it can be one of life's most fulfilling experiences. Precisely what can make toddlers so infuriating can also make them so incomparably cute; what can make them so exasperating can make them so endearing; what can make them so "terrible" can make them so terrific.

## WHAT YOU MAY BE CONCERNED ABOUT

### YOUR ANGER

*"Today, my daughter was having a really bad tantrum and I was having a really bad day, and I completely lost my temper. I feel so guilty."*

Everybody's entitled to blow it sometimes, parents of toddlers more than most. Dealing with toddlers can be ex-
tremely difficult; their irrationality and unreasonableness can often push the best of parents to the brink and, sometimes, even over it. Having lost your temper on a particularly bad day is not only understandable, it's forgivable. Feeling guilty about it not only won't help the situation, it could actually aggravate it by making you feel angrier ("That child makes me feel like such a lousy parent!"). So forgive yourself, but don't stop there. Apologize to your toddler for

your outburst. Tell her, "I was very angry, and I lost my temper. I'm sorry that I yelled at you." If you hit her during the outburst, apologize for that, too: "I'm sorry I hit you. That was wrong." Let her know that your show of anger doesn't mean you don't love her. Make sure she understands that it was what she did—and not her—that you disliked. If it was your mood, and not your toddler's behavior, that made you lose it, explain that: "I was feeling bad so I yelled at you. I'm sorry."

Don't go on and on about how sorry you are or what a bad parent you are, or plead dramatically for forgiveness—all of which may frighten your toddler more than the initial outburst. And don't overcompensate for your slipup by being overindulgent or lax about house rules for the rest of the day. Instead, give your toddler a loving hug and move on quickly to an activity that's fun for both of you.

For tips that may help you control your temper more effectively in the future, even on a really bad day, see page 754. For tips on how to deal with the urge to hit your child, see below.

## OUT-OF-CONTROL HITTING

*"I know I shouldn't hit my son, but when I lose my temper I can't seem to help myself. I don't know what to do."*

Frequently lashing out at a child in anger is a danger sign. Though you may not have seriously hurt your child yet, the potential for physical or emotional damage is there. Now, before your angry outbursts lead to something more serious, is the time to get some professional help. Call your local child-abuse hotline (check your telephone directory for the number) or speak to your clergyperson, to your child's doctor or your own, or to another helping professional, such as a psychologist or family counselor. If alcohol abuse or drug use is contributing to your lack of control, get help in overcoming that problem, too; a substance abuser can't be an effective parent.

If your spouse shows violent tendencies, he or she also needs help from a professional. Don't hesitate to call for such help—before these tendencies get out of hand.

## YOUR DEPRESSION

*"Sometimes, when I'm feeling down in the dumps, I have a really hard time being cheerful for my toddler. I worry how my mood affects her."*

Even the most lighthearted among us can't put on a happy face all the time. And when you're feeling down you don't need to add to your misery by feeling guilty about it. Not only is it okay for your child to know that you feel down once in a while, it's important that she know. Children whose parents always hide their sad feelings can grow up thinking that they're supposed to be happy all the time—an unattainable state of being. Or that if you're sad, you need to hide your feelings. It's healthier for children to grow up knowing that life has its ups and downs and that it's okay to be sad sometimes and good to share your sad feelings with others, even to ask for help ("I bet a hug from you will make me feel better").

While it's okay to let your toddler know how you're feeling, it's not fair to dump your feelings in her lap. A toddler can handle "I'm feeling a little sad today" once in a while, but she shouldn't

# WALK A YARD IN YOUR TODDLER'S SHOES

• • • • • • • • • •

How does it feel to be so small when everyone else is so big? To have a vocabulary that always falls short of expressing your thoughts, needs, and feelings? To have so little control over what you eat, what you wear, when you sleep—over everything? How does it feel to be a toddler?

The next time you find yourself be-

wildered—or annoyed—by something your toddler does, take a moment to step into his or her sneakers. Try to imagine what your child may be feeling, and you may be able to face those confounding or irritating moments with more wisdom, more patience, more understanding, and more effective action.

have to listen to it regularly. Nor should she be burdened with parental problems ("Daddy lost his job. What are we going to do?") or feel responsible for your sadness (let her know that if you're sad, it's not because you're unhappy with her) or for making you feel better (if that hug from her *isn't* going to cheer you up, don't ask for it).

Though an occasional down day is normal, frequent down days can have a negative effect on your toddler as well as on you—and your performance as a parent. To help minimize depression:

**Figure out why you're blue.** Everyone feels down in the dumps once in a while. But depression that comes often, hampers normal functioning, or interferes with relationships needs to be addressed. Try to figure out what's getting you down (for example: not having talked to another adult in weeks, not feeling valuable, or being bored because you're not holding a "real" job; inadequate time with your toddler or your spouse, or for yourself because you are working outside the home). Once you've identified the source, try to do something about it. If your depression seems unrelated to your life, a biochemical cause may be responsible; see your doctor.

**Find an empathetic ear.** Or several ears—your spouse's, a friend's, a rela-

tive's, a therapist's, a clergyperson's, the many ears of a parent support group—and start talking. Often, just unbottling what's bothering you can help you to overcome it. If you don't have some communication time built into your day, add it now. Have dinner and conversation with your spouse after your toddler's in bed (or, if you can't wait that late to eat, just lie in bed and talk). If you're a single parent or your spouse travels a lot or works long hours, bridge the communication gap by spending ten or fifteen minutes a day on the phone with a good friend or a relative you're close with, and when you can manage it (even once in a while can help), meet with a friend for lunch, dinner, or tea.

**Cheer up with your toddler.** Even a toddler who is part of the problem (destructiveness or tantrums are driving you to despair) can become part of the solution. Go somewhere fun with your toddler—the zoo, the children's museum, the playground. Ideally, go with another parent-child duo so you will have some adult companionship, too.

**Cheer up without your toddler.** Whatever it is that gives you a lift, indulge yourself—do it, enjoy it, and don't feel guilty about it. Get a baby-sitter (or exchange-sit with another parent; see page 808) and head for the tennis courts,

# KEEPING YOUR COOL

· · · · · · · · · ·

Nobody is cool, calm, and collected all of the time—particularly when there's a toddler in the house. But since frequent parental tantrums are not good for you or your toddler, it's a good idea to try these simple strategies to help minimize the possibility of such explosions:

**Steer away from stress on "danger" days.** Blow-ups are much more likely on days when your toddler is whiny, overtired, cranky; when you've got problems at work; when you've had a fight with your spouse, your mother, your best friend; when you're experiencing PMS; when the washing machine's given out in the middle of a load and the repair person can't make it until next week. When you've had "one of those days," try to avoid activities that are likely to add to the stress (a trip to the shoe store, for example). Instead, take time out for an activity or outing that promises to be relaxing for both you and your little one (a trip to the park or watching a video with your feet up).

**Choose your issues carefully.** Instead of squaring off with your toddler over every question, save the showdowns for really important matters. As your toddler comes to recognize the innate fairness of this policy (grown-ups don't *always* get their way), he or she will feel less compelled to argue every point. This will reduce blow-ups on both sides and make it easier for you to hold your ground when necessary. (For more on discipline and limit setting see pages 119 and 47.)

**Take a time-out.** When you feel you're about to boil over, step away from the situation for a few minutes. Count to ten (or a hundred, if you need to), take a couple of deep breaths (or use the breathing exercises you learned in childbirth classes), do a meditation, think about something pleasant, repeat over and over to yourself a phrase you find comforting (such as "I am calm and serene")—until you've stopped simmering. Do not, however, leave your toddler alone while you regain your composure.

**Mind your words.** There's nothing wrong with being angry; anger is a natural emotion. But knowing how to express anger without inflicting physical or emotional pain doesn't always come naturally. Instead of automatically exploding when your toddler's doing, or has done, something that makes you angry, train yourself to express your feelings rationally, using words that explain how you feel but aren't hurtful. Instead of saying, "You're so bad—you never listen to me!" say, "When you don't listen to me, I get so angry I feel like screaming."

**Let it out.** If you're so angry you want to strike out, move away from your child immediately and find a less vulnerable target for your aggressive feelings—punch a pillow (but not so violently that you frighten your toddler), jog in place, do a set of jumping jacks, take a few race-walk laps around the room. Explain to your toddler, "I'm really angry at you right now for doing that. But I think I'll walk around the living room two times so I won't feel so angry." Don't express your anger in ways you don't want your toddler to imitate—slamming doors, throwing dishes, or punching walls, for instance. And, again, don't leave your toddler alone.

**Put it in writing.** Keep a notebook handy, and whenever you feel on the verge of losing control, set your angry feelings down on paper. Don't mince words; get them all out

the health club, a dance class, the hiking trails, a ball game, the movies, a restaurant, the beauty salon. Skip the stress of cooking dinner, and order in pizza and salad. Forget the vacuuming;

put your feet up and watch a video.

**Unwind with your toddler.** Spending quiet, quality time together can be very therapeutic for both of you. Try relaxing

of your system. You'll be amazed at the therapeutic power of pen and paper.

**Settle it with music.** Music, too, can be therapeutic—for both adults and children. A favorite tape or CD can help soothe the beast in both of you.

**Embrace.** Not the moment, but your child. Often, hug therapy can magically melt away feelings of anger and effectively stifle the need to lash out. For best results, hug firmly, enveloping your toddler in your arms, while making eye contact. But don't try hug therapy on a toddler who doesn't like to be held; that will only further frustrate and infuriate both of you.

**Don't lose perspective.** Keep handy a photo of your toddler at a particularly sweet moment, and reach for it whenever he or she has done something to provoke your wrath. Or, when a tantrum or other provocative behavior is in progress, close your eyes for a moment and summon up a memory of your toddler at his or her best—offering you a bite of ice cream, smiling ear-to-ear from the top of the slide, "helping" you fold laundry, or angelically asleep.

**Find a shoulder to cry on.** If you're so angry with your toddler that nothing seems to help, call a friend or relative who's a good listener and unload your angst. Do this when your child's napping or out with someone else.

**Don't be a martyr.** Parents who never take the time to be good to themselves have a much harder time being good to their children. When parenthood turns to martyrdom, resentment and hostility build, often resulting in parental loss of control. So make sure you get your share of quality time, too (see page 764).

**Track your blow-ups.** Knowing what prompts a loss of temper can often help you control it. If you think you've been angry too often, try keeping a written record. Once you've regained your composure after an incident, make note of when it occurred; the triggering factors (a specific issue, your mood, your child's mood, a missed meal or not enough sleep for either or both of you, and so on); what your child did; what you did; and how the situation was ultimately resolved. After several such events, read over your notes and try to evaluate what happened as impartially as possible. What did you do right? What did you do wrong? And what might you have done better? If there is a pattern to the outbursts (do they seem to come at the end of the day, when you're both hungry and tired, for example?) that could give you a clue to prevention (a snack and a relaxing activity at the end of the day, for instance, before tempers start flaring). Could there be underlying emotional feelings triggering your outbursts? Are you angry about having to do double-duty—working hard at home and on the job? Or about being "stuck at home" when you'd rather be at work? Are you angry at yourself or someone else, and taking it out on the most convenient and defenseless target, your toddler? Have you set too many limits or provided too many opportunities for your toddler to get into trouble? Have you been "blue" or depressed?

Based on what your analysis turns up, take steps to remedy the situation. If you're angry about giving up your career for your toddler, for example, start easing back into it with part-time or consulting work; see page 768. If you've set so many limits that your toddler can't help but get into trouble, loosen up; see page 123. If you can't seem to figure out the roots of your anger or how to root it out, talk to your child's doctor or your own, your clergyperson, or a therapist (but don't discuss it in front of your toddler). You may benefit from professional help.

together on the front lawn and watching the clouds pass or the stars twinkle in the sky, lying down together on your bed and listening to soothing music, baking cookies together, exercising together, even taking a bath together (wear a bathing suit if you're uncomfortable bathing nude with her)—whatever you find relaxes you. And don't forget the best therapy of all: a loving hug.

**Unwind without your toddler.** Slowing the pace for a while—with a dinner out with your spouse or best friend, a leisurely hot bath, twenty minutes of yoga, a brief meditation, or a relaxation exercise—can often lift the veil of depression.

**Take care of yourself.** What's good for the body is also good for the mind; good health habits can promote good mental health. Make sure that you get enough sleep, eat regularly and correctly (besides following Best-Odds nutrition principles, keep in mind that too much sugar seems to contribute to moodiness in some people); don't abuse alcohol (one or two drinks a day are fine for some people, but for others, that same quantity can lead to depression; more than one or two drinks daily is too much for anyone[1]); get plenty of exercise (the endorphins released during a workout actually do generate an exercise-induced "high"; see page 771 for tips on fitting exercise into your hectic schedule).

**Have a good cry.** One way to shake the blues is to cry them out; studies show that crying can help to improve mood by ridding the body of depression-triggering chemicals, which exit with the tears. So let them flow. When it's possible, do your crying when your toddler is sleeping or out of the house. When it's not, don't worry—occasionally seeing you cry won't be harmful to her; see the next question for more on crying in front of your toddler.

**Have a good laugh.** Psychologists have found that smiling and laughing, even if forced, can lift a person's mood. Rent a funny video, watch a silly situation comedy, smile at your toddler frequently during the day. It will do you both good.

---

1. If you find that you can't stop at one or two drinks, you should seek help from a qualified substance abuse counselor.

**Get help if you need it.** If your slumps come often or the tips above don't help you out of them, if your feelings of sadness interfere with your functioning (either as a parent or a person), and/or if your depression is accompanied by sleeplessness, lack of appetite, loss of interest in yourself and your family, feelings of hopelessness or helplessness, thoughts of hurting yourself, and/or lack of control, get professional help *promptly*—for your sake, as well as for your child's sake. Moods are contagious; if you're depressed, your child could become depressed, too, which could result in growth, behavior, sleep, and other physical and emotional problems.

## CRYING IN FRONT OF YOUR TODDLER

*"My father died recently, and when I was reading a story to my daughter last night, something in it made me think of him—and I started crying. Is that a terrible thing for a parent to let a child see? Could I have traumatized her?"*

Letting your child see that you have emotions—sad as well as happy— and that you're not afraid to express them is not terrible or traumatizing but extremely beneficial. Children who grow up thinking that feelings are something that should be kept under lock and key, even around those they love, can become emotionally handicapped.

But seeing the tears start flowing for no apparent reason can be confusing, so give her a simple explanation: "I felt sad for a minute because I was thinking of my daddy; I miss him, so I started to cry. But I feel better now. And giving you a hug will make me feel even better. Then we can finish reading this book together."

## ONE-ON-ONE FOR FUN

**• • • • • • • • • •**

Family togetherness is terrific, true. But there's also something to be said for one-on-one fun. No matter how big or how small your family is, all members will benefit from some "one-parent, one-child-at-a-time" time. Try to schedule some each week, rotating the partners if there is more than one parent and/or more than one child.

Possible one-on-one adventures include such kid favorites as breakfast at the local pancake house, lunch or dinner at the pizzeria, an afternoon at the pool, a movie and an ice cream cone, and a science or art project at home. Consider, too, some one-on-one sharing of a favorite activity of yours, such as gardening or bird watching.

However, if you find yourself being swept away by your emotions, if weeping turns to wailing, if you're sad a great deal of the time, or if your toddler seems frightened by your behavior, get help dealing with your grief.

## PARENTAL DISAGREEMENT

*"My husband and I don't fight a lot, but we do fight, sometimes in front of our son. I know it's healthy to work out disagreements, but is it something we ought to be doing in front of him?"*

It depends how you fight and how often you're doing it. If your arguments are infrequent and are models of correct conflict resolution—that is, you treat each other and each other's ideas with respect; you give and take (for example, by listening to each other's opinions and gripes without interrupting); you don't resort to name calling, destructive criticism, nagging, humiliation, taunting, or violence; and you practice the art of compromise—then you're doing both your marriage and your toddler a favor. If you get across the notion to your toddler that partners can disagree (even when they care about each other), and

that disagreements can be a constructive and positive force in a relationship, you will have transmitted an invaluable life lesson. Keep all of your disagreements behind closed doors, and your toddler could grow up with unrealistic expectations of what relationships are about.

To be sure that your disagreements remain constructive, observe the following rules: One, make sure that the occasional squabble doesn't turn into constant bickering. Two, don't argue in front of your toddler about subjects that might make him feel insecure, uncomfortable, or unloved (his behavior, for instance, or his beloved grandfather's smoking, or marriage or financial problems). Three, avoid arguments that are clearly destructive and negative; hysterical voices, slammed doors, and banged fists that lead to hurt feelings not only chip away at a marriage but at your child's sense of security. And four, never forget the most important part of an argument: Always kiss and make up to wrap up your arguments, making it clear that even when you argue, you still love each other.

## SHARING THE LOAD

*"Both my husband and I work outside the home, but it seems like I*

*end up doing most of the child care and housework anyway. The load I carry makes me feel resentful and put-upon, yet I can't figure out how to get him to pitch in and do his share."*

Today's fathers do a lot more around the house than their fathers did. They've made tremendous strides in such traditionally female-dominated areas as child care, cooking, and cleaning (handling the diaper, the spatula, the dust rag, the needle and thread more often and more skillfully than their fathers), but apparently they still—on average—do a lot less than mothers do. Studies show that in families in which mothers don't work outside the home, fathers share under 10% of child care and housework. When both parents work outside the home, the statistics stack up a little better (with Dad handling between 20% and 30% of the load), but clearly, in most two-parent homes, moms still shoulder the lioness's share of the work.

There are several reasons why this inequity exists. For one, cultural habit dies hard: Household chores and child care have been considered "women's work" since the beginning of time. During their formative years, most men had paternal role models who didn't make a whole lot of domestic contributions. For another, many men feel fundamentally insecure in these roles—and many women unwittingly feed these feelings by being hypercritical and overly judgmental when Dad does chip in. For still another, while women do tend to complain a lot about their heavy loads, they tend not to do anything about them; instead of sitting down and hammering out a fair division of labor between the spouses, they often suffer with the status quo.

Yet a household in which the load is equally shared doesn't have to be a pie-in-the-sky fantasy—in fact, it's gradually becoming a reality in more and more homes across the country. To make it a reality in yours—both for your sanity and so you will raise children who will be less affected by sexual stereotypes (seeing their fathers pitch in will make little boys much more likely to do their fair share when they grow up):

**Call a parental summit.** Convene at a time when neither of you is preoccupied or in a rush. Express your feelings in a noncombative way; make a concerted effort to stay calm and rational. Let your husband know that carrying the household load is getting you down and wearing you out, and that you feel it's time for a change. Give him some concrete examples of how the burden is affecting you (you've become resentful, you never have time for yourself, you're feeling spent) and how having him share it could bring about positive changes in your home (you'll have more time to spend together as a couple, he'll develop stronger ties with your toddler, having a more involved male role model will be healthy for your child.)

**Form a partnership.** Being a "partner" in house chores and child care is a lot more appealing than being a "mother's helper"—and a partnership is more likely to be productive than an overseer–underling relationship. Work out the terms of the partnership together, rather than you delegating jobs for him to dutifully carry out.

**Divvy up the duties.** Partnerships are most successful when each partner contributes what he or she knows and does best: You're a whiz at vacuuming, he scrubs the floors like no one else; you're unsurpassed at bedtime stories, he's tops at giving baths. But realize that your spouse may need the opportunity to prove himself in areas where he's never before been tested. His prowess in the kitchen may have been limited so far to pouring a bowl of cold cereal. But given half a chance (and a pile of cookbooks), he may be able to earn his Cordon Bleu stripes. Though he may never have tackled giving medicine or taking a temperature, with a little practice, he may easily end up your toddler's Florence Nightingale of choice.

**Hold the criticism.** Allow your spouse to figure out his own way of handling child care and household chores. He'll learn more effectively from his own mistakes and successes—than he would from your standing over his shoulder ready to advise or critique—and will feel more competent and confident sooner. It'll also make him feel less like your sidekick and more like your partner.

**Work as a team.** Group efforts are almost always more enjoyable, and thus more successful, than solo efforts. So plunge into chores together—you wield the dust rag, he pushes the vacuum; you do the peeling, he the chopping; you do the ironing, he does the folding; you do the baths, he does the tucking-in.

**Aim for 50-50, but be flexible.** For a distribution of labor to be fair, each partner need not always do precisely 50% of the work. Depending on your work schedules, your skills, and the needs of the family and the exigencies of the day, what is fair is likely to fluctuate. There'll be days when you do 70% to his 30% or he does 60% to your 40%—as long as there's some balance to the equation, don't keep running calculations.

**Keep a schedule—or keep it loose.** Some couples prefer to schedule chores and child care so that there's no question whose turn it is to cook dinner or pack the lunch box; some couples prefer a looser agenda ("I cooked dinner last night—it's your turn.") Opt for whatever works in your household, as long as both partners consistently do their share.

**Rotate the jobs nobody wants.** Or draw lots. Whether it's washing and drying the lettuce or shampooing your toddler, there are some jobs that are less desirable than others—and some that no one wants at all. Rotating these jobs or choosing chores out of a hat so no one's always stuck with the unwanted jobs will reduce the buildup of resentment.

**Pare down the workload.** Too much to do and not enough time to do it— even with both of you chipping in? Something's got to give. Together, decide what that something—or the many somethings—might be. It could be touching up laundry with an iron, or dusting *all* the bookshelves, but make sure it isn't time spent with your toddler, as a couple, or as a family that suffers.

**As a last resort, strike.** You've stated your case for equal work around the house, but you still find yourself doing an inequitable share? Try making your point with peaceful protest. Stop doing your spouse's laundry, stop clearing the dishes, stop making the bed, picking up the toys, straightening up the bathroom. Letting things go undone for a while may demonstrate just how much you actually do—and convince him to join the team.

# GETTING SICK

*"I've just come down with the flu. I'm achy, I'm feverish, I'm miserable. I don't have to worry about giving it to my toddler—he gave it to me—but I don't see how I can get better if I've got to run around after him all day."*

Having the flu is no picnic under the best of circumstances (as when you have someone to bring you chicken soup in bed, a solid supply of videos, a full box of tissues, and no responsibilities more pressing than the clicking of the remote control). But it can be particularly trying when you're home alone with a toddler. Young children have little understanding of illness, and thus, generally little empathy for the sick. Especially when it's a parent who is sick and the illness is interfering with their receiving the care and attention to which they're accustomed.

But when you're down with the flu, you need your rest at least as much as your toddler needs that care and attention, particularly if you'd like to get better fast. If there's any possibility at all of having someone stay at home with you or of farming your toddler out to a friend or a relative for the day, seize it. If not, and you're stuck home alone with your toddler, you can try to enlist his cooperation by explaining (in simple toddler terms) that you need to stay in bed as much as possible in order to get better. Remind him how awful he felt when he was sick, and how he didn't feel much like running around.

If you can't seem to get your toddler to slow down out of the goodness of his heart (a likely possibility), don't try to instill guilt by playing the martyr ("I'm so sick, and you won't let me lie down for ten minutes!"); remember, he's just a toddler. Instead, try to get him to slow down for the fun of it. Appoint him "doctor for the day" while you play patient. This will make him feel grown-up and important and *may* make him more cooperative. It will also keep him occupied for a while. Let him go at you with the stethoscope and blood pressure cuff from his play doctor's kit; encourage him to plump your pillows, fluff your blanket, feel your head (and then his, so he can feel the difference), bring you the remote control or a magazine, even order you to stay in bed. Don't let him handle any medication you're taking, however, or leave it at your bedside (even an

ostensibly childproof container is not always toddler-proof). Incidentally, if you're taking a cold preparation, be sure to take a nonsedative formula so that you stay alert enough to take care of your toddler.

Make any room where there's a television and a comfortable place to lie down your sick room. And though you might be more in the mood for "An Affair to Remember," bring out a day's supply of children's videos or keep the television tuned to a children's channel; this is one time you shouldn't worry about "too much TV." Have the room stocked with everything you might need (tissues; a thermos of warm soup or warm orangeade; nonperishable snacks and juice packs for your toddler; piles of books, puzzles, crayons and paper, toys, and other amusements). Having your significantly more healthy other make a plate of sandwiches and stow it in the refrigerator for your toddler's lunch will save you from having to slave over a jar of peanut butter later on.

When you're sick with a virus your toddler hasn't already had, it's likely he will catch it. Still, it makes sense to explain the rudiments of germ passing to him and to follow the illness prevention tips on page 606.

# DIFFERING VIEWS ON PARENTING

*"My wife and I see things differently on many child-care issues. That means there's a lot of inconsistency in our daughter's life, and a lot of arguing going on around her."*

Even couples who otherwise have a great deal in common can have trouble finding common ground when it comes to child-rearing philosophy.

## BACK RELIEF

· · · · · · · · · ·

**Y**our toddler may be able to walk, but that doesn't mean you won't still be doing a lot of carrying—carrying that can strain your back. To minimize back strain:

▲ Encourage your toddler to walk whenever possible (see page 317). But don't make it a power struggle, which will only encourage more frequent cries of "Carry me!"

▲ Use the right lifting techniques. Bend at the knees rather than at the waist and lift with your arms and legs rather than your back when picking up your toddler—or anything else.

▲ Use the right carrying techniques. Though it may initially seem comfortable, don't carry your toddler on your hip for long periods. This position could stress your back muscles and spine, especially if you are twisting and turning at the same time. When you do hip-carry, switch back and forth (side to side). Carrying your child close to your body will also ease back stress. For long walks, many parents find a backpack is a good idea.

▲ Watch your posture. Walk with your pelvis thrust forward and your spine as straight as possible; if stroller handles are too short, invest in a pair of extenders; when standing for long periods, keep one knee bent by raising your foot on a stool; when sitting for long periods, use a chair with a supportive back and arms and a firm seat, and try to keep your knees slightly elevated (use a footstool if necessary); sleep on a firm mattress on your side with your knees bent.

▲ Exercise to strengthen the abdominal muscles that support your back. A videotape may be most helpful in learning the recommended exercises, which usually include the pelvic tilt (pushing the pelvis forward), modified leg-lifts (one at a time with knees bent), and sit-ups (lifting the head and shoulders off the floor but not all the way to the upright position).

---

After all, it's rare for a husband and wife to come to parenting with identical backgrounds. The different child-rearing ideas they've evolved often fuel disagreements over how to raise their children.

Too often, however, the loser in parental child-rearing disputes is the child. Children crave consistency; when their parents send different signals, have conflicting policies, and show open disdain for how the other half parents, children are denied that consistency—and the security that goes with it.

Disagreements over one or another parenting area—bedtimes, discipline, or feeding, for example—are inevitable, but destructive consequences needn't be. To resolve disputes before they make a victim of your child, try these approaches:

▲ Talk about it ahead of time. Decide how disagreements will be handled before they come up (see suggestions below). Then stick to your conflict-resolution plan.

▲ Don't disagree in front of your child. Arguing occasionally in front of your toddler about issues that don't directly affect her is healthy for all of you (see page 757), but arguing in front of your toddler *about* your toddler can be confusing, upsetting, and guilt provoking. Instead, resolve such conflicts behind closed doors (but don't take them to bed). When a decision must be made on the spot, try to agree on a contingency plan ahead of time, such as deferring to the person who feels most strongly about the issue until it can be further negotiated later on.

▲ Put safety first. When health, safety, or fairness to a child is concerned, the decision should not be based on opinion, nor should it be one on which you arrive at a compromise. If you and your spouse disagree on what is healthier, safer, or fairer to your child, use this book or another child-rearing resource as referee, or ask the opinion of your child's doctor.

▲ Practice compromise. Common ground can often be found on middle ground: You feel your toddler should pick up his toys by himself, your wife feels he's too young; find a compromise in his picking them up with some adult help. If divergent family traditions are at the root of some of your disagreements (your family always gave mountains of presents at Christmas, your spouse's set limits on extravagant giving), consider creating new family traditions that blend a little of each of the old traditions or are based on a completely new premise.

▲ Divide up areas of responsibility. Assign to each parent the things he or she feels most strongly about. You care about manners, so you make rules related to how your toddler should behave at the table; your spouse cares about diet and health, so the responsibility for deciding what goes on the table is in her court.

▲ Don't give your spouse a bad name. Even under-the-breath mumbles of "Mommy doesn't know how to wash your face," or "Daddy is so slow getting you ready in the morning" can undermine a spouse's authority in a child's eyes and send other undesirable messages ("Daddy doesn't respect Mommy"). Such picking and sniping can also set a model for a more critical, less tolerant child who relates to people in a negative way.

▲ Sometimes, give in. Some issues are not worth making an issue of. It's as true of conflicts with your spouse as it is of conflicts with your toddler. Occasionally

giving in without a fight—and without a sore sport's grumble—can make life much easier while making your spouse more amenable to your opinions in the future.

▲ Be open to learning from each other's insights. Sometimes the parent who spends the most time with the toddler knows what's best; sometimes he or she is too close to be objective. Listen to each other's opinions with open minds—you may have more to learn than you think. And your child will learn something valuable, too: that you respect each other and each other's opinions.

▲ Be consistent. However you decide to settle child-care issues between you, be sure that the rules that are spelled out to your child are consistent. If you insist she wash her hands before eating and your spouse doesn't, or if your spouse allows climbing on the furniture and you don't, she'll feel confused. Worse, she may come to believe she can't do anything right and give up trying. So don't switch back and forth on parental policies depending on who's in charge at the moment.

Finally, keep in mind that there's more than one right way to handle most parenting issues. And that more important to your toddler's future than how any single issue is handled is how you and your spouse respond to each other, show respect for each other, compromise with each other.

# SURVIVING WITH TWO UNDER TWO

*"My son is a year old, and I'm due again in two months. My children will be fourteen months apart, which really has me worried. Do I need one diaper bag, or two? How do I*

*get around? Is there any way to avoid buying a second crib? Help!"*

The logistics of caring for two children under two will be overwhelming enough without adding the stress of worry. So first of all, try not to panic. Countless parents before you have faced and successfully met the challenge of handling a diapered duo—be it composed of twins or closely spaced siblings. And they've lived to tell—and even laugh—about it.

While the next few years won't be a stroll in the park, advance planning, meticulous organization, and realistic expectations will make the parental marathon that lies ahead less grueling. Besides a lot of luck and a lot of help for yourself, you'll need:

**A-crib-to-grow-in for your firstborn.** Your older child won't be ready for a bed yet, but will be soon enough that you won't want to invest in another crib to tide him over. So shop around for a crib that can convert to a junior bed. So that he will be less likely to associate eviction from his present crib with the new arrival, buy and start using the new crib now (talk it up as a "new and special" bed just for him) so that by the time his sibling appears on the scene it will feel like home.

**Double-duty transport.** Though your son will probably be walking by fourteen months (or shortly thereafter), you can't (and shouldn't) count on him walking when you want and/or need him to. Under the circumstances, it's unfair to expect a young toddler to walk long distances (and when your legs are toddler-size, almost every distance looms long). It's particularly unfair when the new baby's being whisked around in a cozy stroller (that the baby usurped from the older child) while he's forced to plod alongside on foot. An ideal solution is a twin stroller—they're available in side-by-side and front-to-back models—which allows one person to push two tots at a time. You can start using a twin stroller (assuming the seat backs recline and you add a padded head support to be sure your newborn's head doesn't slump to one side) right away, and can continue to use it until your firstborn's not only able but willing to walk most of the time (probably at least two or three years down the line). If you don't want to invest in a new stroller, start looking for a used one now. Ask around at the playground, put a notice up on your toddler's doctor's bulletin board and the one at the supermarket, check the newspaper for ads, scout yard sales and "baby exchanges" or secondhand children's stores. When the bulk of a twin stroller is impractical (some supermarket aisles can't accommodate them, for instance), plan on toting your newborn on your person in a baby carrier (or later, in a backpack) while you push your toddler in his stroller or in a shopping cart.

Be sure to get your older child a toddler car seat and use the infant seat for the new arrival. Making a fuss over the new "big-boy" front-facing car seat may make the transition easier. You can put both children in the rear seat of the car, or put the toddler in the rear and the infant (in the rear-facing infant seat) in the middle front (but not if there's a passenger-side airbag).

**A double-duty tote.** One advantage of having two in diapers at the same time (yes, there *are* some) is that you can service both of your offspring with some of the same supplies, eliminating the need to buy two of everything. Buy *one* extra-large diaper bag. (Carrying two separate bags is not a good idea—it will be hard enough to remember you have two tots to tote.) The bag should have at least three compartments: one for your older child's supplies, one for the baby, and one for supplies they can share (such as diaper wipes). A fourth compartment that's waterproof, for carrying wet stuff, is ideal—or keep a sturdy plastic bag tucked in your tote.

In addition to these tangibles, the following intangibles will be invaluable in parenting two under two.

**Time for each baby.** That's a tall order when time is something in perpetually short supply, but it's an absolutely necessary one. The trick: Learn to do double duty. You can't realistically be in two places at the same time, but you can often realistically do two (or more) things at the same time. Use infant-feeding time to read a story to your toddler, infant naptimes to do a puzzle together, diaper-changing time to sing to both of your little ones. While baby watches in fascination from the stroller, give big brother a ride on the swing. When both parents are at home, divvy up the responsibility of giving undivided attention to the older child and care to the younger—Dad can bathe the baby while Mom plays finger songs with the older child. Or, Mom sings to and rocks the new arrival while Dad takes big brother to the park for a romp.

**Time for your first to be a baby.** It's important to keep in mind that a fourteen-month-old is still a baby—even if he is a big brother. Expecting him to be mature beyond his months—to use the toilet, to be responsible for cleaning up his toys or doing other chores, to be cooperative and helpful all of the time, to be totally accepting (and never jealous) of the new baby or of the time and attention you give it—is expecting far too much far too soon. Let your son grow up at his own pace. Praise his maturity whenever he displays it, but never criticize him when he acts his age (or even when he reverts to acting his sibling's age). With the help of plenty of patience on your part and positive reinforcement ("big boys can watch *Sesame Street* . . .

or take a book out of the library . . . or have a cookie with their milk"), he'll eventually wise up to the benefits of not being a baby. For more on a toddler who is regressing, see page 745.

**Time for you to hit your stride.** It takes practice, trial and error, and a sense of humor to make it as a parent, especially as a parent of two under two. In time, you'll fall into a rhythm—just be careful not to fall into the trap of striving for perfection or trying to "do it all" (new parents often do). Relaxed and happy imperfect parents (so what if you can write your name in the dust on the coffee tabe?) are preferable to tense and unhappy perfect ones (which makes them not so perfect after all).

# TIME FOR YOURSELF

*"I love our little boy, but between caring for him and the house, I never seem to have any time for myself. I guess that's part of being a parent, but I must admit that sometimes I feel resentful."*

It's a well-known fact: To be effective at a job, workers need time off. That goes for corporate executives, bookkeepers, assembly-line workers, professional athletes, mechanics, salespeople, lawyers, doctors, dentists, teachers, and equally, if not most of all—considering the emotional and physical challenges of the job—parents. Particularly parents of toddlers.

In other words, not only do you *deserve* a break, but to be effective at your job, you *need* one. Parents whose main work is caring for their children shouldn't be obliged to do so to the exclusion of all other pursuits and pleasures. Being burnt out and resentful doesn't make you a better parent, and being a martyr doesn't make you a better role model. The best parents and best role models are relaxed, reasonably content, and at least somewhat fulfilled. It's important for even young children to see that their parents care for themselves, too.

Of course, finding time for yourself in the context of busy days isn't easy. Trying the tips on page 770 for organizing your time more efficiently might help free up some time for you; so might getting some help—from a spouse (see page 757), a paid worker, or a friend.

Once you've found yourself some time, use it well. Do something that make you feel happy—whether that's an exercise class or an economics class, a nap or a night on the town, a long bath with a good book or a long walk with a good dog, trying your hand at watercolors or trying your feet at roller blades.

Most of all, relax and enjoy. Don't begrudge yourself that precious time away from your precious child and your other responsibilities, and don't feel guilty about spending it on yourself. You're worth it—and you'll be a better parent for it.

## GUILT ABOUT WORKING

*"I enjoy working, and I think I'd go crazy staying home all day with my daughter. I know I should feel good about my decision, but I can't help feeling guilty—especially when I see other mothers at home."*

You're not other mothers—you're you. And what's good for other parents and their children isn't necessarily what's good for you and your child (and vice versa). Your happiness and satisfaction are critical to your child's; if they come from working outside the home, that's what you should be

doing—not just for yourself, but for your child, too.

And don't feel as though your decision to work will compromise your child's future in any way. The most recent studies show that, all other things being fairly equal, children whose mothers work don't suffer more emotional scars or tend to be any less well adjusted than children of mothers who stay home, and they perform on par both socially and academically. So don't feel guilty— feel lucky that you're part of a generation of women who have more than one option open to them, and that you've been able to select an option that makes you happy.

## HOMESICKNESS

*"I went back to work full-time when my son was six months old; he's past a year now and I cry every day. I hate leaving him—I feel I'm missing so much. I know it would be rough on our budget if I quit working, but I think we could manage. On the other hand, I feel like I'd be betraying my feminist ideals by staying home."*

For many, the whole idea behind feminism is that it *expands* choices, rather than limits them. A woman who wants to stay home with her child should no more be forced into out-of-home employment than a woman who wants out-of-home employment should be forced into staying home. If you choose to stay home with your toddler there's no reason to feel less of a feminist—or less of a person. But there's plenty of reason to feel fortunate; many women don't have the luxury of affording that choice, even when that's what they really want.

So go ahead and do what feels right for you. If after being home for a while you find it's difficult making ends meet or that you miss the stimulation of work, you might want to consider some of the compromise options described on page 768.

# MISGIVINGS ABOUT STAYING HOME

*"Most of the time I love staying home with our daughter. But sometimes I stand at the window watching other parents going to work, and I feel like maybe I'm not doing enough with my life."*

Parenting is not a high-profile job: It doesn't put you in line for a promotion, the hours are exhausting, the lunch hours and breaks often nonexistent. You have to pay for your own health insurance, and a vacation is not part of the job description. Yet your work as a full-time parent is at least as worthwhile as anything you could do outside of the home. (What, after all, is more important than raising and nurturing another human being?)

Still, many parents who choose the job of full-time parenting find it hard to shake the nagging feeling that they should be doing more. That's because, as inevitably happens when a pendulum of change swings, it's swung too far. While women in previous generations felt obliged to stay home with their children even if they would have preferred to work outside the home, women in today's generation often feel obliged to work outside the home even if they would prefer to stay home with their children full-time.

If staying home with your child feels like the right choice for you, don't let the pressures that swing the pendulum sway you. And remember, a certain amount of ambivalence and self-doubt

is normal—whether a parent chooses to stay home or go back to work.

If you continue to enjoy staying home but feel the need for some extracurricular stimulation, consider an alternative work arrangement (page 768) that might be available to you. Sometimes, it *is* possible to have your child and your work, too.

# THE FULL-TIME FATHER

*"Since my wife's job pays considerably better than mine, we decided that I would stay home with our son while she works. Everything was great until I started getting out of the house more and going to play dates and toddler classes. I feel out of place being the only father."*

A generation ago, fathers were expected to be the breadwinners, not the sandwich makers. But today the father is the stay-at-home parent of choice for a growing number of families; census statistics indicate that 20% of preschoolers whose mothers work are cared for by their dads. The reason may be financial (Mom's paycheck's bigger, her benefits are better, Dad's been laid off), career-motivated (Mom's headed toward a promotion, Dad's decided to try freelancing), or based on natural bent (Mom goes crazy staying at home, Dad enjoys it). And in most cases, the reversal of traditional roles works well for all concerned.

But though the idea of full-time fathering is becoming progressively more acceptable and respectable, time- and television-honored traditions die hard. Your toddler may well be a father himself before dads who've made the choice to stay home can expect to feel more comfortable in the parenting mainstream.

## WHEN YOUR HEART'S AT HOME, BUT YOU'RE AT WORK

**• • • • • • • • • •**

Even parents who thrive on working often feel a pang or two on heading for the office each morning when they leave their littlest loved one (or loved ones) behind. Here are just a few ideas for staying close to your toddler while you're working nine to five:

**Make rituals a ritual.** Routine is comforting not only to the toddler, but to working parents, whose schedules are often frustratingly and unpredictably frantic. Tailor those rituals to you and your toddler: a snuggle together in bed before getting dressed in the morning, breakfast together while reading a favorite book, a lunchtime phone call, a walk together after work (see page 271 for more on after-work rituals).

**Leave a love note.** Put a special note in the lunch box your toddler takes to day care, on the pillow he or she will be napping on, or taped inside his or her cubby. Express yourself in words for the baby-sitter or teacher to read to your child (but avoid saying "I miss you," or anything else that might unduly upset) or in pictures (a big red heart, some flowers, a photo of you hugging your child.)

**Give your toddler a memento.** A little something of yours (a handkerchief, a picture of you at your desk—or at the beach with your toddler—an expired photo ID, a pen or clipboard from your company) that your toddler can keep nearby all day will help you feel closer to each other when you're apart. A little something that's your toddler's will do the same for you; keep a finger painting on your desk, a little scrap of artwork in your wallet.

**Stay in touch.** Unless a phone call provokes tears, call a toddler who's home with a sitter for a brief chat morning and afternoon. You can also maintain contact with audio- and videotapes (read a story, sing a song).

**Take your toddler to work.** Occasionally, take your toddler to your workplace for a little visit. Introduce him or her to coworkers and explain what you do and where you do it. Let your toddler tap on your computer keys (when the computer is off), scribble on some spare invoices, sit in your chair, or otherwise "try out" your job. Knowing where you go when you go off to work will help your toddler feel more connected to you. To make it clear that being out of sight doesn't put your child out of mind, be sure to point out the photos and drawings that grace your work area or that you carry with you.

**Do lunch.** If your workplace is close enough to where your child spends the day, try having lunch together once a week. Discontinue these lunch dates, however, if your child has trouble going back to the baby-sitter or day care after lunch is over.

Try to remember, however, that while being the only father on the playground, at the play group, in the children's museum on a weekday morning, or at the toddler gymnastics class may attract curious stares from a few, your chosen path is also bound to earn you the admiration and respect of many. No one who's ever cared for a child full-time and knows the challenges and sacrifices involved—as well as the satisfactions—

is going to think any less of you. And chances are, a good many people are going to think more of you.

Still, you may feel in need of some extra moral support (just as many moms do). So look for other fathers who've made the same choice you've made and get together with them in father-dominated play groups. Ask your child's doctor if he or she knows and can give you the names of any other full-time fathers

## HAVING IT ALL—YOUR WAY

··········

**M**any parents find that neither staying home full-time nor working full-time meets their needs. They want it all—and when it's financially feasible, they look for a creative compromise that provides what they see as a sensible balance between work and family. Though these compromise solutions are more commonly used by mothers, some fathers are beginning to take advantage of them, too:

**The slow track.** For those who've found that the fast track leads to exhaustion, burnout, and more stress than they (or their families) can handle, choosing to move up the career ladder more slowly (at least until their children are older) is often sane and sensible. That may mean opting for fewer hours, less travel, less responsibility—and, very probably, less income.

**Flex-time.** More companies are allowing parents to set their own time schedules, which in most cases must include a "core" working period (often 10 A.M. to 3 P.M.). This arrangement allows parents to start and finish work earlier or later (whichever is more convenient and less stressful). As long as the work gets done, these employers aren't sticklers about whether it gets done between 9 and 5, 8 and 3, or 10:30 and 6:30.

Staggered parent working hours (he works 7:30 to 3:30, she works 10:30 to 6:30) may reduce the hours a baby-sitter is required and allow more family time.

**Job sharing.** If part-time work is financially feasible, job sharing can be an excellent way of both keeping in touch with your field and spending the extra time you want with your toddler. The trick is to find someone who's qualified, interested, and dependable with whom to share the job (another parent with a young child often works best). Once done, there are many possible ways to job-share: You each work five half-days (one takes the mornings, the other the afternoons); you each work two-and-a-half days; you each work three days, overlapping one day; or one person works three days, the other two.

**Time-income trade-offs.** Sometimes it's possible to arrange a reduction in working hours (usually of an hour or two) with a commensurate cut in salary. This allows a parent more time at home while giving the employer almost full-time effort. But since many employees are just as productive during the reduced workday as they were during the full one (largely because being able to spend more time with their families decreases stress and increases personal satis-

---

in your neighborhood, and/or put up a notice in the office waiting room and on a few community bulletin boards.

*"I really love staying home with our two kids while my wife works. But when we go to a party and people start asking what I do, I'm embarrassed to tell them."*

**N**o one—man or woman—need be embarrassed about being a full-time parent. Full-time parenting demands at least as much dedication and hard work as any other occupation, while

making at least as much of a contribution to society. The trouble is, society hasn't yet acknowledged this reality—particularly the segment of society one meets at cocktail parties.

The best way to defend your position is to take the offensive. Asked what you do, respond without apology: "I'm taking a daddy-break from my career, and let me tell you, it's the most challenging (exciting, difficult, fascinating, educational—you fill in the blank) job I've ever had." Throw in a few heartwarming or funny anecdotes and you may have your listeners hankering for the same opportunity.

faction, and because they don't work to the point of exhaustion), there may be more inequity for employees than there would be in a flex-time arrangement. Still, for many parents, the trade-off of money for time is well worth it.

**Part-time work.** Whether they're part-day, part-week, or part-year, part-time schedules, when they're logistically and financially workable, can be very appealing to employees with young families. Since part-time workers tend to be highly productive (they usually leave work before exhaustion sets in and before efficiency is reduced), employers, too, benefit from such an arrangement. How your time is best scheduled (if you have a choice) depends on you and your toddler. Some parents and children are happier with, and less disrupted by, longer stretches of time together (two full days in a row, or two weeks in a row) than with half a day together each day; others find comfort in the rhythm of half-days every day and in not being separated for long periods.

**At-home work.** Some parents with young children are able to successfully continue their jobs at home—with the help of computers, modems, faxes, phones, and other modern conveniences. Some opt to start their own businesses out of their homes. Still others (such as travel agents, real-estate agents, commercial artists, editors, writers,

and telemarketers) find it both practical and profitable to freelance in the field they used to work in full-time. Most at-home workers still find they need some kind of child care in order to maintain productivity, but those who have particularly independent or cooperative children (who can be plunked down to play next to the phone or the computer) or are so organized and efficient that they can get all their work done while their children nap may manage to get by without a sitter.

**Consulting work.** Also often home-based, this kind of work can keep you in touch with your field while providing a great deal of flexibility.

**Volunteer work.** For those who don't depend on the financial rewards of employment but do crave the intellectual stimulation and people contact, part-time volunteer work (especially when it's at a place where toddlers are welcome—such as at a children's museum) can fit the bill perfectly.

**Continuing education.** You don't have to be on the job to further your career. Now may be the ideal time to take those continuing education courses that can spell career advancement later on. Look for a program that offers on-site child care, hire a baby-sitter during class hours, or take courses at night or on weekends when your spouse or another family member can be at home with your child.

When a listener nevertheless responds condescendingly, you can again turn the tables: "I know this isn't for everyone. Not everyone can be a good parent—it takes a lot of smarts, good instincts, ingenuity. It's the toughest job around—but also the most rewarding."

# NOT FEELING LIKE A PARENT

*"I've worked full-time since my daughter was three months old.*

*I love her very much, but sometimes I just don't feel like her mother. After all, I spend less awake time with her than her day-care teachers do."*

Feelings of insecurity aren't the exclusive province of working parents. Those who work full-time taking care of their children can be just as uncertain about their parenting role as those who work full-time outside the home. And toddlers, being unpredictable and incomprehensible, can instill more feelings of self-doubt in parents than children of just about any other age group.

## STAYING SANE
## IN THE FAST LANE

· · · · · · · · · ·

**P**arenting has never been easy (just ask your parents), but with more two-pay-check families, more single parents, and the pressure to produce superchildren (and be superparents) seemingly greater than ever before, it's becoming more and more diffi-cult. Still, it is possible to stay sane (at least, relatively sane) in the parenting fast lane. Here's how:

**Learn to handle stress.** Stress is an in-evitable part of life, especially for parents— but it needn't be a debilitating part, *if* you can learn to cope. Start by making a list of the major causes of stress in your life; as you look over the list, assess how much control you have over each stressor, rating each on a scale of 0 to 10. Some you will have no con-trol over (rate those 0), others you will have a moderate amount of control over (rate them 5), still others you will have a great deal of control over (the 10's). Then look at your most controllable stressors (in the 8 to 10 range) and determine how you can get the upper hand over them. Make it a point to try to overcome them during the next couple of weeks.

Occasionally, you can be rid of a par-ticular cause of stress completely. For ex-ample, if the caregiver you've hired to take care of your toddler is making both of you very unhappy, consider trying to find some-one else. If juggling work and parenting is exhausting you and you can afford a change, consider quitting your job and stay-ing home for a while or working part-time (see page 768).

More often, you will have to find ways of coping with the stress. If your toddler has daily tantrums going off to school, spend extra time helping him or her adjust (see page 395). If you've been going through the 5:00 frazzles, take steps to calm things down at that time (see page 271). If your child is having frequent tantrums, learn how to head them off before they get started (see page 338).

**Organize.** Getting organized makes it easier to get things done, which will in turn help you feel more in control. Keep a small note-book with you, and use it to write down everything you need to do on a particular day: household chores, errands, shopping, child-care responsibilities, work-related obligations. Give each item on the list an A, B, or C priority: the A's absolutely have to get done (picking up your toddler at day care, shopping for dinner); the B's you'd *like* to get done today but they can wait till tomorrow (write a thank-you note to Aunt Mary, make an appointment with the den-tist); the C's can wait until later in the week, if necessary (buy new shoes for your sister's wedding next month, clean out the hall closet in preparation for out-of-town visitors a couple of weeks hence).

Always plan to do the A's first. If you can manage it, do one or more B's, too. Save the C's for days (if there are any) when all the A's and B's are miraculously taken care of. You may find that if you wait long enough the C's become even less necessary (it turns out that those satin pumps you bought last year go perfectly with the dress you chose for the wedding, so new shoes aren't needed; the guests cancel and your unnavigatable closet can stay a mess, at least until they reschedule a visit).

**Carpool, or use public transportation.** Either of these options may be more relaxing than struggling with traffic daily (and is bet-ter for the environment). These options may also allow you to use commuting time to your advantage; you might be able to take care of some work, make shopping lists, read a book, meditate, or share stress reducing cama-raderie and conversation with other commut-ing adults.

**Get help anywhere you can.** From networking (get together with other parents and take turns helping each other out with baby-sitting and driving to day care or preschool), teamworking (make sure that if there are two parents in the house, they're both doing their share; see page 757), and/or hired helpers (if you can afford it, have someone in once a week to clean and do some laundry so you can spend more time with your toddler). Putting an older toddler in preschool for half a day or even three mornings a week will give you more time to get things done.

Get emotional support, too. Remember that talking about the problems in your life can help to ease them; if talking to your spouse is hard, talk to other parents in similar situations.

**Double up.** Learn to do two things at once. Fold the laundry while tasting the "soup" your toddler has just made in the play kitchen; return phone calls while you chop vegetables for dinner (use a cordless phone); catch up on bills while you watch a video with your toddler. Involve your toddler in as many of your chores as you can, so that you can spend time together while crossing entries off your to-do list. Cook together, set the table together, match socks together, sort the mail together.

**Cut back.** When you're feeling overwhelmed, look for corners you can cut (dust every other week instead of every week; shop in bulk every two weeks rather than shopping weekly; opt for frozen vegetables over fresh; buy only easy-care clothes that don't need ironing or other special attention).

**Treat yourself.** Do something for yourself every day, or if you can't manage that, at least twice a week (even if it's just watching a favorite sitcom or relaxing in a bubble bath for half an hour; see page 764). Little indulgences can do a lot for your sanity. Stay up late or get up early (depending on your body's natural inclination), if necessary, to make the time.

**Treat your relationship.** At least once a week (or as often as you care to and can swing it), have dinner with your spouse after your toddler is in bed (munch on some vegetables and dip while your toddler dines); be faithful about making "dates" with each other for a movie or dinner out; consider taking a weekend off now and then (see page 773). Time spent as a couple can renew not only your relationship but your mental health as well.

**Practice relaxation.** Use a relaxation technique you learned in childbirth class or devise one of your own (focus on a photo, a picture, or a mental image that relaxes you and repeat over and over a simple calming phrase, such as "I am relaxed . . . I am relaxed"). Practice the technique whenever you feel that stress is getting the better of you. When possible, involve your toddler in your relaxation session, too.

**Get some exercise.** Whether it's walking up the twelve flights to your office, getting off the bus a mile from home and walking the rest of the way, settling your toddler in the stroller and walking the mile and a half to the supermarket, doing fifteen minutes of aerobics with your toddler on the living-room carpet, or taking an intensive exercise class at a local health club, regular exercise will help reawaken your mind, reinvigorate your body, lessen stress, improve your attitude—and offer a pleasant change of pace as a bonus.

**Get healthy.** To keep your mind clear and your stamina at peak levels, eat regularly and nutritiously, avoid smoking and the use of drugs, and limit your consumption of alcohol and caffeine.

**Keep your sense of humor.** Laughter is a well-known stress-buster. When things look grim, look for the humor in the situation (it's virtually always there).

Spending most of your time with a toddler doesn't ensure a good parent–child relationship, any more than spending much of it apart condemns you to a poor one. Time well spent (talking, listening, playing, working alongside your toddler) can more than compensate for time spent away. So, instead of worrying about who spends more time with your toddler, try to relax and make the most out of time *you* spend with her.

# WORKING OUTSIDE THE HOME AND DISCIPLINE

*"My son always acts up when I come home from work. But I'm usually too tired to discipline him— and besides, I want the little time we spend together to be pleasant and conflict-free, so I try to be extra nice to him."*

**M**any working parents feel hesitant about spending the few hours they have with their toddler each day issuing time-outs or denying privileges. But no relationship can be totally conflict-free, especially not one with a toddler. And though neglecting discipline and being "extra nice" to your toddler may assuage any guilt you feel, such an approach isn't in his best interests.

A child needs to know what he can and can't do and what is expected of him. In a *laissez-faire* atmosphere, without limits and expectations (or at least without consistent ones), a child may seem happy as a lark, but underneath he is sure to be insecure and feel out of control (see page 47). He may also be confused after living by limits all day (in day care or with an in-home caregiver) to suddenly find that "anything goes" in the evenings. And he may learn to take

advantage of the lack of limits to manipulate you by playing on your guilt.

So by all means, dish out lavish portions of love and attention at the end of the day—but don't scrimp on the discipline when it's called for. See page 119 for tips on disciplining your toddler and page 271 for making homecomings easier.

*"My wife and I both work, and she feels so guilty about it that she lets our toddler stay up to all hours. Then she lets him sleep with us to make up for the fact that we spend so little time with him during the day. I don't think this is a good practice."*

**I**t may not be a good practice, but it is a common one. Many working parents, trying (consciously or unconsciously) to compensate for lack of time with their child, find it difficult to be firm when it comes to sleep issues. But there are several drawbacks to this lack of firmness. First of all, the child who stays up too late may not be getting enough sleep for healthy growth and development. The result may be increased crankiness and decreased pleasure in the awake time spent together. Second, the child who sleeps in his parents' bed may have some difficulty learning to sleep on his own. And finally, having a child around all evening and night—awake or asleep—can seriously interfere with parental opportunities for intimacy, both verbal and physical.

Though there are legitimate reasons for families to opt for late bedtimes and co-sleeping, guilt is not among them (see page 383 for a discussion of the family bed). Instead of abandoning limits related to sleep, find other ways of improving the time spent with your toddler (see page 757). If your wife is seriously concerned that one or both of you is not spending enough time with your child, perhaps you need to reassess your work schedules.

# TODDLER-FREE TRAVELS

*"Now that our daughter's weaned, we've been thinking about getting away for a little vacation— without her. But we're not sure she'll let us go."*

If you're planning on waiting until your daughter gives you a green light, you may have a long wait ahead of you. Given the choice, just about any young child would prefer to be with her parents than with someone else, and it's a preference that continues well into the early school years. Postponing your maiden voyage away from your child until she's older won't guarantee smooth sailing later on—and it could even make the going rougher. Fact is, a child learns to be more comfortable about separations by experiencing them—in gradually increasing time periods and under the right conditions (see page 23).

So, green light or no, now is as good a time as any to try a short excursion. If you have the right sitter, not only should the experience not be harmful for your toddler, it'll probably be good for her— in no small part because it will be good for you. Once again, happy parents make better parents. See page 774 for tips on making your travels pleasant for all.

And remember, if you're going to spend the entire time away from your toddler worrying about your toddler, you might as well stay home. So relax and enjoy.

*"We're desperate for a little vacation alone, and my parents have even volunteered to take our son. But we're worried about leaving him."*

Stop worrying and start packing. Don't assume that your toddler will be upset by your going away. Toddlers often handle separations better than their parents do, especially if they're left in familiar, loving, and capable hands (a standard that most grandparents easily meet). Getting your toddler used to your taking occasional time off now will make it possible for you to continue taking romantic breaks throughout his childhood. And a vacation alone won't only be good for you as a couple, it will be good for you as parents, too. After a few days of relaxing, you're likely to return rested, refreshed, and ready to resume your parental responsibilities— better able to give to your child, having given to yourselves. Besides, what's good for your marriage (and what could be better for it than a vacation alone together?) can't help but be good for your whole family. So check the tips on page 774 that apply to vacationing parents— and call your travel agent.

*"Everyone's pressuring us to take a vacation alone, but I know I wouldn't enjoy going without our son. Why can't we take him along?"*

While there's nothing wrong with taking a vacation *sans* toddler, there's also nothing wrong with taking a vacation *cum* toddler—if that's your preference. Some parents, especially when they're relatively new to parenting, don't feel any urgency to take off on their own, preferring a family-style holiday to a romantic rendezvous. Different vacation styles are the ticket for different families, and you need to choose the one that suits yours.

So by all means, don't let anyone pressure you into leaving home without your toddler. But make sure that your spouse feels the same way. If he or she craves the toddler-free time you're resisting, it would be wise to seek a compromise, perhaps a vacation at a resort that provides all-day or evening child care, so you can be with your toddler and spend time alone, too.

# LEAVING HOME
# WITHOUT YOUR TODDLER

••••••••••

**B**efore you clean the cobwebs out of your suitcase, consider the following:

▲ Separations should start short (see page 23), and gradually get a little longer as the child adjusts. The general rule: Don't leave children overnight if you haven't left them for several evenings; don't leave them for a weekend if you haven't left them overnight; don't leave them for a week if you haven't left them for a weekend.* Even once trips away from home become routine, try to limit the time away when you can. For example, take a very early flight in the morning and return late at night instead of adding extra overnights to the overall trip. And don't stay away longer than is comfortable for you.

▲ Distances should be short, too. That first sojourn, when possible, should take you only a short distance from home—perhaps a downtown hotel if you live in the suburbs, or a suburban one if you're city dwellers. You'll feel more comfortable knowing that you can get home quickly if your toddler reacts with panic (unlikely, if you set the stage carefully).

▲ Timing is significant. If at all possible, don't plan that first overnight trip when there is anything unsettling going on in your toddler's life—such as a new baby-sitter, a new day-care situation, toilet learning-in-progress, or an illness.

▲ Who you choose to leave your toddler with is even more significant. In most cases, a loving and competent grandparent, another relative, or a close family friend, if available, is the best choice. Next best is a regular baby-sitter or other trusted, responsible person your child knows well, is comfortable with, and likes. Also a good option: a swap with the parent or parents of one of

your toddler's playmates ("You care for our child while we're away, we'll care for yours while you go off"). If none of these options is available to you, then a reputable nanny service (get a recommendation, if possible) should be able to supply a bonded and reliable professional caregiver (see tips for selecting a caregiver on page 809). If you go this route, you should let your child and the caregiver become acquainted before you go—even if it means paying for an extra day or two of the caregiver's time.

▲ There's no place like home. At least for the first separation or two, it's probably best if your toddler stays at home, rather than having to sleep in new, unfamiliar digs. That way, even though your child won't have the comfort of having you around, he or she will still have all the other comforts of home—a familiar bed, familiar toys, familiar dishes, a familiar bathtub. If that's not possible, or if you feel your toddler will miss you less in different surroundings (a possibility when the surroundings are fun and familiar—as Grandma and Grandpa's home or the home of a favorite playmate might be), send along as many personal items as practical (a favorite pillowcase, blanket, toy, even a cereal bowl, if that's very important to your child).

▲ Preparation of the caregiver is crucial. Be sure the person staying with your toddler is well versed in your child's regular routine (provide it in writing)—preferably having been guided through at least one full day with you—and ask that this routine be followed as closely as possible. Consistency is always comforting to toddlers, but even more so in the midst of change. So be sure, too, to relay any of your toddler's little idiosyncrasies (like refusing to eat from any plate but the one with the bunnies, or insisting that a favorite bedtime story be read three times, or having a night-light on and the stuffed kangaroo standing guard over the bed every evening); tried-and-true ways to distract and calm your toddler; a list of your

---

*Occasionally, an emergency trip requires a parent to go off without adequately preparing a child; in such a case, special attention is needed on the return to be sure there are no lingering aftereffects.

toddler's favorite foods, drinks, stories, activities, and toys. Be aware, however, that in-spite of your careful preparations, your toddler may be a lot more flexible with someone else than with you—and may even decide to do things differently. Let the care-giver know that this is okay, too.

In most cases, the sitter should not attempt anything revolutionary (like toilet learning or weaning from the bottle) while you're away. The rare exception is a very close grandparent or sitter, who may be able to accomplish a goal you've had trouble with (but only with your permission).

▲ Preparation of your toddler is crucial, too. Don't make your trip a surprise. Departing on a trip—even an overnighter—without telling your toddler might avoid an unpleas-ant good-bye scene, but it's likely to stir up feelings of insecurity and betrayal. Worse still, it may well heighten future separation anxiety. Begin preparing your toddler two or three days before your planned trip rather than weeks ahead (toddlers have trouble un-derstanding the concept of "future" time, and very early notice could give anxiety too much time to build) or on the way out the door (which wouldn't allow your toddler enough time to get used to the idea).

Let your toddler know, in simple lan-guage, that you're going on a trip, where you're going, when you're going to come back, who will be staying with him or her and where they will be staying.

▲ Trip preparations should take a back seat. Parents are often so preoccupied with last-minute list making, packing, and flight checking that they seem distant even before they've left. To avoid this, try to keep your toddler's routine as normal as possible and spend plenty of time together in the days be-fore you leave. If possible, do your packing when your child's already in bed, so that the frantic flurry of pre-trip activity doesn't be-come unnerving.

▲ Your toddler is entitled to have a good time during this separation. Arrange for some special activities (a trip to the chil-dren's museum, renting a favorite video, playing miniature golf with Grandpa), and let your child know in advance the fun that's in store. Make it clear that it's okay to have fun even when you're not around ("Have lots of fun with Sarah while we are on our trip"), so your child will know that it's not disloyal to enjoy life while you're gone. (And don't forget that you have a right to some fun yourself!)

▲ Parting can be sweet rather than sorrow-ful—if you play your cards right. If you're anxious and nervous as you wave good-bye, your toddler may believe that your leaving is something to really be upset about and will likely feel anxious and nervous, too. On the other hand, chances are good that if you han-dle your departure with aplomb, your tod-dler will, too. For some children, farewells are easier on home turf, where they're sur-rounded by the familiar and friendly. For others, a trip to the airport or the train sta-tion, with all their exciting sights and sounds, might be just the ticket to a smooth farewell. Either way, allot plenty of time in your schedule for calm, attentive, loving good-byes; a frantic dash to the car or to the gate will be frazzling for all. Be generous with the kisses and hugs, but don't cling, weep, or otherwise display anxiety. Reassure your child that you'll be thinking of him or her and that you will be back soon (to make the time period seem more con-crete, you can translate "two days" into "two long sleeps" or "two bedtimes"). Using the same parting phrase you use when going off to work or when dropping your child off at school ("Have fun, play hard, get dirty," for example) may also help make it clear that you will return—just as you always do.

Accept your child's reaction, whatever it is. When a parent leaves, children may scream and cry, plead and cajole, turn their backs in a huff, or seem to ignore their par-ents altogether (either to display their dis-pleasure or because the entire event is beyond their comprehension). Ask for but don't demand a hug and a kiss good-bye. (For more on good-byes, see page 22.)

*(continued on next page)*

*(continued from previous page)*

▲ Coming to associate parental trips with familiar and pleasant "going away" and "coming home" traditions can provide comfort and security—especially if parents travel frequently. So initiate some fun rituals to enjoy with your toddler before you leave on a trip (eating pancakes together at the airport coffee shop before your flight, reading a book about a parent going on a trip, making "cards" to leave under each other's pillow, reciting your own special version of "See you later, alligator" or singing your own special good-bye song). Also establish rituals that your toddler can associate with your homecoming (baking a cake and decorating the house in preparation for your arrival party, visiting the frozen yogurt store or going to the movies together once you're back). Observe these rituals faithfully (make time for them even if you're harried, running late, or dead tired; don't let packing or unpacking, last-minute calls, or catching up on messages and mail get in the way) and your toddler will always have something to look forward to when you go on a trip—and something to look forward to when you return (in addition to you). After a time, this should make your adults-only trips less threatening, maybe even fun, for your child.

▲ Long distance is the next best thing to being there—sometimes. The effect of long-distance phone contact with your toddler while you're away depends on your toddler. Some children get a thrill out of talking to absent parents on the phone, love to hear parental voices on a pre-recorded tape (reading a favorite bedtime story or singing a lullabye, perhaps), enjoy looking at pictures of Mommy and Daddy. With such a child, call like clockwork—at the same time every day, if possible—even if he or she isn't ready to talk back on the telephone. Be upbeat and cheerful; being melancholy ("I'm so sad without you!") will make your toddler feel obliged to be sad as well. Be sure, too, to call at an appropriate time—not when your toddler is watching a favorite TV show or having dinner, for example. For some children, a bedtime call is perfect, but others are upset by the reminder that the parent isn't there to tuck them in.

Some children, in fact, become distraught the minute they are reminded in any way that their parents are not present. For these children, a no-call, out-of-sight, out-of-mind policy is best. You can test your child's reaction by calling on an ordinary evening out—but keep in mind that the reaction may be different when you call from the road. It may change, too, from day to day while you're away; never prod your toddler to talk to you if he or she's clearly not in the mood. Have the sitter pass on your greetings instead.

You can also keep in touch (and give your trip a comfortingly concrete context) by sending colorful postcards from wherever you are—even if they won't arrive home until after you do. Give your child a scrapbook to keep the postcards in and look at them together frequently to provide additional continuity ("Remember when I went to Boston? Then I came back home.")

You can also stay in contact via audio-

# *FREQUENT BUSINESS TRIPS*

*"Now that I've gone back to work, I'm back to traveling—as much as a week every month. I'm used to spending a lot of time with our son, and I'm worried about how he's going to handle my being away so much. I already feel guilty and I haven't even left home yet."*

**M**any parents are required to travel on business. And as long as good child care is in place, business trips don't seem to have any lasting negative effect on their children. And feeling guilty

or videotapes. Record a few of your toddler's favorite bedtime stories and lullabies to be played back to her each night or during times of stress. (Of course, if the sound of your voice seems to make your toddler miss you more instead of less, erase this idea altogether.) Have an older toddler "follow" your trip on a bright map that you post on the wall before you leave. Mark your itinerary with a magic marker or tape and ask the caregiver to help your toddler put stickers or gold stars along the route as you move from place to place. Your child can also put stickers on a calendar to keep track of the time you'll be gone.

▲ Accept that the going may be rough when you first get going. Toddlers who are left for the first time by their parents can react in a wide variety of ways. Some separate without a problem; others withdraw, cry a great deal, or are generally unhappy. Still others seem happy enough while their parents are away, but express their displeasure on their return.

Even toddlers who have had a perfectly wonderful time with grandparents or the baby-sitter may have some conflicted feelings to express when their parents return. They may be especially clingy, whiny, resentful, or spiteful, have more tantrums than usual, experience increased separation anxiety (even crying when the parent leaves the room), refuse to eat the usual "favorite" foods, have trouble settling down for bed, or begin waking during the night.

If you get such reactions on returning from a trip, practice patience, provide plenty of extra love, attention, and reassurance (while reassuring yourself that these reactions are normal and not a sign that you've done something wrong), and these post-trip symptoms will most likely disappear within a few days.

You can expect most negative reactions to parental travel to ease up once your toddler has seen you leave and return a few times—especially if you keep the trips short at first and build up to longer trips only gradually.**

▲ If, however, your toddler seems very sad or becomes very difficult to handle while you're away, when you return, or both, and this doesn't change as trips become routine, look at the child-care situation (for tips on evaluating, see page 822). Is it truly a good situation? Is there a possibility of neglect or abuse? Are there any other problems that could be causing the behavior changes? If you can't solve the problem on your own, turn to your toddler's doctor for help. And if nothing seems to ease your child's distress, look into the possibility of cutting back on or cutting out the travel (at least for a while), or of taking your toddler along—with a sitter—until he or she is older.

---

**Hard-to-beat sleeping problems can develop, however, if a toddler who usually sleeps alone is allowed to come into bed with the caregiver or the grandparents during parental trips away from home, or if parents try to compensate for the absence by offering their bed upon their return.

---

about your traveling isn't only unnecessary, it can be detrimental. Children pick up parental guilt with radar-like precision, and often interpret it as a sign that something *is* wrong. Guilt can also prevent parents and children from enjoying the time they do have together.

Children are amazingly adaptable and remarkably resilient. As long as someone else—ideally, the other parent, a grandparent, or another loving relative—provides your child with the attention and nurturing he needs while you're away, he's likely to adjust to your traveling schedule quickly and with a minimum of problems.

Still, you should do what you can to reduce the number of trips away from

## HAPPY HOLIDAYS

. . . . . . . . . .

For weeks, you've planned, cleaned, shopped, and cooked, and your hard work is apparent in every room in the house. The decorations look as though they leapt right off the pages of a magazine, and the table—resplendent with your good china, your best linens, your wedding crystal, and a seasonal centerpiece of your own creation—sets a magical mood. Nostalgic holiday smells waft in from the kitchen as cousins, aunts, uncles, grandparents, and friends arrive, arms laden with gifts, hearts laden with cheer. It's sure to be a holiday to remember.

That is, until your toddler rebukes Aunt Sarah's advances and makes cousin Jessica cry; spills punch on the sofa and gravy on the linen; knocks over the centerpiece and upends a crystal water glass; balks at the roast-turkey-with-all-the-trimmings and wails loudly for a bowl of Cheerios; plays percussion with the silver while Uncle Jack is trying to tell a story; starts whining for dessert when everyone's still on their salads—then spends the rest of the afternoon cranky from skipping naptime and strung out from the overstimulation and excitement. And your holiday to remember turns into a holiday you wish you could forget.

It *is* possible to have happy holidays with a toddler in the house, but it may mean focusing less on reproducing a Currier and Ives setting and more on accommodating your toddler's needs:

**Lower your expectations.** And then lower them some more. It's just not realistic to expect a toddler, who has no magical memories of holidays past, to appreciate nostalgic re-creations of them—no matter how much time and effort you expend. Your toddler is more likely to be unnerved and confused by the flurry of activity and to find his style cramped ("No, don't touch that!) by the changes around the house than enchanted by your efforts.

**Don't push the holiday traditions.** Forcing a fearful toddler to cuddle up on Santa's lap or come face to face with an overgrown Easter Bunny, to eat turkey with dressing or sit through a lengthy Passover Seder—all in the name of tradition—may create more bad holiday feelings than good ones. Expose your toddler to the traditions that are important to you, by all means, but make participation voluntary.

**Don't lose sight of the rituals.** Not the holiday rituals—your toddler's rituals. Keeping the daily routine as consistent as possible during the holidays will minimize the disruption for your toddler. Try not to skip naps (plan get-togethers accordingly), put off bedtimes, or skimp on bedtime rituals. Feed your toddler breakfast even if there's going to be an 11:00 A.M. brunch, give your toddler lunch even if there's going to be a 3:00 P.M. dinner.

home when possible (use telecommunications when feasible, for example, instead of flying across the country). When trips are unavoidable, try to keep them as brief as possible (for example, take a very early morning flight and return late at night instead of adding an extra overnight to the trip). See the tips on page 22 to make the partings less difficult.

You should also be wary of trying to overcompensate for your absences by being overindulgent between them. Children need consistent limits that aren't lifted when their parents are feeling particularly guilty ("I feel so terrible about going away that I'm going to forget about bedtime"). So be sure that you continue to provide your child with the security he craves when you're home, not only in the form of love and affection, but in the form of fair and effective discipline, consistently enforced (see page 119).

An overly hungry or overly tired toddler doesn't make a happy or cooperative guest.

**Try a little togetherness.** Small children often get sidelined during the holidays as older members of the family prepare and celebrate. This lack of attention not only makes a toddler more likely to start screaming for it (at the worst possible moment), but it keeps him or her from enjoying the holiday. Instead, include your toddler in holiday preparations. Even a two-year-old can help straighten up the living room before the guests arrive, bake cookies, make decorations (the results may be less professional-looking, but will be far more satisfying to your toddler), or put pennies in the charity box. Also include the children in the rituals and celebrations: Read a Thanksgiving picture book at the tail end of your turkey dinner, add some special children's songs to the Passover Seder, arrange an Easter egg hunt in the living room (with the eggs in cellophane bags) while the grown-ups are completing the Easter repast in the dining room.

**Try to slow down.** Instead of the usual stressful hustle and bustle, try setting a slower pace and adopting a lower-key attitude during the holidays. Take on less; you won't feel obligated to overdo.

**Put yourself in your toddler's party shoes.** You may relish a traditional holiday dinner, but your toddler may be more in the mood for spaghetti. A performance of *The Nutcracker* may put you in the holiday spirit, but sitting still for an hour and a half of leaping dancers and unfamiliar music may put your toddler in a distinctly bah-humbug humor. An all-day open house may be your idea of holiday heaven but your toddler's idea of holiday hell—particularly if most of the guests are cheek-pinching, wet-kissing adults. For a happier holiday all around, consider your toddler's natural limitations when making your holiday plans and adjust accordingly: Keep a pot of pasta on the stove alongside the giblet stuffing, hold off on the *The Nutcracker* until your toddler's old enough to appreciate it, scale down holiday entertaining plans.

**Don't go overboard on the giving.** It's tempting to spend a king's ransom on your little prince or princess's holiday gifts, but too many presents can keep your toddler from appreciating any of them. Give sensibly (see page 58), and no matter what you give, don't expect much in the way of gratitude (though you can ask for a "thank you"). Your toddler's eyes may light up on opening that talking bear, but it may be quickly tossed aside as he or she delightedly dives into the collection of discarded boxes and ribbons.

**Get ready for a letdown at holiday's end.** Shifting from high gear to low so suddenly inevitably brings on postholiday letdown for adults. Toddlers, on the other hand, generally take a while to wind down and tantrums and other behavior problems may become more frequent. To help your toddler get down from the holiday high, plan quiet and relaxing activities for the first few days following a major celebration.

---

*"I was away on a two-day business trip, and since I've come back my fifteen-month-old daughter seems desperately afraid of my leaving again."*

To a child without a full grasp of the concept of object permanence (an object is still there even if you can't see it), the disappearance of her most precious "object"—a parent—can be very frightening indeed. That you came back doesn't necessarily offer reassurance to your child: What guarantee does she have, after all, that next time you disappear you won't disappear for good? Working, too, against her sense of security is her improved memory. When she was an infant, she would have forgotten that you'd been absent within moments of your return; now that she's able to remember the past, she can also fear for the future.

But don't worry. With plenty of

## PARENTS VS. GRANDPARENTS

· · · · · · · · · ·

Rare is the family in which there aren't occasional clashes between the generations on the subject of child rearing. This has always been so, but is particularly to be expected when scientific research dramatically and frequently challenges what is believed about what's best for children. To minimize the impact of intergenerational clashes on all three generations involved:

**Encourage family togetherness—up to a point.** Grandparents who either feel excluded from seeing their grandchildren often (once a month at our convenience, thank you!) or who feel pressured to see them too much (baby-sit every Wednesday, or prepare Sunday lunch or Friday night dinner for the clan every week) are more likely to be difficult to deal with. If any grandparents live nearby, sit down and discuss what kind of togetherness would feel right for them and for you. Then come up with a plan that's comfortable for all.

If you find that your busy lives and theirs leave little time for grandparent–grandchild togetherness, discuss with them how to remedy this problem. Explain how much you want your children to have a close relationship with them (if you indeed do) and plan together how to make this a reality. Some possibilities: regular Saturday afternoon visits, religious services together, a weekend meal together (eaten out or take-out, so that no one has to cook), a walk to the park, playing tag, baking cookies, taking trips together.

With grandparents who have ample time to coddle their grandchildren, the problem may be too much familiarity rather than too little. If you're uncomfortable with grandparents appearing on your doorstep without notice any time of the day or night, don't be afraid to say so. That's the only way they will know how you feel. Explain in a loving way your need for privacy, that you like to be able to prepare in advance for a visit, and that you would appreciate a phone call beforehand.

**Accept that there will be disagreements.** You differ with your parents or your in-laws on just a couple of child-care issues—or you seem to disagree on everything. The odds are good that you will disagree on something. Just keep in mind that when it comes to making decisions about child rearing, the child's parents are entitled to the final word. To avoid constant friction and bickering, be clear and firm about this—but be diplomatic. Explain to your parents that they did such a good job raising you that you are now confident and competent enough to do a good job raising your own child. Tell them that you're always willing to hear their suggestions, but that you will also rely on other sources (the doctor, other experts, books) as well as your own instincts when making your choices.

extra attention and loving reassurance, your toddler should once again start feeling secure. And each time you go and come back, that sense of security should increase, making both the trips and the readjustment period when you return home less traumatic for both of you. See page 774 for more on making trips easier on everyone and for suggestions on what to do when or if a child continues to be unhappy about a parent's absence.

## GRANDPARENTS WHO SMOKE

· · · · · · · · · · · · · · · · · · · · · · · · · · · · · · · ·

*"My wife's parents are heavy smokers who refuse to quit. Though that's their decision, I feel that it's our decision whether or not to allow smoking around our son. My wife worries that telling them they can't smoke near him would hurt her parents' feelings."*

**Be flexible.** Children—even young toddlers—are capable of dealing with different house rules in different houses. Before long, they learn that at Grandma's house you can't put your feet on the sofa (like you can at home), but you can watch television after supper (which you can't at home.) As long as the issues aren't major (whether it's your car or theirs, sitting in the car seat should be non-negotiable, for example), allow the grandparents some latitude. If they break one of the rules you feel very strongly about (they give candy to your toddler, for example), think before you react. Calmly and rationally explain why your rule means a lot to you, and that their respecting it would mean a lot to you, too.

**Don't take offense.** It's never easy to accept unsolicited child-care advice gracefully, whether it comes from a nice lady on the bus, a snippy salesperson in the children's department, or your mother (or mother-in-law). Even an off-hand "Oh, the baby needs a sweater"—and especially a pointed "You really shouldn't run to her when she cries"—can get your back up, set your nerves on edge, ready you for conflict. Yet taking the counsel as insult just escalates intergenerational tensions unnecessarily. So, instead, accept it for what it hopefully is—well-meaning advice from someone who cares. Use what you can and let the rest go.

**Be open to learning.** Even if your parenting style and the child rearing choices you've made differ completely from theirs, that doesn't mean you can't learn a thing or two—every once in a while—from your toddler's grandparents. So always listen to what they have to say with an open mind, and be as quick to let them know when you think they're right about something as you are when you think they're wrong.

**Educate grandparents.** Thirty years ago, a child's thumb sucking was thought to be a sign of emotional problems. Today, it's considered a normal self-comforting habit. Then, it was widely believed that getting chilled could lead to a cold. Today, it's known that a virus—not going out without hat and mittens—causes a cold. Child-care and health-care practices have changed radically since you were a toddler and, unless the grandparents are pediatricians, it's likely they haven't kept up. So usher them into the world of contemporary parenting by encouraging them to read this and other child-care books.

**Get a second opinion.** If opinionated grandparents leave you feeling unsure of your own opinions, get a tie-breaking one from your toddler's doctor, this book, or a parenting group. The more you know, the more confidence you can have in standing up for your decisions.

**Present a united front.** You and your spouse should run parental interference together—no matter whose parents have been doing the interfering. And think of your union not as the two of you *against* the grandparents, but the two of you *for* your family.

B etter to hurt their feelings than your toddler's health. The most recent studies show that cigarettes are almost as hazardous to those who breathe their smoke in secondhand as they are to those who do the smoking, causing problems that range from poorer health and lower achievement now to cancer in future years.

Ideally, you'll want to try to protect your toddler's health without putting your relationship with your in-laws in jeopardy. You and your wife (presenting a united front) should sit down with her parents and begin by explaining how much you love them and wish they would stop smoking so that you and your children will have them around for a longer time. Say you know that the decision is their responsibility but that it's your responsibility to safeguard the health and well-being of your child and their grandchild. Detail exactly how their smoking might affect your toddler, showing them the list of secondhand smoke hazards on page 628 to back up your words, if necessary.[2] Then tell them that because of the strong evidence that secondhand smoke is dangerous, and the equally strong recommendations of the medical community and such government agencies as the Environmental Protection Agency that adults refrain from smoking in the presence of children, you must ask them not to light up when your toddler is around. Tell them that if they must smoke during visits to your home, the only really acceptable place to do so is outside. If they balk at not being able to smoke in their own home whenever they want to, let them know, in as nice a way as you can, that since you're not willing to continue putting your toddler's health at risk, you'll have to stop visiting them until they agree to stop smoking around him. Let them know how sad such a drastic step would make both you and your toddler. Make it clear that it's their *smoking*—and not them—that you find objectionable and that the rules are the same for all friends and family, so they shouldn't take your stand personally. Keep your tone empathetic rather than judgmental. Realize that they may well be offended at first—or even incensed—and be prepared to give them some time to think your decision over.

# Moving

*"We're planning on moving out of the city and into a house in the suburbs in a couple of months. How can we help minimize any negative effect on our daughter?"*

**M**oving can be a traumatic experience for anyone. Even if you're happy about where you're going, even if you're happy to leave where you're living, even if the moving company manages not to break your wedding china or scratch the top of your grandmother's heirloom credenza, moving sets nerves on edge and sends emotions off the deep end. Moving can be especially difficult for school-age children, who may be leaving the only home they've ever known, the only school they've ever attended, the only friends they've ever made, the only playgrounds they've ever played in—especially when they have no inkling why they're going, where they're going, and what they're going to do when they get there. For younger children, however, a move is generally less traumatic; their roots are not as deep and they tend to share fewer of the concerns of adults and older children. As long as your toddler has her family, her favorite toys, and any comfort objects she depends on around her, she's likely to do very well. To help make the move even easier for her:

**Don't keep it a secret.** Springing the news on your toddler as the moving truck pulls up won't give her enough time to prepare for the upcoming changes. Waiting until the last minute also leaves open the possibility that she'll hear the news from someone else, which will put your trustworthiness and your intentions in a poor light. Besides, the upheaval and confusion of packing will require some kind of explanation; without one, your toddler's even more liable to become fearful and apprehensive. So start talking about the move ahead of time—before you begin packing, but close enough to the move for your explanation to still be fresh in your toddler's mind when the boxes and suitcases come

---

2. It may help to give the grandparents a copy of the EPA brochure *Secondhand Smoke*, available from the Indoor Air Quality Clearing House (IAQ INFO) by calling (800) 438-4318 or writing to IAQ, P.O. Box 37133, Washington, DC 20013-7133.

out. On a level that your toddler can comprehend, and in as positive terms as possible, explain why you're moving ("Our old house is too small for us now, so we need a bigger one.")

**Be positive.** Talk up the new neighborhood. Tell your toddler about the great playground that's four blocks away, the community swimming pool you can walk to, the children's museum that's nearby, or the beautiful trees that line the streets. Talk up the new house or apartment, too. Tell your toddler about the big yard she'll be able to play in, or her new room, or the playroom you can set up her easel in.

**Give her a preview.** If possible, take her to visit the new house and her new daycare center or preschool (if she will attend one). If you can, arrange for her to meet a couple of neighborhood children. If you can't manage an advance visit, make a scrapbook of pictures of your neighborhood- and home-to-be, so she'll have some idea what to expect before you drive up to the house. Before you leave your old home, ask your toddler what she'd like you to take pictures of, and start a scrapbook of her old home, neighborhood, and friends, too. Looking back at it will help bridge the gap between old and new for her.

**Share your feelings.** Acknowledge that you have some ambivalent feelings about moving—you'll miss the old neighborhood, your friends, the house. But emphasize that you think living in your new house will be a lot of fun.

**When in doubt, *don't* throw it out.** Moving may seem like the ideal time to weed out those worn or outgrown or broken toys and other toddler belongings, but resist the temptation to throw out anything of your toddler's before the move unless you're absolutely positive that she won't ask for it or miss it. Wait

until she's adjusted to her new home before you contemplate any serious tossing.

**Play moving games.** Encourage your toddler to get in the moving mood by playing at moving—with trucks and blocks, dollhouses and dolls, teddy bears and cardboard boxes. Staging some play "moves" will give her an outlet for her mixed feelings and her fears. Read her some picture books about moving, too.

**Don't forget your toddler.** Moving is, undeniably, a time-consuming process. Between wrapping up breakables, boxing books, calling the cable company for a disconnect—and the phone company for a reconnect—the details and demands are endless. But no matter how busy you are, don't forget to attend to a very important and demanding detail not directly related to your move—your toddler. Fail to provide your toddler the attention she needs, and the potential side effects of moving—whining, clinging, irritability—are likely to be be aggravated. Even more than attention, however, your toddler needs supervision; a house in the midst of the packing or unpacking process is highly toddler-unfriendly, particularly if the adults around are preoccupied and distracted. There will be open doors that your toddler could slip through, mover's dollies she could trip over, half-filled cartons full of tempting untouchables, cleaning supplies everywhere. If you can't free yourself up from the packing to give your toddler the attention and supervision she needs, make sure someone else is there to help you out—Grandpa, a friend, a responsible teenager from down the street. Or, if there are two parents around, take turns supervising the movers and supervising your toddler. (The same level of supervision will be necessary after the move, until you have unpacked and your new home is safely childproofed.)

**Don't send your toddler away.** Although the logistics of moving would be a lot less complicated without your toddler underfoot, shipping your toddler off to Grandma's or elsewhere until you've moved out and moved in isn't a terrific idea. The move will be far less confusing and disorienting to your toddler if she's a part of it from start to finish, rather than being excluded until she's suddenly plunked down in the new house.

**Pack up your toddler's room last.** The less time your toddler has to spend without the familiar comforts of her room around her and the less time she has to dwell on the emptiness around her, the better. Packing up her room last will give her a safe place to play (and safe toys to play with) while the rest of the house gets packed up. Be sure that her most treasured possessions—the ones you can't take with you in a tote bag—are in a box that is clearly labeled and will be easy to find once you get to your destination. Also, making sure her cartons and furniture are loaded last will also help ensure that they'll be unloaded first, which will mean her room can be quickly set up.

On moving-in day, make sure you have easy access to a pillow and blanket (so your toddler can take a comfortable nap when she needs to), changes of clothing, several favorite books (so she can have her usual bedtime stories the first night in your new home), and any important toys (so you won't have to start digging for that stuffed beagle the moment the boxes arrive). Also bring along a bag full of nonperishable snacks and drinks (crackers, dried fruit, cookies, juice packs) so that you won't have to dash right out to the grocery store when your toddler becomes cranky with hunger and thirst.

**Leave some packing to your toddler.** To make your toddler feel a part of and more in control of what's going on around her, give her a box to pack her-

self (you can always repack it more efficiently when she's asleep). Provide her, too, with her very own suitcase or backpack, which she can pack with some favorite toys and a comfort object (if she has one) so she can carry them with her on the trip to the new home.

**Settle your toddler in quickly.** Unpack your toddler's room first so she can start feeling at home, surrounded by familiar furnishings and toys. Encourage her to "help" set up her things—even if her help is more of a hindrance. It's probably best to try and re-create her old room as much as possible (using the same comforter and the same throw rug, arranging the furniture in a similar configuration, hanging some of the same pictures on the wall), so that she'll feel at home faster. Unless she's been clamoring for (or expectantly anticipating) new furnishings, wait until she's acclimated to her new environment before attempting any redecorating.

**Hold off on any other changes.** Keep the status as quo as possible during the weeks surrounding the move. Moving is a big enough change without adding the stress of toilet learning (unless your toddler is very ready and extremely motivated, and you're inclined to seize the moment), switching to a bed from a crib, or starting school or day care for the first time. In your new kitchen, set the table with the same placemats and dishes. Offer familiar foods, and serve meals at predictable times.

**Take some time out for exploring.** Even if unpacking in a single day were a realistic goal, the feverish pace it would necessitate would just add to your toddler's anxiety at being in a new place. Instead, after the movers leave, take some time off for some family fun. Explore the new neighborhood, visit a new playground, have dinner at a new restaurant.

## GET A DOCTOR

· · · · · · · · · ·

Don't wait until that first fever spikes. Before you unpack from the move—or preferably, before you move—make sure you have the name of a doctor for your child. Try to get a recommendation from your child's present doctor or someone in your new community (real estate agents can often hook you up with someone who has young children if they don't have any themselves). If you find, after visiting the new doctor a few times, that the chemistry isn't right, switch—but in the meantime, having someone to call is far better than having to run to the emergency room or scan the Yellow Pages when your child suddenly starts throwing up.

**Get in touch.** Become familiar with and involved in your new community. Join a toddler play group, a swim club, a local museum, a house of worship. Go for drives and walks. Tour area attractions and attend local events.

**Stay in touch.** Use the phone, mail, visits, video- and audiotapes to continue ties to any family and friends in the old neighborhood.

**Be extra-patient.** Toddlers in transition need patience and understanding, not admonitions and ultimatums. Though you'll doubtless be busier than ever for a while, don't deprive your toddler of the rituals she's come to expect. If she's accustomed to five stories at night, read all five—without resorting to speed reading. If she's accustomed to having time for splashing in the tub, let her splash to her heart's content. Realize that having to get used to a new room is almost certain to make her bedtime more of an ordeal than usual; being sensitive to her difficulties is likely to be far more effective than reacting with exasperation to them. But don't make the mistake of changing the rules of the bedtime game (or any other routine) "just until she's adjusted" by letting her sleep with you (if you don't favor a family bed) or letting her convince you to sleep with her. Exceptions can quickly become rules that are hard to break.

Though your toddler will probably handle the move well, it will be more difficult when she is older to make such moves, especially if you make them frequently. Five or six moves during a child's school years can lead to both academic and behavior problems. If frequent moves are necessary, be sure that you take extra pains to to ease the transitions for your child.

# AN ADOPTED CHILD

*"We adopted a wonderful little boy when he was just a few days old, and he's been our greatest joy ever since. He just turned one and we wonder if now's the time to tell him he was adopted."*

It's never too early to begin to introduce to your child the idea that he was adopted into, rather than born into, the family. In fact, the earlier the adopted child is exposed to the idea, the more natural it will seem to him. A child who's heard his parents talk about his adoption in positive terms ("We are so lucky we were able to adopt you") since infancy is more likely to feel secure in his standing in the family than a child who is suddenly informed of his history later in childhood.

So by all means talk about your toddler's adoption. But don't expect the discussion to take on much meaning until your child is at least three or four. (While a toddler may be able to parrot the words "I'm adopted," he won't really be able to understand their meaning or the difference between birth and adoption.) Explaining something about how babies are made (see page 420) will help a child grasp the idea that all babies are born to someone. From there you can explain that some children stay with the family they're born into and others, when their birth family can't take care of them, are adopted by families that want them very much.

Tell your child that being adopted is not better or worse than being born into a family, just different. Don't say, "Our family is just like other families." Instead, explain that every family is different from every other family—some families have only a mommy and some only a daddy, some families have children who are birth children, others have children who are adopted, and others have both.

The discussions you have with your child now are only the beginning. Questions about adoption will undoubtedly keep coming, but it won't be until your child is well into his school years that he may begin to wonder about his birth parents and why they gave him up (some children, however, never give this much thought). Until such questions come up, it is unnecessary to provide those answers.

# TWINS—OR MORE

*"We have twin girls who, even at eighteen months, are the best of friends—they'd do everything together if we let them. Our question is: Is that the best way to raise them?"*

The old notion that twins (or triplets or quadruplets) should be treated identically is no longer accepted by child-development experts. Treating them as a unit—as parents of twins past were wont to do—can, it appears, delay physical and emotional growth and slow language development, and may result in the children not reaching their intellectual potential. It's even conceivable that each will develop only half the skills she needs for a future life on her own. Twins (even identical twins) are individuals, and should be treated as such.

To encourage individuality in your twins (without interfering in their very special relationship):

▲ Avoid calling them "the twins." Instead, always call them by name or refer to "the children" or "the girls." Encourage friends, family, and caregivers to do the same.

▲ Make sure you (and everyone else) can tell them apart. If they're identical, try giving them different hair styles (unless they protest), or paint a fingernail on one pink and a fingernail on the other red, or put ankle ID bracelets on them—anything so that they aren't constantly being called by each other's name (though a certain amount of this is inevitable) and so that double doses of vitamins aren't administered to one child, while the other child gets none.

▲ Let them make individual fashion statements. Though it's tempting—almost irresistible—to dress twins in matching outfits, such wardrobe manipulation could prevent them from developing their own sense of self. If your children insist on buying identical clothing (many sets of twins do, right down to the socks), suggest each choose a different color—and continue to encourage (but don't force) them to wear different outfits rather than matching ones.

▲ Provide each twin with her own toys and other possessions. Twin toddlers are slightly more likely to share with each other than are other toddlers (even more so if it's their idea and not yours), but they can still be expected to be age-appropriately possessive some of the time. Asking them to share all is not fair (something you wouldn't ask of two non-twin siblings) and could lead to future rivalries. So give each her own own toys, books, and other personal items, even if there is some duplication, just as you would two siblings of different ages. Mark toys with name labels or with initials in nail polish to avoid confusion.

▲ Treat them equitably but not always the same, respecting differences just as you would in any siblings (see page 733). With identical twins, this may take some extra effort. While their similarities may be obvious, their differences may be less so. Look for what is unique about each child—one loves music, the other art; one is a champion jungle-gym climber, the other a super slider. Even if they're good at some of the same things, try to find different aspects of a talent or skill in each child and nurture them.

▲ Spend time alone with each child. Most parents with more than one child have some trouble finding the time to spend alone with each child, but parents of twins seem to have even more difficulty. And because so many twin siblings enjoy each other's company (at least when they're very young), making the effort almost seems unnecessary. But time alone with Mom or Dad (or both) is important for every child, and it is especially so for twins, who need help in recognizing that they are separate individuals. So make a point of making one-on-one time for each of your twins—whether it's a regularly scheduled pizza lunch or a just-the-two-of-you story session.

▲ Don't necessarily opt for separate classes. Whether to put young twins into separate play groups, day-care classes, or preschool groups depends on the children. Most experts agree that separate classes are best for school-age twins—dividing them up motivates teachers and classmates (as well as the twins themselves) to view the duo as separate individuals. It also minimizes competition. But separating them too early can be traumatic; many—but not all—very young twins find it difficult to function without their "other half." They draw strength from each other when they face a new situation as a team.

Don't, however, discourage occasional separate activities if they're requested, or separate friendships if they develop; a twin who makes a friend has a right to have a play date with that friend without her twin tagging along. As they get older and if they're willing, occasionally expose them solo to new situations (a gymnastics class, for instance), so that they can begin to learn how to handle such situations on their own.

▲ Beware of comparisons. Comparing children ("Tamara always puts her toys away, why can't you?")—whether twins or singletons—denies their individuality, damages their self-esteem, and fuels an unhealthy kind of competitiveness (see page 732 and 747). The widely accepted myth—that when twins are identical, one is the good twin and the other the bad—is just that: a myth. Don't let it color the way you treat your twins or allow it to become a self-fulfilling prophesy.

▲ Beware of other-sibling rivalry. If there are, now or in the future, other siblings on the family scene, be careful not to let the "twin syndrome" exclude them. Since so much attention is paid to twins—if not by the family, then by outsiders—other siblings (particularly older ones) often feel shortchanged or neglected. So take care to pay just as much attention to non-twin siblings. Also keep in mind that twins who are very close may unknowingly shut out a third sibling; though this isn't the twins' fault (they're just doing what comes naturally), it can lead to feelings of insecurity for the odd sibling out. Counteract this with lots of parent-child one-on-one experiences and by providing many opportunities for social interaction with others.

▲ Get all the help you can. With two young children to keep an eye on, you are sure to be even more swamped than other parents of toddlers. So don't be embarrassed to accept or even solicit help from friends, family, or casual acquaintances, and don't feel guilty about it.

And when the double-parenting duty gets you down, remind yourself that twins usually turn out to be somewhat easier to care for than two singletons who are a year or two apart. Because they tend to be close, especially if they are identical (although there are exceptions), they often keep each other entertained; because they generally share a room, they're not as likely to have sleep problems.

As the numbers of twins, triplets, and even quads and quints grow (largely thanks to the increase in older mothers and mothers taking fertility drugs), more attention is being given to their needs and the needs of their parents. A good source of information for parents of twins is the Twin Hotline: (800) 821-5533.

# SINGLE PARENTING

*"I love my daughter and I don't regret my decision to become a single mother for a second. But I do worry that somehow she will suffer because she has only one parent."*

Children who are raised by a loving and attentive single parent can and do thrive, often doing as well as children in happy two-parent households.

But as with every type of family constellation, there's an up and a down side to single parenting. On the up side, the single parent gets to do things her way (there's no arguing over whether to let an infant cry it out, whether to send a toddler to preschool, whether to use time-outs for punishment); the single parent and her children tend to form stronger bonds than exist in a two-parent family; and the children tend to be more mature and independent at an earlier age. On the down side, there may be more financial hardships, more exhaustion, more isolation, less parental personal time, and, sometimes, more behavioral problems in the children. Child rearing also takes twice the effort.

When pondering the negatives, keep in mind that while society romanticizes the traditional nuclear family, no family is immune to problems. While more fathers share the load of child care and house care than ever before, there are still many married women who receive little help from their spouses.

Parenting a child on your own won't be easy, but then, parenting a child *with* a partner isn't always a piece of cake, either. Of course, you will have to put in extra time and effort to compensate for the absence of another adult in the home. But you *can* raise a happy and well-adjusted child. Doing the following will help:

**Abandon the superparent/superworker goal.** No parent can do it all (this is probably doubly true of parents who must do it alone) and no parent is perfect; struggling for "super" status when you're only human just adds pressure you don't need.

**Accept a helping hand.** If it's impossible to do it all, it's next to impossible to do it without help. If you don't get offers, *solicit* help from family and don't wait until you're at the breaking point before you turn to others; not just for your own sake, but for your child's as well. Instead of worrying about "imposing," consider that anyone who lends a hand will probably reap considerable pleasure out of doing so. To avoid wearing out your welcome, try when possible to spread your requests among several different people, instead of calling on the same one or two all the time (unless a very willing grandparent or other close relative is available). And try to return the favors when you can—pick up a few things at the store for the neighbor who stays with your child for a couple of hours a week while you work out at the gym; offer to baby-sit occasionally for the parent who picks your child up when you're late getting home from work; help your mother, who gives unstintingly of her time, with holiday preparations.

Especially important is finding one or two people who live very close by on whom you can call in an emergency—to pick up a prescription at midnight, stay with your child when you have a doctor's appointment, or collect your child at day care when you're stuck with a flat tire.

**Take care of yourself.** You'll need all the vigor you can muster to meet the challenges of single parenthood—and it's important to your child that you stay healthy. So be sure you eat well, exercise at least three times a week (see page 771), get enough rest (a good night's sleep is more important than a clean house), and see a doctor and dentist as necessary.

**Unstress yourself.** Learn stress management techniques. You won't be able to eliminate all the stress in your life, but you can learn better ways to handle it: prioritize (some things you'll just have to let slide), organize (so you won't slide further and further behind), and relax (a few minutes of meditation can renew you for hours). See page 770 for more on coping with stress.

**Give yourself a break.** Giving to your child and ignoring your own needs benefits no one, and can even leave you feeling angry and resentful. So renew

yourself regularly—whether it's going out with a friend once a week or taking in a movie on your own twice a month. And don't feel guilty about it. You deserve it—and, besides, it will make you a more effective parent.

**Give your child plenty of love.** Love *can* make a difference—and can make up for a lot you may not have the time, energy, or means to give to your child. A child in a loving single-parent home who gets adequate attention and is listened to, respected, and disciplined has a better chance of growing up happy and well adjusted than a child in a two-parent home where love is in short supply. And, happily, love—like most of the best things in life—is free and self-replenishing; the more you give, the more there is to give.

**Be generous with your time . . .** For the single parent, love may be easier to lavish than time, but it's nevertheless vital that you spend at least a short time every day doing something fun with your toddler—even if that means that something else less important doesn't get done.

**. . . . but don't "go easy" on your toddler.** Maintaining discipline is as essential (maybe more so) in a single-parent home as in a home with two parents. Don't let any guilt you may feel tempt you to ignore misbehavior. Children of single parents don't need the freedom to be rude, to hit others, or to ignore rules. Nor do they need extra time watching TV, more junk food, or regular reprieves from getting ready for bed. They need what all children need: the security that fair limits and predictable expectations provide (see page 47). But in setting limits, be careful not to make an issue of everything. Limit your "no's" and your rules to what's really important.

**Don't lean on your child.** Children have the right to be children and to enjoy the carefree time that childhood should be, no matter what their parent's problems. Don't burden your toddler with any worries you may have or try to use her to fill your personal needs, such as the need for companionship. And be sure that your toddler understands that whatever your problems are, she's not to blame.

**Find your support elsewhere.** Find a friend or relative who has broad shoulders you can lean on. Better still, join a single-parent support group. Millions of single parents are out there—fathers and mothers, single by choice or because of divorce or death. Getting together individually or as a group with other single parents in your community can improve the quality of your life in many ways. Single-parent support groups— whether they hold formal meetings or simply share social events—can help to alleviate a sense of isolation while allowing you to share feelings, ideas, and support with others in similar circumstances.

Get together with parents from two-parent families, too. What you can learn from them is that all parents, single or not, have the same feelings of inadequacy from time to time, the same feelings of being overwhelmed, the same need for support—that these aren't the sole province of single parents.

**Enlist an opposite-sex role model.** Children do better when they spend time with adults of both genders. So find at least one male relative or friend who is willing to spend some time with your child. (Single fathers, of course, need to enlist a female for this role.)

**Be ready for the inevitable.** If your child is nearing age three, has friends with two-parent families, and there is no second parent in the picture, the question "Why don't I have a daddy (or mommy)?" may have already come up or can be expected to soon. If it doesn't come up spontaneously, it may mean your child is afraid to ask; in that case you may, eventually, want to bring the subject up yourself. Be as honest as you can, but don't get so complicated in your explanation that your child either doesn't understand it or is overwhelmed. The details will depend on your particular situation. For example, if you're a single mother by choice, you can say, "I wanted to have you so much that I didn't want to wait until I found a daddy that I loved." If you've just separated or divorced, see the facing page for possible explanations.

Explain that there are all kinds of families and that not all of them have both a mother and a father. Introduce your child to other children with single parents—both in real life and in books. Get her acquainted with, and talk about, your extended family, if there is one. For how to respond to the "Where do I come from?" question, see page 420.

**And don't take life too seriously.** You'll need your sense of humor—often.

When these suggestions aren't enough to tide you over the rough spots, don't hesitate to seek professional help. Your clergyperson, your child's doctor, or your own physician can help you find the right therapist.

# SINGLE FATHERHOOD

*"I've been my daughter's only parent since she was six months old, when my wife decided she wasn't ready to have a family and left. I've been doing all right, but sometimes I feel terribly inadequate and frustrated that I can't be both a mother and a father to her."*

Pregnancy, childbirth, and breast-feeding aside, there is nothing that caring parents of either gender can't do equally well. In fact, some fathers are by nature more nurturing than some mothers. Your feelings of inadequacy and frustration have less to do with the fact that you're a man than the fact that you're a parent. Almost every parent—married or single, female or male—comes to the job without experience and frequently feels inadequate. Parenting, after all, is not an easy job. Even parents who've already had several children aren't immune to feelings of frustration and inadequacy.

Your feelings are normal and aren't an indication that you're a poor parent. You may not always be able to be both mother and father to your child, but with love and lots of hard work, you can nevertheless raise a happy child. The tips for the single parent in the previous answer can help.

# SEPARATION/DIVORCE

*"Ever since our daughter was born fifteen months ago my relationship with my husband has deteriorated. We are actually talking about divorce because we are worried about our child living in the midst of such turmoil."*

L iving in a household filled with anger, acrimony, and accusations isn't good for a child, but neither, for that matter, is divorce. There are no easy answers in a situation like yours; what's best for the children (and the parents) in one family may not be best for another. One universal truth holds true for all families everywhere: Children do best in happy homes. So the first thing you need to do is to try to improve the atmosphere in yours by trying to make your relationship a better one. Often bandying the word "divorce" around is a cry for help ("I'm desperate, unhappy"). But dissolv-

ing a marriage isn't the only way out of the misery.

It isn't uncommon for couples with a new child to let their relationship fall into disarray, or to neglect their marriage as they nurture their newborn. But the relationship between husband and wife should stay at the top of their priority list, coming even before their relationship with the new baby. Though this may seem selfish on the surface, it's actually very much in the child's best interest; nothing makes a child feel more secure than a secure relationship between her parents and nothing makes her feel more loved than seeing that her parents care about each other.

Still, few new parents take the time that's needed to make their relationships work in a truly satisfying way. If that's been the case in your home, making an effort now to make up for that lost time may well save your marriage—and protect your child. Devote time each and every day to just-the-two-of-you; try to rediscover the intimacy you shared before your child was born. Snuggle in the morning before you get up (if your toddler's been sleeping with you, reclaim your marriage bed); speak on the phone during the day at a time convenient for both of you just to chat and say "I love you." (Ban any "You pick up this, I'll pick up that" transactions during this call.) Have dinner and conversation after your daughter's asleep at night; once a week (religiously) take in dinner, a movie, or another activity you once enjoyed as a twosome (hire a sitter to stay with your toddler, prevail on a relative or friend to sit, or find another parent to exchange favors with). A child-free weekend away could also prove extremely revitalizing to your marriage (see page 773).

Of course, at this point, your marriage may need more skilled mending than a do-it-yourself approach can offer. Often, professional intervention can make the difference. So before you call a lawyer, talk to your clergyperson, your doctor, or someone else you both respect about your marriage and about finding the right therapist for couple's counseling.

While revitalizing your relationship would be better for you, your spouse, and your child than giving up on it, some marriages can't be saved. If you both try hard to make your marriage work, but the discord nevertheless continues, then you need to think about a split (see below). If you do decide to split, counseling can help you build separate lives that will continue to protect your toddler.

*"My husband and I have been unhappy since long before our toddler was born. We've given our marriage every chance, and even spent a year in counseling, but it's become clear that we can't make it work. We're worried about how our splitting up and my husband's moving out will affect our son."*

It's an unfortunate fact that when parents are at odds—whether they live together or are separated or divorced—the children are the victims. Though splitting up won't be easy on your toddler, staying together wouldn't have been, either. Living in an unhappy home with parents who are constantly fighting is often worse for children than adjusting to separation and divorce. It also gives them a model of a poor marriage to emulate and makes it difficult for them to learn what a good relationship is like.

First of all, don't compound your pain with guilt. If you're certain your marriage doesn't stand a chance, getting out of it now is probably a good idea for you and may be less traumatic for your child (younger children tend to be much more resilient in the face of a family split than older ones).

Still, when the only world you've ever known suddenly falls apart, it can be very frightening and distressing.

Studies show that though many children of divorce become happy and well-adjusted adults, they tend to have more behavior problems in childhood than children in happy, intact homes. In many cases these problems appear to have been at least as much a result of the unhappy home as of the divorce. They usually started developing when the marriage first began to fail and simply got worse or more pronounced when the actual breakup came.

It's difficult to predict how any particular child will respond to his parents' divorce. Some children show the effects early but get over the hump within two or three years of the divorce (unless a battle between the exes takes over where the husband–wife feuding left off, keeping up the stress); others seem fine at first and don't show any negative signs until a few years after the split. Some have enduring problems that haunt them into adulthood; others gain strength for having gone through the ordeal. More boys than girls have serious problems adjusting; especially vulnerable are those who displayed a difficult temperament early in life (see page 200). When custody is awarded to the mother, the absence of a caring father at home may be particularly tough for a boy; those who see little of their fathers during their childhoods and have no substitute male presence in their lives may later have trouble making and keeping friends.

Not surprisingly, children who come from homes with high levels of negativity, a lot of conflict, and unsatisfactory conflict-resolution styles (such as those involving verbal or physical attacks or abuse, power assertion, or the use of withdrawal rather than compromise) and who have parents who are disengaged, neglectful, or ineffectively authoritarian (where "Do as I say, or else . . . " is a common warning, but the threat is never carried out) are least likely to do well.

Children who do best come from homes in which the custodial parent pays attention to them, discipline is fair, and limits are consistently enforced. Many of those who turn out to be competent, successful adults have a good, solid relationship with at least one parent (usually the parent they lived with). Some succeed by learning to manipulate others (having learned early to pit one parent against the other in order to survive) and some by becoming very sensitive and empathetic (often having had to care for younger siblings—or even the custodial parent).

Everyone may be better off in the long run if an unhappy marriage breaks up, but the short term may be pretty trying. Toddlers often have a difficult time with transitions of any kind—even leaving the park for home or leaving a game of cars for lunch can spark tears or temper. A transition as major as this one is bound to have a significant effect on your child. But approaching the changes in the following ways can help acclimate your toddler to the family's new dynamics more quickly, and hopefully minimize the mayhem in his life—and yours:

▲ If you can't "stay friends" with your ex-spouse, try to establish a business-like relationship. (Remember, it's possible to do business with someone you don't like.) Meet on neutral territory, without your child when possible, to discuss his needs. Keep meetings short and as stick-to-the-essentials as possible. When you do meet with your toddler in tow, agree to show him that the two of you can still deal with issues concerning him with respect and caring. By treating each other with respect you can teach your child a lot about human relations and also strengthen his self-esteem.

▲ Give it to your toddler straight—but simply. Honesty is always the best policy when it comes to giving a toddler answers to life's tough questions, but it's an especially good policy now. Explain the separation to your toddler before it actually happens, and before he hears it

from someone else or begins to sense that something is horribly wrong (because everyone is whispering, crying, or shouting). Sit down as a family, if possible, and tell your toddler, in words that he can understand, that "Mommy and Daddy aren't happy together. We keep fighting all the time and just can't stop. We think it will be better if Daddy and Mommy don't live in the same house. We can take better care of you that way."

Make it clear that Daddy will still be Daddy, and that your toddler will still see him—just that he'll be living somewhere else (assuming you're the one with custody). Avoid saying "Daddy's going away" or "Daddy's leaving," which may make your toddler fear that each time *you* leave the house, you may not come home, either. (See the next question for help in a family where the departing spouse won't be around.)

Don't toss the term "divorce" around casually. Most toddlers have no idea what it means, and may envision it as even worse than it is. And don't be specific about the disagreements that have led up to it; the details could be very upsetting to a toddler.

▲ Expect confusion. Your toddler may not react at all at first because he doesn't really understand what you're saying. It may not be until *after* the changes actually occur that this will all begin to register for him. That's when he may start to ask questions. Provide the answers he needs and use his questions as springboards for more discussion about both the facts and his feelings.

▲ Let him see that he's not alone. Reading your toddler books on divorce written for very young children will show him that there are other children in the same situation. So may taking him to a support group for young children going through divorce.

▲ Let him know that he's still loved by both of you. Seeing that your love for each other ended may make your toddler worry that you could stop loving him, too. He needs reassurance from both parents that your feelings for him haven't changed and never will—and that you won't abandon him (if one parent abandons the family, see page 796).

▲ Honor promises and stick to agreed-upon schedules—if not for each other, then for your child, who needs to know that he can trust his parents. But make exceptions when it's in your toddler's best interest (one parent might give up a visitation so that the child can attend a special family event with the other parent, for example, then get a make-up visit). Don't make exceptions or threaten your child when he misbehaves ("If you don't behave you can't see Daddy"). Seeing a parent should be an unconditional right.

▲ Ease the time warp. Toddlers don't see time the way adults do. Waiting until Saturday to see Daddy can seem like waiting a lifetime. So try to schedule frequent visits with the noncustodial parent, at least at first, and make the waiting time more tangible, for example, by counting the days on a large wall calendar with special stickers affixed on visiting days.

▲ Stick to the same old same old. Familiar rituals and routines provide a sense of order and control at a time when a child feels helpless and out of control. Keep as many of the traditions your toddler has come to know—from cuddling in bed Sunday morning to reading *Goodnight Moon* before bedtime to Tuesday is pizza night—intact and unaltered. Discuss with your former spouse the importance of keeping with tradition at his new place, too, so that there will be as much continuity as possible when your toddler starts moving back and forth between homes. It will also make it easier for the child if you can replicate his belongings in Dad's home (the bed, the linens, the booster seat, and so on) as much as is practical.

▲ Exorcise any feelings of guilt. The first reaction of many children, particularly naturally self-centered toddlers, to divorce is "What did I do to make this happen?" It's important to make it very clear to your child that he is not responsible for what is happening, that nothing he did made it come to pass—and that nothing he can do will change things back to the way they were.

▲ Deal with denial. Some children go through a period of denial. They pretend that their parents' split-up really isn't happening, that Mommy and Daddy really love each other and will get back together. Respond with sensitivity to this denial, telling your toddler that you understand his feeling that way—and that he can pretend if he wants to—but that pretending won't make it so.

▲ Don't thrust your toddler into the new. If he's never spent a lot of time with his father, don't suddenly send him off to live with Daddy part of the time; long stretches away from the primary parent should be avoided at first. The process of moving toward overnight visitations or joint custody should build gradually, starting with short periods alone with Daddy, then extended periods during the day (some of this time spent at Daddy's home), then finally, a trial overnight. The child doesn't have to sleep in the noncustodial parent's home to be close to him; they can spend time in the evenings and then return to separate homes. When it's time for overnights to begin, they should last no more than one or two days at first.

Of course, if the child has been very close to both parents, each should try to see him every day or two at the beginning. And whatever plan you devise, if your child is beginning to show serious signs of stress, try to alter the plan until he seems more comfortable.

▲ Stick to the old rules. Even in Dad's new house, parental rules (about jumping on the bed, about feet on the sofa, about playing ball in the house) should remain as consistent as possible. If you can't agree on common standards, explain to your child that Daddy does things his way and you do things your way. In your house, you make the rules. In his house, he makes the rules. Not only is now not the time to change the rules, it's also not the time to change the degree of discipline. Don't suddenly crack down (because the separation has made you cranky and impatient) or slack off (because the separation has made you feel guilty).

▲ Don't let your toddler play one parent against the other. Once your child begins spending time with his father, "But Daddy (or Mommy) lets me!" is likely to be a frequent refrain. Don't allow yourselves to be bullied. If you work out common standards (see above), your toddler won't be able to play that game with either of you.

▲ Ease the transition with a transitional object. Comfort from both of you is important, of course, during this transitional time—but you can't be at your toddler's side every minute. A comfort object, such as a special blanket, a teddy bear, or another toy, can stand in for you when you're not around. The object can provide not only comfort but a constant as your toddler tries to get used to two parents in two homes.

▲ Expect hard times. Generally, the times when your toddler was accustomed to having both parents around—usually evenings and weekends—will be the hardest. Sleep disturbances and fears of going to sleep ("Will Mommy still be here when I wake up?") or of the dark, common during any period of change, are not unusual, even in a child who used to sleep well, and particularly on changeover nights (from Mom's to Dad's or back again) or in the nights surrounding changeover nights. Be understanding and patient with your toddler. Continue offering lots of extra attention and love, especially at bedtime, but don't

make the mistake of offering your bed, which could set the stage for a hard-to-break habit as well as lead your toddler to believe he is taking his father's place in your life. When he wakes quaking with fear in the middle of the night, stay with him for a while if you need to, providing quiet reassurance.

Separations from you may also be more difficult than usual. Your toddler may suddenly become afraid when you take your leave, whether at night, when you put him to sleep, or in the morning when you set out for work. Again, extra patience and understanding will help him feel more secure.

Regression—in the form of a lapse in toilet learning, a desire to return to the bottle or to be carried around all the time, and increased dependency—is also common. What this usually reflects is a subconscious wish to go back to the simpler, safer time of babyhood, the good old days. Respond to regression with understanding and reassurance rather than scolding; let it take its natural course and it's not likely to last very long.

▲ Expect more struggles, for a while. Many of toddlerhood's most notorious characteristics may seem accentuated by the separation—you may well see an increase in temper tantrums, irrationality, negativity, aggression. Deal with each kind of behavior as you would at any time (see the selections on individual behaviors for tips), but with added empathy. Say, "I know you don't like it that Daddy and I don't live together anymore. I know it makes you mad and it makes you sad. It makes me sad that you're sad, but it had to happen." Encourage him to talk about how he feels, and give him plenty of safe opportunities to express his feelings nonverbally, too (see page 171).

▲ Watch your tongue. It's very normal to want to blame your spouse for what's happened to your marriage, particularly if the breakup was a messy one. But bitterness won't help you and could hurt your toddler. Just because you've fallen out of love with your spouse doesn't mean your toddler should love his Dad any less. Don't make disparaging remarks about your ex-husband or fight with him in front of your toddler. Your child shouldn't feel that he must choose sides. Don't burden your child, either, by making him a confidant, an informer, or a go-between; don't ask him what his dad has been doing, or don't ask him to give his father messages for you. And never ask your child to decide which parent to spend time with ("Who do you want to see today?"); that's way too much emotional baggage for a young child to handle.

▲ Don't be too hard on yourself. Your toddler isn't the only one who'll have to adjust to the new family dynamics— you'll feel the stress, too. Like anyone living with the stress of learning to be a single person *and* a single parent, you may well find yourself on an uneven emotional keel for a few months or even longer (you may even be angry at your child, wishing you didn't have to be a single parent). Forgive yourself (rest assured that your toddler will forgive you, too) if you can't always keep your cool, can't always hold back the tears, are subject to irrational outbursts on occasion. Just be sure to apologize to your toddler after an explosion, and to give him a loving and gentle hug after you've collected yourself. But don't be overly apologetic, histrionic, or emotional, since that might frighten him. (See page 751 for more on keeping your cool.)

*"My husband just up and deserted me and our two-year-old daughter. She adores her dad and is devastated that he's not around any more."*

Though such abandonment is not that unusual, it *can* be devastating. With a lot of support, however, children who have been abandoned by one parent can recover and do well.

In a way, your child may be better off not seeing her father at all from now on than seeing him sporadically. Noncustodial parents tend to be detached at such isolated visits, and this lack of engagement seems to be worse for a child than total separation. What's important now is for you to continue to develop a strong relationship with your child; the tips for single parents on page 788 may be particularly helpful.

No matter how angry you are at your husband (and you have every right to be), don't burden your child with your feelings. Explain to her that Daddy wasn't happy, that he went away, that you don't know if he will be back. When she asks about him, or wants to talk about him, let her. Reminisce with her— without any editorial comment. If she's angry or she's sad, let her know that's okay. If she fantasizes that he will return, don't feed her fantasy, but don't make fun of it, either. She may need the fantasy to cling to while she adjusts to the reality of his being gone.

Get professional help immediately if your child seems depressed, is always getting into trouble, isn't sleeping or eating well, or is otherwise behaving in a way that worries you. Get support for yourself, too, if you seem to have trouble coping, adjusting, or functioning.

*"My wife and I are divorced and she has custody of our toddler. Every time I pick our son up my ex and I have a fight. I'm beginning to think he may be better off if I don't see him at all."*

Don't underestimate your importance in your child's life. And don't desert him now, when things are already very rough for him. If you can't manage civil exchanges with his mother, work out visitations so that you and she don't have to see each other—for example, have another adult be the go-between, taking your child from her to you and back again. Years from now, you and your son will be glad you made the effort.

# NONCUSTODIAL PARENTHOOD

*"I just went through a divorce and my former wife got custody of our two-year-old son. He is with me every Tuesday and every other weekend but I wonder if I can still keep a good relationship with him that way."*

Being the noncustodial parent is in some ways easier than having custody—but in other ways, of course, it's more difficult. You can, however, maintain a good relationship with your child, if you work hard at it. That means setting up a comfortable space for him in your home; giving him your full attention when he's with you and calling him daily when he's not, if your agreement allows such calls; minimizing discord with his mother (if there is discord, try to keep your toddler out of it); loving him, but disciplining him as needed, too (see tips for single parents on page 788); sharing in decisions about his life (schools, camps, and so on), if this is part of your agreement; taking responsibility for filling his needs (buying clothing, toys, books, and so on), but being careful not to overindulge him (see page 373).

Also see the tips for talking to your child about separation and divorce on page 791, which can be helpful both to custodial and noncustodial parents.

# SAME-SEX PARENTS

*"I am a single mother and a lesbian. There is a special woman in my life and we are talking about living together on a permanent basis. Friends say this won't be good for my little boy."*

An estimated 4,000,000 homosexual family units in the U.S. are raising some 6,000,000 to 14,000,000 children. Most of these families are "invisible" to outsiders; usually neighbors and casual acquaintances aren't even aware the parent or parents are gay. Many of these families include a partner who was involved in a heterosexual relationship before coming out as gay, broke off that relationship, and took the child or children along on leaving. There are also a growing number of gay and lesbian couples who have adopted a child or conceived one through artificial insemination or a surrogate-mother arrangement.

The past belief that having a homosexual parent or parents will damage a child's emotional and sexual development is based on prejudice, not fact. Happily for these children, the most recent research by child-development experts uniformly affirms that children raised by homosexual parents are no more likely to have psychological or social problems than children raised in heterosexual families. Nor are they more likely to be homosexual themselves.

Of course, having a homosexual parent or parents isn't always easy for children, especially if the parent or couple is openly gay. There may be periods of peer teasing and cruelty during the late childhood, preteen, and early teen years, though perhaps as society becomes more accepting, these kinds of social pressures will ease up. In the meantime, gay and lesbian parents (who have almost always experienced such ridicule themselves) are generally quite capable of helping their offspring cope. There are also support groups for teenage children of gay parents in many cities.

When a homosexual parent has a partner in the home, his or her children seem to do slightly better in terms of self-confidence, self-acceptance, and independence. So raising your child with a partner is likely to have a positive rather than a negative effect on your child. All of the tips for single parents are useful for homosexual parents who remain single (see page 788). Particularly important in either case will be finding an opposite-sex relative or friend to spend some time with your child; sometimes the biological father or surrogate mother is willing to play that role).

Homosexual parents can get support for themselves in one of the many support groups springing up around the country; if one doesn't exist in your community, consider starting one.

## A SICK PARENT— COPING WITH SERIOUS ILLNESS

*"My wife is about to go into the hospital for a major operation, and she's likely to be there for several weeks recuperating. We don't know how to explain this to our daughter without frightening her."*

What your toddler doesn't know can frighten her much more than the truth. When potentially upsetting information is withheld from children and they sense that something is wrong (as they usually do), what they imagine is often worse than the reality.

So instead of launching into an involved cover-up to protect your toddler (which would be hard to pull off, anyway, with your wife absent for so long),

give her an explanation that's accurate in substance, but simple enough for her to understand: "Mommy is sick and she has to go to the hospital so the doctor can help her get better." Don't describe the surgery or give other details your toddler doesn't ask for. Make it clear that she will be able to visit Mommy (if that will indeed be possible) and can bring her a picture or a present if she wants to. Tell her who will take care of her while Mommy is away and you're not available (ideally, it should be her regular sitter, a grandparent, or someone else she knows and feels close to). Assure her that you will be with her a lot, too—and make every effort to keep your word.[3]

And most important, let your child know that it isn't her fault or anyone's fault that her mommy's sick; children sometimes blame themselves for bad things that happen to their parents or others ("Mommy's in the hospital because I didn't listen to her" or "Mommy's sick because I had a tantrum in the supermarket").

No matter how reassuring and comforting your explanations, the situation may provoke anxiety in your child. The possible results include sleep problems, eating problems, the development of new fears or problem behaviors (some children act out by acting up; others find security by withdrawing into themselves). Treat these problems as you would at any other time, being particularly understanding and caring—but without letting all limits lapse. Don't, for example, take your toddler into bed with you if she cries at night if that hasn't been your custom in the past, not only because this may set up a hard-to-break pattern, but because it can be scary and unsettling rather than comforting ("Things must be pretty bad if Daddy is letting me sleep in

---

3. Consider requesting family leave for the duration of your wife's illness; in most instances, it will be available to you under the national Family Leave law.

his bed!"). But do sit by her bed a little longer while she's falling asleep and be sure to comfort her when she cries in the middle of the night. It will also help if she follows her regular routine as closely as possible and has plenty to do (play dates, visits to the playground or indoor play area, and so on). And try to see to it that foods she especially likes are on the daily menu at home. She should also have daily hospital visits, if that's possible and her mother's condition isn't too scary for her to see. (Sometimes, when children aren't allowed in the hospital room, a visit can be set up in a waiting room or lobby.) If visits are out entirely, a photo or video taken of a smiling mom in the hospital *prior* to the surgery may be cheering. So may daily phone calls.

# DEALING WITH DEATH

*"My husband had a heart attack last night and died this morning. I don't know how to tell our son, who is nearly three."*

There's no easy way to tell a young child about the death of someone so close to him, but tell you must.

Explain your husband's death as simply and honestly as you can: "Daddy's heart got very sick and he died. The doctors did everything they could to help make him better, but he was too sick. He can't be with us anymore." Your child will probably want to know where his daddy is now; just what your answer will be will depend at least partly on your personal beliefs. See the box on page 800 for help in explaining about death.

Young children often react to news that devastates older children and adults in an unexpected way. Many, at least initially, seem not to react at all; they listen without comment, then toddle off and go about their business. This lack of reaction doesn't reflect a lack of compassion or a lack of love for the person who has died, just a lack of comprehension or the need to defer recognition of the overwhelming news. Others begin crying for Daddy not so much because they understand that he is dead, but because talking about him makes them want him now. Toddlers, after all, usually have trouble grasping any concepts that involve time; it's often not until the school years that children can understand the finality of death. Most young children repeatedly ask for the person who has died, and must be reminded over and over again that the person can't come back before the reality finally sinks in. Letting your child watch you or someone else pack up Daddy's things (clothes from the closet, the robe from the bathroom door, the hat from the coat rack) may help make it clear that he won't be coming back. Resist sending your toddler off to Grandma's or a friend's house in the weeks after the death; not only will being banished from home be unsettling, but it will make the death even more unreal. He will have to deal with the absence of his father eventually anyway, and going through the grieving period together will help both of you come to terms with the death and strengthen the bond between you. Because you will both need emotional support and help dealing with the practical issues of daily life, however, it will probably be comforting to have a good friend or a close relative come and stay at your home to help out.

It's possible that your child may have irrational ideas about why his father died—he didn't have any food or he went out without a coat. Or he may blame it on himself and his "magical" thinking: "Daddy died because I was mad at him because he didn't take me to the zoo." Such misguided notions need to be dug out and dispelled; to do this, you will have to encourage your

## TALKING ABOUT DEATH

· · · · · · · · · ·

While healthier attitudes about other once-suppressed subjects—sexuality, for instance—are on the rise, death is still too often taboo, veiled in euphemisms or voiced in hushed tones.

But this kind of approach is confusing and scary to children. So when the need arises to talk to your child about death—the death of a person your child knows, of a pet or a neighbor's pet, or of someone on a TV program—be honest and open. Avoid all euphemisms, and use the correct terminology as needed. Referring to death as "going away" or "going to sleep" isn't only likely to instill in a child unfounded fears of travel and bedtime, but unfounded hope that the dead person or animal will return or awaken. Eventually, when the child does discover the truth, the pain is compounded by the betrayal of having been lied to.

Shape your explanation in very simple terms that your toddler can make some sense of, keeping in mind that there's no way that a child this young can truly comprehend death. For example, you can say: "Grandma died. Grandma is dead. Grandma can't come and see us anymore. That makes us very sad." This should suffice for a very young toddler, though for many of them even these simple words will have little meaning. For a two- or three-year-old you can add: "When someone dies, their body stops working and stops moving, they don't need to eat, sleep, or breathe, and then they aren't alive anymore." Supply details only if asked for.

An older toddler may wonder, "Where is Grandma now?" Respond (at a moment when you're not too distraught yourself to talk about it) by explaining that her body is in a box called a coffin in a safe place, a cemetery. If you have religious or philosophical ideas about death you want to pass along, you can add those, too. But keep them as simple as you can, and make sure they won't frighten or mislead your child. Before you offer any explanations, you'll need to consider that young children are extremely literal and can misconstrue

almost anything. If you say that "Grandma is in heaven," your child may ask, "Can we go and visit?" Make it clear that only dead people can go there and that they can't come back. Even if you believe it, don't say that a person who died was taken by God because God loved him or her so much; the child may then fear that God will take you or another favorite person, too.

The most difficult—but probably the most important—aspect of death for young children to grasp is its permanence. When told that Mrs. Smith's dog died, a child may ask, "When is he going to stop being dead so I can play with him?" Having mastered the concept of object permanence (things are still there even if we can't see them; Mommy and Daddy go to work but they come back), it's hard to comprehend that there's no coming back from death—that the person or the animal that they knew is permanently gone.

Children often have very farfetched notions about death. If your child is verbal, try to find out what he or she is thinking by asking: "What do you think 'dead' is?" Then try to dispel any misconceptions. Even if your child can't verbalize his or her thoughts, reading some books together that deal with death at a level a young child can understand may help.

Young children sometimes blame themselves for what happens in their lives; it's important for them to know that it isn't their fault when someone close to them dies.

Don't discourage your child from talking about the death or the dead person or animal if he or she wants to, but don't press such conversation, either, if your child doesn't seem interested. Young children should be allowed to mourn in their own way (which is likely to be very different from the way adults mourn). But swapping memories ("Remember the way Aunt Irene used to bring us oatmeal cookies every time she came to visit?") can be therapeutic for both child and parent, helping to evoke pleasant memories of the person.

toddler to talk about (or draw about) what he's feeling. Don't be disturbed if you see yours playing make-believe dead teddy bear or cemetery. Often, children work out their feelings about the loss of a loved one through drawing or play. Such games are appropriate in the context of a recent exposure to death. (If they continue for months or totally occupy your child's time, however, consult his doctor.)

Because young children are so egocentric, they often worry that death will continue to strike their home—that "if Daddy died, then maybe Mommy will too, or even me." Getting the facts (again, in simple language) about the illness that caused his father's death may help keep him from worrying unnecessarily. You may also need to provide reassurance that you won't leave him, that you'll still be here to love him and take care of him, and that when you're not at home, there will always be someone there to take care of him.

Children faced with such a substantial loss may exhibit signs of grief and distress over a brief mourning period or over a long period of time, continuously or in bursts. They often display many of the same behaviors children show following a divorce (another type of traumatic loss). Guilt, fear, regression, increased dependency, loss of appetite, sleep problems, behavior problems (acting out is particularly likely if the child isn't getting enough attention after the death) are all common. There may also be excessive crying, as well as developmental delays and temporary loss of speech. For some children, anger at the dead parent is a major reaction: "Why did he leave me?" Or the anger may be aimed at the remaining parent: "Why did you let Daddy die?" Expect that the toughest times for your toddler will be the times when his father was most often around, for example, dinnertime, bedtime (especially if Daddy gave him his bath or read him stories), weekends.

Anyone who experiences a loss needs to mourn, including a young child. Let your toddler talk about his feelings and cry. Feel free to cry with him (you don't have to keep your grief to yourself), if you feel like it, but try to avoid losing control in front of your child, which could frighten him. Talk to him about his father frequently and remember him together in positive ways, looking through photo albums, taking walks that he always enjoyed, baking his favorite cookies. Don't try to speed your recoveries by removing all reminders of your husband from the house; these reminders (photos, a favorite chair, bowling trophies, and so on) may be painful at first, but eventually they'll offer solace. Give your toddler some memorabilia of his own (a favorite hat of his father's, a T-shirt he always wore, his wallet) to remember him by. Display a photo of his Dad in his room, if he likes.

Mourning is important but it shouldn't be all-consuming. Now more than ever, familiar rituals and routines will bring you and your toddler comfort. Try to maintain as much normalcy as possible in as many ways as you can (keep up play-group meetings, regular mealtimes, and bedtime rituals). Let him be a child; encourage him to play and enjoy himself instead of making him feel guilty for having fun ("Daddy just died, and all you can do is play!"). If he attends day care or preschool, don't wait much more than a week before returning him there (being back in the swing of things will help his life feel more normal and help him feel better, too). If he doesn't, and if you have to go back to work, see that he has the same caring caregiver most, if not all, of the time; if it's at all possible, don't rely on unfamiliar help, or different relatives or friends on different days. Continuity is always important for a young child, but especially so in the face of such major upheaval. If you're at home but are too distraught to be an adequate caregiver,

## DECIDING
## ABOUT THE FUNERAL

· · · · · · · · · ·

Whether a child should attend a loved one's funeral depends on the child and the particular situation. Ask yourself some of these questions before deciding: Is it likely that people attending the funeral (particularly people your child loves and counts on) will lose control? Will the emotions evoked in the child and in others be too powerful for one so young to handle? Will the child be more frightened if left at home, away from the rest of the family? Is there someone your child knows well who can either stay with him or her at home, or who can come along to the funeral and serve as protector—taking the child out if the going gets too rough? Will the casket be open? Will this scare your child, or aid in comprehension? Would you rather the loved one be remembered by your toddler in life rather than death? Will the burial itself (seeing the person they love being lowered into the earth) be traumatic? (In which case, the child could go the funeral but not the burial.) Will attending the funeral make the idea of a permanent loss more tangible and make it more possible for your child to say good-bye?

If a child doesn't attend the funeral of a close family member, then it's a good idea to have another ceremony in which the child can say good-bye. Perhaps you can visit the funeral home privately before the funeral, or have a ceremony at home, or put flowers on the grave together after the funeral. All of these can help a child accept the reality of the death and provide a sense of closure without the public display and ritual aspects of a funeral.

make sure someone else who loves your child is there to care for him and give you the support you need.

Your toddler will also feel more secure if you keep discipline predictable. House rules should stay pretty much the same as they were, though you may need to be particularly gentle and sensitive in enforcing them if your child seems emotionally vulnerable. If your child cries during the night or has a lot of trouble falling asleep (a common problem for children who've experienced a death in the family), go to him and comfort him. Stay with him as long as he needs you for now, but resist the temptation to bring him into your bed—even if you're aching for the company. Letting him take his father's place beside you in your bed may lead him to believe that he's taking his father's place in your life. (Also avoid saying things like "You're the man in the family now, you need to take care of Mommy.")

Allowed to grieve and to recover at their own pace, and given plenty of support and attention, children who've suffered the loss of a parent (or other close family member) usually do just fine. Studies show that problems are only likely to arise if the remaining parent doesn't offset the loss by providing extra nurturing, or if she is so much in need of support herself that the child feels obliged to provide it, placing too heavy a burden on him. It is therefore essential, both for your sake and his, that you get the support you need from other sources. For some children, as well as for some bereaved spouses, a grief support group is extremely beneficial. If group situations make you feel uncomfortable, look to friends or relatives, your clergyperson, your doctor, or a counselor for one-on-one therapy.

If your child seems unable to come to terms with the loss, and is depressed or having serious behavior problems, don't delay in seeking professional counseling.

*"We had to put our cat, whom our daughter loved, to sleep yesterday. We haven't told our daughter yet because we're not sure how to talk to a two-year-old about death."*

First of all, skip the part about the animal being "put to sleep." Though this term is commonly used, it can give rise to all kinds of terrifying ideas about sleep—especially when your toddler learns that the cat is never going to wake up. Instead explain by saying "The cat was very sick and is dead now." Talk honestly, but on your toddler's level, about death (see page 800). Let her react any way that feels right to her, encourage her to talk about her feelings if she wants to, and allow her to be sad. Reminisce about the cat together, looking through pictures, recalling cute behaviors ("Remember the way Whiskers used to climb on your tummy?"). Keep in mind, however, that your toddler may seem not to care one way or the other about the cat's demise. This is a perfectly normal reaction in young children, who have difficulty comprehending the finality of death.

It's possible, though, that your toddler may react to your cat's death as she might to any abrupt and upsetting change in her life—with irritability, sleeping problems, and stepped-up temper tantrums. Be patient and understanding as she adjusts to the change, and if you feel that replacing the cat might help, do so. Having her help select the new pet will help her bond with it more quickly.

A very sensitive toddler may worry that if death can strike her cat, it can strike her, too, or someone else she cares about. If your toddler seems more fearful and clingy than usual after learning of the death, she may need extra reassurance from you for a while.

# CHAPTER TWENTY-SIX

# When Others Care for Your Child

Nobody else can provide the love, the nurturing, the understanding of a parent; nobody else can take a parent's place in a child's heart. But whether it's for a few hours a week or eight hours a day, there will be times when someone else will take your place, if not in your child's heart, then at his or her side. And choosing the person (or people) who will care for your child at those times can be one of the most significant challenges of parenthood. The following chapter will help you meet that challenge, and find the best child-care situation (or preschool) to fill your family's needs.

## WHAT ARE THE CHILD-CARE OPTIONS?

A live-in nanny. A daily baby-sitter. An occasional sitter. Group day care. Home day care. Preschool. There are a variety of options open to parents, but deciding which one (or which combination) is right for you and your toddler requires some exploration. Before you begin to sift through the many options, you should consider several basic factors, including:

**Your child's needs.** A quiet toddler who tends to be shy in groups or a very young one who needs more individualized attention may fare better in a one-on-one situation, or at least in a day-care or family-care setting where there is a low ratio of children to adults and where children are treated with sensitivity. On the other hand, a quiet child who has never spent much time around other children may come out of his or her shell in a supportive group situation. A secure, verbal child who socializes easily will probably be bored at home alone with a nanny and thrive in a group. Most toddlers, however, are relatively adaptable; as long as they're being looked after by a caring person (or caring people), they'll adjust to any type of child care.

**Your needs.** You need to consider your schedule: Do you work? Are your hours irregular—some days until 4:30, some days until 7:30? Do you work different days every week, or work only mornings? Do you need a baby-sitter who is flexible and can come whenever you need help—and stay as long as necessary? What about a home day-care facility that will let you switch days and hours at short notice, or a preschool that provides before- and after-school care? If you don't have a car or access to convenient public transit, then you also need to think about a caregiver who can come to your home, a car pool, or a group program that provides transportation. Location may also be important—a distant day-care program means spending extra hours in the car, hours better spent having fun with your child.

**Financial issues.** Child care in this country does not come cheap. Often, child-care options are limited by what parents can afford. Generally, in-home care by a baby-sitter or nanny is the most expensive choice; family day care, subsidized day care, or cooperative baby-sitting are the most affordable choices. The generalizations may not hold true, however, if you have more than one child; one sitter who cares for two children at home may cost less than two day-care tuitions.

# MOST COMMON OPTIONS

Figuring out what you and your toddler need and what you can afford is just the beginning in determining which child-care situation will work best for your family. Next, you'll have to consider the various options available in your community:

## In-home child care

*What it's like.* A nanny, a baby-sitter, or another child-care worker comes to your home and cares for your child, full- or part-time, or on a flexible schedule.

*Advantages.* For your child, the comfort and consistency of familiar surroundings (a real plus for younger toddlers) and of one-on-one care from the same person each day; improved odds of more personal attention and a chance to form a close bond with the caregiver;[1] less time spent commuting (to and from day care or preschool); probably, fewer illnesses (since he or she is not regularly exposed to a large number of other children—and their germs); and the chance to stay home and rest when ill, rather than having to go back to day care prematurely. For you, fewer logistical complications (no worrying about pickups and drop-offs or taking time off from work when your child is sick); less hurried and harried mornings, maybe even the opportunity for reading a story or playing a game (the baby-sitter can dress and feed your pokey toddler after you leave); and possibly, some relief from household chores (depending on the situation and the job description, the baby-sitter may help with light cleaning, laundry, and/or marketing).

---

1. But no guarantees. A child may, in fact, receive less attention in a one-on-one situation from an uncaring nanny than in a crowded day-care setting with a staff of loving teachers.

*Disadvantages.* For your child, less opportunity to socialize (unless you or the caregiver makes an effort to arrange play dates or set up a play group); possibly, poorer quality care, if you can't find or afford a qualified professional; and the risk of confusion and disappointment (perhaps even a sense of loss if a strong attachment has been formed) should the sitter leave suddenly. For you, the possibility of a potentially job-threatening crisis if the caregiver calls in sick, has transportation trouble, or suddenly quits and you have no back-up arrangement; loss of privacy, if you have a live-in nanny; possibly, added stress if you are uncomfortable having a stranger in your home round-the-clock; higher cost, especially if you hire a trained professional; and possibly, a sense that you have to compete with the caregiver for your child's affections. If you choose a foreign *au pair*, you may find yourself in a bind—you or your child may not like the *au pair* but may be obligated to employ her until her term runs out, or she could

## *SHARING A BABY-SITTER*

.........

For many parents, shouldering the cost of an in-home baby-sitter on their own is financially prohibitive. Yet sharing the cost with another family can make it surprisingly affordable. Before hooking up with another family, however, consider:

▲ Who will hire the sitter? Will one family be in charge of the interviewing process, or will both families share in the decision making?

▲ How well matched are the families' child-care philosophies? You can't expect one sitter to care for each family's child (or children) in a completely different way. Do you have similar ideas about nutrition, discipline, and other significant issues? Or do you feel comfortable compromising?

▲ How well matched are the children? They don't have to be the same age or even have the same temperament, but it's best not to team two children who can't get along.

▲ Where will the sitter sit? Will she switch off between homes? How often? (Consistency is important for toddlers; switching every three months or so might be better than switching daily or weekly, though any schedule that's predictable can work well.)

▲ Who will provide the supplies? Will the visiting family need to bring their own diapers, snacks, and meals, or will the host family always provide these? Will a double stroller be necessary? Do both families chip in to buy it, or will it belong to just one family?

▲ Who will take over when the sitter calls in sick? Will the arrangement be flexible (whoever can spare the day at work more easily stays home) or formal (whoever's house it is will stay home, or parents will alternate the responsibility monthly)?

▲ Will the sitter be able to handle the load? This can be a stretch if there are more than two children, but a well-trained caregiver should be able to handle the job. Arranging play groups and other scheduled activities at least a few times a week may help reduce the stress.

▲ Will the sitter have other responsibilities? It's probably best not to add numerous household chores to the shared sitter's duties, or she may find herself spread too thinly.

▲ How will the financial end be handled? Who will pay the sitter? Who will file the tax forms? How about insurance? Make sure that both households are covered in case your sitter is injured on the job.

## PRESCHOOL: WHO NEEDS IT?

· · · · · · · · · ·

A ctually, no child who's nurtured ade - quately at home *needs* preschool. While children who attend these programs may have a slight initial edge when it comes time for kindergarten, that edge eventually disappears. Still, a well-balanced, stimulating, but pressure-free early childhood program can be enriching and exciting for most two- to five-year-olds—and liberating for their parents, whether they work out of the home or not.

In a quality preschool setting, young children are offered a wide range of experiences that can be beneficial even for those who are thriving at home with a parent or conscientious baby-sitter. They are schooled in such essential skills as how to cooperate, take turns, help with chores, follow rules, make decisions, and get along in a group. Though academics shouldn't be emphasized, a good program will also challenge a child intellectually and creatively while teaching the ABC's of socializing.

---

get homesick and want to return to her country, leaving you in the lurch.[2]

## Family day care (or group home care)

*What it's like.* A caregiver cares for a small number of children (often including her own) in her home.

*Advantages.* For your child, depending on the setting, a cozy, home-like atmosphere; less exposure to infection than in a large day-care center because of the smaller number of children (as long as good hygiene is observed and there is a policy prohibiting attendance by sick children); possibly, more individualized care (though this varies with the skill and dedication of the caregiver); the opportunity to be with other children, usually of varying ages. For you, relatively low cost; possibly, more flexibility as to hours (since the caregiver is at home, she may be more amenable to keeping your child after hours or to early drop-offs).

*Disadvantages.* For your child, possibly,

inadequate safety and health policies, especially common when a facility is unlicensed (see page 815); more infections than in-home care; poorer quality care (though some are excellent, many family caregivers are untrained); a chaotic play situation (such groups have a high turnover rate, with children coming and going throughout the year). For you, lack of back-up (for example, if the caregiver or one of her own children is ill, she may have to close down until they are recovered, leaving parents without child care).

## Group day care

*What it's like.* One or more groups of infants or very young children spend full days (occasionally, part-days) in a relatively formal care program, in the charge of one or more teachers and aides. Hours are usually arranged to fit parental working hours.

*Advantages.* These vary with the quality of the facility, but can include for your child: a better chance of quality care from trained and experienced caregivers than may be found in the average family day care (this is not a given); a program geared to his or her age and development;

---

2. If you do hire a foreign *au pair*, a support group of other *au pairs* may help her adjust.

opportunities for play with a number of other children of the same age; a wide variety of toys and equipment; usually, some state or local regulation, under which health, safety, and other aspects of the program may be monitored. For you, reliability (if a teacher is sick, a replacement is provided—it doesn't become your headache).

*Disadvantages.* These, too, vary with the program, but can include for your child: more exposure to illness, and thus more illness (though this can be reduced when sound health policies are followed); possibly, less individualized care than other child-care choices, especially if there is a high ratio of children to teachers. For you, less flexibility in scheduling (a set schedule may not take parental needs into account); fairly high cost (usually lower than in-home care and higher than family day care, though costs vary).

### Preschool (or nursery school)

*What it's like.* One or more classes of children spend half or full days under the care of one or more teachers in a formal program designed to enhance readiness for school. Some preschools accept children from the age of two years, others not until three; others have acceptance policies based on toileting and other skills.

*Advantages.* Again, these vary with the caliber of the school, but can include for your child: a better chance of quality care from trained and experienced caregivers; a formal program geared to his or her age and development; opportunities for play with lots of other children of the same age; a wide variety of toys and equipment; usually, some state or local regulations, under which health and safety (and sometimes even curriculum) may be monitored. For you, reliability (if a teacher is sick, a substitute is provided).

*Disadvantages.* Again, these vary with the program, but can include for your child: more exposure to illness, and thus more illness (though this can be reduced when sound health policies are followed); toddler burnout, if a preschool program is overly demanding or academically rigorous. For you, less flexibility in scheduling;[3] fairly high cost.

## OTHER OPTIONS

**Cooperative baby-sitting.** Cooperative baby-sitting can involve just two families (you sit for my child on Friday night and I sit for yours on Sunday) or a dozen (parents earn vouchers for each hour spent sitting for other co-op members' children, which they redeem when they need a sitter). It's free (except for the reciprocal obligation of caring for other members' children) and—because you're dealing with other parents, usually parents you know—you can generally trust the care your child will receive. You can set up an informal co-op with friends who have children around the same age, or advertise for members in a doctor's office, house of worship, community center, day-care center, or preschool. Get to know potential parent members before you agree to have them participate and insist they become familiar with child-safety recommendations, such as those in Chapter Twenty-One, and complete a first-aid/CPR course before taking on baby-sitting chores.

For a group cooperative, put together a directory that includes vital information about each child: name, birthdate, address, home phone number, emergency

---

3. Most preschools follow the public school calendar, closing on certain holidays and during school breaks, posing a logistical nightmare for working parents. Many preschools also offer only half a day for young toddlers, mornings or afternoons, which means that parents who work a full day must employ another child-care provider to cover the balance.

phone numbers (including doctor), nap schedule, allergies, favorite foods and hated foods, likes and dislikes, as well as the availability of the parent or parents for sitting. It's a good idea if all members of the co-op have liability coverage so any injuries in the home are covered.

In a large co-op, regular meetings (with kids invited so they can play together) should be held so problems can be worked out and any new parents can be introduced.

**A family-member baby-sitter.** Having a grandparent or another relative who loves your child serve as caregiver can be ideal—but *only* if this family member really wants to take on the job and is really good with kids. Even then, it can sometimes be a decidedly mixed blessing that can lead to family discord. You may, for example, be reluctant to tell the family member when you're unhappy with some aspect of the care, because you don't want to ruffle feelings. You may be particularly hesitant if you aren't paying for the help. To minimize discomfort and prevent resentment, set up house rules in advance (for example, no junk food, no buying gifts on every out-

ing, and so on) and work out a daily schedule (so much TV and no more, so much time at the playground, naps and snacks as specified). Also encourage open communication between baby-sitter and parents.

**Corporate or on-the-job day care**. Though it's unfortunately still rare in the United States (inexplicably, since parents tend to be much more productive on the job when their children are being cared for nearby), corporate on-site day care or preschool facilities can be a boon to working parents. They offer flexibility (you can usually drop off early and pick up late), security (you know your child is nearby and in good hands), and more time together for parents and children (parent and child commute together, and often even take breaks and lunch together). Some corporate day-care programs offer facilities for children whose parents work the night shift, and a few even offer separate care for children when they're sick (see page 825). Hopefully, more companies will start offering day care to their workers with children, either independently or in consortium with other companies.

# Choosing the Right Child Care

## AN IN-HOME CAREGIVER

**Locating candidates.** Often the best way to get the name of a nanny or other in-home caregiver is by tapping into your community's local parents network: ask around at the playground, ask friends with children, ask at the pediatrician's office, or post your needs in appropriate places, such as the doctor's office, your

house of worship, a nearby preschool, or a local hospital. You can also contact an agency that provides baby-sitters or nannies. If you do use an agency, choose one that has been around for years (fly-by-night operations abound, and most states don't license such agencies) or that comes highly recommended (if you don't have an acquaintance who's used the agency, ask for several references). Look for an agency that has a reputation for supplying well trained and well screened

---

## BABY-SITTER PLUS CHILD

· · · · · · · · · ·

A caregiver who has a child or two of her own may be ideal in some ways—certainly, she has some personal experience in child care. But there may also be problems—for example, when her own child-care arrangements break down. Rather than reject an otherwise qualified baby-sitter in this situation, it's often pos-

sible to work out an agreement that allows her to bring along her own child when she's in a bind. Some parents even agree to allow a sitter to care for both her child and theirs full-time, a solution that helps two working parents (or sets of working parents) give their children a good start.

---

applicants, but *never* take the agency's word on any particular applicant. Always follow up yourself with your own screening process (see below). You can also try the jobs-wanted ads in the local newspaper, or run a want ad of your own, but you'll have to be particularly scrupulous about checking references when you go that route.

**What you need to know about an in-home caregiver.** The screening process usually begins with reading resumés, if the candidates have supplied them. It then moves on to an interview process, beginning on the telephone to screen out clearly inappropriate choices and ending with two or three in-person interviews with each of the best finalists. (It's rare that a candidate loosens up enough on the first interview for you to get a good idea of what she's really like.) In your interviews, try to learn the following:

*Why she wants the job.*[4] Is she desperate for work—any kind of work—or does she really love working with children? Does she consider child care an interim position, and only means it to last until another "better" career opportunity comes along?

*Her qualifications.* A caregiver doesn't necessarily have to have a degree in child development (although that would certainly be a nice extra), but she should be: well spoken (even if English is not her native language, she should be fluent in it); bright enough to encourage your child verbally and challenge him or her intellectually; knowledgeable about children and experienced in their care (you'll be able to discern this to some extent from the interview and from observing her interaction with your child or children, but be sure you also carefully check her references); trained in or willing to take a course in first aid, including CPR and the Heimlich maneuver, and concerned with good hygiene (in other words, a hand-washer). Most important, though, are the things that *don't* show up on a resumé, the ones you'll have to trust your instincts and observations, backed up by references, in assessing: energy level, enthusiasm, sensitivity, kindness, and love of children.

*Her age.* Age is less significant on its own than other considerations, but a relatively young baby-sitter may lack maturity and experience (of course, some not-so-young adults may, too) and a much older baby-sitter may lack the vitality necessary to keep up with a toddler—but then again, some older candidates may have more energy than some younger ones.

---

4. Since the vast majority of in-home caregivers are women, we use the feminine pronoun here.

*Previous experience.* Obtain a thorough employment history, especially considering the following: When did she leave her last job, and why? Has she kept jobs for long periods, or tended to flit from job to job? Has there been a lengthy break since the last job, with no good explanation (such as additional education or a new baby)? When there has been a break or when you have another reason to wonder about the candidate's past, you may want to ask for personal references, such as a clergyperson. In some cases, you may even want to check with the state police to be certain the candidate doesn't have a criminal record.

*References.* Narrow your choices down to a few finalists through interviews, then check their references; be thorough and cautious. Insist on talking to previous employers yourself rather than accepting letters of recommendation, which can be faked. If there are no previous employers, ask for references from teachers, clergy, or other objective sources. Do not accept references from family or friends.

*Availability.* Though you won't be able to hold her to a verbal agreement (or, in some cases, even a written one), having a caregiver who is willing to stay with the family for as long as you need her (assuming the situation works out for everyone) offers a certain measure of assurance that there will be continuity of care in your child's life—and that you won't have to hunt for a nanny again in six months.

Also try to determine if there are any factors in her life (such as young children of her own) that might make her less than regularly available on a day-to-day basis, or that could make it difficult for her to work overtime (if that's important to you). See box, facing page for a possible solution to this problem.

*Child-care philosophy.* In general, look for someone who shares as many of your child-rearing philosophies as possible. Discuss with each candidate the issues you consider significant, such as nutrition, discipline, toilet learning, weaning. Ask open-ended questions that require more than "yes" or "no" answers: What do you think is the most important thing a toddler needs? How would you spend a typical day with my toddler? What would you do if you found my toddler climbing on the windowsill? How would you handle a tantrum? What would you do if my toddler had a toileting accident?

*Physical health history.* Make sure that there's nothing about the candidate's health that might interfere with her doing the job. Ask: Has she been tested for tuberculosis? Immunized against hepatitis? Is there anything in her background or present life that could endanger your child?

*Personal habits.* Does the candidate smoke? Since secondhand smoke is linked to so many health problems in children (not to mention safety problems around the home), it's likely that you won't want your toddler cared for by a smoker—or, at least, not by someone who will smoke on the job. A prospective sitter is not liable to admit readily to alcohol or other drug abuse (nor are you liable to feel comfortable asking about it), but if you know what to look for, the signs of such abuse can often be detected; see page 812.

*Transportation to work.* Does she have a way of getting to work each day on time? Does she have a driver's license, if you need her to drive on the job?

Having asked questions of your candidate, also ask some of yourself:

▲ Did the applicant arrive on time for the interview? If she didn't, you can infer that she may sometimes be late for work, too.

▲ Was her appearance neat and clean? If she came to the interview with unwashed

# SIGNS OF SUBSTANCE ABUSE IN A CAREGIVER

Anyone who uses drugs or abuses alcohol is not a suitable caregiver for a child. But since a substance abuser is not likely to announce the fact, parents must be alert to the signs of abuse. They are often readily apparent—if you know what to look for. Consider any of the following signs a red flag:

▲ Slurred speech, staggering, disorientation, poor concentration, and other signs of drunkenness, with or without the smell of liquor on the breath (possible signs of the abuse of alcohol or barbiturates or other "downers").

▲ Restlessness, nervousness, agitation, dilated pupils, poor appetite (possible signs of stimulant abuse—for example, amphetamines or cocaine).

▲ Euphoria, relaxation of inhibitions, increased appetite, memory loss; possibly, dilated pupils and bloodshot eyes; even paranoia (possible signs of marijuana use).

▲ Pinpoint pupils (possible sign of early heroin addiction). Another sign of such addiction, a pronounced craving for sweets, would be next-to-impossible to detect at an interview, or even on the job. It would only be worthy of concern if it were accompanied by the pinpoint pupils.

▲ Watery runny eyes, excessive yawning, irritability, anxiety, tremors, chills and sweating (possible signs of drug withdrawal, which could occur if an addicted person tries not to use drugs on the job).

Any of these could also indicate mental or physical illness. Should you note them in a prospective caregiver, you could insist on a medical checkup to rule out substance abuse as well as any illness, but it may be better to move on to the next candidate.

---

hair or dirty fingernails, you may rightly suspect she will take even less care once she has the job. And a *laissez-faire* attitude about her personal hygiene might well foretell a *laissez-faire* attitude about cleanliness and other important matters when caring for your toddler.

▲ Does her personality seem compatible with yours? Are you comfortable with her? Do you seem able to communicate well? Does she have a sense of humor?

▲ Does your toddler seem comfortable with her? (Keep in mind that a typically reticent toddler may take some time to adjust to a stranger.) More important: Does she seem comfortable with your toddler? Does she seem kind and caring? Is she patient and truly interested in your child or does she seem to be just going through the motions?

▲ Did you notice any warning signs of

mental instability? These could include: lack of eye contact; monosyllabic, evasive, or pat answers; confusion or lack of clarity in conversation; apparent extremist behavior or thinking (religious fanaticism, compulsive cleanliness, excessive rigidity); inappropriate behavior (such as giggling or singsong responses); outlandish dress or makeup; emotional neediness (she's recently broken up with a boyfriend and sees this job as a way of recovering from the loss).

Once you've singled out your best prospect (she's interviewed well, received solid recommendations), consider a trial session so you can see her in action before you make a long-term commitment—such a trial is well worth the cost. Pick a day when you don't have to go to work (on a weekend, perhaps) and plan to be in and out of the house while she's on duty. Take her through your toddler's daily routine as well as any household routines she'll need to be familiar with and give her lots of opportunity to get to know your toddler and your home. Chances are your toddler will loosen up more when you're not around, so make sure you leave for a couple of short stretches (an hour or so at a time) during the day. While you're around, keep your eyes and ears open. If your toddler tends to be shy with new people, pay more attention to how the baby-sitter responds to your child than how your child responds to the sitter (your child will warm up eventually to the right sitter, but the right sitter will already be warm). Follow your instincts; if something tells you that this person is not right for your child, err on the safe side and look elsewhere.

For more information and suggestions, write to the International Nanny Association and/or one of the other caregiver information services (see page 814).

# FAMILY DAY CARE (OR GROUP HOME CARE)

**Locating possibilities.** Again, your child's doctor, parents of other children, friends, and neighbors may be able to provide good leads as well as recommendations. There may also be a local organization that can provide the names of registered family day care facilities; or contact the National Association for the Education of Young Children (NAEYC; see page 814).

**What you need to know about a family day-care situation.** Family day-care facilities can range from wonderful to wretched. To sort out those you are considering, consider:

*Is it licensed or registered?* Not all states regulate or license family care facilities, and requirements are often lax even in

states that do regulate. Inspections are not necessarily required; when they are, they may be few and far between (an inspector may have hundreds of facilities to oversee). Still, some regulation is better than none.

*Health and safety standards.* These are similar to those you'd look for in a day-care or preschool facility: an indoor space that is clean, child-safe, fire-safe (with sprinklers and fire alarm in working order, and with an easy escape route in case of fire), and an enclosed, safe outdoor play space (see page 643).

*The qualifications of the caregiver.* Look for the same qualities you would look for in an in-home caregiver: experience and, preferably, training in child care; training in first aid and basic life support; fondness for and patience with children (see page 810).

*The child-care philosophy of the caregiver.* Evaluate this as you would for an in-home caregiver (see page 811).

*The caregiver-to-child ratio.* For children younger than two, a ratio of 1 adult to 4 (or preferably 3) children is recommended; for ages two and three, at least 1 adult for every 6 children (a 1 to 4 ratio is ideal). These ratios should include any of the caregiver's children who are at home some or all of the time. (Most states allow much higher ratios—as high as 1 adult to 15 children—but such numbers don't make for a safe situation or good care.)

*The setup.* Check to see if the care provider is also running her household (doing laundry, house cleaning, marketing) while caring for your child and the others; if so, attention may be seriously lacking.

*Toys and activities.* There should be an ample supply of well-maintained, age-

## SOURCES OF HELP AND INFORMATION

· · · · · · · · · ·

**National Association for the Education of Young Children (NAEYC)** provides information on child-care options; 1509 16th Street NW, Washington, DC 20036-1826; (800) 424-2460.

**National Academy of Early Childhood Programs** is an independent accrediting agency; 1834 Connecticut Avenue NW, Washington, DC 20009.

**The International Nanny Association** is a professional association; it provides (for a fee) a directory listing affiliated local nanny agencies and nanny schools, as well

as a nanny phone card (see footnote, page 821) and health insurance; 125 S. 4th Street, Norfolk, NE 68701; (402) 691-9628.

**National Association for Childcare Resource and Referral Agencies** is an umbrella group that has 300 member agencies around the country; call them for information about local resources; (507) 287-2220.

**National Association for Family Child Care** can give you a list of accredited child-care providers; (800) 359-3817.

---

appropriate toys (toys meant for older children should not be accessible to younger ones) and plenty of stimulating and safe activities planned (outdoor play, arts and crafts, story time).

Television viewing should *not* be a regular part of the day; though half an hour to an hour a day of shows carefully selected for appropriateness isn't terrible, the television should not be on all of the time (either for the children or the child-care provider to watch).

*Availability of back-up.* Is there back-up if a child of the caregiver or the caregiver herself is ill?

*Insurance.* Make sure the caregiver's home insurance covers injury to any child in the group while in her care.

*References.* Be sure to check these personally; do not rely on written references (see page 811). Make sure they include parents who've had children at the facility in the recent past, as well as those who still have children there.

Once you've located a family day-care center you think will serve your family's needs, plan to spend a few hours

observing the group at a time when all the children are present. If the care provider won't allow you to observe, don't even consider placing your child there.

# GROUP DAY-CARE OR PRESCHOOL PROGRAM

**Locating possibilities.** Again, your child's doctor, parents of other children, friends, and neighbors may be able to provide good leads as well as recommendations. There may also be a local organization that can provide the names of registered day-care or preschool facilities, or you can contact NAEYC (National Association for the Education of Young Children; see above box). If you're really lucky, you won't have to look very far—your employer will supply good-quality on-site day care (see page 809).

**What you need to know about a day-care or preschool program.** Quality varies considerably from program to program; it may take time and effort to find the one that's right for you and your child. Consider the following when making your choice:

*Is it licensed or registered?* Ask to see a current license or registration; if the facility is not licensed, check with your state or local government to see if such licensing is required. Also ask if the program is accredited by any outside organization. The National Academy of Early Childhood Programs and NAEYC both set standards more rigorous than state or local standards. For a list of their accredited programs contact the organizations directly (see box, facing page). Centers that comply with FIDCR (Federal Interagency Day Care Requirements) have also met tougher standards than state licensing would ordinarily demand.

*The safety and health policy.* Are safety precautions taken—are outlets covered, toys age appropriate, stairs gated, playground equipment in good repair, and so on? Is there good ventilation in the facility? (Don't be fooled by air freshening sprays; check for vents.) Are there smoke detectors (ask to see latest inspection certificate), fire extinguishers, window guards (if necessary), and easy egress (with exits clearly marked), in case of fire? Is the parking lot safely away from the play area? Are certified car seats used on field trips? What safety precautions are taken when children take walks outside the school grounds? See Chapter Twenty-One for more on making both indoor and outdoor spaces safe for toddlers.

Are workers trained in first aid, CPR, injury prevention, and infection control? Are emergency numbers posted near every phone? Is there a written policy outlining what to do when a child is ill or injured (ask to see it) and a place that is safe and yet separate from other children where sick children can await their parent or caregiver? If your child must take medication, will the teachers administer it? Is a medical consultant available or at least on call?

Is an effort made to reduce the transmission of infectious organisms? Are toys frequently washed (soft toys in the washing machine, plastic toys in the dishwasher or in hot soapy water)? Are wet surfaces (such as a water-play table), which are most susceptible to germ growth, kept clean and disinfected? Are workers fastidious about hand washing, especially after diaper changes, helping a child at the potty, coming in from outdoors, and cleaning up vomit or blood, and before handling food? Are children expected to wash their hands before eating, after using the toilet, and after playing outside? Is a separate sink used for hand washing and food preparation? Do the same staff members change diapers and prepare food? (It's better if they don't.) Are diaper changing surfaces cleaned after every use? Do children in diapers wear clothes over them? (Contamination of surfaces may be greater if kids wear diapers alone.)

Are the bathroom and kitchen well maintained, with high hygienic and safety standards? Ideally, each child should have his or her own potty chair or seat brought from home; communal seats are difficult to keep sanitary. Are hazardous materials, such as cleaning solutions, inaccessible to children? Does the garbage can have a foot pedal so both the staff and children don't have to touch the lid?

*Scheduling.* Can the available options meet your family's needs? You may need full-time care, or you may just want to start your toddler with a couple of half-day sessions a week and work your way up to five half-days. Most day-care programs and some preschools offer full-day sessions and before- and after-school care to working parents. A full day is not necessary, however, if someone is at home to care for the child. If you sometimes require early drop-off or late pick-up, are these options available at a reasonable additional cost?

*Cost.* The cost of quality day-care programs and preschool programs can be staggeringly high, especially when all the extras are added in (be sure all costs are quoted, including any materials fees or charges for late pickups). Costs can be considerably lower if a program is subsidized (by either the government, a corporation, a house of worship, or another service agency), or if the program is run cooperatively (parents all take turns as classroom volunteers or teaching assistants to keep the personnel costs down). A cooperative arrangement can work well for many families, but isn't ideal for very dependent parents or very dependent children (clinging on either side can interfere with normal social interaction and parental responsibilities). Co-ops, of course, are unrealistic for those parents who don't have a flexible schedule.

*Entrance policy.* Does your child have to "pass" an entrance exam and interview? How much pressure will there be? How much competition? Is it worth it? (See page 818.)

*Teacher-child ratio.* The ratio recommended by the AAP (American Academy of Pediatricians) is: under twenty-four months, 1 adult to 3 children; fifteen to thirty months, 1 adult to 4 children; thirty-one to thirty-five months, 1 adult to 5 children; and for three-year-olds, 1 adult to 7 children. The NAEYC recommends 1 adult to every 5 two-year-olds and every 7 three-year-olds.

*Teacher turnover.* Ask how long each of the teachers has been on the staff. A high turnover rate raises questions about the quality of the program and continuity of care for the children in attendance. It also makes it difficult to assess the present program by talking to parents whose children attended the program in the past.

*Staff qualifications.* The director should have teaching credentials and a degree in early-childhood education. Ideally, teachers should be trained in early-childhood development or education. Unfortunately, many have no training, and most states don't require teacher training for day-care or preschool accreditation. All programs should run criminal background checks and thorough health checks on prospective teacher candidates, but not all do.

*Physical plant.* Is there enough space? (The NAEYC recommends 35 square feet of child-usable indoor space and 75 square feet of outdoor space per child. Many programs do not meet this standard.) Is there an ample selection of toys? Are toys safe and age-appropriate for even the youngest in the room? Are they up-to-date and in good condition—or are puzzles missing pieces, dolls missing heads, and cars missing wheels? Sit on a toddler seat to get a child's-eye view of the room. Is there enough light, a good level of activity (energetic but not frenetic), a comfortable noise level? Are there enough supplies, play areas that encourage imaginative play, natural science materials? Are there lots of pictures on the walls (hung at a child's eye level), and art work that isn't uniform or too neat? (Plenty of individual creativity should be evident.) Is there enough space for afternoon naps—does each child have an individual bed, mattress, or mat to sleep on? Does each have a cubby or another space for personal belongings? Are toilets and sinks child-size or made accessible with the use of sturdy stepstools? Is there a safe playground on the premises or a short, safe walk away? Be sure the play area meets the safety standards on page 644.

*Staff-parent interaction.* Are there regular parent–teacher conferences? Beyond these, can special consultations—either in person or by phone—be arranged when needed? Is there a memo board or other system to facilitate daily parent–teacher communication (especially important in all-day situations)?

*Food and nutrition policy.* Do children eat food brought from home or is it prepared at school? If food is prepared on-site, what is it like? Is it nutritious (see Chapter Eighteen)? Are food safety rules observed (see page 527)? See what meals and snacks look like and how they're prepared; taste them, too, if possible.

*Toileting policy.* Are children who are still in diapers welcome? Day-care programs generally accept children in diapers, but many preschools do not. If your child is in the midst of or about to begin toilet learning, will the staff cooperate in the process?

**Evaluating the program.** To assess any program, you need to use your eyes, nose, and ears, as well as your good sense:

▲ Ask the director about the program's philosophy. A good program is mostly free play, interwoven with noncompetitive group activities, such as circle time, sing-alongs, story time, and playground visits. There should be no pressure to sit still and quietly listen for more than ten or fifteen minutes at a time, and no pressure at all to perform academically. The teachers should, however, have some sort of written daily plan for play and informal learning; ask to see a sample.

The program that's right for your child will depend on your child's personality. Some children do well with a program that has very little structure, others need some structure, still others need a highly structured (but not overly rigid) program. A very active child needs a place with a lot of freedom to move around but may also need clearly defined limits; a quiet child needs small group activities with lots of individual attention

and encouragement to strike out independently; a very curious and bright child may need extra stimulation and challenges. Children for whom adjusting or making transitions is difficult need a flexible preschool program (such children may need to have a parent stay for a few days—or weeks—to help them over the initial adjustment period, or may need special help with transitions from one activity to another). For a child who is sensitive to noise and overstimulation, a relatively quiet atmosphere is preferable (though no day care or preschool will or should be completely quiet), with corners where the child can go to escape the excitement. If very bright and busy surroundings (colors, shapes, patterns) tend to overstimulate your child, select a school that has a more subdued decor.

▲ Ask about the educational aspects of the program. A good program will stimulate a child creatively, intellectually, physically, and socially with a balance of free play, outdoor play, and group activities, but will not set out to teach the three R's. Be wary of schools that promise academic achievement. Young children do not need a formal academic program, and burnout is a strong possibility when children are pushed to learn too much too soon; see page 454. There should, however, be plenty of informal hands-on learning experiences and enriching exposure to the alphabet, numbers, music, literature, art, and science. Television viewing should not be a regular part of the program, though occasional viewing of quality videotapes may be appropriate.

▲ Observe the program yourself. Before you schedule an interview, try to observe the facility without your child. Ask to visit during the day; you can't judge a day-care or preschool program without observing it in action. The best times to visit are when kids are likely to be difficult (e.g., before nap time) or when they are just arriving and may be upset about

# PRESCHOOL ADMISSIONS

··········

Five-page applications, complete with probing essay questions. A grueling series of interviews. Exhaustive checks of background and character. Intensive testing of academic ability and achievement. Submission of writing samples and artwork. Exploration of extracurricular activities. The admissions process for Harvard? Princeton? Yale? No, the admissions process for many of today's preschool programs.

That a toddler should have to endure such an admissions process may seem comical, almost ludicrous, but for many parents and young children, it's a painfully serious reality. And while many preschools still have open admissions—accepting children who apply on a first-to-apply, first-to-be-accepted basis, with an eye only to achieving a healthy balance of boys and girls and a workable mix of ages—more and more seem as demanding as any Ivy League school in their admissions requirements.

If you live in a community where high-pressure preschool admissions tactics aren't the norm, consider yourself lucky. If you don't, and your child must be tested, take the following steps to ease the pressure:

**Look for a pleasant tester.** People who evaluate young children for a living should be empathetic, patient, and kind—but unfor-

tunately, they don't uniformly fit that profile. To ease the potential trauma for your child— as well as to help boost the odds that your child will test well—you should look for a pleasant and understanding tester. If testing is done at the school, you probably won't have much say in the matter. If it's to be done at an independent facility, ask parents who've had their children tested for a recommendation. If possible, ask to meet the tester briefly in advance.

**Consider tagging along.** Some testers allow parents to be present when their children are tested; many others don't. If your child doesn't separate well and is likely to be upset (and uncooperative) without you in the room, petition to come along. If your child might be more responsive without you around (many children are), stay outside. It's also a good idea to wait outside if you think that you might become impatient or upset if your child gives an incorrect answer to a question.

**Use your scheduling smarts.** Schedule testing for a time when your child isn't likely to be hungry or tired (after snack time and after—but not too soon after—naptime). Postpone testing if your child isn't feeling well or is generally out of sorts.

---

separating from their parents (though some schools will not allow visitors at these times, considering them to be disruptive). When visiting, watch how teachers handle disputes, separations, crying, boredom, and behavior problems. How are children like your own handled? Do the kids look happy and occupied? Are teachers cheerful and absorbed in their child-care responsibilities? Is there a lot of interaction between teachers and children and among children? When a child isn't occupied, does a teacher notice and try to draw the child into an activity? Are children allowed to

go off by themselves to do their own thing, whether that's a puzzle, a book, or a daydream? Is space divided into different fun areas (dress-up, books, kitchen, science, blocks, and so on) so the children can play in small groups? Is there constant supervision, indoors and out?

Policies regarding prospective parent visits to a day-care center or preschool vary from facility to facility. Most will require an appointment; many offer a formal tour (often for a group of parents), followed up by a longer visit so that the parents have an opportunity to view the class in action. Dropping in by

**Prepare your child . . .** Make sure your toddler gets plenty of rest the night before. The day before, and the day of the test, mention to your toddler what is going to happen (ask the agency or school ahead of time to outline the routine). Be upbeat, with no hint of pressure or stress in your voice. Explain to your toddler that a person who is like a teacher (you can even describe the person if you've already met) will be talking to him or her, that they're going to play some games together, and that it's going to be fun. If you won't be allowed in the testing room, make that clear so the separation won't take your toddler by surprise—but be sure you emphasize how nice the tester will be and that you will be waiting right outside the door.

**. . . but don't overprepare.** Don't be tempted to quiz your child with flash cards before the testing, or to step up at-home learning. And don't warn your child that the encounter is all-important or that "if you don't answer the questions right, you won't be able to go to that special school"; the more relaxed your toddler is, the better he or she is likely to do. Besides, no young child should feel under pressure to perform.

**Don't show any disappointment.** So what if your toddler—who can identify every animal in the zoo at home—suddenly can't tell a dog from a cat? So what if he or she forgets the alphabet or how to count to ten? These things happen when children are in an uncomfortable, unfamiliar situation (because they panic and go blank; because they aren't in the mood to perform for strangers; because they just want to show off by being silly). Voicing disappointment or disapproval to your toddler because he or she doesn't test as well as you'd like isn't fair, and is likely to compromise future testing.

**Reschedule if your child's upset.** If, once you get to the testing facility, your toddler starts crying and can't be jollied out of it, ask if the test can be postponed. Don't worry about what the school will think; any early childhood center that doesn't consider children's feelings doesn't deserve to be considered by you.

Preschool interviews, like testing, can be traumatic unless you keep them in perspective. Your child is applying for preschool, not for college or an important job. Remain relaxed about the interviews, and your child is likely to be, too. Prepare your child for interviews as you would for testing (see tips above).

And keep in mind that you and your child are not the only ones who are being judged—the school is, too. Ask probing questions during the tour and the interview. Observe what's expected of the children; if you sense that there's too much pressure, this might not be the right school.

---

prospective parents is often discouraged, not only because it can be disruptive, but because it can present security problems. Parents who already have children enrolled in a program may be allowed to drop in unannounced (so they can make periodic evaluations), though, again, policies will vary. However, a day-care program that seems resolutely opposed to an occasional visit by a parent may indeed have something to hide. If this is the case in your child's day-care center, ask for an explanation of the policy—if you don't get a satisfactory one, or if you suspect that the facility is keeping parents away so they won't see what really goes on there, you might want to consider looking elsewhere for child care.

When you do visit a facility, make an effort to avoid disrupting the activities; don't strike up conversations with teachers or children and be careful to stay in the background (ask in advance where to position yourself).

▲ Ask about (and observe) the approach to discipline. Look for a program where the goal of disciplining is to help the children learn self-control rather than to force them to bow to authority. Teachers should discipline with respect for their young charges and in positive ways, using problem solving and discussion, and possibly time-outs as needed (though these shouldn't be overused). Physical or verbal abuse, angry scolding, physical restraint, isolation without supervision, shaming, and ignoring conflicts among children should not be in evidence.

▲ Call some parents with children presently in the program. If you don't know any—and don't know anyone who knows any—you'll have to rely on names and numbers provided by the director. Ask what they like about the program and what they don't like. Also try to talk to a parent or two in the process of dropping off or picking up children (which may be difficult, because they are usually in a hurry).

▲ Listen. What does the place sound like? Is there a happy hum or a piercing cacophony? Is there a lot of crying and scolding or a lot of laughter and cheery voices?

▲ Sniff. Smells may be clues to cleanliness (or lack of it), so use your nose—if you can sniff dirty diapers, tobacco smoke, spoiled food, or other unpleasant odors, you may be smelling unsanitary conditions.

# AN OCCASIONAL SITTER

**Locating candidates.** As with any other kind of child care, a good way of finding a good baby-sitter is to ask friends, acquaintances, and neighbors for recommendations. You can also call a local college placement office, which may have a baby-sitting service, or check a bulletin board that lists students interested in sitting. Or contact the sitter-training program at a local hospital, a local Red Cross affiliate, or Safe Sitter[5] for the names of some trained graduates looking for baby-sitting jobs. If you

know a responsible teenager, speak to her about the possibility of baby-sitting, keeping in mind that she should meet the qualifications below.

**What you need to know about an occasional sitter.** Everyone (unless Grandma is very available and very accommodating), needs a paid sitter occasionally. If you're hiring a baby-sitter, as opposed to asking a family member or friend to stay with your child, there are some important factors to consider.

*Age.* Some much older sitters may not have the energy to keep up if your child is very active (not a concern at nighttime, when your toddler will be sleeping most of the time you're out), although others may be more energetic than younger sitters. Teenagers who love children often make excellent baby-sitters, but just how responsible they'll be will depend on age and maturity.

*Qualifications.* The more experience a caregiver has in child care, obviously, the better. Any sitter you hire should have first aid and CPR training, and be able to respond in an emergency. If you are using teenagers, look for those who have certificates from Safe Sitter, the Red Cross, or another sitter-training program that teaches teens child care, first aid, CPR, and choking rescue procedures.

*References.* Make sure you check out references in person before you hire. Then try to watch the baby-sitter in action (consider paying her for a few hours while she gets to know your child and your routines; see page 22). If you're considering using a teenager who has training but no experience and you don't

---

5. The Safe Sitter program trains teenagers in all baby-sitting fundamentals, including safety and first aid. Call (800) 255-4089 for the number of the Safe Sitter program nearest you.

know her or her family, speak to her teacher, parents, or clergyperson to learn something about her.

Before you leave your toddler alone with a baby-sitter, set basic guidelines; let her know what you expect as far as the use of the phone and the television, the playing of loud music, and entertaining visitors (prohibited unless okayed ahead of time) are concerned. Also make sure she has access to you by phone, and, if she can't drive or doesn't have a car, that she has the phone number of a nearby available neighbor who can drive and has been informed that you're going out, in case of an emergency. Leave a list of other emergency numbers (see the inside back cover) near each phone in your home.

# MAKING CHILD CARE WORK

## WORKING WITH AN IN-HOME CAREGIVER

O nce you have a nanny or baby-sitter you think will do a good job, draw up a work agreement to help avoid misunderstandings. Include in your agreement an initial trial period of two to four weeks during which you both have the option to change your minds. Also specify:

▲ Salary. Will there be a higher rate for overtime? Will the caregiver be paid daily, weekly, or monthly? Will the rate be a flat salary or an hourly rate?

▲ Benefits. Paid vacation of two weeks plus national holidays off is fairly standard; some parents actually cover health insurance as a way of encouraging a good sitter to stay on.

▲ Duties you expect performed. Keep in mind that a sitter who is required to mop floors, sort laundry, and prepare dinner may have less time to devote to your child; on the other hand, if some light household chores do get done while you're at work, you'll have more time to spend with your toddler when you're at home.

▲ The days and the hours you expect your sitter to work, and whether overtime will be expected. Remember that a live-in nanny or *au pair* can't be expected to be on call round the clock. In most cases, they are expected to work five days and get most evenings off, to minimize the risk of burnout.

▲ Accommodations, if the caregiver is to sleep in, as well as the ground rules on the use of the family telephone,[6] television, kitchen, car, and so on. Some families find having live-in help impinges on privacy (though others delight in having another family member); most find such an arrangement works best if a separate "suite" can be set aside (with a separate entrance, a private bathroom, and a mini-kitchen, if possible).

As an employer, you are required to pay withholding and unemployment tax, and need to keep on file a nanny's W4 and I9 (proof of citizenship or possession of a green card). Quarterly, the government requires a 941 form for withholding and Social Security, plus many other forms; check with local government offices or your accountant. The

---

6. A phone card for nannies is available from the International Nanny Association (see page 814) so that family calls and the nanny's personal calls can be separated out.

International Nanny Association (see page 814) offers a health insurance policy for nannies, or speak to your local agent about a policy. Your homeowner's insurance should cover injuries to employees, but you may also want to pay disability insurance. Paying for your nanny's membership in a professional organization may be worthwhile, since it allows her to network with other caregivers who are also serious about their work.

Just as important as your initial agreement with your child's caregiver is continuing communication. Meet regularly with her to talk about how things are going, and supplement these meetings by setting up a chalkboard, journal, or memo system (like some day-care centers do) to pass messages back and forth. Have your sitter jot down notes about naps, meals, play, tantrums, toilet-learning progress, whether a bowel movement was passed (if this is an issue), developmental steps forward (new words spoken, for example), as well as any anecdotes she would like to share with you.

Be alert both during the trial period and later for signs that things aren't right; see below.

# EVALUATING YOUR CURRENT CHILD CARE

You've found the baby-sitter or day-care center of your dreams—or at least, one you're fairly sure you won't have nightmares about. Can you relax? Of course not; a parent's work is never done. Periodic evaluations of a current child-care situation are just as important as the initial selection. So, be watchful for signs that the situation may have soured:

**Your child's behavior.** Clues that your child isn't thriving with present child care may include: the development of new eating or sleeping problems; marked unhappiness when the sitter arrives or when dropped off at day care (beyond normal separation anxiety)— the child seems truly miserable on being left, rather than just sad about your leaving; marked unhappiness at the end of the day; uncharacteristic withdrawal; stepped-up behavior problems. If providing your toddler with plenty of reassurance (see, too, the tips on page 20 for dealing with separation problems) doesn't seem to help, and the behavior difficulties seem directly related to the child-care situation, consider popping home (or into day care or preschool) in the middle of the day on a few occasions to get a behind-the-scenes look. If some of the parents of your child's playmates are available, ask them to try to observe your at-home sitter in action (at play dates, on the playground) and let you know how they feel she's doing. Do not ignore signs of unhappiness in your child that last more than a month, and be especially concerned (and react immediately) if he or she seems truly frightened or has frequent nightmares, unexplained bruises, or other signs of abuse (see page 826).

**The caregiver's behavior.** A good caregiver is responsive, communicative, and respectful of you, your child, and your wishes (as you should be in return). If your child's caregiver displays few or none of these qualities, is chronically late or absent, seems lethargic or uncaring, has mood swings, or exhibits other troubling behavior (see page 812), a problem may exist.

If, on evaluation, you conclude that the behavior of your child, the caregiver, or both is cause for concern, take action. As soon as feasible, meet with the caregiver (or the day-care director) to discuss your concerns. If the discussion doesn't lead to a noticeable improvement, consider revamping your child-care arrangements.

# DEALING WITH A CHANGE IN CHILD CARE

Depending on your child and the situation, a change of caregivers can be insignificant (your child doesn't blink an eye when the switch is made), reason to celebrate (you let go of a poor sitter and hire a good one), or traumatic (a sitter to whom your child has become very attached leaves suddenly).

When the change is traumatic, you can soften the blow by being sensitive to your child's feelings during the adjustment. Ask the departing caregiver for a photo, which your toddler can keep next to the crib or bed if desired. Reminisce with your child about the sitter and encourage a free expression of feelings about the departure. At the same time, keep as many of your child's routines the same as possible, and avoid any other unnecessary upheaval at this point; predictability brings comforting reassurance.

Be patient and understanding while your child gets used to the new caregiver. But don't give your child the impression that you share his or her ambivalence; instead, make it clear that you like the new person and feel confident in her abilities. Don't act overly concerned or hesitant when the two meet (even if your toddler balks). Think, and act, positive, and your toddler will adjust faster and with less fuss.

And hope that this time the caregiver will stay as long as you need her to.

# GETTING READY FOR PRESCHOOL

While there's no formal preparation needed for preschool (except that for some preschools, toilet learning will need to be completed), there's nothing wrong with a little head start. Familiarize your toddler with some of the fundamentals of preschool life by:

**Practicing cooperation.** Cooperation and turn taking will be expected in preschool (though children don't always learn to cooperate immediately). So whenever you get the chance, practice at home. Take turns playing with the same doll and putting pieces into a puzzle; work cooperatively at the kitchen counter and doing laundry (you take the clothes out of the washer, your toddler puts them in the dryer). Don't despair if your toddler doesn't excel in cooperation at home; children are almost always more agreeable when they're *not* with their parents.

**Playing name games.** Your toddler won't be expected to write or read his or her name, but being familiar with what the name looks like (and which letter it starts with) can be helpful when so many things are going to be labeled with it (cubbies, lunch boxes, pictures, and so on). Write your toddler's name on artwork, on the refrigerator in magnetic letters, on the chalkboard, in the sand with a stick. Recite its letters occasionally, in a singsong fashion ("L-I-Z spells Liz"). Don't, however, pressure your toddler to learn to recognize or read letters or words.

**Packing a lunch box.** If your child will be bringing lunch to school, pick out a fun lunch box together. A few days before the first day of preschool or day care, begin packing your child's lunch and letting him or her eat it from the lunch box at the kitchen table. Demonstrate how to take the food out of the containers, pack what's reusable back into the box, and throw out (or recycle) what isn't. Also let your almost-preschooler get used to wearing a backpack if one will be worn to school. (Some children, however, don't like the feeling of a backpack; of course, it's okay to carry the pack by hand instead.) If nap time at child care will be on a mat, having your toddler nap on one at home for several days before trekking off to day care or preschool will increase the odds that he or she will really be able to rest easily in the new environment.

**Sharing the chores.** If you haven't begun giving your toddler some simple chores to do, start now. Concentrate on chores that your child might be asked to do at school, such as putting away toys, clearing the table, or washing paintbrushes (see page 415).

**Giving directions.** Make a game out of following directions (which your toddler will also be expected to be able to do, to a certain extent), calling off several in a row ("Pick up that hairbrush, brush your hair two times, turn around in a circle, and bring me the hairbrush, please.") Again, don't worry if your toddler doesn't follow directions consistently; chances are that he or she will be much more conscientious about following them at school (see page 394). And make sure you keep the game fun and pressure-free.

**Giving choices.** Children are expected to do a certain amount of decision making at school. Provide practice by giving your toddler choices whenever possible ("Do you want to play with the blocks or the puzzles?" "Do you want cereal or grilled cheese for breakfast?"). See page 414 for more on making choices.

**Providing structure.** Some tight-ship families run on a tight schedule; other families have no noticeable structure at all. If yours is the latter kind, begin incorporating a little structure into your toddler's day in the weeks before preschool. You can even post a written schedule (story time right after lunch, clean-up time right after play), illustrating it so your toddler can "read" it (with a picture of a book for story time, a sandwich for lunch, blocks for play, a toy chest for clean-up).

**Stepping up the socializing.** If your child hasn't yet had regular play dates, arrange some in the weeks before preschool to increase comfort with other children. But don't overdo it—your toddler may tire of the social scene before school starts.

# GETTING INTO THE SWING

Adjustments are tough for toddlers. Adjusting to day care or preschool can be especially tough for a child who's never before spent a significant amount of time away from home. Understanding your child's need for extra support while getting into the swing of peer-group life will help make the adjustment happier and smoother. So will getting off to a good start, by:

▲ Preparing for a positive experience. Gradually acclimate your toddler to the idea of embarking on this adventure. Read books together about children in day care or preschool; talk about siblings, cousins, or peers who already attend a program; casually discuss the kinds of activities your toddler will be involved in. Be upbeat and enthusiastic about what's in store, but not so lavish in your descriptions that you prompt suspicion or anxiety or set your toddler up for a disappointment (*nothing* can be *that* good).

▲ Being there for your toddler—in the beginning. Often, knowing that a loving grown-up is nearby gives toddlers the courage to explore an unfamiliar environment. For this reason, most programs invite parents and caregivers to participate during the adjustment period, encouraging them to stay and play with their child for all or part of the first few days (which are often abbreviated). The object is to help toddlers to separate, not to increase clinging. So be available to your child, but don't hover as he or she explores new surroundings and meets new people. It's preferable for the teacher to be the one to say, "Now, do you want to play in the dress-up corner, or would you like to try painting?" Once your toddler has grown comfortable playing at your side, gradually begin moving off—to a chair a few feet away, then to a bench a little further off, then to the doorway.

▲ Saying good-bye. When it comes time to make that move out the door, don't sneak off without a good-bye, even if the good-bye is painful for both of you. Let your toddler know who will pick him or her up and when, being as specific as you can ("I'll be back after lunch" or "Sophie will come and pick you up when you come in from the park"), and plan to keep your word (late pickups can be devastating, particularly during those first days). Leave with a convincing smile on your face that tells your toddler that you're confident he or she will have a good time (even if you're not so sure).

Some toddlers never seem to feel at home in the new environment as long as their parents are around. If you sense this is the case with your child, a swifter separation may actually speed adjustment. Enlisting a teacher's support will help, too.

# SPECIAL CONCERNS

## *THE SICK CHILD AND CHILD CARE*

How sick is too sick for day care or preschool? Many programs have policies about sick children, and criteria vary from facility to facility—be sure to ask when you sign up. Ironically, since most infections are spread *before* a child appears sick or begins exhibiting symptoms, policies that require runny-nosed kids (or kids who aren't contagious at all, such as those with ear infections) to stay at home may not be effective in preventing the spread of illness. Such policies may also keep children who could safely be in school at home, causing parents unnecessary scheduling crises.

Regardless of the school's policy,

it is in everyone's best interest if children stay home if they are feeling very unwell (and therefore can't keep up with the group or can't play outdoors), if they're running fevers or were running fevers within the preceding twenty-four hours; are vomiting or have acute diarrhea; and/or have a red, sore throat, an eye infection that hasn't been treated, infected untreated skin rashes or lesions, rapid or labored breathing, severe pain or discomfort, or a communicable disease (such as chickenpox, measles, flu, strep, hepatitis A, impetigo, scabies, or pertussis) that is still in the contagious stage.

Though it's best for a child who's too sick to go to day care or preschool to be home with a parent, many parents unfortunately can't afford to take time off

# RECOGNIZING ABUSE

. . . . . . . . . .

## Possible Signs of Sexual Abuse

▲ Obsession with the genitals; a little girl may begin poking her vagina with objects.

▲ A sudden spurt in sexual knowledge or vocabulary, unexplained by any teaching in the home; attempts to get other children to perform sexual acts (beyond the normal explorations of "playing doctor"); and for the dropping of subtle remarks, particularly when naked, that might suggest sexual sophistication beyond the child's years.

▲ Nightmares and other fearful behavior; pronounced phobias, particularly of certain people or places, or of a doctor's physical examination; uncharacteristic clinging. Fears may be expressed in frightening drawings, often using the colors black and red.

▲ Depression or abrupt behavior changes, such as sudden, uncontrollable anger or more frequent and more violent temper tantrums.

▲ Physical symptoms. Occasionally, a girl may have redness, swelling, and soreness around the vagina, and may suffer from recurrent, unexplained vaginal or urinary tract infections; a boy may have swelling, redness, and pain around the rectum; either may have abdominal pain, genital pain or bleeding, or signs of a sexually transmitted disease.

If you note any of these signs in your toddler, don't jump to criminal conclusions; these signs could well have a logical explanation, particularly given the typical toddler's erratic and eccentric behavior.

If abuse seems possible, however, face and deal with the issue immediately. If you don't, things can only get worse. The best first step is to take your child to the doctor for a complete examination. If any injuries or signs of abuse are found, the doctor will treat your child and discuss the ramifications of the findings with you, as well as advise you on what to do next. He or she will also have to report the abuse, as required by law. For additional advice and information, you can call (800) 4-A-CHILD or your local child protection agency (check the front of your phone book for Family and Children's Services or Child Abuse Prevention). It's likely that in addition to dealing with any physical injuries, it will be necessary to have your child (and possibly the entire family) counseled for the emotional effects of the ordeal by a qualified and experienced mental health professional.

## Signs of Possible Physical Abuse

Bruises, cuts, and other injuries that your child sustains in someone else's care should be explained. If they can't be explained (or if the explanation is not satisfactory or can't be confirmed by your toddler), show them to your child's doctor. He or she will help you to determine what your next step should be and report any signs of abuse to the authorities. You can also call (800) 4-A-CHILD for additional information and support.

to nurse their child back to health. A few child-care facilities (mostly corporate centers) offer sick care, either in a sick bay at the facility, in a hospital (the unfamiliar setting may be unduly frightening to a sick child), or, rarely, at home (a caregiver is sent to care for the sick child). In some cities, home sick care is available through government subsidy. Universal availability of sick care for children of working parents—or, better still, of a plan that allows the parents to stay home without sacrificing their paychecks—would, of course, be the ideal solution.

# CONCERN ABOUT ABUSE

What was once unthinkable—physical and sexual abuse of young children by their caregivers in day-care centers and preschools—is now very much on the minds of parents across the country, thanks to a handful of highly publicized cases. Although such abuse is relatively rare, when it does take place, it can be traumatizing for both toddler and parents.

Choosing child care according to the guidelines in this chapter will improve the odds that your child will be in good hands, but it isn't a guarantee. The following are some additional precautions that parents can take to help prevent their children from becoming victims of abuse:

▲ Give your child plenty of love, attention, and healthy affection. The children who are most likely to be abused—or who are most likely to suffer abuse in silence—are those who feel as though they aren't receiving enough love at home. Children who feel well loved are also more likely to have a stronger sense of self and higher self-esteem, and are less likely to be emotionally needy; such neediness can make a child more vulnerable to the advances of child abusers.

▲ Keep privates private. For the toddler, the time right around toilet learning is often one of heightened interest in genitals—their own and others. Take this opportunity to introduce your toddler to the concept of body ownership: that the private parts of the body are one's own to touch and one's own to control. Parents and baby-sitters may need to wash a toddler's genitals in the bath, and doctors and nurses will sometimes need to touch them during an examination, but no one else should be allowed to touch them without the child's permission. Since most toddlers know touching their genitals feels "good," it could confuse your

toddler to try to differentiate between "good touch" and "bad touch." And don't worry that letting your toddler explore his or her own genitals will cause sexual overstimulation that might lead to sexual abuse; children who are taught that this kind of self-touching is "bad" are more likely to fall prey to sexual molestation than those who are taught that it's okay, but private.

▲ Ask your child to tell you if someone does something hurtful or that makes him or her feel bad. Always investigate such reports, no matter how farfetched they may seem (see box, facing page).

▲ Avoid authoritarian discipline. Children who are rigidly controlled by domineering parents—who are taught to comply with authority without question—are more liable to accept an adult caregiver's sexual or physical abuse without question. Giving children plenty of opportunities to think for themselves and make their own decisions can help them speak up in such a situation.

# CAN CHILD CARE BE TOO GOOD?

You want the best caregiver you can find for your toddler—someone who's loving, responsive, attentive; someone your toddler dotes on; someone who dotes on your toddler. Someone who's as much like a parent as possible, so your toddler won't miss you so much when you're not there.

Or do you?

Of course you do. But if you've chosen a really good caregiver, and your child has become attached to her—possibly, very attached—you're bound to feel some rivalry and resentment. It's only natural to wonder, as another person takes your child into her arms each morning, whether she's also taking your place in your child's heart. Sure, you want your child to be happy during the day, but sometimes it hurts to see him or her *that* happy. Sure, you want your child to separate easily from you when you leave for work, but it threatens the parental ego when separation is *too* easy.

There's liable to be competition, too, and from both sides. As a parent, you'd like to think that no one can calm, occupy, feed, and amuse your child as well as you can. But it's a child-care provider's job to try—she is paid to focus her attention on your child. When you see the provider has been doing her job well, it's comforting and yet, at the same time, it can be disturbing.

Such feelings are normal—and many parents experience them. But while other people can do a good job of caring for your child—and, hopefully, will continue to, as needed, throughout the growing-up years—no one can take your place. Care providers may come and go, and they often do, but you, the parent, are there for the long haul—and your child, no matter how young, knows it. A child's relationship with a parent may be more complicated and often conflicted, but this intensity makes it all the more meaningful.

If your child is affectionate toward the caregiver, take it as a sign that you've made a good choice. If your child is so engrossed in play with the caregiver that you feel invisible when you walk in the door at the end of the day, take it as a sign that the situation is working. If your child behaves all day for the sitter, saving up the tantrums for you, take it as a sign that your child feels secure enough in your love to misbehave in your presence (see page 244).

In other words, stop worrying and be happy—that your toddler's happy.

# PART FOUR

# *Ready Reference*

# *What Can I Do Now?*

I t doesn't have to be a rainy day for you to run out of activities that keep your toddler busy—and happy. (How many hours can you spend at the park or in the backyard, after all—even under the bluest skies?) The following are a sampling of toddler-tested, time-honored activities that'll prove just as satisfying on a sunny afternoon as they will on a rainy one. Make your selections according to your toddler's age and stage of development.

**Crayons, redux.** What to do with that growing pile of crayon nibs and squibs that your toddler won't touch? Recycle them into multicolor crayon balls. Together peel the paper wraps off the crayons and combine pieces of several different colors together in a plastic sandwich bag. Seal the bag with tape or tie it with a rubber band and leave it in the sun or in a baking dish placed in a just-warm oven until the crayons have softened. Mold the molten mass into balls and refrigerate until firm—and get ready for some colorful coloring.

**Be lyrical.** Compose new lyrics to a favorite song. Pick a song, any song, and take turns singing it with made-up words, the sillier the better. Or try to communicate only in song for a few minutes on the way to the supermarket or while you're making dinner—creating a sort of parent-child operetta.

**Follow the leader.** Take turns being the leader who decides when to crawl, when to run, when to clap hands, when to hop, when to jump. Alternatively, one of you can shout out action directions ("Stretch! Touch your toes! Walk very fast!") while the other performs them. Or play "copy cat," and take turns making funny faces that the other can imitate. A simplified, low-pressure (no losers or winners) form of Simon Says not only can be fun for toddlers, it can improve their coordination and their ability to follow directions.

**Play ball.** Learning to catch isn't easy for toddlers. Make it easier by using a ball that's big enough to eyeball but not so big that it can knock your toddler over. Have your toddler stand with arms out and palms up. Standing close (less than a foot away to start with), toss the ball gently into your toddler's hands and instruct him or her to "hug" it so it won't fall out. Acknowledge unsuccessful attempts with "Good try." Once catching at that distance has been mastered, move a little farther away. Also try bouncing the ball to your toddler at an easy-to-grab height.

**Get gooey.** Mix some cornstarch with water to a gruel-like consistency—then dig in with your hands. Show your toddler how the mixture feels when you squeeze it in your hand and when you let it ooze between your fingers. This activity can be used to pass time when you're in the kitchen cooking or as tension-relaxation therapy.

**String your toddler along.** Once your child's old enough to be trusted with smaller objects, provide a variety of safe stringables (spools, large pasta tubes, cereal circles, big buttons, large wooden beads) to thread onto a piece of thin plastic tubing (because it's relatively rigid, the tubing is easier for small hands to manipulate and safer than ordinary string) or a shoelace.

**Bowl 'em over.** Line up a few empty plastic soda bottles, unopened rolls of paper towels, or stuffed animals (vary the "pins"), and show your toddler how to roll a large rubber ball to knock them over. You can even try knocking over a block pile if the ball is heavy enough.

**Make maracas.** Fill several small, slim-necked, easy-to-grasp plastic bottles with rice, macaroni, and/or dried beans. Secure the bottle cap with masking tape and let your toddler shake, shake, shake to lively Latin tunes. (Allow your toddler to use this instrument only under supervision—given time, most tots can remove the tape and unscrew the cap.)

**Blow bubbles.** Toddlers love to chase bubbles. To add challenge to the chase, blow the bubbles outdoors on a windy day or indoors with a child-safe fan whipping them about.

**Trace a toddler.** Have your toddler stretch out on a sheet of newsprint. Then trace his or her shape with a marker and hand it over for your young artist to decorate before you display it.

**Cross the river.** Lay out two long sticks about six to eight inches apart on a non-slippery surface (sand, carpeting, grass). Pretend that the space between the sticks is a river, and take turns crossing it. You can also try building a "bridge" (using a wide board or a large flat book, for instance) or a pattern of "stepping stones" across your river. For realism, add a few rubber ducks.

**Walk the plank.** Set a smooth plank (about eight or ten inches wide and at least four feet long) flat on the ground or floor, and challenge your toddler to walk it (with shoes on, to avoid splinters) without falling off. Once he or she becomes adept at this, you can raise the challenge a couple of inches by adding another plank on top of the first. Or suggest other ways of walking the plank: crawling, tiptoeing, hopping, inching backward, stepping sideways.

**Play statues.** After a visit to a park or museum or anywhere you and your toddler have seen a statue, play this game: The person who is "it" begins jumping, running, skipping, or dancing. Then suddenly the other player calls out, "Statue." This is the cue to "freeze" in a statue-like position. It'll take plenty of practice before your toddler can manage a perfect freeze-frame (you may not find it so easy yourself), but that's okay—most of the fun of this game is in the practice, and in the laughter when players can't hold a pose.

# Best-Odds Recipes

## SWEET POTATO FRIES

A fast-food favorite, with a nutritious difference. The texture is toddler-perfect—a soft center with an outside that's crunchy but not too crisp.

**Makes 4 servings**

*1 tablespoon vegetable oil*
*2 large sweet potatoes*
*2 egg whites*

1. Preheat the oven to 425°F. Spread the oil evenly over a nonstick baking sheet.

2. Peel the sweet potatoes, and cut them into ¼-inch-thick slices. Cut the slices in half.

3. Whisk the egg whites until frothy. Add the cut potatoes to the egg mixture, and toss until coated.

4. Place the potatoes in one layer on the baking sheet. Bake until soft inside and of desired crispness on the outside (you don't have to turn the potatoes), 30 to 35 minutes. Be careful not to let the fries burn.

5. Allow the fries to cool slightly before serving.

## LITTLE "PUNKINS"

There's no sweeter way to eat your vegetables (or, at least, your Yellow Vegetable Servings).

**Makes 24 muffins**

*Vegetable oil or cupcake liners, for the muffin tins*
*¼ cup vegetable oil*
*2 whole eggs*
*1 egg white*
*⅔ cups raisins*
*½ cup coarsely chopped dried unsweetened pineapple or apricots*
*1¾ cups apple juice concentrate*
*1 cup canned unsweetened solid-pack pumpkin*
*1 cup whole-wheat flour*
*½ cup unbleached all-purpose flour*
*½ cup wheat germ*
*2 teaspoons baking powder*
*1 teaspoon ground cinnamon*

1. Preheat the oven to 350°F. Lightly oil two 12-cup muffin tins, or line with cupcake liners.

2. Beat the oil, eggs, and egg white together in a large mixing bowl. Chop the raisins and other dried fruit with the apple juice concentrate in a

blender or food processor; add the pumpkin and blend. Fold the pumpkin mixture into the egg and oil mixture.

3. Combine the flours, wheat germ, baking powder, and cinnamon in a bowl. Add the flour mixture to the pumpkin mixture; stir until just blended.

4. Pour the batter into the prepared muffin cups, filling each about three-quarters full. Bake until a knife inserted in the center of a muffin comes out clean, about 25 minutes. Cool in the tins for 10 minutes, then turn out onto a rack to cool completely.

## CHOCOLATE MILK CAKE

A preschool favorite, it makes enough for the whole class.

**Makes one 13 × 9-inch cake**

*Butter and flour, for the baking pan*
*1 cup whole-wheat flour*
*¼ cup unbleached all-purpose flour*
*½ cup wheat germ*
*2 teaspoons baking powder*
*⅔ cup unsweetened cocoa*
*¼ cup vegetable oil*
*1¾ cups apple juice concentrate*
*½ cup milk, mixed with 5 tablespoons nonfat dry milk*
*2 whole eggs*
*1 egg white*
*1 teaspoon vanilla extract*
*Whipped cream, for garnishing (optional)*

1. Preheat the oven to 325°F. Lightly butter and flour a 13 × 19-inch baking pan.

2. Place the flours, wheat germ, baking powder, cocoa, oil, juice concentrate, and milk in a large mixing bowl; beat until smooth. Add the eggs, egg white, and vanilla, and beat until thoroughly mixed.

3. Pour the batter into the prepared baking pan. Bake until the top springs back when lightly pressed, about 35 minutes. Cool slightly in the pan before turning out onto a rack to cool completely. Or serve right from the pan, garnished, if desired, with the whipped cream.

## APPLE BUTTER CAKE

A moist and sweet, dark cake that packs a vitamin-A punch.

**Makes two 9-inch cakes or one 9-inch layer cake**

*Butter and flour, for the cake pans*
*1 cup whole-wheat flour*
*½ cup unbleached all-purpose flour*
*½ cup wheat germ*
*2 teaspoons baking soda*
*1 teaspoon ground cinnamon*
*1 cup unsweetened apple butter, plus additional for filling (optional)*
*1 cup plus 2 tablespoons apple juice concentrate*
*2 whole eggs*
*1 egg white*
*1 cup chopped dried apricots*
*Cream Cheese Frosting (optional; recipe follows)*

1. Preheat the oven to 350°F. Lightly butter and flour two 9-inch cake pans.

2. Combine the flours, wheat germ, baking soda, and cinnamon in a large bowl. In another bowl, beat together 1 cup of the apple butter, the juice concentrate, eggs, egg white, and apricots until well blended. Stir the apple butter mixture into the flour mixture until just blended.

3. Pour the batter evenly into the prepared pans. Bake until a toothpick inserted in the center of a layer comes out clean, about 25 minutes. Transfer the pans to a rack to cool; then loosen the sides with a sharp

knife and invert the layers onto plates to cool completely.

4. Frost, if desired. Thickly spread the top of one of the layers with enough apple butter to cover, then place the second layer over the filling. Cover the top of the cake with the cream cheese frosting and refrigerate until serving time.

### Cream Cheese Frosting

*1 package light cream cheese, at room temperature*
*⅓ cup apple butter, or to taste*

Blend together the cream cheese and the apple butter until creamy.

## FRUIT COOKIES

Chewy fruit—and whole-grain nutrition—in every bite.

### Makes about 40 cookies

*1 cup whole-wheat flour*
*¾ cup wheat germ*
*½ cup rolled oats*
*2 teaspoons baking powder*
*2 teaspoons ground cinnamon*
*½ cup golden raisins*
*½ cup coarsely chopped apricots*
*1 cup apple juice concentrate*
*¼ cup vegetable oil*
*1 egg*
*Vegetable oil, for the baking sheets*

1. Mix the flour, wheat germ, oats, baking powder, and cinnamon in a large mixing bowl.

2. Chop the raisins and apricots together in a blender or food processor; add the juice concentrate, oil, and egg, and blend. Add the mixture to the flour mixture and gently stir together. Place the dough in a bowl, cover, and refrigerate until thoroughly chilled, about 1 hour.

3. Preheat the oven to 375°F. Lightly oil two baking sheets.

4. With slightly wet hands, shape the dough into 1-inch balls. Place the balls on the baking sheets, and flatten them with the back of a fork (wet the fork slightly if the mixture sticks). Bake until lightly browned, about 10 minutes. Remove to wire racks and cool completely.

## PEANUT-BUTTER-AND-JELLY BALLS

No-cook cookies that are fun to make, and best of all, don't involve the stove.

### Makes about 30 cookies

*½ cup creamy peanut butter*
*¼ cup nonfat dry milk*
*¼ cup wheat germ*
*1 cup favorite cold cereal, dry*
*½ cup finely chopped dried apricots*
*¼ cup apple juice concentrate*
*Fruit-juice-sweetened jelly or jam*

Mix all the ingredients except the jelly together in a bowl. Shape the mixture into 1-inch balls and place on a baking sheet. Use your index finger to make an indentation in each of the balls. Cover with waxed paper and refrigerate until firm, about 20 minutes. Fill the holes with a dab of jelly and serve.

## FRUIT ICES FOR POPS OR SCOOPING

A sweet treat, particularly refreshing during the summer months. They are fun to eat when made in ice pop molds.

### Makes 6 small pops or scoops

*1¼ cup puréed ripe sweet fruit, such as banana, strawberries, mango, or peaches*

*¼ to ⅓ cup unsweetened fruit juice concentrate, such as apple, orange, pineapple, or a blend*

1. Combine the fruit purée and ¼ cup juice concentrate. Taste, adding additional juice if needed for sweetness.

2. *For ice pops:* Pour the mixture into ice pop molds and freeze.

   *For sorbet:* Freeze the mixture in an ice cream maker, according to the manufacturer's directions; or freeze partially in a mixing bowl, then beat until light and fluffy, and return to the freezer to freeze completely.

# CHEESECAKE PUDDING

A high-protein treat that's sweet to eat.

**Makes 12 individual puddings**

*Vegetable cooking spray*
*½ cup nonfat or low-fat plain yogurt*
*2 cups nonfat or low-fat ricotta cheese*
*½ cup light cream cheese*
*5 teaspoons cornstarch*
*¾ cup apple juice concentrate*
*⅓ cup pineapple juice concentrate*
*2 whole eggs*
*4 egg whites*
*1 tablespoon vanilla extract*
*Sliced banana or berries, or fruit-sweetened jam (your child's favorite flavor)*

1. Preheat the oven to 350°F. Spray 12 individual custard cups or soufflé dishes with nonstick vegetable spray. Arrange on a baking sheet.

2. Combine the yogurt, ricotta, cream cheese, and cornstarch in a food processor, and process until smooth. Add the juice concentrates, eggs, egg whites, and vanilla, and beat until smooth. Spoon into the prepared dishes. Bake until lightly golden and puffed, 30 to 35 minutes. Let rest for 10 minutes, then refrigerate until cool.

3. Sprinkle the pudding with fruit or dollop with a teaspoon of jam and serve.

# BEST-ODDS SHAKE

A quick calcium-loaded snack that toddlers enjoy anytime of the day.

**Makes 1 to 2 servings**

*1 cup nonfat or low-fat milk or plain yogurt*
*½ cup cut-up fruit, such as banana, strawberries, mango, peach, apricots*
*1 to 2 tablespoons wheat germ (optional)*
*Dash of fruit juice concentrate, to taste*

Combine the milk or yogurt, the fruit, and the wheat germ in a blender; blend until smooth. Add the juice concentrate to taste, blend, and serve.

# FRUIT-JUICE GEL

An easy-to-make, easy-to-get-down light dessert.

**Makes 4 toddler portions**

*1 tablespoon unflavored gelatin*
*½ cup water*
*1 cup unsweetened fruit juice, or fruit juice blend*
*½ cup fruit juice concentrate*
*½ cup fruit, such as sliced fresh banana, peach, or apricots; or drained canned juice-sweetened fruit (optional)*

1. Combine the gelatin and the water in a small saucepan. Stir and let stand to soften the gelatin, 1 minute. Heat over medium-high heat just to boiling. Remove from the heat and stir in the juice and juice concentrate, blending until the gelatin is dissolved.

2. Pour the mixture into a shallow bowl or 4 individual custard cups. Place in the freezer until thickened, 10 to 15 minutes. Stir in the fruit, if desired. Chill in the refrigerator until firm.

# Common Home Remedies

Most treatments recommended to handle many of the common ills or injuries of childhood are easy to administer at home—if you know how:[1]

## COLD COMPRESSES

Fill a basin[2] with cold water and add a tray or two of ice cubes. Dip a clean washcloth or towel in the water, wring it out, and apply it to the injury or around the injured part. Rechill the cloth when it's no longer cold. Continue compresses for 15 to 30 minutes or as directed by the doctor or another medical professional. Do not apply ice directly to the skin.

## COLD SOAKS

Fill a basin[2] with cold water and add a tray or two of ice cubes. Immerse the injured part for 15 minutes or as directed by the doctor. Repeat in 30 minutes, if necessary.

## COOL COMPRESSES

Fill a basin[2] with cool water from the tap. Dip a clean washcloth or towel in the water, wring it out, and apply to the injury. Redip when the cloth no longer seems wet and cool. Continue for 15 to 30 minutes or as directed by the doctor.

## EYE SOAKS

Dip a clean washcloth in warm, not hot, water (test temperature for comfort on your inner wrist or forearm), and apply to your child's eye for 5 to 10 minutes every 3 hours.

## HAND WASHING

Proper hand washing by adults *and* children can prevent the spread of infection. It can sometimes even help in treatment, by preventing self-reinfection and secondary infections. Use soap or detergent and warm water (warm enough to cut through grease and grime, but not so hot

---

1. If the specifics (how long to treat, for example) given by the medical professional treating your child differ, follow the professional advice. Of course, how long you *can* treat may be limited by your child's tolerance (see page 678 for kid-friendly approaches to treatment).

2. An ice bucket or cooler will maintain the water temperature longer.

as to burn) and rub vigorously for 10 seconds. Be sure to get under nails, around cuticles, and into creases. Rinse very thoroughly to wash germs away. (Help your child do a thorough job until he or she is old enough to wash solo.)

## HEAD ELEVATION

Cold sufferers breathe easier and sleep better with their heads slightly raised. Raise your toddler's head by putting a pillow, cushion, folded blanket, or telephone book *under* the head of his or her mattress.

## HEATING PAD

If you use a heating pad (a hot-water bottle, which has no cords or heating element, is usually safer to use with a toddler), re-read the manufacturer's directions before each use and follow them carefully. Be sure the pad and cord are in good condition and that the pad has a cover (if it doesn't, wrap a towel or cloth diaper around it). Keep the temperature low and apply the pad for no more than 15 minutes at a time. Do not leave your toddler alone with the heating pad.

## HOMEOPATHIC MEDICINE

Alternative medicine, of which homeopathy is a part, is growing in popularity in the U.S. and elsewhere. Many homeopathic treatments have been around for a very long time and have been used in other parts of the world. Research is now being done in the U.S. to try to find out just how effective such therapies can be. The work is still investigational, but there is some indication that homeopathic remedies can work for at least some illnesses: diarrhea, for example. Check with your doctor before using this

or any other alternative treatment for your child or anyone in your family.

## HOT COMPRESSES

Never use hot compresses on a toddler; use warm compresses instead (see below).

## HOT SOAKS

Fill a basin[2] with water that feels *comfortably* hot on your inner wrist or arm. (Don't test water temperature with your fingers; they can tolerate even excessive heat—and never use water you haven't tested first.) Soak the injured part in the hot water for 15 minutes.

## HOT-WATER BOTTLE

Fill a hot-water bottle with water that is just warm to the touch. Wrap the bottle in a towel or cloth diaper before applying to your child's skin.

## HUMIDIFIER

See "Humidifying," page 838.

## ICE PACK

Use a commercial ice pack (keep one in your freezer at all times) or a plastic bag filled with ice cubes (add a couple of paper towels to absorb melting ice and tie closed with a twist tie or rubber band). Also effective: an unopened can of frozen juice or package of frozen food. Do not apply ice directly to your child's skin; wrap the ice pack in a towel or a cloth diaper. To avoid frostbite, keep the ice pack on for only 20 to 30 minutes at a time.

# HUMIDIFYING

• • • • • • • • • •

I ndoor air that is too dry tends to make for drier skin and scratchier throats, and may even lower resistance to respiratory infections. Some studies have shown that increasing the moisture in the air can reduce the incidence of respiratory infections and allergies. In fact, adding humidity to the air is an often recommended treatment for respiratory illnesses (such as colds and flu)—though whether humidification is effective or not isn't clear.

Air that is *too* moist (humid), on the other hand, may be as unhealthy as air that is too dry. Excess humidity can encourage the growth of bacteria, dust mites, fungi (including molds), and some viruses. You can monitor the relative humidity in your home with an inexpensive hygrometer (available in hardware stores). Most experts suggest that maintaining indoor humidity between 30% and 50% is ideal. (Many airborne bacteria and viruses tend to thrive at levels of humidity that are either higher or lower, and die more quickly at this level.) If your child or anyone in the family suffers from mold allergies, keep the humidity close to 35%.

## The Hows of Humidifying

There are a variety of ways to add moisture to the air in your home:

**Central humidification.** A central system can add humidity to the entire home but is not very useful in a house without a vapor barrier (most pre-1950 homes do not have one), because the humidity can escape through the walls. A central system may also have many of the same problems that other humidifiers have (making the air *too* moist, filling it with microorganisms, minerals, molds, and so on).

**Room humidifiers.*** The array of appliances for humidifying the air in the home can be intimidating. But choosing a good one is important. Options include:

*A cool-mist humidifier.* This kind of humidifier breaks water into tiny droplets, which it then sprays into the air as a cool mist. Because the water is unheated, it may contain potentially harmful germs, fungi, and molds unless the appliance is cleaned and sanitized according to the manufacturer's directions.

*Ultrasonic humidifier.* These humidifiers pulverize bacteria and mold, rendering them harmless. But they also pulverize minerals in the water and send them into the air as "white dust." This white dust can be harmful, especially to those with allergies or asthma. So it's best to use only distilled or demineralized water or demineralization cartridges or filters, if recommended for the unit. This will reduce scale buildup inside the unit as well as the release of white dust.

*Wicking and evaporation-type humidi-*

---

*Many humidifiers that are sold in department or discount stores make no medical claims and are therefore not subject to FDA regulation. A device that claims to help clear congestion is a better bet because it does have to meet FDA standards.

# SALT-WATER NASAL IRRIGATION

• • • • • • • • • • • • • • • • • • • • • • • • • • • •

Though it's possible to use a homemade saline solution (⅛ teaspoon salt to ½ cup boiled water, cooled to body temperature before using), commercial saline solutions are safer and easier to use (but do not use those that contain medication). To soften crusts and thin nasal secretions, put 2 drops of saline solution in each nostril with a clean small dropper. The child should be lying down, or sitting with his or her head back in order for the drops to be effective.

*fiers.* These units, in which a fan blows air through a wet pad or filter, send moisture into the air via evaporation rather than a spray. For this reason, they do not emit white dust and—as long as the filters or pads (which can become a breeding ground for germs) are cleaned regularly—are less likely to spread germs than other humidifiers.

*A steam vaporizer.* This device boils water and sends steam into the air. It doesn't spew germs or large amounts of white dust, but the minerals left behind when the water boils need to be removed periodically, so regular cleaning is necessary. The major drawback: A child can pull the appliance over and be scalded. For this reason, vaporizers are *not recommended* for homes with children; if you do use one, be absolutely certain your toddler can't get to it.

*A warm-mist vaporizer.* This type of unit boils the water, but the steam is cooled slightly before being discharged, resulting in a mist of warm-water droplets instead of real steam. It is still, however, hazardous and *not recommended* for a home with children.

*Therapeutic humidifiers.* Available only by prescription, these are used for treating serious respiratory disorders— asthma, cystic fibrosis, and other chronic pulmonary conditions. Atomizers or non-ventilatory nebulizers can spray an over-the-counter medication (such as a nasal decongestant or cough suppressant) into the air, but use only on the advice of your child's doctor.

**Bathroom steam.** This provides only short-term humidification and is best for dealing with a sudden attack of croup.

**Kitchen steam.** A pot of water simmering on a hot plate or on the stove on the lowest heat (checked regularly to be sure the water hasn't boiled out or a gas flame hasn't flickered out) adds moisture to the kitchen and adjacent areas, but it's risky in homes with young children and *not recommended.* A large coffee maker (without its innards or cover) filled with water and allowed to simmer or a pot of hot water on a radiator or a wood stove can also provide moisture, but again can be *very dangerous* if a toddler can get to it.

### Keeping a Humidifier Clean

A humidifier that's in regular use should be cleaned daily. When cleaning, empty any remaining water, wash according to manufacturer's directions, and thoroughly wipe dry inside and out with a clean, lint-free towel. In addition, the unit in use should be sanitized every 7 days (or 14 days if it has a capacity of 5 gallons or more). To sanitize a humidifier, empty the unit and refill it with a solution of 1 teaspoon bleach to 1 gallon water. Let soak 20 minutes, swishing the water around every few minutes. Empty. Then remove any scale or mineral deposits with a soft brush or towel and a solution of equal parts vinegar and water. Rinse with water until you can no longer smell the bleach. Replace or clean filters or belts as recommended. Always sanitize and thoroughly dry a humidifier before storing. When taking it out of storage, remove any dust on the outside and sanitize the inside again before using.

# STEAM

To provide quick and abundant steam for a child with croup (see page 600), close the bathroom door and turn on the hot water in the tub or shower full blast. The room should fill quickly with steam. Remain with your child in the bathroom until the croupy cough stops.

# WARM COMPRESSES

Fill a basin (see, footnote 2, page 836) with warm, not hot, water (the temperature should feel comfortably warm on your inner arm). Dip a clean washcloth or towel in the water, wring it out, and apply it to the injury as directed by the doctor.

# Common Toddler Illnesses

| DISEASE/SEASON/ SUSCEPTIBILITY | SYMPTOMS | | |
|---|---|---|---|
| | NON-RASH (numbers indicate order of appearance) | | RASH |
| **BRONCHIOLITIS** (Inflammation of the smaller branches of the bronchial tree leading to the lungs) **Season:** For respiratory syncytial viruses (RSV), winter and spring; for parainfluenza viruses (PIV), summer and fall. **Who is susceptible?** Those under 2 years (especially under 6 months); those with a family history of allergy. | 1. Cold symptoms. 2. *A few days later:* Rapid, shallow breathing; wheezing on breathing out; low-grade fever for about 3 days. *Sometimes:* Chest seems not to expand on breathing in; nails and fingertips take on pale or bluish color; loss of appetite; dehydration. | | |
| **BRONCHITIS** (Inflammation of the bronchial tree and often the trachea, or windpipe) **Season:** Varies with causative microorganism. **Who is susceptible?** Mostly children under 4 years. | 1. *Usually:* Cold symptoms. 2. *Abrupt onset of:* Fever, about 102°F (38.9°C); harsh cough, worse at night, sometimes paroxysmal (coming in periodic bursts), with vomiting; greenish or yellowish sputum; wheezing or whistling on breathing out (particularly in those with a family history of respiratory allergy); lips and fingernails tinged blue. | | |

W hen your child is sick, you want to know immediately what is wrong. Though that isn't always possible, skimming the symptoms columns on the illness chart and comparing them to those your child is displaying can often yield some clues. For most illnesses, you should then check with the doctor for a confirmed diagnosis (see the "Call the Doctor" column) and for advice on what to do next. Treatment of many illnesses is symptomatic—you treat just the symptoms (acetaminophen for fever, humidifier for a stuffy nose, and so on) rather than the illness itself. Treatment for the most common symptoms are described starting on page 836; fever is dealt with in depth starting on page 577. When medication is prescribed be sure to give it correctly (see page 592). Note that the most common illnesses (colds, flu, earaches, tummy aches) are covered in Chapter Twenty.

| CAUSE/TRANSMISSION/ INCUBATION/DURATION | CALL THE DOCTOR/ TREATMENT/DIET | PREVENTION/RECURRENCE/ COMPLICATIONS |
|---|---|---|
| **Cause:** Various viruses, most often RSV or PIV; rarely, bacteria. **Transmission:** Usually via respiratory secretions, by direct person-to-person contact, or by contact with contaminated household objects. **Incubation:** Varies with causative organism; usually 2 to 8 days. **Duration:** Acute phase may last only 3 days, cough from 1 to 3 weeks or more. | **Call the doctor immediately or go to the ER** if doctor can't be reached. **Treatment:** Usually hospitalization; possibly, nebulizer treatment, steroids, or antiviral drugs. **Diet:** If food can be taken by mouth, frequent small meals. | **Prevention:** No vaccine available; when possible, take special care to avoid exposure of infants and young toddlers with a family history of respiratory allergy to those with respiratory infections. **Recurrence:** Can recur, but symptoms may be milder with subsequent infections. **Complications:** Rarely heart failure; bronchial asthma. |
| **Cause:** Usually a virus; less often, bacteria, but secondary bacterial infection is common. Cough made worse by tobacco smoke. **Transmission:** Usually via respiratory secretions. **Incubation:** Varies with causative organism. **Duration:** Fever lasts 2 or 3 days; cough 1 or 2 weeks or more. | **Call the doctor** if a cough is severe or lasts more than 3 days. **Treatment:** Symptomatic for fever and/or cough, if needed; in some cases, antibiotics. | **Prevention:** Proper care of child with a common cold (page 596). **Recurrence:** Some children are particularly susceptible and get bronchitis with every cold. **Complications:** Otitis media (ear infection). |

| DISEASE/SEASON/ SUSCEPTIBILITY | SYMPTOMS | |
|---|---|---|
| | NON-RASH   (numbers indicate order of appearance)   RASH | |
| **CAT SCRATCH DISEASE** <br> **Season:** More frequent in fall and winter. <br> **Who is susceptible?** Anyone, but 80% of cases occur in those under 20. | *Usually:* Swollen lymph glands at 1 to 4 weeks after contact, usually under arms or in neck or jaw. Site of glands may be tender, warm, red, hard (sometimes), and may even discharge pus. *Sometimes:* Fever (100.4°F to 102.2°F, or 38C° to 39°C). *Occasionally:* Only fever with no apparent cause, and, possibly, abdominal pain. | *Often,* a red papule (pimple) at site of scratch or bite, 1 or 2 weeks before other symptoms. |
| **CHICKENPOX** <br> **(Varicella)** <br> **Season:** Late winter and early spring in temperate zones. <br> **Who is susceptible?** Anyone who has never been infected; most people are infected as children. | Slight fever; malaise; loss of appetite. Those on steroids or who are immunocompromised can become seriously ill. | Flat red spots turn into pimples, then blister, crust, and scab; new crops continue to develop for 3 or 4 days. Itching is usually intense. |
| **COLDS** | See page 596. | |

| CAUSE/TRANSMISSION/ INCUBATION/DURATION | CALL THE DOCTOR/ TREATMENT/DIET | PREVENTION/RECURRENCE/ COMPLICATIONS |
|---|---|---|
| **Cause:** *Rochalimeaea henselae* or *afipia felis* bacteria. **Transmission:** Usually, kitten scratch, bite, or lick; sometimes, older cat or other animal; rarely, no contact. **Incubation:** 7 to 12 days from scratch to skin lesion (rash); then 5 to 50 days (a median of 12) to swollen glands. **Duration:** Usually 2 to 4 months; fever, about 2 weeks; gland tenderness, 4 to 6 weeks; swelling, several months, but as long as 1 year. | **Call the doctor** for unexplained fever and/or swollen glands following an encounter with a cat. **Treatment:** Disease usually resolves without treatment; antimicrobial drugs may be given if symptoms are severe; pus may be withdrawn from infected lymph nodes with a needle, if necessary, to reduce pain. | **Prevention:** Declawing pet cats; possibly treating infected cats and controlling fleas; keeping toddlers away from kittens. Disposing of cats believed to transmit infection is not warranted. **Recurrence:** Reinfection is very rare. **Complications:** Rarely, brain inflammation with high fever; convulsions; muscle weakness (within 6 weeks of onset); hepatitis; a form of conjunctivitis; usually no residual problems. |
| **Cause:** Varicella-zoster virus. **Transmission:** Primarily, person-to-person; also, airborne droplets from respiratory secretions. Very contagious from 1 to 2 days before onset until all lesions scab (about 6 days). **Incubation:** 11 to 20 days, most often 14 to 16 days; longer if child has had VZIG (immune globulin). **Duration:** First vesicles crust in 6 to 8 hours, scab in 24 to 48; scabs last 5 to 20 days. | **Call the doctor** to confirm diagnosis; **call immediately** for high-risk children; **call again** if symptoms of encephalitis (page 844) appear. Call if nonimmune pregnant woman has been exposed. **Treatment:** For itching (page 612) and fever (page 582). Do not give aspirin or other salicylates. At present, routine use of antiviral drugs is recommended only for high-risk children. | **Prevention:** Vaccine (see page 562); avoidance of exposure for high-risk children and nonimmune expectant mothers; possibly, VZIG or antiviral drugs for exposed family members. **Recurrence:** Extremely rare; but dormant virus may flare up as shingles in future. **Complications:** Rarely, secondary bacterial infection resulting in encephalitis, hepatitis. *In pregnant women,* slight risk to fetus in first or second trimester; greatly increased risk 5 days before to 2 days after delivery. |

| DISEASE/SEASON/ SUSCEPTIBILITY | SYMPTOMS | |
|---|---|---|
| | NON-RASH (numbers indicate order of appearance) | RASH |
| **CONJUNCTIVITIS** (**Pinkeye**; inflammation of the conjunctiva, the membrane lining the eyelids and the eyes) **Season:** Not seasonal. **Who is susceptible?** Depends on cause. | *Depending on cause, may include:* Bloodshot eyes; tearing; eye discharge (lids may be crusted after sleep); burning; itching; light sensitivity. Usually begins in one eye, but may spread to the other. | |
| **CROUP** | See page 600. | |
| **DIARRHEA** | See page 601. | |
| **EAR INFECTION** | See **Otitis Media**, page 605. | |
| **ENCEPHALITIS** (Inflammation of the brain) **Season:** Depends on cause. **Who is susceptible?** Depends on cause. | Fever; drowsiness; headache. *Sometimes:* Neurological impairment (confusion, altered state of consciousness, muscle weakness); progression to coma at a late stage. | |

| CAUSE/TRANSMISSION/ INCUBATION/DURATION | CALL THE DOCTOR/ TREATMENT/DIET | PREVENTION/RECURRENCE/ COMPLICATIONS |
|---|---|---|
| **Cause:** Many, including viruses, bacteria, chlamydia, parasites, fungi, allergens, irritants. **Transmission:** For infectious organisms, eye-hand-eye; towels, bed linens. **Incubation:** Usually brief. **Duration:** Varies with cause; viral, 2 days to 3 weeks (can become chronic); bacterial, about 2 weeks; others, until allergen or irritant is removed. | **Call the doctor** to confirm diagnosis; **call again** if condition worsens or does not begin to improve with treatment. **Treatment:** Eye soaks (page 836); separate bed linens and towels to prevent transmission; elimination of irritants, such as tobacco smoke, when possible; drops or ointment prescribed for bacterial and herpes infections, possibly for viral conjunctivitis (to prevent secondary infection), and to relieve discomfort of allergic reaction. | **Prevention:** Good hygiene (use separate towels and bed linens when a family member is infected); avoidance of allergens and irritants. **Recurrence:** Possible; some children are more susceptible and more likely to have recurrences. **Complications:** Blindness (extremely rare, except with gonorrheal infection); chronic eye inflammation; eye damage from repeated infections. |
| | | |
| | | |
| **Cause:** Bacteria or viruses, often as a complication of another disease. **Transmission:** Depends on cause; some viruses transmitted via insects. **Incubation:** Depends on cause. **Duration:** Varies greatly. | **Call the doctor immediately or go to the ER** if you suspect encephalitis. **Treatment:** Hospitalization is required. | **Prevention:** Immunization against diseases of which encephalitis may be a complication (measles, for example). **Recurrence:** Unlikely. **Complications:** Neurological damage; can be fatal if untreated. |

| DISEASE/SEASON/ SUSCEPTIBILITY | SYMPTOMS | |
|---|---|---|
| | NON-RASH    (numbers indicate order of appearance) | RASH |
| **EPIGLOTTITIS** (Inflammation of the epiglottis—the upper part of the larynx, or voice box) **Season:** Winter months in temperate climates. **Who is susceptible?** Most often children 2 to 4 years old; becoming rare thanks to immunization to a major cause. | Sudden onset of fever over 102°F or 38.9°C (lower in tots under 2); hoarse cough (croupy in under 2's); noisy breathing (stridor); sore throat and difficulty swallowing; drooling. *Sometimes:* protruding tongue; retractions (page 571), blueness of nails and lips. Symptoms worsen rapidly. Child seems ill, agitated, irritable, restless, and may prefer to remain upright, leaning forward with mouth open to get air. On exam, the epiglottis is extremely red and swollen. | |
| **FIFTH DISEASE (Erythema Infectiosum) Season:** Early spring. **Who is susceptible?** Greatest in children 2 to 12 years old. | *Sometimes:* Fever. *Rarely:* Joint pain. | 1. Intense flush on face (slapped-cheek look). 2. *Next day:* Lacy rash on arms and legs. 3. *3 days later:* Rash on inner surfaces, fingers, toes, trunk, and/or buttocks. 4. Rash may reappear on and off with exposure to heat (bath water, sun) for 2 or 3 weeks, even months. |
| **GASTROENTERITIS** | See **Diarrhea**, page 605. | |

| CAUSE/TRANSMISSION/ INCUBATION/DURATION | CALL THE DOCTOR/ TREATMENT/DIET | PREVENTION/RECURRENCE/ COMPLICATIONS |
|---|---|---|
| **Cause:** Bacteria, most often, *hemophilus influenzae* (Hib); sometimes group A *Streptococcus*. **Transmission:** Probably, person-to-person, or inhalation of respiratory droplets. **Incubation:** Uncertain; probably widely variable. **Duration:** 4 to 7 days or longer. | **Call 911 immediately or go to the ER if you suspect epiglottitis.** While waiting for help, keep child upright, leaning forward, with mouth open and tongue out. **Treatment:** Hospitalization; maintenance of open airway; breathing tubes; antibiotics. | **Prevention:** Hib immunization can eliminate at least 75% of cases. **Recurrence:** Slight possibility. **Complications:** Can be fatal without prompt medical attention. |
| **Cause:** Human parvovirus B19. **Transmission:** Probably, respiratory secretions and blood; most cases are most contagious before onset of illness. **Incubation:** Usually, 4 to 14 days, but as long as 20 days. **Duration:** Initial rash, several days to a week; rash can continue to recur for weeks or months. | **Call the doctor** if you need confirmation of the diagnosis, if other symptoms appear, or if child is immuno-suppressed or has sickle-cell disease. **Treatment:** None needed in most cases; for chronic infection in immunodeficient patients, immunoglobulin may be effective. | **Prevention:** Routine hygienic practices (page 606) for control of infection. **Recurrence:** Unlikely. **Complications:** Only in children who are immuno-deficient. *In pregnant women* who are not already immune (most are), can occasionally cause fetal damage in first half of pregnancy; risk may be negligible in second half. |

| DISEASE/SEASON/ SUSCEPTIBILITY | SYMPTOMS | |
|---|---|---|
| | NON-RASH   (numbers indicate order of appearance) | RASH |
| **GERMAN MEASLES (Rubella)** <br> **Season:** Late winter and early spring. <br> **Who is susceptible?** Any person who hasn't had the disease or been immunized against it. | None, in 25% to 50% of cases. <br> 1. *Sometimes:* Slight fever; swollen glands. | 2. Small ($^1/_{10}$ inch), flat, reddish pink spots on face. <br> 3. Rash spreads to body and, sometimes, roof of mouth. |
| **HAND-FOOT-MOUTH DISEASE (Vesicular stomatitis)** <br> **Season:** Summer and fall in temperate climates. <br> **Who is susceptible?** Mostly, babies and young children. | 1. Fever; loss of appetite. <br> *Often:* Sore throat and mouth; difficulty swallowing. | 2. *In 2 or 3 days:* Lesions in mouth (which usually blister). <br> 3. *Then,* lesions on fingers; *sometimes,* feet, buttocks, arms, legs; and *less often,* face. |
| **HERPANGINA** <br> **Season:** Mostly summer and fall in temperate climates; any time in tropical regions. <br> **Who is susceptible?** Primarily, babies and young children. Occurs alone or with other diseases. | 1. Fever: 100°F to 104°F, occasionally to 106°F (37.8°C to 40°C, or 41.1°C); sore throat. A febrile seizure may accompany onset of fever. <br> 1. or 3. Painful swallowing. <br> *Sometimes:* Vomiting; loss of appetite; diarrhea; abdominal pain; lethargy. | 2. Distinct grayish white papules in back of mouth or throat (5 to 10 in number) that blister and ulcerate. |
| **HYDROPHOBIA** | See **Rabies** page 858. | |
| **IMPETIGO** | See page 473. | |

| CAUSE/TRANSMISSION/ INCUBATION/DURATION | CALL THE DOCTOR/ TREATMENT/DIET | PREVENTION/RECURRENCE/ COMPLICATIONS |
|---|---|---|
| **Cause:** Rubella virus. **Transmission:** Via direct contact or droplets from respiratory secretions; most often contagious from a few days before to 5 to 7 days after rash appears. **Incubation:** 14 to 21 days, most often 16 to 18. **Duration:** A few hours to 4 or 5 days. | **Call the doctor** if non-immune pregnant woman has been exposed. **Treatment:** None. | **Prevention:** MMR immunization (see page 560). **Recurrence:** None; one case confers lifetime immunity. **Complications:** Very rarely, thrombocytopenia or encephalitis. |
| **Cause:** Coxsackievirus (an enterovirus). **Transmission:** Mouth-to-mouth; feces-to-hand-to-mouth. **Incubation:** 3 to 6 days. **Duration:** About 1 week. | **Call the doctor** to confirm diagnosis. **Treatment:** Symptomatic. **Diet:** Soft foods will be more comfortable. | **Prevention:** None known. **Recurrence:** Possible. **Complications:** None. |
| **Cause:** Nonpolio enteroviruses, such as Coxsackievirus; occasionally other viruses. **Transmission:** Mouth-to-mouth; feces-to-hand-to-mouth. **Incubation:** 3 to 6 days. **Duration:** 4 to 7 days, but healing can take 2 to 3 weeks. | **Call the doctor** to confirm diagnosis. **Call immediately** if a seizure occurs. **Treatment:** Symptomatic. **Diet:** Soft foods are more comfortable. | **Prevention:** Good hygienic practices. **Recurrence:** Possible. **Complications:** Rare. |

| DISEASE/SEASON/ SUSCEPTIBILITY | SYMPTOMS NON-RASH   (numbers indicate order of appearance)   RASH | |
|---|---|---|
| **INFLUENZA** | See page 604. | |
| **KAWASAKI DISEASE (Mucocutaneous lymph node syndrome, MLNS)** **Season:** Any, but slight increase in winter and spring; occurs in 2- or 3-year cycles. **Who is susceptible?** Mostly infants and children under 5; more boys than girls; more children of Asian (especially Japanese) than of other origin. Living near a body of water *may* also increase risk. | 1. Fever, lasting 5 to 39 days (most often, 7). 2. *Within 3 days of onset of fever:* changes in mucous membranes of nose, mouth, and/or throat (cracked lips, strawberry tongue, throat swollen with excess blood to the area); a swollen gland in the neck; conjunctivitis in both eyes, with no discharge. Usually, other conditions must be ruled out before the diagnosis can be made. | 2. Flat red rash on body; redness and/or swelling or hardening of soles of feet and palms of hands. 3. Peeling of skin on palms and soles during second to third week. |
| **LYME DISEASE (Borrelia burgdorferi)** **Season:** May 1 to November 30, with most cases in June and July. **Who is susceptible?** Anyone; heaviest concentration in Northeast, Midwest, and California, but disease is spreading to other areas of U.S. Also found outside U.S. | 1. or 2. *Often:* Fatigue, headache, fever and chills; generalized achiness; swollen glands near site of bite. *Sometimes:* Conjunctivitis; swelling around the eyes; nervous system involvement (intermittent behavioral changes); swelling of the testicles; sore throat; dry cough. 3. *Weeks to years later, if untreated:* Joint pain; heart abnormalities. *None of these symptoms alone, however, is diagnostic; see under* **Rash**. | 1. *Usually:* A bull's-eye-shaped red rash at site of tick bite, up to 1 month after bite. 2. *Sometimes:* Other rashes, including red blotches or circles, all-over redness, cheek rash, hives. |

| CAUSE/TRANSMISSION/ INCUBATION/DURATION | CALL THE DOCTOR/ TREATMENT/DIET | PREVENTION/RECURRENCE/ COMPLICATIONS |
|---|---|---|
| **Cause:** Unknown; no microorganisms have been identified, but recent research suggests a toxin produced by *Staphylococcus aureus* may be involved; a reported link to rug shampoo is not confirmed, nor is possibility of allergic response. **Transmission:** Unknown. **Incubation:** Unknown. **Duration:** Without treatment, fever lasts about 12 days; appetite loss and irritability can last 2 or 3 weeks. Complications last longer. | **Call the doctor** if signs of Kawasaki appear. **Treatment:** Aspirin** to reduce inflammation; Immune Globulin Intravenous (IGIV) plus aspirin started within 10 days of onset may reduce complications. Frequent evaluation of condition of heart is important.<br><br>**Aspirin therapy is usually stopped if child develops flu or chickenpox. | **Prevention:** None known. **Recurrence:** Unknown. **Complications:** Uveitis (eye inflammation); damage to heart and blood vessels, including coronary artery aneurysms (swellings), ruptured aneurysms, and inflammation of the heart muscle. Also a variety of less common complications affecting the ears, kidneys, brain, and nervous system. Mortality rate: less than 1 in 200. |
| **Cause:** A spirochete, *borrelia burgdorferi.* **Transmission:** Spread by the bite of a pinhead-size deer tick (carried not only by deer but by mice and other animals) and possibly, by other ticks and flying insects. It takes 24 to 48 hours for an attached tick to transmit Lyme disease. **Incubation:** 3 to 32 days; typically, 7 to 10. **Diagnosis:** *Early:* Presence of distinctive rash. *Late:* Blood tests (not always accurate). **Duration:** Without treatment, possibly years. | **Call the doctor** if you remove a tick (see page 661) from your child or anyone in the family, or if a characteristic rash develops. **Treatment:** Antibiotics; usually given only if rash or swollen joints develop, indicating infection; effective even at late stages. | **Prevention:** Protective cover-up clothing when outdoors in infested areas; appropriate use of insect repellent (page 648); checking for, and *prompt* removal of, ticks after such outings. Experimental vaccine being tested. **Recurrence:** Possible; there is no lasting immunity. **Complications:** Arthritic, neurological, cardiac, motor abnormalities. |

| DISEASE/SEASON/ SUSCEPTIBILITY | SYMPTOMS NON-RASH (numbers indicate order of appearance) RASH | |
|---|---|---|
| **MEASLES (Rubeola)** **Season:** Winter and spring. **Who is susceptible?** Anyone not already immune. | 1. *For 1 or 2 days:* Fever; runny nose; red, watery eyes; dry cough. *Sometimes:* Diarrhea; swollen glands. | 2. Tiny white spots like grains of sand appear inside of cheeks (Koplik spots), which may bleed. 3. Dull, red, slightly raised rash begins on forehead and behind ears, then spreads downward, giving a red-all-over appearance. |
| **MENINGITIS** (Inflammation of the membranes around the brain and/or the spinal cord) **Season:** Varies with causative organism; with Hib, winter. **Who is susceptible?** Depends on causative organism. For Hib, mostly infants and children under 3; more often boys, city dwellers, African-Americans, some Native Americans, and children in day-care centers. | Fever; high-pitched cry; drowsiness; irritability; loss of appetite; vomiting; bulging fontanel. *In older toddlers, also:* stiff neck, sensitivity to light, blurred vision, and possibly other neurological symptoms. | |
| **MENINGOENCEPHALITIS** (Combined meningitis and encephalitis) | See **Meningitis** (above) and **Encephalitis**, page 844. | |

| CAUSE/TRANSMISSION/ INCUBATION/DURATION | CALL THE DOCTOR/ TREATMENT/DIET | PREVENTION/RECURRENCE/ COMPLICATIONS |
|---|---|---|
| **Cause:** Measles virus. **Transmission:** Direct contact with respiratory droplets from 2 days before to 4 days after rash appears. **Incubation:** 8 to 12 days. **Duration:** About a week. | **Call the doctor** to confirm diagnosis. **Call again immediately** if cough becomes severe, if convulsions or symptoms of pneumonia, encephalitis, or otitis media occur, or if fever goes up after going down. **Treatment:** Symptomatic; warm soaks for rash; reduced lighting for comfort if eyes are bothered by light, though exposure to bright light is not harmful. In severe cases and in high-risk children, the administration of vitamin A. | **Prevention:** Immunization (MMR); strict isolation of infected persons. **Recurrence:** None. **Complications:** Otitis media, pneumonia, encephalitis; can be fatal, especially in immuno-compromised children. (U.S. mortality rate is 3 in 1,000.) |
| **Cause:** Bacteria, most often Hib; viruses, which cause milder disease. **Transmission:** Depends on organism; with Hib, probably person-to-person, by direct contact or through inhalation of droplets from respiratory secretions. **Incubation:** Varies with organism; for Hib, probably less than 10 days. **Duration:** Varies. | **Call the doctor immediately** if you suspect meningitis; **go to the ER** if the doctor can't be reached. **Treatment:** For viral meningitis, symptomatic; for bacterial, hospitalization and antibiotics. | **Prevention:** Hib immunization, which prevents Hib meningitis; stringent adherence to hygienic rules in day-care centers. **Recurrence:** None with Hib; one attack confers immunity. **Complications:** Hib and other types of bacterial meningitis can do lasting neurological damage; they are sometimes fatal. Viral forms usually do no long-term damage. |

| DISEASE/SEASON/ SUSCEPTIBILITY | SYMPTOMS | |
|---|---|---|
| | NON-RASH (numbers indicate order of appearance) | RASH |
| **MUMPS** **Season:** Late winter and spring. **Who is susceptible?** Anyone not immune. | 1. *Sometimes:* Vague pain; fever; loss of appetite. 2. *Usually*: Swelling of parotid (salivary) glands on one or both sides of jaw, below and in front of ear; ear pain; pain on chewing, or on taking acidic or sour food or drink; swelling of the salivary glands. No symptoms in about 30% of cases. | |
| **NONSPECIFIC VIRAL (NSV) ILLNESSES** **Season:** Mostly summer. **Who is susceptible?** Mostly young children. | *Vary, but may include:* Fever, loss of appetite, diarrhea. | Various types of rashes are seen with NSV. |
| **PERTUSSIS (Whooping Cough)** **Season:** Late winter, early spring. **Who is susceptible?** Mostly unimmunized infants and young children. (If immunized children do contract disease, it is usually mild.) | 1. *Catarrhal stage:* Cold symptoms with dry cough; low-grade fever; irritability. 2. *Paroxysmal stage, 1 or 2 weeks later:* Coughing in explosive bursts with no breaths between; thick mucus expelled. *Often:* Bulging eyes and protruding tongue; pale or reddened skin; vomiting; sweating; exhaustion. *Sometimes:* Hernia, from coughing. 3. *Convalescent stage:* Cessation of whooping and vomiting; reduced coughing; improved appetite and mood. | |

| CAUSE/TRANSMISSION/ INCUBATION/DURATION | CALL THE DOCTOR/ TREATMENT/DIET | PREVENTION/RECURRENCE/ COMPLICATIONS |
|---|---|---|
| **Cause:** A paramyxovirus (mumps virus). **Transmission:** Usually via direct contact with respiratory secretions from 1 or 2 (but as long as 7) days prior to onset until 9 days after. **Incubation:** Usually 16 to 18 days, but can be as few as 12 or as many as 25. **Duration:** 5 to 7 days. | **Call the doctor** to confirm diagnosis; **call back immediately** if there is vomiting, drowsiness, possibility of headache, back or neck stiffness, other signs of meningo-encephalitis, either along with or following mumps. **Treatment:** Symptomatic for fever and pain; cool compresses applied to cheeks. **Diet:** Avoidance of acidic and sour foods; soft foods will be more comfortable. | **Prevention:** Immunization (MMR). **Recurrence:** Very slight chance of recurrence if only one side was affected. **Complications:** Meningoencephalitis; other complications are rare in toddlers but can be serious in adult males. |
| **Cause:** Various enteroviruses, including coxsackieviruses and echoviruses. **Transmission:** Feces-to-hand-to-mouth; possibly, mouth-to-mouth. **Incubation:** 3 to 6 days. **Duration:** Usually a few days. | **Call the doctor** to confirm diagnosis; **call again** if child seems worse or if new symptoms appear. **Treatment:** Symptomatic. **Diet:** Extra fluids for diarrhea, fever (see pages 603, 584). | **Prevention:** None, except good hygienic practices, such as hand washing (see page 606). **Recurrence:** Common. **Complications:** Very rare. |
| **Cause:** *Bordetella pertussis* bacteria. **Transmission:** Direct contact via respiratory droplets; most communicable during catarrhal stage; period of communicability may be reduced when antibiotics are used. **Incubation:** 7 to 10 days; rarely more than 2 weeks. **Duration:** Usually 6 weeks, but can last much longer. | **Call the doctor promptly** for persistent coughing. **Treatment:** Antibiotics may help reduce symptoms in first stage, communicability later; mucus suctioning; humidification; for infants, hospitalization. **Diet:** Frequent small feedings; fluid replacement. For infants, intravenous feeding if necessary. | **Prevention:** Immunization with pertussis vaccine (DTP or DTaP). **Recurrence:** None; one attack confers lifetime immunity. **Complications:** Many, including otitis media; pneumonia; convulsions. Can be fatal, especially in infants. |

| DISEASE/SEASON/ SUSCEPTIBILITY | SYMPTOMS | |
|---|---|---|
| | NON-RASH   (numbers indicate order of appearance)   RASH | |
| **PHARYNGITIS** | See **Sore Throat,** page 610. | |
| **PINWORM INFECTION (Enterobiasis)** **Season:** Not seasonal. **Who is susceptible?** Most often, preschool and school-age children and their mothers. | 1. Pinworms enter and live in lower digestive tract; females lay eggs around anus and on buttocks. 2. Itching begins around the anus. Children may waken at night crying; be irritable, restless, and fatigued. Check for eggs with a flashlight in the middle of night if your child wakes up or first thing in A.M. Anal area may be raw and red. 3. *Occasionally,* in girls, itching of the vulva. If worms enter vagina, may cause vaginitis and a slight vaginal discharge. | |
| **PNEUMONIA** (Inflammation of the lung) **Season:** Varies with causative factor. **Who is susceptible?** Anyone, but especially the very young, the very old, and those with chronic illness. | *Commonly, child with cold or other illness seems suddenly worse.* Often there is: increased fever; productive cough; rapid breathing; bluish skin tone; wheezy, raspy, and/or difficult breathing; shortness of breath; chest retractions (page 571); heavy mucus production; and possibly, abdominal bloating and pain. | |

| CAUSE/TRANSMISSION/ INCUBATION/DURATION | CALL THE DOCTOR/ TREATMENT/DIET | PREVENTION/RECURRENCE/ COMPLICATIONS |
|---|---|---|
| **Cause:** A tiny (¼- to ½-inch), grayish, thread-like parasitic worm, *Enterobius vermicularis.* **Transmission:** Via ova (worm eggs), hand-to-mouth (e.g.: thumb sucking after scratching or wiping) or from toilet seat or other objects; if swallowed, eggs hatch and worms move down to rectum. Communicable as long as females are laying eggs; eggs remain infective for 2 to 3 weeks. **Duration:** Without treatment, cycle can continue indefinitely. | **Call the doctor** if you suspect pinworms. First thing when your toddler awakens in A.M., use a strip of transparent tape to lift any eggs off the area around the anus for the doctor to identify under a microscope. **Treatment:** An oral medication to expel mature pinworms with bowel movements. Entire family may be treated. Vaginitis does not need to be treated separately. | **Prevention:** Scrupulous hand washing plus other preventive hygienic practices (page 606). Hand washing after playing with pets, since pets can carry pinworms. Thorough washing of bed- and nightclothes daily. **Recurrence:** Very common. **Complications:** In severe cases, appetite and weight loss, even anemia. Occasionally, adult worms may migrate to other areas (such as the pelvis) and cause inflammation. |
| **Cause:** Various types of organisms, including bacteria, viruses, mycoplasmas, fungi, and protozoa, as well as inhalation of a chemical, an object, or another irritant. **Transmission:** Varies with cause. **Incubation:** Varies with cause. **Duration:** Varies with cause. | **Call the doctor** for productive or persistent cough; or if a child with cold or flu seems worse or has increased fever, cough, or other signs of pneumonia; **call immediately or go the the ER** if child has difficulty breathing, turns bluish, or seems very sick. **Treatment:** Symptomatic for cough and fever; antibiotics, if appropriate. Possibly, postural drainage to help move mucus. Hospitalization in severe cases. | **Prevention:** Hib immunization for Hib infections; for high-risk children, extra protection against infection (see page 606). **Recurrence:** Many types can recur. **Complications:** More likely in children with impaired immune systems. |

| DISEASE/SEASON/ SUSCEPTIBILITY | SYMPTOMS | | |
|---|---|---|---|
| | NON-RASH (numbers indicate order of appearance) | RASH | |
| **RABIES (Hydrophobia)** **Season:** Anytime, but there are more rabid dogs in summer. **Who is susceptible?** Anyone. | 1. Local or radiating pain, burning, sensation of cold, itching, tingling at site of bite. 2. Slight fever of 101°F to 102°F (38.3°C to 38.9°C); lethargy; headache; loss of appetite; nausea; sore throat; loose cough; irritability; sensitivity to light and noise; dilated pupils; rapid heartbeat; shallow breathing; excessive drooling, tearing, sweating. 3. *2 to 10 days later:* Increased anxiety, restlessness; facial weakness; vision problems; fever to 103°F (39.4°C). *Often:* Fear of water, liquids are often spit out; frothy drooling. 4. *About 3 days later:* Paralysis. | | |
| **RESPIRATORY SYNCYTIAL VIRUS (RSV) ILLNESSES** including the common cold (page 596); bronchiolitis (page 840); and pneumonia (page 856). **Season:** Winter and early spring in temperate climates; rainy season in the tropics. **Who is susceptible?** Anyone, at any age, but most cases occur before age 3. | Range from mild cold symptoms to bronchiolitis and pneumonia, with: Cough; wheezing; sore throat; painful breathing; malaise; inflamed mucous membranes of nose and throat. *Sometimes:* Apnea (breathing lapses), mostly in premature infants. | | |

| CAUSE/TRANSMISSION/ INCUBATION/DURATION | CALL THE DOCTOR/ TREATMENT/DIET | PREVENTION/RECURRENCE/ COMPLICATIONS |
| --- | --- | --- |
| **Cause:** Rabies virus. **Transmission:** From infected animal, via contaminated saliva implanted near nerve tissue by a bite or the licking of an open wound. **Incubation:** 5 days to 1 year or more; 2 months is average. **Duration:** About 2 weeks from start of symptoms to point of paralysis. | **Call the doctor** following a bite by any animal you are not certain has been vaccinated against rabies. **Treatment:** Restraint of animal; first aid for animal bites (see page 660); usually, rabies vaccine and human rabies immune globulin (RIG), if animal can't be found or is rabid; tetanus booster, as needed. Hospitalization if full disease develops. | **Prevention:** Immunization of pets; teaching children caution with strange animals; supervision of children outdoors; community efforts to keep strays off street and wild animal population rabies-free. **Recurrence:** Not an issue; if disease develops it is virtually always fatal. **Complications:** If disease develops, it is invariably fatal if untreated; mortality rate is extremely high, even with treatment, once symptoms occur. |
| **Cause:** Respiratory syncytial virus (RSV). **Transmission:** Via direct or close contact with respiratory secretions or contaminated articles, between 3 days to 4 weeks from onset. **Incubation:** Usually 5 to 8 days. **Duration:** Varies with illness. | **Call the doctor** if a child with a cold has trouble breathing (nostrils flare on breathing in), is wheezing, has a raspy cough or very rapid respiration (page 573). **Treatment:** Symptomatic; in severe cases or high-risk patients, may include antiviral drugs and hospitalization. | **Prevention:** Isolation of infected individuals, careful hand-washing and hygienic measures (page 606); avoidance of exposure to smoke; vaccine and RSV immunoglobulin are under study but not yet available. **Recurrence:** Possibly, but after age 3, usually as upper respiratory infection. **Complications:** Ear infections; more severe illness may develop in infants and in young children with impaired immune systems. |

| DISEASE/SEASON/ SUSCEPTIBILITY | SYMPTOMS | |
|---|---|---|
| | NON-RASH  (numbers indicate order of appearance) | RASH |
| **REYE SYNDROME**<br>**Season:** Not seasonal.<br>**Who is susceptible?** Most often, children who are given aspirin during a viral illness, such as chickenpox or the flu. | 1. *1 to 7 days following a viral infection:* Persistent vomiting (every hour or two, all day); lethargy; rapidly deteriorating and changing mental state (irritability, confusion, delirium, lethargy); rapid heartbeat and respiration.<br>2. *May progress to:* Seizures and coma. | |
| **ROCKY MOUNTAIN SPOTTED FEVER (RMSF)**<br>**Season:** Spring and summer.<br>**Who is susceptible?** Anyone, but most often, children under 15; widespread in U.S. | 1. Fever; headache; muscle pain and weakness; nausea and/or vomiting.<br>*Sometimes:* Abdominal pain; cough. | 2. *Usually before the sixth day:* Flat red spots or splotches appear on palms and soles of feet, spread to wrists and ankles, legs and arms, and finally to trunk.<br>3. Later, papules (pimples) may develop.<br>*Occasionally:* No rash or late-developing rash. |
| **ROSEOLA INFANTUM (Sixth disease; exanthem subitum)**<br>**Season:** Not seasonal.<br>**Who is susceptible?** Primarily babies and young children. | 1. Irritability; loss of appetite; fever of 102°F to 105°F (38.9°C to 40.5°C) for 3 to 7 days.<br>*Sometimes:* Runny nose; swollen glands; convulsions. | 2. *After fever returns to normal:* Faint pink spots that blanch (turn white) upon pressure on body, neck, upper arms, and sometimes, face and legs. *In some cases,* no rash. |
| **SORE THROAT** | See page 610. | |

| CAUSE/TRANSMISSION/ INCUBATION/DURATION | CALL THE DOCTOR/ TREATMENT/DIET | PREVENTION/RECURRENCE/ COMPLICATIONS |
|---|---|---|
| **Cause:** Unknown, but appears related to a reaction to aspirin during a viral illness. **Transmission:** Unknown. **Incubation:** Unknown, but disease seems to develop within days of onset of viral infection. **Duration:** Varies. | **Call the doctor immediately or go to the ER** if you suspect Reye Syndrome. **Treatment:** Hospitalization is vital; transfer to a medical center that specializes in treating Reye Syndrome may be necessary. | **Prevention:** Avoid giving aspirin to children with viral illness, such as chickenpox or flu. **Recurrence:** None. **Complications:** Can be fatal, but survivors usually have no lasting problems. |
| **Cause:** *Rickettsia rickettsii.* **Transmission:** Via the bite of a tick (usually the dog tick); rarely, via blood transfusion. **Incubation:** 1 to 14 days, usually 1 week. **Duration:** Up to 3 weeks. | **Call the doctor** if you suspect RMSF or a tick bite. **Treatment:** Antimicrobials, early in illness. Symptomatic for fever (page 582) and nausea (page 602) as needed. | **Prevention:** Avoidance of tick-infested areas; cover-up clothing in such areas; appropriate use of insect repellents (page 648); safe removal of ticks (page 661). **Recurrence:** Usually none. **Complications:** Involvement of nervous system, heart, lungs, digestive tract, kidneys, and other organs. Fatal shock, especially when untreated. |
| **Cause:** Human herpes virus 6. **Transmission:** Probably via respiratory secretions. **Incubation:** About 9 days. **Duration:** Febrile period, 3 to 7 days; rash, a few hours to a few days. | **Call the doctor** to confirm diagnosis; **call back** if fever persists for 4 or 5 days, or if child develops convulsions or seems ill. **Treatment:** Symptomatic. | **Prevention:** None known. **Recurrence:** Apparently none. **Complications:** Very rare. |
|  |  |  |

| DISEASE/SEASON/ SUSCEPTIBILITY | SYMPTOMS NON-RASH (numbers indicate order of appearance) RASH | |
|---|---|---|
| **TETANUS (Lockjaw)** **Season:** More frequent in warmer climates and months. **Who is susceptible?** Anyone not immunized. | *Localized:* Spasm and increased muscle tone near the entry wound. *Generalized:* Involuntary muscle contractions that can arch back, lock jaw, and twist neck; convulsions; rapid heartbeat; profuse sweating; low-grade fever; difficulty sucking for children still on bottle or breast. | |
| **TONSILLITIS** | See page 610. | |
| **UPPER RESPIRATORY INFECTION (URI)** | See page 596. | |
| **URINARY TRACT INFECTION (UTI)** | See page 612. | |
| **WARTS** **Season:** Not seasonal. **Who is susceptible?** Anyone, but particularly children. | | *Common warts:* Brownish, rough, raised lesions, often on fingers, but elsewhere, too, including genitals (common warts are not sexually transmitted). *Flat warts:* Multiple small, slightly raised lesions, flesh-colored to tan, on face, neck, arms, legs. *Plantar warts:* Speckled, raised, or indented lesions; often painful. *Genital warts:* Soft, flesh-colored papules on genitalia; in children, *may* be sign of sexual abuse. |
| **WHOOPING COUGH** | See **Pertussis,** page 854. | |

| CAUSE/TRANSMISSION/ INCUBATION/DURATION | CALL THE DOCTOR/ TREATMENT/DIET | PREVENTION/RECURRENCE/ COMPLICATIONS |
|---|---|---|
| **Cause:** The spread through the body of the toxin produced by the bacterium *Clostridium tetani.* **Transmission:** Via bacterial contamination of a puncture wound, a burn, or a deep scrape. **Incubation:** 3 days to 3 weeks, but an average of 8 days. **Duration:** Several weeks. | **Call the doctor immediately or go to the ER** if an unvaccinated child incurs a susceptible wound. **Treatment:** Medical treatment is essential, including tetanus toxoid to prevent development of disease; tetanus antitoxins; muscle relaxants; antibiotics; breathing support, if needed. | **Prevention:** Immunization (DTP); shoes outdoors for everyone; supervision of outdoor play. **Recurrence:** None. **Complications:** Many, including: ulcers; pneumonia, abnormal heart rate; blood clot in lung. Can be fatal. |
|  |  |  |
|  |  |  |
| **Cause:** Human papilloma virus (HPV). **Transmission:** Direct person-to-person contact; sexual contact, for genital warts; also transmission from infected mother to newborn during delivery (but lesions may not appear on child for years). **Incubation:** 1 to 20 months. **Duration:** Without treatment, warts resolve in 6 months to 3 years. | **Call the doctor** if the warts are painful, interfere with activity, or otherwise disturb you or your child. **Treatment:** A variety available (try simplest, least painful first). Treatment doesn't always work, but warts always disappear on their own—eventually. | **Prevention:** Avoiding contact with lesions. **Recurrence:** Not unusual. **Complications:** With certain genital warts, a slightly increased risk of cervical cancer developing later. |

# HEIGHT AND WEIGHT CHARTS

G rowth slows noticeably in the toddler years, as you will see when you follow your child's growth on these graphs. To plot growth, find your toddler's age along the bottom of the chart, and your child's height (in cen-

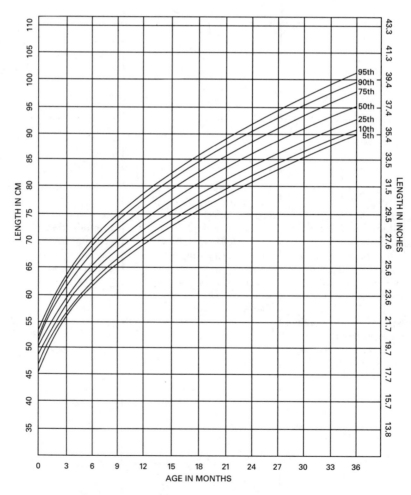

## *GIRLS HEIGHT CHART*

. . . . . . . . . .

### *Percentiles: Birth to 36 Months*

Source: National Center for Health Statistics

timeters or inches) or weight (in kilo-
grams or pounds) along the side. Mark
the point where the two intersect with a
dot—using a colored pen or pencil will
make the dots easier to see. Connect the
dots as you add them at subsequent
checkups. (If you have a copy of your
child's growth from birth to 12 months,
add this information to the chart as well.)
Ninety out of one hundred children fall
within the 5th and 95th percentiles for
height and weight. Though some chil-

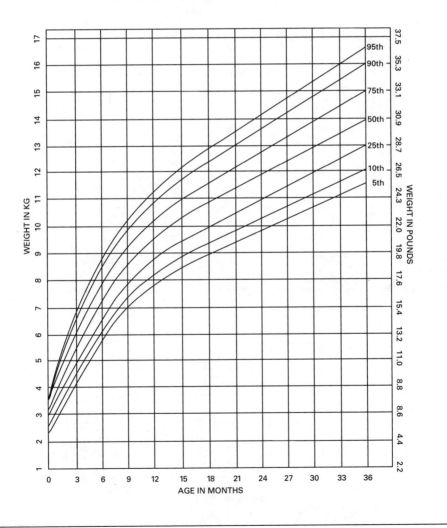

## GIRLS WEIGHT CHART

**Percentiles: Birth to 36 Months**

dren in the top and bottom 5% may come by their size genetically and be growing appropriately, others may be growing too slowly or gaining weight too rapidly. If you're concerned about either in your child, discuss your concerns with the doctor. Check with the doctor, too, about any sudden deviation in your

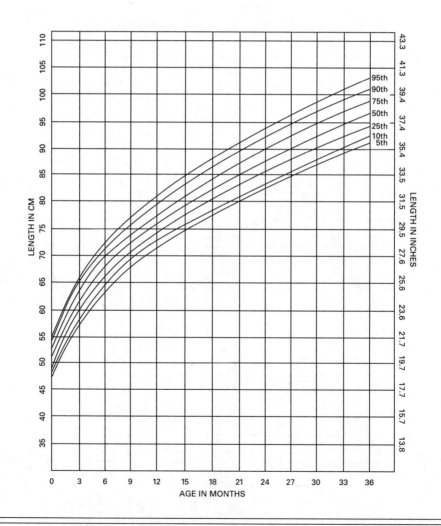

## BOYS HEIGHT CHART

· · · · · · · · · ·

### Percentiles: Birth to 36 Months

child's curve (a sudden spurt up in height, weight, or both, or a sudden dip in growth); though such changes most likely are a sign that your child is moving closer to his or her genetic size, they might also signal a problem. See page 515 for more on growth in the toddler years.

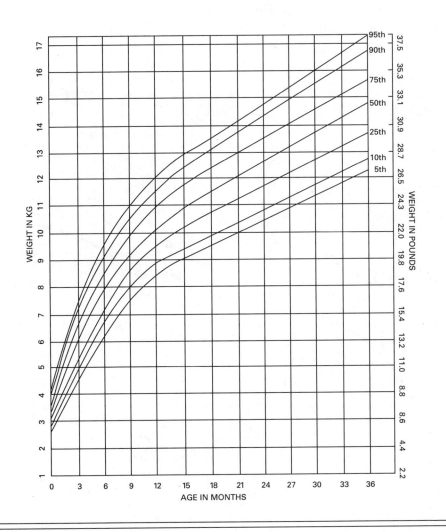

## BOYS WEIGHT CHART

··········

### Percentiles: Birth to 36 Months

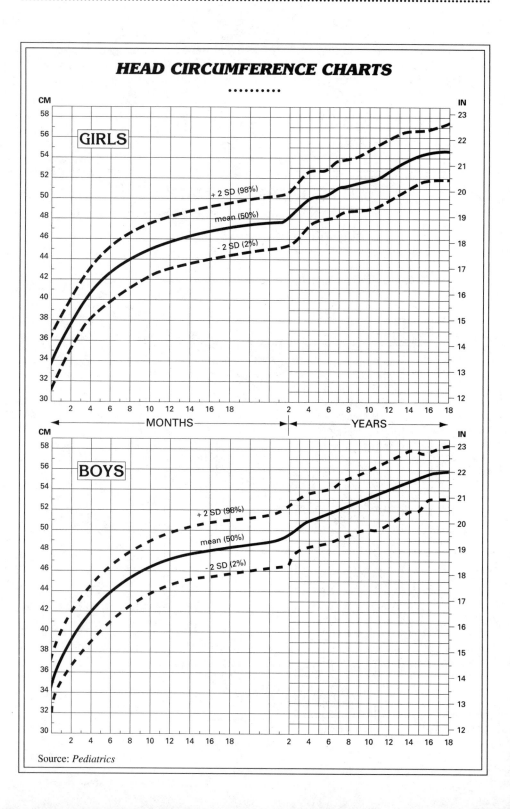

Source: *Pediatrics*

# Health History

# IMPORTANT PERSONAL INFORMATION ABOUT YOUR CHILD:*

Age: _____ Approximate weight: _____

**Chronic illnesses or disabilities, if any:** _____

_____

_____

_____

_____

_____

_____

_____

**Allergies, if any:** _____

_____

_____

_____

_____

_____

_____

**Last tetanus shot:** _____

**Medications:** _____

_____

_____

_____

_____

_____

_____

*Fill these in in pencil and update regularly.

# IMMUNIZATIONS

| AGE | DATE | IMMUNIZATION | REACTION, IF ANY |
|-----|------|--------------|------------------|
|     |      |              |                  |
|     |      |              |                  |
|     |      |              |                  |
|     |      |              |                  |
|     |      |              |                  |
|     |      |              |                  |
|     |      |              |                  |
|     |      |              |                  |
|     |      |              |                  |
|     |      |              |                  |
|     |      |              |                  |
|     |      |              |                  |
|     |      |              |                  |
|     |      |              |                  |
|     |      |              |                  |
|     |      |              |                  |
|     |      |              |                  |
|     |      |              |                  |
|     |      |              |                  |
|     |      |              |                  |
|     |      |              |                  |

# *Illness record*

Date: _____ Diagnosis: _____ Duration: _____

Symptoms: _____

_____

Home treatment: _____

Doctor called: _____

Medical treatment: _____

_____

Medication(s): _____ How long given: _____

Drug reactions, if any: _____

_____

Complications, if any: _____

_____

---

Date: _____ Diagnosis: _____ Duration: _____

Symptoms: _____

_____

_____

Home treatment: _____

Doctor called: _____

Medical treatment: _____

_____

Medication(s): _____ How long given: _____

Drug reactions, if any: _____

_____

Complications, if: _____

_____

# *ILLNESS RECORD*

Date: _____ Diagnosis: _____ Duration: _____

Symptoms: _____

_____

Home treatment: _____

Doctor called: _____

Medical treatment: _____

_____

Medication(s): _____ How long given: _____

Drug reactions, if any: _____

_____

Complications, if any: _____

_____

Date: _____ Diagnosis: _____ Duration: _____

Symptoms: _____

_____

_____

Home treatment: _____

Doctor called: _____

Medical treatment: _____

_____

Medication(s): _____ How long given: _____

Drug reactions, if any: _____

_____

Complications, if: _____

_____

# *ILLNESS RECORD*

Date: _____ Diagnosis: _____ Duration: _____

Symptoms: _____

_____

Home treatment: _____

Doctor called: _____

Medical treatment: _____

_____

Medication(s): _____ How long given: _____

Drug reactions, if any: _____

_____

Complications, if any: _____

_____

---

Date: _____ Diagnosis: _____ Duration: _____

Symptoms: _____

_____

_____

Home treatment: _____

Doctor called: _____

Medical treatment: _____

_____

Medication(s): _____ How long given: _____

Drug reactions, if any: _____

_____

Complications, if: _____

_____

# *ILLNESS RECORD*

**Date:** _____ **Diagnosis:** _____ **Duration:** _____

**Symptoms:** _____

_____

**Home treatment:** _____

**Doctor called:** _____

**Medical treatment:** _____

_____

**Medication(s):** _____ **How long given:** _____

**Drug reactions, if any:** _____

_____

**Complications, if any:** _____

_____

**Date:** _____ **Diagnosis:** _____ **Duration:** _____

**Symptoms:** _____

_____

_____

**Home treatment:** _____

**Doctor called:** _____

**Medical treatment:** _____

_____

**Medication(s):** _____ **How long given:** _____

**Drug reactions, if any:** _____

_____

**Complications, if:** _____

_____

# REGULAR CHECKUPS

## 12-Month Checkup

**Date:** _____ **Doctor:** _____

**Questions to ask:** _____

_____

_____

_____

**What you learned:** _____

_____

_____

_____

**Toddler's weight:** _____ **height:** _____ **head circumference:** _____

## 15-Month Checkup

**Date:** _____ **Doctor:** _____

**Questions to ask:** _____

_____

_____

_____

**What you learned:** _____

_____

_____

_____

**Toddler's weight:** _____ **height:** _____ **head circumference:** _____

# REGULAR CHECKUPS

## 18-Month Checkup

Date: _____ Doctor: _____

Questions to ask: _____

_____

_____

_____

What you learned: _____

_____

_____

_____

Toddler's weight: _____ height: _____ head circumference: _____

## 24-Month Checkup

Date: _____ Doctor: _____

Questions to ask: _____

_____

_____

_____

What you learned: _____

_____

_____

_____

Toddler's weight: _____ height: _____ head circumference: _____

# Regular checkups

## 36-Month Checkup

Date: _____ Doctor: _____

Questions to ask: _____

_____

_____

_____

What you learned: _____

_____

_____

_____

Toddler's weight: _____ height: _____ head circumference: _____

# Moments to Remember

# FIRSTS

(Date, circumstances)

First word: _____

First step: _____

First "no!": _____

First phrase: _____

First sentence: _____

First "I love you": _____

First song: _____

First solo on the slide: _____

First telephone chat: _____

First "success" on the potty: _____

First _____

First _____

First _____

First _____

First _____

First _____

First _____

First _____

First _____

First _____

First _____

First _____

First _____

# THE FIRST BIRTHDAY PARTY

(Guests, gifts, decor, reactions, special moments)

_____

_____

_____

_____

_____

_____

_____

_____

_____

_____

_____

_____

_____

_____

_____

_____

_____

_____

_____

_____

_____

_____

_____

_____

_____

# THE SECOND BIRTHDAY PARTY

(Guests, gifts, decor, games, reactions, special moments)

# THE THIRD BIRTHDAY PARTY

(Guests, gifts, decor, games, reactions, special moments)

_____

_____

_____

_____

_____

_____

_____

_____

_____

_____

_____

_____

_____

_____

_____

_____

_____

_____

_____

_____

_____

_____

_____

_____

_____

_____

_____

# FIRST DAY OF PRESCHOOL OR DAY CARE

Date: _____ School/Center: _____

Your child's reaction: _____

_____

Your reaction: _____

Special moments at school:

_____

_____

_____

_____

_____

_____

_____

_____

_____

_____

_____

_____

_____

_____

_____

_____

_____

_____

_____

_____

# *Index*

·········

Some of the more eccentric toddler behaviors defy being easily categorized in an index (how, after all, would you look up "refusing to eat a broken cookie"). To facilitate the locating of such seemingly strange—but typically toddler—actions and reactions, we've indexed many of them under the catch-all category "Behaviors" (in the case of the broken cookie, you'd find help under "food fetishes"). Other broad categories in which we've placed hard-to-name subjects include: "Sleep problems," "Feeding problems," "Fears," and "Parent issues." Illustrations are listed in bold-face type.

# G

# T